AMERICAN

POLITICAL

THINKING

Readings from the Origins to the
21st Century

For my parents
Margie A. & Robert D.
who first uplifted me with the American spirit

AMERICAN
POLITICAL
THINKING

Readings from the Origins to the 21st Century

Robert Isaak
Pace University

Harcourt Brace College Publishers

Fort Worth Philadelphia San Diego New York Orlando Austin San Antonio
Toronto Montreal London Sydney Tokyo

Publisher	Ted Buchholz
Acquisitions Editor	David Tatom
Editorial Assistant	Kristin Trompeter
Project Editor	Deanna M. Johnson/Kelly Riche
Senior Production Manager	Kathleen Ferguson
Art Director	David A. Day

ISBN: 0-15-500365-8

Library of Congress Number: 93-61230

Printed in the United States of America

4 5 6 7 8 9 0 1 2 0 3 9 9 8 7 6 5 4 3 2

Foreword

Our age is not retrospective. People long to get beyond the past and to think of the
future and how they might prosper in it. It is the age of would-be 'posts': post-
industrialism, post-modernism, post-cold war, post-liberalism. Yet this understandable
but excessive desire to forget the past and to transcend the present ignores the
limits of culture and political tradition that lie just beneath the surface. And these
limits go deep, like riverbeds, usually predetermining the flow of contemporary
currents over the local topography. While trying to see things anew and to constantly
reinvent themselves and their organizations, Americans fall unknowingly back upon certain
habits of mind deeply ingrained in their past. And while attempting to adopt certain
American democratic and economic ways in order to be more successful politically and economically, foreign nations fail to perceive the cultural and political
limits of the unique conservative traditions of liberalism which dominate American
thinking.

This selection of readings aims to dispel the conventional assumption that American political thought is as young, green, and pragmatic as the society which
spawned it. While an effort has been made to cover each of the phases of American
political development with samples from works widely perceived to be "classic," equally
important selection criteria were the sheer quality of the thought or writing, and the
relevance to the founding, maintenance and ultimate crisis in American liberalism.
As the introduction demonstrates, American liberalism is paradoxically dominated
by conservative habit which conspires against social change as much as it fosters
it. By incorporating both the classical laissez-faire anti-state version of liberalism and
the progressive statist version, the dual tradition of American liberalism provides
dynamism and a sense of choice while coopting most people in its status quo framework.

While most Americans are socialized in secondary school with a number of
courses on American history and civics, few, if any, of these courses dwell on
the range or quality of American political thought in any depth. Hence, the majority
may graduate thinking that they "know" about American thought having barely
scratched the surface. If they knew how wide-ranging, exciting and profound the
field was, many more would take a college course in American political thought than is
the case.

My own love affair with American political thinking may serve as an illustration.
It started in the politicized 1960s when I took a graduate course on "American Political
and Social Thought" at New York University with H. Mark Roelofs. The reading
list consisted of 72 provocative and heavy books, none of which had been ordered
at the book store. The search for these books throughout the public and college
libraries of New York City became a physical challenge that all but matched the intellectual
one. In addition to a final exam on *all* of these books (which taught one how to read
any book in an hour and a half), we had to write a short term paper. Mine was
on "The Use of Myth as a Tool in American Foreign Policy" and deservedly received
a mark slightly lower than I had anticipated. Like a jilted lover whose passion had been
(justly) dashed with criticism, I went uptown a few blocks to the New School for
Social Research and submitted the paper to the Dean as a course proposal. He

accepted the idea and my university teaching career began. A decade and a half later when I was asked to come back and teach American Political and Social Thought at NYU to replace Roelofs while he was on a leave, the circle was complete. The gift of Roelofs (in addition to his charismatic oratory) was to link the wide-ranging works on American political thought to the contemporary political situation in the United States.

I have done my best to continue this tradition in the introductory materials that precede each part of the selections which follow by using the phenomenon of liberalism as a touchstone or leitmotif to inform the whole. The stress is upon the contemporary implications for the *process* of American political *thinking* as the basis for action as opposed to the sartorial gravity of American political *thought* (which implies an intimidating, finished edifice more than a spontaneous means). To become fully human, each of us must become political thinkers in our own way, coping with social realities we did not create in order to satisfy our own needs and those of others. By learning the limits of the political thinkers who have gone before us, our own thinking may become more fruitful.

The reader should be aware that many more works of high quality were excluded here than included given the limits of space. This selection represents but the tip of the iceberg in terms of the intellectual riches waiting to be discovered. I am grateful to Torsten Arnswald, Thomas Weissmann, and Alexander Keck for their able research assistance; and to David Tatom, Kathy Ferguson, David Day, Kristin Trompeter, Kelly Riche, and Deanna Johnson for their contributions at Harcourt Brace. I am also grateful to the following reviewers whose comments helped to improve the manuscript: Terence Ball, the University of Minnesota; Booth Fowler, the University of Wisconsin; Joe Kobylka, Southern Methodist University; Joe Kunkel, Mankato State University; Sanford Lakoff, the University of California, San Diego; Michael Lienesch, the University of North Carolina, Chapel Hill; and Robert Thig, the University of New Orleans. Marge Arone was a patient typist. And, finally, I am grateful to my family for tolerating a deprivation of time shared together.

R.I.

Contents

10. Overcoming Slavery and the Civil War

II. Reconstruction through World War II (1865–1945)

1. The American Dream

2. The American Reality for Women and Native Americans

3. Visions of Progress

4. The Frontier, the State, and War

5. The Power of Wealth

6. The Powerless

7. New Nationalism, New Freedom, and Progressivism

4. Critiques from the Left

5. Black Perspectives on Ends and Means

6. The Wisdom of Women

7. From Ecology to Anarchism and Back

8. Native-American Thinking

9. Dialogues on Liberalism and Justice

10. Political Economy Counterpoints

Introduction

The Conservative Tradition of American Liberalism

As the twentieth century comes to an end, Americans wonder to what extent their political system can be changed to be made more effective. And foreign nations ask what elements of the stable, capitalistic democracy represented by the United States they can import to improve their own political frameworks. Although both of these questions are concerned with the future, neither can be answered without looking at the past. The amazing stability of the American political system is no accident, although the reasons for it are complex. They lie in deep-seated conservative traditions of American liberalism that are hard to see if one merely observes the current political situation.

Domestic politicians who would introduce national health, education, or judicial reforms are frustrated by the stability of the very same unbending status quo that often attracts foreigners. The Founding Fathers knew that if they wanted to orchestrate change effectively they needed to go back to the lessons of the past—back, in fact, to the Greek cycle of government. Their writings and speeches are studded with classical references, a grounded solidity of thinking that transcends the past by taking it fully into account. Most contemporary politicians lack this retrospective grounding and wisdom. They tend to be short-term operators—quick studies of policy preoccupied with fund-raising and media time. Still, they are surprised when the short-term successes they have targeted are disrupted by long-term historical obstacles that were never taken into consideration. The past is not necessarily sacred, but it is there, like the tectonic plates that lie beneath the surface of the earth. Political earthquakes have origins deep in the past, as does political stability.

Curiously, Americans may tend to ignore the past because of the very stability that characterizes their political framework. They rarely ask how a political system so devoted to individual freedom can remain so stable, almost to the point of ensuring that no major "revolutionary" reform is possible.

We will assume here, in the spirit of historians Alexis de Tocqueville, Louis Hartz, and Clinton Rossiter, that certain "habits of the heart and mind" characterize the American political tradition—a unique brand of liberalism that has taken on the comfortable guise of a conservative habit. This liberalism has to do with being "born free without having to become so," with a restless, mobile individualism; it has to do with tenacious self-reliance, learning from the school of hard knocks, from one's own experience, rather than being open to learning from others. A pragmatic, naive optimism underlies this spirit, a belief not only in doing things independently and in one's own way but in reinventing the wheel, discovering new things under the sun, extending adolescence, and worshiping a culture of eternal youth. America not only is a young country but wants to remain so.

The American obsession with youth correlates with the American obsession with liberalism. By *liberalism* we mean that Americans tend to look first to the individual as the source of value rather than to an imposed dogmatic creed or hierarchy. American liberalism is an affirmation of individualism, natural rights, and limited government: it assumes that the individual, through the use of reason, is capable not only of self-fulfillment but of becoming a little motor of economic growth as self-interest spurs the natural effort to accumulate or to protect private property. In consequence, liberalism is preoccupied with equal access to this sociopolitical system of individual upward mobility and with the legal protection of natural rights and of private property obtained through individual initiative. Such legal access and protection, in turn, permit Americans to believe that the economic market, if left largely alone, can provide a fair and noncoercive distribution of wealth, status, and power based upon individual accomplishment. Liberalism is a centrist belief system in that it simultaneously advocates human rights and property rights. Those who affirm that property rights, their protection, and free economic markets take precedence over human welfare espouse the *conservative, classical, laissez-faire* strain of liberalism. Those, on the other hand, who put human rights and equality of access to social and economic institutions before property rights as a priority belong to the *progressive* or *populist* strain of liberalism. Because American liberalism embraces both of these classical and progressive strains and evolved without competition from other feudal or long-established ideological frameworks, it has been taken for granted as the basis of Americanism. Liberalism, in short, has become a subconscious "conservative" habit or way of political being. It provides a rather narrow basis for consensus among those on the left (the "progressives"—often called liberals or Democrats today) and on the right (the "conservatives"—often referred to as Republicans today).

Such mainstream liberal beliefs are encouraged by preserving a stable chaos of individual freedom, by keeping the state at arm's length, by maintaining political traditions, and by opening opportunities for the disadvantaged, for entrepreneurship, for "elbow room." In times of global economic crisis, the United States is perceived as the last stronghold of capitalism, where neither right-wing nor left-wing revolutions threaten to seize investments. The protection of private property is the mainstay of the conservative tradition of American liberalism. For although Thomas Jefferson recast English philosopher John Locke's affirmation of the individual's natural right to life, liberty, and property into "life, liberty, and the pursuit of happiness," the American view of happiness has nevertheless continued to be shaped by possession of private property.

Foreigners, therefore, should not be surprised if the United States remains the last stronghold of property-propelled capitalism. Austrian-American economist Joseph Schumpeter called capitalism "creative destruction," a dynamic process in which the new constantly drives out the old as opportunity emerges from discarding obsolescence. The United States is a halfway house of creative destruction that attracts foreign investment with stability and flexibility. America's stability, from this perspective, is based on the belief that U.S. ownership will never be nationalized. Its creative flexibility and opportunities for unlimited speculation permit greater potential return on investment than most other places, given constant changes in the rules and the tempo of U.S. business cycles. Creative, stable disorder, in short, is ideal for investors who want to make money on the roller-coaster ups and downs of creative destruction. It is harder to make money in heavily regulated societies where the ups and downs are flattened out by social insurance of the welfare state that cover risks at the bottom and by high taxes that damper down incomes at the top (as in Western European countries). America's stable chaos of individual freedom and entrepreneurship is the seedbed of economic dynamism and material accumulation.

But, in the words of songwriter Bob Dylan, "the times they are a-changin'." The administration of President Bill Clinton represents an effort to Europeanize the United States, to civilize its capitalism, to shore up the safety net at the bottom of society by expanding medical insurance and job training, and to trim the wings of the speculative rich at the top with higher taxes. Clinton represents not the rejection of the conservative tradition of American liberalism, but the resurrection of its progressive "New Deal" strain. For although the tradition of American liberalism is narrow in comparison to the wide spectrum of ideological positions represented in Europe, it has a dynamic dualism that successfully absorbs Left-wing and Right-wing voters to bring them home to the center.

In summary, the two strains of liberalism subsumed in the tradition of American liberalism are (1) older classical, laissez-faire liberalism with its maximization of individual interests as a source of creating wealth and its negative view of the state ("that government governs best which governs least"); and (2) newer progressive liberalism, which advocates federal-government intervention for the sake of stimulating the economy through government spending and credit, as well as state action to open opportunities for the disadvantaged and to protect the weak. The old view of liberalism has a negative view of the state, while the more recent version sees a positive state. Because the overwhelming majority of Americans identify with one or both of these views, the tradition of American liberalism catches them in the complexity of its dynamic dualism. This cooptation ensures the American liberal tradition's survival and stability by giving citizens a fundamental choice within its "conservative" framework (structurally underpinned by the work of the Founding Fathers—particularly in the Constitution).

By understanding the dual, but narrow, nature of American liberalism, one comes to appreciate what is really new in American political thinking. Movements that transcend the mainstream liberal tradition include the communitarian-Left campaign for social planning; diversity or "gender" politics that advocate group rights rather than individual rights; the diffuse pressure for a new environmental ethic that challenges the traditional belief in continual economic improvement held by both progressive and conservative liberals; and religious-Right efforts to combat secular humanism, the teaching of evolution, abortion, and permissiveness. The flowering, depth, and intensity of these movements make them worthy of Walt Whitman's vision of democratic celebration. And yet, like so many points and counterpoints, moves and countermoves, the end result seems to be yet a new version of American checks and balances. There is much fascinating shifting and philosophical articulation outside the bounds of the conservative tradition of liberalism—a virtual kaleidoscope of multicultural, ideological, and religious hues of political conviction—but the center seems to hold.

But what about multiculturalism? Does not this late twentieth-century movement demonstrate that we have moved to a "post-liberal" age in the United States? Have we not entered an age in which each ethnic minority group brings its own cultural perspective to the national tapestry, making its liberal design unrecognizable?

The multicultural debate, which often slips outside the conservative mainstream of the dualism of the American liberal tradition, paradoxically serves to reconfirm it. Precisely because the United States is such a heterogeneous nation of immigrants, the dominant political ideology of liberalism—usually called Americanism or the American Dream—

functions as an integrating, nationalizing force. Martin Luther King, Jr.'s "I have a Dream!" *was the American Dream*. Other countries that are more ethnically homogeneous lack the same need for an integrating ideology except for "raw" nationalism. But the expanding multicultural diversity of American political thinking, particularly in the twentieth century, usually serves merely as a multicolored background to the American liberal tradition, which is dominant. For many multicultural thinkers come home to liberal ideology at certain points in their lives. Multiculturalism enriches the mother lode of the comparatively narrow tradition of American liberalism, but deepens more than widens it in the process. The selections here from African-Americans, native Americans, and American women sometimes go beyond traditional American thinking, as a river overflows its banks. But much of this thinking, one way or another, seems to work its way back to the mainstream.

In the post–cold war world, defense issues were suddenly pushed to the back burner, and Americans became preoccupied with economic competitiveness. Countries such as Japan, Germany, Singapore, Taiwan, and South Korea, whose political economies were much more heavily steered and subsidized by government, suddenly confronted the United States in a number of markets. This raised the question of whether or not the traditional rules of American liberalism were economically viable in the global economy. With its heritage of loose, laissez-faire liberalism—aside from coordination of Pentagon defense spending—the United States was in head-to-head competition with national strategies based on close coordination of government, business, and labor. American living standards, jobs, and traditional ways of doing business were threatened. Concern mounted in the 1990s as to whether or not the traditional liberal political economic system would "work" in twenty-first century global economic competition. Such doubts inevitably invite us to question the extent that the principles of the conservative tradition of American liberalism can be adapted or changed.

The cultural, religious, intellectual, political, and economic origins of the United States provide a mix so unique that it may be difficult, if not impossible, to duplicate. Yet foreigners who briefly visit the country often mistakenly perceive the political culture to be flat or superficial. Many Americans also fail to appreciate the rich complexities that lie behind the workings of their own political system and traditions. Stable systems are often too easily taken for granted.

Culturally, the United States was founded by European immigrants seeking religious, political, or economic freedom. These settlers longed for an opportunity to construct a new Europe without the traditional constraints of the old Europe. For the most part, these were self-righteous people who had few doubts about the values for which they stood. Those rebelling against the traditional hierarchy of the Anglican church were out to establish a Puritan theocracy, a purer form of social contract influenced by the Protestant Reformation: their "liberalism" was a conservative compact between individuals and their God. Sociologist Max Weber identified one of the main reasons why friendship may not be held in such high esteem in the United States as *gemütlichkeit* (warm comradship) is in Germany: intimacy in Protestant America was supposed to be limited to the individual's relationship with God. It was not to be diluted with family and friends, where a certain emotional reserve was in order. Individual independence was not merely meant to be economic and political but spiritual as well. Thus, the transactional relations between American individuals, often attributed to the dominance of their capitalist economic system, may be furthered by the circumspect religious Protestant heritage of their culture that restrains them from intense emotional involvements over time with other people.

The immigrants who founded the United States were not only interested in the *kind* of religious freedom they wanted to prevail in their utopian social order, but often had strong opinions about their governmental ideals. Many of them embraced John Locke's *Second Treatise on Civil Government*, published in 1690. *The Second Treatise* contended that human beings had intrinsic moral rights and duties that preceded the existence of society and the state. Individuals, thus, have a natural right to life, liberty, and "estate," by which he meant property. In his writing, he used "property" as an analogy for all natural rights, appearing to make it the most important by analyzing it in detail. Locke asserted that to the extent a man mixed his energy and body with the soil, his land became his private property—an extension of himself. And Locke believed that greater production on the land would raise the prosperity of the community. Locke was egalitarian in assuming that all individuals were capable of knowing their natural rights through their use of "right reason." Government was instituted by a contract of individuals to protect the natural rights of all. And particularly, of course, to protect private property. Locke's solution was to make property holders the effective legislative power, while limiting any such power by the natural rights of people (including property rights). Under carefully limited conditions, Locke even proposed the "right of revolution" in case it became necessary to replace a government that failed to fulfill its obligations in terms of natural rights. Functionally, Locke separated the (powerful) legislative branch from the executive branch—an idea deepened and transformed by the Founding Fathers to prevent any one branch of government from overstepping its authority. Locke's liberalism, in short, was an anxious faith that sought to limit the government for the sake of individual rights while providing legitimacy for the government to protect private property.

Locke, of course, was by no means the only European source of liberalism to influence the Founding Fathers. He was merely the dominant influence among the Anglo-Saxon liberals, which included Adam Smith. The Continental liberals—Jean Jacques Rousseau, the Physiocrats (François Quesnay and Vincent de Gournany, to whom the phrase "Laissez-faire, laissez-passer" is attributed), and, later, Immanuel Kant—were also influential.

Nor was the baggage the immigrants brought to the New World limited merely to religious and political aspirations. Most of the immigrants were bourgeois through and through and desired economic success through hard work and upward mobility protected by the government. The United States was a vast land of economic opportunity unrestricted by European feudal traditions and ties. To paraphrase de Tocqueville, Americans were born free without having to become so. Clearly this formula applied more accurately to white Anglo-Saxon Protestant (WASP) males than it did to native Americans, African-Americans, or women at the time, but it still lives on in the mythology of American liberalism. The point is that Americans were born with their liberalism, and their task was to *preserve* or *maintain* it, a conservative task that took the given value context for granted.

The widespread (and continuing) conservative faith in American liberalism is summed up by Clinton Rossiter in his *Conservatism in America*:

> The American political mind has never thought much along consciously radical lines. Its
> Liberal principles, to be sure, are perfectionist and egalitarian, and to many critics from

abroad they have seemed a standing invitation to leveling and anarchy. Such an interpretation of the American faith overlooks three important points: the sobering, stabilizing influence of the conservative elements in this faith; the extent to which Liberal principles have actually been realized in this country and thus have been deradicalized in influence if not in implication; and the fact that this is, after all, a faith, a set of ideals to be realized perfectly only in a far-off future and only by following the teachings of our ancestors.

The immigrants arrived full of optimism and strong beliefs and had the good fortune to have a brilliant group of Founding Fathers emerge to establish a democratic creed and constitution worthy of their progressive yet conservative faith.

Initially, limited economic cooperation among the thirteen colonies was to become the means to preserve the individual freedom of the colonists while assuring their prosperity. But "all the King's men" pushed them too far, and finally the American colonists confronted and displaced the British in increasingly tense disputes regarding monarchical power, taxes, and the desire for individual political, economic, and religious autonomy. Their agenda was largely inherited from European liberals, yet radically transformed by the Founding Fathers with their Enlightenment ideals and knowledge of the classics. Depending upon which of these two elements one emphasizes, the founding of the United States can be called either "The American Replacement" or "The American Revolution." For although the Americans won their freedom through bloodshed, in defeating British imperialism they largely kept the cultural, religious, and ideological heritage of European liberals and merely adapted it to the unique conditions of the New World. It was not a *new* liberalism they had in mind as much as the adaptation of an inherited liberalism (minus its feudal ties) that they wanted to establish and keep in perpetuity. Their pragmatic innovations in checks and balances and separations of power were designed to preserve old liberal ideals.

On the one hand, the brilliance and uniqueness of these innovations cannot be over-emphasized (just consider the remarkable set of authors and readings sampled in Part 1: Paine, Mason, Jefferson, Adams, Henry, Madison, Hamilton). On the other hand, like revolutionaries everywhere, once they had won the war, their objective was to establish the peace. They intended to stabilize the status quo based on their liberal values of maximum individual (and states') rights with minimum state interference by the federal government. Their liberal ideals were briefly expressed in the Declaration of Independence, and their conservative concern with maintaining their hard-earned freedom appeared in the much longer, complex and conservative Constitution. Recall that the Bill of Rights was added to the Constitution later, almost as an afterthought. And although a populist, progressive strain of liberalism was emerging in the era of Presidents Thomas Jefferson and Andrew Jackson, this was balanced by the powerful minority influence of the Federalists, particularly Chief Justice John Marshall, who magnified the influence of the Supreme Court through the invention of constitutional law.

In drawing up the Constitution, the Founding Fathers not only drew upon the assumptions of John Locke's version of liberalism, but went back to the Greek cycle of government as it evolved into the "mixed theory of government." The Greek cycle was first described at length by Plato and adapted into a "mixed theory" by Aristotle and later falsely attributed to the Roman republic by Polybius. The same mixed-government theory was more accurately hypothesized to describe the unwritten British governmental framework of the eighteenth century by Montesquieu. And Aristotle, Polybius, and Montesquieu (in addition to John Locke) made a lasting impression upon the minds of the Founding Fathers, particularly upon James Madison.

Briefly, the Greek cycle described by Plato in the *Republic* deals with the number and quality of governors and assumes that power always corrupts. First comes rule by the one, the benevolent monarch whose power eventually corrupts him into becoming a tyrant. Then comes rule by the few: a noble group of aristocrats overthrow the tyrant only, in time, to be corrupted themselves into a greedy oligarchy. Then the many take over, the masses who throw over the oligarchy to set up a democracy. But the passions of the crowd soon lead to chaos until a heroic leader emerges and establishes rule by the one. The cycle starts again. In *Politics*, Aristotle contends that the secret of the mixed form of government is to combine these potential leaders (each with its own clear economic class interests) into one government that will check and balance the ambitions and corruptions of each, thereby preserving stability.

Madison illustrated his dependence upon the theory of mixed government growing out of the Greek cycle in "Federalist Paper No. 10" and "No. 51," which are widely considered the most important of *The Federalist Papers* underlying the assumptions of the Constitution.

In "Federalist No. 10," Madison makes it clear that he believes conflicting economic factions are inevitable in a free society. Only a government that coopts these factions into a *representative republic* (rather than a direct democracy) will balance them and prevent the dominant majority from oppressing any particular minority. A *republic* divides power among classes, whereas a *democracy* concentrates power in the body of citizens. Madison went on to argue that such a republican system of preserving individual liberty was easier in more extensive or larger states than in smaller ones because of the dilution of majority power. And should something go wrong with a power-hungry faction within the government, Madison proposed in "Federalist No. 51" the dividing up of government into various branches and departments so each could check and balance the potential power of the other, and no tyrannous faction could emerge. The federalist design for the U.S. Constitution was a negative one geared toward preventing evils from occurring rather than a positive one geared toward establishing a democratic utopia. As Madison put it: "But what is government itself, but the greatest of all reflections on human nature? If men were angels, no government would be necessary." And his anxious solution: "Whilst all authority in it [the federal republic of the United States] will be derived from and dependent on the society, the society itself will be broken into so many parts, interests, and classes of citizens, that the rights of individuals, or of the minority, will be in little danger from interested combinations of the majority."

This conservative framework for American liberalism set up all factions against each other in a large state so that none could dictate to others. It set all branches and departments of the federal system against each other so that no majority could lord it over any minority. Through this design, Madison persuaded Americans to give up enough individual freedom and states' rights to establish a central federal government or republic. But this was done at the price of ensuring the stability of the economic status quo to the point of deterring future redistributive change or radical reform. In "Federalist No. 10," Madison made it clear that his basic interest was to assure the established economic classes that their position would not be threatened by the new order: "The diversity in the faculties of men, from which the rights of property originate, is not less an insuperable obstacle to a uniformity of interests. The protection of these faculties is the first object of government.

From the protection of different and unequal faculties of acquiring property and from the influence of these on the sentiments and views of the respective proprietors, ensues a division of the society into different interests and parties."

The assumption that natural inequalities of property were due to the different capacities of human beings—the basic tenet of laissez-faire capitalism—was established by the Founding Fathers. It was a guiding principle to be maintained and safeguarded in perpetuity by the social division of factions and the governmental division of branches and departments, which guaranteed the stability of the status quo above all else.

After the signing of the Constitution in 1789, Benjamin Franklin wrote in a letter to M. Leroy: "Our Constitution is in actual operation; everything appears to promise that it will last; but in this world nothing is certain but death and taxes." When asked by a lady whether he had given the Americans a democracy upon leaving the signing, Franklin was said to have responded: "Madame, we have given you a republic. May you be able to keep it!" The preoccupation, as always, was with stability—maintaining what had been created. The revolutionary creed of the Declaration had been pinned down in the Constitution. The Constitution was designed to make sure that no one person, faction, or branch of government would be able to seize enough power to undo the political system.

The Constitution has since been treated as a sacred document. The original copies are locked up at night deep in the vaults of Washington, D.C. The words are taken largely as scripture by the Supreme Court and innumerable schoolchildren. Although there have been "liberal" judges and "liberal" politicians, they all dance to the constitutional jig. And at its function of dividing power to conquer tyranny the system works—Enlightenment clockwork in a post-Enlightenment world. Even when the government began to intervene in the economy as it became clear that the markets themselves would not pull the United States out of the Great Depression, the political rhetoric touched base with the conservative constitutional framework. Take, for example, President Franklin D. Roosevelt's Annual Message to Congress, January 3, 1936:

> Within democratic nations the chief concern of the people is to prevent the continuation or the rise of autocratic institutions that beget slavery at home and aggression abroad. Within our borders, as in the world at large, popular opinion is at war with a power-seeking minority.
>
> This is no new thing. It was fought out in the Constitutional Convention of 1787. From time to time since then the battle has been continued, under Thomas Jefferson, Andrew Jackson, Theodore Roosevelt and Woodrow Wilson. . . .
>
> . . . In these latter years we have witnessed the domination of government by financial and industrial groups, numerically small but politically dominant in the twelve years that succeeded the World War. . . . As guardians and trustees for great groups of individual stockholders, they wrongfully seek to carry the property and the interest entrusted to them into the arena of partisan politics. They seek—this minority in business and industry—to control, and often do control and use for their own purposes legitimate and highly honored business associations; they engage in vast propaganda to spread fear and discord among the people—they would "gang up" against the people's liberties.

Roosevelt's populist state interventionism draws on progressive liberalism, which dates back at least to Andrew Jackson. Historians such as William Leuchtenberger and

Alan Brinkley have argued Roosevelt's New Deal is a watershed in American political history because it brought the populist-progressive critique to a point at which the state or government gained responsibility for managing the economy, rather than leaving it alone or nationalizing it. And as a result, they contend, the welfare state was established, substituting a safety net for the indifference to poverty and unemployment of classical economic liberalism.

But the overall effect of Roosevelt's ad hoc, halfway steps toward a welfare state served more to rescue the conservative tradition of American liberalism from deep drops in the economic markets than to transform it. His explicit reliance, mentioned above, upon the constitutional framework and the democratic populism of Thomas Jefferson, Andrew Jackson, Theodore Roosevelt, and Woodrow Wilson suggests consolidation of an old tradition, rather than a radical departure. The two world wars and the Great Depression between them called for a more centralized role of management by the state to stabilize the existing liberal order. By providing state insurance for banks, public service jobs for the unemployed, Social Security, and federal spending stimulus for the economy, Franklin Roosevelt was certainly complementing the laissez-faire economic theories of Adam Smith with the state intervention notions of John Maynard Keynes. In this sense, the tradition of American liberalism became more civilized and more mature—a process continued by populist reforms such as the National Service and health care programs launched by Bill Clinton's administration. But this has created no radical transformation. The consistent idea over time is to rely on individual initiative and the private sector as much as possible, and in critical situations to supplement private initiatives with public management. The thrust toward helping those most disadvantaged by unemployment, sickness, old age, or being left out of the economic opportunity structure is aimed to bring everyone back into the mainstream of the liberal order, to help it work as it was supposed to.

Social Darwinism, the survival-of-the-fittest social ethic of William Graham Sumner, was left behind in the era of the New Deal, which might count as a "watershed." And the growth of responsibility by the centralized state certainly represented movement away from the agrarian decentralized democracy envisioned by Thomas Jefferson and toward Alexander Hamilton's vision of a strong federalism with the growing influence of financial elites. But this is maturation *within* the conservative tradition of the Founding Fathers more than a radical break from their design. Indeed, it may just be part of a recurrent cycle between the laissez-faire and progressive strains of liberalism (highlighted by the shift from Reagan and Bush to Clinton) as suggested by historian Arthur Schlessinger. Thus far it is not apparent that the traditional shifting duality of laissez-faire and progressive liberalisms will fail to cope with social change without having to radically transform itself. The New Deal did not go far enough for such radical transformation, nor could it have given the limits of the very conservative tradition of American liberalism it was bending over backwards to restore. The progressive liberalism epitomized by the New Deal is not utopianism, but rather a pragmatic crusade against the vested interests that dominate the historical moment at the expense of those out of power.

Viewed as a whole, American liberalism has become a patriotic creed, a constitutional theology based upon an upbeat individualism aimed at preserving "natural rights." Consider the words with which *The New Republic's* founder, Herbert Croly, began his classic work *The Promise of American Life* in 1909.

> The average American is nothing if not patriotic. . . . The faith of Americans in their own country is religious, if not in its authority. It pervades the air we breathe. Every new stage

of our educational training provides some additional testimony on its behalf. .... The skeptic is not controverted; he is overlooked. It constitutes the kind of faith which is the implication, rather than the object of thought, and consciously or unconsciously it enters largely into our personal lives as a formative influence. We may distrust and dislike much that is done in the name of our country by our fellow-countrymen; but our country itself, its democratic system, and its prosperous future are above suspicion.

Croly maintained that Americans were so optimistic and future-oriented that they were satisfied with the *promise* of the American dream rather than demanding the thing itself in the present. He noted that the so-called Progressive movement accepted the conservative laissez-faire economic doctrines of classical American liberalism, assumptions reinforced by the "Scottish Realism" or pragmatism of the first half of the nineteenth century as legitimized by John Locke and Adam Smith.

The historian Louis Hartz further documented the sources of America's Lockean liberal faith in his classic *The Liberal Tradition in America* published in 1955. Hartz argued that because Americans had experienced neither feudalism nor the reaction to feudalism (socialism) nor the reaction to socialism (fascism), Americans could only perceive such extreme ideologies as anathema. They could not think beyond the mental boundaries of their Lockean liberal heritage. Hartz writes:

> The psychic heritage of a nation "born equal" is . . . a colossal liberal absolutism, the death by atrophy of the philosophic impulse. And in a war of ideas this frame of mind has two automatic effects: it hampers creative action abroad by identifying the alien with the unintelligible, and it inspires hysteria at home by enervating the anxiety that unintelligible things produce. . . . There has been throughout the twentieth century an impulse to transcend the American perspective evoked by the very clash of cultures which it has closed down. . . . "Americanism" is at once heightened and shattered by the crushing impact of the rest of the world upon it. And so, curiously enough, the answer to the national blindness that the new time produces is the national enlightenment that it also produces: the race between the two is a fateful one indeed. Which is to say that America must look to its contact with other nations to provide that spark of philosophy, that grain of relative insight that its own history has denied it.

Hartz pointed out the American tendency to try to export the unique U.S. version of liberalism abroad through foreign policy, a tradition that has by no means abated. But it may be more useful to focus on domestic implications of America's traditional liberal faith. Such implications may have severe effects on America's economic and educational competitiveness in the world economy at the end of the twentieth century.

Might an effective American industrial policy, that is, government coordination and targeting of sectors vital to national economic health and growth, be functionally impossible because of the conservative constitutional framework of American liberalism? Political scientist Theodore Lowi observed in *The End of Liberalism* (1969) that "interest-group liberalism renders government impotent." Comparing the U.S. disadvantages in competing with the Japanese in *The Shadow of the Rising Sun* (1991), business executive and political scientist William Dietrich concludes:

> A strong central state and a top professional bureaucracy are essential preconditions for industrial policy. . . . America is totally lacking the statist traditions of Japan, Germany,

and France. Our political development has been conditioned by an anti-statist tradition. American political institutions are utterly unique. The United States is the only advanced democratic society that lacks a strong central state and a top professional bureaucracy. The only way America can counter the Japanese challenge and regain world economic leadership is through the comprehensive use of industrial policy. . . . But as long as we remain obsessed with our hyperindividualism, anti-statism, and free-market absolutism, we're doomed to decline.

The conservative laissez-faire arguments against industrial policy are well known and widely articulated: individuals and companies in the free market are better decision makers and more flexible in processing changing market condition information than are cumbersome state bureaucracies that choose to subsidize specific sectors (such as high technology) or industries (such as automobiles and semiconductors) at the taxpayer's peril. Politically, it is apt to be most difficult for Americans to achieve the centralized institutional power of Japan, Germany, or France, because as conservative anti-statist liberalism battles progressive interventionist state thinking, stalemate appears more likely than transcendence, short of a cultural revolution that transforms the very meaning of "Americanism."

And given such stalemate, can American education be reformed on a national basis to meet the new high standards in math, science, and applied technology demanded by the most competitive players in the world economy? The institutional inability of Americans to achieve sweeping national educational reforms to match Japanese and German teenage achievement results in math and science raises serious doubts. And the possibility of radical change becomes more remote when one considers the optimistic chauvinism of many Americans toward their local schools. Such schools were, after all, designed to inform immigrant pupils about their democratic liberal creed and to develop *internal* self-expression in this tradition of individual freedom. They were not meant to push all students collectively to meet *external* national achievement standards set by other more hierarchically organized countries. In analyzing the early twentieth century, political scientist Thomas Janoski noted in *The Political Economy of Unemployment* (1990):

> The dominant social problem at the turn of the century was the "immigrant question," soon to be followed by the "race question." Leaders saw the immigrating stranger's lack of socialization as the cause of most social problems. Control and socialization of immigrants was the solution, and training workers became secondary. A substantial minority of urban workers did not need to learn skills; they had brought considerable skills with them. The vast majority of immigrants also did not really need skill training because they were destined for menial jobs. However, this mass of immigrants needed to learn the customs, language, and government of the new country.

The United States had become an assimilation machine, and its public schools socialization factories.

The larger question is whether shortcomings in American economic and educational competitiveness spring in part from optimistic belief in the liberal American creed of individualism. As historian Alexis de Tocqueville wrote in the 1830s in *Democracy in America*, Americans "enjoy explaining almost every act of their lives on the principle of self-interest properly understood. It gives them pleasure to point out how an enlightened self-love continually leads them to help one another and disposes them freely to give part of their time and their wealth for the good of the state." But whether voluntary self-interest and philanthropy—what President George Bush called "a thousand points of light"—can coordinate American educational and economic institutions to compete with hierarchically organized, team-oriented cultures abroad is open to question. What is good in the short run for each individual in a collectivity may not be best for long-term competitive fitness of the whole collectivity. To preserve their liberal tradition, Americans must find a way to turn their plethora of short-run individual incentives into systematic, long-run coordinated efforts. And such standardized institutional coordination may, in the process, involve transcending that very liberal ideology.

The American constitutional framework is designed not for economic nationalism but for economic individualism. The Founding Fathers did not anticipate the domination of the national economy by multinational corporations any more than Adam Smith did. Antitrust legislation has proven a weak antidote to this concentration of power in the traditional scheme of checks and balances, and would, in any case, not address the problem of state-subsidized multinational companies based abroad. As a result, American multinational companies are only checked and balanced by foreign national corporations, a global economic pluralism. But such transnational pluralism does not guarantee the American traditional interest because it is designed to further private profits and corporate interests, interests that may, in themselves, be multinational. In a hypothetical world where all nation-states had constitutions like that of the United States, free world trade and multinational corporate pluralism might be satisfactory in terms of American national economic interests. But few states are so constituted. The mercantilist (or state economic) strategies of Japan and France, for instance, have often illustrated the national interest advantages of targeting business sectors and cultivating national corporate strategies through state subsidies and tax policies. Economic individualism may be a weak match for such collective targeted clout, as the Clinton administration suggested in defending its strategic policies of "managed trade." The understandable domestic resistance to such "strategic trade" decision making by the federal government indicates the vitality of "enlightened" laissez-faire American liberalism.

Maybe this conservative anti-statist heritage of the liberal tradition in the United States destines Americans to use a shotgun approach toward economic and educational objectives in contrast to the rifle style or laser-beam targeting of the Japanese. If this is so, and Americans are "constitutionally" stuck with being individualistic liberals through and through, perhaps Americans should enjoy it more and just accept that other cultures that lack American priorities are apt to outdo Americans on objectives other than individual freedom. This economic and educational celebration of self-interest and self-actualization does have the advantage of stimulating innovation, creativity, and entrepreneurship.

On the other hand, perhaps a new, more mature "communitarian" development is in the offing in which Americans will again find an effective synthesis between their individualist longings and positive state coordination. But most communitarian ideals seem to call for decentralized power and local community self-sufficiency—which would make Thomas Jefferson happy, along with the Germans, Japanese, and other competitors. It seems unimaginable that Americans can overwhelm the Germans and Japanese economically and educationally without a structural revolution that risks undoing the very framework of individualistic stability created in their Enlightenment Constitution. At least until the last decade of the twentieth century Americans generally opted for the stability of individual freedom in their political framework above all else, except in times of war. The dramatic story of how this American priority evolved, from religious, economic, and political desires for autonomy to a stable balance of federalist republicanism with populist democracy, and to dissent from mainstream political thinking, is illustrated in the readings that follow.

Selected Readings

The following titles complement the perspective taken here.

Hartz, Louis. *The Liberal Tradition in America.* New York: Harcourt Brace Jovanovich, 1955.

Hofstadter, Richard. *The American Political Tradition.* New York: Knopf, 1948.

Parrington, Vernon. *Main Currents in American Thought.* 3 vols. New York: Harcourt Brace Jovanovich, 1954.

Roelofs, Mark. *Ideology and Myth in American Politics.* Boston: Little, Brown, 1976.

Rossiter, Clinton. *Conservatism in America.* New York: Knopf, 1955.

Schlesinger, Arthur, Jr., *Cycles of American History.* Burlington, Mass.: Houghton Mifflin, 1978.

Tocqueville, Alexis de. *Democracy in America* (1841). New York: Mentor Editions, 1956.

Other perspectives indicating the richness of alternative interpretations of American political development include:

Abbot, Philip. *Furious Fancies: American Political Thought in the Post-Liberal Era.* Westport, Conn.: Greenwood Press, 1980.

Beard, Charles. *An Economic Interpretation of the Constitution of the United States* (1913). Riverside, N.J.: Free Press, 1968.

Bell, Daniel. *The Cultural Contradictions of Capitalism.* New York: Basic Books, 1976.

Bellah, Robert et al. *Habits of the Heart: Individualism and Commitment in American Life.* New York: Harper Collins, 1986.

Boorstein, Daniel. *The Genius of American Politics.* Chicago: University of Chicago Press, 1953.

Gabriel, Ralph. *The Course of American Thought.* New York: Ronald Press, 1940.

Lasch, Christopher. *The Culture of Narcissism.* New York: W.W. Norton, 1978.

Lowi, Theodore. *The End of Liberalism.* New York: Norton, 1969.

McWilliams, Wilson Carey. *The Idea of Fraternity in America.* Berkeley: University of California Press, 1973.

Potter, David. *People of Plenty: Economic Abundance and the American Character.* Chicago: University of Chicago Press, 1955.

Reisman, David. *The Lonely Crowd: A Study of Changing American Character.* New Haven: Yale University Press, 1950.

Smith, Henry Nash. *Virgin Land: The American West as Symbol and Myth.* Cambridge, Mass.: Harvard University Press, 1950.

I

The Colonial Era through the Civil War
(1630–1865)

Introduction

To understand what it means to be an American requires a look far back in history. This is particularly true given the Founding Fathers' dependence on ancient Christian beliefs and on classical Greek and Roman political thought. However, to distinguish American from European beliefs, a focus on the more immediate origins of American political thinking, principles derived largely from the colonizer Great Britain, may be sufficient. To revolt against one's parents usually means to carry along the cultural baggage of their assumptions for some time to come—if not to return to them consciously in later years.

The feudal heritage in Britain, the hierarchies of wealth, aristocracy, class, and privilege provided the background from which the American spirit would spring. For whether the constraints were religious or economic or territorial, many of those who came to the New World sought the opportunity to create a new and better society—a *novus ordo seclorum* (new order of the ages) while, at the same time, pragmatically making a better life for themselves. In this sense the restlessness and endless striving that characterize the American spirit were products of the desire to escape the Old World or to try something different. Those who were not restless and bold stayed home. As a result, compared with the feudal hierarchies in Europe, colonial America lacked an entrenched hereditary elite in the social structure to form a government. After the first generation had arrived, leaders necessarily emerged as they made their way up the social hierarchy through planting, trade, and the professions. The abundance of opportunities and uncultivated land seemed endless, providing the seedbed for American optimism, Yankee ingenuity, and tolerance for conflicting beliefs and cultural backgrounds.

In looking to the European theorists with the most immediate influence on the thinking of American founders, pointing out a few rather than too many may enable the reader to see the forest, not just the trees.

Two British theorists who were of some importance in preparing the groundwork of early American thinking were Thomas Hobbes and John Locke. Both resorted to the moral fiction of a social contract, and both believed in natural law. Their differences, however, are more important than their similarities, and Hobbes is significant largely to the extent that the Founding Fathers absorbed the residue of Hobbes still left in Locke.

In *Leviathan* (1651), Hobbes argued that life in the state of nature was "nasty, brutish, and short" and that the state of nature was nothing but an egoistic state of war of all against all. With all human beings set to maximize their own material interests out of a natural desire for self-preservation, the only way to prevent chaos was for them to agree in a social contract to surrender their natural rights to everything to a sovereign or state, which would then keep law and order and protect existing property. Life under government was, according to Hobbes, much better than life in the state of nature.

While Locke's theory a few decades later also took up Hobbes's focus on individualism, assumption of natural rights, and notion of social contract with a sovereign, his view of the state of nature was one of "peace, good will, mutual assistance, and preservation." In his *Second Treatise on Civil Government* (1690), Locke defended the Whig-led "Glorious Revolution" of 1688. The only defect in the state of nature according to Locke is that it lacks a common judge to interpret the law of nature and a government to impose sanctions against violators. Right or wrong are eternally so—prior to the existence of law. Governments exist to use their laws to enforce what is naturally and morally right. Locke asserted that the natural right to private property precedes the social compact. The right to property arises because individuals extend their own personalities into the objects produced from the state of nature. And the "life, liberty, and estate" (or property) of one person can only be limited to make effective the equally valid claims of another person to the same rights.

So the natural right of each person to life, liberty, and property was considered self-evident (or derived by a "higher law") by Locke and was so adopted by the Founding Fathers, although Thomas Jefferson converted it to "life, liberty, and the pursuit of happiness." The social contract between individuals thus precedes government, which is obligated to fulfill it. Locke's division of power between the executive and legislative branches of government was purely functional. He maintained that in view of human frailty, the same persons should not hold the power to both make and execute the laws, because the executives would then be able to exempt themselves from obedience to the law. Yet Locke knew that parliamentary England had no neat separation between the executive and legislative. He did not really consider separation of powers in the contemporary sense. He had no theory of the importance of perpetually putting these two powers in separate hands to preserve liberty, guarantee rights, or keep the constitution in harmony. Yet he did advocate a separation of religion and civil government, as noted in his "Letter on Tolerance" of 1689.

Government itself is derived by the consent of the majority, who have a right to revolution if this trust fails to protect their property. Legislative power is supreme in government according to Locke, although the powers of both the executive and legislative branches are limited. Locke provided the American colonists with many justifications and phrases for opposing the imposition of arbitrary power by the state. He did not come to grips, however, with the potential for imposition of arbitrary power by the majority over any particular minority. The Americans had to innovate institutionally to prevent legislative power from getting out of hand. And Locke's contribution to the third branch of government, judicial review (so critical to the success of the American system), is but inferential.

The importance of the judicial branch in the separation of governmental powers and checks and balances to maintain individual rights was derived from Baron de Montesquieu's *The Spirit of the Laws* (1748). Jefferson called Book XI "the most precious gift the present age has received." Founding Father James Madison took this lesson to heart in "Federalist No. 10." Montesquieu asserted that governments are of three kinds: *republican* (a conflation of democracy and aristocracy, based on his idealization of civic virtue in the Roman republic), *monarchical,* and *despotic.* He ascribed liberty in England to the separation of the legislative, executive, and judicial powers, and to the balancing of these powers against each other—the recipe for constructing a liberal constitution. To be convinced of the influence of Montesquieu, one need but read these words from Book XI:

The political liberty of the subject is a tranquillity of mind arising from the opinion each person has of his safety. In order to have this liberty, it is requisite the government be so constituted as one man need not be afraid of another. When the legislative and executive powers are united in the same person, or in the same body of magistrates, there can be no liberty; because apprehensions may arise, lest the same monarch or senate should enact tyrannical laws, to execute them in a tyrannical manner. Again, there is no liberty, if the judiciary power be not separated from the legislative and executive. Were it joined with the legislative, the life and liberty of the subject would be exposed to arbitrary control; for the judge would be then the legislator. Were it joined to the executive power, the judge might behave with violence and oppression.

Montesquieu's heritage involves a number of conservative balances aimed to preserve democratic liberalism: the "republican" balance between representative democracy and aristocracy, the separation of executive, legislative, and judicial powers, and the playing off of these powers one against the other.

Of course, Americans in the eighteenth century had other models for individual liberty and liberal republicanism. The issue of republicanism as against monarchical government was embodied in the diverse works of Algernon Sidney, John Milton, and James Harrington, all admirers of antiquity and the aristocratic republic. But whereas Milton and Sidney defended republicanism on the abstract ground that it was implied by natural law and the sovereign power of the people, Harrington defended republicanism as a consequence of the social shift of economic power in England. John Milton wrote brilliantly against the stupidities and futilities of censorship in *Aeropagitica* (1644) and repeated the ancient principle that resistance to a tyrant is a natural right in *Tenure of Kings and Magistrates* (1649). He asserted that men are born free and set up governments for the sake of mutual defense, and that public authority, embodied in the magistrate, replaces each man's right to protect himself. The law is established to limit and control public authority, whereas the right to protect the common good against a tyrant always resides in the people.

The contribution of seventeenth-century aristocrat James Harrington to republicanism was more original than that of Milton. Founding Father John Adams was much impressed. Harrington advocated a new republican order that would replace the "Gothic balance" ruled by aristocrats with an "equal agrarian" society. Yeoman farmers would compose a broader class of gentry, with an upper limit on landholding, so as to create a new social base for a republican government. In his fictionalized political treatise, *Oceana* (1656), Harrington illustrates (as Adams puts it) that "power always follows property." Other familiar notions from *Oceana* that impressed the founders were the ideal of an "Empire of laws and not of men," the written constitution, the separation of powers, and liberal suffrage combined with short terms of office. For the founders, Harrington's experimental republican thinking made him a model constitutional designer and tinkerer of the sort they must become.

The American literary diet included ample servings of the writings and life story of Algernon Sidney, the "British Brutus," who was beheaded for championing liberal-republican views, only to be venerated as a martyr by Americans. Sidney's *Discourses Concerning Government,* written between 1680 and 1683, but unpublished until 1698, was not original, but impressed Jefferson nevertheless. It argued that all people have a natural right to govern themselves and can select rulers as they see fit. Government, in turn, derives its power from the people, exists for their safety and well-being, and can be held accountable for these purposes. Certain passages make it clear why this text was used as evidence against Sidney for his complicity in the Rye House Plot before he was executed. At one point, for example, he asks men to examine

> whether bawds, whores, thieves, buffoons, parasites, and such vile wretches as are naturally mercenary, have not more power at Whitehall, Versailles, the Vatican, and the Escurial, than in Venice, Amsterdam, and Switzerland: whether Hide, Arlington, Danby, their graces of Cleveland and Portsmouth, Sunderland, Jenkins, or Chiffinch, could probably have attained such power as they have had amongst us, if it had been disposed of by the suffrages of the Parliament and the people.

Let it not be said that liberal republicanism is incapable of being cast as a passionate, populist creed.

Some contemporary scholars, such as J. G. A. Pocock, even go so far as to maintain that the importance of the republican influence on the founders was greater than that of Locke's. Writing in the *Journal of the History of Ideas* in 1987, Pocock argues: "The republican ... discourse of the eighteenth century ... made no significant appeal to Lockean formulae, and neither did many of those who constructed the reply or counter-discourse which it encountered." Pocock's stress on republicanism to the exclusion of Locke's vision of liberalism is too extreme. Nevertheless, it is worth noting that contemporary analysts of American thinking both to the left and the right of the mainstream tradition of American liberalism stress the republican influence because it creates a "usable past." Those to the Left, such as Robert Bellah and Michael Sandel, focus on the values of community, while those to the Right, such as Walter Berns and Hadley Arkes, praise civic virtue as a value with priority over liberty.

What is clear from weighing the contributions of these various European influences on American political thinking is that the thrust is to prevent individual rights from being taken away by arbitrary power and to assert the positive natural rights of all individuals that precede society and the founding of the state. Liberalism connotes human rights (life, liberty) and property rights, which sometimes are in tension. Slavery, for example, was first justified in terms of property rights and later outlawed on the basis of human rights. In cases of tension between human and property rights it often appears administratively easier (and politically more agreeable to the increasing number of people with property) to dwell on individual rights in terms of the adequate protection of private property. Locke did so implicitly in using private property rights as a metaphor for other human rights. Frequent conservative interpretations of the Lockean elements of liberalism absorbed by American government have preserved the status quo based on the constitutional necessity of protecting private property as a primary political objective.

However, this is but one reason why American liberalism may appear to be based on a conservative framework. American institutions that have grown out of inherited republican traditions provide other reasons. Indeed those institutions are haunted with names of Latin derivation in deference to the Roman republic: republic (preferred by the founders to the Greek term "democracy"), president, senate, congress, candidate, nominate, and capitol. To prevent any one person or group from upsetting this government framework by seizing too much power and destabilizing the system, the Founding Fathers further elaborated upon the ideas of Montesquieu by including the separation of powers and checks and balances in drafting the Constitution. Supreme Court justices such as John Marshall extended this diffusion of powers (enhancing particularly those of the judiciary) to legitimate the central authority of the federal government. And as American thinking and Supreme Court decision making shifted more toward human rights than property rights after Franklin Roosevelt's New Deal, this shift merely served to consolidate the strength of the stabilizing Enlightenment framework of American liberalism by integrating minorities into the mainstream. And as the sophisticated religious and republican origins of the American founding fade further into the past, leaving the contemporary focus on the individual freedoms and legal rights of liberalism, the temptation increases for conventional consensus to affirm that what exists today is the best of all possible constitutional frameworks, the best of all possible states—the essential conservative assumption of America's liberal faith. For what could be more conservative than to assume that "the political problem" has been solved, that the constitutional framework has been set up once and for all, and that but for seeing to it that our basic human and property rights are protected, we can leave politics to the politicians and go on about our private business?

Although it is not too difficult to understand the European political thoughts that crossed the Atlantic, it may be more significant to assess the influence of what did *not* cross. The absence of the feudal hierarchy and fixed, traditional ways of doing things left room for and even encouraged the spread of religious, sectional, and ethnic differences and rivalries. Because no one had "won" and anyone white and male could "play," strong contention for position and influence emerged among competing groups.

In Virginia frontier people vied against older Virginia settlements: the Piedmont poor versus the Tidewater aristocracy. New York, Maryland, and Pennsylvania suffered constant conflicts between ethnic and religious minorities (and who is to say that anything fundamental has changed?). With all this group competition about and no feudal or aristocratic order traditionally accepted as superior, deference to the "wisdom" of one's social betters was easily overcome as individuals and groups struggled for their place in the sun.

Colonial life was characterized by rough and ready social turmoil. Civil disobedience started as a subtheme and eventually became the main theme of the New World. By the end of the seventeenth century America had witnessed a number of insurrections by settlers from England and Holland—starting with the "thrusting out" of Virginia's Governor Harvey in 1635, Culpeper's Rebellion in Carolina, the Protestant Association in Maryland, Bacon's Rebellion in Virginia, the seizure of power by Leisler in New York, and the ultimate overthrow of Andros in New England. The stage was set, but every religious and political group was trying to move the props around at the same time.

1. The Colonial Mind: From Religious to Political Autonomy

The emerging tradition of American liberalism can be said to have been embodied by the Englishman Roger Williams, who established the colony of Rhode Island. Williams was a rebel who sided with the congregation's sovereignty over the Puritan church hierarchy and ultimately attacked undemocratic governments. His passionate *The Bloudy Tenent, of*

Persecution, for Cause of Conscience (1644) not only attacked the writings of conservative minister John Cotton, but made a clear case for religious toleration, freedom of conscience, and separation of church and state.

On the other side of the colonial political spectrum, Puritan John Winthrop, first governor of Massachusetts Bay colony, represented Puritan covenantalism. He set up a theocracy in America as Calvin had done in Geneva. Through a loophole in a charter granted from Charles I, a mercantile charter took on the character of a constitution for a self-governed community. On the boat trip over, Winthrop drew up his objectives for the colony—"A Modell of Christian Charity" (1630). This document is a strikingly egalitarian and communitarian statement for its times. As the authority on American Puritanism, Perry Miller, summed it up: "It held that a body politic could be constituted only out of the consent of the governed, yet also out of an agreement not to terms of people's own devising but only to the pre-stated terms of God's eternal law of justice and subordination." This form of Puritan covenantalism established a religious foundation for government by consent, the very essence of modern representative democracy. Winthrop's principle of self-government is contingent upon the condition that God's law is binding on the people. This is not unlike Locke's notion that people who are free to give their consent to government in the social contract are also required to obey the natural law because it is God's law and they are creatures of God. Winthrop had little faith in democracy and believed that representatives selected to govern should have the right to govern on the basis of their own judgment, a view later generations would find too oligarchic, even authoritarian. In "A Little Speech on Liberty" (1645), Winthrop discusses the nature of elected representatives and the distinction between natural and civil liberty.

The positive contribution of Winthrop's democratic thinking of Puritan covenantalism can be contrasted with that of the conservative principal spokesman for American Puritanism, Cotton Mather, who sought to centralize control of church doctrine and practice, particularly in the late part of his life. Mather's classic "An Essay Upon the Good" (1710) illustrates the self-righteousness of a true believer. His insatiable ego could never find enough projects to exhaust its energy.

Not to be outdone when it came to the notion of predestined virtue was Jonathan Edwards. He was an admirer of John Locke and defended strict Calvinism (the doctrine of predestination plus good works on this earth), excluding from full communion members of his congregation who did not live up to his high standard. Edwards inspired the "Great Awakening" among New England Calvinists, an event best summed up by his title: *A Faithful Narrative of the Surprising Work of God in the Conversion of Many Hundred Souls in Northampton and the Neighboring Towns and Villages* (1737).

2. American Values and Pragmatic Self-sufficiency

Puritan morality has always been a deep-seated part of the American value structure and can be best illustrated in terms of its contemporary relevance through the *Autobiography* (1789) of Benjamin Franklin, who was practical enough to make virtue pay off in this world. Unlike Aristotle, who recommended doing good for its own sake, Franklin was more dedicated to doing good for the positive worldly consequences. He was the ultimate busy, virtuous, inventive, pragmatic, witty, and wise American. Self-help was his specialty, and he helped many others on the way with his *Poor Richard's Almanack,* inventions such as the Franklin stove and lightning rod, his plan for the union, an essay on the advantages of preferring old women to young, retouches of Jefferson's draft of the Declaration, and his invisible hand behind the scenes at the constitutional convention.

An answer to "What is an American?" can be found in Hector St. John de Crèvecoeur's essay of the same title, included here from *Letters from an American Farmer* (1782). This writing serves up French agrarian virtue and self-sufficiency in excellent literary style, letting us in on the secrets of "this great American asylum" and illustrating why Jefferson campaigned for agrarian democracy (and perhaps why he seemed partial to French liberalism).

3. Individual Rights and the Declaration of Independence

Proving that nothing is so uncommon as common sense, Thomas Paine's pamphlet "Common Sense" (1776), heavily excerpted here, was timed perfectly to mobilize the independence movement and made the case for reconciliation with Britain appear absurd given American ideals. If anything, this classic is underrated today. "Common Sense" details why the government that governs best governs least. It also makes a penetrating argument for a *negative* concept of government that even at the end of the twentieth century limits possible federal domestic action in the context of constraints underlying American liberalism. At the time, it raised the question whether or not the Declaration of Independence needed an outsider to bring it into being. Paine represented someone who had been in the colonies only thirteen months and was depressed with the repression in Britain, his home country, that same country repressing the colonies. Paine also had the effect of mobilizing conservative reaction in 1776. John Adams, for example, criticized Paine for promoting an excess of democracy. By 1805, Adams had let his critique fester so that he wrote to a correspondent:

> I am willing you should call this the Age of Frivolity, as you do: and would not object if you had named it the Age of Folly, Vice, Frenzy, Fury, Brutality, Demons, Bonaparte, Tom Paine, or the Age of the Burning Brand from the bottomless Pit: or anything but the Age of Reason. I know not whether any man in the world has had more influence on its inhabitants or affairs for the last thirty years than Tom Paine. There can be no severer satire on the age.

Paine died poor and socially excluded in New York City, the coffin containing his remains passed on to a furniture dealer.

George Mason was an intellectual who also furthered greatly the cause of individual rights. He drafted the Virginia Declaration of Rights (1776), which served as a model for other states. Because the Constitution lacked a bill of rights (among other flaws he found), Mason led the unsuccessful fight with Patrick Henry against its ratification.

Thomas Jefferson, who called Mason a great man, was intellectually his superior in ability to synthesize both English and French traditions of liberalism in a harmonious, human way on the behalf of Virginia and then the Union. Virginia, the first British colony in America to alter its political structure, became a blueprint for others. Jefferson was instrumental in this, as in so many other efforts. His idealistic faith in agrarian democracy colored everything he touched, as one can sense in reading "his" Declaration of Independence (1776), excerpts from his *Autobiography* (1821), or his famous letter to John Adams related to the role of the aristocracy (1813).

4. The Constitution: Constructive Conservatism and Its Critics

John Adams responded to Jefferson, of course, with an equally famous letter defending natural aristocracy (1813). Adams was an erudite, conservative Federalist who greatly admired the British parliamentary system. He believed that the aristocracy could through government policy help the poor better than they could help themselves. He wrote "a Defence of the Constitutions of Government of the United States of America" (1787), excerpted here, and devoted himself to the collective interests of the nation, becoming its second president.

Something about Virginia seems to make its partisans love it above everything else, perhaps even above the nation. At least this appeared to be the case with Patrick Henry, the brilliant orator who never wrote down a speech, but rallied the people of Virginia to independence—"Give Me Liberty or Give me Death" (1775)—and then when independence from Britain was achieved, he tried just as persuasively to rally them to oppose ratification of the Constitution in 1788. He believed the Virginians' rights were not sufficiently protected by the Constitution, and he helped pave the way for the first ten amendments added on belatedly as the Bill of Rights.

Richard Henry Lee was another great orator from Virginia who was skeptical of the centralized powers granted to the federal government. Whether he wrote *Letters from a Federal Farmer to the Republican* (1787–1788), excerpted here, is uncertain, but likely. There was a refreshing tradition during the founding of the republic of caring more about the impact of ideas than taking credit for them. Many influential articles and pamphlets were initially published anonymously. A cogent example is "Letters of Brutus, No. 11" (January, 1788) by Anti-Federalist Robert Yates. He was incredibly prescient in his prediction that the power of judicial review could develop into an effective veto over legislative power.

The Federalist Papers (1787–1788) were actually the idea of Alexander Hamilton, Thomas Jefferson's political opponent. Hamilton believed that a financial aristocracy should run the country. However, before his somewhat radical beliefs developed, he settled down to write nearly fifty of *The Federalist* essays in defense of the Constitution. James Madison wrote about thirty, and John Jay, five. These papers represent perhaps the peak of American political thinking and the ultimate statement on the meaning of the Constitution. Eleven are included here. They were published anonymously in newspapers under the name "Publius."

The most famous of *The Federalist Papers* is undoubtedly "No. 10," authored by James Madison. He so desired to separate and to check and balance power that the federal government could hardly do anything without the consensus of all critical groups involved. Madison's structure sought a balance between the powers of the majorities and of the minorities, and between the political equality of all adult citizens and limits upon their sovereignty. On the one hand, Madison feared the potential for tyranny of certain factions of interest groups; on the other, he feared that a dynamic, egalitarian majority in the House of Representatives might ride roughshod over minorities. He and the other brilliant founders were realists who did the best they could in their times, but they overestimated the potential for tyranny of majorities. They also underestimated the power of the presidency, which, starting with President Jackson, could come to symbolize the sole representative of the popular majority, and they neglected the role of the judiciary. Moreover, they relied too much upon checks and balances among government officials and too little upon checks and balances among socioeconomic forces. As political theorist Robert Dahl wrote in *A Preface to Democratic Theory* (1956): "They did not really understand that in an agrarian society lacking feudal institutions and possessing an open and expanding frontier, radical democracy was almost certain to become the dominant and conventional view, almost certain to prevail in politics, and almost certain to be conservative about property." Popular, democratic affirmation of the importance of protecting private property and of protecting individual freedom through a multitude of checks and balances in the government consolidated Madison's design, transforming it, in effect, into a conservative tradition that has shaped American liberal democracy.

Madison was so influential at the Constitutional Convention that he is often referred to as the "father of the Constitution." The Constitution, after all, was more concerned with constraining people from possible tyranny than with giving any branch of government so much power that it could easily do good. Of course Madison was not responsible for the compromise (which he opposed) of giving all states an equal vote in the Senate and of other arrangements that revised his own design. As a whole, the Constitution was more the product of republican planters and merchants than of the radical revolutionaries, who tended to stay home from the Constitutional Convention and fight against the Constitution's ratification in their home states. But, then again, those capable of pulling off a revolution are not always temperamentally the best people to work through the administrative principles necessary to manage a country.

5. Federalism and Constitutional Law

The most noble and symbolic of the Federalists was undoubtedly the first elected president, George Washington, who advised Americans in his "Farewell Address" (1796) to avoid foreign entanglements and to rise above petty disputes and factional interests for the sake of national unity. He struck two main chords of American governance that have been played many times since: the need for individual and interest group sacrifice for national objectives, and the degree to which American can afford to be isolationist and avoid becoming involved in military conflicts in Europe and elsewhere.

Washington's Federalist or national-unity assumptions were reinforced even more strongly by Federalists who followed him, including Chief Justice John Marshall and Daniel Webster in the early nineteenth century. Their task was not an easy one. The spread of populist democracy ideology linked Jefferson's Democrats ultimately to the public appeals of President Andrew Jackson. Recall John Adams's pejorative reference to the beginning of this era as the "Age of Folly" or the "Age of Tom Paine"—clearly the bias of an aristocratic Federalist.

Chief Justice John Marshall invented constitutional law, as illustrated in his two seminal cases excerpted here: *Marbury v. Madison* (1803) and *McCulloch v. Maryland* (1819).

Daniel Webster helped him by making strong appeals in his legal advocacy before Marshall's Court as well as in the Senate for the power of the central government to be included in the Constitution. Never again would the Court exist in the shadows of the executive and legislative branches. Webster's famous "Reply to Hayne" (1830) makes a powerful case for individuals and interest groups to transcend sectional or state interests for the nation's larger community goals as steered by the federal government.

6. Jacksonian Democracy

Populist democracy had its moment in the sun under President Andrew Jackson who took on the power of the Bank of the United States and other interest groups in the name of the average citizen. His strong, disciplinarian leadership style contradicted his democratic ideological objectives, which came to him rather late in life—in his campaign for president.

But no one doubts the lasting influence of his ability to bypass Congress and appeal directly to the people for objectives he believed to be in the national interest. American liberalism had found another way to extend the sense of popular participation without significantly restructuring the existing conservative constitutional framework. Jackson's "Farewell Address" (1837) epitomizes this contribution to American political thinking.

7. Transcendental Individualism

It is but one step from America's liberalism to transcendental idealism or humanism, as in the transcendentalist school of Ralph Waldo Emerson and Henry David Thoreau. Emerson summed up the nature of this moral and radical democratic thinking: "Give me health and a day, and I will make the pomp of emperors ridiculous." Or: "If the single man plant himself indomitably on his instincts, and there abide, the huge world will come round to him." Looking to nature as a guide and having faith in individual instincts and self-reliance, transcendentalism was not comforting for the political status quo. "Let us honestly state the facts, Our America has a bad name for superficialness. Great men, great nations, have not been boasters and buffoons, but perceivers of the terror of life, and have maimed themselves to face it." Thus spoke Emerson as if from his own planet. His essays "Self-Reliance" (1841) and "Politics" (1844) demonstrate the great style and substance of this perspective. Were he to introduce his close friend Henry David Thoreau, he might well have said (as he did in "Self-Reliance"): "Whoso would be a man must be a non-conformist."

Thoreau was truly a man apart—one who would undoubtedly be a militant protesting ecologist, libertarian, or anarchist if alive today. He made a myth of himself by building his hut on Walden Pond on Emerson's property and describing it in truly transcendental terms in his classic *Walden, Or, Life in the Woods* (1854). The immortal message here is to avoid the superficial materialistic goals of society and go back to the simplicity of nature, find resources at hand, and create a self-built nest and social reality worthy of a truly human spirit.

Thoreau went to jail (overnight) for refusing to pay taxes, which he regarded as unjust. He later wrote the essay "Civil Disobedience" (1849), which was to be rediscovered and used to great political effect by Mahatma Gandhi in India's independence movement and by Martin Luther King, Jr. in the American civil rights movement. There was, in short, a practical, whole-earth quality to Thoreau's transcendental individualism: "The Youth gets together his materials to build a bridge to the moon, or, perchance, a palace or temple on the earth, and, at length, the middle-aged man concludes to build a woodshed with them."

8. Neglected Voices: Women and Native Americans

If the voices of Emerson and Thoreau seem too idealistic, too individualistic, almost *too American* to be credible (at least in the mainstream culture of the end of the twentieth century) consider the isolation of such idealism if embodied in anyone but a white male in the nineteenth century. Women could not vote and were discriminated against economically by a male-dominated society. And as for the native American, the white man all but eradicated him and his culture.

Elizabeth Cady Stanton (joining later with Susan B. Anthony) was the leading feminist in the first half of the nineteenth century. Her vibrant energy shows in her first political speech given at the first women's convention organized to demand female suffrage, "The Seneca Falls Declaration" (1848). She had the ability to come to the political point without beating about the bush. For example, in an address to the New York State Legislature in 1854 she said:

> Look at the position of woman as woman. It is not enough for us that by your laws we are permitted to live and breathe, to claim the necessaries of life from our legal protectors— to pay the penalty of our crimes; we demand the full recognition of all our rights as citizens of the Empire State. We are persons; native, free-born citizens; property-holders, tax-payers; yet we are denied the right to the elective franchise. . . . We have every qualification required by the Constitution, necessary to the legal voter, but the one of sex.

Sixty six years later women received the right to vote with the passage of the Nineteenth Amendment.

The perspective from the native American viewpoint is even more depressing. In fact, Chief Seattle's prophetic 1853 speech, nominally entitled here "The Indians' Night Promises to Be Dark," was so perceptive that one almost comes to the conclusion that too much wisdom blocks political action for the sake of social justice. If one can predict the future too clearly, the motive for radical action in the present may be diminished. Seattle's reconciliation with whites can be viewed either this way or from the more typical native American perspective of seeking harmony with nature and one's fellow creatures as the only legitimate moral form of behavior.*

9. Political and Economic Slavery

African-Americans, of course, were not necessarily better off than native Americans, although there were more of them. Therefore, it was more difficult to get around the problem or to eradicate them. One plan, attacked by abolitionist William Lloyd Garrison in *The Liberator* (1831), was to ship the slaves back to Africa (an idea dropped because Americans did not want to bear the cost). Garrison demanded an immediate end to slavery on moral, not political, grounds. He differed in this respect from Frederick Douglass, a slave who managed to work his way into freedom through education, escape, and political activism [see excerpts here from his classic *Narrative of the Life of Frederick Douglass* (1845)]. Douglass wrote his own abolition journals, starting with the *North Star,* and saw the Constitution as potentially antislavery and not a "Covenant with Death" as Garrison viewed it. Douglass joined political organizations and eventually (reluctantly) became a Republican—the party of Lincoln, founded in large part to represent the abolitionist viewpoint.

On the other side of the political spectrum, George Fitzhugh argued in *Cannibals All!* (1857) that to be a slave was better than to be a free laborer and be *truly* exploited.

---

*It is difficult to find the most powerful speeches of native Americans in the adult sections of libraries: they tend to be collected in the children's sections, where their simplicity is no obstacle to communication.

Even more extreme was Orestes A. Brownson, who in "The Laboring Classes" (1840) carried the logic of Jacksonian democracy to its conclusion, arguing that inheritance of private property and the industrial and factory systems ought to be abolished because civil rights can only exist if equality of condition exists. Brownson demonstrated the limits of the traditional mainstream of American liberalism; he was thrown out of the Democratic party upon publication of this essay.

John C. Calhoun deployed a more diplomatic solution for minority representation and states' rights in *A Disquisition on Government* (1851), written in the mature, final years of his life. Starting with the right of suffrage as the primary principle in founding a constitutional government, Calhoun argued that this principle is insufficient to prevent tyranny where diverse and conflicting interests make up a community. A true constitutional government must assess the community's attitude by paying attention to interests as well as numbers. As a result, a "concurrent majority" would permit interests to have veto powers against a mere majority of numbers. In constitutional terms, this would mean that the Union had been formed by the several states combining, but not submerging, their separate sovereignties. States, accordingly, remained free agents with the right to give or withdraw their assent as they saw fit to acts of the federal government. Southern states could maintain slavery even if a majority of states became non–slave owning. Calhoun's proposal would have radically altered the constitutional system, making the United States confederal (or, technically, consociational) rather than federal—like Switzerland.

10. Overcoming Slavery and the Civil War

Last but not least, we come to the climax of the slavery issue: the Lincoln–Douglas Debates of 1858, which made Lincoln famous, although Douglas later won the Senate election. The debates addressed whether or not slavery should be permitted to spread to new states of the Union if the people in those states voted for it. Douglas said yes; Lincoln was opposed. Indeed it was this issue of the potential spread of slavery that called him back into politics from his law practice in Illinois. He then, of course, went on to win the presidential election against Douglas and to free the slaves with "The Emancipation Proclamation" (1863), which he shrewdly labeled a military national security measure during the Civil War. "The Gettysburg Address" (1863), his letter to Henry L. Pierce (1859), and his "Second Inaugural Address" (1865) complete the picture of his efforts to reunite the United States during its greatest crisis—through and after the Civil War— in his typical, rough-hewn, classical style: sparse, practical, self-taught, elegant, and unquestionably American.

Lincoln understood as few politicians do that politics must have a moral edge to it to touch greatness and must never depart from this moral commitment. Yet he was practical, pragmatic, and enigmatic. His words hold as true today as they did in 1862, in his "Second Annual Message to Congress": "If there ever could be a proper time for mere catch arguments, that time surely is not now. In times like the present, men should utter nothing for which they would not willingly be responsible through time and eternity."

Selected Readings

Bailyn, Bernard. *The Ideological Origins of the American Revolution.* Cambridge: Harvard University Press, 1967.

Beard, Charles. *An Economic Interpretation of the American Revolution.* New York: Free
      Press, 1935.

Becker, Carl. *The Declaration of Independence.* New York: Random House, 1958.

Corwin, Edwin S. *The Higher Law Background of American Constitutionalism.* Ithaca, N.Y.:
      Cornell University Press, 1955.

Farrand, Max. *The Framing of the Constitution.* New Haven, Conn.: Yale University Press,
      1913.

Genovese, Eugene. *Roll, Jordan, Roll.* New York: Random House, 1976.

Hofstadter, Richard. *America at 1750.* New York: Random House, 1973.

Lloyd, Arthur Y. *The Slavery Controversy, 1831–1860.* Chapel Hill: University of North
      Carolina Press, 1939.

Lynd, Straughton. *The Intellectual Origins of American Radicalism.* New York: Vintage, 1969.

Miller, Perry. *The New England Mind.* Boston: Beacon Press, 1961.

Miller, Perry. *The Life of the Mind in America.* New York: Harcourt, Brace and World, 1965.

Parrington, Vernon. *The Colonial Mind: 1620–1800.* New York: Harcourt, Brace and World,
      1927.

Parrington, Vernon. *The Beginnings of Critical Realism in America.* New York: Harcourt,
      Brace and World, 1930.

Pocock, J. G. A. *Three British Revolutions: 1641, 1688, 1776.* Princeton, N.J.: Princeton
      University Press, 1980.

Rossiter, Clinton. *Seed-Time of the Republic;.* New York: Harcourt, Brace and World, 1953.

Schlessinger, Arthur M., Jr. *The Age of Jackson.* Boston: Little, Brown, 1945.

Tyler, Alice Felt. *Freedom's Ferment.* Minneapolis: University of Minnesota Press, 1944.

Wolf, Hazel C. *On Freedom's Altar.* Madison: University of Wisconsin Press, 1952.

Wood, Gordon S. *The Confederation and the Constitution: The Critical Issues.* Lanham, Md.:
      University Press of America, 1979.

The Colonial Mind:
From Religious to Political Autonomy

1

Roger Williams

Born in London, most likely in 1603, Roger Williams established the colony of Rhode Island based upon the principles of religious toleration and the separation of church and state. With a natural inclination to study, Williams received his B.A. with honors at Pembroke College, Cambridge. He joined John Cotton and Thomas Hooker in the conference of the founders of the Massachusetts colony and settled there as "a godly minister." But Williams found himself once more where there was no freedom for those who did not conform. His open criticism of the Puritan regime resulted in hostility. He argued that civil governments had no power to enforce the religious injunctions of the Ten Commandments. Accepting a call to teach at Salem Church, Williams was rejected by the authorities and went to Plymouth. He returned to Salem two years later and served as assistant to Reverend Skelton. He became controversial immediately by attacking the clergy meetings as a threat to the liberties of the church congregation.

In Williams one senses the origins of the creed of American liberalism. When Skelton died, Williams took over his spot in defiance of the General Court but with the support of the congregation. Then Williams attacked both England's imperialistic seizure of American lands belonging to the Indians and the oath used by the oligarchy in Massachusetts to keep the lower orders under submissive discipline. With their power position threatened by this growing movement for a more democratic church system, the ministers and magistrates summoned Willliams to the General Court in 1635 and found him guilty of "newe and dangerous opinions, against the aucthoritie of magistrates" and banished him. Williams tried to organize his followers to colonize Narragansett, but was blocked by the authorities. He found cover with friendly Indians at Sowans and eventually gathered enough followers to purchase land from the Indians and found Providence, the earliest Rhode Island settlement, in 1636.

The Pequot War and later conflicts proved that Williams lived up to the tolerance he preached. He helped his former political opponents and consistently demonstrated that he was a friend of the Indians, protesting unfair measures of the Puritan colonies. He preached to the Narrangansetts without trying to convert them, and after a brief interval as a Baptist became a Seeker—accepting no creed, yet maintaining basic Christian principles. Frontier conditions and Williams's liberalism spawned local town governments, primitive early versions of democracy. Heads of family had equal voice, and Williams organized a democratic land association to help settlers obtain land.

Through the New England Confederation, the Puritan colonies attempted to consolidate their position and tried to snuff out fringe colonies that advocated religious and democratic freedom. While Puritan political leaders negotiated in England for the right to control the whole area, an invasion of Rhode Island led to the abduction and jailing of some key settlers. Williams countered the threat by going to London and, with the aid of Sir Henry Vane, obtained a patent for the area to secure Rhode Island's freedoms. It was in England that Williams published the famous *The Bloudy Tenent, of Persecution, for Cause of Conscience* (1644) excerpted here. He boldly proclaimed that all people have a natural right to religious liberty and attacked the undemocratic nature of contemporary governments. He argued that sovereignty lies with the people, not with kings, parliaments, states, or governors.

Upon returning, Williams spent the rest of his life in political struggles, pamphleteering for the sake of democratic principles and religious liberty and serving three terms as president of the Rhode Island colony. While he was in office, Jews and Quakers sought refuge in Rhode Island, and Williams headed off a threat to land owned by the Indians. He died in 1683, after the bitter experience of seeing Providence burned to the ground and the Narragansett tribe split up and enslaved as a result of King Philip's war.

⚜

The Bloudy Tenent, of Persecution, for Cause of Conscience (1644)

(excerpt)

First, That the blood of so many hundred thousand soules of *Protestants and Papists*, split in the *Wars* of *present* and *former Ages*, for their respective *Consciences*, is not *required* nor *accepted* by Jesus Christ the *Prince of Peace.*

Secondly, Pregnant *Scriptures* and *Arguments* are throughout the Worke proposed against the *Doctrine* of *persecution* for *cause* of *Conscience.*

Thirdly, Satisfactorie Answers are given to *Scriptures*, and objections produced by Mr. *Calvin, Beza*, Mr. *Cotton*, and the Ministers of the New English Churches and others former and later, tending to prove the *Doctrine of persecution* for cause of *Conscience.*

Fourthly, The *Doctrine of persecution* for cause of *Conscience*, is proved guilty of all the *blood* of the *Soules* crying for *vengeance* under the *Altar.*

Fifthly, All *Civill States* with their *Officers* of *justice* in their respective *constitutions* and *administrations* are proved *essentially Civill*, and therefore not *Judges, Governours* or *Defendours* of the *Spirituall* or *Christian-state* and *Worship.*

Sixtly, It is the will and command of *God*, that (since the comming of his Sonne the *Lord Jesus*) a *permission* of the most *Paganish, Jewish, Turkish*, or *Antichristian consciences* and *worships*, bee granted to *all* men in all *Nations* and *Countries*: and they are onely to bee *fought* against with that *Sword* which is only (in *Soule matters*) *able* to *conquer*, to wit, the *Sword of Gods Spirit*, the *Word* of *God.*

Seventhly, The slate of the Land of *Israel*, the *Kings* and *people* thereof in *Peace & War*, is proved *figurative* and *ceremoniall*, and no *patterne* nor *president* for any *Kingdome* or *civill state* in the *world* to follow.

Eightly, *God* requireth not an *uniformity* of *Religion* to be *inacted* and *inforced* in any *civill state*; which inforced *uniformity* (sooner or later) is the greatest occasion of *civill Warre, ravishing* of *conscience, persecution* of *Christ Jesus* in his servants, and of the *hypocrisie* and *destruction* of *millions* of souls.

Ninthly, In holding an inforced *uniformity* of *Religion* in a *civill state*, wee must necessarily *disclaime* our desires and hopes of the *Jewes conversion to Christ.*

Tenthly, An inforced *uniformity* of *Religion* throughout a *Nation* or *civill state*, confounds the *Civill* and *Religious*, denies the principles of Christianity and civility, and that *Jesus Christ* is come in the Fifth.

Eleventhly, The permission of other *consciences* and *worships* then a state professeth, only can (according to God) procure a firme and lasting *peace*, (good *assurance* being taken according to the *wisedome* of the *civill state* for *uniformity* of *civill obedience* from all forts.)

Twelfthly, lastly, true *civility* and *Christianity* may both flourish in a *state* or *Kingdome*, notwithstanding the *permission* of divers and contrary *consciences*, either of *Jew* or *Gentile*.

To the Right Honorable,
both Houses of the High Court
of Parliament

Right Honourable and Renowned Patriots:

Next to the saving of your own *soules* (in the lamentable *shipwrack* of *Mankind*) your taske (as *Christians*) is to save the *Soules*, but as *Magistrates*, the *Bodies* and *Goods* of others.

Many excellent *Discourses* have been presented to your *Fathers* hands and Yours in former and present *Parliaments*: I shall be humbly bold to say, that (in what concernes your duties as *Magistrates*, towards others) a more necessary and seasonable *debate* was never yet presented.

Two things your *Honours* here may please to view (in this Controversie of *Persecution* for cause of *Conscience*) beyond what's extant.

First, the whole *Body* of this *Controversie* form'd & pitch'd in true *Battalia*.

Secondly (although in respect of my selfe it be *impar congressus*, yet in the power of that *God* who is *Maximus in Minimis*, Your Honours shall see the Controversie is discussed with men as able as most, eminent for *abilitie* and *pietie*, Mr. *Cotton*, and the *New English Ministers*.

When the *Prophets* in Scripture have given their *Coats of Armes* and *Escutchions* to *Great Men*, Your *Honours* know the *Babylonian Monarch* hath the *Lyon*, the *Persian* the *Beare*, the *Grecian* the *Leopard*, the *Romane* a *compound* of the former 3. most strange and dreadfull, *Dan.* 7.

Their oppressing, plundring, ravishing, murthering, not only of the *bodies*, but the *soules* of Men are large explaining *commentaries* of such similitudes.

Your *Honours* have been famous to the end of the World, for your unparallel'd *wisdome, courage, justice, mercie*, in the vindicating your Civill *Lawes, Liberties*, &c. Yet let it not be grievous to your *Honours* thoughts to ponder a little, why all the *Prayers* and *Teares* and *Fastings* in this Nation have not pierc'd the *Heavens*, and quench'd these *Flames*, which yet who knowes how far they'll spread, and when they'll out!

Your *Honours* have broke the jawes of the *Oppressour*, and taken the prey out of their Teeth (*Iob.* 29.) For which Act I believe it hath pleased the most High *God* to set a *Guard* (not only of Trained Men, but) of mighty *Angels*, to secure your sitting and the Citie.

I feare we are not *pardoned*, though *reprieved*: O that there may be a lengthning of *Londons* tranquilitie, of the *Parliaments* safetie, by *mercy* to the *poore*! Dan. 4.

Right Honorable, *Soule yokes, Soule oppression, plundrings, ravishings*, &c. are of a *crimson* and *deepest dye*, and I believe the chiefe of *Englands* sins, unstopping the Viols of *Englands* presents sorrowes.

This glasse presents your *Honours* with *Arguments* from *Religion, Reason*,

Experience, all proving that the greatest yoakes yet lying upon *English necks*, (the *peoples* and Your *own*) are of a *spirituall* and *soule* nature.

All former *Parliaments* have changed these yoakes according to their *consciences*, (*Popish* or *Protestant*) "Tis now your *Honours* turne at *helme*, and (as your *task*, so I hope your *resolution*, not to change (for that is but to turne the wheele, which another *Parliament*, and the very next may turne againe:) but to ease the Subjects and Your selves from a *yoake* (as was once spoke in a case not unlike *Act.* 15.) which neither Your nor your Fathers were ever able to beare.

Most *Noble Senators*, Your *Fathers* (whose *seats* You fill) are mouldred, and mouldring their *braines*, their *tongues*, &c. to *ashes* in the pit of *rottensse*: They and You must shortly (together with two *worlds* of men) appeare at the great *Barre*: It shall then be no griefe of heart that you have now attended to the *cries* of *Soules, thousands oppressed, millions ravished* by the *Acts* and *Statutes* concerning *Soules*, not yet *repealed*.

Of *Bodies impoverished, imprisoned,* &c. for their *soules* beliefe, yea slaughtered on heapes for *Religions* controversies in the *Warres* of present and former Ages.

mous
of a late
of
nia.

"Notwithstanding the success of later times, (wherein sundry opinions have been hatched about the subject of *Religion*) a man may clearly discerne with his eye, and as it were touch with his finger that according to the verity of holy Scriptures, &c. mens *consciences* ought in no sort to be violated, urged or constrained. And whensoever men have attempted any thing by this violent course, whether openly or by secret meanes, the issue hath beene pernicious, and the cause of great and *wonderfull innovations* in the principallest and mightiest *Kingdomes* and *Countries*, &c."

It cannot be denied to be a pious and prudentiall *act* for Your *Honours* (according to your conscience) to call for the advice of faithfull *Councellours* in the high debates concerning Your owne, and the soules of others.

Yet let it not be imputed as a *crime* for any *suppliant* to the *God* of *Heaven* for You, if in the humble sense of what their soules beleeve, they powre forth (amongst others) these three *requests* at the *Throne* of *Grace*.

First, That neither Your *Honours*, nor those excellent and worthy persons, whose advice you seek, limit the holy *One* of *Israel* to their *apprehensions, debates, conclusions*, rejecting or neglecting the humble and faithfull suggestions of any, though as base as spittle and clay, with which sometimes *Christ Jesus* opens the *eyes* of them that are borne blinde.

Secondly, That the present and future *generations* of the Sons of Men may never have cause to say that such a *Parliament* (as *England* never enjoyed the like) should modell the *worship* of the *living, eternall* and *invisible God* after the *Bias* of any earthly *interest*, though of the highest concernment under the Sunne: And yet, faith that learned Sir *Francis Bacon* (how ever Essays of
Religion. otherwise perswaded, yet thus he confesseth:) "Such as hold *pressure* of *Conscience*, are guided therein "by some private *interests* of their owne."*

Thirdly, What ever way of *worshipping God* Your owne *Consciences* are perswaded to walke in, yet (from any bloody *act* of violence to the consciences of others) it may bee never told at *Rome* nor *Oxford*, that the *Parliament* of *England* hath committed a greater *rape*, then if they had forced or ravished the bodies of all the women in the *World*. It is rarely seen
that ever
persons were
persecuted for
their conscience
but by such
persecution they
were confirmed
and hardened in
their
conscience.

And that *Englands Parliament* (so famous throughout all Europe and the

---

*"It was a notable observation of a wife father, and no less ingenuously confessed; *that those who held and persuaded pressure of conscience, were commonly interested therein themselves for their own ends.*"

World) should at last turne *Papists, Prelatists, Presbyterians, Independents, Socinians, Familists, Antinomians*, &c. by confirming all these sorts of Consciences, by Civill force and violence to their Consciences.

To every Courteous Reader

While I plead the Cause of *Truth* and *Innocencie* against the bloody Doctrine of Persecution for cause of *conscience*, I judge it not unfit to give *alarme* to my selfe, and all men to prepare to be *persecuted* or hunted for cause of *conscience*.

Whether thou standest charged with 10 or but 2 *Talents*, if thou huntest any for cause of *conscience*, how canst thou say thou followest the *Lambe* of *God* who so abhorr'd that practice?

If *Paul*, if *Jesus Christ* were present here at *London*, and the *question* were proposed what *Religion* would they approve of: The *Papists, Prelatists, Presbyterians, Independents*, &c. would each say, Of mine, of mine.

But put the second question, if one of the severall sorts should by *major vote* attaine the *Sword* of steele: what weapons doth Christ Jesus authorize them to fight with in His cause? Doe not all men hate the *persecutor*, and every *conscience* true or false complaine of cruelty, tyranny? &c.

Two *mountaines* of crying *guilt* lye heavie upon the backes of All that name the name of *Christ* in the eyes of *Jewes, Turkes* and *Pagans*.

First, The blasphemies of their *Idolatrous inventions, superstitions*, and most *unchristian conversations*.

Secondly, The bloody irreligious and inhumane *oppressions* and *destructions* under the maske or vaile of the Name of *Christ*, &c.

O how like is the *jealous Jehovah*, the consuming fire to end these present slaugh-

ters in a greater slaughter of the holy Witnesses? *Rev.* 11.

Six yeares preaching of so much Truth of *Christ* (as that time afforded in K. *Edwards* dayes) kindles the flames of Q. *Maries* bloody *persecutions*.

Who can now but expect that after so many scores of yeares *preaching* and *professing* of more Truth, and amongst so many great *contentions* amongst the very best of *Protestants*, a fierie furnace should be heat, and who sees not now the *fires* kindling?

I confesse I have little hopes till those flames are over, that this Discourse against the *doctrine* of *persecution* for cause of *conscience* should passe currant (I say not amongst the *Wolves* and *Lions*, but even amongst the *Sheep* of *Christ* themselves) yet *liberavi animam meam*, I have not hid within my *breast* my *souls* belief: And although sleeping on the bed either of the pleasures or profits of sinne thou thinkest thy conscience bound to smite at him that dares to waken thee? Yet in the middest of all these *civill* and *spirituall Wars* (I hope we shall agree in these particulars.)

First, how ever the proud (upon the advantage of an higher earth or ground) or'elooke the poore and cry out *Schismatickes, Hereticks*, &c. shall *blasphemers* and *seducers* scape unpunished? &c. Yet there is a sorer punishment in the *Gospel* for despising of *Christ* then *Moses*, even when the despiser of Moses was put to death without mercie, *Heb*. 10. 28, 29. He that beleeveth not shall bee damned, *Marke* 16. 16.

Secondly, what ever Worship, Ministry, Ministration, the best and purest are practised without *faith* and true perswasion that they are the true institutions of God, they are sin, sinfull worships, Ministries, &c. And however in Civill things we may be servants unto men, yet in Divine and Spirituall things the poorest *pesant* must disdaine the service of the highest *Prince*:

Be ye not the servants of men, 1 Cor. 14. [vii: 23.]

Thirdly, without search and triall no man attaines this faith and right perswasion, 1 *Thes*. 5. Try all things.

In vaine have *English Parliaments* permitted *English Bibles* in the poorest *English* houses, and the simplest man or woman to search the Scriptures, if yet against their soules perswasion from the Scripture, they should be forced (as if they lived in *Spaine* or *Rome* it selfe without the sight of a *Bible*) to beleeve as the Church beleeves.

Fourthly, having tried, we must hold fast, 1 *Thessal*. 5. upon the losse of a Crowne, *Revel*. 13. [iii: 11.] we must not let goe for all the flea bitings of the present afflictions, &c. having bought Truth deare, we must not sell it cheape, not the least graine of it for the whole World, no not for the saving of Soules, though our owne most precious; least of all for the bitter sweetning of a little vanishing pleasure.

For a little puffe of credit and reputation from the changeable breath of uncertaine sons of men.[:]

For the broken bagges of Riches on Eagles wings: For a dreame of these, any or all of these which on our death-bed vanish and leave tormenting stings behinde them: Oh how much better is it from the love of Truth, from the love of the Father of lights, from whence it comes, from the love of the Sonne of God, who is the way and the Truth, to say as he, *John* 18. 37. For this end was I borne, and for this end came I into the World that I might beare witnesse to the Truth. . . .

John Winthrop

John Winthrop, the first governor of Massachusetts Bay colony, was an important diplomatic force in moving the New England Puritan theocracy, which was governed indirectly by England, towards self-governing colonies. Born in 1587 in Edwardstone, England, into a family of good social position, Winthrop studied at Trinity College, Cambridge, until he left at seventeen to marry. He took his father's profession of law and practiced in London. A Puritan of strong religious and moral beliefs, Winthrop was concerned about economic, political, and religious confusion in England. He ran into financial difficulties and decided to emigrate to the New World when Charles I granted a charter incorporating the Governor and Company of the Massachusetts Bay in New England. Working as one of the executives on this company plan, Winthrop was among those who decided that this colony should be not merely a plantation of settlers operating for the profit of a mercantile company in England, but a permanent settlement of people working for themselves, and that the legal company and its General Court and charter would be moved to America. Suddenly, an ordinary mercantile charter took on the character of a constitution for a self-governed community.

Winthrop was chosen governor and sailed for America with about seven hundred people in his fleet; two to three hundred more arrived simultaneously, and another thousand soon thereafter. On the way he wrote out a plan of what he thought the colony should be as well as the means to achieve these objectives—"A Modell of Christian Charity" (1630)—printed below. He made Boston the center of government and at the beginning was continually elected governor on an annual basis. When the freemen became restive and discovered that the General Court was the only body entitled to legislate, they inquired why the magistrates had usurped some of the powers granted to the General Court. Winthrop argued that it was too awkward for such a body to take on all of these tasks and that the General Court should permanently give up or delegate some of its powers. But the freemen opposed reducing any of the charter's privileges, despite Winthrop's popularity.

Winthrop had no faith in democracy and believed that after representatives were selected they should govern based on their own best judgment. Later political strains caused self-appointed investigators (John Cotton, Governor John Haynes, and others) to arrive in Massachusetts to examine the source of the tensions. They determined that Winthrop was too lenient in discipline and judicial decisions. Bowing to overwhelming political pressures, Winthrop became more severe, especially in making it difficult for followers of the independent-minded Anne Hutchinson to remain in the colony.

After sitting out some occasional terms of being governor, Winthrop started to lose touch with the people in the move toward more democratization. But in 1645, when Winthrop was singled out for impeachment for exceeding the powers granted magistrates in the election of a militia officer, he was totally vindicated. After the verdict, he gave the short, famous "A Little Speech on Liberty" printed here, which distinguished between natural and civil liberty and described the nature of the office of people's elected representatives. He was thereafter reelected governor until his death in 1649.

A Modell of Christian Charity (1630)

Written On Boarde the Arrabella,
On the Attlantick Ocean.
By the Honorable JOHN WINTHROP, Esq.

In His passage, (with the great Company of Religious people, of which Christian Tribes he was the Brave Leader and famous Governor;) from the Island of Great Brittaine, to New-England in the North America.

Anno 1630.

Christian Charities*

A Modell Hereof

God Almightie in his most holy and wise providence hath soe disposed of the Condicion of mankinde, as in all times some must be rich some poore, some highe and eminent in power and dignitie; others meane and in subjeccion.

The Reason Hereof

1. REAS: First, to hold conformity with the rest of his workes, being delighted to shewe forthe the glory of his wisdome in the variety and differance of the Creatures and the glory of his power, in ordering all these differences for the preservacion and good

---

Isaak, *American Political Thinking.*

Editor's Note: For ease in reading, the typographical setting of the letters *u, v,* and *s* has been modernized in this selection.

of the whole, and the glory of his greatnes that as it is the glory of princes to have many officers, soe this great King will have many Stewards counting himselfe more honoured in dispenceing his guifts to man by man, then if hee did it by his owne immediate hand.

2. REAS: Secondly, That he might have the more occasion to manifest the worke of his Spirit: first, upon the wicked in moderateing and restraineing them: soe that the riche and mighty should not eate upp the poore, nor the poore, and dispised rise upp against theire superiours, and shake off theire yoake: 2ly in the regenerate in exerciseing his graces in them, as in the greate ones, theire love mercy, gentlenes, temperance etc., in the poore and inferiour sorte, theire faithe patience, obedience etc:

3. REAS: Thirdly, That every man might have need of other, and from hence they might be all knitt more nearly together in the Bond of brotherly affeccion; from hence it appears plainely that noe man is made more honourable than another or more wealthy etc., out of any perticuler and singuler respect to himselfe but for the glory of his Creator and the Common good of the Creature. Man; Therefore God still reserves the propperty of these guifts to himselfe as Ezek. 16:17. he there calls wealthe his gold and his silver etc. Prov. 3:9, he claimes theire service as his due[.] honour the Lord with thy riches etc. . . . There is likewise a double Lawe by which wee are regulated in our conversacion one towardes another: in both the former respects, the lawe of nature and the lawe of grace, or the morrall lawe or the lawe of the gospell, to omitt the rule of Justice as not propperly belonging to this purpose otherwise then it may fall into consideracion in some perticuler Cases; By the first of these lawes man as he was enabled soe withall [is] commaunded to love his neighbour as himselfe[.] upon this ground stands all the precepts of the morrall lawe, which

concernes our dealings with men. To apply this to the works of mercy this lawe requires two things[,] first that every man afford his help to another in every want or distresse Secondly, That hee performe this out of the same affeccion, which makes him carefull of his owne good according to that of our Saviour Math. [7:12] Whatsoever ye would that men should doe to you. This was practised by Abraham and Lott in entertaineing the Angells and the old man of Gibea.

The Lawe of Grace or the Gospell hath some differance from the former as in these respectes first the lawe of nature was given to man in the estate of innocency; this of the gospell in the estate of regeneracy: 2ly, the former propounds one man to another, as the same fleshe and Image of god, this as a brother in Christ allsoe, and in the Communion of the same spirit and soe teacheth us to put a difference betweene Christians and others. Doe good to all especially to the household of faith [Gal. 6:10]; upon this ground the Israelites were to putt a difference betweene the brethren of such as were strangers though not of the Canaanites. 3ly. The Lawe of nature could give noe rules for dealeing with enemies for all to be considered as freinds in the estate of innocency, but the Gospell commaunds love to an enemy. proofe. If thine Enemie hunger feede him; Love your Enemies doe good to them that hate you Math. 5:44.

This Laawe of the Gospell propoundes likewise a difference of seasons and occasions: there is a time when a christian must sell all and give to the poore as they did in the Apostles times. There is a tyme allsoe when a christian (though they give not all yet) must give beyond theire abillity as they of Macedonia Cor. 2:6. likewise community of perills calls for extraordinary liberallity and soe doth Community in some speciall service for the Churche. Lastly, when there is noe other meanes whereby our Christian brother may be releived in this distresse wee must help him beyond our ability, rather than tempt God, in putting him upon help by miraculous or extraordinary meanes.

This duty of mercy is exercised in the kindes, Giveing, lending, and forgiveing. . . .

QUESTION: What rule must wee observe in lending?

ANSWER: Thou must observe whether thy brother hath present or probable, or possible meanes of repayeing thee, if ther be none of these, thou must give him according to his necessity, rather than lend him as hee requires: if he hath present meanes of repayeing thee, thou art to looke at him, not as an Act of mercy, but by way of Commerce; wherein thou arte to walke by the rule of Justice, but, if his meanes of repayeing thee be onely probable or possible then is hee an object of thy mercy thou must lend him, though there be danger of looseing it Deut. 15:7. If any of thy brethren be poore etc. thou shalt lend him sufficient that men might not shift off this duty by the apparent hazzard, he tells them that though the Yeare of Jubile were at hand (when he must remitt it., if hee were not able to repay it before) yet he must lend him and that chearefully; it may not greive thee to give him (saith hee) and because some might object, why soe I should soone impoverishe my selfe and my family, he adds with all thy Worke etc. for our Saviour Math. 5:42. From him that would borrow of thee turne not away.

QUESTION: What rule must wee observe in forgiveing?

ANSWER: Whether thou didst lend by way of Commerce or in mercy, if he have noething to pay thee [thou] must forgive him (except in cause where thou hast a surety or a lawfull pledge) Deut. 15:2. Every seaventh yeare the Creditor was to quitt that which hee lent to his brother if hee were poore as appeares ver: 8[4]:save when there shall be noe poore with thee. In all these and like Cases Christ was a generall rule Math. 7:22. Whatsoever ye would that men should doe to you doe yee the same to them allsoe.

QUESTION: What rule must wee observe and walke by in cause of Community of perill?

ANSWER: The same as before, but with more enlargement towardes others and lesse respect towards our selves, and our owne right hence it was that in the primitive Churche they sold all [.] had all things in Common, neither did any man say that that which he possessed was his owne [Acts 2:44–45; 4:32–35] likewise in theire returne out of the Capituity, because the worke was greate for the restoreing of the church and the danger of enemies was Common to all Nehemiah exhortes the Jewes to liberallity and readiness in remitting theire debtes to theire brethren, and disposeth liberally of his owne to such as wanted and stands not upon his owne due, which hee might have demaunded of them, thus did some of our forefathers in times of persecucion here in England, and soe did many of the faithfull in other Churches whereof wee keepe an honourable remembrance of them. . . .

The diffinition which the Scripture gives us of love is this Love is the bond of perfection [Col. 3:14]. First, it is a bond, or ligament. 21v, it makes the worke perfect. There is noe body but consistes of partes and that which knitts these partes together gives the body its perfeccion, because it makes each parte soe contiguous to other as thereby they doe mutually participate with eache other, both in st:engthe and infirmity in pleasure and paine, to instance in the most perfect of all bodies, Christ and his church make one body: the severall parties of this body considered aparte before they were united were as disproportionate and as much disordering as soe many contrary quallities or elements but when christ comes and by his spirit and love knitts all these partes to himselfe and each to other, it become the most perfect and best proportioned body in the world

Eph. 4:16. Christ by whome all the body being knitt together by every ioynt for the furniture thereof according to the effectuall power which is in the measure of every perfeccion of partes a glorious body without spott or wrinckle the ligaments hereof being Christ or his love for Christ is love 1 John 4:8. Soe this definition is right Love is the bond of perfeccion.

From hence wee may frame these Conclusions.

1. first all true Christians are of one body in Christ 1. Cor. 12:12–13. 17. [27.] Ye are the body of Christ and members of [your?] parte.

2ly. The ligamentes of this body which knitt together are love.

31y. Noe body can be perfect which wants its propper ligamentes.

4ly. All the partes of this body being thus united are made soe contiguous in a speciall relacion as they must needes partake of each others strength and infirmity, ioy, and sorrowe, weale and woe. 1. Cor. 12:26. If one member suffers all suffer with it, if one be in honour, all reioyce with it.

5ly. This sensiblenes and Sympathy of each others Condicions will necessarily infuse into each parte a native desire and endeavour, to strengthen defend preserve and comfort the other.

To insist a little on this Conclusion being the product of all the former the truthe hereof will appeare both by precept and patterne i. John 3:10. yee ought to lay downe your lives for the brethren Gal. 6:2. beare ye one anothers burthens and soe fulfill the lawe of Christ. . . .

The next consideracion is how this love comes to be wrought; Adam in his first estate was a perfect modell of mankinde in all theire generacions, and in him this love was perfected in regard of the habit, but Adam Rent in himselfe from his Creator, rent all his posterity allsoe one from another, whence it comes that every man is borne with this principle in him, to love and seeke himselfe onely and thus a man continueth till Christ comes and takes possession of the soule, and infuseth another principle of love to God and our brother, and this latter haveing continuall supply from Christ, as the head and roote by which hee is united get the predominency in the soule, soe by little and little expells the former 1 John 4:7. love cometh of god and every one that loveth is borne of god, soe that this love is the fruite of the new birthe, and none can have it but the new Creature, now when this quality is thus formed in the soules of men it workes like the Spirit upon the drie bones Ezek. 37:[7] bone came to bone, it gathers together the scattered bones or perfect old man Adam and knitts them into one body againe in Christ whereby a man is become againe a liveing soule.

The third Consideracion is concerning the exercise of this love, which is twofold, inward or outward, the outward hath beene handled in the former preface of this discourse, for unfolding the other wee must take in our way that maxime of philosophy, Simile simili gaudet or like will to like; for as it is things which are carried with disafeccion to eache other, the ground of it is from a dissimilitude or [*blank*] ariseing from the contrary or different nature of the things themselves, soe the ground of love is an apprehension of some resemblance in the things loved to that which affectes it, this is the cause why the Lord loves the Creature, soe farre as it hath any of his Image in it, he loves his elect because they are like himselfe, he beholds them in his beloved sonne; soe a mother loves her childe, because shee throughly conceiues a resemblance of herselfe in it. Thus it is betweene the members of Christ, each discernes by the worke of the spirit his owne Image and resemblance in another, and therefore cannot but love him as he loves himselfe: Now when the soule which is of a sociable nature findes anything like to it selfe, it is like Adam when Eve was brought to him, shee must have it one with herselfe this is fleshe of my fleshe (saith shee) and bone of my bone shee conceives a great delighte in it, therefore shee desire nearenes and familiarity with it: . . .

From the former Consideracions ariseth these Conclusions.

1. First. This love among Christians is a reall thing not Imaginarie.

2ly. This love is as absolutely necessary to the being of the body of Christ, as the sinewes and other ligaments of a naturall body are to the being of that body.

3ly. This love is a divine Spirituall nature free, active strong Couragious permanent under valueing all things beneathe its propper object, and of all the graces this makes us nearer to resemble the virtues of our heavenly father.

4ly. It restes in the love and welfare of its beloved, for the full and certaine knowledge of these truthes concerning the nature use, [and] excellency of this grace, that which the holy ghost hath left recorded 1. Cor. 13. may give full satisfaccion which is needful for every true member of this lovely body of the Lord Jesus, to worke upon theire heartes, by prayer meditacion continuall exercise at least of the speciall [*blank*] of this grace till Christ be formed in them and they in him all in eache other knitt together by this bond of love.

It rests now to make some application of this discourse by the present designe which gave the occasion of writeing of it. Herein are 4 things to be propounded: first the persons. 2ly, the worke, 3ly, the end, 4ly the meanes.

1. For the persons, wee are a Company professing our selves fellow members of Christ, In which respect only though wee were absent from eache other many miles, and had our ilmploymentes as farre distant, yet wee ought to account our selves knitt together by this bond of love, and live in the exercise of it, if wee would have com-

forte of our being in Christ, this was notorious in the practise of the Christians in former times. . . .

2ly. for the Worke wee have in hand, it is by a mutuall consent through a speciall over-ruleing providence, and a more then an ordinary approbation of the Churches of Christ to seeke out a place of Cohabitation and Consorteshipp under a due forme of Government both civill and ecclesiasticall. In such cases as this the care of the publique must oversway all private respects, by which not onely conscience, but meare Civill pollicy doth binde us; for it is a true rule that perticuler Estates cannott subsist in the ruine of the publique.

3ly. The end is to improve our lives to doe more service to the Lord the comforte and encrease of the body of christe whereof wee are members that our selves and posterity may be the better preserved from the Common corrupcions of this evill world to serve the Lord and worke out our Salvacion under the power and purity of his holy Ordinances.

4ly. for the meanes whereby this must bee effected, they are 2fold, a Conformity with the worke and end wee aime at, these wee see are extraordinary, therefore wee must not content our selves with usuall ordinary meanes whatsoever wee did or ought to have done when wee lived in England, the same must wee doe and more allsoe where wee goe; That which the most in theire Churches maineteine as a truthe in profession onely, wee must bring into familiar and constant practise, as in this duty of love wee must love brotherly without dissimulation, wee must love one another with a pure hearte fervently wee must beare one anothers burtheens, wee must not looke onely on our owne things, but allsoe on the things of our brethren, neither must wee think that the lord will beare with such faileings at our hands as hee dothe from those among whome wee have lived, and that for 3 Reasons.

1. In regard of the more neare bond of mariage, betweene him and us wherein he hath taken us to be his after a most strickt and peculiar manner which will make him the more Jealous of our love and obedience soe he tells the people of Israell, you onely have I knowne of all the families of the Earthe therefore will I punishe you for your Transgressions.

2ly. because the lord will be sanctified in them that come neare him. Wee know that there were many that corrupted the service of the Lord some setting upp Alters before his owne, others offering both strange fire and strange Sacrifices allsoe; yet there came noe fire from heaven, or other sudden Judgment upon them as did upon Nadab and Abihu [Lev. 10:1–2] whoe yet wee may thinke did not sinne presumptuously.

3ly. When God gives a speciall Commission he lookes to have it strictly observed in every Article, when hee gave Saule a Commission to destroy Amaleck hee indented with him upon certaine Articles and because hee failed in one of the least, and that upon a faire pretence, it lost him the kingdome, which should have been his reward, if hee had observed his Commission [I Sam. 15; 28:16–18]; Thus stands the cause betweene God and us. wee are entered into Covenant with him for this worke, wee have taken out a Commission. the Lord hath given us leave to drawe our owne Articles wee have professed to enterprise these Accions upon these and these ends, we have hereupon besought him of favour and blessing; Now if the Lord shall please to heare us, and bring us in peace to the place wee desire, then hath hee ratified this Covenant and sealed our Commission, [and] will expect a strickt performance of the Articles contained in it, but if wee shall neglect the observacion of these Articles which are the ends wee have propounded, and dissembling with our God, shall fall to embrace this present world and

prosecute our carnall intencions, seekeing greate things for our selves and our posterity, the Lord will surely breake out in wrathe against us be revenged of such a periured people and make us knowe the price of the breache of such a Covenant.

Now the onely way to avoyde this shipwracke and to provide for our posterity is to followe the Counsell of Micah, to doe Justly, to love mercy, to walke humbly with our God, for this end wee must be knitt together in this worke as one man, wee must entertainee each other in brotherly Affeccion, wee must be willing to abridge our selves of our superfluities, for the supply of others necessities, wee must uphold a familiar Commerce together in all meekenes, gentlenes, patience and liberallity, wee must delight in eache other, make others Condicions our owne reioyce together, mourne together, labour, and suffer together, allwayes haveing before our eyes our Commission and Community in the worke, our Community as members of the same body, soe shall wee keepe the unitie of the spirit in the bond of peace, the Lord will be our God and delight to dwell among us, as his owne people and will commaund a blessing upon us in all our wayes, soe that wee shall see much more of his wisdome power goodnes and truthe then formerly wee have beene acquainted with, wee shall finde that the God of Israel is among us. when tenn of us shall be able to resist a thousand of our enemies, when hee shall make us a prause and glory, that men shall say of succeeding plantacions: the lord make it like that of New England; for wee must Consider that wee shall be as a Citty upon a Hill, the Eies of all people are upoon us; soe that if wee shall deale falsely with our god in this worke wee have undertaken and soe cause him to withdrawe his present help from us, wee shall be made a story and a by-word through the world, wee shall open the mouthes of enemies to speake evill of the wayes of god and all professours for Gods sake; wee shall shame the faces of many of gods worthy servants, and cause theire prayers to be turned into Cursses upon us till wee be consumed out of the good land whether wee are goeing; And to shutt upp this Discourse with that exhortacion of Moses that faithfull servant of the Lord in his last farewell to Israell Deut. 30: [15–19]. Beloved there is now sett before us life, and good, deathe and evill in that wee are Commaunded this day to love the Lord our God, and to love one another to walke in his wayes and to keepe his Commaundements and his Ordinance, and his lawes, and the Articles of our Covenant with him that wee may live and be multiplyed, and

that the Lord our God may blesse us in the land whether wee goe to possesse it: But if our heartes shall turne away soe that wee will not obey, but shall be seduced and worshipp other Gods our pleasures, and proffitts, and serve them; it is propounded unto us this day, wee shall surely perishe out of the good Land whether wee passe over this vast Sea to possesse it;

> Therefore lett us choose life,
> that wee, and our Seede,
> may live; by obeying his
> voyce, and cleaveing to him,
> for hee is our life, and
> our prosperity.

A Little Speech on Liberty (1645)

I suppose something may be expected from me. upon this charge that is befallen me, which moves me to speak now to you. Yet I intend not to intermeddle in the proceedings of the Court, or with any of the persons concerned therein. Only I bless God that I see an issue of this troublesome business. I also acknowledge the justice of the Court, and, for mine own part, I am well satisfied, I was publicly charged, and I am publicly and legally acquitted, which is all I did expect or desire. . . .

The great questions that have troubled the country are about the authority of the magistrates and the liberty of the people. It is yourselves who have called us to this office; and being called by you, we have our authority from God, in way of an ordinance, such as hath the image of God eminently stamped upon it, the contempt and violation whereof hath been vindicated with examples of divine vengeance. I

entreat you to consider that when you choose magistrates, you take them from among yourselves, men subject to like passions as you are. Therefore, when you see infirmities in us, you should reflect upon your own; and that would make you bear the more with us, and not be severe censurers of the failings of your magistrates, when you have continual experience of the like infirmities in yourselves and others. We account him a good servant who breaks not his covenant. The covenant between you and us is the oath you have taken of us, which is to this purpose, that we shall govern you and judge your causes by the rules of God's law and our own, according to our best skill. When you agree with a workman to build you a ship or house, etc., he undertakes as well for his skill as for his faithfulness, for it is his profession, and you pay him for both. But when you call one to be a magistrate, he doth not profess

Isaak, *American Political Thinking*.

nor undertake to have sufficient skill for that office, nor can you furnish him with gifts, etc.; therefore you must run the hazard of his skill and ability. But if he fail in faithfulness, which by his oath he is bound unto, that he must answer for. If it fall out that the case be clear to common apprehension and the rule clear also, if he transgress here, the error is not in the skill but in the evil of the will: it must be required of him. But if the case be doubtful or the rule doubtful to men of such understanding and parts as your magistrates are, if your magistrates should err here, yourselves must bear it.

For the other point concerning liberty, I observe a great mistake in the country about that. There is a twofold liberty—natural (I mean as our nature is now corrupt), and civil or federal. The first is common to man, with beasts and other creatures. By this, man, as he stands in relation to man simply, hath liberty to do what he lists; it is a liberty to evil as well as to good. This liberty is incompatible and inconsistent with authority, and cannot endure the least restraint of the most just authority. The exercise and maintaining of this liberty makes men grow more evil and in time to be worse than brute beasts: *omnes sumus licentia deteriores*. This is that great enemy of truth and peace, and wild beast, which all the ordinances of God are bent against to restrain and subdue it.

The other kind of liberty I call civil or federal: it may also be termed moral, in reference to the covenant between God and man in the moral law, and the politic covenants and constitutions amongst men themselves. This liberty is the proper end and object of authority and cannot subsist without it; and it is a liberty to that only which is good, just, and honest. This liberty you are to stand for, with the hazard not only of your goods, but of your lives, if need be. Whatsoever crosseth this is not authority, but distemper thereof. This liberty is maintained and exercised in a way of subjection to authority; it is of the same kind of liberty wherewith Christ hath made us free. The woman's own choice makes such a man her husband; yet being so chosen, he is her lord, and she is to be subject to him, yet in a way of liberty, not of bondage; and a true wife accounts her subjection her honor and freedom, and would not think her condition safe and free but in her subjection to her husband's authority. Such is the liberty of the church under the authority of Christ, her king and husband; his yoke is so easy and sweet to her as a bride's ornaments; and if through frowardness or wantonness, etc., she shake it off at any time, she is at no rest in her spirit until she take it up again; and whether her lord smiles upon her and embraceth her in his arms, or whether he frowns or rebukes, or smites her, she apprehends the sweetness of his love in all, and is refreshed, supported, and instructed by every such dispensation of his authority over her. On the other side, ye know who they are that complain of this yoke and say, let us break their bands, etc., we will not have this man to rule over us.

Even so, brethren, it will be between you and your magistrates. If you stand for your natural, corrupt liberties and will do what is good in your own eyes, you will not endure the least weight of authority, but will murmur, and oppose, and be always striving to shake off that yoke. But if you will be satisfied to enjoy such civil and lawful liberties, such as Christ allows you, then will you quietly and cheerfully submit unto that authority which is set over you, in all the administrations of it, for your good. Wherein, if we fail at any time, we hope we shall be willing, by God's assistance, to hearken to good advice from any of you or in any other way of God. So shall your liberties be preserved, in upholding the honor and power of authority amongst you.

Cotton Mather

Known as the principal spokesperson of American Puritanism in the early eighteenth century, Cotton Mather led a movement with his father to centralize control of church doctrine and practices. He had previously served actively in the 1689 rebellion against the royal governor Sir Edmund Andros of Massachusetts and had written the manifesto of insurgents. Born in Boston as the eldest son of the Puritan leader Increase Mather in 1663, Cotton Mather received his B.A. and M.A. from Harvard and then joined his father at the Second Church in Boston, where he served until his death in 1728.

Mather became renowned not only as a preacher, but as a man of letters, a scientist, and a scholar in many fields, writing more than 450 books. In his early years he became preoccupied with witchcraft, arguing in the witchcraft excitement of 1692 that judges should be cautious in their use of "spectral evidence" against those accused and that prayer and fasting might be more appropriate than punitive legal action. Nevertheless, his preoccupation with witches in his writing and preaching before he was thirty probably helped to stimulate the hysterical fear of witches in Salem, Massachusetts.

Mather's most celebrated book is *Magnalia Christi Americana* (1702), an ecclesiastical history of New England. His diaries reveal a vain man with a cosmic ego and pedantic turn of mind. He self-righteously sought out opportunities to exercise "devices for the good" in which he could magnify self in the process of presumed self-abasement. As historian Vernon Parrington summed him up: "He was a primitive Puritan in Boston that was fast becoming Yankee, and his love for the theocracy grew stronger with every defeat."

Politically, Mather represented an ambitious leader for the forces of reaction upon whom the traditional authority of the ministry had focused public attention. Although he worked tirelessly for moral reform and bookish erudition, his hot temper and vindictive nature made him more enemies than friends, and he became a tempting target for the growing numbers of reformers who would decentralize and democratize the power of the Puritan theocracy.

An Essay upon the Good (1710)
(excerpt)

Such *glorious things are spoken* in the oracle of our good God, concerning them who *devise good*, that A BOOK OF GOOD DEVICES may very reasonably demand attention and acceptance from them that have any impressions of the most *reasonable religion* upon them. I am *devising* such a BOOK; but at the same time offering a sorrowful demonstration, that if men would set themselves to *devise good*, a world of *good* might be done, more than there is, in this *present evil world*. It is very sure, the world has *need enough*. There needs abundance to be done, that the great GOD and

His CHRIST may be more known and served in the world; and that the *errors* which are *impediments* to the *acknowledgments* wherewith men ought to glorify their Creator and Redeemer, may be rectified. There needs abundance to be done, that the *evil manners* of the world, by which men are *drowned in perdition*, may be reformed; and mankind rescued from the epidemical corruption and slavery which has overwhelmed it. There needs abundance to be done, that the *miseries* of the world may have *remedies* and *abatements* provided for them; and that miserable people may be relieved and comforted. The world has according to the computation of some, above seven hundred millions of people now living in it. What an ample field among all these, to *do good* upon! In a word, *the kingdom of God* in the world calls for innumerable *services* from us. To do SUCH THINGS is to DO GOOD. Those men DEVISE GOOD, who shape any DEVICES to do things of such a tendency; whether the things be of a *spiritual* importance, or of a *temporal*. You see, Sirs, the general matter, appearing as yet but as a *chaos*, which is to be wrought upon. *Oh! that the good Spirit of God may now fall upon us, and carry on the glorious work which lies before us!*

2. 'Tis to be supposed, my readers will readily grant, that it is an excellent, a virtuous, a laudable thing to be full of *devices*, to bring about such *noble purposes*. For any man to deride, or to despise my proposal, *that we resolve and study to do as much good in the world as we can*, would be so black a character, that I am not willing to make a supposal of it in any of those with when I am concerned. Let no man pretend unto the name of *a Christian*, who does not approve the proposal of *a perpetual endeavor to do good in the world*. What pretension can such a man have to be *a follower of the Good One*? The primitive *Christians* gladly accepted and improved

the name, when the pagans by a mistake styled them, *Chrestians*; because it signified, *useful ones*. The *Christians* who have no ambition to be so, shall be condemned by the pagans, among whom it was a term of the highest honor, to be termed, *a benefactor*; to have *done good*, was accounted *honorable*. The philosopher being asked why everyone desired so much to look upon a fair object, he answered, that *it was a question of a blind man*. If any man ask, as wanting the sense of it, "What is it worth the while to *do good* in the world?," I must say, "It sounds not like the question of a good man." The Αισθησις πνευματικη, as *Origen* calls it, the *spiritual taste* of every good man will make him have an unspeakable *relish* for it. Yea, unworthy to be discoursed as a *man*, is he, who is not for *doing of good among men*. An *enemy* to the proposal, *that mankind may be the better for us*, deserves to be reckoned, little better than, *a common enemy of mankind*. How cogently do I bespeak, a good reception of what is now designed! I produce not only *religion*, but even *humanity* itself, as full of a *fiery indignation against the adversaries of the design*. Excuse me, Sirs; I declare, that if I could have my choice, I would never *eat* or *drink*, or *walk*, with such an one as long as I live; or, look on him as any other than one by whom *humanity* itself is debased and blemished. A very *wicked writer*, has yet found himself compelled by the force of *reason*, to publish this confession. "To love the public, to study an universal good, and to promote the interest of the whole world, as far as is in our power, is surely the highest of goodness, and makes that temper, which we call Divine." And, he goes on: "Is the doing of good for glory's sake so divine a thing? [Alas, too much *humane*, Sir!] Or, is it not a diviner to do good, even where it may be thought inglorious? Even unto the ungrateful, and unto those who are wholly insensible of the good they receive!" A man must be far gone in *wickedness*, who will open his mouth, against such *maxims* and *actions*! A better pen has remarked it; yea, the man must be much a stranger in history, who has not made the remark. *To speak truth, and to do good, were in the esteem even of the heathen world, most God-like qualities.* God forbid, that in the esteem of the *Christian world* for those qualities, there should be any abatement!

3. I won't yet propose the *reward* of *well-doing*, and the glorious things which the *mercy* and *truth* of God will do, for them who *devise good*, because I would have to do with such, as will esteem it, a sufficient *Reward* unto itself. I will imagine that generous ingenuity, in my readers, which will dispose them to count themselves *well-rewarded* in the thing itself, if God will accept them to *do good* in the world. It is an invaluable *honor*, to *do good*; it is an incomparable *pleasure*. A man must look upon himself as *dignified* and *gratified* by GOD, when an *opportunity* to *do good* is put into his hands. He must embrace it with *rapture*, as enabling him directly to answer the great END of his being. He must manage it with *rapturous delight*, as a most suitable business, as a most precious privilege. He must *sing in those ways of the Lord*, wherein he cannot but find himself, while he is *doing of good*. As the saint of old sweetly sang, "I was glad, when they said unto me, Let us go into the House of the Lord." Thus ought we to be *glad*, when any *opportunity* to *do good*, is offered unto us. We should need no *arguments*, to make us entertain the offer; but we should *naturally* fly into the matter, as most agreeable to the *divine nature* whereof we are *made partakers*. It should *oblige* us wonderfully! An ingot of gold presented unto us, not more obliging! Think, Sirs, *Now I enjoy what I am for! Now I attain what I wish for!* Some servants of God have been so strongly disposed this way, that they have cheerfully made a tender of any *recom-*

pense that could be desired (yea, rather than fail, a *pecuniary* one) unto any friend that would *think* for them, and *supply* the *barrenness* of their thoughts, and *suggest* unto them any special and proper *methods*, wherein they may be *serviceable*. Certainly, to *do good*, is a thing that brings its own *recompense*, in the opinion of those, who reckon a kind *information* of a point wherein they may *do good*, worthy to be by them requited with a *recompense* to the *informer*. I will only say: "If any of you are strangers unto such a disposition as this, to look upon an *opportunity* to *do good*, as a thing that *enriches* you, and to look upon yourselves as *enriched*, and *favored* of God, when He does employ you to *do good*: I have done with you." I would pray them, to lay the *book* aside; it will disdain to carry on any further conversation with 'em! It handles a subject on which the wretches of the house of *Caleb*, will not be conversed withal. It is content with one of Dr. *Stoughton's* Introductions: "It is enough to me, that I speak to wise men, whose reason shall be my rhetoric, to Christians, whose conscience shall be my eloquence."

4. Though the assertion fly never so much like a *chainshot* among us, and rake down all before it, I will again, and again assert it; *that we might every one of us do more good than we do.* And therefore, this is the FIRST PROPOSAL, to be made unto us: *to be exceedingly humbled, that we have done so little good in the world.* I am not *uncharitable*, in saying: I know not that *assembly* of Christians upon earth, which ought not to be a *Bochim*, in this consideration. Oh! tell me, what *Utopia* I shall find it in! Sirs, let us begin to bring forth some *good fruit*, by lamenting our own *great unfruitfulness*. Verily, *sins of omission* must be confessed and bewailed; else we add unto the number of them. The most *useful* men in the world, have gone out of it, crying to God, "Lord, let my sins of omission be forgiven to me!" Men that have made more than ordinary conscience about well-spending of their *time*, have had their death-bed made uneasy by this reflection: *The loss of time now sits heavy upon me*. Be sure, all *unregenerate* persons are, as our Bible has told us, *unprofitable* persons. 'Tis not for nothing, that the comparison of *thorns*, and *briars*, has been used, to *teach* us, what they are. An unrenewed sinner, alas, he never did *one good work* in all his *life*! In all his *life*, did I say? You must give me that word again! He is *dead* while he *lives*; he is *dead in sins*; he has never yet begun to *live unto God*: and, as is he, so are *all the works of his hands*; they are *dead works*. Ah! wretched *good-for-nothing*. Wonder, wonder at the patience of Heaven, which yet forbears *cutting down* such a *cumberer of the ground*. The best, and the first advice, to be given unto such persons, is, *immediately to do their best, that they may get out of their woeful unregeneracy*. Let them *immediately* acknowledge the *necessity* of their turning to God, but how *unable* they are to do it, and how *unworthy* that God should make them *able*. *Immediately* let them lift up their *cry* unto sovereign *grace*, to *quicken* them; and let them then *try*, whether they cannot with *quickened* Souls, *plead* the *sacrifice* and *righteousness* of a glorious CHRIST for their happy reconciliation to God; seriously resolve upon a life of *obedience* to God, and *serious religion*; and resign themselves up unto the *Holy Spirit*, that He may possess them, instruct them, strengthen them, and *for His name's sake lead them in the paths of holiness*. There will no *good* be done, till this be done. The very *first-born* of all *devices* to *do good*, is in being *born again*, and in *devising means, that a banished* soul may no longer be *expelled* from the presence of God. But you that have been brought home to God, have sad cause, not only to deplore the *dark days* of your unregeneracy, wherein you did none but the *unfruitful*

works of darkness; but also, that you have done so *little*, since God has quickened you and enabled you, to *do*, the things that should be done. How little, how little have you lived up, to the strains of *gratitude*, which might have been justly expected, since God has brought you *into His marvelous light!* The best of us may mourn in our complaint: "Lord, how little good have I done, to what I might have done!" Let the sense of this cause us to *loathe* and *judge* ourselves before the Lord: let it fill us with shame, and abase us wonderfully! How can we do any other, than with *David*, even make a cauldron of our couch, and a bath of our tears, when we consider how little *good* we have done! *Oh! that our heads were waters*, because they have been so *dry* of all thoughts to *do good!* *Oh! that our eyes were a fountain of tears*, because they have been so little upon the *lookout* for objects and methods to *do good* upon! For the *pardon* of this *evil-doing*, let us fly to the Great *Sacrifice*, which is our only *expiation*. Plead the *blood* of that *Lamb of God*, whose universal *usefulness* is one of those admirable properties, for which He has been called, *a lamb*. The *pardon* of our *barrenness* at *good works* being thus obtained, by faith in that *blood which cleanses from all sin*, that is the way for us to be rescued from a condemnation to *perpetual barrenness*. The dreadful sentence of, *Let no fruit grow on thee forever!* will be reversed and prevented, by such a *pardon*. Sirs, a true, right, evangelical procedure to *do good*, must have this *repentance* laid in the foundation of it! We do not *handle the matter wisely*, if a *foundation* be not laid thus *low*, and in the deepest *self-abasement*.

5. How full, how full of *devices* are we, for our own *secular advantage*! And how *expert* in *devising* many *little things*, to be done for ourselves! We apply our thoughts, with a mighty assiduity, unto the old question, *What shall I eat and drink,* *and wherewithal shall I be clothed*? It is with a very strong application of our thoughts, that we study, what we shall do for ourselves, in our *marriages*, in our *voyages*, in our *bargains*, and in many, many other concerns, wherein we are solicitous to have our condition easy. We solicitously *contrive*, that we may accomplish *good bargains*, and that we may steer clear of ten thousand *inconveniences*, to which, without some *contrivance*, we may lie obnoxious. The *business* of our *personal callings* we carry on with numberless thoughts, how we may *do well*, in what is to be done. To accomplish our temporal *business*, in affairs that cannot be numbered, we *find out witty inventions*. But, O rational, immortal, Heaven-born SOUL, are thy wonderous faculties capable of no greater improvements, no better employments? Why should a *soul* of such high capacities, a *soul* that may arrive to be clothed in the bright *scarlet* of *angels*, yet *embrace a dunghill*! O let a *blush* coloring

beyond *scarlet*, be thy clothing for thy being found so meanly occupied! Alas, *in the multitude of thy thoughts within thee*, hast thou no dispositions to raise thy soul, unto some thoughts, *what may be done for* GOD, *and* CHRIST, *and for my own* SOUL, *and for the most considerable interests*? How many hundreds of *thoughts* have we, how to obtain or secure some trifle for ourselves; to *one*, how we may serve the interests of the glorious LORD, and of His people in the world? How can we now pretend, that we *love Him*, or, that a carnal, and criminal *self-love*, has not the dominion over us? I again come in, upon a *soul* of an Heavenly extract, and *smite* it, as the angel did the sleeping prisoner: *Awake, shake off thy shackles, lie no longer fettered in a base confinement unto nothing but a meaner sort of business*. Assume and assert the liberty of now and then thinking on the *noblest question* in the world: *What good may I do in the world*? ...

Jonathan Edwards

Born in East Windsor, Connecticut, in 1703, Jonathan Edwards became an influential nineteenth-century philosopher, inspiring the Great Awakening Calvinist movement in New England. Graduating from Yale at seventeen, he studied theology and preached in New York City, tutored at Yale, and then joined his grandfather in the Northhampton, Massachusetts, ministry, which he eventually took over in 1729 upon his grandfather's death.

In his youth he revolted against Calvinism as it was being practiced and admired by Locke and Berkeley, gaining a wide following because of his clear logic and forceful speaking. He focused upon predestination and the absolute dependence of man upon God and divine grace, which alone could lead to salvation. Defending strict or consistent Calvinism from Arminian and deist modifications, he denied the freedom of human will and held a religious revival in Northhampton in 1734–35, initiating the Great Awakening. Stern and strictly orthodox, he excluded from full participation in communion those members of his congregation who did not quite live up to his ideals, so his parishioners dismissed him in 1750. He turned to caring for the Indians at the mission in Stockbridge, Massachusetts, and wrote his masterpiece, *The Freedom of the Will* (1754), in which he discusses his metaphysical and ethical case for determinism.

In 1757 he was elected president of the College of New Jersey (now Princeton University) and died a few months later in 1758. Known as the last of the great New England Calvinists, Edwards had great impact for a while upon American Christian thought. His belief in personal religious experience paradoxically stimulated evangelical revivalism, countering Calvinism in its assertion that salvation was possible without predestined election.

∽✿∾

A Faithful Narrative
of the Surprising Work of God
in the Conversion of Many Hundred Souls
in Northhampton and the Neighboring Towns
and Villages (1737)
(excerpt)

Reverend and Honored Sir,

Having seen your letter to my honored Uncle Williams of Hatfield of July 20 [1736], wherein you inform him of the notice that has been taken of the late wonderful work of God, in this and some other towns in this country; by the Rev. Dr. Watts and Dr. Guyse of London, and the congregation to which the last of these preached on a monthly day of solemn prayer; as also, of your desire to be more perfectly acquainted with it, by some of us on the spot: and having been since informed by my Uncle Williams that you desire me to undertake it; I would now do it in as just and faithful a manner as in me lies.

The people of the county, in general, I suppose, are as sober, and orderly, and good sort of people, as in any part of New England; and I believe they have been preserved the freest by far, of any part of the country, from error and variety of sects and opinions. Our being so far within the land, at a distance from seaports, and in a corner of the country, has doubtless been one reason why we have not been so much corrupted with vice, as most other parts. But without question, the religion and good order of the country, and their purity in doctrine, has, under God, been very much owing to the great abilities and eminent piety of my venerable and honored grandfather Stoddard. I suppose we have been the freest of any part of the land from unhappy divisions and quarrels in our ecclesiastical and religious affairs, till the late lamentable Springfield contention.

We being much separated from other parts of the province, and having comparatively but little intercourse with them, have from the beginning till now, always managed our ecclesiastical affairs within ourselves: 'tis the way in which the county, from its infancy, has gone on, by the practical agreement of all, and the way in which our peace and good order has hitherto been maintained.

The town of Northhampton is of about 82 years standing, and has now about 200 families; which mostly dwell more compactly together than any town of such a bigness in these parts of the country; which probably has been an occasion that both our corruptions and reformations have been, from time to time, the more swiftly propagated from one to another through the town. Take the town in general, and so far as I can judge, they are as rational and understanding a people as most I have been acquainted with: many of them have been noted for religion, and particularly have been remarkable for their distinct knowledge in things that relate to heart religion and Christian experience, and their great regards thereto.

I am the third minister that has been settled in the town: the Rev. Mr. Eleazar Mather, who was the first, was ordained in [July 1661 and died] July 1669. He was one whose heart was much in his work, abundant in labors for the good of precious souls; he had the high esteem and great love of his people, and was blessed with no small success. The Rev. Mr. Stoddard, who succeeded him, came first to the town the November after his death, but was not ordained till September 11, 1672, and died February 11, 1728/9. So that he continued in the work of the ministry here, from his first coming to town, near sixty years. And as he was eminent and renowned for his gifts and grace; so he was blessed, from the beginning, with extraordinary success in his ministry in the conversion of many souls. He had five harvests, as he called them: the first was about 57 years ago; the second about 53 years; the third about 40; the fourth about 24; the fifth and last about 18 years ago. Some of these times were much more remarkable than others, and the ingathering of souls more plentiful. Those that were about 53, and 40, and 24 years ago were much greater than either the first or the last: but in each of them, I have heard my grandfather say, the bigger part of the young people in the town seemed to be mainly concerned for their eternal salvation.

After the last of these came a far more degenerate time (at least among the young people), I suppose, than ever before. Mr. Stoddard, indeed, had the comfort before he died, of seeing a time where there were no small appearances of a divine work amongst some, and a considerable ingathering of souls, even after I was settled with him in the ministry, which was about two years before his death; and I have reason to bless God for the great advantage I had by it. In these two years there were near twenty that Mr. Stoddard hoped to be savingly converted; but there was nothing of any general awakening. The greater part seemed to be at that time very insensible of the things of religion, and engaged in other cares and pursuits. Just after my grandfather's death, it seemed to be a time of extraordinary dullness in religion: licentiousness for some years greatly prevailed among the youth of the town; they were many of them very much addicted to night-walking, and frequenting the tavern, and lewd practices, wherein some, by their example exceedingly corrupted others. It was their manner very frequently to get together in conventions of both sexes, for mirth and jollity, which they called frolics; and they would often spend the greater part of the night in them, without regard to any order in the families they belonged to: and indeed family government did too much fail in the town. It was become very customary with many of our young people, to be indecent in their carriage at meeting, which doubtless would not have prevailed to such a degree, had it not been that my grandfather, through his great age (though he retained his powers surprisingly to the last) was not so able to observe them. There had also long prevailed in the town a spirit of contention between two parties, into which they had for many years been divided, by which was maintained a jealousy one of the other, and they were prepared to oppose one another in all public affairs.

But in two or three years after Mr. Stoddard's death, there began to be a sensible amendment of these evils; the young people shewed more of a disposition to hearken to counsel and by degrees left off their frolicking, and grew observably more decent in their attendance on the public worship, and there were more than manifested a religious concern than there used to be.

[A New Awakening Begins]

At the latter end of the year 1733, there appeared a very unusual flexibleness, and yielding to advice, in our young people. It had been too long their manner to make the evening after the Sabbath, and after our public lecture, to be especially the times of their mirth and company-keeping. But a sermon was now preached on the Sabbath before the lecture, to shew the evil tendency of the practice, and to persuade them to reform it; and it was urged on heads of families, that it should be a thing agreed upon among them, to govern their families and keep their children at home at these times; and withal it was more privately moved that they should meet together the next day, in their several neighborhoods, to know each other's minds; which was accordingly done, and the motion complied with throughout the town. But parents found little or no occasion for the exercise of government in the case: the young people declared themselves convinced by what they had heard from the pulpit, and were willing of themselves to comply with the counsel that had been given: and it was immediately, and I suppose, almost universally complied with; and there was a thorough reformation of these disorders thenceforward, which has continued ever since.

Presently after this, there began to appear a remarkable religious concern at a little village belonging to the congregation, called Pascommuck, where a few families were settled at about three miles distance from the main body of the town. At this place, a number of persons seemed to be savingly wrought upon. In the April following, *anno* 1734, there happened a very sudden and awful death of a young man in the bloom of his youth; who being violently seized with a pleurisy and taken immediately very delirious, died in about two days; which (together with what was preached publicly on that occasion) much affected many young people. This was followed with another death of a young married woman, who had been considerably exercised in mind about the salvation of her soul before she was ill, and was in great distress in the beginning of her illness; but seemed to have satisfying evidences of God's saving mercy to her before her death; so that she died very full of comfort, in a most earnest and moving manner warning and counseling others. This seemed much to contribute to the solemnizing of the spirits of many young persons: and there began evidently to appear more of a religious concern on people's minds.

In the fall of that year, I proposed it to the young people, that they should agree among themselves to spend the evenings after lectures in social religion, and to that end divide themselves into several companies to meet in various parts of the town; which was accordingly done, and those meetings have been since continued, and the example imitated by elder people. This was followed with the death of an elderly person, which was attended with many unusual circumstances, by which many were much moved and affected.

About this time, began the great noise that was in this part of the country about Arminianism, which seemed to appear with a very threatening aspect upon the interest of religion here. The friends of vital piety trembled for fear of the issue; but it seemed, contrary to their fear, strongly to be overruled for the promoting of religion. Many who looked on themselves as in a Christless condition, seemed to be awakened by it, with fear that God was about to withdraw from the land, and that we should be given up to heterodoxy and corrupt principles;

and that then their opportunity for obtaining salvation would be past; and many who were brought a little to doubt about the truth of the doctrines they had hitherto been taught, seemed to have a kind of trembling fear with their doubts, lest they should be led into bypaths, to their eternal undoing: and they seemed with much concern and engagedness of mind, to inquire what was indeed the way in which they must come to be accepted with God. There were then some things said publicly on that occasion concerning justification by faith alone.

Although great fault was found with meddling with the controversy in the pulpit, by such a person and at that time, and though it was ridiculed by many elsewhere, yet it proved a word spoken in season here; and was most evidently attended with a very remarkable blessing of heaven to the souls of the people in this town. They received thence a general satisfaction with respect to the main thing in question, which they had been in trembling doubts and concern about; and their minds were engaged the more earnestly to seek that they might come to be accepted of God, and saved in the way of the Gospel, which had been made evident to them to be the true and only way. And then it was, in the latter part of December, that the Spirit of God began extraordinarily to set in, and wonderfully to work amongst us; and there were, very suddenly, one after another, five or six persons who were to all appearance savingly converted, and some of them wrought upon in a very remarkable manner.

Particularly, I was surprised with the relation of a young woman, who had been one of the greatest company-keepers in the whole town. When she came to me, I had never heard that she was become in any wise serious, but by the conversation I then had with her, it appeared to me that what she gave an account of was a glorious work of God's infinite power and sovereign grace; and that God had given her a new

heart, truly broken and sanctified. I could not then doubt of it, and have seen much in my acquaintance with her since to confirm it.

Though the work was glorious, yet I was filled with concern about the effect it might have upon others: I was ready to conclude (though too rashly) that some would be hardened by it, in carelessness and looseness of life; and would take occasion from it to open their mouths in reproaches of religion. But the event was the reverse, to a wonderful degree; God made it, I suppose, the greatest occasion of awakening to others, of anything that ever came to pass in the town. I have had abundant opportunity to know the effect it had, by my private conversation with many. The news of it seemed to be almost like a flash of lightning, upon the hearts of young people all over the town, and upon many others. Those persons amongst us who used to be farthest from seriousness, and that I most feared would make an ill improvement of it, seemed greatly to be awakened with it; many went to talk with her, concerning what she had met with; and what appeared in her seemed to be the satisfaction of all that did so.

Presently upon this, a great and earnest concern about the great things of religion and the eternal world became universal in all parts of the town, and among persons of all degrees and all ages; the noise amongst the dry bones waxed louder and louder. All other talk about spiritual and eternal things was soon thrown by; all the conversation in all companies and upon all occasions, was upon these things only, unless so much as was necessary for people, carrying on their ordinary secular business. Other discourse than of the things of religion would scarcely be tolerated in any company. The minds of people were wonderfully taken off from the world; it was treated amongst us as a thing of very little consequence. They seemed to follow their worldly business more as a part of their duty than from any disposition they had to it; the temptation now seemed to lie on that hand, to neglect worldly affairs too much, and to spend too much time in the immediate exercise of religion: which thing was exceedingly misrepresented by reports that were spread in distant parts of the land, as though the people here had wholly thrown by all worldly business, and betook themselves entirely to reading and praying, and such like religious exercises.

But although people did not ordinarily neglect their worldly business; yet there then was the reverse of what commonly is: religion was with all sorts the great concern, and the world was a thing only by the bye. The only thing in their view was to get the kingdom of heaven, and everyone appeared pressing into it. The engagedness of their hearts in this great concern could not be hid; it appeared in their very countenances. It then was a dreadful thing amongst us to lie out of Christ, in danger every day of dropping into hell; and what persons' minds were intent upon was to escape for their lives, and to fly from the wrath to come. All would eagerly lay hold of opportunities for their souls; and were wont very often to meet together in private houses for religious purposes: and such meetings when appointed were wont greatly to be thronged.

There was scarcely a single person in the town, either old or young, that was left unconcerned about the great things of the eternal world. Those that were wont to be the vainest and loosest, and those that had been most disposed to think and speak slightly of vital and experimental religion, were now generally subject to great awakenings. And the work of conversion was carried on in a most astonishing manner, and increased more and more; souls did as it were come by flocks to Jesus Christ. From day to day, for many months together, might be seen evident instances of sinners brought out of darkness into marvelous light, and delivered out of an horrible pit, and from the miry clay, and set upon a rock with a new song of praise to God in their mouths [cf. I Pet. 2:9 and Ps. 40:2–3].

This work of God, as it was carried on, and the number of true saints multiplied, soon made a glorious alteration in the town; so that in the spring and summer following, *anno* 1735, the town seemed to be full of the presence of God: it never was so full of love, nor so full of joy; and yet so full of distress, as it was then. There were remarkable tokens of God's presence in almost every house. It was a time of joy in families on the account of salvation's being brought unto them; parents rejoicing over their children as newborn, and husbands over their wives, and wives over their husbands. The goings of God were then seen in his sanctuary [Ps. 68:24]. God's day was a delight, and his tabernacles were amiable [Ps. 84:1]. Our public assemblies were then beautiful; the congregation was alive in God's service, everyone earnestly intent on the public worship, every hearer eager to drink in the words of the minister as they came from his mouth; the assembly in general were, from time to time, in tears while the Word was preached; some weeping with sorrow and distress, others with joy and love, others with pity and concern for the souls of their neighbors. . . .

American Values and Pragmatic Self-Sufficiency

Benjamin Franklin

Often viewed as the model American character—self-made, hard-working, pragmatic, inventive, shrewd in business and politics, and wise in the ways of the world—Benjamin Franklin helped define the traditional conservative limits of American liberalism and individualism. Born a Boston candlemaker's son of pious Puritan stock in 1706, Franklin had less than two years of formal schooling and went to work for his father. Self-taught, he read every book he could get his hands on. At twelve, he was apprenticed to his brother James, printer of *The New England Courant*. Franklin absorbed the books of the English Enlightenment and memorized the essays of Joseph Addison in the *Spectator*, thereby adding urbanity and tolerance to his inherited Puritan earnestness. At sixteen, he wrote satirical essays concerning Boston authorities and society under the pseudonym "Silence Dogood." In 1723, suffering under his domineering brother, Franklin ran away to Philadelphia, penniless. He found a job as a printer. A year later he went to England and became a master printer, swimmer, and worldly bachelor. He returned to Philadelphia in 1726, soon owned his own newspaper, and started to print *Poor Richard's Almanack* (1732).

Getting the contracts for the public printing for the province helped Franklin expand his business, establish partnerships with printers in other colonies, open a book shop, and become clerk of the Pennsylvania Assembly and postmaster of Philadelphia. At 42, his businesses managed by others, he retired to live off the proceeds. His plan for achieving moral virtue through pragmatic steps is spelled out in his one book, the famous *Autobiography* excerpted here. Franklin also founded the Junto, a club of upwardly mobile tradesmen that met weekly for intellectual and moral development, business planning, and for planning improvement of the city of Philadelphia. The Junto became Franklin's vehicle for founding a library, a fire company, a learned society, a college (later the University of Pennsylvania), an insurance company, and a hospital. In 1740, Franklin invented the Pennsylvania fireplace, or Franklin stove, which was used throughout America and Europe. He experimented with electricity and showed that lightning was a form of electricity, invented the lightning rod, and became world famous. Later he invented bifocal lenses, a theory of heat absorption, ship designs, storm-path tracking techniques, and ways to measure the Gulf Stream.

Elected to the Pennsylvania Assembly in 1751, Franklin was to serve about forty years as a public official. A generation before the Declaration of Independence, Franklin was anonymously writing the principles of the Quaker Party and defending the powers of the elected representatives of the people. At first he opposed separation from Britain, which he thought to have the best system of government in the world. In 1754 Franklin produced the Plan of Union presented to the Albany Congress, proposing partial self-government by the colonies. Serving in a military expedition for the sake of the empire, Franklin observed that the colonies and England were growing apart. In 1757 while acting as Pennsylvania's agent in England, he was upset to hear Lord Granville, president of the Privy Council, announce that the king's order for the colonies were "the law of the land: for the king is the legislator of the Colonies." While in London, Franklin worked to limit the proprietary power of British officials in Pennsylvania.

When he returned home, Franklin reorganized the U.S. postal service in the 1760s. Following Pontiac's Rebellion of 1763, Franklin used his political influence to oppose revenge of the frontier people against innocent native Americans. After losing his seat in the assembly, he was sent to London to petition that Pennsylvania become a royal colony, but the Stamp Act crisis of 1765 transformed him to the American defender of colonial rights in Britain. He advised compliance with the act until it could be repealed. But Franklin reversed his stand when he heard of the violence it was precipitating. In 1767 he warned the British against enforcement of the Townshend Acts, arguing that such "acts of oppression" could lead Americans into open revolt. Finally, when the British Tea Act of 1773 was passed, Franklin protested orally and in writing with such sharply aimed essays as "Rules by Which a Great Empire May Be Reduced to a Small One." After the Boston Tea Party, Franklin gave up efforts at conciliation and went back home, serving on the Pennsylvania Committee of Safety and in the Continental Congress. He drafted articles of confederation for the united colonies, suggested a new constitution for Pennsylvania, and helped write the Declaration of Independence.

In 1776 Franklin went to France and won critical support for the American side in the Revolutionary War. He was an international sensation in literary, scientific, and political circles. Meanwhile, he guided French war supplies over the seas to the American rebels. Together with two other American representatives, he helped cultivate the relations that led to the signing of the French alliance in 1778. Franklin became the first American minister to France, where for seven years he served to rally French money, supplies, and goodwill for the American cause. When the British loss in Yorktown in 1781 persuaded the English that they could not win, Franklin met secretly with British negotiators to suggest treaty terms that were later largely adopted—complete U.S. independence, evacuation of all British troops from all occupied areas, a western boundary along the Mississippi River, and access to fishing grounds in Newfoundland. Franklin then joined John Jay in signing the 1783 Treaty of Paris by which France recognized the United States.

Upon returning home, Franklin served as president of Pennsylvania for three years, was active in the Pennsylvania Society for Promoting the Abolition of Slavery, and contributed goodwill and wisdom to the Constitutional Convention of 1787. He died in 1790.

ojo

Autobiography (1789)
(excerpts)

... It was about this time I conceiv'd the bold and arduous project of arriving at moral perfection. I wish'd to live without commiting any fault at any time; I would conquer all that either natural inclination, custom, or company might lead me into. As I knew, or thought I knew, what was right and wrong, I did not see why I might not always do the one and avoid the other. But I soon found I had undertaken a task of more difficulty than I had imagined. While my care was employ'd in guarding against one fault, I was often surprised by another; habit took the advantage of inattention; inclination was sometimes too strong for reason. I concluded, at length, that the mere speculative conviction that it was our interest to be completely virtuous, was not sufficient to prevent our slipping; and that the contrary habits must be broken, and good ones acquired and established, before we can have any dependence on a steady, uniform rectitude of conduct. For this purpose I therefore contrived the following method.

In the various enumerations of the moral virtues I had met with in my reading, I found the catalogue more or less numerous, as different writers included more or fewer ideas under the same name. Temperance, for example, was by some confined to eating and drinking, while by others it was extended to mean the moderating [of] every other pleasure, appetite, inclination, or passion, bodily or mental, even to our avarice and ambition. I propos'd to myself, for the sake of clearness, to use rather more names, with fewer ideas annex'd to each, than a few names with more ideas; and I included under thirteen names of virtues all that at that time occurr'd to me as necessary or desirable, and annexed to each a short precept, which fully express'd the extent I gave to its meaning.

These names of virtues, with their precepts, were:

1. Temperance
Eat not to dullness; drink not to elevation.

2. Silence
Speak not but what may benefit others or yourself: avoid trifling conversation.

3. Order
Let all your things have their places; let each part of your business have its time.

4. Resolution
Resolve to perform what you ought; perform without fail what you resolve.

5. Frugality
Make no expense but to do good to others or yourself; i.e., waste nothing.

6. Industry
Lose no time; be always employ'd in something useful; cut off all unnecessary actions.

7. Sincerity
Use no hurtful deceit; think innocently and justly; and if you speak, speak accordingly.

8. Justice
Wrong none by doing injuries, or omitting the benefits that are your duty.

9. Moderation
Avoid extreams; forbear resenting injuries so much as you think they deserve.

10. Cleanliness
Tolerate no uncleanliness in body, cloaths, or habitation.

11. Tranquillity
Be not disturbed at trifles, or at accidents common or unavoidable.

---

13. Humility
Imitate Jesus and Socrates.

My intention being to acquire the *habitude* of all these virtues, I judg'd it would be well not to distract my attention by attempting the whole at once, but to fix it on one of them at a time; and, when I should be master of that, then proceed to another, and so on till I had gone thro' the thirteen; and, as the previous acquisition of some might facilitate the acquisition of certain others, I arrang'd them with that view, as they stand above. Temperance first, as it tends to procure that coolness and clearness of head, which is so necessary where constant vigilance was to be kept up, and guard maintained against the unremitting attraction of ancient habits, and the force of perpetual temptations. This being acquir'd and establish'd, Silence would be more easy; and my desire being to gain knowledge at the same time that I improv'd in virtue, and considering that in conversation it was obtain'd rather by the use of the ears than of the tongue, and therefore wishing to break a habit I was getting into of prattling, punning, and joking, which only made me acceptable to trifling company, I gave *Silence* the second place. This and the next, *Order*, I expected would allow me more time for attending to my project and my studies. *Resolution*, once become habitual, would keep me firm in my endeavors to obtain all the subsequent virtues; *Frugality* and Industry freeing me from my remaining debt, and producing affluence and independence, would make more easy the practice of Sincerity and Justice, etc, etc. Conceiving, then, that, agreeably to the advice of Pythagoras in his *Golden Verses,* daily examination would be necessary, I contrived the following method for conducting that examination.

I made a little book, in which I allotted each of the virtues. I rul'd each page with red ink, so as to have seven columns, one for each day of the week, marking each column with a letter for the day. I cross'd these columns with thirteen red lines, marking the beginning of each line with the first letter of one of the virtues, on which line, and in its proper column, I might mark, by a little black spot, every fault I found upon examination to have been committed respecting that virtue upon that day.

I determined to give a week's strict attention to each of the virtues successively. Thus, in the first week, my great guard was to avoid every day the least offence against *Temperance,* leaving the

Form of the Pages

TEMPERANCE						
EAT NOT TO DULLNESS; DRINK NOT TO ELEVATION.						
	S.	M.	T.	W.	T.	F.	S.
T							
S	*	*		*		*	
O	* *	*	*		*	*	*
R			*			*	
F		*			*		
I			*				
S							
J							
M							
C							
T							
H							

other virtues to their ordinary chance, only marking every evening the faults of the day. Thus, if in the first week I could keep my first line, marked T, clear of spots, I suppos'd the habit of that virtue so much strengthen'd, and its opposite weaken'd, that I might venture extending my attention to include the next, and for the following week keep both lines clear of spots. Proceeding thus to the last, I could go thro' a course compleat in thirteen weeks, and four courses in a year. And like him who, having a garden to weed, does not attempt to eradicate all the bad herbs at once, which would exceed his reach and his strength, but works on one of the beds at a time, and, having accomplish'd the first, proceeds to a second, so I should have, I hoped, the encouraging pleasure of seeing on my pages the progress I made in virtue, by clearing successively my lines of their spots, till in the the end, by a number of courses, I should be happy in viewing a clean book, after a thirteen weeks' daily examination.

I should have mentioned before, that, in the autumn of the preceding year, I had form'd most of my ingenious acquaintance into a club of mutual improvement which we called the JUNTO; we met on Friday evenings. The rules that I drew up required that every member in his turn should produce one or more queries on any point of Morals, Politics, or Natural Philosophy, to be discuss'd by the company; and once in three months produce and read an essay of his own writing, on any subject he pleased. Our debates were to be under the direction of a president, and to be conducted in the sincere spirit of inquiry after truth, without fondness for dispute or desire of victory; and, to prevent warmth, all expressions of positiveness in opinions or direct contradiction were after some time made contraband and prohibited under small pecuniary penalties.

The first members were Joseph Breintnal, a copyer of deeds for the scriveners, a good-natur'd, friendly, middle-ag'd man, a great lover of poetry, reading all he could meet with, and writing some that was tolerable; very ingenious in many little Nicknackeries, and of sensible conversation.

Thomas Godfrey, a self-taught mathematician, great in his way, and afterward inventor of what is now called Hadley's Quadrant. But he knew little out of his way, and was not a pleasing companion; as, like most great mathematicians I have met with, he expected universal precision in every thing said, or was for ever denying or distinguishing upon trifles, to the disturbance of all conversation. He soon left us.

Nicholas Scull, a surveyor, afterward surveyor-general, who lov'd books and sometimes made a few verses.

William Parsons, bred a shoemaker, but, loving reading, had acquir'd a considerable share of mathematics, which he first studied with a view to astrology, that he afterwards laught at. He also became surveyor-general.

William Maugridge, a joiner, a most exquisite mechanic, and a solid, sensible man.

Hugh Meredith, Stephen Potts, and George Webb I have characteriz'd before.

Robert Grace, a young gentleman of some fortune, generous, lively and witty; a lover of punning and of his friends.

And William Coleman, then a merchant's clerk, about my age, who had the coolest, clearest head, the best heart, and the exactest morals of almost any man I ever met with. He became afterwards a merchant of great note, and one of our provincial judges. Our friendship continued without interruption to his death, upward of forty years; and the club continued almost as long, and was the best school of philosophy, morality, and politics that then existed in the province; for our queries, which were read the week preceding their discussion, put us upon reading with attention upon the several subjects, that we might speak more to the purpose; and here, too, we acquired better habits of conversation, every thing being studied in our rules which might prevent our disgusting each other. From hence the long continuance of the club, which I shall have frequent occasion to speak further of hereafter.

But my giving this account of it here is to show something of the interest I had, every one of these exerting themselves in recommending business to us.

In 1754, war with France being again apprehended, a congress of commissioners from the different colonies was, by an order of the Lords of Trade, to be assembled at Albany, there to confer with the chiefs of the Six Nations concerning the means of defending both their country and ours. Governor Hamilton, having receiv'd this order, acquainted the House with it, requesting they would furnish proper presents for the Indians, to be given on this occasion; and naming the Speaker (Mr.

Norris) and myself to join Mr. Thomas Penn and Mr. Secretary Peters as commissioners to act for Pennsylvania. The House approv'd the nomination, and provided the goods for the present, tho' they did not much like treating out of the provinces, and we met the other commissioners at Albany about the middle of June.

In our way thither, I projected and drew a plan for the union of all the colonies under one government, so far as might be necessary for defense, and other important general purposes. As we pass'd thro' New York, I had there shown my project to Mr. James Alexander and Mr. Kennedy, two gentlemen of great knowledge in public affairs and, being fortified by their approbation I ventur'd to lay it before the Congress. It then appeared that several of the commissioners had form'd plans of the same kind. A previous question was first taken whether a union should be established, which pass'd in the affirmative unanimously. A committee was then appointed, one member from each colony, to consider the several plans and report. Mine happen'd to be preferr'd, and, with a few amendments, was accordingly reported.

By this plan the general government was to be administered by a president-general, appointed and supported by the crown, and a grand council was to be chosen by the representatives of the people of the several colonies, met in their respective assemblies. The debates upon it in Congress went on daily hand in hand with the Indian business. Many objections and difficulties were started but at length they were all overcome and the plan was unanimously agreed to and copies ordered to be transmitted to the Board of Trade and to the assemblies of the several provinces. Its fate was singular; the assemblies did not adopt it as they all thought there was too much *prerogative* in it, and in England it was judg'd to have too much of the *democratic*. The Board of Trade therefore did not approve of it nor recommend it for the approbation of his majesty; but another scheme was form'd, supposed to answer the same purpose better, whereby the governors of the provinces, with some members of their respective councils, were to meet and order the raising of troops, building of forts, etc., and to draw on the treasury of Great Britain for the expense which was afterwards to be refunded by an act of Parliament laying a tax on America. My plan with my reasons in support of it is to be found among my political papers that are printed.

Being the winter following in Boston, I had much conversation with Governor Shirley upon both the plans. Part of what passed between us on the occasion may also be seen among those papers. The different and contrary reasons of dislike to my plan make me suspect that it was really the true medium; and I am still of opinion it would have been happy for both sides of the water if it had been adopted. The colonies, so united, would have been sufficiently strong to have defended themselves; there would then have been no need of troops from England; of course, the subsequent pretence for taxing America, and the bloody contest it occasioned, would have been avoided. But such mistakes are not new; history is full of the errors of states and princes.

> Look round the habitable world,
>   how few
> Know their own good, or, knowing
>   it, pursue!

Those who govern, having much business on their hands do not generally like to take the trouble of considering and carrying into execution new projects. The best public measures are therefore seldom *adopted from previous wisdom but forc'd by the occasion.* . . .

Hector St. John de Crèvecoeur

"Here nature opens her broad lap to receive the perpetual accession of new comers, and to supply them with food. I am sure I cannot be called a partial American when I say, that the spectacle afforded by these pleasing scenes must be more entertaining, and more philosophical than that which arises from beholding the musty ruins of Rome," wrote Hector St. John de Crèvecoeur (1735–1813) in *Letters from an American Farmer* (1782), most of which was written before the American Revolution.

Crèvecoeur was born in Normandy, France, and accompanied the French forces to Canada as a cartographer during the French and Indian War. After the British defeated the French, Crèvecoeur, married to an Anglo-American wife, settled on a 371-acre farm twenty-five miles west of the Hudson in Orange County, New York. There he farmed and wrote about American life until his death in 1813. He viewed the provinces of North America as "the asylum for freedom, as the cradle of future nations, and the refuge of distressed Europeans." America was for Crèvecoeur a potential agrarian utopia. He embodied the agrarian hopes later expressed by both Franklin and Jefferson, who praised the virtues of the simpler, natural society made up of people living off the land, with the promise of westward expansion reinforcing native optimism and democratic equality. The absence of the inherited titles and crowding typical of Europe represented an ideal environment for a new race of man. To a certain extent, Crèvecoeur reinforced French romantic and physiocratic traditions, which partly complemented the notion of individualistic natural rights and partly contradicted it.

The ecological movement of the late twentieth century—often moved by a longing for natural, rural living free from the complexity and corruption of modern industrial life—is but one outgrowth of the tradition represented by Hector St. John de Crèvecoeur.

Letters from an American Farmer (1782)
(excerpt)

What Is an American

I wish I could be acquainted with the feelings and thoughts which must agitate the heart and present themselves to the mind of an enlightened Englishman, when he first lands on this continent. He must greatly rejoice that he lived at a time to see this fair country discovered and settled; he must necessarily feel a share of national pride, when he views the chain of settlements which embellishes these extended shores. When he says to himself, this is the work of my countrymen, who, when convulsed by factions, afflicted by a variety of miseries and wants, restless and impatient, took refuge here. They brought along with them their national genius, to which they principally owe what liberty they enjoy, and what substance they possess. Here he sees the industry of his native country displayed in a new manner, and traces in their works the embryos of all the arts, sciences, and ingenuity which flourish in Europe. Here he beholds fair cities, substantial villages, extensive fields, an immense country filled with decent houses, good roads, orchards, meadows, and bridges, where an hundred years ago all was wild, woody, and uncultivated! What a train of pleasing ideas this fair spectacle must suggest; it is a prospect which must inspire a good citizen with the most heartfelt pleasure. The difficulty consists in the manner of viewing so extensive a scene. He is arrived on a new continent; a modern society offers itself to his contemplation, different from what he had hitherto seen. It is not composed, as in Europe, of great lords who possess everything, and of a herd of people who have nothing. Here are no aristocratical families, no courts, no kings, no bishops, no ecclesiastical dominion, no invisible power giving to a few a very visible one; no great manufacturers employing thousands, no great refinements of luxury. The rich and the poor are not so far removed from each other as they are in Europe. Some few towns excepted, we are all tillers of the earth, from Nova Scotia to West Florida. We are a people of cultivators, scattered over an immense territory, communicating with each other by means of good roads and navigable rivers, united by the silken bands of mild government, all respecting the laws, without dreading their power, because they are equitable. We are all animated with the spirit of an industry which is unfettered and unrestrained, because each person works for himself. If he travels through our rural districts he views not the hostile castle, and the haughty mansion, contrasted with the clay-built hut and miserable cabin, where cattle and men help to keep each other warm, and dwell

in meanness, smoke, and indigence. A pleasing uniformity of decent competence appears throughout our habitations. The meanest of our log houses is a dry and comfortable habitation. Lawyer or merchant are the fairest titles our towns afford; that of a farmer is the only appellation of the rural inhabitants of our country. It must take some time ere he can reconcile himself to our dictionary, which is but short in words of dignity, and names of honour. There, on a Sunday, he sees a congregation of respectable farmers and their wives, all clad in neat homespun, well mounted, or riding in their own humble waggons. There is not among them an esquire, saving the unlettered magistrate. There he sees a parson as simple as his flock, a farmer who does not riot on the labour of others. We have no princes, for whom we toil, starve, and bleed: we are the most perfect society now existing in the world. Here man is free as he ought to be; nor is this pleasing equality so transitory as many others are. Many ages will not see the shores of our great lakes replenished with inland nations, nor the unknown bounds of North America entirely peopled. Who can tell how far it extends? Who can tell the millions of men whom it will feed and contain? for no European foot has as yet travelled half the extent of this mighty continent!

The next wish of this traveller will be to know whence came all these people? They are a mixture of English, Scotch, Irish, French, Dutch, Germans, and Swedes. From this promiscuous breed, that race now called Americans have arisen. The eastern provinces must indeed be excepted as being the unmixed descendants of Englishmen. I have heard many wish that they had been more intermixed also: for my part, I am no wisher, and think it much better as it has happened. They exhibit a most conspicuous figure in this great and variegated picture; they too enter for a great share in the pleasing perspective displayed in these thirteen provinces. I know it is fashionable to reflect on them, but I respect them for what they have done; for the accuracy and wisdom with which they have settled their territory; for the decency of their manners; for their early love of letters; their ancient college, the first in this hemisphere; for their industry; which to me who am but a farmer, is the criterion of everything. There never was a people, situated as they are, who with so ungrateful a soil have done more in so short a time. Do you think that the monarchical ingredients which are more prevalent in other governments, have purged them from all foul stains? Their histories assert the contrary.

In this great American asylum, the poor of Europe have by some means met together, and in consequence of various causes; to what purpose should they ask one another what countrymen they are? Alas, two thirds of them had no country. Can a wretch who wanders about, who works and starves, whose life is a continual scene of sore affliction or pinching penury; can that man call England or any other kingdom his country? A country that had no bread for him, whose fields procured him no harvest, who met with nothing but the frowns of the rich, the severity of the laws, with jails and punishments, who owned not a single foot of the extensive surface of this planet? No! urged by a variety of motives, here they came. Every thing has tended to regenerate them; new laws, a new mode of living, a new social system; here they are become men: in Europe they were as so many useless plants, wanting vegetative mould, and refreshing showers; they withered, and were mowed down by want, hunger, and war; but now by the power of transplantation, like all other plants they have taken root and flourished! Formerly they were not numbered in any civil lists of their country, except in those of the poor; here they rank as citizens. By

what invisible power has this surprising metamorphosis been performed? By that of the laws and that of their industry. The laws, the indulgent laws, protect them as they arrive, stamping on them the symbol of adoption; they receive ample rewards for their labours; these accumulated rewards procure them lands; those lands confer on them the title of freemen, and to that title every benefit is affixed which men can possibly require. This is the great operation daily performed by our laws. From whence proceed these laws? From our governments. Whence the government? It is derived from the original genius and strong desire of the people ratified and confirmed by the crown. This is the great chain which links us all, this is the picture which every province exhibits, Nova Scotia excepted. There the crown has done all; either there were no people who had genius, or it was not much attended to: the consequence is, that the province is very thinly inhabited indeed; the power of the crown in conjunction with the musketos has prevented men from settling there. Yet some parts of it flourished once, and it contained a mild harmless set of people. But for the fault of a few leaders, the whole were banished. The greatest political error the crown ever committed in America, was to cut off men from a country which wanted nothing but men!

What attachment can a poor European emigrant have for a country where he had nothing? The knowledge of the language, the love of a few kindred as poor as himself, were the only cords that tied him: his country is now that which gives him land, bread, protection, and consequence: *Ubi panis ibi patria,* is the motto of emigrants. What then is the American, this new man? He is either an European, or the descendant of an European, hence that strange mixture of blood, which you will find in no other country. I could point out to you a family whose grandfather was an Englishman, whose wife was Dutch, whose son married a French woman, and whose present four sons have now four wives of different nations. *He* is an American, who, leaving behind him all his ancient prejudices and manners, receives new ones from the new mode of life he has embraced, the new government he obeys, and the new rank he holds. He becomes an American by being received in the broad lap of our great *Alma Mater.* Here individuals of all nations are melted into a new race of men, whose labours and posterity will one day cause great changes in the world. Americans are the western pilgrims, who are carrying along with them that great mass of arts, sciences, vigour, and industry which began long since in the east; they will finish the great circle. The Americans were once scattered all over Europe; here they are incorporated into one of the finest systems of population which has ever appeared, and which will hereafter become distinct by the power of the different climates they inhabit. The American ought therefore to love this country much better than that wherein either he or his forefathers were born. Here the rewards of his industry follow with equal steps the progress of his labour; his labour is founded on the basis of nature, *self-interest;* can it want a stronger allurement? Wives and children, who before in vain demanded of him a morsel of bread, now, fat and frolicsome, gladly help their father to clear those fields whence exuberant crops are to arise to feed and to clothe them all; without any part being claimed, either by a despotic prince, a rich abbot, or a mighty lord. Here religion demands but little of him; a small voluntary salary to the minister, and gratitude to God; can he refuse these? The American is a new man, who acts upon new principles; he must therefore entertain new ideas, and form new opinions. From involuntary idleness, servile dependence, penury, and useless labour, he has passed to toils of a very different nature, rewarded by ample subsistence.—This is an American.

British America is divided into many provinces, forming a large association, scattered along a coast 1500 miles extent and about 200 wide. This society I would fain examine, at least such as it appears in the middle provinces; if it does not afford that variety of tinges and gradations which may be observed in Europe, we have colours peculiar to ourselves. For instance, it is natural to conceive that those who live near the sea, must be very different from those who live in the woods; the intermediate space will afford a separate and distinct class.

Men are like plants; the goodness and flavour of the fruit proceeds from the peculiar soil and exposition in which they grow. We are nothing but what we derive from the air we breathe, the climate we inhabit, the government we obey, the system of religion we profess, and the nature of our employment. Here you will find but few crimes; these have acquired as yet no root among us. I wish I was able to trace all my ideas; if my ignorance prevents me from describing them properly, I hope I shall be able to delineate a few of the outlines, which are all I propose.

Those who live near the sea, feed more on fish than on flesh, and often encounter that boisterous element. This renders them more bold and enterprising; this leads them to neglect the confined occupations of the land. They see and converse with a variety of people, their intercourse with mankind becomes extensive. The sea inspires them with a love of traffic, a desire of transporting produce from one place to another; and leads them to a variety of resources which supply the place of labour. Those who inhabit the middle settlements, by far the most numerous, must be very different; the simple cultivation of the earth purifies them, but the indulgences of the government, the soft remonstrances of religion, the rank of independent freeholders, must necessarily inspire them with sentiments, very little known in Europe among people of the same class. What do I say? Europe has no such class of men; the early knowledge they acquire, the early bargains they make, give them a great degree of sagacity. As freemen they will be litigious; pride and obstinacy are often the cause of law suits; the nature of our laws and governments may be another. As citizens it is easy to imagine, that they will carefully read the newspapers, enter into every political disquisition, freely blame or censure governors and others. As farmers they will be careful and anxious to get as much as they can, because what they get is their own. As northern men they will love the cheerful cup. As Christians, religion curbs them not in their opinions; the general indulgence leaves every one to think for themselves in spiritual matters; the laws inspect our actions, our thoughts are left to God. Industry, good living, selfishness, litigiousness, country politics, the pride of freemen, religious indifference, are their characteristics. If you recede still farther from the sea, you will come into more modern settlements; they exhibit the same strong lineaments, in a ruder appearance. Religion seems to have still less influence, and their manners are less improved.

Now we arrive near the great woods, near the last inhabited districts; there men seem to be placed still farther beyond the reach of government, which in some measure leaves them to themselves. How can it pervade every corner; as they were driven there by misfortunes, necessity of beginnings, desire of acquiring large tracts of land, idleness, frequent want of economy, ancient debts; the re-union of such people does not afford a very pleasing spectacle. When discord, want of unity and friendship; when either drunkenness or idleness prevail in such remote districts; contention, inactivity, and wretchedness must ensue.

There are not the same remedies to these evils in a long established community. The few magistrates they have, are in general little better than the rest; they are often in a perfect state of war; that of man against man, sometimes decided by blows, sometimes by means of the law; that of man against every wild inhabitant of these venerable woods, of which they are come to dispossess them. There men appear to be no better than carnivorous animals of a superior rank, living on the flesh of wild animals when they can catch them, and when they are not able, they subsist on grain. He who would wish to see America in its proper light, have a true idea of its feeble beginnings and barbarous rudiments, must visit our extended line of frontiers where the last settlers dwell, and where he may see the first labours of settlement, the mode of clearing the earth, in all their different appearances; where men are wholly left dependent on their native tempers, and on the spur of uncertain industry, which often fails when not sanctified by the efficacy of a few moral rules. There, remote from the power of example and check of shame, many families exhibit the most hideous parts of our society. They are a kind of forlorn hope, preceding by ten or twelve years the most respectable army of veterans which come after them. In that space, prosperity will polish some, vice and the law will drive off the rest, who uniting again with others like themselves will recede still farther; making room for more industrious people, who will finish their improvements, convert the loghouse into a convenient habitation, and rejoicing that the first heavy labours are finished, will change in a few years that hitherto barbarous country into a fine fertile, well regulated district. Such is our progress, such is the march of the Europeans toward the interior parts of this continent. In all societies there are off-casts; this impure part serves as our precursors or pioneers; my father himself was one of that class, but he came upon honest principles, and was therefore one of the few who held fast; by good conduct and temperance, he transmitted to me his fair inheritance, when not above one in fourteen of his contemporaries had the same good fortune.

Forty years ago this smiling country was thus inhabited; it is now purged, a general decency of manners prevails throughout, and such has been the fate of our best countries.

Exclusive of those general characteristics, each province has its own, founded on the government, climate, mode of husbandry, customs, and peculiarity of circumstances. Europeans submit insensibly to these great powers, and become, in the course of a few generations, not only Americans in general, but either Pennsylvanians, Virginians, or provincials under some other name. Whoever traverses the continent must easily observe those strong differences, which will grow more evident in time. The inhabitants of Canada, Massachusetts, the middle provinces, the southern ones will be as different as their climates; their only points of unity will be those of religion and language.

As I have endeavoured to show you how Europeans become Americans; it may not be disagreeable to show you likewise how the various Christian sects introduced, wear out, and how religious indifference becomes prevalent. When any considerable number of a particular sect happen to dwell contiguous to each other, they immediately erect a temple, and there worship the Divinity agreeably to their own peculiar ideas. Nobody disturbs them. If any new sect springs up in Europe it may happen that many of its professors will come and settle in American. As they bring their zeal with them, they are at liberty to make proselytes if they can, and to build a meeting and to follow the dictates of their consciences; for neither the government nor any other power interferes. If they are peaceable subjects, and are industrious, what is it to their neighbours how and in what manner they think fit to address their prayers to the Supreme Being? But if the sectaries are not settled close together, if they are mixed with other denominations, their zeal will cool for want of fuel, and will be extinguished in a little time. Then the Americans become as to religion, what they are as to country, allied to all. In them the name of Englishman, Frenchman and European is lost, and in like manner, the strict modes of Christianity as practised in Europe are lost also. This effect will extend itself still farther hereafter, and though this may appear to you as a strange idea, yet it is a very true one. I shall be able perhaps hereafter to explain myself better; in the meanwhile, let the following example serve as my first justification.

Let us suppose you and I to be travelling; we observe that in this house, to the right, lives a Catholic, who prays to God as he has been taught, and believes in transubstantiation; he works and raises wheat, he has a large family of children, all hale and robust; his belief, his prayers offend nobody. About one mile farther on the same road, his next neighbour may be a good honest plodding German Lutheran, who addresses himself to the same God, the God of all, agreeably to the modes he has been educated in, and believes in consubstantiation; by so doing he scandalises nobody; he also works in his fields, embellishes the earth, clears swamps, etc. What has the world to do with his Lutheran principles? He persecutes nobody, and nobody persecutes him, he visits his neighbours, and his neighbours visit him. Next to him lives a seceder; the most enthusiastic of all sectaries; his zeal is hot and fiery, but separated as he is from others of the same complexion, he has no congregation of his own to resort to, where he might cabal and mingle religious pride with worldly obstinacy. He likewise raises good crops, his house is handsomely painted, his orchard is one of the fairest in the neighbourhood. How does it concern the welfare of the country, or of the province at large, what this man's religious sentiments are, or really whether he has any at all? He is a good farmer, he is a sober, peaceable, good citizen: William Penn himself would not wish for more. This is the visible character, the invisible one is only guessed at, and is nobody's business. Next again lives a Low Dutchman, who implicitly believes the rules laid down by the synod of Dort. He conceives no other idea of a clergyman than that of an hired man; if he does his work well he will pay him the stipulated sum; if not he will dismiss him, and do without his sermons, and let his church be shut up for years. But notwithstanding this coarse idea, you will find his house and farm to be the neatest in all the country; and you will judge by his waggon and fat horses, that he thinks more of the affairs of this world than of those of the next. He is sober and laborious, therefore he is all he ought to be as to the affairs of this life; as for those of the next, he must trust to the great Creator. Each of these people instruct their children as well as they can, but these instructions are feeble compared to those which are given to the youth of the poorest class in Europe. Their children will therefore grow up less zealous and more indifferent in matters of religion than their parents. The foolish vanity, or rather the fury of making Proselytes, is unknown here; they have no time, the seasons call for all their attention, and thus in a few years, this mixed neighbourhood will exhibit a strange religious medley, that will be neither pure Catholicism nor pure Calvinism. A very perceptible indifference even in the first generation,

will become apparent; and it may happen that the daughter of the Catholic will marry the son of the seceder, and settle by themselves at a distance from their parents. What religious education will they give their children? A very imperfect one. If there happens to be in the neighbourhood any place of worship, we will suppose a Quaker's meeting; rather than not show their fine clothes, they will go to it, and some of them may perhaps attach themselves to that society. Others will remain in a perfect state of indifference; the children of these zealous parents will not be able to tell what their religious principles are, and their grandchildren still less. The neighbourhood of a place of worship generally leads them to it, and the action of going thither, is the strongest evidence they can give of their attachment to any sect. The Quakers are the only people who retain a fondness for their own mode of worship; for be they ever so far separated from each other, they hold a sort of communion with the society, and seldom depart from its rules, at least in this country. Thus all sects are mixed as well as all nations; thus religious indifference is imperceptibly disseminated from one end of of the continent to the other; which is at present one of the strongest characteristics of the Americans. Where this will reach no one can tell, perhaps it may leave a vacuum fit to receive other systems. Persecution, religious pride, the love of contradiction, are the food of what the world commonly calls religion. These motives have ceased here; zeal in Europe is confined; here it evaporates in the great distance it has to travel; there it is a grain of powder inclosed, here it burns away in the open air, and consumes without effect. . . .

Individual Rights
and the Declaration of Independence

3

Thomas Paine

Born the son of a Quaker corsetmaker in Thetford, England, Thomas Paine came to write "Common Sense," the most influential political pamphlet ever published in America, to persuade Americans that reconciliation with England was impossible to achieve, unworthy of a free people, and of no advantage. They must go for independence. Arguing for a republican form of government, Paine was the first person to designate the thirteen colonies as the "United States of America."

Family poverty required Paine to leave school at thirteen to become his father's apprentice. In and out of various trades (including, ironically, tax collection) for the next twenty years, Paine finally got in trouble with the authorities for activities involving organization of workers and left for the New World to try his luck. In 1774 he took up journalism in Philadelphia with letters of introduction from Benjamin Franklin, whom he had met in England. He wrote about inventions and the abolition of slavery and edited the new *Pennsylvania Magazine.* He became outspokenly partisan for the patriot cause, benefiting from the English Whig liberalism heritage: a belief in self-government by the well-to-do, which included a balance of great interests such as crown, nobility, church, and commonality. But Paine believed that the monarchy was the root of the evils of society.

When Ben Franklin returned from England in 1775, he suggested to Paine that he might write a history of the American-British conflict. But Dr. Benjamin Rush, a Pennsylvania patriot, suggested that Paine turn from history to work that would convince the Americans of the need for independence; this he did, publishing "Common Sense" (1776) only thirteen months after arriving in the United States. Knowing when Parliament would meet and guessing what the King would say, Paine contrived to have his anonymously authored pamphlet published at the same time the speech arrived in the colonies—magnifying its effect with perfect timing. Within three months, 120,000 copies were circulated. Paine was soon the acknowledged author. The pamphlet helped transform thirteen divergent rebellions into a revolution and to steer the independence versus reconciliation-with-Britain debate into the drafting of the Declaration of Independence.

Paine enlisted in the army later that year and began to edit the revolutionary journal *The Crisis,* beginning the first section with the immortal words: "These are the times that try men's souls. . . ." After serving in several governmental positions in the late 1770s, Paine went to France and actively supported the French Revolution. He wrote *Rights of Man* (1791) to counter Edmund Burke's attack on the Revolution. Here Paine maintains "*the unity of man;* by which I mean that men are all *of one degree,* and consequently that all men are born equal, and with equal natural right. . . ." And further, he argued that a constitution "is a thing *antecedent* to government, and government is only the creature of a constitution. The constitution of a country is not the act of its government, but of the people constituting its government."

Paine served in the French National Convention, but in the next turn of French history, his book was suppressed and he was imprisoned by Robespierre. Later he was freed at the request of American minister James Monroe as a favor to the United States. But his strong defense of the French Revolution and Deism (in *Age of Reason*) and egalitarianism (in *Agrarian Justice,* which advocated progressive state taxes and a form of social security) had turned American public opinion against him. He became hated for his religious views, which were misinterpreted as atheism. In 1809, Paine died in New York City—broke, lonely, and socially ostracized.

Common Sense (1776)
(excerpts)

Introduction

Perhaps the sentiments contained in the following pages, are not *yet* sufficiently fashionable to procure them general favor; a long habit of not thinking a thing *wrong,* gives it a superficial appearance of being *right,* and raises at first a formidable outcry in defence of custom. But the tumult soon subsides. Time makes more converts than reason.

As a long and violent abuse of power, is generally the Means of calling the right of it in question (and in Matters too which might never have been thought of, had not the Sufferers been aggravated into the inquiry) and as the King of England hath undertaken in his *own Right,* to support the Parliament in what he calls *Theirs,* and as the good people of this country are grievously oppressed by the combination, they have an undoubted privilege to inquire into the pretensions of both, and equally to reject the usurpation of either. . . .

The cause of America is in a great measure the cause of all mankind. Many circumstances hath, and will arise, which are not local, but universal, and through which the principles of all Lovers of Mankind are affected, and in the Event of which, their Affections are interested. The laying a Country desolate with Fire and Sword, declaring War against the natural rights of all Mankind, and extirpating the Defenders thereof from the Face of the Earth, is the Concern of every Man to whom Nature hath given the Power of feeling. . . .

Of the origin and design of government in general. With concise remarks on the English constitution.

Some writers have so confounded society with government, as to leave little or no distinction between them; whereas they are not only different, but have different origins. Society is produced by our wants, and government by our wickedness; the former promotes our happiness *positively* by uniting our affections, the latter *negatively* by restraining our vices. The one encourages intercourse, the other creates distinctions. The first is a patron, the last a punisher.

Society in every state is a blessing, but government even in its best state is but a necessary evil; in its worst state an intolerable one; for when we suffer, or are exposed to the same miseries *by a government,* which we might expect in a country *without government,* our calamity is heightened by reflecting that we furnish the means by which we suffer. Government, like dress, is the badge of lost innocence; the palaces of kings are built on the ruins of the bowers of paradise. For were the impulses of conscience clear, uniform, and irresistibly obeyed, man would need no other lawgiver; but that not being the case, he finds it necessary to surrender up a part of his property to furnish means for the protection of the rest; and this he is induced to do by the same prudence which in every other case advises him out of two evils to choose the least. *Wherefore,* security being the true design and end of government, it unanswerably follows, that whatever *form* thereof appears most likely to ensure it to us, with the least expence and greatest benefit, is preferable to all others.

In order to gain a clear and just idea of the design and end of government, let us suppose a small number of persons settled in some sequestered part of the earth, unconnected with the rest, they will then represent the first peopling of any country, or of the world. In this state of natural liberty, society will be their first thought. A thousand motives will excite them thereto, the strength of one man is so unequal to his wants, and his mind so unfitted for perpetual solitude, that he is soon obliged to seek assistance and relief of another, who in his turn requires the same. Four or five united would be able to raise a tolerable dwelling in the midst of a wilderness, but *one* man might labour out the common period of life without accomplishing any thing; when he had felled his timber he could not remove it, nor erect it after it was removed; hunger in the mean time would urge him from his work, and every different want call him a different way. Disease, nay even misfortune would be death, for though neither might be mortal, yet either would disable him from living, and reduce him to a state in which he might rather be said to perish than to die.

Thus necessity, like a gravitating power, would soon form our newly arrived emigrants into society, the reciprocal blessings of which, would supersede, and render the obligations of law and government unnecessary while they remained perfectly just to each other; but as nothing but heaven is impregnable to vice, it will unavoidably happen, that in proportion as they surmount the first difficulties of emigration, which bound them together in a common cause, they will begin to relax in their duty and attachment to each other; and this remissness will point out the necessity of establishing some form of government to supply the defect of moral virtue.

Some convenient tree will afford them a State-House, under the branches of which, the whole colony may assemble to deliberate on public matters. It is more than probable that their first laws will have the title only of REGULATIONS, and be enforced by no other penalty than public disesteem. In this first parliament every man, by natural right, will have a seat.

But as the colony increases, the public concerns will increase likewise, and the distance at which the members may be separated, will render it too inconvenient for all of them to meet on every occasion as at first, when their number was small, their habitations near, and the public concerns few and trifling. This will point out the convenience of their consenting to leave the legislative part to be managed by a select number chosen from the whole body, who are supposed to have the same concerns at stake which those have who appointed them, and who will act in the same manner as the whole body would act, were they present. If the colony continue increasing, it will become necessary to augment the number of the representatives, and that the interest of every part of the colony may be attended to, it will be found best to divide the whole into convenient parts, each part sending its proper number; and that the *elected* might never form to themselves an interest separate from the *electors,* prudence will point out the propriety of having elections often; because as the *elected* might by that means return and mix again with the general body of the *electors* in a few months, their fidelity to the public will be secured by the prudent reflexion of not making a rod for themselves. And as this frequent interchange will establish a common interest with every part of the community, they will mutually and naturally support each other, and on this (not on the unmeaning name of king) depends the *strength of government, and the happiness of the governed.*

Here then is the origin and rise of government; namely a mode rendered necessary by the inability of moral virtue to govern the world; here too is the design and end of government, viz. freedom and security. And however our eyes may be dazzled with show, or our ears deceived by sound; however prejudice may warp our wills, or interest darken our understanding, the simple voice of nature and of reason will say, it is right.

I draw my idea of the form of government from a principle in nature, which no art can overturn, viz. that the more simple any thing is, the less liable it is to be disordered, and the easier repaired when disordered; and with this maxim in view, I offer a few remarks on the so much boasted constitution of England. That it was noble for the dark and slavish times in which it was erected, is granted. When the world was overrun with tyranny the least remove therefrom was a glorious rescue. But that it is imperfect, subject to convulsions, and

incapable of producing what it seems to promise, is easily demonstrated.

Absolute governments (tho' the disgrace of human nature) have this advantage with them, that they are simple; if the people suffer, they know the head from which their suffering springs, know likewise the remedy, and are not bewildered by a variety of causes and cures. But the constitution of England is so exceedingly complex, that the nation may suffer for years together without being able to discover in which part the fault lies; some will say in one and some in another, and every political physician will advise a different medicine.

I know it is difficult to get over local or long standing prejudices, yet if we will suffer ourselves to examine the component parts of the English constitution, we shall find them to be the base remains of two ancient tyrannies, compounded with some new republican materials.

First.—The remains of monarchical tyranny in the person of the king.

Secondly.—The remains of aristocraticial tyranny in the persons of the peers.

Thirdly.—The new republican materials in the persons of the commons, on whose virtue depends the freedom of England.

The two first, by being hereditary, are independent of the people; wherefore in a *constitutional sense* they contribute nothing towards the freedom of the state.

To say that the constitution of England is a *union* of three powers reciprocally *checking* each other, is farcical, either the words have no meaning, or they are flat contradictions.

To say that the commons is a check upon the king, presupposes two things:

First.—That the king is not to be trusted without being looked after, or in other words, that a thirst for absolute power is the natural disease of monarchy.

Secondly.—That the commons, by being appointed for that purpose, are either wiser or more worthy of confidence than the crown.

But as the same constitution which gives the commons a power to check the king by withholding the supplies, gives afterwards the king a power to check the commons, by empowering him to reject their other bills; it again supposes that the king is wiser than those whom it has already supposed to be wiser than him. A mere absurdity!

There is something exceedingly ridiculous in the composition of monarchy; it first excludes a man from the means of information, yet empowers him to act in cases where the highest judgment is required. The state of a king shuts him from the world, yet the business of a king requires him to know it thoroughly; wherefore the different parts, by unnaturally opposing and destroying each other, prove the whole character to be absurd and useless. . . .

In the early ages of the world, according to the scripture chronology, there were no kings; the consequence of which was, there were no wars; it is the pride of kings which throw mankind into confusion. Holland without a king hath enjoyed more peace for this last century than any of the monarchical governments in Europe. Antiquity favours the same remark; for the quiet and rural lives of the first patriarchs hath a happy something in them, which vanishes away when we come to the history of Jewish royalty.

Government by kings was first introduced into the world by the Heathens, from whom the children of Israel copied the custom. It was the most prosperous invention the Devil ever set on foot for the promotion of idolatry. The Heathens paid divine honors to their deceased kings, and the Christian world hath improved on the plan, by doing the same to their living ones. How impious is the title of sacred majesty applied to a worm, who in the midst of his splendor is crumbling into dust! . . .

To the evil of monarchy we have added that of hereditary succession; and as the first is a degradation and lessening of ourselves, so the second, claimed as a matter of right, is an insult and an imposition on posterity. For all men being originally equals, no *one* by *birth* could have a right to set up his own family in perpetual preference to all others for ever, and though himself might deserve *some* decent degree of honors of his contemporaries, yet his descendants might be far too unworthy to inherit them. One of the strongest *natural* proofs of the folly of hereditary right in kings, is, that nature disapproves it, otherwise she would not so frequently turn it into ridicule by giving mankind an *Ass for a Lion.*

Secondly, as no man at first could possess any other public honors than were bestowed upon him, so the givers of those honors could have no power to give away the right of posterity. And though they might say, "We choose you for *our* head," they could not, without manifest injustice to their children, say "that your children and your childrens children shall reign over *ours* for ever." Because such an unwise, unjust, unnatural compact might (perhaps) in the next succession put them under the government of a rogue or a fool. Most wise men in their private sentiments, have ever treated hereditary right with contempt; yet it is one of those evils, which when once established is not easily removed; many submit from fear, others from superstition, and the more powerful part shares with the king the plunder of the rest. . . .

Thoughts on the Present State of American Affairs

. . . As much has been said of the advantages of reconciliation, which, like an agreeable dream, has passed away and left us as we were, it is but right that we should examine the contrary side of the argument and inquire into some of the many material injuries which these colonies sustain, and always will sustain, by being connected with and dependent on Great Britain. To examine that connection and dependence on the principles of nature and common sense; to see what we have to trust to, if separated, and what we are to expect, if dependent.

I have heard it asserted by some that, as America has flourished under her former connection with Great Britain, the same connection is necessary toward her future happiness and will always have the same effect. Nothing can be more fallacious than this kind of argument. We may as well assert that because a child has thrived upon milk that it is never to have meat, or that the first twenty years of our lives is to become a precedent for the next twenty. But even this is admitting more than is true; for I answer roundly that America would have flourished as much, and probably much more, had no European power had anything to do with her. The commerce by which she has enriched herself are the necessaries of life and will always have a market while eating is the custom of Europe.

But she has protected us, say some. That she has engrossed us is true, and defended the continent at our expense as well as her own is admitted; and she would

have defended Turkey from the same motive, viz., for the sake of trade and dominion.

Alas! we have been long led away by ancient prejudices and made large sacrifices to superstition. We have boasted the protection of Great Britain without considering that her motive was *interest,* not *attachment;* and that she did not protect us from *our enemies* on *our account* but from *her enemies* on *her own account,* from those who had no quarrel with us on any *other account* and who will always be our enemies on the *same account.* Let Britain waive her pretensions to the continent or the continent throw off the dependence, and we should be at peace with France and Spain, were they at war with Britain. The miseries of Hanover's last war ought to warn us against connections.

It has lately been asserted in Parliament that the colonies have no relation to each other but through the parent country, i.e., that Pennsylvania and the Jerseys, and so on for the rest, are sister colonies by the way of England; this is certainly a very roundabout way of proving relationship, but it is the nearest and only true way of proving enemyship, if I may so call it. France and Spain never were, nor perhaps ever will be, our enemies as *Americans,* but as our being the *subjects of Great Britain.*

But Britain is the parent country, say some. Then the more shame upon her conduct. Even brutes do not devour their young nor savages make war upon their families; wherefore the assertion, if true, turns to her reproach; but it happens not to be true, or only partly so, and the phrase "parent" or "mother country" has been jesuitically adopted by the king and his parasites with a low papistical design of gaining an unfair bias on the credulous weakness of our minds. Europe, and not England, is the parent country of America. This New World has been the asylum for the persecuted lovers of civil and religious liberty from *every part* of Europe. Hither have they fled, not from the tender embraces of the mother, but from the cruelty of the monster; and it is so far true of England that the same tyranny which drove the first emigrants from home pursues their descendants still.

In this extensive quarter of the globe, we forget the narrow limits of three hundred and sixty miles (the extent of England) and carry our friendship on a larger scale; we claim brotherhood with every European Christian, and triumph in the generosity of the sentiment.

It is pleasant to observe by what regular gradations we surmount the force of local prejudices as we enlarge our acquaintance with the world. A man born in any town in England divided into parishes will naturally associate most with his fellow parishioners (because their interests in many cases will be common) and distinguish him by the name of "neighbor"; if he meet him but a few miles from home, he drops the narrow idea of a street and salutes him by the name of "townsman"; if he travel out of the country and meet him in any other, he forgets the minor divisions of street and town, and calls him "countryman," i.e., "countyman"; but if in their foreign excursions they should associate in France, or any other part of *Europe,* their local remembrance would be enlarged into that of "Englishmen." And by a just parity of reasoning, all Europeans meeting in America, or any other quarter of the globe, are "countrymen"; for England, Holland, Germany, or Sweden, when compared with the whole, stand in the same places on the larger scale which the divisions of street, town, and county do on the smaller ones—distinctions too limited for continental minds. Not one third of the inhabitants, even of this province,[1] are of English descent. Wherefore I reprobate the phrase of parent or mother country applied to England only as being false, selfish, narrow, and ungenerous.

But, admitting that we were all of English descent, what does it amount to? Nothing. Britain, being now an open enemy, extinguishes every other name and title; and to say that reconciliation is our duty is truly farcical. The first king of England of the present line (William the Conqueror) was a Frenchman, and half the peers of England are descendants from the same country; wherefore, by the same method of reasoning, England ought to be governed by France.

Much has been said of the united strength of Britain and the colonies, that in conjunction they might bid defiance to the world. But this is mere presumption; the fate of war is uncertain, neither do the expressions mean anything; for this continent would never suffer itself to be drained of inhabitants to support the British arms in either Asia, Africa, or Europe.

Besides, what have we to do with setting the world at defiance? Our plan is commerce, and that, well attended to, will secure us the peace and friendship of all Europe; because it is the interest of all Europe to have America a free port. Her trade will always be a protection, and her barrenness of gold and silver secure her from invaders.

I challenge the warmest advocate for reconciliation to show a single advantage that this continent can reap by being connected with Great Britain. I repeat the challenge; not a single advantage is derived. Our corn will fetch its price in any market in Europe, and our imported goods must be paid for, buy them where we will.

But the injuries and disadvantages we sustain by that connection are without number, and our duty to mankind at large, as well as to ourselves, instruct us to

---

[1][Pennsylvania]

renounce the alliance; because any submission to or dependence on Great Britain tends directly to involve this continent in European wars and quarrels and sets us at variance with nations who would otherwise seek our friendship and against whom we have neither anger nor complaint. As Europe is our market for trade, we ought to form no partial connection with any part of it. It is the true interest of America to steer clear of European contentions, which she never can do while, by her dependence on Britain, she is made the makeweight in the scale of British politics.

Europe is too thickly planted with kingdoms to be long at peace; and whenever a war breaks out between England and any foreign power, the trade of America goes to ruin *because of her connection with Britain.* The next war may not turn out like the last; and should it not, the advocates for reconciliation now will be wishing for separation then, because neutrality in that case would be a safer convoy than a man-of-war. Everything that is right or natural pleads for separation. The blood of the slain, the weeping voice of nature cries, " *'Tis time to part.*" Even the distance at which the Almighty has placed England and America is a strong and natural proof that the authority of the one over the other was never the design of heaven. The time likewise at which the continent was discovered adds weight to the argument, and the manner in which it was peopled increases the force of it. The Reformation was preceded by the discovery of America—as if the Almighty graciously meant to open a sanctuary to the persecuted in future years, when home should afford neither friendship nor safety.

The authority of Great Britain over this continent is a form of government which sooner or later must have an end. And a serious mind can draw no true pleasure by looking forward, under the painful and positive conviction that what he calls "the present constitution" is merely temporary. As parents, we can have no joy, knowing that this government is not sufficiently lasting to insure anything which we may bequeath to posterity. And by a plain method of argument, as we are running the next generation into debt, we ought to do the work of it; otherwise we use them meanly and pitifully. In order to discover the line of our duty rightly, we should take our children in our hand and fix our station a few years farther into life; that eminence will present a prospect which a few present fears and prejudices conceal from our sight. . . .

A government of our own is our natural right: And when a man seriously reflects on the precariousness of human affairs, he will become convinced, that it is infinitely wiser and safer, to form a constitution of our own in a cool deliberate manner, while we have it in our power, than to trust such an interesting event to time and chance. If we omit it now, some Massanello[2] may hereafter arise, who laying hold of popular disquietudes, may collect together the desperate and the discontented, and by assuming to themselves the powers of government, may sweep away the liberties of the continent like a deluge. Should the government of America return again into the hands of Britain, the tottering situation of things will be a temptation for some desperate adventurer to try his fortune; and in such a case, what relief can Britain give? Ere she could hear the news, the fatal business might be done; and ourselves suffering like the wretched Britons under

---

[2]Thomas Anello, otherwise Massanello, a fisherman of Naples who, after spiriting up his countrymen in the public marketplace against the oppressions of the Spaniards, to whom the place was then subject, prompted them to revolt, and in the space of a day became king.

the oppression of the Conqueror. Ye that oppose independence now, ye know not what ye do; ye are opening a door to eternal tyranny, by keeping vacant the seat of government. There are thousands, and tens of thousands, who would think it glorious to expel from the continent that barbarous and hellish power, which hath stirred up the Indians and Negroes to destroy us; the cruelty hath a double guilt, it is dealing brutally by us, and treacherously by them.

To talk of friendship with those in whom our reason forbids us to have faith, and our affections wounded through a thousand pores instruct us to detest, is madness and folly. Every day wears out the little remains of kindred between us and them, and can there be any reason to hope, that as the relationship expires, the affection will increase, or that we shall agree better, when we have ten times more and greater concerns to quarrel over than ever?

Ye that tell us of harmony and reconciliation, can ye restore to us the time that is past? Can ye give to prostitution its former innocence? Neither can ye reconcile Britain and America. The last cord now is broken, the people of England are presenting addresses against us. There are injuries which nature cannot forgive; she would cease to be nature if she did. As well can the lover forgive the ravisher of his mistress, as the continent forgive the murders of Britain. The Almighty hath implanted in us these unextinguishable feelings for good and wise purposes. They are the guardians of his image in our hearts. They distinguish us from the herd of common animals. The social compact would dissolve, and justice be extirpated [from] the earth, or have only a casual existence were we callous to the touches of affection. The robber, and the murderer, would often escape unpunished, did not the injuries which our tempers sustain, provoke us into justice.

O ye that love mankind! Ye that dare oppose, not only the tyranny, but the tyrant, stand forth! Every spot of the old world is overrun with oppression. Freedom hath been hunted round the globe. Asia, and Africa, have long expelled her—Europe regards her like a stranger, and England hath given her warning to depart. O! receive the fugitive, and prepare in time an asylum for mankind. . . .

To Conclude, however strange it may appear to some, or however unwilling they may be to think so, matters not, but many strong and striking reasons may be given, to shew, that nothing can settle our affairs so expeditiously as an open and determined declaration for independence. Some of which are,

First.—It is the custom of nations, when any two are at war, for some other powers, not engaged in the quarrel, to step in as mediators, and bring about the preliminaries of a peace: but while America calls herself the Subject of Great Britain, no power, however well disposed she may be, can offer her mediation. Wherefore, in our present state we may quarrel on for ever.

Secondly.—It is unreasonable to suppose, that France or Spain will give us any kind of assistance, if we mean only, to make use of that assistance for the purpose of repairing the breach, and strengthening the connection between Britain and America; because, those powers would be sufferers by the consequences.

Thirdly.—While we profess ourselves the subjects of Britain, we must, in the eye of foreign nations, be considered as rebels. The precedent is somewhat dangerous to *their peace,* for men to be in arms under the name of subjects; we, on the spot, can solve the paradox: but to unite resistance and subjection, requires an idea much too refined for common understanding.

Fourthly.—Were a manifesto to be published, and despatched to foreign courts, setting forth the miseries we have endured, and the peaceable methods we have ineffectually used for redress; declaring, at the same time, that not being able, any longer, to live happily or safely under the cruel disposition of the British court, we had been driven to the necessity of breaking off all connections with her; at the same time, assuring all such courts of our peaceable disposition towards them, and of our desire of entering into trade with them: Such a memorial would produce more good effects to this Continent, than if a ship were freighted with petitions to Britain.

Under our present denomination of British subjects, we can neither be received nor heard abroad: The custom of all courts is against us, and will be so, until, by an independence, we take rank with other nations.

These proceedings may at first appear strange and difficult; but, like all other steps which we have already passed over, will in a little time become familiar and agreeable; and, until an independence is declared, the Continent will feel itself like a man who continues putting off some unpleasant business from day to day, yet knows it must be done, hates to set about it, wishes it over, and is continually haunted with the thoughts of its necessity.

George Mason

George Mason (1725–1792) became a prominent political figure in Virginia and is known for drafting the "Virginia Declaration of Rights" (1776)—copied by other American states. He also led the fight with Patrick Henry against ratifying the Constitution, which he had helped to draft, because its final version failed to include bills of rights, compromised on tariff and slave trade issues, and contained provisions for the centralization of power. Born in Fairfax County, Virginia, and educated by a private tutor, Mason grew up with access to a private library on a well-endowed family plantation. With influential neighbors such as George Washington, Mason learned to respect intellectual qualities over material ones and valued a man's intellectual skills not less than the quality of his tobacco leaves— but more. He became one of the wealthiest plantation owners in Virginia, and Thomas Jefferson said he was "of the first order of greatness."

At twenty-three, Mason unsuccessfully sought a seat in the House of Burgesses. The next year he was elected vestryman of Truro Parish and admitted to partnership in the Ohio company. He served as justice of Fairfax County Court and was elected to the House of Burgesses in 1759. In the mid-1760s, he joined the resistance to the enforcement of the Stamp Act. He became known as an early opponent of British colonial policy, drafting the 1769 nonimportation resolutions by the burgesses against the British, as well as the Fairfax Resolves five years later, which recast the constitutional relations between the colonies and the British monarchy. His political service was extensive, given family obligations and ill health. As a member of the Virginia committee on safety at the Virginia Constitutional Convention of 1776, he drafted the famous Virginia Bill of Rights, a model for other states and for Thomas Jefferson in writing the first part of the Declaration of Independence. Always a passionate defender of human rights, Mason was easily bored with the "Bablers" (as he called them) on issues of local provincial politics and treated them curtly. Also a member of the Federal Constitution Convention in Philadelphia in 1787, he helped to draft the Constitution, but then refused to sign it because the end result was not to his liking.

Because of his Anti-Federalist stance, Mason's contributions to the Constitution are difficult to pinpoint. However, he showed his courage as a slaveholder in declaring in 1787 that "every master of slaves is born a petty tyrant." And he even went so far as to make an accurate prophecy: unless heavy restrictions were put upon slavery, it would bring "the judgment of heaven on a Country."

Mason's position on slavery won as few converts as did his fight for taxes on luxuries—though both stances showed that he would take public policy positions that went against his own private interests. Mason wanted to allow state legislators to tax exports to prevent Northern industrial states from taking advantage of agrarian states in the South. For similar reasons he demanded that Congress approve an act regulating commerce between the United States and foreign powers to check the hated "navigation laws." All goods had to be carried back and forth in British ships, and Mason wanted to safeguard Northern shipping firms from demanding subsidies from Southern states. When this provision failed to pass and the bill of rights he submitted was not included, Mason was convinced that the Northern states would succeed in dominating the Constitution politically, refused to sign it and led the opposition to its ratification together with Patrick Henry.

Final Draft of the
Virginia Declaration of Rights (1776)

[12 June 1776]

A DECLARATION OF RIGHTS made by the Representatives of the good people of VIRGINIA, assembled in full and free Convention; which rights do pertain to (them and their) posterity, as the basis and foundation of Government.

1. That all men are (by nature) equally free and independent, and have certain inherent rights, of which, (when they enter into a state of society,) they cannot, by any compact, deprive or divest their posterity; (namely,) the enjoyment of life and liberty, with the means of acquiring and possessing property, and pursuing and obtaining happiness and safety.

2. That all power is vested in, and consequently derived from, the People; that magistrates are their trustees and servants, and at all times amenable to them.

3. That Government is, or ought to be, instituted for the common benefit, protection and security of the people, nation, or community;—of all the various modes and forms of Government that is best which is capable of producing the greatest degree of happiness and safety, and is most effectually secured against the danger of maladministration;—and that, whenever any Government shall be found inadequate or contrary to these purposes, a majority of the community hath an indubitable, unalienable, and indefeasible right, to reform, alter, or abolish it, in such manner as shall be judged most conducive to the publick weal.

4. That no man, or set of men, are entitled to exclusive or separate emoluments and privileges from the community, but in consideration of publick services; which, not being descendible, (neither ought the offices) of Magistrate, Legislator, or Judge, (to be hereditary).

5. That the Legislative and Executive powers of the State should be separate and distinct from the Judicative; and, that the members of the first two may be restrained from oppression, by feeling and participating the burdens of the people, they should, at fixed periods, be reduced to a private station, return into the body from which they were originally taken, and the vacancies be supplied by frequent, certain, and regular elections, (in which all, or any part of the former members, to be again eligible, or ineligible, as the law shall direct).

6. That elections of members to serve as Representatives of the people, in Assembly, ought to be free; and that all men, having sufficient evidence of permanent common interest with, and attachment to, the community, have the right of suffrage, (and cannot be taxed or deprived of their property for) publick uses without their own consent or that of their Representative (so elected,) nor bound by any law to which they have not, in like manner, assented, for the publick good.

7. That all power of suspending laws, or the execution of laws, by any authority, without consent of the Representatives of the people, is injurious to their rights, and ought not to be exercised.

8. That in all capital or criminal prosecutions a man hath a right to demand the cause and nature of his accusation, to be confronted with the accusers and witnesses, to call for evidence in his favour, and to a speedy trial by an impartial jury of his vicinage, without whose unanimous consent he cannot be found guilty, nor can

he be compelled to give evidence against himself; that no man be deprived of his liberty except by the law of the land, or the judgment of his peers.

9. That excessive bail ought not to be required, nor excessive fines imposed, nor cruel and unusual punishments inflicted.

10. That (general) warrants, whereby any officer or messenger may be commanded to search suspected places (without evidence of a fact committed,) or to seize any person or persons (not named, or whose offence is) not particularly described (and supported by evidence,) are grievous and oppressive, and ought not to be granted.

11. That in controversies respecting property, and in suits between man and man, the ancient trial by Jury is preferable to any other, and ought to be held sacred.

12. That the freedom of the Press is one of the greatest bulwarks of liberty, and can never be restrained but by despotick Governments.

13. That a well-regulated Militia, composed of the body of the people, trained to arms, is the proper, natural, and safe defence of a free State; that Standing Armies, in time of peace, should be avoided as dangerous to liberty; and that, in all cases, the military should be under strict subordination to, and governed by, the civil power.

14. That the people have a right to uniform Government; and, therefore, that no Government separate from, or independent of, the Government of *Virginia,* ought to be erected or established within the limits thereof.

15. That no free Government, or the blessing of liberty, can be preserved to any people but by a firm adherence to justice, moderation, temperance, frugality, and virtue, and by frequent recurrence to fundamental principles.

16. That Religion, or the duty which we owe to our *Creator,* and the manner of discharging it, can be directed only by reason and conviction, not by force or violence; and, therefore, all men (are equally entitled to the free) exercise of religion, according to the dictates of conscience; and that it is the mutual duty of all to practise Christian forbearance, love, and charity, towards each other.

Thomas Jefferson

"The care of human life and happiness, and not their destruction, is the first and only legitimate object of good government" wrote the ultimate agrarian democrat. Thomas Jefferson drafted the Declaration of Independence and transformed John Locke's realistic objectives of life, liberty, and *property* into the wider sociological idealism of life, liberty, and *the pursuit of happiness.* Equally wary of aristocratic oppression and mass mob rule, Jefferson combined both the English and French theories of liberalism to adapt them to Virginia and to American frontier country. Born in 1743 into a well-established Virginia frontier family, he received a classical education and later read fifteen hours a day with enthusiasm. During his first eighteen years Jefferson probably never saw a village of more than twenty houses. Graduating from the College of William and Mary in two years, in the next decade he studied, passed the Virginia bar exam, and opened his own law practice.

Jefferson became a member of the Virginia House of Burgesses in 1769 and became known throughout his state. By 1775 he was a delegate to the Continental Congress, impressing all with his knowledge and skills. Five men were appointed in June 1776 to draft the Declaration of Independence: as chairman, Jefferson wrote the first draft, which stayed intact but for slight changes made by Benjamin Franklin and John Adams (see excerpt from Jefferson's *Autobiography*).

Resigning his seat in Congress to return to his sick wife in Virginia, Jefferson worked at revising the laws of Virginia to fit with the emerging republican government. He was elected governor of Virginia in 1779—an arduous task given the historical turmoil.

Notes on Virginia (1782) expressed his agrarian ideals:

> The political economists of Europe have established it as a principle, that every State should endeavor to manufacture for itself; and this principle, like many others, we transfer to America. . . . But we have an immensity of land courting the industry of the husbandman. . . . Those who labor in the earth are chosen people of God, if ever he had a chosen people, whose breasts he has made his peculiar deposit for substantial and genuine virtue. It is the focus in which he keeps alive the sacred fire, which otherwise might escape from the face of the earth. Corruption of morals in the mass of cultivators is a phenomenon of which no age nor nation has furnished an example. . . . Dependence begets subservience and venality, suffocates the germ of virtue, and prepares fit tools for the design of ambition. . . . It is the manner and spirit of a people which preserves a republic in vigor. A degeneracy in these is a canker which soon eats to the heart of its laws and constitution.

Elected to the Confederation in 1783, Jefferson chaired a committee on currency and was responsible, in large part, for the decimal currency still used. In 1785 Jefferson began five years as minister to France, returning in 1790 to become the first secretary of state. His partisan disagreements with Hamilton, who dominated Washington's cabinet (advocating a centralized government of monied aristocracy), were so profound that he resigned in 1794 over Washington's objections. Two years later, Jefferson ran a close second to John Adams in the presidential election, becoming vice president (as the Constitution then stipulated). Four years later, Jefferson was elected on a popular movement affirming his vision of democracy as opposed to the conservative Federalism typified by Hamilton and Adams. By purchasing the Louisiana Territory, Jefferson greatly expanded American lands. In his second term, he faced continual difficulties in attempting to maintain American neutrality in the Napoleonic wars. Upon retiring to his home in Monticello, Jefferson devoted the remainder of his life to education, overseeing development of the University of Virginia until his death in 1826 on the same day that John Adams died.

Autobiography (1821)
(excerpts)

January 6–July 21, 1821

... In 1769, I became a member of the legislature by the choice of the county in which I live, and so continued until it was closed by the Revolution. I made one effort in that body for the permission of the emancipation of slaves, which was rejected: and indeed, during the regal government, nothing liberal could expect success. Our minds were circumscribed within narrow limits, by an habitual belief that it was our duty to be subordinate to the mother country in all matters of government, to direct all our labors in subservience to her interests, and even to observe a bigoted intolerance for all religions but hers. The difficulties with our representatives were of habit and despair, not of reflection and conviction. Experience soon proved that they could bring their minds to rights, on the first summons of their attention. But the King's Council, which acted as another house of legislature, held their places at will, and were in most humble obedience to that will: the Governor too, who had a negative on our laws, held by the same tenure, and with still greater devotedness to it: and, last of

all, the Royal negative closed the last door to every hope of amelioration.

On the 1st of January, 1772, I was married to Martha Skelton, widow of Bathurst Skelton, and daughter of John Wayles, then twenty-three years old. Mr. Wayles was a lawyer of much practice, to which he was introduced more by his great industry, punctuality, and practical readiness, than by eminence in the science of his profession. He was a more agreeable companion, full of pleasantry and good humor, and welcomed in every society. He acquired a handsome fortune, and died in May, 1773, leaving three daughters: the portion which came on that event to Mrs. Jefferson, after the debts should be paid, which were very considerable, was about equal to my own patrimony, and consequently doubled the ease of our circumstances.

When the famous Resolutions of 1765, against the Stamp-act were proposed, I was yet a student of law in Williamsburgh. I attended the debate, however, at the door at the lobby of the House of Burgesses, and heard the splendid display of Mr. Henry's talents as a popular orator. They were great indeed; such as I have never heard from any other man. He appeared to me to speak as Homer wrote. Mr. Johnson, a lawyer, and member from the Northern Neck, seconded the resolutions, and by him the learning and the logic of the case were chiefly maintained. My recollections of these transactions may be seen page 60 of the life of Patrick Henry, by Wirt, to whom I furnished them.

In May, 1769, a meeting of the General Assembly was called by the Governor, Lord Botetourt. I had then become a member; and to that meeting became known the joint resolutions and address of the Lords and Commons, of 1768–9, on the proceedings in Massachusetts. Counter-resolutions, and an address to the King by the House of Burgesses, were agreed to with little opposition, and a spirit manifestly displayed itself of considering the cause of Massachusetts as a common one. The Governor dissolved us: but we met the next day in the Apollo of the Raleigh tavern, formed ourselves into a voluntary convention, drew up articles of association against the use of any merchandise imported from Great Britain, signed and recommended them to the people, repaired to our several counties, and were re-elected without any other exception than of the very few who had declined assent to our proceedings.

Nothing of particular excitement occurring for a considerable time, our countrymen seemed to fall into a state of insensibility to our situation; the duty on tea, not yet repealed, and the declaratory act of a right in the British Parliament to bind us by their laws in all cases whatsoever, still suspended over us. But a court of inquiry held in Rhode Island in 1762, with a power to send persons to England to be tried for offences committed here, was considered, at our session of the spring of 1773, as demanding attention. Not thinking our old and leading members up to the point of forwardness and zeal which the times required, Mr. Henry, Richard Henry Lee, Francis L. Lee, Mr. Carr and myself agreed to meet in the evening, in a private room of the Raleigh, to consult on the state of things. There may have been a member or two more whom I do not recollect. We were all sensible that the most urgent of all measures was that of coming to an understanding with all the other colonies, to consider the British claims as a common cause to all, and to produce a unity of action: and, for this purpose, that a committee of correspondence in each colony would be the best instrument for intercommunication: and that their first measure would probably be, to propose a meeting of deputies from every colony, at some central place, who should be charged with the direction of the measures which should be taken by all. We, therefore, drew up the resolutions which may be seen in Wirt, page 87. The consulting members proposed to me to move them, but I urged that it should be done by Mr. Carr, my friend and brother-in-law, then a new member, to whom I wished an opportunity should be given of making known to the house his great worth and talents. It was so agreed; he moved them, they were agreed to *nem. con.*, and a committee of correspondence appointed, of whom Peyton Randolph, the speaker, was chairman. The Governor (then Lord Dunmore) dissolved us, but the committee met the next day, prepared a circular letter to the speakers of the other colonies, inclosing to each a copy of the resolutions, and left it in charge with their chairman to forward them by expresses.

The origination of these committees of correspondence between the colonies has been since claimed for Massachusetts, and Marshall has given into this error, although the very note of his appendix to which he refers, shows that their establishment was confined to their own towns. This matter will be seen clearly stated in a letter of

Samuel Adams Wells to me of April 2nd, 1819, and my answer of May 12th. I was corrected by the letter of Mr. Wells in the information I had given Mr. Wirt, as stated in his note, page 87, that the messengers of Massachusetts and Virginia crossed each other on the way, bearing similar propositions; for Mr. Wells shows that Massachusetts did not adopt the measure, but on the receipt of our proposition, delivered at their next session. Their message, therefore, which passed ours, must have related to something else, for I well remember Peyton Randolph's informing me of the crossing of our messengers.

The next event which excited our sympathies for Massachusetts, was the Boston port bill, by which that port was to be shut up on the 1st of June, 1774. This arrived while we were in session in the spring of that year. The lead in the House, on these subjects, being no longer left to the old members, Mr. Henry R. H. Lee, Fr. L. Lee, three or four other members, whom I do not recollect, and myself, agreeing that we must boldly take an unequivocal stand in the line with Massachusetts, determined to meet and consult on the proper measures, in the council-chamber, for the benefit of the library in that room. We were under conviction of the necessity of arousing our people from the lethargy into which they had fallen, as to passing events; and thought that the appointment of a day of general fasting and prayer would be most likely to call up and alarm their attention. No example of such a solemnity had existed since the days of our distresses in the war of '55, since which a new generation had grown up. With the help, therefore, of Rushworth, whom we rummaged over for the revolutionary precedents and forms of the Puritans of that day, preserved for him, we cooked up a resolution, somewhat modernizing their phrases for appointing the 1st day of June, on which the port bill was to commence, for a day of fasting,

humiliation, and prayer, to implore Heaven to avert from us the evils of civil war, to inspire us with firmness in support of our rights, and to turn the hearts of the King and Parliament to moderation and justice. To give greater emphasis to our proposition, we agreed to wait the next morning on Mr. Nicholas, whose grave and religious character was more in unison with the tone of our resolution, and to solicit him to move it. We accordingly went to him in the morning. He moved it the same day; the 1st of June was proposed; and it passed without opposition. The Governor dissolved us, as usual. We retired to the Apollo, as before, agreed to an association, and instructed the committee of correspondence to propose to the corresponding committees of the other colonies, to appoint deputies to meet in Congress at such place, *annually,* as should be convenient, to direct from time to time, the measures required by the general interest: and we declared that an attack on any one colony, should be considered as an attack on the whole. This was in May. We further recommended to the several counties to elect deputies to meet at Williamsburgh, the 1st of August ensuing, to consider the state of the colony, and particularly to appoint delegates to a general Congress, should that measure be acceded to by the committees of correspondence generally. It was acceded to; Philadelphia was appointed for the place, and the 5th of September for the time of meeting. We returned home, and in our several counties invited the clergy to meet assemblies of the people on the 1st of June, to perform the ceremonies of the day, and to address to them discourses suited to the occasion. The people met generally, with anxiety and alarm in their countenances, and the effect of the day, through the whole colony, was like a shock of electricity, arousing every man, and placing him erect and solidly on his centre. They chose, universally, delegates for the convention. Being elected one for my own county, I prepared a draught of instructions to be given to the delegates whom we should send to the Congress, which I meant to propose at our meeting. In this I took the ground that, from the beginning, I had thought the only one orthodox or tenable, which was, that the relation between Great Britain and these colonies was exactly the same as that of England and Scotland, after the accession of James, and until the union, and the same as her present relations with Hanover, having the same executive chief, but no other necessary political connection; and that our emigration from England to this country gave her no more rights over us, than the emigrations of the Danes and Saxons gave to the present authorities of the mother country, over England. In this doctrine, however, I had never been able to get anyone to agree with me but Mr. Wythe. He concurred in it from the first dawn of the question. What was the political relation between us and England? Our other patriots, Randolph, the Lees, Nicholas, Pendleton, stopped at the half-way house of John Dickinson, who admitted that England had a right to regulate our commerce, and to lay duties on it for the purposes of regulation, but not of raising revenue. But for this ground there was no foundation in compact, in any acknowledged principles of colonization, nor in reason: expatriation being a natural right, and acted on as such, by all nations, in all ages. I set out for Williamsburgh some days before that appointed for our meeting, but was taken ill of a dysentery on the road, and was unable to proceed. I sent on, therefore, to Williamsburgh, two copies of my draught, the one under cover to Peyton Randolph, who I knew would be in the chair of the convention, the other to Patrick Henry. Whether Mr. Henry disapproved the ground taken, or was too lazy to read it (for he was the laziest man in reading I ever knew) I never learned: but he communicated it to nobody. Peyton Randolph informed the convention he had received such a paper from a member, prevented by sickness from offering it in his place, and he laid it on the table for perusal. It was read generally by the members, approved by many, though thought too bold for the present state of things; but they printed it in pamphlet form, under the title of "A Summary View of the Rights of British America." It found its way to England, was taken up by the opposition, interpolated a little by Mr. Burke so as to make it answer opposition purposes, and in that form ran rapidly through several editions. This information I had from Parson Hurt, who happened at the time to be in London, whither he had gone to receive clerical orders; and I was informed afterwards by Peyton Randolph, that it had procured me the honor of having my name inserted in a long list of proscriptions, enrolled in a bill of attainder commenced in one of the Houses of Parliament, but suppressed in embryo by the hasty step of events, which warned them to be a little cautious. Montague, agent of the House of Burgesses in England, made extracts from the bill, copied the names, and sent them to Peyton Randolph. The names, I think, were about twenty, which he repeated to me, but I recollect those only of Hancock, the two Adamses, Peyton Randolph himself, Patrick Henry, and myself. The convention met on the 1st of August, renewed their association, appointed delegates to the Congress, gave them instructions very temperately and properly expressed, both as to style and matter; and they repaired to Philadelphia at the time appointed. The splendid proceedings of that Congress, at their first session, belong to general history, are known to everyone, and need not therefore be noted here. They terminated their session on the 26th of October, to meet again on the 10th of May ensuing. The convention, at their ensuing session of March, '75, approved of the proceedings of Congress, thanked their delegates, and re-appointed the same persons to represent the colony at the meeting to be held in May: and foreseeing the probability that Peyton Randolph, their president, and speaker also of the House of Burgesses, might be called off, they added me, in that event, to the delegation.

Mr. Randolph was, according to expectation, obliged to leave the chair of Congress, to attend the General Assembly summoned by Lord Dunmore, to meet on the 1st day of June, 1775. Lord North's conciliatory propositions, as they were called, had been received by the Governor, and furnished the subject for which this assembly was convened. Mr. Randolph accordingly attended, and the tenor of these propositions being generally known, as having been addressed to all the governors, he was anxious that the answer of our Assembly, likely to be the first, should harmonize with what he knew to be the sentiments and wishes of the body he had recently left. He feared that Mr. Nicholas, whose mind was not yet up to the mark of the times, would undertake the answer, and therefore pressed me to prepare it. I did so, and, with his aid, carried it through the House, with long and doubtful scruples from Mr. Nicholas and James Mercer, and a dash of cold water on it here and there, enfeebling it somewhat, but finally with unanimity, or a vote approaching it. This being passed, I repaired immediately to Philadelphia, and conveyed to Congress the first notice they had of it. It was entirely approved there. I took my seat with them on the 21st of June. On the 24th, a committee which had been appointed to prepare a declaration of the causes of taking up arms, brought in their report (drawn I believe by J. Rutledge) which, not being liked, the House recommitted it, on the 26th, and added Mr. Dickinson and myself to the committee. On the rising of the House, the

committee having not yet met, I happened to find myself near Governor W. Livingston, and proposed to him to draw the paper. He excused himself and proposed that I should draw it. On my pressing him with urgency, "we are as yet but new acquaintances, sir," said he, "why are you so earnest for my doing it?" "Because," said I, "I have been informed that you drew the Address to the people of Great Britain, a production, certainly, of the finest pen in America." "On that," says he, "perhaps, sir, you may not have been correctly informed." I had received the information in Virginia from Colonel Harrison on his return from that Congress. Lee, Livingston, and Jay had been the committee for that draught. The first, prepared by Lee, had been disapproved and recommitted. The second was drawn by Jay, but being presented by Governor Livingston, had led Colonel Harrison into the error. The next morning, walking in the hall of Congress, many members being assembled, but the House not yet formed, I observed Mr. Jay speaking to R. H. Lee, and leading him by the button of his coat to me. "I understand, sir," said he to me, "that this gentleman informed you, that Governor Livingston drew the Address to the people of Great Britain." I assured him, at once, that I had not received that information from Mr. Lee, and that not a word had ever passed on the subject between Mr. Lee and myself; and after some explanations the subject was dropped. These gentlemen had had some sparrings in debate before, and continued ever very hostile to each other.

I prepared a draught of the declaration committed to us. It was too strong for Mr. Dickinson. He still retained the hope of reconciliation with the mother country, and was unwilling it should be lessened by offensive statements. He was so honest a man, and so able a one, that he was greatly indulged even by those who could not feel his scruples. We therefore requested him to take the paper, and put it into a form he could approve. He did so, preparing an entire new statement, and preserving of the former only the last four paragraphs and half of the preceding one. We approved and reported it to Congress, who accepted it. Congress gave a signal proof of their indulgence to Mr. Dickinson, and of their great desire not to go too fast for any respectable part of our body, in permitting him to draw their second petition to the King according to his own ideas, and passing it with scarcely any amendment. The disgust against this humility was general; and Mr. Dickinson's delight at its passage was the only circumstance which reconciled them to it. The vote being passed, although further observation on it was out of order, he could not refrain from rising and expressing his satisfaction, and concluded by saying, "there is but one word, Mr. President, in the paper which I disapprove, and that is the word *Congress*;" on which Ben Harrison rose and said, "There is but one word in the paper, Mr. President, of which I approve, and that is the word *Congress.*"

On the 22d of July, Dr. Franklin, Mr. Adams, R.H. Lee, and myself were appointed a committee to consider and report on Lord North's conciliatory resolution. The answer of the Virginia Assembly on that subject having been approved, I was requested by the committee to prepare this report, which will account for the similarity of feature in the two instruments.

On the 15th of May, 1776, the convention of Virginia instructed their delegates in Congress, to propose to that body to declare the colonies independent of Great Britain, and appointed a committee to prepare a declaration of rights and plan of government.

In Congress, Friday, June 7, 1776. The delegates from Virginia moved, in obedience to instructions from their constituents, that the Congress should declare that these United colonies are, and of right ought to be, free and independent states, that they are absolved from all allegiance to the British crown, and that all political connection between them and the state of Great Britain is, and ought to be, totally dissolved; that measures should be immediately taken for procuring the assistance of foreign powers, and a Confederation be formed to bind the colonies more closely together.

The House being obliged to attend at that time to some other business, the proposition was referred to the next day, when the members were ordered to attend punctually at ten o'clock.

Saturday, June 8. They proceeded to take it into consideration, and referred it to a committee of the whole, into which they immediately resolved themselves, and passed that day and Monday, the 10th, in debating on the subject.

It was argued by Wilson, Robert R. Livingston, E. Rutledge, Dickinson, and others—

That, though they were friends to the measures themselves, and saw the impossibility that we should ever again be united with Great Britain, yet they were against adopting them at this time:

That the conduct we had formerly observed was wise and proper now, of deferring to take any capital step till the voice of the people drove us into it:

That they were our power, and without them our declarations could not be carried into effect:

That the people of the middle colonies (Maryland, Delaware, Pennsylvania, the Jerseys and New York) were not yet ripe for bidding adieu to British connection, but that they were fast ripening, and, in a short time, would join in the general voice of America:

That the resolution, entered into by this House on the 15th of May, for suppressing the exercise of all powers derived from the crown, had shown, by the ferment into which it had thrown these middle colonies, that they had not yet accommodated their minds to a separation from the mother country:

That some of them had expressly forbidden their delegates to consent to such a declaration, and others had given no instructions, and consequently no powers to give such consent:

That if the delegates of any particular colony had no power to declare such colony independent, certain they were, the others could not declare it for them; the colonies being as yet perfectly independent of each other:

That the assembly of Pennsylvania was now sitting above stairs, their convention would sit within a few days, the convention of New York was now sitting, and those of the Jerseys and Delaware counties would meet on the Monday following, and it was probable these bodies would take up the question of Independence, and would declare to their delegates the voice of their state:

That if such a declaration should now be agreed to, these delegates must retire, and possibly their colonies might secede from the Union:

That such a secession would weaken us more than could be compensated by any foreign alliance:

That in the event of such a division, foreign powers would either refuse to join themselves to our fortunes, or, having us so much in their power as that desperate declaration would place us, they would insist on terms proportionately more hard and prejudicial:

That we had little reason to expect an alliance with those to whom alone, as yet, we had cast our eyes:

That France and Spain had reason to be jealous of that rising power, which would one day certainly strip them of all their American possessions:

That it was more likely they should form a connection with the British court, who, if they should find themselves unable otherwise to extricate themselves from their difficulties, would agree to a partition of our territories, restoring Canada to France, and the Floridas to Spain, to accomplish for themselves a recovery of these colonies:

That it would not be long before we should receive certain information of the disposition of the French court, from the agent whom we had sent to Paris for that purpose:

That if this disposition should be favorable, by waiting the event of the present campaign, which we all hoped would be successful, we should have reason to expect an alliance on better terms:

That this would in fact work no delay of any effectual aid from such ally, as, from the advance of the season and distance of our situation, it was impossible we could receive any assistance during this campaign:

That it was prudent to fix among ourselves the terms on which we should form alliance, before we declared we would form one at all events:

And that if these were agreed on, and our Declaration of Independence ready by the time our Ambassador should be prepared to sail, it would be as well as to go into that Declaration at this day.

On the other side, it was urged by J. Adams, Lee, Wythe, and others, that no gentleman had argued against the policy or the right of separation from Britain, nor had supposed it possible we should ever renew our connection; that they had only opposed its being now declared:

That the question was not whether, by a Declaration of Independence, we should make ourselves what we are not; but whether we should declare a fact which already exists:

That, as to the people or parliament of England, we had always been independent of them, their restraints on our trade deriving efficacy from our acquiescence only, and not from any rights they possessed of imposing them, and that so far, our connection had been federal only, and was now dissolved by the commencement of hostilities:

That, as to the King, we had been bound to him by allegiance, but that this bond was now dissolved by his assent to the last act of Parliament, by which he declares us out of his protection, and by his levying war on us, a fact which had long ago proved us out of his protection; it being a certain position in law, that allegiance and protection are reciprocal, the one ceasing when the other is withdrawn:

That James the II never declared the people of England out of his protection, yet his actions proved it, and the Parliament declared it:

No delegates then can be denied, or ever want, a power of declaring an existing truth:

That the delegates from the Delaware counties having declared their constituents ready to join, there are only two colonies, Pennsylvania and Maryland, whose delegates are absolutely tied up, and that these had, by their instructions, only reserved a right of confirming or rejecting the measure:

That the instructions from Pennsylvania might be accounted for from the times in which they were drawn, near a twelve-month ago, since which the face of affairs has totally changed:

That within that time, it had become apparent that Britain was determined to accept nothing less than a *carte-blanche,* and that the King's answer to the Lord Mayor, Alderman and Common Council of London, which had come to hand four days ago, must have satisfied everyone of this point:

That the people wait for us to lead the way:

That *they* are in favor of the measure, though the instructions given by some of their *representatives* are not:

That the voice of the representatives is not always consonant with the voice of the people, and that this is remarkably the case in these middle colonies:

That the effect of the resolution of the 15th of May has proved this, which, raising the murmurs of some in the colonies of Pennsylvania and Maryland, called forth the opposing voice of the freer part of the people, and proved them to be the majority even in these colonies:

That the backwardness of these two colonies might be ascribed, partly to the influence of proprietary power and connections, and partly, to their having not yet been attacked by the enemy:

That these causes were not likely to be soon removed, as there seemed no probability that the enemy would make either of these the seat of this summer's war:

That it would be vain to wait either weeks or months for perfect unanimity, since it was impossible that all men should ever become of one sentiment on any question:

That the conduct of some colonies, from the beginning of this contest, had given reason to suspect it was their settled policy to keep in the rear of the confederacy, that their particular prospect might be better, even in the worst event:

That, therefore, it was necessary for those colonies who had thrown themselves forward and hazarded all from the beginning, to come forward now also, and put all again to their own hazard:

That the history of the Dutch Revolution, of whom three states only confederated at first, proved that a secession of some colonies would not be so dangerous as some apprehended:

That a declaration of Independence alone could render it consistent with European delicacy, for European powers to treat with us, or even to receive an Ambassador from us:

That till this, they would not receive our vessels into their ports, nor acknowledge the adjudications of our courts of admiralty to be legitimate, in cases of capture of British vessels:

That though France and Spain may be jealous of our rising power, they must think it will be much more formidable with the addition of Great Britain; and will therefore see it their interest to prevent a coalition; but should they refuse, we shall be but where we are; whereas without trying, we shall never know whether they will aid us or not:

That the present campaign may be unsuccessful, and therefore we had better propose an alliance while our affairs wear a hopeful aspect:

That to wait the event of this campaign will certainly work delay, because, during the summer, France may assist us effectually, by cutting off those supplies of provisions from England and Ireland, on which the enemy's armies here are to depend; or by setting in motion the great power they have collected in the West Indies, and calling our enemy to the defence of the possessions they have there:

That it would be idle to lose time in settling the terms of alliance, till we had first determined we would enter into alliance:

That it is necessary to lose no time in opening a trade for our people, who will want clothes, and will want money too, for the payment of taxes:

And that the only misfortune is, that we did not enter into alliance with France six months sooner, as, besides opening her ports for the vent of our last year's produce she might have marched an army into Germany, and prevented the petty princes there, from selling their unhappy subjects to subdue us.

It appearing in the course of their debates, that the colonies of New York, New Jersey, Pennsylvania, Delaware, Maryland, and South Carolina were not yet matured for falling from the parent stem, but that they were fast advancing to that state, it was thought most prudent to wait a while for them, and to postpone the final decision to July 1st; but, that this might occasion as little delay as possible, a committee was appointed to prepare a Declaration of Independence. The committee were John Adams, Dr. Franklin, Roger Sherman, Robert R. Livingston, and myself. Committees were also appointed, at the same time, to prepare a plan of confederation for the colonies, and to state the terms proper to be proposed for foreign alliance. The committee for drawing the Declaration of Independence, desired me to do it. It was accordingly done, and being approved by them, I reported it to the House on Friday, the 28th of June, when it was read, and ordered to lie on the table. On Monday, the 1st of July, the House resolved itself into a committee of the whole, and resumed the consideration of the original motion made by the delegates of Virginia, which, being again debated through the day, was carried in the affirmative by the votes of New Hampshire, Connecticut, Massachusetts, Rhode Island, New Jersey, Maryland, Virginia, North Carolina and Georgia. South Carolina and Pennsylvania voted against it. Delaware had but two members present, and they were divided. The delegates from New York declared they were for it themselves, and were assured their constituents were for it; but that their instructions having been drawn near a twelvemonth before, when reconciliation was still the general object, they were enjoined by them to do nothing which should impede that object. They, therefore, thought themselves not justifiable in voting on either side, and asked leave to withdraw from the question; which was given them. The committee rose and reported their resolution to the House. Mr. Edward Rutledge, of South Carolina, then requested the determination might be put off to the next day, as he believed his colleagues, though they disapproved of the resolution, would then join in it for the sake of unanimity. The ultimate question, whether the House would agree to the resolution of the committee, was accordingly postponed to the next day, when it was again moved, and South Carolina concurred in voting for it. In the meantime, a third member had come post from the Delaware counties, and turned the vote of that colony in favor of the resolution. Members of a different sentiment attending that morning from Pennsylvania also, her vote was changed, so that the whole twelve colonies who were authorized to vote at all, gave their voices for it; and, within a few days, the convention of New York approved of it, and thus supplied the void occasioned by the withdrawing of her delegates from the vote.

Congress proceeded the same day to consider the Declaration of Independence, which had been reported and lain on the table the Friday preceding, and on Monday referred to a committee of the whole. The pusillanimous idea that we had friends in England worth keeping terms with, still haunted the minds of many. For this reason, those passages which conveyed censures on the people of England were struck out, lest they should give them offence. The clause too, reprobating the enslaving the inhabitants of Africa, was struck out in complaisance to South Carolina and Georgia, who had never attempted to restrain the importation of slaves, and who, on the contrary, still wished to continue it. Our northern brethren also, I believe, felt a little tender under those censures; for though their people had very few slaves themselves, yet they had been pretty considerable carriers of them to others. The debates, having taken up the greater parts of the 2d, 3d, and 4th days of July, were, on the evening of the last, closed; the Declaration was reported by the committee, agreed to by the House, and signed by every member present, except Mr. Dickinson. As the sentiments of men are known not only by what they receive, but what they reject also, I will state the form of the Declaration as originally reported. The parts struck out by Congress shall be distinguished by [italics within brackets] and those inserted by them shall be placed in the margin, or in a concurrent column.

A Declaration by the Representatives of the United States of America in General Congress Assembled*

July 4, 1776

When, in the course of human events, it becomes necessary for one people to dissolve the political bands which have connected them with another, and to assume among the powers of the earth the separate and equal station to which the laws of nature and of

---

*This was Jefferson's original title. Congress changed it, on July 19, 1776, to "The Unanimous Declaration of the thirteen united States of America." Since this is Jefferson's most famous paper, the text is given here as he first wrote it and as it was finally corrected. The parts stricken out by Congress are shown in italics within brackets, and insertions are given in the margin or in a parallel column.

nature's God entitle them, a decent respect to the opinions of mankind requires that they should declare the causes which impel them to the separation.

certain

We hold these truths to be self-evident; that all men are created equal; that they are endowed by their creator with [*inherent and*] inalienable rights; that among these are life, liberty, and the pursuit of happiness; that to secure these rights, governments are instituted among men, deriving their just powers from the consent of the governed; that whenever any form of government becomes destructive of these ends, it is the right of the people to alter or to abolish it, and to institute new government, laying its foundation on such principles, and organizing its powers in such form, as to them shall seem most likely to effect their safety and happiness. Prudence, indeed, will dictate that governments long established should not be changed for light and transient causes; and accordingly all experience hath shown that mankind are more disposed to suffer while evils are sufferable, than to right themselves by abolishing the forms to which they are accustomed. But when a long train of abuses and usurpations [*begun at a distinguished period and*] pursuing invariably the same object, evinces a design to reduce them under absolute despotism, it is their right, it is their duty to throw off such government, and to provide new guards for their future security. Such has been the patient sufferance of these Colonies; and such

alter
repeated

is now the necessity which constrains them to [*expunge*] their former systems of government. The history of the present King of Great Britain is a history of [*unremitting*] injuries and usurpations, [*among which appears no solitary fact to contradict the uniform tenor*

all having

of the rest, but all have] in direct object the establishment of an absolute tyranny over these States. To prove this, let facts be submitted to a candid world [*for the truth of which we pledge a faith yet unsullied by falsehood*].

He has refused his assent to laws the most wholesome and necessary for the public good.

He has forbidden his governors to pass laws of immediate and pressing importance, unless suspended in their operation till his assent should be obtained; and, when so suspended, he has utterly neglected to attend to them.

He has refused to pass other laws for the accommodation of large districts of people, unless those people would relinquish the right of representation in the Legislature, a right inestimable to them, and formidable to tyrants only.

He has called together legislative bodies at places unusual, uncomfortable, and distant from the depository of their public records, for the sole purpose of fatiguing them into compliance with his measures.

He has dissolved representative houses repeatedly [*and continually*] for opposing with manly firmness his invasions on the rights of the people.

He has refused for a long time after such dissolutions to cause others to be elected, whereby the legislative powers, incapable of annihilation, have returned to the people at large for their exercise, the State remaining, in the meantime, exposed to all the dangers of invasion from without and convulsions within.

He has endeavored to prevent the population of these States; for that purpose obstructing the laws for naturalization of foreigners, refusing to pass others to encourage their migrations hither, and raising the conditions of new appropriations of lands.

obstructed
by

He has [*suffered*] the administration of justice [*totally to cease in some of these States*] refusing his assent to laws for establishing judiciary powers.

He has made [*our*] judges dependent on his will alone for the tenure of their offices, and the amount and payment of their salaries.

He has erected a multitude of new offices, [*by a self-assumed power*] and sent hither swarms of new officers to harass our people and eat out their substance.

He has kept among us in times of peace standing armies [*and ships of war*] without the consent of our Legislatures.

He has affected to render the military independent of, and superior to, the civil power.

He has combined with others to subject us to a jurisdiction foreign to our constitutions and unacknowledged by our laws, giving his assent to their acts of pretended legislation for quartering large bodies of armed troops among us; for protecting them by a mock trial from punishment for any murders which they should commit on the inhabitants of these States; for cutting off our trade with all parts of the world; for imposing taxes on us without our consent; for depriving us [ ] of the benefits of trial by jury; for transporting us beyond seas to be tried for pretended offences; for abolishing the free system of English laws in a neighboring province, establishing therein an arbitrary government, and enlarging its boundaries, so as to render it at once an example and fit instrument for introducing the same absolute rule into these [*States*] for taking away our charters, abolishing our most valuable laws, and altering fundamentally the forms of our governments; for suspending our own Legislatures, and declaring themselves invested with power to legislate for us in all cases whatsoever.

He has abdicated government here [*withdrawing his governors, and declaring us out of his allegiance and protection*].

He has plundered our seas, ravaged our coasts, burnt our towns, and destroyed the lives of our people.

He is at this time transporting large armies of foreign mercenaries to complete the works of death, desolation, and tyranny already begun with circumstances of cruelty and perfidy [ ] unworthy the head of a civilized nation.

He has constrained our fellow-citizens taken captive on the high seas to bear arms against their country, to become the executioners of their friends and brethren, or to fall themselves by their hands.

He has [ ] endeavored to bring on the inhabitants of our frontiers the merciless Indian savages, whose known rule of warfare is an undistinguished destruction of all ages, sexes, and conditions [*of existence*].

[*He has incited treasonable insurrections of our fellow-citizens, with the allurements of forfeiture and confiscation of our property.*

He has waged cruel war against human nature itself, violating its most sacred rights of life and liberty in the persons of a distant people who never offended him, captivating and carrying them into slavery in another hemisphere, or to incur miserable death in their transportation thither. This piratical warfare, the opprobrium of INFIDEL *powers, is the warfare of the* CHRISTIAN *King of Great Britain. Determined to keep open a market where* MEN *should be bought and sold, he has prostituted his negative for suppressing every legislature attempt to prohibit or to restrain this execrable commerce. And that this assemblage of horrors might want no fact of distinguished die, he is now exciting those very people to rise in arms among us, and to purchase that liberty of which he has deprived them, by murdering the people on whom he also obtruded them: thus paying off former crimes committed against the* LIBERTIES *of one people with crimes which he urges them to commit against the* LIVES *of another.*]

In every stage of these oppressions we have petitioned for redress in the most humble terms: our repeated petitions have been answered only by repeated injuries.

A Prince whose character is thus marked by every act which may define a tyrant is unfit to be the ruler of a [ ] people [*who mean to be free. Future ages will scarcely believe that the hardiness of one man adventured, within the short compass of twelve years only, to lay a foundation so broad and so undisguised for tyranny over a people fostered and fixed in principles of freedom.*]

Nor have we been wanting in attentions to our British brethren. We have warned them from time to time of attempts by their legislature to extend [*a*] jurisdiction over [*these our States*]. We have reminded them of the circumstances of our emigration and settlement here, [*no one of which could warrant so strange a pretension: that these were effected at the expense of our own blood and treasure, unassisted by the wealth or the strength of Great Britain: that in constituting indeed our several forms of government, we had adopted one common king, thereby laying a foundation for perpetual league and amity with them: but that submission to their parliament was no part of our Constitution,*

have

nor ever in idea, if history may be credited: and,] we [ ] appealed to their native justice

and we have conjured them

and magnanimity *[as well as to]* the ties of our common kindred to disavow these

by

usurpations which *[were likely to]* interrupt our connection and correspondence. They too

would inevitably

have been deaf to the voice of justice and of consanguinity, *[and when occasions have been given them, by the regular course of their laws, of removing from their councils the disturbers of our harmony, they have, by their free election, re-established them in power. At this very time too, they are permitting their chief magistrate to send over not only*

We must therefore

soldiers of our common blood, but Scotch and foreign mercenaries to invade and destroy us. These facts have given the last stab to agonizing affection, and manly spirit bids us to renounce forever these unfeeling brethren. We must endeavor to forget our former love for them, and hold them as we hold the rest of mankind, enemies in war, in peace friends.

and hold them as we hold the rest of mankind, enemies in war, in peace friends.

We might have been a free and a great people together; but a communication of grandeur and of freedom, it seems, is below their dignity. Be it so, since they will have it. The road to happiness and to glory is open to us too. We will tread it apart from them, and] acquiesce in the necessity which denounces our *[eternal]* separation [ ]!

We therefore the representatives of the United States of America in General Congress assembled, appealing to the supreme judge of the world for the rectitude of our intentions, do in the name, and by the authority of the good people of these Colonies, solemnly publish and declare, that these united Colonies are, and of right ought to be, free and independent States; that they are absolved from all allegiance to the British crown, and that all political connection between them and the state of Great Britain is, and ought to be, totally dissolved; and that as free and independent States, they have full power to levy war, conclude peace, contract alliances, establish commerce, and to do all other acts and things which independent States may of right do.

And for the support of this declaration, with a firm reliance on the protection of divine providence, we mutually pledge to each other our lives, our fortunes, and our sacred honor.

We therefore the representatives of the United States of America in General Congress assembled, do in the name, and by the authority of the good people of these [*States reject and renounce all allegiance and subjection to the kings of Great Britain and all others who may hereafter claim by, through, or under them; we utterly dissolve all political connection which may heretofore have subsisted between us and the people or parliament of Great Britain: and finally we do assert and declare these Colonies to be free and independent States,*] and that as free and independent States, they have full power to levy war, conclude peace, contract alliances, establish commerce, and to do all other acts and things which independent States may of right do.

And for the support of this declaration, we mutually pledge to each other our lives, our fortunes, and our sacred honor.

Letter to John Adams (1813)

Monticello Oct. 28. 13.

DEAR SIR

According to the reservation between us, of taking up one of the subjects of our correspondence at a time, I turn to your letters of Aug. 16 and Sep. 2.

The passage you quote from Theognis, I think has an Ethical, rather than a political object. The whole piece is a moral *exhortation*, παραίνεσις, and this passage particu-

larly seems to be a reproof to man, who, while with his domestic animals he is curious to improve the race by employing always the finest male, pays no attention to the improvement of his own race, but intermarries with the vicious, the ugly, or the old, for considerations of wealth or ambition. It is in conformity with the principle adopted afterwards by the Pythagoreans, and expressed by Ocellus in another form. Περι δε τῆς ἐκ τῶν αλληλων ανθρω-πων γενεσεως etc.—ουχ ἡδονης ἐνεκα ἡ μιξις. Which, as literally as intelligibility will admit, may be thus translated. "Concerning the interprocreation of men, how, and of whom it shall be, in a perfect manner, and according to the laws of modesty and sanctity, conjointly, this is what I think right. First to lay it down that we do not commix for the sake of pleasure, but of the procreation of children. For the powers, the organs and desires for coition have not been given by god to man for the sake of pleasure, but for the procreation of the race. For as it were incongruous for a mortal born to partake of divine life, the immortality of the race being taken away, god fulfilled the purpose by making the generations uninterrupted and continuous. This therefore we are especially to lay down as a principle, that coition is not for the sake of pleasure." But Nature, not trusting to this moral and abstract motive, seems to have provided more securely for the perpetuation of the species by making it the effect of the oestrum implanted in the constitution of both sexes. And not only has the commerce of love been indulged on this unhallowed impulse, but made subservient also to wealth and ambition by marriages without regard to the beauty, the healthiness, the understanding, or virtue of the subject from which we are to breed. The selecting the best male for a Haram of well chosen females also, which Theognis seems to recommend from the example of our sheep and asses, would doubtless improve the human, as it does the brute animal, and produce a race of veritable αριστοι ["aristocrats"]. For experience proves that the moral and physical qualities of man, whether good or evil, are transmissible in a certain degree from father to son. But I suspect that the equal rights of men will rise up against this privileged Solomon, and oblige us to continue acquiescence under the Ἀμαυρωσις γενεος ἀστων ["the degeneration of the race of men"] which Theognis complains of, and to content ourselves with the accidental aristoi produced by the fortuitous concourse of breeders. For I agree with you that there is a natural aristocracy among men. The grounds of this are virtue and talents. Formerly bodily powers gave place among the aristoi. But since the invention of gunpowder has armed the weak as well as the strong with missile death, bodily strength, like beauty, good humor, politeness and other accomplishments, has become but an auxiliary ground of distinction. There is also an artificial aristocracy founded on wealth and birth, without either virtue or talents; for with these it would belong to the first class. The natural aristocracy I consider as the most precious gift of nature for the instruction, the trusts, and government of society. And indeed it would have been inconsistent in creation to have formed man for the social state, and not to have provided virtue and wisdom enough to manage the concerns of the society. May we not even say that that form of government is the best which provides the most effectually for a pure selection of these natural aristoi into the offices of government? The artificial aristocracy is a mischievous ingredient in government, and provision should be made to prevent it's ascendancy. On the question, What is the best provision, you and I differ; but we differ as rational friends, using the free exercise of our own reason, and mutually indulging it's errors. *You* think it best to put the Pseudo-aristoi into a separate chamber of legislation where they may be hindered from doing mischief by their coordinate branches, and where also they may be a protection to wealth against the Agrarian and plundering enterprises of the Majority of the people. I think that to give them power in order to prevent them from doing mischief, is arming them for it, and increasing instead of remedying the evil. For if the coordinate branches can arrest their action, so may they that of the coordinates. Mischief may be done negatively as well as positively. Of this a cabal in the Senate of the U.S. has furnished many proofs. Nor do I believe them necessary to protect the wealthy; because enough of these will find their way into every branch of the legislation to protect themselves. From 15. to 20. legislatures of our own, in action for 30. years past, have proved that no fears of an equalisation of property are to be apprehended from them.

I think the best remedy is exactly that provided by all our constitutions, to leave to the citizens the free election and separation of the aristoi from the pseudo-aristoi, of the wheat from the chaff. In general they will elect the real good and wise. In some instances, wealth may corrupt, and birth blind them; but not in sufficient degree to endanger the society.

It is probable that our difference of opinion may in some measure be produced by a difference of character in those among whom we live. From what I have seen in Massachusetts and Connecticut myself, and still more from what I have heard, and the character given of the former by yourself, who know them so much better, there seems to be in those two states a traditionary reverence for certain families, which has rendered the offices of the government nearly hereditary in those families. I presume that from an early period of your history, members of these families happening to possess virtue and talents, have honestly exercised them for the good of the people, and by their services have endeared their names to them.

In coupling Connecticut with you, I mean it politically only, not morally. For having made the Bible the Common law of their land they seem to have modelled their morality on the story of Jacob and Leban. But altho' this hereditary succession to office with you may in some degree be founded in real family merit, yet in a much higher degree it has proceeded from your strict alliance of church and state. These families are canonised in the eyes of the people on the common principle "you tickle me, and I will tickle you." In Virginia we have nothing of this. Our clergy, before the revolution, having been secured against rivalship by fixed salaries, did not give themselves the trouble of acquiring influence over the people. Of wealth, there were great accumulations in particular families, handed down from generation to generation under the English law of entails. But the only object of ambition for the wealthy was a seat in the king's council. All their court then was paid to the crown and it's creatures; and they Philipised in all collisions between the king and people. Hence they were unpopular; and that unpopularity continues attached to their names. A Randolph, a Carter, or a Burwell must have great personal superiority over a common competitor to be elected by the people, even at this day.

At the first session of our legislature after the Declaration of Independence, we passed a law abolishing entails. And this was followed by one abolishing the privilege of Primogeniture, and dividing the lands of interstates equally among all their children, or other representatives. These laws, drawn by myself, laid the axe to the root of Pseudo-aristocracy. And had another which I prepared been adopted by the legislature, our work would have been compleat. It was a Bill for the more general diffusion of learning. This proposed to divide every county into wards of 5. or 6. miles square, like your townships; to establish in each ward a free school for reading, writing and common arithmetic; to provide for the annual selection of the best subjects from these schools who might recieve at the public expence a higher degree of education at a district school; and from these district schools to select a certain number of the most promising subjects to be compleated at an University, where all the useful sciences should be taught. Worth and genius would thus have been sought out from every condition of life, and compleatly prepared by education for defeating the competition of wealth and birth for public trusts.

My proposition had for a further object to impart to these wards those portions of self-government for which they are best qualified, by confining to them the care of their poor, their roads, police, elections, the nomination of jurors, administration of justice in small cases, elementary exercises of militia, in short, to have made them little republics, with a Warden at the head of each, for all those concerns which, being under their eye, they would better manage than the larger republics of the county or state. A general call of ward-meetings by their Wardens on the same day thro' the state would at any time produce the genuine sense of the people on any required point, and would enable the state to act in mass, as your people have so often done, and with so much effect, by their town meetings. The law for religious freedom, which made a part of this system, having put down the aristocracy of the clergy, and restored to the citizen the freedom of the mind, and those of entails and descents nurturing an equality of condition among them, this on Education would have raised the mass of the people to the high ground of moral respectability necessary to their own safety, and to orderly government; and would have compleated the great object of qualifying them to select the veritable aristoi, for the trusts of government, to the exclusion of the Pseudalists: and the same Theognis who has furnished the epigraphs of your two letters assures us that "ουδεμιαν πω, Κυρν' ἀγαθοι πολιν ὢλεσαν ἀνδρες ["Curnis, good men have never harmed any city"]." Altho' this law has not yet been acted on but in a small and inefficient degree, it is still considered as before the legislature, with other bills of the revised code, not yet taken up, and I have great hope that some patriotic spirit will, at a favorable moment, call it up, and make it the key-stone of the arch of our government.

With respect to Aristocracy, we should further consider that, before the establishment of the American states, nothing was known to History but the Man of the old world, crouded within limits either small or overcharged, and steeped in the vices which that situation generates. A government adapted to such men would be one thing; but a very different one that for the Man of these states. Here every one may have land to labor for himself if he chuses; or, preferring the exercise of any other industry, may exact for it such compensation as not only to afford a comfortable subsistence, but wherewith to provide for a cessation from labor in old age. Every one, by his property, or by his satisfactory situation, is interested in the support of law and order. And such men may safely and advantageously reserve to themselves a wholsome controul over their public affairs, and a degree of freedom, which in the hands of the Canaille of the cities of Europe, would be instantly perverted to the demolition and destruction of every thing public and private. The history of the last 25. years of France, and of the last 40. years in America, nay of it's last 200. years, proves the truth of both parts of this observation.

But even in Europe a change has sensibly taken place in the mind of Man. Science had liberated the ideas of those who read and reflect, and the American example had kindled feelings of right in the people. An insurrection has consequently begun, of science, talents and courage against rank and birth, which have fallen into contempt. It has failed in it's first effort, because the mobs of the cites, the instrument used for it's accomplishment, debased by ignorance, poverty and vice, could not be restrained to rational action. But the world will recover from the panic of this first catastrophe. Science is progressive, and talents and enterprize on the alert. Resort may be had to the people of the country, a more governable power from their principles and subordination; and rank, and birth, and tinsel-aristocracy will finally shrink into insignificance, even there. This however we have no right to meddle with. It suffices for us, if the moral and physical condition of our own citizens qualifies them to select the able and good for the direction of their government with a recurrence of elections at such short periods as will enable them to displace an unfaithful servant before the mischief he mediates may be irremediable.

I have thus stated my opinion on a point on which we differ, not with a view to controversy, for we are both too old to change opinions which are the result of a long life of inquiry and reflection; but on the suggestion of a former letter of yours, that we ought not to die before we have explained ourselves to each other. We acted in perfect harmony thro' a long and perilous contest for our liberty and independance. A constitution has been acquired which, tho neither of us think perfect, yet both consider as competent to render our fellow-citizens the happiest and securest on whom the sun has ever shone. If we do not think exactly alike as to it's imperfections, it matters little to our country which, after devoting to it long lives of disinterested labor, we have delivered over to our successors in life, who will be able to take care of it, and of themselves.

Of the pamphlet on aristocracy which has been sent to you, or who may be it's author, I have heard nothing but thro' your letter. If the person you suspect it may be known from the quaint, mystical and hyperbolical ideas involved in affected, new-fangled and pedantic terms, which stamp his writings. Whatever it be, I hope your quiet is not to be affected at this day by the rudeness of intemperance of scribblers; but that you may continue in tranquility to live and to rejoice in the prosperity of our country until it shall be your own wish to take your seat among the Aristoi who have gone before you. Ever and affectionately yours.

Th: Jefferson

The Constitution:
Constructive Conservatism and Its Critics

4

John Adams

Active in opposing the Stamp Act and in the revolutionary activities of Boston and Philadelphia, as well as in founding the republic, John Adams became the first vice president and second president of the United States. Adams opposed democracy because he distrusted the people, and he worked selflessly for the welfare of the entire nation, arguing that an aristocratic class could provide for the interests of the poor more adequately than the masses of ordinary people whose interests might be at stake.

Born in 1735 in Braintree (Quincy), Massachusetts, Adams received his B.A. at Harvard College and then began teaching in Worcester, Massachusetts. He decided to become a lawyer, apprenticed under Worcester's most distinguished lawyer, and began legal work in Boston as well, where he helped found "Sodalitas," a group of lawyers who debated issues, including the Stamp Act of 1765. Out of these meetings, Adams published anonymous articles in the Boston *Gazette* tracing the origins of freedom—rights derived from God, not king or Parliament. He drew up a protest against the Stamp Act for Braintree that became a model for other New England towns.

Willing always to speak out for liberty, Adams kept his political independence and served as a Boston representative in the legislature. After sixteen months of semiretirement, he returned to Boston and became associated with the radicals and their patriotic maneuvers. Elected by the radicals to the Governor's Council in 1773, he was rejected by the governor for his partisanship. He then became a delegate to the First Continental Congress in 1774. While in Philadelphia, Adams pushed Congress into action that would lead to the separation of the colonies from Britain and successfully promoted the appointment of George Washington as commander in chief of the colonial forces. He helped formulate principles of foreign policy, helped write resolutions declaring America independent, and supported the Declaration of Independence in congressional debate.

Helping to equip the army as chairman of the Board of War and Ordinance, Adams also aided the revolutionary cause by writing his *Novanglus* papers (1774–75) and *Thoughts on Government* (1776) proposing American principles of liberty and order. Adams represented American commercial and military interests in France and was part of the negotiating team that concluded the Treaty of Paris, ending the War of Independence in 1783. As the first U.S. minister to Britain, Adams became well acquainted with Jefferson, then U.S. minister to France. While in London, he wrote *A Defense of the Constitutions of Government of the United States of America* (1787), excerpted here, in which he praised balanced government and the British parliamentary system (the "most stupendous fabric of human invention"). After returning home, he was chosen vice president of the United States and was reelected to the position in 1792. An attempt to remain a nonpartisan led to a serious rift with Alexander Hamilton, who then took over leadership of the Federalists, Nevertheless, Adams was second president of the United States as the Federalist candidate.

As president, Adams declared his faith in republicanism and asked the people to give up partisan politics. In his administration he established the Department of the Navy;

passed the Alien and Sedition Acts of 1798, which imposed penalties on those criticizing the government; and in 1800 concluded a treaty with France that averted war. He then lost the presidential election to Thomas Jefferson. Adams left the capital bitter about Hamilton and the Federalists and remarked that a "fine load of manure was a fair exchange for the honors and virtues of the world." In retirement, his correspondence on the need to maintain the principles of 1776 continued to reveal his erudition before he died in 1826.

 oj(o

Letter to Thomas Jefferson (1813)

Quincy November 15.13

Dear Sir

I cannot appease my melancholy commiseration for our Armies in this furious snow storm in any way so well as by studying your Letter of Oct. 28.

We are now explicitly agreed, in one important point, vizt. That "there is a natural Aristocracy among men; the grounds of which are Virtue and Talents."

You very justly indulge a little merriment upon this solemn subject of Aristocracy. I often laugh at it too, for there is nothing in this laughable world more ridiculous than the management of it by almost all the nations of the Earth. But while We smile, Mankind have reason to say to Us, as the froggs said to the Boys, What is Sport to you is Wounds and death to Us. When I consider the weakness, the folly, the Pride, the Vanity, the Selfishness, the Artifice, the low craft and meaning cunning, the want of Principle, the Avarice the unbounded Ambition, the unfeeling Cruelty of a majority of those (in all Nations) who are allowed an aristocratical influence; and on the other hand, the Stupidity with which the more numerous multitude, not only become their Dupes, but even love to be Taken in by their Tricks: I feel a stronger

disposition to weep at their destiny, than to laugh at their Folly.

But tho' We have agreed in one point, in Words, it is not yet certain that We are perfectly agreed in Sense. Fashion has introduced an indeterminate Use of the Word "Talents." Education, Wealth, Strength, Beauty, Stature, Birth, Marriage, graceful Attitudes and Motions, Gait, Air, Complexion, Physiognomy, are Talents, as well as Genius and Science and learning. Any one of these Talents, that in fact commands or influences true Votes in Society, gives to the Man who possesses it, the Character of an Aristocrat, in my Sense of the Word.

Pick up, the first 100 men you meet, and make a Republick. Every Man will have an equal Vote. But when deliberations and discussions are opened it will be found that 25, by their Talents, Virtues being equal, will be able to carry 50 Votes. Every one of these 25, is an Aristocrat, in my Sense of the Word; whether he obtains his one Vote in Addition to his own, by his Birth Fortune, Figure, Eloquence, Science, learning, Craft Cunning, or even his Character for good fellowship and a bon vivant.

What gave Sir William Wallace his amazing Aristocratical Superiority? His Strength. What gave Mrs. Clark, her Aristocratical Influence to create Generals Admirals and Bishops? her Beauty. What gave Pompadour and Du Barry the Power of making Cardinals and Popes? their Beauty. You have seen the Palaces of Pompadour and Du Barry: and I have lived for years in the Hotel de Velentinois, with Franklin who had as many Virtues as any of them. In the investigation of the meaning of the Word "Talents" I could write 630 Pages, as pertinent as John Taylors of Hazelwood. But I will select a single Example: for female Aristocrats are nearly as formidable in Society as male.

A daughter of a green Grocer, walks the Streets in London dayly with a baskett of Cabbage, Sprouts, Dandlions and Spinage on her head. She is observed by the Painters to have a beautiful Face, an elegant figure, a graceful Step and a debonair. They hire her to Sitt. She complies, and is painted by forty Artists in a Circle around her. The scientific Sir William Hamilton outbids the Painters, sends her to Schools for a genteel Education and Marries her. This Lady not only causes the Tryumphs of the Nile of Copinhagen and Trafalgar, but seperates Naples from France and finally banishes the King and Queen from Sicilly. Such is the Aristocracy of the natural Talent of Beauty. Millions of Examples might be quoted from History sacred and profane, from Eve, Hannah, Deborah Susanna Abigail, Judith, Ruth, down to Hellen Madame de Maintenon and Mrs. Fitcherbert. For mercy's sake do not compell me to look to our chaste States and Territories, to find Women, one of whom lett go, would, in the Words of Holopherne's Guards "deceive the whole Earth."

The Proverbs of Theognis, like those of Solomon, are Observations on human nature, ordinary life, and civil Society, with moral reflections on the facts. I quoted him as a Witness of the Fact, that there was as much difference in the races of Men as in the breeds of Sheep; and as a sharp reprover and censurer of the sordid mercenary practice of disgracing Birth by preferring gold

to it. Surely no authority can be more expressly in point to prove the existence of Inequalities, not of rights, but of moral intellectual and physical inqualities in Families, descents and Generations. If a descent from, pious, virtuous, wealthy litterary or scientific Ancestors is a letter of recommendation, or introduction in a Mans his favour, and enables him to influence only one vote in Addition to his own, he is an Aristocrat, for a democrat can have but one Vote. Aaron Burr had 100,000 Votes from the single Circumstance of his descent from President Burr and President Edwards.

Your commentary on the Proverbs of Theognis reminded me of two solemn Charactors, the one resembling John Bunyan, the other Scarron. The one John Torrey: the other Ben. Franklin. Torrey a Poet, an Enthusiast, a superstitious Bigot, once very gravely asked my Brother Cranch, "whether it would not be better for Mankind, if Children were always begotten from religious motives only"? Would not religion in this sad case, have as little efficacy in encouraging procreation, as it has now in discouraging it? I should apprehend a decrease of population even in our Country where it increases so rapidly. In 1775 Franklin made a morning Visit, at Mrs. Yards to Sam. Adams and John. He was unusually loquacious. "Man, a rational Creature"! said Franklin. "Come, Let Us suppose a rational Man. Strip him of all his Appetites, especially of his hunger and thirst. He is in his Chamber, engaged in making Experiments, or in pursuing some Problem. He is highly entertained. At this moment a Servant Knocks, "Sir dinner is on Table." "Dinner! Pox! Pough! But what have you for dinner?" Ham and Chickens. "Ham"! "And must I break the chain of my thoughts, to go down and knaw a morsel of a damn'd Hogs Arse"? "Put aside your Ham." "I will dine tomorrow."

Take away Appetite and the present generation would not live a month and no future generation would ever exist. Thus the exalted dignity of human Nature would be annihilated and lost. And in my opinion, the whole loss would be of no more importance, than putting out a Candle, quenching a Torch, or crushing a Firefly, *if in this world only We have hope.*

Your distinction between natural and artificial Aristocracy does not appear to me well founded. Birth and Wealth are conferred on some Men, as imperiously by Nature, as Genius, Strength or Beauty. The Heir is honours and Riches, and power has often no more merit in procuring these Advantages, than he has in obtaining an handsome face or an elegant figure. When Aristocracies, are established by human Laws and honour Wealth and Power are made hereditary by municipal Laws and political Institutions, then I acknowledge artificial Aristocracy to commence: but this never commences, till Corruption in Elections becomes dominant and uncontroulable. But this artificial Aristocracy can never last. The everlasting Envys, Jealousies, Rivalries and quarrells among them, their cruel rapacities upon the poor ignorant People their followers, compel these to sett up Caesar, a Demagogue to be a Monarch and Master, pour mettre chacun a sa place ["to put each one in his place"]. Here you have the origin of all artificial Aristocracy, which is the origin of all Monarchy. And both artificial Aristocracy, and Monarchy, and civil, military, political and hierarchical Despotism, have all grown out of the natural Aristocracy of "Virtues and Talents." We, to be sure, are far remote from this. Many hundred years must roll away before We shall be corrupted. Our pure, virtuous, public spirited federative Republick will last for ever, govern the Globe and introduce the perfection of Man, his perfectability being already proved by Price Priestly, Condorcet Rousseau Diderot and Godwin.

"Mischief has been done by the Senate of U.S." I have known and felt more of this mischief, than Washington, Jefferson and Madison altoge[the]r. But this has been all caused by the constitutional Power of the Senate in Executive Business, which ought to be immediately, totally and eternally abolished.

Your distinction between the aristoi and pseudo aristoi, will not help the matter. I would trust one as soon as the other with unlimited Power. The Law wisely refuses an Oath as a witness in his own cause to the Saint as well as to the Sinner.

No Romance would be more amusing, than the History of your Virginian and our new England Aristocratical Families. Yet even in Rhode Island, where there has been no Clergy, no Church, and I had almost said, no State, and some People say no religion, there has been a constant respect for certain old Families. 57 or 58 years ago, in company with Col. Counsellor, Judge, John Chandler, whom I have quoted before, a Newspaper was brought in. The old Sage asked me to look for the News from Rhode Island and see how the Elections had gone there. I read the List of Wantons, Watsons, Greens, Whipples, Malbones etc. "I expected as much" said the aged Gentleman, "for I have always been of Opinion, that in the most popular Governments, the Elections will generally go in favour of the most ancient families." To this day when any of these Tribes and We may Add Ellerys, Channings Champlins etc are pleased to fall in with the popular current, they are sure to carry all before them.

You suppose a difference of Opinion between You and me, on the Subject of Aristocracy. I can find none. I dislike and detest hereditary honours, Offices Emoluments established by Law. So do you. I am for ex[c]luding legal hereditary distinctions from the U.S. as long as possible. So are you. I only say that Mankind have not yet discovered any remedy against irresistable Corruption in Elections to Offices of great Power and Profit, but making them hereditary.

But will you say our Elections are pure? Be it so; upon the whole. But do you recollect in history, a more Corrupt Election than that of Aaron Burr to be President, or that of De Witt Clinton last year. By corruption, here I mean a sacrifice of every national Interest and honour, to private and party Objects.

I see the same Spirit in Virginia, that you and I see in Rhode Island and the rest of New England. In New York it is a struggle of Family Feuds. A fewdal Aristocracy. Pensylvania is a contest between German, Irish and old English Families. When Germans and Irish Unite, they give 30,000 majorities. There is virtually a White Rose and a Red Rose a Caesar and a Pompey in every State in this Union and Contests and dissentions will be as lasting. The Rivalry of Bourbons and Noailleses produced the French Revolution, and a similar Competition for Consideration and Influence, exists and prevails in every Village in the World.

Where will terminate the Rabies Agri ["madness for land"]? The Continent will be scattered over with Manors, much larger than Livingstons, Van Ranselaers or Phillips's. Even our Deacon Strong will have a Principality among you Southern Folk. What Inequality of Talents will be produced by these Land Jobbers?

Where tends the Mania for Banks? At my Table in Philadelphia, I once proposed to you to unite in endeavours to obtain an Amendment of the Constitution, prohibiting to the separate States the Power of creating Banks; but giving Congress Authority to establish one Bank, with a branch in each State; the whole limited to Ten Millions of dollars. Whether this Project was wise or unwise, I know not, for I had deliberated little on it then and have never thought it worth thinking much of since. But you spurned the Proposition from you with disdain.

This System of Banks begotten, hatched and brooded by Duer, Robert and Governeur Morris, Hamilton and Washington, I have always considered as a System of national Injustice. A Sacrifice of public and private Interest to a few Aristocratical Friends and Favourites. My scheme could have had no such Effect.

Verres plundered Temples and robbed a few rich Men; but he never made such ravages among private property in general, nor swindled so much out of the pocketts of the poor and the middle Class of People as these Banks have done. No people but this would have borne the Imposition so long. The People of Ireland would not bear Woods half pence. What Inequalities of Talent, have been introduced into this Country by these Aristocratical Banks!

Our Winthrops, Winslows, Bradfords, Saltonstalls, Quincys, Chandlers, Leonards Hutchinsons Olivers, Sewalls etc are precisely in the Situation of your Randolphs, Carters and Burwells, and Harrisons. Some of them unpopular for the part they took in the late revolution, but all respected for their names and connections and whenever they fall in with the popular Sentiments, are preferred, cetoris paribus to all others. When I was young, the Summum Bonum in Massachusetts, was to be worth ten thousand pounds Sterling, ride in a Chariot, be Colonel of a Regment of Militia and hold a seat in his Majesty's Council. No Mans Imagination aspired to any thing higher beneath the Skies. But these Plumbs, Chariots, Colonelships and counsellorships are recorded and will never be forgotten. No great Accumulations of Land were made by our early Settlers. Mr. Bausoin a French Refugee, made the first great Purchases and your General Dearborne, born under a fortunate Starr is now enjoying a large Portion of the Aristocratical sweets of them.

As I have no Amanuenses but females, and there is so much about generation in this letter that I dare not ask any one of them to copy it, and I cannot copy it myself I must beg of you to return it to me, your old Friend

John Adams

A Defence of the Constitutions of Government of the United States of America (1787)

(excerpt)

It is undoubtedly honourable in any man, who has acquired a great influence, unbounded confidence, and unlimited power, to resign it voluntarily; and odious to take advantage of such an opportunity to destroy a free government: but it would be madness in a legislator to frame his policy upon a supposition that such magnanimity would often appear. It is his business to contrive his plan in such a manner, that such unlimited influence, confidence, and power, shall never be obtained by any man. The laws alone can be trusted with unlimited confidence:—Those laws, which alone can secure equity between all and every one; which are the bond of that dignity which we enjoy in the commonwealth; the foundation of liberty, and the fountain of equity; the mind, the soul, the counsel, and judgment of the city; whose ministers are the magistrates, whose interpreters the judges, whose servants are all men who mean to be free:—Those laws, which are right reason, derived from the Divinity, commanding honesty, and forbidding iniquity; which are silent magistrates, where the magistrates are only speaking laws; which, as they are founded in eternal morals, are emanations of the Divine mind.

If, "the life of liberty, and the only remedy against self-interest, lies in succession of powers and persons," the United States of America have taken the most effectual measures to secure that life and that remedy, in establishing annual elections of their governors, senators, and representatives. This will probably be allowed to be as perfect an establishment of a succession of powers and persons as human laws can make: but in what manner annual elections of governors and senators will operate remains to be ascertained. It should always be remembered, that this is not the first experiment that was ever made in the world of elections to great offices of state: how they have hitherto operated in every great nation, and what has been their end, is very well known. Mankind have universally discovered that chance was preferable to a corrupt choice, and have trusted Providence rather than themselves. First magistrates and senators had better be made hereditary at once, than that the people should be universally debauched and bribed, go to loggerheads, and fly to arms regularly every year. Thank Heaven! Americans understand calling conventions; and if the time should come, as it is very possible it may, when hereditary descent shall become a less evil than annual fraud and violence, such a convention may still prevent the first magistrate from becoming absolute as well as hereditary.—But if this argument of our author is considered as he intended it, as a proof that a succession of powers and persons in one assembly is the most perfect commonwealth, it is totally fallacious.

Though we allow benevolence and generous affections to exist in the human breast, yet every moral theorist will allow the selfish passions in the generality of men to be the strongest. There are few who love the public better than themselves, though all may have some affection for the public. We are not, indeed, commanded to love our neighbour better than ourselves. Self-interest, private avidity, ambition, and avarice, will exist in every state of society, and under every form of government. A

Isaak, *American Political Thinking.*

succession of powers and persons, by frequent elections, will not lessen these passions in any case, in a governor, senator, or representative; nor will the apprehension of an approaching election restrain them from indulgence if they have the power. The only remedy is to take away the power, by controuling the selfish avidity of the governor, by the senate and house; of the senate, by the governor and house; and of the house, by the governor and senate. Of all possible forms of government, a sovereignty in one assembly, successively chosen by the people, is perhaps the best calculated to facilitate the gratification of self-love, and the pursuit of the private interest of a few individuals; a few eminent conspicuous characters will be continued in their seats in the sovereign assembly, from one election to another, whatever changes are made in the seats around them; by superior art, address, and opulence, by more splendid birth, reputations, and connections, they will be able to intrigue with the people and their leaders out of doors, until they worm out most of their opposers, and introduce their friends: to this end they will bestow all offices, contracts, privileges in commerce, and other emoluments, on the latter and their connections, and throw every vexation and disappointment in the way of the former, until they establish such a system of hopes and fears throughout the state as shall enable them to carry a majority in every fresh election of the house. The judges will be appointed by them and their party, and of consequence will be obsequious enough to their inclinations. The whole judicial authority, as well as the executive, will be employed, perverted, and prostituted to the purposes of electioneering. No justice will be attainable, nor will innocence or virtue be safe, in the judicial courts, but for the friends of the prevailing leaders: legal prosecutions will be instituted and carried on against opposers, to their vexation and ruin, and as they have the public purse at command, as well as

the executive and judicial power, the public money will be expended in the same way. No favours will be attainable but by those who will court the ruling demagogues in the house, by voting for their friends and instruments; and pensions and pecuniary rewards and gratifications, as well as honours and offices of every kind, voted to friends and partisans. The leading minds and most influential characters among the clergy will be courted, and the views of the youth in this department will be turned upon those men, and the road to promotion and employment in the church will be obstructed against such as will not worship the general idol. Capital characters among the physicians will not be forgotten, and the means of acquiring reputation and practice in the healing art will be to get the state trumpeters on the side of youth. The bar too will be made so subservient, that a young gentleman will have no chance to obtain a character or clients, but by falling in with the views of the judges and their creators. Even the theatres, and actors and actresses, must become politicians, and convert the public pleasures into engines of popularity for the governing members of the house. The press, that great barrier and bulwark of the rights of mankind, when it is protected in its freedom by law, can now no longer be free: if the authors, writers, and printers, will not accept of the hire that will be offered them, they must submit to the ruin that will be denounced against them. The presses, with much secrecy and concealment, will be made the vehicles of calumny against the minority, and of panegyric and empirical applauses of the leaders of the majority, and no remedy can possibly be obtained. In one word, the whole system of affairs, and every conceivable motive of hope and fear, will be employed to promote the private interests of a few, and their obsequious majority: and there is no remedy but in arms. Accordingly we find in all the Italian republics the minority always were driven to arms in despair. "The attaining of particular ends requires length of time; designs must lie in fermentation to gain the opportunity to bring matters to perfection." It is true; but less time will be necessary in this case, in general, than even in a simple hereditary monarchy or aristocracy.

An aristocracy, like the Roman senate, between the abolition of royalty and the institution of the tribunate, is of itself a faction, a private partial interest. Yet it was less so than an assembly annually chosen by the people, and vested with all authority, would be; for such an assembly runs faster and easier into an oligarchy than an hereditary aristocratical assembly. The leading members having, as has been before shewn in detail, the appointment of judges, and the nomination to all lucrative and honourable offices, they have thus the power to bend the whole executive and judicial authority to their own private interest, and by these means to increase their own reputations, wealth and influence, and those of their party, at every new election: whereas in a simple hereditary aristocracy, it is the interest of the members in general to preserve an equality among themselves as long as they can; and as they are smaller in number, and have more knowledge, they can more easily unite for that purpose, and there is no opportunity for any one to increase his power by any annual elections. An aspiring aristocratic therefore must take more time, and use more address, to augment his influence: yet we find in experience, that even hereditary aristocracies have never been able to prevent oligarchies rising up among them, but by the most rigorous, severe, and tyrannical regulations, such as the institution of inquisitions, &c.

It may sound oddly to say that the majority is a faction; but it is, nevertheless, literally just. If the majority are partial in their own favour, if they refuse to deny a perfect equality to every member of the minority, they are a faction: and as a popular assembly, collective or representative, cannot act, or will, but by a vote, the first step they take, if they are not unanimous, occasions a division into majority and minority, that is into two parties, and the moment the former is unjust it is a faction. The Roman decemvirs themselves were set up by the people, not by the senate: much longer time would have been required for an oligarchy to have grown up among the patricians and in the senate, if the people had not interposed and demanded a body of laws, that is, a constitution. The senate opposed the requisition as long as they could, but at last appointed the decemvirs, much against their own inclinations, and merely in compliance with the urgent clamours of the people. Nedham thinks, that "as the first founders of the Roman liberty did well in driving out their kings; so on the other side, they did very ill in settling a standing authority within themselves." It is really very injudicious, and very ridiculous, to call those Roman nobles who expelled their kings, founders of the Roman liberty: nothing was farther from their heads or their hearts than national liberty; it was merely a struggle for power between a king and a body of haughty envious nobles; the interests of the people and of liberty had no share in it. The Romans might do well in driving out their king: he might be a bad and incorrigible character; and in such a case any people may do well in expelling or deposing a king. But they did not well in demolishing the single executive magistracy: they should have then demanded a body of laws, a definite constitution, and an integral share in the legislature for the people, with a precise delineation of the powers of the first magistrate and senate. In this case they would have been entitled to the praise of founders of Roman liberty: but as it was, they only substituted one system of tyranny for another, and the new one was worse than the old. They certainly "did very ill in settling a standing sovereign supreme authority within themselves." Thus far our author is perfectly in the right, and the reason he gives for this opinion is very well founded: it is the fame that was given thousands of years before him, by Plato, Socrates, and others, and has been constantly given by all succeeding writers in favour of mixed governments, and against simple ones, "because, lying open to the temptations of honour and profit," or, in other words, having their ambition and vanity, avarice and lust, hatred and resentment, malice and revenge, in short, their self-love, and all their passions ("which are sails too big for any human bulk") unrestrained by any controuling power, they were at once transported by them; made use of their public power not for the good of the commonwealth, but for the gratification of their private passions, whereby they put the commonwealth, into frequent flames of discontent and sedition. Thus far is very well: but when our author goes on, "which might all have been prevented, could they have settled the slate free, indeed, by placing an orderly succession of supreme authority in the hands of the people," he can be followed by no one who knows what is in man, and in society—because that supreme authority falls out of the whole body into a majority at the first vote. To expect self-denial from men, when they have a majority in their favour, and consequently power to gratify themselves, is to disbelieve all history and universal experience; it is to disbelieve Revelation and the Word of God, which informs us, the heart is deceitful above all things, and desperately wicked. There have been examples of self-denial, and will be again; but such exalted virtue never yet existed in any large body of men and lasted long: and our authors argument requires it to be proved, not only that individuals, but that nations and majorities of nations, are capable not only of a

single act, or a few acts of disinterested justice and exalted self-denial, but of a course of such heroic virtue for ages and generations; and not only that they are capable of this, but that it is probable they will practice it. There is no man so blind as not to see, that to talk of founding a government upon a supposition that nations and great bodies of men, left to themselves, will practice a course of self-denial, is either to babble like a new-born infant, or to deceive like an unprincipled impostor. Nedham has himself acknowledged, in several parts of this work, the depravity of men in very strong terms. In this fifth reason he avers "temptations of honour and profit to be sails too big for any human bulk." Why then does he build a system on a foundation which he owns to be so unstable? If his mind had been at liberty to follow his own ideas and principles, he must have seen, that a succession of supreme authority in the hands of the people, by their house of representatives, is at first an aristocracy as despotical as a Roman senate, and becomes an oligarchy even sooner than that assembly fell into the decemvirate. There is this infallible disadvantage in such a government, even in comparison with an hereditary aristocracy, that it lets in vice, profligacy, and corruption, like a torrent, with tyranny; whereas the latter often guards the morals of the people with the utmost severity:—even the despotism of aristocracy preserves the morals of the people.

It is pretended by some, that a sovereignty in a single assembly, annually elected, is the only one in which there is any responsibility for the exercise of power. In the mixed government we contend for, the ministers, at least of the executive power, are responsible for every instance of the exercise of it; and if they dispose of a single commission by corruption, they are responsible to a house of representatives, who may, by impeachment, make them responsible before a senate, where they may be accused, tried, condemned, and punished, by independent judges. But in a single sovereign assembly, each member, at the end of his year, is only responsible to his constituents: and the majority of members who have been in one party, and carried all before them, are to be responsible only to their constituents, not to the constituents of the minority who have been overborne, injured, and plundered. And who are these constituents to whom the majority are accountable? Those very persons to gratify whom they have prostituted the honours, rewards, wealth, and justice of the state. These, instead of punishing, will applaud; instead of discarding, will re-elect, with still greater eclat, and a more numerous majority; for the losing cause will be deserted by numbers: and this will be done in hopes of having still more injustice done, still more honours and profits divided among themselves, to the exclusion and mortification of the minority. It is then astonishing that such a simple government should be preferred to a mixed one, by any rational creature, on the score of responsibility. There is in short, no possible way of defending the minority in such a government, from the tyranny of the majority, but by giving the former a negative on the latter, the most absurd institution that ever took place among men. As the major may bear all possible relations of proportion to the minor part, it may be fifty-one against forty-nine in an assembly of an hundred, or it may be ninety-nine against one only:

it becomes therefore necessary to give the negative to the minority, in all cases, though it be ever so small. Every member must possess it, or he can never be secure that himself and his constituents shall not be sacrificed by all the rest. This is the true ground and original of the liberum veto in Poland; but the consequence has been ruin to that noble but ill-constituted republic. One fool, or one knave, one member of the diet which is a single sovereign assembly, bribed by an intriguing ambassador of some foreign power, has prevented measures the most essential to the defense, safety, and existence of the nation. Hence humiliations and partitions! This also is the reason on which is founded the law of the United Netherlands, that all the seven provinces must be unanimous in the assembly of the States General; and all the cities and other voting bodies in the assemblies of the separate states. Having no sufficient checks in their uncouth constitution, nor any mediating power possessed of the whole executive, they have been driven to demand unanimity instead of a balance: and this must be done in every government of a single assembly, or the majority will instantly oppress the minority. But what kind of government would that be in the United States of America, or any one of them, that should require unanimity, or allow of the liberum veto? It is sufficient to ask the question, for every man will answer it alike. . . .

Patrick Henry

A revolutionary leader and orator renowned for his "Give me liberty or give me death" rallying cry that assured the mobilization of the Virginia militia, Patrick Henry was perhaps the best orator in American history. Born in 1736 in Hanover County, Virginia, Henry spent more time with the streams and woods in the countryside than he did with books. Indeed, Jefferson called Henry, when he first listened to him, the greatest orator he had ever heard and later called him the laziest reader he ever knew. At sixteen Henry operated a country store with his brother. The store failed, and two years later he married and his parents set him up on a farm with a small number of slaves. But Henry preferred the pleasures of farming to the duties involved and sold it after two years, opening another store. This venture failed as well, and he decided to become a lawyer. Studying for the exam on his own, he passed the oral bar exam in 1760 to the surprise of his examiners. He was a success at his new profession, handling more than 1,100 cases in the first three years.

At twenty-seven, Henry took over the defense in the "Parson's Cause" case, which was to establish his reputation as a speaker and advocate of colonial rights. In 1758 the Virginia Assembly passed an act setting the value of tobacco at two pence a pound to pay the Anglican clergy. But this value was far below the market price. The established Anglican church protested to King George II, who disallowed the act. Then the clergy sued for back salary, and everyone took for granted that they would win. But though awkward and shabbily dressed, Henry argued powerfully that the Virginia act of 1758 was just and that the king was not the father but the enemy of his people for disallowing it. He contended that the clergy who opposed the act were enemies, as well. Henry won, and the clergy were awarded one penny for damages.

Elected to Virginia's House of Burgesses, he immediately proposed resolutions condemning the Stamp Act just passed by the British. He argued that only colonial legislatures could levy taxes on the colonists. His position culminated in his famous "tyranny" speech, ending: "Caesar had his Brutus; Charles the First, his Cromwell; and George the Third [interruption with cries of "Treason!"] may profit by their example. If this be treason, make the most of it." (It should be noted that versions of Henry's speeches vary greatly because he never wrote them down.) Henry's resolutions were adopted, and Virginia became the first colony to officially come out against the Stamp Act. Suddenly Henry was the most popular person in his state. Serving as a delegate to the First Continental Congress in 1774, Henry was called to protest against coercive British measures against Boston and Massachusetts. He realized the need for armed resistance, and in 1775, at the second revolutionary convention held in his state, he called for organization of a Virginia militia, concluding: "Is life so dear, or peace so sweet as to be purchased at the price of chains and slavery? Forbid it, Almighty God! I know not what course others may take, but as for me, give me liberty, or give me death!" Following his prophetic words ("The war is actually begun. . . ."), the British and colonists clashed militarily at Lexington and Concord.

Although he anticipated war with Britain, Henry opposed separation until the colonies had a strong government and firm alliances with France and Spain. Therefore, he opposed independence at the Second Continental Congress and lost his cutting edge in political leadership nationally. He was elected the first governor of the new Commonwealth of Virginia in 1776 and thereafter reelected. Later he declined a number of appointments, including one as minister to France and as a delegate to the Constitutional Convention in Philadelphia in 1787, which he boycotted with the words: "I smelt a rat." In 1788 he led the opposition to the ratification of the Constitution in Virginia, arguing that the rights of the state and of its people were insufficiently protected. While he lost this campaign, it helped to prepare the way for the first ten amendments, the Bill of Rights. Henry returned to his law practice. He became more of a Federalist in his later years, and accepted Washington's request to run for the state legislature, which gave him a chance to oppose the states' rights doctrine. Although elected, he died in 1799 before he could take his seat.

✺

Give Me Liberty or Give Me Death (1775)

(Delivered at Richmond, in the Virginia Convention, on a Resolution to put the Commonwealth into a State of Defense, March 23d, 1775)

Mr. President:—

No man thinks more highly than I do of the patriotism, as well as abilities, of the very worthy gentlemen who have just addressed the house. But different men often see the same subject in different lights; and, therefore, I hope it will not be thought disrespectful to those gentlemen, if, entertaining as I do opinions of a character very opposite to theirs, I shall speak forth my sentiments freely and without reserve. This is no time for ceremony. The question before the house is one of awful moment to this country. For my own part, I consider it as nothing less than a question of freedom or slavery; and in proportion to the magnitude of the subject ought to be the freedom of the debate. It is only in this way that we can hope to arrive at truth, and fulfill the great responsibility which we hold to God and our country. Should I keep back my opinions at such a time, through fear of giving offense, I should consider myself as guilty of treason towards my country, and of an act of disloyalty toward the Majesty of Heaven, which I revere above all earthly kings.

Mr. President, it is natural to man to indulge in the illusions of hope. We are apt to shut our eyes against a painful truth, and listen to the song of that siren, till she transforms us into beasts. Is this the part of wise men, engaged in a great and arduous struggle for liberty? Are we disposed to be of the number of those, who, having eyes, see not, and having ears, hear not, the things which so nearly concern their temporal salvation? For my part, whatever anguish of spirit it may cost, I am willing to know the whole truth; to know the worst, and to provide for it.

I have but one lamp by which my feet are guided, and that is the lamp of experience. I know of no way of judging of the future but by the past. And judging by the past, I wish to know what there has been in the conduct of the British ministry for the last ten years to justify those hopes with which gentlemen have been pleased to solace themselves and the house. Is it that insidious smile with which our petition has been lately received? Trust it not, sir; it will prove a snare to your feet. Suffer not yourselves to be betrayed with a kiss. Ask yourselves how this gracious reception of our petition comports with those warlike preparations which cover our waters and darken our land. Are fleets and armies necessary to a work of love and reconciliation? Have we shown ourselves so unwilling to be reconciled, that force must be called in to win back our love? Let us not deceive ourselves, sir. These are the implements of war and subjugation; the last arguments to which kings resort. I ask gentlemen, sir,

What means this martial array, if its purpose be not to force us to submission? Can gentlemen assign any other possible motive for it? Has Great Britain any enemy, in this quarter of the world, to call for all this accumulation of navies and armies? No, sir, she has none. They are meant for us: they can be meant for no other. They are sent over to bind and rivet upon us those chains which the British ministry have been so long forging. And what have we to oppose to them? Shall we try argument? Sir, we have been trying that for the last ten years. Have we anything new to offer upon the subject? Nothing. We have held the subject up in every light of which it is capable; but it has been all in vain. Shall we resort to entreaty and humble supplication? What terms shall we find, which have not been already exhausted? Let us not, I beseech you, sir, deceive ourselves longer. Sir, we have done everything that could be done, to avert the storm which is now coming on. We have petitioned; we have remonstrated; we have supplicated; we have prostrated ourselves before the throne, and have implored its interposition to arrest the tyrannical hands of the ministry and Parliament. Our petitions have been slighted; our remonstrances have produced additional violence and insult; our supplications have been disregarded; and we have been spurned, with contempt, from the foot of the throne! In vain, after these things, may we indulge the fond hope of peace and reconciliation. There is no longer any room for hope. If we wish to be free—if we mean to preserve inviolate those inestimable privileges for which we have been so long contending—if we mean not basely to abandon the noble struggle in which we have been so long engaged, and which we have pledged ourselves never to abandon, until the glorious object of our contest shall be obtained—we must fight! I repeat it, sir, we must fight! An appeal to arms and to the God of Hosts is all that is left us!

They tell us, sir, that we are weak; unable to cope with so formidable an adversary. But when shall we be stronger? Will it be the next week, or the next year? Will it be when we are totally disarmed, and when a British guard shall be stationed in every house? Shall we gather strength by irresolution and inaction? Shall we acquire the means of effectual resistance by lying supinely on our backs and hugging the delusive phantom of hope, until our enemies shall have bound us hand and foot? Sir, we are not weak, if we make a proper use of those means which the God of nature hath placed in our power. Three millions of people, armed in the holy cause of liberty, and in such a country as that which we possess, are invincible by any force which our enemy can send against us. Besides, sir, we shall not fight our battles alone. There is a just God who presides over the destinies of nations, and who will raise up friends to fight our battles for us. The battle, sir, is not to the strong alone; it is to the vigilant, the active, the brave. Besides, sir, we have no election. If we were base enough to desire it, it is now too late to retire from the contest. There is no retreat, but in submission and slavery! Our chains are forged! Their clanking may be heard on the plains of Boston! The war is inevitable—and let it come! I repeat it, sir, let it come.

It is in vain, sir, to extenuate the matter. Gentlemen may cry, Peace, Peace—but there is no peace. The war is actually begun! The next gale that sweeps from the north will bring to our ears the clash of resounding arms! Our brethren are already in the field! Why stand we here idle? What is it that gentlemen wish? What would they have? Is life so dear, or peace so sweet, as to be purchased at the price of chains and slavery? Forbid it, Almighty God! I know not what course others may take; but as for me, give me liberty or give me death!

"We the People" or "We the States"?

(Delivered in the Virginia Convention, June 4th, 1788, on the Preamble and the First Two Sections of the First Article of the Federal Constitution)

Mr. Chairman:—

The Public mind, as well as my own, is extremely uneasy at the proposed change of government. Give me leave to form one of the number of those who wish to be thoroughly acquainted with the reasons of this perilous and uneasy situation, and why we are brought hither to decide on this great national question. I consider myself as the servant of the people of this Commonwealth, as a sentinel over their rights, liberty, and happiness. I represent their feelings when I say that they are exceedingly uneasy, being brought from that state of full security, which they enjoy, to the present delusive appearance of things. Before the meeting of the late Federal Convention at Philadelphia, a general peace and a universal tranquillity prevailed in this country, and the minds of our citizens were at perfect repose; but since that period, they are exceedingly uneasy and disquieted. When I wished for an appointment to this convention, my mind was extremely agitated for the situation of public affairs. I conceive the Republic to be in extreme danger. If our situation be thus uneasy, whence has arisen this fearful jeopardy? It arises from this fatal system; it arises from a proposal to change our government—a proposal that goes to the utter annihilation of the most solemn engagements of the States—a proposal of establishing nine States into a confederacy, to the eventual exclusion of four States. It goes to the annihilation of those solemn treaties we have formed with foreign nations. The present circumstances of France, the good offices rendered us by that kingdom, require our most faithful and most punctual adherence to our treaty with her. We are in alliance with the Spaniards, the Dutch, the Prussians: those treaties bound us as thirteen States, confederated together. Yet here is a proposal to sever that confederacy. Is it possible that we shall abandon all our treaties and national engagements? And for what? I expected to have heard the reasons of an event so unexpected to my mind, and many others. Was our civil polity, or public justice, endangered or sapped? Was the real existence of the country threatened, or was this preceded by a mournful progression of events? This proposal of altering our Federal Government is of a most alarming nature; make the best of this new Government—say it is composed of anything but inspiration—you ought to be extremely cautious, watchful, jealous of your liberty; for, instead of securing your rights, you may lose them forever. If a wrong step be now made, the Republic may be lost forever. If this new Government will not come up to the expectation of the people, and they should be disappointed, their liberty will be lost, and tyranny must and will arise. I repeat it again, and I beg gentlemen to consider, that a wrong step, made now, will plunge us into misery, and our Republic will be lost. It will be necessary for this convention to have a faithful historical detail of the facts that preceded the session of the Federal Convention, and the reasons that actuated its members in proposing an entire alteration of government—and to

Isaak, *American Political Thinking.*

demonstrate the dangers that awaited us. If they were of such awful magnitude as to warrant a proposal so extremely perilous as this, I must assert that this convention has an absolute right to a thorough discovery of every circumstance relative to this great event. And here I would make this inquiry of those worthy characters who composed a part of the late Federal Convention. I am sure they were fully impressed with the necessity of forming a great consolidated government, instead of a confederation. That this is a consolidated government is demonstrably clear, and the danger of such a government is, to my mind, very striking. I have the highest veneration for those gentlemen; but, sir, give me leave to demand what right had they to say, "We, the People"? My political curiosity, exclusive of my anxious solicitude for the public welfare, leads me to ask who authorized them to speak the language of "We, the People," instead of "We, the States"? States are the characteristics and the soul of a confederation. If the States be not the agents of this compact, it must be one great consolidated national government of the people of all the States. I have the highest respect for those gentlemen who formed the convention; and were some of them not here, I would express some testimonial of esteem for them. America had, on a former occasion, put the utmost confidence in them—a confidence which was well placed; and I am sure, sir, I would give up anything to them; I would cheerfully confide in them as my representatives.

But, sir, on this great occasion, I would demand the cause of their conduct. Even from that illustrious man, who saved us by his valor, I would have a reason for his conduct; that liberty which he has given us by his valor tells me to ask this reason, and sure I am, were he here, he would give us that reason: but there are other gentlemen here who can give us this information. The people gave them no power to use their name. That they exceeded their power is perfectly clear. It is not mere curiosity that actuates me; I wish to bear the real, actual, existing danger, which should lead us to take those steps so dangerous in my conception. Disorders have arisen in other parts of America, but here, sir, no dangers, no insurrection or tumult, has happened; everything has been calm and tranquil. But notwithstanding this, we are wandering on the great ocean of human affairs. I see no landmark to guide us. We are running we know not whither. Difference in opinion has gone to a degree of inflammatory resentment in different parts of the country, which has been occasioned by this perilous innovation. The Federal Convention ought to have amended the old system; for this purpose they were solely delegated: the object of their mission extended to no other consideration. You must therefore forgive the solicitation of one unworthy member to know what danger could have arisen under the present confederation, and what are the causes of this proposal to change our government.

Richard Henry Lee

Although Richard Henry Lee is the presumed author of two controversial Anti-Federalist pamphlets entitled "Letters from the Federal Farmer to the Republican" (1787–1788), the question of authorship is still not a settled matter. A Virginia delegate to Congress when Congress received the Constitution from the Philadelphia Convention, Lee was clearly the main instigator of the drive to have Congress amend the document before it was transmitted to the states for ratification. However, his specific proposals for a bill of rights were pushed aside by Congress, which decided to send on the Constitution to the states in its original form.

Lee was born in 1732 in Stratford, Virginia, and educated in England. He returned to Virginia to enter the House of Burgesses and, together with Patrick Henry, he led the opposition to British colonial regulations. His oratorical skills were so great that he was called the "Virginia Cicero" by his contemporaries. As a delegate to the First Continental Congress of 1774, Lee pressed strong measures against England. On June 7, 1776, he introduced a resolution calling for independence of the American colonies from Britain, which the Second Continental Congress adopted on July 2. Joining Samuel Adams, he opposed the active French role in American peacemaking attempts.

Following the Revolution, Lee returned to Congress and was elected its president for the 1784–85 session. He vehemently opposed a new strong central government before he died in 1794.

Letters from the Federal Farmer
to the Republican (1787)
(excerpts)

Essentials of a Free Government

October 9, 1787.

Dear Sir,

The essential parts of a free and good government are a full and equal representation of the people in the legislature, and the jury trial of the vicinage in the administration of justice—a full and equal representation, is that which possesses the same interests, feelings, opinions, and views the people themselves would were they all assembled—a fair representation, therefore, should be so regulated, that every order of men in the community, according to the common course of elections, can have a share in it—in order to allow professional men, merchants, traders, farmers, mechanics, &c. to bring a just proportion of their best informed men respectively into the legislature, the representation must be considerably numerous—We have about 200 state senators in the United States, and a less number than that of federal representatives cannot, clearly, be a full representation of this people, in the affairs of internal taxation and police, were there but one legislature for the whole union. The representation cannot be equal, or the situation of the people proper for one government only—if the extreme parts of the society cannot be represented as fully as the central—It is apparently impracticable that this should be the case in this extensive country—it would be impossible to collect a representation of the parts of the country five, six, and seven hundred miles from the seat of government.

Under one general government alone, there could be but one judiciary, one

Isaak, *American Political Thinking.*

supreme and a proper number of inferior courts. I think it would be totally impracticable in this case to preserve a due administration of justice, and the real benefits of the jury trial of the vicinage—there are now supreme courts in each state in the union; and a great number of county and other courts subordinate to each supreme court—most of these supreme and inferior courts are itinerant, and hold their sessions in different parts every year of their respective states, counties and districts—with all these moving courts, our citizens, from the vast extent of the country must travel very considerable distances from home to find the place where justice is administered. I am not for bringing justice so near to individuals as to afford them any temptation to engage in law suits; though I think it one of the greatest benefits in a good government, that each citizen should find a court of justice within a reasonable distance, perhaps, within a day's travel of his home; so that, without great inconveniences and enormous expenses, he may have the advantages of his witnesses and jury—it would be impracticable to derive these advantages from one judiciary—the one supreme court at most could only set in the centre of the union, and move once a year into the centre of the eastern and southern extremes of it—and, in this case, each citizen, on an average, would travel 150 or 200 miles to find this court—that however inferior courts might be properly placed in the different counties, and districts of the union, the appellate jurisdiction would be intolerable and expensive.

If it were possible to consolidate the states, and preserve the features of a free government, still it is evident that the middle states, the parts of the union, about the seat of government, would enjoy great advantages, while the remote states would experience the many inconveniences of remote provinces. Wealth, offices, and the benefits of government would collect in the centre: and the extreme states, and their principal towns, become much less important.

There are other considerations which tend to prove that the idea of one consolidated whole, on free principles, is ill-founded—the laws of a free government rest on the confidence of the people, and operate gently—and never can extend their influence very far—if they are executed on free principles, about the centre, where the benefits of the government induce the people to support it voluntarily, yet they must be executed on the principles of fear and force in the extremes—This has been the case with every extensive republic of which we have any accurate account.

There are certain unalienable and fundamental rights, which in forming the social compact, ought to be explicitly ascertained and fixed—a free and enlightened people in forming this compact, will not resign all their rights to those who govern, and they will fix limits to their legislators and rulers, which will soon be plainly seen by those who are governed, as well as by those who govern: and the latter will know they cannot be passed unperceived by the former, and without giving a general alarm—These rights should be made the basis of every constitution; and if a people be so situated or have such different opinions that they cannot agree in ascertaining and fixing them, it is a very strong argument against their attempting to form one entire society, to live under one system of laws only.—I confess, I never thought the people of these states differed essentially in these respects; they having derived all these rights from one common source, the British systems; and having in the formation of their state constitutions, discovered that their ideas relative to these rights are very similar. However, it is now said that the states differ so essentially in these respects, and even in the important article of the trial by jury, that when assembled in convention, they can agree to no words by which to establish that trial, or by which to ascertain and establish many other of these rights, as fundamental articles in the social compact. If so, we proceed to consolidate the states on no solid basis whatever.

But I do not pay much regard to the reasons given for not bottoming the new constitution on a better bill of rights. I still believe a complete federal bill of rights to be very practicable. Nevertheless I acknowledge the proceedings of the convention furnish my mind with many new and strong reasons, against a complete consolidation of the states. They tend to convince me, that it cannot be carried with propriety very far—that the convention have gone much farther in one respect than they found it practicable to go in another; that is, they propose to lodge in the general government very extensive powers—*powers* nearly, if not altogether, complete and unlimited, over the purse and the sword. But, in its organization, they furnish the strongest proof that the proper limbs, or parts of a government, to support and execute those powers on proper principles (or in which they can be safely lodged) cannot be formed. These powers must be lodged somewhere in every society; but then they should be lodged where the strength and guardians of the people are collected. They can be wielded, or safely used, in a free country only by an able executive and judiciary, a respectable senate, and a secure, full, and equal representation of the people. I think the principles I have premised or brought into view, are well founded—I think they will not be denied by any fair reasoner. It is in connection with these, and other solid principles, we are to examine the constitution. It is not a few democratic phrases, or a few well formed features, that will prove its merits; or a few small omissions that will produce its rejection among men of sense; they will enquire what are the essential powers in a community, and

what are nominal ones; where and how the essential powers shall be lodged to secure government, and to secure true liberty.

In examining the proposed constitution carefully, we must clearly perceive an unnatural separation of these powers from the substantial representation of the people. The state governments will exist, with all their governors, senators, representatives, officers and expenses; in these will be nineteen twentieths of the representatives of the people; they will have a near connection, and their members an immediate intercourse with the people; and the probability is, that the state governments will possess the confidence of the people, and be considered generally as their immediate guardians.

The general government will consist of a new species of executive, a small senate, and a very small house of representatives. As many citizens will be more than three hundred miles from the seat of this government as will be nearer to it, its judges and officers cannot be very numerous, without making our governments very expensive. Thus will stand the state and the general governments, should the constitution be adopted without any alterations in their organization; but as to powers, the general governments will possess all essential ones, at least on paper, and those of the states a mere shadow of power. And therefore, unless the people shall make some great exertions to restore to the state governments their powers in matters of internal police; as the powers to lay and collect, exclusively, internal taxes, to govern the militia, and to hold the decisions of their own judicial courts upon their own laws final, the balance cannot possibly continue long; but the state governments must be annihilated, or continue to exist for no purpose.

It is however to be observed, that many of the essential powers given the national government are not exclusively given; and the general government may have prudence enough to forbear the exercise of those which may still be exercised by the respective states. But this cannot justify the impropriety of giving powers, the exercise of which prudent men will not attempt, and imprudent men will, or probably can, exercise only in a manner destructive of free government. The general government, organized as it is, may be adequate to many valuable objects, and be able to carry its laws into execution on proper principles in several cases; but I think its warmest friends will not contend, that it can carry all the powers proposed to be lodged in it into effect, without calling to its aid a military force, which must very soon destroy all elective governments in the country, produce anarchy, or establish despotism. Though we cannot have now a complete idea of what will be the operations of the proposed system, we may, allowing things to have their common course, have a very tolerable one. The powers lodged in the general government, if exercised by it, must intimately affect the internal police of the states, as well as external concerns;

and there is no reason to expect the numerous state governments, and their connections, will be very friendly to the execution of federal laws in those internal affairs, which hitherto have been under their own immediate management. There is more reason to believe, that the general government, far removed from the people, and none of its members elected oftener than once in two years, will be forgot or neglected, and its laws in many cases disregarded, unless a multitude of officers and military force be continually kept in view, and employed to enforce the execution of the laws, and to make the government feared and respected. No position can be truer than this. That in this country either neglected laws, or a military execution of them, must lead to a revolution, and to the destruction of freedom. Neglected laws must first lead to anarchy and confusion; and a military execution of laws is only a shorter way to the same point—despotic government.

Your's, &c.
The Federal Farmer

Organization and Powers
of the Proposed Government I

October 10th, 1787.

Dear Sir,

The great object of a free people must be so to form their government and laws and so to administer them, as to create a confidence in, and respect for the laws; and thereby induce the sensible and virtuous part of the community to declare in favor of the laws, and to support them without an expensive military force. I wish, though I confess I have not much hope, that this

may be the case with the laws of congress under the new constitution. I am fully convinced that we must organize the national government on different principles, and make the parts of it more efficient, and secure in it more effectually the different interests in the community; or else leave in the state governments some powers proposed to be lodged in it—at least till such an organization shall be found to be practicable. Not sanguine in my expectations of a good federal administration, and satisfied, as I am, of the impracticability of consolidating the states, and at the same time of preserving the rights of the people at large. I believe we ought still to leave some of those powers in the state governments, in which the people, in fact, will still be represented—to define some other powers proposed to be vested in the general government, more carefully, and to establish a few principles to secure a proper exercise of the powers given it. It is not my object to multiply objections, or to contend about inconsiderable powers or amendments; I wish the system adopted with a few alterations; but those, in my mind, are essential ones; if adopted without, every good citizen will acquiesce though I shall consider the duration of our governments, and the liberties of this people, very much dependant on the administration of the general government. A wise and honest administration, may make the people happy under any government; but necessity only can justify even our leaving open avenues to the abuse of power, by wicked, unthinking, or ambitious men. I will examine, first, the organization of the proposed government, in order to judge; 2d. with propriety, what powers are improperly, at least prematurely lodged in it. I shall examine, 3d, the undefined powers; and 4th, those powers, the exercise of which is not secured on safe and proper ground.

First. As to the organization—the house of representatives, the democrative branch, as it is called, is to consist of 65 members: that is, about one representative for fifty thousand inhabitants, to be chosen biennially—the federal legislature may increase this number to one for each thirty thousand inhabitants, abating fractional numbers in each state.—Thirty-three representatives will make a quorum for doing business, and a majority of those present determine the sense of the house.—I have no idea that the interests, feelings, and opinions of three or four millions of people, especially touching internal taxation can be collected in such a house.—In the nature of things, nine times in ten, men of the elevated classes in the community only can be chosen—Connecticut, for instance, will have five representatives—not one man in a hundred of those who form the democrative branch in the state legislature, will, on a fair computation, be one of the five—. The people of this country, in one sense, may all be democratic; but if we make the proper distinction between the few men of wealth and abilities, and consider them, as we ought, as the natural aristocracy of the country, and the great body of the people, the middle and lower classes, as the democracy, this federal representative branch will have but very little democracy in it, even this small representation is not secured on proper principles.—The branches of the legislature are essential parts of the fundamental compact, and ought to be so fixed by the people, that the legislature cannot alter itself by modifying the elections of its own members. This, by a part of Art. 1. Sect. 4, the general legislature may do, it may evidently so regulate elections as to secure the choice of any particular description of men.—It may make the whole state one district—make the capital, or any places in the state, the place or places of election—it may declare that the five men (or whatever the number may be the state may chuse) who shall have the most votes shall be considered as chosen—In this case it is easy to perceive how the people who live scattered in the inland towns will bestow their votes on different men—and how a few men in a city, in any order or profession, may unite and place any five men they please highest among those that may be voted for—and all this may be done constitutionally, and by those silent operations, which are not immediately perceived by the people in general.—I know it is urged, that the general legislature will be disposed to regulate elections on fair and just principles:—This may be true—

good men will generally govern well with almost any constitution: but why in laying the foundation of the social system, need we unnecessarily leave a door open to improper regulations?—This is a very general and unguarded clause, and many evils may flow from that part which authorises the congress to regulate elections—Were it omitted, the regulations of elections would be solely in the respective states, where the people are substantially represented; and where the elections ought to be regulated, otherwise to secure a representation from all parts of the community, in making the constitution, we ought to provide for dividing each state into a proper number of districts, and for confining the electors in each district to the choice of some men, who shall have a permanent interest and residence in it; and also for this essential object, that the representative elected shall have a majority of the votes of those electors who shall attend and give their votes.

In considering the practicability of having a full and equal representation of the people from all parts of the union, not only distances and different opinions, customs, and views common in extensive tracts of country, are to be taken into view, but many differences peculiar to Eastern, Middle, and Southern states. These differences are not so perceivable among the members of congress, and men of general information in the states, as among the men who would properly form the democratic branch. The Eastern states are very democratic, and composed chiefly of moderate freeholders; they have but few rich men and no slaves; the Southern states are composed chiefly of rich planters and slaves; they have but few moderate freeholders, and the prevailing influence, in them, is generally a dissipated aristocracy: The Middle states partake partly of the Eastern and partly of the Southern character.

Perhaps, nothing could be more disjointed, unweildly and incompetent to doing business with harmony and dispatch, than a federal house of representatives properly numerous for the great objects of taxation, &c. collected from the several states; whether such men would ever act in concert; whether they would not worry along a few years, and then be the means of separating the parts of the union, is very problematical?—View this system in whatever form we can, propriety brings us still to this point, a federal government possessed of general and complete powers, as to those national objects which cannot well come under the cognizance of the internal laws of the respective states, and this federal government, accordingly, consisting of branches not very numerous.

The house of representatives is on the plan of consolidation, but the senate is entirely on the federal plan; and Delaware will have as much constitutional influence in the senate, as the largest state in the union: and in this senate are lodged legislative, executive and judicial powers: Ten states in this union urge that they are small states, nine of which were present in the convention.—They were interested in collecting large powers into the hands of the senate, in which each state still will have its equal share of power. I suppose it was impracticable for the three large states, as they were called, to get the senate formed on any other principles: But this only proves, that we cannot form one general government on equal and just principles— and proves, that we ought not to lodge in it such extensive powers before we are convinced of the practicability of organizing it on just and equal principles. . . .

Robert Yates

Robert Yates was an Anti-Federalist leader famous for his attacks on the Constitution, which were published in a series of letters signed "Brutus." Born in 1738 in Schenectady, New York, Yates received a classical education in New York City, was admitted to the bar, and then moved to Albany, where he served on the board of aldermen.

Before the Revolution, Yates was a radical Whig and represented the county of Albany in the four provincial conferences and the convention meeting from 1775 through 1777. Even before the new state government was established, Yates was appointed a justice of the Supreme Court, where he served with impartiality to the point of receiving criticism by members of his own party for being fair to the Loyalists. He was later made chief justice.

In the mid-1780s, Yates emerged as a leader of the Anti-Federalists. He was appointed with fellow Anti-Federalist John Lansing and Federalist Alexander Hamilton to represent New York at the convention of 1787. Yates served with Lansing as a member of the compromise committee and then left the convention after giving his report with Lansing. He left because he thought the convention, called to revise the Articles of Confederation, had overstepped its authority in devising a plan to consolidate the separate states into one national state that would impair the sovereignty of New York. When the Federal Constitution was published, Yates attacked it in a series of letters signed "Brutus." Also, some of the Anti-Federalist papers signed "Rough Hewer" have been attributed to Yates. He voted against ratification at the Poughkeepsie Convention which ratified the Constitution on behalf of New York. Yates accepted the results, even running (unsuccessfully) for governor with the support of the Federalists. After losing a second time in a race for governor, Yates retired as chief justice at sixty, as required by law. He died in the modest circumstances in which he had always lived in 1801.

Nobody forecast the importance the judicial branch would have in the Constitution with such uncanny accuracy as Robert Yates in the following excerpt. To answer this powerful attack, Alexander Hamilton felt obliged to write Nos. 78 and 81 of *The Federalist Papers* to head off fears raised by Yates's predictions of the potential superiority of judicial review over legislative power.

Letters of Brutus (1788)

(excerpts)

31 January 1788

Brutus, No. 11

... Much has been said and written upon the subject of this new system on both sides, but I have not met with any writer, who has discussed the judicial powers with any degree of accuracy. And yet it is obvious, that we can form but very imperfect ideas of the manner in which this government will work, or the effect it will have in changing the internal police and mode of distributing justice at present subsisting in the respective states, without a thorough investigation of the powers of the judiciary and of the manner in which they will operate. This government is a complete system, not only for making, but for executing laws. And the courts of law, which will be constituted by it, are not only to decide upon the constitution and the laws made in pursuance of it, but by officers subordinate to them to execute all their decisions. The real effect of this system of government, will therefore be brought home to the feelings of the people, through the medium of the judicial power. It is, moreover, of great importance, to examine with care the nature and extent of the judicial power, because those who are to be vested with it, are to be placed in a situation altogether unprecedented in a free country. They are to be rendered totally independent, both of the people and the legislature, both with respect to their offices and salaries. No errors they may commit can be corrected by any power above them, if any such power there be, nor can they be removed from office for making ever so many erroneous adjudications.

The only causes for which they can be displaced, is, conviction of treason, bribery, and high crimes and misdemeanors.

This part of the plan is so modelled, as to authorize the courts, not only to carry into execution the powers expressly given, but where these are wanting or ambiguously expressed, to supply what is wanting by their own decisions. ... They [the courts] will give the sense of every article of the constitution, that may from time to time come before them. And in their decisions they will not confine themselves to any fixed or established rules, but will determine, according to what appears to them, the reason and spirit of the constitution. The opinions of the supreme court, whatever they may be, will have the force of law; because there is no power provided in the constitution, that can correct their errors, or controul their adjudications.

From this court there is no appeal. And I conceive the legislature themselves, cannot set aside a judgment of this court, because they are authorized by the constitution to decide in the last resort. The legislature must be controuled by the constitution, and not the constitution by them. They have therefore no more right to set aside any judgment pronounced upon the construction of the constitution, than they have to take from the president, the chief command of the army and navy, and commit it to some other person. The reason is plain; the judicial and executive derive their authority from the same source, that the legislature do theirs; and therefore in all cases, where the constitution does not make the one responsible to, or controulable by the other, they are altogether independent of each other.

The judicial power will operate to effect, in the most certain, but yet silent and imperceptible manner, what is evidently the tendency of the constitution:— I mean, an entire subversion of the legislative, executive and judicial powers of the individual states. Every adjudication of the supreme court on any question that may arise upon the nature and extent of the general government, will affect the limits of the state jurisdiction. In proportion as the former enlarge the exercise of their powers, will that of the latter be restricted.

That the judicial power of the United States will lean strongly in favour of the general government, and will give such an explanation to the constitution, as will favour an extension of its jurisdiction, is very evident from a variety of considerations.

1st. The constitution itself strongly countenances such a mode of construction. Most of the articles in this system, which convey powers of any considerable importance, are conceived in general and indefinite terms, which are either equivocal, ambiguous, or which require long definitions to unfold the extent of their meaning.

The two most important powers committed to any government, those of raising money, and of raising and keeping up troops, have already been considered, and shewn to be unlimited by anything but the discretion of the legislature. The clause which vests the power to pass all laws which are proper and necessary, to carry the powers given into execution, it has been shewn, leaves the legislature at liberty, to do every thing, which in their judgment is best. It is said, I know, that this clause confers no power on the legislature, which they would not have had without it—though I believe this is not the fact, yet, admitting it to be, it implies that the constitution is not to receive an explanation strictly, according to its letter; but more power is implied than is expressed. And this clause, if it is to be considered, as explanatory of the extent of the powers given, rather than giving a new power, is to be understood as declaring, that in construing any of the articles conveying power, the spirit, intent and design of the clause, should be attended to, as well as the words in their common acceptation.

This constitution gives sufficient colour for adopting an equitable construction, if we consider the great end and design it professedly has in view—this appears from its preamble to be, "to form a more perfect union, establish justice, insure domestic tranquility, provide for the common defense, promote the general welfare, and secure the blessings of liberty to ourselves and posterity." The design of this system is here expressed, and it is proper to give such a meaning to the various parts, as will best promote the accomplishment of the end; this idea suggests itself naturally upon reading the preamble, and will countenance the court in giving the several articles such a sense, as will the most effectually promote the ends of the constitution had in view—how this manner of explaining the constitution will operate in practice, shall be the subject of future enquiry.

2d. Not only will the constitution jus-

tify the courts in inclining to this mode of explaining it, but they will be interested in using this latitude of interpretation. Every body of men invested with office are tenacious of power; they feel interested, and hence it has become a kind of maxim, to hand down their offices, with all its rights and privileges, unimpaired to their successors; the same principle will influence them to extend their power, and increase their rights: this of itself will operate strongly upon the courts to give such a meaning to the constitution in all cases where it can possibly be done, as will enlarge the sphere of their own authority. Every extension of the power of the general legislature, as well as of the judicial powers, will increase the powers of the courts; and the dignity and importance of the judges, will be in proportion to the extent and magnitude of the powers they exercise. I add, it is highly probable that emolument of the judges will be increased, with the increase of the business they will have to transact and its importance. From these considerations the judges will be interested to extend the powers of the courts, and to construe the constitution as much as possible, in such a way as to favour it; and that they will do it, appears probable.

3d. Because they will have precedent to plead, to justify them in it. It is well known, that the courts in England, have by their own authority, extended their jurisdiction far beyond the limits set them in their original institution, and by the laws of the land. . . .

When the courts will have a president [precedent] before them of a court which extended its jurisdiction in opposition to an act of the legislature, is it not to be expected that they will extend theirs, especially when there is nothing in the constitution expressly against it? and they are authorized to construe its meaning, and are not under any controul?

This power in the judicial, will enable them to mould the government, into almost any shape they please. . . .

James Madison

James Madison is known as the "father of the Constitution" and particularly for his "Federalist Paper No. 10." He stands for the principle of checks and balances which, added to the separation of powers, means that American government cannot act decisively unless all significant interests are in agreement. This "interest-group liberalism" (as political scientist Theodore Lowi called it) is the basis of the framework of American liberalism.

Born in 1751 into a wealthy Virginia family, Madison graduated from Princeton and eight years later became a delegate to the Continental Congress. He soon became leader of the House of Delegates from Orange County and attended the Annapolis Convention of 1786 as a delegate from Virginia, where he lobbied for calling the Philadelphia Convention. Representing Virginia at the Philadelphia Convention, he advocated a strong central government so effectively that many called him the "Father of the Constitution." For example, he drafted the Virginia plan, which attempted to avert the evils suffered under the Articles of Confederation by permitting the new government to act directly on individuals rather than states. Madison authored about thirty of *The Federalist* essays (1787–88), which were signed by "Publius" and published in New York newspapers designed by the Federalists to build support for the ratification of the Constitution. (Hamilton conceived the idea and wrote about fifty of the eighty-five essays; John Jay authored five.) Although used as propaganda to promote the Constitution, the essays of *The Federalist* are often considered the greatest examples of American political thinking and the clearest statement of the intentions of the Founders and of the meaning of the Constitution. Madison was also the principal author of the Bill of Rights and steered it through Congress.

He was elected to the House of Representatives, where he became increasingly critical of Hamilton's economic policies and emerged as a leader of the Jeffersonian party.

Madison voluntarily retired to do some farming, but was called back to become secretary of state when Jefferson was elected in 1800. Eight years later, Madison was elected the fourth president of the United States, but became bogged down with the War of 1812, which he failed to manage well. He died in 1836.

The Federalist No. 10 (1787)

November 22, 1787

To the People of the State of New York:

Among the numerous advantages promised by a well constructed Union, none deserves to be more accurately developed than its tendency to break and control the violence of faction. The friend of popular governments, never finds himself so much alarmed for their character and fate, as when he contemplates their propensity to this dangerous vice. He will not fail therefore to set a due value on any plan which, without violating the principles to which he is attached, provides a proper cure for it. The instability, injustice and confusion introduced into the public councils, have in truth been the mortal diseases under which popular governments have every where perished; as they continue to be the favorite and fruitful topics from which the adversaries to liberty derive their most specious declamations. The valuable improvements made by the American constitutions on the popular models, both ancient and modern, cannot certainly be too much admired; but it would be an unwarrantable partiality, to contend that they have as effectually obviated the danger on this side as was wished and expected. Complaints are every where heard from our most considerate and virtuous citizens, equally the friends of public and private faith, and of public and personal liberty; that our governments are too unstable; that the public good is disregarded in the conflicts of rival parties; and that measures are too often decided, not according to the rules of justice, and the rights of the minor party; but by the superior force of an interested and over-bearing majority. However anxiously we may wish that these complaints had no foundation, the evidence of known facts will not permit us to deny that they are in some degree true. It will be found indeed, on a candid review of our situation, that some of the distresses under which we labor, have been erroneously charged on the operation of our governments; but it will be found, at the same time, that other causes will not alone account for many of our heaviest misfortunes; and particularly, for that prevailing and increasing distrust of public engagements, and alarm for private rights, which are echoed from one end of the continent to the other. These must be chiefly, if not wholly, effects of the unsteadiness and injustice, with which a factious spirit has tainted our public administrations.

By a faction I understand a number of citizens, whether amounting to a majority or minority of the whole, who are united and actuated by some common impulse of passion, or of interest, adverse to the rights of other citizens, or to the permanent and aggregate interests of the community.

There are two methods of curing the mischiefs of faction: the one, by removing its causes; the other, by controling its effects.

There are again two methods of removing the causes of faction: the one by destroying the liberty which is essential to its existence; the other, by giving to every citizen the same opinions, the same passions, and the same interests.

It could never be more truly said than of the first remedy, that it is worse than the disease. Liberty is to faction, what air is to fire, an aliment without which it instantly expires. But it could not be a less folly to abolish liberty, which is essential to political life, because it nourishes faction, than it would be to wish the annihilation of air, which is essential to animal life, because it imparts to fire its destructive agency.

The second expedient is as impracticable, as the first would be unwise. As long as the reason of man continues fallible, and he is at liberty to exercise it, different opinions will be formed. As long as the connection subsists between his reason and his self-love, his opinions and his passions will have a reciprocal influence on each other; and the former will be objects to which the latter will attach themselves. The diversity in the faculties of men from which the rights of property originate, is not less an insuperable obstacle to a uniformity of interests. The protection of these faculties is the first object of Government. From the protection of different and unequal faculties of acquiring property, the possession of different degrees and kinds of property immediately results: and from the influence of these on the sentiments and views of the respective proprietors, ensues a division of the society into different interests and parties.

The latent causes of faction are thus sown in the nature of man; and we see them every where brought into different degrees of activity, according to the different circumstances of civil society. A zeal for different opinions concerning religion, concerning Government and many other points, as well of speculation as of practice; an attachment to different leaders ambitiously contending for pre-eminence and power; or to persons of other descriptions whose fortunes have been interesting to the human passions, have in turn divided mankind into parties, inflamed them with mutual animosity, and rendered them much more disposed to vex and oppress each other, than to co-operate for their common good. So strong is this propensity of mankind to fall into mutual animosities, that where no substantial occasion presents itself, the most frivolous and fanciful distinctions have been sufficient to kindle their unfriendly passions, and excite their most violent conflicts. But the most common and durable source of factions, has been the various and unequal distribution of property. Those who hold, and those who are without property, have ever formed distinct interests in society. Those who are creditors, and those who are debtors, fall under a like discrimination. A landed interest, a manufacturing interest, a mercantile interest, a monied interest, with many lesser interests, grow up of necessity in civilized nations, and divide them into different classes, actuated by different sentiments and views. The regulation of these various and interfering interests forms the principal task of modern Legislation, and involves the spirit of party and faction in the necessary and ordinary operations of Government.

No man is allowed to be a judge in his own cause; because his interest would certainly bias his judgment, and, not improbably, corrupt his integrity. With equal, nay with greater reason, a body of men, are unfit to be both judges and parties, at the same time; yet, what are many of the most important acts of legislation, but so many judicial determinations, not indeed concerning the rights of single persons, but concerning the rights of large bodies of citizens; and what are the different classes of legislators, but advocates and parties to the causes which they determine? Is a law proposed concerning private debts? It is a question to which the creditors are parties on one side, and the debtors on the other. Justice ought to hold the balance between them. Yet the parties are and must be themselves the judges; and the most numerous party, or, in other words the most powerful faction must be expected to prevail. Shall domestic manufactures be encouraged, and in what degree, by restrictions on foreign manufactures? are questions which would be differently decided by the landed and the manufacturing classes; and probably by neither, with a sole regard to justice and the public good. The apportionment of taxes on the various descriptions of property, is an act which seems to require the most exact impartiality; yet, there is perhaps no legislative act in which greater opportunity and temptation are given to a predominant party, to trample on the rules of justice. Every shilling with which they over-burden the inferior number, is a shilling saved to their own pockets.

It is in vain to say, that enlightened statesmen will be able to adjust these clashing interests, and render them all subservient to the public good. Enlightened statesmen will not always be at the helm. Nor, in many cases, can such an adjustment be made at all, without taking into view indirect and remote considerations, which will rarely prevail over the immediate interest which one party may find in disregarding the rights of another, or the good of the whole.

The inference to which we are brought, is, that the *causes* of faction cannot be removed; and that relief is only to be sought in the means of controling its *effects.*

If a faction consists of less than a majority, relief is supplied by the republican principle, which enables the majority to defeat its sinister views by regular vote: It may clog the administration, it may convulse the society; but it will be unable to execute and mask its violence under the forms of the Constitution. When a majority is included in a faction, the form of popular government on the other hand enables it to sacrifice to its ruling passion or interest, both the public good and the rights of other citizens. To secure the public good, and private rights, against the danger of such a faction, and at the same time to preserve the spirit and the form of popular government, is then the great object to which our enquiries are directed: Let me add that it is the great desideratum, by which alone this form of government can be rescued from the opprobrium under which it has so long labored, and be recommended to the esteem and adoption of mankind.

By what means is this object attainable? Evidently by one of two only. Either the existence of the same passion or interest in a majority at the same time, must be prevented; or the majority, having such co-existent passion or interest, must be tendered, by their number and local situation, unable to concert and carry into effect schemes of oppression. If the impulse and the opportunity be suffered to coincide, we well know that neither moral nor religious motives can be relied on as an adequate control. They are not found to be such on the injustice and violence of individuals, and lose their efficacy in proportion to the number combined together; that is, in proportion as their efficacy becomes needful.

From this view of the subject, it may be concluded, that a pure Democracy, by which I mean, a Society, consisting of a small number of citizens, who assemble and administer the Government in person, can admit of no cure for the mischiefs of faction. A common passion or interest will, in almost every case, be felt by a majority of the whole; a communication and concert results from the form of Government itself; and there is nothing to check the inducements to sacrifice the weaker party, or an obnoxious individual. Hence it is, that such Democracies have ever been spectacles of turbulence and contention; have ever been found incompatible with personal security, or the rights of property; and have in general been as short in their lives, as they have been violent in their deaths. Theoretic politicians, who have patronized this species of Government, have erroneously supposed, that by reducing mankind to a perfect equality in their political rights, they would, at the same time, be perfectly equalized and assimilated in their possessions, their opinions, and their passions.

A Republic, by which I mean a Government in which the scheme of representation takes place, opens a different prospect, and promises the cure for which we are seeking. Let us examine the points in which it varies from pure Democracy, and we shall comprehend both the nature of the cure, and the efficacy which it must derive from the Union.

The two great points of difference between a Democracy and a Republic are, first, the delegation of the Government, in the latter, to a small number of citizens elected by the rest: secondly, the greater number of citizens, and greater sphere of country, over which the latter may be extended.

The effect of the first difference is, on the one hand to refine and enlarge the public views, by passing them through the medium of a chosen body of citizens, whose wisdom may best discern the true interest of their country, and whose patriotism and love of justice, will be least likely to sacrifice it to temporary or partial considerations. Under such a regulation, it may well happen that the public voice pronounced by the representatives of the people, will be more consonant to the public good, than if pronounced by the people themselves convened for the purpose. On the other hand, the effect may be inverted. Men of factious tempers, of local prejudices, or of sinister designs, may by intrigue, by corruption or by other means, first obtain the suffrages, and then betray the interests of the people. The question resulting is, whether small or extensive Republics are most favorable to the election of proper guardians of the public weal: and it is clearly decided in favor of the latter by two obvious considerations.

In the first place it is to be remarked that however small the Republic may be, the Representatives must be raised to a certain number, in order to guard against the cabals of a few; and that however large it may be, they must be limited to a certain number, in order to guard against the confusion of a multitude. Hence the number of Representatives in the two cases, not being in proportion to that of the Constituents, and being proportionally greatest in the small Republic, it follows, that if the proportion of fit characters, be not less, in the large than in the small Republic, the former will present a greater option, and consequently a greater probability of a fit choice.

In the next place, as each Representative will be chosen by a greater number of citizens in the large than in the small Republic, it will be more difficult for unworthy candidates to practice with success the vicious arts, by which elections are too often carried; and the suffrages of the people being more free, will be more likely to centre on men who possess the most attractive merit, and the most diffusive and established characters.

It must be confessed, that in this, as in most other cases, there is a mean, on both sides of which inconveniences will be found to lie. By enlarging too much the number of electors, you render the representative too little acquainted with all their local circumstances and lesser interests; as by reducing it too much, you render him unduly attached to these, and too little fit to comprehend and pursue great and national objects. The Federal Constitution forms a happy combination in this respect; the great and aggregate interests being referred to the national, the local and particular, to the state legislatures.

The other point of difference is, the greater number of citizens and extent of territory which may be brought within the compass of Republican, than of Democratic Government; and it is this circumstance principally which renders factious combinations less to be dreaded in the former, than in the latter. The smaller the society, the fewer probably will be the distinct parties and interests composing it; the fewer the distinct parties and interests, the more frequently will a majority be found of the same party; and the smaller the number of individuals composing a majority, and the smaller the compass within which they are placed, the more easily will they concert and execute their plans of oppression. Extend the sphere, and you take in a greater variety of parties and interests; you make it less probable that a majority of the whole will have a common motive to invade the rights of other citizens; or if such a common motive exists, it will be more difficult for all who feel it to discover their own strength, and to act in unison with each other. Besides other impediments, it may be remarked, that where there is a consciousness of unjust or dishonorable purposes, communication is always checked by distrust, in proportion to the number whose concurrence is necessary.

Hence it clearly appears, that the same advantage, which a Republic has over a Democracy, in controling the effects of faction, is enjoyed by a large over a small Republic—is enjoyed by the Union over the States composing it. Does this advantage consist in the substitution of Representatives, whose enlightened views and virtuous sentiments render them superior to local prejudices, and to schemes of injustice? It will not be denied, that the Representation of the Union will be most likely to possess these requisite endowments. Does it consist in the greater security afforded by a greater variety of parties, against the event of any one party being able to outnumber and oppress the rest? In an equal degree does the increased variety of parties, comprised within the Union, increase this security. Does it, in fine, consist in the greater obstacles opposed to the concert and accomplishment of the secret wishes of an unjust and interested majority? Here, again, the extent of the Union gives it the most palpable advantage.

The influence of factious leaders may kindle a flame within their particular States, but will be unable to spread a general conflagration through the other States: a religious sect, may degenerate into a political faction in a part of the Confederacy; but the variety of sects dispersed over the entire fact of it, must secure the national Councils against any danger from that source: a rage for paper money, for an abolition of debts, for an equal division of property, or for any other improper or wicked project, will be less apt to pervade the whole body of the Union, than a particular member of it; in the same proportion as such a malady is more likely to taint a particular county or district, than an entire State.

In the extent and proper structure of the Union, therefore, we behold a Republican remedy for the diseases most incident to Republican Government. And according to the degree of pleasure and pride, we feel in being Republicans, ought to be our zeal in cherishing the spirit, and supporting the character of Federalists.

PUBLIUS.

The Federalist No. 37 (1788)
(excerpts)

January 11, 1788

To the People of the State of New York:

In reviewing the defects of the existing Confederation, and showing that they cannot be supplied by a government of less energy than that before the public, several of the most important principles of the latter fell of course under consideration. But as the ultimate object of these papers is to determine clearly and fully the merits of this Constitution and the expediency of adopting it, our plan cannot be complete without taking a more critical and thorough survey of the work of the convention, without examining it on all its sides, comparing it in all its parts, and calculating its probable effects. . . .

Among the difficulties encountered by the convention a very important one must have lain in combining the requisite stability and energy in government with the inviolable attention due to liberty and to the republican form. Without substantially accomplishing this part of their undertaking, they would have very imperfectly fulfilled the object of their appointment or the expectation of the public; yet that it could not be easily accomplished will be denied by no one who is unwilling to betray his ignorance of the subject. Energy in government is essential to that security against external and internal danger, and to that prompt and salutary execution of the laws which enter into the very definition of good government. Stability in government is essential to national character and to the advantages annexed to it, as well as to that repose and confidence in the minds of the people, which are among the chief blessings of civil society. An irregular and mutable legislation is not more an evil in itself than it is odious to the people; and it may be pronounced with assurance that the people of this country, enlightened as they are with regard to the nature, and interested, as the great body of them are, in the effects of good government, will never be satisfied till some remedy be applied to the vicissitudes and uncertainties which characterize the State administrations. On comparing, however, these valuable ingredients with the vital principles of liberty, we must perceive at once the difficulty of mingling them together in their due proportions. The genius of republican liberty seems to demand on one side, not only that all power should be derived from the people, but that those intrusted with it should be kept in dependence on the people, by a short duration of their appointments; and that even during this short period the trust should be placed not in a few, but a number of hands. Stability, on the contrary, requires that the hands in which power is lodged should continue for a length of time the same. A frequent change of men will result from a frequent return of elections; and a frequent change of measures from a frequent change of men; whilst energy in government requires not only a certain duration of power, but the execution of it by a single hand.

How far the convention may have succeeded in this part of their work will better appear on a more accurate view of it. From the cursory view here taken, it must clearly appear to have been an arduous part.

Not less arduous must have been the task of marketing the proper line of partition between the authority of the general and that of the State governments. . . .

When we pass from the works of nature, in which all the delineations are perfectly accurate, and appear to be otherwise only from the imperfection of the eye which surveys them, to the institutions of man, in which the obscurity arises as well from the object itself as from the organ by which it is contemplated, we must perceive the necessity of moderating still further our expectations and hopes from the efforts of human sagacity. Experience has instructed us that no skill in the science of government has yet been able to discriminate and define with sufficient certainty its three great provinces—the legislative, executive, and judiciary; or even the privileges and powers of the different legislative branches. Questions daily occur in the course of practice, which prove the obscurity which reigns in these subjects, and which puzzle the greatest adepts in political science.

The experience of ages, with the continued and combined labors of the most enlightened legislators and jurists, has been equally unsuccessful in delineating the several objects and limits of different codes of laws and different tribunals of justice. The precise extent of the common law, and the statute law, the maritime law, the ecclesiastical law, the law of corporations, and other local laws and customs, remains still to be clearly and finally established in Great Britain, where accuracy in such subjects has been more industriously pursued than in any other part of the world. The jurisdiction of her several courts, general and local, of law, of equity, of admiralty, etc., is not less a source of frequent and intricate discussions, sufficiently denoting the indeterminate limits by which they are respectively circumscribed. All new laws, though penned with the greatest technical skill, and passed on the fullest and most mature deliberation, are considered as more or less obscure and equivocal until their meaning be liquidated and ascertained by a series of particular discussions and adjudications. Besides the obscurity arising from the complexity of objects, and the imperfection of the human faculties, the medium through which the conceptions of men are conveyed to each other adds a fresh embarrassment. The use of words is to express ideas. Perspicuity, therefore, requires not only that the ideas should be distinctly formed, but that they should be expressed by words distinctly and exclusively appropriate to them. But no language is so copious as to supply words and phrases for every complex idea, or so correct as not to include many equivocally denoting different ideas. Hence it must happen that however accurately objects may be discriminated in themselves and however accurately the discrimination may be considered, the definition of them may be rendered inaccurate by the inaccuracy of the terms in which it is delivered. And this unavoidable inaccuracy must be greater or less, according to the complexity and novelty of the objects defined. When the Almighty himself condescends to address mankind in their own language, his meaning, luminous as it must be, is rendered dim and doubtful by the cloudy medium through which it is communicated.

Here, then, are three sources of vague and incorrect definitions: indistinctness of the object, imperfection of the organ of conception, inadequateness of the vehicle of ideas. Any one of these must produce a certain degree of obscurity. The convention, in delineating the boundary between the federal and State jurisdictions, must have experienced the full effect of them all.

To the difficulties already mentioned may be added the interfering pretensions of the larger and smaller States. We cannot err in supposing that the former would contend for a participation in the government, fully proportioned to their superior wealth and importance; and that the latter would not be less tenacious of the equality at present enjoyed by them. We may well suppose that neither side would entirely yield to the other, and consequently that the struggle could be terminated only by compromise. It is extremely probable, also, that after the ratio of representation had been adjusted, this very compromise must have produced a fresh struggle between the same parties, to give such a turn to the organization of the government and to the distribution of its powers, as would increase the importance of the branches, in forming which they had respectively obtained the greatest share of influence. There are features in the Constitution which warrant each of these suppositions; and as far as either of them is well founded, it shows that the convention must have been compelled to sacrifice theoretical propriety to the force of extraneous considerations.

Nor could it have been the large and small States only which would marshal themselves in opposition to each other on various points. Other combinations, resulting from a difference of local position and policy, must have created additional difficulties. As every State may be divided into different districts and its citizens into different classes, which give birth to contending interests and local jealousies, so the different parts of the United States are distinguished from each other by a variety of circumstances, which produce a like effect on a larger scale. And although this variety of interests, for reasons sufficiently explained in a former paper [*No. 10*], may have a salutary influence on the administration of the government when formed, yet every one must be sensible of the contrary influence which must have been experienced in the task of forming it.

Would it be wonderful if under the pressure of all these difficulties, the convention should have been forced into some deviations from that artificial structure and regular symmetry which an abstract view of the subject might lead an ingenious theorist to bestow on a Constitution planned in his closet or in his imagination? The real wonder is that so many difficulties should have been surmounted, and surmounted with a unanimity almost as unprecedented as it must have been unexpected. It is impossible for any man of candor to reflect on this circumstance without partaking of the astonishment. It is impossible for the man of pious reflection not to perceive in it a finger of that Almighty hand which has been so frequently and signally extended to our relief in the critical stages of the revolution.

We had occasion, in a former paper [*No. 20*], to take notice of the repeated trials which have been unsuccessfully made in the United Netherlands for reforming the baneful and notorious vices of their constitution. The history of almost all the great councils and consultations held among mankind for reconciling their discordant opinions, assuaging their mutual jealousies, and adjusting their respective interests, is a history of factions, contentions, and disappointments, and may be classed among the most dark and degraded pictures which display the infirmities and depravities of the human character. If, in a few scattered instances, a brighter aspect is presented, they serve only as exceptions to admonish us of the general truth; and by their lustre to darken the gloom of the adverse prospect to which they are contrasted. In revolving the causes from which these exceptions result, and applying them to the particular instances before us, we are necessarily led to two important conclusions. The first is that the convention must have enjoyed, in a very singular degree, an exemption from the pestilential influence of party animosities—the disease most incident to deliberative bodies, and most apt to contaminate their proceedings. The second conclusion is that all the deputations composing the convention were satisfactorily accommodated by the final act, or were induced to accede to it by a deep conviction of the necessity of sacrificing private opinions and partial interests to the public good, and by a despair of seeing this necessity diminished by delays or by new experiments.

PUBLIUS.

The Federalist No. 39 (1788)
(excerpts)

January 16, 1788

To the People of the State of New York:

... The first question that offers itself is whether the general form and aspect of the government be strictly republican. It is evident that no other form would be reconcilable with the genius of the people of America; with the fundamental principles of the Revolution; or with that honorable determination which animates every votary of freedom to rest all our political experiments on the capacity of mankind for self-government. If the plan of the convention, therefore, be found to depart from the republican character, its advocates must abandon it as no longer defensible.

What, then, are the distinctive characters of the republican form? Were an answer to this question to be sought, not by recurring to principles but in the application of the term by political writers to the constitutions of different States, no satisfactory one would ever be found. Holland, in which no particle of the supreme authority is derived from the people, has passed almost universally under the denomination of a republic. The same title has been bestowed on Venice, where absolute power over the great body of the people is exercised in the most absolute manner by a small body of hereditary nobles. Poland, which is a mixture of aristocracy and of monarchy in their worst forms, has been dignified with the same appellation. The government of England, which has one republican branch only, combined with an hereditary aristocracy and monarchy, has with equal impropriety been frequently placed on the list of republics. These examples, which are nearly as dissimilar to each other as to a genuine republic, show the extreme inaccuracy with which the term has been used in political disquisitions.

If we resort for a criterion to the different principles on which different forms of government are established, we may define a republic to be, or at least may bestow that name on, a government which derives all its powers directly or indirectly from the great body of the people, and is administered by persons holding their offices during pleasure for a limited period, or during good behavior. It is *essential* to such a government that it be derived from the great body of the society, not from an inconsiderable proportion or a favored class of it; otherwise a handful of tyrannical nobles, exercising their oppressions by a delegation of their powers, might aspire to the rank of republicans and claim for their government the honorable title of republic. It is *sufficient* for such a government that the persons administering it be appointed, either directly or indirectly, by the people;

and that they hold their appointments by either of the tenures just specified; otherwise every government in the United States, as well as every other popular government that has been or can be well organized or well executed, would be degraded from the republican character. ... The House of Representatives, like that of one branch at least of all the State legislatures, is elected immediately by the great body of the people. The Senate, like the present Congress and the Senate of Maryland, derives its appointment indirectly from the people. The President is indirectly derived from the choice of the people, according to the example in most of the States. Even the judges, with all other officers of the Union, will, as in the several States, be the choice, though a remote choice, of the people themselves. The duration of the appointments is equally conformable to the republican standard and to the model of State constitutions. The House of Representatives is periodically elective, as in all the States; and for the period of two years, as in the State of South Carolina. The Senate is elective for the period of six years, which is but one year more than the period of the Senate of Maryland, and but two more than that of the Senates of New York and Virginia. The President is to continue in office for the period of four years; as in New York and Delaware the chief magistrate is elected for three years, and in South Carolina for two years. In the other States the election is annual. In several of the States, however, no explicit provision is made for the impeachment of the chief magistrate. And in Delaware and Virginia he is not impeachable till out of office. The President of the United States is impeachable at any time during his continuance in office. The tenure by which the judges are to hold their places is, as it unquestionably ought to be, that of good behavior. The tenure of the ministerial offices generally will be a subject of legal regulation, conformably to the reason of the case and the example of the State constitutions.

Could any further proof be required of the republican complexion of this system, the most decisive one might be found in its absolute prohibition of titles of nobility, both under the federal and the State governments; and in its express guaranty of the republican form to each of the latter.

"But it was not sufficient," say the adversaries of the proposed Constitution, "for the convention to adhere to the republican form. They ought with equal care to have preserved the *federal* form, which regards the Union as a *Confederacy* of sovereign states; instead of which they have framed a *national* government, which regards the Union as a *consolidation* of the States." And it is asked by what authority this bold and radical innovation was undertaken? The handle which has been made of this objection requires that it should be examined with some precision. . . .

The next relation is to the sources from which the ordinary powers of government are to be derived. The House of Representatives will derive its powers from the people of America; and the people will be represented in the same proportion and on the same principle as they are in the legislature of a particular State. So far the government is *national,* not *federal.* The Senate, on the other hand, will derive its powers from the States as political and coequal societies; and these will be represented on the principle of equality in the Senate, as they now are in the existing Congress. So far the government is *federal,* not *national.* The executive power will be derived from a very compound source. The immediate election of the President is to be made by the States in their political characters. The votes allotted to them are in a compound ratio, which considers them partly as distinct and coequal societies, partly as

unequal members of the same society. The eventual election, again, is to be made by that branch of the legislature which consists of the national representatives; but in this particular act they are to be thrown into the form of individual delegations from so many distinct and coequal bodies politic. From this aspect of the government it appears to be of a mixed character, presenting at least as many *federal* as *national* features.

The difference between a federal and national government, as it relates to the *operation of the government,* is by the adversaries of the plan of the convention supposed to consist in this, that in the former the powers operate on the political bodies composing the Confederacy in their political capacities; in the latter, on the individual citizens composing the nation in their individual capacities. On trying the Constitution by this criterion, it falls under the *national* not the *federal* character; though perhaps not so completely as has been understood. In several cases, and particularly in the trial of controversies to which States may be parties, they must be viewed and proceeded against in their collective and political capacities only. But the operation of the government on the people in their individual capacities, in its ordinary and most essential proceedings, will, in the sense of its opponents, on the whole, designate it, in this relation, a *national* government.

But if the government be national with regard to the *operation* of its powers, it changes its aspect again when we contemplate it in relation to the extent of its powers. The idea of a national government involves in it not only an authority over the individual citizens, but an indefinite supremacy over all persons and things, so far as they are objects of lawful government. Among a people consolidated into one nation, this supremacy is completely vested in the national legislature. Among communities united for particular purposes, it is vested partly in the general and partly in the municipal legislatures. In the former case, all local authorities are subordinate to the supreme; and may be controlled, directed, or abolished by it at pleasure. In the latter, the local or municipal authorities form distinct and independent portions of the supremacy, no more subject, within their respective spheres, to the general authority than the general authority is subject to them, within its own sphere. In this relation, then, the proposed government cannot be deemed a *national* one; since its jurisdiction extends to certain enumerated objects only, and leaves to the several States a residuary and inviolable sovereignty over all other objects. It is true that in controversies relating to the boundary between the two jurisdictions, the tribunal which is ultimately to decide is to be established under the general government. But this does not change the principle of the case. The decision is to be impartially made, according to the rules of the Constitution; and all the usual and most effectual precautions are taken to secure this impartiality. Some such tribunal is clearly essential to prevent an appeal to the sword and a dissolution of the compact; and that it ought to be established under the general rather than under the local governments, or, to speak more properly, that it could be safely established under the first alone, is a position not likely to be combated.

If we try the Constitution by its last relation to the authority by which amendments are to be made, we find it neither wholly *national* nor wholly *federal.* Were it wholly national, the supreme and ultimate authority would reside in the *majority* of the people of the Union; and this authority would be competent at all times, like that of a majority of every national society to alter or abolish its established government. Were it wholly federal, on the other hand, the concurrence of each State in the Union would be essential to every alteration that would be binding on all. The mode provided by the plan of the convention is not founded on either of these principles. In requiring more than a majority, and particularly in computing the proportion by *States,* not by *citizens,* it departs from the national and advances towards the *federal* character; in rendering the concurrence of less than the whole number of States sufficient, it loses again the *federal* and partakes of the *national* character.

The proposed Constitution, therefore, even when tested by the rules laid down by its antagonists, is, in strictness, neither a national nor a federal Constitution, but a composition of both. In its foundation it is federal, not national; in the sources from which the ordinary powers of the government are drawn, it is partly federal and partly national; in the operation of these powers, it is national, not federal; in the extent of them, again, it is federal, not national; and, finally in the authoritative mode of introducing amendments, it is neither wholly federal nor wholly national.

PUBLIUS.

The Federalist No. 44 (1788)

(excerpts)

January 25, 1788

To the People of the State of New York:

A *fifth* class of provisions in favor of the federal authority consists of the following restrictions on the authority of the several States.

1. "No State shall enter into any treaty, alliance, or confederation; grant letters of marque and reprisal; coin money; emit bills of credit; make anything but gold and silver a legal tender in payment of debts; pass any bill of attainder, *ex-post-facto* law, or law impairing the obligation of contracts; or grant any title of nobility."

The prohibition against treaties, alliances, and confederations makes a part of the existing articles of Union; and for reasons which need no explanation, is copied into the new Constitution. The prohibition of letters of marque is another part of the old system, but is somewhat extended in the new. According to the former, letters of marque could be granted by the States after a declaration of war; according to the latter, these licenses must be obtained, as well during war as previous to its declaration, from the government of the United States. This alteration is fully justified by the advantage of uniformity in all points which relate to foreign powers; and of immediate responsibility to the nation in all those for whose conduct the nation itself is to be responsible.

The right of coining money, which is here taken from the States, was left in their hands by the Confederation, as a concurrent right with that of Congress, under an exception in favor of the exclusive right of Congress to regulate the alloy and value. In this instance, also, the new provision is an improvement on the old. Whilst the alloy and value depended on the general authority, a right of coinage in the particular States could have no other effect than to multiply expensive mints and diversify the forms and weights of the circulating pieces. The latter inconveniency defeats one purpose for which the power was originally submitted to the federal head; and as far as the former might prevent an inconvenient remittance of gold and silver to the central mint for recoinage, the end can be as well attained by local mints established under the general authority.

The extension of the prohibition to bills of credit must give pleasure to every citizen, in proportion to his love of justice and his knowledge of the true springs of public prosperity. The loss which America has sustained since the peace, from the pestilent effects of paper money on the necessary confidence between man and man, on the necessary confidence in the public councils, on the industry and morals of the people, and on the character of republican government, constitutes an enormous debt against the States chargeable with this unadvised measure, which must long remain unsatisfied; or rather an accumulation of guilt, which can be expiated no otherwise than by a voluntary sacrifice on the altar of justice, of the power which has been the instrument of it. In addition to these persuasive considerations, it may be observed, that the same reasons which show the necessity of denying to the States the power of regulating coin prove with equal force that they ought not to be at liberty to substitute a paper medium in the place of coin. Had every State a right to regulate the value of its coin, there might be as many different currencies as States, and thus the intercourse among them would be impeded; retrospective alterations in its value might be made, and thus the citizens of other States be injured, and animosities be kindled among the States themselves. The subjects of foreign powers might suffer from the same cause, and hence the Union be discredited and embroiled by the indiscretion of a single member. No one of these mischiefs is less incident to a power in the States to emit paper money than to coin gold or silver. The power to make anything but gold and silver a tender in payment of debts is withdrawn from the States, on the same principle with that of issuing a paper currency.

Bills of attainder, *ex-post-facto* laws, and laws impairing the obligation of contracts are contrary to the first principles of the social compact, and to every principle of sound legislation. The two former are expressly prohibited by the declarations prefixed to some of the State constitutions, and all of them are prohibited by the spirit and scope of these fundamental charters. Our own experience has taught us, nevertheless, that additional fences against these dangers ought not to be omitted. Very properly, therefore, have the convention added this constitutional bulwark in favor of personal security and private rights; and I am much deceived if they have not, in so doing, as faithfully consulted the genuine sentiments as the undoubted interests of their constituents. The sober people of America are weary of the fluctuating policy which has directed the public councils. They have seen with regret and indignation that sudden changes and legislative interferences, in cases affecting personal rights, become jobs in the hands of enterprising and influential speculators, and snares to the more-industrious and less-informed part of the community. They have seen, too, that one legislative interference is but the first link of a long chain of repetitions, every subsequent interference being naturally produced by the effects of the preceding. They very rightly infer, therefore, that some thorough reform is wanting, which will banish speculations on public measures, inspire a general prudence and industry, and give a regular course to the business of society. The prohibition with respect to titles of nobility is copied from the articles of Confederation, and needs no comment. . . .

The *sixth* and last class consists of the several powers and provisions by which efficacy is given to all the rest.

1. Of these the first is, the . . . power "To make all laws which shall be necessary and proper for carrying into execution the foregoing powers, and all other powers vested by this Constitution in the Government of the United States, or in any department or office thereof."

Few parts of the Constitution have been assailed with more intemperance than this; yet on a fair investigation of it, no part can appear more completely invulnerable.

Without the *substance* of this power the whole Constitution would be a dead letter. Those who object to the article . . . can only mean that the *form* of the provision is improper. But have they considered whether a better form could have been substituted?

There are four other possible methods which the Constitution might have taken on this subject. They might have copied the second article of the existing Confederation, which would have prohibited the exercise of any power not *expressly* delegated; they might have attempted a positive enumeration of the powers comprehended under the general terms "necessary and proper"; they might have attempted a negative enumeration of them by specifying the powers excepted from the general definition; they might have been altogether silent on the subject, leaving these necessary and proper powers to construction and inference.

Had the convention taken the first method of adopting the second article of Confederation, it is evident that the new Congress would be continually exposed, as their predecessors have been, to the alternative of construing the term "*expressly*" with so much rigor as to disarm the government of all real authority whatever, or with so much latitude as to destroy altogether the force of the restriction. It would be easy to show . . . that no important power delegated by the articles of Confederation has been or can be executed by Congress without recurring more or less to the doctrine of *construction* or *implication*. As the powers delegated under the new system are more extensive, the government which is to administer it would find itself still more distressed with the alternative of betraying the public interests by doing nothing, or of violating the Constitution by exercising powers indispensably necessary and proper, but, at the same time, not *expressly* granted.

Had the convention attempted a positive enumeration of the powers necessary and proper for carrying their other powers into effect, the attempt would have involved a complete digest of laws on every subject to which the Constitution relates; accommodated too, not only to the existing state of things, but to all the possible changes which futurity may produce; for in every new application of a general power, the *particular powers,* which are the means of attaining the *object* of the general power, must always necessarily vary with that object and be often properly varied whilst the object remains the same.

Had they attempted to enumerate the particular powers or means not necessary or proper for carrying the general powers into execution, the task would have been no less chimerical; and would have been liable to this further objection, that every defect in the enumeration would have been equivalent to a positive grant of authority. If, to avoid this consequence, they had attempted a partial enumeration of the exceptions and described the residue by the general terms, *not necessary or proper,* it must have happened that the enumeration would comprehend a few of the excepted powers only; that these would be such as would be least likely to be assumed or tolerated, because the enumeration would of course select such as would be least necessary or proper; and that the unnecessary and improper powers included in the residuum, would be less forcibly excepted, than if no partial enumeration had been made.

Had the Constitution been silent on this head, there can be no doubt that all the particular powers requisite as means of executing the general powers would have resulted to the government by unavoidable implication. No axiom is more clearly established in law or in reason, than that wherever the end is required, the means are authorized; wherever a general power to do a thing is given, every particular power necessary for doing it is included. Had this last method, therefore, been pursued by the convention, every objection now urged against their plan would remain in all its plausibility; and the real inconveniency would be incurred of not removing a pretext which may be seized on critical occasions for drawing into question the essential powers of the Union.

If it be asked what is to be the consequence, in case the Congress shall misconstrue this part of the Constitution and exercise powers not warranted by its true meaning, I answer, the same as if they should misconstrue or enlarge any other power vested in them; as if the general power had been reduced to particulars, and any one of these were to be violated; the same, in short, as if the State legislatures should violate their respective constitutional authorities. In the first instance, the success of the usurpation will depend on the executive and judiciary departments, which are to expound and give effect to the legislative acts; and in the last resort a remedy must be obtained from the people, who can, by the election of more faithful representatives, annul the acts of the usurpers. The truth is that this ultimate redress may be more confided in against unconstitutional acts of the federal than of the State legislatures for this plain reason, that as every such act of the former will be an invasion of the rights of the latter, these will be ever ready to mark the innovation, to sound the alarm to the people, and to exert their local influence in effecting a change of federal representatives. There being no such intermediate body between the State legislatures and the people interested in watching the conduct of the former, violations of the State constitutions are more likely to remain unnoticed and unredressed.

2. "This Constitution and the laws of the United States which shall be made in pursuance thereof, and all treaties made, or which shall be made, under the authority of the United States, shall be the supreme law of the land, and the Judges in every State shall be bound thereby, anything in the Constitution or laws of any State to the contrary notwithstanding."

The indiscreet zeal of the adversaries to the Constitution has betrayed them into an attack on this part of it also, without which it would have been evidently and radically defective. To be fully sensible of this, we need only suppose for a moment that the supremacy of the State constitutions had been left complete by a saving clause in their favor.

In the first place, as these constitutions invest the State legislatures with absolute sovereignty in all cases not excepted by the existing articles of Confederation, all the authorities contained in the proposed Constitution, so far as they exceed those enumerated in the Confederation, would have been annulled, and the new Congress would have been reduced to the same impotent condition with their predecessors.

In the next place, as the constitutions of some of the States do not even expressly and fully recognize the existing powers of the Confederacy, an express saving of the supremacy of the former would . . . have brought into question every power contained in the proposed Constitution.

In the third place, as the constitutions of the States differ much from each other, it might happen that a treaty or national law of great and equal importance to the States would interfere with some and not with other constitutions, and would consequently be valid in some of the States at the same time that it would have no effect in others.

In fine, the world would have seen for the first time a system of government founded on an inversion of the fundamental principles of all government; it would have seen the authority of the whole society everywhere subordinate to the authority of the parts; it would have seen a monster in which the head was under the direction of the members.

3. "The Senators and Representatives and the members of the several State Legislatures, and all Executive and Judicial officers, both of the United States and [of] the several States, shall be bound by oath or affirmation, to support this Constitution."

It has been asked why it was thought necessary that the State magistracy should be bound to support the federal Constitution, and unnecessary that a like oath should be imposed on the officers of the United States in favor of the State constitutions.

Several reasons might be assigned for the distinction. I content myself with one, which is obvious and conclusive. The members of the federal government will have no agency in carrying the State constitutions into effect. The members and officers of the State governments, on the contrary, will have an essential agency in giving effect to the federal Constitution. The election of the President and Senate will depend in all cases on the legislatures of the several States. And the election of the House of Representatives will equally depend on the same authority in the first instance; and will probably forever be conducted by the officers and according to the laws of the States.

4. Among the provisions for giving efficacy to the federal powers might be added those which belong to the executive and judiciary departments; but as these are reserved for particular examination in another place [67–83], pass them over in this.

We have now received in detail all the articles composing the sum or quantity of power delegated by the proposed Constitution to the federal government, and are brought to this undeniable conclusion, that no part of the power is unnecessary or improper for accomplishing the necessary objects of the Union. The question, therefore, whether this amount of power shall be granted or not resolves itself into another question, whether or not a government commensurate to the exigencies of the Union shall be established; or in other words, whether the Union itself shall be preserved.

PUBLIUS.

The Federalist No. 48 (1788)

February 1, 1788

To the People of the State of New York:

IT was shown in the last paper that the political apothegm there examined does not require that the legislative, executive, and judiciary departments should be wholly unconnected with each other. I shall undertake, in the next place, to show that unless these departments be so far connected and blended as to give each a constitutional control over the others, the degree of separation which the maximum requires, as essential to a free government, can never in practice be duly maintained.

It is agreed on all sides that the powers properly belonging to one of the departments ought not to be directly and completely administered by either of the other departments. It is equally evident that none of them ought to possess, directly or indirectly, an overruling influence over the others in the administration of their respective powers. It will not be denied that power is of an encroaching nature, and that it ought to be effectually restrained from passing the limits assigned to it. After discriminating therefore in theory the several classes of power as they may in their nature be legislative, executive, or judiciary, the next and most difficult task is to provide some practical security for each, against the invasion of the others. What this security ought to be is the great problem to be solved.

Will it be sufficient to mark with precision the boundaries of these departments in the constitution of the government, and to trust to these parchment barriers against the encroaching spirit of power? This is the security which appears to have been principally relied on by the compilers of most of the American constitutions. But experience assures us that the efficacy of the provision has been greatly overrated; and that some more adequate defence is indispensably necessary for the more feeble, against the most powerful, members of the government. The legislative department is everywhere extending the sphere of its activity, and drawing all power into its impetuous vortex.

The founders of our republics have so much merit for the wisdom which they have displayed that no task can be less pleasing than that of pointing out the errors into which they have fallen. A respect for truth, however, obliges us to remark that they seem never for a moment to have turned their eyes from the danger to liberty from the overgrown and all-grasping prerogative of an hereditary magistrate, supported and fortified by an hereditary branch of the legislative authority. They seem never to have recollected the danger from legislative usurpations, which, by assembling all power in the same hands, must lead to the same tyranny as is threatened by executive usurpations.

In a government where numerous and

extensive prerogatives are placed in the hands of an hereditary monarch, the executive department is very justly regarded as the source of danger, and watched with all the jealousy which a zeal for liberty ought to inspire. In a democracy, where a multitude of people exercise in person the legislative functions, and are continually exposed, by their incapacity for regular deliberation and concerted measures, to the ambitious intrigues of their executive magistrates, tyranny may well be apprehended, on some favorable emergency, to start up in the same quarter. But in a representative republic, where the executive magistracy is carefully limited, both in the extent and the duration of its power; and where the legislative power is exercised by an assembly, which is inspired by a supposed influence over the people, with an intrepid confidence in its own strength; which is sufficiently numerous to feel all the passions which actuate a multitude, yet not so numerous as to be incapable of pursuing the objects of its passions, by means which reason prescribes; it is against the enterprising ambition of this department that the people ought to indulge all their jealousy and exhaust all their precautions.

The legislative department derives a superiority in our governments from other circumstances. Its constitutional powers being at once more extensive and less susceptible of precise limits, it can with the greater facility mask under complicated and indirect measures the encroachments which it makes on the coördinate departments. It is not unfrequently a question of real nicety in legislative bodies, whether the operation of a particular measure will, or will not, extend beyond the legislative sphere. On the other side, the executive power being restrained within a narrower compass and being more simple in its nature, and the judiciary being described by landmarks still less uncertain, projects of usurpation by either of these depart-

ments would immediately betray and defeat themselves. Nor is this all; as the legislative department alone has access to the pockets of the people, and has in some constitutions full discretion and in all prevailing influence, over the pecuniary rewards of those who fill the other departments, a dependence is thus created in the latter, which gives still greater facility to encroachments of the former.

I have appealed to our own experience for the truth of what I advance on this subject. Were it necessary to verify this experience by particular proofs, they might be multiplied without end. I might find a witness in every citizen who has shared in, or been attentive to, the course of public administrations. I might collect vouchers in abundance from the records and archives of every State in the Union. But as a more concise, and at the same time equally satisfactory, evidence, I will refer to the example of two States, attested by two unexceptionable authorities.

The first example is that of Virginia, a State which, as we have seen, has expressly declared in its constitution, that the three great departments ought not to be intermixed. The authority in support of it is Mr. Jefferson, who, besides his other advantages for remarking the operation of the government, was himself the chief magistrate of it. In order to convey fully the ideas with which his experience had impressed him on this subject, it will be necessary to quote a passage of some length from his very interesting "Notes on the State of Virginia," p. 195. "All the powers of government, legislative, executive, and judiciary, result to the legislative body. The concentrating these in the same hands, is precisely the definition of despotic government. It will be no alleviation, that these powers will be exercised by a plurality of hands, and not by a single one. One hundred and seventy-three despots would surely be as oppressive as one. Let those who doubt it, turn their eyes on the republic of Venice. As little will it avail us, that they are chosen by ourselves. An *elective despotism* was not the government we fought for; but one which should not only be founded on free principles, but in which the powers of government should be so divided and balanced among several bodies of magistracy, as that no one could transcend their legal limits, without being effectually checked and restrained by the others. For this reason, that convention which passed the ordinance of government, laid its foundation on this basis, that the legislative, executive, and judiciary departments should be separate and distinct, so that no person should exercise the powers of more than one of them at the same time. *But no barrier was provided between these several powers.* The judiciary and the executive members were left dependent on the legislative for their subsistence in office, and some of them for their continuance in it. If, therefore, the legislature assumes executive and judiciary powers, no opposition is likely to be made; nor, if made, can be effectual; because in that case they may put their proceedings into the form of an act of Assembly, which will render them obligatory on the other branches. They have accordingly, *in many* instances, *decided rights* which should have been left to *judiciary controversy,* and *the direction of the executive, during the whole time of their session, is becoming habitual and familiar."*

The other State which I shall take for an example is Pennsylvania; and the other authority, the Council of Censors, which assembled in the years 1783 and 1784. A part of the duty of this body as marked out by the constitution was "to inquire whether the constitution had been preserved inviolate in every part; and whether the legislative and executive branches of government had performed their duty as guardians of the people, or assumed to themselves, or exercised, other or greater powers than they

are entitled to by the constitution" [*sic*]. In the execution of this trust the council were necessarily led to a comparison of both the legislative and executive proceedings with the constitutional powers of these departments; and from the facts enumerated, and to the truth of most of which both sides in the council subscribed, it appears that the constitution had been flagrantly violated by the legislature in a variety of important instances.

A great number of laws had been passed, violating, without any apparent necessity, the rule requiring that all bills of a public nature shall be previously printed for the consideration of the people; although this is one of the precautions chiefly relied on by the constitution against improper acts of the legislature.

The constitutional trial by jury had been violated, and powers assumed which had not been delegated by the constitution.

Executive powers had been usurped.

The salaries of the judges, which the constitution expressly requires to be fixed, had been occasionally varied; and cases belonging to the judiciary department frequently drawn within legislative cognizance and determination.

Those who wish to see the several particulars falling under each of these heads may consult the journals of the council, which are in print. Some of them . . . may be imputable to peculiar circumstances connected with the war, but the greater part of them may be considered as the spontaneous shoots of an ill-constituted government.

It appears, also, that the executive department had not been innocent of frequent breaches of the constitution. There are three observations, however, which ought to be made on this head: *first,* a great proportion of the instances were either immediately produced by the necessities of the war, or recommended by Congress or the commander-in-chief; *secondly,* in most of the other instances, they conformed either to the declared or the known sentiments of the legislative department; *thirdly,* the executive department of Pennsylvania is distinguished from that of the other States by the number of members composing it. In this respect, it has as much affinity to a legislative assembly as to an executive council. And being at once exempt from the restraint of an individual responsibility for the acts of the body, and deriving confidence from mutual example and joint influence, unauthorized measures would, of course, be more freely hazarded than where the executive department is administered by a single hand or by a few hands.

The conclusion which I am warranted in drawing from these observations is, that a mere demarcation on parchment of the constitutional limits of the several departments, is not sufficient guard against those encroachments which lead to a tyrannical concentration of all the powers of government in the same hands.

PUBLIUS.

The Federalist No. 51 (1788)

February 6, 1788

To the People of the State of New York:

To what expedient, then, shall we finally resort, for maintaining in practice the necessary partition of power among the several departments as laid down in the Constitution? The only answer that can be given is that as all these exterior provisions are found to be inadequate the defect must be supplied, by so contriving the interior structure of the government as that its several constituent parts may, by their mutual relations, be the means of keeping each other in their proper places. Without presuming to undertake a full development of this important idea I will hazard a few general observations which may perhaps place it in a clearer light, and enable us to form a more correct judgment of the principles and structure of the government planned by the convention.

In order to lay a due foundation for that separate and distinct exercise of the different powers of government, which to a certain extent is admitted on all hands to be essential to the preservation of liberty, it is evident that each department should have a will of its own: and consequently should be so constituted that the members of each should have as little agency as possible in the appointment of the members of the others. Were this principle rigorously adhered to, it would require that all the appointments for the supreme executive, legislative, and judiciary magistracies should be drawn from the same fountain of authority, the people, through channels having no communication whatever with one another. Perhaps such a plan of constructing the several departments would be less difficult in practice than it may in contemplation appear. Some difficulties, however, and some additional expense would attend the execution of it. Some deviations, therefore, from the principle must be admitted. In the constitution of the judiciary department in particular, it might be inexpedient to insist rigorously on the principle: first, because peculiar qualifications being essential in the members, the primary consideration ought to be to select that mode of choice which best secures these qualifications; second, because the permanent tenure by which the appointments are held in that department must soon destroy all sense of dependence on the authority conferring them.

It is equally evident that the members of each department should be as little dependent as possible on those of the others for the emoluments annexed to their offices. Were the executive magistrate, or the judges, not independent of the legislature in this particular, their independence in every other would be merely nominal.

But the great security against a gradual concentration of the several powers in the same department consists in giving to those who administer each department the necessary constitutional means and personal motives to resist encroachments of the other. The provision for defense must in this, as in all other cases, be made commensurate to the danger of attack. Ambition must be made to counteract ambition. The interest of the man must be connected with the constitutional rights of the place. It may be a reflection on human nature that such devices should be necessary to control the abuses of government. But what is government itself but the greatest of all reflections on human nature? If men were angels, no government would be necessary. If angels were to govern men, neither external nor internal controls on government would be necessary. In framing a government which is to be administered by men over men, the great difficulty lies in this: you must first enable the government to control the governed: and in the next place oblige it to control itself. A dependence on the people is, no doubt, the primary control on the government; but experience has taught mankind the necessity of auxiliary precautions.

This policy of supplying, by opposite and rival interests, the defect of better motives, might be traced through the whole system of human affairs, private as well as public. We see it particularly displayed in all the subordinate distributions of power, where the constant aim is to divide and arrange the several offices in such a manner as that each may be a check on the other— that the private interest of every individual may be a sentinel over the public rights. These inventions of prudence cannot be less requisite in the distribution of the supreme powers of the State.

But it is not possible to give to each department an equal power of self-defense. In republican government, the legislative authority necessarily predominates. The remedy for this inconveniency is to divide the legislature into different branches: and to render them, by different modes of election and different principles of action, as little connected with each other as the nature of their common functions and their common dependence on the society will admit. It may even be necessary to guard against dangerous encroachments by still further precautions. As the weight of the legislative authority requires that it should be thus divided, the weakness of the executive may require, on the other hand, that it should be fortified. An absolute negative on the legislature appears, at first view, to be the natural defense with which the executive magistrate should be armed. But perhaps it would be neither altogether safe nor alone sufficient. On ordinary occasions it might not be exerted with the requisite firmness, and on extraordinary occasions it might be perfidiously abused. May not this defect of an absolute negative be supplied by some qualified connection between this weaker department and the weaker branch of the stronger department, by which the latter may be led to support the constitutional rights of the former, without being too much detached from the rights of its own departments?

If the principles on which these observations are founded be just, as I persuade myself they are, and they be applied as a criterion to the several State constitutions, and to the federal Constitution, it will be found that if the latter does not perfectly correspond with them, the former are infinitely less able to bear such a test.

There are, moreover, two considerations particularly applicable to the federal system of America, which place that system in a very interesting point of view.

First. In a single republic, all the power surrendered by the people is submitted to the administration of a single government; and the usurpations are guarded against by a division of the government into distinct and separate departments. In the compound republic of America, the power surrendered by the people is first divided between two distinct governments, and then the portion allotted to each subdivided among distinct and separate departments. Hence a double security arises to the rights of the people. The different governments will control each other, at the same time that each will be controlled by itself.

Second. It is of great importance in a republic not only to guard the society against the oppression of its rulers, but to guard one part of the society against the injustice of the other part. Different interests necessarily exist in different classes of citizens. If a majority be united by a common interest, the rights of the minority will be insecure. There are but two methods of providing against this evil: the one by creating a will in the community independent of the majority—that is, of the society itself; the other, by comprehending in the society so many separate descriptions of citizens as will render an unjust combination of a majority of the whole very improbable if not impracticable. The first method prevails in all governments possessing an hereditary or self-appointed authority. This, at best, is but a precarious security; because a power independent of the society may as well espouse the unjust views of the major as the rightful interests of the minor party, and may possibly be turned against both parties. The second method

will be exemplified in the federal republic of the United States. Whilst all authority in it will be derived from and dependent on the society, the society itself will be broken into so many parts, interests and classes of citizens, that the rights of individuals, or of the minority, will be in little danger from interested combinations of the majority. In a free government the security for civil rights must be the same as that for religious rights. It consists in the one case in the multiplicity of interests, and in the other in the multiplicity of sects. The degree of security in both cases will depend on the number of interests and sects; and this may be presumed to depend on the extent of country and number of people comprehended under the same government. This view of the subject must particularly recommend a proper federal system to all the sincere and considerate friends of republican government, since it shows that in exact proportion as the territory of the Union may be formed into more circumscribed Confederacies, or States, oppressive combinations of a majority will be facilitated; the best security, under the republican forms, for the rights of every class of citizen, will be diminished; and consequently the stability and independence of some member of the government, the only other security, must be proportionally increased. Justice is the end of government. It is the end of civil society. It ever has been and ever will be pursued until it be obtained, or until liberty be lost in the pursuit. In a society under the forms of which the stronger faction can readily unite and oppress the weaker, anarchy may as truly be said to reign as in a state of nature, where the weaker individual is not secured against the violence of the stronger; and as, in the latter state, even the stronger individuals are prompted, by the uncertainty of their condition, to submit to a government which may protect the weak as well as themselves; so, in the former state, will the more powerful factions or parties be gradually induced, by a like motive, to wish for a government which will protect all parties, the weaker as well as the more powerful. It can be little doubted that if the State of Rhode Island was separated from the Confederacy and left to itself, the insecurity of rights under the popular form of government within such narrow limits would be displayed by such reiterated oppressions of factious majorities that some power altogether independent of the people would soon be called for by the voice of the very factions whose misrule had proved the necessity of it. In the extended republic of the United States, and among the great variety of interests, parties, and sects which it embraces, a coalition of a majority of the whole society could seldom take place on any other principles than those of justice and the general good; whilst there being thus less danger to a minor from the will of a major party, there must be less pretext, also, to provide for the security of the former, by introducing into the government a will not dependent on the latter, or, in other words, a will independent of the society itself. It is no less certain than it is important, notwithstanding the contrary opinions which have been entertained, that the larger the society, provided it lie within a practicable sphere, the more duly capable it will be of self-government. And happily for the *republican cause,* the practicable sphere may be carried to a very great extent by a judicious modification and mixture of the *federal principle.*

PUBLIUS.

Alexander Hamilton

"Money is the vital principle of the body politic," said Alexander Hamilton. This was the basic philosophy of the energetic Federalist who sought to increase the power of a federal government allied with the financial aristocracy at the time the Constitution was framed. Born in 1757 on the British West Indies island of Nevis, Hamilton's education was brief. At age twelve, he was put to work in the office of a West Indian merchant. Relatives provided him with the money to go to New York to study, where he became absorbed with the revolutionary developments in progress.

Hamilton soon published two pamphlets, "A Full Vindication of the Measures of the Congress" and "The Farmer Refuted," which attracted attention. Appointed to command a company of artillery, he proved so skillful at organization that he was asked to join Washington's staff, where he became equally effective. Although he played an active role leading up to the Philadelphia Convention in 1787, Hamilton had no significant part at the convention itself (despite his advocacy there of a quasi-monarchical executive). Thereafter he thought up *The Federalist Papers* and wrote fifty-one articles, coauthoring three others with James Madison. Hamilton envisioned a strong government by "the wise, the good, and the rich,"—a dynamic, centralized form of aristocracy that would strive for industrial and financial power. In 1789, Washington appointed Hamilton the first secretary of the treasury. In this role his speeches and reports strove for mercantilistic Federalism. He envisioned a government led by men of financial and industrial property. Hamilton was extreme in his conservative agenda, striving for state industrial power regardless of current conditions or the potential social instability caused by such a preoccupation with industrial progress over all other objectives.

One result of the debate over Hamilton's economic policies was the emergence of political parties. Overwhelmed with criticism, Hamilton left Washington's cabinet but continued to advise that group unofficially. Hamilton split his party in an unsuccessful attempt to swing the election of 1796 to Thomas Pinckney rather than John Adams. His political career ended completely in 1800 when he preferred his old Republican enemy Thomas Jefferson over Aaron Burr when the election was thrown into the House. He retired to his law practice. Presumably, he later insulted Aaron Burr, who challenged him to a duel. In 1804 Burr's bullet killed Hamilton.

The Federalist No. 9 (1787)

November 21, 1787

To the People of the State of New York:

A Firm Union will be of the utmost moment to the peace and liberty of the States as a barrier against domestic faction and insurrection. It is impossible to read the history of the petty Republics of Greece and Italy, without feeling sensations of horror and disgust at the distractions with which they were continually agitated, and at the rapid succession of revolutions, by which they were kept in a state of perpetual vibration, between the extremes of tyranny and anarchy. If they exhibit occasional calms, these only serve as short-lived contrasts to the furious storms that are to succeed. If now and then intervals of felicity open themselves to view, we behold them with a mixture of regret arising from the reflection that the pleasing scenes before us are soon to be overwhelmed by the tempestuous waves of sedition and party-rage. If momentary rays of glory break forth from the gloom, while they dazzle us with a transient and fleeting brilliancy, they at the same time admonish us to lament that the vices of government should pervert the direction and tarnish the lustre of those

bright talents and exalted endowments, for which the favoured soils, that produced them, have been so justly celebrated.

From the disorders that disfigure the annals of those republics, the advocates of despotism have drawn arguments, not only against the forms of republican government, but against the very principles of civil liberty. They have decried all free government, as inconsistent with the order of society, and have indulged themselves in malicious exultation over its friends and partizans. Happily for mankind, stupendous fabrics reared on the basis of liberty, which have flourished for ages, have in a few glorious instances refuted their gloomy sophisms. And, I trust, America will be the broad and solid foundation of other edifices not less magnificent, which will be equally permanent monuments of their errors.

But it is not to be denied that the portraits, they have sketched of republican government, were too just copies of the originals from which they were taken. If it had been found impracticable, to have devised models of a more perfect structure, the enlightened friends to liberty would have been obliged to abandon the cause of that species of government as indefensible. The science of politics, however, like most other sciences has received great improvement. The efficacy of various principles is now well understood, which were either not known at all, or imperfectly known to the ancients. The regular distribution of power into distinct departments—the introduction of legislative balances and checks—the institution of courts composed of judges, holding their offices during good behaviour—the representation of the people in the legislature of deputies of their own election—these are either wholly new discoveries or have made their principal progress towards perfection in modern times. They are means, and powerful means, by which the excellencies of republican government may be retained and its imperfections lessened or avoided. To this catalogue of circumstances, that tend to the amelioration of popular systems of civil government, I shall venture, however novel it may appear to some, to add one more on a principle, which has been made the foundation of an objection to the New Constitution, I mean the ENLARGEMENT of the ORBIT within which such systems are to revolve either in respect to the dimensions of a single State, or to the consolidation of several smaller States into one great confederacy. The latter is that which immediately concerns the object under consideration. It will however be of use to examine the principle in its application to a single State which shall be attended to in another place.

The utility of a confederacy, as well to suppress faction and to guard the internal tranquillity of States, as to increase their external force and security, is in reality not a new idea. It has been practiced upon in different countries and ages, and has received the sanction of the most applauded writers, on the subjects of politics. The opponents of the PLAN proposed have with great assiduity cited and circulated the observations of Montesquieu on the necessity of a contracted territory for a republican government. But they seem not to have

been apprised of the sentiments of that great man expressed in another part of his work, nor to have adverted to the consequences of the principle to which they subscribe, with such ready acquiescence.

When Montesquieu recommends a small extent for republics, the standards he had in view were of dimensions, far short of the limits of almost every one of these States. Neither Virginia, Massachusetts, Pennsylvania, New York, North Carolina, nor Georgia, can by any means be compared with the models, from which he reasoned and to which the terms of his description apply. If we therefore take his ideas on this point, as the criterion of truth, we shall be driven to the alternative, either of taking refuge at once in the arms of monarchy, or of splitting ourselves into an infinity of little jealous, clashing, tumultuous commonwealths, the wretched nurseries of unceasing discord and the miserable objects of universal pity or contempt. Some of the writers, who have come forward on the other side of the question, seem to have been aware of the dilemma; and have even been bold enough to hint at the division of the larger States, as a desirable thing. Such an infatuated policy, such a desperate expedient, might, by the multiplication of petty offices, answer the views of men, who possess not qualifications to extend their influence beyond the narrow circles of personal intrigue, but it could never promote the greatness or happiness of the people of America.

Referring the examination of the principle itself to another place, as has been already mentioned, it will be sufficient to remark here, that in the sense of the author who has been most emphatically quoted upon the occasion, it would only dictate a reduction of the SIZE of the more considerable MEMBERS of the Union; but would not militate against their being all comprehended in one Confederate Government. And this is the true question, in the discussion of which we are at present interested.

So far are the suggestions of Montesquieu from standing in opposition to a general Union of the States, that he explicitly treats of a CONFEDERATE REPUBLIC as the expedient for extending the sphere of popular government and reconciling the advantages of monarchy with those of republicanism.

"It is very probable (says he)[1] that mankind would have been obliged, at length, to live constantly under the government of a SINGLE PERSON, had they not contrived a kind of constitution, that has all the internal advantages of a republican, together with the external force of a monarchical government. I mean a CONFEDERATE REPUBLIC.

"This form of Government is a Convention, by which several smaller *States* agree to become members of a larger *one,* which they intend to form. It is a kind of assemblage of societies, that constitute a new one, capable of increasing by means of new associations, till they arrive to such a degree of power as to be able to provide for the security of the united body.

"A republic of this kind, able to withstand an external force, may support itself without any internal corruption. The form of this society prevents all manner of inconveniences.

"If a single member should attempt to usurp the supreme authority, he could not be supposed to have an equal authority and credit, in all the confederate states. Were he to have too great influence over one, this would alarm the rest. Were he to subdue a part, that which would still remain free might oppose him with forces, independent of those which he had usurped, and overpower him before he could be settled in his usurpation.

"Should a popular insurrection happen, in one of the confederate States, the others are able to quell it. Should abuses

creep into one part, they are reformed by those that remain sound. The State may be destroyed on one side, and not on the other; the confederacy may be dissolved and the confederates preserve their sovereignty.

"As this government is composed of small republics it enjoys the internal happiness of each, and with respect to its external situation it is possessed, by means of the association of all the advantages of large monarchies."

I have thought it proper to quote at length these interesting passages, because they contain a luminous abridgement of the principal arguments in favour of the Union, and must effectually remove the false impressions, which a misapplication of other parts of the work was calculated to produce. They have at the same time an intimate connection with the more immediate design of this Paper; which is to illustrate the tendency of the Union to repress domestic faction and insurrection.

A distinction, more subtle than accurate has been raised between a *confederacy* and a *consolidation* of the States. The essential characteristic of the first is said to be, the restriction of its authority to the members in their collective capacities, without reaching to the individuals of whom they are composed. It is contended that the national council ought to have no concern with any object of internal administration. An exact equality of suffrage between the members has also been insisted upon as a leading feature of a Confederate Government. These positions are in the main arbitrary; they are supported neither by principle nor precedent. It has indeed happened that governments of this kind have generally operated in the manner, which the distinction, taken notice of, supposes to be inherent in their nature—but there have been in most of them extensive exceptions to the practice, which serve to

---

[1]Spirit of Laws, Vol. 1. Book IX. Chap. 1.

prove as far as example will go, that there is no absolute rule on the subject. And it will be clearly shewn, in the course of this investigation, that as far as the principle contended for has prevailed, it has been the cause of incurable disorder and imbecility in the government.

The definition of a *Confederate Republic* seems simply to be, an "assemblage of societies" or an association of two or more States into one State. The extent, modifications and objects of the Federal authority are mere matters of discretion. So long as the separate organisation of the members be not abolished, so long as it exists by a constitutional necessity for local purposes, though it should be in perfect subordination to the general authority of the Union, it would still be, in fact and in theory, an association of States, or a confederacy. The proposed Constitution, so far from implying an abolition of the State Governments, makes them constituent parts of the national sovereignty by allowing them a direct representation in the Senate, and leaves in their possession certain exclusive and very important portions of sovereign power. This fully corresponds, in every rational import of the terms, with the idea of a Federal Government.

In the Lycian confederacy, which consisted of twenty three CITIES, or republics, the largest were intitled to *three* votes in the COMMON COUNCIL, those of the middle class to *two* and the smallest to *one*. The COMMON COUNCIL had the appointment of all the judges and magistrates of the respectives CITIES. This was certainly the most delicate species of interference in their internal administration; for if there be any thing, that seems exclusively appropriated to the local jurisdictions, it is the appointment of their own offices. Yet Montesquieu, speaking of this association, says "Were I to give a model of an excellent confederate republic, it would be that of Lycia." Thus we perceive that the distinctions insisted upon were not within the contemplation of this enlightened civilian, and we shall be led to conclude that they are the novel refinements of an erroneous theory.

PUBLIUS.

The Federalist No. 15 (1787)

December 1, 1787

To the People of the State of New York:

IN the course of the preceding papers, I have endeavoured, my Fellow Citizens, to place before you in a clear and convincing light, the importance of Union to your political safety and happiness. I have unfolded to you a complication of dangers to which you would be exposed should you permit that sacred knot which binds the people of America together to be severed or dissolved by ambition or by avarice, by jealousy or by misrepresentation. In the sequel of the inquiry, through which I propose to accompany you, the truths intended to be inculcated will receive further confirmation from facts and arguments hitherto unnoticed. If the road, over which you will still have to pass, should in some places appear to you tedious or irksome, you will recollect, that you are in quest of information on a subject the most momentous which can engage the attention of a free people: that the field through which you have to travel is in itself spacious, and that the difficulties of the journey have been unnecessarily increased by the mazes with which sophistry has beset the way. It will be my aim to remove the obstacles to your progress in as compendious a manner, as it can be done, without sacrificing utility to dispatch.

In pursuance of the plan, which I have laid down for the discussion of the subject, the point next in order to be examined is the "insufficiency of the present confederation to the preservation of the Union." It may perhaps be asked, what need is there of reasoning or proof to illustrate a position, which is not either controverted or doubted; to which the understandings and feelings of all classes of men assent; and which in substance is admitted by the opponents as well as by the friends of the New Constitution? It must in truth be acknowledged that however these may differ in other respects, they in general appear to harmonise in this sentiment at least, that there are material imperfections in our national system, and that something is necessary to be done to rescue us from impending anarchy. The facts that support this opinion are no longer objects of speculation. They have forced themselves upon the sensibility of the people at large, and have at length extorted from those, whose mistaken policy has had the principal share in precipitating the extremity, at which we are arrived, a reluctant confession of the reality of those defects in the scheme of our Federal Government, which have been long pointed out and regretted by the intelligent friends of the Union.

We may indeed with propriety be said to have reached almost the last stage of national humiliation. There is scarcely any thing that can wound the pride, or degrade the character of an independent nation, which we do not experience. Are there engagements to the performance of which we are held by every tie respectable among men? These are the subjects of constant and unblushing violation. Do we owe debts to foreigners and to our own citizens contracted in a time of imminent peril, for the preservation of our political existence? These remain without any proper or satisfactory provision for their discharge. Have we valuable territories and important posts in the possession of a foreign power, which by express stipulations ought long since to have been surrendered? These are still retained, to the prejudice of our interests not less than of our rights. Are we in a condition to resent, or to repel the aggression? We have neither troops nor treasury nor government.* Are we even in a condition to remonstrate with dignity? The just imputations on our own faith, in respect to the same treaty, ought first to be removed. Are we entitled by nature and compact to a free participation in the navigation of the Mississippi? Spain excludes us from it. Is public credit an indispensable resource in time of public danger? We seem to have abandoned its cause as desperate and irretrievable. Is commerce of importance to national wealth? Ours is at the lowest point of declension. Is respectability in the eyes of foreign powers a safe guard against foreign encroachments? The imbecility of our Government even forbids them to treat with us: Our ambassadors abroad are the mere pageants of mimic sovereignty. Is a violent and unnatural decrease in the value of land a symptom of national distress? The price of improved land in most parts of the country is much lower than can be accounted for by the quantity of waste land at market, and can only be fully explained by that want of private and public confidence, which are so alarmingly prevalent among all ranks and which have a direct tendency to depreciate property of every kind. Is private credit the friend and patron of industry? That most useful kind which relates to borrowing and lending is reduced within the narrowest limits, and this still

---

*I mean for the Union.

more from an opinion of insecurity than from the scarcity of money. To shorten an enumeration of particulars which can afford neither pleasure nor instruction it may in general be demanded, what indication is there of national disorder, poverty and insignificance that could befal a community so peculiarly blessed with natural advantages as we are, which does not form a part of the dark catalogue of our public misfortunes?

This is the melancholy situation to which we have been brought by those very maxims and councils, which would now deter us from adopting the proposed constitution; and which not content with having conducted us to the brink of the precipice, seem resolved to plunge us into the abyss, that awaits us below. Here, my Countrymen, impelled by every motive that ought to influence an enlightened people, let us make a firm stand for our safety, our tranquillity, our dignity, our reputation. Let us at last break the fatal charm which has too long seduced us from the paths of felicity and prosperity.

It is true, as has been before observed, that facts too stubborn to be resisted have produced a species of general assent to the abstract proposition that there exist material defects in our national system; but the usefulness of the concession, on the part of the old adversaries of federal measures, is destroyed by a strenuous opposition to a remedy, upon the only principles, that can give it a chance of success. While they admit that the Government of the United States is destitute of energy; they contend against conferring upon it those powers which are requisite to supply that energy: They seem still to aim at things repugnant and irreconcilable—at an augmentation of Federal authority without a diminution of State authority—at sovereignty in the Union and complete independence in the members. They still in fine seem to cherish with blind devotion the political monster

of an *imperium in imperio*. This renders a full display of the principal defects of the confederation necessary, in order to shew, that the evils we experience do not proceed from minute or partial imperfections, but from fundamental errors in the structure of the building which cannot be amended otherwise than by an alteration in the first principles and main pillars of the fabric.

The great and radical vice in the construction of the existing Confederation is in the principle of LEGISLATION for STATES or GOVERNMENTS, in their CORPORATE or COLLECTIVE CAPACITIES and as contradistinguished from the INDIVIDUALS of whom they consist. Though this principle does not run through all the powers delegated to the Union; yet it pervades and governs those, on which the efficacy of the rest depends. Except as to the rule of apportionment, the United States have an indefinite discretion to make requisitions for men and money; but they have no authority to raise either by regulations extending to the individual citizens of America. The consequence of this is, that though in theory their resolutions concerning those objects are laws, constitutionally binding on the members of the Union, yet in practice they are mere recommendations, which the States observe or disregard at their option.

It is a singular instance of the capriciousness of the human mind, that after all the admonitions we have had from experience on this head, there should still be found men, who object to the New Constitution for deviating from a principle which has been found the bane of the old; and which is in itself evidently incompatible with the idea of GOVERNMENT; a principle in short which if it is to be executed at all must substitute the violent and sanguinary agency of the sword to the mild influence of the Magistracy.

There is nothing absurd or impracticable in the idea of a league or alliance between independent nations, for certain defined purposes precisely stated in a treaty; regulating all the details of time, place, circumstance and quantity; leaving nothing to future discretion; and depending for its execution on the good faith of the parties. Compacts of this kind exist among all civilized nations subject to the usual vicissitudes of peace and war, of observance and non observance, as the interests or passions of the contracting powers dictate. In the early part of the present century, there was an epidemical rage in Europe for this species of compacts; from which the politicians of the times fondly hoped for benefits which were never realised. With a view to establishing the equilibrium of power and the peace of that part of the world, all the resources of negotiation were exhausted, and triple and quadruple alliances were formed; but they were scarcely formed before they were broken, giving an instructive but afflicting lesson to mankind how little dependence is to be placed on treaties which have no other sanction than the obligations of good faith; and which oppose general considerations of peace and justice to the impulse of any immediate interest and passion.

If the particular States in this country are disposed to stand in a similar relation to each other, and to drop the project of a general DISCRETIONARY SUPERINTENDENCE, the scheme would indeed be pernicious, and would entail upon us all the mischiefs that have been enumerated under the first head; but it would have the merit of being at least consistent and practicable. Abandoning all views towards a confederate Government, this would bring us to a simple alliance offensive and defensive; and would place us in a situation to be alternately friends and enemies of each other as our mutual jealousies and rivalships nourished by the intrigues of foreign nations should prescribe to us.

But if we are unwilling to be placed in this perilous situation; if we will still adhere to the design of a national government, or which is the same thing of a superintending power under the direction of a common Council, we must resolve to incorporate into our plan those ingredients which may be considered as forming the characteristic difference between a league and a government; we must extend the authority of the union to the persons of the citizens,—the only proper objects of government.

Government implies the power of making laws. It is essential to the idea of a law, that it be attended with a sanction; or, in other words, a penalty or punishment for disobedience. If there be no penalty annexed to disobedience, the resolutions or commands which pretend to be laws will in fact amount to nothing more than advice or recommendation. This penalty, whatever it may be, can only be inflicted in two ways; by the agency of the Courts and Ministers of Justice, or by military force; by the COERTION of the magistracy, or by the COERTION of arms. The first kind can evidently apply only to men—the last kind must of necessity be employed against bodies politic, or communities or States. It is evident, that there is no process of a court by which their observance of the laws can in the last resort be enforced. Sentences may be denounced against them for violations of their duty; but these sentences can only be carried into execution by the sword. In an association where the general authority is confined to the collective bodies of the communities that compose it, every breach of the laws must involve a state of war, and military execution must become the only instrument of civil obedience. Such a state of things can certainly not deserve the name of government, nor would any prudent man choose to commit his happiness to it.

There was a time when we were told that breaches, by the States, of the regulations of the federal authority were not to be expected—that a sense of common interest would preside over the conduct of the respective members, and would beget a full compliance with all the constitutional requisitions of the Union. This language at the present day would appear as wild as a great part of what we now hear from the same quarter will be thought, when we shall have received further lessons from that best oracle of wisdom, experience. It at all times betrayed an ignorance of the true springs by which human conduct is actuated, and belied the original inducements to the establishment of civil power. Why has government been instituted at all? Because the passions of men will not conform to the dictates of reason and justice, without constraint. Has it been found that bodies of men act with more rectitude or greater disinterestedness than individuals? The contrary of this has been inferred by all accurate observers of the conduct of mankind; and the inference is founded upon obvious reasons. Regard to reputation has a less active influence, when the infamy of a bad action is to be divided among a number, than when it is to fall singly upon one. A spirit of faction which is apt to mingle its poison in the deliberations of all bodies of men, will often hurry the persons of whom they are composed into improprieties and excesses, for which they would blush in a private capacity.

In addition to all this, there is in the nature of sovereign power an impatience of controul, that disposes those who are invested with the exercise of it, to look with an evil eye upon all external attempts to restrain or direct its operations. From this spirit it happens that in every political association which is formed upon the principle of uniting in a common interest a number of lesser sovereignties, there will be found a kind of eccentric tendency in the subordinate or inferior orbs, by the operation of which there will be a perpetual effort in each to fly off from the common center. This tendency is not difficult to be accounted for. It has its origin in the love of power. Power controuled or abridged is almost always the rival and enemy of that power by which it is controuled or abri[d]ged. This simple proposition will teach us how little reason there is to expect, that the persons, entrusted with the administration of the affairs of the particular members of a confederacy, will at all times be ready, with perfect good humour, and an unbiassed regard to the public weal, to execute the resolutions or decrees of the general authority. The reverse of this results from the constitution of human nature.

If therefore the measures of the confederacy cannot be executed, without the intervention of the particular administrations, there will be little prospect of their being executed at all. The rulers of the respective members, whether they have a constitutional right to do it or not, will undertake to judge of the propriety of the measures themselves. They will consider the conformity of the thing proposed or required to their immediate interests or aims, the momentary conveniences or inconveniences that would attend its adoption. All this will be done, and in a spirit of interested and suspicious scrutiny, without that knowledge of national circumstances and reasons of state, which is essential to a right judgment, and with that strong predilection in favour of local objects, which can hardly fail to mislead the decision. The same process must be repeated in every member of which the body is constituted; and the execution of the plans, framed by the councils of the whole, will always fluctuate on the discretion of the ill-informed and prejudiced opinion of every part. Those who have been conversant in the proceedings of popular assemblies; who have seen how difficult it often is when there is no exterior pressure of circumstances, to bring them to harmonious resolutions on important points, will readily conceive how impossible it must be to induce a number of such assemblies, deliberating at a distance from each other, at different times, and under different impressions, long to cooperate in the same views and pursuits.

In our case, the concurrence of thirteen distinct sovereign wills is requisite under the confederation to the complete execution of every important measure, that proceeds from the Union. It has happened as was to have been foreseen. The measures of the Union have not been executed; and the delinquencies of the States have step by step matured themselves to an extreme; which has at length arrested all the wheels of the national government, and brought them to an awful stand. Congress at this time scarcely possess the means of keeping up the forms of administration; 'till the States can have time to agree upon a more substantial substitute for the present shadow of a federal government. Things did not come to this desperate extremity at once. The causes which have been speci-fied produced at first only unequal and disproportionate degrees of compliance with the requisitions of the Union. The greater deficiencies of some States furnished the pretext of examples and the temptation of interest to the complying, or to the least delinquent States. Why should we do more in proportion than those who are embarked with us in the same political voyage? Why should we consent to bear more than our proper share of the common burthen? These were suggestions which human selfishness could not withstand, and which even speculative men, who looked forward to remote consequences, could not, without hesitation, combat. Each State yielding to the persuasive voice of immediate interest and convenience has successively withdrawn its support, 'till the frail and tottering edifice seems ready to fall upon our heads and to crush us beneath its ruins.

PUBLIUS.

The Federalist No. 70 (1788)

March 15, 1788

To the People of the State of New York:

There is an idea, which is not without its advocates, that a vigorous executive is inconsistent with the genius of republican government. The enlightened well wishers to this species of government must at least hope that the supposition is destitute of foundation; since they can never admit its truth, without at the same time admitting the condemnation of their own principles. Energy in the executive is a leading character in the definition of good government. It is essential to the protection of the community against foreign attacks: It is not less essential to the steady administration of the laws, to the protection of property against those irregular and high handed combinations, which sometimes interrupt the ordinary course of justice to the security of liberty against the enterprises and assaults of ambition, of faction and of anarchy. Every man the least conversant in Roman [hi]story knows how often that republic was obliged to take refuge in the absolute power of a single man, under the formidable title of dictator, as well [as] against the intrigues of ambitious individuals, who aspired to the tyranny, and the seditions of whole classes of the community, whose conduct threatened the existence of all government, as against the invasions of external enemies, who menaced the conquest and destruction of Rome.

There can be no need however to multiply arguments or examples on this head. A feeble executive implies a feeble execution of the government. A feeble execution is but another phrase for a bad execution: And a government ill executed, whatever it may be in theory, must be in practice a bad government.

Taking it for granted, therefore, that all men of sense will agree in the necessity of an energetic executive; it will only remain to inquire, what are the ingredients which constitute this energy—how far can they be combined with those other ingredients which constitute safety in the republican sense? And how far does this combination characterize the plan, which has been reported by the convention?

The ingredients, which constitute energy in the executive, are first unity, secondly duration, thirdly an adequate provision for its support, fourthly competent powers.

The circumstances which constitute safety in the republican sense are, Ist. a due dependence on the people, secondly a due responsibility.

Those politicians and statesmen, who have been the most celebrated for the soundness of their principles, and for the justness of their views, have declared in favor of a single executive and a numerous legislature. They have with great propriety considered energy as the most necessary qualification of the former, and have regarded this as most applicable to power in a single hand; while they have with equal propriety considered the latter as best adapted to deliberation and wisdom, and best calculated to conciliate the confidence of the people and to secure their privileges and interests.

That unity is conducive to energy will not be disputed. Decision, activity, secrecy, and dispatch will generally characterize the proceedings of one man, in a much more eminent degree, than the proceedings of any greater number; and in proportion as the number is increased, these qualities will be diminished.

This unity may be destroyed in two ways; either by vesting the power in two or more magistrates of equal dignity and authority; or by vesting it ostensibly in one man, subject in whole or in part to the controul and co-operation of others, in the capacity of counsellors to him. Of the first the two consuls of Rome may serve as an example; of the last we shall find examples in the constitutions of several of the states. New York and New Jersey, if I recollect right, are the only states, which have entrusted the executive authority wholly to single men.[1] Both these methods of destroying the unity of the executive have their partisans; but the votaries of an executive council are the most numerous. They are both liable, if not to equal, to similar objections; and may in most lights be examined in conjunction.

The experience of other nations will afford little instruction on this head. As far however as it teaches any thing, it teaches us not to be inamoured of plurality in the executive. We have seen that the Achaeans on an experiment of two Praetors, were induced to abolish one. The Roman history records many instances of mischiefs to the republic from the dissentions between the consuls, and between the military tribunes, who were at times substituted to the consuls. But it gives us no specimens of any peculiar advantages derived to the state, from the circumstance of the plurality of those magistrates. That the dissentions between them were not more frequent, or

---

[1] New-York has no council except for the single purpose of appointing to offices; New-Jersey has a council, whom the governor may consult. But I think from the terms of the constitution their resolutions do not bind him.

more fatal, is matter of astonishment; until we advert to the singular position in which the republic was almost continually placed and to the prudent policy pointed out by the circumstances of the state, and pursued by the consuls, of making a division of the government between them. The Patricians engaged in a perpetual struggle with the Plebeians for the preservation of their ancient authorities and dignities; the consuls, who were generally chosen out of the former body, were commonly united by the personal interest they had in the defence of the privileges of their order. In addition to this motive of union, after the arms of the republic had considerably expanded the bounds of its empire, it became an established custom with the consuls to divide the administration between themselves by lot; one of them remaining at Rome to govern the city and its environs; the other taking the command in the more distant provinces. This expedient must no doubt have had great influence in preventing those collisions and rivalships, which might otherwise have embroiled the peace of the republic.

But quitting the dim light of historical research, and attaching ourselves purely to the dictates of reason and good sense, we shall discover much greater cause to reject than to approve the idea of plurality in the executive, under any modification whatever.

Wherever two or more persons are engaged in any common enterprize or pursuit, there is always danger of difference of opinion. If it be a public trust or office in which they are cloathed with equal dignity and authority, there is peculiar danger of personal emulation and even animosity. From either and especially from all these causes, the most bitter dissentions are apt to spring. Whenever these happen, they lessen the respectability, weaken the authority, and distract the plans and operations of those whom they divide. If they should

unfortunately assail the supreme executive magistracy of a country, consisting of a plurality of persons, they might impede or frustrate the most important measures of the government, in the most critical emergencies of the state. And what is still worse, they might split the community into the most violent and irreconcilable factions, adhering differently to the different individuals who composed the magistracy.

Men often oppose a thing merely because they have had no agency in planning it, or because it may have been planned by those whom they dislike. But if they have been consulted and have happened to disapprove, opposition then becomes in their estimation an indispensable duty of self love. They seem to think themselves bound in honor, and by all the motives of personal infallibility to defeat the success of what has been resolved upon, contrary to their sentiments. Men of upright, benevolent tempers have too many opportunities of remarking with horror, to what desperate lengths this disposition is sometimes carried, and how often the great interests of society are sacrificed to the vanity, to the conceit and to the obstinacy of individuals, who have credit enough to make their passions and their caprices interesting to mankind. Perhaps the question now before the public may in its consequences afford melancholy proofs of the effects of this despicable frailty, or rather detestable vice in the human character.

Upon the principles of a free government, inconveniences from the source just mentioned must necessarily be submitted to in the formation of the legislature; but it is unnecessary and therefore unwise to introduce them into the constitution of the executive. It is here too that they may be most pernicious. In the legislature, promptitude of decision is oftener an evil than a benefit. The differences of opinion, and the jarrings of parties in that department of the government, though they may sometimes obstruct salutary plans, yet often promote deliberations and circumspection; and serve to check excesses in the majority. When a resolution too is once taken, the opposition must be at an end. That resolution is a law, and resistance to it punishable. But no favourable circumstances palliate or atone for the disadvantages of dissention in the executive department. Here they are pure and unmixed. There is no point at which they cease to operate. They serve to embarrass and weaken the execution of the plan or measure, to which they relate, from the first step to the final conclusion of it. They constantly counteract those qualities in the executive, which are the most necessary ingredients in its composition, vigour and expedition, and this without any counterballancing good. In the conduct of war, in which the energy of the executive is the bulwark of the national security, every thing would be to be apprehended from its plurality.

It must be confessed that these observations apply with principal weight to the first case supposed, that is to a plurality of magistrates of equal dignity and authority; a scheme the advocates for which are not likely to form a numerous sect: But they apply, though not with equal, yet with considerable weight, to the project of a council, whose concurrence is made constitutionally necessary to the operations of the ostensible executive. An artful cabal in that council would be able to distract and to enervate the whole system of administration. If no such cabal should exist, the mere diversity of views and opinions would alone be sufficient to tincture the exercise of the executive authority with a spirit of habitual feebleness and delatoriness.

But one of the weightiest objections to a plurality in the executive, and which lies as much against the last as the first plan, is that it tends to conceal faults, and destroy responsibility. Responsibility is of two kinds, to censure and to punishment.

The first is the most important of the two; especially in an elective office. Man, in public trust, will much oftener act in such a manner as to render him unworthy of being any longer trusted, than in such a manner as to make him obnoxious to legal punishment. But the multiplication of the executive adds to the difficulty of detection in either case. It often becomes impossible, amidst mutual accusations, to determine on whom the blame or the punishment of a pernicious measure, or series of pernicious measures ought really to fall. It is shifted from one to another with so much dexterity, and under such plausible appearances, that the public opinion is left in suspense about the real author. The circumstances which may have led to any national miscarriage or misfortune are sometimes so complicated, that where there are a number of actors who may have had different degrees and kinds of agency, though we may clearly see upon the whole that there has been mismanagement, yet it may be impracticable to pronounce to whose account the evil which may have been incurred is truly chargeable.

"I was overruled by my council. The council were so divided in their opinions, that it was impossible to obtain any better resolution on the point." These and similar pretexts are constantly at hand, whether true or false. And who is there that will either take the trouble or incur the odium of a strict scrutiny into the secret springs of the transactions? Should there be found a citizen zealous enough to undertake the unpromising task, if there happen to be a collusion between the parties concerned, how easy is it to cloath the circumstances with so much ambiguity, as to render it uncertain what was the precise conduct of any of those parties?

In the single instance in which the governor of this state is coupled with a council, that is in the appointment to offices, we have seen the mischiefs of it in the view now under consideration. Scandalous appointments to important offices have been made. Some cases indeed have been so flagrant, that ALL PARTIES have agreed in the impropriety of the thing. When enquiry has been made, the blame has been laid by the governor on the members of the council; who on their part have charged it upon his nomination: While the people remain altogether at a loss to determine by whose influence their interests have been committed to hands so unqualified, and so manifestly improper. In tenderness to individuals, I forbear to descend to particulars.

It is evident from these considerations, that the plurality of the executive tends to deprive the people of the two greatest securities they can have for the faithful exercise of any delegated power; first, the restraints of public opinion, which lose their efficacy as well on account of the division of the censure attendant on bad measures among a number, as on account of the uncertainty on whom it ought to fall; and secondly, the opportunity of discovering with facility and clearness the misconduct of the persons they trust, in order either to their removal from office, or to their actual punishment, in cases which admit of it.

In England the king is a perpetual magistrate; and it is a maxim, which has obtained for the sake of the public peace, that he is unaccountable for his administration, and his person sacred. Nothing therefore can be wiser in that kingdom than to annex to the king a constitutional council, who may be responsible to the nation for the advice they give. Without this there would be no responsibility whatever in the executive department; an idea inadmissible in a free government. But even there the king is not bound by the resolutions of his council, though they are answerable for the advice they give. He is the absolute master of his own conduct, in the exercise of his office; and may observe or disregard the council given to him at his sole discretion.

But in a republic, where every magistrate ought to be personally responsible for his behaviour in office, the reason which in the British constitution dictates the propriety of a council not only ceases to apply, but turns against the institution. In the monarchy of Great Britain, it furnishes a substitute for the prohibited responsibility of the chief magistrate; which serves in some degree as a hostage to the national justice for his good behaviour. In the American republic it would serve to destroy, or would greatly diminish the intended and necessary responsibility of the chief magistrate himself.

The idea of a council to the executive, which has so generally obtained in the state constitutions, has been derived from that maxim of republican jealousy, which considers power as safer in the hands of a number of men than of a single man. If the maxim should be admitted to be applicable to the case, I should contend that the advantage on that side would not counterballance the numerous disadvantages on the opposite side. But I do not think the rule at all applicable to the executive power. I clearly concur in opinion in this particular with a writer whom the celebrated Junius pronounces to be "deep, solid and ingenious," that, "the executive power is more easily confined when it is one:"[2] That it is far more safe there should be a single object for the jealousy and watchfulness of the people; and in a word that all multiplication of the executive is rather dangerous than friendly to liberty.

A little consideration will satisfy us, that the species of security sought for in the multiplication of the executive is unattainable. Numbers must be so great as to render combination difficult; or they are rather a source of danger than of security.

---

[2]De Lome.

The united credit and influence of several individuals must be more formidable to liberty than the credit and influence of either of them separately. When power therefore is placed in the hands of so small a number of men, as to admit of their interests and views being easily combined in a common enterprise, by an artful leader, it becomes more liable to abuse and more dangerous when abused, than if it be lodged in the hands of one man; who from the very circumstance of his being alone will be more narrowly watched and more readily suspected, and who cannot unite so great a mass of influence as when he is associated with others. The Decemvirs of Rome, whose name denotes their number,[3] were more to be dreaded in their usurpation than any ONE of them would have been. No person would think of proposing an executive much more numerous than that body, from six to a dozen have been suggested for the number of the council. The extreme of these numbers is not too great for an easy combination; and from such a combination America would have more to

fear, than from the ambition of any single individual. A council to a magistrate, who is himself responsible for what he does, are generally nothing better than a clog upon his good intentions; are often the instruments and accomplices of his bad, and are almost always a cloak to his faults.

I forbear to dwell upon the subject of expence; though it be evident that if the council should be numerous enough to answer the principal end, aimed at by the institution, the salaries of the members, who must be drawn from their homes to reside at the seat of government, would form an item in the catalogue of public expenditures, too serious to be incurred for an object of equivocal utility.

I will only add, that prior to the appearance of the constitution, I rarely met with an intelligent man from any of the states, who did not admit as the result of experience, that the UNITY of the Executive of this state was one of the best of the distinguishing features of our constitution.

PUBLIUS.

The Federalist No. 78 (1788)

May 28, 1788

To the People of the State of New York:
We proceed now to an examination of the judiciary department of the proposed government.

In unfolding the defects of the existing confederation, the utility and necessity of a federal judicature have been clearly pointed out. It is the less necessary to recapitulate the considerations there urged; as the propriety of the institution in the abstract is not disputed: The only questions which have been raised being relative to the manner of constituting it, and to its

extent. To these points therefore our observations shall be confined.

The manner of constituting it seems to embrace these several objects—1st. The mode of appointing the judges—2d. The tenure by which they are to hold their places—3d. The partition of the judiciary authority between different courts, and their relations to each other.

First. As to the mode of appointing the judges: This is the same with that of appointing the officers of the union in general, and has been so fully discussed in the two last numbers, that nothing can be

[3]Ten.

Isaak, *American Political Thinking.*

said here which would not be useless repetition.

Second. As to the tenure by which the judges are to hold their places: This chiefly concerns their duration in office; the provisions for their support; and the precautions for their responsibility.

According to the plan of the convention, all the judges who may be appointed by the United States are to hold their offices *during good behaviour,* which is conformable to the most approved of the state constitutions; and among the rest, to that of this state. Its propriety having been drawn into question by the adversaries of that plan, is no light symptom of the rage for objection which disorders their imaginations and judgments. The standard of good behaviour for the continuance in office of the judicial magistracy is certainly one of the most valuable of the modern improvements in the practice of government. In a monarchy it is an excellent barrier to the despotism of the prince: In a republic it is a no less excellent barrier to the encroachments and oppressions of the representative body. And it is the best expedient which can be devised in any government, to secure a steady, upright and impartial administration of the laws.

Whoever attentively considers the different departments of power must perceive, that in a government in which they are separated from each other, the judiciary from the nature of its functions, will always be the least dangerous to the political rights of the constitution; because it will be least in a capacity to annoy or injure them. The executive not only dispenses the honors, but holds the sword of the community. The legislature not only commands the purse, but prescribes the rules by which the duties and rights of every citizen are to be regulated. The judiciary on the contrary has no influence over either the sword or the purse, no direction either of the strength or of the wealth of the society, and can take no active resolution whatever. It may truly be said to have neither FORCE nor WILL, but merely judgment; and must ultimately depend upon the aid of the executive arm even for the efficacy of its judgments.

This simple view of the matter suggests several important consequences. It proves incontestibly that the judiciary is beyond comparison the weakest of the three departments of power;[1] that it can never attack with success either of the other two; and that all possible care is requisite to enable it to defend itself against their attacks. It equally proves, that though individual oppression may now and then proceed from the courts of justice, the general liberty of the people can never be endangered from that quarter; I mean, so long as the judiciary remains truly distinct from both the legislative and executive. For I agree that "there is no liberty, if the power of judging be not separated from the legislative and executive powers."[2] And it proves, in the last place, that as liberty can have nothing to fear from the judiciary alone, but would have every thing to fear from its union with either of the other departments; that as all the effects of such an union must ensue from a dependence of the former on the latter, notwithstanding a nominal and apparent separation; that as from the natural feebleness of the judiciary, it is in continual jeopardy of being overpowered, awed or influenced by its coordinate branches; and that as nothing can contribute so much to its firmness and independence, as permanency in office, this

---

[1] The celebrated Montesquieu speaking of them says, "of the three powers above mentioned, the JUDICIARY is next to nothing." Spirit of Laws, vol. I, page 186.

[2] Idem. page 181.

quality may therefore be justly regarded as an indispensable ingredient in its constitution; and in a great measure as the citadel of the public justice and the public security.

The complete independence of the courts of justice is peculiarly essential in a limited constitution. By a limited constitution I understand one which contains certain specific exceptions to the legislative authority; such for instance as that it shall pass no bills of attainder, no *ex post facto* laws, and the like. Limitations of this kind can be preserved in practice no other way than through the medium of the courts of justice; whose duty it must be to declare all acts contrary to the manifest tenor of the constitution void. Without this, all the reservations of particular rights or privileges would amount to nothing.

Some perplexity respecting the right of the courts to pronounce legislative acts void, because contrary to the constitution, has arisen from an imagination that the doctrine would imply a superiority of the judiciary to the legislative power. It is urged that the authority which can declare the acts of another void, must necessarily be superior to the one whose acts may be declared void. As this doctrine is of great importance in all the American constitutions, a brief discussion of the grounds on which it rests cannot be unacceptable.

There is no position which depends on clearer principles, than that every act of a delegated authority, contrary to the tenor of the commission under which it is exercised, is void. No legislative act therefore contrary to the constitution can be valid. To deny this would be to affirm that the deputy is greater than his principal; that the servant is above his master; that the representatives of the people are superior to the people themselves; that men acting by virtue of powers may do not only what their powers do not authorise, but what they forbid.

If it be said that the legislative body are themselves the constitutional judges of their own powers, and that the construction they put upon them is conclusive upon the other departments, it may be answered, that this cannot be the natural presumption, where it is not to be collected from any particular provision in the constitution. It is not otherwise to be supposed that the constitution could intend to enable the representatives of the people to substitute their *will* to that of their constituents. It is far more rational to suppose that the courts were designed to be an intermediate body between the people and the legislature, in order, among other things, to keep the latter within the limits assigned to their authority. The interpretation of the laws is the proper and peculiar province of the courts. A constitution is in fact, and must be, regarded by the judges as a fundamental law. It therefore belongs to them to ascertain its meaning as well as the meaning of any particular act proceeding from the legislative body. If there should happen to be an irreconcileable variance between the two, that which has the superior obligation and validity ought of course to be preferred; or in other words, the constitution ought to be preferred to the statute, the intention of the people to the intention of their agents.

Nor does this conclusion by any means suppose a superiority of the judicial to the legislative power. It only supposes that the power of the people is superior to both; and that where the will of the legislature declared in its statutes, stands in opposition to that of the people declared in the constitution, the judges ought to be governed by the latter, rather than the former. They ought to regulate their decisions by the fundamental laws, rather than by those which are not fundamental.

This exercise of judicial discretion in determining between two contradictory laws, is exemplified in a familiar instance. It not uncommonly happens, that there are two statutes existing at one time, clashing in whole or in part with each other, and neither of them containing any repealing clause or expression. In such a case, it is the province of the courts to liquidate and fix their meaning and operation: So far as they can by any fair construction be reconciled to each other; reason and law conspire to dictate that this should be done: Where this is impracticable, it becomes a matter of necessity to give effect to one, in exclusion of the other. The rule which has obtained in the courts for determining their relative validity is that the last in order of time shall be preferred to the first. But this is mere rule of construction, not derived from any positive law, but from the nature and reason of the thing. It is a rule not enjoined upon the courts by legislative provision, but adopted by themselves, as consonant to truth and propriety, for the direction of their conduct as interpreters of the law. They thought it reasonable, that between the interfering acts of an *equal* authority, that which was the last indication of its will, should have the preference.

But in regard to the interfering acts of a superior and subordinate authority, of an original and derivative power, the nature and reason of the thing indicate the converse of that rule as proper to be followed. They teach us that the prior act of a superior ought to be prefered to the subsequent act of an inferior and subordinate authority; and that, accordingly, whenever a particular statute contravenes the constitution, it will be the duty of the judicial tribunals to adhere to the latter, and disregard the former.

It can be of no weight to say, that the courts on the pretense of a repugnancy, may substitute their own pleasure to the constitutional intentions of the legislature. This might as well happen in the case of two contradictory statutes; or it might as well happen in every adjudication upon any single statute. The courts must declare the sense of the law; and if they should be disposed to exercise *will* instead of *judgment,* the consequence would equally be the substitution of their pleasure to that of the legislative body. The observation, if it proved any thing, would prove that there ought to be no judges distinct from that body.

If then the courts of justice are to be considered as the bulwarks of a limited constitution against legislative encroachments, this consideration will afford a strong argument for the permanent tenure of judicial offices, since nothing will contribute so much as this to that independent spirit in the judges, which must be essential to the faithful performance of so arduous a duty.

This independence of the judges is equally requisite to guard the constitution and the rights of individuals from the effects of those ill humours which the arts of designing men, or the influence of particular conjunctures, sometimes disseminate among the people themselves, and which, though they speedily give place to better information and more deliberate reflection, have a tendency in the mean time to occasion dangerous innovations in the government, and serious oppressions of the minor party in the community. Though I trust the friends of the proposed constitution will never concur with its enemies[3] in questioning that fundamental principle of republican government, which admits the right of the people to alter or abolish the established constitution whenever they find it inconsistent with their happiness; yet it is not to be inferred from this principle, that the representatives of the people, whenever a momentary inclination happens to lay hold of a majority of their constituents incompatible with the provisions in the existing constitution, would on that account be justifiable in a violation of those provisions; or

---

[3]Vide Protest of the minority of the convention of Pennsylvania, Martin's speech, &c.

that the courts would be under a greater obligation to connive at infractions in this shape, than when they had proceeded wholly from the cabals of the representative body. Until the people have by some solemn and authoritative act annulled or changed the established form, it is binding upon themselves collectively, as well as individually; and no presumption, or even knowledge of their sentiments, can warrant their representatives in a departure from it, prior to such an act. But it is easy to see that it would require an uncommon portion of fortitude in the judges to do their duty as faithful guardians of the constitution, where legislative invasions of it had been instigated by the major voice of the community.

But it is not with a view to infractions of the constitution only that the independence of the judges may be an essential safeguard against the effects of occasional ill humours in the society. These sometimes extend no farther than to the injury of the private rights of particular classes of citizens, by unjust and partial laws. Here also the firmness of the judicial magistracy is of vast importance in mitigating the severity, and confining the operation of such laws. It not only serves to moderate the immediate mischiefs of those which may have been passed, but it operates as a check upon the legislative body in passing them; who, perceiving that obstacles to the success of an iniquitous intention are to be expected from the scruples of the courts, are in a manner compelled by the very motives of the injustice they mediate, to qualify their attempts. This is a circumstance calculated to have more influence upon the character of our governments, than but few may be aware of. The benefits of the integrity and moderation of the judiciary have already been felt in more states than one; and though they may have displeased those whose sinister expectations they may have disappointed, they must

have commanded the esteem and applause of all the virtuous and disinterested. Considerate men of every description ought to prize whatever will tend to beget or fortify that temper in the courts; as no man can be sure that he may not be to-morrow the victim of a spirit of injustice, by which he may be a gainer to-day. And every man must now feel that the inevitable tendency of such a spirit is to sap the foundations of public and private confidence, and to introduce in its stead, universal distrust and distress.

That inflexible and uniform adherence to the rights of the constitution and of individuals, which we perceive to be indispensable in the courts of justice, can certainly not be expected from judges who hold their offices by a temporary commission. Periodical appointments, however regulated, or by whomsoever made, would in some way or other be fatal to their necessary independence. If the power of making them was committed either to the executive or legislature, there would be danger of an improper complaisance to the branch which possessed it; if to both, there would be an unwillingness to hazard the displeasure of either; if to the people, or to persons chosen by them for the special purpose, there would be too great a disposition to consult popularity, to justify a reliance that nothing would be consulted but the constitution and the laws.

There is yet a further and a weighty reason for the permanency of the judicial offices; which is deductible from the nature of the qualifications they require. It has been frequently remarked with great propriety, that a voluminous code of laws is one of the inconveniences necessarily connected with the advantages of a free government. To avoid an arbitrary discretion in the courts, it is indispensable that they should be bound down by strict rules and precedents, which serve to define and point out their duty in every particular case that comes before them; and it will readily be conceived from the variety of controversies which grow out of the folly and wickedness of mankind, that the records of those precedents must unavoidably swell to a very considerable bulk, and must demand long and laborious study to acquire a competent knowledge of them. Hence it is that there can be but few men in the society, who will have sufficient skill in the laws to qualify them for the stations of judges. And making the proper deductions for the ordinary depravity of human nature, the number must be still smaller of those who unite the requisite integrity with the requisite knowledge. These considerations apprise us, that the government can have no great option between fit characters; and that a temporary duration in office, which would naturally discourage such characters from quitting a lucrative line of practice to accept a seat on the bench, would have a tendency to throw the administration of justice into hands less able, and less well qualified to conduct it with utility and dignity. In the present circumstances of this country, and in those in which it is likely to be for a long time to come, the disadvantages on this score would be greater than they may at first sight appear; but it must be confessed that they are far inferior to those which present themselves under the other aspects of the subject.

Upon the whole there can be no room to doubt that the convention acted wisely in copying from the models of those constitutions which have established *good behaviour* as the tenure of their judicial offices in point of duration; and that so far from being blameable on this account, their plan would have been inexcuseably defective if it had wanted this important feature of good government. The experience of Great Britain affords an illustrious comment on the excellence of the institution.

PUBLIUS.

The Federalist No. 84 (1788)

May 28, 1788

To the People of the State of New York:

In the course of the foregoing review of the constitution I have taken notice of, and endeavoured to answer, most of the objections which have appeared against it. There however remain a few which either did not fall naturally under any particular head, or were forgotten in their proper places. These shall not be discussed; but as the subject has been drawn into great length, I shall so far consult brevity as to compromise all my observations on these miscellaneous points in a single paper.

The most considerable of these remaining objections is, that the plan of the convention contains no bill of rights. Among other answers given to this, it has been upon different occasions remarked, that the constitutions of several of the states are in a similar predicament. I add, that New York is of this number. And yet the opposers of the new system in this state, who profess an unlimited admiration for its constitution, are among the most intemperate partizans of a bill of rights. To justify their zeal in this matter, they allege two things; one is, that though the constitution of New York has no bill of rights prefixed to it, yet it contains in the body of it various provisions in favour of particular privileges and rights, which in substance amount to the same thing; the other is, that the constitution adopts in their full extent the common and statute law of Great-Britain, by which many other rights not expressed in it are equally secured.

To the first I answer, that the constitution proposed by the convention contains, as well as the constitution of this state, a number of such provisions.

Independent of those, which relate to the structure of the government, we find the following: Article I. section 3. clause 7. "Judgment in cases of impeachment shall not extend further than to removal from office, and disqualification to hold and enjoy any office of honour, trust or profit under the United States; but the party convicted shall nevertheless be liable and subject to indictment, trial, judgment and punishment, according to law." Section 9. of the same article, clause 2. "The privilege of the writ of *habeas corpus* shall not be suspended, unless when in cases of rebellion or invasion the public safety may require it." Clause 3. "No bill of attainer or *ex post facto* law shall be passed." Clause 7. "No title of nobility shall be granted by the United States: And no person holding any office of profit or trust under them, shall, without the consent of congress, accept of any present, emolument, office or title, of any kind whatever, from any king, prince or foreign state." Article III. section 2. clause 3. "The trial of all crimes, except in cases of impeachment, shall be by jury; and such trial shall be held in the state where the said crimes shall have been committed; but when not committed within any state, the trial shall be at such place or places as the congress may by law have directed." Section 3, of the same article, "Treason against the United States shall consist only in levying war against them, or in adhering to their enemies, giving them aid and comfort. No person shall be convicted of treason unless on the testimony of two witness to the same overt act, or on confession in open court." And clause 3, of the same section. "The congress shall have power to declare the punishment of treason, but no attainder of treason shall work corruption of blood, or forfeiture, except during the life of the person attainted."

It may well be a question whether these are not upon the whole, of equal importance with any which are to be found in the constitution of this state. The establishment of the writ of *habeas corpus,* the prohibition of *ex post facto* laws, and of TITLES OF NOBILITY, *to which we have no corresponding provisions in our constitution,* are perhaps greater securities to liberty and republicanism than any it contains. The creation of crimes after the commission of the fact, or in other words, the subjecting of men to punishment for things which, when they were done, were breaches of no law, and the practice of arbitrary imprisonments have been in all ages the favourite and most formidable instruments of tyranny. The observations of the judicious Blackstone[1] in reference to the latter, are well worthy of recital. "To bereave a man of life (says he) or by violence to confiscate his estate, without accusation or trial, would be so gross and notorious an act of despotism, as must at once convey the alarm of tyranny throughout the whole nation; but confinement of the person by secretly hurrying to goal, where his sufferings are unknown or forgotten, is a less public, a less striking, and therefore *a more dangerous engine* of arbitrary government." And as a remedy for this fatal evil, he is every where peculiarly emphatical in his encomiums on the *habeas corpus* act, which in one place he calls "the BULWARK of the British constitution."[2]

---

[1]Vide Blackstone's Commentaries, vol. I, page 136.

[2]Idem, vol. 4, page 438.

Nothing need be said to illustrate the importance of the prohibition of titles of nobility. This may truly be denominated the corner stone of republican government; for so long as they are excluded, there can never be serious danger that the government will be any other than that of the people.

To the second, that is, to the pretended establishment of the common and statute law by the constitution, I answer, that they are expressly made subject "to such alterations and provisions as the legislature shall from time to time make concerning the same." They are therefore at any moment liable to repeal by the ordinary legislative power, and of course have no constitutional sanction. The only use of the declaration was to recognize the ancient law, and to remove doubts which might have been occasioned by the revolution. This consequently can be considered as no part of a declaration of rights, which under our constitutions must be intended as limitations of the power of the government itself.

It has been several times truly remarked, that bills of rights are in their origin, stipulations between kings and their subjects, abridgments of prerogative in favor of privilege, reservations of rights not surrendered to the prince. Such was MAGNA CHARTA, obtained by the Barons, sword in hand, from king John. Such were the subsequent confirmations of that charter by subsequent princes. Such was the *petition of right* assented to by Charles the First, in the beginning of his reign. Such also was the declaration of right presented by the lords and commons to the prince of Orange in 1688, and afterwards thrown into the form of an act of parliament, called the bill of rights. It is evident, therefore, that according to their primitive signification, they have no application to constitutions professedly founded upon the power of the people, and executed by their immediate representatives and servants. Here, in

strictness, the people surrender nothing, and as they retain every thing, they have no need of particular reservations. "WE THE PEOPLE of the United States, to secure the blessings of liberty to ourselves and our posterity, do *ordain* and *establish* this constitution for the United States of America." Here is a better recognition of popular rights than volumes of those aphorisms which make the principal figure in several of our state bills of rights, and which would sound much better in a treatise of ethics than in a constitution of government.

But a minute detail of particular rights is certainly far less applicable to a constitution like that under consideration, which is merely intended to regulate the general political interests of the nation, than to a constitution which has the regulation of every species of personal and private concerns. If therefore the loud clamours against the plan of the convention on this score, are well founded, no epithets of reprobation will be too strong for the constitution of this state. But the truth is, that both of them contain all, which in relation to their objects, is reasonably to be desired.

I go further, and affirm that bills of rights, in the sense and in the extent in which they are contended for, are not only unnecessary in the proposed constitution, but would even be dangerous. They would contain various exceptions to powers which are not granted; and on this very account, would afford a colourable pretext to claim more than were granted. For why declare that things shall not be done which there is no power to do? Why for instance, should it be said, that the liberty of the press shall not be restrained, when no power is given by which restrictions may be imposed? I will not contend that such a provision would confer a regulating power; but it is evident that it would furnish, to men disposed to usurp, a plausible pretence for claiming that power. They might urge with a semblance of reason, that the constitution ought not to be charged with the absurdity of providing against the abuse of an authority, which was not given, and that the provision against restraining the liberty of the press afforded a clear implication, that a power to prescribe proper regulations concerning it, was intended to be vested in the national government. This may serve as a specimen of the numerous handles which would be given to the doctrine of constructive powers, by the indulgence of an injudicious zeal for bills of rights.

On the subject of the liberty of the press, as much has been said, I cannot forbear adding a remark or two: In the first place, I observe that there is not a syllable concerning it in the constitution of this state, and in the next, I contend that whatever has been said about it in that of any other state, amounts to nothing. What signifies a declaration that "the liberty of the press shall be inviolably preserved?" What is the liberty of the press? Who can give it any definition which would not leave the utmost latitude for evasion? I hold it to be impracticable; and from this, I infer, that its security, whatever fine declarations may be inserted in any constitution respecting it, must altogether depend on public opinion, and on the general spirit of the people and of the government.[3] And here, after all, as intimated upon another occasion, must we seek for the only solid basis of all our rights.

There remains but one other view of this matter to conclude the point. The truth is, after all the declamation we have heard, that the constitution is itself in every ratio-nal sense, and to every useful purpose A BILL OF RIGHTS. The several bills of rights, in Great-Britain, form its constitution, and conversely the constitution of each state is its bill of rights. And the proposed constitution, if adopted, will be the bill of rights of the union. Is it one object of a bill of rights to declare and specify the political privileges of the citizens in the structure and administration of the government? This is done in the most ample and precise manner in the plan of the convention, comprehending various precautions for the public security, which are not to be found in any of the state constitutions. Is another object of a bill of rights to define certain immunities and modes of proceeding, which are relative to personal and private concerns? This we have seen has also been attended to, in a variety of cases, in the same plan. Adverting therefore to the substantial meaning of a bill of rights, it is absurd to allege that it is not to be found in the work of the convention. It may be said that it does not go far enough, though it will not be easy to make this appear; but it can with no propriety be contended that there is no such thing. It certainly must be immaterial what mode is observed as to the order of declaring the rights of the citizens, if they are to be found in any part of the instrument which establishes the government. And hence it must be apparent that much of what has been said on this subject rests merely on verbal and nominal distinctions, which are entirely foreign from the substance of the thing.

---

[3]To show that there is a power in the constitution by which the liberty of the press may be affected, recourse has been had to the power of taxation. It is said that duties may be laid upon publications so high as to amount to a prohibition. I know not by what logic it could be maintained that the declarations in the state constitutions, in favour of the freedom of the press, would be a constitutional impediment to the imposition of duties upon publications by the state legislatures. It cannot certainly be pretended that any degree of duties, however low, would be an abrigement of the liberty of the press. We know that newspapers are taxed in Great-Britain, and yet it is notorious that the press no where enjoys greater liberty than in that country. And if duties of any kind may be laid without a violation of that liberty, it is evident that the extent must depend on legislative discretion, regulated by public opinion; so that after all, general declarations respecting the liberty of the press will give it no greater security than it will have without them. The same invasions of it may be effected under the state constitutions which contain those declarations through the means of taxation, as under the proposed constitution which has nothing of the kind. It would be quite as significant to declare that government ought to be free, that taxes ought not be excessive, &c., as that the liberty of the press ought not to be restrained.

Another objection, which has been made, and which from the frequency of its repetition it is to be presumed is relied on, is of this nature: It is improper (say the objectors) to confer such large powers, as are proposed, upon the national government; because the seat of that government must of necessity be too remote from many of the states to admit of a proper knowledge on the part of the constituent, of the conduct of the representative body. This argument, if it proves any thing, proves that there ought to be no general government whatever. For the powers which it seems to be agreed on all hands, ought to be vested in the union, cannot be safely intrusted to a body which is not under every requisite controul. But there are satisfactory reasons to shew that the objection is in reality not well founded. There is in most of the arguments which relate to distance a palpable illusion of the imagination. What are the sources of information by which the people in Montgomery county must regulate their judgment of the conduct of their representatives in the state legislature? Of personal observation they can have no benefit. This is confined to the citizens on the spot. They must therefore depend on the information of intelligent men, in whom they confide— and how must these men obtain their information? Evidently from the complection of public measures, from the public prints, from correspondences with their representatives, and with other persons who reside at the place of their deliberation. This does not apply to Montgomery county only, but to all the counties, at any considerable distance from the seat of government.

It is equally evident that the same sources of information would be open to the people, in relation to the conduct of their representatives in the general government; and the impediments to a prompt communication which distance may be supposed to create, will be overbalanced by the effects of the vigilance of the state governments. The executive and legislative bodies of each state will be so many centinels over the persons employed in every department of the national administration; and as it will be in their power to adopt and pursue a regular and effectual system of intelligence, they can never be at a loss to know the behaviour of those who represent their constituents in the national councils, and can readily communicate the same knowledge to the people. Their disposition to apprise the community of whatever may prejudice its interests from another quarter, may be relied upon, if it were only from the rivalship of power. And we may conclude with the fullest assurance, that the people, through that channel, will be better informed of the conduct of their national representatives, than they can be by any means they now possess of that of their state representatives.

It ought also to be remembered, that the citizens who inhabit the country at and near the seat of government, will in all questions that affect the general liberty and prosperity, have the same interest with those who are at a distance; and that they will stand ready to sound the alarm when necessary, and to point out the actors in any pernicious project. The public papers will be expeditious messengers of intelligence to the most remote inhabitants of the union.

Among the many extraordinary objections which have appeared against the proposed constitution, the most extracdinary and the least colourable one, is derived from the want of some provision respecting the debts due *to* the United States. This has been represented as a tacit relinquishment of those debts, and as a wicked contrivance to screen public defaulters. The newspapers have teemed with the most inflammatory railings on this head; and yet there is nothing clearer than that the suggestion is entirely void of foundation, and is the offspring of extreme ignorance or extreme dishonesty. In addition to the remarks I have made upon the subject in another place, I shall only observe, that as it is a plain dictate of common sense, so it is also an established doctrine of political law, that *"States neither lose any of their rights, nor are discharged from any of their obligations by a change in the form of their civil government."*[4]

The last objection of any consequence which I at present recollect turns upon the article of expense. If it were even true that the adoption of the proposed government would occasion a considerable increase of expense, it would be an objection that ought to have no weight against the plan. The great bulk of the citizens of America, are with reason convinced that union is the basis of their political happiness. Men of sense of all parties now, with few exceptions, agree that it cannot be preserved under the present system, nor without radical alterations; that new and extensive powers ought to be granted to the national head, and that these require a different organization of the federal government, a single body being an unsafe depository of such ample authorities. In conceding all this, the question of expense must be given up, for it is impossible, with any degree of safety, to narrow the foundation upon which the system is to stand. The two branches of the legislature are in the first instance, to consist of only sixty-five persons, which is the same number of which congress, under the existing confederation, may be composed. It is true that this number is intended to be increased; but this is to keep pace with the increase of the population and resources of the country. It is evident, that a less number would, even in the first instance, have been unsafe; and that a continuance of the present number would, in a more advanced stage of population, be a very inadequate representation of the people.

Whence is the dreaded augmentation of expense to spring? One source pointed out, is the multiplication of offices under the new government. Let us examine this a little.

It is evident that the principal departments of the administration under the present government are the same which will be required under the new. There are now a secretary at war, a secretary for foreign affairs, a secretary for domestic affairs, a board of treasury consisting of three persons, a treasurer, assistants, clerks, &c. These offices are indispensable under any system, and will suffice under the new as well as under the old. As to ambassadors and other ministers and agents in foreign countries, the proposed constitution can make no other difference, than to render their characters, where they reside, more respectable, and their services more useful. As to persons to be employed in the collection of the revenues, it is unquestionably true that these will form a very considerable addition to the number of federal officers; but it will not follow, that this will occasion an increase of public expence. It will be in most cases nothing more than an exchange of state officers for national officers. In the collection of all duties, for instance, the persons employed will be wholly of the latter description. The states individually will stand in no need for any for this purpose. What difference can it make in point of expense, to pay officers of the customs appointed by the state, or those appointed by the United States? There is no good reason to suppose, that either the number or the salaries of the latter, will be greater than those of the former.

Where then are we to seek for those additional articles of expense which are to

---

[4]Vide Rutherford's Institutes, vol. 2. book II. chap. x. see. xiv, and xv.—Vide also Grotius, book II, chap. ix, sect. viii, and ix.

swell the account to the enormous size that has been represented to us? The chief item which occurs to me, respects the support of the judges of the United States. I do not add the president, because there is now a president of congress, whose expences may not be far, if any thing, short of those which will be incurred on account of the president of the United States. The support of the judges will clearly be an extra expense, but to what extent will depend on the particular plan which may be adopted in practice in regard to this matter. But it can upon no reasonable plan amount to a sum which will be an object of material consequence.

Let us now see what there is to counterballance any extra expences that may attend the establishment of the proposed government. The first thing that presents itself is, that a great part of the business, which now keeps congress sitting through the year, will be transacted by the president. Even the management of foreign negotiations will naturally devolve upon him according to general principles concerted with the senate, and subject to their final concurrence. Hence it is evident, that a portion of the year will suffice for the session of both the senate and the house of representatives: We may suppose about a fourth for the latter, and a third or perhaps a half for the former. The extra business of treaties and appointments may give this extra occupation to the senate. From this circumstance we may infer, that until the house of representatives shall be increased greatly beyond its present number, there will be a considerable saving of expense from the difference between the constant session of the present, and the temporary session of the future congress.

But there is another circumstance, of great importance in the view of the economy. The business of the United States has hitherto occupied the state legislatures as well as congress. The latter has made requisitions which the former have had to provide for. Hence it has happened that the sessions of the state legislatures have been protracted greatly beyond what was necessary for the execution of the mere local business of the states. More than half their time has been frequently employed in matters which related to the United States. Now the members who compose the legislatures of the several states amount to two thousand and upwards; which number has hitherto performed what under the new system will be done in the first instance by sixty-five persons, and probably at no future period by above a fourth or a fifth of that number. The congress under the proposed government will do all the business of the United States themselves, without the intervention of the state legislatures, who thenceforth will have only to attend to the affairs of their particular states, and will not have to sit in any proportion as long as they have heretofore done. This difference, in the time of the sessions of the state legislatures, will be all clear gain, and will alone form an article of saving, which may be regarded as an equivalent for any additional objects of expense that may be occasioned by the adoption of the new system.

The result from these observations is, that the sources of additional expense from the establishment of the proposed constitution are much fewer than may have been imagined, that they are counterbalanced by considerable objects of saving, and that while it is questionable on which side the scale will preponderate, it is certain that a government less expensive would be incompetent to the purposes of the union.

PUBLIUS.

George Washington

George Washington (1732–1799) was the nonpartisan "father" of the country. His legacy to American political thought lies in his noble, patriotic behavior as a reserved statesman and in the intellectual principles of his "Farewell Address" (1976), which asked for unity over selfish factions and advised the avoidance of entangling alliances abroad.

Born in Westmoreland County, Virginia, Washington's skills at military leadership emerged in the French and Indian War, in which he commanded the Continental army. His effort to avoid partisan positions despite his usual conservative inclination to side with the Federalists made him an easy first choice as American president. His image was carefully crafted, leaving little to chance. In government he managed to maintain his cool reserve, attempting to remain above conflict and petty intrigue. Personally he embodied gentility, integrity, and a deep sense of duty, which in action reflected as loyal service, patriotism, and a high standard of morality. His request for isolationism for the United States in his farewell address was a natural outgrowth of his desire for a national politics of unity that transcended petty disputes.

☙❦❧

Farewell Address (1796)

September 19, 1796

To the People of the United States

Friends, and Fellow-Citizens:

The period for a new election of a Citizen, to administer the Executive Government of the United States, being not far distant, and the time actually arrived, when your thoughts must be employed in designating the person, who is to be clothed with that important trust, it appears to me proper, especially as it may conduce to a more distinct expression of the public voice, that I should now apprise you of the resolution I have formed, to decline being considered among the number of those, out of whom a choice is to be made.

I beg you, at the same time, to do me the justice to be assured, that this resolution has not been taken, without a strict regard to all the considerations appertaining to the relation, which binds a dutiful citizen to his country—and that, in withdrawing the tender of service which silence in my situation might imply, I am influenced by no diminution of zeal for your future interest, no deficiency of grateful respect for your past kindness; but am supported by a full conviction that the step is compatible with both.

The acceptance of, and continuance hitherto in, the office to which your suffrages have twice called me, have been a uniform sacrifice of inclination to the opinion of duty, and to a deference for what appeared to be your desire.—I constantly hoped, that it would have been much earlier in my power, consistently with motives, which I was not at liberty to disregard, to return to that retirement, from which I had been reluctantly drawn.—The strength of my inclination to do this, previous to the last election, had even led to the preparation of an address to declare to you; but mature reflection on the then perplexed and critical posture of our affairs with foreign Nations, and the unanimous advice of persons entitled to my confidence, impelled me to abandon the idea.—

I rejoice that the state of your concerns, external as well as internal, no longer renders the pursuit of inclination incompatible with the sentiment of duty, or propriety; and am persuaded, whatever partiality may be retained for my service, that in the present circumstances of our country, you will not disapprove my determination to retire.

The impressions, with which I first undertook the arduous trust, were explained on the proper occasion.—In the discharge of this trust, I will only say, that I have, with good intentions, contributed towards the organization and administration of the government, the best exertions of which a very fallible judgment was capable.—Not unconscious, in the outset, of the inferiority of my qualifications, experience in my own eyes, perhaps still more in the eyes of others, has strengthened the motives to diffidence of myself; and every day the increasing weight of years admonishes me more and more, that the shade of retirement is as necessary to me as it will be welcome.—Satisfied, that, if any circumstances have given peculiar value to my services, they were temporary, I have the consolation to believe, that, while choice and prudence invite me to quit the political scene, patriotism does not forbid it.

In looking forward to the moment, which is intended to terminate the career of my public life, my feelings do not permit me to suspend the deep acknowledgment of that debt of gratitude, which I owe to my beloved country,—for the many honors it has conferred upon me; still more for the steadfast confidence with which it has supported me; and for the opportunities I have thence enjoyed of manifesting my inviolable attachment, by services faithful and perserving, though in usefulness unequal to my zeal.—If benefits have resulted to our country from these services, let it always be remembered to your praise, and as an instructive example in our annals, that under circumstances in which the Passions agitated in every direction were liable to mislead, amidst appearances sometimes dubious,—vicissitudes of fortune often discouraging,—in situations in which not unfrequently want of success has countenanced the spirit of criticism, the constancy of your support was the essential prop of the efforts and a guarantee of the plans by which they were effected.—Profoundly penetrated with this idea, I shall carry it with me to the grave, as a strong incitement to unceasing vows that Heaven may continue to you the choicest tokens of its beneficence—that your union and brotherly affection may be perpetual—that the free constitution, which is the work of your hands, may be sacredly maintained—that its administration in every department may be stamped with wisdom and virtue—that, in fine, the happiness of the people of these States, under the auspices of liberty, may be made complete, by so careful a preservation and so prudent a use of this blessing as will acquire to them the glory of recommending it to the applause, the affection, and adoption of every nation, which is yet a stranger to it.

Here, perhaps, I ought to stop.—But a solicitude for your welfare, which cannot end but with my life, and the apprehension of danger, natural to that solicitude, urge me on an occasion like the present, to offer to you solemn contemplation, and to recommend to your frequent review, some sentiments; which are the result of much reflection, of no inconsiderable observation, and which appear to me all-important to the permanency of your felicity as a People.—These will be offered to you with the more freedom, as you can only see in them the disinterested warnings of a parting friend, who can possibly have no personal motive to bias his counsels.—Nor can I forget, as an encouragement to it your indulgent reception of my sentiments on a former and not dissimilar occasion.

Interwoven as is the love of liberty with every ligament of your hearts, no recommendation of mine is necessary to fortify or confirm the attachment.—

The Unity of Government which constitutes you one people, is also now dear to you.—It is justly so;—for it is a main Pillar in the Edifice of your real independence; the support of your tranquillity at home; your peace abroad; of your safety; of your prosperity; of that very Liberty, which you so highly prize.—But as it is easy to foresee, that from different causes, and from different quarters, much pains will be taken, many artifices employed, to weaken in your minds the conviction of this truth;—as this is the point in your political fortress against which the batteries of internal and external enemies will be most constantly and actively (though often covertly and insidiously) directed, it is of infinite moment, that you should properly estimate the immense value of your national Union to your collective and individual happiness;—that you should cherish a cordial, habitual, and immoveable attachment to it;

accustoming yourself to think and speak of it as of the Palladium of your political safety and prosperity; watching for its preservation with jealous anxiety; discountenancing whatever may suggest even a suspicion that it can in any event be abandoned, and indignantly frowning upon the first dawning of every attempt to alienate any portion of our Country from the rest, or to enfeeble the sacred ties which now link together the various parts.

For this you have every inducement of sympathy and interest.—Citizens by birth or choice of a common country, that country has a right to concentrate your affections.—The name of AMERICAN, which belongs to you, in your national capacity, must always exalt the just pride of Patriotism, more than any appellation derived from local discriminations.—With slight shades of difference, you have the same Religion, Manners, Habits, and political Principles.—You have in common cause fought and triumphed together.—The Independence and Liberty you possess are the work of joint councils, and joint efforts—of common dangers, sufferings and successes.—

But these considerations, however powerfully they address themselves to your sensibility, are greatly outweighed by those which apply more immediately to your Interest.—Here every portion of our country finds the most commanding motives for carefully guarding and preserving the Union of the whole.

The *North* in an unrestrained intercourse with the *South,* protected by the equal Laws of a common government, finds in the productions of the latter great additional resources of maritime and commercial enterprise—and precious materials of manufacturing industry.—The *South* in the same intercourse, benefiting by the agency of the *North,* sees its agriculture grow and its commerce expand. Turning partly into its own channels the seamen of the *North,* it finds its particular navigation envigorated;—and, while it contributes, in different ways, to nourish and increase the general mass of the national navigation, it looks forward to the protection of a maritime strength to which itself is unequally adopted.—The *East,* in a like intercourse with the *West,* already finds, and in the progressive improvement of interior communications, by land and water, will more and more find, a valuable vent for the commodities which it brings from abroad, or manufactures at home.—The *West* derives from the *East* supplies requisite to its growth and comfort,—and what is perhaps of still greater consequence, it must of necessity owe the *secure* enjoyment of indispensable *outlets* for its own productions to the weight, influence, and the future maritime strength of the Atlantic side of the Union, directed by an indissoluble community of interest, as *one Nation.*— Any other tenure by which the *West* can hold this essential advantage, whether derived from its own separate strength, or from an apostate and unnatural connexion with any foreign power, must be intrinsically precarious.

While then every part of our Country thus feels an immediate and particular interest in Union, all the parts combined cannot fail to find in the united mass of means and efforts, greater strength, greater resource, proportionably greater security from external danger, a less frequent interruption of their Peace by foreign Nations; and, what is of inestimable value! they must derive from Union an exemption from those broils and wars between themselves, which so frequently afflict neighbouring countries, not tied together by the same government; which their own rivalships alone would be sufficient to produce; but which opposite foreign alliances, attachments, and intrigues would stimulate and embitter.—Hence likewise they will avoid the necessity of those overgrown Military

establishments, which under any form of government, are inauspicious to liberty, and which are to be regarded as particularly hostile to Republican Liberty: In this sense it is, that your Union ought to be considered as a main prop of your liberty, and that the love of the one ought to endear to you the preservation of the other.

These considerations speak a persuasive language to every reflecting and virtuous mind,—and exhibit the continuance of the UNION as a primary object of Patriotic desire.—Is there a doubt, whether a common government can embrace so large a sphere?—Let experience solve it.—To listen to mere speculation in such a case were criminal.—We are authorized to hope that a proper organization of the whole, with the auxiliary agency of governments for the respective subdivisions, will afford a happy issue to the experiment. 'Tis well worth a fair and full experiment. With such powerful and obvious motives to Union, affecting all parts of our country, while experience shall not have demonstrated its impracticability, there will always be reason to distrust the patriotism of those, who in any quarter may endeavor to weaken its bands.—

In contemplating the causes which may disturb our Union, it occurs as matter of serious concern, that any ground should have been furnished for characterizing parties by *Geographical* discriminations— *Northern* and *Southern*—*Atlantic* and *Western;* whence designing men may endeavor to excite a belief, that there is a real difference of local interests and views. One of the expedients of Party to acquire influence, within particular districts, is to misrepresent the opinions and aims of other districts.—You cannot shield yourselves too much against the jealousies and heartburnings which spring from these misrepresentations;—They tend to render alien to each other those who ought to be bound together by fraternal affection.—The inhabitants of our Western country have lately had a useful lesson on this head.— They have seen, in the negotiation by the Executive, and in the unanimous ratification by the Senate, of the Treaty with Spain, and in the universal satisfaction at that event, throughout the United States, a decisive proof how unfounded were the suspicions propagated among them of a policy in the General Government and in the Atlantic States unfriendly to their interests in regard to the MISSISSIPPI.—They have been witnesses to the formation of two Treaties, that with G. Britain, and that with Spain, which secure to them every thing they could desire, in respect to our Foreign Relations, towards confirming their prosperity.—Will it not be their wisdom to rely for the preservation of these advantages on the UNION by which they were procured?— Will they not henceforth be deaf to those advisers, if such there are, who would sever them from their Brethren, and connect them with Aliens?—

To the efficacy and permanency of your Union, a Government for the whole is indispensable.—No alliances however strict between the parts can be an adequate substitute.—They must inevitably experience the infractions and interruptions which all alliances in all times have experienced.—Sensible of this momentous truth, you have improved upon your first essay, by the adoption of a Constitution of Government, better calculated than your former for an intimate Union, and for the efficacious management of your common concerns.—This government, the offspring of our own choice uninfluenced and unawed, adopted upon full investigation and mature deliberation, completely free in its principles, in the distribution of its powers, uniting security with energy, and containing within itself a provision for its own amendment, has a just claim to your confidence and your support.—Respect for its authority, compliance with its Laws, acquiescence in its measures, are duties enjoined by the fundamental maxims of true Liberty.—The basis of our political systems is the right of the people to make and to alter their Constitutions of Government.— But the Constitution which at any time exists, 'till changed by an explicit and authentic act of the whole people, is sacredly obligatory upon all.—The very idea of the power and the right of the people to establish Government, presupposes the duty of every individual to obey the established Government.

All obstructions to the execution of the Laws, all combinations and associations, under whatever plausible character, with the real design to direct, controul, counteract, or awe the regular deliberation and action of the constituted authorities, are destructive of this fundamental principle, and of fatal tendency.—They serve to organize faction, to give it an artificial and extraordinary force—to put, in the place of the delegated will of the Nation, the will of a party;—often a small but artful and enterprizing minority of the community;— and, according to the alternate triumphs of different parties, to make the public administration the mirror of the ill-concerted and incongruous projects of faction, rather than the organ of consistent and wholesome plans digested by common councils, and modified by mutual interests.—However combinations or associations of the above description may now and then answer popular ends, they are likely, in the course of time and things, to become potent engines, by which cunning, ambitious, and unprincipled men will be enabled to subvert the Power of the People and to usurp for themselves the reins of Government; destroying afterwards the very engines which have lifted them to unjust dominion.—

Towards the preservation of your Government and the permanency of your present happy state, it is requisite, not only that you steadily discountenance irregular oppositions to its acknowledged authority, but also that you resist with care the spirit of innovation upon its principles, however specious the pretexts.—One method of assault may be to effect, in the forms of the Constitution, alterations which will impair the energy of the system, and thus to undermine what cannot be directly overthrown.—In all the changes to which you may be invited, remember that time and habit are at least as necessary to fix the true character of Governments, as of other human institutions—that experience is the surest standard, by which to test the real tendency of the existing Constitution of a Country—that facility in changes upon the credit of mere hypothesis and opinion exposes to perpetual change, from the endless variety of hypothesis and opinion:— and remember, especially, that for the efficient management of your common interests, in a country so extensive as ours, a Government of as much vigour as is consistent with the perfect security of Liberty is indispensable.—Liberty itself will find in such a Government, with powers properly distributed and adjusted, its surest Guardian.—It is indeed little else than a name, where the Government is too feeble to withstand the enterprise of faction, to confine each member of the Society within the limits prescribed by the laws, and to maintain all in the secure and tranquil enjoyment of the rights of person and property.

I have already intimated to you the danger of Parties in the State, with particular reference to the founding of them on Geographical discriminations.—Let me now take a more comprehensive view, and warn you in the most solemn manner against the baneful effects of the Spirit of Party, generally.

This Spirit, unfortunately, is inseparable from our nature, having its roots in the strongest passions of the human mind.—It exists under different shapes in all Govern-

ments, more or less stifled, controuled, or repressed; but, in those of the popular form, it is seen in its greatest rankness, and is truly their worst enemy.—

The alternate domination of one faction over another, sharpened by the spirit of revenge natural to party dissension, which in different ages and countries has perpetrated the most horrid enormities, is itself a frightful despotism.—But this leads at length to a more formal and permanent despotism.—The disorders and miseries, which result, gradually incline the minds of men to seek security and repose in the absolute power of an Individual: and sooner or later the chief of some prevailing faction, more able or more fortunate than his competitors, turns this disposition to the purposes of his own elevation, on the ruins of Public Liberty.

Without looking forward to an extremity of this kind, (which nevertheless ought not to be entirely out of sight,) the common and continual mischiefs of the spirit of Party are sufficient to make it the interest and duty of a wise People to discourage and restrain it.—

It serves always to distract the Public Councils, and enfeeble the Public administration.—It agitates the community with ill-founded jealousies and false alarms, kindles the animosity of one part against another, foments occasionally riot and insurrection.—It opens the doors to foreign influence and corruption, which find a facilitated access to the Government itself through the channels of party passions. Thus the policy and the will of one country, are subjected to the policy and will of another.

There is an opinion that parties in free countries are useful checks upon the Administration of the Government, and serve to keep alive the Spirit of Liberty.— This within certain limits is probably true—and in Governments of a Monarchical cast, Patriotism may look with indulgence, if not with favour, upon the spirit of party.—But in those of the popular character, in Governments purely elective, it is a spirit not to be encouraged.—From their natural tendency, it is certain there will always be enough of that spirit for every salutary purpose,—and there being constant danger of excess, the effort ought to be, by force of public opinion, to mitigate and assuage it.—A fire not to be quenched; it demands a uniform vigilance to prevent its bursting into a flame, lest, instead of warming, it should consume.—

It is important, likewise, that the habits of thinking in a free country should inspire caution in those entrusted with its administration, to confine themselves within their respective constitutional spheres; avoiding in the exercise of the powers of one department to encroach upon another.—The spirit of encroachment tends to consolidate the powers of all the departments in one, and thus to create, whatever the form of government, a real despotism.—A just estimate of that love of power, and proneness to abuse it, which predominates in the human heart, is sufficient to satisfy us of the truth of this position.—The necessity of reciprocal checks in the exercise of political power, by dividing and distributing it into different depositories, and constituting each the Guardian of the Public Weal against invasions by the others, has been evinced by experiments ancient and modern; some of them in our country and under our own eyes.—To preserve them must be as necessary as to institute them. If in the opinion of the People, the distribution or modification of the Constitutional powers be in any particular wrong, let it be corrected by an amendment in the way which the Constitution designates.—But let there be no change by usurpation; for though this, in one instance, may be the instrument of good, it is the customary weapon by which free governments are destroyed.— The precedent must always greatly overbalance in permanent evil any partial or transient benefit which the use can at any time yield.—

Of all the dispositions and habits, which lead to political prosperity, Religion and morality are indispensable supports.— In vain would that man claim the tribute of Patriotism, who should labour to subvert these great Pillars of human happiness, these firmest props of the duties of Men and Citizens.—The mere Politician, equally with the pious man, ought to respect and to cherish them.—A volume could not trace all their connexions with private and public felicity.—Let it simply be asked where is the security for property, for reputation, for life, if the sense of religious obligation *desert* the oaths, which are the instruments of investigation in Courts of Justice? And let us with caution indulge the supposition, that morality can be maintained without religion.—Whatever may be conceded to the influence of refined education on minds of peculiar structure— reason and experience both forbid us to expect, that national morality can prevail in exclusion of religious principle.—

'Tis substantially true, that virtue or morality is a necessary spring of popular government.—The rule indeed extends with more or less force to every species of Free Government.—Who that is a sincere friend to it, can look with indifference upon attempts to shake the foundation of the fabric?—

Promote, then, as an object of primary importance, institutions for the general diffusion of knowledge.—In proportion as the structure of a government gives force to public opinion, it is essential that public opinion should be enlightened.—

As a very important source of strength and security, cherish public credit.—One method of preserving it is to use it as sparingly as possible:—avoiding occasions of expense by cultivating peace, but remembering also that timely disbursements to prepare for danger frequently prevent much greater disbursements to repel it—avoiding likewise the accumulation of debt, not only by shunning occasions of expense, but by vigorous exertions in time of Peace to discharge the debts which unavoidable wars may have occasioned, not ungenerously throwing upon posterity the burthen which we ourselves ought to bear. The execution of these maxims belongs to your Representatives, but it is necessary that public opinion should coöperate.—To facilitate to them the performance of their duty, it is essential that you should practically bear in mind, that towards the payment of debts there must be Revenue—that to have Revenue there must be taxes—that no taxes can be devised which are not more or less inconvenient and unpleasant—that the intrinsic embarrassment inseparable from the selection of the proper objects (which is always a choice of difficulties) ought to be a decisive motive for a candid construction of the conduct of the Government in making it, and for a spirit of acquiescence in the measures for obtaining Revenue which the public exigencies may at any time dictate.—

Observe good faith and justice towards all Nations. Cultivate peace and harmony with all.—Religion and Morality enjoin this conduct; and can it be that good policy does not equally enjoin it?—It will be worthy of a free, enlightened, and, at no distant period, a great nation, to give to mankind the magnanimous and too novel example of a People always guided by an exalted justice and benevolence.—Who can doubt that in the course of time and things, the fruits of such a plan would richly repay any temporary advantages, which might be lost by a steady adherence to it? Can it be, that Providence has not connected the permanent felicity of a Nation with its virtue? The experiment, at least, is recommended by every sentiment which ennobles human nature.—Alas! is it rendered impossible by its vices?

In the execution of such a plan nothing is more essential than that permanent, inveterate antipathies against particular nations and passionate attachments for others should be excluded; and that in place of them just and amicable feelings towards all should be cultivated.—The Nation, which indulges towards another an habitual hatred or an habitual fondness, is in some degree a slave. It is a slave to its animosity or to its affection, either of which is sufficient to lead it astray from its duty and its interest.—Antipathy in one nation against another disposes each more readily to offer insult and injury, to lay hold of slight causes of umbrage, and to be haughty and intractable, when accidental or trifling occasions of dispute occur.—Hence frequent collisions, obstinate, envenomed and bloody contests.—The Nation promoted by ill-will and resentment sometimes impels to War the Government, contrary to the best calculations of policy.—The Government sometimes participates in the national propensity, and adopts through passion what reason would reject;—at other times, it makes the animosity of the Nation subservient to projects of hostility instigated by pride, ambition, and other sinister and pernicious motives.—The peace often, sometimes perhaps the Liberty, of Nations has been the victim.—

So likewise a passionate attachment of one Nation for another produces a variety of evils.—Sympathy for the favourite nation, facilitating the illusion of an imaginary common interest in cases where no real common interest exists, and infusing into one the enmities of the other, betrays the former into a participation in the quarrels and wars of the latter, without adequate inducement or justification: It leads also to concessions to the favourite Nation of privileges denied to others, which is apt doubly to injure the Nation making the concessions; by unnecessarily parting with what ought to have been retained, and by exciting jealousy, ill-will, and a disposition to retaliate, in the parties from whom equal privileges are withheld; and it gives to ambitious, corrupted, or deluded citizens, (who devote themselves to the favourite Nation) facility to betray, or sacrifice the interests of their own country, without odium, sometimes even with popularity:— gilding with the appearances of a virtuous sense of obligation, a commendable deference for public opinion, or a laudable zeal for public good, the base or foolish compliances of ambition, corruption or infatuation.—

As avenues to foreign influence in innumerable ways, such attachments are particularly alarming to the truly enlightened and independent Patriot.—How many opportunities do they afford to tamper with domestic factions, to practise the arts of seduction, to mislead public opinion, to influence or awe the public councils! Such an attachment of a small or weak, towards a great and powerful nation, dooms the former to be the satellite of the latter.

Against the insidious wiles of foreign influence, I conjure you to believe me, fellow-citizens, the jealousy of a free people ought to be *constantly* awake, since history and experience prove that foreign influence is one of the most baneful foes of Republican Government.—But that jealousy to be useful must be impartial; else it becomes the instrument of the very influence to be avoided, instead of a defence against it.— Excessive partiality for one foreign nation and excessive dislike of another, cause those whom they actuate to see danger only on one side, and serve to veil and even second the arts of influence on the other.— Real Patriots, who may resist the intrigues of the favourite, are liable to become suspected and odious; while its tools and dupes usurp the applause and confidence of the people, to surrender their interests.—

The great rule of conduct for us, in regard to foreign Nations, is, in extending our commercial relations, to have with them as little *Political* connection as possible.—So far as we have already formed engagements, let them be fulfilled with perfect good faith.—Here let us stop.—

Europe has a set of primary interests, which to us have none, or a very remote relation.—Hence she must be engaged in frequent controversies, the causes of which are essentially foreign to our concerns.— Hence therefore it must be unwise in us to implicate ourselves, by artificial ties in the ordinary vicissitudes of her politics, or the ordinary combinations and collisions of her friendships, or enmities.

Our detached and distant situation invites and enables us to pursue a different course.—If we remain one People, under an efficient government, the period is not far off, when we may defy material injury from external annoyance; when we may take such an attitude as will cause the neutrality we may at any time resolve upon to be scrupulously respected.—When belligerent nations, under the impossibility of making acquisitions upon us, will not lightly hazard the giving us provocation; when we may choose peace or war, as our interest guided by our justice shall counsel.—

Why forego the advantages of so peculiar a situation?—Why quit our own to stand upon foreign ground?—Why, by interweaving our destiny with that of any part of Europe, entangle our peace and prosperity, in the toils of European ambition rivalship, interest, humour, or caprice?—

'Tis our true policy to steer clear of permanent alliances, with any portion of the foreign world;—so far, I mean, as we are now at liberty to do it—for let me not be understood as capable of patronizing infidelity to existing engagements, (I hold the maxim no less applicable to public than to private affairs, that honesty is always the best policy).—I repeat it therefore let those engagements be observed in their genuine sense.—But in my opinion it is unnecessary and would be unwise to extend them.—

Taking care always to keep ourselves, by suitable establishments, on a respectably defensive posture, we may safely trust to temporary alliances for extraordinary emergencies.—

Harmony, liberal intercourse with all nations, are recommended by policy, humanity, and interest.—But even our commercial policy should hold an equal and impartial hand:—neither seeking nor granting exclusive favours or preferences;—consulting the natural course of things;—diffusing and diversifying by gentle means the streams of commerce, but forcing nothing;—establishing with Powers so disposed—in order to give trade a stable course, to define the rights of our Merchants, and to enable the Government to support them—conventional rules of intercourse, the best that present circumstances and mutual opinion will permit; but temporary, and liable to be from time to time abandoned or varied, as experience and circumstances shall dictate; constantly keeping in view, that 'tis folly in one nation to look for disinterested favors from another,—that it must pay with a portion of its independence for whatever it may accept under that character—that by such acceptance, it may place itself in the condition of having given equivalents for nominal favours and yet of being reproached with ingratitude for not giving more.— There can be no greater error than to expect, or calculate upon real favours from Nation to Nation.—'Tis an illusion which experience must cure, which a just pride ought to discard.

In offering to you, my Countrymen, these counsels of an old and affectionate friend, I dare not hope they will make the strong and lasting impression, I could wish,—that they will controul the usual current of the passions, or prevent our Nation from running the course which has hitherto marked the destiny of Nations.— But if I may even flatter myself, that they may be productive of some partial benefit; some occasional good; that they may now and then recur to moderate the fury of party spirit, to warn against the mischiefs of foreign intrigue, to guard against the impostures of pretended patriotism, this hope will be a full recompense for the solicitude for your welfare, by which they have been dictated.—

How far in the discharge of my official duties, I have been guided by the principles which have been delineated, the public Records and other evidences of my conduct must witness to You, and to the World.— To myself, the assurance of my own conscience is, that I have at least believed myself to be guided by them.

In relation to the still subsisting War in Europe, my Proclamation of the 22d of April 1793 is the index to my plan.—Sanctioned by your approving voice and by that of Your Representatives in both Houses of Congress, the spirit of that measure has continually governed me:—uninfluenced by any attempts to deter or divert me from it.

After deliberate examination with the aid of the best lights I could obtain, I was well satisfied that our country, under all the circumstances of the case, had a right to take, and was bound in duty and interest, to take a Neutral position.—Having taken it, I determined, as far as should depend upon me, to maintain it, with moderation, perseverance, and firmness.—

The considerations which respect the right to hold this conduct, it is not necessary on this occasion to detail. I will only observe, that according to my understanding of the matter, that right, so far from being denied by any of the Belligerent Powers, has been virtually admitted by all.—

The duty of holding a neutral conduct may be inferred, without any thing more, from the obligation which justice and humanity impose on every Nation, in cases in which it is free to act, to maintain inviolate the relations of Peace and Amity towards other Nations.—

The inducements of interest for observing that conduct will best be referred to your own reflections and experience.— With me, a predominant motive has been to endeavour to gain time to our country to settle and mature its yet recent institutions, and to progress without interruption to that degree of strength and consistency, which is necessary to give it, humanly speaking, the command of its own fortunes.

Though, in reviewing the incidents of my Administration, I am unconscious of intentional error—I am nevertheless too sensible of my defects not to think it probable that I may have committed many errors.—Whatever they may be I fervently beseech the Almightly to avert or mitigate the evils to which they may tend.—I shall also carry with me the hope that my country will never cease to view them with indulgence; and that after forty-five years of my life dedicated to its service, with an upright zeal, the faults of incompetent abilities will be consigned to oblivion, as myself must soon be to the mansions of rest.

Relying on its kindness in this as in other things, and actuated by that fervent love towards it, which is so natural to a man, who views in it the native soil of himself and his progenitors for several generations;—I anticipate with pleasing expectation that retreat, in which I promise myself to realize, without alloy, the sweet enjoyment of partaking, in the midst of my fellow-citizens, the benign influence of good Laws under a free Government,—the ever favourite object of my heart, and the happy reward, as I trust, of our mutual cares, labours, and dangers.

John Marshall

John Marshall, chief justice of the United States, created the American system of constitutional law through the opinions he wrote for the whole court in the first third of the nineteenth century. Born in 1755 in Virginia, Marshall obtained a good education in Virginia outside the colleges and lived the hardy frontier life. At twenty, he drilled a company of soldiers and served in the Revolution, first as lieutenant, then as captain. In this capacity he also served as judge advocate and came to know Washington and Hamilton.

Marshall was admitted to the Virginia bar and soon rose to head it. He served in the Virginia Legislature and at the Federal Ratification Convention in Virginia. Having declined the positions of U.S. attorney general and minister to France, he was made a special envoy to France in 1797. There, with two others, he authored the American side of the famous XYZ correspondence. In 1787 he began a term in Congress for Virginia. He turned down an appointment as associate justice of the Supreme Court, tendered by President John Adams, but later accepted the position of secretary of war. He later served as secretary of state.

Marshall's public life was devoted to the Federalist party and the Union: "I had grown up at a time . . . when the maxim 'United we stand, divided we fall,' was the maxim of every orthodox American, and I had imbibed those sentiments so thoroughly that they constituted a part of my being." In 1801, at the end of his term, Adams appointed

Marshall chief justice of the United States. The principles of Washington's and Hamilton's beliefs in the need for a strong federal government had begun to fade with the founding of new communities along the Ohio and Mississippi rivers and with the spread of democratic principles. Jefferson's election as president in 1800 was thus symbolic of vast change in political and social life. The Federalist party began its rapid disintegration as Federalists were ousted from the federal government bureaucracy.

Up to the time of Marshall's appointment, the Supreme Court had played a small part in the American governmental system, with limited jurisdiction and judges of limited powers. Just before the transition from the administration of Adams to the Jeffersons, the Federalists passed an amendment to the Judiciary Act creating a system of inferior federal courts, requiring new judges to be appointed in a great hurry for the District of Columbia before Jefferson took over—the "Midnight Appointments." The Jeffersonians, naturally, repealed this amendment and denied commissions to these judges. One of the judges, Marbury, brought the case of receiving his commission to the Supreme Court in the famous case of *Marbury v. Madison* (1803). Marshall was confronted here with a conflict of interest; he was the secretary of state who failed to deliver the commissions.

Marshall's famous opinion in the case marked the beginning of American constitutional law. He proclaimed the right of the Supreme Court to review the constitutionality of acts of the national legislature and the executive branch—the other two branches of government (see excerpts). Such court-held power was nowhere to be found within the Constitution and was a stunning addition to the American governmental framework, which infuriated Jefferson no end. Marshall's second great court opinion was in the case of *McCulloch v. The State of Maryland* (1819), in which the broad powers of the U.S. government were first declared and established. The case dealt with the attempt of the state of Maryland to tax the operations of the Bank of the United States in the city of Baltimore. The Bank of the United States was hated by many as a remnant of Federalism and as the disciplinarian that called for a stable national currency in a widespread money crisis. Land speculation and irresponsible printing of local currencies had led the South and the West to near bankruptcy. An effort to repeal the Bank's charter failed, and state legislatures became determined to tax it out of existence. Accordingly, the cashier of the Bank, McCulloch, refused to obey the Maryland act, which required all notes issued by banks not operating by authority of the state to be issued upon stamped paper and taxed according to the denomination of the notes. Marshall's opinion clearly established the basis for the primacy of the federal government over state governments in key constitutional areas, although it was resisted for years to come. Marshall died in 1835.

Marbury *v.* Madison (1803)

(excerpts)

The question, whether an act, repugnant to the constitution, can become the law of the land, is a question deeply interesting to the United States; but, happily, not of an intricacy proportioned to its interest. It seems only necessary to recognize certain principles, supposed to have been long and well established, to decide it.

Isaak, *American Political Thinking.*

That the people have an original right to establish, for their future government, such principles, as, in their opinion, shall most conduce to their own happiness is the basis on which the whole American fabric has been erected. The exercise of this original right is a very great exertion; nor can it, nor ought it, to be frequently repeated. The principles, therefore, so established, are deemed fundamental. And as the authority from which they proceed is supreme, and can seldom act, they are designed to be permanent.

This original and supreme will organizes the government, and assigns to different departments their respective powers. It may either stop here, or establish certain limits not to be transcended by those departments.

The government of the United States is of the latter description. The powers of the legislature are defined and limited; and that those limits may not be mistaken, or forgotten, the constitution is written. To what purpose are powers limited, and to what purpose is that limitation committed to writing, if these limits may, at any time, be passed by those intended to be restrained? The distinction between a government with limited and unlimited powers is abolished, if those limits do not confine the persons on whom they are imposed, and if acts prohibited and acts allowed, are of equal obligation. It is a proposition too plain to be contested, that the constitution controls any legislative act repugnant to it; or, that the legislature may alter the constitution by an ordinary act.

Between these alternatives there is no middle ground. The constitution is either a superior paramount law, unchangeable by ordinary means, or it is on a level with ordinary legislative acts, and, like other acts, is alterable when the legislature shall please to alter it.

If the former part of the alternative be true, then a legislative act contrary to the constitution is not law: if the latter part be true, then written constitutions are absurd attempts, on the part of the people, to limit a power in its own nature illimitable.

Certainly all those who have framed written constitutions contemplate them as forming the fundamental and paramount law of the nation, and, consequently, the theory of every such government must be, that an act of the legislature, repugnant to the constitution, is void.

This theory is essentially attached to a written constitution, and, is consequently, to be considered, by this court, as one of the fundamental principles of our society. It is not therefore to be lost sight of in the further consideration of this subject.

If an act of the legislature, repugnant to the constitution, is void, does it, notwithstanding its invalidity, bind the courts, and oblige them to give it effect? Or, in other words, though it be not law, does it constitute a rule as operative as if it was a law? This would be to overthrow in fact what was established in theory; and would seem, at first view, an absurdity too gross to be insisted on. It shall, however, receive a more attentive consideration.

It is emphatically the province and duty of the judicial department to say what the law is. Those who apply the rule to particular cases, must of necessity expound and interpret that rule. If two laws conflict with each other, the courts must decide on the operation of each.

So if a law be in opposition to the constitution; if both the law and the constitution apply to a particular case, so that the court must either decide that case conformably to the law, disregarding the constitution; or conformably to the constitution, disregarding the law; the court must determine which of these conflicting rules governs the case. This is of the very essence of judicial duty.

If, then, the courts are to regard the constitution, and the constitution is superior to any ordinary act of the legislature, the constitution, and not such ordinary act, must govern the case to which they both apply.

Those, then, who controvert the principle that the constitution is to be considered, in court, as a paramount law, are reduced to the necessity of maintaining that courts must close their eyes on the constitution, and see only the law.

This doctrine would subvert the very foundation of all written constitutions. It would declare that an act which, according to the principles and theory of our government, is entirely void, is yet, in practice, completely obligatory. It would declare that if the legislature shall do what is expressly forbidden, such act, notwithstanding the express prohibition, is in reality effectual. It would be giving to the legislature a practical and real omnipotence, with the same breath which professes to restrict their powers within narrow limits. It is prescribing limits, and declaring that those limits may be passed at pleasure.

That it thus reduces to nothing what we have deemed the greatest improvement on political institutions, a written constitution would of itself be sufficient, in America, where written constitutions have been viewed with so much reverence, for rejecting the construction. But the peculiar expressions of the constitution of the United States furnish additional arguments in favour of its rejection.

The judicial power of the United States is extended to all cases arising under the constitution.

Could it be the intention of those who gave this power, to say that in using it the constitution should not be looked into? That a case arising under the constitution should be decided without examining the instrument under which it arises?

This is too extravagant to be maintained.

In some cases, then, the constitution must be looked into by the judges. And if

they can open it at all, what part of it are they forbidden to read or to obey?

There are many other parts of the constitution which serve to illustrate this subject.

It is declared that "no tax or duty shall be laid on articles exported from any state." Suppose a duty on the export of cotton, of tobacco, or of flour; and a suit instituted to recover it. Ought judgment to be rendered in such a case? ought the judges to close their eyes on the constitution, and only see the law?

The constitution declares "that no bill of attainder or ex post facto law shall be passed."

If, however, such a bill should be passed, and a person should be prosecuted under it; must the court condemn to death those victims whom the constitution endeavours to preserve?

"No person," says the constitution, "shall be convicted of treason unless on the testimony of two witnesses to the same overt act, or on confession in open court."

Here the language of the constitution is addressed especially to the courts. It prescribes, directly for them, a rule of evidence not to be departed from. If the legislature should change that rule, and declare one witness, or a confession out of court, sufficient for conviction, must the constitutional principle yield to the legislative act?

From these, and many other selections which might be made, it is apparent, that the framers of the constitution contemplated that instrument as a rule for the government of courts, as well as of the legislature.

Why otherwise does it direct the judges to take an oath to support it? This oath certainly applies in an especial manner, to their conduct in their official character. How immoral to impose it on them, if they were to be used as the instruments, and the knowing instruments, for violating what they swear to support!

The oath of office, too, imposed by the legislature, is completely demonstrative of the legislative opinion on this subject. It is in these words: "I do solemnly swear that I will administer justice without respect to persons, and do equal right to the poor and to the rich; and that I will faithfully and impartially discharge all the duties incumbent on me as _____, according to the best of my abilities and understanding, agreeably to the constitution and laws of the United States."

Why does a judge swear to discharge his duties agreeably to the constitution of the United States, if that constitution forms no rule for his government? if it is closed upon him, and cannot be inspected by him?

If such be the real state of things, this is worse than solemn mockery. To pre-scribe, or to take this oath, becomes equally a crime.

It is also not entirely unworthy of observation, that in declaring what shall be the supreme law of the land, the constitution itself is first mentioned; and not the laws of the United States generally, but those only which shall be made in pursuance of the constitution, have that rank.

Thus, the particular phraseology of the constitution of the United States confirms and strengthens the principle, supposed to be essential to all written constitutions, that a law repugnant to the constitution is void; and that courts, as well as other departments, are bound by that instrument. . . .

McCulloch *v.* The State of Maryland *et al.* (1819)
(excerpts)

. . . In the case now to be determined, the defendant, a sovereign state, denies the obligation of a law enacted by the legislature of the Union, and the plaintiff, on his part, contests the validity of an act which has been passed by the legislature of that state. The constitution of our country, in its most interesting and vital parts, is to be considered; the conflicting powers of the government of the Union and of its members, as marked in that constitution, are to be discussed; and an opinion given, which may essentially influence the great operations of the government. No tribunal can approach such a question without a deep sense of its importance, and of the awful responsibility involved in its decision. But it must be decided peacefully, or remain a source of hostile legislation, perhaps of hostility of a still more serious nature; and if it is to be so decided, by this tribunal alone can the decision be made. On the Supreme Court of the United States has the constitution of our country devolved this important duty.

The first question made in the cause is, has Congress power to incorporate a bank? . . .

In discussing this question, the counsel for the state of Maryland have deemed it of some importance in the construction of the constitution, to consider that instrument not as emanating from the people, but as the act of sovereign and independent states. The powers of the general government, it has been said, are delegated by the states, who alone are truly sovereign; and must be exercised in subordination to the states, who alone possess supreme dominion.

It would be difficult to sustain this proposition. The convention which framed the constitution was indeed elected by the state legislatures. But the instrument, when it came from their hands, was a mere proposal, without obligation, or pretensions to it. It was reported to the then existing Congress of the United States, with a request that it might "be submitted to a convention of delegates, chosen in each state by the people thereof, under the recommendation of its legislature, for their assent and ratification." This mode of proceeding was adopted; and by the convention by Congress, and by the state legislatures, the instrument was submitted to the people. They acted upon it in the only manner in which they can act safely, effectively, and wisely, on such a subject, by assembling in convention. It is true, they assembled in their several states—and where else should they have assembled? No political dreamer was ever wild enough to think of breaking down the lines which separate the states, and of compounding the American people into one common mass. Of consequence, when they act, they act in their states. But the measures they adopt do not, on that account, cease to be the measures of the people themselves, or become the measures of the state governments.

From these conventions the constitution derives its whole authority. The government proceeds directly from the people; is "ordained and established" in the name of the people; and is declared to be ordained, "in order to form a more perfect union, establish justice, insure domestic tranquillity, and secure the blessings of liberty to themselves and to their posterity." The assent of the states, in their sovereign capacity, is implied in calling a convention, and thus submitting that instrument to the people. But the people were at perfect liberty to accept or reject it; and their act was final. It required not the affirmance, and could not be negatived, by the state governments. The constitution, when thus

adopted, was of complete obligation, and bound the state sovereignties. . . .

The government of the Union, then (whatever may be the influence of this fact on the case), is, emphatically, and truly, a government of the people. In form and in substance it emanates from them. Its powers are granted by them, and are to be exercised directly on them, and for their benefit.

This government is acknowledged by all to be one of enumerated powers. The principle, that it can exercise only the powers granted to it, would seem too apparent to have required to be enforced by all those arguments which its enlightened friends, while it was depending before the people, found it necessary to urge. That principle is now universally admitted. . . .

If any one proposition could command the universal assent of mankind, we might expect it would be this—that the government of the Union, though limited in its powers, is supreme within its sphere of action. This would seem to result necessarily from its nature. It is the government of all; its powers are delegated by all; it represents all, and acts for all. Though any one state may be willing to control its operations, no state is willing to allow others to control them. The nation, on those subjects on which it can act, must necessarily bind its component parts. But this question is not left to mere reason; the people have, in express terms, decided it by saying, "this constitution, and the laws of the United States, which shall be made in pursuance thereof," "shall be the supreme law of the land," and by requiring that the members of the state legislatures, and the officers of the executive and judicial departments of the states shall take the oath of fidelity to it. . . .

Among the enumerated powers, we do not find that of establishing a bank or creating a corporation. But there is no phrase in the instrument which, like the articles of confederation, excludes incidental or implied powers; and which requires that everything granted shall be expressly and minutely described. Even the 10th amendment, which was framed for the purpose of quieting the excessive jealousies which had been excited, omits the word "expressly," and declares only that the powers "not delegated to the United States, nor prohibited to the states, are reserved to the states or to the people;" thus leaving the question, whether the particular power which may become the subject of contest has been delegated to the one government, or prohibited to the other, to depend on a fair construction of the whole instrument. The men who drew and adopted this amendment had experienced the embarrassments resulting from the insertion of this word in the articles of confederation, and probably omitted it to avoid these embarrassments. A constitution, to contain an accurate detail of all the subdivisions of which its great powers will admit, and of all the means by which they may be carried into execution, would partake of a prolixity of a legal code, and could scarcely be embraced by the human mind. It would probably never be understood by the public. Its nature, therefore, requires, that only its great outlines should be marked, its important objects designated, and the minor ingredients which compose those objects be deduced from the nature of the objects themselves. That this idea was entertained by the framers of the American constitution, is not only to be inferred from the nature of the instrument, but from the

language. Why else were some of the limitations, found in the ninth section of the 1st article, introduced? It is also, in some degree, warranted by their having omitted to use any restrictive term which might prevent its receiving a fair and just interpretation. In considering this question, then, we must never forget that it is a constitution we are expounding.

Although, among the enumerated powers of government, we do not find the word "bank" or "incorporation," we find the great powers to lay and collect taxes; to borrow money; to regulate commerce; to declare and conduct a war; and to raise and support armies and navies. The sword and the purse, all the external relations, and no inconsiderable portion of the industry of the nation, are entrusted to its government. It can never be pretended that these vast powers draw after them others of inferior importance, merely because they are inferior. Such an idea can never be advanced. But it may with great reason be contended, that a government, entrusted with such ample powers, on the due execution of which the happiness and prosperity of the nation so vitally depends, must also be entrusted with ample means for their execution. The power being given, it is the interest of the nation to facilitate its execution. It can never be their interest, and cannot be presumed to have been their intention, to clog and embarrass its execution by withholding the most appropriate means. . . . Can we adopt that construction (unless the words imperiously require it) which would impute to the framers of that instrument, when granting these powers for the public good, the intention of impending their exercise by withholding a choice of means? If, indeed, such be the mandate of the constitution, we have only to obey; but that instrument does not profess to enumerate the means by which the powers it confers may be executed; nor does it prohibit the creation of a corporation, if the existence of such a being be essential to the beneficial exercise of those powers. It is, then, the subject of fair inquiry, how far such means may be employed. It is not denied that the powers given to the government imply the ordinary means of execution. . . . But it is denied that the government has its choice of means; or, that it may employ the most convenient means, if, to employ them, it be necessary to erect a corporation.

On what foundation does this argument rest? On this alone: The power of creating a corporation, is one appertaining to sovereignty, and is not expressly conferred on Congress. This is true. But all legislative powers appertain to sovereignty. The original power of giving the law on any subject whatever, is a sovereign power; and if the government of the Union is restrained from creating a corporation, as a means for performing its functions, on the single reason that the creation of a corporation is an act of sovereignty; if the sufficiency of this reason be acknowledged, there would be some difficulty in sustaining the authority of Congress to pass other laws for the accomplishment of the same objects.

The government which has a right to do an act, and has imposed on it the duty of performing that act, must, according to the dictates of reason, be allowed to select the means; and those who contend that it may not select any appropriate means, that one particular mode of effecting the object is excepted, take upon themselves the burden of establishing that exception.

The creation of a corporation, it is said, appertains to sovereignty. This is admitted. But to what portion of sovereignty does it appertain? Does it belong to one more than to another? In America, the powers of sovereignty are divided between the government of the Union, and those of the States. They are each sovereign, with respect to the objects committed to it, and neither

sovereign with respect to the objects committed to the other. We cannot comprehend that train of reasoning which would maintain that the extent of power granted by the people is to be ascertained, not by the nature and terms of the grant, but by its date. Some state constitutions were formed before, some since that of the United States. We cannot believe that their relation to each other is in any degree dependent upon this circumstance. Their respective powers must, we think, be precisely the same as if they had been formed at the same time. Had they been formed at the same time, and had the people conferred on the general government the power contained in the constitution, and on the states the whole residuum of power, would it have been asserted that the government of the Union was not sovereign with respect to those objects which were entrusted to it, in relation to which its laws were declared to be supreme? If this could not have been asserted, we cannot well comprehend the process of reasoning which maintains that a power appertaining to sovereignty cannot be connected with that vast portion of it which is granted to the general government, so far as it is calculated to subserve the legitimate objects of that government. The power of creating a corporation, though appertaining to sovereignty, is not, like the power of making war, or levying taxes, or of regulating commerce, a great substantive and independent power, which cannot be implied as incidental to other powers, or used as a means of executing them. It is never the end for which other powers are exercised, but a means by which other objects are accomplished. No contributions are made to charity for the sake of an incorporation, but a corporation is created to administer the charity; no seminary of learning is instituted in order to be incorporated, but the corporate character is conferred to subserve the purposes of education. No city was ever built with the sole object of being incorporated, but is incorporated as affording the best means of being well governed. The power of creating a corporation is never used for its own sake, but for the purpose of effecting something else. No sufficient reason is, therefore, perceived, why it may not pass as incidental to those powers which are expressly given, if it be a direct mode of executing them.

But the constitution of the United States has not left the right of Congress to employ the necessary means for the execution of the powers conferred on the government to general reasoning. To its enumeration of powers is added that of making "all laws which shall be necessary and proper, for carrying into execution the foregoing powers, and all other powers vested by this constitution, in the government of the United States, or in any department thereof."

The counsel for the State of Maryland have urged various arguments, to prove that this clause, though in terms a grant of power, is not so in effect; but is really restrictive of the general right, which might otherwise be implied, of selecting means for executing the enumerated powers.

In support of this proposition, they have found it necessary to contend, that this clause was inserted for the purpose of conferring on Congress the power of making laws. . . .

But could this be the object for which it was inserted? A government is created by the people, having legislative, executive, and judicial powers. Its legislative powers are vested in a Congress, which is to consist of a senate and house of representatives. Each house may determine the rule of its proceedings; and it is declared that every bill which shall have passed both houses, shall, before it becomes a law, be presented to the President of the United States. . . . Could it be necessary to say that a legislature should exercise legislative powers in the shape of legislation? . . . That a legislature, endowed with legislative powers, can legislate, is a proposition too self-evident to have been questioned.

But the argument on which most reliance is placed, is drawn from the peculiar language of this clause. Congress is not empowered by it to make all laws, which may have relation to the powers conferred on the government, but such only as may be "necessary and proper" for carrying them into execution. The word "necessary" is considered as controlling the whole sentence, and as limiting the right to pass laws for the execution of the granted powers, to such as are indispensable, and without which the power would be nugatory. That it excludes the choice of means, and leaves to Congress, in each case, that only which is most direct and simple.

Is it true that this is the sense in which the word "necessary" is always used? Does it always import an absolute physical necessity, so strong that one thing, to which another may be termed necessary, cannot exist without that other? We think it does not. If reference be had to its use, in the common affairs of the world, or in approved authors, we find that it frequently imports no more than that one thing is convenient, or useful, or essential to another. To employ the means necessary to an end, is generally understood as employing any means calculated to produce the end, and not as being confined to those single means, without which the end would be entirely unattainable. Such is the character of human language, that no word conveys to the mind, in all situations, one single definite idea; and nothing is more common than to use words in a figurative sense. Almost all compositions contain words, which, taken in their rigorous sense, would convey a meaning different from that which is obviously intended. It is essential to just construction, that many words which import something excessive should be understood in a more mitigated sense—in that sense which common usage justifies. The word "necessary" is of this description. It has not a fixed character peculiar to itself. It admits of all degrees of comparison; and is often connected with other words, which increase or diminish the impression the mind receives of the urgency it imports. A thing may be necessary, very necessary, absolutely or indispensably necessary. To no mind would the same idea be conveyed by these several phrases. . . . This word, then, like others, is used in various senses; and, in its construction, the subject, the context, the intention of the person using them, are all to be taken into view.

Let this be done in the case under consideration. The subject is the execution of those great powers on which the welfare of a nation essentially depends. It must have been the intention of those who gave these powers, to insure, as far as human prudence could insure, their beneficial execution. This could not be done by confining the choice of means to such narrow limits as not to leave it in the power of Congress to adopt any which might be appropriate, and which were conducive to the end. This provision is made in a constitution intended to endure for ages to come, and, consequently, to be adapted to the various crises of human affairs. To have prescribed the means by which government should, in all future time, execute its powers, would have been to change, entirely, the character of the instrument, and give it the properties of a legal code. It would have been an unwise attempt to provide, by immutable rules, for exigencies which if foreseen at all, must have been seen dimly, and which can be best provided for as they occur. To have declared that the best means shall not be used, but those alone without which the power given would be nugatory, would have been to deprive the legislature of the capacity to avail itself of experience, to exercise its reason, and to accommodate

its legislation to circumstances. If we apply this principle of construction to any of the powers of the government, we shall find it so pernicious in its operation that we shall be compelled to discard it. . . .

But the argument which most conclusively demonstrates the error of the construction contended for by the counsel for the state of Maryland, is founded on the intention of the convention, as manifested in the whole clause. To waste time and argument in proving that without it Congress might carry its powers into execution, would be not much less idle than to hold a lighted taper to the sun. As little can it be required to prove, that in the absence of this clause, Congress would have some choice of means. That it might employ those which, in its judgment, would most advantageously effect the object to be accomplished. That any means adapted to the end, any means which tended directly to the execution of the constitutional powers of the government, were in themselves constitutional. This clause, as construed by the state of Maryland, would abridge, and almost annihilate this useful and necessary right of the legislature to select its means. That this could not be intended, is, we should think, had it not been already controverted, too apparent for controversy. We think so for the following reasons:

1st. The clause is placed among the powers of Congress, not among the limitations on these powers.

2d. Its terms purport to enlarge, not to diminish the powers vested in the government. It purports to be an additional power, not a restriction on those already granted. . . .

The result of the most careful and attentive consideration bestowed upon this clause is, that if it does not enlarge, it cannot be construed to restrain the powers of

Congress, or to impair the right of the legislature to exercise its best judgment in the selection of measures to carry into execution the constitutional powers of the government. If no other motive for its insertion can be suggested, a sufficient one is found in the desire to remove all doubts respecting the right to legislate on that vast mass of incidental powers which must be involved in the constitution, if that instrument be not a splendid bauble.

We admit, as all must admit, that the powers of the government are limited, and that its limits are not to be transcended. But we think the sound construction of the constitution must allow to the national legislature that discretion, with respect to the means by which the powers it confers are to be carried into execution, which will enable that body to perform the high duties assigned to it, in the manner most beneficial to the people. Let the end be legitimate, let it be within the scope of the constitution, and all means which are appropriate, which are plainly adapted to that end, which are not prohibited, but consist with the letter and spirit of the constitution, are constitutional. . . .

If a corporation may be employed indiscriminately with other means to carry into execution the powers of the government, no particular reason can be assigned for excluding the use of a bank, if required for its fiscal operations. To use one, must be within the discretion of Congress, if it be an appropriate mode of executing the powers of government. That it is a convenient, a useful, and essential instrument in the prosecution of its fiscal operations, is not now a subject of controversy. . . .

It being the opinion of the court that the act incorporating the bank is constitutional, and that the power of establishing a branch in the state of Maryland might be properly exercised by the bank itself, we proceed to inquire:

. . .Whether the state of Maryland may, without violating the constitution, tax that branch?

That the power of taxation is one of vital importance; that it is retained by the states; that it is not abridged by the grant of a similar power to the government of the Union; that it is to be concurrently exercised by the two governments: are truths which have never been denied. But, such is the paramount character of the constitution that its capacity to withdraw any subject from the action of even this power, is admitted. . . .

On this ground the counsel for the bank places its claim to be exempted from the power of a state to tax its operations. There is no express provision for the case, but the claim has been sustained on a principle which so entirely pervades the constitution, is so intermixed with the materials which compose it, so interwoven with its web, so blended with its texture, as to be incapable of being separated from it without rending it into shreds.

This great principle is, that the constitution and the laws made in pursuance thereof are supreme; that they control the constitution and laws of the respective states, and cannot be controlled by them. From this, which may be almost termed an axiom, other propositions are deduced as corollaries, on the truth or error of which, and on their application to this case, the cause has been supposed to depend. These are, 1st. That a power to create implies a power to preserve. 2d. That a power to destroy if wielded by a different hand, is hostile to, and incompatible with these powers to create and to preserve. 3d. That where this repugnancy exists, that authority which is supreme must control, not yield to that over which it is supreme. . . .

That the power of taxing it by the states may be exercised so as to destroy it, is too obvious to be denied. But taxation is said to be an absolute power, which acknowledges no other limits than those expressly prescribed in the constitution, and like sovereign power of every other description, is trusted to the discretion of those who use it. But the very terms of this argument admit that the sovereignty of the state, in the article of taxation itself, is subordinate to, and may be controlled by the constitution of the United States. How far it has been controlled by that instrument must be a question of construction. . . .

The sovereignty of a state extends to everything which exists by its own authority, or is introduced by its permission; but does it extend to those means which are employed by Congress to carry into execution—powers conferred on that body by the people of the United States? We think it demonstrable that it does not. Those powers are not given by the people of a single state. They are given by the people of the United States, to a government whose laws, made in pursuance of the constitution, are declared to be supreme. Consequently, the people of a single state cannot confer a sovereignty which will extend over them. . . .

We find, then, on just theory, a total failure of this original right to tax the means employed by the government of the Union, for the execution of its powers. The right never existed, and the question whether it has been surrendered, cannot arise.

But, waiving this theory for the present, let us resume the inquiry, whether this power can be exercised by the respective states, consistently with a fair construction of the constitution. That the power to tax involves the power to destroy; that the power to destroy may defeat and render useless the power to create; that there is plain repugnance, in conferring on one government a power to control the constitutional measures of another, which other, with respect to those very measures, is declared to be supreme over that which exerts the control, are propositions not to be denied. But all inconsistencies are to be reconciled by the magic of the word CONFIDENCE. Taxation, it is said, does not necessarily and unavoidably destroy. To carry to the excess and destruction would be an abuse, to presume which, would banish that confidence which is essential to all government.

But is this a case of confidence? Would the people of any one state trust those of another with a power to control the most insignificant operations of their state government? We know they would not. Why, then, should we suppose that the people of any one state should be willing to trust those of another with a power to control the operations of a government to which they have confided the most important and most valuable interests? In the legislature of the Union alone, are all represented. The legislature of the Union alone, therefore, can be trusted by the people with the power of controlling measures which concern all, in the confidence that it will not be abused. This, then, is not a case of confidence, and we must consider it as it really is.

If we apply the principle for which the state of Maryland contends, to the constitution generally, we shall find it capable of changing totally the character of that instrument. We shall find it capable of arresting all the measures of the government, and of prostrating it at the foot of the states. The American people have declared their constitution, and the laws made in pursuance thereof, to be supreme; but this principle would transfer the supremacy, in fact, to the states.

If the states may tax one instrument, employed by the government in the execution of its powers, they may tax any and every other instrument. They may tax the mail; they may tax the mint; they may tax patent-rights; they may tax the papers of the custom-house; they may tax judicial process; they may tax all the means employed by the government, to an excess which would defeat all the ends of government. . . . This is not all. If the controlling power of the states be established; if their supremacy as to taxation be acknowledged; what is to restrain their exercising this control in any shape they may please to give it? Their sovereignty is not confined to taxation. That is not the only mode in which it might be displayed. The question is, in truth, a question of supremacy; and if the right of the states to tax the means employed by the general government be conceded, the declaration that the constitution, and the laws made in pursuance thereof, shall be the supreme law of the land, is empty and unmeaning declamation. . . .

It has also been insisted, that, as the power of taxation in the general and state governments is acknowledged to be concurrent, every argument which would sustain the right of the general government to tax banks chartered by the states, will equally sustain the right of the states to tax banks chartered by the general government.

But the two cases are not on the same reason. The people of all the states have created the general government, and have conferred upon it the general power of taxation. The people of all the states, and the states themselves, are represented in Congress, and, by their representatives, exercise this power. When they tax the chartered institutions of the states, they tax their constituents; and these taxes must be uniform. But, when a state taxes the operations of the government of the United States, it acts upon institutions created, not by their own constituents, but by people over whom they claim no control. It acts upon the measures of a government created by others as well as themselves, for the benefit of others in common with themselves. The difference is that which always exists, and always must exist, between the action of the whole on a part, and the action of a part on the whole—between the laws of a government declared to be supreme, and those of a government which, when in opposition to those laws, is not supreme. . . .

Daniel Webster

As an orator and statesman, Daniel Webster was best known for legal positions and political speeches on behalf of strengthening the federal Union and at the expense of sectionalists and extremists in the critical historical era preceding the Civil War. Born in 1782 in Salisbury, New Hampshire, Webster attended the Phillips Exeter Academy and graduated from Dartmouth College. While apprenticing to practice law, he briefly taught at the Frybury Academy in Maine. Thereafter, he practiced law, first in Boscaswen and Portsmouth, New Hampshire, and later in Boston.

As a Federalist, he denounced Jefferson's policies and the War of 1812 against Great Britain. His vigorous speeches soon brought him into the opposition in Congress. Later, as a lawyer arguing before the Supreme Court, Webster became known as "the Expounder of the Constitution," serving somewhat as the alter ego of Supreme Court Justice Marshall in arguing cases such as *McCulloch v. The State of Maryland* (1819) (see excerpts under "John Marshall"). Webster's significance at this historical turning point is comparable to that of Alexander Hamilton's role at the time of the founding.

His famous "Reply to Hayne" was made when, as senator from Massachusetts, Webster countered South Carolina Senator Robert Hayne's arguments for sectionalism, states' rights, and the proposition that "there is no evil more to be deprecated than the consolidation of this government." Webster contended that the federal Union was not established by the states severally but by the people as a governmental unit with limited powers yet superior in some ways to state governments. He ended with the famous words: "Liberty and Union, now and forever, one and inseparable!"

Although Webster and Andrew Jackson were on the same side in terms of support for the Union, they parted company on the issue of the Bank of the United States, which Webster supported and Jackson opposed. Webster was a candidate for president in 1836 for the ill-fated Whig party and campaigned in the next election for William Henry Harrison—with the reward of being appointed secretary of state. He also served in this post briefly under President John Tyler after Harrison's death, and once again later, under President Millard Fillmore. Near the end of his illustrious career in the Senate, Webster persuasively sponsored Henry Clay's Fugitive Slave Act, called the "Compromise of 1850," which probably staved off disunion and postponed the Civil War for a decade. Webster died in 1852, leaving behind a monumental tradition of defense of the Founders' constitutional framework in establishing a strong central government.

Reply to Hayne (1830)
(excerpts)

I spoke, sir, of the Ordinance of 1787, which prohibits slavery, in all future times, northwest of the Ohio, as a measure of great wisdom and foresight, and one which had been attended with highly beneficial and permanent consequences. I supposed that on this point, no two gentlemen in the Senate could entertain different opinions. But the simple expression of this sentiment has led the gentleman not only into a labored defense of slavery, in the abstract and on principle, but also into a warm accusation against me, as having attacked the system of domestic slavery now existing in the Southern States. For all this there was not the slightest foundation in anything said or intimated by me. I did not utter a single word which any ingenuity could torture into an attack on the slavery of the South. I said only that it was highly wise and useful, in legislating for the Northwestern country while it was yet a wilderness, to prohibit the introduction of slaves; and added that I presumed there was no reflecting and intelligent person in the neighboring State of Kentucky who would doubt that, if the same prohibition had been extended at the same early period over that commonwealth, her strength and population would at this day have been far greater than they are. If these opinions be thought doubtful, they are nevertheless, I trust, neither extraordinary nor disrespectful. They attack nobody and menace nobody. And yet, sir, the gentleman's optics have discovered, even in the mere expression of this sentiment, what he calls the very spirit of the Missouri question! He represents me as making an onset on the whole South, and manifesting a spirit which would interfere with and disturb their domestic condition!

Sir, this injustice no otherwise surprises me than as it is committed here, and committed without the slightest pretense of ground for it. I say it only surprises me as being done here; for I know full well that it is and has been the settled policy of some persons in the South, for years, to represent the people of the North as disposed to interfere with them in their own exclusive and peculiar concerns. This is a delicate and sensitive point in Southern feeling; and of late years it has always been touched, and generally with effect, whenever the object has been to unite the whole South against Northern men or Northern measures. This feeling, always carefully kept alive, and maintained at too intense a heat to admit discrimination or reflection, is a lever of great power in our political machine. It moves vast bodies, and gives to them one and the same direction. But it is without adequate cause, and the suspicion which exists is wholly groundless. There is not, and never has been, a disposition in the North to interfere with these interests of the South. Such interference has never been supposed to be within the power of government; nor has it been in any way attempted. The slavery of the South has always been regarded as a matter of domestic policy left with the States themselves, and with which the federal government had nothing to do.

Certainly, sir, I am, and ever have been, of that opinion. The gentleman, indeed, argues that slavery in the abstract is no evil. Most assuredly I need not say I differ with him altogether and most widely on that point. I regard domestic slavery as one of the greatest evils, both moral and political. But whether it be a malady, and whether it be curable, and, if so, by what means; or, on the other hand, whether it be the *rulnus immedicabile* of the social system, I leave it to those whose right and duty it is to inquire and to decide. And this I believe, sir, is, and uniformly has been, the sentiment of the North. Let us look a little at the history of this matter.

When the present Constitution was submitted for the ratification of the people, there were those who imagined that the powers of the government which it proposed to establish might, in some possible mode, be exerted in measures tending to the abolition of slavery. This suggestion would of course attract much attention in the Southern conventions. In that of Virginia, Governor Randolph[1] said:—

"I hope there is none here who, considering the subject in the calm light of philosophy, will make an objection dishonorable to Virginia; that, at the moment they are securing the rights of their citizens, an objection is started that there is a spark of hope that those unfortunate men now held in bondage may, by the operation of the general government, be made free."

At the very first Congress, petitions on the subject were presented, if I mistake not, from different States. The Pennsylvania Society for promoting the abolition of slavery took a lead, and laid before Congress a memorial praying Congress to promote the abolition by such powers as it possessed. This memorial was referred, in the House of Representatives, to a select committee consisting of Mr. Foster of New

---

[1]Edmund Randolph.

Hampshire, Mr. Gerry of Massachusetts, Mr. Huntington of Connecticut, Mr. Lawrence of New York, Mr. Sinnickson of New Jersey, Mr. Hartley of Pennsylvania, and Mr. Parker of Virginia; all of them, sir, as you will observe, Northern men but the last. This committee made a report, which was referred to a committee of the whole House, and there considered and discussed for several days; and being amended, although without material alteration, it was made to express three distinct propositions on the subject of slavery and the slave-trade. First, in the words of the Constitution, that Congress could not, prior to the year 1808, prohibit the migration or importation of such persons as any of the States then existing should think proper to admit; and, secondly, that Congress had authority to restrain the citizens of the United States from carrying on the African slave-trade for the purpose of supplying foreign countries. On this proposition our early laws against those who engage in that traffic are founded. The third proposition, and that which bears on the present question, was expressed in the following terms:—

"*Resolved*, That Congress have no authority to interfere in the emancipation of slaves, or in the treatment of them in any of the States; it remaining with the several States alone to provide rules and regulations therein, which humanity and true policy may require."

This resolution received the sanction of the House of Representatives so early as March, 1790. And now, sir, the honorable member will allow me to remind him that not only were the select committee who reported the resolution, with a single exception, all Northern men, but also that, of the members then composing the House of Representatives, a large majority, I believe nearly two thirds, were Northern men also.

The House agreed to insert these resolutions in its journal; and from that day to this it has never been maintained or contended at the North that Congress had any authority to regulate or interfere with the condition of slaves in the several States. No Northern gentleman, to my knowledge, has moved any such question in either house of Congress.

The fears of the South, whatever fears they might have entertained, were allayed and quieted by this early decision; and so remained till they were excited afresh, without cause, but for collateral and indirect purposes. When it became necessary, or was thought so by some political persons, to find an unvarying ground for the exclusion of Northern men from confidence and from lead in the affairs of the republic, then, and not till then, the cry was raised, and the feeling industriously excited, that the influence of Northern men in the public councils would endanger the relation of master and slave. For myself, I claim no other merit than that this gross and enormous injustice towards the whole North has not wrought upon me to change my opinions or my political conduct. I hope I am above violating my principles, even under the smart of injury and false imputations. Unjust suspicions and undeserved reproach, whatever pain I may experience from them, will not induce me, I trust, to overstep the limits of constitutional duty, or to encroach on the rights of others. The domestic slavery of the Southern States I leave where I find it,—in the hands of their own governments. It is their affair, not mine. Nor do I complain of the peculiar effect which the magnitude of that population has had in the distribution of power under this federal government. We know, sir, that the representation of the States in the other house is not equal. We know that great advantage in that respect is enjoyed by the slave-holding States; and we know, too, that the intended equivalent for that advantage, that is to say, the imposition of direct taxes in the same ratio, has become merely nominal, the habit of the government being almost invariably to collect its revenue from other sources and in other modes. Nevertheless, I do not complain; nor would I countenance any movement to alter this arrangement of representation. It is the original bargain, the compact; let it stand; let the advantage of it be fully enjoyed. The Union itself is too full of benefit to be hazarded in propositions for changing its original basis. I go for the Constitution as it is, and for the Union as it is. But I am resolved not to submit in silence to accusations, either against myself individually or against the North, wholly unfounded and unjust; accusations which impute to us a disposition to evade the constitutional compact, and to extend the power of the government over the internal laws and domestic condition of the States. All such accusations, wherever and whenever made, all insinuations of the existence of any such purposes, I know and feel to be groundless and injurious. And we must confide in Southern gentlemen themselves; we must trust to those whose integrity of heart and magnanimity of feeling will lead them to a desire to maintain and disseminate truth, and who possess the means of its diffusion with the Southern public; we must leave it to them to disabuse that public of its prejudices. But in the mean time, for my own part, I shall continue to act justly, whether those towards whom justice is exercised receive it with candor or with contumely.

Having had occasion to recur to the Ordinance of 1787, in order to defend myself against the inferences which the honorable member has chosen to draw from my former observations on that subject, I am not willing now entirely to take leave of it without another remark. It need hardly be said that that paper expresses just sentiments on the great subject of civil and religious liberty. Such sentiments were common, and abound in all our state papers of that day. But this Ordinance did that which was not so common, and which is not, even now, universal; that is, it set forth and declared it to be a high and binding duty of government itself to encourage schools, and advance the means of education, on the plain reason that religion, morality, and knowledge are necessary to good government, and to the happiness of mankind. One observation further. The important provision incorporated into the Constitution of the United States, and into several of those of the States, and recently, as we have seen, adopted into the reformed Constitution of Virginia, restraining legislative power in questions of private right, and from impairing the obligation of contracts, is first introduced and established, as far as I am informed, as matter of express written constitutional law, in this Ordinance of 1787. And I must add, also, in regard to the author of the Ordinance, who has not had the happiness to attract the gentleman's notice heretofore, nor to avoid his sarcasm now, that he was chairman of that select committee of the old Congress whose report first expressed the strong sense of that body that the old Confederation was not adequate to the exigencies of the country, and recommended to the States to send delegates to the convention which formed the present Constitution.

An attempt has been made to transfer from the North to the South the honor of this exclusion of slavery from the Northwestern Territory. The journal, without argument or comment, refutes such attempt. The cession by Virginia was made in March, 1784. On the 19th of April following, a committee, consisting of Messrs. Jefferson, Chase, and Howell, reported a plan for a temporary government of the Territory, in which was this article: "That, after the year 1800, there shall be neither slavery nor involuntary servitude in any of the said States, otherwise than in punishment of crimes whereof the party shall have been convicted." Mr. Spaight of North

Carolina moved to strike out this paragraph. The question was put, according to the form then practiced: "Shall these words stand as a part of the plan?" New Hampshire, Massachusetts, Rhode Island, Connecticut, New York, New Jersey, and Pennsylvania—seven States—voted in the affirmative; Maryland, Virginia, and South Carolina, in the negative. North Carolina was divided. As the consent of nine States was necessary, the words could not stand, and were struck out accordingly. Mr. Jefferson voted for the clause, but was overruled by his colleagues.

In March of the next year (1785), Mr. King of Massachusetts, seconded by Mr. Ellery of Rhode Island, proposed the formerly rejected article, with this addition: "And that this regulation shall be an article of compact, and remain a fundamental principle of the Constitutions between the thirteen original States and each of the States described in the resolve." On this clause, which provided the adequate and thorough security, the eight Northern States at that time voted affirmatively, and the four Southern States negatively. The votes of nine States were not yet obtained, and thus the provision was again rejected by the Southern States. The perseverance of the North held out, and two years afterwards the object was attained. It is no derogation from the credit, whatever that may be, of drawing the Ordinance, that its principles had before been prepared and discussed in the form of resolutions. If one should reason in that way, what would become of the distinguished honor of the author of the Declaration of Independence? There is not a sentiment in that paper which had not been voted and resolved in the assemblies and other popular bodies in the country over and over again. . . .

I need not repeat at large the general topics of the honorable gentleman's speech. When he said yesterday that he did not attack the Eastern States, he certainly must have forgotten, not only particular remarks, but the whole drift and tenor of his speech; unless he means, by not attacking, that he did not commence hostilities, but that another had preceded him in the attack. He in the first place disapproved of the whole course of the government for forty years in regard to its disposition of the public lands; and then, turning northward and eastward, and fancying he had found a cause for alleged narrowness and niggardliness in the "accursed policy" of the tariff, to which he represented the people of New England as wedded, he went on for a full hour with remarks the whole scope of which was to exhibit the results of this policy in feelings and in measures unfavorable to the West. I thought his opinions unfounding and erroneous as to the general course of the government, and ventured to reply to them.

The gentleman had remarked on the analogy of other cases, and quoted the conduct of European governments towards their own subjects settling on this continent as in point, to show that we had been harsh and rigid in selling, when we should have given the public lands to settlers without price. I thought the honorable member had suffered his judgment to be betrayed by a false analogy; that he was struck with an appearance of resemblance where there was no real similitude. I think so still. The first settlers of North America were enterprising spirits, engaged in private adventure, or fleeing from tyranny at home. When arrived here, they were forgotten by the mother country, or remembered only to be oppressed. Carried away again by the appearance of analogy, or struck with the eloquence of the passage, the honorable member yesterday observed that the conduct of government toward the Western emigrants, or my representation of it, brought to his mind a celebrated speech in the British Parliament. It was sir, the speech of Colonel Barré. On the question of the Stamp Act,[2] or tea tax, I forget which, Colonel Barré had heard a member on the Treasury bench argue that the people of the United States, being British colonists, planted by the maternal care, nourished by the indulgence and protected by the arms of England, would not grudge their mite to relieve the mother country from the heavy burden under which she groaned. The language of Colonel Barré in reply to this was: "They planted by your care? Your oppression planted them in America. They fled from your tyranny, and grew by your neglect of them. So soon as you began to care for them, you showed your care by sending persons to spy out their liberties, misrepresent their character, prey upon them, and eat out their substance."

And how does the honorable gentleman mean to maintain that language like this is applicable to the conduct of the government of the United States toward the Western emigrants, or to any representation given by me of that conduct? Were the settlers in the West driven thither by our oppression? Have they flourished only by our neglect of them? Has the government done nothing but prey upon them and eat out their substance? Sir, this fervid eloquence of the British speaker, just when and where it was uttered, and fit to remain an exercise for the schools, is not a little out of place when it is brought thence to be applied here to the conduct of our own country toward her own citizens. From America to England, it may be true; from Americans to their own government, it would be strange language. Let us leave it to be recited and declaimed by our boys against a foreign nation; not introduce it

here, to recite and declaim ourselves against our own.

But I come to the point of the alleged contradiction. In my remarks on Wednesday I contended that we could not give away gratuitously all the public lands; that we held them in trust; that the government had solemnly pledged itself to dispose of them as a common fund for the common benefit, and to sell and settle them as its discretion should dictate. Now, sir, what contradiction does the gentleman find to this sentiment in the speech of 1825? He quotes me as having then said that we ought not to hug these lands as a very great treasure. Very well, sir, supposing me to be accurately reported in that expression, what is the contradiction? I have not now said that we should hug these lands as a favorite source of pecuniary income. No such thing. It is not my view. What I have said, and what I do say, is, that they are a common fund, to be disposed of for the common benefit, to be sold at low prices for the accommodation of settlers, keeping the object of settling the lands as much in view as that of raising money from them. This I say now, and this I have always said. Is this hugging them as a favorite treasure? Is there no difference between hugging and hoarding this fund, on the one hand, as a great treasure, and on the other of disposing of it at low prices, placing the proceeds in the general treasury of the Union? My opinion is that as much is to be made of the land as fairly and reasonably may be, selling it all the while at such rates as to give the fullest effect to settlement. This is not giving it all away to the States, as the gentleman would propose; nor is it hugging the fund closely and tenaciously, as a favorite treasure; but it is, in my judgment, a

---

[2]This was the speech of Colonel Isaac Barré in reply to Grenville during the passage of the Stamp Act (*Parliamentary History of England,* xvi. 38). In this speech occurred the expression "sons of liberty," which was speedily adopted by the famous society of that name.

just and wise policy, perfectly according with all the various duties which rest on government. So much for my contradiction. And what is it? Where is the ground of the gentleman's triumph? What inconsistency in word or doctrine has he been able to detect? Sir, if this be a sample of that discomfiture with which the honorable gentleman threatened me, commend me to the word "discomfiture" for the rest of my life.

But, after all, this is not the point of the debate, and I must now bring the gentleman back to that which is the point.

The real question between me and him is, Has the doctrine been advanced at the South or at the East that the population of the West should be retarded, or at least need not be hastened, on account of its effect to drain off the people from the Atlantic States? Is this doctrine, as has been alleged, of Eastern origin? That is the question. Has the gentleman found anything by which he can make good his accusation? I submit to the Senate that he has entirely failed; and, as far as this debate has shown, the only person who has advanced such sentiments is a gentleman from South Carolina, and a friend to the honorable member himself. . . .

So then, sir, New England is guiltless of the policy of retarding Western population, and of all envy and jealousy of the growth of the new States. Whatever there be of that policy in the country, no part of it is hers. If it has a local habitation, the honorable member has probably seen by this time where to look for it; and if it now has received a name, he has himself christened it.

We approach at length, sir, to a more important part of the honorable gentleman's observations. Since it does not accord with my views of justice and policy to give away the public lands altogether, as a mere matter of gratuity, I am asked by the honorable gentleman on what ground it is that I consent to vote them away in

particular instances. How, he inquires, do I reconcile with these professed sentiments my support of measures appropriating portions of the lands to particular roads, particular canals, particular rivers, and particular institutions of education in the West? This leads, sir, to the real and wide difference in political opinion between the honorable gentleman and myself. On my part, I look upon all these objects as connected with the common good, fairly embraced in its object and its terms; he, on the contrary, deems them all, if good at all, only local good. This is our difference. The interrogatory, which he proceeded to put, at once explains this difference. "What interest," asks he, "has South Carolina in a canal in Ohio?" Sir, this very question is full of significance. It develops the gentleman's whole political system, and its answer expounds mine. Here we differ. I look upon a road over the Alleghanies, a canal round the falls of the Ohio, or a canal or railway from the Atlantic to the western waters, as being an object large and extensive enough to be fairly said to be for the common benefit. The gentleman thinks otherwise, and this is the key to his construction of the powers of the government. He may well ask what interest has South Carolina in a canal in Ohio. On his system, it is true, she has no interest. On that system, Ohio and Carolina are different governments and different countries, connected here, it is true, by some slight and ill-defined bond of union, but in all main respects separate and diverse. On that system, Carolina has no more interest in a canal in Ohio than in Mexico. The gentleman, therefore, only follows out his own principles; he does no more than arrive at the natural conclusions of his own doctrines; he only announces the true results of that creed which he has adopted himself, and would persuade others to adopt, when he thus declares that South Carolina has no interest in a public work in Ohio.

Sir, we narrow-minded people of New England do not reason thus. Our *notion* of things is entirely different. We look upon the States, not as separated, but as united. We love to dwell on that union, and on the mutual happiness which it has so much promoted, and the common renown which it has so greatly contributed to acquire. In our contemplation, Carolina and Ohio are parts of the same country; States united under the same general government, having interests common, associated, intermingled. In whatever is within the proper sphere of the constitutional power of the government, we look upon the States as one. We do not impose geographical limits to our patriotic feeling or regard; we do not follow rivers and mountains and lines of latitude to find boundaries beyond which public improvements do not benefit us. We, who come here as agents and representatives of these narrow-minded and selfish men of New England, consider ourselves as bound to regard with an equal eye the good of the whole, in whatever is within our power of legislation. Sir, if a railroad or canal, beginning in South Carolina and ending in South Carolina, appeared to me to be of national importance and national magnitude, believing, as I do, that the power of government extends to the encouragement of works of that description, if I were to stand up here and ask, What interest has Massachusetts in a railroad in South Carolina? I should not be willing to face my constituents. These same narrow-minded men would tell me that they had sent me to act for the whole country, and that one who possessed too little comprehension, either of intellect or feeling, one who was not large enough, both in mind and in heart, to embrace the whole, was not fit to be intrusted with the interest of any part.

Sir, I do not desire to enlarge the powers of the government by unjustifiable construction, nor to exercise any not within a fair interpretation. But when it is believed that a power does exist, then it is, in my judgment, to be exercised for the general benefit of the whole. So far as respects the exercise of such a power, the States are one. It was the very object of the Constitution to create unity of interests to the extent of the powers of the general government. In war and peace we are one; in commerce one; because the authority of the general government reaches to war and peace, and to the regulation of commerce. I have never seen any more difficulty in erecting lighthouses on the lakes than on the ocean; in improving the harbors of inland seas than if they were within the ebb and flow of the tide; or in removing obstructions in the vast streams of the West, more than in any work to facilitate commerce on the Atlantic coast. If there be any power for one, there is power also for the other; and they are all and equally for the common good of the country.

There are other objects apparently more local, or the benefit of which is less general, towards which, nevertheless, I have concurred with others to give aid by donations of land. It is proposed to construct a road in or through one of the new States in which this government possesses large quantities of land. Have the United States no right, or, as a great and untaxed proprietor, are they under no obligation to contribute to an object thus calculated to promote the common good of all the proprietors, themselves included? And even with respect to education, which is the extreme case, let the question be considered. In the first place, as we have seen, it was made matter of compact with these States that they should do their part to promote education. In the next place, our whole system of land laws proceeds on the idea that education is for the common good, because, in every division, a certain portion is uniformly reserved and appropriated for the use of schools. And, finally, have not these new States singularly strong claims, founded on the ground already stated, that the government is a great untaxed proprietor in the ownership of the soil? It is a consideration of great importance that probably there is in no part of the country or of the world so great a call for the means of education as in those new States, owing to the vast number of persons within those ages in which education and instruction are usually received, if received at all. This is the natural consequence of recency of settlement and rapid increase. The census of these States shows how great a proportion of the whole population occupies the classes between infancy and manhood. These are the wide fields, and here is the deep and quick soil for the seeds of knowledge and virtue; and this is the favored season, the springtime for sowing them. Let them be disseminated without stint. Let them be scattered with a bountiful hand broadcast. Whatever the government can fairly do towards these objects, in my opinion, ought to be done. . . .

6

Andrew Jackson

Andrew Jackson was the seventh president of the United States and the symbol of populist egalitarianism and individualism during his era. However, until he became president and embraced the concept as a focus for political leadership, Jackson had little to do with the development of American popular rule.

Born in 1767 in Waxhaw, South Carolina, the son of Irish immigrants killed during the American Revolution, Jackson had little formal education and served in the Revolutionary army from 1780–81. He studied law in Salisbury, North Carolina, and was admitted to the bar. After serving as a public prosecutor in North Carolina, he sought his fortune on the frontier of Tennessee. He succeeded through trade, speculation, and politics, settling at The Hermitage as a cotton planter. In 1796 he served as delegate to the Tennessee Constitutional Convention and was elected to the House of Representatives. The next year he was elected to the Senate but soon had to resign due to financial problems. He then turned to success in a military career, becoming renowned in the War of 1812 in the campaign against the Creek Indians and in the successful defense of New Orleans from British attacks. As a military commander, Jackson was an uncompromising disciplinarian and would think nothing of executing a young recruit for insubordination. Following a brutal 1818 campaign against the Indians on the borders of Alabama and Florida, President Monroe named him governor of the new territory of Florida.

In 1822 Jackson was nominated for the presidency by the Tennessee Legislature and was again elected to the Senate the following year. In 1824–25, he received the plurality of electoral votes in the presidential election, but lost to John Quincy Adams in the House of Representatives. Representative Henry Clay had used his influence to ensure the election of Adams in the House, and when Adams appointed Clay secretary of state, the Jacksonians accused both of a "corrupt bargain." This charge became the basis for the claim that Jackson, the people's choice, had been unjustly denied the presidency by the political tricks of an unrepresentative minority. Jackson rose to power as states were expanding the right to vote to include poor white males. Jackson's name became synonymous with democracy, and he swept the presidential election of 1828. There was a Jacksonian Democratic movement much larger than Jackson or his immediate following.

Although Jackson's democratic faith may have been triggered by political expediency, he preached and practiced this philosophy with enthusiasm during his two presidential terms. He used republican rhetoric to promote individualism, nationalism, and limited government. At the same time he anticipated the majority position on upcoming issues to expand the powers of the presumably virtuous public realm to include all areas affecting the economic marketplace. Once in power, Jackson utilized the tradition of the spoils system to turn out those representing the minority in the federal bureaucracy who lost the election, arguing that such turnovers prevented corruption in public servants and were in the public interest. In vetoing a congressional bill to recharter the Second Bank of the United States, Jackson described the issue as one of the few against the many, and he sided with the many, demonstrating that the people could be a factor in the legislative process. The excerpts below are from Jackson's "Farewell Address" and summarize the principles upon which American institutions that preserve freedom were founded.

Farewell Address of Andrew Jackson to the People of the United States (1837)

Fellow-Citizens: Being about to retire finally from public life, I beg leave to offer you my grateful thanks for the many proofs of kindness and confidence which I have received at your hands. It has been my fortune, in the discharge of public duties, civil and military, frequently to have found myself in difficult and trying situations where prompt decision and energetic action were necessary and where the interest of the country required that high responsibilities should be fearlessly encountered; and it is with the deepest emotions of gratitude that I acknowledge the continued and unbroken confidence with which you have sustained me in every trial. My public life has been a long one, and I cannot hope that it has, at all times, been free from errors. But I have the consolation of knowing that, if mistakes have been committed, they have not seriously injured the country I so anxiously endeavored to serve; and, at the moment when I surrender my last public trust, I leave this great people prosperous and happy, in the full enjoyment of liberty and peace, and honored and respected by every nation of the world.

If my humble efforts have in any degree contributed to preserve to you these blessings, I have been more than rewarded by the honors you gave heaped upon me and above all, by the generous confidence with which you have supported me in every peril and with which you have continued to animate and cheer my path to the closing hour of my political life. The time has now come when advanced age and a broken frame warn me to retire from public concerns; but the recollection of the many favors you have bestowed upon me is engraven upon my heart, and I have felt that I could not part from your service without making this public acknowledgment of the gratitude I owe you. And if I use the occasion to offer to you the counsels of age and experience, you will, I trust, receive them with the same indulgent kindness which you have so often extended to me; and will, at least, see in them an earnest desire to perpetuate, in this favored land, the blessings of liberty and equal law.

We have now lived almost fifty years under the Constitution framed by the sages and patriots of the Revolution. The conflicts in which the nations of Europe were engaged during a great part of this period, the spirit in which they waged war against each other, and our intimate commercial connections with every part of the civilized world, rendered it a time of much difficulty for the Government of the United States. We have had our seasons of peace and of war, with all the evils which precede or follow a state of hostility with powerful nations. We encountered these trials with our Constitution yet in its infancy, and under the disadvantages which a new and untried Government must always feel when it is called upon to put forth its whole strength, without the lights of experience to guide it or the weight of precedents to justify its measures. But we have passed triumphantly through all these difficulties. Our Constitution is no longer a doubtful

Isaak, *American Political Thinking.*

experiment; and, at the end of nearly half a century, we find that it has preserved unimpaired the liberties of the people, secured the rights of property, and that our country has improved and is flourishing beyond any former example in the history of nations.

In our domestic concerns there is everything to encourage us, and if you are true to yourselves, nothing can impede your march to the highest point of national prosperity. The States which had so long been retarded in their improvement by the Indian tribes residing in the midst of them are at length relieved from the evil; and this unhappy race—the original dwellers in our land—are now placed in a situation where we may well hope that they will share in the blessings of civilization and be saved from that degradation and destruction to which they were rapidly hastening while they remained in the States; and while the safety and comfort of our own citizens have been greatly promoted by their removal, the philanthropist will rejoice that the remnant of that ill-fated race has been at length placed beyond the reach of injury or oppression, and that the paternal care of the General Government will hereafter watch over them and protect them.

If we turn to our relations with foreign Powers, we find our condition equally gratifying. Actuated by the sincere desire to do justice to every nation and to preserve the blessings of peace, our intercourse with them has been conducted on the part of this Government in the spirit of frankness, and I take pleasure in saying that it has generally been met in a corresponding temper. Difficulties of old standing have been surmounted by friendly discussion and the mutual desire to be just; and the claims of our citizens, which had been long withheld, have at length been acknowledged and adjusted, and satisfactory arrangements made for their final payment; and with a limited and, I trust, a temporary exception,

our relations with every foreign Power are now of the most friendly character, our commerce continually expanding, and our flag respected in every quarter of the world.

These cheering and grateful prospects and these multiplied favors we owe, under Providence, to the adoption of the Federal Constitution. It is no longer a question whether this great country can remain happily united and flourish under our present form of government. Experience, the unerring test of all human undertakings, has shown the wisdom and foresight of those who formed it; and has proved that in the union of these States there is a sure foundation for the brightest hopes of freedom and for the happiness of the people. At every hazard and by every sacrifice, this Union must be preserved.

The necessity of watching with jealous anxiety for the preservation of the Union was earnestly pressed upon his fellow citizens by the Father of his country in his farewell address. He has there told us that "while experience shall not have demonstrated its impracticability, there will always be reason to distrust the patriotism of those who, in any quarter, may endeavor to weaken its bonds"; and he has cautioned us, in the strongest terms, against the formation of parties on geographical discriminations, as one of the means which might disturb our union, and to which designing men would be likely to resort.

The lessons contained in this invaluable legacy of Washington to his countrymen should be cherished in the heart of every citizen to the latest generation; and, perhaps, at no period of time could they be more usefully remembered than at the present moment. For when we look upon the scenes that are passing around us, and dwell upon the pages of his parting address, his paternal counsels would seem to be not merely the offspring of wisdom and foresight, but the voice of prophecy foretelling events and warning us of the evil to come. Forty years have passed since this imperishable document was given to his countrymen. The Federal Constitution was then regarded by him as an experiment, and he so speaks of it in his address; but an experiment upon the success of which the best hopes of his country depended, and we all know that he was prepared to lay down his life, if necessary, to secure to it a full and a fair trial. The trial has been made. It has succeeded beyond the proudest hopes of those who framed it. Every quarter of this widely extended nation has felt its blessings and shared in the general prosperity produced by its adoption. But amid this general prosperity and splendid success, the dangers of which he warned us are becoming every day more evident and the signs of evil are sufficiently apparent to awaken the deepest anxiety in the bosom of the patriot. We behold systematic efforts publicly made to sow the seeds of discord between different parts of the United States and to place party divisions directly upon geographical distinctions; to excite the *South* against the *North* and the *North* against the *South* and to force into the controversy the most delicate and exciting topics—topics upon which it is impossible that a large portion of the Union can ever speak without strong emotion. Appeals, too, are constantly made to sectional interests in order to influence the election of the Chief Magistrate, as if it were desired that he should favor a particular quarter of the country instead of fulfilling the duties of his station with impartial justice to all; and the possible dissolution of the Union has at length become an ordinary and familiar subject of discussion. Has the warning voice of Washington been forgotten? or have designs already been formed to sever the Union? Let it not be supposed that I impute to all of those who have taken an active part in these unwise and unprofitable discussions a want of patriotism or of public virtue. The honorable feeling of

State pride and local attachments find a place in the bosoms of the most enlightened and pure. But while such men are conscious of their own integrity and honesty of purpose, they ought never to forget that the citizens of other States are their political brethren; and that, however mistaken they may be in their views, the great body of them are equally honest and upright with themselves. Mutual suspicions and reproaches may in time create mutual hostility, and artful and designing men will always be found who are ready to foment these fatal divisions and to inflame the natural jealousies of different sections of the country. The history of the world is full of such examples and especially the history of republics.

What have you to gain by division and dissension? Delude not yourselves with the belief that a breach once made may be afterwards repaired. If the Union is once severed, the line of separation will grow wider and wider, and the controversies which are now debated and settled in the halls of legislation will then be tried in fields of battle and determined by the sword. Neither should you deceive yourselves with the hope that the first line of separation would be the permanent one, and that nothing but harmony and concord would be found in the new associations formed upon the dissolution of this Union. Local interests would still be found there, and unchastened ambition. And if the recollection of common dangers in which the people of these United States stood side by side against the common foe; the memory of victories won by their united valor; the prosperity and happiness they have enjoyed under the present Constitution; the proud name they bear as citizens of this great republic: if all these recollections and proofs of common interest are not strong enough to bind us together as one people, what tie will hold united the new divisions of empire, when these bonds have been broken and this Union dissevered? The first line of separation would not last for a single generation; new fragments would be torn off; new leaders would spring up; and this great and glorious republic would soon be broken into a multitude of petty states, without commerce, without credit; jealous of one another; armed for mutual aggression; loaded with taxes to pay armies and leaders; seeking aid against each other from foreign powers; insulted and trampled upon by the nations of Europe, until, harassed with conflicts and humbled and debased in spirit, they would be ready to submit to the absolute dominion of any military adventurer and to surrender their liberty for the sake of repose. It is impossible to look on the consequences that would inevitably follow the destruction of this Government and not feel indignant when we hear cold calculations about the value of the Union and have so constantly before us a line of conduct so well calculated to weaken its ties.

There is too much at stake to allow pride or passion to influence your decision. Never for a moment believe that the great body of the citizens of any State or States can deliberately intend to do wrong. They may, under the influence of temporary excitement or misguided opinions, commit mistakes; they may be misled for a time by the suggestions of self-interest; but in a community so enlightened and patriotic as the people of the United States, argument will soon make them sensible of their errors; and, when convinced, they will be ready to repair them. If they have no higher or better motives to govern them, they will at least perceive that their own interest requires them to be just to others as they hope to receive justice at their hands.

But in order to maintain the Union unimpaired, it is absolutely necessary that the laws passed by the constituted authorities should be faithfully executed in every part of the country, and that every good citizen should at all times stand ready to put down with the combined force of the nation every attempt at unlawful resistance under whatever pretext it may be made or whatever shape it may assume. Unconstitutional or oppressive laws may no doubt be passed by Congress, either from erroneous views or the want of due consideration; if they are within the reach of judicial authority, the remedy is easy and peaceful; and if from the character of the law it is an abuse of power not within the control of the judiciary, then free discussion and calm appeals to reason and to the justice of the people will not fail to redress the wrong. But until the law shall be declared void by the courts or repealed by Congress, no individual or combination of individuals can be justified in forcibly resisting its execution. It is impossible that any Government can continue to exist upon any other principles. It would cease to be a Government and be unworthy of the name if it had not the power to enforce the execution of its own laws within its own sphere of action.

It is true that cases may be imagined disclosing such a settled purpose of usurpation and oppression on the part of the Government as would justify an appeal to arms. These, however, are extreme cases, which we have no reason to apprehend in a Government where the power is in the hands of a patriotic people; and no citizen who loves his country would in any case whatever resort to forcible resistance unless he clearly saw that the time had come when a freeman should prefer death to submission; for if such a struggle is once begun and the citizens of one section of the country arrayed in arms against those of another in doubtful conflict, let the battle result as it may, there will be an end of the Union and, with it an end to the hopes of freedom. The victory of the injured would not secure to them the blessings of liberty; it would avenge their wrongs, but they would themselves share in the common ruin.

But the Constitution cannot be maintained nor the Union preserved in opposition to public feeling by the mere exertion of the coercive powers confided to the General Government. The foundations must be laid in the affections of the people; in the security it gives to life, liberty, character, and property, in every quarter of the country; and in the fraternal attachment which the citizens of the several States bear to one another as members of one political family, mutually contributing to promote the happiness of each other. Hence the citizens of every State should studiously avoid everything calculated to wound the sensibility or offend the just pride of the people of other States; and they should frown upon any proceedings within their own borders likely to disturb the tranquillity of their political brethren in other portions of the Union. In a country so extensive as the United States and with pursuits so varied, the internal regulations of the several States must frequently differ from one another in important particulars; and this difference is unavoidably increased by the varying principles upon which the American colonies were originally planted; principles which had taken deep root in their social relations before the Revolution, and, therefore, of necessity influencing their policy since they became free and independent States. But each State has the unquestionable right to regulate its own internal concerns according to its own pleasure; and while it does not interfere with the rights of the people of other States or the rights of the Union, every State must be the sole judge of the measures proper to secure the safety of its citizens and promote their happiness; and all efforts on the part of people of other States to cast odium upon their institutions, and all measures calculated to disturb their rights of property or to put in jeopardy their peace and internal tranquillity are in direct opposition to the spirit in which the Union was formed, and must

endanger its safety. Motives of philanthropy may be assigned for this unwarrantable interference; and weak men may persuade themselves for a moment that they are laboring in the cause of humanity and asserting the rights of the human race; but everyone upon sober reflection will see that nothing but mischief can come from these improper assaults upon the feelings and rights of others. Rest assured that the men found busy in this work of discord are not worthy of your confidence and deserve your strongest reprobation.

In the legislation of Congress also and in every measure of the General Government, justice to every portion of the United States should be faithfully observed. No free Government can stand without virtue in the people and a lofty spirit of patriotism; and if the sordid feelings of mere selfishness shall usurp the place which ought to be filled by public spirit, the legislation of Congress will soon be converted into a scramble for personal and sectional advantages. Under our free institutions the citizens of every quarter of our country are capable of attaining a high degree of prosperity and happiness without seeking to profit themselves at the expense of others; and every such attempt must in the end fail to succeed, for the people in every part of the United States are too enlightened not to understand their own rights and interests and to detect and defeat every effort to gain undue advantages over them; and when such designs are discovered, it naturally provokes resentments which cannot always be easily allayed. Justice, full and ample justice, to every portion of the United States should be the ruling principle of every freeman and should guide the deliberations of every public body, whether it be State or national.

It is well known that there have always been those amongst us who wish to enlarge the powers of the General Government; and experience would seem to indicate that there is a tendency on the part of this Government to overstep the boundaries marked out for it by the Constitution. Its legitimate authority is abundantly sufficient for all the purposes for which it was created; and its powers being expressly enumerated, there can be no justification for claiming anything beyond them. Every attempt to exercise power beyond these limits should be promptly and firmly opposed. For one evil example will lead to other measures still more mischievous; and if the principle of constructive powers, or supposed advantages, or temporary circumstances, shall ever be permitted to justify the assumption of a power not given by the Constitution, the General Government will before long absorb all the powers of legislation, and you will have in effect but one consolidated Government. From the extent of our country, its diversified interests, different pursuits, and different habits, it is too obvious for argument that a single consolidated Government would be wholly inadequate to watch over and protect its interests; and every friend of our free institutions should be always prepared to maintain unimpaired and in full vigor the rights and sovereignty of the States and to confine the action of the General Government strictly to the sphere of its appropriate duties.

There is, perhaps, no one of the powers conferred on the Federal Government so liable to abuse as the taxing power. The most productive and convenient sources of revenue were necessarily given to it, that it might be able to perform the important duties imposed upon it; and the taxes which it lays upon commerce being concealed from the real payer in the price of the article, they do not so readily attract the attention of the people as smaller sums demanded from them directly by the tax gatherer. But the tax imposed on goods enhances by so much the price of the commodity to the consumer; and, as many of these duties are imposed on articles of necessity which are daily used by the great body of the people, the money raised by these imposed on articles of necessity which are daily used by the great body of the people, the money raised by these imposts is drawn from their pockets. Congress has no right, under the Constitution, to take money from the people unless it is required to execute some one of the specific powers intrusted to the Government; and if they raise more than is necessary for such purposes, it is an abuse of the power of taxation and unjust and oppressive. It may, indeed, happen that the revenue will sometimes exceed the amount anticipated when the taxes were laid. When, however, this is ascertained, it is easy to reduce them; and, in such a case, it is unquestionably the duty of the Government to reduce them, for no circumstances can justify it in assuming a power not given to it by the Constitution nor in taking away the money of the people when it is not needed for the legitimate wants of the Government.

Plain as these principles appear to be, you will yet find that there is a constant effort to induce the General Government to go beyond the limits of its taxing power and to impose unnecessary burdens upon the people. Many powerful interests are continually at work to procure heavy duties on commerce and swell the revenue beyond the real necessities of the public service; and the country has already felt the injurious effects of their combined influence. They succeeded in obtaining a tariff of duties bearing most oppressively on the agricultural and laboring classes of society and producing a revenue that could not be usefully employed within the range of the powers conferred upon Congress; and, in order to fasten upon the people this unjust and unequal system of taxation, extravagant schemes of internal improvement were got up in various quarters to squander the money and to purchase support. Thus, one unconstitutional measure was intended to be upheld by another, and the abuse of the power of taxation was to be maintained by usurping the power of expending the money in internal improvements. You cannot have forgotten the severe and doubtful struggle through which we passed when the Executive Department of the Government, by its veto, endeavored to arrest this prodigal scheme of injustice, and to bring back the legislation of Congress to the boundaries prescribed by the Constitution. The good sense and practical judgment of the people, when the subject was brought before them, sustained the course of the Executive; and this plan of unconstitutional expenditure for the purpose of corrupt influence is, I trust, finally overthrown.

The result of this decision has been felt in the rapid extinguishment of the public debt and the large accumulation of a surplus in the Treasury, notwithstanding the tariff was reduced and is now very far below the amount originally contemplated by its advocates. But, rely upon it, the design to collect an extravagant revenue and to burden you with taxes beyond the economical wants of the Government is not yet abandoned. The various interests which have combined together to impose a heavy tariff and to produce an overflowing treasury are too strong and have too much at stake to surrender the contest. The corporations and wealthy individuals who are engaged in large manufacturing establishments desire a high tariff to increase their gains. Designing politicians will support it to conciliate their favor and to obtain the means of profuse expenditure for the purpose of purchasing influence in other quarters; and since the people have decided that the Federal Government cannot be permitted to employ its income in internal improvements, efforts will be made to seduce and mislead the citizens of the several States by holding out to them the deceitful prospect of benefits to be derived from a surplus revenue collected by the General Government and annually divided among the States. And if, encouraged by these fallacious hopes, the States should disregard the republican Government and should indulge in lavish expenditures exceeding their resources, they will, before long, find themselves oppressed with debts which they are unable to pay, and the temptation will become irresistible to support a high tariff in order to obtain a surplus for distribution. Do not allow yourselves, my fellow-citizens, to be misled on this subject. The Federal Government cannot collect a surplus for such purposes without violating the principles of the Constitution and assuming powers which have not been granted. It is, moreover, a system of injustice, and, if persisted in, will inevitably lead to corruption and must end in ruin. The surplus revenue will be drawn from the pockets of the people, from the farmer, the mechanic, and the laboring classes of society; but who will receive it when distributed among the States, where it is to be disposed of by leading State politicians who have friends to favor and political partisans to gratify? It will certainly not be returned to those who paid it and who have most need of it and are honestly entitled to it. There is but one safe rule, and that is to confine the General Government rigidly within the sphere of its appropriate duties. It has no power to raise a revenue or impose taxes except for the purposes enumerated in the Constitution; and if its income is found to exceed these wants, it should be forthwith reduced, and the burdens of the people so far lightened.

In reviewing the conflicts which have taken place between different interests in the United States and the policy pursued since the adoption of our present form of government, we find nothing that has produced such deep-seated evil as the course of legislation in relation to the currency. The Constitution of the United States unquestionably intended to secure to the people a circulating medium of gold and silver. But the establishment of a national bank by Congress with the privilege of issuing paper money receivable in the payment of the public dues, and the unfortunate course of legislation in the several States upon the same subject, drove from general circulation the constitutional currency and substituted one of paper in its place.

It was not easy for men engaged in the ordinary pursuits of business, whose attention had not been particularly drawn to the subject, to foresee all the consequences of a currency exclusively of paper; and we ought not on that account to be surprised at the facility with which laws were obtained to carry into effect the paper system. Honest and even enlightened men are sometimes misled by the specious and plausible statements of the designing. But experience has now proved the mischiefs and dangers of a paper currency, and it rests with you to determine whether the proper remedy shall be applied.

The paper system being founded on public confidence and having of itself no intrinsic value, it is liable to great and sudden fluctuations, thereby rendering property insecure and the wages of labor unsteady and uncertain. The corporations which create the paper money cannot be relied upon to keep the circulating medium uniform in amount. In times of prosperity, when confidence is high, they are tempted by the prospect of gain, or by the influence of those who hope to profit by it, to extend their issues of paper beyond the bounds of discretion and the reasonable demands of business. And when these issues have been pushed on from day to day until public confidence is at length shaken, then a reaction takes place, and they immediately withdraw the credits they have given; suddenly curtail their issues; and produce an unexpected and ruinous contraction of the circulating medium which is felt by the whole community. The banks by this

means save themselves, and the mischievous consequences of their imprudence or cupidity are visited upon the public. Nor does the evil stop here. These ebbs and flows in the currency and these indiscreet extensions of credit naturally engender a spirit of speculation injurious to the habits and character of the people. We have already seen its effects in the wild spirit of speculation in the public lands and various kinds of stock which, within the last year or two, seized upon such a multitude of our citizens and threatened to pervade all classes of society and to withdraw their attention from the sober pursuits of honest industry. It is not by encouraging this spirit that we shall best preserve public virtue and promote the true interests of our country. But if your currency continues as exclusively paper as it now is, it will foster this eager desire to amass wealth without labor; it will multiply the number of dependents on bank accommodations and bank favors; the temptation to obtain money at any sacrifice will become stronger and stronger, and inevitably lead to corruption which will find its way into your public councils and destroy, at no distant day, the purity of your Government. Some of the evils which arise from this system of paper press with peculiar hardship upon the class of society least able to bear it. A portion of this currency frequently becomes depreciated or worthless, and all of it is easily counterfeited in such a manner as to require peculiar skill and much experience to distinguish the counterfeit from the genuine note. These frauds are most generally perpetrated in the smaller notes, which are used in the daily transactions of ordinary business; and the losses occasioned by them are commonly thrown upon the laboring classes of society whose situation and pursuits put it out of their power to guard themselves from these impositions and whose daily wages are necessary for their subsistence. It is the duty of every Government so to regulate its currency as to protect this numerous class as far as practicable from the impositions of avarice and fraud. It is more especially the duty of the United States where the Government is emphatically the Government of the people, and where this respectable portion of our citizens are so proudly distinguished from the laboring classes of all other nations by their spirit, their love of liberty, their intelligence, and their high tone of moral character. Their industry in peace is the source of our wealth; and their bravery in war has covered us with glory; and the Government of the United States will but ill discharge its duties if it leaves them a prey to such dishonest impositions. Yet it is evident that their interests cannot be effectually protected unless silver and gold are restored to circulation.

These views alone of the paper currency are sufficient to call for immediate reform; but there is another consideration which should still more strongly press it upon your attention.

Recent events have proved that the paper money system of this country may be used as an engine to undermine your free institutions, and that those who desire to engross all power in the hands of the few and to govern by corruption of force are aware of its power and prepared to employ it. Your banks now furnish your only circulating medium, and money is plenty or scarce according to the quantity of notes issued by them. While they have capitals not greatly disproportioned to each other, they are competitors in business, and no one of them can exercise dominion over the rest; and although, in the present state of the currency, these banks may and do operate injuriously upon the habits of business, the pecuniary concerns, and the moral tone of society; yet, from their number and dispersed situation, they cannot combine for the purpose of political influence; and whatever may be the dispositions of some

of them, their power of mischief must necessarily be confined to a narrow space and felt only in their immediate neighborhoods.

But when the charter for the Bank of the United States was obtained from Congress, it perfected the schemes of the paper system and gave to its advocates the position they have struggled to obtain from the commencement of the Federal Government down to the present hour. The immense capital and peculiar privileges bestowed upon it enabled it to exercise despotic sway over the other banks in every part of the country. From its superior strength it could seriously injure, if not destroy, the business of any one of them which might incur its resentment; and it openly claimed for itself the power of regulating the currency throughout the United States. In other words, it asserted (and it undoubtedly possessed) the power to make money plenty or scarce, at its pleasure, at any time, and in any quarter of the Union by controlling the issues of other banks and permitting an expansion or compelling a general contraction of the circulating medium according to its own will. The other banking institutions were sensible of its strength, and they soon generally became its obedient instruments, ready, at all times, to execute its mandates; and with the banks necessarily went, also, that numerous class of persons in our commercial cities who depend altogether on bank credits for their solvency and means of business; and who are, therefore, obliged for their own safety to propitiate the favor of the money power by distinguished zeal and devotion in its service. The result of the ill-advised legislation which established this great monopoly was to concentrate the whole moneyed power of the Union, with its boundless means of corruption and its numerous dependents, under the direction and command of one acknowledged head; thus organizing this particular interest as one body and securing to it unity and concert of action throughout the United States and enabling it to bring forward, upon any occasion, its entire and undivided strength to support of defeat any measure of the Government. In the hands of this formidable power, thus perfectly organized, was also placed unlimited dominion over the amount of the circulating medium, giving it the power to regulate the value of property and the fruits of labor in every quarter of the Union and to bestow prosperity or bring ruin upon any city or section of the country as might best comport with its own interest or policy.

We are not left to conjecture how the moneyed power, thus organized and with such a weapon in its hands, would be likely to use it. The distress and alarm which pervaded and agitated the whole country when the Bank of the United States waged war upon the people in order to compel them to submit to its demands cannot yet be forgotten. The ruthless and unsparing temper with which whole cities and communities were oppressed, individuals impoverished and ruined, and a scene of cheerful prosperity suddenly changed into one of gloom and despondency ought to be indelibly impressed on the memory of the people of the United States. If such was its power in a time of peace, what would it not have been in a season of war with an enemy at your doors? No nation but the freemen of the United States could have come out victorious from such a contest; yet, if you had not conquered, the Government would have passed from the hands of the many to the hands of the few; and this organized money power, from its secret conclave, would have dictated the choice of your highest officers and compelled you to make peace or war as best suited their own wishes. The forms of your government might for a time have remained, but its living spirit would have departed from it.

The distress and sufferings inflicted on the people by the bank are some of the fruits of that system of policy which is continually striving to enlarge the authority of the Federal Government beyond the limits fixed by the Constitution. The powers enumerated in that instrument do not confer on Congress the right to establish such a corporation as the Bank of the United States; and the evil consequences which followed may warn us of the danger of departing from the true rule of construction and of permitting temporary circumstances or the hope of better promoting the public welfare to influence, in any degree, our decisions upon the extent of the authority of the General Government. Let us abide by the Constitution as it is written or amend it in the constitutional mode if it is found to be defective.

The severe lessons of experience will, I doubt not, be sufficient to prevent Congress from again chartering such a monopoly, even if the Constitution did not present an insuperable objection to it. But you must remember, my fellow-citizens, that eternal vigilance by the people is the price of liberty; and that you must pay the price if you wish to secure the blessing. It behooves you, therefore, to be watchful in your States as well as in the Federal Government. The power which the moneyed interest can exercise, when concentrated under a single head, and with our present system of currency, was sufficiently demonstrated in the struggle made by the Bank of the United States. Defeated in the General Government, the same class of intriguers and politicians will now resort to the States and endeavor to obtain there the same organization which they failed to perpetuate in the Union; and with specious and deceitful plans of public advantages and State interests and State pride they will endeavor to establish in the different States one moneyed institution with overgrown capital and exclusive privileges sufficient to enable it to control the operations of the other banks. Such an institution will be pregnant with the same evils produced by the Bank of the United States, although its sphere of action is more confined; and in the State in which it is chartered the money power will be able to embody its whole strength and to move together with undivided force to accomplish any object it may wish to attain. You have already had abundant evidence of its power to inflict injury upon the agricultural, mechanical, and laboring classes of society; and over those whose engagements in trade or speculation render them dependent on bank facilities, the dominion of the State monopoly will be absolute, and their obedience unlimited. With such a bank and a paper currency the money power would in a few years govern the State and control its measures, and if a sufficient number of States can be induced to create such establishments, the time will soon come when it will again take the field against the United States and succeed in perfecting and perpetuating its organization by a charter from Congress.

It is one of the serious evils of our present system of banking that it enables one class of society, and that by no means a numerous one, by its control over the currency to act injuriously upon the interests of all the others and to exercise more than its just proportion of influence in political affairs, The agricultural, the mechanical, and the laboring classes have little or no share in the direction of the great moneyed corporations; and from their habits and the nature of their pursuits, they are incapable of forming extensive combinations to act together with united force. Such concert of action may sometimes be produced in a single city or in a small district of country by means of personal communications with each other; but they have no regular or active correspondence with those who are engaged in similar pursuits in distant places; they have but little patronage to give to the press and exercise but a small share of influence over it; they have no crowd of dependents above them who hope

to grow rich without labor by their countenance and favor and who are, therefore, always ready to exercise their wishes. The planter, the farmer, the mechanic, and the laborer all know that their success depends upon their own industry and economy and that they must not expect to become suddenly rich by the fruits of their toil. Yet these classes of society form the great body of the people of the United States; they are the bone and sinew of the country; men who love liberty and desire nothing but equal rights and equal laws and who, moreover, hold the great mass of our national wealth, although it is distributed in moderate amounts among the millions of freemen who possess it. But, with overwhelming numbers and wealth on their side, they are in constant danger of losing their fair influence in the Government and with difficulty maintain their just rights against the incessant efforts daily made to encroach upon them. The mischief springs from the power which the moneyed interest derives from a paper currency which they are able to control; from the multitude of corporations with exclusive privileges which they have succeeded in obtaining in the different States and which are employed altogether for their benefit; and unless you become more watchful in your States and check this spirit of monopoly and thirst for exclusive privileges, you will, in the end, find that the most important powers of Government have been given or bartered away, and the control over your dearest interests has passed into the hands of these corporations.

The paper money system and its natural associates—monopoly and exclusive privileges—have already struck their roots deep in the soil; and it will require all your efforts to check its further growth and to eradicate the evil. The men who profit by the abuses and desire to perpetuate them will continue to besiege the halls of legislation in the General Government as well as in the States and will seek, by every artifice, to mislead and deceive the public servants. It is to yourselves that you must look for safety and the means of guarding and perpetuating your free institutions. In your hands is rightfully placed the sovereignty of the country and to you every one placed in authority is ultimately responsible. It is always in your power to see that the wishes of the people are carried into faithful execution, and their will, when once made known, must sooner or later be obeyed. And while the people remain, as I trust they ever will, uncorrupted and incorruptible and continue watchful and jealous of their rights, the Government is safe, and the cause of freedom will continue to triumph over all its enemies.

But it will require steady and persevering exertions on your part to rid yourselves of the iniquities and mischiefs of the paper system and to check the spirit of monopoly and other abuses which have sprung up with it and of which it is the main support. So many interests are united to resist all reform on this subject that you must not hope the conflict will be a short one nor success easy. My humble efforts have not been spared, during my administration of the Government, to restore the constitutional currency of gold and silver; and something, I trust, has been done towards the accomplishment of this most desirable object. But enough yet remains to require all your energy and perseverance. The power, however, is in your hands, and the remedy must and will be applied, if you determine upon it.

While I am thus endeavoring to press upon your attention the principles which I deem of vital importance in the domestic concerns of the country, I ought not to pass over without notice the important considerations which should govern your policy towards foreign Powers, It is, unquestionably, our true interest to cultivate the most friendly understanding with every nation and to avoid by every honorable means the calamities of war; and we shall best attain this object by frankness and sincerity in our foreign intercourse by the prompt and faithful execution of treaties and by justice and impartiality in our conduct to all. But no nation, however desirous of peace, can hope to escape occasional collisions with other Powers; and the soundest dictates of policy require that we should place ourselves in a condition to assert our rights if a resort to force should ever become necessary. Our local situation, our long line of seacoast indented by numerous bays with deep rivers opening into the interior, as well as our extended and still increasing commerce, point to the navy as our natural means of defense. It will, in the end, be found to be the cheapest and most effectual; and now is the time, in a season of peace, and with an overflowing revenue, that we can, year after year, add to its strength without increasing the burdens of the people. It is your true policy. For your navy will not only protect your rich and flourishing commerce in distant seas, but will enable you to reach and annoy the enemy and will give to defense its greatest efficiency by meeting danger at a distance from home. It is impossible by any line of fortifications to guard every point from attack against a hostile force advancing from the ocean and selecting its object; but they are indispensable to protect cities from bombardment, dock yards and naval arsenals from destruction; to give shelter to merchant vessels in time of war, and to single ships or weaker squadrons when pressed by superior force. Fortifications of this description cannot be too soon completed and armed and placed in a condition of the most perfect preparation. The abundant means we now possess cannot be applied in any manner more useful to the country; and when this is done and our naval force sufficiently strengthened and our militia armed, we need not fear that any nation will wantonly insult us or needlessly provoke hostilities.

We shall more certainly preserve peace when it is well understood that we are prepared for war.

In presenting to you, my fellow-citizens, these parting counsels, I have brought before you the leading principles upon which I endeavored to administer the Government in the high office with which you twice honored me. Knowing that the path of freedom is continually beset by enemies who often assume the disguise of friends, I have devoted the last hours of my public life to warn you of the danger. The progress of the United States under our free and happy institutions has surpassed the most sanguine hopes of the founders of the Republic. Our growth has been rapid beyond all former example, in numbers, in wealth, in knowledge, and all the useful arts which contribute to the comforts and convenience of man; and from the earliest ages of history to the present day, there never have been thirteen millions of people associated together in one political body who enjoyed so much freedom and happiness as the people of these United States. You have no longer any cause to fear danger from abroad; your strength and power are well known throughout the civilized world, as well as the high and gallant bearing of your sons. It is from within, among yourselves, from cupidity, from corruption, from disappointed ambition, and inordinate thirst for power, that factions will be formed and liberty endangered. It is against such designs, whatever disguise the actors may assume, that you have especially to guard yourselves. You gave the highest of human trusts committed to your care. Providence has showered on this favored land blessings without number and has chosen you as the guardians of freedom to preserve it for the benefit of the human race. May He who holds in his hands the destinies of nations make you worthy of the favors He has bestowed and enabled you, with pure hearts and and pure hands and sleepless vigilance, to guard and defend to the end of time the great charge he has committed to your keeping.

My own race is nearly run; advanced age and failing health warn me that before long I must pass beyond the reach of human events and cease to feel the vicissitudes of human affairs. I thank God that my life has been spent in a land of liberty and that He has given me a heart to love my country with the affection of a son. And, filled with gratitude for your constant and unwavering kindness, I bid you a last and affectionate farewell.

Andrew Jackson

March 4, 1837

Ralph Waldo Emerson

Ralph Waldo Emerson was America's leading transcendental philosopher. He affirmed the infinite capacities of the individual (partaking of the whole universe) and provided a cultural basis for the individualistic democratic liberalism of the United States. The transcendentalists were so called because they went beyond experience and rational analysis by developing the individual's intuitive and spiritual qualities. Born in 1803 in Boston, son of a pastor, Emerson entered Harvard at fourteen and graduated four years later in the upper half of his class, but without distinction. He then taught at a finishing school for young women in Boston and later at other schools before entering Harvard Divinity School. In 1829 Emerson became assistant pastor, and then pastor, of the Second Church, where his father had preached. In 1832, Emerson informed his congregation that he no longer believed Christ had intended for the sacrament to be administered as a general, regular observance. The church, however, wanted the tradition of the Lord's Supper to continue, so Emerson resigned. He traveled to Europe to recover from the death of his wife and his own poor health and while there he visited those whose writings appealed to him—Landor in Italy and Coleridge, Wordsworth, and Carlyle in England.

Emerson returned to the States to remarry and settle in Concord, Massachusetts, for the next forty-seven years. He was proud of Concord's historical role in America's fight for independence and participated in local life, serving as a member of the Fire Association, preaching occasionally at the church, and directing the Concord Athenaeum, which maintained a public reading room and where he served with his friend Henry David Thoreau to stimulate intellectual life in Concord. He planted a garden and orchard and bought a tract in Walden woods, where Thoreau later built his celebrated hut. Concord is not far from Boston, America's intellectual center at that time.

In addition to occasional preaching and lecturing, Emerson published anonymously a poetic book of philosophy, *Nature* (1836), which dealt with the influence of Nature on the life of mankind. Emerson's "The American Scholar" address in 1837 before the Harvard Phi Beta Kappa Society was an influential event in American cultural history. In it Emerson maintains "the scholar is the delegated intellect. In the right state he is *Man Thinking*. In the degenerate state, when the victim of society, he tends to become a mere thinker, or still worse, the parrot of other men's thinking. ... I had better never see a book than to be warped by its attraction clean out of my own orbit, and made a satellite instead of a system." Oliver Wendell Holmes called this lecture "Our intellectual Declaration of Independence." When Emerson addressed the graduating class of the Divinity School and openly criticized the inherited version of historical Christianity and uninspired, formal preaching, he was called an atheist and opposed by the clergy, who no longer invited him to preach as before. After he discovered that he could lecture to people on Wednesday and say things that on Sunday would be considered blasphemous, he spent the rest of his life on the lecture circuit and traveled throughout the United States as a master orator. Almost all of his famous essays were first tried out as lectures and then revised and polished before being published in books. In 1847 he lectured in England and visited France as an American celebrity, resulting in his book *English Traits.*

After the Fugitive Slave Act was passed, Emerson actively associated himself with abolitionist political forces despite his reluctance to become involved in politics and his skepticism regarding his own practical political abilities. He entertained John Brown and spoke in his defense after the Harpers Ferry incident. Emerson lectured at Harvard, 1879–81, and died in 1882.

Below are excerpts from his essay "Self-Reliance" (1841). In another essay, "The Conservative" (1841) (not excerpted here), Emerson distinguishes between the two parties in America: the party of memory—the conservatives—and the party of hope—the radicals. His principles in "Self-Reliance" epitomize the cultural basis underlying American liberalism. "Politics" was an address delivered at an anti-annexation meeting in New England when the pro-slavery movement was fighting for the annexation of Texas. Emerson called on New England to resist "tooth and nail."

❧❦

Self-Reliance (1841)
(excerpt)

"Ne te quaesiveris extra."

Man is his own star; and the soul that can
Render an honest and a perfect man,
Commands all light, all influence, all fate;
Nothing to him falls early or too late.
Our acts our angels are, or good or ill,
Our fatal shadows that walk by us still.

Epilogue to Beaumont and Fletcher's Honest Man's Fortune

Cast the bantling on the rocks,
Suckle him with the she-wolf's teat,
Wintered with the hawk and fox,
Power and speed be hands and feet.

I read the other day some verses written by an eminent painter which were original and not conventional. The soul always hears an admonition in such lines, let the subject be what it may. The sentiment they instil is of more value than any thought they may contain. To believe your own thought, to believe that what is true for you

in your private heart is true for all men—
that is genius. Speak your latent conviction,
and it shall be the universal sense; for the
inmost in due time becomes the outmost,
and our first thought is rendered back to
us by the trumpets of the Last Judgment.
Familiar as the voice of the mind is to each,
the highest merit we ascribe to Moses, Plato
and Milton is that they set at naught books
and traditions, and spoke not what men,
but what *they* thought. A man should learn
to detect and watch that gleam of light
which flashes across his mind from within,
more than the lustre of the firmament of
bards and sages. Yet he dismisses without
notice his thought, because it is his. In
every work of genius we recognize our own
rejected thoughts; they come back to us
with a certain alienated majesty. Great
works of art have no more affecting lesson
for us than this. They teach us to abide
by our spontaneous impression with good-
humored inflexibility then most when the
whole cry of voices is on the other side.
Else to-morrow a stranger will say with
masterly good sense precisely what we
have thought and felt all the time, and we
shall be forced to take with shame our own
opinion from another.

There is a time in every man's education when he arrives at the conviction that
envy is ignorance; that imitation is suicide;
that he must take himself for better for
worse as his portion; that though the wide
universe is full of good, no kernel of nourishing corn can come to him but through
his toil bestowed on that plot of ground
which is given to him to till. The power
which resides in him is new in nature, and
none but he knows what that is which he
can do, nor does he know until he has tried.
Not for nothing one face, one character,
one fact, makes much impression on him,
and another none. This sculpture in the
memory is not without preëstablished harmony. The eye was placed where one ray

should fall, that it might testify of that particular ray. We but half express ourselves,
and are ashamed of that divine idea which
each of us represents. It may be safely trusted as proportionate and of good issues, so
it be faithfully imparted, but God will not
have his work made manifest by cowards.
A man is relieved and gay when he has put
his heart into his work and done his best;
but what he has said or done otherwise
shall give him no peace. It is a deliverance
which does not deliver. In the attempt his
genius deserts him; no muse befriends; no
invention, no hope.

Trust thyself: every heart vibrates to
that iron string. Accept the place the divine
providence has found for you, the society
of your contemporaries, the connection of
events. Great men have always done so,
and confided themselves childlike to the
genius of their age, betraying their perception that the absolutely trustworthy was
seated at their heart, working through their
hands, predominating in all their being.
And we are now men, and must accept
in the highest mind the same transcendent
destiny; and not minors and invalids in a
protected corner, not cowards fleeing
before a revolution, but guides, redeemers
and benefactors, obeying the Almighty
effort and advancing on Chaos and the
Dark.

What pretty oracles nature yields us
on this text in the face and behavior of
children, babes, and even brutes! That
divided and rebel mind, that distrust of a
sentiment because our arithmetic has com-
puted the strength and means opposed to
our purpose, these have not. Their mind
being whole, their eye is as yet uncon-
quered; and when we look in their faces
we are disconcerted. Infancy conforms to
nobody; all conform to it; so that one babe
commonly makes four or five out of the
adults who prattle and play to it. So God
has armed youth and puberty and manhood

no less with its own piquancy and charm, and made it enviable and gracious and its claims not to be put by, if it will stand by itself. Do not think the youth has no force, because he cannot speak to you and me. Hark! in the next room his voice is sufficiently clear and emphatic. It seems he knows how to speak to his contemporaries. Bashful or bold then, he will know how to make us seniors very unnecessary.

The nonchalance of boys who are sure of a dinner, and would disdain as much as a lord to do or say aught to conciliate one, is the healthy attitude of human nature. A boy is in the parlor what the pit is in the playhouse; independent, irresponsible, looking out from his corner on such people and facts as pass by, he tries and sentences them on their merits, in the swift, summary way of boys, as good, bad, interesting, silly, eloquent, troublesome. He cumbers himself never about consequences, about interests; he gives an independent, genuine verdict. You must court him; he does not court you. But the man is as it were clapped into jail by his consciousness. As soon as he has once acted or spoken with *éclat* he is a committed person, watched by the sympathy or the hatred of hundreds, whose affections must now enter into his account. There is no Lethe for this. Ah, that he could pass again into his neutrality! Who can thus avoid all pledges and, having observed, observe again from the same unaffected, unbiased, unbribable, unaffrighted innocence—must always be formidable. He would utter opinions on all passing affairs, which being seen to be not private but necessary, would sink like darts into the ear of men and put them in fear.

These are the voices which we hear in solitude, but they grow faint and inaudible as we enter into the world. Society everywhere is in conspiracy against the manhood of every one of its members. Society is a joint-stock company, in which the mem-

bers agree, for the better securing of his breed to each share-holder, to surrender the liberty and culture of the eater. The virtue in most request is conformity. Self-reliance is its aversion. It loves not realities and creators, but names and customs.

Whoso would be a man, must be a nonconformist. He who would gather immortal palms must not be hindered by the name of goodness, but must explore if it be goodness. Nothing is at last sacred but the integrity of your own mind. Absolve you to yourself, and you shall have the suffrage of the world. I remember an answer which when quite young I was prompted to make to a valued adviser who was wont to importune me with the dear old doctrines of the church. On my saying, "What have I to do with the sacredness of traditions, if I live wholly from within?" my friend suggested—"But these impulses may be from below, not from above." I replied, "They do not seem to me to be such; but if I am the Devil's child, I will live then from the Devil." No law can be sacred to me but that of my nature. Good and bad are but names very readily transferable to that or this; the only right is what is after my constitution; the only wrong what is against it. A man is to carry himself in the presence of all opposition as if every thing were titular and ephemeral but he. I am ashamed to think how easily we capitulate to badges and names, to large societies and dead institutions. Every decent and well-spoken individual affects and sways me more than is right. I ought to go upright and vital, and speak the rude truth in all ways. If malice and vanity wear the coat of philanthropy, shall that pass? If an angry bigot assumes this bountiful cause of Abolition, and comes to me with his last news from Barbadoes, why should I not say to him, "Go love thy infant; love thy wood-chopper; be good-natured and modest; have that grace; and never varnish your hard, uncharitable ambition with this incredible tenderness for black folk a thousand miles off. Thy love afar is spite at home." Rough and graceless would be such greeting, but truth is handsomer than the affectation of love. Your goodness must have some edge to it—else it is none. The doctrine of hatred must be preached, as the counteraction of the doctrine of love, when that pules and whines. I shun father and mother and wife and brother when my genius calls me. I would write on the lintels of the door-post, *Whim.* I hope it is somewhat better than whim at last, but we cannot spend the day in explanation. Expect me not to show cause why I seek or why I exclude company. Then again, do not tell me, as a good man did to-day, of my obligation to put all poor men in good situations. Are they *my* poor? I tell thee, thou foolish philanthropist, that I grudge the dollar, the dime, the cent I give to such men as do not belong to me and to whom I do not belong. There is a class of persons to whom by all spiritual affinity I am bought and sold; for them I will go to prison if need be; but your miscellaneous popular charities; the education at college of fools; the building of meeting-houses to the vain end to which many now stand; alms to sots, and the thousand-fold Relief Societies; though I confess with shame I sometimes succumb and give the dollar, it is a wicked dollar, which by and by I shall have the manhood to withhold.

Virtues are, in the popular estimate, rather the exception than the rule. There is the man *and* his virtues. Men do what is called a good action, as some piece of courage or charity, much as they would pay a fine in expiation of daily non-appearance on parade. Their works are done as an apology or extenuation of their living in the world—as invalids and the insane pay a high board. Their virtues are penances. I do not wish to expiate, but to live. My life is for itself and not for a spectacle. I much prefer that it should be of a lower strain, so it be genuine and equal, than that it should be glittering and unsteady. I wish it to be sound and sweet, and not to need diet and bleeding. I ask primary evidence that you are a man, and refuse this appeal from the man to his actions. I know that for myself it makes no difference whether I do or forbear those actions which are reckoned excellent. I cannot consent to pay for a privilege where I have intrinsic right. Few and mean as my gifts may be, I actually am, and do not need for my own assurance or the assurance of my fellows any secondary testimony.

What I must do is all that concerns me, not what the people think. This rule, equally arduous in actual and in intellectual life, may serve for the whole distinction between greatness and meanness. It is the harder because you will always find those who think they know what is your duty better than you know it. It is easy in the world to live after the world's opinion; it is easy in solitude to live after our own; but the great man is he who in the midst of the crowd keeps with perfect sweetness the independence of solitude. . . .

Politics (1844)

Gold and iron are good
To buy iron and gold;
All earth's fleece and food
For their like are sold.
Boded Merlin wise,
Proved Napoleon great—
Nor kind nor coinage buys
Aught above its rate.
Fear, Craft and Avarice
Cannot rear a State.
Out of dust to build
What is more than dust—
Walls Amphion piled

Phoebus stablish must.
When the Muses nine
With the Virtues meet,
Find to their design
An Atlantic seat,
By green orchard boughs
Fended from the heat,
Where the statesman ploughs
Furrow for the wheat;
When the Church is social worth,
When the state-house is the hearth
Then the perfect State is come,
The republican at home.

In dealing with the State we ought to remember that its institutions are not aboriginal, though they existed before we were born; that they are not superior to the citizen; that every one of them was once the act of a single man; every law and usage was a man's expedient to meet a particular case; that they all are imitable, all alterable; we may make as good, we may make better. Society is an illusion to the young citizen. It lies before him in rigid repose, with certain names, men and institutions rooted like oak-trees to the centre, round which all arrange themselves the best they can. But the old statesman knows that society is fluid; there are no such roots and centres, but any particle may suddenly become the centre of the movement and compel the system to gyrate around it; as every man of strong will, like Pisistratus or Cromwell, does for a time, and every man of truth, like Plato or Paul, does forever. But politics rest on necessary foundations, and cannot be treated with levity. Republics abound in young civilians who believe that the laws make the city, that grave modifications of the policy and modes of living and employments of the population, that commerce, education and religion may be voted in or out; and that any measure, though it were absurd, may be imposed on a people if only you can get sufficient voices to make it a law. But the wise know that foolish legislation is a rope of sand which perishes in the twisting; that the State must follow and not lead the character and progress of the citizen; the strongest usurper is quickly got rid of; and they only who build on Ideas, build for eternity; and that the form of government which prevails is the expression of what cultivation exists in the population which permits it. The law is only a memorandum. We are superstitious, and esteem the statute somewhat: so much life as it has in the character of living men is its force. The statute stands there to say, Yesterday we agreed so and so, but how feel ye this article to-day? Our statute is a currency which we stamp with our own portrait: it soon becomes unrecognizable, and in process of time will return to the mint. Nature is not democratic, nor limited-monarchical, but despotic, and will not be fooled or abated of any jot of her authority by the pertest of her sons; and as fast as the public mind is opened to more intelligence, the code is seen to be brute and stammering. It speaks not articulately, and must be made to. Meantime the education of the general mind never stops. The reveries of the true and simple are prophetic. What the tender poetic youth dreams, and prays, and paints to-day, but shuns the ridicule of saying aloud, shall presently be the resolutions of public bodies; then shall be carried as grievance and bill of rights through conflict and war, and then shall be triumphant law and establishment for a hundred years, until it gives place in turn to new prayers and pictures. The history of the State sketches in coarse outline the progress of thought, and follows at a distance the delicacy of culture and of aspiration.

The theory of politics which has possessed the mind of men, and which they have expressed the best they could in their laws and in their revolutions, considers persons and property as the two objects for whose protection government exists. Of persons, all have equal rights, in virtue of being identical in nature. This interest of course with its whole power demands a democracy. Whilst the rights of all as persons are equal, in virtue of their access to reason, their rights in property are very unequal. One man owns his clothes, and another owns a county. This accident, depending primarily on the skill and virtue of the parties, of which there is every degree, and secondarily on patrimony, falls unequally, and its rights of course are unequal. Personal rights, universally the same, demand a government framed on the ratio of the census; property demands a government framed on the ratio of owners and of owing. Laban, who has flocks and herds, wishes them looked after by an officer on the frontiers, lest the Midianites shall drive them off; and pays a tax to that end. Jacob has no flocks or herds and no fear of the Midianites, and pays no tax to the officer. It seems fit that Laban and Jacob should have equal rights to elect the officer who is to defend their persons, but that Laban and not Jacob should elect the officer who is to guard the sheep and cattle. And if question arise whether additional

officers or watch-towers should be provided, must not Leban and Isaac, and those who must sell part of their herds to buy protection for the rest, judge better of this, and with more right, than Jacob, who, because he is a youth and a traveller, eats their bread and not his own?

In the earliest society the proprietors made their own wealth, and so long as it comes to the owners in the direct way, no other opinion would arise in any equitable community than that property should make the law for property, and persons the law for persons.

But property passes through donation or inheritance to those who do not create it. Gift, in one case, makes it as really the new owner's, as labor made it the first owner's: in the other case, of patrimony, the law makes an ownership which will be valid in each man's view according to the estimate which he sets on the public tranquillity.

It was not, however, found easy to embody the readily admitted principle that property should make law for property and persons for persons; since persons and property mixed themselves in every transaction. At last it seemed settled that the rightful distinction was that the proprietors should have more elective franchise than non-proprietors, on the Spartan principle of "calling that which is just, equal; not that which is equal, just."

That principle no longer looks so self-evident as it appeared in former times, partly because doubts have arisen whether too much weight had not been allowed in the laws to property, and such a structure given to our usages as allowed the rich to encroach on the poor, and to keep them poor; but mainly because there is an instinctive sense, however obscure and yet inarticulate, that the whole constitution of property, on its present tenures, is injurious, and its influence on persons deteriorating and degrading; that truly the only interest for the consideration of the State is persons;

that property will always follow persons; that the highest end of government is the culture of men; and that if men can be educated, the institutions will share their improvement and the moral sentiment will write the law of the land.

If it be not easy to settle the equity of this question, the peril is less when we take note of our natural defences. We are kept by better guards than the vigilance of such magistrates as we commonly elect. Society always consists in greatest part of young and foolish persons. The old, who have seen through the hypocrisy of courts and statesmen, die and leave no wisdom to their sons. They believe their own newspaper, as their fathers did at their age. With such an ignorant and deceivable majority, States would soon run to ruin, but that there are limitations beyond which the folly and ambition of governors cannot go. Things have their laws, as well as men; and things refuse to be trifled with. Property will be protected. Corn will not grow unless it is planted and manured; but the farmer will not plant or hoe it unless the chances are a hundred to one that he will cut and harvest it. Under any forms, persons and property must and will have their just sway. They exert their power, as steadily as matter its attraction. Cover up a pound of earth ever so cunningly, divide and subdivide it; melt it to liquid, convert it to gas; it will always weigh a pound; it will always attract and resist other matter by the full virtue of one pound weight: and the attributes of a person, his wit and his moral energy, will exercise, under any law or extinguishing tyranny, their proper force, if not overtly, then covertly; if not for the law, then against it; if not wholesomely, then poisonously; with right, or by might.

The boundaries of personal influence it is impossible to fix, as persons are organs of moral or supernatural force. Under the dominion of an idea which possesses the minds of multitudes, as civil freedom, or the religious sentiment, the powers of persons are no longer subjects of calculation. A nation of men unanimously bent on freedom or conquest can easily confound the arithmetic of statists, and achieve extravagant actions, out of all proportion to their means; as the Greeks, the Saracens, the Swiss, the Americans, and the French have done.

In like manner to every particle of property belongs its own attraction. A cent is the representative of a certain quantity of corn or other commodity. Its value is in the necessities of the animal man. It is so much warmth, so much bread, so much water, so much land. The law may do what it will with the owner of property; its just power will still attach to the cent. The law may in a mad freak say that all shall have power except the owners of property; they shall have no vote. Nevertheless, by a higher law, the property will, year after year, write every statute that respects property. The non-proprietor will be the scribe of the proprietor. What the owners wish to do, the whole power of property will do, either through the law or else in defiance of it. Of course I speak of all the property, not merely of the great estates. When the rich are outvoted, as frequently happens, it is the joint treasury of the poor which exceeds their accumulations. Every man owns something, if it is only a cow, or a wheelbarrow, or his arms, and so has that property to dispose of.

The same necessity which secures the rights of person and property against the malignity or folly of the magistrate, determines the form and methods of governing, which are proper to each nation and to its habit of thought, and nowise transferable to other states of society. In this country we are very vain of our political institutions, which are singular in this, that they sprung, within the memory of living men, from the character and conditions of the people, which they still express with sufficient fidelity—and we ostentatiously prefer them to any other in history. They are not better, but only fitter for us. We may be wise in asserting the advantage in modern times of the democratic form, but to other states of society, in which religion consecrated the monarchical, that and not this was expedient. Democracy is better for us, because the religious sentiment of the present time accords better with it. Born democrats, we are nowise qualified to judge of monarchy, which, to our fathers living in the monarchical idea, was also relatively right. But our institutions, though in coincidence with the spirit of the age, have not any exemption from the practical defects which have discredited other forms. Every actual State is corrupt. Good men must not obey the laws too well. What satire on government can equal the severity of censure conveyed in the word *politic,* which now for ages has signified *cunning,* intimating that the State is a trick?

The same benign necessity and the same practical abuse appear in the parties, into which each State divides itself, of opponents and defenders of the administration of the government. Parties are also founded on instincts, and have better guides to their own humble aims than the sagacity of their leaders. They have nothing perverse in their origin, but rudely mark some real and lasting relation. We might as wisely reprove the east wind or the frost, as a political party, whose members, for the most part, could give no account of their position, but stand for the defence of those interests in which they find themselves. Our quarrel with them begins when they quit this deep natural ground at the bidding of some leader, and obeying personal considerations, throw themselves into the maintenance and defence of points nowise belonging to their system. A party is perpetually corrupted by personality. Whilst we absolve the association from dishonesty, we cannot extend the same charity to their leaders. They reap the rewards of the docility and zeal of the masses which they direct. Ordinarily our parties are parties of circumstance, and not of principle; as the planting interest in conflict with the commercial; the party of capitalists and that of operatives: parties which are identical in their moral character, and which can easily change ground with each other in the support of many of their measures. Parties of principle, as, religious sects, or the party of free-trade, of universal suffrage, of abolition of slavery, of abolition of capital punishment—degenerate into personalities, or would inspire enthusiasm. The vice of our leading parties in this country (which may be cited as a fair specimen of these societies of opinion) is that they do not plant themselves on the deep and necessary grounds to which they are respectively entitled, but lash themselves to fury in the carrying of some local and momentary measure, nowise useful to the commonwealth. Of the two great parties which at this hour almost share the nation between them, I should say that one has the best cause, and the other contains the best men. The philosopher, the poet, or the religious man, will of course wish to cast his vote with the democrat, for free-trade, for wide suffrage, for the abolition of legal cruelties in the penal code, and for facilitating in every manner the access of the young and the poor to the sources of wealth and power. But he can rarely accept the persons whom the so-called popular party propose to him as representatives of these liberties. They have not at heart the ends which give to the name of democracy what hope and virtue are in it. The spirit of our American radicalism is destructive and aimless: it is not loving; it has no ulterior and divine ends, but is destructive only out of hatred and selfishness. On the other side, the conservative party, composed of the most moderate, able and cultivated part of the population, is timid, and merely defensive of property. It vindicates no right, it aspires to no real good, it brands no crime, it proposes no generous policy; it does not build, nor write, nor cherish the arts, nor foster religion, nor establish schools, nor encourage science, nor emancipate the slave, nor befriend the poor, or the Indian, or the immigrant. From neither party, when in power, has the world any benefit to expect in science, art, or humanity, at all commensurate with the resources of the nation.

I do not for these defects despair of our republic. We are not at the mercy of any waves of chance. In the strife of ferocious parties, human nature always finds itself cherished; as the children of the convicts at Botany Bay are found to have as healthy a moral sentiment as other children. Citizens of feudal states are alarmed at our democratic institutions lapsing into anarchy, and the older and more cautious among ourselves are learning from Europeans to look with some terror at our turbulent freedom. It is said that in our license of construing the Constitution, and in the despotism of public opinion, we have no anchor; and one foreign observer thinks he has found the safeguard in the sanctity of Marriage among us; and another thinks he has found it in our Calvinism. Fisher Ames expressed the popular security more wisely, when he compared a monarchy and a republic saying that a monarchy is a merchantman, which sails well, but will sometimes strike on a rock and go to the bottom; whilst a republic is a raft, which would never sink, but then your feet are always in water. No forms can have any dangerous importance whilst we are befriended by the laws of things. It makes no difference how many tons' weight of atmosphere presses on our heads, so long as the same pressure resists it within the lungs. Augment the mass a thousand-fold, it cannot begin to crush us, as long as reaction is equal to action. The fact of two poles, of two forces, centripetal and centrifugal, is universal,

and each force by its own activity develops the other. Wild liberty develops from conscience. Want of liberty, by strengthening law and decorum, stupefies conscience. "Lynch-law" prevails only where there is greater hardihood and self-subsistency in the leaders. A mob cannot be a permanency; everybody's interest requires that it should not exist, and only justice satisfies all.

We must trust infinitely to the beneficent necessity which shines through all laws. Human nature expresses itself in them as characteristically as in statues, or songs or railroads; and an abstract of the codes of nations would be a transcript of the common conscience. Governments have their origin in the moral identity of men. Reason for one is seen to be reason for another, and for every other. There is a middle measure which satisfies all parties, be they never so many or so resolute for their own. Every man finds a sanction for his simplest claims and deeds, in decisions of his own mind, which he calls Truth and Holiness. In these decisions all the citizens find a perfect agreement, and only in these; not in what is good to eat, good to wear, good use of time, or what amount of land or of public aid each is entitled to claim. This truth and justice men presently endeavor to make application of to the measuring of land, the apportionment of service, the protection of life and property. Their first endeavors no doubt, are very awkward. Yet absolute right is the first governor; or, every government is an impure theocracy. The idea after which each community is aiming to make and mend its law, is the will of the wise man. The wise man it cannot find in nature, and it makes awkward but earnest efforts to secure his government by contrivance; as by causing the entire people to give their voices on every measure; or by a double choice to get the representation of the whole; or by a selection of the best citizens; or to secure the advantages of efficiency and internal peace by confiding the government to one, who may himself select his agents. All forms of government symbolize an immortal government, common to all dynasties and independent of numbers, perfect where two men exist, perfect where there is only one man.

Every man's nature is a sufficient advertisement to him of the character of his fellows. My right and my wrong is their right and their wrong. Whilst I do what is fit for me, and abstain from what is unfit, my neighbor and I shall often agree in our means, and work together for a time to one end. But whenever I find my dominion over myself not sufficient for me, and undertake the direction of him also, I overstep the truth, and come into false relations to him. I may have so much more skill or strength than he that he cannot express adequately his sense of wrong, but it is a lie, and hurts like a lie both him and me. Love and nature cannot maintain the assumption; it must be executed by a practical lie, namely by force. This undertaking for another is the blunder which stands in colossal ugliness in the governments of the world. It is the same thing in numbers, as in a pair, only not quite so intelligible. I can see well enough a great difference between my setting myself down to a self-control, and my going to make somebody else act after my views; but when a quarter of the human race assume to tell me what I must do, I may be too much disturbed by the circumstances to see so clearly the absurdity of their command. Therefore all public ends look vague and quixotic beside private ones. For any laws but those which men make for themselves are laughable. If I put myself in the place of my child, and we stand in one thought and see that things are thus or thus, that perception is law for him and me. We are both there, both act. But if, without carrying him into the thought, I look over into his plot, and, guessing how it is with

him, ordain this or that, he will never obey me. This is the history of governments—one man does something which is to bind another. A man who cannot be acquainted with me, taxes me; looking from afar at me ordains that a part of my labor shall go to this or that whimsical end—not as I, but as he happens to fancy. Behold the consequence. Of all debts men are least willing to pay the taxes. What a satire is this on government! Everywhere they think they get their money's worth, except for these.

Hence the less government we have the better—the fewer laws, and the less confided power. The antidote to this abuse of formal government is the influence of private character, the growth of the Individual; the appearance of the principal to supersede the proxy; the appearance of the wise man; of whom the existing government is, it must be owned, but a shabby imitation. That which all things tend to educe; which freedom, cultivation, intercourse, revolutions, go to form and deliver, is character; that is the end of Nature, to reach unto this coronation of her king. To educate the wise man the State exists, and with the appearance of the wise man the State expires. The appearance of character makes the State unnecessary. The wise man is the State. He needs no army, fort, or navy—he loves men too well; no bribe, or feast, or palace, to draw friends to him; no vantage ground, no favorable circumstance. He needs no library, for he has not done thinking; no church, for he is a prophet; no statute-book, for he has the lawgiver; no money, for he is value; no road, for he is at home where he is; no experience, for the life of the creator shoots through him, and looks from his eyes. He has no personal friends, for he who has the spell to draw the prayer and piety of all men unto him needs not husband and educate a few to share with him a select and poetic life. His relation to men is angelic; his memory is myrrh to them; his presence, frankincense and flowers.

We think our civilization near its meridian, but we are yet only at the cock-crowing and the morning star. In our barbarous society the influence of character is in its infancy. As a political power, as the rightful lord who is to tumble all rulers from their chairs, its presence is hardly yet suspected. Malthus and Ricardo quite omit it; the Annual Register is silent; in the Conversations' Lexicon it is not set down; the President's Message, the Queen's Speech, have not mentioned it; and yet it is never nothing. Every thought which genius and piety throw into the world, alters the world. The gladiators in the lists of power feel, through all their frocks of force and simulation, the presence of worth. I think the very strife of trade and ambition is confession of this divinity; and successes in those fields are the poor amends, the fig-leaf with which the shamed soul attempts to hide its nakedness. I find the like unwilling homage in all quarters. It is because we know how much is due from us that we are impatient to show some petty talent as a substitute for worth. We are haunted by a conscience of this right to grandeur of character, and are false to it. But each of us has some talent, can do somewhat useful, or graceful, or formidable, or amusing, or lucrative. That we do, as an apology to others and to ourselves for not reaching the mark of a good and equal life. But it does not satisfy *us,* whilst we thrust it on the notice of our companions. It may throw dust in their eyes, but does not smooth our own brow, or give us the tranquillity of the strong when we walk abroad. We do penance as we go. Our talent is a sort of expiation, and we are constrained to reflect on our splendid moment with a certain humiliation, as somewhat too fine, and not as one act of many acts, a fair expression of our permanent energy. Most persons of ability meet in society with a kind of tacit appeal.

Each seems to say, "I am not all here." Senators and presidents have climbed so high with pain enough, not because they think the place specially agreeable, but as an apology for real worth, and to vindicate their manhood in our eyes. This conspicuous chair is their compensation to themselves for being of a poor, cold, hard nature. They must do what they can. Like one class of forest animals, they have nothing but a prehensile tail; climb they must, or crawl. If a man found himself so rich-natured that he could enter into strict relations with the best persons and make life serene around him by the dignity and sweetness of his behavior, could he afford to circumvent the favor of the caucus and the press, and covet relations so hollow and pompous as those of a politician? Surely nobody would be a charlatan who could afford to be sincere.

The tendencies of the times favor the idea of self-government, and leave the individual, for all code, to the rewards and penalties of his own constitution; which work with more energy than we believe whilst we depend on artificial restraints. The movement in this direction has been very marked in modern history. Much has been blind and discreditable, but the nature of the revolution is not affected by the vices of the revolters; for this is a purely moral force. It was never adopted by any party in history, neither can be. It separates the individual from all party, and unites him at the same time to the race. It promises a recognition of higher rights than those of personal freedom, or the security of property. A man has a right to be employed, to be trusted, to be loved, to be revered. The power of love, as the basis of a State, has never been tried. We must not imagine that all things are lapsing into confusion if every tender protestant be not compelled to bear his part in certain social conventions; nor doubt that roads can be built, letters carried, and the fruit of labor secured, when the government of force is at an end. Are our methods now so excellent that all competition is hopeless? could not a nation of friends even devise better ways? On the other hand, let not the most conservative and timid fear anything from a premature surrender of the bayonet and the system of force. For, according to the order of nature, which is quite superior to our will, it stands thus; there will always be a government of force where men are selfish; and when they are pure enough to abjure the code of force they will be wise enough to see how these public ends of the post-office, of the highway, of commerce and the exchange of property, of museums and libraries, of institutions of art and science can be answered.

We live in a very low state of the world, and pay unwilling tribute to governments founded on force. There is not, among the most religious and instructed men of the most religious and civil nations, a reliance on the moral sentiment and a sufficient belief in the unity of things, to persuade them that society can be maintained without artificial restraints, as well as the solar system; or that the private citizen might be reasonable and a good neighbor, without the hint of a jail or a confiscation. What is strange too, there never was in any man sufficient faith in the power of rectitude to inspire him with the broad design of renovating the State on the Principle of right and love. All those who have pretended this design have been partial reformers, and have admitted in some manner the supremacy of the bad State. I do not call to mind a single human being who has steadily denied the authority of the laws, on the simple ground of his own moral nature. Such designs, full of genius and full of faith as they are, are not entertained except avowedly as air-pictures. If the individual who exhibits them dare to think them practicable, he disgusts scholars and churchmen; and men of talent and women of superior sentiments cannot hide their contempt. Not the less does nature continue to fill the heart of youth with suggestions of this enthusiasm, and there are now men—if indeed I can speak in the plural number—more exactly, I will say, I have just been conversing with one man, to whom no weight of adverse experience will make it for a moment appear impossible that thousands of human beings might exercise towards each other the grandest and simplest sentiments, as well as a knot of friends, or a pair of lovers.

Henry David Thoreau

"It is not of much importance to inquire of a man what actions he performed at one and what at another period of his life, as what manner of man he was at every period"—thus spoke Henry David Thoreau. A leader of the transcendentalist movement, together with Ralph Waldo Emerson, Thoreau represents perhaps the ultimate spokesman for the value of the individual and natural living in contrast with the materialism of society. He lambasted the repressive potential of the state in "Civil Disobedience" (1849). With his classic *Walden or, Life in the Woods* (1854), he became a forerunner of the ecology movement if not of the libertarians.

Born in Concord, Massachusetts, in 1817, Thoreau graduated from Harvard. He taught in public school in Concord for a few weeks before teaching for three years in a successful experimental private school with his brother. When his brother's sickness forced him to give up the private school, Thoreau wrote *A Week on the Concord and Merrimack Rivers* (1840), dedicated to his brother's memory. To write this book describing their joint excursion on the rivers and to overcome the necessity of earning a living to accomplish this task, Thoreau worked out a deal with his neighbor Ralph Waldo Emerson in 1845 for the use of his land and built a hut on Walden Pond. He did write the book he planned during the twenty-six months he lived on Walden Pond. Although that book was a commercial failure, the notes he took there for the only other book he wrote, *Walden,* were to make the pond and hut immortal (see excerpt).

In 1846 Thoreau was arrested for refusing to pay his poll tax (not a voting tax, but a head tax on all males between twenty and seventy). He was extremely upset when someone paid his tax and he was released after but one night in jail. He had hoped that his imprisonment would attract attention to his reason for protest, which, at the time, included advocacy of abolition. The government that sanctioned slavery had become the problem, as he saw it, and he wrote "Civil Disobedience" to spell out the higher moral law of the individual which, at times, makes it inevitable to engage in civil disobedience and to go to jail for what one believes. This essay was largely ignored until Mahatma Gandhi rediscovered its importance and was heavily influenced by it in his successful nonviolent protest movement leading to India's independence. Martin Luther King, Jr. was also impressed by this moral tract. The power of Thoreau's perspective continues to resurface. In the late 1960s, for example, U.S. Solicitor General E. N. Griswold and Undersecretary of State Eugene Rostow both found Thoreau dangerous enough to be worth attacking. But nevertheless the U.S. Post Office issued a Thoreau stamp in his honor in 1967. Thoreau died in 1862 at 45, but his political influence and haunting, modern prose live on in the American imagination and in the longing for natural self-sufficiency and ecological integrity.

ৡৡ

Walden or, Life in the Woods (1854)
(excerpt)

. . . Near the end of March, 1845, I borrowed an axe and went down to the woods by Walden Pond, nearest to where I intended to build my house, and began to cut down some tall arrowy white pines, still in their youth, for timber. It is difficult to begin without borrowing, but perhaps it is the most generous course thus to permit your fellow-men to have an interest in your enterprise. The owner of the axe, as he released his hold on it, said that it was the apple of his eye; but I returned it sharper than I received it. It was a pleasant hillside where I worked, covered with pine woods, through which I looked out on the pond, and a small open field in the woods where pines and hickories were springing up. The ice in the pond was not yet dissolved, though there were some open spaces, and it was all dark colored and saturated with water. There were some slight flurries of snow during the days that I worked there; but for the most part when I came out on to the railroad, on my way home, its yellow sand heap stretched away gleaming in the hazy atmosphere, and the rails shone in the spring sun, and I heard the lark and pewee and other birds already come to commence

---

another year with us. They were pleasant spring days, in which the winter of man's discontent was thawing as well as the earth, and the life that had lain torpid began to stretch itself. One day, when my axe had come off and I had cut a green hickory for a wedge, driving it with a stone, and had placed the whole to soak in a pond hole in order to swell the wood, I saw a striped snake run into the water, and he lay on the bottom, apparently without inconvenience, as long as I staid there, or more than a quarter of an hour; perhaps because he had not yet fairly come out of the torpid state. It appeared to me that for a like reason men remain in their present low and primitive condition; but if they should feel the influence of the spring of springs arousing them, they would of necessity rise to a higher and more ethereal life. I had previously seen the snakes in frosty mornings in my path with portions of their bodies still numb and inflexible, waiting for the sun to thaw them. On the 1st of April it rained and melted the ice, and the early part of the day, which was very foggy, I heard a stray goose groping about over the pond and cackling as if lost, or like the spirit of the fog.

So I went on for some days cutting and hewing timber, and also studs and rafters, all with my narrow axe, not having many communicable or scholar-like thoughts, singing to myself,—

> Men say they know many things;
> But lo! they have taken wings,—
> The arts and sciences,
> And a thousand appliances;
> The wind that blows
> Is all that any body knows.

I hewed the main timbers six inches square, most of the studs on two sides only, and the rafters and floor timbers on one side, leaving the rest of the bark on, so that they were just as straight and much stronger than sawed ones. Each stick was carefully mortised or tenoned by its stump, for I had borrowed other tools by this time. My days in the woods were not very long ones; yet I usually carried my dinner of bread and butter, and read the newspaper in which it was wrapped, at noon, sitting amid the green pine boughs which I had cut off, and to my bread was imparted some of their fragrance, for my hands were covered with a thick coat of pitch. Before I had done I was more the friend than the foe of the pine tree, though I had cut down some of them, having become better acquainted with it. Sometimes a rambler in the wood was attracted by the sound of my axe, and we chatted pleasantly over the chips which I had made.

By the middle of April, for I made no haste in my work, but rather made the most of it, my house was framed and ready for the raising. I had already bought the shanty of James Collins, an Irishman who worked on the Fitchburg Railroad, for boards. James Collins' shanty was considered an uncommonly fine one. When I called to see it he was not at home. I walked about the outside, at first unobserved from within, the window was so deep and high. It was of small dimensions, with a peaked cottage roof, and not much else to be seen, the dirt being raised five feet all around as if it were a compost heap. The roof was the soundest part, though a good deal warped and made brittle by the sun. Doorsill there was none, but a perennial passage for the hens under the door board. Mrs. C. came to the door and asked me to view it from the inside. The hens were driven in by my approach. It was dark, and had a dirt floor for the most part, dank, clammy, and aguish, only here a board and there a board which would not bear removal. She lighted a lamp to show me the inside of the roof and the walls, and also that the board floor extended under the bed, warning me not to step into the cellar, a sort of dust hole two feet deep. In her own words, they were "good boards overhead, good boards all around, and a good window,"—of two whole squares originally, only the cat had passed out that way lately. There was a stove, a bed, and a place to sit, an infant in the house where it was born, a silk parasol, gilt-framed looking-glass, and a patent new coffee mill nailed to an oak sapling, all told. The bargain was soon concluded, for James had in the meanwhile returned. I to pay four dollars and twenty-five cents tonight, he to vacate at five tomorrow morning, selling to nobody else meanwhile: I to take possession at six. It were well, he said, to be there early, and anticipate certain indistinct but wholly unjust claims on the score of ground rent and fuel. This he assured me was the only encumbrance. At six I passed him and his family on the road. One large bundle held their all,—bed, coffee-mill, looking-glass, hens,—all but the cat, she took to the woods and became a wild cat, and, as I learned afterward, trod in a trap set for woodchucks, and so became a dead cat at last.

I took down this dwelling the same morning, drawing the nails, and removed it to the pond side by small cart-loads, spreading the boards on the grass there to bleach and warp back again in the sun. One early thrush gave me a note or two as I drove along the woodland path. I was informed treacherously by a young Patrick that neighbor Seeley, an Irishman, in the interval of the carting, transferred the still tolerable, straight, and drivable nails, staples, and spikes to his pocket, and then stood when I came back to pass the time of day, and look freshly up, unconcerned, with spring thoughts, at the devastation; there being a dearth of work, as he said. He was there to represent spectatordom, and help make this seemingly insignificant event one with the removal of the gods of Troy.

I dug my cellar in the side of a hill sloping to the south, where a woodchuck had formerly dug his burrow, down through sumach and blackberry roots, and the lowest stain of vegetation, six feet square by seven deep, to a fine sand where potatoes would not freeze in any winter. The sides were left shelving, and not stoned; but the sun having never shone on them, the sand still keeps its place. It was but two hours' work. I took particular pleasure in this breaking of ground, for in almost all latitudes men dig into the earth for an equable temperature. Under the most splendid house in the city is still to be found the cellar where they store their roots as of old, and long after the superstructure has disappeared posterity remark its dent in the earth. The house is still but a sort of porch at the entrance of a burrow.

At length, in the beginning of May, with the help of some of my acquaintances, rather to improve so good an occasion for neighborliness than from any necessity, I set up the frame of my house. No man was ever more honored in the character of his raisers than I. They are destined, I trust, to assist at the raising of loftier structures one day. I began to occupy my house on the 4th of July, as soon as it was boarded and roofed, for the boards were carefully feather-edged and lapped, so that it was perfectly impervious to rain; but before boarding I laid the foundation of a chimney at one end, bringing two cartloads of stones up the hill from the pond in my arms. I built the chimney after my hoeing in the fall, before a fire became necessary for warmth, doing my cooking in the mean while out of doors on the ground, early in the morning: which mode I still think is in some respects more convenient and agreeable than the usual one. When it stormed before my bread was baked, I fixed a few boards over the fire, and sat under them to watch my loaf, and passed some pleasant hours in that way. In those days, when my hands were much employed, I read but little, but the least scraps of paper which lay on the ground, my holder, or tablecloth, afforded me as much entertainment, in fact answered the same purpose as the Iliad.

It would be worth the while to build still more deliberately than I did, considering, for instance, what foundation a door, a window, a cellar, a garret, have in the nature of man, and perchance never raising any superstructure until we found a better reason for it than our temporal necessities even. There is some of the same fitness in a man's building his own house that there is in a bird's building its own nest. Who knows but if men constructed their dwelling with their own hands, and provided food for themselves and families simply and honestly enough, the poetic faculty would be universally developed, as birds universally sing when they are so engaged? But alas! we do like cowbirds and cuckoos, which lay their eggs in nests which other birds have built, and cheer no traveller with their chattering and unmusical notes. Shall we forever resign the pleasure of construction to the carpenter? What does architecture amount to in the experience of the mass of men? I never in all my walks came across a man engaged in so simple and natural an occupation as building his house. We belong to the community. It is not the tailor alone who is the ninth part of a man, it is as much the preacher, and the merchant, and the farmer. Where is this division of labor to end? and what object does it finally serve? No doubt another *may* also think for me; but it is not therefore desirable that he should do so to the exclusion of my thinking for myself.

True, there are architects so called in this country, and I have heard of one at least possessed with the idea of making architectural ornaments have a core of truth, a necessity, and hence a beauty, as if it were a revelation to him. All very well perhaps from his point of view, but only a little better than the common dilettantism.

A sentimental reformer in architecture, he began at the cornice, not at the foundation. It was only how to put a core of truth within the ornaments, that every sugar plum in fact might have an almond or caraway seed in it,—though I hold that almonds are most wholesome without the sugar,—and not how the inhabitant, the indweller, might build truly within and without, and let the ornaments take care of themselves. What reasonable man ever supposed that ornaments were something outward and in the skin merely,—that the tortoise got his spotted shell, or the shellfish its mother-o'-pearl tints by such a contract as the inhabitants of Broadway their Trinity Church? But a man has no more to do with the style of architecture of his house than a tortoise with that of its shell: nor need the soldier be so idle as to try to paint the precise *color* of his virtue on his standard. The enemy will find it out. He may turn pale when the trial comes. This man seemed to me to lean over the cornice, and timidly whisper his half truth to the rude occupants who really knew it better than he. What of architectural beauty I now see, I know has gradually grown from within outward, out of the necessities and character of the indweller, who is the only builder,—out of some unconscious truthfulness, and nobleness, without ever a thought for the appearance; and whatever additional beauty of this kind is destined to be produced will be preceded by a like unconscious beauty of life. The most interesting dwellings in this country, as the painter knows, are the most unpretending, humble log huts and cottages of the poor commonly; it is the life of the inhabitants whose shells they are, and not any peculiarity in their surfaces merely, which makes them *picturesque;* and equally interesting will be the citizen's suburban box, when his life shall be as simple and as agreeable to the imagination, and there is as little straining after effect in the style of his dwelling. A great proportion of architectural ornaments are literally hollow, and a September gale would strip them off, like borrowed plumes, without injury to the substantials. They can do without *architecture* who have no olives nor wines in the cellar. What if an equal ado were made about the ornaments of style in literature, and the architects of our bibles spent as much time about their cornices as the architects of our churches do? So are made the *belles-lettres* and the *beaux-arts* and their professors. Much it concerns a man, forsooth, how a few sticks are slanted over him or under him and what colors are daubed upon his box. It would signify somewhat, if, in any earnest sense, *he* slanted them and daubed it; but the spirit having departed out of the tenant, it is of a piece with constructing his own coffin,—the architecture of the grave, and "carpenter," is but another name for "coffin-maker." One man says, in his despair or indifference to life, take up a handful of the earth at your feet, and paint your house that color. Is he thinking of his last and narrow house? Toss up a copper for it as well. What an abundance of leisure he must have! Why

do you take up a handful of dirt? Better paint your house your own complexion; let it turn pale or blush for you. An enterprise to improve the style of cottage architecture! When you have got my ornaments ready I will wear them.

Before winter I built a chimney, and shingled the sides of my house, which were already impervious to rain, with imperfect and sappy shingles made of the first slice of the log, whose edges I was obliged to straighten with a plane.

I have thus a tight shingled and plastered house, ten feet wide by fifteen long, and eight-feet posts, with a garret and a closet, a large window on each side, two trap doors, one door at the end, and a brick fireplace opposite. The exact cost of my house, paying the usual price for such materials as I used, but not counting the work, all of which was done by myself, was as follows; and I give the details because very few are able to tell exactly what their houses cost, and fewer still, if any, the separate cost of the various materials which compose them:—

Boards, ...	$8 03½,	mostly shanty boards.
Refuse shingles for roof and sides,	4 00	
Laths, ...	1 25	
Two second-hand windows with		
glass, ...	2 43	
One thousand old brick, ...	4 00	
Two casks of lime, ...	2 40	That was high.
Hair, ...	0 31	More than I needed.
Mantle-tree iron, ...	0 15	
Nails, ...	3 90	
Hinges and screws, ...	0 14	
Latch, ...	0 10	
Chalk, ...	0 01	
Transportation, ...	1 40	I carried a good part on my back.
In all, ...	$28 12½	

These are all the materials excepting the timber, stones and sand, which I claimed by squatter's right. I have also a small wood-shed adjoining, made chiefly of the stuff which was left after building the house.

I intend to build me a house which will surpass any on the main street in Concord in grandeur and luxury, as soon as it pleases me as much and will cost me no more than my present one.

I thus found that the student who wishes for a shelter can obtain one for a lifetime at an expense not greater than the rent which he now pays annually. If I seem to boast more than is becoming, my excuse is that I brag for humanity rather than for myself; and my shortcomings and inconsistencies do not affect the truth of my statement. Notwithstanding much cant and hypocrisy,—chaff which I find it difficult to separate from my wheat, but for which I am as sorry as any man,—I will breathe freely and stretch myself in this respect, it is such a relief to both the moral and physical system; and I am resolved that I will not through humility become the devil's attorney. I will endeavor to speak a good word for the truth. At Cambridge College the mere rent of a student's room, which is only a little larger than my own, is thirty dollars each year, though the corporation had the advantage of building thirty-two side by side and under one roof, and the occupant suffers the inconvenience of many and noisy neighbors, and perhaps a residence in the fourth story. I cannot but think that if we had more true wisdom in these respects, not only less education would be needed, because, forsooth, more would already have been acquired, but the pecuniary expense of getting an education would in a great measure vanish. Those conveniences which the student requires at Cambridge or elsewhere cost him or somebody else ten times as great a sacrifice of life as they would with proper management

on both sides. Those things for which the most money is demanded are never the things which the student most wants. Tuition, for instance, is an important item in the term bill, while for the far more valuable education which he gets by associating with the most cultivated of his contemporaries no charge is made. The mode of founding a college is, commonly, to get up a subscription of dollars and cents, and then following blindly the principles of a division of labor to its extreme, a principle which should never be followed but with circumspection,—to call in a contractor who makes this a subject of speculation, and he employs Irishmen or other operatives actually to lay the foundation, while the students that are to be are said to be fitting themselves for it; and for these oversights successive generations have to pay. I think that it would be *better than this,* for the students, or those who desire to be benefited by it, even to lay the foundation themselves. The student who secures his coveted leisure and retirement by systematically shirking any labor necessary to man obtains but an ignoble and unprofitable leisure, defrauding himself of the experience which alone can make leisure fruitful. "But," says one, "you do not mean that the students should go to work with their hands instead of their heads?" I do not mean that exactly, but I mean something which he might think a good deal like that; I mean that they should not *play* life, or *study* it merely, while the community supports them at this expensive game, but earnestly *live* it from beginning to end. How could youths better learn to live than by at once trying the experiment of living? Methinks this would exercise their minds as much as mathematics. If I wished a boy to know something about the arts and sciences, for instance, I would not pursue the common course, which is merely to send him into the neighborhood of some professor, where any thing is professed and practised but the art of life;—to survey the world through a telescope or a microscope, and never with his natural eye; to study chemistry, and not learn how his bread is made, or mechanics, and not learn how it is earned; to discover new satellites to Neptune, and not detect the motes in his eyes, or to what vagabond he is a satellite himself; or to be devoured by the monsters that swarm all around him, while contemplating the monsters in a drop of vinegar. Which would have advanced the most at the end of a month,—the boy who had made his own jackknife from the ore which he had dug and smelted, reading as much as would be necessary for this,— or the boy who had attended the lectures on metallurgy at the Institute in the mean while, and had received a Rogers' penknife from his father? Which would be most likely to cut his fingers? ... To my astonishment I was informed on leaving college that I had studied navigation!— why, if I had taken one turn down the harbor I should have known more about it. Even the *poor* student studies and is taught only *political* economy, while that economy of living which is synonymous with philosophy is not even sincerely professed in our colleges. The consequence is, that while he is reading Adam Smith, Ricardo, and Say, he runs his father in debt irretrievably. . . .

Civil Disobedience (1849)

I heartily accept the motto,—"That government is best which governs least"; and I should like to see it acted up to more rapidly and systematically. Carried out, it finally amounts to this, which also I believe,— "That government is best which governs not at all"; and when men are prepared for it, that will be the kind of government which they will have. Government is at best but an expedient; but most governments are usually, and all governments are sometimes, inexpedient. The objections which have been brought against a standing army, and they are many and weighty, and deserve to prevail, may also at last be brought against a standing government. The standing army is only an arm of the standing government. The government itself, which is only the mode which the people have chosen to execute their will, is equally liable to be abused and perverted before the people can act through it. Witness the present Mexican war, the work of comparatively a few individuals using the standing government as their tool; for, in the outset, the people would not have consented to this measure.

This American government,—what is it but a tradition, though a recent one, endeavoring to transmit itself unimpaired to posterity, but each instant losing some of its integrity? It has not the vitality and force of a single living man; for a single man can bend it to his will. It is a sort of wooden gun to the people themselves. But it is not the less necessary for this; for the people must have some complicated machinery or other, and hear its din, to satisfy that idea of government which they have. Governments show thus how successfully men can be imposed on, even impose on themselves, for their own advantage. It is excellent, we must all allow. Yet this government never of itself furthered any enterprise, but by the alacrity with which it got out of its way. *It* does not keep the country free. *It* does not settle the West. *It* does not educate. The character inherent in the American people has done all that has been accomplished; and it would have done somewhat more, if the government had not sometimes got in its way. For government is an expedient by which men would fain succeed in letting one another alone; and, as has been said, when it is most expedient, the governed are most let alone by it. Trade and commerce, if they were not made of India-rubber, would never manage to bounce over the obstacles which legislators are continually putting in their way; and, if one were to judge these men wholly by the effects of their actions and not partly by their intentions, they would deserve to be classed and punished with those mischievous persons who put obstructions on the railroads.

But, to speak practically and as a citizen, unlike those who call themselves no-government men, I ask for, not at once no government, but *at once* a better government. Let every man make known what kind of government would command his respect, and that will be one step toward obtaining it.

After all, the practical reason why, when the power is once in the hands of the people, a majority are permitted, and for a long period continue, to rule, is not because they are most likely to be in the right, nor because this seems fairest to the minority, but because they are physically the strongest. But a government in which the majority rule in all cases cannot be based on justice, even as far as men understand it. Can there not be a government in which majorities do not virtually decide right and wrong, but conscience?—in which majorities decide only those questions to which the rule of expediency is applicable? Must the citizen ever for a moment, or in the least degree, design his conscience to the legislator? Why has every man a conscience, then? I think that we should be men first, and subjects afterward. It is not desirable to cultivate a respect for the law, so much as for the right. The only obligation which I have a right to assume, is to do at any time what I think right. It is truly enough said, that a corporation has no conscience; but a corporation of conscientious men is a corporation *with* a conscience. Law never made men a whit more just; and, by means of their respect for it, even the well-disposed are daily made the agents of injustice. A common and natural result of an undue respect for law is, that you may see a file of soldiers, colonel, captain, corporal, privates, powder-monkeys, and all, marching in admirable order over hill and dale to the wars, against their wills, ay, against their common sense and consciences, which makes it very steep marching indeed, and produces a palpitation of the heart. They have no doubt that it is a damnable business in which they are concerned; they are all peaceably inclined. Now, what are they? Men at all? or small movable forts and magazines, at the service of some unscrupulous man in power? Visit the Navy-Yard, and behold a marine, such man as an American government can make, or such as it can make a man with its black arts,—a mere shadow and reminiscence of humanity, a man laid out alive and standing, and already, as one may say, buried under arms with funeral accompaniments, though it may be,—

> "Not a drum was heard, not a funeral note,
>   As his corse to the rampart we hurried;
> Not a soldier discharged his farewell shot
>   O'er the grave where our hero we buried."

The mass of men serve the state thus, not as men mainly, but as machines, with their bodies. They are the standing army, and the militia, jailers, constables, posse comitatus, &c. In most cases there is no free exercise whatever of the judgment or of the moral sense; but they put themselves on a level with wood and earth and stones; and wooden men can perhaps be manufactured that will serve the purpose as well. Such command no more respect than men of straw or a lump of dirt. They have the same sort of worth only as horses and dogs. Yet such as these even are commonly esteemed good citizens. Others,—as most legislators, politicians, lawyers, ministers, and office-holders,—serve the state chiefly with their heads; and, as they rarely make any moral distinctions, they are as likely to serve the Devil, without *intending* it, as God. A very few, as heroes, patriots, martyrs, reformers in the great sense, and *men,* serve the state with their consciences also, and so necessarily resist it for the most part; and they are commonly treated as enemies by it. A wise man will only be useful as a man, and will not submit to be "clay," and "stop a hole to keep the wind away," but leave that office to his dust at least:—

> "I am too high-born to be propertied,
> To be a secondary at control,
> Or useful serving-man and instrument
> To any sovereign state throughout the world."

He who gives himself entirely to his fellow-men appears to them useless and selfish; but he who gives himself partially to them is pronounced a benefactor and philanthropist.

How does it become a man to behave toward this American government to-day? I answer, that he cannot without disgrace be associated with it. I cannot for an instant recognize that political organization as *my* government which is the *slave's* government also.

All men recognize the right of revolution; that is, the right to refuse allegiance to, and to resist, the government, when its tyranny or its inefficiency are great and unendurable. But almost all say that such

is not the case now. But such was the case, they think in the Revolution of '75. If one were to tell me that this was a bad government because it taxed certain foreign commodities brought to its ports, it is most probable that I should not make an ado about it, for I can do without them. All machines have their friction; and possibly this does enough good to counterbalance the evil. At any rate, it is a great evil to make a stir about it. But when the friction comes to have its machine, and oppression and robbery are organized, I say, let us not have such a machine any longer. In other words, when a sixth of the population of a nation which has undertaken to be the refuge of liberty are slaves, and a whole country is unjustly overrun and conquered by a foreign army, and subjected to military law, I think that it is not too soon for honest men to rebel and revolutionize. What makes this duty the more urgent is the fact, that the country so overrun is not our own, but ours is the invading army.

Paley, a common authority with many on moral questions, in his chapter on the "Duty of Submission to Civil Government," resolves all civil obligation into expediency; and he proceeds to say, "that so long as the interest of the whole society requires it, that is, so long as the established government cannot be resisted or changed without public inconveniency, it is the will of God that the established government be obeyed, and no longer. . . . This principle being admitted, the justice of every particular case of resistance is reduced to a computation of the quantity of the danger and grievance on the one side, and of the probability and expense of redressing it on the other." Of this, he says, every man shall judge for himself. But Paley appears never to have contemplated those cases to which the rule of expediency does not apply, in which a people, as well as an individual, must do justice, cost what it may. If I have unjustly wrested a plank from a drowning man, I must restore it to him though I drown myself. This, according to Paley, would be inconvenient. But he that would save his life, in such a case, shall lose it. This people must cease to hold slaves, and to make war on Mexico, though it cost them their existence as a people.

In their practice, nations agree with Paley; but does any one think that Massachusetts does exactly what is right at the present crisis?

> "A drab of state, a cloth-o'-silver
>   slut,
> To have her train borne up, and her
>   soul trail in the dirt."

Practically speaking, the opponents to a reform in Massachusetts are not a hundred thousand politicians at the South, but a hundred thousand merchants and farmers here, who are more interested in commerce and agriculture than they are in humanity, and are not prepared to do justice to the slave and to Mexico, *cost what it may*. I quarrel not with far-off foes, but with those who, near at home, co-operate with, and do the bidding of, those far away, and without whom the latter would be harmless. We are accustomed to say, that the mass of men are unprepared; but improvement is slow, because the few are not materially wiser or better than the many. It is not so important that many should be as good as you, as that there be some absolute goodness somewhere; for that will leaven the whole lump. There are thousands who are *in opinion* opposed to slavery and to the war, who yet in effect do nothing to put an end to them; who, esteeming themselves children of Washington and Franklin, sit down with their hands in their pockets, and say that they know not what to do, and do nothing; who even postpone the question of freedom to the question of free-trade, and quietly read the prices-current along with the latest advices from Mexico, after dinner, and, it may, fall asleep over them

both. What is the price-current of an honest man and patriot to-day? They hesitate and they regret, and sometimes they petition; but they do nothing in earnest and with effect. They will wait, well disposed, for others to remedy the evil, that they may no longer have it to regret. At most, they give only a cheap vote, and a feeble countenance and God-speed, to the right, as it goes by them. There are nine hundred and ninety-nine patrons of virtue to one virtuous man. But it is easier to deal with the real possessor of a thing than with the temporary guardian of it.

All voting is a sort of gaming, like checkers or backgammon, with a slight moral tinge to it, a playing with right and wrong, with moral questions; and betting naturally accompanies it. The character of the voters is not staked. I cast my vote, perchance, as I think right; but I am not vitally concerned that that right should prevail. I am willing to leave it to the majority. Its obligation, therefore, never exceeds that of expediency. Even voting *for the right* is *doing* nothing for it. It is only expressing to men feebly your desire that it should prevail. A wise man will not leave the right to the mercy of chance, nor wish it to prevail through the power of the majority. There is but little virtue in the action of masses of men. When the majority shall at length vote for the abolition of slavery, it will be because they are indifferent to slavery, or because there is but little slavery left to be abolished by their vote. *They* will then be the only slaves. Only *his* vote can hasten the abolition of slavery who asserts his own freedom by his vote.

I hear of a convention to be held at Baltimore, or elsewhere, for the selection of a candidate for the Presidency, made up chiefly of editors, and men who are politicians by profession; but I think, what is it to any independent, intelligent, and respectable man what decision they may come to? Shall we not have the advantage of his wisdom and honesty nevertheless? Can we not count upon some independent votes? Are there not many individuals in the country who do not attend conventions? But no: I find that the respectable man, so called, has immediately drifted from his position, and despairs of his country, when his country has more reason to despair of him. He forthwith adopts one of the candidates thus selected as the only *available* one, thus proving that he is himself *available* for any purposes of the demagogue. His vote is of no more worth than that of any unprincipled foreigner or hireling native, who may have been bought. O for a man who is a *man,* and, as my neighbor says, has a bone in his back which you cannot pass your hand through! Our statistics are at fault: the population has been returned too large. How many *men* are there to a square thousand miles in this country? Hardly one. Does not America offer any inducement for men to settle here? The American has dwindled into an Odd Fellow,—one who may be known by the development of his organ of gregariousness, and a manifest lack of intellect and cheerful self-reliance; whose first and chief concern, on coming into the world, is to see that the Almshouses are in good repair; and, before yet he has lawfully donned the virile garb, to collect a fund for the support of the widows and orphans that may be; who, in short, ventures to live only by the aid of the Mutual Insurance Company, which has promised to bury him decently.

It is not a man's duty, as a matter of course, to devote himself to the eradication of any, even the most enormous wrong; he may still properly have other concerns to engage him; but it is his duty, at least, to wash his hands of it, and, if he gives it no thought longer, not to give it practically his support. If I devote myself to other pursuits and contemplations, I must first see, at least, that I do not pursue them sitting upon another man's shoulders. I

must get off him first, that he may pursue his contemplations too. See what gross inconsistency is tolerated. I have heard some of my townsmen say, "I should like to have them order me out to help put down an insurrection of the slaves, or to march to Mexico;—see if I would go"; and yet these very men have each, directly by their allegiance, and so indirectly, at least, by their money, furnished a substitute. The soldier is applauded who refuses to serve in an unjust war by those who do not refuse to sustain the unjust government which makes the war; is applauded by those whose own act and authority he disregards and sets at naught; as if the State were penitent to that degree that it hired one to scourge it while it sinned, but not to that degree that it left off sinning for a moment. Thus, under the name of Order and Civil Government, we are all made at last to pay homage to and support our own meanness. After the first blush of sin comes its indifference; and from immoral it becomes, as it were, *un*moral, and not quite unnecessary to that life which we have made.

The broadest and most prevalent error requires the most disinterested virtue to sustain it. The slight reproach to which the virtue of patriotism is commonly liable, the noble are most likely to incur. Those who, while they disapprove of the character and measures of a government, yield to it their allegiance and support, are undoubtedly its most conscientious supporters, and so frequently the most serious obstacles to reform. Some are petitioning the State to dissolve the Union, to disregard the requisitions of the President. Why do they not dissolve it themselves,—the union between themselves and the State,—and refuse to pay their quota into its treasury? Do not they stand in the same relation to the State, that the State does to the Union? And have not the same reasons prevented the State from resisting the Union, which have prevented them from resisting the State?

How can a man be satisfied to entertain an opinion merely, and enjoy *it?* Is there any enjoyment in it, if his opinion is that he is aggrieved? If you are cheated out of a single dollar by your neighbor, you do not rest satisfied with knowing that you are cheated, or with saying that you are cheated, or even with petitioning him to pay you your due; but you take effectual steps at once to obtain the full amount, and see that you are never cheated again. Action from principle, the perception and the performance of right, changes things and relations; it is essentially revolutionary, and does not consist wholly with anything which was. It not only divides states and churches, it divides families; ay, it divides the *individual,* separating the diabolical in him from the divine.

Unjust laws exist: shall we be content to obey them, or shall we endeavor to amend them, and obey them until we have succeeded, or shall we transgress them at once? Men generally, under such a government as this, think that they ought to wait until they have persuaded the majority to alter them. They think that, if they should resist, the remedy would be worse than the evil. But it is the fault of the government itself that the remedy *is* worse than the evil. *It* makes it worse. Why is it not more apt to anticipate and provide for reform? Why does it not cherish its wise minority? Why does it cry and resist before it is hurt? Why does it not encourage its citizens to be on the alert to point out its faults, and *do* better than it would have them? Why does it always crucify Christ, and excommunicate Copernicus and Luther, and pronounce Washington and Franklin rebels?

One would think, that a deliberate and practical denial of its authority was the only offence never contemplated by government; else, why has it not assigned its definite, its suitable and proportionate penalty? If a man who has no property refuses but once to earn nine shillings for the State, he is put in prison for a period unlimited by any law that I know, and determined only by the discretion of those who placed him there; but if he should steal ninety times nine shillings from the State, he is soon permitted to go at large again.

If the injustice is part of the necessary friction of the machine of government, let it go, let it go: perchance it will wear smooth,—certainly the machine will wear out. If the injustice has a spring, or a pulley, or a rope, or a crank, exclusively for itself, then perhaps you may consider whether the remedy will not be worse than the evil; but if it is of such a nature that it requires you to be the agent of injustice to another, then, I say, break the law. Let your life be a counter friction to stop the machine. What I have to do is to see, at any rate, that I do not lend myself to the wrong which I condemn.

As for adopting the ways which the State has provided for remedying the evil, I know not of such ways. They take too much time, and a man's life will be gone. I have other affairs to attend to. I came into this world, not chiefly to make this a good place to live in, but to live in it, be it good or bad. A man has not everything to do, but something; and because he cannot do *everything,* it is not necessary that he should do *something* wrong. It is not my business to be petitioning the Governor or the Legislature any more than it is theirs to petition me; and, if they should not hear my petition, what should I do then? But in this case the State has provided no way: its very Constitution is the evil. This may seen to be harsh and stubborn and unconciliatory; but it is to treat with the utmost kindness and consideration the only spirit that can appreciate or deserves it. So is all change for the better, like birth and death, which convulse the body.

I do not hesitate to say, that those who call themselves Abolitionists should at once effectually withdraw their support, both in person and property, from the government of Massachusetts, and not wait till they constitute a majority of one, before they suffer the right to prevail through them. I think that it is enough if they have God on their side, without waiting for that other one. Moreover, any man more right than his neighbors constitutes a majority of one already.

I meet this American government, or its representative, the State government, directly, and face to face, once a year—no more—in the person of its tax-gatherer; this is the only mode in which a man situated as I am necessarily meets it; and it then says distinctly, Recognize me; and the simplest, the most effectual, and, in the present posture of affairs, the indispensablest mode of treating with it on this head, of expressing your little satisfaction with and love for it, is to deny it then. My civil neighbor, the tax-gatherer, is the very man I have to deal with,—for it is, after all, with men and not with parchment that I quarrel,—and he has voluntarily chosen to be an agent of the government. How shall he ever know well what he is and does as an officer of the government, or as a man, until he is obliged to consider whether he shall treat me, his neighbor, for whom he has respect, as a neighbor and well-disposed man, or a maniac and disturber of the peace, and see if he can get over this obstruction to his neighborliness without a ruder and more impetuous thought or speech corresponding with his action. I know this well, that if one thousand, if one hundred, if ten men whom I could name,— if ten *honest* men only,—ay, if *one* HONEST man, in this State of Massachusetts, *ceasing to hold slaves,* were actually to withdraw from this copartnership, and be locked up in the county jail therefor, it would be the abolition of slavery in America. For it matters not how small the beginning may seem to be: what is once well done is done forever. But we love

better to talk about it: that we say is our mission. Reform keeps many scores of newspapers in its service, but not one man. If my esteemed neighbor, the State's ambassador, who will devote his days to the settlement of the question of human rights in the Council Chamber, instead of being threatened with the prisons of Carolina, were to sit down the prisoner of Massachusetts, that State which is so anxious to foist the sin of slavery upon her sister,— though at present she can discover only an act of inhospitality to be the ground of a quarrel with her,—the Legislature would not wholly waive the subject the following winter.

Under a government which imprisons any unjustly, the true place for a just man is also a prison. The proper place to-day, the only place which Massachusetts has provided for her freer and less desponding spirits, is in her prisons, to be put out and looked out of the State by her own act, as they have already put themselves out by their principles. It is there that the fugitive slave, and the Mexican prisoner on parole, and the Indian come to plead the wrongs of his race, should find them; on that separate, but more free and honorable ground, where the State places those who are not *with* her, but *against* her,—the only house in a slave State in which a free man can abide with honor. If any think that their influence would be lost there, and their voices no longer afflict the ear of the State, that they would not be as an enemy within its walls, they do not know by how much truth is stronger than error, nor how much more eloquently and effectively he can combat injustice who has experienced a little in his own person. Cast your whole vote, not a strip of paper merely, but your whole influence. A minority is powerless while it conforms to the majority; it is not even a minority then; but it is irresistible when it clogs by its whole weight. If the alternative is to keep all just men in prison, or give up war and slavery, the State will not hesitate which to choose. If a thousand men were not to pay their tax-bills this year that would not be a violent and bloody measure, as it would be to pay them, and enable the State to commit violence and shed innocent blood. This is, in fact, the definition of a peaceable revolution, if any such is possible. If the tax-gatherer, or any other public officer, asks me, as one has done, "But what shall I do?" my answer is, "If you really wish to do anything, resign your office." When the subject has refused allegiance, and the officer has resigned his office, then the revolution is accomplished. But even suppose blood should flow. Is there not a sort of blood shed when the conscience is wounded? Through this wound a man's real manhood and immortality flow out, and he bleeds to an everlasting death. I see this blood flowing now.

I have contemplated the imprisonment of the offender, rather than the seizure of his goods,—though both will serve the same purpose,—because they who assert the purest right, and consequently are most dangerous to a corrupt State, commonly have not spent much time in accumulating property. To such the State renders comparatively small service, and a slight tax is wont to appear exorbitant, particularly if they are obliged to earn it by special labor with their hands. If there were one who lived wholly without the use of money, the State itself would hesitate to demand it of him. But the rich man,—not to make any invidious comparison,—is always sold to the institution which makes him rich. Absolutely speaking, the more money, the less virtue; for money comes between a man and his objects, and obtains them for him; and it was certainly no great virtue to obtain it. It puts to rest many questions which he would otherwise be taxed to answer; while the only new question which it puts is the hard but superfluous one, how to spend it. Thus his moral ground is taken from under

his feet. The opportunities of living are diminished in proportion as what are called the "means" are increased. The best thing a man can do for his culture when he is rich is to endeavor to carry out those schemes which he entertained when he was poor. Christ answered the Herodians according to their condition. "Show me the tribute-money," said he;—and one took a penny out of his pocket;—if you use money which has the image of Caesar on it, and which he has made current and valuable, that is, *if you are men of the State,* and gladly enjoy the advantages of Caesar's government, then pay him back some of his own when he demands it; "Render therefore to Caesar that which is Caesar's, and to God those things which are God's,"—leaving them no wiser than before as to which was which; for they did not wish to know.

When I converse with the freest of my neighbors, I perceive that, whatever they may say about the magnitude and seriousness of the question, and their regard for the public tranquillity, the long and the short of the matter is, that they cannot spare the protection of the existing government, and they dread the consequences to their property and families of disobedience to it. For my own part, I should not like to think that I ever rely on the protection of the State. But, if I deny the authority of the State when it presents its tax-bill, it will soon take and waste all my property, and so harass me and my children without end. This is hard. This makes it impossible for a man to live honestly, and at the same time comfortably, in outward respects. It will not be worth the while to accumulate property; that would be sure to go again. You must hire or squat somewhere, and raise but a small crop, and eat that soon. You must live within yourself, and depend upon yourself always tucked up and ready for a start and not have many affairs. A man may grow rich in Turkey even, if he will be in all respects a good subject of the

Turkish government. Confucius said: "If a state is governed by the principles of reason, poverty and misery are subjects of shame; if a state is not governed by the principles of reason, riches and honors are the subjects of shame." No; until I want the protection of Massachusetts to be extended to me in some distant Southern port, where my liberty is endangered, or until I am bent solely on building up an estate at home by peaceful enterprise. I can afford to refuse allegiance to Massachusetts, and her right to my property and life. It costs me less in every sense to incur the penalty of disobedience to the State, than it would to obey. I should feel as if I were worth less in that case.

Some years ago, the State met me in behalf of the Church, and commanded me to pay a certain sum toward the support of a clergyman whose preaching my father attended, but never I myself. "Pay," it said, "or be locked up in the jail." I declined to pay. But, unfortunately, another man saw fit to pay it. I did not see why the schoolmaster should be taxed to support the priest, and not the priest the schoolmaster; for I was not the State's schoolmaster, but I supported myself by voluntary subscription. I did not see why the lyceum should not present its tax-bill, and have the State to back its demand, as well as the Church. However, at the request of the selectmen, I condescended to make some such statement as this in writing:—"Know all men by these presents, that I, Henry Thoreau,— do not wish to be regarded as a member of any incorporated society which I have not joined." This I gave to the town clerk; and he has it. The State, having thus learned that I did not wish to be regarded as a member of that church, has never made a like demand on me since; though it said that it must adhere to its original presumption that time. If I had known how to name them, I should then have signed off in detail from all the societies which I never signed on to; but I did not know where to find a complete list.

I have paid no poll-tax for six years. I was put into a jail once on this account, for one night; and, as I stood considering the walls of solid stone, two or three feet thick, the door of wood and iron, a foot thick, and the iron grating which strained the light, I could not help being struck with the foolishness of that institution which treated me as if I were mere flesh and blood and bones, to be locked up. I wondered that it should have concluded at length that this was the best use it could put me to, and had never thought to avail itself of my services in some way. I saw that, if there was a wall of stone between me and my townsmen, there was a still more difficult one to climb or break through, before they could get to be as free as I was. I did not for a moment feel confined, and the walls seemed a great waste of stone and mortar. I felt as if I alone of all my townsmen had paid my tax. They plainly did not know how to treat me, but behaved like persons who are underbred. In every threat and in every compliment there was a blunder; for they thought that the chief desire was to stand the other side of that stone wall. I could not but smile to see how industriously they locked the door on my meditations, which followed them out again without let or hindrance, and *they* were really all that was dangerous. As they could not reach me, they had resolved to punish my body; just as boys, if they cannot come at some person against whom they have a spite, will abuse his dog. I saw that the State was half-witted, that it was timid as a lone woman with her silver spoons, and that it did not know its friends from its foes, and I lost all my remaining respect for it, and pitied it.

Thus the State never intentionally confronts a man's sense, intellectual or moral, but only his body, his senses. It is not armed with superior wit or honesty, but with superior physical strength. I was not born to be forced. I will breathe after my own fashion. Let us see who is the strongest. What force has a multitude? They only can force me who obey a higher law than I. They force me to become like themselves. I do not hear of *men* being *forced* to live this way or that by masses of men. What sort of life were that to live? When I meet a government which says to me, "Your money or your life," why should I be in haste to give it my money? It may be in a great strait, and not know what to do; I cannot help that. It must help itself; do as I do. It is not worth the while to snivel about it. I am not responsible for the successful working of the machinery of society. I am not the son of the engineer. I perceive that, when an acorn and a chestnut fall side by side, the one does not remain inert to make way for the other, but both obey their own laws, and spring and grow and flourish as best they can, till one, perchance, overshadows and destroys the other. If a plant cannot live according to its nature, it dies; and so a man.

The night in prison was novel and interesting enough. The prisoners in their shirt-sleeves were enjoying a chat and the evening air in the doorway, when I entered. But the jailer said, "Come, boys, it is time to lock up"; and so they dispersed, and I heard the sound of their steps returning into the hollow apartments. My room-mate was introduced to me by the jailer, as "a first-rate fellow and a clever man." When the door was locked, he showed me where to hang my hat, and how he managed matters there. The rooms were whitewashed once a month; and this one, at least, was the whitest, most simply furnished, and probably the neatest apartment in the town. He naturally wanted to know where I came from, and what brought me there; and, when I had told him, I asked him in my turn how he came there, presuming him to

be an honest man, of course; and, as the world goes, I believe he was. "Why," said he, "they accuse me of burning a barn; but I never did it." As near as I could discover, he had probably gone to bed in a barn when drunk, and smoked his pipe there; and so a barn was burnt. He had the reputation of being a clever man, had been there some three months waiting for his trial to come on, and would have to wait as much longer; but he was quite domesticated and contented, since he got his board for nothing, and thought that he was well treated.

He occupied one window, and I the other; and I saw, that, if one stayed there long, his principal business would be to look out the window. I had soon read all the tracts that were left there, and examined where former prisoners had broken out, and where a grate had been sawed off, and heard the history of the various occupants of that room; for I found that even here there was a history and a gossip which never circulated beyond the walls of the jail. Probably this is the only house in the town where verses are composed, which are afterwards printed in a circular form, but not published. I was shown quite a long list of verses which were composed by some young men who had been detected in an attempt to escape, who avenged themselves by singing them.

I pumped my fellow-prisoner as dry as I could, for fear I should never see him again; but at length he showed me which was my bed, and left me to blow out the lamp.

It was like travelling into a far country, such as I had never expected to behold, to lie there for one night. It seemed to me that I never had heard the town-clock strike before, nor the evening sounds of the village; for we slept with the windows open, which were inside the grating. It was to see my native village in the light of the Middle Ages, and our Concord was turned into a Rhine stream, and visions of knights and castles passed before me. They were the voices of old burghers that I heard in the streets. I was an involuntary spectator and auditor of whatever was done and said in the kitchen of the adjacent village-inn,— a wholly new and rare experience to me. It was a closer view of my native town. I was fairly inside of it. I never had seen its institutions before. This is one of its peculiar institutions; for it is a shire town. I began to comprehend what its inhabitants were about.

In the morning, our breakfasts were put through the hole in the door, in small oblong-square tin pans, made to fit, and holding a pint of chocolate, with brown bread, and an iron spoon. When they called for the vessels again, I was green enough to return what bread I had left; but my comrade seized it, and said that I should lay up for lunch or dinner. Soon after he was let out to work at haying in a neighboring field, whither he went every day, and would not be back till noon; so he bade me good-day, saying that he doubted if he should see me again.

When I came out of prison,—for some one interfered, and paid that tax,—I did not perceive that great changes had taken place on the common, such as he observed who went in a youth, and emerged a tottering and gray-headed man; and yet a change had to my eyes come over the scene,—the town, and State, and country,—greater than any that mere time could effect. I saw yet more distinctly the State in which I lived. I saw to what extent the people among whom I lived could be trusted as good neighbors and friends; that their friendship was for summer weather only; that they did not greatly propose to do right; that they were a distinct race from me by their prejudices and superstitions, as the Chinamen and Malays are; that in their sacrifices to humanity, they ran no risks, not even to their property; that, after all, they were not so noble but they treated the thief as he

had treated them, and hoped, by a certain outward observance and a few prayers, and by walking in a particular straight though useless path from time to time, to save their souls. This may be to judge my neighbors harshly; for I believe that many of them are not aware that they have such an institution as the jail in their village.

It was formerly the custom in our village, when a poor debtor came out of jail, for his acquaintances to salute him, looking through their fingers, which were crossed to represent the grating of a jail window, "How do ye do?" My neighbors did not thus salute me, but first looked at me, and then at one another, as if I had returned from a long journey. I was put into jail as I was going to the shoemaker's to get a shoe which was mended. When I was let out the next morning, I proceeded to finish my errand, and having put on my mended shoe, joined a huckleberry party, who were impatient to put themselves under my conduct; and in half an hour,—for the horse was soon tackled,—was in the midst of a huckleberry field, on one of our highest hills, two miles off, and then the State was nowhere to be seen.

This is the whole history of "My Prisons."

I have never declined paying the highway tax, because I am as desirous of being a good neighbor as I am of being a bad subject; and, as for supporting schools, I am doing my part to educate my fellow-countrymen now. It is for no particular item in the tax-bill that I refuse to pay it. I simply wish to refuse allegiance to the State, to withdraw and stand aloof from it effectually. I do not care to trace the course of my dollar, if I could, till it buys a man or a musket to shoot one with,—the dollar is innocent,—but I am concerned to trace the effects of my allegiance. In fact, I quietly declare war with the State, after my fashion, though I will still make what use and get what advantage of her I can, as is usual in such cases.

If others pay the tax which is demanded of me, from a sympathy with the State, they do but what they have already done in their own case, or rather they abet injustice to a greater extent than the State requires. If they pay the tax from a mistaken interest in the individual taxed, to save his property, or prevent his going to jail, it is because they have not considered wisely how far they let their private feelings interfere with the public good.

This, then, is my position at present. But one cannot be too much on his guard in such a case, lest his action be biassed by obstinacy, or an undue regard for the opinions of men. Let him see that he does only what belongs to himself and to the hour.

I think sometimes, Why, this people mean well; they are only ignorant; they would do better if they knew how: why give your neighbors this pain to treat you as they are not inclined to? But I think again, this is no reason why I should do as they do, or permit others to suffer much greater pain of a different kind. Again, I sometimes say to myself, When many millions of men, without heat, without ill will, without personal feeling of any kind, demand of you a few shillings only, without the possibility, such is their constitution, of retracting or altering their present demand, and without the possibility, on your side, of appeal to any other millions, why expose yourself to this overwhelming brute force? You do not resist cold and hunger, the winds and the waves, thus obstinately; you quietly submit to a thousand similar necessities. You do not put your head into the fire. But just in proportion as I regard this as not wholly a brute force, but partly a human force, and consider that I have relations to those millions as to so many millions of men, and not of mere brute or inanimate things, I see that

appeal is possible, first and instantaneously, from them to the Maker of them, and secondly, from them to themselves. But, if I put my head deliberately into the fire, there is no appeal to fire or to the Maker of fire, and I have only myself to blame. If I could convince myself that I have any right to be satisfied with men as they are, and to treat them accordingly, and not according, in some respects, to my requisitions and expectations of what they and I ought to be, then, like a good Mussulman and fatalist, I should endeavor to be satisfied with things as they are, and say it is the will of God. And, above all, there is this difference between resisting this and a purely brute or natural force, that I can resist this with some effect; but I cannot expect, like Orpheus, to change the nature of the rocks and trees and beasts.

I do not wish to quarrel with any man or nation. I do not wish to split hairs, to make fine distinctions, or set myself up as better than my neighbors. I seek rather, I may say, even an excuse for conforming to the laws of the land. I am but too ready to conform to them. Indeed, I have reason to suspect myself on this head; and each year, as the tax-gatherer comes round, I find myself disposed to review the acts and position of the general and State governments, and the spirit of the people, to discover a pretext for conformity.

> "We must affect our country as our
>   parents;
> And if at any time we alienate
> Our love or industry from doing it
>   honor,
> We must respect effects and teach
>   the soul
> Matter of conscience and religion,
> And not desire of rule or benefit."

I believe that the State will soon be able to take all the work of this sort out of my hands, and then I shall be no better a patriot than my fellow-countrymen. Seen from a lower point of view, the Constitution, with all its faults, is very good; the law and the courts are very respectable; even this State and this American government are, in many respects, very admirable and rare things, to be thankful for, such as a great many have described them; but seen from a point of view a little higher, they are what I have described them; seen from a higher still, and the highest, who shall say what they are, or that they are worth looking at or thinking of at all?

However, the government does not concern me much, and I shall bestow the fewest possible thoughts on it. It is not many moments that I live under a government, even in this world. If a man is thought-free, fancy-free, imagination-free, that which *is not* never for a long time appearing *to be* to him, unwise rulers or reformers cannot fatally interrupt him.

I know that most men think differently from myself; but those whose lives are by profession devoted to the study of these of kindred subjects, content me as little as any. Statesmen and legislators, standing so completely within the institution, never distinctly and nakedly behold it. They speak of moving society, but have no resting-place without it. They may be men of a certain experience and discrimination, and have no doubt invented ingenious and even useful systems, for which we sincerely thank them; but all their wit and usefulness lie within certain not very wide limits. They are wont to forget that the world is not governed by policy and expediency. Webster never goes behind government, and so cannot speak with authority about it. His words are wisdom to those legislators who contemplate no essential reform in the existing government; but for thinkers, and those who legislate for all time, he never once glances at the subject. I know of those whose serene and wise speculations on this theme would soon reveal the limits of his mind's range and hospitality. Yet, com-

pared with the cheap professions of most reformers, and the still cheaper wisdom and eloquence of politicians in general, his are almost the only sensible and valuable words, and we thank Heaven for him. Comparatively, he is always strong, original, and, above all, practical. Still his quality is not wisdom, but prudence. The lawyer's truth is not Truth, but consistency, or a consistent expediency. Truth is always in harmony with herself, and is not concerned chiefly to reveal the justice that may consist with wrong-doing. He well deserves to be called, as he has been called, the Defender of the Constitution. There are really no blows to be given by him but defensive ones. He is not a leader, but a follower. His leaders are the men of '87. "I have never made an effort," he says, "and never propose to make an effort; I have never countenanced an effort, and never mean to countenance an effort, to disturb the arrangement as originally made, by which the various States came into the Union." Still thinking of the sanction which the Constitution gives to slavery, he says, "Because it was a part of the original compact,—let it stand." Notwithstanding his special acuteness and ability, he is unable to take a fact out of its merely political relations, and behold it as it lies absolutely to be disposed of by the intellect,—what, for instance, it behooves a man to do here in America to-day with regard to slavery, but ventures or is driven, to make some desperate answer as the following, while professing to speak absolutely, and as a private man,—from which what new and singular code of social duties might be inferred? "The manner," says he, "in which the governments of those States where slavery exists are to regulate it, is for their own consideration, under their responsibility to their constituents, to the general laws of propriety, humanity, and justice, and to God. Associations formed elsewhere, springing from a feeling of humanity, or any other cause, have nothing whatever to do with it. They have never received any encouragement from me, and they never will."*

They who know of no purer sources of truth, who have traced up its stream no higher, stand, and wisely stand, by the Bible and the Constitution, and drink at it there with reverence and humility; but they who behold where it comes trickling into this lake or that pool, gird up their loins once more, and continue their pilgrimage toward its fountainhead.

No man with a genius for legislation has appeared in America. They are rare in the history of the world. There are orators, politicians, and eloquent men, by the thousand; but the speaker has not yet opened his mouth to speak, who is capable of settling the much-vexed questions of the day. We love eloquence for its own sake, and not for any truth which it may utter, or any heroism it may inspire. Our legislators have not yet learned the comparative value of free-trade and of freedom, of union, and of rectitude, to a nation. They have no genius or talent for comparatively humble questions of taxation and finance, commerce and manufactures and agriculture. If we were left solely to the wordy wit of legislators in Congress for our guidance, uncorrected by the seasonable experience and the effectual complaints of the people, America would not long retain her rank among the nations. For eighteen hundred years, though perchance I have no right to say it, the New Testament has been written; yet where is the legislator who has wisdom and practical talent enough to avail himself of the light which it sheds on the science of legislation?

The authority of government, even such as I am willing to submit to,—for I will cheerfully obey those who know and can do better than I, and in many things even those who neither know nor can do so well,—is still an impure one: to be strictly just, it must have the sanction and consent of the governed. It can have no pure right over my person and property but what I concede to it. The progress from an absolute to a limited monarchy, from a limited monarchy to a democracy, is a progress toward a true respect for the individual. Even the Chinese philosopher was wise enough to regard the individual as the basis of the empire. Is a democracy, such as we know it, the last improvement possible in government? Is it not possible to take a step further towards recognizing and organizing the rights of man? There will never be a really free and enlightened State, until the State comes to recognize the individual as a higher and independent power, from which all its own power and authority are derived, and treats him accordingly. I please myself with imagining a State at last which can afford to be just to all men, and to treat the individual with respect as a neighbor; which even would not think it inconsistent with its own repose, if a few were to live aloof from it, not meddling with it, nor embraced by it, who fulfilled all the duties of neighbors and fellow-men. A State which bore this kind of fruit, and suffered it to drop off as fast as it ripened, would prepare the way for a still more perfect and glorious State, which also I have imagined, but not yet anywhere seen.

*These extracts have been inserted since the Lecture was read [Thoreau's footnote].

Elizabeth Cady Stanton

Epitomizing the vanguard of the feminist movement in the nineteenth century, Elizabeth Cady Stanton was born in 1815, daughter of a judge who headed a "blue-blooded first family" in New York. Her heritage gave her a tendency towards elitism and self-confidence. Attending Emma Willard's Troy Seminary, she obtained perhaps the best education available to a woman at that time. She overcame what she called an "epidemic" of religious revivalism, which caused emotional breakdowns among many young women who could not experience spiritual conversion and were left feeling depraved and dependent on God. In its place, she grounded her beliefs on a secular rationality, read law in her father's law office, and became a student of legal and constitutional history.

Her cousin, Gerrit Smith, introduced her to the abolitionist movement and the need for practical political organization to further social reform. She married Henry Stanton, a lawyer and political organizer in the abolitionist movement who helped found the antislavery Liberty party. In London, she met Lucretia Mott, a feminist who was refused admission to the World's Anti-Slavery Convention because of the bitter split in the abolitionist movement concerning women's rights. By 1848 her feminist apprenticeship under Mott was complete, and Stanton organized the first women's rights convention at Seneca Falls, New York. This was the year of revolutionary movements spreading throughout Europe demanding the extension of democratic political rights, and the year the New York Legislature passed a law (for which Stanton had lobbied) giving married women control over their inherited property.

Stanton not only conceived of the convention but suggested the Declaration of Independence be adapted to function as a manifesto for women's rights. And she collected a number of grievances aimed to demonstrate that "the history of mankind is the history of repeated injuries and usurpations on the part of man toward women." Most importantly, Stanton was responsible for the focus on political equality and the demand for women's suffrage, which distinguished the Seneca Falls Convention from activities organized by women before that time.

It took two years after the Seneca Falls Convention for women's rights conventions to be held outside New York—in Salem, Ohio, and in Worcester, Massachusetts. By 1851 women in Indiana and Pennsylvania had organized such conventions. Unable to attend because of the household duties involved with three children, Stanton nevertheless wrote, first for the women's temperance newspaper *The Lily* and later for a long-term book project on women's history, which she strove to complete with Susan B. Anthony. Stanton died in 1902 after a lifetime dedicated to speaking and writing on feminist issues.

The Seneca Falls Declaration (1848)
(excerpts)

I should feel exceeding diffident to appear before you at this time, having never before spoken in public, were I not nerved by a sense of right and duty, did I not feel the time had fully come for the question of woman's wrongs to be laid before the public, did I not believe that woman herself must do this work; for woman alone can understand the height, the depth, the length, and the breadth of her own degradation. Man cannot speak for her, because he has been educated to believe that she differs from him so materially, that he cannot judge of her thoughts, feelings, and opinions by his own. Moral beings can only judge of others by themselves. The moment they assume a different nature for any of their own kind, they utterly fail. . . .

Among the many important questions which have been brought before the public, there is none that more vitally affects the whole human family than that which is technically called Woman's Rights. Every allusion to the degraded and inferior position occupied by women all over the world has been met by scorn and abuse. From the man of highest mental cultivation to the most degraded wretch who staggers in the streets do we meet ridicule, and coarse jests, freely bestowed upon those who dare assert that woman stands by the side of man, his equal, placed here by her God, to enjoy with him the beautiful earth, which is her home as it is his, having the same sense of right and wrong, and looking to the same Being for guidance and support. So long has man exercised tyranny over her, injurious to himself and benumbing to her faculties, that few can nerve themselves to meet the storm; and so long has the chain been about her that she knows not there is a remedy. . . .

As the nations of the earth emerge from a state of barbarism, the sphere of woman gradually becomes wider, but not even under what is thought to be the full blaze of the sun of civilization, is it what God designed it to be. In every country and clime does man assume the responsibility of marking out the path for her to tread. In every country does he regard her as a being inferior to himself, and one whom he is to guide and control. From the Arabian Kerek, whose wife is obliged to steal from her husband to supply the necessities of life; from the Mahometan who forbids pigs, dogs, women and other impure animals, to enter a Mosque, and does not allow a fool, madman or woman to proclaim the hour of prayer; from the German who complacently smokes his meerschaum, while his wife, yoked with the ox, draws the plough through its furrow; from the delectable carpet-knight, who thinks an inferior style of conversation adapted to woman; to the legislator, who considers her incapable of saying what laws shall govern her, is the same feeling manifested. . . .

Let us consider . . . man's superiority, intellectually, morally, physically.

Man's intellectual superiority cannot be a question until woman has had a fair trial. When we shall have had our freedom to find our own sphere, when we shall have had our colleges, our professions, our trades, for a century, a comparison then may be justly instituted. When woman, instead of being taxed to endow colleges where she is forbidden to enter—instead of forming sewing societies to educate "poor, but pious," young men, shall first educate herself, when she shall be just to herself before she is generous to others; improving the talents God has given her, and leaving her neighbor to do the same for himself, we shall not hear so much about this boasted superiority. . . .

In consideration of man's claim to moral superiority, glance now at our theological seminaries, our divinity students, the long line of descendants from our Apostolic fathers, the immaculate priesthood, and what do we find there? Perfect moral rectitude in every relation of life, a devoted spirit of self-sacrifice, a perfect union of thought, opinion and feeling among those who profess to worship the one God, and whose laws they feel themselves called upon to declare to a fallen race? Far from it. . . . Is the moral and religious life of this class what we might expect from minds said to be fixed on such mighty themes? By no means. . . . The lamentable want of principle among our lawyers, generally, is too well known to need comment. The everlasting backbiting and bickering of our physicians is proverbial. The disgraceful riots at our polls, where man, in performing the highest duty of citizenship, ought surely to be sober-minded, the perfect rowdyism that now characterizes the debates in our national Congress,—all these are great facts which rise up against man's claim for moral superiority. In my opinion, he is infinitely woman's inferior in every moral quality, not by nature, but made so by a false education. In carrying out his own selfishness, man has greatly improved woman's moral nature, but by an almost total shipwreck of his own. Woman has now the noble virtues of the martyr. She is early schooled to self-denial and suffering. But man is not so wholly buried in selfishness that he does not sometimes get a glimpse of the narrowness of his soul, as compared with woman. Then he says, by way of an excuse for his degradation, "God

made woman more self-denying than man. It is her nature. It does not cost her as much to give up her wishes, her will, her life, even, as it does him. He is naturally selfish. God man him so."

No, I think not. . . . God's commands rest upon man as well as woman. It is as much his duty to be kind, self-denying and full of good works, as it is hers. As much his duty to absent himself from scenes of violence as it is hers. A place or position that would require the sacrifice of the delicacy and refinement of woman's nature is unfit for man, for these virtues should be as carefully guarded in him as in her. The false ideas that prevail with regard to the purity necessary to constitute the perfect character in woman, and that requisite for man, has done an infinite deal of mischief in the world. I would not have woman less pure, but I would have man more so. I would have the same code of morals for both. . . .

Let us now consider man's claim to physical superiority. Methinks I hear some say, surely, you will not contend for equality here. Yes, we must not give an inch, lest you take an ell. We cannot accord to man even this much, and he has no right to claim it until the fact has been fully demonstrated. . . . We cannot say what the woman might be physically, if the girl were allowed all the freedom of the boy in romping, climbing, swimming, playing whoop and ball. Among some of the Tartar tribes of the present day, women manage a horse, hurl a javelin, hunt wild animals, and fight an enemy as well as a man. The Indian women endure fatigues and carry burdens that some of our fair-faced, soft-handed, moustached young gentlemen would consider quite impossible for them to sustain. The Croatian and Wallachian women perform all the agricultural operations in addition to their domestic labors, and it is no uncommon sight in our cities, to see the German immigrant with his hands in his pockets, walking complacently by the side of his wife, whilst she bears the weight of some huge package or piece of furniture upon her head. Physically, as well as intellectually, it is use that produces growth and development.

But there is a class of objectors who say they do not claim superiority, they merely assert a difference. But you will find by following them up closely, that they soon run this difference into the old groove of superiority. . . .

We have met here to-day to discuss our rights and wrongs, civil and political, and not, as some have supposed, to go into the detail of social life alone. We do not propose to petition the legislature to make our husbands just, generous and courteous, to seat every man at the head of a cradle, and to clothe every woman in male attire. None of these points, however important they may be considered by leading men, will be touched in this Convention. . . .

We are assembled to protest against a form of government, existing without the consent of the governed—to declare our right to be free as man is free, to be represented in the government which we are taxed to support, to have such disgraceful laws as give man the power to chastise and imprison his wife, to take the wages which she earns, the property which she inherits, and, in case of separation, the children of her love; laws which make her the mere dependent on his bounty. It is to protest against such unjust laws as these that we are assembled to-day, and to have them, if possible, forever erased from our statute-books, deeming them a shame and a disgrace to a Christian republic in the nineteenth century. . . .

And, strange as it may seem to many, we now demand our right to vote according to the declaration of the government under which we live. . . . We have no objection to discuss the question of equality, for we feel that the weight of argument lies wholly with us, but we wish the question of equality kept distinct from the question of rights, for the proof of the one does not determine the truth of the other. All white men in this country have the same rights, however they may differ in mind, body or estate. The right is ours. The question now is, how shall we get possession of what rightfully belongs to us. We should not feel so sorely grieved if no man who had not attained the full stature of a Webster, Clay, Van Buren, or Gerrit Smith could claim the right of the elective franchise. But to have drunkards, idiots, horse-racing, rumselling rowdies, ignorant foreigners, and silly boys fully recognized, while we ourselves are thrust out from all the rights that belong to citizens, it is too grossly insulting to the dignity of woman to be longer quietly submitted to. The right is ours. Have it we must. Use it we will. The pens, the tongues, the fortunes, the indomitable wills of many women are already pledged to secure this right. The great truth, that no just government can be formed without the consent of the governed, we shall echo and re-echo in the ears of the unjust judge, until by continual coming we shall weary him. . . .

But what would woman gain by voting? Men must know the advantages of voting, for they all seem very tenacious about the right. Think you, if woman had a vote in this government, that all those laws affecting her interests would so entirely violate every principle of right and justice? Had woman a vote to give, might not the office-holders and seekers propose some change in her condition? Might not Woman's Rights become as great a question as free soil?

"But you are already represented by your fathers, husbands, brothers and sons?" Let your statute books answer the question. We have had enough of such representation. In nothing is woman's true happiness consulted. Men like to call her an angel—to feed her on what they think sweet food—

nourishing her vanity; to make her believe that her organization is so much finer than theirs, that she is not fitted to struggle with the tempests of public life, but needs their care and protection!! Care and protection— such as the wolf gives the lamb—such as the eagle the hare he carries to his eyrie!! Most cunningly he entraps her, and then takes from her all those rights which are dearer to him than life itself—rights which have been baptized in blood—and the maintenance of which is even now rocking to their foundations the kingdoms of the Old World.

The most discouraging, the most lamentable aspect our cause wears is the indifference, indeed, the contempt, with which women themselves regard the movement. Where the subject is introduced, among those even who claim to be intelligent and educated, it is met by the scornful curl of the lip, and by expression of ridicule and disgust. But we shall hope better things of them when they are enlightened in regard to their present position. When women know the laws and constitutions under which they live, they will not publish their degradation by declaring themselves satisfied, nor their ignorance, by declaring they have all the rights they want. . . .

Let woman live as she should. Let her feel her accountability to her Maker. Let her know that her spirit is fitted for as high a sphere as man's, and that her soul requires food as pure and exalted as his. Let her live *first* for God, and she will not make imperfect man an object of reverence and awe. Teach her her responsibility as a being of conscience and reason, that all earthly support is weak and unstable, that her only safe dependence is the arm of omnipotence, and that true happiness springs from duty accomplished. Thus will she learn the lesson of individual responsibility for time and eternity. That neither father, husband, brother, or son, however willing they may be, can discharge her high duties of life,

or stand in her stead when called into the presence of the great Searcher of Hearts at the last day. . . .

Let me here notice one of the greatest humbugs of the day, which has long found for itself the most valuable tool in woman—"The Education Society." The idea to me, is simply absurd, for women, in their present degradation and ignorance, to form sewing societies for the education of young men for the ministry. An order of beings above themselves, claiming to be gifted with superior powers, having all the avenues to learning, wealth and distinction thrown freely open to them, who, if they had but the energy to avail themselves of all these advantages, could easily secure an education for themselves, while woman herself, poor, friendless, robbed of all her rights, oppressed on all sides, civilly, religiously and socially, must needs go ignorant herself. Now, is not the idea preposterous, for such a being to educate a great, strong, lazy man, by working day and night with her needle, stitch, stitch, and the poor widow always throws in her mite, being taught to believe that all she gives for the decoration of churches and their black-coated gentry, is given unto the Lord. I think a man, who, under such conditions, has the moral hardihood to take an education at the hands of woman, and at such an expense to her, should, as soon as he graduates, with all his honors thick upon him, take the first ship for Turkey, and there pass his days in earnest efforts to rouse the inmates of the harems to a true sense of their degradation, and not, as is his custom, immediately enter our pulpits to tell us of his superiority to us, "weaker vessels,"—his prerogative to command, ours to obey, his duty to preach, ours to keep silence. . . . The last time when an appeal of this kind was made to me, I told the young girl that I would send her to school a year, if she would go, but I would never again give one red cent to the Education Society. And I do hope that every Christian woman, who has the least regard for her sex, will make the same resolve. We have worked long enough for man, and at a most unjust and unwarrantable sacrifice of self, yet he gives no evidence of gratitude, but has, thus far, treated his benefactors with scorn, ridicule and neglect. . . .

One common objection to this movement is, that if the principles of freedom and equality which we advocate were put into practice, it would destroy all harmony in the domestic circle. Here let me ask, how many truly harmonious households have we now? . . . The only happy households we now see are those in which husband and wife share equally in counsel and government. There can be no true dignity or independence where there is subordination to the absolute will of another, no happiness without freedom. Let us then have no fears that the movement will disturb what is seldom found, a truly united and happy family. . . .

There seems now to be a kind of moral stagnation in our midst. Philanthropists have done their utmost to rouse the nation to a sense of its sins. . . . Our churches are multiplying on all sides, our missionary societies, Sunday schools, and prayer meetings and innumerable charitable and reform organizations are all in operation, but still the tide of vice is swelling, and threatens the destruction of everything, and the battlements of righteousness are weak against the raging elements of sin and death. Verily, the world waits the coming of some new element, some purifying power, some spirit of mercy and love. The voice of woman has been silenced in the state, the church, and the home, but man cannot fulfill his destiny alone, he cannot redeem his race unaided. There are deep and tender chords of sympathy and love in the heart of the down-fallen and oppressed that woman can touch more skillfully than man. The world has never yet seen a truly great and virtuous nation, because in the degradation of woman the very fountains of life are poisoned at their source. It is vain to look for silver and gold from mines of copper and lead. It is the wise mother that has the wise son. So long as your women are slaves you may throw your colleges and churches to the winds. . . . Truly are the sins of the fathers visited upon the children to the third and fourth generation. God, in his wisdom, has so linked the whole human family together that any violence done at one end of the chain is felt throughout its length, and here, too, is the law of restoration, as in woman all have fallen, so in her elevation shall the race be recreated.

. . .We do not expect our path will be strewn with flowers of popular applause, but over the thorns of bigotry and prejudice will be our way, and on our banners will beat the dark storm-clouds of opposition from those who have entrenched themselves behind the stormy bulwarks of custom and authority, and who have fortified their position by every means, holy and unholy. But we will steadfastly abide the result. Unmoved we will bear it aloft. Undaunted we will unfurl it to the gale, for we know that the storm cannot rend from it a shred, that the electric flash will but more clearly show to us the glorious words inscribed upon it, "Equality of Rights."

Seattle

Seattle became chief of the Suquamish and Duwamish tribes in Washington and Oregon and was known for accommodating the whites whenever he could. Born in 1786, this chief received honors that few other native Americans have ever received. The city of Seattle, Washington, was named after him. His prophecy for the Indians in the United States was so accurately pessimistic that realistic compliance with the white man struck Seattle as the ultimate wisdom.

Seattle was converted by Catholic missionaries in the 1830s, and he changed his lifestyle accordingly. In 1855 he signed the Port Elliott Treaty giving Washington tribes a reservation. In 1853 the Washington Territory was organized, and the town of Seattle was officially registered. When Governor Stevens visited settlers and Indians in Seattle soon thereafter, Seattle made the following reply to the governor's talk. Seattle died in 1866.

❧❦❧

The Indians' Night
Promises to Be Dark (1853)

Yonder sky that has wept tears of compassion upon my people for centuries untold, and which to us appears changeless and eternal, may change. Today is fair. Tomorrow it may be overcast with clouds. My words are like the stars that never change. Whatever Seattle says the great chief at Washington can rely upon with as much certainty as he can upon the return of the sun or the seasons. The White Chief says that Big Chief at Washington sends us greetings of friendship and goodwill. This is kind of him for we know he has little need of our friendship in return. His people are many. They are like the grass that covers vast prairies. My people are few. They resemble the scattering trees of a storm-swept plain. The great—and I presume—good White Chief sends us word that he wishes to buy our lands but is willing to allow us enough to live comfortably. This indeed appears just, even generous, for the Red Man no longer has rights that he need respect, and the offer may be wise also, as we are no longer in need of an extensive country.

There was a time when our people covered the land as the waves of a wind-ruffled sea cover its shell-paved floor, but that time long since passed away with the greatness of tribes that are now but a mournful memory. I will not dwell on, nor mourn over, our untimely decay, nor reproach my paleface brothers with hastening it as we too may have been somewhat to blame.

Youth is impulsive. When our young men grow angry at some real or imaginary wrong, and disfigure their faces with black paint, it denotes that their hearts are black, and that they are often cruel and relentless, and our old men and old women are unable to restrain them. Thus it has ever been. Thus it was when the white man first began to push our forefathers westward. But let us hope that the hostilities between us may never return. We would have everything to lose and nothing to gain. Revenge by young men is considered gain, even at the cost of their own lives, but old men who stay at home in times of war, and mothers who have sons to lose, know better.

Our good father at Washington—for I presume he is now our father as well as yours, since King George has moved his boundaries further north—our great and good father, I say, sends us word that if we do as he desires he will protect us. His brave warriors will be to us a bristling wall

Isaak, *American Political Thinking.*

of strength, and his wonderful ships of war will fill our harbors so that our ancient enemies far to the northward—the Hydas and Tsimpsians—will cease to frighten our women, children and old men. Then in reality will he be our father and we his children. But can that ever be? Your God is not our God! Your God loves your people and hates mine. He folds his strong protecting arms lovingly about the paleface and leads him by the hand as a father leads his infant son—but He has forsaken His red children—if they really are His. Our God, the Great Spirit, seems also to have forsaken us. Your God makes your people wax strong every day. Soon they will fill all the land. Our people are ebbing away like a rapidly receding tide that will never return. The white man's God cannot love our people or He would protect them. They seem to be orphans who can look nowhere for help. How then can we be brothers? How can your God become our God and renew our prosperity and awaken in us dreams of returning greatness. If we have a common heavenly father He must be partial—for He came to His paleface children. We never saw Him. He gave you laws but had no word for his red children whose teeming multitudes once filled this vast continent as stars fill the firmament. No; we are two distinct races with separate origins and separate destinies. There is little in common between us.

To us the ashes of our ancestors are sacred and their resting place is hallowed ground. You wander far from the graves of your ancestors and seemingly without regret. Your religion was written upon tables of stone by the iron finger of your God so that you could not forget. The Red Man could never comprehend nor remember it. Our religion is the tradition of our ancestors—the dreams of our old men, given them in the solemn hours of night by the Great Spirit; and the visions of our sachems, and is written in the hearts of our people.

Your dead cease to love you and the land of their nativity as soon as they pass the portals of the tomb and wander way beyond the stars. They are soon forgotten and never return. Our dead never forget the beautiful world that gave them being. They still love its verdant valleys, its murmuring rivers, its magnificent mountains, sequestered vales and verdant lined lakes and bays, and even yearn in tender, fond affection over the lonely hearted living, and often return from the Happy Hunting Ground to visit, guide, console and comfort them.

Day and night cannot dwell together. The Red Man has ever fled the approach of the White Man, as the morning mist flees before the morning sun.

However, your proposition seems fair and I think that my people will accept it and will retire to the reservation you offer them. Then we will dwell in peace, for the words of the Great White Chief seem to be the words of nature speaking to my people out of dense darkness.

It matters little where we pass the remnant of our days. They will not be many. The Indians' night promises to be dark. Not a single star of hope hovers above his horizon. Sad-voiced winds moan in the distance. Grim fate seems to be on the Red Man's trail, and wherever he goes he will hear the approaching footsteps of his fell destroyer and prepare stolidly to meet his doom, as does the wounded doe that hears the approaching footsteps of the hunter.

A few more moons. a few more winters—and not one of the descendants of the mighty hosts that once moved over this broad land or lived in happy homes, protected by the Great Spirit, will remain to mourn over the graves of a people—once more powerful and hopeful than yours. But why should I mourn at the untimely fate of my people? Tribe follows tribe, and nation follows nation, like the waves of the sea. It is the order of nature, and regret is useless.

Your time of decay may be distant, but it will surely come, for even the White Man whose God walked and talked with him as friend with friend, cannot be exempt from the common destiny. We may be brothers after all. We will see.

We will ponder your proposition and when we decide we will let you know. But should we accept it, I here and now make this condition that we will not be denied the privilege without molestation of visiting at any time the tombs of our ancestors, friends and children. Every part of this soil is sacred in the estimation of my people. Every hillside, every valley, every plain and grove, has been hallowed by some sad or happy event in days long vanished. Even the rocks, which seem to be dumb and dead as they swelter in the sun along the silent shore, thrill with memories of stirring events connected with the lives of my people, and the very dust upon which you now stand responds more lovingly to their footsteps than to yours, because it is rich with the blood of our ancestors and our bare feet are conscious of the sympathetic touch. Our departed braves, fond mothers, glad, happy-hearted maidens, and even our little children who lived here and rejoiced here for a brief season, will love these somber solitudes and at eventide they greet shadowy returning spirits. And when the last Red Man shall have perished, and the memory of my tribe shall have become a myth among the White Men, these shores will swarm with the invisible dead of my tribe, and when your children's children think themselves alone in the field, the store, the shop, upon the highway, or in the silence of the pathless woods, they will not be alone. In all the earth there is no place dedicated to solitude. At night when the streets of your cities and villages are silent and you think them deserted, they will throng with the returning hosts that once filled them and still love this beautiful land. The White Man will never be alone.

Let him be just and deal kindly with my people, for the dead are not powerless. Dead, did I say? There is no death, only a change of worlds.

Frederick Douglass

The foremost black spokesman for black political rights in the first half of the nineteenth century, Frederick Douglass is known today mainly for his famous *Narrative of the Life of Frederick Douglass* (1845), excerpted here. Born Frederick W. Bailey, a slave in Talbot County, Maryland, about 1817, he was sent to Baltimore at age seven, where the wife of his master taught him basic literacy. He worked as a house servant there until he received training in Baltimore as a ship caulker. Seeking physical dignity and spiritual freedom, he tried unsuccessfully to escape in 1835, and then was returned to his job as houseboy.

In 1838 he managed to escape to New York, moved to New Bedford, Massachusetts, and changed his name to Frederick Douglass. Attending a lecture of the Massachusetts Anti-Slavery Society in 1841, he stood up and gave a spontaneous speech, which impressed the society enough to ask him to become a lecturer for them. His career as a black activist was launched. Four years later, he wrote his famous autobiography, which sold thirty thousand copies within five years.

Once his book came out, his identity was revealed, and he sailed to Europe to avoid capture, lecturing in England, Scotland, and Ireland. In 1846, a couple from England purchased his freedom for $700. Upon returning to the United States in 1847, Douglass founded the *North Star,* the leading abolition journal apart from William Garrison's *The Liberator.* Slavery was a moral and religious issue for Garrison, and he viewed the Constitution as hopelessly proslavery. Douglass was interested in slavery primarily as a political issue and believed the Constitution could be understood to outlaw slavery if enough people could be brought to perceive it so. Accordingly, he joined the Free Soil party and later the Republican party.

After the *North Star,* Douglass published *Frederick Douglass Weekly, Frederick Douglass' Paper, Douglass' Monthly,* and the *New National Era* in quick succession. He fought for African-American rights even after the Civil War ended. In his later life, Douglas served as president of the ill-fated Freedmen's Savings Bank, marshal and then recorder of deeds for the District of Columbia, resident minister and consul general to the Republic of Haiti, and *chargé d'affaires* for Santo Domingo. He died in 1895.

Narrative of the Life of Frederick Douglass (1845)
(excerpts)

I was born in Tuckahoe, near Hillsborough, and about twelve miles from Easton, in Talbot county, Maryland. I have no accurate knowledge of my age, never having seen any authentic record containing it. By far the larger part of the slaves know as little of their ages as horses know of theirs, and it is the wish of most masters within my knowledge to keep their slaves thus ignorant. I do not remember to have ever met a slave who could tell of his birthday. They seldom come nearer to it than planting-time, harvest-time, cherry-time, spring-time, or fall-time. A want of information concerning my own was a source of unhappiness to me even during childhood. The white children could tell their ages. I could not tell why I ought to be deprived of the same privilege. I was not allowed to make any inquiries of my master concerning it. He deemed all such inquiries on the part of a slave improper and impertinent, and evidence of a restless spirit. The nearest estimate I can give makes me now between twenty-seven and twenty-eight years of age. I come to this, from hearing my master say, some time during 1835, I was about seventeen years old.

My mother was named Harriet Bailey. She was the daughter of Isaac and Betsey Bailey, both colored, and quite dark. My mother was of a darker complexion than either my grandmother or grandfather.

My father was a white man. He was admitted to be such by all I ever heard speak of my parentage. The opinion was also whispered that my master was my father; but of the correctness of this opinion, I know nothing; the means of knowing was withheld from me. My mother and I were separated when I was but an infant— before I knew her as my mother. It is a common custom, in the part of Maryland from which I ran away, to part children from their mothers at a very early age. Frequently, before the child has reached its twelfth month, its mother is taken from it, and hired out on some farm a considerable distance off, and the child is placed under the care of an old woman, too old for field labor. For what this separation is done, I do not know, unless it be to hinder the development of the child's affection toward its mother, and to blunt and destroy the natural affection of the mother for the child. This is the inevitable result.

I never saw my mother, to know her as such, more than four or five times in my life; and each of those times was very short in duration, and at night. She was hired by a Mr. Stewart, who lived about twelve miles from my home. She made her journeys to see me in the night, travelling the whole distance on foot, after the performance of her day's work. She was a field hand, and a whipping is the penalty of not being in the field at sunrise, unless a slave has special permission from his or her master to the contrary—a permission which they seldom get, and one that gives to him that gives it the proud name of being a kind master. I do not recollect of ever seeing my mother by the light of day. She was with me in the night. She would lie down with me, and get me to sleep, but long before I waked she was gone. Very little communication ever took place between us. Death soon ended what little we could have while she lived, and with it her hardships and suffering. She died when I was about seven years old, on one of my master's farms, near Lee's Mill. I was not allowed to be present during her illness, at her death, or burial. She was gone long before I knew any thing about it. Never having enjoyed, to any considerable extent, her soothing presence, her tender and watchful care, I received the tidings of her death with much the same emotions I should have probably felt at the death of a stranger.

Called thus suddenly away, she left me without the slightest intimation of who my father was. The whisper that my master was my father, may or may not be true; and, true or false, it is of but little consequence to my purpose whilst the fact remains, in all its glaring odiousness, that slaveholders have ordained, and by law established, that the children of slave women shall in all cases follow the condition of their mothers; and this is done too obviously to administer to their own lusts, and make a gratification of their wicked desires profitable as well as pleasurable; for by this cunning arrangement, the slaveholder, in cases not a few, sustains to his slaves the double relation of master and father.

I know of such cases; and it is worthy of remark that such slaves invariably suffer greater hardships, and have more to contend with, than others. They are, in the first place, a constant offence to their mistress. She is ever disposed to find fault with them; they can seldom do any thing to please her; she is never better pleased than when she sees them under the lash, especially when she suspects her husband of showing to his mulatto children favors which he withholds from his black slaves. The master is frequently compelled to sell this class of his slaves, out of deference to the feelings of his white wife; and, cruel as the deed may strike any one to be, for a man to sell his own children to human flesh-mongers, it is often the dictate of humanity for him to do so; for, unless he does this, he must not only whip them himself, but must stand by and see one white son tie up his brother, of but few shades darker complexion than himself, and ply the gory lash to his naked back; and if he lisp one word of disapproval, it is set down to his parental partiality, and only makes a bad matter worse, both for himself and the slave whom he would protect and defend.

Every year brings with it multitudes of this class of slaves. It was doubtless in consequence of a knowledge of this fact, that one great statesman of the south predicted the downfall of slavery by the inevitable laws of population. Whether this prophecy is ever fulfilled or not, it is nevertheless plain that a very different-looking class of people are springing up at the south, and are now held in slavery, from those originally brought to this country from Africa; and if their increase will do no other good, it will do away the force of the argument, that God cursed Ham, and therefore American slavery is right. If the lineal descendants of Ham are alone to be scripturally enslaved, it is certain that slavery at the south must soon become unscriptural; for thousands are ushered into the world, annually, who, like myself, owe their existence to white fathers, and those fathers most frequently their own masters.

I have had two masters. My first master's name was Anthony. I do not remember his first name. He was generally called Captain Anthony—a title which, I presume, he acquired by sailing a craft on the Chesapeake Bay. He was not considered a rich slaveholder. He owned two or three farms, and about thirty slaves. His farms and slaves were under the care of an overseer. The overseer's name was Plummer. Mr. Plummer was a miserable drunkard, a profane swearer, and a savage monster. He always went armed with a cowskin and a heavy cudgel. I have known him to cut and slash the women's heads so horribly, that even master would be enraged at his cruelty, and would threaten to whip him if he did not mind himself. Master, however, was not a humane slaveholder. It required extraordinary barbarity on the part of an overseer to affect him. He was a cruel man, hardened by a long life of slaveholding. He would at times seem to take great pleasure in whipping a slave. I have often been awakened at the dawn of day by the most heart-rending shrieks of an own aunt of mine, whom he used to tie up to a joist, and whip upon her naked back till she was literally covered with blood. No words, no tears, no prayers, from his gory victim, seemed to move his iron heart from its bloody purpose. The louder she screamed, the harder he whipped; and where the blood ran fastest, there he whipped longest. He would whip her to make her scream, and whip her to make her hush; and not until overcome by fatigue, would he cease to swing the blood-clotted cowskin. I remember the first time I ever witnessed this horrible exhibition. I was quite a child, but I well remember it. I never shall forget it whilst I remember any thing. It was the first of a long series of such outrages, of which I was doomed to be a witness and a participant. It struck me with awful force. It was the blood-stained gate, the entrance to the hell of slavery, through which I was about to pass. It was a most terrible spectacle. I wish I could commit to paper the feelings with which I beheld it.

This occurrence took place very soon after I went to live with my old master, and under the following circumstances. Aunt Hester went out one night,—where or for what I do not know,—and happened to be absent when my master desired her presence. He had ordered her not to go out evenings, and warned her that she must never let him catch her in company with a young man, who was paying attention to her belonging to Colonel Lloyd. The young man's name was Ned Roberts, generally called Lloyd's Ned. Why master was so careful of her, may be safely left to conjecture. She was a woman of noble form, and of graceful proportions, having very few equals, and fewer superiors, in personal appearance, among the colored or white women of our neighborhood.

Aunt Hester had not only disobeyed his orders in going out, but had been found in company with Lloyd's Ned; which circumstance, I found, from what he said while whipping her, was the chief offence. Had he been a man of pure morals himself, he might have been thought interested in protecting the innocence of my aunt; but those who knew him will not suspect him of any such virtue. Before he commenced whipping Aunt Hester, he took her into the kitchen, and stripped her from neck to waist, leaving her neck, shoulders, and back entirely naked. He then told her to cross her hands, calling her at the same time a d———d b———h. After crossing

her hands, he tied them with a strong rope, and led her to a stool under a large hook in the joist, put in for the purpose. He made her get upon the stool, and tied her hands to the hook. She now stood fair for his infernal purpose. Her arms were stretched up at their full length, so that she stood upon the ends of her toes. He then said to her, "Now, you d———d b———h, I'll learn you how to disobey my orders!" and after rolling up his sleeves, he commenced to lay on the heavy cowskin, and soon the warm, red blood (amid heart-rending shrieks from her, and horrid oaths from him) came dripping to the floor. I was so terrified and horror-stricken at the sight, that I hid myself in a closet, and dared not venture out till long after the bloody transaction was over. I expected it would be my turn next. It was all new to me. I had never seen any thing like it before. I had always lived with my grandmother on the outskirts of the plantation, where she was put to raise the children of the younger women. I had therefore been, until now, out of the way of the bloody scenes that often occurred on the plantation. . . .

I now come to that part of my life during which I planned, and finally succeeded in making, my escape from slavery. But before narrating any of the peculiar circumstances, I deem it proper to make known my intention not to state all the facts connected with the transaction. My reasons for pursuing this course may be understood from the following: First, were I to give a minute statement of all the facts, it is not only possible, but quite probable, that others would thereby be involved in the most embarrassing difficulties. Secondly, such a statement would most undoubtedly induce greater vigilance on the part of slaveholders than has existed heretofore among them; which would, of course, be the means of guarding a door whereby some dear brother bondman might escape his galling chains. I deeply regret the necessity that impels me to suppress any thing of importance connected with my experience in slavery. It would afford me great pleasure indeed, as well as materially add to the interest of my narrative, were I at liberty to gratify a curiosity, which I know exists in the minds of many, by an accurate statement of all the facts pertaining to my most fortunate escape. But I must deprive myself of this pleasure, and the curious of the gratification which such a statement would afford. I would allow myself to suffer under the greatest imputations which evil-minded men might suggest, rather than exculpate myself, and thereby run the hazard of closing the slightest avenue by which a brother slave might clear himself of the chains and fetters of slavery.

I have never approved of the very public manner in which some of our western friends have conducted what they call the *underground railroad,* but which, I think, by their open declarations, has been made most emphatically the *upperground railroad.* I honor those good men and women for their noble daring, and applaud them for willingly subjecting themselves to bloody persecution, by openly avowing their participation in the escape of slaves. I, however, can see very little good resulting from such a course, either to themselves or the slaves escaping; while, upon the other hand, I see and feel assured that those open declarations are a positive evil to the slaves remaining, who are seeking to escape. They do nothing towards enlightening the slave, whilst they do much towards enlightening the master. They stimulate him to greater watchfulness, and enhance his power to capture his slave. We owe something to the slaves south of the line as well as to those north of it; and in aiding the latter on their way to freedom, we should be careful to do nothing which would be likely to hinder the former from escaping from slavery. I would keep the merciless slaveholder profoundly ignorant of the means of flight adopted by the slave. I would leave him to imagine himself surrounded by myriads of invisible tormentors, ever ready to snatch from his infernal grasp his trembling prey. Let him be left to feel his way in the dark; let darkness commensurate with his crime hover over him; and let him feel that at every step he takes, in pursuit of the flying bondman, he is running the frightful risk of having his hot brains dashed out by an invisible agency. Let us render the tyrant no aid; let us not hold the light by which he can trace the footprints of our flying brother. But enough of this. I will not proceed to the statement of those facts, connected with my escape, for which I am alone responsible, and for which no one can be made to suffer but myself.

In the early part of the year 1838, I became quite restless. I could see no reason why I should, at the end of each week, pour the reward of my toil into the purse of my master. When I carried to him my weekly wages, he would, after counting the money, look me in the face with a robber-like fierceness, and ask, "Is this all?" He was satisfied with nothing less than the last cent. He would, however, when I made him six dollars, sometimes give me six cents, to encourage me. It had the opposite effect. I regarded it as a sort of admission of my right to the whole. The fact that he gave me any part of my wages was proof, to my mind, that he believed me entitled to the whole of them. I always felt worse for having received any thing; for I feared that the giving me a few cents would ease his conscience, and make him feel himself to be a pretty honorable sort of robber. My discontent grew upon me. I was ever on the look-out for means of escape; and, finding no direct means, I determined to try to hire my time, with a view of getting money with which to make my escape. In the spring of 1838, when Master Thomas came to Baltimore to purchase his spring goods, I got an opportunity, and applied to him to allow me to hire my time. He unhesitatingly refused my request, and told me this was another stratagem by which to escape. He told me I could go nowhere but that he could get me; and that, in the event of my running away, he should spare no pains in his efforts to catch me. He exhorted me to content myself, and be obedient. He told me, if I would be happy, I must lay out no plans for the future. He said, if I behaved myself properly, he would take care of me. Indeed, he advised me to complete thoughtlessness of the future, and taught me to depend solely upon him for happiness. He seemed to see fully the pressing necessity of setting aside my intellectual nature, in order to [achieve] contentment in slavery. But in spite of him, and even in spite of myself, I continued to think, and to think about the injustice of my enslavement, and the means of escape.

About two months after this, I applied to Master Hugh for the privilege of hiring my time. He was not acquainted with the fact that I had applied to Master Thomas, and had been refused. He too, at first, seemed disposed to refuse; but, after some reflection, he granted me the privilege, and proposed the following terms: I was to be allowed all my time, make all contracts with those for whom I worked, and find my own employment; and, in return for this liberty, I was to pay him three dollars at the end of each week; find myself in calking tools, and in board and clothing. My board was two dollars and a half per week. This, with the wear and tear of clothing and calking tools, made my regular expenses about six dollars per week. This amount I was compelled to make up, or relinquish the privilege of hiring my time. Rain or shine, work or no work, at the end of each week the money must be forthcoming, or I must give up my privilege. This arrangement, it will be perceived, was

decidedly in my master's favor. It relieved him of all need of looking after me. His money was sure. He received all the benefits of slaveholding without its evils; while I endured all the evils of a slave, and suffered all the care and anxiety of a freeman. I found it a hard bargain. But, hard as it was, I thought it better than the old mode of getting along. It was a step towards freedom to be allowed to bear the responsibilities of a freeman, and I was determined to hold on upon it. I bent myself to the work of making money. I was ready to work at night as well as day, and by the most untiring perseverance and industry, I made enough to meet my expenses, and lay up a little money every week. I went on thus from May till August. Master Hugh then refused to allow me to hire my time longer. The ground for his refusal was a failure on my part, one Saturday night, to pay him for my week's time. This failure was occasioned by my attending a camp meeting about ten miles from Baltimore. During the week, I had entered into an engagement with a number of young friends to start from Baltimore to the camp ground early Saturday evening; and being detained by my employer, I was unable to get down to Master Hugh's without disappointing the company. I knew that Master Hugh was in no special need of the money that night. I therefore decided to go to camp meeting, and upon my return pay him the three dollars. I staid [sic] at the camp meeting one day longer than I intended when I left. But as soon as I returned, I called upon him to pay him what he considered his due. I found him very angry; he could scarce restrain his wrath. He said he had a great mind to give me a severe whipping. He wished to know how I dared go out of the city without asking his permission. I told him I hired my time, and while I paid him the price which he asked for it, I did not know that I was bound to ask him when and where I should go. This reply troubled him; and, after reflecting a few moments, he turned to me, and said I should hire my time no longer; that the next thing he should know of, I would be running away. Upon the same plea, he told me to bring my tools and clothing home forthwith. I did so; but instead of seeking work, as I had been accustomed to do previously to hiring my time, I spent the whole week without the performance of a single stroke of work. I did this in retaliation. Saturday night, he called upon me as usual for my week's wages. I told him I had no wages; I had done no work that week. Here we were upon the point of coming to blows. He raved, and swore his determination to get hold of me. I did not allow myself a single word; but was resolved, if he laid the weight of his hand upon me, it should be blow for blow. He did not strike me, but told me that he would find me in constant employment in future. I thought the matter over during the next day, Sunday, and finally resolved upon the third day of September, as the day upon which I would make a second attempt to secure my freedom. I now had three weeks during which to prepare for my journey. Early on Monday morning, before Master Hugh had time to make any engagement for me, I went out and got employment of Mr. Butler, at his ship-yard near the draw-bridge, upon what is called the City Block, thus making it unnecessary for him to seek employment for me. At the end of the week, I brought him between eight and nine dollars. He seemed very well pleased, and asked me why I did not do the same the week before. He little knew what my plans were. My object in working steadily was to remove any suspicion he might entertain of my intent to run away; and in this I succeeded admirably. I suppose he thought I was never better satisfied with my condition than at the very time during which I was planning my escape. The second week passed, and again I carried him my full wages; and so well pleased was he, that he gave me twenty-five cents, (quite a large

sum for a slaveholder to give a slave,) and bade me to make a good use of it. I told him I would.

Things went on without very smoothly indeed, but within there was trouble. It is impossible for me to describe my feelings as the time of my contemplated start drew near. I had a number of warm-hearted friends in Baltimore,—friends that I loved almost as I did my life,—and the thought of being separated from them forever was painful beyond expression. It is my opinion that thousands would escape from slavery, who now remain, but for the strong cords of affection that bind them to their friends. The thought of leaving my friends was decidedly the most painful thought with which I had to contend. The love of them was my tender point, and shook my decision more than all things else. Besides the pain of separation, the dread and apprehension of a failure exceeded what I had experienced at my first attempt. The appalling defeat I then sustained returned to torment me. I felt assured that, if I failed in this attempt, my case would be a hopeless one—it would seal my fate as a slave forever. I could not hope to get off with any thing less than the severest punishment, and being placed beyond the means of escape. It required no very vivid imagination to depict the most frightful scenes through which I should have to pass, in case I failed. The wretchedness of slavery, and the blessedness of freedom, were perpetually before me. It was life and death with me. But I remained firm, and, according to my resolution, on the third day of September, 1838, I left my chains, and succeeded in reaching New York without the slightest interruption of any kind. How I did so,—what means I adopted,—what direction I travelled, and by what mode of conveyance,—I must leave unexplained, for the reasons before mentioned.

I have been frequently asked how I felt when I found myself in a free State. I have never been able to answer the question with any satisfaction to myself. It was a moment of the highest excitement I ever experienced. I suppose I felt as one may imagine the unarmed mariner to feel when he is rescued by a friendly man-of-war from the pursuit of a pirate. In writing to a dear friend, immediately after my arrival at New York, I said I felt like one who had escaped a den of hungry lions. This state of mind, however, very soon subsided; and I was again seized with a feeling of great insecurity and loneliness. I was yet liable to be taken back, and subjected to all the tortures of slavery. This in itself was enough to damp the ardor of my enthusiasm. But the loneliness overcame me. There I was in the midst of thousands, and yet a perfect stranger; without home and without friends, in the midst of thousands of my own brethren—children of a common Father, and yet I dared not to unfold to any one of them my sad condition. I was afraid to speak to any one for fear of speaking to the wrong one, and thereby falling into the hands of money-loving kidnappers, whose business it was to lie in wait for the panting fugitive, as the ferocious beasts of the forest lie in wait for their prey. The motto which I adopted when I started from slavery was this—"Trust no man!" I saw in every white man an enemy, and in almost every colored man cause for distrust. It was a most painful situation; and, to understand it, one must needs experience it, or imagine himself in similar circumstances. Let him be a fugitive slave in a strange land—a land given up to be the hunting-ground for slaveholders—whose inhabitants are legalized kidnappers—where he is every moment subjected to the terrible liability of being seized upon by his fellow-men, as the hideous crocodile seizes upon his prey!—I say, let him place himself in my situation—without home or friends—without money or credit—wanting shelter, and no one to give it—wanting bread, and no money to buy it,—and at the

same time let him feel that he is pursued by merciless men-hunters, and in total darkness as to what to do, where to go, or where to stay,—perfectly helpless both as to the means of defence and means of escape,—in the midst of plenty, yet suffering the terrible gnawings of hunger,—in the midst of houses, yet having no home,—among fellow-men, yet feeling as if in the midst of wild beasts, whose greediness to swallow up the trembling and half-famished fugitive is only equalled by that with which the monsters of the deep swallow up the helpless fish upon which they subsist,—I say, let him be placed in this most trying situation,—the situation in which I was placed,—then, and not till then, will he fully appreciate the hardships of, and know how to sympathize with, the toil-worn and whip-scarred fugitive slave.

Thank Heaven, I remained but a short time in this distressed situation. I was relieved from it by the humane hand of Mr. DAVID RUGGLES, whose vigilance, kindness, and perseverance, I shall never forget. I am glad of an opportunity to express, as far as words can, the love and gratitude I bear him. Mr. Ruggles is now afflicted with blindness, and is himself in need of the same kind offices which he was once so forward in the performance of toward others. I had been in New York but a few days, when Mr. Ruggles sought me out, and very kindly took me to his boarding-house at the corner of Church and Lespenard Streets. Mr. Ruggles was then very deeply engaged in the memorable *Darg* case, as well as attending to a number of other fugitive slaves, devising ways and means for their successful escape; and, though watched and hemmed in on almost every side, he seemed to be more than a match for his enemies.

Very soon after I went to Mr. Ruggles, he wished to know of me where I wanted to go; as he deemed it unsafe for me to remain in New York. I told him I was a calker, and should like to go where I could get work. I thought of going to Canada; but he decided against it, and in favor of my going to New Bedford, thinking I should be able to get work there at my trade. At this time, Anna,[1] my intended wife, came on; for I wrote to her immediately after my arrival at New York, (notwithstanding my homeless, houseless, and helpless condition,) informing her of my successful flight, and wishing her to come on forthwith. In a few days after her arrival, Mr. Ruggles called in the Rev. J. W. C. Pennington, who, in the presence of Mr. Ruggles, Mrs. Michaels, and two or three others, performed the marriage ceremony, and gave us a certificate, of which the following is an exact copy:—

"THIS may certify, that I joined together in holy matrimony Frederick Johnson[2] and Anna Murray, as man and wife, in the presence of Mr. David Ruggles and Mrs. Michaels.

"JAMES W. C. PENNINGTON.
"New York, Sept. 15, 1838."

Upon receiving this certificate, and a five-dollar bill from Mr. Ruggles, I shouldered one part of our baggage, and Anna took up the other, and we set out forthwith to take passage on board of the steamboat John W. Richmond for Newport, on our way to New Bedford. Mr. Ruggles gave me a letter to a Mr. Shaw in Newport, and told me, in case my money did not serve me to New Bedford, to stop in Newport and obtain further assistance; but upon our arrival at Newport, we were so anxious to get to a place of safety, that, notwithstanding we lacked the necessary money to pay our fare, we decided to take seats in the stage, and promise to pay when we got to

New Bedford. We were encouraged to do this by two excellent gentlemen, residents of New Bedford, whose names I afterward ascertained to be Joseph Ricketson and William C. Taber. They seemed at once to understand our circumstances, and gave us such assurance of their friendliness as put us fully at ease in their presence. It was good indeed to meet with such friends, at such a time. Upon reaching New Bedford, we were directed to the house of Mr. Nathan Johnson, by whom we were kindly received, and hospitably provided for. Both Mr. and Mrs. Johnson took a deep and lively interest in our welfare. They proved themselves quite worthy of the name of abolitionists. When the stage-driver found us unable to pay our fare, he held on upon our baggage as security for the debt. I had but to mention the fact to Mr. Johnson, and he forthwith advanced the money.

We now began to feel a degree of safety, and to prepare ourselves for the duties and responsibilities of a life of freedom. On the morning after our arrival at New Bedford, while at the breakfast-table, the question arose as to what name I should be called by. The name given me by my mother was, "Frederick Augustus Washington Bailey." I, however, had dispensed with the two middle names long before I left Maryland so that I was generally known by the name of "Frederick Bailey." I started from Baltimore bearing the name of "Stanley." When I got to New York, I again changed my name to "Frederick Johnson," and thought that would be the last change. But when I got to New Bedford, I found it necessary again to change my name. The reason of this necessity was, that there were so many Johnsons in New Bedford it was already quite difficult to distinguish between them. I gave Mr. Johnson the privilege of choosing me a name,

[1]She was free.

[2]I had changed my name from Frederick *Bailey* to that of *Johnson*.

but told him he must not take from me the name of "Frederick." I must hold on to that, to preserve a sense of my identity. Mr. Johnson had just been reading the "Lady of the Lake," and at once suggested that my name be "Douglass." From that time until now I have been called "Frederick Douglass;" and as I am more widely known by that name than by either of the others, I shall continue to use it as my own.

I was quite disappointed at the general appearance of things in New Bedford. The impression which I had received respecting the character and condition of the people of the north, I found to be singularly erroneous. I had very strangely supposed, while in slavery, that few of the comforts, and scarcely any of the luxuries, of life were enjoyed at the north, compared with what were enjoyed by the slaveholders of the south. I probably came to this conclusion from the fact that northern people owned no slaves. I supposed that they were about upon a level with the non-slaveholding population of the south. I knew *they* were exceedingly poor, and I had been accustomed to regard their poverty as the necessary consequence of their being non-slaveholders. I had somehow imbibed the opinion that, in the absence of slaves, there could be no wealth, and very little refinement. And upon coming to the north, I expected to meet with a rough, hard-handed, and uncultivated population, living in the most Spartan-like simplicity, knowing nothing of the ease, luxury, pomp, and grandeur of southern slaveholders. Such being my conjectures, any one acquainted with the appearance of New Bedford may very readily infer how palpably I must have seen my mistake.

In the afternoon of the day when I reached New Bedford, I visited the wharves, to take a view of the shipping. Here I found myself surrounded with the strongest proofs of wealth. Lying at the wharves, and riding in the stream, I saw many ships of the finest model, in the best order, and of the largest size. Upon the right and left, I was walled in by granite warehouses of the widest dimensions, stowed to their utmost capacity with the necessaries and comforts of life. Added to this, almost every body seemed to be at work, but noiselessly so, compared with what I had been accustomed to in Baltimore. There were no loud songs heard from those engaged in loading and unloading ships. I heard no deep oaths or horrid curses on the laborer. I saw no whipping of men; but all seemed to go smoothly on. Every man appeared to understand his work, and went at it with a sober, yet cheerful earnestness, which betokened the deep interest which he felt in what he was doing, as well as a sense of his own dignity as a man. To me this looked exceedingly strange. From the wharves I strolled around and over the town, gazing with wonder and admiration at the splendid churches, beautiful dwellings, and finely-cultivated gardens; evincing an amount of wealth, comfort, taste and refinement, such as I had never seen in any part of slaveholding Maryland.

Every thing looked clean, new, and beautiful. I saw few or no dilapidated houses, with poverty-stricken inmates; no half-naked children and barefooted women, such as I had been accustomed to see in Hillsborough, Easton, St. Michael's, and Baltimore. The people looked more able, stronger, healthier, and happier, than those of Maryland. I was for once made glad by a view of extreme wealth, without being saddened by seeing extreme poverty. But the most astonishing as well as the most interesting thing to me was the condition of the colored people, a great many of whom, like myself, had escaped thither as a refuge from the hunters of men. I found many, who had not been seven years out of their chains, living in finer houses, and evidently enjoying more of the comforts of life, than the average of slave-holders in Maryland.

I will venture to assert that my friend Mr. Nathan Johnson (of whom I can say with a grateful heart, "I was hungry, and he gave me meat; I was thirsty, and he gave me drink; I was a stranger, and he took me in") lived in a neater house; dined at a better table; took, paid for, and read, more newspapers; better understood the moral, religious, and political character of the nation,—than nine tenths of the slaveholders in Talbot county Maryland. Yet Mr. Johnson was a working man. His hands were hardened by toil, and not his alone, but those also of Mrs. Johnson. I found the colored people much more spirited than I had supposed they would be. I found among them a determination to protect each other from the blood-thirsty kidnapper, at all hazards. Soon after my arrival, I was told of a circumstance which illustrated their spirit. A colored man and a fugitive slave were on unfriendly terms. The former was heard to threaten the latter with informing his master of his whereabouts. Straightway a meeting was called among the colored people, under the stereotyped notice, "Business of importance!" The betrayer was invited to attend. The people came at the appointed hour, and organized the meeting by appointing a very religious old gentleman as president, who, I believe, made a prayer, after which he addressed the meeting as follows: *"Friends, we have got him here, and I would recommend that you young men just take him outside the door, and kill him!"* With this a number of them bolted at him; but they were intercepted by some more timid than themselves, and the betrayer escaped their vengeance, and has not been seen in New Bedford since. I believe there have been no more such threats, and should there be hereafter, I doubt not that death would be the consequence.

I found employment, the third day after my arrival, in stowing a sloop with a load of oil. It was new, dirty, and hard work for me; but I went at it with a glad heart and a willing hand. I was now my own master. It was a happy moment, the rapture of which can be understood only by those who have been slaves. It was the first work, the rewards of which was to be entirely my own. There was no Master Hugh standing ready, the moment I earned the money, to rob me of it. I worked that day with a pleasure I had never before experienced. I was at work for myself and newly-married wife. It was to me the starting-point of a new existence. When I got through with that job, I went in pursuit of a job of calking; but such was the strength of prejudice against color, among the white calkers, that they refused to work with me, and of course I could get no employment.[3] Finding my trade of no immediate benefit, I threw off my calking habiliments, and prepared myself to do any kind of work I could get to do. Mr. Johnson kindly let me have his wood-horse and saw, and I very soon found myself a plenty of work. There was no work too hard—none too dirty. I was ready to saw wood, shovel coal, carry the hod, sweep the chimney, or roll oil casks,—all of which I did for nearly three years in New Bedford, before I became known to the anti-slavery world.

In about four months after I went to New Bedford, there came a young man to me, and inquired if I did not wish to take the "Liberator." I told him I did; but, just having made my escape from slavery, I remarked that I was unable to pay for it then. I, however, finally became a subscriber to it. The paper came, and I read it from week to week with such feelings as it would be quite idle for me to attempt to describe. The paper became my meat and

[3] I am told that colored persons can now get employment at calking in New Bedford—a result of anti-slavery effort.

my drink. My soul was set all on fire. Its sympathy for my brethren in bonds—its scathing denunciations of slaveholders—its faithful exposures of slavery—and its powerful attacks upon the upholders of the institution—sent a thrill of joy through my soul, such as I had never felt before!

I had not long been a reader of the "Liberator," before I got a pretty correct idea of the principles, measures and spirit of the anti-slavery reform. I took right hold of the cause. I could do but little; but what I could, I did with a joyful heart, and never felt happier than when in an anti-slavery meeting. I seldom had much to say at the meetings, because what I wanted to say was said so much better by others. But, while attending an anti-slavery convention at Nantucket, on the 11th of August, 1841, I felt strongly moved to speak, and was at the same time much urged to do so by Mr. William C. Coffin, a gentleman who had heard me speak in the colored people's meeting at New Bedford. It was a severe cross, and I took it up reluctantly. The truth was, I felt myself a slave, and the idea of speaking to white people weighed me down. I spoke but a few moments, when I felt a degree of freedom, and said what I desired with considerable ease. From that time until now, I have been engaged in pleading the cause of my brethren—with what success, and with what devotion, I leave those acquainted with my labors to decide.

William Lloyd Garrison

An unrelenting moral crusader for the abolition of slavery, William Lloyd Garrison was known mainly through his journal, *The Liberator,* the journal he published from 1831 to 1865. Born in 1805 to a poor family in Newburyport, Massachusetts, Garrison became a printer's apprentice at thirteen for the *Newburyport Herald.* By the time he was seventeen, he was contributing essays to the paper. At twenty-one Garrison tried to publish a paper of his own, the *Free Press,* in partnership with another printer, but it soon failed. He then worked in Boston as an editor for the *National Philanthropist,* a journal promoting temperance.

Benjamin Lundy inspired Garrison to become active in the antislavery movement, and he edited the Bennington, Vermont, *Journal of the Times,* which supported the gradual emancipation of the slaves and the colonization of freed African-Americans in Africa. But Garrison disagreed with Lundy on the colonization policy, and was soon convicted for libel and jailed for seven weeks for writing with a violent tone against slave traders. He then started *The Liberator* in 1831. This was an uncompromising antislavery editorial weapon supported largely by free African-Americans. Subscriber numbers never surpassed three thousand. Garrison considered slaveholding a crime and demanded immediate abolition. He believed strongly that it was immoral to accept slavery as a legitimate institution. The Southern states blamed Garrison's provocation in part for the Nat Turner slave uprising in Virginia in 1831. They outlawed his paper and tried to prosecute him (see his reaction to the uprising in *The Liberator* printed here).

The next year he founded the New England Anti-Slavery Society on "immediatist" principles. Members included not only those of the Boston aristocracy, but also local African-Americans of ordinary background. Simultaneously he published *Thoughts on*

African Colonization, helping to undermine that plan. In 1833, after visiting England as the leader of American abolitionists, he aided in the founding of the American Anti-Slavery Society in Philadelphia. His life was threatened in the 1835 anti-abolitionist riot in Boston.

As antislavery sentiment grew in the North, Garrison continued to advocate his moral approach, even condemning the U.S. Constitution and federal government for being proslavery. Disagreements between him and the "political" anti-abolitionists split the American Anti-Slavery Society. Although Garrison gained control, the society declined as the Liberty party picked up the antislavery crusade as part of its electoral platform.

In the 1850s, Garrison's moral approach gained new support as it became clear through the Fugitive Slave Act compromise legislation that political action was not about to end slavery. Garrison was viewed as the image of uncompromising integrity in the North, even after he publicly burned a copy of the Constitution on July 4, 1854, in Framingham, Massachusetts. His position amounted to a call for states or individuals to secede from the Union over slavery. A pacifist who accepted the Civil War as a necessary means, he published *The Liberator* until the Thirteenth Amendment prohibited slavery in 1865. Thereafter, until his death in 1879, he helped out in reform movements focused upon suffrage for women, prohibition, and securing the rights of native Americans.

Garrison's style of political thinking is illustrated by the famous defiant lines from the first issue of *The Liberator:* "I will be as harsh as truth, and as uncompromising as justice. On this subject, I do not wish to think, or speak, or write, with moderation. . . . I am in earnest—I will not retreat a single inch—AND I WILL BE HEARD."

The Liberator (1831)
(excerpts)

January 1, 1831

BLACK LIST
Horrible News—Domestic and Foreign

The Ship Francis.

This ship, as I mentioned in our last number,* sailed a few weeks since from this port [Baltimore—T.N.] with a cargo of slaves for the New Orleans market. I do not repeat the fact because it is a rare instance of domestic piracy, or because the case was attended with extraordinary circumstances; for the horrible traffic is briskly carried on, and the transaction was effected in the ordinary manner. I merely wish to illustrate New England humanity and morality. I am determined to cover with thick infamy all who are concerned in this nefarious business.

I have stated that the ship Francis hails from my native place, Newburyport (Massachusetts,) is commanded by a yankee captain, and owned by a townsman named

---

Isaak, *American Political Thinking.*

*In *Genius of Universal Emancipation,* Nov. 13, 1829.[T.N.]

Francis Todd.

Of Captain Nicholas Brown I should have expected better conduct. It is no worse to fit out piratical cruisers, or to engage in the foreign slave trade, than to pursue a similar trade along our coasts; and the men who have the wickedness to participate therein, for the purpose of heaping up wealth, should be ☞ SENTENCED TO SOLITARY CONFINEMENT FOR LIFE; ☞ *they are the enemies of their own species—highway robbers and murderers;* and their final doom will be, unless they speedily repent, *to occupy the lowest depths of perdition.* I know that our laws make a distinction in this matter. I know that the man who is allowed to freight his vessel with slaves at home, for a distant market, would be thought worthy of death if he should take a similar freight on the coast of Africa; but I know, too, that this distinction is absurd, and at war with the common sense of mankind, and that God and good men regard it with abhorrence.

I recollect that it was always a mystery in Newburyport how Mr. Todd contrived to make profitable voyages to New Orleans and other places, when other merchants, with as fair an opportunity to make money, and sending at the same ports at the same time, invariably made fewer successful speculations. The mystery seems to be unravelled. Any man can gather up riches, if he does not care by what means they are obtained.

The Francis carried off *seventy-five* slaves, chained in a narrow place between decks. Captain Brown originally intended to take *one hundred and fifty* of these unfortunate creatures; but another hard-hearted shipmaster underbid him in the price of passage for the remaining moiety. Captain B., we believe, is a *mason.* Where was his charity or brotherly kindness?

I respectfully request the editor of the Newburyport Herald to copy this article or publish a statement of the facts contained herein—not for the purpose of giving information to Mr. Todd, for I shall send him a copy of this number, but in order to enlighten the public mind in that quarter—
G.

July 30, 1831

WHAT SHALL BE DONE?

The solemn inquiries are often anxiously made, what shall be done for the abolition of slavery, and wherein can the people of the free States act efficiently? A full and satisfactory reply to these inquiries demands a series of numbers. In the present essay, I shall sketch out only the outlines of a few feasible schemes.

First of all, I want every man and every woman to discard their criminal prejudices, their timorous fears, and their paralyzing doubts. I want them to feel that two millions of their brothers and sisters are groaning under the thraldom of slavery; that they are bound, by every conceivable motive, to assist in breaking their fetters; and that they are capable of effecting their desires, through divine assistance.—The work of reform must commence with *ourselves.* Until *we* are purified, it will be fruitless and intrusive for *us* to cleanse *others.* I say, then, that the *entire abstinence* from the products of slavery is the duty of every individual. . . .

In England, more is doing, perhaps, by females towards overthrowing slavery in the British Colonies, than by the other sex. Each member of a Free Produce Society pays annually a few shillings into the treasury thereof—with which money, tracts, illustrative of the horrors of slavery, and filled with pathetic entreaties, are circulated far and wide. . . . The ladies of this country ought not to be outdone in this benevolent and holy enterprise.

2dly. Religious professors, of all denominations, must bear unqualified testimony against slavery. They must not support, they must not palliate it. . . .

"For this thing which it cannot bear, the earth is disquieted." The Gospel of Peace and Mercy preached by him who steals, buys and sells the purchase of the Messiah's blood! . . .

3dly. The formation of an American Anti-Slavery Society is of the utmost importance; and it is now, I am happy to say, in embryo. The objects of this Society will be, to consolidate the moral power of the nation, so that Congress and the State Legislatures may be inundated with petitions;—to scatter tracts, like rain-drops, over the land, on the subject of slavery;— to employ active and eloquent agents to plead the cause constantly, and to form auxiliaries;—to encourage planters to cultivate their lands by freemen, by offering large premiums;—to promote education and the mechanical arts among the free

people of color, and to recover their lost rights. The people, at large, are astonishingly ignorant of the horrors of slavery. Let information be circulated among them as prodigally as the light of heaven, and they cannot long act and reason as they now do.

4thly. Slavery in the District of Columbia is sustained in our national capacity: it ought, therefore, to be prostrated at a blow.

5thly. The clause in the Constitution should be erased, which tolerates, greatly to the detriment and injustice of the free states, a slave representation in Congress. Why should property be represented from the impoverished south, and not from the opulent north?

6thly. We want, at this moment, at least one hundred periodicals over the land, expressly devoted to the cause of emancipation. . . . 'What more shall we do?' It will be seasonable enough to answer this question, when we shall have done what has been already suggested.

September 3, 1831

THE INSURRECTION

What we have long predicted,—at the peril of being stigmatized as an alarmist and declaimer,—has commenced its fulfillment. The first step of the earthquake, which is ultimately to shake down the fabric of oppression, leaving not one stone upon the other, has been made. The first drops of blood, which are but the prelude to a deluge from the gathering clouds, have fallen. The first flash of lightning, which is to ignite and consume, has been felt. The first wailings of a bereavement, which is to clothe the earth in sackcloth, have broken upon our ears.

In the first number of the Liberator, we alluded to the hour of vengeance in the following lines:

Wo if it come with storm, and blood, and fire,
When midnight darkness veils the earth and sky!
Wo to the innocent babe—the guilty sire—
Mother and daughter—friends of kindred tie!
Stranger and citizen alike shall die!
Red-handed Slaughter his revenge shall feed,

And Havoc yell his ominous death-
cry,
And wild Despair in vain for mercy
plead—
While hell itself shall shrink and
sicken at the deed!

Read the account of the insurrection
in Virginia, and say whether our prophecy
be not fulfilled. What was poetry—imagination—in January, is now a bloody reality.
"Wo to the innocent babe—to mother and
daughter!" Is it not true? Turn again to the
record of slaughter! Whole families have
been cut off—not a mother, not a daughter,
not a babe left. Dreadful retaliation! "The
dead bodies of white and black lying just as
they were slain, unburied"—the oppressor
and the oppressed equal at last in death—
what a spectacle!

True, the rebellion is quelled. Those
of the slaves who were not killed in combat,
have been secured, and the prison is
crowded with victims destined for the gal-
lows!

"Yet laugh not in your carnival of
crime
Too proudly, ye oppressors!"

You have seen, it is to be feared, but the
beginning of sorrows. All the blood which
has been shed will be required at your
hands. At your hands alone? No—but at
the hands of the people of New-England
and of all the free states. The crime of
oppression is national. The south is only
the agent in this guilty traffic. But, remember! the same causes are at work which
must inevitably produce the same effects;
and when the contest shall have again
begun, it must be again a war of extermination. In the present instance, no quarters
have been asked or given.

But we have killed and routed them
now—we can do it again and again—we
are invincible! A dastardly triumph, well
becoming a nation of oppressors. Detestable complacency, that can think, without

emotion, of the extermination of the blacks!
We have the power to kill *all*—let us, therefore, continue to apply the whip and forge
new fetters!

In his fury against the revolters, who
will remember their wrongs? What will it
avail them, though the catalogue of their
sufferings, dripping with warm blood fresh
from their lacerated bodies, be held up to
extenuate their conduct? It is enough that
the victims were black—that circumstance
makes them less precious than the dogs
which have been slain in our streets! They
were black—brutes, pretending to be
men—legions of curses on their memories!
They were black—God made them to serve
us!

Ye patriotic hypocrites! ye panegyrists
of Frenchmen, Greeks, and Poles! ye fus-
tian declaimers for liberty! ye valient [*sic*]
sticklers for equal rights among yourselves! ye haters of aristocracy! ye assail-
ants of monarchies! ye republican
nullifiers! ye treasonable disunionists! be
dumb! Cast no reproach upon the conduct
of the slaves, but let your lips and cheeks
wear the blisters of condemnation!

Ye accuse the pacific friends of emancipation of instigating the slaves to revolt.
Take back the charge as a foul slander.
The slaves need no incentives at our hands.
They will find them in their stripes—in
their emaciated bodies—in their ceaseless
toil—in their ignorant minds—in every
field, in every valley, on every hill-top and
mountain, wherever you and your fathers
have fought for liberty—in your speeches,
your conversations, your celebrations, your
pamphlets, your newspapers—voices in
the air, sounds from across the ocean, in
resistance above, below, around them!
What more do they need? Surrounded by
such influences, and smarting under their
newly made wounds, is it wonderful that
they should rise to contend—as other
"heroes" have contended—for their lost
rights? It is *not* wonderful.

In all that we have written, is there aught to justify the excesses of the slaves? No. Nevertheless, they deserve no more censure than the Greeks in destroying the Turks, or the Poles in exterminating the Russians, or our fathers in slaughtering the British. Dreadful, indeed, is the standard erected by worldly patriotism!

For ourselves, we are horror-struck at the late tidings. We have exerted our utmost efforts to avert the calamity. We have warned our countrymen of the danger of persisting in their unrighteous conduct. We have preached to the slaves the pacific precepts of Jesus Christ. We have appealed to christians, philanthropists and patriots, for their assistance to accomplish the great work of national redemption through the agency of moral power—of public opinion—of individual duty. How have we been received? We have been threatened, proscribed, vilified and imprisoned—a laughing-stock and a reproach. Do we falter, in view of these things? Let time answer. If we have been hitherto urgent, and bold, and denunciatory in our efforts,—hereafter we shall grow vehement and active with the increase of danger. We shall cry, in trumpet tones, night and day,—Wo to this guilty land, unless she speedily repents of her evil doings! The blood of millions of her sons cries aloud for redress! IMMEDIATE EMANCIPATION can alone save her from the vengeance of Heaven, and cancel the debt of ages!

September 3, 1831

George Fitzhugh

A proslavery advocate who argued that the so-called free laborer is emotionally and morally worse off than the slave, George Fitzhugh was a sociologist whose extreme views carved out a niche in the abolitionist debate preceding the Civil War. Born in Prince William County, Virginia, in 1807, Fitzhugh was largely self-taught, going to "field schools" where he often managed the class when no teacher showed up. Nevertheless, he obtained a good education, studied law, and then set up a law practice in Port Royal, Virginia, specializing in criminal cases.

During the administration of President Buchanan, Fitzhugh served in the land claims department of the attorney general's office. He made his only visit to the North, meeting Mrs. Harriet Beecher Stowe. He published a number of articles in the *New York Day-Book*, the *Richmond Examiner*, and *DeBow's Review*, as well as other periodicals.

Fitzhugh was much impressed with Thomas Carlyle's essay "The Present Age," which stimulated some of the ideas and the title and subtitle of *Cannibals All! or, Slaves Without Masters* (1857) (see excerpts). Not only was Carlyle's attack on British abolitionists and West Indian emancipation attractive to Fitzhugh, but he was carried away by Carlyle's diatribes against the "Mammonism" of the industrialists and the "wicked" economics of Manchester.

Arguing that slavery is the natural and rightful condition of society, which, without it, results in (economic) cannibalism, Fitzhugh believed that the laboring classes, regardless of color, should be slaves on the model of ancient Greece and Rome. In his book *Sociology for the South* (1854), he wrote:

Slavery without domestic affection would be a curse, and so would marriage and parental authority. The free laborer is excluded from its holy and charmed circle. Shelterless, naked, and hungry, he is exposed to the bleak winds, the cold rains and hot sun of heaven, with none that love him, none that care for him. His employer hates him because he asks high wages or joins strikes, his fellow-laborer hates him because he competes with him for employment. Foolish abolitionists! Bring him back, like the prodigal son. Let him fare at least as well as the dog, and the horse, and the sheep. Better to lie down with the kids and the goats, than stand naked and hungry without. As a slave, he will be beloved and protected. Whilst free, he will be hated, despised, and persecuted.

Fitzhugh died in 1881 after losing his battle to preserve slavery.

Cannibals All!
or, Slaves without Masters (1857)
(excerpts)

The Universal Trade

We are all, North and South, engaged in the White Slave Trade, and he who succeeds best is esteemed most respectable. It is far more cruel than the Black Slave Trade, because it exacts more of its slaves, and neither protects nor governs them. We boast that it exacts more when we say, "that the *profits* made from employing free labor are greater than those from slave labor." The profits, made from free labor, are the amount of the products of such labor, which the employer, by means of the command which capital or skill gives him, takes away, exacts, or "exploitates" from the free laborer. The profits of slave labor are that portion of the products of such labor which the power of the master enables him to appropriate. These profits are less, because the master allows the slave to retain a larger share of the results of his own labor than do the employers of free labor. But we not only boast that the White Slave Trade is more exacting and fraudulent (in fact, though not in intention) than Black Slavery; but we also boast that it is more cruel in leaving the laborer to take care of himself and family out of the pittance which skill or capital have allowed him to retain. When the day's labor is ended, he is free, but is overburdened with the cares of family and household, which make his freedom an empty and delusive mockery. But his employer is really free, and may enjoy the profits made by others' labor, without a care, or a trouble, as to their well-being. The negro slave is free, too, when the labors of the day are over, and free in mind as well as body; for the master provides food, raiment, house, fuel, and everything else necessary to the physical well-being of himself and family. The master's labors commence just when the slave's end. No wonder men should prefer white slavery to capital, to negro slavery, since it is more profitable, and is free from all the cares and labors of black slave-holding.

Isaak, *American Political Thinking.*

Now, reader, if you wish to know your-self—to "descant on your own deformity"—read on. But if you would cherish self-conceit, self-esteem, or self-appreciation, throw down our book; for we will dispel illusions which have promoted your happiness, and show you that what you have considered and practiced as virtue is little better than moral Cannibalism. But you will find yourself in numerous and respectable company; for all good and respectable people are "Cannibals all" who do not labor, or who are successfully trying to live without labor, on the unrequited labor of other people:—Whilst low, bad, and disreputable people, are those who labor to support themselves, and to support said respectable people besides. Throwing the negro slaves out of the account, and society is divided in Christendom into four classes: the rich, or independent respectable people, who live well and labor not at all, the professional and skillful respectable people, who do a little light work, for enormous wages; the poor hard-working people, who support everybody, and starve themselves; and the poor thieves, swindlers, and sturdy beggars, who live like gentlemen, without labor, on the labor of other people. The gentlemen exploitate, which being done on a large scale and requiring a great many victims, is highly respectable—whilst the rogues and beggars take so little from others that they fare little better than those who labor.

But, readers, we do not wish to fire into the flock. "Thou art the man!" You are a Cannibal! and if a successful one, pride yourself on the number of your victims quite as much as any Fiji chieftain, who breakfasts, dines, and sups on human flesh—and your conscience smites you, if you have failed to succeed, quite as much as his, when he returns from an unsuccessful foray.

Probably, you are a lawyer, or a merchant, or a doctor, who has made by your business fifty thousand dollars, and retired to live on your capital. But, mark! not to spend your capital. That would be vulgar, disreputable, criminal. That would be, to live by your own labor; for your capital is your amassed labor. That would be to do as common working men do; for they take the pittance which their employers leave them to live on. They live by labor; for they exchange the results of their own labor for the products of other people's labor. It is, no doubt, an honest, vulgar way of living, but not at all a respectable way. The respectable way of living is to make other people work for you, and to pay them nothing for so doing—and to have no concern about them after their work is done. Hence, white slave-holding is much more respectable than negro slavery—for the master works nearly as hard for the negro as he for the master. But you, my virtuous, respectable reader, exact three thousand dollars per annum from white labor (for your income is the product of white labor) and make not one cent of return in any form. You retain your capital, and never labor, and yet live in luxury on the labor of others. Capital commands labor, as the master does the slave. Neither pays for labor; but the master permits the slave to retain a larger allowance from the proceeds of his own labor, and hence "free labor is cheaper than slave labor." You, with the command over labor which your capital gives you, are a slave owner—a master, without the obligations of a master. They who work for you, who create your income, are slaves, without the rights of slaves. Slaves without a master! Whilst you were engaged in amassing your capital, in seeking to become independent, you were in the White Slave Trade. To become independent is to be able to make other people support you, without being obliged to labor for *them*. Now, what man in society is not seeking to attain this situation? He who attains it is a slave owner, in the worst sense. He who is in pursuit of it is engaged in the slave trade. You, reader, belong to the one or other class. The men without property, in free society, are theoretically in a worse condition than slaves. Practically, their condition corresponds with this theory, as history and statistics everywhere demonstrate. The capitalists, in free society, live in ten times the luxury and show that Southern masters do, because the slaves to capital work harder and cost less than negro slaves.

The negro slaves of the South are the happiest, and, in some sense, the freest people in the world. The children and the aged and infirm work not at all, and yet have all the comforts and necessaries of life provided for them. They enjoy liberty, because they are oppressed neither by care nor labor. The women do little hard work, and are protected from the despotisim of their husbands by their masters. The negro men and stout boys, on the average, in good weather, not more than nine hours a day. The balance of their time is spent in perfect abandon. Besides, they have their Sabbaths and holidays. White men, with so much of license and liberty, would die of ennui; but negroes luxuriate in corporeal and mental repose. With their faces upturned to the sun, they can sleep at any hour; and quiet sleep is the greatest of human enjoyments. "Blessed be the man who invented sleep." 'Tis happiness in itself—and results from contentment with the present, and confident assurance of the future. We do not know whether free laborers ever sleep. They are fools to do so; for, whilst they sleep, the wily and watchful capitalist is devising means to ensnare and exploitate them. The free laborer must work or starve. He is more of a slave than the negro, because he works longer and harder for less allowance than the slave, and has no

holiday, because the cares of life with him begin when its labors end. He has no liberty, and not a single right. We know, 'tis often said, air and water are common property, which all have equal right to participate and enjoy; but this is utterly false. The appropriation of the lands carries with it the appropriation of all on or above the lands, *usque ad coelum, aut ad inferos.*[1] A man cannot breathe the air without a place to breathe it from, and all places are appropriated. All water is private property "to the middle of the stream," except the ocean, and that is not fit to drink.

Free laborers have not a thousandth part of the rights and liberties of negro slaves. Indeed, they have not a single liberty, unless it be the right or liberty to die. But the reader may think that he and other capitalists and employers are freer than negro slaves. Your capital would soon vanish, if you dared indulge in the liberty and abandon of negroes. You hold your wealth and position by the tenure of constant watchfulness, care, and circumspection. You never labor; but you are never free.

Where a few own the soil, they have unlimited power over the balance of society, until domestic slavery comes in to compel them to permit this balance of society to draw a sufficient and comfortable living from *terra mater.* Free society asserts the right of a few to the earth— slavery maintains that it belongs, in different degrees, to all.

But, reader, well may you follow the slave trade. It is the only trade worth following, and slaves the only property worth owning. All other is worthless, a mere *caput mortuum,*[2] except in so far as it vests the owner with the power to command the labors of others—to enslave them. Give you a palace, ten thousand acres of land, sumptuous clothes, equipage, and every

---

[1] "Even to heaven or to hell."

[2] "Worthless residue."

other luxury; and with your artificial wants you are poorer than Robinson Crusoe, or the lowest working man, if you have no slaves to capital, or domestic slaves. Your capital will not bring you an income of a cent, nor supply one of your wants, without labor. Labor is indispensable to give value to property and if you owned every thing else, and did not own labor, you would be poor. But fifty thousand dollars means, and is, fifty thousand dollars worth of slaves. You can command, without touching on that capital, three thousand dollars' worth of labor per annum. You could do no more were you to buy slaves with it, and then you would be cumbered with the cares of governing and providing for them. You are a slaveholder now, to the amount of fifty thousand dollars, with all the advantages, and none of the cares and responsibilities of a master.

"Property in man" is what all are struggling to obtain. Why should they not be obliged to take care of man, their property, as they do of their horses and their hounds, their cattle and their sheep. Now, under the delusive name of liberty, you work him "from morn to dewy eve"—from infancy to old age—then turn him out to starve. You treat your horses and hounds better. Capital is a cruel master. The free slave trade, the commonest, yet the cruellest of trades.

Negro Slavery

Until the lands of America are appropriated by a few, population becomes dense, competition among laborers active, employment uncertain, and wages low, the personal liberty of all the whites will continue to be a blessing. We have vast unsettled territories; population may cease to increase slowly, as in most countries, and many centuries may elapse before the question will be practically suggested, whether slavery to capital be preferable to slavery to human masters. But the negro has neither energy nor enterprise, and, even in our sparser population, finds, with his improvident habits, that his liberty is a curse to himself, and a greater curse to the society around him. These considerations, and others equally obvious, have induced the South to attempt to defend negro slavery as an exceptional institution, admitting, nay asserting, that slavery, in the general or in the abstract, is morally wrong, and against common right. With singular inconsistency, after making this admission, which admits away the authority of the Bible, of profane history, and of the almost universal practice of mankind—they turn round and attempt to bolster up the cause of negro slavery by these very exploded authorities. If we mean not to repudiate all divine, and almost all human authority in favor of slavery, we must vindicate that institution in the abstract.

To insist that a status of society, which has been almost universal, and which is expressly and continually justified by Holy Writ, is its natural, normal, and necessary status, under the ordinary circumstances, is on its face a plausible and probable proposition. To insist on less, is to yield our cause, and to give up our religion; for if white slavery be morally wrong, be a violation of natural rights, the Bible cannot be true. Human and divine authority do seem in the general to concur, in establishing the expediency of having masters and slaves of different races. The nominal servitude of the Jews to each other, in its temporary character, and no doubt in its mild character, more nearly resembled our wardship and apprenticeship, than ordinary domestic slavery. In very many nations of antiquity, and in some of modern times, the law has permitted the native citizens to become slaves to each other. But few take advantage of such laws; and the infrequency of the practice, establishes the general truth that master and slave should be of different national descent. In some respects, the wider the difference the better, as the slave will feel less mortified by his position. In other respects, it may be that too wide a difference hardens the hearts and brutalizes the feelings of both master and slave. The civilized man hates the savage, and the savage returns the hatred with interest. Hence, West India slavery of newly caught negroes is not a very humane, affectionate, or civilizing institution. Virginia negroes have become moral and intelligent. They love their master and his family, and the attachment is reciprocated. Still, we like the idle, but intelligent house-servants, better than the hard-used, but stupid outhands; and we like the mulatto better than the negro; yet the negro is generally more affectionate, contented and faithful.

The world at large looks on negro slavery as much the worst form of slavery; because it is only acquainted with West India slavery. Abolition never arose till negro slavery was instituted; and now abolition is only directed against negro slavery. This is no philanthropic crusade attempting to set free the white slaves of Eastern Europe and of Asia. The world, then is prepared for the defence of slavery in the abstract—it is prejudiced only against negro slavery. These prejudices were in their origin well founded. The Slave Trade, the horrors of the Middle Passage, and West India slavery were enough to rouse the most torpid philanthropy.

But our Southern slavery has become a benign and protective institution, and our negroes are confessedly better off than any free laboring population in the world.

How can we contend that white slavery is wrong, whilst all the great body of free laborers are starving; and slaves, white or black, throughout the world, are enjoying comfort?

We write in the cause of Truth and Humanity, and will not play the advocate for master or for slave.

The aversion to negroes, the antipathy of race, is much greater at the North than at the South; and it is very probable that this antipathy to the person of the negro, is confounded with or generates hatred of the institution with which he is usually connected. Hatred to slavery is very generally little more than hatred of negroes.

There is one strong argument in favor of negro slavery over all other slavery: that he, being unfitted for the mechanic arts, for trade, and all skillful pursuits, leaves those pursuits to be carried on by the whites; and does not bring all industry into disrepute, as in Greece and Rome, where the slaves were not only the artists and mechanics, but also the merchants.

Whilst, as a general and abstract question, negro slavery has no other claims over other forms of slavery, except that from inferiority, or rather peculiarity, of race, almost all negroes require masters, whilst only the children, the women, the very weak, poor, and ignorant, &c., among the whites, need some protective and governing relation of this kind; yet as a subject of temporary, but worldwide importance, negro slavery has become the most necessary of all human institutions.

The African slave trade to America commenced three centuries and a half since. By the time of the American Revolution, the supply of slaves had exceeded the demand for slave labor, and the slaveholders, to get rid of a burden and to prevent the increase of a nuisance, became violent opponents of the slave trade, and many of them abolitionists. New England, Bristol, and Liverpool, who reaped the profits of the trade, without suffering from the nuisance, stood out for a long time against its abolition. Finally, laws and treaties were made, and fleets fitted out to abolish it; and after a while, the slaves of most of South America, of the West Indies, and of Mexico were liberated. In the meantime, cotton, rice, sugar, coffee, tobacco, and other products of slave labor, came into universal use as necessaries of life. The population of Western Europe, sustained and stimulated by those products, was trebled, and that of the North increased tenfold. The products of slave labor became scarce and dear, and famines frequent. Now, it is obvious, that to emancipate all the negroes would be to starve Western Europe and our North. Not to extend and increase negro slavery, *pari passu,* with the extension and multiplication of free society, will produce much suffering. If all South America, Mexico, the West Indies, and our Union south of Mason and Dixon's line, of the Ohio and Missouri, were slaveholding, slave products would be abundant and cheap in free society; and their market for their merchandise, manufactures, commerce, &c., illimitable. Free white laborers might live in comfort and luxury on light work, but for the exacting and greedy landlords, bosses and other capitalists.

We must confess, that overstock the world as you will with comforts and with luxuries, we do not see how to make capital relax its monopoly—how to do aught but tantalize the hireling. Capital, irresponsible capital, begets, and ever will beget, the *immedicabile vulnus*[3] of so-called Free Society. It invades every recess of domestic life, infects its food, its clothing, its drink, its very atmosphere, and pursues the hireling, from the hovel to the poor-house, the prison and the grave. Do what he will, go where he will, capital pursues and persecutes him. "Haeret lateri lethalis arundo!"[4]

Capital supports and protects the domestic slave; taxes, oppresses and persecutes the free laborer. . . .

Orestes A. Brownson

A powerful writer, and a Jeffersonian Democrat in his radical phase, Orestes Brownson argued that equality of civil rights must lead to equality of conditions. Therefore, the inheritance of private property, the system of bank credit, the modern industrial company, and the factory system must be abolished. When this radical argument was published in the "Essay on the Laboring Classes" in 1840, an election year, Brownson was expelled from the Democratic party because of his great influence as a writer and editor at the time.

Born into poverty in 1803 and largely self-taught with little formal education, Brownson became a moving target for his opponents. He went through a number of social, political, and religious transformations as he worked things through the hard way. Starting as a Presbyterian, Brownson went through Universalism, humanitarianism, Unitarianism, and transcendentalism, and finally converted permanently to Catholicism in 1844. He served as a Universalist preacher, then a Unitarian preacher, then an activist in Robert Owen's socialistic endeavors. Even after joining the Catholics, he was never totally happy with the church hierarchy, nor it with him because of his sharp pen. His political views went through the same kind of cycle: beginning as a Chartist (a member of a British social reform movement for improving conditions of the working class), becoming a

---

[3]"Irreparable injury."

[4]"The lethal arrow clings to her side." Virgil, *Aeneid,* IV, 73

Jacksonian Democrat, then joining the Workingman's party, and finally ending up as an unaffiliated conservative after 1844, placing authority and duties before rights.

Courting no man's favor, Brownson was a forthright, uncompromising political thinker. He founded the *Boston Quarterly Review* in 1836, which later merged with the *Democratic Review*. When Brownson's views became too conservative for the Jacksonian journal, he was forced to resign. As a result he founded the *Brownson Quarterly Review*, editing it from 1844 until 1865 and from 1872 to 1875. In his later conservative phase, Brownson, who had been a socialist before Marx was known, said that socialism is the application of the theory of pure democracy to economic life and that it must end in the destruction of both economic prosperity and of true social justice. He died in 1876. Note Brownson's radical economic position in the following essay, which clearly placed him outside the mainstream tradition of American liberalism.

❧❦

The Laboring Classes (1840)

Art. IV.—*Chartism,* by Thomas Carlyle.
Boston: C. C. Little & James Brown. 1840. 12 mo. pp. 113.

Thomas Carlyle unquestionably ranks among the ablest writers of the day. His acquaintance with literature seems to be almost universal, and there is apparently no art or science with which he is not familiar. He possesses an unrivalled mastery over the resources of the English tongue, a remarkably keen insight into the mysteries of human nature, and a large share of genuine poetic feeling. His works are characterized by freshness and power, as well as by strangeness and singularity, and must be read with interest, even when they cannot be with approbation.

The little work, named at the head of this article, is a fair sample of his peculiar excellences, and also of his peculiar defects. As a work intended to excite attention and lead the mind to an investigation of a great subject, it possesses no ordinary value; but as a work intended to throw light on a difficult question, and to afford some positive directions to the statesman and the philanthropist, it is not worth much. Car-

lyle, like his imitators in this country, though he declaims against the destructives, possesses in no sense a constructive genius. He is good as a demolisher, but pitiable enough as a builder. No man sees more clearly that the present is defective and unworthy to be retained; he is a brave and successful warrior against it, whether reference be had to its literature, its politics, its philosophy, or its religion; but when the question comes up concerning what ought to be, what should take the place of what is, we regret to say, he affords us no essential aid, scarcely a useful hint. He has fine spiritual instincts, has outgrown materialism, loathes skepticism, sees clearly the absolute necessity of faith in both God and man, and insists upon it with due sincerity and earnestness; but with feelings very nearly akin to despair. He does not appear to have found as yet a faith for himself, and his writings have almost invariably a skeptical tendency. He has doubtless a sort of faith in God, or an overwhelming

Necessity, but we cannot perceive that he has any faith in man or in man's efforts. Society is wrong, but he mocks at our sincerest and best directed efforts to right it. It cannot subsist as it is; that is clear: but what shall be done to make it what it ought to be, that he saith not. Of all writers we are acquainted with, he is the least satisfactory. He is dissatisfied with everything himself, and he leaves his readers dissatisfied with everything. Hopeless himself, he makes them also hopeless, especially if they have strong social tendencies, and are hungering and thirsting to work out the regeneration of their race.

Mr. Carlyle's admirers, we presume, will demur to this criticism. We have heard some of them speak of him as a sort of soul-quickener, and profess to derive from his writings fresh life and courage. We know not how this may be. It may be that they derive advantage from him on the homeopathic principle, and that he curses their diseases by exaggerating them; but for ourselves we must say that we have found him anything but a skilful physician. He disheartens and enfeebles us; and while he emancipates us from the errors of tradition, he leaves us without strength or courage to engage in the inquiry after truth. We rise from his writings with the weariness and exhaustion one does from the embraces of the Witch Mara. It is but slowly that our blood begins to circulate again, and it is long before we recover the use of our powers. Whether his writings produce this effect on others or not, we are unable to say; but this effect they do produce on us. We almost dread to encounter them.

Mr. Carlyle would seem to have great sympathy with man. He certainly is not wanting in the sentiment of humanity; nor is he deceived by external position, or dazzled by factitious glare. He can see worth in the socially low as well as in the socially high; in the artisan as well as the noble. This is something, but no great merit in

one who can read the new Testament. Still it is something, and we are glad to meet it. But after all, he has no true reverence for Humanity. He may offer incense to a Goethe, a Jean Paul, a Mirabeau, a Danton, a Napoleon, but he nevertheless looks down upon his fellows, and sneers at the mass. He looks down upon man as one of his admirers has said, "as if man were a mouse." But we do not wish to look upon man in that light. We would look upon him as a brother, an equal, entitled to our love and sympathy. We would feel ourselves neither above him nor below him, but standing up by his side, with our feet on the same level with his. We would also love and respect the common-place mass, not merely heroes and sages, prophets and priests.

We are moreover no warm admirers of Carlyle's style of writing. We acknowledge his command over the resources of our language, and we enjoy the freshness, and occasional strength, beauty, and felicity of his style and expression, but he does not satisfy us. He wants clearness and precision, and that too when writing on topics where clearness and precision are all but indispensable. We have no patience with his mistiness, vagueness, and singularity. If a man must needs write and publish his thoughts to the world, let him do it in as clear and as intelligible language as possible. We are not aware of any subject worth writing on at all, that is already so plain that it needs to be rendered obscure. Carlyle can write well if he chooses; no man better. He is not necessarily misty, vague, nor fantastic. The antic tricks he has been latterly playing do not spring from the constitution of his mind, and we must say do by no means become him. We are disposed ourselves to assume considerable latitude in both thought and expression; but we believe every scholar should aim to keep within the general current of his language. Every language receives certain laws from the genius of the people who use it, and it is no mark of wisdom to transgress them; nor is genuine literary excellence to be attained but by obeying them. An Englishman, if he would profit Englishmen, must write English, not French nor German. If he wishes his writings to become an integral part of the literature of his language, he must keep within the steady current of what has ever been regarded as classical English style, and deny himself the momentary eclat he might gain by affectation and singularity.

We can, however, pardon Carlyle altogether more easily than we can his American imitators. Notwithstanding his manner of writing, when continued for any considerable length, becomes monotonous and wearisome, as in his History of the French Revolution,—a work which, with all its brilliant wit, inimitable humor, deep pathos, and graphic skill, can scarcely be read without yawning,—yet in his case it is redeemed by rare beauties, and marks a mind of the highest order, and of vast attainments. But in the hands of his American imitators, it becomes puerile and disgusting; and what is worthy of note is, that it is adopted and most servilely followed by the men among us who are loudest in their boasts of originality, and the most intolerant to its absence. But enough of this. For our consolation, the race of imitators is feeble and shortlived.

The object of the little work before us, is one of the weightiest which can engage the attention of the statesman or the philanthropist. It is indeed, here, discussed only in relation to the working classes of England, but it in reality involves the condition of the working classes throughout the world,—a great subject, and one never yet worthily treated. Chartism, properly speaking, is no local or temporary phenomenon. Its germ may be found in every nation in Christendom; indeed whenever man has approximated a state of civilization, wherever there is inequality in social condition, and in the distribution of the products of industry. And where does not this inequality obtain? Where is the spot on earth, in which the actual producer of wealth is not one of the lower class, shut out from what are looked upon as the main advantages of the social state?

Mr. Carlyle, though he gives us few facts, yet shows us that the condition of the workingmen in England is deplorable, and every day growing worse. It has already become intolerable, and hence the outbreak of the Chartists. Chartism is the protest of the working classes against the injustice of the present social organization of the British community, and a loud demand for a new organization which shall respect the rights and well-being of the laborer.

The movements of the Chartists have excited considerable alarm in the higher classes of English society, and some hope in the friends of Humanity among ourselves. We do not feel competent to speak with any decision on the extent or importance of these movements. If our voice could reach the Chartists we would bid them be bold and determined; we would bid them persevere even unto death; for their cause is that of justice, and in fighting for it they will be fighting the battles of God and man. But we look for no important results from their movements. We have little faith in a John Bull mob. It will bluster, and swagger, and threaten much; but give it plenty of porter and roast-beef, and it will sink back to its kennel, as quiet and as harmless as a lamb. The lower classes in England have made many a move since the days of Wat Tyler for the betterment of their condition, but we cannot perceive that they have ever effected much. They are doubtless nearer the day of their emancipation, than they were, but their actual condition is scarcely superior to what it was in the days of Richard the Second.

There is no country in Europe, in which the condition of the laboring classes seems to us so hopeless as in that of England. This is not owing to the fact, that the aristocracy is less enlightened, more powerful, or more oppressive in England than elsewhere. The English laborer does not find his worst enemy in the nobility, but in the middling class. The middle class is much more numerous and powerful in England than in any other European country, and is of a higher character. It has always been powerful; for by means of the Norman Conquest it received large accessions from the old Saxon nobility. The Conquest established a new aristocracy, and degraded the old to the condition of Commoners. The superiority of the English Commons is, we suppose, chiefly owing to this fact.

The middle class is always a firm champion of equality, when it concerns humbling a class above it; but it is its inveterate foe, when it concerns elevating a class below it. Manfully have the British Commoners struggled against the old feudal aristocracy, and so successfully that they now constitute the dominant power in the state. To their struggles against the throne and the nobility is the English nation indebted for the liberty it so loudly boasts, and which, during the last half of the last century, so enraptured the friends of Humanity throughout Europe.

But this class has done nothing for the laboring population, the real *proletarii*. It has humbled the aristocracy; it has raised itself to dominion, and it is now conservative,—conservative in fact, whether it call itself Whig or Radical. From its near relation to the workingmen, its kindred pursuits with them, it is altogether more hostile to them than the nobility ever were or ever can be. This was seen in the conduct of England towards the French Revolution. So long as that Revolution was in the hands of the middle class, and threatened merely to humble monarchy and nobility, the English nation applauded it; but as soon as it descended to the mass of the people, and

promised to elevate the laboring classes, so soon as the starving workingman began to flatter himself, that there was to be a Revolution for him too as well as for his employer, the English nation armed itself and poured out its blood and treasure to suppress it. Everybody knows that Great Britain, boasting of her freedom and of her love of freedom, was the life and soul of the opposition to the French Revolution; and on her head almost alone should fall the curses of Humanity for the sad failure of that glorious uprising of the people in behalf of their imprescriptible, and inalienable rights. Yet it was not the English monarchy, nor the English nobility, that was alone in fault. Monarchy, and nobility would have been powerless, had they not had with them the great body of the English Commoners. England fought in the ranks, nay, at the head of the allies, not for monarchy, not for nobility, nor yet for religion; but for trade and manufactures, for her middle class, against the rights and well-being of the workingman; and her strength and efficiency consisted in the strength and efficiency of this class.

Now this middle class, which was strong enough to defeat nearly all the practical benefit of the French Revolution, is the natural enemy of the Chartists. It will unite with the monarchy and nobility against them; and spare neither blood nor treasure to defeat them. Our despair for the poor Chartists arises from the number and power of the middle class. We dread for them neither monarchy nor nobility. Nor should they. Their only real enemy is in the employer. In all countries is it the same. The only enemy of the laborer is your employer, whether appearing in the shape of the master mechanic, or in the owner of a factory. A Duke of Wellington is much more likely to vindicate the rights of labor than an Abbot Lawrence, although the latter may be a very kind-hearted man, and liberal citizen, as we always find Blackwood's Magazine more true to the interests of the poor, than we do the Edinburgh Review, or even the London and Westminster.

Mr. Carlyle, contrary to his wont, in the pamphlet we have named, commends two projects for the relief of the working-men, which he finds others have suggested,—universal education, and general emigration. Universal education we shall not be thought likely to depreciate; but we confess that we are unable to see in it that sovereign remedy for the evils of the social state as it is, which some of our friends do, or say they do. We have little faith in the power of education to elevate a people compelled to labor from twelve to sixteen hours a day, and to experience for no mean portion of the time a paucity of even the necessaries of life, let alone its comforts. Give your starving boy a breakfast before you send him to school, and your tattered beggar a cloak before you attempt his moral and intellectual elevation. A swarm of naked and starving urchins crowded into a schoolroom will make little proficiency in the "Humanities." Indeed, it seems to us most bitter mockery for the well-dressed and well-fed to send the schoolmaster and priest to the wretched hovels of squalid poverty,—a mockery at which devils may laugh, but over which angels must weep. Educate the working classes of England; and what then? Will they require less food and less clothing when educated than they do now? Will they be more contented or more happy in their condition? For God's sake beware how you kindle within them the intellectual spark, and make them aware that they too are men, with powers of thought and feeling which ally them by the bonds of brotherhood to their betters. If you will doom them to the external condition of brutes, do in common charity keep their minds and hearts brutish. Render them as insensible as possible, that they may feel the less acutely their degradation, and see the less clearly the monstrous injustice which is done them.

General emigration can at best afford only a temporary relief, for the colony will soon become an empire, and reproduce all the injustice and wretchedness of the mother country. Nor is general emigration necessary. England, if she would be just, could support a larger population than she now numbers. The evil is not from over population, but from the unequal repartition of the fruits of industry. She suffers from over production, and from over production, because her workmen produce not for themselves but for their employers. What then is the remedy? As it concerns England, we shall leave the English statesman to answer. Be it what it may, it will not be obtained without war and bloodshed. It will be found only at the end of one of the longest and severest struggles the human race has ever been engaged in, only by that most dreaded of all wars, the war of the poor against the rich, a war which, however long it may be delayed, will come, and come with all its horrors. The day of vengeance is sure; for the world after all is under the dominion of a Just Providence.

No one can observe the signs of the times with much care, without perceiving that a crisis as to the relation of wealth and labor is approaching. It is useless to shut our eyes to the fact, and like the ostrich fancy ourselves secure because we have so concealed our heads that we see not the danger. We or our children will have to meet this crisis. The old war between the King and the Barons is well nigh ended, and so is that between the Barons and the Merchants and Manufacturers,—landed capital and commercial capital. The business man has become the peer of my Lord. And now commences the new struggle between the operative and his employer, between wealth and labor. Every day does this struggle extend further and wax stronger and fiercer; what or when the end will be God only knows.

In this coming contest there is a deeper question at issue than is commonly imagined; a question which is but remotely touched in your controversies about United States Banks and Sub Treasuries, chartered Banking and free Banking, free trade and corporations, although these controversies may be paving the way for it to come up. We have discovered no presentiment of it in any king's or queen's speech, nor in any president's message. It is embraced in no popular political creed of the day, whether christened Whig or Tory, *Juste-milieu* or Democratic. No popular senator, or deputy, or peer seems to have any glimpse of it; but it is working in the hearts of the million, is struggling to shape itself, and one day it will be uttered, and in thunder tones. Well will it be for him, who, on that day, shall be found ready to answer it.

What we would ask is, throughout the Christian world, the actual condition of the laboring classes, viewed simply and exclusively in their capacity of laborers? They constitute at least a moiety of the human race. We exclude the nobility, we exclude also the middle class, and include only actual laborers, who are laborers and not proprietors, owners of none of the funds of production, neither houses, shops, nor lands, nor implements of labor, being therefore solely dependent on their hands. We have no means of ascertaining their precise proportion to the whole number of the race; but we think we may estimate them at one half. In any contest they will be as two to one, because the large class of proprietors who are not employers, but laborers on their own lands or in their own shops will make common cause with them.

Now we will not so belie our acquaintance with political economy, as to allege that these alone perform all that is necessary to the production of wealth. We are not ignorant of the fact, that the merchant, who is literally the common carrier and exchange dealer, performs a useful service, and is therefore entitled to a portion of the proceeds of labor. But make all necessary deductions on his account, and then ask what portion of the remainder is retained, either in kind or in its equivalent, in the hands of the original producer, the workingman? All over the world this fact stares us in the face, the workingman is poor and depressed, while a large portion of the non-workingmen, in the sense we now use the term, are wealthy. It may be laid down as a general rule, with but few exceptions, that men are rewarded in an inverse ratio to the amount of actual service they perform. Under every government on earth the largest salaries are annexed to those offices, which demand of their incumbents the least amount of actual labor either mental or manual. And this is in perfect harmony with the whole system of repartition of the fruits of industry, which obtains in every department of society. Now here is the system which prevails, and here is its result. The whole class of simple laborers are poor, and in general unable to procure anything beyond the bare necessaries of life.

In regard to labor two systems obtain; one that of slave labor, the other that of free labor. Of the two, the first is, in our judgment, except so far as the feelings are concerned, decidedly the least oppressive. If the slave has never been a free man, we think, as a general rule, his sufferings are less than those of the free laborer at wages. As to actual freedom one has just about as much as the other. The laborer at wages has all the disadvantages of freedom and none of its blessings, while the slave, if denied the blessings, is freed from the disadvantages. We are no advocates of slavery, we are as heartily opposed to it as any modern abolitionist can be; but we say frankly that, if there must always be a laboring population distinct from proprietors and employers, we regard the slave system as decidedly preferable to the system at wages. It is no pleasant thing to go days without food, to lie idle for weeks, seeking work and finding none, to rise in the morning with a wife and children you love, and know not where to procure them a breakfast, and to see constantly before you no brighter prospect than the almshouse. Yet these are no unfrequent incidents in the lives of our laboring population. Even in seasons of general prosperity, when there was only the ordinary cry of "hard times," we have seen hundreds of people in a not very populous village, in a wealthy portion of our common country, suffering for the want of the necessaries of life, willing to work, and yet finding no work to do. Many and many is the application of a poor man for work, merely for his food, we have seen rejected. These things are little thought of, for the applicants are poor; they fill no conspicuous place in society, and they have no biographers. But their wrongs are chronicled in heaven. It is said there is no want in this country. There may be less than in some other countries. But death by actual starvation in this country is, we apprehend, no uncommon occurrence. The sufferings of a quiet, unassuming but useful class of females in our cities, in general sempstresses, too proud to beg or to apply to the alms-house, are not easily told. They are industrious; they do all that they can find to do; but yet the little there is for them to do, and the miserable pittance they receive for it, is hardly sufficient to keep soul and body together. And yet there is a man who employs them to make shirts, trousers &c., and grows rich on their labors. He is one of our respectable citizens, perhaps is praised in the newspapers for his liberal donations to some charitable institution. He passes among us as a pattern of morality, and is honored as a worthy Christian. And why should he not be, since our *Christian* community is made up of such as he, and since our clergy would not dare question his piety, lest they should incur the reproach of infidelity, and lose their standing, and their salaries? Nay, since our clergy are raised up, educated, fashioned, and sustained by such as he? Not a few of our churches rest on Mammon for their

foundation. The basement is a trader's shop.

We pass through our manufacturing villages, most of them appear neat and flourishing. The operatives are well dressed, and we are told, well paid. They are said to be healthy, contented, and happy. This is the fair side of the picture; the side exhibited to distinguished visitors. There is a dark side, moral as well as physical. Of the common operatives, few, if any, by their wages, acquire a competence. A few of what Carlyle terms not inaptly the *body-servants* are well paid, and now and then an agent or an overseer rides in his coach. But the great mass wear out their health, spirits, and morals, without becoming one whit better off than when they commenced labor. The bills of mortality in these factory villages are not striking, we admit, for the poor girls, when they can toil no longer go home to die. The average life, working life we mean, of the girls that come to Lowell, for instance, from Maine, New Hampshire, and Vermont, we have been assured, is only about three years. What becomes of them then? Few of them ever marry; fewer still ever return to their native places with reputations unimpaired. "She has worked in a Factory," is almost enough to damn to infamy the most worthy and virtuous girl. We know no sadder sight on earth than one of our factory villages presents, when the bell at break of day, or at the hour of breakfast, or dinner, calls out its hundreds or thousands of operatives. We stand and look at these hard working men and women hurrying in all directions, and ask ourselves, where go the proceeds of their labors? The man who employs them, and for whom they are toiling as so many slaves, is one of our city nabobs, revelling in luxury; or he is a member of our legislature, enacting laws to put money in his own pocket; or he is a member of Congress, contending for a high Tariff to tax the poor for the benefit of the rich; or in these times he is shedding crocodile tears over the deplorable condition of the poor laborer, while he docks his wages twenty-five per cent.; building miniature log cabins, shouting Harrison and "hard cider." And this man too would fain pass for a Christian and a republican. He shouts for liberty, stickles for equality, and is horrified at a Southern planter who keeps slaves.

One thing is certain; that of the amount actually produced by the operative, he retains a less proportion than it costs the master to feed, clothe, and lodge his slave. Wages is a cunning device of the devil, for the benefit of tender consciences, who would retain all the advantages of the slave system, without the expense, trouble, and odium of being slave-holders.

Messrs. Thome and Kimball, in their account of emancipation in the West Indies, establish the fact that the employer may have the same amount of labor done, twenty-five per cent cheaper than the master. What does this fact prove, if not that wages is a more successful method of taxing labor than slavery? We really believe our Northern system of labor is more oppressive and even more mischievous to morals, than the Southern. We, however, war against both. We have no toleration for either system. We would see the slave a man, but a free man, not a mere operative at wages. This he would not be were he now emancipated. Could the abolitionists effect all they propose, they would do the slave no service. Should emancipation work as well as they say, still it would do the slave no good. He would be a slave still, although with the title and cares of a freeman. If then we had no constitutional objections to abolitionism, we could not, for the reason here implied, be abolitionists.

The slave system, however, in name and form, is gradually disappearing from Christendom. It will not subsist much longer. But its place is taken by the system of labor at wages, and this system, we hold, is no improvement upon the one it supplants. Nevertheless the system of wages will triumph. It is the system which in name sounds honester than slavery, and in substance is more profitable to the master. It yields the wages of iniquity, without its opprobrium. It will therefore supplant slavery, and be sustained—for a time.

Now, what is the prospect of those who fall under the operation of this system? We ask, is there a reasonable chance that any considerable portion of the present generation of laborers, shall ever become owners of a sufficient portion of the funds of production, to be able to sustain themselves by laboring on their own capital, that is, as independent laborers? We need not ask this question, for everybody knows there is not. Well, is the condition of a laborer at wages the best that the great mass of the working people ought to be able to aspire to? Is it a condition,—nay can it be made a condition,—with which a man should be satisfied; in which he should be contented to live and die?

In our own country this condition has existed under its most favorable aspects, and has been made as good as it can be. It has reached all the excellence of which it is susceptible. It is now not improving but growing worse. The actual condition of the working-man to-day, viewed in all its bearings, is not so good as it was fifty years ago. If we have not been altogether misinformed, fifty years ago, health and industrious habits, constituted no mean stock in trade, and with them almost any man might aspire to competence and independence. But it is so no longer. The wilderness has receded, and already the new lands are beyond the reach of the mere laborer, and the employer has him at his mercy. If the present relation subsist, we see nothing better for him in reserve than what he now possesses, but something altogether worse.

We are not ignorant of the fact that men born poor become wealthy, and that men born to wealth become poor; but this fact does not necessarily diminish the numbers of the poor, nor augment the numbers of the rich. The relative numbers of the two classes remain, or may remain, the same. But be this as it may; one fact is certain, no man born poor has ever, by his wages, as a simple operative, risen to the class of the wealthy. Rich he may have become, but it has not been by his own manual labor. He has in some way contrived to tax for his benefit the labor of others. He may have accumulated a few dollars which he has placed at usury, or invested in trade; or he may, as a master workman, obtain a premium on his journeymen; or he may have from a clerk passed to a partner, or from a workman to an overseer. The simple market wages for ordinary labor, has never been adequate to raise him from poverty to wealth. This fact is decisive of the whole controversy, and proves that the system of wages must be supplanted by some other system, or else one half of the human race must forever be the virtual slaves of the other.

Now the great work for this age and the coming, is to raise up the laborer, and to realize in our own social arrangements and in the actual condition of all men, that equality between man and man, which God has established between the rights of one and those of another. In other words, our business is to emancipate the proletaries, as the past has emancipated the slaves. This is our work. There must be no class of our fellow men doomed to toil through life as mere workmen at wages. If wages are tolerated it must be, in the case of the individual operative, only under such conditions that by the time he is of a proper age to settle in life, he shall have accumulated enough to be an independent laborer on his own capital,—on his own farm or in his own shop. Here is our work. How is it to be done?

Reformers in general answer this question, or what they deem its equivalent, in a manner which we cannot but regard as very unsatisfactory. They would have all men wise, good, and happy; but in order to make them so, they tell us that we want not external changes, but internal; and therefore instead of declaiming against society and seeking to disturb existing social arrangements, we should confine ourselves to the individual reason and conscience; seek merely to lead the individual to repentance, and to reformation of life; make the individual a practical, a truly religious man, and all evils will either disappear, or be sanctified to the spiritual growth of the soul.

This is doubtless a capital theory, and has the advantage that kings, hierarchies, nobilities,—in a word, all who fatten on the toil and blood of their fellows, will feel no difficulty in supporting it. Nicholas of Russia, the Grand Turk, his Holiness the Pope, will hold us their especial friends for advocating a theory, which secures to them the odor of sanctity even while they are sustaining by their anathemas or their armed legions, a system of things of which the great mass are and must be the victims. If you will only allow me to keep thousands toiling for my pleasure or my profit, I will even aid you in your pious efforts to convert their souls. I am not cruel; I do not wish either to cause, or to see suffering; I am therefore disposed to encourage your labors for the souls of the workingman, providing you will secure to me the products of his bodily toil. So far as the salvation of his soul will not interfere with my income, I hold it worthy of being sought; and if a few thousand dollars will aid you, Mr. Priest, in reconciling him to God, and making fair weather for him hereafter, they are at your service. I shall not want him to work for me in the world to come, and I can indemnify myself for what your salary costs me, by paying him less wages. A capital theory this, which one may advocate without incurring the reproach of a disorganizer, a jacobin, a leveller, and without losing the friendship of the rankest aristocrat in the land.

This theory, however, is exposed to one slight objection, that of being condemned by something like six thousand years' experience. For six thousand years its beauty has been extolled, its praises sung, and its blessings sought, under every advantage which learning, fashion, wealth, and power can secure; and yet under its practical operations, we are assured, that mankind, though totally depraved at first, have been growing worse and worse ever since.

For our part, we yield to none in our reverence for science and religion; but we confess that we look not for the regeneration of the race from priests and pedagogues. They have had a fair trial. They cannot construct the temple of God. They cannot conceive its plan, and they know not how to build. They daub with untempered mortar, and the walls they erect tumble down if so much as a fox attempt to go up, thereon. In a word they always league with the people's masters, and seek to reform without disturbing the social arrangements which render reform necessary. They would change the consequents without changing the antecedents, secure to men the rewards of holiness, while they continue their allegiance to the devil. We have no faith in priests and pedagogues. They merely cry peace, peace, and that too when there is no peace, and can be none.

We admit the importance of what Dr. Channing, in his lectures on the subject we are treating recommends as "self-culture." Self-culture is a good thing, but it cannot abolish inequality, nor restore men to their rights. As a means of quickening moral and intellectual energy, exalting the sentiments,

and preparing the laborer to contend manfully for his rights, we admit its importance, and insist as strenuously as any one on making it as universal as possible; but as constituting in itself a remedy for the vices of the social state, we have no faith in it. As a means it is well, as the end it is nothing.

The truth is, the evil we have pointed out is not merely individual in its character. It is not, in the case of any single individual, of any one man's procuring, nor can the efforts of any one man, directed solely to his own moral and religious perfection, do aught to remove it. What is purely individual in its nature, efforts of individuals to perfect themselves, may remove. But the evil we speak of is inherent in all our social arrangements, and cannot be cured without a radical change of those arrangements. Could we convert all men to Christianity in both theory and practice, as held by the most enlightened sect of Christians among us, the evils of the social state would remain untouched. Continue our present system of trade, and all its present evil consequences will follow, whether it be carried on by your best men or your worst. Put your best men, your wisest, most moral, and most religious men, at the head of your paper money banks, and the evils of the present banking system will remain scarcely diminished. The only way to get rid of its evils is to change the system, not its managers. The evils of slavery do not result from the personal characters of slave masters. They are inseparable from the system, not who will be masters. Make all your rich men good Christians, and you have lessened not the evils of existing inequality in wealth. The mischievous effects of this inequality do not result from the personal characters of either rich or poor, but from itself, and they will continue, just so long as there are rich men and poor men in the same community. You must abolish the system or accept its consequences. No man can serve both God and Mammon. If you will serve the devil, you must look to the devil for your wages; we know no other way.

Let us not be misinterpreted. We deny not the power of Christianity. Should all men become good Christians, we deny not that all social evils would be cured. But we deny in the outset that a man, who seeks merely to save his own soul, merely to perfect his own individual nature, can be a good Christian. The Christian forgets himself, buckles on his armor, and goes forth to war against principalities and powers, and against spiritual wickedness in high places. No man can be a Christian who does not begin his career by making war on the mischievous social arrangements from which his brethren suffer. He who thinks he can be a Christian and save his soul, without seeking their radical change, has no reason to applaud himself for his proficiency in Christian science, nor for his progress towards the kingdom of God. Understand Christianity, and we will admit, that should all men become good Christians, there would be nothing to complain of. But one might as well undertake to dip the ocean dry with a clam-shell, as to undertake to cure the evils of the social state by converting men to the Christianity of the Church.

The evil we have pointed out, we have said, is not of individual creation, and it is not to be removed by individual effort, saving so far as individual effort induces the combined effort of the mass. But whence has this evil originated? How comes it that all over the world the working classes are depressed, are the low and vulgar, and virtually the slaves of the non-working classes? This is an inquiry which has not yet received the attention it deserves. It is not enough to answer, that it has originated entirely in the inferiority by nature of the working classes; that they

have less skill and foresight, and are less able than the upper classes, to provide for themselves, or less susceptible of the highest moral and intellectual cultivation. Nor is it sufficient for our purpose to be told, that Providence has decreed that some shall be poor and wretched, ignorant and vulgar; and that others shall be rich and vicious, learned and polite, oppressive and miserable. We do not choose to charge this matter to the will of God. "The foolishness of man perverteth his way, and his heart fretteth against the Lord." God has made of one blood all the nations of men to dwell on all the face of the earth, and to dwell there as brothers, as members of one and the same family; and although he has made them with a diversity of powers, it would perhaps, after all, be a bold assertion to say that he has made them with an inequality of powers. There is nothing in the actual difference of the powers of individuals, which accounts for the striking inequalities we everywhere discover in their condition. The child of the plebeian, if placed early in the proper circumstances, grows up not less beautiful, active, intelligent, and refined, than the child of the patrician; and the child of the patrician may become as coarse, as brutish as the child of any slave. So far as observation on the original capacities of individuals goes, nothing is discovered to throw much light on social inequalities.

The cause of the inequality, we speak of, must be sought in history, and be regarded as having its root in Providence, or in human nature, only in that sense in which all historical facts have their origin in these. We may perhaps trace it in the first instance to conquest, but not to conquest as the ultimate cause. The Romans in conquering Italy no doubt reduced many to the condition of slaves, but they also found the great mass of the laboring population already slaves. There is everywhere a class distinct from the reigning class, bearing the same relation to it, that the Gibbeonites did to the Jews. They are principally *Colons,* the cultivators for foreign masters, of a soil of which they seemed to have been dispossessed. Who has dispossessed them? Who has reduced them to their present condition,—a condition which under the Roman dominion is perhaps even ameliorated? Who were this race? Whence came they? They appear to be distinct from the reigning race, as were the Helotae from the Doric-Spartan. Were they the aborigines of the territory? Had they once been free? By what concurrence of events have they been reduced to their present condition? By a prior conquest? But mere conquest does not so reduce a population. It may make slaves of the prisoners taken in actual combat, and reduce the whole in tributaries, but it leaves the mass of the population free, except in its political relations. Were they originally savages, subjugated by a civilized tribe? Savages may be exterminated, but they never, so far as we can ascertain, become to any considerable extent "the hewers of wood and drawers of water" to their conquerors. For our part we are disposed to seek the cause of the inequality of conditions of which we speak, in religion, and to charge it to the priesthood. And we are confirmed in this, by what appears to be the instinctive tendency of every, or almost every, social reformer. Men's instincts, in a matter of this kind, are worthier of reliance than their reasonings. Rarely do we find in any age or country, a man feeling himself commissioned to labor for a social reform, who does not feel that he must begin it by making war upon the priesthood. This was the case with the old Hebrew reformers, who are to us the prophets of God; with Jesus, the Apostles, and the early Fathers of the Church; with the French democrats of the last century; and is the case with the Young Germans, and the Socialists, as they call themselves in England, at the present moment. Indeed it

is felt at once that no reform can be effected without resisting the priests and emancipating the people from their power.

Historical research, we apprehend, will be found to justify this instinct, and to authorize the eternal hostility of the reformer, the advocate of social progress, to the priesthood. How is it, we ask, that man comes out of the savage state? In the savage state, properly so called, there is no inequality of the kind of which we speak. The individual system obtains there. Each man is his own centre, and is a whole in himself. There is no community, there are no members of society; for society is not. This individuality, which, if combined with the highest possible moral and intellectual cultivation, would be the perfection of man's earthly condition, must be broken down before the human race can enter into the path of civilization, or commence its career of progress. But it cannot be broken down by material force. It resists by its own nature the combination of individuals necessary to subdue it. It can be successfully attacked only by a spiritual power, and subjugated only by the representatives of that power, that is to say, the priests.

Man is naturally a religious being, and disposed to stand in awe of invisible powers. This makes, undoubtedly, under certain relations, his glory; but when coupled with his ignorance, it becomes the chief source of his degradation and misery. He feels within the workings of a mysterious nature, and is conscious that hidden and superior powers are at work all around him, and perpetually influencing his destiny; now wafting him onward with a prosperous gale, or now resisting his course, driving him back, defeating his plans, blasting his hopes, and wounding his heart. What are his relations to these hidden, mysterious, and yet all-influencing forces? Can their anger be appeased? Can their favor be secured? Thus he asks himself. Unable to answer, he goes to the more aged and experienced of his tribe, and asks them the same questions. They answer as best they can. What is done by one is done by another, and what is done once is done again. The necessity of instruction, which each one feels in consequence of his own feebleness and inexperience, renders the recurrence to those best capable of giving it, or supposed to be the best capable of giving it, frequent and uniform. Hence the priest. He who is consulted prepares himself to answer, and therefore devotes himself to the study of man's relations to these invisible powers, and the nature of these invisible powers themselves. Hence religion becomes a special object of study, and the study of it a profession. Individuals whom a thunderstorm, an earthquake, an eruption of a volcano, an eclipse of the sun or moon, any unusual appearance in the heavens or earth, has frightened, or whom some unforeseen disaster has afflicted, go to the wise-man for explanation, to know what it means, or what they shall do in order to appease the offended powers. When reassured they naturally feel grateful to this wise-man; they load him with honors, and in the access of their gratitude raise him far above the common level, and spare him the common burdens of life. Once thus distinguished, he becomes an object of envy. His condition is looked upon as superior to that of the mass. Hence a multitude aspire to possess themselves of it. When once the class has become somewhat numerous, it labors to secure to itself the distinction it has received, its honors and its emoluments, and to increase them. Hence the establishment of priesthoods or sacerdotal corporations, such as the Egyptian, the Braminical, the Ethiopian, the Jewish, the Scandinavian, the Druidical, the Mexican, and Peruvian.

The germ of these sacerdotal corporations is found in the savage state, and exists there in that formidable personage called a *jongleur,* juggler, or conjurer. But as the tribe or people advances, the juggler becomes a priest and the member of a corporation. These sacerdotal corporations are variously organized, but everywhere organized for the purpose, as that arch rebel, Thomas Paine, says, "of monopolizing power and profit." The effort is unceasing to elevate them as far above the people as possible, to enable them to exert the greatest possible control over the people, and to derive the greatest possible profit from the people.

Now if we glance over the history of the world, we shall find, that at the epoch of coming out of the savage state, these corporations are universally instituted. We find them among every people; and among every people, at this epoch, they are the dominant power, ruling with an iron despotism. The real idea at the bottom of these institutions, is the control of individual freedom by moral laws, the assertion of the supremacy of moral power over physical force,—a great truth, and one which can never be too strenuously insisted on; but a truth which at this epoch can only enslave the mass of the people to its professed representatives, the priests. Through awe of the gods, through fear of divine displeasure, and dread of the unforeseen chastisements that displeasure may inflict, and by pretending, honestly or not, to possess the secret of averting it, and of rendering the gods propitious, the priests are able to reduce the people to the most wretched subjection, and to keep them there; at least for a time.

But these institutions must naturally be jealous of power, and ambitious of confining it to as few hands as possible. If the sacerdotal corporations were thrown open to all the world, all the world would rush into them, and then there would be no advantage in being a priest. Hence the number who may be priests must be limited. Hence again a distinction of clean and unclean is introduced. Men can be admitted into these corporations only as they descend from the priestly race. As in India, no man can aspire to the priesthood unless of Braminical descent, and among the Jews unless he be of the tribe of Levi. The priestly race was the ruling race; it dealt with science, it held communion with the Gods, and therefore was the purer race. The races excluded from the priesthood were not only regarded as inferior, but as unclean. The Gib[b]eonite to a Jew was both an inferior and an impure. The operation of the principles involved in these considerations, has, in our judgment, begun and effected the slavery of the great mass of the people. It has introduced distinctions of blood or race, founded privileged orders, and secured the rewards of industry to the few, while it has reduced the mass to the most degrading and hopeless bondage.

Now the great mass enslaved by the sacerdotal corporations, are not emancipated by the victories which follow by the warrior caste, even when those victories are said to be in behalf of freedom. The military order succeeds the priestly; but in establishing, as it does in Greece and Rome, the supremacy of the state over the church, it leaves the great mass in the bondage in which it finds them. The Normans conquer England, but they scarcely touch the condition of the old Saxon bondmen. The Polish serf lost his freedom before began the Russian dominion, and he would have recovered none of it, had Poland regained, in her late struggle, her former political independence. The subjection of a nation is in general merely depriving one class of its population of its exclusive right to enslave the people; and the recovery of political independence, is little else than the recovery of this right. The Germans call their rising against Napoleon a rising for liberty, and so it was, liberty for German princes and German nobles; but the German people were more free under Napoleon's supremacy than they are now, or will be very soon. Conquest may undoubtedly increase the number of slaves; but in general it merely adds to the number and power of the middle class. It institutes a new nobility, and degrades the old to the rank of commoners. This is its general effect. We cannot therefore ascribe to conquest, as we did in a former number of this journal, the condition in which the working classes are universally found. They have been reduced to their condition by the priest, not by the military chieftain.

Mankind came out of the savage state by means of the priests. Priests are the first civilizers of the race. For the wild freedom of the savage, they substitute the iron despotism of the theocrat. This is the first step in civilization, in man's career of progress. It is not strange then that some should prefer the savage state to the civilized. Who would not rather roam the forest with a free step and unshackled limb, though exposed to hunger, cold, and nakedness, than crouch an abject slave beneath the whip of a master? As yet civilization has done little but break and subdue man's natural love of freedom; but tame his wild and eagle spirit. In what a world does man even now find himself, when he first awakes and feels some of the workings of his manly nature? He is in a cold, damp, dark dungeon, and loaded all over with chains, with the iron entering into his very soul. He cannot make one single free movement. The priest holds his conscience, fashion controls his tastes, and society with her forces invades the very sanctuary of his heart, and takes command of his love, that which is purest and best in his nature, which alone gives reality to his existence, and from which proceeds the only ray which pierces the gloom of his prison-house. Even that he cannot enjoy in peace and quietness, nor scarcely at all. He is wounded on every side, in every part of his being, in every relation in life, in every idea of his mind, in every sentiment of his heart. O, it is a sad world, a sad world to the young soul just awakening to its diviner instincts! A sad world to him who is not gifted with the only blessing which seems compatible with life as it is—absolute insensibility. But no matter. A wise man never murmurs. He never kicks against the pricks. What is it, and there is an end of it; what can be may be, and will do what we can to make life what it ought to be. Though man's first step in civilization is slavery, his last step shall be freedom. The free soul can never be wholly subdued; the etherial fire in man's nature may be smothered, but it cannot be extinguished. Down, down deep in the centre of his heart it burns inextinguishable and forever, glowing intenser with the accumulating heat of centuries; and one day the whole mass of Humanity shall become ignited, and be full of fire within and all over, as a live coal; and then—slavery, and whatever is foreign to the soul itself, shall be consumed.

But, having traced the inequality we complain of to its origin, we proceed to ask again what is the remedy? The remedy is first to be sought in the destruction of the priest. We are not mere destructives. We delight not in pulling down; but the bad must be removed before the good can be introduced. Conviction and repentance precede regeneration. Moreover we are Christians, and it is only by following out the Christian law, and the example of the early Christians, that we can hope to effect anything. Christianity is the sublimest protest against the priesthood ever uttered, and a protest uttered by both God and man; for he who uttered it was God-Man. In the person of Jesus both God and Man protest against the priesthood. What was the mission of Jesus but a solemn summons of every priesthood on earth to judgment, and of the human race to freedom? He discomfited the learned doctors, and with whips of small cords drove the priests, degenerated into mere money changers, from the

temple of God. He instituted himself no priesthood, no form of religious worship. He recognised no priest but a holy life, and commanded the construction of no temple but that of the pure heart. He preached no formal religion, enjoined no creed, set apart no day for religious worship. He preached fraternal love, peace on earth, and good will to men. He came to the soul enslaved, "cabined, cribbed, confined," to the poor child of mortality, bound hand and foot, unable to move, and said in the tones of a God, "Be free; be enlarged; be there room for thee to grow, expand, and overflow with the love thou wast made to overflow with."

In the name of Jesus we admit there has been a priesthood instituted, and considering how the world went, a priesthood could not be instituted; but the religion of Jesus repudiates it. It recognises no mediator between God and man but him who dies on the cross to redeem man; no propitiation for sin but a pure love, which rises in a living flame to all that is beautiful and good, and spreads out in light and warmth for all the chilled and benighted sons of mortality. In calling every man to be a priest, it virtually condemns every possible priesthood, and in recognising the religion of the new covenant, the religion written on the heart, of a law put within the soul, it abolishes all formal worship.

The priest is universally a tyrant, universally the enslaver of his brethren, and therefore it is Christianity condemns him. It could not prevent the reestablishment of a hierarchy, but it prepared for its ultimate destruction, by denying the inequality of blood, by representing all men as equal before God, and by insisting on the celibacy of the clergy. The best feature of the Church was in its denial to the clergy of the right to marry. By this it prevented the new hierarchy from becoming hereditary, as were the old sacerdotal corporations of India and Judea.

We object not to religious instruction; we object not to the gathering together of the people on one day in seven, to sing and pray, and listen to a discourse from a religious teacher; but we object to everything like an outward, visible church; to everything that in the remotest degree partakes of the priest. A priest is one who stands as a sort of mediator between God and man; but we have one mediator, Jesus Christ, who gave himself a ransom for all, and that is enough. It may be supposed that we, protestants, have no priests; but for ourselves we know no fundamental difference between a catholic priest and a protestant clergyman, as we know no difference of any magnitude, in relation to the principles on which they are based, between a protestant church and the catholic church. Both are based on the principle of authority; both deny in fact, however it may be in manner, the authority of reason, and war against freedom of mind; both substitute dead works for true righteousness, a vain show for the reality of piety, and are sustained as the means of reconciling us to God without requiring us to become godlike. Both therefore ought to go by the board.

We may offend in what we say, but we cannot help that. We insist upon it, that the complete and final destruction of the priestly order, in every practical sense of the word priest, is the first step to be taken towards elevating the laboring classes. Priests are, in their capacity of priests, necessarily enemies to freedom and equality. All reasoning demonstrates this, and all history proves it. There must be no class of men set apart and authorized, either by law or fashion, to speak to us in the name of God, or to be the interpreters of the word of God. The word of God never drops from the priest's lips. He who redeemed man did not spring from the priestly class, for it is evident that our Lord sprang out of Juda, of which tribe Moses spake nothing concerning the priesthood. Who in fact were the authors of the Bible, the book which Christendom professes to receive as the word of God? The priests? Nay, they were the inveterate foes of the priests. No man ever berated the priests more soundly than did Jeremiah and Ezekiel. And who were they who heard Jesus the most gladly? The priests? The chief priests were at the head of those who demanded his crucifixion. In every age the priests, the authorized teachers of religion, are the first to oppose the true prophet of God, and to condemn his prophecies as blasphemies. They are always a let and a hindrance to the spread of truth. Why then retain them? Why not abolish the priestly office? Why continue to sustain what the whole history of man condemns as the greatest of all obstacles to intellectual and social progress?

We say again, we have no objection to teachers of religion, as such; but let us have no class of men whose profession it is to minister at the altar. Let us leave this matter to Providence. When God raises up a prophet, let that prophet prophesy as God gives him utterance. Let every man speak out of his own full heart, as he is moved by the Holy Ghost, but let us have none to prophesy for hire, to make preaching a profession, a means of gaining a livelihood. Whoever has a word pressing upon his heart for utterance, let him utter it, in the stable, the market-place, the street, in the grove, under the open canopy of heaven, in the lowly cottage, or the lordly hall. No matter who or what he is, whether a graduate of a college, a shepherd from the hill sides, or a rustic from the plough. If he feels himself called to go forth in the name of God, he will speak words of truth and power, for which Humanity shall fare the better. But none of your hireling priests, your "dumb dogs" that will not bark. What are the priests of Christendom as they now are? Miserable panders to the prejudices of the age, loud in condemning sins nobody is guilty of, but silent as the grave when it concerns the crying sin of the times; bold as bold can be when there is no danger, but miserable cowards when it is necessary to speak out for God and outraged Humanity. As a body they never preach a truth till there is none whom it will indict. Never do they as a body venture to condemn sin in the concrete, and make each sinner feel "thou art the man." When the prophets of God have risen up and proclaimed the word of God, and, after persecution and death, led the people to acknowledge it to be the word of God, then your drivelling priest comes forward, and owns it to be a truth, and cries, "cursed of God and man is he who believes it not." But enough. The imbecility of an organized priesthood, of a hireling clergy, for all good, and its power only to demoralize the people and misdirect their energies, is beginning to be seen, and will one day be acknowledged. Men are beginning to speak out on this subject, and the day of reckoning is approaching. The people are rising up and asking of these priests whom they have fed, clothed, honored, and followed, What have ye done for the poor and friendless, to destroy oppression, and establish the kingdom of God on earth? A fearful question for you, O ye priests, which we leave you to answer as best ye may.

The next step in this work of elevating the working class will be to resuscitate the Christianity of Christ. The Christianity of the Church has done its work. We have had enough of that Christianity. It is powerless for good, but by no means powerless for evil. It now unmans us and hinders the growth of God's kingdom. The moral energy which is awakened it misdirects, and makes its deluded disciples believe that they have done their duty to God when they have joined the church, offered a prayer, sung a psalm, and contributed of the means to send out a missionary to preach unintelligible dogmas to the poor heathen, who, God knows have unintelligible dogmas enough already, and more than enough. All this must be abandoned, and Christianity, as it came from Christ, be taken up, and preached, and preached in simplicity and in power.

According to the Christianity of Christ no man can enter the kingdom of God, who does not labor with all zeal and diligence to establish the kingdom of God on the earth; who does not labor to bring down the high, and bring up the low; to break the fetters of the bound and set the captive free; to destroy all oppression, establish the reign of justice, which is the reign of equality, between man and man; to introduce new heavens and a new earth, wherein dwelleth righteousness, wherein all shall be as brothers, loving one another, and no one possessing what another lacketh. No man can be a Christian who does not labor to reform society, to mould it according to the will of God and the nature of man; so that free scope shall be given to every man to unfold himself in all beauty and power, and to grow up into the stature of a perfect man in Christ Jesus. No man can be a Christian who does not refrain from all practices by which the rich grow richer and the poor poorer, and who does not do all, in his power to elevate the laboring classes, so that one man shall not be doomed to toil while another enjoys the fruits; so that each man shall be free and independent, sitting under "his own vine and figtree with none to molest or to make afraid." We grant the power of Christianity in working out the reform we demand; we agree that one of the most efficient means of elevating the workingmen is to christianize the community. But you must christianize it. It is the Gospel of Jesus you must preach, and not the gospel of the priests. Preach the Gospel of Jesus, and that will turn every man's attention to the crying evil we have designated, and will arm every Christian with power to effect those changes in social arrangements, which shall secure to all men the equality of position and condition, which it is already acknowledged they possess in relation to their rights. But let it be the genuine Gospel that you preach, and not that pseudo-gospel, which lulls the conscience asleep, and permits men to feel that they may be servants of God while they are slaves to the world, the flesh, and the devil; and while they ride roughshod over the hearts of their prostrate brethren. We must preach no Gospel that permits men to feel that they are honorable men and good Christians, although rich and with eyes standing out with fatness, while the great mass of their brethren are suffering from iniquitous laws, from mischievous social arrangements, and pining away for the want of the refinements and even the necessaries of life.

We speak strongly and pointedly on this subject, because we are desirous of arresting attention. We would draw the public attention to the striking contrast which actually exists between the Christianity of Christ, and the Christianity of the Church. That moral and intellectual energy which exists in our country, indeed throughout Christendom, and which would, if rightly directed, transform this wilderness world into a blooming paradise of God, is now by the pseudo-gospel, which is preached, rendering wholly inefficient, by being wasted on that which, even if effected, would leave all the crying evils of the times untouched. Under the influence of the Church, our efforts are not directed to the reörganization of society, to the introduction of equality between man and man, to the removal of the corruptions of the rich, and the wretchedness of the poor. We think only of saving our own souls, as if a man must not put himself so out of the case, as to be willing to be damned before he can be saved. Paul was willing to be accursed from Christ, to save his brethren from the vengeance which hung over them. But nevertheless we think only of saving our own souls; or if perchance our benevolence is awakened and we think it desirable to labor for the salvation of others, it is

merely to save them from imaginary sins and the tortures of an imaginary hell. The redemption of the world is understood to mean simply the restoration of mankind to the favor of God in the world to come. Their redemption from the evils of inequality, of factitious distinctions, and iniquitous social institutions, counts for nothing in the eyes of the Church. And this is its condemnation.

We cannot proceed a single step, with the least safety, in the great work of elevating the laboring classes, without the exaltation of sentiment, the generous sympathy and the moral courage which Christianity alone is fitted to produce or quicken. But it is lamentable to see how, by means of the mistakes of the Church, the moral courage, the generous sympathy, the exaltation of sentiment, Christianity does actually produce or quicken, is perverted, and made efficient only in producing evil, or hindering the growth of good. Here is wherefore it is necessary on the one hand to condemn in the most pointed terms the Christianity of the Church, and to bring out on the other hand in all its clearness, brilliancy, and glory the Christianity of Christ.

Having, by breaking down the power of the priesthood and the Christianity of the priests, obtained an open field and freedom for our operations, and by preaching the true Gospel of Jesus, directed all minds to the great social reform needed, and quickened in all souls the moral power to live for it or to die for it; our next resort must be to government, to legislate enactments. Government is instituted to be the agent of society, or more properly the organ through which society may perform its legitimate functions. It is not the master of society; its business is not to control society, but to be the organ through which society effects its will. Society has never to petition government; government is its servant, and subject to its commands.

Now the evils of which we have complained are of a social nature. That is, they have their root in the constitution of society as it is, and they have attained to their present growth by means of social influences, the action of government, of laws and of systems and institutions upheld by society, and of which individuals are the slaves. This being the case, it is evident that they are to be removed only by the action of society, that is, by government, for the action of society is government.

But what shall government do? Its first doing must be an *undoing*. There has been thus far quite too much government, as well as government of the wrong kind. The first act of government we want, is a still further limitation of itself. It must begin by circumscribing within narrower limits its powers. And then it must proceed to repeal all laws which bear against the laboring classes, and then to enact such laws as are necessary to enable them to maintain their equality. We have no faith in those systems of elevating the working classes, which propose to elevate them without calling in the aid of the government. We must have government, and legislation expressly directed to this end.

But again what legislation do we want so far as this country is concerned? We want first the legislation which shall free the government, whether State or Federal, from the control of the Banks. The Banks represent the interest of the employer, and therefore of necessity interests adverse to those of the employed; that is, they represent the interests of the business community in opposition to the laboring community. So long as the government remains under the control of the Banks, so long it must be in the hands of the natural enemies of the laboring classes and may be made, nay, will be made, an instrument of depressing them yet lower. It is obvious then that, if our object be the elevation of the laboring classes, we must destroy the power of the Banks over the government, and place the government in the hands of

the laboring classes themselves, or in the hands of those, if such there be, who have an identity of interest with them. But this cannot be done so long as the Banks exist. Such is the subtle influence of credit, and such the power of capital, that a banking system like ours, if sustained, necessarily and inevitably becomes the real and efficient government of the country. We have been struggling for ten years in this country against the power of the banks, struggling to free merely the Federal government from their grasp, but with humiliating success. At this moment, the contest is almost doubtful,—not indeed in our mind, but in the minds of a no small portion of our countrymen. The partizans of the Banks count on certain victory. The Banks discount freely to build "log cabins," to purchase "hard cider," and to defray the expense of manufacturing enthusiasm for a cause which is at war with the interests of the people. That they will succeed, we do not for one moment believe; but that they could maintain the struggle so long, and be as strong as they now are, at the end of ten years' constant hostility, proves but all too well the power of the Banks, and their fatal influence on the political action of the community. The present character, standing, and resources of the Bank party, prove to a demonstration that the Banks must be destroyed, or the laborer not elevated. Uncompromising hostility to the whole banking system should therefore be the motto of every working man, and of every friend of Humanity. The system must be destroyed. On this point their must be no misgiving, no subterfuge, no palliation. The system is at war with the rights and interest of labor, and it must go. Every friend of the system must be marked as an enemy to his race, to his country, and especially to the laborer. No matter who he is, in what party he is found, or what name he bears, he is, in our judgment, no true democrat, as he can be no true Christian.

Following the destruction of the Banks, must come that of all monopolies, of all PRIVILEGE. There are many of these. We cannot specify them all; we therefore select only one, the greatest of them all, the privilege which some have of being born rich while others are born poor. It will be seen at once that we allude to the hereditary descent of property, an anomaly in our American system, which must be removed, or the system itself will be destroyed. We cannot now go into a discussion of this subject, but we promise to resume it at our earliest opportunity. We only say now, that as we have abolished hereditary monarchy and hereditary nobility, we must complete the work by abolishing hereditary property.* A man shall have all he honestly acquires, so long as he himself belongs to the world in which he acquires it. But his power over his property must cease with his life, and his property must then become the property of the state, to be disposed of by some equitable law for the use of the generation which takes his place. Here is the principle without any of its details, and this is the grand legislative measure to which we look forward.

We see no means of elevating the laboring classes which can be effectual without this. And is this a measure to be easily carried? Not at all. It will cost infinitely more than it cost to abolish either hereditary monarchy or hereditary nobility. It is a great measure, and a startling one. The rich, the business community, will never voluntarily consent to it, and we think we know too much of human nature to believe that it will ever be effected peaceably. It will be effected only by the strong arm of physical force. It will come, if it ever come at all, only at the conclusion of war, the like of which the world as yet has never witnessed, and from which, however inevitable it may seem to the eye of philosophy, the heart of Humanity recoils with horror.

We are not ready for this measure yet. There is much previous work to be done, and we should be the last to bring it before the legislature. The time, however has come for its free and full discussion. It must be canvassed in the public mind, and society prepared for acting on it. No doubt they who broach it, and especially they who support it, will experience a due share of contumely and abuse. They will be

---

*I am aware that I broach in this place a delicate subject, though I by no means advance a novel doctrine. In justice to those friends with whom I am in the habit of thinking and acting on most subjects, as well as to the political party with which I am publicly connected, I feel bound to say, that my doctrine, on the hereditary descent of property, is put forth by myself alone, and on my own responsibility. There are to my knowledge, none of my friends who entertain the doctrine, and who would not, had I consulted them, have labored to convince me of its unsoundness. Whatever then may be the measure of condemnation the community in its wisdom may judge it proper to mete out for its promulgation, that condemnation should fall on my head alone. I hold not myself responsible for others' opinions, and I wish not others to be held responsible for mine.

I cannot be supposed to be ignorant of the startling nature of the proposition I have made, nor can I, if I regard myself of the least note in the commonwealth, expect to be able to put forth such propositions, and go scathless. Because I advance singular doctrines, it is not necessary to suppose that I am ignorant of public opinion, or that I need to be informed as to the manner in which my doctrines are likely to be received. I have made the proposition, which I have, deliberately, with what I regard a tolerably clear view of its essential bearings, and after having meditated it, and been satisfied of its soundness, for many years. I make it then with my eyes open, if the reader please, "with malice prepense." I am then entitled to no favor, and I ask as I expect none. But I am not quite so unfortunate as to be wholly without friends in this world. There are those to whom I am linked by the closest ties of affection, and whose approbation and encouragement, I have ever found an ample reward for all the labors I could perform. Their reputations are dear to me. For their sake I add this note, that they may not be in the least censured for the fact that one whom they have honored with their friendship, and in a journal which, in its general character, they have not hesitated to commend, has been proper to put forth a doctrine, which, to say the least, for long years to come must be condemned almost unanimously.

O. A. B.

regarded by the part of the community they oppose, or may be thought to oppose, as "graceless varlets," against whom every man of substance should set his face. But this is not, after all, a thing to disturb a wise man, nor to deter a true man from telling his whole thought. He who is worthy of the name of man, speaks what he honestly believes the interests of his race demand, and seldom disquiets himself about what may be the consequences to himself. Men have, for what they believed the cause of God or man, endured the dungeon, the scaffold, the stake, the cross, and they can do it again, if need be. This subject must be freely, boldly, and fully discussed, whatever may be the fate of those who discuss it.

Editor.

John C. Calhoun

Arguing that the function of political order is the preservation and establishment of social order, John C. Calhoun is perhaps best remembered as the senator who inspired the Southern bloc in presenting their position on slavery in the 1830s. Born in 1782 in South Carolina, Calhoun gave up plans to become a planter, ultimately to graduate from Yale and to study for the bar. In 1808 he was elected to the South Carolina Legislature, and then to Congress in 1810, becoming nationally known for his outspoken support of the war with Great Britain.

National solidarity and nationalism were his creeds at this time. He served as secretary of the War Department under President Monroe, greatly improving its organization. Then he became vice president under Adams in 1824, serving in the same post under Andrew Jackson in 1828. After conflicts with Jackson on a number of questions, Calhoun resigned in 1832 to return to the Senate. There he represented the minority interests of the South against what he perceived as the developing industrial and financial culture and power of the North. Calhoun argued that the North's domination of the federal government was a potential threat to all minorities and that "What was once a constitutional federal republic, is now converted, in reality, into one as absolute as that of the Autocrat of Russia, and as despotic in its tendency as any absolute government that ever existed."

When President Tyler's secretary of state died, Calhoun was appointed to the post, but was not asked to remain when President Polk took office. Toward the end of his life, Calhoun wrote two major works on political thought: *A Disquisition on Government* and *A Discourse on the Constitution and Government of the United States.* He died in 1850, a year before *A Disquisition on Government* was published. Here he explains his famous concept of concurrent majority, which would permit veto powers to interests against a mere majority of numbers (theoretically giving states the right to give or withdraw their assent to acts of the federal government).

A Disquisition on Government (1851)

(excerpts)

In order to have a clear and just conception of the nature and object of government, it is indispensable to understand correctly what that constitution or law of our nature is, in which government originates; or, to express it more fully and accurately,—that law, without which government would not, and with which, it must necessarily exist. Without this, it is as impossible to lay any solid foundation for the science of government, as it would be to lay one for that of astronomy, without a like understanding of that constitution or law of the material world, according to which the several bodies composing the solar system mutually act on each other, and by which they are kept in their respective spheres. The first question, accordingly, to be considered is,—What is that constitution or law of our nature, without which government would not exist, and with which its existence is necessary?

In considering this, I assume, as an incontestable fact, that man is so constituted as to be a social being. His inclinations and wants, physical and moral, irresistibly impel him to associate with his kind; and he has, accordingly, never been found, in any age or country, in any state other than the social. In no other, indeed, could he exist; and in no other,—were it possible for him to exist,—could he attain to a full development of his moral and intellectual faculties, or raise himself, in the scale of being, much above the level of the brute creation.

I next assume, also, as a fact not less incontestable, that, while man is so constituted as to make the social state necessary to his existence and the full development of his faculties, this state itself cannot exist without government. The assumption rests on universal experience. In no age or country has any society or community ever been found, whether enlightened or savage, without government of some description.

Having assumed these, as unquestionable phenomena of our nature, I shall, without further remark, proceed to the investigation of the primary and important question,—What is that constitution of our nature, which, while it impels man to associate with his kind, renders it impossible for society to exist without government?

The answer will be found in the fact, (not less incontestable than either of the others,) that, while man is created for the social state, and is accordingly so formed as to feel what affects others, as well as what affects himself, he is, at the same time, so constituted as to feel more intensely what affects him directly, than what affects him indirectly through others; or, to express it differently, he is so constituted, that his direct or individual affections are stronger than his sympathetic or social feelings. I intentionally avoid the expression, *selfish* feelings, as applicable to the former; because, as commonly used, it implies an unusual excess of the individual over the social feelings, in the person to whom it is applied; and, consequently, something depraved and vicious. My object is, to exclude such inference, and to restrict the inquiry exclusively to facts in their bearings on the subject under consideration, viewed as mere phenomena appertaining to our nature,—constituted as it is;

and which are as unquestionable as is that of gravitation, or any other phenomenon of the material world.

In asserting that our individual are stronger than our social feelings, it is not intended to deny that there are instances, growing out of peculiar relations,—as that of a mother and her infant,—or resulting from the force of education and habit over peculiar constitutions, in which the latter have overpowered the former; but these instances are few, and always regarded as something extraordinary. The deep impression they make, whenever they occur, is the strongest proof that they are regarded as exceptions to some general and well understood law of our nature; just as some of the minor powers of the material world are apparently to gravitation.

I might go farther, and assert this to be a phenomenon, not of our nature only, but of all animated existence, throughout its entire range, so far as our knowledge extends. It would, indeed, seem to be essentially connected with the great law of self-preservation which pervades all that feels, from man down to the lowest and most insignificant reptile or insect. In none is it stronger than in man. His social feelings may, indeed, in a state of safety and abundance, combined with high intellectual and moral culture, acquire great expansion and force; but not so great as to overpower this all-pervading and essential law of animated existence.

But that constitution of our nature which makes us feel more intensely what affects us directly than what affects us indirectly through others, necessarily leads to conflict between individuals. Each, in consequence, has a greater regard for his own safety or happiness, than for the safety or happiness of others; and, where these come in opposition, is ready to sacrifice the interests of others to his own. And hence, the tendency to a universal state of conflict, between individual and individual; accompanied by the connected passions of suspicion, jealousy, anger and revenge,—followed by insolence, fraud and cruelty;—and, if not prevented by some controlling power, ending in a state of universal discord and confusion, destructive of the social state and the ends for which it is ordained. This controlling power, wherever vested, or by whomsoever exercised, is GOVERNMENT.

It follows, then, that man is so constituted, that government is necessary to the existence of society, and society to his existence, and the perfection of his faculties. It follows, also, that government has its origin in this twofold constitution of his nature; the sympathetic or social feelings constituting the remote,—and the individual or direct, the proximate cause.

If man had been differently constituted in either particular;—if, instead of being social in his nature, he had been created without sympathy for his kind, and independent of others for his safety and existence; or if, on the other hand, he had been so created, as to feel more intensely what affected others than what affected himself (if that were possible,) or, even, had this supposed interest been equal,—it is manifest that, in either case, there would have been no necessity for government, and that none would ever have existed. But, although society and government are thus intimately connected with and dependent on each other,—of the two society is the greater. It is the first in the order of things, and in the dignity of its object; that of society being primary,—to preserve and perfect our race; and that of government secondary and subordinate, to preserve and perfect society. Both are, however, necessary to the existence and well-being of our race, and equally of Divine ordination.

I have said,—if it were possible for man to be so constituted, as to feel what affects others more strongly than what affects himself, or even as strongly,—because, it may be well doubted, whether the stronger feeling or affection of individuals for themselves, combined with a feebler and subordinate feeling or affection for others, is not, in beings of limited reason and faculties, a constitution necessary to their preservation and existence. If reversed,—if their feelings and affections were stronger for others than for themselves, or even as strong, the necessary result would seem to be, that all individuality would be lost; and boundless and remediless disorder and confusion would ensue. For each, at the same moment, intensely participating in all the conflicting emotions of those around him, would, of course, forget himself and all that concerned him immediately, in his officious intermeddling with the affairs of all others; which, from his limited reason and faculties, he could neither properly understand nor manage. Such a state of things would, as far as we can see, lead to endless disorder and confusion, not less destructive to our race than a state of anarchy. It would, besides, be remediless,—for government would be impossible; or, if it could by possibility exist, its object would be reversed. Selfishness would have to be encouraged, and benevolence discouraged. Individuals would have to be encouraged, by rewards, to become more selfish, and deterred, by punishments, from being too benevolent; and this, too, by a government, administered by those who, on the supposition, would have the greatest aversion for selfishness and the highest admiration for benevolence.

To the Infinite Being, the Creator of all, belongs exclusively the care and superintendence of the whole. He, in his infinite wisdom and goodness, has allotted to every class of animated beings its condition and appropriate functions; and has endowed each with feelings, instincts, capacities, and faculties, best adapted to its allotted condition. To man, he has assigned the social and political state, as best adapted to develop the great capacities and faculties, intellectual and moral, with which he has endowed him; and has, accordingly, constituted him so as not only to impel him into the social state, but to make government necessary for his preservation and well-being.

But government, although intended to protect and preserve society, has itself a strong tendency to disorder and abuse of its powers, as all experience and almost every page of history testify. The cause is to be found in the same constitution of our nature which makes government indispensable. The powers which it is necessary for government to possess, in order to repress violence and preserve order, cannot execute themselves. They must be administered by men in whom, like others, the individual are stronger than the social feelings. And hence, the powers vested in them to prevent injustice and oppression on the part of others, will, if left unguarded, be by them converted into instruments to oppress the rest of the community. That, by which this is prevented, by whatever name called, is what is meant by CONSTITUTION, in its most comprehensive sense, when applied to GOVERNMENT.

Having its origin in the same principle of our nature, *constitution* stands to *government,* as *government* stands to *society;* and, as the end for which society is ordained, would be defeated without government, so that for which government is ordained would, in a great measure, be defeated without constitution. But they differ in this striking particular. There is no difficulty in forming government. It is not even a matter of choice, whether there shall be one or not. Like breathing, it is not permitted to depend on our volition. Necessity will force it on all communities in some one form or another. Very different is the case as to constitution. Instead of a matter of necessity, it is one of the most difficult tasks imposed on man to form a constitution worthy of the name; while, to form a perfect one,—one that would completely counteract the tendency of government to oppression and abuse, and hold it strictly to the great ends for which it is ordained,—has thus far exceeded human wisdom, and possibly ever will. From this, another striking difference results. Constitution is the contrivance of man, while government is of Divine ordination. Man is left to perfect what the wisdom of the Infinite ordained, as necessary to preserve the race.

With these remarks, I proceed to the consideration of the important and difficult question: How is this tendency of government to be counteracted? Or, to express it more fully,—How can those who are invested with the powers of government be prevented from employing them, as the means of aggrandizing themselves, instead of using them to protect and preserve society? It cannot be done by instituting a higher power to control the government, and those who administer it. This would be but to change the seat of authority, and to make this higher power in reality, the government; with the same tendency, on the part of those who might control its powers, to pervert them into instruments of aggrandizement. Nor can it be done by limiting the powers of government, so as to make it too feeble to be made an instrument of abuse; for, passing by the difficulty of so limiting its powers, without creating a power higher than the government itself to enforce the observance of the limitations, it is a sufficient objection that it would, if practicable, defeat the end for which government is ordained, by making it too feeble to protect and preserve society. The powers necessary for this purpose will ever prove sufficient to aggrandize those who

control it, at the expense of the rest of the community.

In estimating what amount of power would be requisite to secure the objects of government, we must take into the reckoning, what would be necessary to defend the community against external, as well as internal dangers. Government must be able to repel assaults from abroad, as well as to repress violence and disorders within. . . .

Self-preservation is the supreme law, as well with communities as individuals. And hence the danger of withholding from government the full command of the power and resources of the state; and the great difficulty of limiting its powers consistently with the protection and preservation of the community. And hence the question recurs,—By what means can government, without being divested of the full command of the resources of the community, be prevented from abusing its powers? . . .

There is but one way in which this can possibly be done; and that is, by such an organism as will furnish the ruled with the means of resisting successfully this tendency on the part of the rulers to oppression and abuse. Power can only be resisted by power,—and tendency by tendency. Those who exercise power and those subject to its exercise,—the rulers and the ruled,—stand in antagonistic relations to each other. The same constitution of our nature which leads rulers to oppress the ruled,—regardless of the object for which government is ordained,—will, with equal strength, lead the ruled to resist, when possessed of the means of making peaceable and effective resistance. Such an organism, then, as will furnish the means by which resistance may be systematically and peaceably made on the part of the ruled, to oppression and abuse of power on the part of the rulers, is the first and indispensable step towards *forming* a constitutional government. And as this can only be effected by or through the right of suffrage,—(the right on the part of the ruled to choose their rulers at proper intervals, and to hold them thereby responsible for their conduct,)—the responsibility of the rulers to the ruled, through the right of suffrage, is the indispensable and primary principle in the *foundation* of a constitutional government. When this right is properly guarded, and the people sufficiently enlightened to understand their own rights and the interests of the community, and duly to appreciate the motives and conduct of those appointed to make and execute the laws, it is all-sufficient to give to those who elect, effective control over those they have elected.

I call the right of suffrage the indispensible and primary principle; for it would be a great and dangerous mistake to suppose, as many do, that it is, of itself, sufficient to form constitutional governments. . . .

The right of suffrage, of itself, can do no more than give complete control to those who elect, over the conduct of those they have elected. In doing this, it accomplishes all it possibly can accomplish. This is its aim,—and when this is attained, its end is fulfilled. It can do no more, however enlightened the people, or however widely extended or well guarded the right may be. The sum total, then, of its effects, when most successful, is, to make those elected, the true and faithful representatives of those who elected them,—instead of irresponsible rulers,—as they would be without it; and thus, by converting it into an agency, and the rulers into agents, to divest government of all claims to sovereignty, and to retain it unimpaired to the community. But it is manifest that the right of suffrage, in making these changes, transfers, in reality, the actual control over the government, from those who make and execute the laws, to the body of the community; and, thereby, places the powers of the government as fully in the mass of the community, as they would be if they, in fact, had assembled, made, and executed the laws themselves, without the intervention of representatives or agents. The more perfectly it does this, the more perfectly it accomplishes its ends; but in doing so, it only changes the seat of authority, without counteracting, in the least, the tendency of the government to oppression and abuse of its powers.

If the whole community had the same interests, so that the interests of each and every portion would be so affected by the action of the government, that the laws which oppressed or impoverished one portion, would necessarily oppress and impoverish all others,—or the reverse,—then the right of suffrage, of itself, would be all-sufficient to counteract the tendency of the government to oppression and abuse of its powers; and, of course, would form, of itself, a perfect constitutional government. The interest of all being the same, by supposition, as far as the action of the government was concerned, all would have like interests as to what laws should be made, and how they should be executed. All strife and struggle would cease as to who should be elected to make and execute them. The only question would be, who was most fit; who the wisest and most capable of understanding the common interest of the whole. This decided, the election would pass off quietly, and without party discord; as no one portion could advance its own peculiar interest without regard to the rest, by electing a favorite candidate.

But such is not the case. On the contrary, nothing is more difficult than to equalize the action of the government, in reference to the various and diversified interests of the community; and nothing more easy than to pervert its powers into instruments to aggrandize and enrich one or more interests by oppressing and impoverishing the others; and this too, under the operation of laws, couched in general terms;—and which, on their face, appear fair and equal. Nor is this the case in some particular communities only. It is so in all; the small and the great,—the poor and the rich,—irrespective of pursuits, productions, or degrees of civilization;—with, however, this difference, that the more extensive and populous the country, the more diversified the condition and pursuits of its population, and the richer, more luxurious, and dissimilar the people, the more difficult it is to equalize the action of the government,—and the more easy for one portion of the community to pervert its powers to oppress, and plunder the other.

Such being the case, it necessarily results, that the right of suffrage, by placing the control of the government in the community must, from the same constitution of our nature which makes government necessary to preserve society, lead to conflict among its different interests,—each striving to obtain possession of its powers, as the means of protecting itself against the others;—or of advancing its respective interests, regardless of the interests of others. For this purpose, a struggle will take place between the various interests to obtain a majority, in order to control the government. If no one interest be strong enough, of itself, to obtain it, a combination will be formed between those whose interests are most alike;—each conceding something to the others, until a sufficient number is obtained to make a majority. The process may be slow, and much time may be required before a compact, organized majority can be thus formed; but formed it will be in time, even without preconcert or design, by the sure workings of that principle or constitution of our nature in which government itself originates. When once formed, the community will be divided into two great parties,—a major and minor,—between which there will be incessant struggles on the one side to retain,

and on the other to obtain the majority,— and, thereby, the control of the government and the advantages it confers. . . .

As, then, the right of suffrage, without some other provision, cannot counteract this tendency of government, the next question for consideration is—What is that other provision? This demands the most serious consideration; for of all the questions embraced in the science of government, it involves a principle, the most important, and the least understood; and when understood, the most difficult of application in practice. It is, indeed, emphatically, that principle which *makes* the constitution, in its strict and limited sense.

From what has been said, it is manifest, that this provision must be of a character calculated to prevent any one interest, or combination of interests, from using the powers of government to aggrandize itself at the expense of the others. Here lies the evil: and just in proportion as it shall prevent, or fail to prevent it, in the same degree it will effect, or fail to effect the end intended to be accomplished. There is but one certain mode in which this result can be secured; and that is, by the adoption of some restriction or limitation, which shall so effectually prevent any one interest, or combination of interests, from obtaining the exclusive control of the government, as to render hopeless all attempts directed to that end. There is, again, but one mode in which this can be effected; and that is, by taking the sense of each interest or portion of the community, which may be unequally and injuriously affected by the action of the government, separately, through its own majority, or in some other way by which its voice may be fairly expressed; and to require the consent of each interest, either to put or to keep the government in action. This, too, can be accomplished only in one way,—and that is, by such an organism of the government,—and, if necessary for the purpose, of the community also,—as will, by dividing and distributing the powers of government, give to each division or interest, through its appropriate organ, either a concurrent voice in making and executing the laws, or a veto on their execution. It is only by such an organism, that the assent of each can be made necessary to put the government in motion; or the power made effectual to arrest its action, when put in motion;—and it is only by the one or the other that the different interests, orders, classes, or portions, into which the community may be divided, can be protected, and all conflict and struggle between them prevented,—by rendering it impossible to put or to keep it in action, without the concurrent consent of all.

Such an organism as this, combined with the right of suffrage, constitutes, in fact, the elements of constitutional government. The one, by rendering those who make and execute the laws responsible to those on whom they operate, prevents the rulers from oppressing the ruled; and the other, by making it impossible for any one interest or combination of interests or class, or order, or portion of the community, to obtain exclusive control, prevent any one of them from oppressing the other. It is clear, that oppression and abuse of power must come, if at all, from the one or the other quarter. From no other can they come. It follows, that the two, suffrage and proper organism combined, are sufficient to counteract the tendency of government to oppression and abuse of power; and to restrict it to the fulfillment of the great ends for which it is ordained.

... Where the organism is perfect, every interest will be truly and fully represented, and of course the whole community must be so. It may be difficult, or even impossible, to make a perfect organism,— but, although this be true, yet even when,

instead of the sense of each and of all, it takes that of a few great and prominent interests only, it would still, in a great measure, if not altogether, fulfil the end intended by a constitution. For, in such case, it would require so large a portion of the community, compared with the whole, to concur, or acquiesce in the action of the government, that the number to be plundered would be too few, and the number to be aggrandized too many, to afford adequate motives to oppression and the abuse of its powers. Indeed, however imperfect the organism, it must have more or less effect in diminishing such tendency.

It may be readily inferred, from what has been stated, that the effect of organism is neither to supersede nor diminish the importance of the right of suffrage; but to aid and perfect it. The object of the latter is, to collect the sense of the community. The more fully and perfectly it accomplishes this, the more fully and perfectly it fulfills its end. But the most it can do, of itself, is to collect the sense of the greater number; that is, of the stronger interests, or combination of interests; and to assume this to be the sense of the community. It is only when aided by a proper organism, that it can collect the sense of the entire community,—of each and all its interests; of each, through its appropriate organ, and of the whole, through all of them united. This would truly be the sense of the entire community; for whatever diversity each interest might have within itself,—as all would have the same interest in reference to the action of the government, the individuals composing each would be fully and truly represented by its own majority or appropriate organ, regarded in reference to the other interests. In brief, every individual of every interest might trust, with confidence, its majority or appropriate organ, against that of every other interest.

It results, from what has been said, that there are two different modes in which the sense of the community may be taken; one, simply by the right of suffrage, unaided; the other, by the right through a proper organism. Each collects the sense of the majority. But one regards numbers only, and considers the whole community as a unit, having but one common interest throughout; and collects the sense of the greater number of the whole, as that of the community. The other, on the contrary, regards interests as well as numbers;—considering the community as made up of different and conflicting interests, as far as the action of the government is concerned; and takes the sense of each, through its majority or appropriate organ, and the united sense of all, as the sense of the entire community. The former of these I shall call the numerical, or absolute majority; and the latter, the concurrent, or constitutional majority. I call it the constitutional majority, because it is an essential element in every constitutional government,—be its form what it may. So great is the difference, politically speaking, between the two majorities, that they cannot be confounded, without leading to great and fatal errors; and yet the distinction between them has been so entirely overlooked, that when the term *majority* is used in political discussions, it is applied exclusively to designate the numerical,—as if there were no other. Until this distinction is recognized, and better understood, there will continue to be great liability to error in properly constructing constitutional governments, especially of the popular form, and of preserving them when properly constructed. Until then, the latter will have a strong tendency to slide, first, into the government of the numerical majority, and, finally, into absolute government of some other form. To show that such must be the case, and at the same time to mark more strongly the difference between the two, in order to guard against the danger of overlooking it, I propose to consider the subject more at length.

The first and leading error which naturally arises from overlooking the distinction referred to, is, to confound the numerical majority with the people; and this so completely as to regard them as identical. This is a consequence that necessarily results from considering the numerical as the only majority. All admit, that a popular government, or democracy, is the government of the people; for the terms imply this. A perfect government of the kind would be one which would embrace the consent of every citizen or member of the community; but as this is impracticable, in the opinion of those who regard the numerical as the only majority, and who can perceive no other way by which the sense of the people can be taken,—they are compelled to adopt this as the only true basis of popular government, in contradistinction to governments of the aristocratical or monarchical form. Being thus constrained, they are, in the next place, forced to regard the numerical majority, as, in effect, the entire people; that is, the greater part as the whole; and the government of the greater part as the government of the whole. It is thus the two come to be confounded, and a part made identical with the whole. And it is thus, also, that all the rights, powers, and immunities of the whole people come to be attributed to the numerical majority; and, among others, the supreme, sovereign authority of establishing and abolishing governments at pleasure.

This radical error, the consequence of confounding the two, and of regarding the numerical as the only majority, has contributed more than any other cause, to prevent the formation of popular constitutional governments,—and to destroy them even when they have been formed. It leads to the conclusion that, in their formation and establishment nothing more is necessary than the right of suffrage,—and the allotment to each division of the community a representation in the government, in proportion to numbers. If the numerical majority were really the people; and if, to take its sense truly, were to take the sense of the people truly, a government so consti-tuted would be a true and perfect model of a popular constitutional government; and every departure from it would detract from its excellence. But, as such is not the case,—as the numerical majority, instead of being the people, is only a portion of them,—such a government, instead of being a true and perfect model of the people's govern-ment, that is, a people self-governed, is but the government of a part, over a part,—the major over the minor portion.

But this misconception of the true ele-ments of constitutional government does not stop here. It leads to others equally false and fatal, in reference to the best means of preserving and perpetuating them, when, from some fortunate combination of cir-cumstances, they are correctly formed. For they who fall into these errors regard the restrictions which organism imposes on the will of the numerical majority as restric-tions on the will of the people, and, there-fore, as not only useless, but wrongful and mischievous. And hence they endeavor to destroy organism, under the delusive hope of making government more democratic. . . .

A written constitution certainly has many and considerable advantages; but it is a great mistake to suppose, that the mere insertion of provisions to restrict and limit the powers of the government, without investing those for whose protection they are inserted with the means of enforcing their observance, will be sufficient to pre-vent the major and dominant party from abusing its powers. Being the party in pos-session of the government, they will, from the same constitution of man which makes government necessary to protect society, be in favor of the powers granted by the constitution, and opposed to the restrictions intended to limit them. As the major and dominant party, they will have no need of

these restrictions for their protection. The ballot-box, of itself, would be ample pro-tection to them. Needing no other, they would come, in time, to regard these limita-tions as unnecessary and improper restraints;—and endeavor to elude them, with the view of increasing their power and influence.

The minor, or weaker party, on the contrary, would take the opposite direc-tion;—and regard them as essential to their protection against the dominant party. And, hence, they would endeavor to defend and enlarge the restrictions, and to limit and contract the powers. But where there are no means by which they could compel the major party to observe the restrictions, the only resort left them would be, a strict con-struction of the constitution,—that is, a construction which would confine these powers to the narrowest limits which the meaning of the words used in the grant would admit.

To this the major party would oppose a liberal construction,—one which would give to the words of the grant the broadest meaning of which they were susceptible. It would then be construction against con-struction; the one to contract, and the other to enlarge the powers of the government to the utmost. But of what possible avail could the strict construction of the minor party be, against the liberal interpretation of the major, when the one would have all the powers of the government to carry its construction into effect,—and the other be deprived of all means of enforcing its con-struction? In a contest so unequal, the result would not be doubtful. The party in favor of the restrictions would be overpowered. At first, they might command some respect, and do something to stay the march of encroachment; but they would, in the prog-ress of the contest, be regarded as mere abstractionists; and, indeed, deservedly, if they should indulge the folly of supposing that the party in possession of the ballot-box and the physical force of the country, could be successfully resisted by an appeal to reason, truth, justice, or the obligations imposed by the constitution. For when these, of themselves, shall exert sufficient influence to stay the hand of power, then government will be no longer necessary to protect society, nor constitutions needed to prevent government from abusing its powers. The end of the contest would be the subversion of the constitution, either by the undermining process of construction,—where its meaning would admit of possible doubt,—or by substituting in practice what is called party-usage, in place of its provisions;—or, finally, when no other contrivance would subserve the purpose, by openly and boldly setting them aside. By the one or the other, the restrictions would ultimately be annulled, and the government be converted into one of unlimited powers. . . .

The necessary consequence of taking the sense of the community by the concurrent majority is, as has been explained, to give to each interest or portion of the community a negative on the others. It is this mutual negative among its various conflicting interests, which invests each with the power of protecting itself;—and places the rights and safety of each, where only they can be securely placed, under its own guardianship. Without this there can be no systematic, peaceful, or effective resistance to the natural tendency of each to come into conflict with the others: and without this there can be no constitution. It is this negative power,—the power of preventing or arresting the action of the government,—be it called by what term it may,—veto, interposition, nullification, check, or balance of power,—which, in fact, forms the constitution. They are all but different names for the negative power. In all its forms, and under all its names, it results

from the concurrent majority. Without this there can be no negative; and, without a negative, no constitution. The assertion is true in reference to all constitutional governments, be their forms what they may. It is, indeed, the negative power which makes the constitution,—and the positive which makes the government. The one is the power of acting;—and the other the power of preventing or arresting action. The two, combined, make constitutional governments.

But, as there can be no constitution without the negative power, and no negative power without the concurrent majority;—it follows, necessarily, that where the numerical majority has the sole control of the government, there can be no constitution; as constitution implies limitation or restriction,—and, of course, is inconsistent with the idea of sole or exclusive power. And hence, the numerical, unmixed with the concurrent majority, necessarily forms, in all cases, absolute government.

It is, indeed, the single, or *one power,* which excludes the negative, and constitutes absolute government; and not the *number* in whom the power is vested. The numerical majority is as truly a *single power,* and excludes the negative as completely as the absolute government of one, or of the few. The former is as much the absolute government of the democratic, or popular form, as the latter of the monarchical or aristocratical. It has, accordingly, in common with them, the same tendency to oppression and abuse of power. . . .

The concurrent majority, then, is better suited to enlarge and secure the bounds of liberty, because it is better suited to prevent government from passing beyond its proper limits, and to restrict it to its primary end,—the protection of the community. But in doing this, it leaves, necessarily, all beyond it open and free to individual exertions; and thus enlarges and secures the sphere of liberty to the greatest extent which the condition of the community will admit, as has been explained. The tendency of government to pass beyond its proper limits is what exposes liberty to danger, and renders it insecure; and it is the strong counteraction of governments of the concurrent majority to this tendency which makes them so favorable to liberty. . . .

Such are the many and striking advantages of the concurrent over the numerical majority. Against the former but two objections can be made. The one is, that it is difficult of construction, which has already been sufficiently noticed; and the other, that it would be impracticable to obtain the concurrence of conflicting interests, where they were numerous and diversified; or, if not, that the process for this purpose, would be too tardy to meet, with sufficient promptness, the many and dangerous emergencies, to which all communities are exposed. This objection is plausible; and deserves a fuller notice than it has yet received.

The diversity of opinion is usually so great, on almost all questions of policy, that it is not surprising, on a slight view of the subject, it should be thought impracticable to bring the various conflicting interests of a community to unite on any one line of policy;—or, that a government, founded on such a principle, would be too slow in its movements and too weak in its foundation to succeed in practice. But, plausible as it may seem at the first glance, a more deliberate view will show, that this opinion is erroneous. It is true, that, when there is no urgent necessity, it is difficult to bring those who differ, to agree on any one line of action. Each will naturally insist on taking the course he may think best;—and, from pride of opinion, will be unwilling to yield to others. But the case is different when there is an urgent necessity to unite on some common course of action; as reason and experience both prove. When something *must* be done,—and when it can be done only by the united consent of all,— the necessity of the case will force to a compromise;—be the cause of that necessity what it may. On all questions of acting, necessity, where it exists, is the overruling motive; and where, in such cases, compromise among the parties is an indispensable condition to acting, it exerts an overruling influence in predisposing them to acquiesce in some one opinion or course of action. Experience furnishes many examples in confirmation of this important truth. Among these, the trial by jury is the most familiar. . . .

Overcoming Slavery and the Civil War $\quad$ 10

Stephen A. Douglas

Known today primarily as Lincoln's opponent in the Lincoln–Douglas debates of 1858 in Galesburg, Illinois, and in senatorial and presidential elections, Stephen A. Douglas consistently supported the rights of states to pass legislation that was either unfriendly or friendly toward slavery on the principle of local "popular sovereignty."

Born in Brandon, Vermont, in 1813, Douglas served as an apprentice cabinetmaker and then went to the Canandaigua Academy in New York. Epitomizing the restless American moving westward to see new opportunity, Douglas went to Cleveland, St. Louis, and, finally, Jacksonville, Illinois, where he studied law and passed his bar exam at age twenty. His rise in the new and growing Democratic party was phenomenal.

Elected to the Illinois General Assembly in 1836, Douglas lost in his first run for Congress. He served as secretary of state of Illinois before becoming a judge, and at age 27 he was sitting on the Illinois Supreme Court. Finally, in 1842 he was elected to Congress (for two terms), and then became a U.S. senator for fourteen years, where he became influential as chairman of the Senate Committee on Territories. Douglas worked to get the Illinois Central Railroad Bill passed in 1850, making Chicago the railroad's northern-end station. The same year, he worked to help enact the Compromise of 1850 (which in effect postponed the Civil War by permitting new territories admitted to the Union to be "open" to slavery). In 1854 Douglas was the chief sponsor of the controversial Kansas-Nebraska Act, which prepared the territories of Kansas and Nebraska for statehood, permitting them to pass local friendly or unfriendly legislation in regard to slavery based on the principle of popular sovereignty. Many Northerners (including abolitionists, Whigs, and some of the Democrats) were so upset with legislation that could lead to the spread of slavery to all new territories that the Republican party emerged to oppose this position. In 1857, Kansas submitted a proslavery constitution to Congress, which President Buchanan supported. Douglas opposed it for violating the principle of popular sovereignty and causing a split in the Democratic party.

That same year the Dred Scott decision emerged from the Supreme Court, giving Southerners the right to take slaves with them as property if they moved westward. Douglas argued that the people of Kansas could still keep out slavery by passing local "unfriendly" legislation on the basis of popular sovereignty, which cost him much political support in the South. In 1858, when Douglas ran for reelection to the Senate, Abraham Lincoln opposed him. Representing the Republicans, Lincoln pointed out the contradiction between the Dred Scott decision and Douglas's notion of popular sovereignty in the famous Lincoln-Douglas debates (see excerpts below). Douglas won the Senate race. However, Lincoln had made his name and defeated Douglas in his bid for the presidency in 1860 largely because the southern wing of the Democrats split off from Douglas and ran a candidate of their own. As the Civil War approached, Douglas worked to support Lincoln and the Union until he died in 1861.

The Lincoln–Douglas Debates (1858)
(excerpt)

. . . In a speech in reply to me at Chicago in July last, Mr. Lincoln, in speaking of the equality of the negro with the white man used the following language:

> I should like to know, if taking this old Declaration of Independence, which declares that all men are equal upon principle, and making exceptions to it, where will it stop? If one man says it does not mean a negro, why may not another man say it does not mean another man? (Laughter.) If the Declaration is not the truth, let us get the statute book in which we find it and tear it out. Who is so bold as to do it? If it is not true, let us tear it out.

You find that Mr. Lincoln there proposed that if the doctrine of the Declaration of Independence, declaring all men to be born equal, did not include the negro and put him on an equality with the white man, that we should take the statute book and tear it out. (Laughter and cheers.) He there took the ground that the negro race is included in the Declaration of Independence as the equal of the white race, and that there could be no such thing as a distinction in the races, making one superior and the other inferior. I read now from the same speech:

> My friends, [he says,] I have detained you about as long as I desire to do, and I have only to say let us discard all this quibbling about this man and the other man—this race and that race, and the other race being inferior and therefore they must be placed in an inferior position, discarding our standard that we have left us. Let us discard

all these things, and unite as one people throughout this land, until we shall once more stand up declaring that all men are created equal.

("That's right," &c.)

Yes, I have no doubt that you think it is right, but the Lincoln men down in Coles, Tazewell and Sangamon counties *do not* think it is right. (Immense applause and laughter. "Hit him again," &c.) In the conclusion of the same speech, talking to the Chicago Abolitionists, he said: "I leave you, hoping that the lamp of liberty will burn in your bosoms until there shall no longer be a doubt that all men are created free and equal." ("Good," "good," "shame," &c.) Well, you say good to that, and you are going to vote for Lincoln because he holds that doctrine. ("That's so.") I will not blame you for supporting him on that ground, but I will show you in immediate contrast with that doctrine, what Mr. Lincoln said down in Egypt in order to get votes in that locality where they do not hold to such a doctrine. In a joint discussion between Mr. Lincoln and myself, at Charleston, I think, on the 18th of last month, Mr. Lincoln referring to this subject used the following language:

> I will say then, that I am not nor ever have been in favor of bringing about in any way, the social and political equality of the white and black races; that I am not nor ever have been in favor of making voters of the free negroes, or jurors, or qualifying them to hold office, or having them to marry with white people. I will say in addition,

that there is a physical difference between the white and black races, which, I suppose, will forever forbid the two races living together upon terms of social and political equality, and inasmuch as they cannot so live, that while they do remain together, there must be the position of superior and inferior, that I as much as any other white man am in favor of the superior position being assigned to the white man.

("Good for Lincoln.")

Fellow-citizens, here you find men hurrahing for Lincoln and saying that he did right, when in one part of the state he stood up for negro equality, and in another part for political effect, discarded the doctrine and declared that there always must be a superior and inferior race. ("They're not men. Put them out," &c.) Abolitionists up north are expected and required to vote for Lincoln because he goes for the equality of the races, holding that by the Declaration of Independence the white man and the negro were created equal and endowed by the Divine law with that equality, and down south he tells the old Whigs, the Kentuckians, Virginians, and Tennesseeans, that there is a physical difference in the races, making one superior and the other inferior, and that he is in favor of maintaining the superiority of the white race over the negro. Now, how can you reconcile those two positions of Mr. Lincoln? He is to be voted for in the south as a pro-slavery man, and he is to be voted for in the north as an Abolitionist. ("Give it to him." "Hit him again.") Up here he thinks it is all nonsense to talk about a difference between the races, and says that we must "discard all quibbling about this race and that race and the other race being inferior, and therefore they must be placed in an inferior position." Down south he makes this "quibble" about this race and that race and the other race being inferior as the creed of his party, and declares that the negro can never be elevated to the position of the white man.

You find that his political meetings are called by different names in different counties in the state. Here they are called Republican meetings, but in old Tazewell, where Lincoln made a speech last Tuesday, he did not address a *Republican* meeting, but "a grand rally of the *Lincoln men.*" (Great laughter.) There are very few Republicans there, because Tazewell County is filled with old Virginians and Kentuckians, all of whom are Whigs or Democrats, and if Mr. Lincoln had called an Abolition or Republican meeting there, he would not get many votes. (Laughter.) Go down into Egypt and you find that he and his party are operating under an alias there, which his friend Trumbull has given them, in order that they may cheat the people. When I was down in Monroe County a few weeks ago addressing the people, I saw handbills posted announcing that Mr. Trumbull was going to speak in behalf of Lincoln, and what do you think the name of his party was there? Why the *"Free Democracy."* (Great laughter.) Mr. Trumbull and Mr. Jehu Baker were announced to address the Free Democracy of Monroe Country, and the bill was signed "Many Free Democrats." The reason that Lincoln and his party adopted the name of "Free Democracy" down there was because Monroe County has always been an old fashioned Democratic county, and hence it was necessary to make the people believe that they were Democrats, sympathized with them, and were fighting for Lincoln as Democrats. ("That's it," &c.) Come up to Springfield, where Lincoln now lives and always has lived, and you find that the convention of his party which assembled to nominate candidates for legislature, who are expected to vote for him if elected, dare not adopt the name of Republican, but assembled under the title of "all opposed to the Democracy." (Laughter and cheers.) Thus you find that Mr. Lincoln's creed cannot travel through even one half of the counties of this state, but that it changes its hues and becomes lighter and lighter, as it travels from the extreme north, until it is nearly white, when it reaches the extreme south end of the state. ("That's so, it's true," etc.) I ask you, my friends, why cannot Republicans avow their principles alike everywhere? I would despise myself if I thought that I was procuring your votes by concealing my opinions, and by avowing one set of principles in one part of the state, and a different set in another part. If I do not truly and honorably represent your feelings and principles, then I ought not to be your Senator; and I will never conceal my opinions, or modify or change them a hair's breadth in order to get votes. I tell you that this Chicago doctrine of Lincoln's—declaring that the negro and the white man are made equal by the Declaration of Independence and by Divine Providence—is a monstrous heresy. ("That's so," and terrific applause.) The signers of the Declaration of Independence never dreamed of the negro when they were writing that document. They referred to white men, to men of European birth and European descent, when they declared the equality of all men. I see a gentleman there in the crowd shaking his head. Let me remind him that when Thomas Jefferson wrote that document he was the owner, and so continued until his death, of a large number of slaves. Did he intend to say in that Declaration that his negro slaves, which he held and treated as property, were created his equals by Divine law, and that he was violating the law of God every day of his life by holding them as slaves? ("No, no.") It must be borne in mind that when that Declaration was put forth every one of the thirteen colonies were slave-holding colonies, and every man who signed that instrument represented a slaveholding constituency. Recollect, also, that no one of them emancipated his slaves, much less put them on an equality with himself, after he signed the Decla-

ration. On the contrary, they all continued to hold their negroes as slaves during the Revolutionary war. Now, do you believe—are you willing to have it said—that every man who signed the Declaration of Independence declared the negro his equal, and then was hypocrite enough to continue to hold him as a slave, in violation of what he believed to be the divine law? ("No, no.") And yet when you say that the Declaration of Independence includes the negro, you charge the signers of it with hypocrisy.

I say to you, frankly, that in my opinion this government was made by our fathers on the white basis. It was made by white men for the benefit of white men and their posterity forever, and was intended to be administered by white men in all time to come. ("That's so," and cheers.) But while I hold that under our constitution and political system the negro is not a citizen, cannot be a citizen, and ought not to be a citizen, it does not follow by any means that he should be a slave. On the contrary it does follow that the negro, as an inferior race, ought to possess every right, every privilege, every immunity which he can safely exercise consistent with the safety of the society in which he lives. ("That's so," and cheers.) Humanity requires, and Christianity commands that you shall extend to every inferior being, and every dependent being, all the privileges, immunities and advantages that can be granted to them consistent with the safety of society. If you ask me the nature and extent of these privileges, I answer that that is a question which the people of each state must decide for themselves. ("That's it.") Illinois has decided that question for herself. We have said that in this state the negro shall not be a slave, nor shall he be a citizen. Kentucky holds a different doctrine. New York holds one different from either, and Maine one different from all. Virginia, in her policy on this question, differs in many respects from the others, and so on, until there is hardly two states whose policy is exactly alike in regard to the relation of the white man and the negro. Nor can you reconcile them and make them alike. Each state must do as it pleases. Illinois had as much right to adopt the policy which we have on that subject as Kentucky had to adopt a different policy. The great principle of this government is that each state has the right to do as it pleases on all these questions, and no other state, or power on earth has the right to interfere with us, or complain of us merely because our system differs from theirs. In the compromise measures of 1850, Mr. Clay declared that this great principle ought to exist in the territories as well as in the states, and I reasserted his doctrine in the Kansas and Nebraska Bill in 1854.

But Mr. Lincoln cannot be made to understand, and those who are determined to vote for him, no matter whether he is a pro-slavery man in the south and a negro equality advocate in the north, cannot be made to understand how it is that in a territory the people can do as they please on the slavery question under the Dred Scott decision. Let us see whether I cannot explain it to the satisfaction of all impartial men. Chief Justice Taney has said in his opinion in the Dred Scott case, that a negro slave being property, stands on an equal footing with other property, and that the owner may carry them into United States territory the same as he does other property. ("That's so.") Suppose any two of you, neighbors, should conclude to go to Kansas, one carrying $100,000 worth of negro slaves and the other $100,000 worth of mixed merchandise, including quantities of liquors. You both agree that under that decision you may carry your property to Kansas, but when you get it there, the merchant who is possessed of the liquors is met by the Maine liquor law, which prohibits the sale or use of his property, and the owner of the slaves is met with equally unfriendly legislation, which makes his property worthless after he gets it there. What is the right to carry your property into the territory worth to either, when unfriendly legislation in the territory renders it worthless after you get it there? The slaveholder when he gets his slaves there finds that there is no local law to protect him in holding them, no slave code, no police regulation maintaining and supporting him in his right, and he discovers at once that the absence of such friendly legislation excludes his property from the territory, just as irresistibly as if there was a positive constitutional prohibition excluding it. Thus you find it is with any kind of property in a territory, it depends for its protection on the local and municipal law. If the people of a territory want slavery, they make friendly legislation to introduce it, but if they do not want it, they withhold all protection from it, and then it cannot exist there. Such was the view taken on the subject by different Southern men when the Nebraska Bill passed. See the speech of Mr. Orr, of South Carolina, the present Speaker of the House of Representatives of Congress made at that time, and there you will find this whole doctrine argued out at full length. Read the speeches of other Southern congressmen, Senators and Representatives, made in 1854, and you will find that they took the same view of the subject as Mr. Orr—that slavery could never be forced on a people who did not want it. I hold that in this country there is no power on the face of the globe that can force any institution on an unwilling people. The great fundamental principle of our government is that the people of each state and each territory shall be left perfectly free to decide for themselves what shall be the nature and character of their institutions. When this government was made, it was based on that principle. At the time of its formation there were twelve slaveholding states and one free state in this Union. Suppose this doctrine of Mr.

Lincoln and the Republicans, of uniformity of the laws of all states on the subject of slavery, had prevailed; suppose Mr. Lincoln himself had been a member of the convention which framed the Constitution, and that he had risen in that august body, and addressing the father of his country, had said as he did in Springfield:

> A house divided against itself cannot stand. I believe this government cannot endure permanently half slave and half free. I do not expect the Union to be dissolved—I do not expect the house to fall, but I do expect it will cease to be divided. It will become all one thing or all the other.

What do you think would have been the result? ("Hurrah for Douglas.") Suppose he had made that convention believe that doctrine and they had acted upon it, what do you think would have been the result? Do you believe that the one free state would have outvoted the twelve slaveholding states, and thus abolished slavery? ("No! no!" and cheers.) On the contrary, would not the twelve slaveholding states have outvoted the one free state, and under his doctrine have fastened slavery by an irrevocable constitutional provision upon every inch of the American Republic? Thus you see that the doctrine he now advocates,

if proclaimed at the beginning of the government, would have established slavery everywhere throughout the American continent, and are you willing, now that we have the majority section, to exercise a power which we never would have submitted to when we were in the minority? ("No, no," and great applause.) If the Southern states had attempted to control our institutions, and make the states all slave when they had the power, I ask would you have submitted to it? If you would not, are you willing now that we have become the strongest under that great principle of self-government that allows each state to do as it pleases—to attempt to control the Southern institutions? ("No, no.") Then, my friends, I say to you that there is but one path of peace in this republic, and that is to administer this government as our fathers made it, divided into free and slave states, allowing each state to decide for itself whether it wants slavery or not. If Illinois will settle the slavery question for herself, mind her own business and let her neighbors alone, we will be at peace with Kentucky, and every other Southern state. If every other state in the Union will do the same there will be peace between the North and the South, and in the whole Union.

I am told that my time has expired. (Nine cheers for Douglas.)

Lincoln's Reply

My Fellow Citizens:

A very large portion of the speech which Judge Douglas has addressed to you has previously been delivered and put in print. [Laughter.] I do not mean that for a hit upon the Judge at all. [Renewed laughter.] If I had not been interrupted, I was going to say that such an answer as I was able to make to a very large portion of it, had already been more than once made and

published. There has been an opportunity afforded to the public to see our respective views upon the topics discussed in a large portion of the speech which he has just delivered. I make these remarks for the purpose of excusing myself for not passing over the entire ground that the Judge has traversed. I however desire to take up some of the points that he has attended to, and ask your attention to them, and I shall follow him backwards upon some notes which

I have taken, reversing the order by beginning where he concluded.

The Judge has alluded to the Declaration of Independence, and insisted that negroes are not included in that Declaration; and that it is a slander upon the framers of that instrument, to suppose that negroes were meant therein; and he asks you: Is it possible to believe that Mr. Jefferson, who penned the immortal paper, could have supposed himself applying the language of that instrument to the negro race, and yet hold a portion of that race in slavery? Would he not at once have freed them? I only have to remark upon this part of the Judge's speech, (and that, too, very briefly, for I shall not detain myself, or you, upon that point for any great length of time,) that I believe the entire records of the world, from the date of the Declaration of Independence up to within three years ago, may be searched in vain for one single affirmation, from one single man, that the negro was not included in the Declaration of Independence. I think I may defy Judge Douglas to show that he ever said so, that Washington ever said so, that any President ever said so, that any member of Congress ever said so, or that any living man upon the whole earth ever said so, until the necessities of the present policy of the Democratic party, in regard to slavery, had to invent that affirmation. [Tremendous applause.] And I will remind Judge Douglas and this audience, that while Mr. Jefferson was the owner of slaves, as undoubtedly he was, in speaking upon this very subject, he used the strong language that "he trembled for his country when he remembered that God was just;" and I will offer the highest premium in my power to Judge Douglas if he will show that he, in all his life, ever uttered a sentiment at all akin to that of Jefferson. [Great applause and cries of "Hit him again," "good," "good."]

The next thing to which I will ask your attention is the Judge's comments upon the fact, as he assumes it to be, that we cannot call our public meetings as Republican meetings; and he instances Tazewell County as one of the places where the friends of Lincoln have called a public meeting and have not dared to name it a Republican meeting. He instances Monroe County as another where Judge Trumbull and Jehu Baker addressed the persons whom the Judge assumes to be the friends of Lincoln, calling them the "Free Democracy." I have the honor to inform Judge Douglas that he spoke in that very county of Tazewell last Saturday, and I was there on Tuesday last, and when he spoke there he spoke under a call not venturing to use the word "Democrat." [Cheers and laughter.] (Turning to Judge Douglas.) What do you think of this? [Immense applause and roars of laughter.]

So again, there is another thing to which I would ask the Judge's attention upon this subject. In the contest of 1856 his party delighted to call themselves together as the "National Democracy," but now, if there should be a notice put up anywhere for a meeting of the "National Democracy," Judge Douglas and his friends would not come. [Laughter.] They would not suppose themselves invited. [Renewed laughter and cheers.] They would understand that it was a call for those hateful postmasters whom he talks about. [Uproarious laughter.]

Now a few words in regard to these extracts from speeches of mine, which Judge Douglas has read to you, and which he supposes are in very great contrast to each other. Those speeches have been before the public for a considerable time, and if they have any inconsistency in them, if there is any conflict in them the public have been able to detect it. When the Judge says, in speaking on this subject, that I make speeches of one sort for the people of the northern end of the state, and of a different sort for the southern people, he assumes that I do not understand that my speeches will be put in print and read north and south. I knew all the while that the speech that I made at Chicago and the one I made at Jonesboro and the one at Charleston, would all be put in print and all the reading and intelligent men in the community would see them and know all about my opinions. And I have not supposed, and do not now suppose, that there is any conflict whatever between them. ["They are all good speeches!" "Hurrah for Lincoln!"] But the Judge will have it that if we do not confess that there is a sort of inequality between the white and black races, which justifies us in making them slaves, we must, then, insist that there is a degree of equality that requires us to make them our wives. [Loud applause, and cries, "Give it to him;" "Hit him again."] Now, I have all the while taken a broad distinction in regard to that matter; and that is all there is in these different speeches which he arrays here, and the entire reading of either of the speeches will show that that distinction was made. Perhaps by taking two parts of the same speech, he could have got up as much of a conflict as the one he has found. I have all the while maintained, that in so far as it should be insisted that there was an equality between the white and black races that should produce a perfect social and political equality, it was an impossibility. This you have seen in my printed speeches, and with it I have said, that in their right to "life, liberty and the pursuit of happiness," as proclaimed in that old Declaration, the inferior races are our equals. [Long-continued cheering.] And these declarations I have constantly made in reference to the abstract moral question, to contemplate and consider when we are legislating about any new country which is not already cursed with the actual presence of the evil—slavery. I have never manifested any impatience with the necessities that spring from the actual presence of black people amongst us, and the actual existence of slavery amongst us where it does already exist; but I have insisted that, in legislating for new countries, where it does not exist, there is no just rule other than that of moral and abstract right! With reference to those new countries, those maxims as to the right of a people to "life, liberty and the pursuit of happiness," were the just rules to be constantly referred to. There is no misunderstanding this, except by men interested to misunderstand it. [Applause.] . . .

Abraham Lincoln

Considered the greatest American president by many historians, Abraham Lincoln freed the slaves and led the United States successfully through its greatest crisis, the Civil War.

Lincoln was born in 1809 in a log cabin in Hardin (now Larue) County, Kentucky. He symbolized "the American story" for many by working his way up from poverty and ignorance to a successful law practice and political career. He was a wily practitioner of politics with a stern moral base, and a teller of jokes and tales in the midst of tragic historical circumstances. For example, when he fired a cabinet minister and was asked by senators to get rid of the rest of his cabinet, he said it reminded him of the farmer who, when confronted with seven skunks in his barn, killed one, which raised such an awful stench that he decided to let the others go. His practical politics always had a moral edge, no matter how difficult the times—and his era was one of the most trying Americans have ever experienced on their own soil.

Lincoln's parents belonged to a Baptist sect that disapproved of slavery, perhaps accounting for Lincoln's later statement that he was "naturally anti-slavery." He grew up farming in a fight "with trees and logs and grubs," clearing the wild forest. He had less than a year of formal education in various so-called schools and was largely self-taught. In 1830, the Lincolns moved to Illinois. A year later, Lincoln became estranged from his father and went to New Salem to try out various occupations, serving in 1832 briefly in the Black Hawk War. Elected captain of his volunteer company, Lincoln gained self-confidence. That same year he ran for the Illinois Legislature, but lost. Elected as a Whig to the legislature one year later, Lincoln served four terms. He could identify with the Whig platform of national economic development after the hardships of his rural past. He backed the Second Bank of the United States, government-sponsored infrastructure projects, and protective tariffs. Although he was unsentimental with agricultural workers, whom he perceived as neither better nor worse than anyone else, his own hard-working past caused him to sympathize with workers in general, whom he viewed to be "prior to, and independent of, capital." Lincoln was publicly critical of slavery as early as 1837.

In 1836 Lincoln became a lawyer and moved to Springfield, Illinois, to join in a law practice with a fellow Whig legislator. Shifting from partner to partner, Lincoln soon became successful. From 1847–49, he served as a member of the U.S. House of Representatives, opposing the Mexican War with the other Whigs. He supported the Wilmot Proviso, which prohibited slavery from any area incorporated into the United States as a result of the Mexican War. He returned voluntarily to his law practice as his interest in politics declined. But the Kansas–Nebraska Act was suddenly passed, which opened areas previously closed to slavery by popular sovereignty or local preference. Lincoln thought the provisions of this legislation were immoral. His view of the legality of slavery was complex. He thought it was clearly constitutional in the original states that had it when the Constitution was signed and that it naturally would tend toward extinction if not permitted to spread to other territories. So he was not an abolitionist.

Nevertheless, when Senator Stephen Douglas sponsored the Kansas–Nebraska Act, Lincoln felt morally concerned and moved to act. National Republican leaders wanted to leave Douglas unopposed for reelection. But Lincoln persuaded them that the Act compelled them morally to oppose Douglas and ran against him, pushing Douglas into the famous Lincoln–Douglas debates (excerpts here). Lincoln supported the Fugitive Slave Acts, confessing that he had no idea how to abolish slavery even if empowered to do so. He argued that "A house divided against itself cannot stand" in his 1858 debates with Douglas, asserting that the nation would go all slave or all free eventually. The next year, abolitionist John Brown was hanged, and Lincoln told Southerners in his campaigning that if they rebelled, they would be dealt with as John Brown had been. He stressed the moral principles of the Republicans in opposing slavery in contrast with the moral indifference of the Democrats who, under Douglas's leadership, argued that each state should leave the issue of slavery up to popular sovereignty. Lincoln won the debates and gained national fame, although he lost the Senate race. Well enough known to be a presidential candidate, Lincoln captured the Republican nomination in 1860 and went on to win the election.

His election triggered the South's secession from the Union by the time Lincoln was inaugurated. His conciliatory speech had no effect in the South. Against the advice of his cabinet, he sent provisions to Fort Sumter in Charleston, South Carolina. On April 12, 1861, the Civil War began when South Carolina fired on the fort. As commander in chief, Lincoln often took strong measures that went against the advice of his military commanders and were, at times, at odds with the Constitution. He used Republican-party organization to satisfy his administrative needs, while dividing military appointments between Republicans and Democrats. Lincoln was accused of being a tyrant by Democrats because of his wartime restrictions on civil liberties (such as the writ of *habeas corpus*). But he tolerated extreme criticism from the press and rival politicians and restrained his commanders from arresting more people than necessary.

Although the Constitution protected slavery in peacetime, Lincoln interpreted it to permit him to abolish slavery during war as a military necessity. His preliminary Emancipation Proclamation of 1862 made use of a military justification, as did all of his racial measures. By the presidential election of 1864, the Republicans clearly stood on the side of the Thirteenth Amendment to the Constitution, abolishing slavery. The Democrats, led by Lincoln's former chief general, George B. McClellan, promised to give the Southern states the same rights they held in 1860. By winning the election, Lincoln thus determined the future of the race issue in the United States. This victory also provoked John Wilkes Booth, Southern sympathizer and Black-hater, to assassinate Lincoln in 1865, five days after Confederate General Robert E. Lee surrendered to Union General Ulysses S. Grant.

The Emancipation Proclamation

January 1, 1863

By the President of the United States of America:

A Proclamation.

Whereas, on the twentysecond day of September, in the year of our Lord one thousand eight hundred and sixty two, a proclamation was issued by the President of the United States, containing, among other things, the following, to wit:

"That on the first day of January, in the year of our Lord one thousand eight hundred and sixty-three, all persons held as slaves within any State or designated part of a State, the people whereof shall then be in rebellion against the United States, shall be then, thenceforward, and forever free; and the Executive Government of the United States, including the military and naval authority thereof, will recognize and maintain the freedom of such persons, and will do no act or acts to repress such persons, or any of them, in any efforts they may make for their actual freedom.

"That the Executive will, on the first day of January aforesaid, by proclamation, designate the States and parts of States, if any, in which the people thereof, respectively, shall then be in rebellion against the United States; and the fact that any State, or the people thereof, shall on that day be, in good faith, represented in the Congress of the United States by members chosen thereto at elections wherein a majority of the qualified voters of such State shall have participated, shall, in the absence of strong countervailing testimony, be deemed conclusive evidence that such State, and the people thereof, are not then in rebellion against the United States."

Now, therefore, I, Abraham Lincoln, President of the United States, by virtue of the power in me vested as Commander-in-Chief, of the Army and Navy of the United

States in time of actual armed rebellion against authority and government of the United States, and as a fit and necessary war measure for suppressing said rebellion, do, on this first day of January, in the year of our Lord one thousand eight hundred and sixty three, and in accordance with my purpose so to do publicly proclaimed for the full period of one hundred days, from the day first above mentioned, order and designate as the States and parts of States wherein the people thereof respectively, are this day in rebellion against the United States, the following, to wit:

Arkansas, Texas, Louisiana, (except the Parishes of St. Bernard, Plaquemines, Jefferson, St. Johns, St. Charles, St. James[,] Ascension, Assumption, Terrebonne, Lafourche, St. Mary, St. Martin, and Orleans, including the City of New-Orleans) Mississippi, Alabama, Florida, Georgia, South-Carolina, North-Carolina, and Virginia, (except the fortyeight counties designated as West Virginia, and also the counties of Berkley, Accomac, Northampton, Elizabeth-City, York, Princess Ann, and Norfolk, including the cities of Norfolk & Portsmouth [)]; and which excepted parts are, for the present, left precisely as if this proclamation were not issued.

And by virtue of the power, and for the purpose aforesaid, I do order and declare that all persons held as slaves within said designated States, and parts of States, are, and henceforward shall be free; and that the Executive government of the United States, including the military and naval authorities thereof, will recognize and maintain the freedom of said persons.

And I hereby enjoin upon the people so declared to be free to abstain from all violence, unless in necessary self-defence; and I recommend to them that, in all cases when allowed, they labor faithfully for reasonable wages.

And I further declare and make known, that such persons of suitable condition, will be received into the armed service of the United States to garrison forts, positions, stations, and other places, and to man vessels of all sorts in said service.

And upon this act, sincerely believed to be an act of justice, warranted by the Constitution, upon military necessity, I invoke the considerate judgment of mankind, and the gracious favor of Almighty God.

The Gettysburg Address*

November 19, 1863

Four score and seven years ago our fathers brought forth on this continent, a new nation, conceived in Liberty, and dedicated to the proposition that all men are created equal.

Now we are engaged in a great civil war, testing whether that nation, or any nation so conceived and so dedicated, can long endure. We are met on a great battle-field of that war. We have come to dedicate a portion of that field, as a final resting place for those who here gave their lives that that nation might live. It is altogether fitting and proper that we should do this.

But, in a larger sense, we can not dedicate—we can not consecrate—we can not hallow—this ground. The brave men, living and dead, who struggled here, have consecrated it, far above our poor power to add or detract. The world will little note,

---

Isaak, *American Political Thinking.*

*Address delivered at the dedication of the Cemetery at Gettysburg.

nor long remember what we say here, but it can never forget what they did here. It is for us the living, rather, to be dedicated here to the unfinished work which they who fought here have thus far so nobly advanced. It is rather for us to be here dedicated to the great task remaining before us—that from these honored dead we take increased devotion to that cause for which they gave the last full measure of devotion—that we here highly resolve that these dead shall not have died in vain—that this nation, under God, shall have a new birth of freedom—and that government of the people, by the people, for the people, shall not perish from the earth.

Abraham Lincoln.

Letter to Henry L. Pierce and Others

Springfield, Ills.
April 6. 1859

Messrs. Henry L. Pierce, & others.
Gentlemen

Your kind note inviting me to attend a Festival in Boston, on the 13th. Inst. in honor of the birth-day of Thomas Jefferson, was duly received. My engagements are such that I can not attend.

Bearing in mind that about seventy years ago, two great political parties were first formed in this country, that Thomas Jefferson was the head of one of them, and Boston the head-quarters of the other, it is both curious and interesting that those supposed to descend politically from the party opposed to Jefferson, should now be celebrating his birth-day in their own original seat of empire, while those claiming political descent from him have nearly ceased to breathe his name everywhere.

Remembering too, that the Jefferson party were formed upon their supposed superior devotion to the *personal* rights of men, holding the rights of *property* to be secondary only, and greatly inferior, and then assuming that the so-called democracy of to-day, are the Jefferson, and their opponents, the anti-Jefferson parties, it will be equally interesting to note how completely the two have changed hands as to the principle upon which they were originally supposed to be divided.

The democracy of to-day hold the *liberty* of one man to be absolutely nothing, when in conflict with another man's right of *property*. Republicans, on the contrary, are for both the *man* and the *dollar;* but in cases of conflict, the man *before* the dollar.

I remember once being much amused at seeing two partially intoxicated men engage in a fight with their great-coats on, which fight, after a long, and rather harmless contest, ended in each having fought himself *out* of his own coat, and *into* that of the other. If the two leading parties of this day are really identical with the two in the days of Jefferson and Adams, they have performed about the same feat as the two drunken men.

But soberly, it is now no child's play to save the principles of Jefferson from total overthrow in this nation.

One would start with great confidence that he could convince any sane child that the simpler propositions of Euclid are true; but, nevertheless, he would fail, utterly, with one who should deny the definitions and axioms. The principles of Jefferson are the definitions and axioms of free society. And yet they are denied, and evaded, with no small show of success. One dashingly calls them "glittering generalities"; another bluntly calls them "self evident lies"; and

still others insidiously argue that they apply only to "superior races."

These expressions, differing in form, are identical in object and effect—the supplanting the principles of free government, and restoring those of classification, caste, and legitimacy. They would delight a convocation of crowned heads, plotting against the people. They are the van-guard—the miners, and sappers—of returning despotism. We must repulse them, or they will subjugate us.

This is a world of compensations; and he who would *be* no slave, must consent to *have* no slave. Those who deny freedom to others, deserve it not for themselves; and, under a just God, can not long retain it.

All honor to Jefferson—to the man who, in the concrete pressure of a struggle for national independence by a single people, had the coolness, forecast, and capacity to introduce into a merely revolutionary document, an abstract truth, applicable to all men and all times, and so to embalm it there, that to-day, and in all coming days, it shall be a rebuke and a stumbling-block to the very harbingers of re-appearing tyrany and oppression. Your obedient Servant

A. Lincoln—

Second Inaugural Address

March 4, 1865

[*Fellow Countrymen*:]

At this second appearing to take the oath of the presidential office, there is less occasion for an extended address than there was at the first. Then a statement, somewhat in detail, of a course to be pursued, seemed fitting and proper. Now, at the expiration of four years, during which public declarations have been constantly called forth on every point and phase of the great contest which still absorbs the attention, and engrosses the enerergies [*sic*] of the nation, little that is new could be presented. The progress of our arms, upon which all else chiefly depends, is as well known to the public as to myself; and it is, I trust, reasonably satisfactory and encouraging to all. With high hope for the future, no prediction in regard to it is ventured.

On the occasion corresponding to this four years ago, all thoughts were anxiously directed to an impending civil-war. All dreaded it—all sought to avert it. While the inaugeral [*sic*] address was being delivered from this place, devoted altogether to *saving* the Union without war, insurgent agents were in the city seeking to *destroy* it without war—seeking to dissol[v]e the Union, and divide effects, by negotiation. Both parties deprecated war; but one of them would *make* war rather than let the nation survive; and the other would *accept* war rather than let it perish. And the war came.

One eighth of the whole population were colored slaves, not distributed generally over the Union, but localized in the Southern part of it. These slaves constituted a peculiar and powerful interest. All knew that this interest was, somehow, the cause of the war. To strengthen, perpetuate, and extend this interest was the object for which the insurgents would rend the Union, even by war; while the government claimed no right to do more than to restrict the territorial enlargement of it. Neither party expected for the war, the magnitude, or the duration, which it has already attained.

Neither anticipated that the *cause* of the conflict might cease with, or even before, the conflict itself should cease. Each looked for an easier triumph, and a result less fundamental and astounding. Both read the same Bible, and pray to the same God; and each invokes His aid against the other. It may seem strange that any men should dare to ask a just God's assistance in wringing their bread from the sweat of other men's faces; but let us judge not that we be not judged. The prayers of both could not be answered; that of neither has been answered fully. The Almighty has His own purposes. "Woe unto the world because of offences! for it must needs be that offences come; but woe to that man by whom the offence cometh!" If we shall suppose that American Slavery is one of those offences which, in the providence of God, must needs come, but which, having continued through His appointed time, He now wills to remove, and that He gives to both North and South, this terrible war, as the woe due to those by whom the offence came, shall we discern therein any departure from those divine attributes which the believers in a Living God always ascribe to Him? Fondly do we hope—fervently do we pray—that this mighty scourge of war may speedily pass away. Yet, if God wills that it continue, until all the wealth piled by the bond-man's two hundred and fifty years of unrequited toil shall be sunk, and until every drop of blood drawn with the lash, shall be paid by another drawn with the sword, as was said three thousand years ago, so still it must be said "the judgments of the Lord, are true and righteous altogether[.]"

With malice toward none; with charity for all; with firmness in the right, as God gives us to see the right, let us strive on to finish the work we are in; to bind up the nation's wounds; to care for him who shall have borne the battle, and for his widow, and his orphan—to do all which may achieve and cherish a just, and a lasting peace, among ourselves, and with all nations.

[Endorsement]

A. Lincoln

II

Reconstruction through World War II
(1865–1945)

Introduction

The American liberalism of the Founding Fathers, which assumed a balance between natural rights for individual citizens, states' rights, and a minimalist federal government, was overwhelmed by the Civil War, its aftermath, and the ongoing Industrial Revolution in the late nineteenth century. Idealists who believed in Thomas Jefferson–era republicanism, that is, representative democracy stemming from a decentralized condition of equality and local participation, faced sharply growing inequalities as the agrarian economy was industrialized. No one had anticipated the sudden rise of large corporations that could monopolize certain economic sectors and create great concentrations of wealth and power. The industries that build the country's infrastructure—railroads, iron, and steel—became the basis of great fortunes for wealthy tycoons such as Commodore Vanderbilt, Andrew Carnegie, and J. P. Morgan. In contrast, an urban working class had evolved without property or economic security. Procedural political equality was no longer enough: people began to demand equality of economic opportunity.

The Civil War dramatized that not everyone was "born free." Not only those representing former slaves, but women, too, demanded their "natural rights." Traditional American liberalism did not take into account the need for strong government intervention for the sake of bringing equal rights to those excluded from the political system, nor for the sake of ensuring market competition free from domination by corporate monopolies or trusts. Laissez-faire economics stimulated economic growth, but the rich got richer, and the gap between the rich and poor widened. Those who at the beginning of the nineteenth century would have advocated decentralization and populism against the Federalists (who sought greater power for the central government) now argued for the reverse—government intervention for equal rights and to protect fair economic opportunity. First the Populists and then the Progressives offered proposals for the government to break up corporate monopolies. Results included the Sherman Antitrust Act of 1890 and the antitrust agenda of the "New Freedom" movement represented by Woodrow Wilson. American socialism reached its zenith, symbolized by the leadership of Eugene V. Debs. On the other hand, the rich industrialists picked up the doctrine of laissez-faire and argued for the least possible government intervention for the sake of economic growth and national prosperity. The Social Darwinism theory became attractive here, handed down from biologist Charles Darwin and sociologist Herbert Spencer to Yale sociologist William Graham Sumner, whose motto was: "liberty, inequality, survival of the fittest; non-liberty, equality, survival of the unfittest."

In the years of World War I, the Great Depression, and World War II, the ideology of "negative state," or laissez-faire liberalism, which provided minimal protection of the existing order for the sake of individual rights, was undermined by a vision of "positive state," or progressive liberalism, which provided increasing positive government intervention in the economy and society. This evolution culminated in Franklin Roosevelt's New Deal, in which the federal government established its legitimate role in the economy in a desperate bid to turn around the country's condition following the stock market crash of 1929 and subsequent Great Depression. Roosevelt's brain trust, which included thinkers such as Adolph Berle, argued that individuals not only have the right to speak and to vote but the right to work and to have economic opportunity. Some historians have called the New Deal a "watershed" in American political thinking. And to the extent that even 1970s Republican President Richard Nixon was to say "We are all Keynesians now" (meaning that even the conservatives saw the need for government intervention in the economy), they may have a point. But the reality of the laissez-faire liberalism of the 1980s illustrates that even watersheds can be subject to tidal cycles, if not rip-tide movements, and that the conservative tradition of American liberalism (the seesaw between the classical laissez-faire and progressive strains of liberalism) has outlived the New Deal, the presidency of Bill Clinton notwithstanding.

At the end of the Civil War in 1865, the main political issue in the United States became reconstruction, how to restore the states of the Confederate South to the Union and how to protect the newly freed slaves in the process. Recall that at the birth of the republic, slaves, freedmen, and women did not count as voting citizens. Black suffrage became a legal reality only with the passing of the Fourteenth, Fifteenth, and Twentieth Amendments to the Constitution. Women could vote only as of 1920 with the passage of the Nineteenth Amendment. Eighteen-year-olds had to wait until 1971 for the Twenty-sixth Amendment. The first ten amendments established the Bill of Rights as an afterthought to the Constitution at the founding of the Republic, but it applied only to older white males.

Before the Civil War, the U.S. Supreme Court ruled in the 1857 Dred Scott case that black people "had no rights which the white man was bound to respect." This ruling caused an uproar that helped elect Abraham Lincoln, who opposed the spread of slavery. The Southern states left the Union; the Civil War was fought; and afterwards, the "radical" antislavery element of Lincoln's Republican party pushed through three "Civil War amendments"—the Thirteenth (1865), Fourteenth (1868), and Fifteenth (1870)—which aimed to give blacks legal citizenship and to protect their status. But the decade of Reconstruction after the Civil War was largely devoted to efforts by the Southern states to undermine or water down the legal rights of freedmen with inconsistent efforts by the Northern states to fight back and try to get the Southern states to obey the letter, if not the spirit, of the law. For example, the Thirteenth Amendment, which simply banned slavery in the United States, was more or less nullified by "black codes" passed by Southern state legislatures. Public opinion in the North, angered by these codes, forced passage of the Reconstruction Act (1867) and the Fourteenth and Fifteenth Amendments. The sweeping shifts of powers from the states to the national government mandated in the Fourteenth Amendment initially led to its rejection by the Southern states. Later, however, they were forced to ratify it through new laws passed in Congress by the radical Republicans. Some Southerners reacted in bitter opposition in other ways, such as in the organization of the Ku Klux Klan, which started a violent campaign against black Americans to keep them from voting or asserting other legal rights they presumably had attained.

The radical Republicans countered in 1870 with the Fifteenth Amendment: "The right of citizens of the U.S. to vote shall not be denied or abridged by the U.S. or by any state on account of race, color or previous condition of servitude." This amendment worked until 1877, the watershed year of political uncertainty and labor strikes, when the federal government stopped supervising elections in the South and the amendment was effectively nullified. Corruption, fraud, and the threat of organized racial violence were enough to discourage potential black voters. And by the 1890s, the Northern states had become so indifferent that eleven state legislatures passed ingenious laws that served to exclude the great majority of Southern black Americans from the right to vote (effectively through the 1960s) particularly those in rural areas. These laws required literacy, a "poll tax," or demonstrations of "good character." Although the selections of W. E. B. Du Bois's *The Souls of Black Folk* (1903) gives a balanced black-American perspective on the government's efforts to help bring black Americans into the mainstream after the Civil War, clearly these efforts were not nearly up to the task. Given the political obstacles of the Reconstruction, it was hard to envision practical alternatives at the time. Most American political thinkers did not even attempt it. The radical Republicans worried about consolidating votes and the support of financial and business interests given the economic boom in the North and the West precipitated by the war. The concern for equal rights for African-Americans dimmed into indifference. The national government gained power at the expense of the states, as the national focus turned slowly from Reconstruction politics to economic issues of industrialism, and suffrage and civil rights issues were postponed for decades.

1. The American Dream

Indeed, most Americans wished only to get beyond the horrors of the Civil War. The popular escapist novels of Horatio Alger, which celebrated the American dream of the worthy poor boy going from rags to riches through "pluck, luck, and hard work," epitomized how many Americans wanted to think (and continue to want to think). Here, excerpts from Alger's *Ragged Dick* (1867) illustrate this optimistic American urge toward upward mobility through hard work and the belief in the triumph of good over evil, resulting in material rewards that are then philanthropically shared to help out those on their way up the social ladder. This is patriotism for the conservative frame of American liberalism at work—affirmation of the honest, rugged individual triumphing over social obstacles without any help from the state, using honorable business practices and compassion (see Irving Kristol's "Horatio Alger and Profits" in Part III for evidence of the abiding contemporary belief in the American Horatio Alger myth).

Walt Whitman viewed the Civil War era more darkly than Alger, having seen the suffering firsthand as a nurse. Yet he affirms the American dream in "Democracy" (1871) as a celebration of individual liberalism and small property holdings, looking to the divine spark in each man and woman as the source of democratic being. His assumption of absolute human equality set the political agenda as perhaps only a poet could. Thus, in his best-selling *Leaves of Grass,* he wrote: "The United States themselves are essentially the greatest poem. ... Here at last is something in the doing of man that corresponds with the broadcast doings of the day and night," and, "I celebrate myself and sing myself, / And what I assume you shall assume." Politically speaking, this celebration of the potential genius of each *individual* is critical for its importance in affirming the Lockean individualism of traditional liberalism. The free unit is an individual unit, not a collective. It is a freedom *to be* as an individual, with equal democratic rights. Thus, the agenda is set for the expansion of individual rights—to women, to African-Americans, to Native Americans—*within* the conservative liberal framework of American liberalism, that system of checks and balances that stabilizes the rights to individual freedom for those who have already attained it.

2. The American Reality for Women and Native Americans

The issue of women's suffrage heated up as the slaves became free and received the legal right to vote. One political leader who kept the issue hot was Susan B. Anthony. She opposed granting suffrage to freed men unless women were granted suffrage at the same time. Although she lost many former supporters through this position, her uncompromising stance helped to prepare the ground for passage of the Nineteenth Amendment in 1920, granting women the right to vote. But as the speech "Suffrage and the Working Woman" (1871) points out, Anthony was not merely asking for suffrage but for the right of women to an independent source of subsistence, for economic as well as political dignity. From this perspective, although women have come a long way, by the end of the twentieth century Anthony still would not have achieved the ideal economic and political equality she envisioned.

As for Native Americans, they were by far the worst off of the minorities in terms of economic and social justice in the United States. Standing Bear's testimony of 1879, included here, the veracity of which was confirmed by a Senate committee, illustrates the dark forecast that Chief Seattle made for the Indian people. Most of Standing Bear's Ponca tribe died or were permanently disabled from the U.S. government's policy forcing them off their lands. In most cases, Native American speeches and writings are found in "children's" libraries where they have been relegated. The simple, poetic, oral prose of the Native American evidently appeared too childish for the adult section in the late twentieth century. Presumably they never attained the means of Susan Anthony, who used her own money to make sure her *History of Women's Suffrage* made it into adult libraries. But the deceptive "one with the earth" simplicity of the native American mind may be more where the political world is going than where it has been, toward ecological integrity and a sense of sharing and responsibility in terms of the sacredness of place.

3. Visions of Progress

The socioeconomic crisis of the Civil War was followed by the traumatic change of the industrial revolution and the subsequent consolidation of business into monopolies and trusts that could take advantage of technological advances. The gap between the rich and poor became more striking than ever, particularly in the metropolitan areas where the high life was celebrated a stone's throw from slum areas. Henry George analyzed these problems in *Progress and Poverty* (1880), arguing that land monopoly canceled out any potential gain the laborer might reap from rising wages by raising rents.

The novelist Edward Bellamy went even further in *Looking Backward, 2000–1887* (1888), envisioning the arrival of a socialist utopia in the United States by the end of the twentieth century. This was the most widely read novel of its time, a blueprint that led John Dewey, Charles Beard, and Edward Weeks, in separate surveys conducted in 1935, to name Bellamy's work as the most influential book written by an American in the past fifty years. The reader is encouraged to go beyond the excerpts here to read the whole of this young Boston gentleman's voyage in sleep from his war-torn nineteenth-century world of economic deprivation to a peaceful twenty-first century where efforts correlated with moral worth and basic economic needs are satisfied for all human beings.

The final vision of progress excerpted here is that of John Dewey himself, a philosopher whom many have identified as America's greatest. His *Democracy and Education* (1916) experienced a rebirth of popularity on college campuses at the end of the twentieth century among students and faculty searching for practical, hands-on solutions to educational reform. Dewey seeks solutions which are consistent with a participatory democracy aiming to provide for all of its members on equal terms. The efforts of the Clinton administration to bring apprenticeship and pragmatic educational reform back to life in the United States can still be measured by Dewey's standards.

4. The Frontier, the State, and War

Frederick Jackson Turner, Randolph Bourne, and Mark Twain provide us with readings that are not merely prescient, but disturbingly contemporary. Their works explore the anticipation of dwindling frontiers, the temptation to find new frontiers in imperialistic thrusts abroad, the rise of the national security state with its monopoly of force and power, and the inevitable wars between states that result from these developments. Turner stressed the frontier's positive support of egalitarian democracy and asked what would happen when Americans ran out of the "safety valve" of more frontier to expand to. His famous "frontier thesis" of American development (1894) was to have widespread influence on American studies in the twentieth century. Much less optimistic than Turner, Twain would not let "The War Prayer" (1904–05) be published in his lifetime, so savagely biting is its truth: To read "The War Prayer" is never to think of Mark Twain or the patriotic war in the same way again. And the excerpt from "The State" by Randolph Bourne (1918) summed up the end of illusions as to where the "liberal" state could lead as World War I came to an end: "War is the health of the state. . . . The state is the organization of the herd to act offensively or defensively against another herd similarly organized."

5. The Power of Wealth

The survival of the fittest as an ethos, the trophies of war as status, the gospel of wealth, these are universal themes that led into World War I and from it into World War II and from it to today. One interpretation is that the *reductio ad absurdum* of liberalism—the absurd result of waiting to see what happens if conservative laissez-faire liberalism is followed to its logical conclusion—is Social Darwinism, the argument that only the fittest individuals *should* survive in the egotistic competition between free individuals and that the weak *should* be left to die off for the sake of long-term racial health.

Is America a "money culture" as John Dewey once suggested? Industrial millionaire and philanthropist Andrew Carnegie, a Horatio Alger in the flesh, seems to say yes, and why not? By becoming rich through effective individualism in the laissez-faire liberal, capitalistic culture, one creates wealth. As a millionaire, one becomes "a trustee for the poor." Carnegie in "Gospel of Wealth" (1890) argues that it is immoral to die with money in the bank; it must be spent or given away for worthy projects.

In this late nineteenth-century era of the concentration of capital into monopolies and trusts, Carnegie's kind of business success was no accident, argued sociologist Lester Ward.

In *Plutocracy and Paternalism* (1895) he claims that the state specializes in subsidizing the plutocracy—the rich and powerful, who could not do without it. For the sake of social justice, the state's intervention must be extended to aid the poor. Otherwise, the state will continue to subsidize not the qualities best designed for strengthening the species but those that create the pampered rich who monopolize the state's paternalism.

When it comes to casting a critical eye upon the wealthy, no one has a sharper vision than Thorstein Veblen, whose *The Theory of the Leisure Class* (1899) contends that status depends upon conspicuous consumption and upon the flagrant exhibition of doing useless things for a living. Foremost among those representing useless vocations are politicians, generals, priests, and athletes. Veblen's *The Theory of Business Enterprise* (1904) suggests that the business system is destined for self-destruction given society's other tendencies. And later he praised a system in which craftsmen and engineers would rule, those who made real things with competence and pride, rather than speculators, money managers, and others of dubious social value.

Finally, we come to the sociologist who took Charles Darwin's *Origin of Species* thesis literally, transforming it from an "is" to an "ought." In *What Social Classes Owe to Each Other* (1903) William Graham Sumner argues that people should mind their own business and let laissez-faire liberalism run full tilt. He approved of free trade, letting the wealthy get wealthy for the sake of the economic strength of society, letting the natural law of selection and inequity be, and not having governmental intervention to upset this process lest the plutocracy take advantage for its own interests and seize control of democracy.

6. The Powerless

Of course, leaving laissez-faire liberalism alone without any government intervention to help create a "fair start" or "level playing field" means that the weak stay weak and the powerless, powerless unless they somehow manage to pull themselves up by their own flimsy bootstraps. In *Women and Economics* (1898), sociologist and feminist Charlotte Perkins Gilman demonstrated the great economic status differences between men and women in American society at the end of the nineteenth century. Her ironical recipe for feminine success and survival was for women to marry rich, for men are their meal ticket.

From the perspective of powerless African-Americans, two major views emerged. Booker T. Washington, a former slave who became a great educator, argued in *Up from Slavery* (1901) that blacks must try to fit into the mainstream of white society, not demanding political and economic equality immediately, but learning useful, applied trades to become self-sufficient through hard work and to attract white sponsors for black educational development. W. E. B. Du Bois, author of *The Souls of Black Folk* (1903), believed that segregation and discrimination inhibited the self-confidence of blacks and would have none of Washington's diplomatic compromises. He argued for socioeconomic equality and dignity for African-Americans and a solid liberal arts education rather than mere vocational training and emphasized the uplifting role and responsibility of the "talented tenth." Du Bois planted the seeds for the twentieth-century civil rights movement, ending his life as a Communist in self-imposed exile in Africa.

7. New Nationalism, New Freedom, and Progressivism

At the end of the nineteenth century, Populist William Jennings Bryan used his oratorical gifts (as in his "Cross of Gold" speech reprinted here) to argue for popular reforms and to prepare the way for the Progressive movement. The early twentieth century was marked by debate about the nature of government intervention. Such involvement had become inevitable given the strengthening of the federal government at the expense of the states after the Civil War. The debate also concerned the role of government in the indirect subsidy and regulation of big business as the industrial revolution consolidated economic power with advances in communications, transportation, and technology. On one side of this debate were Progressive Herbert Croly (in *The Promise of American Life* (1909)) and Republican and later Progressive Theodore Roosevelt (see his 1910 speech "The New Nationalism"), who argued for a new dedication to national purpose in which a strengthened state would push for community values that transcended private or sectional interests. On the other side, but clearly influenced by his opponents, was Democrat Woodrow Wilson. He argued for a New Freedom in which the role of the government would be as a just arbiter to ensure that all groups were equally free and that no group had special privileges. Monopolies or trusts, he argued, must be much more heavily regulated by the government for the sake of free competition (see his 1910 campaign address here). Ultimately, Wilson won the 1912 presidential election, if not the debate, putting many of his proposed reforms into practice and further strengthening the role of the federal government not just through reform but through the reluctant entrance of the United States into World War I. Coming to epitomize the "progressive" himself, Wilson introduced the idea for the League of Nations (through his famous Fourteen-Points peace proposal), which paved the way for the United Nations.

8. Management versus the Gospel of Socialism

The early twentieth century was dominated not merely by the inevitable growth in power of the federal government—and the debate as to how this might best be rationalized within the structure of traditional American liberalism—but also by the increasing power of corporations in the economy and social realms. Frederick W. Taylor, often called the "father of scientific management," makes the case for its inevitability in *The Principles of Scientific Management* (1912). At congressional hearings (excerpted here) he makes the case that labor-saving devices and management techniques increase wealth and jobs rather than reduce them, as presumably misinformed labor unions claimed at the time. We sense here the groundwork for the late twentieth-century call to increase American economic competitiveness for the sake of jobs and the American standard of living in the creative destruction of global economic competitiveness. Taylor "won" the debate.

On the other side, the strengthening of capital through new technology and management practices inevitably seemed to mean increasing the power differential between capital and labor, between the rich and the poor, between the corporate manager and the farm or factory worker. Walter Rauschenbusch argues in *A Theology for the Social Gospel* (1917) that Christianity could no longer afford to turn the other cheek when confronted with these social problems, but must adapt its theology to social reform. Five-time Socialist presidential candidate Eugene Debs went even further, organizing labor and arguing for a socialist revolution based on Marx and others (see his 1905 speech here). Debs claimed that workers were being used as cheap tools by management and must stand up for themselves and seize power to recover their dignity and rightful place in society.

9. Individualism, Materialism, and Idealism

Of course, Debs and the socialist and union movements eventually lost in the twentieth century. The socialists peaked in power before World War I, the unions after World War II. The American people continued to revert to their tradition of laissez-faire liberalism, represented here by Republican President Herbert Hoover (*American Individualism,* 1922). Hoover makes a strong case for the innovative genius springing from individuals and the need for freedom and leadership to bring out such dynamic economic and social potential, pointing to the failures of statist theories in Russia, Germany, and Europe. He is the ultimate advocate of voluntarism, what President George Bush was to proclaim in 1988 as "a thousand points of light." Hoover saw individual philanthropy rather than state intervention as the solution to social problems. Despite his strong business credentials and noble food-relief organizational efforts, the Great Depression discredited Hoover and his theories, at least temporarily, when he lost to Democrat Franklin D. Roosevelt in 1932.

Fiction and philosophy of this era offer intriguing views of social and political thought. Enthusiastic business materialism, voluntarism, and naiveté in American society are epitomized by Sinclair Lewis's novel *Babbitt* (1922), which created mythical American George Babbitt to match Horatio Alger's heroes. However, this hero is etched with a sharp pen that leaves no weakness in American middle-class society unobserved. Spanish-American philosopher George Santayana casts a worldly eye on American character in *Character and Opinion in the United States* (1920), differentiating between American materialism and idealism by suggesting that being an American may, in itself, be a full-time vocation.

10. Conservative Critics of Democratic Liberalism

The traditional laissez-faire, or Lockean, liberalism of American democracy was clearly having a difficult time coping with the challenges of world wars, corporate monopolies, and economic depressions, among other things, and conservative critiques illustrated its weaknesses. H. L. Mencken's classic barbs in *Notes on Democracy* (1926) imply that the only hope is in a return to some form of elitist aristocracy or "royalism." Theologian Reinhold Niebuhr led the Social Gospel movement after experiencing inner-city poverty and also helped found "Americans for Democratic Action." Later Niebuhr became the Social Gospel movement's sharpest critic, arguing in *Moral Man And Immoral Society* (1932) for political realism as the only sound basis for individual morality. He questioned the naiveté of liberals who supposed they could apply a belief in man's basic goodness to the behavior of states. Conservative iconoclast Albert Jay Nock sums up the American shift from laissez-faire liberalism to statist liberalism in his introduction to Herbert Spencer's *The Man versus the State* (1940). Clearly Nock prefers the old liberalism to the new.

11. Corporations, Society, and the State

American liberalism became interventionist in no small part because of corporate-business domination of the American economy. In their classic *The Modern Corporation and Private Property* (1932), Adolf Berle and Gardiner Means demonstrate how this came about through the effort to create a neutral class of technocratic managers who neither own the corporations nor are "workers" in it. The book was so persuasive that President Franklin Roosevelt recruited Adolf Berle into his brain trust in the White House to help develop and explain the New Deal. Roosevelt's "Commonwealth Club Address" (1932) illustrates his view on the need for government action to remedy the dislocations of the Great Depression by creating a new economic constitutional order.

We end on the critical cautionary note of anarchist Emma Goldman, who would have none of this state interventionist recipe, but who claimed in "The Individual, Society and the State" (1940) that the state is a name only, not an organic thing, and that society should exist for man, not man for society. "Red Emma" has continued to inspire anarchist and feminist thinkers in the United States and has thrown into sharp relief the question: What does it really mean to be an individual with freedom in society?

Selected Readings

Arnold, Thurman. *The Folklore of Capitalism*. New Haven, Conn.: Yale University Press, 1937.
Egbert, Donald D., and Stow Persons, eds. *Socialism and American Life*. Princeton: Princeton University Press, 1952.
Destler, Chester. *American Radicalism, 1865–1901*. Chicago: Quadrangle, 1966.
Fine, Sidney. *Laissez-faire and the General Welfare State*. Ann Arbor: University of Michigan Press, 1956.
Forcey, Charles. *The Crossroads of Liberalism*. New York: Oxford University Press, 1961.
Hays, Samuel. *The Response to Industrialism, 1885–1914*. Chicago: University of Chicago Press, 1957.
Hofstadter, Richard. *Social Darwinism in America*. Boston: Beacon Press, 1944.
———. *The Age of Reform*. New York: Knopf, 1966.
Hopkins, Charles H. *The Rise of the Social Gospel in American Protestantism, 1865–1915*. New Haven, Conn.: Yale University Press, 1940.
Josephson, Matthew. *The Robber Barons*. Boston: Beacon Press, 1944.
Kolko, Gabriel, *Main Currents in Modern American History*. New York: Harper & Row, 1976.
Lasch, Christopher. *The New Radicalism in America*. New York: Random House, 1967.
McCloskey, Robert. *American Conservatism in an Age of Enterprise*. Cambridge: Harvard University Press, 1951.
Schumpeter, Joseph. *Capitalism, Socialism and Democracy*. New York: Harper & Row, 1942.
Simon, Rita, James, ed. *As We Saw the Thirties*. Champaign: University of Illinois Press, 1966.
Spitz, David. *The Liberal Idea of Freedom*. Phoenix: University of Arizona Press, 1964.
Weinstein, James. *The Corporate Ideal in the Liberal State, 1900–1925*. Boston: Beacon Press, 1968.
White, Morton. *Social Thought in America*. New York: Viking Press, 1949.
Zinn, Howard, ed. *New Deal Thought*. Indianapolis: Bobbs-Merrill, 1966.

Horatio Alger

Horatio Alger published about 120 influential books (which sold 17 million copies) epitomizing the American Dream of going from rags to riches through pluck, luck, and the Protestant ethic. In these short, how-to-do-it novels for boys, egalitarianism was praised in cardboard prose, and the struggle for material success was properly viewed as a basis for social responsibility.

Alger was born in 1832 in Revere, Massachusetts, and named after his father, a Unitarian minister. After studying foreign languages at Harvard, Alger followed his father's wishes and completed his graduate degree at the Harvard Divinity School. During that time, his elderly landlord was threatened with foreclosure for not keeping up his house payments. Alger entered an essay, "Athens at the Time of Socrates," in a Harvard competition, won the first prize of forty dollars and gave it to the landlord. Soon thereafter the landlord died, bequeathing Alger two thousand dollars. Alger skipped meeting his parents at graduation to go to Paris to learn about life and literature with friends. After the army failed to accept him for medical reasons during the Civil War, Alger briefly became a pastor of a Unitarian church in Massachusetts. There, an editor of a children's monthly and author of juvenile books, William Adams, attended a service and asked Alger to submit a manuscript. Soon after "Squire Pitman's Peaches" and "Deacon Baxter's Cow" were accepted, Alger completed *Ragged Dick,* the novel from which the following excerpts were drawn. When episodes from the novel appeared, Charles O'Connor, superintendent of the Newboys' Lodging House in New York City, a residence for homeless boys displaced by the war, invited Alger to live there. Alger accepted and there discovered numerous inspirations for his writing. He became well-acquainted with the city, grew famous, and was appointed to political commissions on urban problems. Discovering a contract-labor system that misused young street musicians imported from Calabria, Italy, for a begging network, Alger published *Phil, the Fiddler* in 1871 to expose their plight and led a life-threatening public campaign to free the boys. After a brutal case of child mistreatment, the Society for the Prevention of Cruelty to Animals filed suit on behalf of the victim. Consequently, the state legislature passed in 1874 the first law in the United States for the prevention of cruelty to children.

Horatio Alger has become a mythical symbol of the individual American success story. He epitomizes the optimism, hard work, belief in the main chance and in the triumph of good over evil, the desire for material rewards, and compassion for those less fortunate that many Americans still identify as their values. Alger wrote his own epitaph, made up of some of his titles, which his family declined to use when he died in 1899: "Six feet underground reposes Horatio Alger, *Helping Himself* to a part of the earth, not *Digging for Gold* or *In Search of Treasure,* but *Struggling Upward* and *Bound to Rise* at last *In a New World* where it shall be said he is *Risen from the Ranks.*"

⚛

Ragged Dick (1867)

(excerpts)

"Wake up there, youngster," said a rough voice.

Ragged Dick opened his eyes slowly, and stared stupidly in the face of the speaker, but did not offer to get up.

"Wake up, you young vagabond!" said the man, a little impatiently; "I suppose you'd lay there all day, if I hadn't called you."

"What time is it?" asked Dick.

"Seven o'clock."

"Seven o'clock! I oughter 've been up an hour ago. I know what 'twas made me so precious sleepy. I went to the Old Bowery last night, and didn't turn in till past twelve."

"You went to the Old Bowery? Where'd you get your money?" asked the man, who was a porter in the employ of a firm doing business on Spruce Street.

"Made it by shines, of course. My guardian don't allow me no money for theatres, so I have to earn it."

"Some boys get it easier than that," said the porter significantly.

"You don't catch me stealin', if that's what you mean," said Dick.

"Don't you ever steal, then?"

"No, and I wouldn't. Lots of boys does it, but I wouldn't."

"Well, I'm glad to hear you say that. I believe there's some good in you, Dick, after all."

"Oh, I'm a rough customer!" said Dick. "But I wouldn't steal. It's mean."

"I'm glad you think so, Dick," and the rough voice sounded gentler than at first. "Have you got any money to buy your breakfast?"

"No, but I'll soon get some."

While this conversation had been going on, Dick had got up. His bedchamber had been a wooden box half full of straw, on which the young bootblack had reposed his weary limbs, and slept as soundly as if it had been a bed of down. He dumped down into the straw without taking the trouble of undressing. Getting up too was an equally short process. He jumped out of the box, shook himself, picked out one or two straws that had found their way into the rents of his clothes, and, drawing a well-worn cap over his uncombed locks, he was all ready for the business of the day.

Dick's appearance as he stood beside the box was rather peculiar. His pants were torn in several places, and had apparently belonged in the first instance to a boy two sizes larger than himself. He wore a vest, all the bottoms of which were gone except two, out of which peeped a shirt which looked as if it had been worn a month. To complete his costume he wore a coat too long for him, dating back, if one might judge from its general appearance, to a remote antiquity.

Washing the face and hands is usually considered proper in commencing the day, but Dick was above such refinement. He had no particular dislike to dirt, and did not think it necessary to remove several dark streaks on his face and hands. But in spite of his dirt and rags there was something about Dick that was attractive. It was easy to see that if he had been clean and well dressed he would have been decidedly good-looking. Some of his companions were sly, and their faces inspired distrust; but Dick had a frank, straight-forward manner that made him a favorite.

Dick's business hours had commenced. He had no office to open. His little blacking-box was ready for use, and he looked sharply in the faces of all who passed, addressing each with, "Shine yer boots, sir?"

"How much?" asked a gentleman on his way to his office.

"Ten cents," said Dick, dropping his box, and sinking upon his knees on the sidewalk, flourishing his brush with the air of one skilled in his profession.

"Ten cents! Isn't that a little steep?"

"Well, you know 'taint all clear profit," said Dick, who had already set to work. "There's the *blacking* costs something, and I have to get a new brush pretty often."

"And you have a large rent too," said the gentleman quizzically, with a glance at a large hole in Dick's coat.

"Yes, sir," said Dick, always ready to joke; "I have to pay such a big rent for my manshun up on Fifth Avenoo, that I can't afford to take less than ten cents a shine. I'll give you a bully shine, sir."

"Be quick about it, for I am in a hurry. So your house is on Fifth Avenue, is it?"

"It isn't anywhere else," said Dick, and Dick spoke the truth there.

"What tailor do you patronize?" asked the gentleman, surveying Dick's attire.

"Would you like to go to the same one?" asked Dick, shrewdly.

"Well, no; it strikes me that he didn't give you a very good fit."

"This coat once belonged to General Washington," said Dick comically. "He wore it all through the Revolution, and it got torn some, 'cause he fit so hard. When he died he told his widder to give it to some smart young feller that hadn't got none of his own; so she gave it to me. But if you'd like it, sir, to remember General Washington by, I'll let you have it reasonable."

"Thank you but I wouldn't want to deprive you of it. And did your pants come from General Washington too?"

"No, they was a gift from Lewis Napoleon. Lewis had outgrown 'em and sent 'em to me,—he's bigger than me, and that's why they don't fit."

"It seems you have distinguished friends. Now, my lad, I suppose you would like your money."

"I shouldn't have any objection," said Dick. . . .

"What did you do next?"

"I went into the match business," said Dick; "but it was small sales and small profits. Most of the people I called on had just laid in a stock, and didn't want to buy. So one cold night, when I hadn't money enough to pay for a lodgin', I burned the last of my matches to keep me from freezin'. But it cost too much to get warm that way, and I couldn't keep it up."

"You've seen hard times, Dick," said Frank, compassionately. . . .

"So you didn't stay long in the match business, Dick?"

"No, I couldn't sell enough to make it pay. Then there was some folks that wanted me to sell cheaper to them; so I couldn't make any profit. There was one old lady— she was rich, too, for she lived in a big brick house—beat me down so, that I didn't make no profit at all; but she wouldn't buy without, and I hadn't sold none that day; so I let her have them. I don't see why rich folks should be so hard upon a poor boy that wants to make a livin'."

"There's a good deal of meanness in the world, I'm afraid, Dick."

"If everybody was like you and your uncle," said Dick, "there would be some chance for poor people. If I was rich I'd try to help 'em along."

"Perhaps you will be rich someday, Dick." . . .

"Frank's been very kind to me," said Dick, who, rough street-boy as he was, had a heart easily touched by kindness, of which he had never experienced much. "He's a tip-top fellow."

"I believe he is a good boy," said Mr. Whitney. "I hope, my lad, you will prosper and rise in the world. You know in this free country poverty in early life is no bar to a man's advancement. I haven't risen very high myself," he added, with a smile, "but have met with moderate success in life; yet there was a time when I was as poor as you."

"Were you, sir?" asked Dick, eagerly.

"Yes, my boy, I have known the time when I have been obliged to go without my dinner because I didn't have enough money to pay for it."

"How did you get up in the world?" asked Dick, anxiously.

"I entered a printing-office as an apprentice, and worked for some years. Then my eyes gave out and I was obliged to give that up. Not knowing what else to do, I went into the country, and worked on a farm. After a while I was lucky enough to invent a machine, which has brought me a great deal of money. But there was one thing I got while I was in the printing-office which I value more than money."

"What was that, sir?"

"A taste for reading and study. During my leisure hours I improved myself by study, and acquired a large part of the knowledge which I now possess. Indeed, it was one of my books that first put me on the track of the invention, which I afterwards made. So you see, my lad, that my studious habits paid me in money, as well as in another way. . . .

"Good-by, my lad," said Mr. Whitney. "I hope to hear good accounts of you sometime. Don't forget what I have told you. Remember that your future position depends mainly upon yourself, and that it will be high or low as you choose to make it." . . .

A question now came up for consideration. For the first time in his life Dick possessed two suits of clothes. Should he put on the clothes Frank had given him, or resume his old rags?

Now, twenty-four hours before, at the time Dick was introduced to the reader's notice, no one could have been less fastidious as to his clothing than he. Indeed, he had rather a contempt for good clothes, or at least he thought so. But now, as he surveyed the ragged and dirty coat and the patched pants, Dick felt ashamed of them. He was unwilling to appear in the streets with them. Yet, if he went to work in his new suit, he was in danger of spoiling it, and he might not have it in his power to purchase a new one. Economy dictated a return to the old garments. Dick tried them on, and surveyed himself in the cracked glass; but the reflection did not please him.

"They don't look 'spectable," he decided; and, forthwith taking them off again, he put on the new suit of the day before.

"I must try to earn a little more," he thought, "to pay for my room, and to buy some new clo'es when these is wore out." . . .

Dick's change of costume was liable to lead to one result of which he had not thought. His brother boot-blacks might think he had grown aristocratic, and was putting on airs,—that, in fact, he was getting above his business, and desirous to outshine his associates. Dick had not dreamed of this, because in fact, in spite of his new-born ambition, he entertained no such feelings. There was nothing of what boys call "big-feeling" about him. He was a thorough democrat, using the word not politically, but in its proper sense, and was disposed to fraternize with all whom he styled "good fellows," without regard to their position. It may seem a little unnecessary to some of my readers to make this explanation; but they must remember that pride and "big feeling" are confined to no age or class, but may be found in boys as well as men, and in boot-blacks as well as those of a higher rank. . . .

But Dick had gained something more valuable than money. He had studied regularly every evening, and his improvement had been marvelous. He could now read well, write a fair hand, and had studied arithmetic as far as Interest. Besides this he had obtained some knowledge of grammar and geography. If some of my boy readers, who have been studying for years, and got no farther than this, should think it incredible that Dick, in less than a year, and studying evenings only, should have accomplished it, they must remember that our hero was very much in earnest in his desire to improve. He knew that, in order to grow up respectable, he must be well advanced, and he was willing to work. But then the reader must not forget that Dick was naturally a smart boy. His street education had sharpened his faculties, and taught him to rely upon himself. He knew that it would take him a long time to reach the goal which he had set before him, and he had patience to keep on trying. He knew that he had only himself to depend upon, and he determined to make the most of himself,—a resolution which is the secret of success in nine cases out of ten. . . .

Returning to the City Hall Park, Dick soon fell in with Tom Wilkins.

"How are you, Tom?" he said. "How's your mother?"

"She's better, Dick, thank you. She felt worried about bein' turned out into the street; but I gave her that money from you, and now she feels a good deal easier."

"I've got some more for you, Tom," said Dick, producing a two-dollar bill from his pocket.

"I ought not to take it from you, Dick."

"Oh, it's all right, Tom. Don't be afraid."

"But you may need it yourself."

"There's plenty more where that came from."

"Any way, one dollar will be enough. With that we can pay the rent."

"You'll want the other to buy something to eat."

"You're very kind, Dick."

"I'd ought to be. I've only got myself to take care of."

"Well, I'll take it for my mother's sake. When you want anything done just call on Tom Wilkins."

"All right. Next week, if your mother doesn't get better, I'll give you some more."

Tom thanked our hero very gratefully, and Dick walked away, feeling the self-approval which always accompanies a generous and disinterested action. He was generous by nature, and, before the period at which he is introduced to the reader's notice, he frequently treated his friends to cigars and oyster-stews. Sometimes he invited them to accompany him to the theatre at his expense. But he never derived from these acts of liberality the same degree of satisfaction as from this timely gift to Tom Wilkins. He felt that his money was well bestowed, and would save an entire family from privation and discomfort. Five dollars would, to be sure, make something of a difference in the amount of his savings. It was more than he was able to save up in a week. But Dick felt fully repaid for what he had done, and he felt prepared to give as much more, if Tom's mother should continue to be sick, and should appear to him to need it.

Besides all this, Dick felt a justifiable pride in his financial ability to afford so handsome a gift. A year before, however much he might have desired to give, it would have been quite out of his power to give five dollars. His cash balance never reached that amount. It was seldom, indeed, that it equalled one dollar. In more ways than one Dick was beginning to reap the advantage of his self-denial and judicious economy. . . .

Walt Whitman

Walt Whitman is ranked by many as the greatest American poet. He praised democracy and the dignity of the individual and has had a lasting influence upon American culture and the belief in individualism. His major volume of poetry, *Leaves of Grass* (1855), is often considered the most influential book of poetry in the history of American literature. For example, it opens with: "One's Self I sing, a simple separate person, / Yet utter the word Democratic, the word En-Masse."

Whitman was born in 1819 in West Hills, Huntington, Long Island, and was educated at public schools in Brooklyn, New York. Dismissing all further formal education, he dropped out of school to enter the printer's trade. He briefly taught school on Long Island and edited the *Long Islander,* a newspaper. As a journalist writing prose and verse for New York papers, he developed an interest in politics and edited the Brooklyn *Daily Eagle,* a Democratic party paper. However, he lost this job because of his strong stands for abolition and the Free-Soil movement.

Continuing as a journalist and then carpenter in Brooklyn, Whitman published twelve poems in a volume at his own expense in 1855: *Leaves of Grass.* Although critics noticed his new, unique voice, Whitman paid for his exaltation of bodily and sexual love and his innovative free-verse forms. The first edition of the book failed commercially, as did the expanded 1856 and 1860 editions.

During the Civil War, Whitman volunteered as a hospital nurse in Washington. His Civil War poetry appeared in *Drum-Taps* and *Sequel to Drum-Taps* (1865–66). Whitman then was appointed a clerk in the Department of the Interior, until he was dismissed for the "immorality" of *Leaves of Grass. Democratic Vistas* (1871) was based on two essays Whitman published in *The Galaxy:* "Democracy" (1867)—printed below—and "Personalism" (1868). "Democracy" was initially a response to Thomas Carlyle's "Shooting Niagara and After" (1867), which attacked democracy as a "Gathering of Men in Swarms" and equally as "delirious absurdity"—"any man equal to any other; Quashee Nigger to Socrates or Shakespeare shall we say?", and, "By far the notablest case of Swarmery, in these times is that of the late American War, with Settlement of the Nigger Question for results." Carlyle's attack was largely aimed at the British Reform Bill of 1867, which extended suffrage to large sections of the working class. Whitman addressed Carlyle in this essay as "my venerable friend" and "venerable and eminent person" while defending the cultural equality and independence of each individual. Whitman's last book, *November Boughs,* appeared in 1888. He died in 1892.

※

Democracy (1867)

After the rest is said—after many time-honored and really true things for subordination, experience, rights of property, etc., have been listened to, and acquiesced in—after the valuable and well-settled statement of our duties and relations in society is thoroughly conned over and exhausted—it remains to bring forward and modify everything else with the idea of that Something a man is, standing apart from all else, divine in his own right, and a woman in hers, sole and untouchable by any canons of religion, politics, or what is called modesty or art.

The radiation of this truth, practically a modern one, is the history and key of the most significant doings of our immediately preceding three centuries, and has been the political genesis and life of America. Advancing visibly, it still more advances invisibly. Underneath the fluctuations of the expressions of society, as well as the movements of the politics of the leading nations, we see steadily pressing ahead, and strengthening itself, even in the midst of immense tendencies toward aggregation, this image of completeness in separatism, of individual personal dignity, of a single person, either male or female, characterized in the main, not from extrinsic acquirements or position, but in the pride of himself or herself alone; and, as an eventual conclusion and summing-up, the simple, but tremendous and revolutionary, idea that the last, best dependence is to be upon Humanity itself, and its own inherent, normal, full-grown qualities, without any superstitious support whatever.

The purpose of Democracy—supplanting old belief in the necessary absoluteness of established dynastic rulership, temporal, ecclesiastical, and scholastic, as furnishing the only security against chaos, crime, and ignorance—is, through many transmigrations, and amid endless ridicules, arguments, and ostensible failures, to illustrate, at all hazards, this doctrine of the sovereignty and sacredness of the individual, coequal with the balance-doctrine that man, properly trained, may and must become a law, and series of laws, unto himself, surrounding and providing for, not only his own personal control, but all his relations to other individuals, and to the State; and that, while other theories, as in the past histories of nations, have proved wise enough, and indispensable perhaps for their conditions, *this,* as matters now stand in our civilized world, is the only Scheme worth working from, as warranting results like those of Nature's laws, reliable, when once established, to carry on themselves.

With such for outset, and a silent, momentary prayer that we may be enabled to tell what is worthy the faith within us, we follow on.

Leaving unsaid much that should properly prepare the way for the treatment of this many-sided matter of Democracy—leaving the whole history and consideration of the Feudal Plan and its products, embodying Humanity, its politics and civilization, through the retrospect of past time (which Plan and products, indeed, make up all of the past, and a major part of the present)—leaving unanswered, at least by any specific and local answer, many a well-wrought argument and instance, and many a conscientious declamatory cry and warning—as, very lately, from an eminent and venerable person abroad—things, problems, full of doubt, dread, suspense, (not new to me, but old occupiers of many an anxious hour in city's din, or night's silence), we still may give a paragraph or so, whose drift is opportune. Time alone can finally answer these things. But as a substitute in passing let us, even if fragmentarily, throw forth a thought or two—a short direct or indirect suggestion of the premises of the theory, that other Plan, in the new spirit, under the new forms, started here in our America.

As to the political section of Democracy, which introduces and breaks ground for further and vaster sections, few probably are the minds, even in these republican States, that fully comprehend the aptness of that phrase, "THE GOVERNMENT OF THE PEOPLE, BY THE PEOPLE, FOR THE PEOPLE," which we inherit from the lips of Abraham Lincoln; a formula whose verbal shape is homely wit, but whose scope includes both the totality and all minutiae of the lesson.

The People! Like our huge earth itself, which, to ordinary scansion, is full of vulgar contradictions and offence, Man, viewed in the lump, displeases, and is a constant puzzle and affront to the merely educated classes. The rare, cosmical, artist-mind, lit with the Infinite, alone confronts his manifold and oceanic qualities; but taste, intelligence and culture (so-called), have been against the masses, and remain so. There is plenty of glamour about the most damnable crimes and hoggish meannesses, special and general, of the Feudal and dynastic world, with its *personnel* of lords and queens and courts, so well-dressed and so handsome. But the People are ungrammatical, untidy, and their sins are gaunt and ill-bred.

Literature has never recognized the People, and, whatever may be said, does not to-day. Speaking generally, the tendencies of literature, as pursued, are to make mostly critical and querulous men. It seems as if, so far, there were some natural repugnance between a literary and professional life, and the rude spirit of the Democracies. There is, in later literature, a treatment of benevolence, a charity business, rife enough; but I know nothing more rare, even in this country, than a fit scientific estimate and reverent appreciation of the People—of their measureless wealth of latent power and capacity, their vast, artistic contrasts of lights and shades—and in America, their entire reliability in emergencies, and a certain breadth of historic grandeur, of peace or war, surpassing all the vaunted samples of the personality of book-heroes, in all the records of the world.

The movements of the late war, and their results, to any sense that studies well and comprehends them, show that Popular Democracy practically justifies itself beyond the proudest claims and wildest hopes of its enthusiasts. Probably no future age can know, as we well know, how the gist of this fiercest and most resolute of the world's warlike contentions resided exclusively in the unnamed, unknown rank and file; and how the brunt of its labor of death was, to all essential purposes, Volunteered. The People, of their own choice, fighting, dying for their own idea, insolently attacked by the Secession-Slave-Power, and its very existence imperilled. Descending to detail, entering any of the armies, and mixing with the private soldiers, we see and have seen august spectacles. We have seen the alacrity with which the American-born populace, the peaceablest and most good-natured race in the world, and the most personally independent and intelligent, and the least fitted to submit to the irksomeness and exasperation of regimental discipline, sprang, at the first tap of the drum, to arms—not for gain, nor even glory, nor to repel invasion—but for an emblem, a mere abstraction—for the life, *the safety of the Flag.* We have seen the unequalled docility and obedience of these soldiers. We have seen them tried long and long by hopelessness, mismanagement, and by defeat; have seen the incredible slaughter toward or through which the armies (as at first Fredericksburg, and afterward at the Wilderness), still unhesitatingly obeyed orders to advance. We have seen them in trench, or crouching behind breastwork, or tramping in deep mud, or amid pouring rain or snow, or under forced marches in hottest Summer (as on the road to get to Gettysburg), vast suffocating swarms, divisions, corps, with every single man so grimed and black with sweat and dust, his own mother would not have known him; his clothes all dirty, stained and torn, with sour, accumulated sweat for perfume, many a comrade, perhaps a brother, sunstruck, staggering out, dying, by the roadside, of exhaustion—yet the great bulk bearing steadily on, cheery enough, hollow-bellied from hunger, but sinewy with unconquerable resolution.

We have seen this race proved by wholesale by drearier, yet more fearful tests—the wound, the amputation, the shattered face or limb, the slow, hot fever, long, impatient anchorage in bed, and all the forms of maiming, operation and disease. Alas! America have we seen, though only in her early youth, already to hospital brought. There have we watched these soldiers, many of them only boys in years—marked their decorum, their religious nature and fortitude, and their sweet affection. Wholesale, truly! For at the front, and through the camps, in countless tents, stood the regimental, brigade and division hospitals; while everywhere amid the land, in or near cities, rose clusters of huge, whitewashed, crowded, wooden barracks, (Washington City alone, at one period, containing in her Army hospitals of this kind, 50,000 wounded and sick men)—and there ruled Agony with bitter scourge, yet seldom brought a cry; and there stalked Death by day and night along the narrow aisles between the rows of cots, or by the blankets on the ground, and touched lightly many a poor sufferer, often with blessed, welcome touch.

I know not whether I shall be understood, but I realize that it is finally from what I learned in such scenes that I am now penning this article. One night in the gloomiest period of the war, in the Patent Office Hospital, as I stood by the bedside of a Pennsylvania soldier, who lay, conscious of quick approaching death, yet perfectly calm, and with noble, spiritual manner, the veteran surgeon, Dr. Stone (Horatio Stone, the sculptor), turning aside, said to me that though he had witnessed many, many deaths of soldiers, and had been a worker at Bull Run, Antietam, Fredericksburg, etc., he had not seen yet the first case of man or boy that met the approach of dissolution with cowardly qualms or terror. My own observation fully bears out the remark.

What have we here, if not, towering above all talk and argument, the plentifully-supplied, last-needed proof of Democracy, in its personalities?

Grand, common stock! to me the accomplished and convincing growth, prophetic of the future; proof undeniable to sharpest sense, of perfect beauty, tenderness and pluck, that never Feudal lord, nor Greek nor Roman breed, yet rivalled. Let no tongue ever speak in disparagement of the American races, North or South, to one who has been through the war in the great Army hospitals.

—Meantime, Humanity (for we will not shirk anything) has always, in every department, been full of perverse maleficence, and is so yet. In downcast hours the Soul thinks it always will be—but soon recovers from such sickly moods. I, as Democrat, see clearly enough (none more clearly), the crude, defective streaks in all the strata of the common people; the specimens and vast collections of the ignorant, the credulous, the unfit and uncouth, the incapable and the very low and poor. The eminent person in his conscientious cry just mentioned, sneeringly asks whether we expect to elevate and improve politics by absorbing such morbid collections and qualities therein. The point is a formidable one, and there will doubtless always be numbers of solid citizens who will never get over it. Our answer is general, and is involved in the scope and letter of this article. We believe the object of political and all other government (having, of course, provided for the police, the safety of life, property, and the basic common and civil law, always first in order) to be, among the rest, not merely to rule, to repress disorder, etc., but to develop, to open up to cultivation, to encourage the possibilities of all beneficent and manly outcroppage, and of that aspiration for independence, and the pride and self-respect latent in all characters. (Or, if there be exceptions, we cannot, fixing our eyes on them alone, make theirs the rule for all.)

The mission of government, henceforth, in civilized lands, is not authority alone, not even of law, nor by that favorite standard of the eminent writer, the rule of the best men, the born heroes and captains of the race (as if such ever, or one time out of a hundred, got into the big places, elective or dynastic!)—but, higher than the highest arbitrary rule, to train communities through all their grades, beginning with individuals and ending there again, to rule themselves.

What Christ appeared for in the moral-spiritual field for Human-kind, namely, that in respect to the absolute Soul, there is in the possession of such by each single individual, something so transcendent, so incapable of gradations (like life), that, to that extent, it places all beings on a common level, utterly regardless of the distinctions of intellect, station, or any height or lowliness whatever—is tallied in like manner, in this other field, by Democracy's rule that men, the Nation, as a common

aggregate of living identities, affording in each a separate and complete subject for freedom, worldly thrift and happiness, and for a fair chance for growth, and for protection, in citizenship, etc., must, to the political extent of the suffrage or vote, if no further, be placed, in each and in the whole, on one broad, primary, universal, common platform.

The purpose is not altogether direct; perhaps it is more indirect. To be a voter with the rest is not so much; and this, like every institute, will have its imperfections. But to become an enfranchised man, and now to stand and start without humiliation, and equal with the rest; to commence, or have the road cleared to commence, the grand experiment of development, whose end, perhaps requiring several generations, may be the forming of a full-grown manly or womanly Personality—that *is* something. To ballast the state is also secured, and in our times is to be secured, in no other way.

We do not (at any rate I do not) put it either so much on the ground that the People, the masses, even the best of them are, in their latent or exhibited qualities, essentially sensible and good—nor on the ground of their rights; but that, good or bad, rights or no rights, the Democratic formula is the only safe and preservative one for coming times. We endow the masses with the suffrage for their own sake, no doubt; then, still more, from another point of view, for community's sake. Leaving the rest to the sentimentalists, we present Freedom as sufficient in its scientific aspects, cold as ice, reasoning, clear and passionless as crystal.

Democracy too is law, and of the strictest, amplest kind. Many suppose (and often in its own ranks the error) that it means a throwing aside of law, and running riot. But, briefly, it is the superior law, not alone that of physical force, the body, which, adding to, it supersedes with that of the spirit. Law is the unshakable order of the universe forever; and the law over all, and law of laws, is the law of successions; that of the superior law, in time, gradually supplanting and overwhelming the inferior one. (While, for myself, I would cheerfully agree—first covenanting that the formative tendencies shall be administered in favor, or, at least not against it, and that this reservation be closely construed—that until the individual or community show due signs, or be so minor and fractional as not to endanger the State, the condition of tutelage may continue, and self-government must abide its time.)

—Nor is the esthetic point, always an important one, without fascination for highest aiming souls. The common ambition strains for common elevations, to become some privileged exclusive. The master sees greatness and health in being part of the mass. Nothing will do as well as common ground. Would you have in yourself the divine, vast, general law? Then merge yourself in it.

And, topping Democracy, this most alluring record, that it alone can bind, and ever seeks to bind, all nations, all men, of however various and distant lands, into a brotherhood, a family. It is the old, yet ever-modern dream of Earth, out of her eldest and her youngest, her fond philosophers and poets. Not this half only, this Individualism, which isolates. There is another half, which is Adhesiveness or Love, that fuses, ties and aggregates, making the races comrades, and fraternizing all. Both are to be vitalized by Religion (sole worthiest elevator of man or State) breathing into the proud, material tissues, the breath of life. For at the core of Democracy, finally, is the Religious element. All the Religions, old and new, are there. Nor may the Scheme step forth, clothed in resplendent beauty and command, till these, bearing the best, the latest fruit, the

Spiritual, the aspirational, shall fully appear.

—Portions of our pages we feel to indite with reference toward Europe more than our own land, and thus, perhaps not absolutely needed for the home reader. But the whole question hangs together, and fastens and links all peoples. The Liberalist of to-day has this advantage over antique or medieval times, that his doctrine seeks both to universalize as well as individualize. The great sword Solidarity has arisen.

How, then (for in that shape forebodes the current deluge)—how shall we, good-class folk, meet the rolling, mountainous surges of "swarmery" that already beat upon and threaten to overwhelm us? What disposal, short of wholesale throat-cutting and extermination (which seems not without its advantages), offers, for the countless herds of "hoofs and hobnails," that will somehow, and so perversely get themselves born, and grow up to annoy and vex us? What under heaven is to become of "nigger Cushee," that imbruted and lazy being— now, worst of all, preposterously free? etc. Never before such a yawning gulf; never such danger as now from incarnated Democracy advancing, with the laboring classes at its back. Woe the day; woe the doings, the prospects thereof! England, or any respectable land, giving the least audience to these "servants of the mud gods," or, utterly infatuate, extending to them the suffrage, takes swift passage therewith, bound for the infernal pit. Ring the alarm bell! Put the flags at half mast! Or, rather, let each man spring for the nearest loose spar or plank. The ship is going down!

Be not so moved, not to say distraught, my venerable friend. Spare those spasms of dread and disgust. England, after her much-widened suffrage, as she did before, will still undergo troubles and tribulations, without doubt; but they will be as nothing to what (in the judgment of all heads not quite careened and addled), would certainly follow the spirit, carried out in any modern nation, these days, of your appeal or diatribe. Neither by berating them, nor twitting them with their low condition of ignorance and misery, nor by leaving them as they are, nor by turning the screws still tighter, nor by taking even the most favorable chances for "the noble Few" to come round with relief, will the demon of that "unanimous vulgar" (paying very heavy taxes) be pacified and made harmless any more. Strangely enough, about the only way to really lay the fiend appears to be this very way—the theme of these your ravings. A sort of fate and antique Nemesis, of the highest old Greek tragedy sort, is in it (as in our own Play, or affair, rapidly played of late here in the South, through all the acts—indeed a regular, very wondrous Eschuylean piece—to that old part First, that bound and chained unkillable Prometheus, now, after twenty-three hundred years, very grandly and epico-dramatically supplementing and fully supplying the lost, or never before composed, Second and Third parts). Your noble, hereditary, Anglo-Saxon-Norman institutions (still here so loudly championed and battled for in your argument) having been, through some seven or eight centuries, thriftily engaged in cooking up this mess, have now got to eat it. The only course eligible, it is plain, is to plumply confront, embrace, absorb, swallow (O, big and bitter pill!) the entire British "swarmery," demon, "loud roughs" and all. These ungrateful men, not satisfied with the poor-house for their old age, and the charity-school for their infants, evidently mean business—may-be of bloody kind. By all odds, my friend, the thing to do is to make a flank movement, surround them, disarm them, give them their first degree, incorporate them in the State as voters, and then—wait for the next emergency.

Nor may I permit myself to dismiss this utterance of the eminent person without pronouncing its laboriously-earned and fully-deserved credit for about the highest eminence attained yet, in a certain direction, of any linguistic product, written or spoken, to me known. I have had occasion in my past life (being born, as it were, with propensities, from my earliest years, to attend popular American speech-gatherings, conventions, nominations, camp-meetings, and the like, and also as a reader of newspapers, foreign and domestic)—I therefore know that trial to one's ears and brains from divers creatures, alluded to by sample, and well-hetchelled in this diatribe, crow-cawing the words Liberty, loyalty, human rights, constitutions, etc. I, too, have heard the ceaseless braying, screaming blatancy (on behalf of my own side), making noisiest threats and clatter stand for sense. But I must now affirm that such a comic-painful hullabaloo and vituperative cat-squalling as this about "the Niagara leap," "swarmery," "Orsonism," etc. (meaning, in point, as I make out, simply extending to full-grown British working-folk, farmers, mechanics, clerks, and so on—the "industrial aristocracy," indeed, there named—the privilege of the ballot, or vote, deciding, by popular majorities, who shall be designated to sit in one of the two Houses of Parliament, if it mean anything), I never yet encountered; no, not even in extremest hour of midnight, in whooping Tennessee revival, or Bedlam let loose in crowded, colored Carolina bush-meeting.

But to proceed, and closer to our text.

The curse and canker of Nations politically has been—or, at any rate, will be, as things have come to exist in our day—the having of certain portions of the people set off from the rest by a line drawn—they not privileged as others, but degraded, humiliated, made of no account. We repeat it, the question is, finally, one of Science—the science of the present and the future. Much quackery teems, of course, yet does not really affect the orbic quality of the matter. To work in, if we may so term it, and justify God, his divine aggregate, the People (or, the veritable horned and fluke-tailed Devil, *his* aggregate, then, since you so convulsively insist upon it, O, eminence!)—this, without doubt, is what Democracy is for; and this is what our America means, and is doing—may I not say, has done? If not, she means nothing more, and does nothing more than any other land. And as, by virtue of its cosmical, antiseptic power, Nature's stomach is fully strong enough not only to digest the morbific matter always presented, not to be turned aside, and perhaps, indeed, intuitively gravitating thither—but even to change such contributions into nutriment for highest use and life—so American Democracy's. That is the lesson we, these days, send over to European lands by every western breeze.

And, truly, whatever may be said in the way of abstract argument, for or against the theory of a wider democratizing of institutions in any civilized country, much trouble might well be saved to those European lands by recognizing this palpable fact (for a palpable fact it is), that some form of such democratizing is about the only resource now left. *That,* or chronic dissatisfaction continued, mutterings which grow annually louder and louder, till, in due course, and pretty swiftly in most cases, the inevitable crisis, crash, dynastic ruin. Anything worthy to be called statesmanship in the Old World, I should say, among the advanced students, adepts, or men of any brains, does not debate to-day whether to hold on, attempting to lean back and monarchize, or to look forward and democratize—but *how,* and in what degree and part, most prudently to democratize. The difficulties of the transfer may be fearful; perhaps none here in our America can truly

know them. I, for one, fully acknowledge them, and sympathize deeply. But there is Time, and must be Faith; and Opportunities, though gradual and slow, will everywhere be born. And beaming like a star, to any and to all, whatever else may for a while be quenched, shines not the eternal signal in the West?

—There is (turning home again) a thought, or fact, I must not forget—subtle and vast, dear to America, twin-sister of its Democracy—so ligatured indeed to it, that either's death, if not the other's also, would make that other live out life, dragging a corpse, a loathsome, horrid tag and burden forever at its feet. What the idea of Messiah was to the ancient race of Israel, through storm and calm, through public glory and their name's humiliation, tenacious, refusing to be argued with, shedding all shafts of ridicule and disbelief, undestroyed by captivities, battles deaths—for neither the scalding blood of war, nor the rotted ichor of peace could ever wash it out, nor has yet—a great Idea, bedded in Judah's heart—source of the loftiest Poetry the world yet knows—continuing on the same, though all else varies—the spinal thread of the incredible romance of that people's career along five thousand years—so runs this thought, this fact, amid our own land's race and history. It is the thought of Oneness, averaging, including all; of Identity—the indissoluble Union of These States.

—The eager and often inconsiderate appeals of reformers and revolutionists are indispensable to counterbalance the inertness and fossilism making so large a part of human institutions. The latter will always take care of themselves. The former is to be treated with indulgence, and even respect. As circulation to air, so is agitation and a plentiful degree of speculative license to political and moral sanity. Indirectly, but surely, goodness, virtue, law (of the very best) follow Freedom. These, to Democracy, are what the keel is to the ship, or saltness to the ocean.

The gravitation-hold of Liberalism will be a more universal ownership of property, general homesteads, general comfort—a vast, intertwining reticulation of wealth. No community furnished throughout with homes, and substantial, however moderate, incomes, commits suicide, or "shoots Niagara." As the human frame, or, indeed, any object in this manifold Universe, is best kept together by the simple miracle of its own cohesion, and the necessity and profit thereof, so a great and varied Nationality, occupying millions of square miles, were firmest held and knit by the principle of the safety and endurance of the aggregate of its middling property owners.

So that, from another point of view, ungracious as it may sound, and a paradox after what we have been saying, Democracy looks with suspicious, ill-satisfied eye upon the very poor, and on the ignorant. She asks for men and women well-off, owners of houses and acres, and with cash in the bank—and with some cravings for literature, too; and must have them, and hastens to make them. Luckily, the seed is already well-sown, and has taken ineradicable root.

—Huge and mighty are our Days, our republican lands—and most in their rapid shiftings, their changes, all in the interest of the Cause. As I write, the din of disputation rages around me. Acrid the temper of the parties, vital the pending questions. Congress convenes; the President sends his Message; Reconstruction is still in abeyance; the nominations and the contest for the twenty-first Presidentiad draw close, with loudest threat and bustle. Of these, and all the like of these, the eventuations I know not; but well I know that behind them, and whatever their eventuations, the really vital things remain safe and certain,

and all the needed work goes on. Time, with soon or later superciliousness, disposes of Presidents, Congressmen, party platforms, and such. Anon, it clears the stage of each and any mortal shred that thinks itself so potent to its day; and at and after which (with precious, golden exceptions once or twice in a century), all that relates to sire potency is flung to moulder in a burial-vault, and no one bothers himself the least bit about it afterward. But the People ever remains, tendencies continue, and all the idiocratic transfers in unbroken chain go on. In a few years the dominion-heart of America will be far inland, toward the West. Our future National Capitol will not be where the present one is. I should say that certainly, in less than fifty years, it will migrate a thousand or two miles, will be re-founded, and every thing belonging to it made on a different plan, original, far more superb. The main social, political spine-character of The States will probably run along the Ohio, Missouri and Mississippi Rivers, and west and north of them, including Canada. Those regions, with the group of powerful brothers toward the Pacific (destined to the mastership of that sea and its countless Paradises of islands), will compact and settle the traits of America, with all the old retained, but more expanded, grafted on newer, hardier, purely native stock. A giant growth, composite from the rest, getting their contribution, absorbing it to make it more illustrious. From the North, Intellect, the sun of things—also the idea of unswayable Justice, anchor amid the last, the wildest tempests. From the South, the living Soul, the animus of good and bad, haughtily admitting no demonstration but its own. While from the West itself comes solid Personality, with blood and brawn, and the deep quality of all-accepting fusion.

Political Democracy, as it exists and practically works in America, supplies a training-school for making grand young men. It is life's gymnasium, not of good only, but of all. We try often, though we fall back often. A brave delight, fit for freedom's athletes, fills these arenas, and fully satisfies, out of the action in them, irrespective of success. Whatever we do not attain, we at any rate attain the experiences of the fight, the hardening of the strong campaign, and throb with currents of attempt at least. Time is ample. Let the victors come after us. Not for nothing does evil play its part among men. *Vive,* the attack—the perennial assault! *Vive,* the unpopular cause—the spirit that audaciously aims—the courage that dies not—the never-abandoned efforts, pursued the same amid opposing proofs and precedents.

—Once, before the war, I, too, was filled with doubt and gloom. A traveller, an acute and good man, had impressively said to me, that day—putting in form, indeed, my own observations: I have traveled much in the United States, and watched their politicians, and listened to the speeches of the candidates, and read the journals, and gone into the public houses, and heard the unguarded talk of men. And I have found your vaunted America honey-combed from top to toe with infidelism, even to itself and its own programme. I have marked the brazen hell-faces of succession and slavery gazing defiantly from all the windows and doorways. I have everywhere found, primarily, thieves and scalliwags arranging the nominations to offices and sometimes filling the offices themselves. I have found the North just as full of bad stuff as the South. Of the holders of public offices in the Nation, or in the States, or their municipalities, I have found that not one in a hundred has been chosen by any spontaneous selection of the outsiders, the people, but all have been nominated and put through by little or large caucuses of the politicians, and have got in by electioneering, not desert. I have noticed how

the millions of sturdy farmers and mechanics are thus the helpless supple-jacks of comparatively few politicians. And I have noticed more and more, the alarming spectacle of parties usurping the Government, and openly and shamelessly wielding it for party purposes.

Sad, serious, deep truths. Yet are there other, still deeper, amply confronting, dominating truths. Over those politicians, and over all their insolence and wiles, and over the powerfulest parties, looms a Power, too sluggish may-be, but ever holding decisions and decrees in hand, ready, with stern process to execute them as soon as plainly needed, and at times, indeed, summarily crushing to atoms the mightiest parties, even in the hour of their pride.

Far different are the amounts of these things from what, at first sight, they appear. Though it is no doubt important who is elected President or Governor, Mayor or Legislator, there are other, quieter contingencies, infinitely more important. Shams, etc., will always be the show, like ocean's scum; enough if waters deep and clear make up the rest. Enough, that while the piled embroidered shoddy gaud and fraud spreads to the superficial eye, the hidden warp and weft are genuine, and will wear forever. Enough, in short, that the race, the land which could raise such as the late rebellion, could also put it down.

The average man of a land at last only is important. He, in These States, remains immortal owner and boss, deriving good uses, somehow, out of any sort of servant in office, even the basest; because (certain universal requisites, and their settled regularity and protection, being first secured), a Nation like ours, in the formation state, trying continually new experiments, choosing new delegations, is not served by the best men only, but sometimes more by those that provoke it—by the combats they arouse. Thus national rage, fury, discussion, etc., sublimer than content. Thus, also, the warning signals, invaluable for after times.

What is more dramatic than the spectacle we have seen repeated, and doubtless long shall see—the popular judgment taking the successful candidates on trial in the offices—standing off, as it were and observing them and their doing for a while, and always giving, finally, the fit, exactly due reward.

—When I pass to and fro, different latitudes, different seasons, beholding the crowds of the great cities, New York, Boston, Philadelphia, Cincinnati, Chicago, St. Louis, San Francisco, New Orleans, Baltimore—when I mix with these interminable swarms of alert, turbulent, good-natured, independent citizens, mechanics, clerks, young persons—at the idea of this mass of men, so fresh and free, so loving and so proud, a singular awe falls upon me. I feel, with dejection and amazement, that among our geniuses and talented writers or speakers, few or none have yet really spoken to this people, or absorbed the central spirit and the idiosyncrasies which are theirs, and which, thus, in highest ranges, so far remain entirely uncelebrated, unexpressed.

Dominion strong is the body's; dominion strong is the mind's. What has filled, and fills to-day our intellect, our fancy, furnishing the standards therein, is yet foreign. The great poems, Shakespeare included, are poisonous to the idea of the pride and dignity of the common people, the life-blood of Democracy. The models of our literature, as we get it from other lands, ultramarine, have had their birth originally in courts, and basked and grown in castle sunshine; all smells of princes' favors. For aesthetic Europe is yet exclusively feudal.

The literature of These States, a new projection, when it comes, must be the born outcrop, through all rich and luxuriant forms, but stern and exclusive, of the sole Idea of The States, belonging here alone.

Of course, of workers of a certain sort, we have already plenty, contributing after their kind; many elegant, many learned, all complacent. But, touched by the National test, they wither to ashes. I say I have not seen one single writer, artist, lecturer, or what not, that has confronted the voiceless but ever erect and active, pervading, underlying will and typic Aspiration of the land, in a spirit kindred to itself. Do you call those genteel little creatures American poets? Do you term that perpetual, pistareen, pasteboard work, American art, American opera, drama, taste, verse? I think I hear, echoed as from some mountain-top afar in the West, the scornful laugh of the Genius of These States.

—Democracy, in silence, biding its time, ponders its own ideals, not of men only, but of women. The idea of the women of America (extricated from this daze, this fossil and unhealthy air which hangs about the word, Lady), developed raised to become the robust equals, workers, and even practical and political deciders with the men—greater than man, we may admit, through their divine maternity, always their towering, emblematical attribute—but great, at any rate, as man, in all departments; or, rather, capable of being so, soon as they realize it, and can bring themselves to give up toys and fictions, and launch forth, as men do, amid real, independent, stormy life.

—Then, as toward finale (and, in that, overarching the true scholar's lesson), we have to say there can be no complete or epical presentation of Democracy, or any thing like it, at this day, because its doctrines will only be effectually incarnated in any one branch, when, in all, their spirit is at the root and centre. How much is still to be disentangled, freed! How long it takes to make this world see that it is, in itself, the final authority and reliance!

Did you, too, suppose Democracy was only for elections, for politics, and for a party name? I say Democracy is only of use there that it may pass on and come to its flower and fruits in manners, in the highest forms of interaction between men, and their beliefs—Democracy in all public and private life, and in the Army and Navy. I have intimated that, as a paramount scheme, it has yet few or no full realizers and believers. I do not see, either, that it owes any serious thanks to noted propagandists or champions, or has been essentially helped, though often harmed, by them. It has been and is carried on by all the moral forces, and by trade, finance, machinery, intercommunications, etc., and can no more be stopped than the tides, or the earth in its orbit. Doubtless, also, it resides, crude and latent, well down in the hearts of the fair average of the American-born people, mainly in the agricultural regions. But it is not yet, there or anywhere, the fully-received, the fervid, the absolute faith.

I submit, therefore, that the fruition of Democracy, on aught like a grand scale, resides altogether in the future. As, under any profound and comprehensive view of the gorgeous-composite Feudal world, we see in it, through the long ages and cycles of ages, the results of a deep, integral, human and divine principle, or fountain, from which issued laws, ecclesia, manners, institutes, costumes, personalities, poems (hitherto unequalled), faithfully partaking of their source, and indeed only arising either to betoken it, or to furnish parts of that varied-flowing display, whose centre was one and absolute—so, long ages hence, shall the due historian or critic make at least an equal retrospect, an equal History for the Democratic principle. It, too, must be adorned, credited with its results; then, when it, with imperial power, through amplest time, has dominated mankind— has been the source and test of all the moral, aesthetic, social, political, and religious expressions and institutes of the civilized world—has begotten them in spirit and in form, and carried them to its own unprecedented heights—has had monastics and ascetics, more numerous, more devout than the monks and priests of all previous creeds—has swayed the ages with a breadth and rectitude tallying Nature's own—has fashioned, systematized, and triumphantly finished and carried out, in its own interest, and with unparalleled success, a New Earth and a New Man.

—Thus we presume to write, as it were, upon things that exist not, and travel by maps yet unmade, and a blank. But the throes of birth are upon us; and we have something of this advantage in seasons of strong formations, doubts, suspense—for then the afflatus of such themes haply may fall upon us, more or less; and then, hot from surrounding revolution, our speech, though without polished coherence, and a failure by the standard called criticism, comes forth, real at least, as the lightnings.

And may-be, we, these days, have, too, our own reward (for there are yet some, in all lands, worthy to be so encouraged). Though not for us the joy of entering at the last the conquered city—nor ours the chance ever to see with our own eyes the peerless power and splendid *eclat* of the Democratic principle, arrived at meridian, filling the world with effulgence and majesty far beyond those of past history's kings, or all dynastic sway; there is yet, to whoever is eligible among us, the prophetic vision; the joy of being tossed in the brave turmoil of these times—the promulgation and the path, obedient, lowly reverent to the voice; the gesture of the god, or holy ghost, which others see not, hear not—with the proud consciousness that amid whatever clouds, seductions, or heart-wearying postponements, we have never deserted, never despaired, never abandoned the Faith.

Susan B. Anthony

The daughter of a Quaker abolitionist, Susan B. Anthony was raised to believe that men and women were equal in the eyes of God. Born in 1820 in Adams, Massachusetts, she became a leader in the women's suffrage movement in the United States. At seventeen she taught in rural New York state where she pushed for equal pay for female teachers, for coeducation, and for college education for girls.

Refused admittance to the Sons of Temperance because she was a woman, Anthony organized the Daughters of Temperance—the first woman's temperance association. She met Elizabeth Cady Stanton at a temperance meeting, and they became lifelong friends. Her lecturing on the rights of women and abolition, together with Stanton's support, brought about the first legislation in New York guaranteeing women rights over their children, property, and wages.

During the Civil War, Anthony was a co-organizer of the Woman's Loyalty League to support emancipation and Lincoln's government. After the war, she opposed granting suffrage to freed men unless women were also granted suffrage. This issue caused many sympathetic to woman's suffrage to stop supporting her. In 1869 Anthony and Stanton organized the National Woman Suffrage Association, which united two decades later with the American Woman Suffrage Association to create the National American Women Suffrage Association, which Anthony headed from 1892 to 1900.

In 1872 in Rochester, New York, Anthony led a group of women in a futile attempt to vote, testing woman's rights under the Fourteenth Amendment. She was arrested, tried, and sentenced to a fine. This made her a national figure (see the speech printed here). A number of other women followed her example until the Supreme Court decided against them. During the final three decades of the nineteenth century, Anthony lectured throughout the United States and Europe, bringing the feminist movement respectability. With Elizabeth Cady Stanton and Matilda Joslyn Gage, Anthony compiled the first three volumes of the *History of Woman Suffrage* (1881–86) and used her own money to buy most of the first edition. She distributed it to colleges throughout the United States and Europe. Later, Ida Husted Harper completed volumes four through six (1900–22), with Anthony contributing to volume four. Anthony died in 1906.

Suffrage and the Working Woman (1871)
(excerpts)

I come tonight . . . as a representative of the working women. I lay down my doctrine that the first step for the alleviation of their oppression is to secure to them pecuniary independence. Alexander Hamilton said 100 years ago "take my right over my subsistence and you possess absolute power over my moral being." That is applicable to the working women of the present day. Others possess the right over their subsistence. What is the cause of this? I will tell you. It is because of a false theory having been in the minds of the human family for ages that woman is born to be supported by man and to accept such circumstances as he chooses to accord to her. She not like him is not allowed to control her own circumstances. The pride of every man is that he is free to carve out his own destiny. A woman has no such pride.

A little circumstance happened at this hall last night which illustrates this. A mother and daughter came to the ticket office to purchase tickets, when they were confronted by a man who exclaimed, "Didn't I forbid you to come here to-night?" He had a heavy cane in his hand which he flourished over them, and finally drove them away from the hall.

I appeal to you men. If you were under such control of another man would you not consider it an absolute slavery? But you say that man was a brute. Suppose he is a brute, he is no more of a brute than the law permits him to be.

But to go back. Is it true that women are supported by men? If I was to go home with you all to-night, I should find ample proof of falsity. I should find among your homes many who support themselves. Then if I should go into your manufactories . . . I should find hundreds and thousands who support themselves by the industry of their own hands. In Boston there are 10,000 women engaged in shoemaking. You say these are extreme cases. So they are, but it is in these large cities that the hardship and wrong is most apparent. . . .

If you will take the stand with me on the main thoroughfares of New York, on the Bowery, at the ferries, you will see troops and troops of women going to their daily work. There are not quite so many as there are men, but the men think it is

not disreputable to work. Not so with woman. If she makes an effort to support herself, she always makes an effort to conceal it. The young girl has her satchel as though going to the depot, or has her books as though going to school.

Some years ago we had a Woman's Benevolent Society in New York and appointed a committee to visit all over the city among the poor. The committee visited among others a family of rag pickers. . . . In one little garret was a mother and five little children. The committee appealed to the mother to allow them to put her in a way to support her children and send them to school. They pleaded with her for some time without avail and finally she straightened herself up and exclaimed, "No indeed, ladies. I'll have you to understand my husband is a gintleman and no gintleman allows his wife to go out to work." [Laughter]

That society is wrong which looks on labor as being any more degrading to woman than to man.

It was no more ridiculous for the rag picker's wife to scout the idea of going to work out than it is for the daughter of a well-to-do farmer to scout the idea of supporting herself. . . .

I am proud of San Francisco that she is an exception to the rule, and that she has raised a woman to the position of Principal of one of the cosmopolitan schools with a full salary of $1,200 a year. But if to-morrow, the same model girl, whom I have just referred to, were to marry a banker and live a life of idleness, with horses, carriages, and house finely furnished, able to take her trip to Europe with all the advantages wealth could purchase, though her husband were a drunkard, a libertine and a vile and depraved wretch, the woman would never again receive pity. Now we want this rule changed.

The first result of this false theory is this: no woman is even educated to work. Sons are educated while daughters are allowed to grow up mere adornments, and when the hour of necessity comes, then comes cruelty in the extreme. The woman has to skill her hands for labor, and has to compete with men who have been skilled from boyhood; and not only this but when she has attained ability to compete with them and to do just as well in every respect she is placed at work, if at all, on half pay. Society dooms her always to a subordinate position, as inferior. . . .

Nowhere can woman hold head offices and the reason is this, politicians can't afford to give an office to one who can't pay back in votes. If in New York the women could decide the fate of elections, don't you think they could afford to make women County Clerks or Surrogate Clerks or even Surrogate Judges? Said a Surrogate Judge to me, "Miss Anthony, I was almost converted by your lecture last night. I have one son and one daughter. The son is at college." I asked him, "Is your son possessed of the requisite ability to place him in your position?" "No," he replied; "he will spend his days in a garrett daubing paints on a canvass. But my daughter has a splendid legal mind, and understands already much of my duties. What a pity she was not a boy!" Only think, a brain wasted because it happens to be a woman's. For this reason one half the brain in the world will remain undeveloped. How will we remedy this? Give woman an equal chance to compete with men, educate her and surround her with the same legal advantages. Every one knows that the great stimulus for activity is to be paid for in having that activity recognized by promotion.

How will the ballot cure the evil? You tell me the ballot is not going to alleviate this. I will tell you how it is going to alleviate it. Never have the disfranchised classes had equal chances with the enfranchised. What is the difference between the working classes of the United States and Europe? Simply that, here the workman has the bal-

lot and there he has not. Here, if he has the brains or energy, his chances are quite equal with the son of the millionaire. That is American Republicanism—the ballot in the hand of every man. [Applause] . . . See how it works. Take the St. Crispins for example. . . . Well these three hundred St. Crispins strike against a reduction of wages, and not only they, but twenty other St. Crispin Societies, and not only they but other workmen. Now, suppose the New York *World* denounced those men, and the Democratic party manifested prejudice, not only those 300 men would vote against the party but all the other societies: the hod carriers, brick layers, the masons, the carpenters and the tailors would vote solidly against the party which opposed them, and that party would go to the wall.

No political party can hope for success and oppose the interests of the working class. You can all see that neither of the great parties dared to put a plank in the platform directly opposed. Both wrote a paragraph on finance, but nobody knew what it meant. They did this not because of a desire to do justice to the workingmen, but simply because of the power of the workingmen to do them harm. . . .

Now what do women want? Simply the same ballot. In this city, they, the women hat and cap makers, 2,000 of them, made a strike and held out three weeks, but finally they were forced to yield. Their employers said "Take that or nothing," and although "that" was *almost* "nothing" they had to take it or starve. Until two weeks ago I never heard of a successful strike among women. I'll tell you why this was successful. The employers of the Daughters of St. Crispin at Baltimore undertook to cut their wages down, and the Daughters struck. They were about to be defeated when the men St. Crispins came to the rescue and said to the employers, "If you don't accede we will strike," and they carried their point. How happened the workmen to do this? Because they are beginning to see that as long as women work, the capitalists are able to use them to undermine the workmen. . . .

In '68 the collar laundry women organized into a trades union. Their wages had once been but from $6 to $8 per week, but they gradually got them raised to $11 to $21 per week. You may all say that this is very good wages and so it was, compared with what they had been getting, but they thought they were poorly paid in proportion to the profits of their employers, and struck for an advance. Their employers said they must put a stop to this. Give women an inch and they will take an ell. The women called the men trades unions into counsel. The men said "Now is your time to make a strike; you are organized and your employers will come to terms." So one May morning in '69 the 1,000 women threw down their work. For three long months these women held out. They exhausted all their money. From all over the United States trade unions sent money to help them to carry the day. But their employers laughed at them; not a single paper advocated their cause, and they had to yield.

Not long ago I met the President of the organization and I asked her "If you were men you would have won?" "O yes," she said, "the men always win when they strike." "What was the cause of your defeat?" She said: "I guess it was the newspapers. They said if the women were not satisfied, they had better get married." [Laughter] "What made the newspapers oppose you?" "I guess our employers paid them money." "How much?" "I think $10,000." I asked her if the five hundred collar workers had had votes, would the newspapers dared to have opposed them? She said they would not. When the men strike, the employers try to bribe the newspapers in just the same way, but the newspapers dare not sell. The political editor of a party paper puts the votes in one scale and the cash in the other, and the cash

knocks the beam every time. [Laughter] Simply because those five hundred women were helpless and powerless and represented the whole half of a country who were helpless and powerless, they failed. . . .

Now let me give you an example for teachers. In a certain city in the East, the women teachers petitioned for an advance of salary. The School Board finding it necessary to retrench, instead of advancing their salaries deducted from the salaries of the women intermediate teachers $25 a month. They did not dare to reduce the salaries of the male teachers because they had votes.

I have a sister somewhat younger than I who has been in those schools for twenty years. [Laughter] Suppose six or seven women were members of the Board, do you believe the Board would have failed to receive that petition?. . .

A few years ago in this house a colored woman would not have been allowed a seat. Now the negro is enfranchised and what is the result? We see the black man walk the streets as proud as any man, simply because he has the ballot. Now black men are mayors of cities, legislators and office holders. Nobody dares to vent his spleen on negroes to-day.

We always invite the mayor and governor to our conventions, but they always have important business which keeps them from attending. The negro invites them and they come. Two years ago they did not. . . . To-day the conservative Republicans bid the negro good morning, and even the Democrats look wistfully at him.

I visited last year the Legislature of Tennessee. I inquired, "Who is that negro member?" I was answered that it was the honorable gentleman of Lynchburg, and that is the honorable gentleman of Hampton County, and that is the honorable gentleman of somewhere else. There were 20 of them. They did not occupy the black man's corner. They were seated with the white members. One black member was sitting on the same cushion on which sat his master three or four years ago.

I thought it would be nice to ask this Legislative body to attend my lecture; and when I extended my invitation, a gentleman asked that the courtesy of the Legislature be extended to me, and that I be allowed the use of the Legislative Hall. This called forth derisive laughter. The question was put on a suspension of the rules and was lost by a vote of 18 to 38. For the benefit of the Democracy, I will state that the negroes voted in favor of the suspension. A man stood near, who, from his appearance, might have been a slave-driver, and he launched out in a tirade of oaths and ended with, "If that had been a damned nigger who wanted the House, he could have had it." [Laughter] And so he could.... I believe that women have now the legal right to vote, and I believe that they should go to the polls and deposit their ballot, and if refused carry the officers and inspectors before the Supreme Court.

When we get the ballot those men who now think we are angels just before election will actually see our wings cropping out. [Laughter]

You say the women and the negro are not parallel cases. The negro was a down trodden race, but for the women there is no such necessity for they are lovely and beloved, and the men will guard them from evil. I suppose they will guard their own wives and daughters and mothers and sisters, but is every man as careful to guard another man's wife, daughter, mother and sister? It is not a question of safety to women in general. It is simply "Is she *my* property?" . . . You women who have kind brothers and husband and sons, I ask you to join with us in this movement so that woman can protect herself.

Standing Bear

Born in 1819, Standing Bear became chief of the Ponca tribe and inspired the Indian rights movement by traveling throughout the United States in the late 1870s telling the story of U.S. government policies that served to eradicate many of his people.

Under President Thomas Jefferson, the U.S. government initiated a policy of removing Indians from their homelands to consolidate them into one large, homogenous reservation and make room for white settlers—a policy carried out by President Andrew Jackson. This policy proved ineffective and, by the mid-nineteenth century, U.S. government policy had shifted toward forming a number of small, fixed reservations. Initially, this blueprint seemed to work, but as these fixed reservations became surrounded by white settlers, conflicts inevitably arose. Therefore, during the Lincoln administration, the commissioner of Indian affairs pushed for larger areas to be targeted for Indians. In the late 1860s, under the Grant administration, the "Grant Peace Policy" (ultimately executed by primarily Protestant "missionary" or religious field officers and backed up by the army) went into effect. This policy had several goals: to pacify Indian conflicts, to resettle all Indians on designated reservations, to turn Indians into farmers, and to teach Indian children English and integrate them into mainstream American culture.

The Peace Policy shifted to a more individualized approach toward Indians under President Rutherford B. Hayes in 1877, emphasizing smaller reserves for private ownership and farming. This resulted in the forced removal of the small, peaceful Ponca tribe from their Missouri River Reservation in South Dakota to a designated Indian territory. Carrying the body of his only son, Standing Bear left with some of his tribe for the former burial grounds, but they were arrested in Nebraska for leaving their designated reservation without permission. At court the Indians were freed after *Standing Bear vs. Crook* went to trial. An assistant editor of the *Omaha Daily Herald* quit after the trial to organize a speaking tour for Standing Bear, which turned his story into a hot public issue. Standing Bear's speeches were particularly effective in the northeast, leading to the creation of the Boston Indian Citizenship Committee, which pushed for recognition of the rights of the Ponca and other tribes. Helen Hunt Jackson was one of the Indian-rights militants inspired by Standing Bear.

The 1879 speech reprinted here describes the five-hundred mile journey of 1877 in which one third of the Ponca died of starvation and disease, and most survivors were disabled. Standing Bear's speeches represent the first Indian grievance to receive serious national attention, triggered by angry letters to Congress in response to the case of the Ponca. A Senate investigating committee later confirmed Standing Bear's description of events. The Ponca were allowed to return to their Nebraska homeland. Those who wanted to stay received land in Indian territory, and those who had property taken during the forced move were given some compensation. Standing Bear died in 1908.

ᏨᎥᏨ

The Land Was Owned by Our Tribe (1879)

We lived on our land as long as we can remember. No one knows how long ago we came there. The land was owned by our tribe as far back as memory of men goes. We were living quietly on our farms. All of a sudden one white man came. We had no idea what for. This was the inspector. He came to our tribe with Rev. Mr. Hinman. These two, with the agent, James Lawrence, they made our trouble.

They said the President told us to pack up—that we must move to the Indian Territory.

The inspector said to us: "The President says you must sell this land. He will buy it and pay you the money, and give you new land in the Indian Territory."

We said to him: "We do not know your authority. You have no right to move us till we have had council with the President."

We said to him: "When two persons wish to make a bargain, they can talk together and find out what each wants, and then make their agreement."

We said to him: "We do not wish to go. When a man owns anything, he does not let it go till he has received payment for it."

We said to him: "We will see the President first."

He said to us: "I will take you to see the new land. If you like it, then you can see the President, and tell him so. If not, then you can see him and tell him so." And he took all ten of our chiefs down. I went, and Bright Eyes' uncle went. He took us to look at three different pieces of land. He said we must take one of the three pieces, so the President said. After he took us down there, he said: "No pay for the land you left."

Isaak, *American Political Thinking.*

We said to him: "You have forgotten what you said before we started. You said we should have pay for our land. Now you say not. You told us then you were speaking truth."

All these three men took us down there. The man got very angry. He tried to compel us to take one of the three pieces of land. He told us to be brave. He said to us: "If you do not accept these, I will leave you here alone. You are one thousand miles from home. You have no money. You have no interpreter, and you cannot speak the language." And he went out and slammed the door. The man talked to us from long before sundown till it was nine o'clock at night.

We said to him: "We do not like this land. We could not support ourselves. The water is bad. Now send us to Washington, to tell the President, as you promised."

He said to us: "The President did not tell me to take you to Washington; neither did he tell me to take you home."

We said to him: "You have the Indian money you took to bring us down here. That money belongs to us. We would like to have some of it. People do not give away food for nothing. We must have money to buy food on the road."

He said to us: "I will not give you a cent."

We said to him: "We are in a strange country. We cannot find our way home. Give us a pass, that people may show us our way."

He said: "I will not give you any."

We said to him: "The interpreter is ours. We pay him. Let him go with us."

He said: "You shall not have the interpreter. He is mine, and not yours."

We said to him: "Take us at least to the railroad; show us the way to that."

And he would not. He left us right there. It was winter. We started for home on foot. At night we slept in haystacks. We barely lived till morning, it was so cold.

We had nothing but our blankets. We took the ears of corn that had dried in the fields; we ate it raw. The soles of our moccasins wore out. We went barefoot in the snow. We were nearly dead when we reached the Otoe Reserve. It had been fifty days. We stayed there ten days to strengthen up, and the Otoes gave each of us a pony. The agent of the Otoes told us he had received a telegram from the inspector, saying that the Indian chiefs had run away; not to give us food or shelter, or help in any way. The agent said: "I would like to understand. Tell me all that has happened. Tell me the truth. . . ."

Then we told our story to the agent and to the Otoe chiefs—how we had been left down there to find our way.

The agent said: "I can hardly believe it possible that anyone could have treated you so. The inspector was a poor man to have done this. If I had taken chiefs in this way, I would have brought them home; I could not have left them there."

In seven days we reached the Omaha Reservation. Then we sent a telegram to the President; asked him if he had authorized this thing. We waited three days for the answer. No answer came.

In four days we reached our own home. We found the inspector there. While we were gone, he had come to our people and told them to move.

Our people said: "Where are our chiefs? What have you done with them? Why have you not brought them back? We will not move till our chiefs come back."

Then the inspector told them: "Tomorrow you must be ready to move. If you are not ready you will be shot. Then the soldiers came to the doors with their bayonets, and ten families were frightened. The soldiers brought wagons, they put their things in and were carried away. The rest of the tribe would not move. . . .

Then, when he found that we would not go, he wrote for more soldiers to come.

Then the soldiers came, and we locked our doors, and the women and children hid in the woods. Then the soldiers drove all the people [to] the other side of the river, all but my brother Big Snake and I. We did not go, and the soldiers took us and carried us away to a fort and put us in jail. There were eight officers who held council with us after we got there. The commanding officer said: "I have received four messages telling me to send my soldiers after you. Now, what have you done?"

Then we told him the whole story. Then the officer said: "You have done no wrong. The land is yours; they had no right to take it from you. Your title is good. I am here to protect the weak, and I have no right to take you; but I am a soldier, and I have to obey orders."

He said: "I will telegraph to the President, and ask him what I shall do. We do not think these three men had any authority to treat you as they have done. When we own a piece of land, it belongs to us till we sell it and pocket the money."

Then he brought a telegram, and said he had received answer from the President. The President said he knew nothing about it.

They kept us in jail ten days. Then they carried us back to our home. The soldiers collected all the women and children together; then they called all the chiefs together in council; and then they took wagons and went round and broke open the houses. When we came back from the council, we found the women and children surrounded by a guard of soldiers.

They took our reapers, mowers, hay rakes, spades, ploughs, bedsteads, stoves cupboards, everything we had on our farms, and put them in one large building. Then they put into the wagons such things as they could carry., We told them that we would rather die than leave our lands; but we could not help ourselves. They took us down. Many died on the road. Two of my children died. After we reached the new land, all my horses died. The water was very bad. All our cattle died; not one was left. I stayed till one hundred and fifty-eight of my people had died. Then I ran away with thirty of my people, men and women and children. Some of the children were orphans. We were three months on the road. We were weak and sick and starved. When we reached the Omaha Reserve the Omahas gave us a piece of land, and we were in a hurry to plough it and put in wheat. While we were working, the soldiers came and arrested us. Half of us were sick. We would rather have died than have been carried back; but we could not help ourselves.

STANDING BEAR, *Ponca*

Henry George

Henry George became famous in the United States and Europe as an economist and reformer arguing for a single tax on land as a solution to the social problem of large-scale wealth in the midst of widespread poverty. Born in 1839, George left school at thirteen. By sixteen he was working as a deck hand on a ship headed to Calcutta and Melbourne. In his journal he expressed his shock at the disparity between the concentrations of wealth and the massive poverty that he observed in India. Back in the United States, George went west to Oregon and California to seek his fortune. He worked for a while in gold mines, but nothing came of it. He then worked as a printer and reporter in California.

George advocated free trade after the Civil War in opposition to industrialists who pressed for protectionism. In New York, George was again struck by the stark contrasts between rich and poor. He blamed Monopoly power—particularly in terms of land ownership and rents—for social and political inequities. He thought the western part of the United States provided the greatest opportunity because land there was not yet monopolized. Returning to California in time for the land speculation that spread with the railroad expansion, George described, in his pamphlet "Our Land and Land Policy" (1871), the huge land price rises that benefited those who held property and locked out those who owned none. This theme was developed in detail in *Progress and Poverty* (1880), a book that made George famous at home and abroad. Because all people had a natural right to apply their labor to the land, private ownership of property unjustly limited this right. Therefore, a "single tax" on land would regain for the community the value it had added to the property and from which the owner was benefiting, even though he had not created it. Such a tax would reduce other taxes on the people.

John Dewey called Henry George "one of the world's greatest social philosophers, certainly the greatest which our country has produced." Although few Americans have agreed with Dewey, "Land and Labor" clubs were founded in the United States, Scotland, and Ireland advocating George's ideas after the publication of his book. George came in a close second in the running for mayor of New York in 1886. He finished ahead of Theodore Roosevelt. George died in 1897.

Progress and Poverty (1880)
(excerpts)

The Persistence of Poverty amid Advancing Wealth

The great problem, of which these recurring seasons of industrial depression are but peculiar manifestations, is now, I think, fully solved, and the social phenomena which all over the civilized world appall the philanthropist and perplex the statesman, which hang with clouds the future of the most advanced races, and suggest doubts of the reality and ultimate goal of what we have fondly called progress, are now explained.

The reason why, in spite of the increase of productive power, wages constantly tend to a minimum which will give but a bare living, is that, with increase in productive power, rent tends to even greater increase, thus producing a constant tendency to the forcing down of wages.

In every direction, the direct tendency of advancing civilization is to increase the power of human labor to satisfy human desires—to extirpate poverty, and to banish want and the fear of want. All the things in which progress consists, all the conditions which progressive communities are striving for, have for their direct and natural result the improvement of the material (and consequently the intellectual and moral) condition of all within their influence. The growth of population, the increase and extension of exchanges, the discoveries of science, the march of invention, the spread of education, the improvement of government, and the amelioration of manners, considered as material forces, have all a direct tendency to increase the productive power of labor—not of some labor but of all labor; not in some departments of industry, but in all departments of industry; for the law of the production of wealth in society is the law of "each for all, and all for each."

But labor cannot reap the benefits which advancing civilization thus brings, because they are intercepted. Land being necessary to labor, and being reduced to private ownership, every increase in the productive power of labor but increases rent—the price that labor must pay for the opportunity to utilize its powers; and thus all the advantages gained by the march of progress go to the owners of land, and wages do not increase. Wages cannot increase; for the greater the earnings of labor the greater the price that labor must pay out of its earnings for the opportunity to make any earnings at all. The mere laborer has thus no more interest in the general advance of productive power than the Cuban slave has in advance in the price of sugar. And just as an advance in the price of sugar may make the condition of the slave worse, by inducing the master to drive him harder, so may the condition of the free laborer be positively, as well as relatively, changed for the worse by the increase in the productive power of his labor. For, begotten of the continuous advance of rents, arises a speculative tendency which discounts the effect of future improvements by a still further advance of rent, and thus tends, where this has not occurred from the normal advance of rent, to drive wages down to the slave point— the point at which the laborer can just live.

And thus robbed of all the benefits of the increase in productive power, labor is exposed to certain effects of advancing civilization which, without the advantages that naturally accompany them, are positive evils, and of themselves tend to reduce the free laborer to the helpless and degraded condition of the slave.

For all improvements which add to productive power as civilization advances consist in, or necessitate, a still further subdivision of labor, and the efficiency of the whole body of laborers is increased at the expense of the independence of the constituents. The individual laborer acquires knowledge of and skill in but an infinitesimal part of the varied processes which are required to supply even the commonest wants. The aggregate produce of the labor of a savage tribe is small, but each member is capable of an independent life. He can build his own habitation, hew out or stitch together his own canoe, make his own clothing, manufacture his own weapons, snares, tools and ornaments. He has all the knowledge of nature possessed by his tribe—knows what vegetable productions are fit for food, and where they may be found; knows the habits and resorts of beasts, birds, fishes, and insects; can pilot himself by the sun or the stars, by the turning of blossoms or the mosses on the trees; is, in short, capable of supplying all his wants. He may be cut off from his fellows and still live; and thus possesses an independent power which makes him a free contracting party in his relations to the community of which he is a member.

Compare with this savage the laborer in the lowest ranks of civilized society, whose life is spent in producing but one thing, or oftener but the infinitesimal part of one thing, out of the multiplicity of things that constitute the wealth of society and go to supply even the most primitive wants; who not only cannot make even the tools required for his work, but often works with tools that he does not own, and can never hope to own. Compelled to even closer and more continuous labor than the savage, and gaining by it no more than the savage gets—the mere necessaries of life—he loses the independence of the savage. He is not only unable to apply his own powers to the direct satisfaction of his own wants, but, without the concurrence of many others, he is unable to apply them indirectly to the satisfaction of his wants. He is a mere link in an enormous chain of producers and consumers, helpless to separate himself, and helpless to move, except as they move. The worse his position in society, the more dependent is he on society; the more utterly unable does he become to do anything for himself. The very power of exerting his labor for the satisfaction of his wants passes from his own control, and may be taken away or restored by the actions of others, or by general causes over which he has no more influence than he has over the motions of the solar system. The primeval curse comes to be looked upon as a boon, and men think, and talk, and clamor, and legislate, as though monotonous manual labor in itself were a good and not an evil, an end and not a means. Under such circumstances, the man loses the essential quality of manhood—the godlike power of modifying and controlling conditions. He becomes a slave, a machine, a commodity—a thing, in some respects, lower than the animal.

I am no sentimental admirer of the savage state. I do not get my ideas of the untutored children of nature from Rousseau, or Chateaubriand, or Cooper. I am conscious of its material and mental poverty, and its low and narrow range. I believe that civilization is not only the natural destiny of man, but the enfranchisement, elevation, and refinement of all his powers, and think that it is only in such moods as may lead him to envy the cud-chewing cattle, that a man who is free to the advantages of civilization could look with regret upon the savage state. But, nevertheless, I think no one who will open his eyes to the facts can resist the conclusion that there are in the heart of our civilization large classes with whom the veriest savage could not afford to exchange. It is my deliberate opinion that if, standing on the threshold of being, one were given the choice of entering life as a Tierra del Fuegan, a black fellow of Australia, an Esquimaux in the Arctic Circle, or among the lowest classes in such a highly civilized country as Great Britain, he would make infinitely the better choice in selecting the lot of the savage. For those classes who in the midst of wealth are condemned to want suffer all the privations of the savage, without his sense of personal freedom; they are condemned to more than his narrowness and littleness, without opportunity for the growth of his rude virtues; if their horizon is wider, it is but to reveal blessings that they cannot enjoy.

There are some to whom this may seem like exaggeration, but it is only because they have never suffered themselves to realize the true condition of those classes upon whom the iron heel of modern civilization presses with full force. As De Tocqueville observes, in one of his letters to Mme. Swetchine, "we so soon become used to the thought of want that we do not feel that an evil which grows greater to the sufferer the longer it lasts becomes less to the observer by the very fact of its duration;" and perhaps the best proof of the justice of this observation is that in cities where there exists a pauper class and a criminal class, where young girls shiver as they sew for bread, and tattered and barefooted children make a home in the streets, money is regularly raised to send missionaries to the heathen! Send missionaries to the heathen! It would be laughable if it were not so sad. Baal no longer stretches forth his hideous, sloping arms; but in Christian lands mothers slay their infants for a burial fee! And I challenge the production from any authentic accounts of savage life of such descriptions of degradation as are to be found in official documents of highly civilized countries—in reports of Sanitary Commissioners and of inquiries into the condition of the laboring poor.

The simple theory which I have outlined (if indeed it can be called a theory which is but the recognition of the most obvious relations) explains this conjunction of poverty with wealth, of low wages with high productive power, of degradation amid enlightenment, of virtual slavery in political liberty. It harmonizes, as results flowing from a general and inexorable law, facts otherwise most perplexing, and exhibits the sequence and relation between phenomena that without reference to it are diverse and contradictory. It explains why interest and wages are higher in new than in older communities, though the average, as well as the aggregate, production of wealth is less. It explains why improvements which increase the productive power of labor and capital increase the reward of neither. It explains what is commonly called the conflict between labor and capital, while proving the real harmony of interest between them. It cuts the last inch of ground from under the fallacies of protection, while showing why free trade fails to benefit permanently the working classes. It explains why want increases with abundance, and wealth tends to greater and greater aggregations. It explains the periodically recurring depressions of industry without recourse either to the absurdity of "over-production" or the absurdity of "over-consumption." It explains the enforced idleness of large numbers of would-be producers, which wastes the productive force of advanced communities, without the absurd assumption that there is too little work to do or that there are too many to do it. It explains the ill effects upon the laboring classes which often follow the introduction of machinery, without denying the natural advantages which the use of machinery gives. It explains the vice and misery which show themselves amid dense population, without attributing to the laws of the All-Wise and All-Beneficent defects which belong only to the short-sighted and selfish enactments of men.

This explanation is in accordance with all the facts.

Look over the world to-day. In countries the most widely differing—under conditions the most diverse as to government, as to industries, as to tariffs, as to currency—you will find distress among the working classes; but everywhere that you thus find distress and destitution in the midst of wealth you will find that the land is monopolized; that instead of being treated as the common property of the whole people, it is treated as the private property of individuals; that, for its use by labor, large revenues are extorted from the earnings of labor. Look over the world to-day, comparing different countries with each other, and you will see that it is not the abundance of capital or the productiveness of labor that makes wages high or low; but the extent to which the monopolizers of land can, in rent, levy tribute upon the earnings of labor. Is it not a notorious fact, known to the most ignorant, that new countries, where the aggregate wealth is small, but where land is cheap, are always better countries for the laboring classes than the rich countries, where land is dear? Wherever you find land relatively low, will you not find wages relatively high? And wherever land is high, will you not find wages low? As land increases in value, poverty deepens and pauperism appears. In the new settlements, where land is cheap, you will find no beggars, and the inequalities in condition are very slight. In the great cities, where land is so valuable that it is measured by the foot, you will find the extremes of poverty and of luxury. And this disparity in condition between the two extremes of the social scale may always be measured by the price of land. Land in New York is more valuable than in San Francisco; and in New York, the San Franciscan may see squalor and misery that will make him stand aghast. Land is more valuable in London than in New York; and in London, there is squalor and destitution worse than that of New York. . . .

But it were as well to cite historical illustrations of the attraction of gravitation. The principle is as universal and as obvious. That rent *must* reduce wages, is as clear as that the greater the subtractor the less the remainder. That rent *does* reduce wages, any one, wherever situated, can see by merely looking around him.

There is no mystery as to the cause which so suddenly and so largely raised wages in California in 1849, and in Australia in 1852. It was the discovery of the placer mines in unappropriated land to which labor was free that raised the wages of cooks in San Francisco restaurants to $500 a month, and left ships to rot in the harbor without officers or crew until their owners would consent to pay rates that in any other part of the globe seemed fabulous. Had these mines been on appropriated land, or had they been immediately monopolized so that rent could have arisen, it would have been land values that would have leaped upward, not wages. The Comstock lode has been richer than the placers, but the Comstock lode was readily monopolized, and it is only by virtue of the strong organization of the Miners' Association and the fears of the damage which it might do, that enables men to get four dollars a day for parboiling themselves two thousand feet underground, where the air that they breathe must be pumped down to them. The wealth of the Comstock lode has added to rent. The selling price of these mines runs up into hundreds of millions, and it has produced individual fortunes whose monthly returns can be estimated only in hundreds of thousands, if not in millions. Nor is there any mystery about the cause which has operated to reduce wages in California from the maximum of the early days to very nearly a level of wages in the Eastern States, and that is still operating to reduce them. The productiveness of labor has not decreased, on the contrary it has increased, as I have before shown; but, out of what it produces labor has now to pay rent. As the placer deposits were exhausted, labor had to resort to the deeper mines and to agricultural land, but monopolization of these being permitted, men now walk the streets of San Francisco ready to go to work for almost anything—for natural opportunities are now no longer free to labor.

The truth is self-evident. Put to any one capable of consecutive thought this question:

"Suppose there should arise from the English Channel or the German Ocean a No-man's land on which common labor to an unlimited amount should be able to make ten shillings a day and which should remain unappropriated and of free access, like the commons which once compromised so large a part of English soil. What would be the effect upon wages in England?"

He would at once tell you that common wages throughout England must soon increase to ten shillings a day.

And in response to another question, "What would be the effect on rents?" he would at a moment's reflection say that rents must necessarily fall; and if he thought out the next step he would tell you that all this would happen without any very large part of English labor being diverted to the new natural opportunities, or the forms and direction of industry being much changed; only that kind of production being abandoned which now yields to labor and to landlord together has less than labor could secure on the new opportunities. The great rise in wages would be at the expense of rent.

Take now the same man or another—some hard-headed business man, who has no theories, but knows how to make money. Say to him: "Here is a little village; in ten years it will be a great city—in ten years the railroad will have taken the place of the stage coach, the electric light of the candle; it will abound with all the machinery and improvements that so enormously multiply the effective power of labor. Will, in ten years, interest be any higher?"

He will tell you, "No!"

"Will the wages of common labor be any higher; will it be easier for a man who has nothing but his labor to make an independent living?"

He will tell you, "No; the wages of common labor will not be any higher; on the contrary, all the chances are that they will be lower; it will not be easier for the mere laborer to make an independent living; the chances are that it will be harder."

"What, then, will be higher?"

"Rent; the value of land. Go, get yourself a piece of ground, and hold possession."

And if, under such circumstances, you take his advice, you need do nothing more. You may sit down and smoke your pipe; you may lie around like the lazzaroni of Naples or the leperos of Mexico; you may go up in a balloon, or down a hole in the ground; and without doing one stroke of work, without adding one iota to the wealth of the community, in ten years you will be rich! In the new city you may have a luxurious mansion; but among its public buildings will be an almshouse.

In all our long investigation we have been advancing to this simple truth: That as land is necessary to the exertion of labor in the production of wealth, to command the land which is necessary to labor, is to command all the fruits of labor save enough to enable labor to exist. We have been advancing as through an enemy's country, in which every step must be secured, every position fortified, and every by-path explored; for this simple truth, in its application to social and political problems, is hid from the great masses of men partly by its very simplicity, and in greater part by widespread fallacies and erroneous habits of thought which lead them to look in every direction but the right one for an explanation of the evils which oppress and threaten the civilized world. And back of these elaborate fallacies and misleading theories is an active, energetic power, a power that in every country, be its political forms what they may, writes laws and molds thought—the power of a vast and dominant pecuniary interest.

But so simple and so clear is this truth, that to see it fully once is always to recognize it. There are pictures which, though looked at again and again, present only a confused labyrinth of lines or scroll work—a landscape, trees, or something of the kind—until once the attention is called to the fact that these things make up a face or a figure. This relation once recognized, is always afterward clear. It is so in this case. In the light of this truth all social facts group themselves in an orderly relation, and the most diverse phenomena are seen to spring from one great principle. It is not in the relations of capital and labor; it is not in the pressure of population against subsistence, that an explanation of the unequal development of our civilization is to be found. The great cause of inequality in the distribution of wealth is inequality in the ownership of land. The ownership of land is the great fundamental fact which ultimately determines the social, the political, and consequently the intellectual and moral condition of a people. And it must be so. For land is the habitation of man, the storehouse upon which he must draw for all his needs, the material to which his labor must be applied for the supply of all his desires; for even the products of the sea cannot be taken, the light of the sun enjoyed, or any of the forces of nature utilized, without the use of land or its products. On the land we are born, from it we live, to it we return again—children of the soil as truly as is the blade of grass or the flower of the field. Take away from man all that belongs to land, and he is but a disembodied spirit. Material progress cannot rid us of our dependence upon land; it can but add to the power of producing wealth from land; and hence, when land is monopolized, it might go on to infinity without increasing wages or improving the condition of those who have but their labor. It can but add to the value of land and the power which its possession gives. Everywhere, in all times, among all peoples, the possession of land is the base of aristocracy, the foundation of great fortunes, the source of power. As said the Brahmins, ages ago—

> *"To whomsoever the soil at any time belongs, to him belong the fruits of it. White parasols and elephants mad with pride are the flowers of a grant of land." [. . .]*

Edward Bellamy

On a tour of urban slum areas in Germany in 1868, Edward Bellamy was overwhelmed by "the extent and consequences of Man's inhumanity to man" and returned to the United States to become an influential utopian socialist writer of the late nineteenth century. Born in Chicopee Falls, Massachusetts, in 1850, Bellamy studied toward a law degree after his trip to Germany. Then he went into journalism, writing for the New York *Evening Post* before returning to Massachusetts to become editor of the Springfield *Union*. Together with his brother, he founded the Springfield *Daily News*. At the same time, Bellamy published his first novel, *Dr. Heidenhoff's Process* (1880). He then wrote a romantic novel about psychic phenomena, *Mrs. Ludington's Sister* (1884).

Bellamy's main work, however, was *Looking Backward: 2000–1887* (1888)—the most influential American novel of its time. Not only did he predict inventions such as radio, motion pictures, and television, he attempted to sketch out a solution for problems of political and social inequality. "Bellamy Clubs" sprang up across the nation, providing him with springboards for speaking tours. The book led to the founding of the Nationalist party based on Bellamy's ideas. Founding *The New Nation* to express his views, he published a sequel to his famous novel titled *Equality* (1897) just before he died in 1898. Bellamy's utopia described in *Looking Backward* is a gentle form of socialism in which a classless society comes into existence without a class struggle. Bellamy's fictional community enjoyed complete equality of income, state control of all production, a national party, and a credit card system replacing money. (Critics, of course, find an authoritarian "Big Brother" lurking in the background.)

Bellamy is significant not only for his prophetic intuitions, but for epitomizing a systematic socialist dissent from the traditional liberal mainstream.

ᐁᑳᐉ

Looking Backward: 2000–1887 (1888)
(excerpts)

[DR. LEETE:] "It was in 1887 that you fell into this sleep, I think you said."

[MR. WEST:] "Yes, May 30th, 1887."

My companion regarded me musingly for some moments. Then he observed, "And you tell me that even then there was no general recognition of the nature of the crisis which society was nearing? Of course, I fully credit your statement. The singular blindness of your contemporaries to the signs of the times is a phenomenon commented on by many of our historians, but few facts of history are more difficult for us to realize, so obvious and unmistakable as we look back seem the indications, which must also have come under your eyes, of the transformation about to come to pass. I should be interested. Mr. West, if you would give me a little more definite idea of the view which you and men of your grade of intellect took of the state and prospects of society in 1887. You must, at least, have realized that the widespread industrial and social troubles, and the underlying dissatisfaction of all classes with the inequalities of society, and the general misery of mankind, were portents of great changes of some sort."

"We did, indeed, fully realize that," I replied. "We felt that society was dragging anchor and in danger of going adrift. Whither it would drift nobody could say, but all feared the rocks."

"Nevertheless," said Doctor Leete, "the set of the current was perfectly perceptible if you had but taken pains to observe it, and it was not toward the rocks, but toward a deeper channel." . . .

". . . The Bostonians of your day had the reputation of being great askers of questions, and I am going to show my descent by asking you one to begin with. What should you name as the most prominent feature of the labor troubles of your day?"

"Why, the strikes, of course," I replied.

"Exactly. But what made the strikes so formidable?"

"The great labor organizations."

"And what was the motive of these great organizations?"

"The workmen claimed they had to organize to get their rights from the big corporations," I replied.

"That is just it," said Doctor Leete. "The organization of labor and the strikes were an effect, merely, of the concentration of capital in greater masses than had ever been known before. Before this concentration began, while as yet commerce and industry were conducted by innumerable petty concerns with small capital, instead of a small number of great concerns with vast capital, the individual workman was relatively important and independent in his relations to the employer. Moreover, when a little capital or a new idea was enough to start a man in business for himself, workingmen were constantly becoming employers and there was no hard and fast line between the two classes. Labor unions were needless then, and general strikes out of the question. But when the era of small concerns with small capital was succeeded by that of the great aggregations of capital, all this was changed. The individual laborer, who had been relatively important to the small employer, was reduced to insignificance and powerlessness over against the great corporation, while at the same time the way upward to the grade of employer was closed to him. Self-defense drove him to union with his fellows.

"The records of the period show that the outcry against the concentration of capital was furious. Men believed that it threatened society with a form of tyranny more abhorrent than it had ever endured. They believed that the great corporations were preparing for them the yoke of a baser servitude than had ever been imposed on the race, servitude not to men but to soulless machines incapable of any motive but insatiable greed. Looking back, we cannot wonder at their desperation, for certainly humanity was never confronted with a fate more sordid and hideous than would have been the era of corporate tyranny which they anticipated.

"Meanwhile, without being in the smallest degree checked by the clamor against it, the absorption of business by ever-larger monopolies continued. In the United States there was not, after the beginning of the last quarter of the century, any

opportunity whatever for individual enterprise in any important field of industry, unless backed by a great capital. During the last decade of the century, such small businesses as still remained were fast-failing survivals of a past epoch, or mere parasites on the great corporations, or else existed in fields too small to attract the great capitalists. Small businesses, as far as they still remained, were reduced to the condition of rats and mice, living in holes and corners, and counting on evading notice for the enjoyment of existence. The railroads had gone on combining till a few great syndicates controlled every rail in the land. In manufactories, every important staple was controlled by a syndicate. These syndicates, pools, trusts, or whatever their name, fixed prices and crushed all competition except when combinations as vast as themselves arose. Then a struggle, resulting in a still greater consolidation, ensued. The great city bazaar crushed its country rivals with branch stores, and in the city itself absorbed its smaller rivals till the business of a whole quarter was concentrated under one roof, with a hundred former proprietors of shops serving as clerks. Having no business of his own to put his money in, the small capitalist, at the same time that he took service under the corporation, found no other investment for his money but its stocks and bonds, thus becoming doubly dependent upon it.

"The fact that the desperate popular opposition to the consolidation of business in a few powerful hands had no effect to check it proves that there must have been a strong economical reason for it. The small capitalists, with their innumerable petty concerns, had in fact yielded the field to the great aggregations of capital, because they belonged to a day of small things and were totally incompetent to the demands of an age of steam and telegraphs and the gigantic scale of its enterprises. To restore the former order of things, even if possible, would have involved returning to the day of stagecoaches. Oppressive and intolerable as was the regime of the great consolidations of capital, even its victims, while they cursed it, were forced to admit the prodigious increase of efficiency which had been imparted to the national industries, the vast economies effected by concentration of management and unity of organization, and to confess that since the new system had taken the place of the old the wealth of the world had increased at a rate before undreamed of. To be sure this vast increase had gone chiefly to make the rich richer, increasing the gap between them and the poor; but the fact remained that, as a means merely of producing wealth, capital had been proved efficient in proportion to its consolidation. The restoration of the old system with the subdivision of capital, if it were possible, might indeed bring back a greater equality of conditions, with more individual dignity and freedom, but it would be the price of general poverty and the arrest of material progress.

"Was there, then, no way of commanding the services of the mighty wealth-producing principle of consolidated capital without bowing down to a plutocracy like that of Carthage? As soon as men began to ask themselves these questions, they found the answer ready for them. The movement toward the conduct of business by larger and larger aggregations of capital, the tendency toward monopolies, which had been so desperately and vainly resisted, was recognized at last, in its true significance, as a process which only needed to complete its logical evolution to open a golden future to humanity.

("Early in the last century the evolution was completed by the final consolidation of the entire capital of the nation. The industry and commerce of the country, ceasing to be conducted by a set of irresponsible corporations and syndicates of private persons at their caprice and for their profit, were entrusted to a single syndicate representing the people, to be conducted in the common interest for the common profit.)" The nation, that is to say, organized as the one great business corporation in which all other corporations were absorbed; it became the one capitalist in the place of all other capitalists, the sole employer, the final monopoly in which all previous and lesser monopolies were swallowed up, a monopoly in the profits and economies of which all citizens shared. The epoch of trusts had ended in The Great Trust. In a word, the people of the United States concluded to assume the conduct of their own business, just as one hundred-odd years before they had assumed the conduct of their own government, organizing now for industrial purposes on precisely the same grounds that they had then organized for political purposes. At last, strangely late in the world's history, the obvious fact was perceived that no business is so essentially the public business as the industry and commerce on which the people's livelihood depends, and that to entrust it to private persons to be managed for private profit is a folly similar in kind, though vastly greater in magnitude, to that of surrendering the functions of political government to kings and nobles to be conducted for their personal glorification."

"Such a stupendous change as you describe," said I, "did not, of course, take place without great bloodshed and terrible convulsions."

"On the contrary," replied Doctor Leete, "there was absolutely no violence. The change had been long foreseen. Public opinion had become fully ripe for it, and the whole mass of the people was behind it. There was no more possibility of opposing it by force than by argument. On the other hand the popular sentiment toward the great corporations and those identified with them had ceased to be one of bitterness, as they came to realize their necessity as a link, a transition phase, in the evolution of the true industrial system. The most violent foes of the great private monopolies were now forced to recognize how invaluable and indispensable had been their office in educating the people up to the point of assuming control of their own business. Fifty years before, the consolidation of the industries of the country under national control would have seemed a very daring experiment to the most sanguine. But by a series of object lessons, seen and studied by all men, the great corporations had taught the people an entirely new set of ideas on this subject. They had seen for many years syndicates handling revenues greater than those of states, and directing the labors of hundreds of thousands of men with an efficiency and economy unattainable in smaller operations. It had come to be recognized as an axiom that the larger the business the simpler the principles that can be applied to it; that, as the machine is truer than the hand, so the system, which in a great concern does the work of the master's eye in a small business, turns out more accurate results. Thus it came about that, thanks to the corporations themselves, when it was proposed that the nation should assume their functions, the suggestion implied nothing which seemed impracticable even to the timid. To be sure, it was a step beyond any yet taken, a broader generalization, but the very fact that the nation would be the sole corporation in the field would, it was seen, relieve the undertaking of many difficulties with which the partial monopolies had contended." . . .

Doctor Leete ceased speaking, and I remained silent, endeavoring to form some general conception of the changes in the arrangements of society implied in the tremendous revolution which he had described.

Finally I said, "The idea of such an extension of the functions of government is, to say the least, rather overwhelming."

"Extension!" he repeated. "Where is the extension?"

"In my day," I replied, "it was considered that the proper functions of government, strictly speaking, were limited to keeping the peace and defending the people against the public enemy, that is, to the military and police powers."

"And, in heaven's name, who are the public enemies?" exclaimed Doctor Leete. "Are they France, England, Germany, or hunger, cold, and nakedness? In your day governments were accustomed, on the slightest international misunderstanding, to seize upon the bodies of citizens and deliver them over by hundreds of thousands to death and mutilation, wasting their treasures the while like water; and all this oftenest for no imaginable profit to the victims. We have no wars now, and our governments no war powers, but in order to protect every citizen against hunger, cold, and nakedness, and provide for all his physical and mental needs, the function is assumed of directing his industry for a term of years. No, Mr. West, I am sure on reflection you will perceive that it was in your age, not in ours, that the extension of the functions of governments was extraordinary. Not even for the best ends would men now allow their governments such powers as were then used for the most maleficent."

"Leaving comparisons aside," I said, "the demagoguery and corruption of our public men would have been considered, in my day, insuperable objections to any assumption by government of the charge of the national industries. We should have thought that no arrangement could be worse than to entrust the politicians with control of the wealth-producing machinery of the country. Its material interests were quite too much the football of parties as it was."

"No doubt you were right," rejoined Doctor Leete, "but all that is changed now. We have no parties or politicians, and as for demagoguery and corruption, they are words having only an historical significance."

"Human nature itself must have changed very much," I said.

"Not at all," was Doctor Leete's reply, "but the conditions of human life have changed, and with them the motives of human action. The organization of society with you was such that officials were under a constant temptation to misuse their power for the private profit of themselves or others. Under such circumstances it seems almost strange that you dared entrust them with any of your affairs. Nowadays, on the contrary, society is so constituted that there is absolutely no way in which an official, however ill-disposed, could possibly make any profit for himself or any one else by a misuse of his power. Let him be as bad an official as you please, he cannot be a corrupt one. There is no motive to be. The social system no longer offers a premium on dishonesty. . . ."

"But you have not yet told me how you have settled the labor problem. It is the problem of capital which we have been discussing," I said. "After the nation had assumed conduct of the mills, machinery, railroads, farms, mines, and capital in general of the country, the labor question still remained. In assuming the responsibilities of capital the nation had assumed the difficulties of the capitalist's position."

"The moment the nation assumed the responsibilities of capital those difficulties vanished," replied Doctor Leete. "The national organization of labor under one direction was the complete solution of what was, in your day and under your system, justly regarded as the insoluble labor problem. When the nation became the sole employer, all the citizens, by virtue of their citizenship, became employees, to be distributed according to the needs of industry."

"That is," I suggested, "you have simply applied the principle of universal military service, as it was understood in our day, to the labor question."

"Yes," said Doctor Leete, "that was something which followed as a matter of course as soon as the nation had become the sole capitalist. The people were already accustomed to the idea that the obligation of every citizen, not physically disabled, to contribute his military services to the defense of the nation was equal and absolute. That it was equally the duty of every citizen to contribute his quota of industrial or intellectual services to the maintenance of the nation was equally evident, though it was not until the nation became the employer of labor that citizens were able to render this sort of service with any pretense either of universality or equity. No organization of labor was possible when the employing power was divided among hundreds or thousands of individuals and corporations, between which concert of any kind was neither desired, nor indeed feasible. It constantly happened then that vast numbers who desired to labor could find no opportunity, and on the other hand, those who desired to evade a part or all of their debt could easily do so."

"Service, now, I suppose, is compulsory upon all," I suggested.

"It is rather a matter of course than of compulsion," replied Doctor Leete. "It is regarded as so absolutely natural and reasonable that the idea of its being compulsory has ceased to be thought of. He would be thought to be an incredibly contemptible person who should need compulsion in such a case. Nevertheless, to speak of service being compulsory would be a weak way to state its absolute inevitableness. Our entire social order is so wholly based upon and deduced from it that if it were conceivable that a man could escape it, he would be left with no possible way to provide for his existence. He would have excluded himself from the world, cut himself off from his kind, in a word, committed suicide."

"Is the term of service in this industrial army for life?"

"Oh, no; it both begins later and ends earlier than the average working period in your day. Your workshops were filled with children and old men, but we hold the period of youth sacred to education, and the period of maturity, when the physical forces begin to flag, equally sacred to ease and agreeable relaxation. The period of industrial service is twenty-four years, beginning at the close of the course of education at twenty-one and terminating at forty-five. After forty-five, while discharged from labor, the citizen still remains liable to special calls, in case of emergencies causing a sudden great increase in the demand for labor, till he reaches the age of fifty-five, but such calls are rarely, in fact almost never, made. The fifteenth day of October of every year is what we call Muster Day, because those who have reached the age of twenty-one are then mustered into the industrial service, and at the same time those who, after twenty-four years' service, have reached the age of forty-five are honorably mustered out. It is the great day of the year with us, whence we reckon all other events, our Olympiad, save that it is annual." . . .

"It is after you have mustered your industrial army into service," I said, "that I should expect the difficulty to arise, for there its analogy with a military army must cease. Soldiers have all the same thing, and a very simple thing, to do, namely, to practice the manual of arms, to march and stand guard. But the industrial army must learn and follow two or three hundred diverse trades and advocations. What

administrative talent can be equal to determine wisely what trade or business every individual in a great nation shall pursue?"

"The administration has nothing to do with determining that point."

"Who does determine it, then?" I asked.

"Every man for himself in accordance with his natural aptitude, the utmost pains being taken to enable him to find out what his natural aptitude really is. The principle on which our industrial army is organized is that a man's natural endowments, mental and physical, determine what he can work at most profitably to the nation and most satisfactorily to himself. While the obligation of service in some form is not to be evaded, voluntary election, subject only to necessary regulation, is depended on to determine the particular sort of service every man is to render. As an individual's satisfaction during his term of service depends on his having an occupation to his taste, parents and teachers watch from early years for indications of special aptitudes in children. A thorough study of the national industrial system, with the history and rudiments of all the great trades, is an essential part of our educational system. While manual training is not allowed to encroach on the general intellectual culture to which our schools are devoted, it is carried far enough to give our youth, in addition to their theoretical knowledge of the national industries, mechanical and agricultural, a certain familiarity with their tools and methods. Our schools are constantly visiting our workshops, and often are taken on long excursions to inspect particular industrial enterprises. In your day a man was not ashamed to be grossly ignorant of all trades except his own, but such ignorance would not be consistent with our idea of placing every one in a position to select intelligently the occupation for which he has most taste. Usually long before he is mustered into service a young man has found out the pursuit he wants to follow, has acquired a great deal of knowledge about it, and is waiting impatiently the time when he can enlist in its ranks."

"Surely," I said, "it can hardly be that the number of volunteers for any trade is exactly the number needed in that trade. It must be generally either under or over the demand."

"The supply of volunteers is always expected to fully equal the demand," replied Doctor Leete. "It is the business of the administration to see that this is the case. The rate of volunteering for each trade is closely watched. If there be a noticeably greater excess of volunteers over men needed in any trade, it is inferred that the trade offers greater attractions than others. On the other hand, if the number of volunteers for a trade tends to drop below the demand, it is inferred that it is thought more arduous. It is the business of the administrations to seek constantly to equalize the attractions of the trades, so far as the conditions of labor in them are concerned, so that all trades shall be equally attractive to persons having natural tastes for them. This is done by making the hours of labor in different trades to differ according to their arduousness. The lighter trades, prosecuted under the most agreeable circumstances, have in this way the longest hours, while an arduous trade, such as mining, has very short hours. There is no theory, no a priori rule, by which the respective attractiveness of industries is determined. The administration, in taking burdens off one class of workers and adding them to other classes, simply follows the fluctuations of opinion among the workers themselves as indicated by the rate of volunteering. The principle is that no man's work ought to be, on the whole, harder for him than any other man's for him, the workers themselves to be the judges. There are no limits to the application of this rule. If any particular occupation is in itself so arduous or so oppressive

that, in order to induce volunteers, the day's work in it had to be reduced to ten minutes, it would be done. If, even then, no man was willing to do it, it would remain undone. But of course, in point of fact, a moderate reduction in the hours of labor, or addition of other privileges, suffices to secure all needed volunteers for any occupation necessary to men. . . ."

"You were surprised," he said, "at my saying that we got along without money or trade, but a moment's reflection will show that trade existed and money was needed in your day simply because the business of production was left in private hands, and that, consequently, they are superfluous now."

"I do not at once see how that follows," I replied.

"It is very simple," said Doctor Leete. "When innumerable different and independent persons produced the various things needful to life and comfort, endless exchanges between individuals were requisite in order that they might supply themselves with what they desired. These exchanges constituted trade, and money was essential as their medium. But as soon as the nation became the sole producer of all sorts of commodities, there was no need of exchanges between individuals that they might get what they required. Everything was procurable from one source, and nothing could be procured anywhere else. A system of direct distribution from the national storehouses took the place of trade, and for this money was unnecessary."

"How is the distribution managed?" I asked.

"On the simplest possible plan," replied Doctor Leete. "A credit corresponding to his share of the annual product of the nation is given to every citizen on the public books at the beginning of each year, and a credit card issued him with which he procures at the public storehouses, found in every community, whatever he desires whenever he desires it. This arrangement, you will see, totally obviates the necessity for business transactions of any sort between individuals and consumers. Perhaps you would like to see what our credit cards are like.

"You observe," he pursued as I was curiously examining the piece of pasteboard he gave me, "that this card is issued for a certain number of dollars. We have kept the old word, but not the substance. The term, as we use it, answers to no real thing, but merely serves as an algebraical symbol for comparing the values of products with one another. For this purpose they are all priced in dollars and cents, just as in your day. The value of what I procure on this card is checked off by the clerk, who pricks out of these tiers of squares the price of what I order."

"If you wanted to buy something of your neighbor, could you transfer part of your credit to him as consideration?" I inquired.

"In the first place," replied Doctor Leete, "our neighbors have nothing to sell us, but in any event our credit would not be transferable, being strictly personal. Before the nation could even think of honoring such transfer as you speak of, it would be bound to inquire into all the circumstances of the transaction, so as to be able to guarantee its absolute equity. It would have been reason enough, had there been no other, for abolishing money, that its possession was no indication of rightful title to it. In the hands of the man who had stolen it or murdered for it, it was as good as in those which had earned it by industry. People nowadays interchange gifts and favors out of friendship, but buying and selling is considered absolutely inconsistent with the mutual benevolence and disinterestedness which should prevail between

citizens and the sense of community of interest which supports our social system. According to our ideas, buying and selling is essentially anti-social in all its tendencies. It is an education in self-seeking at the expense of others, and no society whose citizens are trained in such a school can possibly rise above a very low grade of civilization."

"What if you have to spend more than your card in any one year?" I asked.

"The provision is so ample that we are more likely not to spend it all," replied Doctor Leete. "But if extraordinary expenses should exhaust it, we can obtain a limited advance on the next year's credit, though this practice is not encouraged, and a heavy discount is charged to check it. Of course if a man showed himself a reckless spendthrift he would receive his allowance monthly or weekly instead of yearly, or if necessary not be permitted to handle it at all."

"If you don't spend your allowance, I suppose it accumulates?"

"That is also permitted to a certain extent when a special outlay is anticipated. But unless notice to the contrary is given, it is presumed that the citizen who does not fully expend his credit did not have occasion to do so, and the balance is turned into the general surplus."

"Such a system does not encourage saving habits on the part of citizens," I said.

"It is not intended to," was the reply. "The nation is rich, and does not wish the people to deprive themselves of any good thing. In your day, men were bound to lay up goods and money against coming failure of the means of support and for their children. This necessity made parsimony a virtue. But now it would have no such laudable object, and, having lost its utility, it has ceased to be regarded as a virtue. No man any more has any care for the morrow, either for himself or his children, for the nation guarantees the nurture, education, and comfortable maintenance of every citizen from the cradle to the grave."

"That is a sweeping guarantee!" I said. "What certainty can there be that the value of a man's labor will recompense the nation for its outlay on him? On the whole, society may be able to support all its members, but some must earn less than enough for their support, and others more; and that brings us back once more to the wages question, on which you have hitherto said nothing. It was at just this point, if you remember, that our talk ended last evening; and I say again, as I did then, that here I should suppose a national industrial system like yours would find its main difficulty. How, I ask once more, can you adjust satisfactorily the comparative wages or remuneration of the multitude of avocations, so unlike and so incommensurable, which are necessary for the service of society? In our day the market rate determined the price of labor of all sorts, as well as of goods. The employer paid as little as he could, and the worker got as much. It was not a pretty system ethically, I admit; but it did, at least, furnish us a rough-and-ready formula for settling a question which must be settled ten thousand times a day if the world was ever going to get forward. There seemed to us no other practicable way of doing it."

"Yes," replied Doctor Leete, "it was the only practicable way under a system which made the interests of every individual antagonistic to those of every other; but it would have been a pity if humanity could never have devised a better plan, for yours was simply the application to the mutual relations of men of the devil's maxim, 'Your necessity is my opportunity.' The reward of any service depended not upon its difficulty, danger, or hardship, for throughout the world it seems that the most perilous, severe, and repulsive labor was done by the worst-paid classes, but solely upon the straits of those who needed the service."

"All that is conceded," I said. "But, with all its defects, the plan of settling prices by the market rate was a practical plan; and I cannot conceive what satisfactory substitute you can have devised for it. The government being the only possible employer, there is of course no labor market or market rate. Wages of all sorts must be arbitrarily fixed by the government. I cannot imagine a more complex and delicate function than that must be, or one, however performed, more certain to breed universal dissatisfaction."

"I beg your pardon," replied Doctor Leete, "but I think you exaggerate the difficulty. Suppose a board of fairly sensible men were charged with settling the wages for all sorts of trades under a system which, like ours, guaranteed employment to all, while permitting the choice of avocations. Don't you see that, however unsatisfactory the first adjustment might be, the mistakes would soon correct themselves? The favored trades would have too many volunteers, and those discriminated against would lack them till the errors were set right. But this is aside from the purpose, for, though this plan would, I fancy, be practicable enough, it is no part of our system."

"How, then, do you regulate wages?" I once more asked.

Doctor Leete did not reply till after several moments of meditative silence. "I know, of course," he finally said, "enough of the old order of things to understand just what you mean by that question; and yet the present order is so utterly different at this point that I am a little at a loss how to answer you best. You ask me how we regulate wages; I can only reply that there is no idea in the modern social economy which at all corresponds with what was meant by wages in your day."

"I suppose you mean that you have no money to pay wages in," said I. "But the credit given the worker at the government storehouse answers to his wages with us. How is the amount of the credit given respectively to the workers in different lines determined? By what title does the individual claim his particular share? What is the basis of allotment?"

"His title," replied Doctor Leete, "is his humanity. The basis of his claim is the fact that he is a man."

"The fact that he is a man!" I repeated, incredulously. "Do you possibly mean that all have the same share?"

"Most assuredly."

The readers of this book never having practically known any other arrangement, or perhaps very carefully considered the historical accounts of former epochs in which a very different system prevailed, cannot be expected to appreciate the stupor of amazement into which Doctor Leete's simple statement plunged me.

"You see," he said, smiling, "that it is not merely that we have no money to pay wages in, but, as I said, we have nothing at all answering to your idea of wages."

By this time I had pulled myself together sufficiently to voice some of the criticisms which, man of the nineteenth century as I was, came uppermost in my mind, upon this, to me, astounding arrangement. "Some men do twice the work of others!" I exclaimed. "Are the clever workmen content with a plan that ranks them with the indifferent?"

"We leave no possible ground for any complaint of injustice," replied Doctor Leete, "by requiring precisely the same measure of service from all."

"How can you do that, I should like to know, when no two men's powers are the same?"

"Nothing could be simpler," was Doctor Leete's reply. "We require of each that he shall make the same effort; that is, we demand of him the best service it is in his power to give."

"And supposing all do the best they can," I answered, "the amount of the product resulting is twice greater from one man than from another."

"Very true," replied Doctor Leete, "but the amount of the resulting product has nothing whatever to do with the question, which is one of desert. Desert is a moral question, and the amount of the product a material quantity. It would be an extraordinary sort of logic which should try to determine a moral question by a material standard. The amount of the effort alone is pertinent to the question of desert. All men who do their best, do the same. A man's endowments, however godlike, merely fix the measure of his duty. The man of great endowments who does not do all he might, though he may do more than a man of small endowments who does his best, is deemed a less deserving worker than the latter, and dies a debtor to his fellows. The Creator sets men's tasks for them by the faculties he gives them; we simply exact their fulfillment." [. . .]

John Dewey

John Dewey, generally recognized as America's leading philosopher, was born on a farm in Burlington, Vermont, in 1859—the year of publication of Charles Darwin's *Origin of Species,* Karl Marx's *Critique of Political Economy,* and J. S. Mill's *On Liberty.* Reared in a Protestant household by a mother socially ambitious for her sons, Dewey completed his B.A. (Phi Beta Kappa) at the University of Vermont. He taught at a high school for several years thereafter while studying the philosophical classics under guidance of H. A. P. Torrey at the University of Vermont. At twenty-three he published two articles in the *Journal of Speculative Philosophy.* He obtained his Ph.D. at Johns Hopkins University, writing his thesis on the philosophy of Kant.

Teaching philosophy at the University of Michigan, the University of Minnesota, the University of Chicago, and Columbia University, Dewey became known for his theory of instrumentalism; his repudiation of the separation of the individual and the social (both concrete traits and capacities of human beings); and for his pragmatism, particularly in the application of democratic ideals to education. Extremely prolific before he died in 1952, a few of Dewey's works include *Studies in Logical Theory* (1903), *Democracy and Education* (1916), *Essays in Experimental Logic* (1917), *Reconstruction in Philosophy* (1920), *Human Nature and Conduct* (1922), *The Quest for Certainty* (1929), and *Logic: The Theory of Inquiry* (1938). Strongly emphasizing the social aspects of philosophy and of intelligence in action, Dewey wrote of American liberalism in *Individualism Old and New* (1929): "Anthropologically speaking, we are living in a money culture. Its cults and rites dominate. . . . Instead of development of individualities which it prophetically set forth, there is a perversion of the whole ideal of individualism to conform to the practices of a pecuniary culture."

In the following essay, "The Democratic Conception in Education" from *Democracy and Education,* Dewey illustrates his revolt against German philosophy; the limitations of Platonism; and the democratic ideals for education in American liberalism, which would have to be fulfilled in an existing social context to ensure that "each individual is doing that for which he has aptitude by nature in such a way as to be useful to others," transcending limitations of class or income.

Democracy and Education (1916)
(excerpt)

The Democratic Conception in Education

For the most part, save incidentally, we have hitherto been concerned with education as it may exist in any social group. We have now to make explicit the differences in the spirit, material, and method of education as it operates in different types of community life. To say that education is a social function, securing direction and development in the immature through their participation in the life of the group to which they belong, is to say in effect that education will vary with the quality of life which prevails in a group. Particularly is it true that a society which not only changes but which has the ideal of such change as will improve it, will have different standards and methods of education from one which aims simply at the perpetuation of its own customs. To make the general ideas set forth applicable to our own educational practice, it is, therefore, necessary to come to closer quarters with the nature of present social life.

1. The Implications of Human Association. Society is one word, but many things. Men associate together in all kinds of ways and for all kinds of purposes. One man is concerned in a multitude of diverse groups, in which his associates may be quite different. It often seems as if they had nothing in common except that they are modes of associated life. Within every larger social organization there are numerous minor groups: not only political subdivisions, but industrial, scientific, religious, associations. There are political parties with differing aims, social sets, cliques, gangs, corporations, partnerships, groups bound closely together by ties of blood, and so on in endless variety. In many modern states and in some ancient, there is great diversity of populations, of varying languages, religions, moral codes, and traditions. From this standpoint, many a minor political unit, one of our large cities, for example, is a congeries of loosely associated societies, rather than an inclusive and permeating community of action and thought.

The terms society, community, are thus ambiguous. They have both a eulogistic or normative sense, and a descriptive sense; a meaning *de jure* and a meaning *de facto.* In social philosophy, the former connotation is almost always uppermost. Society is conceived as one by its very nature. The qualities which accompany this unity, praiseworthy community of purpose and welfare, loyalty to public ends, mutuality of sympathy, are emphasized. But when we look at the facts which the term *denotes* instead of confining our attention to its intrinsic *connotation,* we find not unity, but a plurality of societies, good and bad. Men banded together in a criminal conspiracy,

business aggregations that prey upon the public while serving it, political machines held together by the interest of plunder, are included. If it is said that such organizations are not societies because they do not meet the ideal requirements of the notion of society, the answer, in part, is that the conception of society is then made so "ideal" as to be of no use, having no reference to facts; and in part, that each of these organizations, no matter how opposed to the interests of other groups, has something of the praiseworthy qualities of "Society" which hold it together. There is honor among thieves, and a band of robbers has a common interest as respects its members. Gangs are marked by fraternal feeling, and narrow cliques by intense loyalty to their own codes. Family life may be marked by exclusiveness, suspicion, and jealousy as to those without, and yet be a model of amity and mutual aid within. Any education given by a group tends to socialize its members, but the quality and value of the socialization depends upon the habits and aims of the group.

Hence, once more, the need of a measure for the worth of any given mode of social life. In seeking this measure, we have to avoid two extremes. We cannot set up, out of our heads, something we regard as an ideal society. We must base our conception upon societies which actually exist, in order to have any assurance that our ideal is a practicable one. But, as we have just seen, the ideal cannot simply repeat the traits which are actually found. The problem is to extract the desirable traits of forms of community life which actually exist, and employ them to criticize undesirable features and suggest improvement. Now in any social group whatever, even in a gang of thieves, we find some interest held in common, and we find a certain amount of interaction and coöperative intercourse with other groups. From these two traits we derive our standard. How numerous and varied are the interests which are consciously shared? How full and free is the interplay with other forms of association? If we apply these considerations to, say, a criminal band, we find that the ties which consciously hold the members together are few in number, reducible almost to a common interest in plunder; and that they are of such a nature as to isolate the group from other groups with respect to give and take of the values of life. Hence, the education such a society gives is partial and distorted. If we take, on the other hand, the kind of family life which illustrates the standard, we find that there are material, intellectual, aesthetic interests in which all participate and that the progress of one member has worth for the experience of other members—it is readily communicable—and that the family is not an isolated whole, but enters intimately into relationships with business groups, with schools, with all the agencies of culture, as well as with other similar groups, and that it plays a due part in the political organization and in return receives support from it. In short, there are many interests consciously communicated and shared; and there are varied and free points of contact with other modes of association.

I. Let us apply the first element in this criterion to a despotically governed state. It is not true there is no common interest in such an organization between governed and governors. The authorities in command must make some appeal to the native activities of the subjects, must call some of their powers into play. Talleyrand said that a government could do everything with bayonets except sit on them. This cynical declaration is at least a recognition that the bond of union is not merely one of coercive force. It may be said, however, that the activities appealed to are themselves unworthy and degrading—that such a government calls into functioning activity simply capacity for fear. In a way, this

statement is true. But it overlooks the fact that fear need not be an undesirable factor in experience. Caution, circumspection, prudence, desire to foresee future events so as to avert what is harmful, these desirable traits are as much a product of calling the impulse of fear into play as is cowardice and abject submission. The real difficulty is that the appeal to fear is *isolated*. In evoking dread and hope of specific tangible reward—say comfort and ease—many other capacities are left untouched. Or rather, they are affected, but in such a way as to pervert them. Instead of operating on their own account they are reduced to mere servants of attaining pleasure and avoiding pain.

This is equivalent to saying that there is no extensive number of common interests; there is no free play back and forth among the members of the social group. Stimulation and response are exceedingly one-sided. In order to have a large number of values in common, all the members of the group must have an equable opportunity to receive and to take from others. There must be a large variety of shared undertakings and experiences. Otherwise, the influences which educate some into masters, educate others into slaves. And the experience of each party loses in meaning, when the free interchange of varying modes of life-experience is arrested. A separation into a privileged and a subject-class prevents social endosmosis. The evils thereby affecting the superior class are less material and less perceptible, but equally real. Their culture tends to be sterile, to be turned back to feed on itself; their art becomes a showy display and artificial; their wealth luxurious; their knowledge overspecialized; their manners fastidious rather than humane.

Lack of the free and equitable intercourse which springs from a variety of shared interests makes intellectual stimulation unbalanced. Diversity of stimulation means novelty, and novelty means challenge to thought. The more activity is restricted to a few definite lines—as it is when there are rigid class lines preventing adequate interplay of experiences—the more action tends to become routine on the part of the class at a disadvantage, and capricious, aimless, and explosive on the part of the class having the materially fortunate position. Plato defined a slave as one who accepts from another the purposes which control his conduct. This condition obtains even where there is no slavery in the legal sense. It is found wherever men are engaged in activity which is socially serviceable, but whose service they do not understand and have no personal interest in. Much is said about scientific management of work. It is a narrow view which restricts the science which secures efficiency of operation to movements of the muscles. The chief opportunity for science is the discovery of the relations of a man to his work—including his relations to others who take part—which will enlist his intelligent interest in what he is doing. Efficiency in production often demands division of labor. But it is reduced to a mechanical routine unless workers see the technical, intellectual, and social relationships involved in what they do, and engage in their work because of the motivation furnished by such perceptions. The tendency to reduce such things as efficiency of activity and scientific management to purely technical externals is evidence of the one-sided stimulation of thought given to those in control of industry—those who supply its aims. Because of their lack of all-round and well-balanced social interest, there is not sufficient stimulus for attention to the human factors and relationships in industry. Intelligence is narrowed to the factors concerned with technical production and marketing of goods. No doubt, a very acute and intense intelligence in these narrow lines can be developed, but the fail-

ure to take into account the significant social factors means none the less an absence of mind, and a corresponding distortion of emotional life.

II. This illustration (whose point is to be extended to all associations lacking reciprocity of interest) brings us to our second point. The isolation and exclusiveness of a gang or clique brings its antisocial spirit into relief. But this same spirit is found wherever one group has interests "of its own" which shut it out from full interaction with other groups, so that its prevailing purpose is the protection of what it has got, instead of reorganization and progress through wider relationships. It marks nations in their isolation from one another; families which seclude their domestic concerns as if they had no connection with a larger life; schools when separated from the interest of home and community; the divisions of rich and poor; learned and unlearned. The essential point is that isolation makes for rigidity and formal institutionalizing of life, for static and selfish ideals within the group. That savage tribes regard aliens and enemies as synonymous is not accidental. It springs from the fact that they have identified their experience with rigid adherence to their past customs. On such a basis it is wholly logical to fear intercourse with others, for such contact might dissolve custom. It would certainly occasion reconstruction. It is a commonplace that an alert and expanding mental life depends upon an enlarging range of contact with the physical environment. But the principle applies even more significantly to the field where we are apt to ignore it—the sphere of social contacts.

Every expansive era in the history of mankind has coincided with the operation of factors which have tended to eliminate distance between peoples and classes previously hemmed off from one another. Even the alleged benefits of war, so far as more than alleged, spring from the fact that conflict of peoples at least enforces inter-course between them and thus accidentally enables them to learn from one another, and thereby to expand their horizons. Travel, economic and commercial tendencies, have at present gone far to break down external barriers; to bring peoples and classes into closer and more perceptible connection with one another. It remains for the most part to secure the intellectual and emotional significance of this physical annihilation of space.

2. The Democratic Ideal. The two elements in our criterion both point to democracy. The first signifies not only more numerous and more varied points of shared common interest, but greater reli-ance upon the recognition of mutual inter-ests as a factor in social control. The second means not only freer interaction between social groups (once isolated so far as inten-tion could keep up a separation) but change in social habit—its continuous readjust-ment through meeting the new situations produced by varied intercourse. And these two traits are precisely what characterize the democratically constituted society.

Upon the educational side, we note first that the realization of a form of social life in which interests are mutually inter-penetrating, and where progress, or read-justment, is an important consideration, makes a democratic community more inter-ested than other communities have cause to be in deliberate and systematic educa-tion. The devotion of democracy to educa-tion is a familiar fact. The superficial explanation is that a government resting upon popular suffrage cannot be successful unless those who elect and who obey their governors are educated. Since a democratic society repudiates the principle of external authority, it must find a substitute in volun-tary disposition and interest; these can be created only by education. But there is a deeper explanation. A democracy is more than a form of government; it is primarily

a mode of associated living, of conjoint communicated experience. The extension in space of the number of individuals who participate in an interest so that each has to refer his own action to that of others, and to consider the action of others to give point and direction to his own, is equivalent to the breaking down of those barriers of class, race, and national territory which kept men from perceiving the full import of their activity. These more numerous and more varied points of contact denote a greater diversity of stimuli to which an individual has to respond; they conse-quently put a premium on variation in his action. They secure a liberation of powers which remain suppressed as long as the incitations to action are partial, as they must be in a group which in its exclusiveness shuts out many interests.

The widening of the area of shared concerns, and the liberation of a greater diversity of personal capacities which char-acterize a democracy, are not of course the product of deliberation and conscious effort. On the contrary, they were caused by the development of modes of manufacture and commerce, travel, migration, and inter-communication which flowed from the command of science over natural energy. But after greater individualization on one hand, and a broader community of interest on the other have come into existence, it is a matter of deliberate effort to sustain and extend them. Obviously a society to which stratification into separate classes would be fatal, must see to it that intellec-tual opportunities are accessible to all on equitable and easy terms. A society marked off into classes need be specially attentive only to the education of its ruling elements. A society which is mobile, which is full of channels for the distribution of a change occurring anywhere, must see to it that its members are educated to personal initiative and adaptability. Otherwise, they will be overwhelmed by the changes in which they are caught and whose significance or connections they do not perceive. The result will be a confusion in which a few will appropriate to themselves the results of the blind and externally directed activities of others.

3. The Platonic Educational Philosophy. Subsequent chapters will be devoted to making explicit the implications of the democratic ideas in education. In the remaining portions of this chapter, we shall consider the educational theories which have been evolved in three epochs when the social import of education was especially conspicuous. The first one to be considered is that of Plato. No one could better express than did he the fact that a society is stably organized when each individual is doing that for which he has aptitude by nature in such a way as to be useful to others (or to contribute to the whole to which he belongs); and that it is the business of education to discover these aptitudes and progressively to train them for social use. Much which has been said so far is borrowed from what Plato first consciously taught the world. But conditions which he could not intellectually control led him to restrict these ideas in their application. He never got any conception of the indefinite plurality of activities which may characterize an individual and a social group, and consequently limited his view to a limited number of *classes* of capacities and of social arrangements.

Plato's starting point is that the organization of society depends ultimately upon knowledge of the end of existence. If we do not know its end, we shall be at the mercy of accident and caprice. Unless we know the end, the good, we shall have no criterion for rationally deciding what the possibilities are which should be promoted, nor how social arrangements are to be ordered. We shall have no conception of the proper limits and distribution of activities—what he called justice—as a trait of both individual and social organization. But how is the knowledge of the final and permanent good to be achieved? In dealing with this question we come upon the seemingly insuperable obstacle that such knowledge is not possible save in a just and harmonious social order. Everywhere else the mind is distracted and misled by false valuations and false perspectives. A disorganized and factional society sets up a number of different models and standards. Under such conditions it is impossible for the individual to attain consistency of mind. Only a complete whole is fully self-consistent. A society which rests upon the supremacy of some factor over another irrespective of its rational or proportionate claims, inevitably leads thought astray. It puts a premium on certain things and slurs over others, and creates a mind whose seeming unity is forced and distorted. Education proceeds ultimately from the patterns furnished by institutions, customs, and laws. Only in a just state will these be such as to give the right education; and only those who have rightly trained minds will be able to recognize the end, and ordering principle of things. We seem to be caught in a hopeless circle. However, Plato suggested a way out. A few men, philosophers or lovers of wisdom—or truth—may by study learn at least in outline the proper patterns of true existence. If a powerful ruler should form a state after these patterns, then its regulations could be preserved. An education could be given which would sift individuals, discovering what they were good for, and supplying a method of assigning each to the work in life for which his nature fits him. Each doing his own part, and never transgressing, the order and unity of the whole would be maintained.

It would be impossible to find in any scheme of philosophic thought a more adequate recognition on one hand of the educational significance of social arrangements and, on the other, of the dependence of those arrangements upon the means used to educate the young. It would be impossible to find a deeper sense of the function of education in discovering and developing personal capacities, and training them so that they would connect with the activities of others. Yet the society in which the theory was propounded was so undemocratic that Plato could not work out a solution for the problem whose terms he clearly saw.

While he affirmed with emphasis that the place of the individual in society should not be determined by birth or wealth or any conventional status, but by his own nature as discovered in the process of education, he had no perception of the uniqueness of individuals. For him they fall by nature into classes, and into a very small number of classes at that. Consequently the testing and sifting function of education only shows to which one of three classes an individual belongs. There being no recognition that each individual constitutes his own class, there could be no recognition of the infinite diversity of active tendencies and combinations of tendencies of which an individual is capable. There were only three types of faculties or powers in the individual's constitution. Hence education would soon reach a static limit in each class, for only diversity makes change and progress.

In some individuals, appetites naturally dominate; they are assigned to the laboring and trading class, which expresses and supplies human wants. Others reveal, upon education, that over and above appetites, they have a generous, outgoing, assertively courageous disposition. They become the citizen-subjects of the state; its defenders in war; its internal guardians in peace. But their limit is fixed by their lack of reason, which is a capacity to grasp the universal. Those who possess this are capable of the highest kind of education, and become in time the legislators of the state—

for laws are the universals which control the particulars of experience. Thus it is not true that in intent, Plato subordinated the individual to the social whole. But it is true that lacking the perception of the uniqueness of every individual, his incommensurability with others, and consequently not recognizing that a society might change and yet be stable, his doctrine of limited powers and classes came in net effect to the idea of the subordination of individuality.

We cannot better Plato's conviction that an individual is happy and society well organized when each individual engages in those activities for which he has a natural equipment, nor his conviction that it is the primary office of education to discover this equipment to its possessor and train him for its effective use. But progress in knowledge has made us aware of the superficiality of Plato's lumping of individuals and their original powers into a few sharply marked-off classes; it has taught us that original capacities are indefinitely numerous and variable. It is but the other side of this fact to say that in the degree in which society has become democratic, social organization means utilization of the specific and variable qualities of individuals, not stratification by classes. Although his educational philosophy was revolutionary, it was none the less in bondage to static ideals. He thought that change or alteration was evidence of lawless flux; that true reality was unchangeable. Hence while he would radically change the existing state of society, his aim was to construct a state in which change would subsequently have no place. The final end of life is fixed; given a state framed with this end in view, not even minor details are to be altered. Though they might not be inherently important, yet if permitted they would inure the minds of men to the idea of change, and hence be dissolving and anarchic. The breakdown of his philosophy is made apparent in the fact that he could not trust to gradual improvements in education to bring about a better society which should then improve education, and so on indefinitely. Correct education could not come into existence until an ideal state existed, and after that education would be devoted simply to its conservation. For the existence of this state he was obliged to trust to some happy accident by which philosophic wisdom should happen to coincide with possession of ruling power in the state.

4. The "Individualistic" Ideal of the Eighteenth Century. In the eighteenth-century philosophy we find ourselves in a very different circle of ideas. "Nature" still means something antithetical to existing social organization; Plato exercised a great influence upon Rousseau. But the voice of nature now speaks for the diversity of individual talent and for the need of free development of individuality in all its variety. Education in accord with nature furnishes the goal and the method of instruction and discipline. Moreover, the native or original endowment was conceived, in extreme cases, as nonsocial or even as antisocial. Social arrangements were thought of as mere external expedients by which these nonsocial individuals might secure a greater amount of private happiness for themselves.

Nevertheless, these statements convey only an inadequate idea of the true significance of the movement. In reality its chief interest was in progress and in social progress. The seeming antisocial philosophy was a somewhat transparent mask for an impetus toward a wider and freer society—toward cosmopolitanism. The positive ideal was humanity. In membership in humanity, as distinct from a state, man's capacities would be liberated; while in existing political organizations his powers were hampered and distorted to meet the requirements and selfish interests of the rulers of the state. The doctrine of extreme individualism was but the counterpart, the

obverse, of ideals of the indefinite perfectibility of man and of a social organization having a scope as wide as humanity. The emancipated individual was to become the organ and agent of a comprehensive and progressive society.

The heralds of this gospel were acutely conscious of the evils of the social estate in which they found themselves. They attributed these evils to the limitations imposed upon the free powers of man. Such limitation was both distorting and corrupting. Their impassioned devotion to emancipation of life from external restrictions which operated to the exclusive advantage of the class to whom a past feudal system consigned power, found intellectual formulation in a worship of nature. To give "nature" full swing was to replace an artificial, corrupt, and inequitable social order by a new and better kingdom of humanity. Unrestrained faith in Nature as both a model and a working power was strengthened by the advances of natural science. Inquiry freed from prejudice and artificial restraints of church and state had revealed that the world is a scene of law. The Newtonian solar system, which expressed the reign of natural law, was a scene of wonderful harmony, where every force balanced with every other. Natural law would accomplish the same result in human relations, if men would only get rid of the artificial man-imposed coercive restrictions.

Education in accord with nature was thought to be the first step in insuring this more social society. It was plainly seen that economic and political limitations were ultimately dependent upon limitations of thought and feeling. The first step in freeing men from external chains was to emancipate them from the internal chains of false beliefs and ideals. What was called social life, existing institutions, were too false and corrupt to be intrusted with this work. How could it be expected to undertake it when the undertaking meant its own destruction? "Nature" must then be the power to which the enterprise was to be left. Even the extreme sensationalistic theory of knowledge which was current derived itself from this conception. To insist that mind is originally passive and empty was one way of glorifying the possibilities of education. If the mind was a wax tablet to be written upon by objects, there were no limits to the possibility of education by means of the natural environment. And since the natural world of objects is a scene of harmonious "truth," this education would infallibly produce minds filled with the truth.

5. Education as National and as Social. As soon as the first enthusiasm for freedom waned, the weakness of the theory upon the constructive side became obvious. Merely to leave everything to nature was, after all, but to negate the very idea of education; it was to trust to the accidents of circumstance. Not only was some method required but also some positive organ, some administrative agency for carrying on the process of instruction. The "complete and harmonious development of all powers," having as its social counterpart an enlightened and progressive humanity, required definite organization for its realization. Private individuals here and there could proclaim the gospel; they could not execute the work. A Pestalozzi could try experiments and exhort philanthropically inclined persons having wealth and power to follow his example. But even Pestalozzi saw that any effective pursuit of the new educational ideal required the support of the state. The realization of the new education destined to produce a new society was, after all, dependent upon the activities of existing states. The movement for the democratic idea inev-

itably became a movement for publicly conducted and administered schools.

So far as Europe was concerned, the historic situation identified the movement for a state-supported education with the nationalistic movement in political life—a fact of incalculable significance for subsequent movements. Under the influence of German thought in particular, education became a civic function and the civic function was identified with the realization of the ideal of the national state. The "state" was substituted for humanity; cosmopolitanism gave way to nationalism. To form the citizen, not the "man," became the aim of education.[1] The historic situation to which reference is made is the after-effects of the Napoleonic conquests, especially in Germany. The German states felt (and subsequent events demonstrate the correctness of the belief) that systematic attention to education was the best means of recovering and maintaining their political integrity and power. Externally they were weak and divided. Under the leadership of Prussian statesmen they made this condition a stimulus to the development of an extensive and thoroughly grounded system of public education.

This change in practice necessarily brought about a change in theory. The individualistic theory receded into the background. The state furnished not only the instrumentalities of public education but also its goal. When the actual practice was such that the school system, from the elementary grades through the university faculties, supplied the patriotic citizen and soldier and the future state official and administrator and furnished the means for military, industrial, and political defense and expansion, it was impossible for theory

---

[1] There is a much neglected strain in Rousseau tending intellectually in this direction. He opposed the existing state of affairs on the ground that it formed *neither* the citizen nor the man. Under existing conditions, he preferred to try for the latter rather than for the former. But there are many sayings of his which point to the formation of the citizen as ideally the higher, and which indicate that his own endeavor, as embodied in the *Émile,* was simply the best makeshift the corruption of the times permitted him to sketch.

not to emphasize the aim of social efficiency. And with the immense importance attached to the nationalistic state, surrounded by other competing and more or less hostile states, it was equally impossible to interpret social efficiency in terms of a vague cosmopolitan humanitarianism. Since the maintenance of a particular national sovereignty required subordination of individuals to the superior interests of the state both in military defense and in struggles for international supremacy in commerce, social efficiency was understood to imply a like subordination. The educational process was taken to be one of disciplinary training rather than of personal development. Since, however, the ideal of culture as complete development of personality persisted, educational philosophy attempted a reconciliation of the two ideas. The reconciliation took the form of the conception of the "organic" character of the state. The individual in his isolation is nothing; only in and through an absorption of the aims and meaning of organized institutions does he attain true personality. What appears to be his subordination to political authority and the demand for sacrifice of himself to the commands of his superiors is in reality but making his own the objective reason manifested in the state—the only way in which he can become truly rational. The notion of development which we have seen to be characteristic of institutional idealism (as in the Hegelian philosophy) was just such a deliberate effort to combine the two ideas of complete realization of personality and thorough-going "disciplinary" subordination to existing institutions.

The extent of the transformation of educational philosophy which occurred in Germany in the generation occupied by the struggle against Napoleon for national independence, may be gathered from Kant, who well expresses the earlier individual-cosmopolitan ideal. In his treatise on Pedagogics, consisting of lectures given in the later years of the eighteenth century, he defines education as the process by which man becomes man. Mankind begins its history submerged in nature—not as Man who is a creature of reason, while nature furnishes only instinct and appetite. Nature offers simply the germs which education is to develop and perfect. The peculiarity of truly human life is that man has to create himself by his own voluntary efforts; he has to make himself a truly moral, rational, and free being. This creative effort is carried on by the educational activities of slow generations. Its acceleration depends upon men consciously striving to educate their successors not for the existing state of affairs but so as to make possible a future better humanity. But there is the great difficulty. Each generation is inclined to educate its young so as to get along in the present world instead of with a view to the proper end of education: the promotion of the best possible realization of humanity as humanity. Parents educate their children so that they may get on; princes educate their subjects as instruments of their own purposes.

Who, then, shall conduct education so that humanity may improve? We must depend upon the efforts of enlightened men in their private capacity. "All culture begins with private men and spreads outward from them. Simply through the efforts of persons of enlarged inclinations, who are capable of grasping the ideal of a future better condition, is the gradual approximation of human nature to its end possible. . . . Rulers are simply interested in such training as will make their subjects better tools for their own intentions." Even the subsidy by rulers of privately conducted schools must be carefully safeguarded. For the rulers' interest in the welfare of their own nation instead of in what is best for humanity, will make them, if they give money for the schools, wish to draw their plans. We have in this view an express statement of the points characteristic of the eighteenth century individualistic cosmopolitanism. The full development of private personality is identified with the aims of humanity as a whole and with the idea of progress. In addition we have an explicit fear of the hampering influence of a state-conducted and state-regulated education upon the attainment of these ideas. But in less than two decades after this time, Kant's philosophic successors, Fichte and Hegel, elaborated the idea that the chief function of the state is educational; that in particular the regeneration of Germany is to be accomplished by an education carried on in the interests of the state, and that the private individual is of necessity an egoistic, irrational being, enslaved to his appetites and to circumstances unless he submits voluntarily to the educative discipline of state institutions and laws. In this spirit, Germany was the first country to undertake a public, universal, and compulsory system of education extending from the primary school through the university, and to submit to jealous state regulation and supervision all private educational enterprises.

Two results should stand out from this brief historical survey. The first is that such terms as the individual and the social conceptions of education are quite meaningless taken at large, or apart from their context. Plato had the ideal of an education which should equate individual realization and social coherency and stability. His situation forced his ideal into the notion of a society organized in stratified classes, losing the individual in the class. The eighteenth century educational philosophy was highly individualistic in form, but this form was inspired by a noble and generous social ideal: that of a society organized to include humanity, and providing for the indefinite perfectibility of mankind. The idealistic philosophy of Germany in the early nineteenth century endeavored again to equate the ideals of a free and complete development of cultured personality with social discipline and political subordination. It made the national state an intermediary between the realization of private personality on one side and of humanity on the other. Consequently, it is equally possible to state its animating principle with equal truth either in the classic terms of "harmonious development of all the powers of personality" or in the more recent terminology of "social efficiency." All this reënforces the statement which opens this chapter: The conception of education as a social process and function has no definite meaning until we define the kind of society we have in mind.

These considerations pave the way for our second conclusion. One of the fundamental problems of education in and for a democratic society is set by the conflict of a nationalistic and a wider social aim. The earlier cosmopolitan and "humanitarian" conception suffered both from vagueness and from lack of definite organs of execution and agencies of administration. In Europe, in the Continental states particularly, the new idea of the importance of education for human welfare and progress was captured by national interests and harnessed to do a work whose social aim was definitely narrow and exclusive. The social aim of education and its national aim were identified, and the result was a marked obscuring of the meaning of a social aim.

This confusion corresponds to the existing situation of human intercourse. On the one hand, science, commerce, and art transcend national boundaries. They are largely international in quality and method. They involve interdependencies and coöperation among the peoples inhabiting different countries. At the same time, the idea of national sovereignty has never been as accentuated in politics as it is at the present time. Each nation lives in a state of suppressed hostility and incipient war with its neighbors. Each is supposed to be the supreme judge of its own interests, and it is assumed as matter of course that each has interests which are exclusively its own. To question this is to question the very idea of national sovereignty which is assumed to be basic to political practice and political science. This contradiction (for it is nothing less) between the wider sphere of associated and mutually helpful social life and the narrower sphere of exclusive and hence potentially hostile pursuits and purposes, exacts of educational theory a clearer conception of the meaning of "social" as a function and test of education than has yet been attained.

Is it possible for an educational system to be conducted by a national state and yet the full social ends of the educative process not be restricted, constrained, and corrupted? Internally, the question has to face the tendencies, due to present economic conditions, which split society into classes some of which are made merely tools for the higher culture of others. Externally, the question is concerned with the reconciliation of national loyalty, of patriotism, with superior devotion to the things which unite men in common ends, irrespective of national political boundaries. Neither phase of the problem can be worked out by merely negative means. It is not enough to see to it that education is not actively used as an instrument to make easier the exploitation of one class by another. School facilities must be secured of such amplitude and efficiency as will in fact and not simply in name discount the effects of economic inequalities, and secure to all the wards of the nation equality of equipment for their future careers. Accomplishment of this end demands not only adequate administrative provision of school facilities, and such supplementation of family resources as will enable youth to take advantage of them,

but also such modification of traditional ideals of culture, traditional subjects of study and traditional methods of teaching and discipline as will retain all the youth under educational influences until they are equipped to be masters of their own economic and social careers. The ideal may seem remote of execution, but the democratic ideal of education is a farcical yet tragic delusion except as the ideal more and more dominates our public system of education.

The same principle has application on the side of the considerations which concern the relations of one nation to another. It is not enough to teach the horrors of war and to avoid everything which would stimulate international jealousy and animosity. The emphasis must be put upon whatever binds people together in coöperative human pursuits and results, apart from geographical limitations. The secondary and provisional character of national sovereignty in respect to the fuller, freer, and more fruitful association and intercourse of all human beings with one another must be instilled as a working disposition of mind. If these applications seem to be remote from a consideration of the philosophy of education, the impression shows that the meaning of the idea of education previously developed has not been adequately grasped. This conclusion is bound up with the very idea of education as a freeing of individual capacity in a progressive growth directed to social aims. Otherwise a democratic criterion of education can only be inconsistently applied.

Summary. Since education is a social process, and there are many kinds of societies, a criterion for educational criticism and construction implies a *particular* social ideal. The two points selected by which to measure the worth of a form of social life are the extent in which the interests of a group are shared by all its members, and the fullness and freedom with which it interacts with other groups. An undesirable society, in other words, is one which internally and externally sets up barriers to free intercourse and communication of experience. A society which makes provision for participation in its good of all its members on equal terms and which secures flexible readjustment of its institutions through interaction of the different forms of associated life is in so far democratic. Such a society must have a type of education which gives individuals a personal interest in social relationships and control, and the habits of mind which secure social changes without introducing disorder.

Three typical historic philosophies of education were considered from this point of view. The Platonic was found to have an ideal formally quite similar to that stated, but which was compromised in its working out by making a class rather than an individual the social unit. The so-called individualism of the eighteenth-century enlightenment was found to involve the notion of a society as broad as humanity, of whose progress the individual was to be the organ. But it lacked any agency for securing the development of its ideal as was evidenced in its falling back upon Nature. The institutional idealistic philosophies of the nineteenth century supplied this lack by making the national state the agency, but in so doing narrowed the conception of the social aim to those who were members of the same political unit, and reintroduced the idea of the subordination of the individual to the institution.

Frederick Jackson Turner

Frederick Jackson Turner proposed the thesis that the expanding frontier explained American development as well as the inventiveness, practicality, inquisitiveness, restlessness, optimism, and individualism of the American intellect. His viewpoint had a profound influence on subsequent interpretations of the growth of American civilization.

Born in 1861 in Portage, Wisconsin, Turner received his B.A. and M.A. from the University of Wisconsin and his Ph.D. from Johns Hopkins University, where his dissertation was titled "The Character and Influence of the Indian Trade in Wisconsin." He began teaching at the University of Wisconsin when he was twenty-eight years old and stayed there until moving to Harvard in 1910. After retiring from teaching, he worked for the Huntington Library in California from 1924 until his death in 1932.

His single analytical essay has probably had more influence than any other in terms of how American historians have interpreted American development. At the Chicago World's Fair in 1893, Turner read his paper, "The Significance of the Frontier in American History," at the meeting of the American Historical Association. The paper generated much controversy and influenced theories of American development for years to come. Reading a census report of 1890, asserting that the "frontier of settlement" existed no longer and would not have a "place in the census reports" in the future, Turner recognized the end of a great historic movement. He wrote: "Up to our day American history has been in a large degree the history of the colonization of the Great West. The existence of an area of free land, its continuous recession, and the advance of American settlement westward, explain American development."

The Significance of the Frontier in American History (1893)

(excerpts)

The American frontier is sharply distinguished from the European frontier—a fortified boundary line running through dense populations. The most significant thing about the American frontier is, that it lies at the hither edge of free land. In the census reports it is treated as the margin of that settlement which has a density of two or more to the square mile. The term is an elastic one, and for our purposes does not need sharp definition. We shall consider the whole frontier belt, including the Indian country and the outer margin of the "settled area" of the census reports. This paper will make no attempt to treat the subject exhaustively; its aim is simply to call attention to the frontier as a fertile field for investigation, and to suggest some of the problems which arise in connection with it.

In the settlement of America we have to observe how European life entered the continent, and how America modified and

Isaak, *American Political Thinking*.

developed that life and reacted on Europe. Our early history is the study of European germs developing in an American environment. Too exclusive attention has been paid by institutional students to the Germanic origins, too little to the American factors. The frontier is the line of most rapid and effective Americanization. The wilderness masters the colonist. It finds him a European in dress, industries, tools, modes of travel, and thought. It takes him from the railroad car and puts him in the birch canoe. It strips off the garments of civilization and arrays him in the hunting shirt and the moccasin. It puts him in the log cabin of the Cherokee and Iroquois and runs an Indian palisade around him. Before long he has gone to planting Indian corn and plowing with a sharp stick; he shouts the war cry and takes the scalp in orthodox Indian fashion. In short, at the frontier the environment is at first too strong for the man. He must accept the conditions which it furnishes, or perish, and so he fits himself into the Indian clearings and follows the Indian trails. Little by little he transforms the wilderness, but the outcome is not the old Europe, not simply the development of Germanic germs, any more than the first phenomenon was a case of reversion to the Germanic mark. The fact is, that here is a new product that is American. At first, the frontier was the Atlantic coast. It was the frontier of Europe in a very real sense. Moving westward, the frontier became more and more American. As successive terminal moraines result from successive glaciations, so each frontier leaves its traces behind it, and when it becomes a settled area the region still partakes of the frontier characteristics. Thus the advance of the frontier has meant a steady movement away from the influence of Europe, a steady growth of independence on American lines. And to study this advance, the men who grew up under these conditions,

and the political, economic, and social results of it, is to study the really American part of our history. . . .

. . . Loria, the Italian economist, has urged the study of colonial life as an aid in understanding the stages of European development, affirming that colonial settlement is for economic science what the mountain is for geology, bringing to light primitive stratifications. "America," he says, "has the key to the historical enigma which Europe has sought for centuries in vain, and the land which has no history reveals luminously the course of universal history." There is much truth in this. The United States lies like a huge page in the history of society. Line by line as we read this continental page from west to east we find the record of social evolution. It begins with the Indian and the hunter; it goes on to tell of the disintegration of savagery by the entrance of the trader, the pathfinder of civilization; we read the annals of the pastoral stage in ranch life; the exploitation of the soil by the raising of unrotated crops of corn and wheat in sparsely settled farming communities; the intensive culture of the denser farm settlement; and finally the manufacturing organization with city and factory system. This page is familiar to the student of census statistics, but how little of it has been used by our historians. Particularly in eastern States this page is a palimpsest. What is now a manufacturing State was in an earlier decade an area of intensive farming. Earlier yet it had been a wheat area, and still earlier the "range" had attracted the cattle-herder. Thus Wisconsin, now developing manufacture, is a State with varied agricultural interests. But earlier it was given over to almost exclusive grain-raising, like North Dakota at the present time.

Each of these areas has had an influence in our economic and political history; the evolution of each into a higher stage has worked political transformations. But what constitutional historian has made any adequate attempt to interpret political facts by the light of these social areas and changes?

The Atlantic frontier was compounded of fisherman, fur-trader, miner, cattle-raiser, and farmer. Excepting the fisherman, each type of industry was on the march toward the West, impelled by an irresistible attraction. Each passed in successive waves across the continent. Stand at Cumberland Gap and watch the procession of civilization, marching single file— the buffalo following the trail to the salt springs, the Indian, the fur-trader and hunter, the cattle-raiser, the pioneer farmer—and the frontier has passed by. Stand at South Pass in the Rockies a century later and see the same procession with wider intervals between. The unequal rate of advance compels us to distinguish the frontier into the trader's frontier, the rancher's frontier, or the miner's frontier, and the farmer's frontier. When the mines and the cow pens were still near the fall line the traders' pack trains were tinkling across the Alleghanies, and the French on the Great Lakes were fortifying their posts, alarmed by the British trader's birch canoe. When the trappers sealed the Rockies the farmer was still near the mouth of the Missouri.

The Indian Trader's Frontier

Why was it that the Indian trader passed so rapidly across the continent? What effects followed from the trader's frontier? The trade was coeval with American discovery. The Norsemen, Vespuccius, Verrazani, Hudson, John Smith, all trafficked for furs. The Plymouth pilgrims settled in Indian cornfields, and their first return cargo was of beaver and lumber. The records of the various New England colonies show how steadily exploration was carried into the wilderness by this trade. What is true for New England is, as would be expected, even plainer for the rest of the colonies. All along the coast from Maine to Georgia the Indian trade opened up the river courses. Steadily the trader passed westward, utilizing the older lines of French trade. The Ohio, the Great Lakes, the Mississippi, the Missouri, and the Platte, the lines of western advance, were ascended by traders. They found the passes in the Rocky Mountains and guided Lewis and Clark,[1] Fremont, and Bidwell. The explanation of the rapidity of this advance is connected with the effects of the trader on the Indian. The trading post left the unarmed tribes at the mercy of those that had purchased fire-arms—a truth which the Iroquois Indians wrote in blood, and so the remote and unvisited tribes gave eager welcome to the trader. "The savages," wrote La Salle, "take better care of us French than of their own children; from us only can they get guns and goods." This accounts for the trader's power and the rapidity of his advance. Thus the disintegrating forces of civilization entered the wilderness. Every river valley and Indian trail became a fissure in Indian society, and so that society became honeycombed. Long before the pioneer farmer appeared on the scene, primitive Indian life had passed away. The farmers met Indians armed with guns. The trading

[1]But Lewis and Clark were the first to explore the route from the Missouri to the Columbia.

frontier, while steadily undermining Indian power by making the tribes ultimately dependent on the whites, yet, through its sale of guns, gave to the Indians increased power of resistance to the farming frontier. French colonization was dominated by its trading frontier; English colonization by its farming frontier. There was an antagonism between the two frontiers as between the two nations. Said Duquesne to the Iroquois, "Are you ignorant of the difference between the king of England and the king of France? Go see the forts that our king has established and you will see that you can still hunt under their very walls. They have been placed for your advantage in places which you frequent. The English, on the contrary, are no sooner in possession of a place than the game is driven away. The forest falls before them as they advance, and the soil is laid bare so that you can scarce find the wherewithal to erect a shelter for the night."

And yet, in spite of this opposition of the interests of the trader and the farmer, the Indian trade pioneered the way for civilization. The buffalo trail became the Indian trail, and this became the trader's "trace"; the trails widened into roads, and the roads into turnpikes, and these in turn were transformed into railroads. The same origin can be shown for the railroads of the South, the far West, and the Dominion of Canada. The trading posts reached by these trails were on the sites of Indian villages which had been placed in positions suggested by nature; and these trading posts, situated so as to command the water systems of the country, have grown into such cities as Albany, Pittsburgh, Detroit, Chicago, St. Louis, Council Bluffs, and Kansas City. Thus civilization in America has followed the arteries made by geology, pouring an ever richer tide through them, until at last the slender paths of aboriginal intercourse have been broadened and interwoven into the complex mazes of modern commercial lines; the wilderness has been interpenetrated by lines of civilization growing ever more numerous. It is like the steady growth of a complex nervous system for the originally simple, inert continent. If one would understand why we are today one nation, rather than a collection of isolated states, he must study this economic and social consolidation of the country. In this progress from savage conditions lie topics for the evolutionist.

The effect of the Indian frontier as a consolidating agent in our history is important. From the close of the seventeenth century various intercolonial congresses have been called to treat with Indians and establish common measures of defense. Particularism was strongest in colonies with no Indian frontier. This frontier stretched along the western border like a cord of union. The Indian was a common danger, demanding united action. Most celebrated of these conferences was the Albany congress of 1754, called to treat with the Six Nations, and to consider plans of union. Even a cursory reading of the plan proposed by the congress reveals the importance of the frontier. The powers of the general council and the officers were, chiefly, the determination of peace and war with the Indians, the regulation of Indian trade, the purchase of Indian lands, and the creation and government of new settlements as a security against the Indians. It is evident that the unifying tendencies of the Revolutionary period were facilitated by the previous cooperation in the regulation of the frontier. In this connection may be mentioned the importance of the frontier, from that day to this, as a military training school, keeping alive the power of resistance to aggression, and developing the stalwart and rugged qualities of the frontiersman. . . .

Salt Springs

... From the time the mountains rose between the pioneer and the seaboard, a new order of Americanism arose. The West and the East began to get out of touch of each other. The settlements from the sea to the mountains kept connection with the rear and had a certain solidarity. But the over-mountain men grew more and more independent. The East took a narrow view of American advance, and nearly lost these men. Kentucky and Tennessee history bears abundant witness to the truth of this statement. The East began to try to hedge and limit westward expansion. Though Webster could declare that there were no Alleghanies in his politics, yet in politics in general they were a very solid factor.

Land

The exploitation of the beasts took hunter and trader to the west, the exploitation of the grasses took the rancher west, and the exploitation of the virgin soil of the river valleys and prairies attracted the farmer. Good soils have been the most continuous attraction to the farmer's frontier. The land hunger of the Virginians drew them down the rivers into Carolina, in early colonial days; the search for soils took the Massachusetts men to Pennsylvania and to New York. As the eastern lands were taken up migration flowed across them to the west. Daniel Boone, the great backwoodsman, who combined the occupations of hunter, trader, cattle-raiser, farmer, and surveyor— learning, probably from the traders, of the fertility of the lands on the upper Yadkin; where the traders were wont to rest as they took their way to the Indians, left his Pennsylvania home with his father, and passed down the Great Valley road to that stream. Learning from a trader whose posts were on the Red River in Kentucky of its game and rich pastures, he pioneered the way for the farmers to that region. Thence he passed to the frontier of Missouri, where his settle-ment was long a landmark on the frontier. Here again he helped to open the way for civilization, finding salt licks, and trails, and land. His son was among the earliest trappers in the passes of the Rocky Mountains, and his party are said to have been the first to camp on the present site of Denver. His grandson, Col. A. J. Boone, of Colorado, was a power among the Indians of the Rocky Mountains, and was appointed an agent by the Government. Kit Carson's mother was a Boone. Thus this family epitomizes the backwoodsman's advance across the continent.

The farmer's advance came in a distinct series of waves. In Peck's *New Guide to the West,* published in Boston in 1837, occurs this suggestive passage:

> Generally, in all the western settlements, three classes, like the waves of the ocean, have rolled one after the other. First comes the pioneer, who depends for the subsistence of his family chiefly upon the natural growth of vegetation, called the "range," and the proceeds of hunting. His implements of agriculture are rude, chiefly of his own make, and his efforts directed

mainly to a crop of corn and a "truck patch." The last is a rude garden for growing cabbage, beans, corn for roasting ears, cucumbers, and potatoes. A log cabin, and, occasionally, a stable and corn-crib, and a field of a dozen acres, the timber girdled or "deadened," and fenced, are enough for his occupancy. It is quite immaterial whether he ever becomes the owner of the soil. He is the occupant for the time being, pays no rent, and feels as independent as the "lord of the manor." With a horse, cow, and one or two breeders of swine, he strikes into the woods with his family, and becomes the founder of a county, or perhaps state. He builds his cabin, gathers around him a few other families of similar tastes and habits, and occupies till the range is somewhat subdued, and hunting a little precarious, or, which is more frequently the case, till the neighbors crowd around, roads, bridges, and fields annoy him, and he lacks elbow room. The preemption law enables him to dispose of his cabin and cornfield to the next class of emigrants; and, to employ his own figures, he "breaks for the high timber," "clears out for the New Purchase," or migrates to Arkansas or Texas, to work the same process over.

The next class of emigrants purchase the lands, add field to field, clear out the roads, throw rough bridges over the streams, put up hewn log houses with glass windows and brick or stone chimneys, occasionally plant orchards, build mills, schoolhouses, court-houses, etc., and exhibit the picture and forms of plain, frugal, civilized life.

Another wave rolls on. The men of capital and enterprise come. The settler is ready to sell out and take the advantage of the rise in property, push farther in turn. The small village rises to a spacious town or city; substantial edifices of brick, extensive fields, orchards, gardens, colleges, and churches are seen. Broadcloths, silks, leghorns, crapes, and all the refinements, luxuries, elegancies, frivolities, and fashions are in vogue. Thus wave after wave is rolling westward; the real Eldorado is still farther on.

A portion of the two first classes remain stationary amidst the general movement, improve their habits and condition, and rise in the scale of society.

The writer has traveled much amongst the first class, the real pioneers. He has lived many years in connection with the second grade; and now the third wave is sweeping over large districts of Indiana, Illinois, and Missouri. Migration has become almost a habit in the West. Hundreds of men can be found, not over 50 years of age, who have settled for the fourth, fifth, or sixth time on a new spot. To sell out and remove only a few hundred miles makes up a portion of the variety of backwoods life and manners.

Omitting those of the pioneer farmers who move from the love of adventure, the advance of the more steady farmer is easy to understand. Obviously the immigrant was attracted by the cheap lands of the frontier, and even the native farmer felt their influence strongly. Year by year the farmers who lived on soil whose returns were diminished by unrotated crops were offered the virgin soil of the frontier at nominal prices. Their growing families demanded more lands, and these were dear. The competition of the unexhausted, cheap, and easily tilled prairie lands compelled the farmer either to go west and continue the exhaustion of the soil on a new frontier, or to adopt intensive culture. Thus the census of 1890 shows, in the Northwest, many counties in which there is an absolute or a relative decrease of population. These States have been sending farmers to advance the frontier on the plains, and have themselves begun to turn to intensive farming and to manufacture. A decade before this, Ohio had shown the same transition stage. Thus the demand for land and the love of wilderness freedom drew the frontier ever onward. . . .

The Public Domain

The public domain has been a force of profound importance in the nationalization and development of the Government. The effects of the struggle of the landed and the landless States, and of the ordinance of 1787, need no discussion. Administratively the frontier called out some of the highest and most vitalizing activities of the General Government. The purchase of Louisiana was perhaps the constitutional turning point in the history of the Republic, inasmuch as it afforded both a new area for national legislation and the occasion of the downfall of the policy of strict construction. But the purchase of Louisiana was called out by frontier needs and demands. As frontier States accrued to the Union the national power grew. In a speech on the dedication of the Calhoun monument Mr. Lamar explained: "In 1789 the States were the creators of the Federal Government; in 1861 the Federal Government was the creator of a large majority of the States."

When we consider the public domain from the point of view of the sale and disposal of the public lands we are again brought face to face with the frontier. The policy of the United States in dealing with its lands is in sharp contrast with the European system of scientific administration. Efforts to make this domain a source of revenue, and to withhold it from emigrants in order that settlement might be compact, were in vain. The jealousy and the fears of the East were powerless in the face of the demands of the frontiersmen. John Quincy Adams was obliged to confess: "My own system of administration, which was to make the national domain the inexhaustible fund for progressive and unceasing internal improvement, has failed." The reason is obvious; a system of administration was not what the West demanded; it wanted land. Adams states the situation as follows: "The slaveholders of the South have bought the cooperation of the western country by the bribes of the western lands, abandoning to the new Western States their own proportion of the public property and aiding them in the design of grasping all the lands into their own hands. Thomas H. Benton was the author of this system, which he brought forward as a substitute of the American system of Mr. Clay, and to supplant him as the leading statesman to the West. Mr. Clay, by his tariff compromise with Mr. Calhoun, abandoned his own American system. At the same time he brought forward a plan for distributing among all the States of the Union the proceeds of the sales of the public lands. His bill for that purpose passed both Houses of Congress, but was vetoed by President Jackson, who, in his annual message of December, 1832, formally recommended that all public lands should be gratuitously given away to individual adventurers and to the States in which the lands are situated."

"No subject," said Henry Clay, "which has presented itself to the present, or perhaps any preceding, Congress, is of greater magnitude than that of the public lands." When we consider the far-reaching effects of the Government's land policy upon political, economic, and social aspects of American life, we are disposed to agree with him. But this legislation was framed under frontier influences, and under the lead of Western statesmen like Benton and Jackson. Said Senator Scott of Indiana in 1841: "I consider the preemption law merely declaratory of the custom or common law of the settlers."

National Tendencies of the Frontier

It is safe to say that the legislation with regard to land, tariff, and internal improvements—the American system of the nationalizing Whig party—was conditioned on frontier ideas and needs. But it was not merely in legislative action that the frontier worked against the sectionalism of the coast. The economic and social characteristics of the frontier worked against sectionalism. The men of the frontier had closer resemblances to the Middle region than to either of the other sections. Pennsylvania had been the seed-plot of frontier emigration, and, although she passed on her settlers along the Great Valley into the west of Virginia and the Carolinas, yet the industrial society of these Southern frontiersmen was always more like that of the Middle region than like that of the tide-water portion of the South, which later came to spread its industrial type throughout the South.

The Middle region, entered by New York harbor, was an open door to all Europe. The tide-water part of the South represented typical Englishmen, modified by a warm climate and servile labor, and living in baronial fashion on great plantations; New England stood for a special English movement—Puritanism. The Middle region was less English than the other sections. It had a wide mixture of nationalities, a varied society, the mixed town and county system of local government, a varied economic life, many religious sects. In short, it was a region mediating between New England and the South, and the East and the West. It represented that composite nationality which the contemporary United States exhibits, that juxtaposition of non-English groups, occupying a valley or a little settlement, and presenting reflections of the map of Europe in their variety. It was democratic and nonsectional, if not national; "easy, tolerant, and contented";

rooted strongly in material prosperity. It was typical of the modern United States. It was least sectional, not only because it lay between North and South, but also because with no barriers to shut out its frontiers from its settled region, and with a system of connecting waterways, the Middle region mediated between East and West as well as between North and South. Thus it became the typically American region. Even the New Englander, who was shut out from the frontier by the Middle region, tarrying in New York or Pennsylvania on his westward march, lost the acuteness of his sectionalism on the way.

The spread of cotton culture into the interior of the South finally broke down the contrast between the "tide-water" region and the rest of the State, and based Southern interests on slavery. Before this process revealed its results the western portion of the South, which was akin to Pennsylvania in stock, society, and industry, showed tendencies to fall away from the faith of the fathers into internal improvement legislation and nationalism. . . .

It was this nationalizing tendency of the West that transformed the democracy of Jefferson into the national republicanism of Monroe and the democracy of Andrew Jackson. The West of the War of 1812, the West of Clay, and Benton, and Harrison, and Andrew Jackson, shut off by the Middle States and the mountains from the coast sections, had a solidarity of its own with national tendencies. On the tide of the Father of Waters, North and South met and mingled into a nation. Interstate migration went steadily on—a process of cross-fertilization of ideas and institutions. The fierce struggle of the sections over slavery on the western frontier does not diminish the truth of this statement; it proves the truth of it. Slavery was a sectional trait that would not down, but in the West it could not remain sectional. It was the greatest of frontiersmen who declared: "I believe this Government can not endure permanently half slave and half free. It will become all of one thing or all of the other." Nothing works for nationalism like intercourse within the nation. Mobility of population is death to localism, and the western frontier worked irresistibly in unsettling population. The effects reached back from the frontier and affected profoundly the Atlantic coast and even the Old World.

Growth of Democracy

But the most important effect of the frontier has been in the promotion of democracy here and in Europe. As has been indicated, the frontier is productive of individualism. Complex society is precipitated by the wilderness into a kind of primitive organization based on the family. The tendency is anti-social. It produces antipathy to control, and particularly to any direct control. The tax-gatherer is viewed as a representative of oppression. Prof. Osgood, in an able article, has pointed out that the frontier conditions prevalent in the colonies are important factors in the explanation of the American Revolution, where individual liberty was sometimes confused with absence of all effective government. The same conditions aid in explaining the difficulty of instituting a strong government in the period of the confederacy. The frontier individualism has from the beginning promoted democracy.

The frontier States that came into the Union in the first quarter of a century of its existence came in with democratic suffrage provisions, and had reactive effects of the highest importance upon the older States whose peoples were being attracted there. An extension of the franchise became essential. It was *western* New York that forced an extension of suffrage in the constitutional convention of that State in 1821; and it was *western* Virginia that compelled the tide-water region to put a more liberal suffrage provision in the constitution framed in 1830, and to give to the frontier region a more nearly proportionate representation with the tide-water aristocracy.

The rise of democracy as an effective force in the nation came in with western preponderance under Jackson and William Henry Harrison, and it meant the triumph of the frontier—with all of its good and with all of its evil elements. An interesting illustration of the tone of frontier democracy in 1830 comes from the same debates in the Virginia convention. . . . A representative from western Virginia declared:

But, sir, it is not the increase of population in the West which this gentleman ought to fear. It is the energy which the mountain breeze and western habits impart to those emigrants. They are regenerated, politically I mean, sir. They soon become *working politicans;* and the difference, sir, between a *talking* and a *working* politician is immense. The Old Dominion has long been celebrated for producing great orators; the ablest metaphysicians in policy; men that can split hairs in all abstruse questions of political economy. But at home, or when they return from Congress they have negroes to fan them asleep. But a Pennsylvania, a New York, an Ohio, or a western Virginia statesman, though far inferior in logic, metaphysics, and rhetoric to an old Virginia statesman, has this advantage, that when he returns home he takes off his coat and takes hold of the plow. This gives him bone and muscle, sir, and preserves his republican principles pure and uncontaminated.

So long as free land exists, the opportunity for a competency exists, and economic power secures political power. But the democracy born of free land, strong in selfishness and individualism, intolerant of administrative experience and education, and pressing individual liberty beyond its proper bounds, has its dangers as well as it benefits. Individualism in American has allowed a laxity in regard to governmental affairs which has rendered possible the spoils system and all the manifest evils that follow from the lack of a highly developed civic spirit. In this connection may be noted also the influence of frontier conditions in permitting lax business honor, inflated paper currency and wild-cat banking. The colonial and revolutionary frontier was the region whence emanated many of the worst forms of an evil currency. The West in the War of 1812 repeated the phenomenon on the frontier of that day, while the speculation and wild-cat banking of the period of

the Crisis of 1837 occurred on the new frontier belt of the next tier of States. Thus each one of the periods of lax financial integrity coincides with periods when a new set of frontier communities had arisen, and coincides in area with these successive frontiers, for the most part. The recent Populist agitation is a case in point. Many a State that now declines any connection with the tenets of the Populists, itself adhered to such ideas in an earlier stage of the development of the State. A primitive society can hardly be expected to show the intelligent appreciation of the complexity of business interests in a developed society. The continual recurrence of these areas of paper-money agitation is another evidence that the frontier can be isolated and studied as a factor in American history of the highest importance. . . .[2]

Missionary Activity

The most effective efforts of the East to regulate the frontier came through its educational and religious activity, exerted by interstate migration and by organized societies. Speaking in 1835, Dr. Lyman Beecher declared: "It is equally plain that the religious and political destiny of our nation is to be decided in the West," and he pointed out that the population of the West "is assembled from all the States of the Union and from all the nations of Europe, and is rushing in like the waters of the flood, demanding for its moral preservation the immediate and universal action of those institutions which discipline the mind and arm the conscience and the heart. And so various are the opinions and habits, and so recent and imperfect is the acquaintance,

and so sparse are the settlements of the West, that no homogeneous public sentiment can be formed to legislate immediately into being the requisite institutions. And yet they are all needed immediately in their utmost perfection and power. A nation is being 'born in a day.' . . . But what will become of the West if her prosperity rushes up to such a majesty of power, while those great institutions linger which are necessary to form the mind and the conscience and the heart of that vast world. It must not be permitted. . . . Let no man at the East quiet himself and dream of liberty, whatever may become of the West. . . . Her destiny is our destiny."

With the appeal to the conscience of New England, he adds appeals to her fears

---

[2]I have refrained from dwelling on the lawless characteristics of the frontier, because they are sufficiently well known. The gambler and desperado, the regulators of the Carolinas and the vigilantes of California, are types of that line of scum that the waves of advancing civilization bore before them, and of the growth of spontaneous organs of authority where legal authority was absent. . . . The humor, bravery, and rude strength, as well as the vices of the frontier in its worst aspect, have left traces on American character, language, and literature, not soon to be effaced.

lest other religious sects anticipate her own. The New England preacher and school-teacher left their mark in the West. The dread of Western emancipation from New England's political and economic control was paralled by her fears lest the West cut loose from her religion. Commenting in 1850 on reports that settlement was rapidly extending northward in Wisconsin, the editor of the Home Missionary writes: "We scarcely know whether to rejoice or mourn over this extension of our settlements. While we sympathize in whatever tends to increase the physical resources and prosperity of our country, we can not forget that with all these dispersions into remote and still remoter corners of the land the supply of the means of grace is becoming relatively less and less." Acting in accordance with such ideas, home missions were established and Western colleges were erected. As seaboard cities like Philadelphia, New York, and Baltimore strove for the mastery of Western trade, so the various denominations strove for the possession of the West. Thus an intellectual stream from New England sources fertilized the West. Other sections sent their missionaries; but the real struggle was between sects. The contest for power and the expansive tendency furnished to the various sects by the existence of a moving frontier must have had important results on the character of religious organization in the United States. The multiplication of rival churches in the little frontier towns had deep and lasting social effects. The religious aspects of the frontier make a chapter in our history which needs study.

Intellectual Traits

From the conditions of frontier life came intellectual traits of profound importance. The works of travelers along each frontier from colonial days onward describe certain common traits, and these traits have, while softening down, still persisted as survivals in the place of their origin, even when a higher social organization succeeded. The result is that to the frontier the American intellect owes its striking characteristics. That coarseness and strength combined with acuteness and inquisitiveness; that practical, inventive turn of mind, quick to find expedients; that masterful grasp of material things, lacking in the artistic but powerful to effect great ends; that restless, nervous energy, that dominant individualism, working for good and for evil, and withal that buoyancy and exuberance which comes with freedom—these are traits of the frontier, or traits called out elsewhere because of the existence of the frontier. Since the days when the fleet of Columbus sailed into the waters of the New World, America has been another name for opportunity, and the people of the United States have taken their tone from the incessant expansion which has not only been open but has even been forced upon them. He would be a rash prophet who should assert that the expansive character of American life has now entirely ceased. Movement has been its dominant fact, and, unless this training has no effect upon a people, the American energy will continually demand a wider field for its exercise. But never again will such gifts of free land offer themselves. For a moment, at the frontier, the bonds of custom are broken and unrestraint is triumphant. There is not *tabula rasa*. The stubborn American environment is there with its imperious summons to accept its conditions; the inherited ways of doing things are also there; and yet, in spite of environment, and in spite of custom, each frontier did indeed furnish a new field of opportunity, a gate of escape from the bondage of the past; and freshness, and confidence, and scorn of older society, impatience of its restraints and its ideas, and indifference to its lessons, have accompanied the frontier. What the Mediterranean Sea was to the Greeks, breaking the bond of custom, offering new experiences, calling out new institutions and activities, that, and more, the ever retreating frontier has been to the United States directly, and to the nations of Europe more remotely. And now, four centuries from the discovery of America, at the end of a hundred years of life under the Constitution, the frontier has gone, and with its going has closed the first period of American history.

Mark Twain (Samuel Clemens)

Born in 1835 in Florida, Missouri, Samuel Clemens became apprenticed to a printer in Hannibal, Missouri. He first wrote for his brother's newspaper there and later worked as a printer elsewhere. In 1857, Clemens took a river trip to New Orleans on his way to make his fortune in South America. He got sidetracked and became a Mississippi River pilot, a line of work he pursued until it ended with the Civil War. From this came the pseudonym "Mark Twain," which was the river call for a two-fathom water depth. His youth at Hannibal and experiences on the Mississippi River generated what has been called the first modern American novel, *The Adventures of Huckleberry Finn*, a masterpiece that many believe has not been surpassed in American literature. Within the novel, a raft is used as an outpost for realistic social observations on nineteenth-century life through the eyes of a boy and the words of the vernacular of the times. Some have found all the typical values of American society epitomized in this classical narrative.

Twain moved to Nevada and began a lifetime pattern of failing at get-rich schemes that landed him heavily in debt. That and grief over the deaths of his two daughters and wife led him into a state of misanthropic pessimism late in his life. As a newspaperman, Twain developed a reputation for humor as a teller of tall tales, as exemplified in "The Celebrated Jumping Frog of Calaveras County." Successful as a humorous lecturer, Twain wrote a great deal, including *The Innocents Abroad* (1869), *Roughing It* (1872), *The Gilded Age* (1873) with Charles Warner, *The Adventures of Tom Sawyer* (1876), *A Tramp Abroad* (1880), *The Prince and the Pauper* (1882), *Life on the Mississippi* (1883), *The Adventures of Huckleberry Finn* (1884), *A Connecticut Yankee at King Arthur's Court* (1889), *The Tragedy of Pudd'nhead Wilson* (1894), *Following the Equator* (1897), *What Is Man?* (1905), *Europe and Elsewhere* (1923), and *Letters from the Earth*, (1962). Twain died in 1910.

Twain's basic principle was that the individual should be able to exercise independent choice and that any attempt to impose the views of others on anyone was unjust. Asked if he was going to publish "The War Prayer" (reprinted here from *Europe and Elsewhere*), Twain responded: "No. I have told the whole truth in that, and only dead men can tell the truth in this world. It can be published after I am dead."

Perhaps his most clear-cut political statement, "The War Prayer," represents a sophisticated radical humanitarianism—a forerunner of American peace movements to follow throughout the twentieth century.

❧

The War Prayer (1905)

It was a time of great and exalting excitement. The country was up in arms, the war was on, in every breast burned the holy fire of patriotism; the drums were beating, the bands playing, the toy pistols popping, the bunched firecrackers hissing and spluttering; on every hand and far down the receding and fading spread of roofs and balconies a fluttering wilderness of flags flashed in the sun; daily the young volunteers marched down the wide avenue gay and fine in their new uniforms, the proud fathers and mothers and sisters and sweethearts cheering them with voices choked with happy emotion as they swung by; nightly the packed mass meetings listened, panting, to patriot oratory which stirred the deepest deeps of their hearts, and which they interrupted at briefest intervals with cyclones of applause, the tears running down their cheeks the while; in the churches the pastors preached devotion to flag and country, and invoked the God of Battles, beseeching His aid in our good cause in outpouring of fervid eloquence which moved every listener. It was indeed a glad and gracious time, and the half dozen rash spirits that ventured to disapprove of the war and cast a doubt upon its righteousness straightway got such a stern and angry warning that for their personal safety's sake they quickly shrank out of sight and offended no more in that way.

Sunday morning came—next day the battalions would leave for the front; the church was filled; the volunteers were there, their young faces alight with martial dreams—visions of the stern advance, the gathering momentum, the rushing charge, the flashing sabers, the flight of the foe, the tumult, the enveloping smoke, the fierce pursuit, the surrender!—them home from the war, bronzed heroes, welcomed, adored, submerged in golden seas of glory! With the volunteers sat their dear ones, proud, happy, and envied by the neighbors and friends who had no sons and brothers to send forth to the field of honor, there to win for the flag, or, failing, die the noblest of noble deaths. The service proceeded; a war chapter from the Old Testament was read; the first prayer was said; it was followed by an organ burst that shook the building, and with one impulse the house rose, with glowing eyes and beating hearts, and poured out that tremendous invocation—

> "God the all-terrible! Thou who ordainest,
> Thunder thy clarion and lightning thy sword!"

Then came the "long" prayer. None could remember the like of it for passionate pleading and moving and beautiful language. The burden of its supplication was, that an ever-merciful and benignant Father of us all would watch over our noble young soldiers, and aid, comfort, and encourage them in their patriotic work; bless them, shield them in the day of battle and the hour of peril, bear them in His mighty hand, make them strong and confident, invincible in the bloody onset; help them to crush the foe, grant to them and to their flag and country imperishable honor and glory—

An aged stranger entered and moved with slow and noiseless step up the main aisle, his eyes fixed upon the minister, his long body clothed in a robe that reached to his feet, his head bare, his white hair descending in a frothy cataract to his shoulders, his seamy face unnaturally pale, pale even to ghastliness. With all eyes following him and wondering, he made his silent way; without pausing, he ascended to the preacher's side and stood there, waiting. With shut lids the preacher, unconscious of his presence, continued his moving prayer, and at last finished it with the words, uttered in fervent appeal, "Bless our arms, grant us the victory, O Lord our God, Father and Protector of our land and flag!"

The stranger touched his arm, motioned him to step aside—which the startled minister did—and took his place. During some moments he surveyed the spellbound audience with solemn eyes, in which burned an uncanny light; then in a deep voice he said:

"I come from the Throne—bearing a message from Almighty God!" The words smote the house with a shock; if the stranger perceived it he gave no attention. "He has heard the prayer of His servant your shepherd, and will grant it if such shall be your desire after I, His messenger, shall have explained to you its import— that is to say, its full import. For it is like unto many of the prayers of men, in that it asks for more than he who utters it is aware of —except he pause and think.

"God's servant and yours has prayed his prayer. Has he paused and taken thought? Is it one prayer? No, it is two— one uttered, the other not. Both have reached the ear of Him Who heareth all supplications, the spoken and the unspoken. Ponder this—keep it in mind. If you would beseech a blessing upon yourself, beware! lest without intent you invoke a curse upon a neighbor at the same time. If you pray for the blessing of rain upon your crop which needs it, by that act you are possibly praying for a curse upon some neighbor's crop which may not need rain and can be injured by it.

"You have heard your servant's prayer—the uttered part of it. I am commissioned of God to put into words the other part of it—that part which the pastor—and also you in your hearts—fervently prayed silently. And ignorantly and unthinkingly? God grant that it was so! You heard these words: 'Grant us the victory, O Lord our God!' That is sufficient. The *whole* of the uttered prayer is compact into those pregnant words. Elaborations were not necessary. When you have prayed for victory you have prayed for many unmentioned results which follow victory—*must* follow it, cannot help but follow it. Upon the listening spirit of God the Father fell also the unspoken part of the prayer. He commandeth me to put it into words. Listen!

"O Lord our Father, our young patriots, idols of our hearts, go forth to battle— be Thou near them! With them—in spirit— we also go forth from the sweet peace of our beloved firesides to smite the foe. O Lord our God, help us to tear their soldiers to bloody shreds with our shells; help us to cover their smiling fields with the pale forms of their patriot dead; help us to drown the thunder of the guns with the shrieks of their wounded, writhing in pain; help us to lay waste their humble homes with a hurricane of fire; help us to wring the hearts of their unoffending widows with unavailing grief; help us to turn them out roofless with their little children to wander unfriended the wastes of their desolated land in rags and hunger and thirst, sports of the sun flames of summer and the icy winds of winter, broken in spirit, worn with travail, imploring Thee for the refuge of the grave and denied it—for our sakes who adore Thee, Lord, blast their hopes, blight their lives, protract their bitter pilgrimage, make heavy their steps, water their way with their tears, stain the white snow with the blood of their wounded feet! We ask it, in the spirit of love, of Him Who is the Source of Love, and Who is the ever-faithful refuge and friend of all that are sore beset and seek His aid with humble and contrite hearts. Amen."

(After a pause.) "Ye have prayed it; if ye still desire it, speak! The messenger of the Most High waits."

It was believed afterward that the man was a lunatic, because there was no sense in what he said.

Randolph Bourne

In his short life, before he died in the influenza epidemic of 1918, Randolph Bourne came to symbolize a "new youth movement." His radical essays grew beyond the liberal pragmatism of Dewey into an original critique, symbolized by his classic unfinished fragment on the state (1918). Born in 1886 in Bloomfield, New Jersey, Bourne attended public school and then worked for a company producing player-piano music. At twenty-three he went to Columbia University. He published a collection of essays, *Youth and Life,* in 1913, the year of his graduation. He traveled to Europe on a Gilder Fellowship, but returned out of concern for the growing chances of war there, and voiced his concerns in his essays.

After a brief phase under the influence of John Dewey's liberal pragmatism on educational issues, Bourne gained some reputation as a progressive writer for *The New Republic.* But with the outbreak of World War I, he soon became critical of progressives such as Herbert Croly who looked to the promise of war to strengthen a sense of national community and purpose. After "War and the Intellectuals," his essay attacking this position, was published, he became increasingly isolated, finding it difficult to publish even a book review given his views on the war.

Labeled an emerging "proletarian-aristocrat" by Van Wyck Brooks, Bourne was sensitive to art, psychology, and philosophy in his critiques of conventional assumptions of American life and politics (illustrated by his radical essays in *The Masses* and *The Seven Arts).* When he died, he was in the midst of his greatest work, *The State,* excerpted here.

The State (1918)
(excerpts)

Government is synonymous with neither State nor Nation. It is the machinery by which the nation, organized as a State, carries out its State functions. Government is a framework of the administration of laws, and the carrying out of the public force. Government is the idea of the State put into practical operation in the hands of definite, concrete, fallible men. It is the visible sign of the invisible grace. It is the word made flesh. And it has necessarily the limitations inherent in all practicality. Government is the only form in which we can envisage the State, but it is by no means identical with it. That the State is a mystical conception is something that must never be forgotten. Its glamor and its significance linger behind the framework of Government and direct its activities.

Wartime brings the ideal of the State out into very clear relief, and reveals attitudes and tendencies that were hidden. In times of peace the sense of the State flags in a republic that is not militarized. For war is essentially the health of the State. The ideal of the State is that within its territory its power and influence should be universal. As the Church is the medium for the spiritual salvation of men, so the State is thought of as the medium for his political salvation. Its idealism is a rich blood flowing to all the members of the body politic. And it is precisely in war that the urgency for union seems greatest, and the necessity for universality seems most unquestioned. The State is the organization of the herd to act offensively or defensively against another herd similarly organized. The more terrifying the occasion for defense, the closer will become the organization and the more coercive the influence upon each member of the herd. War sends the current of purpose and activity flowing down to the lowest level of the herd, and to its most remote branches. All the activities of society are linked together as fast as possible to this central purpose of making a military offensive or a military defense, and the State becomes what in peace times it has vainly struggled to become—the inexorable arbiter and determinant of men's businesses and attitudes and opinions. The slack is taken up, the cross-currents fade out, and the nation moves lumberingly and slowly, but with ever accelerated speed and

integration, towards the great end, towards that "peacefulness of being at war," of which L.P. Jacks has so unforgetably spoken.

The classes which are able to play an active and not merely a passive rôle in the organization for war get a tremendous liberation of activity and energy. Individuals are jolted out of their old routine, many of them are given new positions of responsibility, new techniques must be learnt. Wearing home ties are broken and women who would have remained attached with infantile bonds are liberated for service overseas. A vast sense of rejuvenescence pervades the significant classes, a sense of new importance in the world. Old national ideals are taken out, re-adapted to the purpose and used as universal touchstones, or molds into which all thought is poured. Every individual citizen who in peacetimes had no function to perform by which he could imagine himself an expression or living fragment of the State becomes an active amateur agent of the Government in reporting spies and disloyalists, in raising Government funds, or in propagating such measures as are considered necessary by officialdom. Minority opinion, which in times of peace, was only irritating and could not be dealt with by law unless it was conjoined with actual crime, becomes, with the outbreak of war, a case for outlawry. Criticism of the State, objections to war, lukewarm opinions concerning the necessity or the beauty of conscription, are made subject to ferocious penalties, far exceeding in severity those affixed to actual pragmatic crimes. Public opinion, as expressed in the newspapers, and the pulpits and the schools, becomes one solid block. "Loyalty," or rather war orthodoxy, becomes the sole test for all professions, techniques, occupations. Particularly is this true in the sphere of the intellectual life, There the smallest taint is held to spread over the whole soul, so that a professor of physics is *ipso facto* disqualified to teach physics or to hold honorable place in a university—the republic of learning—if he is at all unsound on the war. Even mere association with persons thus tainted is considered to disqualify a teacher. Anything pertaining to the enemy becomes taboo. His books are suppressed wherever possible, his language is forbidden. His artistic products are considered to convey in the subtlest spiritual way taints of vast poison to the soul that permits itself to enjoy them. So enemy music is suppressed, and energetic measures of opprobrium taken against those whose artistic consciences are not ready to perform such an act of self-sacrifice. The rage for loyal conformity works impartially, and often in diametric opposition to other orthodoxies and traditional conformities, or even ideals. The triumphant orthodoxy of the State is shown at its apex perhaps when Christian preachers lose their pulpits for taking [in] more or less literal terms the Sermon on the Mount, and Christian zealots are sent to prison for twenty years for distributing tracts which argue that war is unscriptural.

War is the health of the State. It automatically sets in motion throughout society those irresistible forces for uniformity, for passionate cooperation with the Government in coercing into obedience the minority groups and individuals which lack the larger herd sense. The machinery of government sets and enforces the drastic penalties, the minorities are either intimidated into silence, or brought slowly around by a subtle process of persuasion which may seem to them really to be converting them. Of course the ideal of perfect loyalty, perfect uniformity is never really attained. The classes upon whom the amateur work of coercion falls are unwearied in their zeal, but often their agitation instead of converting, merely serves to stiffen their resistance. Minorities are rendered sullen, and some intellectual opinion bitter and satiri-cal. But in general, the nation in war-time attains a uniformity of feeling, a hierachy of values culminating at the undisputed apex of the State ideal, which could not possibly be produced through any other agency than war. Other values such as artistic creation, knowledge, reason, beauty, the enhancement of life, are instantly and almost unanimously sacrificed, and the significant classes who have constituted themselves the amateur agents of the State, are engaged not only in sacrificing these values for themselves but in coercing all other persons into sacrificing them.

War—or at least modern war waged by a democratic republic against a powerful enemy—seems to achieve for a nation almost all that the most inflamed political idealist could desire. Citizens are no longer indifferent to their Government, but each cell of the body politic is brimming with life and activity. We are at last on the way to full realization of that collective community in which each individual somehow contains the virtue of the whole. In a nation at war, every citizen identifies himself with the whole, and feels immensely strengthened in that identification. The purpose and desire of the collective community live in each person who throws himself wholeheartedly into the cause of war. The impeding distinction between society and the individual is almost blotted out. At war, the individual becomes almost identical with his society. He achieves a superb self-assurance, an intuition of the rightness of all his ideas and emotions, so that in the suppression of opponents or heretics he is invincibly strong; he feels behind him all the power of the collective community. The individual as social being in war seems to have achieved almost his apotheosis. Not for any religious impulse could the American nation have been expected to show such devotion *en masse,* such sacrifice and labor. Certainly not for any secular good, such as universal education or the subjugation of

nature, would it have poured forth its treasure and its life, or would it have permitted
such stern coercive measures to be taken
against it, such as conscripting its money
and its men. But for the sake of a war of
offensive self-defense, undertaken to support a difficult cause to the slogan of
"democracy" it would reach the highest
level ever known of collective effort.

For these secular goods, connected
with the enhancement of life, the education
of man and the use of the intelligence to
realize reason and beauty in the nation's
communal living, are alien to our traditional ideal of the State. The State is intimately connected with war, for it is the
organization of the collective community
when it acts in a political manner, and to
act in a political manner towards a rival
group has meant, throughout all history—
war.

There is nothing invidious in the use
of the term, "herd," in connection with the
State. It is merely an attempt to reduce
closer to first principles the nature of this
institution in the shadow of which we all
live, move and have our being. Ethnolo-
gists are generally agreed that human society made its first appearance as the human
pack and not as a collection of individuals
or of couples. The herd is in fact the original unit, and only as it was differentiated
did personal individuality develop. All the
most primitive surviving tribes of men are
shown to live in a very complex but very
rigid social organization where opportunity
for individuation is scarcely given. These
tribes remain strictly organized herds, and
the difference between them and the modern State is one of degree of sophistication
and variety of organization, and not of kind.

Psychologists recognize the gregarious impulse as one of the strongest primitive pulls which keeps together the herds
of the different species of higher animals.
Mankind is no exception. Our pugnacious

evolutionary history has prevented the
impulse from ever dying out. This gregarious impulse is the tendency to imitate, to
conform, to coalesce together, and is most
powerful when the herd believes itself
threatened with attack. Animals crowd
together for protection, and men become
most conscious of their collectivity at the
threat of war. Consciousness of collectivity
brings confidence and a feeling of massed
strength, which in turn arouses pugnacity
and the battle is on. In civilized man, the
gregarious impulse acts not only to produce
concerted action for defense, but also to
produce identity of opinion. Since thought
is a form of behavior, the gregarious
impulse floods up into its realms and
demands that sense of uniform thought
which wartime produces so successfully.
And it is in this flooding of the conscious
life of society that gregariousness works
its havoc.

For just as in modern societies the sex-
instinct is enormously over-supplied for the
requirements of human propagation, so the
gregarious impulse is enormously over-
supplied for the work of protection which
it is called upon to perform. It would be
quite enough if we were gregarious enough
to enjoy the companionship of others, to
be able to coöperate with them, and to feel
a slight malaise at solitude. Unfortunately,
however, this impulse is not content with
these reasonable and healthful demands,
but insists that like-mindedness shall prevail everywhere, in all departments of life.
So that all human progress, all novelty, and
non-conformity, must be carried against the
resistance of this tyrannical herd-instinct
which drives the individual into obedience
and conformity with the majority. Even in
the most modern and enlightened societies
this impulse shows little sign of abating. As
it is driven by inexorable economic demand
out of the sphere of utility, it seems to
fasten itself ever more fiercely in the realm

of feeling and opinion, so that conformity comes to be a thing aggressively desired and demanded.

The gregarious impulse keeps its hold all the more virulently because when the group is in motion or is taking any positive action, this feeling of being with and supported by the collective herd very greatly feeds that will to power, the nourishment of which the individual organism so constantly demands. You feel powerful by conforming, and you feel forlorn and helpless if you are out of the crowd. While even if you do not get any access of power by thinking and feeling just as everybody else in your group does, you get at least the warm feeling of obedience, the soothing irresponsibility of protection.

Joining as it does to these very vigorous tendencies of the individual—the pleasure in power and the pleasure in obedience—this gregarious impulse becomes irresistible in society. War stimulates it to the highest possible degree, sending the influences of its mysterious herd-current with its inflations of power and obedience to the farthest reaches of the society, to every individual and little group that can possibly be affected. And it is these impulses which the State—the organization of the entire herd, the entire collectivity—is founded on and makes use of. . . .

The members of the working-classes, that portion at least which does not identify itself with the significant classes and seek to imitate it and rise to it, are notoriously less affected by the symbolism of the State, or, in other words, are less patriotic than the significant classes. For theirs is neither the power nor the glory. The State in wartime does not offer them the opportunity to regress, for, never having acquired social adulthood, they cannot lose it. If they have

been drilled and regimented, as by the industrial regime of the last century, they go out docilely enough to do battle for their State, but they are almost entirely without that filial sense and even without that herd-intellect sense which operates so powerfully among their "betters." They live habitually in an industrial serfdom, by which though nominally free, they are in practice as a class bound to a system of machine-production the implements of which they do not own, and in the distribution of whose product they have not the slightest voice, except what they can occasionally exert by a veiled intimidation which draws slightly more of the product in their direction. From such serfdom, military conscription is not so great a change. But into the military enterprise they go, not with those hurrahs of the significant classes whose instincts war so powerfully feeds, but with the same apathy with which they enter and continue in the industrial enterprise.

From this point of view, war can be called almost an upper-class sport. The novel interests and excitements it provides, the inflations of power, the satisfaction it gives to those very tenacious human impulses—gregariousness and parent-regression—endow it with all the qualities of a luxurious collective game which is felt intensely just in proportion to the sense of significant rule the person has in the class-division of his society. A country at war—particularly our own country at war—does not act as a purely homogeneous herd. The significant classes have all the herd-feeling in all its primitive intensity, but there are barriers, or at least differentials of intensity, so that this feeling does not flow freely without impediment throughout the entire nation. A modern country represents a long historical and social process of disaggregation of the herd. The nation at peace is not a group, it is a network of myriads of groups representing the cooperation and similar feeling of men on all sorts of planes and in all sorts of human interests and enterprises. In every modern industrial country, there are parallel planes of economic classes with divergent attitudes and institutions and interests—bourgeois and proletariat, with their many subdivisions according to power and function, and even their interweaving, such as those more highly skilled workers who habitually identify themselves with the owning and the significant classes and strive to raise themselves to the bourgeois level, imitating their cultural standards and manners. Then there are religious groups with a certain definite, though weakening sense of kinship, and there are the powerful ethnic groups which behave almost as cultural colonies in the New World, clinging tenaciously to language and historical tradition, though their herdishness is usually founded on cultural rather than State symbols. There are even certain vague sectional groupings. All these small sects, political parties, classes, levels, interests, may act as foci for herd-feelings. They intersect and interweave, and the same person may be a member of several different groups lying at different planes. Different occasions will set off his herd-feeling in one direction or another. In a religious crisis he will be intensely conscious of the necessity that his sect (or sub-herd) may prevail; in a political campaign, that his party shall triumph.

To the spread of herd-feeling, therefore, all these smaller herds offer resistance. To the spread of that herd-feeling which arises from the threat of war, and which would normally involve the entire nation, the only groups which make serious resistance are those, of course, which continue to identify themselves with the other nation from which they or their parents have come. In times of peace they are for all practical purposes citizens of their new country. They keep alive their ethnic traditions more as a luxury than anything. Indeed these traditions tend rapidly to die out except where they connect with some still unresolved nationalistic cause abroad, with some struggle for freedom, or some irredentism. If they are consciously opposed by a too invidious policy of Americanism, they tend to be strengthened. And in time of war, these ethnic elements which have any traditional connection with the enemy, even though most of the individuals may have little real sympathy with the enemy's cause, are naturally lukewarm to the herd-feeling of the nation which goes back to State traditions in which they have no share. But to the natives imbued with State-feeling, any such resistance or apathy is intolerable. This herd-feeling, this newly awakened consciousness of the State, demands universality. The leaders of the significant classes, who feel most intensely this State-compulsion, demand a one hundred per cent. Americanism, among one hundred per cent of the population. The State is a jealous God and will brook no rivals. Its sovereignty must pervade every one, and all feeling must be run into the stereotyped forms of romantic patriotic militarism which is the traditional expression of the State herd-feeling. . . .

. . . The punishment for opinion has been far more ferocious and unintermittent than the punishment of pragmatic crime. Unimpeachable Anglo-Saxon Americans who were freer of pacifist or socialist utterance than the State-obsessed ruling public opinion, received heavier penalties and even greater opprobrium, in many instances, than the definitely hostile German plotter. A public opinion which, almost without protest, accepts as just, adequate, beautiful, deserved and in fitting harmony with ideals of liberty and freedom of speech, a sentence of twenty years in prison for mere utterances, no matter what they may be, shows itself to be suffering from a kind of social derangement of values, a sort of social neurosis, that deserves analysis and comprehension.

On our entrance into the war, there were many persons who predicted exactly this derangement of values, who feared lest democracy suffer more at home from an America at war than could be gained for democracy abroad. That fear has been amply justified. The question whether the American nation would act like an enlightened democracy going to war for the sake of high ideals, or like a State-obsessed herd, has been decisively answered. The record is written and cannot be erased. History will decide whether the terrorization of opinion, and the regimentation of life was justified under the most idealistic of democratic administrations. It will see that when the American nation had ostensibly a chance to conduct a gallant war, with scrupulous regard to the safety of democratic values at home, it chose rather to adopt all the most obnoxious and coercive techniques of the enemy and of the other countries at war, and to rival in intimidation and ferocity of punishment the worst governmental systems of the age. For its former unconsciousness and disrespect of the State ideal, the nation apparently paid the penalty in a violent swing to the other extreme. It acted so exactly like a herd in its irrational coercion of minorities that there is no artificiality in interpreting the progress of the war in terms of the herd psychology. It unwittingly brought out into the strongest relief the true characteristics of the State and its intimate alliance with war. It provided for the enemies of war and the critics of the State the most telling arguments possible. The new passion for the State ideal unwittingly set in motion and encouraged forces that threaten very materially to reform the State. It has shown those who are really determined to end war that the problem is not the mere simple one of finishing a war that will end war. . . .

Andrew Carnegie

Born in Scotland, Andrew Carnegie (1835–1909) came to the United States with his family as a boy and became one of the leading businessmen and philanthropists of his time. He was a free thinker who believed it immoral for the wealthy to die rich. His climb from poverty to wealth could have been a Horatio Alger rags-to-riches novel: With only a grammar school education, he worked as a bobbin boy in a cotton mill, then as a telegraph messenger boy for the Pennsylvania Railroad, where he quickly worked his way up. Eventually he founded his own company, the Keystone Bridge Company.

Investing in the Bessemer steel process and surviving the Panic of 1893, Carnegie came to possess the most successful steel company in the United States. A few years after the violent Homestead Steel Strike of 1894, Carnegie sold out. All of his energy then went into philanthropy and writing, and he became renowned for his generous gifts to educational institutions and charities. The *North American Review* published his essay "Wealth" in 1889. The piece was later known as "Gospel of Wealth" (printed here). In it Carnegie defends the unequal accumulation of wealth and argues for the elimination of inheritance and for the obligation of the wealthy to give to social causes.

Gospel of Wealth (1889)
(excerpts)

The problem of our age is the proper administration of wealth, so that the ties of brotherhood may still bind together the rich and poor in harmonious relationship. The conditions of human life have not only been changed, but revolutionized, within the past few hundred years. In former days there was little difference between the dwelling, dress, food, and environment of the chief and those of his retainers. The Indians are to-day where civilized man then was. When visiting the Sioux, I was led to the wigwam of the chief. It was just like the others in external appearance, and even within the difference was trifling between it and those of the poorest of his braves. The contrast between the palace of the millionaire and the cottage of the laborer with us to-day measures the change which has come with civilization.

This change, however, is not to be deplored, but welcomed as highly beneficial. It is well, nay, essential for the progress of the race, that the houses of some should be homes for all that is highest and best in literature and the arts, and for all the refinements of civilization, rather than that none should be so. Much better this great irregularity than universal squalor. Without wealth there can be no Maecenas. The "good old times" were not good old times. Neither master nor servant was as well situated then as to-day. A relapse to old conditions would be disastrous to both—not the least so to him who serves—and would sweep away civilization with it.

But whether the change be for good or ill, it is upon us, beyond our power to alter, and therefore to be accepted and made the best of. It is a waste of time to criticise the inevitable.

It is easy to see how the change has come. One illustration will serve for almost every phase of the cause. In the manufacture of products we have the whole story. It applies to all combinations of human industry, as stimulated and enlarged by the inventions of this scientific age. Formerly articles were manufactured at the domestic hearth or in small shops which formed part of the household. The master and his apprentices worked side by side, the latter living with the master, and therefore subject to the same conditions. When these apprentices rose to be masters, there was little or no change in their mode of life, and they, in turn, educated in the same routine succeeding apprentices. There was, substantially, social equality, and even political equality, for those engaged in industrial pursuits had then little or no political voice in the State.

But the inevitable result of such a mode of manufacture was crude articles at high prices. To-day the world obtains commodities of excellent quality at prices which even the generation preceding this would have deemed incredible. In the commercial world similar causes have produced similar results, and the race is benefited thereby. The poor enjoy what the rich could not before afford. What were the luxuries have become the necessaries of life. The laborer has now more comforts than the farmer had a few generations ago. The farmer has more luxuries than the landlord had, and is more richly clad and better housed. The landlord has books and pictures rarer, and appointments more artistic, than the King could then obtain.

The price we pay for this salutary change is, no doubt, great. We assemble thousands of operatives in the factory, in the mine, and in the counting-house, of whom the employer can know little or nothing, and to whom the employer is little better than a myth. All intercourse between them is at an end. Rigid Castes are formed, and, as usual, mutual ignorance breeds mutual distrust. Each Caste is without sympathy for the other, and ready to credit anything disparaging in regard to it. Under the law of competition, the employer of thousands is forced into the strictest economies, among which the rates paid to labor figure prominently, and often there is friction between the employer and the employed, between capital and labor, between rich and poor. Human society loses homogeneity.

The price which society pays for the law of competition, like the price it pays for cheap comforts and luxuries, is also great; but the advantages of this law are also greater still, for it is to this law that we owe our wonderful material development, which brings improved conditions in its train. But, whether the law be benign or not, we must say of it, as we say of the change in the conditions of men to which we have referred: It is here; we cannot evade it; no substitutes for it have been found; and while the law may be sometimes hard for the individual, it is best for the race, because it insures the survival of the fittest in every department. We accept and welcome, therefore, as conditions to which we must accommodate ourselves, great inequality of environment, the concentration of business, industrial and commercial, in the hands of a few, and the law of competition between these, as being not only beneficial, but essential for the future progress of the race. Having accepted these, it follows that there must be great scope for the exercise of special ability in the merchant and in the manufacturer who has to conduct affairs upon a great scale. That this talent for organization and management is rare among men is proved by the fact that it invariably secures for its possessor enormous rewards, no matter where or under what laws or conditions. The experienced in affairs always rate the MAN whose services can be obtained as a partner as not only the first consideration, but such as to render the question of his capital scarcely worth considering, for such men soon create capital; while, without the special talent required, capital soon takes wings. Such men become interested in firms or corporations using millions; and estimating only simple interest to be made upon the capital invested, it is inevitable that their income must exceed their expenditures, and that they must accumulate wealth. Nor is there any middle ground which such men can occupy, because the great manufacturing or commercial concern which does not earn at least interest upon its capital soon becomes bankrupt. It must either go forward or fall behind: to stand still is impossible. It is a condition essential for its successful operation that it should be thus far profitable, and even that, in addition to interest on capital, it should make profit. It is a law, as certain as any of the others named, that men possessed of this peculiar talent for affairs, under the free play of economic forces, must, of necessity, soon be in receipt of more revenue than can be judiciously expended upon themselves; and this law is as beneficial for the race as the others.

Objections to the foundations upon which society is based are not in order, because the condition of the race is better with these than it has been with any others which have been tried. Of the effect of any new substitutes proposed we cannot be sure. The Socialist or Anarchist who seeks to overturn present conditions is to be regarded as attacking the foundation upon which civilization itself rests, for civilization took its start from the day that the capable, industrious workman said to his incompetent and lazy fellow, "If thou dost not sow, thou shalt not reap," and thus ended primitive Communism by separating the drones from the bees. One who studies this subject will soon be brought face to face with the conclusion that upon the sacredness of property civilization itself depends—the right of the laborer to his hundred dollars in the savings bank, and equally the legal right of the millionaire to his millions. To those who propose to substitute Communism for this intense Individualism the answer, therefore, is: The race has tried that. All progress from that barbarous day to the present time has resulted from its displacement. Not evil, but good, has come to the race from the accumulation of wealth by those who have the ability and energy that produce it. . . . We might as well urge the destruction of the highest existing type of man because he failed to reach our ideal as to favor the destruction of Individualism, Private Property, the Law of Accumulation of Wealth, and the Law of Competition; for these are the highest results of human experience, the soil in which society so far has produced the best fruit. Unequally or unjustly, perhaps, as these laws sometimes operate, and imperfect as they appear to the Idealist, they are, nevertheless, like the highest type of man, the best and most valuable of all that humanity has yet accomplished.

We start, then, with a condition of affairs under which the best interests of the race are promoted, but which inevitably gives wealth to the few. Thus far, accepting conditions as they exist, the situation can be surveyed and pronounced good. The question then arises,—and, if the foregoing be correct, it is the only question with which we have to deal,—What is the proper mode of administering wealth after the laws upon which civilization is founded have thrown it into the hands of the few? And it is of this great question that I believe I offer the true solution. It will be understood that *fortunes* are here spoken of, not moderate sums saved by many years of effort, the returns from which are required for the comfortable maintenance and education of families. This is not *wealth* but only *competence,* which it should be the aim of all to acquire.

There are but three modes in which surplus wealth can be disposed of. It can be left to the families of the decedents; or it can be bequeathed for public purposes; or, finally, it can be administered during their lives by its possessors. Under the first and second modes most of the wealth of the world that has reached the few has hitherto been applied. Let us in turn consider each of these modes. The first is the most injudicious. In monarchical countries, the estates and the greatest portion of the wealth are left to the first son, that the vanity of the parent may be gratified by the thought that his name and title are to descend to succeeding generations unimpaired. The condition of this class in Europe to-day teaches the futility of such hopes or ambitions. The successors have become impoverished through their follies or from the fall in the value of land. . . .

Why should men leave great fortunes to their children? If this is done from affection, is it not misguided affection? Observation teaches that, generally speaking, it is not well for the children that they should be so burdened. Neither is it well for the state. Beyond providing for the wife and daughters moderate sources of income, and very moderate allowances indeed, if any, for the sons, men may well hesitate, for it is no longer questionable that great sums bequeathed oftener work more for the injury than for the good of the recipients. Wise men will soon conclude that, for the best interests of the members of their families and of the state, such bequests are an improper use of their means.

It is not suggested that men who have failed to educate their sons to earn a liveli-

hood shall cast them adrift in poverty. If any man has seen fit to rear his sons with a view to their living idle lives, or, what is highly commendable, has instilled in them the sentiment that they are in a position to labor for public ends without reference to pecuniary considerations, then, of course, the duty of the parent is to see that such are provided for *in moderation.* There are instances of millionaires' sons unspoiled by wealth, who, being rich, still perform great services in the community. Such are the very salt of the earth, as valuable as, unfortunately, they are rare; still it is not the exception, but the rule, that men must regard, and, looking at the usual result of enormous sums conferred upon legatees, the thoughtful man must shortly say, "I would as soon leave to my son a curse as the almighty dollar," and admit to himself that it is not the welfare of the children, but family pride, which inspires these enormous legacies.

The growing disposition to tax more and more heavily large estates left at death is a cheering indication of the growth of a salutary change in public opinion. The State of Pennsylvania now takes—subject to some exceptions—one-tenth of the property left by its citizens. The budget presented in the British Parliament the other day proposes to increase the death-duties; and, most significant of all, the new tax is to be a graduated one. Of all forms of taxation, this seems the wisest. Men who continue hoarding great sums all their lives, the proper use of which for public ends would work good to the community, should be made to feel that the community, in the form of the state, cannot thus be deprived of its proper share. By taxing estates heavily at death the state marks its condemnation of the selfish millionaire's unworthy life.

It is desirable that nations should go much further in this direction. Indeed, it is difficult to set bounds to the share of a rich man's estate which should go at his death to the public through the agency of the state, and by all means such taxes should be graduated, beginning at nothing upon moderate sums to dependents and increasing rapidly as the amounts swell, until of the millionaire's hoard, as of Shylock's, at least

> —The other half
> Comes to the privy coffer of the
> state.

This policy would work powerfully to induce the rich man to attend to the administration of wealth during his life, which is the end that society should always have in view, as being that by far most fruitful for the people. Nor need it be feared that this policy would sap the root of enterprise and tender men less anxious to accumulate, for to the class whose ambition it is to leave great fortunes and be talked about after their death, it will attract even more attention, and, indeed, be a somewhat nobler ambition to have enormous sums paid over to the state from their fortunes.

There remains, then, only one mode of using great fortunes: but in this we have the true antidote for the temporary unequal distribution of wealth, the reconciliation of the rich and the poor—a reign of harmony—another ideal, differing, indeed, from that of the Communist in requiring only the further evolution of existing conditions, not the total overthrow of our civilization. It is founded upon the present most intense individualism, and the race is prepared to put it in practice by degrees whenever it pleases. Under its sway we shall have an ideal state, in which the surplus wealth of the few will become, in the best sense, the property of the many, because administered for the common good, and this wealth, passing through the hands of the few, can be made a much more potent force for the elevation of our race than if it had been distributed in small sums to the people themselves. Even the poorest can

be made to see this, and to agree that great sums gathered by some of their fellow-citizens and spent for public purposes, from which the masses reap the principal benefit, are more valuable to them than if scattered among them through the course of many years in trifling amounts.

If we consider what results flow from the Cooper Institute, for instance, to the best portion of the race in New York not possessed of means, and compare these with those which would have arisen for the good of the masses from an equal sum distributed by Mr. Cooper in his lifetime in the form of wages, which is the highest form of distribution, being for work done and not for charity, we can form some estimate of the possibilities for the improvement of the race which lie embedded in the present law of the accumulation of wealth. Much of this sum, if distributed in small quantities among the people, would have been wasted in the indulgence of appetite, some of it in excess, and it may be doubted whether even the part put to the best use, that of adding to the comforts of the home, would have yielded results for the race, as a race, at all comparable to those which are flowing and are to flow from the Cooper Institute from generation to generation. Let the advocate of violent or radical change ponder well this thought.

We might even go so far as to take another instance, that of Mr. Tilden's bequest of five millions of dollars for a free library in the city of New York, but in referring to this one cannot help saying involuntarily. How much better if Mr. Tilden had devoted the last years of his own life to the proper administration of this immense sum; in which case neither legal contest nor any other cause of delay could have interfered with his aims. But let us assume that Mr. Tilden's millions finally become the means of giving to this city a noble public library, where the treasures of the world contained in books will be open to all forever, without money and without price. Considering the good of that part of the race which congregates in and around Manhattan Island, would its permanent benefit have been better promoted had these millions been allowed to circulate in small sums through the hands of the masses? Even the most strenuous advocate of Communism must entertain a doubt upon this subject. Most of those who think will probably entertain no doubt whatever. . . .

This, then, is held to be the duty of the man of Wealth: First, to set an example of modest, unostentatious living, shunning display or extravagance; to provide moderately for the legitimate wants of those dependent upon him; and after doing so to consider all surplus revenues which come to him simply as trust funds, which he is called upon to administer, and strictly bound as a matter of duty to administer in the manner which, in his judgment, is best calculated to produce the most beneficial results for the community—the man of wealth thus becoming the mere agent and trustee for his poorer brethren, bringing to their service his superior wisdom, experience, and ability to administer, doing for them better than they would or could do for themselves. . . .

The best uses to which surplus wealth can be put have already been indicated. Those who would administer wisely must, indeed, be wise, for one of the serious obstacles to the improvement of our race is indiscriminate charity. It were better for mankind that the millions of the rich were thrown into the sea than to spend as to encourage the slothful, the drunken, the unworthy. Of every thousand dollars spent in so called charity to-day, it is probable that $950 is unwisely spent; so spent, indeed, as to produce the very evils which it proposes to mitigate or cure. A well-known writer of philosophic books admitted the other day that he had given a quarter of a dollar to a man who approached him as he was coming to visit the house of his

friend. He knew nothing of the habits of this beggar; knew not the use that would be made of this money, although he had every reason to suspect that it would be spent improperly. This man professed to be a disciple of Herbert Spencer; yet the quarter-dollar given that night will probably work more injury than all the money which its thoughtless donor will ever be able to give in true charity will do good. He only gratified his own feelings, saved himself from annoyance—and this was probably one of the most selfish and very worst actions of his life, for in all respects he is most worthy.

In bestowing charity, the main consideration should be to help those who will help themselves; to provide part of the means by which those who desire to improve may do so; to give those who desire to rise the aid by which they may rise; to assist, but rarely or never to do all. Neither the individual nor the race is improved by alms-giving. Those worthy of assistance, except in rare cases, seldom require assistance. The really valuable men of the race never do, except in cases of accident or sudden change. Every one has, of course, cases of individuals brought to his own knowledge where temporary assistance can do genuine good, and these he will not overlook. But the amount which can be wisely given by the individual for individuals is necessarily limited by his lack of knowledge of the circumstances connected with each. He is the only true reformer who is as careful and as anxious not to aid the unworthy as he is to aid the worthy, and, perhaps, even more so, for in alms-giving more injury is probably done by rewarding vice than by relieving virtue. . . .

Thus is the problem of Rich and Poor to be solved. The laws of accumulation will be left free; the laws of distribution free. Individualism will continue, but the millionaire will be but a trustee for the poor; intrusted for a season with a great part of the increased wealth of the community, but administering it for the community far better than it could or would have done for itself. The best minds will thus have reached a stage in the development of the race in which it is clearly seen that there is no mode of disposing of surplus wealth creditable to thoughtful and earnest men into whose hands it flows save by using it year by year for the general good. This day already dawns. But a little while, and although, without incurring the pity of their fellows, men may die sharers in great business enterprises from which their capital cannot be or has not been withdrawn, and is left chiefly at death for public uses, yet the man who dies leaving behind him millions of available wealth which was his to administer during life, will pass away "unwept, unhonored, and unsung," no matter to what uses he leaves the dross which he cannot take with him. Of such as these the public verdict will then be: "The man who dies thus rich dies disgraced."

Such, in my opinion, is the true Gospel concerning Wealth, obedience to which is destined some day to solve the problem of the Rich and the Poor, and to bring "Peace on earth, among men Good-Will."

Lester Ward

Lester Ward represented one of the major trends in sociology in the nineteenth century. He countered William Graham Sumner's philosophy of Social Darwinism by arguing that the state must transcend classical liberalism to protect the weak and the poor from the plutocracy of the rich that had come to dominate the American political system in the industrial era.

Born in 1841 in Joliet, Illinois, Ward was largely self-taught and ultimately earned degrees in medicine and law. From 1881 to 1906, Ward worked as a geologist and paleontologist for the government. He then became a professor of sociology at Brown University, where he developed a theory of "telesis" whereby human beings could use education and intellectual development to direct social evolution for the sake of planned progress. His books include: *Dynamic Sociology* (1883), *Psychic Factors of Civilization* (1893), *Pure Sociology* (1903), and *Glimpses of the Cosmos* (1913–18; in six volumes). In the following article, "Plutocracy and Paternalism" (1895), Ward argues that although "nothing is more obvious than the inability of capital or private enterprise to take care of itself unaided by the state," the state must, for the sake of social justice, extend its paternalism to those who are poor.

Plutocracy and Paternalism (1895)
(excerpts)

To judge from the tone of the popular press, the country would seem to be between the devil of state interference and the deep sea of gold. The two epithets, "plutocracy" and "paternalism," so freely applied, are intended to characterize the worst tendencies of the times in these two opposite directions, and are calculated to engender the bitterest feelings in the public mind. If such a thing were possible, it would certainly be useful, standing aloof from the contest, to make a cool, unbiased analysis of the true meaning of these terms in their relation to the existing state of affairs. . . .

Justly or unjustly, society has made wealth a measure of worth. It is easy on general principles to prove that it is not such a measure. Every one is personally cognizant of numerous cases to the contrary. All will admit that, taken in the abstract, the principle is unsound, and yet all act upon it. Not rationally, not perhaps consciously, but still they do it. It is "human nature" to respect those who have, and to care little for those who have not. There is a sort of feeling that if one is destitute there must be a reason for it. It is inevitably ascribed to some personal deficit. In a word, absence of means is, in one form or another, made to stand for absence of merit. Its cause is looked for in character. This is most clearly seen in the marked contrast between the indisposition to help the unsuccessful, and the willingness to help the successful. Aside from the prospect of a *quid pro quo,* no one wants to waste time, energy, or money on what is worthless,—and possession is the primary test of worth. . . .

Thus it comes about that wealth, in the existing state of society, is a tremendous power. It gives not only ease, plenty, luxury, but, what is infinitely more, the respect of all and the envy of the less favored. It gives, in a word, superiority; and the strongest craving of man's nature is, in one way or another, to be set over his fellows. When all this is considered, the futility of the proposal of certain reformers to eradicate the passion for proprietary acquisition becomes apparent. It may be assumed that this passion will continue for an indefinite period to be the ruling element of the industrial state. That it has done and is still doing incalculable service to society few will deny. That it may continue to be useful to the end of our present industrial era will probably be admitted by all but a small class.

If the accumulation of wealth, even for the benefit of individuals, were all that is involved in the term "plutocracy," the indictment would not be serious. If the governing power implied in the last component of the word were nothing more than the normal influence that wealth exerts, no great injury to society could accrue. Even the amassing of colossal fortunes is not an evil in itself, since the very activity which it requires stimulates industry and benefits a large number. There is, it is true, a danger—in the transmission of such fortunes to inactive and non-productive heirs—of creating a non-industrial class in perpetuity; but this could be remedied, without hardship to any worthy person, by a wise limitation of inheritance.

So much for plutocracy. Let us now turn to the other pole of public opinion and inquire into the meaning of "paternalism." Literally, of course, paternalism in government would be restricted to cases in which the governing power is vested in a single person, who may be regarded as well-disposed and seeking to rule his subjects for their own good, as a father governs his children. But a ruling family, or even a large ruling class, may be supposed to govern from similar motives. In either case the governed are not supposed to have any voice in the matter, but are cared for like children by the assumed wisdom of their rulers. How far from true paternalism is anything that exists in this or any other civilized country to-day may therefore be readily seen. No one will claim that there is any danger, in a representative government with universal suffrage, of any such state being brought about. This shows at the outset that the term is not used in its original and correct sense, but is merely borrowed and applied as a stigma to certain tendencies in republican governments which the users of it do not approve. What are these tendencies? In general it may be said that they are tendencies toward the assumption by the state of functions that are now entrusted to private enterprise.

On the one hand it is logically argued that the indefinite extension of such powers would eventuate in the most extreme socialistic system,—the conduct of all business by the state. On the other hand it is shown with equal logic that the entire relinquishment of the functions which the state has already assumed would be the abolition of government itself. The extremists of one party would land us in socialism; those of the other, in anarchy. But on one side it is said by the more moderate that the true function of government is the protection of society; to which it is replied by the other that such extension of governmental powers is in the interest of protection, viz., protection against the undue rapacity of private enterprise. Here, as almost everywhere else in the realm of politics, it is a question of quantity and not of quality. It is not a difference in principle, but in policy. It is the degree to which the fundamental principle of all government is to be carried out.

If we look for precedents and historical examples we find great diversity. If we take the question of government telegraphy we find that the United States is almost the only country in the civilized world that has not adopted it, while the reports from other countries are practically unanimous in its favor. That such a movement should be called paternalism is therefore quite gratuitous, and must spring from either pecuniary interest or unenlightened prejudice. From this on, up to the question of abolishing the private ownership of land, there is a multitude of problems presenting all shades of difference in the degree to which

the principle of state action is to be applied in their solution. They need to be fearlessly investigated, coolly considered, and wisely decided in the true interests of the public. It was not the purpose of this article to discuss any of these questions, but simply to mention them in illustration of the popular use of the term "paternalism." It is clear that that term is employed solely to excite prejudice against the extension of the functions of the state, just as the term "plutocracy" is used to arouse antagonism to the wealthy classes. The words have in these senses no natural meaning, and, with intelligent persons, should have no argumentative weight.

Are there, then, no dangerous or deleterious tendencies in modern society? There certainly are such, and they may be said to be in the direction of both plutocracy and paternalism, giving to these terms not a literal, but a real or scientific meaning, as denoting respectively the too great power of wealth, and the too great solicitude for and fostering of certain interests on the part of government.

The first law of economics is that every one may be depended upon at all times to seek his greatest gain. It is both natural and right that the individual should be ever seeking to acquire for himself and his; and this rather irrespective of the rest of the world. It was so in the olden time, when physical strength was almost the only force. It is so to-day, when business shrewdness is practically supreme. Government was instituted to protect the weak from the strong in this universal struggle to possess; or, what is the same thing, to protect society at large. Originally it was occupied solely with abuses caused by brute force. It is still, so far as this primary function of enforcing justice is concerned, practically limited to this class of abuses, relatively trifling as they are. Crime still means this, as it did in the days of King Arthur, and as it does to-day in barbaric countries. Any advantage gained by force is promptly met by the law; but advantage gained by cunning, by superior knowledge,—if it be only of the technicalities of the law,—is not a crime, though its spirit be as bad as that of highway robbery and its consequences a thousand times worse.

From this point of view, then, modern society is suffering from the very opposite of paternalism,—from undergovernment, from the failure of government to keep pace with the change which civilization has wrought in substituting intellectual for physical qualities as the workers of injustice. Government to-day is powerless to perform its primary and original function of protecting society. There was a time when brigandage stalked abroad throughout Europe and no one was safe in life or property. This was due to lack of adequate government. Man's nature has not changed, but brigandage has succumbed to the strong arm of the law. Human rapacity now works in subtler ways. Plutocracy is the modern brigandage and can be dislodged only by the same power,—the power of the state. All the evils of society are the result of the free flow of natural propensities. The purpose of government is, as far as may be, to prevent this from causing injustice. The physical passions of men are natural and healthy, but they cannot be allowed to go unbridled. Government was established, not to lessen or even to alter them. Exactly the same is needed to be done with the higher acquisitive faculty. It need not be condemned; it cannot be suppressed: but it can and should be directed into harmless ways and restricted to useful purposes. Properly viewed, too, this is to secure its maximum exercise and greatest freedom, for unrestrained license soon leads to conflict, chokes its own free operation, and puts an end to its activity. The true function of government is not to fetter but to liberate the forces of society, not to diminish but to increase their effectiveness. Unbridled

competition destroys itself. The only competition that endures is that which goes on under judicious regulations.

If, then, the danger of plutocracy is so largely due to insufficient government, where is the tendency to paternalism in the sense of too much government? This opens up the last and most important aspect of the subject. If there were no influences at work in society but those of unaided nature; if we had a pure physiocracy or government of nature, such as prevails among wild animals, and the weak were thereby sacrificed that the strong might survive to beget the strong, and thus elevate the race along the lines of evolution,—however great the hardship, we might resign ourselves to it as part of the great cosmic scheme. But unfortunately this is not the case. Without stopping to show that, from the standpoint of a civilized society, the qualities which best fit men to gain advantage over their fellows are the ones least useful to society at large, it will be sufficient for the present purpose to point out that in the actual state of society it is not even those who, from this biological point of view, are the fittest, that become in fact the recipients of the greatest favors at the hands of society. This is due to the creation, by society itself, of artificial conditions that destroy the balance of forces and completely nullify all the beneficial effects that are secured by the operation of the natural law on the lower plane. Indeed, the effect is reversed, and instead of developing strength, either physical or mental, through activity incident to emulation, it tends to parasitic degeneracy through the pampered idleness of the favored classes.

What, in the last analysis, are these social conditions? They are at bottom integral parts of government. They are embodied in law. Largely they consist of statute law. Where this is wanting they rest on judicial decisions, often immemorial, and belonging to the *lex non scripta*. In a word, they constitute the great system of jurisprudence relating to property and business, gradually built up through the ages to make men secure in their possessions and safe in their business transactions, but which in our day, owing to entirely changed industrial conditions, has become the means of throwing unlimited opportunities in the way of some and of barring out the rest from all opportunities. This system of artificial props, bolsterings, and scaffoldings has grown so perfect as to make exertion needless for the protected class and hopeless for the neglected mass. . . .

And thus we have the remarkable fact, so persistently overlooked in all the discussions of current question, that government, which fails to protect the weak, is devoting all its energies to protecting the strong. It legalizes and promotes trusts and combinations; subsidizes corporations, and then absolves them from their obligations; sustains stockwatering schemes and all forms of speculation; grants without compensation the most valuable franchises, often in perpetuity; and in innumerable ways creates, defends, and protects a vast array of purely parasitic enterprises, calculated directly to foster the worst forms of municipal corruption. The proofs of each one of these counts lie about us on every hand. Only those who are blinded by interest or prejudice can fail to see them.

There is no greater danger to civilization than the threatened absorption by a few individuals of all the natural resources of the earth, so that they can literally extort tribute from the rest of mankind. If half a dozen persons could get possession of all the breadstuffs of a country, it would justify a revolution. Fortunately, from the nature of this product, this is impossible, although long strides in that direction have from time to time been taken. But it is otherwise with some other products which, if less indispensable, are still among the modern necessities of life. All the petroleum of this

country is owned by a single trust. If men could not live without it there is no telling how high the price would be raised. Nothing limits it but the question of how much the public will pay rather than do without. That indispensable product, coal, has well-nigh reached the same stage through the several railroad combinations that now control it. That which costs sixty cents to mine, and as much more to transport, cannot be obtained by the consumer for less than five or six dollars. Does it speak well for the common sense of a great people that they should continue to submit to such things? There seems to be no remedy except in the power of the nation. . . .

The very possession of wealth is only made possible by government. The safe conduct of all business depends upon the certain protection of law. The most powerful business combinations take place under legal forms. Even dishonest and swindling schemes, so long as they violate no penal statute, are protected by law. Speculation in the necessaries of life is legitimate business, and is upheld by the officers of the law though it result in famine; and even then bread riots are put down by the armed force of the state. Thus has society become the victim of its own system, against the natural effects of which it is powerless to protect itself. It has devised the best possible scheme for satisfying the rapacity of human nature.

And now, mark: The charge of paternalism is chiefly made by the class that enjoys the largest share of government protection. Those who denounce state interference are the ones who most frequently and successfully invoke it. The cry of *laissez-faire* mainly goes up from the ones who, if really "let alone," would instantly lose their wealth-absorbing power. . . .

Nothing is more obvious to-day than the signal inability of capital and private enterprise to take care of themselves unaided by the state; and while they are incessantly denouncing "paternalism,"—by which they mean the claim of the defenceless laborer and artisan to a share in this lavish state protection,—they are all the while besieging legislatures for relief from their own incompetency, and "pleading the baby act" through a trained body of lawyers and lobbyists. The dispensing of national pap to this class should rather be called "maternalism," to which a square, open, and dignified paternalism would be infinitely preferable.

Still all these things must be regarded as perfectly natural, that is, inherent in the nature of man, and not as peculiar to any class. Therefore personalities and vituperation are entirely out of place. It is simply a question of whether they are going to be permitted to go on. The fault is altogether with the system. Nor should any one object to state protection of business interests. Even monopoly may be defended against aggressive competition on the ground of economy. The protection of the strong may not be too great, but there should be at the same time protection of the weak against the protected strong. It is not the purpose of this article to point out remedies, but tendencies, and it seems clear that right here are to be located the two greatest dangers to modern society. Here lies the only plutocracy, and here the only paternalism. The two are really one, and are embodied in the joint fact of state-protected monopoly. . . .

Thorstein Veblen

Born in 1857 on a farm in Wisconsin, a son of Norwegian immigrants, Thorstein Veblen became a radical social critic and profound American economist with a biting wit and great disdain for the capitalist business system and American social norms. Alienated from society to the point of living as a hermit, his unconventional private life forced him to move from university to university. Veblen was a radical with such a detached, anthropological stance and ironic style that it was difficult to tell whether he was conservative, socialist or nihilist. He was an enigma symbolizing American individualism gone to the extreme. Much of Veblen's life was spent loafing and reading; the rest was spent in writing and indifferent teaching.

Veblen was sent to study at Carleton College Academy, a school with a strong religious flavor. At his weekly declaration, instead of calling for a conversion of sinners, he shocked the faculty with "A Plea for Cannibalism," arguing later that he was merely making scientific observations. He studied at Johns Hopkins and earned his Ph.D. at Yale. Plagued by bad luck in looking for professional positions, Veblen returned to his clannish Norwegian family, married, but remained isolated, and focused on reading for the next seven years. He later secured a position teaching at the University of Chicago.

His essays and first two books earned him a national reputation. The first book, *The Theory of the Leisure Class* (1899), had a fermenting effect on economic and social thinking in the United States and became a classic. Largely devoted to the economic psychopathology of daily life, the book became famous for its thesis that social status among the leisure class depends upon wasteful, conspicuous consumption and pecuniary emulation.

His second book, *The Theory of Business Enterprise* (1904), constituted a radical attack upon business capitalists who built a superstructure of credit, loans, and imaginary capitalizations and presumably acted as saboteurs of the economic system, aiming to turn the ups and downs of their disruptions into profits. Veblen praised engineers, technicians, and craftsmen and was enamored by the machine. His view of social change predicted that the capitalists would do themselves in and be forced to call in an engineering or technocratic elite to save the system, or would watch the system revert to the authoritarianism of war lords (fascism). His vague alternative was a vision of industrial democracy. Having edited one of the most prestigious of economic journals, *Journal of Political Economy,* he left Chicago to teach at Stanford, the University of Missouri, and The New School for Social Research, never transcending the level of assistant professor despite his growing renown. He died in 1929.

Today Veblen's perceptive analysis of the split between the money economy and the goods economy and of the American habit of competitive emulation still ring true, as the following excerpts illustrate.

ꙮ

The Theory of
the Leisure Class (1899)
(excerpts)

Introductory

The institution of a leisure class is found in its best development at the higher stages of the barbarian culture; as, for instance, in feudal Europe or feudal Japan. In such communities the distinction between classes is very rigorously observed; and the feature of most striking economic significance in these class differences is the distinction maintained between the employments proper to the several classes. The upper classes are by custom exempt or excluded from industrial occupations, and are reserved for certain employments to which a degree of honor attaches. Chief among the honorable employments in any feudal community is warfare; and priestly service is commonly second to warfare. If the barbarian community is not notably warlike, the priestly office may take precedence, with that of the warrior second. But the rule holds with but slight exceptions that, whether warriors or priests, the upper classes are exempt from industrial employments, and this

exemption is the economic expression of their superior rank. Brahmin India affords a fair illustration of the industrial exemption of both these classes. In the communities belonging to the higher barbarian culture there is a considerable differentiation of sub-classes within what may be comprehensively called the leisure class; and there is a corresponding differentiation of employments between these sub-classes. The leisure class as a whole comprises the noble and the priestly classes, together with much of their retinue. The occupations of the class are correspondingly diversified; but they have the common economic characteristic of being non-industrial. These non-industrial upper-class occupations may be roughly comprised under government, warfare, religious observances, and sports.

At an earlier, but not the earliest, stage of barbarism, the leisure class is found in a less differentiated form. Neither the class distinctions nor the distinctions between leisure-class occupations are so minute and intricate. The Polynesian islanders generally show this stage of the development in good form, with the exception that, owing to the absence of large game, hunting does not hold the usual place of honor in their scheme of life. The Icelandic community in the time of the Sagas also affords a fair instance. In such a community there is a rigorous distinction between classes and between the occupations peculiar to each class. Manual labor, industry, whatever has to do directly with the everyday work of getting a livelihood, is the exclusive occupation of the inferior class. This inferior class includes slaves and other dependents, and ordinarily also all the women. If there are several grades of aristocracy, the women of high rank are commonly exempt from industrial employment, or at least from the more vulgar kinds of manual labor. The men of the upper classes are not only exempt, but by prescriptive custom they are debarred, from all industrial occupations. The range of employments open to them is rigidly defined. As on the higher plane already spoken of, these employments are government, warfare, religious observances, and sports. These four lines of activity govern the scheme of life of the upper classes, and for the highest rank—the kings or chieftains—these are the only kinds of activity that custom or the common sense of the community will allow. Indeed, where the scheme is well developed even sports are accounted doubtfully legitimate for the members of the highest rank. To the lower grades of the leisure class certain other employments are open, but they are employments that are subsidiary to one or another of these typical leisure-class occupations. Such are, for instance, the manufacture and care of arms and accoutrements and of war canoes, the dressing and handling of horses, dogs, and hawks, the preparation of sacred apparatus,

etc. The lower classes are excluded from these secondary honorable employments, except from such as are plainly of an industrial character and are only remotely related to the typical leisure-class occupations.

If we go a step back of this exemplary barbarian culture, into the lower stages of barbarism, we no longer find the leisure class in fully developed form. But this lower barbarism shows the usages, motives, and circumstances out of which the institution of a leisure class has arisen, and indicates the steps of its early growth. Nomadic hunting tribes in various parts of the world illustrate these more primitive phases of the differentiation. Any one of the North American hunting tribes may be taken as a convenient illustration. These tribes can scarcely be said to have a defined leisure class. There is a differentiation of function, and there is a distinction between classes on the basis of this difference of function, but the exemption of the superior class from work has not gone far enough to make the designation "leisure class" altogether applicable. The tribes belonging on this economic level have carried the economic differentiation to the point at which a marked distinction is made between the occupations of men and women, and this distinction is of an invidious character. In nearly all these tribes the women are, by prescriptive custom, held to those employments out of which the industrial occupations proper develop at the next advance. The men are exempt from these vulgar employments and are reserved for war, hunting, sports, and devout observances. A very nice discrimination is ordinarily shown in this matter.

This division of labor coincides with the distinction between the working and the leisure class as it appears in the higher barbarian culture. As the diversification and specialization of employments proceed, the line of demarcation so drawn comes to divide the industrial from the non-industrial employments. The man's occupation as it stands at the earlier barbarian stage is not the original out of which any appreciable portion of later industry has developed. In the later development it survives only in employments that are not classed as industrial—war, politics, sports, learning, and the priestly office. The only notable exceptions are a portion of the fishery industry and certain slight employments that are doubtfully to be classed as industry; such as the manufacture of arms, toys, and sporting goods. Virtually the whole range of industrial employments is an outgrowth of what is classed as woman's work in the primitive barbarian community.

The work of the men in the lower barbarian culture is no less indispensable to the life of the group than the work done by the women. It may even be that the men's work contributes as much to the food supply and the other necessary consumption of the group. Indeed, so obvious is this "productive" character of the men's work that in the conventional economic writings the hunter's work is taken as the type of primitive industry. But such is not the barbarian's sense of the matter. In his own eyes he is not a laborer, and he is not to be classed with the women in this respect; nor is his effort to be classed with the women's drudgery, as labor or industry, in such a sense as to admit of its being confounded with the latter. There is in all barbarian communities a profound sense of the disparity between man's and woman's work. His work may conduce to the maintenance of the group, but it is felt that it does so through an excellence and an efficacy of a kind that cannot without derogation be compared with the uneventful diligence of the women. . . .

Pecuniary Emulation

In the sequence of cultural evolution the emergence of a leisure class coincides with the beginning of ownership. This is necessarily the case, for these two institutions result from the same set of economic forces. In the inchoate phase of their development they are but different aspects of the same general facts of social structure.

It is as elements of social structure—conventional facts—that leisure and ownership are matters of interest for the purpose in hand. An habitual neglect of work does not constitute a leisure class; neither does the mechanical fact of use and consumption constitute ownership. The present inquiry, therefore, is not concerned with the beginning of indolence, nor with the beginning of the appropriation of useful articles to individual consumption. The point in question is the origin and nature of a conventional leisure class on the one hand and the beginnings of individual ownership as a conventional right or equitable claim on the other hand.

The early differentiation out of which the distinction between a leisure and a working class arises is a division maintained between men's and women's work in the lower stages of barbarism. Likewise the earliest form of ownership is an ownership of the women by the able-bodied men of the community. The facts may be expressed in more general terms, and truer to the import of the barbarian theory of life, by saying that it is an ownership of the woman by the man.

There was undoubtedly some appropriation of useful articles before the custom of appropriating women arose. The usages of existing archaic communities in which there is no ownership of women is warrant for such a view. In all communities the members, both male and female, habitually appropriate to their individual use a variety of useful things; but these useful things are not thought of as owned by the person who appropriates and consumes them. The habitual appropriation and consumption of certain slight personal effects goes on without raising the question of ownership; that is to say, the question of a conventional, equitable claim to extraneous things.

The ownership of women begins in the lower barbarian stages of culture, apparently with the seizure of female captives. The original reason for the seizure and appropriation of women seems to have been their usefulness as trophies. The practice of seizing women from the enemy as trophies, gave rise to a form of ownership-marriage, resulting in a household with a male head. This was followed by an extension of slavery to other captives and inferiors, besides women, and by an extension of ownership-marriage to other women than those seized from the enemy. The outcome of emulation under the circumstances of a predatory life, therefore, has been on the one hand a form of marriage resting on coercion, and on the other hand the custom of ownership. The two institutions are not distinguishable in the initial phase of their development; both arise from the desire of the successful men to put their prowess in evidence by exhibiting some durable result in their exploits. Both also minister to that propensity for mastery which pervades all predatory communities. From the ownership of women the concept of ownership extends itself to include the products of their industry, and so there arises the ownership of things as well as of persons.

In this way a consistent system of property in goods is gradually installed. And although in the latest stages of the development, the serviceability of goods for consumption has come to be the most obtrusive element of their value, still, wealth has by no means yet lost its utility as an honorific evidence of the owner's prepotence.

Wherever the institution of private property is found, even in a slightly developed form, the economic process bears the character of a struggle between men for the possession of goods. It has been customary in economic theory, and especially among those economists who adhere with least faltering to the body of modernized classical doctrines, to construe this struggle for wealth as being substantially a struggle for subsistence. Such is, no doubt, its character in large part during the earlier and less efficient phases of industry. Such is also its character in all cases where the "niggardliness of nature" is so strict as to afford but a scanty livelihood to the community in return for strenuous and unremitting application to the business of getting the means of subsistence. But in all progressing communities an advance is presently made beyond this early stage of technological development. Industrial efficiency is presently carried to such a pitch as to afford something appreciably more than a bare livelihood to those engaged in the industrial process. It has not been unusual for economic theory to speak of the further struggle for wealth on this new industrial basis as a competition for an increase of the comforts of life—primarily for an increase of the physical comforts which the consumption of goods affords.

The end of acquisition and accumulation is conventionally held to be the consumption of the goods accumulated—whether it is consumption directly by the owner of the goods or by the household attached to him and for this purpose identified with him in theory. This is at least felt to be the economically legitimate end of acquisition, which alone it is incumbent on the theory to take account of. Such consumption may of course be conceived to serve the consumer's physical wants—his physical comfort—or his so-called higher wants—spiritual, aesthetic, intellectual, or what not; the latter class of wants being served indirectly by an expenditure of goods, after the fashion familiar to all economic readers.

But it is only when taken in a sense far removed from its naïve meaning that consumption of goods can be said to afford the incentive from which accumulation invariably proceeds. The motive that lies at the root of ownership is emulation; and the same motive of emulation continues active in the further development of the institution to which it has given rise and in the development of all those features of the social structure which this institution of ownership touches. The possession of wealth confers honor; it is an invidious distinction. Nothing equally cogent can be said for the consumption of goods, nor for any other conceivable incentive to acquisition, and especially not for any incentive to the accumulation of wealth.

It is of course not to be overlooked that in a community where nearly all goods are private property the necessity of earning a livelihood is a powerful and ever-present incentive for the poorer members of the community. The need of subsistence and of an increase of physical comfort may for a time be the dominant motive of acquisition for those classes who are habitually employed at manual labor, whose subsistence is on a precarious footing, who possess little and ordinarily accumulate little; but it will appear in the course of the discussion that even in the case of these impecunious classes the predominance of the motive of physical want is not so decided as has sometimes been assumed. On the other hand, so far as regards those members and classes of the community who are chiefly concerned in the accumulation of wealth, the incentive of subsistence or of physical comfort never plays a considerable part. Ownership began and grew into a human institution on grounds unrelated to the subsistence minimum. The dominant incentive was from the outset the invidious distinction attaching to wealth, and, save temporarily and by exception, no other motive has usurped the primacy at any stage of the development.

Property set out with being booty held as trophies of the successful raid. So long as the group had departed but little from the primitive communal organization, and so long as it still stood in close contact with other hostile groups, the utility of things or persons owned lay chiefly in an invidious comparison between their possessor and the enemy from whom they were taken. The habit of distinguishing between the interests of the individual and those of the group to which he belongs is apparently a later growth. Invidious comparison between the possessor of the honorific booty and his less successful neighbors within the group was no doubt present early as an element of the utility of the things possessed, though this was not at the outset the chief element of their value. The man's prowess was still primarily the group's prowess, and the possessor of the booty felt himself to be primarily the keeper of the honor of his group. This appreciation of exploit from the communal point of view is met with also at later stages of social growth, especially as regards the laurels of war.

But so soon as the custom of individual ownership begins to gain consistency, the point of view taken in making the invidious comparison on which private property rests will begin to change. Indeed, the one change is but the reflex of the other. The initial phase of ownership, the phase of acquisition by naïve seizure and conversion, begins to pass into the subsequent stage of an incipient organization of industry on the basis of private property (in slaves); the horde develops into a more or less self-sufficing industrial community; possessions then come to be valued not so much as evidence of successful foray, but rather as evidence of the prepotence of the possessor of these goods over other individuals within the community. The invidious comparison now becomes primarily a comparison of the owner with the other members of the group. Property is still of the nature of trophy, but, with the cultural advance, it becomes more and more a trophy of successes scored in the game of ownership carried on between the members of the group under the quasi-peaceable methods of nomadic life.

Gradually, as industrial activity further displaces predatory activity in the community's everyday life and in men's habits of thought, accumulated property more and more replaces trophies of predatory exploit as the conventional exponent of prepotence and success. With the growth of settled industry, therefore, the possession of wealth gains in relative importance and effectiveness as a customary basis of repute and esteem. Not that esteem ceases to be awarded on the basis of other, more direct evidence of prowess; not that successful predatory aggression or warlike exploit ceases to call out the approval and admiration of the crowd, or to stir the envy of the less successful competitors; but the opportunities for gaining distinction by means of this direct manifestation of superior force grow less available both in scope and frequency. At the same time opportunities for industrial aggression, and for the accumulation of property by the quasi-peaceable methods of nomadic industry, increase in scope and availability. And it is even more to the point that property now becomes the most easily recognized evidence of a reputable degree of success as distinguished from heroic or signal achievement. It therefore becomes the conventional basis of esteem. Its possession in some amount becomes necessary in order to have any reputable standing in the community. It becomes indispensable to accumulate, to acquire property, in order to retain one's good name. When accumulated goods have in this way once become the accepted badge of efficiency, the possession of wealth presently assumes the character of an independent and definitive basis of esteem. The possession of goods, whether acquired aggressively by one's own exertion or passively by transmission through inheritance from others, becomes a conventional basis of reputability. The possession of wealth, which was at the outset valued simply as an evidence of efficiency, becomes, in popular apprehension, itself a meritorious act. Wealth is now itself intrinsically honorable and confers honor on its possessor. By a further refinement, wealth acquired passively by transmission from ancestors or other antecedents presently becomes even more honorific than wealth acquired by the possessor's own effort; but this distinction belongs at a later stage in the evolution of the pecuniary culture and will be spoken of in its place. . . .

The Theory of Business Enterprise (1904)
(excerpts)

The material framework of modern civilization is the industrial system, and the directing force which animates this framework is business enterprise. To a greater extent than any other known phase of culture, modern Christendom takes its complexion from its economic organization. This modern economic organization is the "Capitalistic System" or "Modern Industrial System," so called. Its characteristic features, and at the same time the forces by virtue of which it dominates modern culture, are the machine process and investment for a profit.

The scope and method of modern industry are given by the machine. This may not seem to hold true for all industries, perhaps not for the greater part of industry as rated by the bulk of the output or by the aggregate volume of labor expended. But it holds true to such an extent and in such a pervasive manner that a modern industrial community cannot go on except by the help of the accepted mechanical appliances and processes. The machine industries—those portions of the industrial system in which the machine process is paramount—are in a dominant position; they set the pace for the rest of the industrial system. In this sense the present is the age of the machine process. This dominance of the machine process in industry marks off the present industrial situation from all else of its kind.

In a like sense the present is the age of business enterprise. Not that all industrial activity is carried on by the rule of investment for profits, but an effective majority of the industrial forces are organized on that basis. There are many items of great volume and consequence that do not fall within the immediate scope of these business principles. The housewife's work, *e.g.,* as well as some appreciable portion of the work on farms and in some handicrafts, can scarcely be classed as business enterprise. But those elements in the industrial world that take the initiative and exert a far-reaching coercive guidance in matters of industry go to their work with a view to profits on investment, and are guided by the principles and exigencies of business. The business man, especially the business

man of wide and authoritative discretion, has become a controlling force in industry, because, through the mechanism of investments and markets, he controls the plants and processes, and these set the pace and determine the direction of movement for the rest. His control in those portions of the field that are not immediately under his hand is, no doubt, somewhat loose and uncertain; but in the long run his discretion is in great measure decisive even for these outlying portions of the field, for he is the only large self-directing economic factor. His control of the motions of other men is not strict, for they are not under coercion from him except through the coercion exercised by the exigencies of the situation in which their lives are cast; but as near as it may be said of any human power in modern times, the large business man controls the exigencies of life under which the community lives. Hence, upon him and his fortunes centers the abiding interest of civilized mankind.

For a theoretical inquiry into the course of civilized life as its runs in the immediate present, therefore, and as it is running into the proximate future, no single factor in the cultural situation has an importance equal to that of the business man and his work. . . .

The largest and most promising factor of cultural discipline—most promising as a corrective of iconoclastic vagaries—over which business principles rule is national politics. . . . Business interests urge an aggressive national policy and business men direct it. Such a policy is warlike as well as patriotic. The direct cultural value of a warlike business policy is unequivocal. It makes for a conservative animus on the part of the populace. During war time, and within the military organization at all times, under martial law, civil rights are in abeyance; and the more warfare and armament the more abeyance. Military training is a training in ceremonial precedence, arbitrary command, and unquestioning obedience. A military organization is essentially a servile organization. Insubordination is the deadly sin. The more consistent and the more comprehensive this military training, the more effectually will the members of the community be trained into habits of subordination and away from that growing propensity to make light of personal authority that is the chief infirmity of democracy. This applies first and most decidedly, of course, to the soldiery, but it applies only in a less degree to the rest of the population. They learn to think in warlike terms of rank, authority, and subordination, and so grow progressively more patient of encroachments upon their civil rights. Witness the change that has latterly been going on in the temper of the German people.

The modern warlike policies are entered upon for the sake of peace, with a view to the orderly pursuit of business. In their initial motive they differ from the warlike dynastic politics of the sixteenth, seventeenth, and eighteenth centuries. But the disciplinary effects of warlike pursuits and of warlike preoccupations are much the same whatever may be their initial motive or ulterior aim. The end sought in the one case was warlike mastery and high repute in the matter of ceremonial precedence; in the other, the modern case, it is pecuniary mastery and high repute in the matter of commercial solvency. But in both cases alike the pomp and circumstance of war and armaments, and the sensational appeals to patriotic pride and animosity made by victories, defeats, or comparisons of military and naval strength, act to rehabilitate lost ideals and weakened convictions of the chauvinistic or dynastic order. At the same stroke they direct the popular interest to other, nobler, institutionally less hazardous matters than the unequal distribution of wealth or of creature comforts. Warlike and patriotic preoccupations fortify the barbarian virtues of subordination and prescriptive authority. Habituation to a warlike, predatory scheme of life is the strongest disciplinary factor that can be brought to counteract the vulgarization of modern life wrought by peaceful industry and the machine process, and to rehabilitate the decaying sense of status and differential dignity. Warfare, with the stress on subordination and mastery and the insistence on gradations of dignity and honor incident to a militant organization, has always proved an effective school in barbarian methods of thought.

In this direction, evidently, lies the hope of a corrective for "social unrest" and similar disorders of civilized life. There can, indeed, be no serious question but that a consistent return to the ancient virtues of allegiance, piety, servility, graded dignity, class prerogative, and prescriptive authority would greatly conduce to popular content and to the facile management of affairs. Such is the promise held out by a strenuous national policy.

The reversional trend given by warlike experience and warlike preoccupations, it is plain, does not set backward to the régime of natural liberty. Modern business principles and the modern scheme of civil rights and constitutional government rest on natural-rights ground. But the system of natural rights is a halfway house. The warlike culture takes back to a more archaic situation that preceded the scheme of natural rights, viz. the system of absolute government, dynastic politics, devolution of rights and honors, ecclesiastical authority, and popular submission and squalor. It makes not for a reinstatement of the Natural Rights of Man but for a reversion to the Grace of God.

The barbarian virtues of fealty and patriotism run on national or dynastic exploit and aggrandizement, and these archaic virtues are not dead. In those modern communities whose hearts beat with the pulsations of the world-market they find expression in an enthusiasm for the commercial aggrandizement cf the nation's business men. But when once the policy of warlike enterprise has been entered upon for business ends, these loyal affections gradually shift from the business interests to the warlike and dynastic interests, as witness the history of imperialism in Germany and England. The eventual outcome should be a rehabilitation of the ancient patriotic animosity and dynastic loyalty, to the relative neglect of business interests. This may easily be carried so far as to sacrifice the profits of the business men to the exigencies of the higher politics.

The disciplinary effect of war and armaments and imperialist politics is complicated with a selective effect. War not only affords a salutary training, but it also acts to eliminate certain elements of the population. The work of campaigning and military tenure, such as is carried on by England, America, or the other civilizing powers, lies, in large part, in the low latitudes, where the European races do not find a favorable habitat. The low latitudes are particularly unwholesome for that dolicho-blond racial stock that seems to be the chief bearer of the machine industry. It results that the viability and the natural increase of the soldiery is perceptibly lowered. The service in the low latitudes, as contrasted with Europe, for instance, is an extra-hazardous occupation. The death rate, indeed, exceeds the birth rate. But in the more advanced industrial communities, of which the English and American are typical, the service is a volunteer service; which means that those who go to the wars seek this employment by their own choice. That is to say, the human material so drawn off is automatically selected on the basis of a peculiar spiritual fitness for this predatory employment; they are, on the whole, of a more malevolent and vagabond temper, have more of the ancient barbarian animus, than those who are left at home to carry on the work of the home community and propagate the home population. And since the troops and ships are offered by the younger sons of the conservative leisure class and by the buccaneering scions of the class of professional politicians, a natural selection of the same character takes effect also as regards the officers. There results a gradual selective elimination of that old-fashioned element of the population that is by temperament best suited for the old-fashioned institutional system of status and servile organization.

This selective elimination of conservative elements would in the long run leave each succeeding generation of the community less predatory and less emulative in temper, less well endowed for carrying on its life under the servile institutions proper to a militant régime. But, for the present and the nearer future, there can be little doubt but that this selective shaping of the community's animus is greatly outweighed by the contrary trend given by the discipline of warlike preoccupations. What helps to keep the balance in favor of the reversional trend is the cultural leaven carried back into the home community by the veterans. These presumptive past masters in the archaic virtues keep themselves well in the public eye and serve as exemplars to the impressionable members of the community, particularly to the less mature.

The net outcome of the latter-day return to warlike enterprise is, no doubt, securely to be rated as fostering a reversion to national ideals of servile status and to institutions of a despotic character. On the whole and for the present, it makes for conservatism, ultimately for reversion.

The quest of profits leads to a predatory national policy. The resulting large fortunes call for a massive government apparatus to secure the accumulations, on the one hand, and for large and conspicuous opportunities to spend the resulting income, on the other hand; which means a militant, coercive home administration and something in the way of an imperial court life—a dynastic fountain of honor and a courtly bureau of ceremonial amenities. Such an ideal is not simply a moralist's day-dream; it is a sound business proposition, in that it lies on the line of policy along which the business interests are moving in their own behalf. If national (that is to say dynastic) ambitions and warlike aims, achievements, spectacles, and discipline be given a large place in the community's life, together with the concomitant coercive police surveillance, then there is a fair hope that the disintegrating trend of the machine discipline may be corrected. The régime of status, fealty, prerogative, and arbitrary command would guide the institutional growth back into the archaic conventional ways and give the cultural structure something of that secure dignity and stability which it had before the times, not only of socialistic vapors, but of natural rights as well. Then, too, the rest of the spiritual furniture of the ancient régime shall presumably be reinstated; materialistic skepticism may yield the ground to a romantic philosophy, and the populace and the scientists alike may regain something of that devoutness and faith in preternatural agencies which they have recently been losing. As the discipline of prowess again comes to its own, conviction and contentment with whatever is authentic may return to distracted Christendom, and may once more give something of a sacramental serenity to men's outlook on the present and the future.

But authenticity and sacramental dignity belong neither with the machine technology, nor with modern science, nor with business traffic. In so far as the aggressive politics and the aristocratic ideals currently furthered by the business community are worked out freely, their logical outcome is an abatement of those cultural features that distinguish modern times from what went before, including a decline of business enterprise itself.

How imminent such a consummation is to be accounted is a question of how far the unbusinesslike and unscientific discipline brought in by aggressive politics may be expected to prevail over the discipline of the machine industry. It is difficult to believe that the machine technology and the pursuit of the material sciences will be definitely superseded, for the reason, among others, that any community which loses these elements of its culture thereby loses that brute material force that gives it strength against its rivals. And it is equally difficult to imagine how any one of the communities of Christendom can avoid entering the funnel of business and dynastic politics, and so running through the process whereby the materialistic animus is eliminated. Which of the two antagonistic factors may prove the stronger in the long run is something of a blind guess; but the calculable future seems to belong to the one or the other. It seems possible to say this much, that the full dominion of business enterprise is necessarily a transitory dominion. It stands to lose in the end whether the one or the other of the two divergent cultural tendencies wins, because it is incompatible with the ascendancy of either. . . .

William Graham Sumner

Born in 1840 in Paterson, New Jersey, William Graham Sumner was reared by an outspoken, uneducated, immigrant workman father who read a great deal and strongly influenced his son. After attending public school, Sumner became an excellent student at Yale and was supported by friends in studying for the ministry at Geneva, Göttingen, and Oxford. Once back in the United States he taught at Yale while serving as the deaconate of the Episcopal church. Briefly he was rector of a church in New Jersey.

Sumner found life as a clergyman a constraint on his growing interests in social and political issues. He believed that the importance of the clergy was declining in the industrial era. He accepted appointment to a new chair in political economy at Yale in 1872 and taught and wrote there the rest of his life. As a member of New Haven's board of alderman and later the Connecticut State Board of Education, Sumner assisted in reforming public schools. Specializing in the origins of institutions, he helped cultivate the academic study of sociology before his death in 1910.

Sumner is known for his Americanization of Herbert Spencer's philosophy of Social Darwinism. According to Social Darwinism, the fittest ought to survive and become wealthy if they can, generating economic and technical progress. Free citizens in a free democracy should have no duties toward others of the same rank and standing but respect and goodwill. People (particularly would-be social reformers) should mind their own business—allow laissez-faire to work—lest the plutocracy seize control of government for its own interests, undermining democracy. He praised inequality, social stratification, and free trade.

His books include *Folkways* (1906) and *The Science of Society* (1927). The following excerpts are taken from *What Social Classes Owe to Each Other* (1883).

What Social Classes Owe to Each Other (1883)
(excerpts)

. . . I now propose to try to find out whether there is any class in society which lies under the duty and burden of fighting the battles of life for any other class, or of solving social problems for the satisfaction of any other class; also, whether there is any class which has the right to formulate demands on "society"—that is, on other classes; also, whether there is anything but a fallacy and a superstition in the notion that "the State" owes anything to anybody except peace, order, and the guarantees of rights. . . .

Certain ills belong to the hardships of human life. They are natural. They are a part of the struggle with Nature for existence. We cannot blame our fellow-men for our share of these. My neighbor and I are both struggling to free ourselves from these ills. The fact that my neighbor has succeeded in this struggle better than I constitutes no grievance for me. Certain other ills are due to the malice of men, and to the imperfections or errors of civil institutions. These ills are an object of agitation, and a subject of discussion. The former class of ills is to be met only by manly effort and energy; the latter may be corrected by associated effort. The former class of ills is constantly grouped and generalized, and made the object of social schemes. We shall see, as we go on, what that means. The second class of ills may fall on certain social classes, and reform will take the form of interference by other classes in favor of that one. The last fact is, no doubt, the reason why people have been led, not noticing distinctions, to believe that the same method was applicable to the other class of ills. The distinction here made between the ills which belong to the struggle for existence and those which are due to the faults of human institutions is of prime importance.

It will also be important, in order to clear up our ideas about the notions which are in fashion, to note, the relation of the economic to the political significance of assumed duties of one class to another. That is to say, we may discuss the question whether one class owes duties to another by reference to the economic effects which will be produced on the classes and society; or we may discuss the political expediency of formulating and enforcing rights and duties respectively between the parties. In the former case we might assume that the givers of aid were willing to give it, and we might discuss the benefit or mischief of their activity. In the other case we must assume that some at least of those who were forced to give aid did so unwillingly. Here, then, there would be a question of rights. The question whether voluntary charity is mischievous or not is one thing; the question whether legislation which forces one man to aid another is right and

wise, as well as economically beneficial, is quite another question. Great confusion and consequent error is produced by allowing these two questions to become entangled in the discussion. Especially we shall need to notice the attempts to apply legislative methods of reform to the ills which belong to the order of Nature.

There is no possible definition of "a poor man." A pauper is a person who cannot earn his living; whose producing powers have fallen positively below his necessary consumption; who cannot, therefore, pay his way. A human society needs the active co-operation and productive energy of every person in it. A man who is present as a consumer, yet who does not contribute either by land, labor, or capital to the work of society, is a burden. On no sound political theory ought such a person to share in the political power of the State. He drops out of the ranks of workers and producers. Society must support him. It accepts the burden, but he must be cancelled from the ranks of the rulers likewise. So much for the pauper. About him no more need be said. But he is not the "poor man." The "poor man" is an elastic term, under which any number of social fallacies may be hidden.

Neither is there any possible definition of "the weak." Some are weak in one way, and some in another; and those who are weak in one sense are strong in another. In general, however, it may be said that those whom humanitarians and philanthropists call the weak are the ones through whom the productive and conservative forces of society are wasted. They constantly neutralize and destroy the finest efforts of the wise and industrious, and are a dead-weight on the society in all its struggles to realize any better things. Whether the people who mean no harm, but are weak in the essential powers necessary to the performance of one's duties in life, or those who are malicious and vicious, do the more mischief, is a question not easy to answer.

Under the names of the poor and the weak, the negligent, shiftless, inefficient, silly, and imprudent are fastened upon the industrious and prudent as a responsibility and a duty. On the one side, the terms are extended to cover the idle, intemperate, and vicious, who, by the combination, gain credit which they do not deserve, and which they could not get if they stood alone. On the other hand, the terms are extended to include wage-receivers of the humblest rank, who are degraded by the combination. The reader who desires to guard himself against fallacies should always scrutinize the terms "poor" and "weak" as used, so as to see which or how many of these classes they are made to cover.

The humanitarians, philanthropists, and reformers, looking at the facts of life as they present themselves, find enough which is sad and unpromising in the condition of many members of society. They see wealth and poverty side by side. They note great inequality of social position and social chances. They eagerly set about the attempt to account for what they see, and to devise schemes for remedying what they do not like. In their eagerness to recommend the less fortunate classes to pity and consideration they forget all about the rights of other classes; they gloss over all the faults of the classes in question, and they exaggerate their misfortunes and their virtues. They invent new theories of property, distorting rights and perpetrating injustice, as any one is sure to do who sets about the re-adjustment of social relations with the interests of one group distinctly before his mind, and the interests of all other groups thrown into the background. When I have read certain of these discussions I have thought that it must be quite disreputable to be respectable, quite dishonest to own property, quite unjust to go one's own way and earn one's own living,

and that the only really admirable person was the good-for-nothing. The man who by his own effort raises himself above poverty appears, in these discussions, to be of no account. The man who has done nothing to raise himself above poverty finds that the social doctors flock about him, bringing the capital which they have collected from the other class, and promising him the aid of the State to give him what the other had to work for. In all these schemes and projects the organized intervention of society through the State is either planned or hoped for, and the State is thus made to become the protector and guardian of certain classes. . . .

In our modern state, and in the United States more than anywhere else, the social structure is based on contract, and status is the least importance. Contract, however, is rational—even rationalistic. It is also realistic, cold, and matter-of-fact. A contract relation is based on a sufficient reason, not on custom, or prescription. It is not permanent. It endures only so long as the reason for it endures. In a state based on contract sentiment is out of place in any public or common affairs. It is relegated to the sphere of private and personal relations, where it depends not at all on class types, but on personal acquaintance and personal estimates. The sentimentalists among us always seize upon the survivals of the old order. They want to save them and restore them. Much of the loose thinking also which troubles us in our social discussions arises from the fact that men do not distinguish the elements of status and of contract which may be found in our society. . . .

A society based on contract is a society of free and independent men, who form ties without favor or obligation, and cooperate without cringing or intrigues. A society based on contract, therefore, gives the utmost room and chance for individual development, and for all the self-reliance and dignity of a free man. That a society of free men, co-operating under contract, is by far the strongest society which has ever yet existed; that no such society has ever yet developed the full measure of strength of which it is capable; and that the only social improvements which are now conceivable lie in the direction of more complete realization of a society of free men united by contract, are points which cannot be controverted. It follows, however, that one man, in a free state, cannot claim help from, and cannot be charged to give help to, another. To understand the full meaning of this assertion it will be worth while to see what a free democracy is. . . .

The notion of a free state is entirely modern. It has been developed with the development of the middle class, and with the growth of a commercial and industrial civilization. Horror at human slavery is not a century old as a common sentiment in a civilized state. The idea of the "free man," as we understand it, is the product of a revolt against medieval and feudal ideas; and our notion of equality, when it is true and practical, can be explained only by that revolt. It was in England that the modern idea found birth. It has been strengthened by the industrial and commercial development of that country. It has been inherited by all the English-speaking nations, who have made liberty real because they have inherited it, not as a notion, but as a body of institutions. . . .

The notion of civil liberty which we have inherited is that of a *status created for the individual by laws and institutions, the effect of which is that each man is guaranteed the use of all his own powers exclusively for his own welfare.* It is not at all a matter of elections, or universal suffrage, or democracy. All institutions are to be tested by the degree to which they guarantee liberty. It is not to be admitted for a moment that liberty is a means to social ends, and that it may be impaired for major

considerations. Any one who so argues has lost the bearing and relations of all the facts and factors in a free state. A human being has a life to live, a career to run. He is a centre of powers to work, and of capacities to suffer. What his powers may be— whether they can carry him far or not; what his chances may be, whether wide or restricted; what his fortune may be, whether to suffer much or little—are questions of his personal destiny which he must work out and endure as he can; but for all that concerns the bearing of the society and its institutions upon that man, and upon the sum of happiness to which he can attain during his life on earth, the product of all history and all philosophy up to this time is summed up in the doctrine, that he should be left free to do the most for himself that he can, and should be guaranteed the exclusive enjoyment of all that he does. If the society, that is to say, in plain terms, if his fellow-men, either individually, by groups, or in a mass—impinge upon him otherwise than to surround him with neutral conditions of security, they must do so under the strictest responsibility to justify themselves. Jealousy and prejudice against all such interferences are high political virtues in a free man. It is not at all the function of the State to make men happy. They must make themselves happy in their own way, and at their own risk. The functions of the State lie entirely in the conditions or chances under which the pursuit of happiness is carried on, so far as those conditions or chances can be affected by civil organization. Hence, liberty for labor and security for earnings are the ends for which civil institutions exist, not means which may be employed for ulterior ends. . . .

A free man in a free democracy has no duty whatever toward other men of the same rank and standing, except respect, courtesy, and good will. We cannot say that there are no classes, when we are speaking politically, and then say that there are classes, when we are telling A what it is his duty to do for B. In a free state every man is held and expected to take care of himself and his family, to make no trouble for his neighbor, and to contribute his full share to public interests and common necessities. If he fails in this he throws burdens on others. He does not thereby acquire rights against the others. On the contrary, he only accumulates obligations toward them; and if allowed to make his deficiencies a ground of new claims, he passes over into the position of a privileged or petted person—emancipated from duties, endowed with claims. This is the inevitable result of combining democratic political theories with humanitarian social theories. It would be aside from my present purpose to show, but it is worth noticing in passing, that one result of such inconsistency must surely be to undermine democracy, to increase the power of wealth in the democracy, and to hasten the subjection of democracy to plutocracy; for a man who accepts any share which he has not earned in another man's capital cannot be an independent citizen. . . .

The aggregation of large fortunes is not at all a thing to be regretted. On the contrary, it is a necessary condition of many forms of social advance. If we should set a limit to the accumulation of wealth, we should say to our most valuable producers, "We do not want you to do us the services which you best understand how to perform, beyond a certain point." It would be like killing off our generals in war. A great deal is said, in the cant of a certain school, about "ethical views of wealth," and we are told that some day men will be found of such public spirit that, after they have accumulated a few millions, they will be willing to go on and labor simply for the pleasure of paying the taxes of their fellow-citizens. Possibly this is true. It is a prophecy. It is as impossible to deny it as it is silly to affirm it. For if a time ever comes when there are men of this kind, the

men of that age will arrange their affairs accordingly. There are no such men now, and those of us who live now cannot arrange our affairs by what men will be a hundred generations hence. . . .

In the United States the opponent of plutocracy is democracy. Nowhere else in the world has the power of wealth come to be discussed in its political aspects as it is here. Nowhere else does the question arise as it does here. . . . Nowhere in the world is the danger of a plutocracy as formidable as it is here. To it we oppose the power of numbers as it is presented by democracy. Democracy itself, however, is new and experimental. It has not yet existed long enough to find its appropriate forms. It has no prestige from antiquity such as aristocracy possesses. It has, indeed, none of the surroundings which appeal to the imagination. On the other hand, democracy is rooted in the physical, economic, and social circumstances of the United States. This country cannot be other than democratic for an indefinite period in the future. Its political processes will also be republican. The affection of the people for democracy makes them blind and uncritical in regard to it, and they are as fond of the political fallacies to which democracy lends itself as they are of its sound and correct interpretation, or fonder. Can democracy develop itself and at the same time curb plutocracy?

Already the question presents itself as one of life or death to democracy. Legislative and judicial scandals show us that the conflict is already opened, and that it is serious. The lobby is the army of the plutocracy. An elective judiciary is a device so much in the interest of plutocracy, that it must be regarded as a striking proof of the toughness of the judicial institution that it has resisted the corruption so much as it has. The caucus, convention, and committee lend themselves most readily to the purposes of interested speculators and jobbers. It is just such machinery as they might have invented if they had been trying to make political devices to serve their purpose, and their processes call in question nothing less than the possibility of free self-government under the forms of a democratic republic.

For now I come to the particular point which I desire to bring forward against all the denunciations and complainings about the power of chartered corporations and aggregated capital. If charters have been given which confer undue powers, who gave them? Our legislators did. Who elected these legislators? We did. If we are a free, self-governing people, we must understand that it costs vigilance and exertion to be self-governing. It costs far more vigilance and exertion to be so under the democratic form, where we have no aids from tradition or prestige, than under other forms. If we are a free, self-governing people, we can blame nobody but ourselves for our misfortunes. No one will come to help us out of them. It will do no good to heap law upon law, or to try by constitutional provisions simply to abstain from the use of powers which we find we always abuse. How can we get bad legislators to pass a law which shall hinder bad legislators from passing a bad law? That is what we are trying to do by many of our proposed remedies. The task before us, however, is one which calls for fresh reserves of moral force and political virtue from the very foundations of the social body. Surely it is not a new thing to us to learn that men are greedy and covetous, and that they will be selfish and tyrannical if they dare. The plutocrats are simply trying to do what the generals, nobles, and priests have done in the past—get the power of the State into their hands, so as to bend the rights of others to their own advantage; and what we need to do is to recognize the fact that we are face to face with the same old foes—the vices and passions of human nature. . . .

The new foes must be met, as the old ones were met—by institutions and guarantees. The problem of civil liberty is constantly renewed. Solved once, it re-appears in a new form. The old constitutional guarantees were all aimed against king and nobles. New ones must be invented to hold the power of wealth to that responsibility without which no power whatever is consistent with liberty. The judiciary has given the most satisfactory evidence that it is competent to the new duty which devolves upon it. The courts have proved, in every case in which they have been called upon, that there are remedies, that they are adequate and that they can be brought to bear upon the cases. The chief need seems to be more power of voluntary combination and co-operation among those who are aggrieved. Such co-operation is a constant necessity under free self-government; and when, in any community, men lose the power of voluntary co-operation in furtherance or defence of their own interests, they deserve to suffer, with no other remedy than newspaper denunciations and platform declamations. Of course, in such a state of things, political mountebanks come forward and propose fierce measures which can be paraded for political effect. Such measures would be hostile to all our institutions, would destroy capital, overthrow credit, and impair the most essential interests of society. On the side of political machinery there is no ground for hope, but only for fear. On the side of constitutional guarantees and the independent action of self-governing free men there is every ground for hope. . . .

The amateur social doctors are like the amateur physicians—they always begin with the question of remedies, and they go at this without any diagnosis or any knowledge of the anatomy or physiology of society. They never have any doubt of the efficacy of their remedies. They never take account of any ulterior effects which may be apprehended from the remedy itself. It generally troubles them not a whit that their remedy implies a complete reconstruction of society, or even a reconstitution of human nature. Against all such social quackery the obvious injunction to the quacks is, to mind their own business. . . .

Society . . . does not need any care or supervision. If we can acquire a science of society, based on observation of phenomena and study of forces, we may hope to gain some ground slowly toward the elimination of old errors and the re-establishment of a sound and natural social order. Whatever we gain that way will be by growth, never in the world by any reconstruction of society on the plan of some enthusiastic social architect. The latter is only repeating the old error over again and postponing all our chances of real improvement. Society needs first of all to be freed from these meddlers—that is, to be let alone. Here we are, then, once more back at the old doctrine—*laissez-faire.* Let us translate it into blunt English, and it will read, Mind your own business. It is nothing but the doctrine of liberty. Let every man be happy in his own way. . . .

It no doubt wounds the vanity of a philosopher who is just ready with a new solution of the universe to be told to mind his own business. So he goes on to tell us that if we think that we shall, by being let alone, attain to perfect happiness on earth, we are mistaken. The half-way men—the professorial socialists—join him. They solemnly shake their heads, and tell us that he is right—that letting us alone will never secure us perfect happiness. Under all this lies the familiar logical fallacy, never expressed, but really the point of the whole, that we *shall* get perfect happiness if we put ourselves in the hands of the world-reformer. We never supposed that *laissez-faire* would give us perfect happiness. We have left perfect happiness entirely out of our account. If the social doctors will mind their own business, we shall have no troubles but what belong to Nature. Those we will endure or combat as we can. What we desire is, that the friends of humanity

should cease to add to them. Our disposition toward the ills which our fellow-man inflicts on us through malice or meddling is quite different from our disposition toward the ills which are inherent in the conditions of human life.

To mind one's business is a purely negative and unproductive injunction, but, taking social matters as they are just now, it is a sociological principle of the first importance. . . .

Social improvement is not to be won by direct effort. It is secondary, and results from physical or economic improvements. That is the reason why schemes of direct social amelioration always have an arbitrary, sentimental, and artificial character, while true social advance must be a product and a growth. The efforts which are being put forth for every kind of progress in the arts and sciences are, therefore, contributing to true social progress. Let any one learn what hardship was involved, even for a wealthy person, a century ago, in crossing the Atlantic, and then let him compare that hardship even with a steerage passage at the present time, considering time and money cost. This improvement in transportation by which "the poor and weak" can be carried from the crowded centres of population to the new land is worth more to them than all the schemes of all the social reformers. An improvement in surgical instruments or in anaesthetics really does more for those who are not well off than all the declamations of the orators and pious wishes of the reformers. Civil service reform would be a greater gain to the laborers than innumerable factory acts and eight-hour laws. Free trade would be a greater blessing to "the poor man" than all the devices of all the friends of humanity if they could be realized. . . .

We each owe it to the other to guarantee rights. Rights do not pertain to *results,* but only to *chances.* They pertain to the *conditions* of the struggle for existence, not to any of the results of it; to the *pursuit* of happiness, not to the possession of happiness. It cannot be said that each one has a right to have some property, because if one man had such a right some other man or men would be under a corresponding obligation to provide him with some property. Each has a right to acquire and possess property if he can. It is plain what fallacies are developed when we overlook this distinction. Those fallacies run through *all* socialistic schemes and theories. If we take rights to pertain to results, and then say that rights must be equal, we come to say that men have a right to be equally happy, and so on in all the details. Rights should be equal, because they pertain to chances, and all ought to have equal chances so far as chances are provided or limited by the action of society. This, however, will not produce equal rights, but it is right just because it will produce unequal results— that is, results which shall be proportioned to the merits of individuals. . . .

. . . If there be liberty, some will profit by the chances eagerly and some will neglect them altogether. Therefore, the greater the chances the more unequal will be the fortune of these two sets of men. So it ought to be, in all justice and right reason. The yearning after equality is the offspring of envy and covetousness, and there is no possible plan for satisfying that yearning which can do aught else than rob A to give to B; consequently all such plans nourish some of the meanest vices of human nature, waste capital, and overthrow civilization. . . .

The Powerless

6

Charlotte Perkins Gilman

Charlotte Perkins Gilman, born in 1860 in Hartford, Connecticut, was a noted feminist and reformer who focused particularly on the economic and social conditions of women. In her lifetime she served as an effective lecturer and writer on the labor movement and on feminism. Gilman preferred to be known as a sociologist rather than a feminist, though she was called the "Militant Madonna."

She was self-educated for the most part and was well read in anthropology, sociology, and economics. After marrying and divorcing artist Charles Stetson, she married George Gilman. Her best piece of fiction is her short story *The Yellow Wall-Paper* (1899).

Gilman single-handedly edited and published a liberal journal, *The Forerunner*, but went beyond the classic version of American liberalism by arguing that if the state left all individuals to their private lives, women would remain restrained from fulfilling their potential due to their heavy household and family duties and their disadvantageous economic position. She called for reform while maintaining a nineteenth-century faith in progress, attacking social wrongs where she found them. Of her many works on social and economic problems, the most important was *Women and Economics: A Study of the Economic Relation between Men and Women as a Factor in Social Evolution* (1898), from which the following excerpts are taken.

Gilman committed suicide in 1935 after contracting an incurable illness. Her autobiography was published later that year.

Women and Economics (1898)
(excerpt)

. . . We are the only animal species in which the female depends on the male for food, the only animal species in which the sex-relation is also an economic relation. With us an entire sex lives in a relation of economic dependence upon the other sex, and the economic relation is combined with the sex-relation. The economic status of the human female is relative to the sex-relation.

It is commonly assumed that this condition also obtains among other animals, but such is not the case. There are many birds among which, during the nesting sea-son, the male helps the female feed the young, and partially feeds her; and, with certain of the higher carnivora, the male helps the female feed the young, and partially feeds her. In no case does she depend on him absolutely, even during this season, save in that of the hornbill, where the female, sitting on her nest in a hollow tree, is walled in with clay by the male, so that only her beak projects; and then he feeds her while the eggs are developing. But even the female hornbill does not expect to be fed at any other time. The female bee and ant are economically dependent, but not on the male. The workers are females, too, specialized to economic functions solely. And with the carnivora, if the young are to lose one parent, it might far better be the father: the mother is quite competent to take care of them herself. With many species, as in the case of the common cat, she not only feeds herself and her young, but has to defend the young against the male as well. In no case is the female throughout her life supported by the male.

In the human species the condition is permanent and general, though there are exceptions, and though the present century is witnessing the beginnings of a great change in this respect. We have not been accustomed to face this fact beyond our loose generalization that it was "natural," and that other animals did so, too.

To many this view will not seem clear at first; and the case of working peasant women or females of savage tribes, and the general household industry of women, will be instanced against it. Some careful and honest discrimination is needed to make plain to ourselves the essential facts of the relation, even in these cases. The horse, in his free natural condition, is economically independent. he gets his living by his own exertions, irrespective of any other creature. The horse, in his present condition of slavery, is economically dependent. He gets his living at the hands of his master; and his exertions, though strenuous, bear no direct relation to his living. In fact, the horses who are the best fed and cared for and the horses who are the hardest worked are quite different animals. The horse works, it is true; but what he gets to eat depends on the power and will of his master. His living comes through another. He is economically dependent. So with the hard-worked savage or peasant women. Their labor is the property of another: they work under another will; and what they receive depends not on their labor, but on the power and will of another. They are economically dependent. This is true of the human female both individually and collectively.

In studying the economic position of the sexes collectively, the difference is most marked. As a social animal, the economic status of man rests on the combined and exchanged services of vast numbers of progressively specialized individuals. The economic progress of the race, its maintenance at any period, its continued advance, involve the collective activities of all the trades, crafts, arts, manufactures, inventions, discoveries, and all the civil and military institutions that go to maintain them. The economic status of any race at any time, with its involved effect on all the constituent individuals, depends on their world-wide labors and their free exchange. Economic progress, however, is almost exclusively masculine. Such economic processes as women have been allowed to exercise are of the earliest and most primitive kind. Were men to perform no economic services save such as are still performed by women, our racial status in economics would be reduced to most painful limitations.

To take from any community its male workers would paralyze it economically to a far greater degree than to remove its female workers. The labor now performed by the women could be performed by the men, requiring only the setting back of many advanced workers into earlier forms of industry; but the labor now performed by the men could not be performed by the women without generations of effort and adaptation. Men can cook, clean, and sew as well as women; but the making and managing of the great engines of modern industry, the threading of earth and sea in our vast systems of transportation, the handling of our elaborate machinery of trade, commerce, government—these things could not be done so well by women in their present degree of economic development.

This is not owing to lack of the essential human faculties necessary to such achievements, nor to any inherent disability of sex, but to the present condition of woman, forbidding the development of this degree of economic ability. The male human being is thousands of years in advance of the female in economic status. Speaking collectively, men produce and distribute wealth; and women receive it at their hands. As men hunt, fish, keep cattle, or raise corn, so do women eat game, fish, beef, or corn. As men go down to the sea in ships, and bring coffee and spices and silks and gems from far away, so do women partake of the coffee and spices and silks and gems the men bring.

The economic status of the human race in any nation, at any time, is governed mainly by the activities of the male: the female obtains her share in the racial advance only through him.

Studied individually, the facts are even more plainly visible, more open and familiar. From the day laborer to the millionnaire, the wife's worn dress or flashing jewels, her low roof or her lordly one, her weary feet or her rich equipage,—these speak of the economic ability of the husband. The comfort, the luxury, the necessities of life itself, which the woman receives, are obtained by the husband, and given her by him. And, when the woman, left alone with no man to "support" her, tries to meet her own economic necessities, the difficulties which confront her prove conclusively what the general economic status of the woman is. None can deny these patent facts,—that the economic status of women generally depends upon that of men generally, and that the economic status of women individually depends upon that of men individually, those men to whom they are related. But we are instantly confronted by the commonly received opinion that, although it must be admitted that men make and distribute the wealth of the world, yet women earn their share of it as wives. This assumes either that the husband is in the position of employer and the wife as employee. or that marriage is a "partnership," and the wife an equal factor with the husband in producing wealth.

Economic independence is a relative condition at best. In the broadest sense, all living things are economically dependent upon others,—the animals upon the vegetables, and man upon both. In a narrower sense, all social life is economically interdependent, man producing collectively what he could by no possibility produce separately. But, in the closest interpretation, individual economic independence among human beings means that the individual pays for what he gets, works for what he gets, gives to the other an equivalent for what the other gives him. I depend on the shoemaker for shoes, and the tailor for coats; but, if I give the shoemaker and the tailor enough of my own labor as a house-builder to pay for the shoes and coats they give me, I retain my personal independence. I have not taken of their product, and given nothing of mine. As long as what I get is obtained by what I give, I am economically independent.

Women consume economic goods. What economic product do they give in exchange for what they consume? The claim that marriage is a partnership, in which the two persons married produce wealth which neither of them, separately, could produce, will not bear examination. A man happy and comfortable can produce more than one unhappy and uncomfortable, but this is as true of a father or son as of a husband. To take from a man any of the conditions which make him happy and strong is to cripple his industry, generally speaking. But those relatives who make him happy are not therefore his business partners, and entitled to share his income.

Grateful return for happiness conferred is not the method of exchange in a partnership. The comfort a man takes with his wife is not in the nature of a business partnership, nor are her frugality and industry. A housekeeper, in her place, might be as frugal, as industrious, but would not therefore be a partner. Man and wife are partners truly in their mutual obligation to their children,—their common love, duty, and service. But a manufacturer who marries, or a doctor, or a lawyer, does not take a partner in his business, when he takes a partner in parenthood, unless his wife is also a manufacturer, a doctor, or a lawyer. In his business, she cannot even advise wisely without training and experience. To love her husband, the composer, does not enable her to compose; and the loss of a man's wife, though it may break his heart, does not cripple his business, unless his mind is affected by grief. She is in no sense a business partner, unless she contributes capital or experience or labor, as a man would in like relation. Most men would hesitate very seriously before entering a business partnership with any woman, wife or not.

If the wife is not, then, truly a business partner, in what way does she earn from her husband the food, clothing, and shelter she receives at his hand? By house service, it will be instantly replied. This is the general misty idea upon the subject,— that women earn all they get, and more, by house service. Here we come to a very practical and definite economic ground. Although not producers of wealth, women serve in the final processes of preparation and distribution. Their labor in the household has a genuine economic value.

For a certain percentage of persons to serve other persons, in order that the ones so served may produce more, is a contribution not to be overlooked. The labor of women in the house, certainly, enables men to produce more wealth than they otherwise could; and in this way women are economic factors in society. But so are horses. The labor of horses enables men to produce more wealth than they otherwise could. The horse is an economic factor in society. But the horse is not economically independent, nor is the woman. If a man plus a valet can perform more useful service than he could minus a valet, then the valet is performing useful service. But, if the valet is the property of the man, is obliged to perform this service, and is not paid for it, he is not economically independent.

The labor which the wife performs in the household is given as part of her functional duty, not as employment. The wife of the poor man, who works hard in a small house, doing all the work for the family, or the wife of the rich man, who wisely and gracefully manages a large house and administers its functions, each is entitled to fair pay for services rendered.

To take this ground and hold it honestly, wives, as earners through domestic service, are entitled to the wages of cooks, housemaids, nursemaids, seamstresses, or housekeepers, and to no more. This would of course reduce the spending money of the wives of the rich, and put it out of the power of the poor man to "support" a wife at all, unless, indeed, the poor man faced the situation fully, paid his wife her wages as house servant, and then she and he combined their funds in the support of their children. He would be keeping a servant: she would be helping keep the family. But nowhere on earth would there be "a rich woman" by these means. Even the highest class of private housekeeper, useful as her services are, does not accumulate a fortune. She does not buy diamonds and sables and keep a carriage. Things like these are not earned by house service.

But the salient fact in this discussion is that, whatever the economic value of the domestic industry of women is, they do not get it. The women who do the most work get the least money, and the women who have the most money do the least work.

Their labor is neither given nor taken as a factor in economic exchange. It is held to be their duty as women to do this work; and their economic status bears no relation to their domestic labors, unless an inverse one. Moreover, if they were thus fairly paid,—given what they earned, and no more,—all women working in this way would be reduced to the economic status of the house servant. Few women—or men either—care to face this condition. The ground that women earn their living by domestic labor is instantly forsaken, and we are told that they obtain their livelihood as mothers. This is a peculiar position. We speak of it commonly enough, and often with deep feeling, but without due analysis.

In treating of an economic exchange, asking what return in goods or labor women make for the goods and labor given them,—either to the race collectively or to their husbands individually,—what payment women make for their clothes and shoes and furniture and food and shelter, we are told that the duties and services of the mother entitle her to support.

If this is so, if motherhood is an exchangeable commodity given by women in payment for clothes and food, then we must of course find some relation between the quantity or quality of the motherhood and the quantity and quality of the pay. This being true, then the women who are not mothers have no economic status at all; and the economic status of those who are must be shown to be relative to their motherhood. This is obviously absurd. The childless wife has as much money as the mother of many,—more; for the children of the latter consume what would otherwise be hers; and the inefficient mother is no less provided for than the efficient one. Visibly, and upon the face of it, women are not maintained in economic prosperity proportioned to their motherhood. Motherhood bears no relation to their economic status. Among primitive races, it is true,—

in the patriarchal period, for instance,—there was some truth in this position. Women being of no value whatever save as bearers of children, their favor and indulgence did bear direct relation to maternity; and they had reason to exult on more grounds than one when they could boast a son. To-day, however, the maintenance of the woman is not conditioned upon this. A man is not allowed to discard his wife because she is barren. The claim of motherhood as a factor in economic exchange is false to-day. But suppose it were true. Are we willing to hold this ground, even in theory? Are we willing to consider motherhood as a business, a form of commercial exchange? Are the cares and duties of the mother, her travail and her love, commodities to be exchanged for bread?

It is revolting so to consider them; and, if we dare face our own thoughts, and force them to their logical conclusion, we shall see that nothing could be more repugnant to human feeling, or more socially and individually injurious, than to make motherhood a trade. Driven off these alleged grounds of women's economic independence; shown that women, as a class, neither produce nor distribute wealth; that women, as individuals, labor mainly as house servants, are not paid as such, and would not be satisfied with such an economic status if they were so paid; that wives are not business partners or co-producers of wealth with their husbands, unless they actually practise the same profession; that they are not salaried as mothers, and that it would be unspeakably degrading if they were,—what remains to those who deny that women are supported by men? This (and a most amusing position it is),—that the function of maternity unfits a woman for economic production, and, therefore, it is right that she should be supported by her husband.

The ground is taken that the human female is not economically independent, that she is fed by the male of her species. In denial of this, it is first alleged that she is economically independent,—that she does support herself by her own industry in the house. It being shown that there is no relation between the economic status of woman and the labor she performs in the home, it is then alleged that not as house servant, but as mother, does woman earn her living. It being shown that the economic status of woman bears no relation to her motherhood, either in quantity or quality, it is then alleged that motherhood renders a woman unfit for economic production, and that, therefore, it is right that she be supported by her husband. Before going farther, let us seize upon this admission,—that she *is* supported by her husband.

Without going into either the ethics or the necessities of the case, we have reached so much common ground: the female of genus homo is supported by the male. Whereas, in other species of animals, male and female alike graze and browse, hunt and kill, climb, swim, dig, run, and fly for their livings, in our species the female does not seek her own living in the specific activities of our race, but is fed by the male.

Now as to the alleged necessity. Because of her maternal duties, the human female is said to be unable to get her own living. As the maternal duties of other females do not unfit them for getting their own living and also the livings of their young, it would seem that the human maternal duties require the segregation of the entire energies of the mother to the service of the child during her entire adult life, or so large a proportion of them that not enough remains to devote to the individual interests of the mother.

Such a condition, did it exist, would of course excuse and justify the pitiful dependence of the human female, and her support by the male. As the queen bee, modified entirely to maternity, is sup-

ported, not by the male, to be sure, but by her co-workers, the "old maids," the barren working bees, who labor so patiently and lovingly in their branch of the maternal duties of the hive, so would the human female, modified entirely to maternity, become unfit for any other exertion, and a helpless dependant.

Is this the condition of human motherhood? Does the human mother, by her motherhood, thereby lose control of brain and body, lose power and skill and desire for any other work? Do we see before us the human race, with all its females segregated entirely to the uses of motherhood, consecrated, set apart, specially developed, spending every power of their nature on the service of their children?

We do not. We see the human mother worked far harder than a mare, laboring her life long in the service, not of her children only, but of men; husbands, brothers, fathers, whatever male relatives she has; for mother and sister also; for the church a little, if she is allowed; for society, if she is able; for charity and education and reform,—working in many ways that are not the ways of motherhood.

It is not motherhood that keeps the housewife on her feet from dawn till dark; it is house service, not child service. Women work longer and harder than most men, and not solely in maternal duties. The savage mother carries the burdens, and does all menial service for the tribe. The peasant mother toils in the fields, and the working-man's wife in the home. Many mothers, even now, are wage-earners for the family, as well as bearers and rearers of it. And the women who are not so occupied, the women who belong to rich men,—here perhaps is the exhaustive devotion to maternity which is supposed to justify an admitted economic dependence. But we do not find it even among these. Women of ease and wealth provide for their children better care than the poor woman can; but they do not spend more time upon it themselves, nor more care and effort. They have other occupation.

In spite of her supposed segregation to maternal duties, the human female, the world over, works at extra-maternal duties for hours enough to provide her with an independent living, and then is denied independence on the ground that motherhood prevents her working!

If this ground were tenable, we should find a world full of women who never lifted a finger save in the service of their children, and of men who did *all* the work besides, and waited on the women whom motherhood prevented from waiting on themselves. The ground is not tenable. A human female, healthy, sound, has twenty-five years of life before she is a mother, and should have twenty-five years more after the period of such maternal service as is expected of her has been given. The duties of grandmotherhood are surely not alleged as preventing economic independence.

The working power of the mother has always been a prominent factor in human life. She is the worker *par excellence*, but her work is not such as to affect her economic status. Her living, all that she gets,— food, clothing, ornaments, amusements, luxuries,—these bear no relation to her power to produce wealth, to her services in the house, or to her motherhood. These things bear relation only to the man she marries, the man she depends on,—to how much he has and how much he is willing to give her. The women whose splendid extravagance dazzles the world, whose economic goods are the greatest, are often neither houseworkers nor mothers, but simply the women who hold most power over the men who have the most money. The female of genus homo is economically dependent on the male. He is her food supply. . . .

Booker T. Washington

Born a slave in 1856 in Franklin County, Virginia, Booker T. Washington became the foremost black leader of his era, advocating educational reform and economic opportunity for black Americans as a tradeoff for temporary acceptance of political inequality. This compromise contradicted the egalitarian position of Frederick Douglass and was sharply attacked by later black leaders such as W. E. B. Du Bois.

As a boy after emancipation, Washington worked in West Virginia in a salt furnace and in coal mines. He then went to the Hampton Institute, a school for freedmen, working his way through as a janitor. He taught school, became a Baptist minister, and returned to Hampton to teach in a program for Native Americans. In 1881 Washington was appointed the first principal of the Tuskegee Institute in Alabama, where he used his social and speaking skills and principles of accommodation with whites in positions of influence to raise money for his school and build it into a selective institution. In his famous "Cotton States Exposition" address in Atlanta, he endeared himself to whites at this segregated fair by stating: "In all things that are purely social we shall be as separate as the fingers, yet one as the hand in all things essential to mutual progress." His writings include *Up from Slavery* (1901), excerpted here, and *My Larger Education* (1911). The following pages illustrate why Washington opposed liberal-arts education for black Americans, arguing instead for vocational training for the majority at that stage in their development.

ojo

Up from Slavery:
An Autobiography (1901)
(excerpts)

A Slave among Slaves

I was born a slave on a plantation in Franklin County, Virginia. I am not quite sure of the exact place or exact date of my birth, but at any rate I suspect I must have been born somewhere and at some time. As nearly as I have been able to learn, I was born near a cross-roads post-office called Hale's Ford, and the year was 1858 or 1859. I do not know the month or the day. The earliest impressions I can now recall are of the plantation and the slave quarters—the latter being part of the plantation where the slaves had their cabins.

My life had its beginning in the midst of the most miserable, desolate, and discouraging surroundings. This was so, however, not because my owners were especially cruel, for they were not, as compared with many others. I was born in a typical log cabin, about fourteen by sixteen feet square. In this cabin I lived with my mother and a brother and sister till after the Civil War, when we were all declared free.

Of my ancestry I know almost nothing. In the slave quarters, and even later, I heard whispered conversations among the coloured people of the tortures which the slaves, including, no doubt, my ancestors on my mother's side, suffered in the middle passage of the slave ship while being conveyed from Africa to America. I have been unsuccessful in securing any information that would throw any accurate light upon the history of my family beyond my mother. She, I remember, had a half-brother and half-sister. In the days of slavery not very much attention was given to family history and family records—that is, black family records. My mother, I suppose, attracted the attention of a purchaser who was afterwards my owner and hers. Her addition to the slave family attracted about as much attention as the purchase of a new horse or cow. Of my father I know even less than of my mother. I do not even know his name. I have heard reports to the effect that he was a white man who lived on one of the near-by plantations. Whoever he was, I never heard of his taking the least interest in me or providing in any way for my rearing. But I do not find especial fault with him. He was simply another unfortunate victim of the institution which the Nation unhappily had engrafted upon it at that time.

The cabin was not only our living-place, but was also used as the kitchen for the plantation. My mother was the plantation cook. The cabin was without glass windows; it had only openings in the side which let in the light, and also the cold, chilly air of winter. There was a door to the cabin—that is, something that was called a door—but the uncertain hinges by which it was hung, and the large cracks in it, to say nothing of the fact that it was too small, made the room a very uncomfortable one. In addition to these openings there was, in the lower right-hand corner of the room, the "cat-hole,"—a contrivance which almost every mansion or cabin in Virginia possessed during the ante-bellum period. The "cat-hole" was a square opening, about seven by eight inches, provided for the purpose of letting the cat pass in and out of the house at will during the night. In the case of our particular cabin I could never understand the necessity for this convenience, since there were at least a half-dozen other places in the cabin that would have accommodated the cats. There was no wooden floor in our cabin, the naked earth being used as a floor. In the centre of the earthen floor there was a large, deep opening covered with boards, which was used as a place in which to store sweet potatoes during the winter. An impression of this potato-hole is very distinctly engraved upon my memory, because I recall that during the process of putting the potatoes in or taking them out I would often come into possession of one or two, which I roasted and thoroughly enjoyed. There was no cooking-stove on our plantation, and all the cooking for the whites and slaves my mother had to do over an open fireplace, mostly in pots and "skillets." While the poorly built cabin caused us to suffer with cold in the winter, the heat from the open fireplace in summer was equally trying.

The early years of my life, which were spent in the little cabin, were not very different form those of thousands of other slaves. My mother, of course, had little time in which to give attention to the training of her children during the day. She snatched a few moments for our care in the early morning before her work began, and at night after the day's work was done. One of my earliest recollections is that of my mother cooking a chicken late at night, and awakening her children for the purpose of feeding them. How or where she got it I do not know. I presume, however, it was procured from our owner's farm. Some people may call this

theft. If such a thing were to happen now, I should condemn it as theft myself. But taking place at the time it did, and for the reason that it did, no one could ever make me believe that my mother was guilty of thieving. She was simply a victim of the system of slavery. I cannot remember having slept in a bed until after our family was declared free by the Emancipation Proclamation. Three children—John, my older brother, Amanda, my sister, and myself—had a pallet on the dirt floor, or, to be more correct, we slept in and on a bundle of filthy rags laid upon the dirt floor.

I was asked not long ago to tell something about the sports and pastimes that I engaged in during my youth. Until that question was asked it had never occurred to me that there was no period of my life that was devoted to play. From the time that I can remember anything, almost every day of my life has been occupied in some kind of labour; though I think I would now be a more useful man if I had had time for sports. During the period that I spent in slavery I was not large enough to be of much service, still I was occupied most of the time in cleaning the yards, carrying water to the men in the fields, or going to the mill, to which I used to take corn, once a week, to be ground. The mill was about three miles from the plantation. This work I always dreaded. The heavy bag of corn would be thrown across the back of the horse, and the corn divided about evenly on each side; but in some way, almost without exception, on these trips, the corn would so shift as to become unbalanced and would fall off the horse, and often I would fall with it. As I was not strong enough to reload the corn upon the horse, I would have to wait, sometimes for many hours, till a chance passer-by came along who would help me out of my trouble. The hours while waiting for some one were usually spent in crying. The time consumed in this way made me late in reaching the mill, and by the time I got my corn ground and reached home it would be far into the night. The road was a lonely one, and often led through dense forests. I was always frightened. The woods were said to be full of soldiers who had deserted from the army, and I had been told that the first thing a deserter did to a Negro boy when he found him alone was to cut off his ears. Besides, when I was late in getting home I know I would always get a severe scolding or a flogging.

I had no schooling whatever while I was a slave, though I remember on several occasions I went as far as the schoolhouse door with one of my young mistresses to carry her books. The picture of several dozen boys and girls in a schoolroom engaged in study made a deep impression upon me, and I had the feeling that to get into a schoolhouse and study in this way would be about the same as getting into paradise.

So far as I can now recall, the first knowledge that I got of the fact that we were slaves, and that freedom of the slaves was being discussed, was early one morning before day, when I was awakened by my mother kneeling over her children and fervently praying that Lincoln and his armies might be successful, and that one day she and her children might be free. In this connection I have never been able to understand how the slaves throughout the South, completely ignorant as were the masses so far as books or newspapers were concerned, were able to keep themselves so accurately and completely informed about the great National questions that were agitating the country. From the time that Garrison, Lovejoy, and others began to agitate for freedom, the slaves throughout the South kept in close touch with the progress of the movement. Though I was a mere child during the preparation for the Civil War and during the war itself, I now recall the many late-at-night whispered discussions that I heard my mother and the other slaves on the plantation indulge in. These discussions showed that they understood the situation, and that they kept themselves informed of events by what was termed the "grape-vine" telegraph.

During the campaign when Lincoln was first a candidate for the Presidency, the slaves on our far-off plantation, miles from any railroad or large city or daily newspaper, knew what the issues involved were. When war was begun between the North and the South, every slave on our plantation felt and knew that, though other issues were discussed, the primal one was that of slavery. Even the most ignorant members of my race on the remote plantations felt in their hearts, with a certainty that admitted of no doubt, that the freedom of the slaves would be the one great result of the war, if the Northern armies conquered. Every success of the Federal armies and every defeat of the Confederate forces was watched with the keenest and most intense interest. Often the slaves got knowledge of the results of great battles before the white people received it. This news was usually gotten from the coloured man who was sent to the post-office for the mail. In our case the post-office was about three miles from the plantation and the mail came once or twice a week. The man who was sent to the office would linger about the place long enough to get the drift of the conversation from the group of white people who naturally congregated there, after receiving their mail, to discuss the latest news. The mail-carrier on his way back to our master's house would as naturally retail the news that he had secured among the slaves, and in this way they often heard of important events before the white people at the "big house," as the master's house was called. . . .

Helping Others

It was while my home was at Malden that what was known as the "Ku Klux Klan" was in the height of its activity. The "Ku Klux" were bands of men who had joined themselves together for the purpose of regulating the conduct of the coloured people, especially with the object of preventing the members of the race from exercising any influence in politics. They corresponded somewhat to the "patrollers" of whom I used to hear a great deal during the days of slavery, when I was a small boy. The "patrollers" were bands of white men— usually young men—who were organized largely for the purpose of regulating the conduct of the slaves at night in such matters as preventing the slaves from going from one plantation to another without passes, and for preventing them from holding any kind of meetings without permission and without the presence at these meetings of at least one white man.

Like the "patrollers" the "Ku Klux" operated almost wholly at night. They were, however, more cruel than the "patrollers." Their objects, in the main, were to crush out the political aspirations of the Negroes, but they did not confine themselves to this, because schoolhouses as well as churches were burned by them, and many innocent persons were made to suffer. During this period not a few coloured people lost their lives.

As a young man, the acts of these lawless bands made a great impression upon me. I saw one open battle take place at Malden between some of the coloured and white people. There must have been not far from a hundred persons engaged on each side; many on both sides were seriously injured, among them being General Lewis Ruffner, the husband of my friend Mrs. Viola Ruffner. General Ruffner tried to defend the coloured people, and for this he was knocked down and so seriously wounded that he never completely recovered. It seemed to me as I watched this struggle between members of the two races, that there was no hope for our people in this country. The "Ku Klux" period was, I think, the darkest part of the Reconstruction days. . . .

The Reconstruction Period

It could not have been expected that a people who had spent generations in slavery, and before that generations in the darkest heathenism, could at first form any proper conception of what an education meant. In every part of the South, during the Reconstruction period, schools, both day and night, were filled to overflowing with people of all ages and conditions, some being as far along in age as sixty and seventy years. The ambition to secure an education was most praiseworthy and encouraging.

The idea, however, was too prevalent that, as soon as one secured a little education, in some unexplainable way he would be free from most of the hardships of the world, and, at any rate, could live without manual labour. There was a further feeling that a knowledge however little, of the Greek and Latin languages would make one a very superior human being, something bordering almost on the supernatural. I remember that the first coloured man whom I saw who knew something about foreign languages impressed me at that time as being a man of all others to be envied.

Naturally, most of our people who received some little education became teachers or preachers. While among these two classes there were many capable, earnest, godly men and women, still a large proportion took up teaching or preaching as an easy way to make a living. Many became teachers who could do little more than write their names. I remember there came into our neighbourhood one of this class, who was in search of a school to teach, and the question arose while he was there as to the shape of the earth and how he would teach the children concerning this subject. He explained his position in the matter by saying that he was prepared to teach that the earth was either flat or round, according to the preference of a majority of his patrons.

The ministry was the profession that suffered most—and still suffers, though there has been great improvement—on account of not only ignorant but in many cases immoral men who claimed that they were "called to preach." In the earlier days of freedom almost every coloured man who learned to read would receive "a call to preach" within a few days after he began reading. At my home in West Virginia the process of being called to the ministry was a very interesting one. Usually the "call" came when the individual was sitting in church. Without warning the one called would fall upon the floor as if struck by a bullet, and would lie there for hours, speechless and motionless. Then the news would spread all through the neighbourhood that this individual had received a "call." If he were inclined to resist the summons, he would fall or be made to fall a second or third time. In the end he always yielded to the call. While I wanted an education badly, I confess that in my youth I had a fear that when I had learned to read

and write well I would receive one of these "calls"; but, for some reason, my call never came.

When we add the number of wholly ignorant men who preached or "exhorted" to that of those who possessed something of an education, it can be seen at a glance that the supply of ministers was large. In fact, some time ago I knew a certain church that had a total membership of about two hundred, and eighteen of that number were ministers. But, I repeat, in many communities in the South the character of the ministry is being improved, and I believe that within the next two or three decades a very large proportion of the unworthy ones will have disappeared. The "calls" to preach, I am glad to say, are not nearly so numerous now as they were formerly, and the calls to some industrial occupation are growing more numerous. The improvement that has taken place in the character of the teachers is even more than in the case of the ministers.

During the whole of the Reconstruction period our people throughout the South looked to the Federal Government for everything, very much as a child looks to its mother. This was not unnatural. The central government gave them freedom, and the whole Nation had been enriched for more than two centuries by the labour of the Negro. Even as a youth, and later in manhood, I had the feeling that it was cruelly wrong in the central government, at the beginning of our freedom, to fail to make some provision for the general education of our people in addition to what the states might do, so that the people would be the better prepared for the duties of citizenship.

It is easy to find fault, to remark what might have been done, and perhaps, after all, and under all the circumstances, those in charge of the conduct of affairs did the only thing that could be done at the time. Still, as I look back now over the entire period of our freedom, I cannot help feeling that it would have been wiser if some plan could have been put in operation which would have made the possession of a certain amount of education or property, or both, a test for the exercise of the franchise, and a way provided by which this test should be made to apply honestly and squarely to both the white and black races.

Though I was but little more than a youth during the period of Reconstruction, I had the feeling that mistakes were being made, and that things could not remain in the condition that they were in then very long. I felt that the Reconstruction policy, so far as it related to my race, was in a large measure on a false foundation, was artificial and forced. In many cases it seemed to me that the ignorance of my race was being used as a tool with which to help white men into office, and that there was an element in the North which wanted to punish the Southern white men by forcing the Negro into positions over the heads of the Southern whites. I felt that the Negro would be the one to suffer for this in the end. Besides, the general political agitation drew the attention of our people away from the more fundamental matters of perfecting themselves in the industries at their doors and in securing property.

The temptations to enter political life were so alluring that I came very near yielding to them at one time, but I was kept from doing so by the feeling that I would be helping in a more substantial way by assisting in the laying of the foundation of the race through a generous education of the hand, head, and heart. I saw coloured men who were members of the state legislatures, and county officers, who, in some cases, could not read or write, and whose morals were as weak as their education. Not long ago, when passing through the streets of a certain city in the South, I heard some brick-masons calling out, from the top of a two-story brick building on which

they were working, for the "Governor" to "hurry up and bring up some more bricks." Several times I heard the command, "Hurry up, Governor!" My curiosity was aroused to such an extent that I made inquiry as to who the "Governor" was, and soon found that he was a coloured man who at one time had held the position of Lieutenant-Governor of his state.

But not all the coloured people who were in office during Reconstruction were unworthy of their positions, by any means. Some of them, like the late Senator B. K. Bruce, Governor Pinchback, and many others, were strong, upright, useful men. Neither were all the class designated as carpetbaggers dishonourable men. Some of them, like ex-Governor Bullock, of Georgia, were men of high character and usefulness.

Of course the coloured people, so largely without education, and wholly without experience in government, made tremendous mistakes, just as any people similarly situated would have done. Many of the Southern whites have a feeling that, if the Negro is permitted to exercise his political rights now to any degree, the mistakes of the Reconstruction period will repeat themselves. I do not think this would be true, because the Negro is a much stronger and wiser man than he was thirty-five years ago, and he is fast learning the lesson that he cannot afford to act in a manner that will alienate his Southern white neighbours from him. More and more I am convinced that the final solution of the political end of our race problem will be for each state that finds it necessary to change the law bearing upon the franchise to make the law apply with absolute honesty, and without opportunity for double dealing or evasion, to both races alike. Any other course my daily observation in the South convinces me, will be unjust to the Negro, unjust to the white man, and unfair to the rest of the states in the Union, and will be, like slavery, a sin that at some time we shall have to pay for.

In the fall of 1878, after having taught school in Malden for two years, and after I had succeeded in preparing several of the young men and women, besides my two brothers, to enter the Hampton Institute, I decided to spend some months in study at Washington, D.C. I remained there for eight months. I derived a great deal of benefit from the studies which I pursued, and I came into contact with some strong men and women. At the institution I attended there was no industrial training given to the students, and I had an opportunity of comparing the influence of an institution with no industrial training with that of one like the Hampton Institute, that emphasized the industries. At this school I found the students, in most cases, had more money, were better dressed, wore the lastest style of all manner of clothing, and in some cases were more brilliant mentally. At Hampton it was a standing rule that, while the institution would be responsible for securing some one to pay the tuition for the students, the men and women themselves must provide for their own board, books, clothing, and room wholly by work, or partly by work and partly in cash. At the institution at which I now was, I found that a large proportion of the students by some means had their personal expenses paid for them. At Hampton the student was constantly making the effort through the industries to help himself, and that very effort was of immense value in character-building. The students at the other school seemed to be less self-dependent. They seemed to give more attention to mere outward appearances. In a word, they did not appear to me to be beginning at the bottom, on a real, solid foundation, to the extent that they were at Hampton. They knew more about Latin and Greek when they left school, but they seemed to know less about life and its conditions as they would meet it at their

homes. Having lived for a number of years in the midst of comfortable surroundings, they were not as much inclined as the Hampton students to go into the country districts of the South, where there was little of comfort, to take up work for our people, and they were more inclined to yield to the temptation to become hotel waiters and Pullman-car porters as their life-work.

During the time I was a student in Washington the city was crowded with coloured people, many of whom had recently come from the South. A large proportion of these people had been drawn to Washington because they felt that they could lead a life of ease there. Others had secured minor government positions, and still another large class was there in the hope of securing Federal positions. A number of coloured men—some of them very strong and brilliant—were in the House of Representatives at that time, and one, the Hon. B. K. Bruce, was in the Senate. All this tended to make Washington an attractive place for members of the coloured race. Then, too, they knew that at all times they could have the protection of the law in the District of Columbia. The public schools in Washington for coloured people were better than they were elsewhere. I took great interest in studying the life of our people there closely at that time. I found that while among them there was a large element of substantial, worthy citizens, there was also a superficiality about the life of a large class that greatly alarmed me. I saw young coloured men who were not earning more than four dollars a week spend two dollars or more for a buggy on Sunday to ride up and down Pennsylvania Avenue in order that they might try to convince the world that they were worth thousands. I saw other young men who received seventy-five or one hundred dollars per month from the Government, who were in debt at the end of every month. I saw men who but a few months previous were members of Congress, then without employment and in poverty. Among a large class there seemed to be a dependence upon the Government for every conceivable thing. The members of this class had little ambition to create a position for themselves, but wanted the Federal officials to create one for them. How many times I wished then, and have often wished since, that by some power of magic I might remove the great bulk of these people into the country districts and plant them upon the soil, upon the solid and never deceptive foundation of Mother Nature, where all nations and races that have ever succeeded have gotten their start—a start that at first may be slow and toilsome, but one that nevertheless is real.

In Washington I saw girls whose mothers were earning their living by laundrying. These girls were taught by their mothers, in rather a crude way it is true, the industry of laundrying. Later, these girls entered the public schools and remained there perhaps six or eight years. When the public-school course was finally finished, they wanted more costly dresses, more costly hats and shoes. In a word, while their wants had been increased, their ability to supply their wants had not been increased in the same degree. On the other hand, their six or eight years of book education had weaned them away from the occupation of their mothers. The result of this was in too many cases that the girls went to the bad. I often thought how much wiser it would have been to give these girls the same amount of mental training—and I favour any kind of training, whether in the languages or mathematics, that gives strength and culture to the mind—but at the same time to give them the most thorough training in the latest and best methods of laundrying and other kindred occupations. . . .

Last Words

. . . Twenty years have now passed since I made the first humble effort at Tuskegee, in a broken-down shanty and an old henhouse, without owning a dollar's worth of property, and with but one teacher and thirty students. At the present time the institution owns twenty-three hundred acres of land, one thousand of which are under cultivation each year, entirely by student labour. There are now upon the grounds, counting large and small, sixty-six buildings; and all except four of these have been almost wholly erected by the labour of our students. While the students are at work upon the land and in erecting buildings, they are taught, by competent instructors, the latest methods of agriculture and the trades connected with the building.

There are in constant operation at the school, in connection with thorough academic and religious training, thirty industrial departments. All of these teach industries at which our men and women can find immediate employment as soon as they leave the institution. The only difficulty now is that the demand for our graduates from both white and black people in the South is so great that we cannot supply more than one-half the persons for whom applications come to us. Neither have we the buildings nor the money for current expenses to enable us to admit to the school more than one-half the young men and women who apply to us for admission.

In our industrial teaching we keep three things in mind: first, that the student shall be so educated that he shall be enabled to meet conditions as they exist *now*, in the part of the South where he lives—in a word, to be able to do the thing which the world wants done; second, that every student who graduates from the school shall have enough skill, coupled with intelligence and moral character, to enable him to make a living for himself and others; third, to send every graduate out feeling and knowing that labour is dignified and beautiful—to make each one love labour instead of trying to escape it. . . .

W. E. B. Du Bois

William Edward Burghardt Du Bois (1868–1963) became a famous black political activist, sociologist, and historian, noted for his criticism of Booker T. Washington and his demands for absolute social and political equality and rigorous liberal-arts education for black Americans. Born in Great Barrington, Massachusetts, Du Bois received a B.A. from Fisk University and a B.A., M.A., and Ph.D from Harvard. His famous doctoral thesis, *The Suppression of the African Slave Trade in the U.S. 1638–1870,* was later published. He also studied at the University of Berlin.

Du Bois taught Greek and Latin at Wilberforce University, and then sociology at the University of Pennsylvania and Atlanta University. At the turn of the century, he was so upset with the disfranchisement and segregation stemming from racist backlash that he founded the Niagara Movement (1905–09), a group of northern black intellectuals, to protest the accommodationist views symbolized by Booker T. Washington and others willing to compromise rather than demand political and social equality. This movement consisted of a short series of annual conferences with published proceedings. Du Bois was the director of publicity and research of the National Association for the Advancement of Colored People (NAACP) from 1909 to 1934, editing its paper, *The Crisis.* He resigned in a disagreement over policy toward the Great Depression in 1934, but returned later as director of special research for a short period.

Disenchanted with the failure of Theodore Roosevelt's Progressives to include a plank on African-American rights in their 1912 election platform, he supported Woodrow Wilson, the Democratic nominee. But Wilson's antiblack policies led Du Bois to support the Socialist party's candidate in 1916. By the 1940s and 1950s, Du Bois turned further to the Left. He was linked with Communist groups and indicted by the U.S. Justice Department on charges of acting as an agent for a foreign power, though he was acquitted. At the age of 93, he joined the American Communist party and then moved to Ghana at the invitation of prime minister Kwame Nkrumah, where he spent the last two years of his life directing the creation of an encyclopedia of Africa.

A prolific writer, some of Du Bois's works include: *The Philadelphia Negro* (1899), *The Souls of Black Folk* (1903), *John Brown* (1909), *Quest of the Silver Fleece* (1911), *The Negro* (1915), *Darkwater* (1920), *The Gift of Black Folk* (1924), *Dark Princess* (1928), *Black Reconstruction* (1935), *Black Folk Then and Now* (1939), *Dusk of Dawn* (1940), *Color and Democracy* (1945), and *The World and Africa* (1946). Du Bois was a life-long critic of the American social order and its suppression of African-Americans. He advocated a variety of solutions including egalitarian democracy, pan-Africanism, cultural and economic self-determinism, and Marxian socialism.

❦

The Souls of Black Folk (1903)
(excerpts)

... The Nation has not yet found peace from its sins; the freedman has not yet found in freedom his promised land. Whatever of good may have come in these years of change, the shadow of a deep disappointment rests upon the Negro people,—a disappointment all the more bitter because the unattained ideal was unbounded save by the simple ignorance of a lowly people.

The first decade was merely a prolongation of the vain search for freedom, the boon that seemed ever barely to elude their grasp,—like a tantalizing will-o'-the-wisp, maddening and misleading the headless host. The holocaust of war, the terrors of the Ku-Klux Klan, the lies of carpet-baggers, the disorganization of industry, and the contradictory advice of friends and foes, left the bewildered serf with no new watchword beyond the old cry for freedom. As the time flew, however, he began to grasp a new idea. The ideal of liberty demanded for its attainment powerful means, and these the Fifteenth Amendment gave him. The ballot, which before he had looked upon as a visible sign of freedom, he now regarded as the chief means of gaining and perfecting the liberty with which war had partially endowed him. And why not? Had not votes made war and emancipated millions? Had not votes enfranchised the freedmen? Was anything impossible to a power that had done all this? A million black men started with renewed zeal to vote themselves into the kingdom. So the decade flew away, the revolution of 1876 came, and left the half-free serf weary, wondering, but still inspired. Slowly but steadily, in the following years, a new vision began gradually to replace the dream of political power,—a powerful movement, the rise of another ideal to guide the unguided, another pillar of fire by night after a clouded day. It was the ideal of "book-learning"; the curiosity, born of compulsory ignorance, to know and test the power of the cabalistic letters of the white man, the longing to know. Here at last seemed to have been discovered the mountain path to Canaan; longer than the highway of Emancipation and law, steep and rugged, but straight, leading to heights high enough to overlook life.

Up the new path the advance guard toiled, slowly, heavily, doggedly; only those who have watched and guided the faltering feet, the misty minds, the dull understandings, of the dark pupils of these schools know how faithfully, how piteously, this people strove to learn. It was weary work. The cold statistician wrote down the inches of progress here and there, noted also where here and there a foot had slipped or some one had fallen. To the tired climbers, the horizon was ever dark, the mists were often cold, the Canaan was always dim and far away. If, however, the vistas disclosed as yet no goal, no resting-place, little but flattery and criticism, the journey at least gave leisure for reflection and self-examination; it changed the child of Emancipation to the youth with dawning self-consciousness, self-realization, self-respect. In those sombre forests of his striving his own soul rose before him, and he saw himself,—darkly as through a veil; and yet he saw in himself some faint revelation of his power, of his mission. He began to have a dim feeling that, to attain his place in the world, he must be himself, and not another. For the first time he sought to analyze the burden he bore upon his back, that dead-weight of social degradation partially masked behind a half-named Negro problem. He felt his poverty; without a cent, without a home, without land, tools, or savings, he had entered into competition with rich, landed, skilled neighbors. To be a poor man is hard, but to be a poor race in a land of dollars is the very bottom of hardships. He felt the weight of his ignorance,—not simply of letters, but of life, of business, of the humanities; the accumulated sloth and shirking and awkwardness of decades and centuries shackled his hands and feet. Nor was his burden all poverty and ignorance. The red stain of bastardy, which two centuries of systematic legal defilement of Negro women had stamped upon his race, meant not only the loss of ancient African chastity, but also the hereditary weight of a mass of corruption from white adulterers, threatening almost the obliteration of the Negro home.

A people thus handicapped ought not to be asked to race with the world, but rather allowed to give all its time and thought to its own social problems. But alas! while sociologists gleefully count his bastards and his prostitutes, the very soul of the toiling, sweating black man is darkened by the shadow of a vast despair. Men call the shadow prejudice, and learnedly explain it as the natural defence of culture against barbarism, learning against ignorance, purity against crime, the "higher" against the "lower" races. To which the Negro cries Amen! and swears that to so much of this strange prejudice as is founded on just homage to civilization, culture, righteousness, and progress, he humbly bows and meekly does obeisance. But before that nameless prejudice that leaps beyond all this he stands helpless, dismayed, and well-nigh speechless; before that personal disrespect and mockery, the ridicule and systematic humiliation, the

distortion of fact and wanton license of fancy, the cynical ignoring of the better and the boisterous welcoming of the worse, the all-pervading desire to inculcate disdain for everything black, from Toussaint to the devil,—before this there rises a sickening despair that would disarm and discourage any nation save that black host to whom "discouragement" is an unwritten word.

But the facing of so vast a prejudice could not but bring the inevitable self-questioning, self-disparagement, and lowering of ideals which ever accompany repression and breed in an atmosphere of contempt and hate. Whisperings and portents came borne upon the four winds: Lo! we are diseased and dying, cried the dark hosts; we cannot write, our voting is vain; what need of education, since we must always cook and serve? And the Nation echoed and enforced this self-criticism, saying: Be content to be servants, and nothing more; what need of higher culture for half-men? Away with the black man's ballot, by force or fraud,—and behold the suicide of a race! Nevertheless, out of the evil came something of good,—the more careful adjustment of education to real life, the clearer perception of the Negroes' social responsibilities, and the sobering realization of the meaning of progress. . . .

The act of 1866 gave the Freedmen's Bureau its final form,—the form by which it will be known to posterity and judged of men. It extended the existence of the Bureau to July, 1868; it authorized additional assistant commissioners, the retention of army officers mustered out of regular service, the sale of certain forfeited lands to freedmen on nominal terms, the sale of Confederate public property for Negro schools, and a wider field of judicial interpretation and cognizance. The government of the unreconstructed South was thus put very largely in the hands of the Freed-men's Bureau, especially as in many cases the departmental military commander was now made also assistant commissioner. It was thus that the Freedmen's Bureau became a full-fledged government of men. It made laws, executed them and interpreted them; it laid and collected taxes, defined and punished crime, maintained and used military force, and dictated such measures as it thought necessary and proper for the accomplishment of its varied ends. Naturally, all these powers were not exercised continuously nor to their fullest extent; and yet, as General Howard has said, "scarcely any subject that has to be legislated upon in civil society failed, at one time or another, to demand the action of this singular Bureau.

To understand and criticise intelligently so vast a work, one must not forget an instant the drift of things in the later sixties. Lee had surrendered, Lincoln was dead, and Johnson and Congress were at loggerheads; the Thirteenth Amendment was adopted, the Fourteenth pending, and the Fifteenth declared in force in 1870. Guerrilla raiding, the ever-present flickering after-flame of war, was spending its forces against the Negroes, and all the Southern land was awakening as from some wild dream to poverty and social revolution. In a time of perfect calm, amid willing neighbors and streaming wealth, the social uplifting of four million slaves to an assured and self-sustaining place in the body politic and economic would have been a herculean task; but when to the inherent difficulties of so delicate and nice a social operation were added the spite and hate of conflict, the hell of war; when suspicion and cruelty were rife, and gaunt Hunger wept beside Bereavement,—in such a case, the work of any instrument of social regeneration was in large part foredoomed to failure. The very name of the Bureau stood for a thing in the South which for two centuries and better men had refused even to argue,—that life amid free Negroes was simply unthinkable, the maddest of experiments.

The agents that the Bureau could command varied all the way from unselfish philanthropists to narrow-minded busybodies and thieves; and even though it be true that the average was far better than the worst, it was the occasional fly that helped spoil the ointment.

Then amid all crouched the freed slave, bewildered between friend and foe. He had emerged from slavery,—not the worst slavery in the world, not a slavery that made all life unbearable, rather a slavery that had here and there something of kindliness, fidelity, and happiness,—but withal slavery, which, so far as human aspiration and desert were concerned, classed the black man and the ox together. And the Negro knew full well that, whatever their deeper convictions may have been, Southern men had fought with desperate energy to perpetuate this slavery under which the black masses, with half-articulate thought, had writhed and shivered. They welcomed freedom with a cry. They shrank from the master who still strove for their chains; they fled to the friends that had freed them, even though those friends stood ready to use them as a club for driving the recalcitrant South back into loyalty. So the cleft between the white and black South grew. Idle to say it never should have been; it was as inevitable as its results were pitiable. Curiously incongruous elements were left arrayed against each other,—the North, the government, the carpet-bagger, and the slave, here; and there, all the South that was white, whether gentleman or vagabond, honest man or rascal, lawless murderer or martyr to duty.

Thus it is doubly difficult to write of this period calmly, so intense was the feeling, so mighty the human passions that swayed and blinded men. Amid it all, two figures ever stand to typify that day to coming ages,—the one, a gray-haired gentleman, whose fathers had quit themselves like men, whose sons lay in nameless graves; who bowed to the evil of slavery because its abolition threatened untold ill to all; who stood at last, in the evening of life, a blighted, ruined form, with hate in his eyes;—and the other, a form hovering dark and mother-like, her awful face black with the mists of centuries, had aforetime quailed at that white master's command, had bent in love over the cradles of his sons and daughters, and closed in death the sunken eyes of his wife,—aye, too, at his behest had laid herself low to his lust, and borne a tawny man-child to the world, only to see her dark boy's limbs scattered to the winds by midnight marauders riding after "damned Niggers." These were the saddest sights of that woeful day; and no man clasped the hands of these two passing figures of the present-past; but, hating, they went to their long home, and, hating, their children's children live to-day.

Here, then, was the field of work for the Freedmen's Bureau; and since, with some hesitation, it was continued by the act of 1868 until 1869, let us look upon four years of its work as a whole. There were, in 1868, nine hundred Bureau officials scattered from Washington to Texas, ruling, directly and indirectly, many millions of men. The deeds of these rulers fall mainly under seven heads: the relief of physical suffering, the overseeing of the beginnings of free labor, the buying and selling of land, the establishment of schools, the paying of bounties, the administration of justice, and the financiering of all these activities.

Up to June, 1869, over half a million patients had been treated by Bureau physicians and surgeons, and sixty hospitals and asylums had been in operation. In fifty months twenty-one million free rations were distributed at a cost of over four million dollars. Next came the difficult question of labor. First, thirty thousand black men were transported from the refuges and relief stations back to the farms, back to the critical trial of a new way of working. Plain instructions went out from Washington: the laborers must be free to choose their employers, no fixed rate of wages was prescribed, and there was to be no peonage or forced labor. So far, so good; but where local agents differed *toto coelo* in capacity and character, where the *personnel* was continually changing, the outcome was necessarily varied. The largest element of success lay in the fact that the majority of the freedmen were willing, even eager, to work. So labor contracts were written,— fifty thousand in a single State,—laborers advised, wages guaranteed, and employers supplied. In truth, the organization became a vast labor bureau,—not perfect, indeed, notably defective here and there, but on the whole successful beyond the dreams of thoughtful men. The two great obstacles which confronted the officials were the tyrant and the idler,—the slaveholder who was determined to perpetuate slavery under another name; and the freedman who regarded freedom as perpetual rest,—the Devil and the Deep Sea.

In the work of establishing the Negroes as peasant proprietors, the Bureau was from the first handicapped and at last absolutely checked. Something was done, and larger things were planned; abandoned lands were leased so long as they remained in the hands of the Bureau, and a total revenue of nearly half a million dollars derived from black tenants. Some other lands to which the nation had gained title were sold on easy terms, and public lands were opened for settlement to the very few freedmen who had tools and capital. But the vision of "forty acres and a mule"—the righteous and reasonable ambition to become a landholder, which the nation had all but categorically promised the freedmen—was destined in most cases to bitter disappointment. And those men of marvellous hindsight who are today seeking to preach the Negro back to the present peonage of the soil know well, or ought to know, that the opportunity of binding the Negro peasant willingly to the soil was lost on that day when the Commissioner of the Freedmen's Bureau had to go to South Carolina and tell the weeping freedmen, after their years of toil, that their land was not theirs, that there was a mistake—somewhere. If by 1874 the Georgia Negro alone owned three hundred and fifty thousand acres of land, it was by grace of his thrift rather than by bounty of the government.

The greatest success of the Freedmen's Bureau lay in the planting of the free school among Negroes, and the idea of free elementary education among all classes in the South. It not only called the school-mistresses through the benevolent agencies and built them schoolhouses, but it helped discover and support such apostles of human culture as Edmund Ware, Samuel Armstrong, and Erastus Cravath. The opposition to Negro education in the South was at first bitter, and showed itself in ashes, insult, and blood; for the South believed an educated Negro to be a dangerous Negro. And the South was not wholly wrong; for education among all kinds of men always has had, and always will have, an element of danger and revolution, of dissatisfaction and discontent. Nevertheless, men strive to know. Perhaps some inkling of this paradox, even in the unquiet days of the Bureau, helped the bayonets allay an opposition to human training which still to-day lies smouldering in the South, but not flaming. Fisk, Atlanta, Howard, and Hampton were founded in these days, and six million dollars were expended for educational work, seven hundred and fifty thousand dollars of which the freedmen themselves gave of their poverty.

Such contributions, together with the buying of land and various other enterprises, showed that the ex-slave was handling some free capital already. The chief initial source of this was labor in the army, and his pay and bounty as a soldier. Payments to Negro soldiers were at first complicated by the ignorance of the recipients, and the fact that the quotas of colored regiments from Northern States were largely filled by recruits from the South, unknown to their fellow soldiers. Consequently, payments were accompanied by such frauds that Congress, by joint resolution in 1867, put the whole matter in the hands of the Freedmen's Bureau. In two years six million dollars was thus distributed to five thousand claimants, and in the end the sum exceeded eight million dollars. Even in this system fraud was frequent; but still the work put needed capital in the hands of practical paupers, and some, at least, was well spent.

The most perplexing and least successful part of the Bureau's work lay in the exercise of its judicial functions. The regular Bureau court consisted of one representative of the employer, one of the Negro, and one of the Bureau. If the Bureau could have maintained a perfectly judicial attitude, this arrangement would have been ideal, and must in time have gained confidence; but the nature of its other activities and the character of its *personnel* prejudiced the Bureau in favor of the black litigants, and led without doubt to much injustice and annoyance. On the other hand, to leave the Negro in the hands of Southern courts was impossible. In a distracted land where slavery had hardly fallen, to keep the strong from wanton abuse of the weak, and the weak from bloating insolently over the half-shorn strength of the strong, was a thankless, hopeless task. The former masters of the land were peremptorily ordered about, seized, and imprisoned, and punished over and again, with scant courtesy from army officers. The former slaves were intimidated, beaten, raped, and butchered by angry and revengeful men. Bureau courts tended to become centres simply for punishing whites, while the regular civil courts tended to become solely institutions for perpetuating the slavery of blacks. Almost every law and method ingenuity could devise was employed by the legislatures to reduce the Negroes to serfdom,—to make them the slaves of the State, if not of individual owners; while the Bureau officials too often were found striving to put the "bottom rail on top," and gave the freedmen a power and independence which they could not yet use. It is all well enough for us of another generation to wax wise with advice to those who bore the burden in the heat of the day. It is full easy now to see that the man who lost home, fortune, and family at a stroke, and saw his land ruled by "mules and niggers," was really benefited by the passing of slavery. It is not difficult now to say to the young freedman, cheated and cuffed about who has seen his father's head beaten to a jelly and his own mother namelessly assaulted, that the meek shall inherit the earth. Above all, nothing is more convenient than to heap on the Freedmen's Bureau all the evils of that evil day, and damn it utterly for every mistake and blunder that was made.

All this is easy, but it is neither sensible nor just. Some one had blundered, but that was long before Oliver Howard was born; there was criminal aggression and heedless neglect, but without some system of control there would have been far more than there was. Had that control been from within, the Negro would have been re-enslaved, to all intents and purposes. Coming as the control did from without, perfect men and methods would have bettered all things; and even with imperfect agents and questionable methods, the work accomplished was not undeserving of commendation.

Such was the dawn of Freedom; such

was the work of the Freedmen's Bureau, which, summed up in brief, may be epitomized thus: for some fifteen million dollars, beside the sums spent before 1865, and the dole of benevolent societies, this Bureau set going a system of free labor, established a beginning of peasant proprietorship, secured the recognition of black freedmen before courts of law, and founded the free common school in the South. On the other hand, it failed to begin the establishment of good-will between ex-masters and freedmen, to guard its work wholly from paternalistic methods which discouraged self-reliance, and to carry out to any considerable extent its implied promises to furnish the freedmen with land. Its successes were the result of hard work, supplemented by the aid of philanthropists and the eager striving of black men. Its failures were the result of bad local agents, the inherent difficulties of the work, and national neglect.

Such an institution, from its wide powers, great responsibilities, large control of moneys, and generally conspicuous position, was naturally open to repeated and bitter attack. It sustained a searching Congressional investigation at the instance of Fernando Wood in 1870. Its archives and few remaining functions were with blunt discourtesy transferred from Howard's control, in his absence, to the supervision of Secretary of War Belknap in 1872, on the Secretary's recommendation. Finally, in consequence of grave intimations of wrong-doing made by the Secretary and his subordinates, General Howard was court-martialed in 1874. In both of these trials the Commissioner of the Freedmen's Bureau was officially exonerated from any wilful misdoing, and his work commended. Nevertheless, many unpleasant things were brought to light,—the methods of transacting the business of the Bureau were faulty; several cases of defalcation were proved, and other frauds strongly suspected; there were some business transactions which savored of dangerous speculation, if not dishonesty; and around it all lay the smirch of the Freedmen's Bank.

Morally and practically the Freedmen's Bank was part of the Freedmen's Bureau, although it had no legal connection with it. With the prestige of the government back of it, and a directing board of unusual respectability and national reputation, this banking institution had made a remarkable start in the development of that thrift among black folk which slavery had kept them from knowing. Then in one sad day came the crash,—all the hard-earned dollars of the freedmen disappeared; but that was the least of the loss,—all the faith in saving went too, and much of the faith in men; and that was a loss that a Nation which to-day sneers at Negro shiftlessness has never yet made good. Not even ten additional years of slavery could have done so much to throttle the thrift of the freedmen as the mismanagement and bankruptcy of the series of savings banks chartered by the Nation for their especial aid. Where all the blame should rest, it is hard to say; whether the Bureau and the Bank died chiefly by reason of the blows of its selfish friends or the dark machinations of its foes, perhaps even time will never reveal, for here lies unwritten history.

Of the foes without the Bureau, the bitterest were those who attacked not so much its conduct or policy under the law as the necessity for any such institution at all. Such attacks came primarily from the Border States and the South; and they were summed up by Senator Davis, of Kentucky, when he moved to entitle the act of 1866 a bill "to promote strife and conflict between the white and black races . . . by a grant of unconstitutional power." The argument gathered tremendous strength South and North; but its very strength was its weakness. For, argued the plain common-sense of the nation, if it is unconstitu-

tional, unpractical, and futile for the nation to stand guardian over its helpless wards, then there is left but one alternative,—to make those wards their own guardians by arming them with the ballot. Moreover, the path of the practical politician pointed the same way; for, argued this opportunist, if we cannot peacefully reconstruct the South with white votes, we certainly can with black votes. So justice and force joined hands.

The alternative thus offered the nation was not between full and restricted Negro suffrage; else every sensible man, black and white, would easily have chosen the latter. It was rather a choice between suffrage and slavery, after endless blood and gold had flowed to sweep human bondage away. Not a single Southern legislature stood ready to admit a Negro, under any conditions, to the polls; not a single Southern legislature believed free Negro labor was possible without a system of restrictions that took all its freedom away; there was scarcely a white man in the South who did not honestly regard Emancipation as a crime, and its practical nullification as a duty. In such a situation, the granting of the ballot to the black man was a necessity, the very least a guilty nation could grant a wronged race, and the only method of compelling the South to accept the results of the war. Thus Negro suffrage ended a civil war by beginning a race feud. And some felt gratitude toward the race thus sacrificed in its swaddling clothes on the altar of national integrity; and some felt and feel only indifference and contempt.

Had political exigencies been less pressing, the opposition to government guardianship of Negroes less bitter, and the attachment to the slave system less strong, the social seer can well imagine a far better policy,—a permanent Freedmen's Bureau, with a national system of Negro schools; a carefully supervised employment and labor office; a system of impartial protection before the regular courts; and such institutions for social betterment as savings-banks, land and building associations, and social settlements. All this vast expenditure of money and brains might have formed a great school of prospective citizenship, and solved in a way we have not yet solved the most perplexing and persistent of the Negro problems.

That such an institution was unthinkable in 1870 was due in part to certain acts of the Freedmen's Bureau itself. It came to regard its work as merely temporary, and Negro suffrage as a final answer to all present perplexities. The political ambition of many of its agents and *protégés* led it far afield into questionable activities, until the South, nursing its own deep prejudices, came easily to ignore all the good deeds of the Bureau and hate its very name with perfect hatred. So the Freedmen's Bureau died, and its child was the Fifteenth Amendment.

The passing of a great human institution before its work is done, like the untimely passing of a single soul, but leaves a legacy of striving for other men. The legacy of the Freedmen's Bureau is the heavy heritage of this generation. To-day, when new and vaster problems are destined to strain every fibre of the national mind and soul, would it not be well to count this legacy honestly and carefully? For this much all men know: despite compromise, war, and struggle, the Negro is not free. In the backwoods of the Gulf States, for miles and miles, he may not leave the plantation of his birth; in well-nigh the whole rural South the black farmers are peons, bound by law and custom to an economic slavery, from which the only escape is death or the penitentiary. In the most cultured sections and cities of the South the Negroes are a segregated servile caste, with restricted rights and privileges. Before the courts, both in law and custom, they stand on a different and peculiar basis. Taxation without representation is the rule of their political life. And the result of all this is, and in nature must have been, lawlessness and crime. That is the large legacy of the Freedmen's Bureau, the work it did not do because it could not.

I have seen a land right merry with the sun, where children sing, and rolling hills lie like passioned women wanton with harvest. And there in the King's Highway sat and sits a figure veiled and bowed, by which the traveller's footsteps hasten as they go. On the tainted air broods fear. Three centuries' thought has been the raising and unveiling of that bowed human heart, and now behold a century new for the duty and the deed. The problem of the Twentieth Century is the problem of the color-line.

Jane Addams

Born in 1860 in Cedarville, Illinois, daughter of a prosperous Quaker, Jane Addams became a symbol of the influence volunteerism can have in improving lives. She became an influential political reformer of factory working conditions, child-labor laws, the control of narcotics, and sanitary environmental conditions, not to mention her antiwar activities during World War I. Addams also sympathized with the handicapped; she herself had a crooked spine resulting from childhood tuberculosis.

Addams graduated from Rockford Seminary, one of the first U.S. colleges for women, and inherited enough money at her father's death to support herself. She traveled to

Europe and visited Toynbee Hall in the slums of London, the world's first "settlement house," established by Oxford students for the needy. Toynbee Hall offered courses in music, shorthand, and French and English literature, and provided a library, athletic field, and meeting room.

Back in America, Addams decided to create her own settlement house in Chicago. She rented the Hull-House, in a poor industrial section of the city, together with Ellen Gates Starr, her traveling companion. There, without a plan, they spontaneously reacted to whatever was needed. They opened a nursery in their home, followed by a kindergarten, a boys' club, and a coffeehouse for working-class adults in the evening. They taught English, music, and acting, recruiting college volunteers attracted by the reputation of Hull-House. An art museum and book bindery followed as wealthy Chicago patrons began to donate money.

Addams began to make enemies, as well as friends, by lobbying to clean up the "sweatshops" of Chicago—factories with unsanitary working conditions that exploited children under age fourteen. Partly due to her activities, the 1893 Workshop and Factories bill was passed in Illinois prohibiting the exploitation of minors in the workplace. Addams became the district garbage inspector to clean up the streets in her area, significantly lowering the death rate, and was instrumental in controlling the sale of drugs and impure milk, which resulted in a decline in infant mortality.

During World War I, Addams organized the Women's International League for Peace and Freedom, which supported ending the war and caused many American patriots to view her as an enemy and a radical. Despite this, Addams in 1931 was awarded the Nobel Peace Prize. She died in 1935, leaving behind an inspiration for volunteerism and the Hull-House Association, which still runs inner-city neighborhood centers. Addams's writings include *Democracy and Social Ethics* (1902), *Newer Ideals of Peace* (1907), *The Spirit of Youth and the City Streets* (1909), *If Men Were Seeking the Franchise* (1913), and *Twenty Years at Hull-House* (1910), from which the following is excerpted.

❦

Twenty Years at Hull-House (1910)
(excerpts)

Subjective Necessity for Social Settlements

The Ethical Culture Societies held a summer school at Plymouth, Massachusetts, in 1892, to which they invited several people representing the then new Settlement movement, that they might discuss with others the general theme of Philanthropy and Social Progress.

I venture to produce here parts of a lecture I delivered in Plymouth, both because I have found it impossible to formulate with the same freshness those early motives and strivings, and because, when published with other papers given that summer, it was received by the Settlement people themselves as a satisfactory statement. . . .

[The Lecture]

This paper is an attempt to analyze the motives which underlie a movement based, not only upon conviction, but upon genuine emotion, wherever educated young people are seeking an outlet for that sentiment of universal brotherhood, which the best spirit of our times is forcing from an emotion into a motive. These young people accomplish little toward the solution of this social problem, and bear the brunt of being cultivated into unnourished, oversensitive lives. They have been shut off from the common labor by which they live which is a great source of moral and physical health. They feel a fatal want of harmony between their theory and their lives, a lack of coordination between thought and action. I think it is hard for us to realize how seriously many of them are taking to the notion of human brotherhood, how eagerly they long to give tangible expression to the democratic ideal. These young men and women, longing to socialize their democracy, are animated by certain hopes which may be thus loosely formulated; that if in a democratic country nothing can be permanently achieved save through the masses of the people, it will be impossible to establish a higher political life than the people themselves crave; that it is difficult to see how the notion of a higher civic life can be fostered save through common intercourse; that the blessing which we associate with a life of refinement and cultivation can be made universal and must be made universal if they are to be permanent; that the good we secure for ourselves is precarious and uncertain, is floating in mid-air, until it is secured for all of us and incorporated into our common life. It is easier to state these hopes than to formulate the line of motives, which I believe to constitute the trend of the subjective pressure toward the Settlement. There is something primordial about these motives, but I am perhaps over-bold in designating them as a great desire to share the race life. We all bear traces of the starvation struggle which for so long made up the life of the race. Our very organism holds memories and glimpses of that long life of our ancestors which still goes on among so many of our contemporaries. Nothing so deadens the sympathies and shrivels the power of enjoyment, as the persistent keeping away from the great opportunities for helpfulness and a continual ignoring of the starvation struggle which makes up the life of at least half the race. To shut one's self away from that half of the race life is to shut one's self away from the most vital part of it; it is to live out but half the humanity to which we have been born heir and to use but half our faculties. We have all had longings for a fuller life which should include the use of these faculties. These longings are the physical component of the "Intimations of Immortality," on which no ode has yet been written. To portray these would be the work of a poet, and it is hazardous for any but a poet to attempt it.

You may remember the forlorn feeling which occasionally seizes you when you arrive early in the morning a stranger in a great city: the stream of laboring people goes past you as you gaze through the plate-glass window of your hotel; you see hard working men lifting great burdens; you hear the driving and jostling of huge carts and your heart sinks with a sudden sense of futility. The door opens behind you and you turn to the man who brings you in your breakfast with a quick sense of human fellowship. You find yourself praying that you may never lose your hold on it all. A more poetic prayer would be that the great mother breasts of our common humanity, with its labor and suffering and its homely comforts, may never be withheld from you. You turn helplessly to the waiter and feel that it would be almost grotesque to claim from him the sympathy you crave because civilization has placed you apart, but you resent your position with a sudden sense of snobbery. Literature is full of portrayals of these glimpses: they come to ship-wrecked men on rafts; they overcome the differences of an incongruous multitude when in the presence of a great danger or when moved by a common enthusiasm. They are not, however, confined to such moments, and if we were in the habit of telling them to each other, the recital would be as long as the tales of children are, when they sit down on the green grass and confide to each other how many times they have remembered that they lived once before. If these childish tales are the stirring of inherited impressions, just so surely is the other the striving of inherited powers.

"It is true that there is nothing after disease, indigence and a sense of guilt, so fatal to health and to life itself as the want of a proper outlet for active faculties." I have seen young girls suffer and grow sensibly lowered in vitality in the first years after they leave school. In our attempt then to give a girl pleasure and freedom from care we succeed, for the most part, in making her pitifully miserable. She finds "life" so different from what she expected it to be. She is besotted with innocent little ambitions, and does not understand this apparent waste of herself, this elaborate preparation, if no work is provided for her. There is a heritage of noble obligation which young people accept and long to perpetuate. The desire for action, the wish to right wrong and alleviate suffering haunts them daily. Society smiles at it indulgently instead of making it of value to itself. The wrong to them begins even farther back, when we restrain the first childish desires for "doing good" and tell them that they must wait until they are older and better fitted. We intimate that social obligation begins at a fixed date, forgetting that it begins with birth itself. We treat them as children who, with strong-growing limbs, are allowed to use their legs but not their arms, or whose legs are daily carefully exercised that after a while their arms may be put to high use. We do this in spite of the protest of the best educators,

Locke and Pestalozzi. We are fortunate in the meantime if their unused members do not weaken and disappear. They do sometimes. There are a few girls who, by the time they are "educated," forget their old childish desires to help the world and to play with poor little girls "who haven't playthings." Parents are often inconsistent: they deliberately expose their daughters to knowledge of the distress in the world; they send them to hear missionary addresses on famines in India and China; they accompany them to lectures on suffering in Siberia; they agitate together over the forgotten region of East London. In addition to this, from babyhood the altruistic tendencies of these daughters are persistently cultivated. They are taught to be self-forgetting and self-sacrificing, to consider the good of the whole before the good of the ego. But when all this information and culture show results, when the daughter comes back from college and begins to recognize her social claim to the "submerged tenth," and to evince a disposition to fulfill it, the family claim is strenuously asserted; she is told that she is unjustified, ill-advised in her efforts. If she persists, the family too often are injured and unhappy unless the efforts are called missionary and the religious zeal of the family carry them over their sense of abuse. When this zeal does not exist, the result is perplexing. It is a curious violation of what we would fain believe a fundamental law—that the final return of the deed is upon the head of the doer. The deed is that of exclusiveness and caution, but the return, instead of falling upon the head of the exclusive and cautious, falls upon a young head full of generous and unselfish plans. The girl loses something vital out of her life to which she is entitled. She is restricted and unhappy; her elders, meanwhile, are unconscious of the situation and we have all the elements of a tragedy.

We have in America a fast-growing number of cultivated young people who have no recognized outlet for their active faculties. They hear constantly of the great social maladjustment, but no way is provided for them to change it, and their uselessness hangs about them heavily. Huxley declares that the sense of uselessness is the severest shock which the human system can sustain, and that if persistently sustained, it results in atrophy of function. These young people have had advantages of college, of European travel, and of economic study, but they are sustaining this shock of inaction. They have pet phrases, and they tell you that the things that make us all alike are stronger than the things that make us different. They say that all men are united by needs and sympathies far more permanent and radical than anything that temporarily divides them and sets them in opposition to each other. If they affect art, they say that the decay in artistic expression is due to the decay in ethics, that art when shut away from the human interests and from the great mass of humanity is self-destructive. They tell their elders with all the bitterness of youth that if they expect success from them in business or politics or in whatever lines their ambition for them has run, they must let them consult all of humanity; that they must let them find out what the people want and how they want it. It is only the stronger young people, however, who formulate this. Many of them dissipate their energies in so-called enjoyment. Others not content with that, go on studying and go back to college for their second degrees; not that they are especially fond of study, but because they want something definite to do, and their powers have been trained in the direction of mental accumulation. Many are buried beneath this mental accumulation with lowered vitality and discontent. Walter Besant says they have had the vision that Peter had when he saw the great sheet let down from heaven, wherein was neither clean nor unclean. He calls it the sense of humanity.

It is not philanthropy nor benevolence, but a thing fuller and wider than either of these.

This young life, so sincere in its emotion and good phrases and yet so undirected, seems to me as pitiful as the other great mass of destitute lives. One is supplementary to the other, and some method of communication can surely be devised. Mr. Barnett, who urged the first Settlement,—Toynbee Hall, in East London,—recognized this need of outlet for the young men of Oxford and Cambridge, and hoped that the Settlement would supply the communication. It is easy to see why the Settlement movement originated in England, where the years of education are more constrained and definite than they are here, where class distinctions are more rigid. The necessity of it was greater there, but we are fast feeling the pressure of the need and meeting the necessity for Settlements in America. Our young people feel nervously the need of putting theory into action, and respond quickly to the Settlement form of activity.

Other motives which I believe make toward the Settlement are the result of a certain renaissance going forward in Christianity. The impulse to share the lives of the poor, the desire to make social service, irrespective of propaganda, express the spirit of Christ, is as old as Christianity itself. We have no proof from the records themselves that the early Roman Christians, who strained their simple art to the point of grotesqueness in their eagerness to record a "good news" on the walls of the catacombs, considered this good news a religion. Jesus had no set of truths labeled Religious. On the contrary, his doctrine was that all truth is one, that the appropriation of it is freedom. His teaching had no dogma to mark it off from truth and action in general. He himself called it a revelation—a life. These early Roman Christians received the Gospel message, a command to love all men, with a certain joyous simplicity. The image of the Good Shepherd is blithe and gay beyond the gentlest shepherd of Greek mythology; the hart no longer pants, but rushes to the water brooks. The Christians looked for the continuous revelation, but believed what Jesus said, that this revelation, to be retained and made manifest, must be put into terms of action; that action is the only medium man has for receiving and appropriating truth; that the doctrine must be known through the will.

That Christianity has to be revealed and embodied in the line of social progress is a corollary to the simple proposition, that man's action is found in his social relationships in the way in which he connects with his fellows; that his motives for action are the zeal and affection with which he regards his fellows. By this simple process was created a deep enthusiasm for humanity, which regarded man as at once the organ and the object of revelation; and by this process came about the wonderful fellowship, the true democracy of the early Church, that so captivates the imagination. The early Christians were preeminently nonresistant. They believed in love as a cosmic force. There was no iconoclasm during the minor peace of the Church. They did not yet denounce nor tear down temples, nor preach the end of the world. They grew to a mighty number, but it never occurred to them, either in their weakness or in their strength, to regard other men for an instant as their foes or as aliens. The spectacle of the Christians loving all men was the most astounding Rome had ever seen. They were eager to sacrifice themselves for the weak, for children, and for the aged; they identified themselves with slaves and did not avoid the plague; they longed to share the common lot that they might receive the constant revelation. It was a new treasure which the early Christians added to the sum of all treasures, a joy hitherto unknown in the world—the joy of finding the Christ which lieth in each man,

but which no man can unfold save in fellowship. A happiness ranging from the heroic to the pastoral enveloped them. They were to possess a revelation as long as life had new meaning to unfold, new action to propose.

I believe that there is a distinct turning among many young men and women toward this simple acceptance of Christ's message. They resent the assumption that Christianity is a set of ideas which belong to the religious consciousness, whatever that may be. They insist that it cannot be proclaimed and instituted apart from the social life of the community and that it must seek a simple and natural expression in the social organism itself. The Settlement movement is only one manifestation of that wider humanitarian movement which throughout Christendom, but preeminently in England, is endeavoring to embody itself, not in a sect, but in society itself.

I believe that this turning, this renaissance of the early Christian humanitarianism, is going on in America, in Chicago, if you please, without leaders who write or philosophize, without much speaking, but with a bent to express in social service and in terms of action the spirit of Christ. Certain it is that spiritual force is found in the Settlement movement, and it is also true that this force must be evoked and must be called into play before the success of any Settlement is assured. There must be the overmastering belief that all that is noblest in life is common to men as men, in order to accentuate the likenesses and ignore the differences which are found among the people whom the Settlement constantly brings into juxtaposition. It may be true, as the Positivists insist, that the very religious fervor of man can be turned into love for his race, and his desire for a future life into content to live in the echo of his deeds; Paul's formula of seeking for the Christ which lieth in each man and founding our likenesses on him, seems a simpler formula to many of us.

In a thousand voices singing the Hallelujah Chorus in Handel's "Messiah," it is possible to distinguish the leading voices, but the differences of training and cultivation between them and the voices of the chorus, are lost in the unity of purpose and in the fact that they are all human voices lifted by a high motive. This is a weak illustration of what a Settlement attempts to do. It aims, in a measure, to develop whatever of social life its neighborhood may afford, to focus and give form to that life, to bring to bear upon it the results of cultivation and training; but it receives in exchange for the music of isolated voices the volume and strength of the chorus. It is quite impossible for me to say in what proportion or degree the subjective necessity which led to the opening of Hull-House combined the three trends: first, the desire to interpret democracy in social terms; secondly, the impulse beating at the very source of our lives, urging us to aid in the race progress; and, thirdly, the Christian movement toward humanitarianism. It is difficult to analyze a living thing; the analysis is at best imperfect. Many more motives may blend with the three trends; possibly the desire for a new form of social success due to the nicety of imagination, which refuses worldly pleasures unmixed with the joys of self-sacrifice; possibly a love of approbation, so vast that it is not content with the treble clapping of delicate hands, but wishes also to hear the bass notes from toughened palms, may mingle with these.

The Settlement, then, is an experimental effort to aid in the solution of the social and industrial problems which are engendered by the conditions of life in a great city. It insists that these problems are not confined to any one portion of a city. It is an attempt to relieve, at the same time, the overaccumulation at one end of society and the destitution at the other; but it assumes that this overaccumulation and destitution is most sorely felt in the things that pertain to social and educational advantages. From its very nature it can stand for no political or social propaganda. It must, in a sense, give the warm welcome of an inn to all such propaganda, if perchance one of them be found an angel. The one thing to be dreaded in the Settlement is that it lose its flexibility, its power of quick adaptation, its readiness to change its methods as its environment may demand. It must be open to conviction and must have a deep and abiding sense of tolerance. It must be hospitable and ready for experiment. It should demand from its residents a scientific patience in the accumulation of facts and the steady holding of their sympathies as one of the best instruments for that accumulation. It must be grounded in a philosophy whose foundation is on the solidarity of the human race, a philosophy which will not waver when the race happens to be represented by a drunken woman or an idiot boy. Its residents must be emptied of all conceit of opinion and all self-assertion, and ready to arouse and interpret the public opinion of their neighborhood. They must be content to live quietly side by side with their neighbors, until they grow into a sense of relationship and mutual interests. Their neighbors are held apart by differences of race and language which the residents can more easily overcome. They are bound to see the needs of their neighborhood as a whole, to furnish data for legislation, and to use their influence to secure it. In short, residents are pledged to devote themselves to the duties of good citizenship and to the arousing of the social energies which too largely lie dormant in every neighborhood given over to industrialism. They are bound to regard the entire life of their city as organic, to make an effort to unify it, and to protest against its over-differentiation.

It is always easy to make all philosophy point one particular moral and all history adorn one particular tale; but I may be forgiven the reminder that the best speculative philosophy sets forth the solidarity of the human race; that the highest moralists have taught that without the advance and improvement of the whole, no man can hope for any lasting improvement in his own moral or material individual condition; and that the subjective necessity for Social Settlements is therefore identical with that necessity, which urges us on toward social and individual salvation.

William Jennings Bryan

Populist William Jennings Bryan became a perennial Democratic candidate for president whose major reforms were adopted although he was never elected: the income tax, woman suffrage, popular election of senators, public knowledge of ownership of newspapers, and Prohibition. Born in 1860 in Salem, Illinois, Bryan practiced law in Illinois until moving to Nebraska, where he served as a U.S. representative from 1891 to 1895. After being defeated in a race for the Senate, he served briefly as editor in chief of the Omaha *World-Herald.*

Bryan became the chief advocate of the Free Silver movement, arguing that the unlimited coinage of silver would cure the economic problems of farmers and industrial workers. His "Cross of Gold" speech at the 1896 Democratic Convention was so compelling that he was nominated for president at age thirty-six with $100 in his pocket and no influential backers or large funds—just shrewdness, luck, and a golden tongue. He lost to Republican William McKinley. Four years later, with a campaign focused on anti-imperialism, Bryan again lost to McKinley. Bryan then founded the widely read *Commoner,* and in 1908 was again nominated by the Democrats to run for president, this time losing to William H. Taft. In 1912 Bryan switched to support Woodrow Wilson, giving Wilson the Democratic nomination. Wilson, in turn, appointed Bryan secretary of state when the Democrats won the election, although Bryan's antiwar sentiments led him to resign rather than sign the strong language Wilson used in the second note to the Germans on the sinking of the *Lusitania.*

In later life, a Presbyterian, Bryan devoted himself to fundamentalism, urging legislatures to oppose the teaching of evolution and acting as prosecutor in the famous Scopes trial in Tennessee in 1925, which he won, although he was ridiculed severely by the opposing counsel, Clarence Darrow. Bryan died five days after the trial ended.

❧❦❧

Cross of Gold Speech (1896)

Mr. Chairman and Gentlemen of the Convention:

I would be presumptuous, indeed, to present myself against the distinguished gentlemen to whom you have listened if this were a mere measuring of abilities; but this is not a contest between persons. The humblest citizen in all the land, when clad in the armor of a righteous cause, is stronger than all the hosts of error. I come to speak to you in defense of a cause as holy as the cause of liberty—the cause of humanity.

When this debate is concluded, a motion will be made to lay upon the table the resolution offered in commendation of the administration, and also the resolution offered in condemnation of the administration. We object to bringing this question down to the level of persons. The individual is but an atom; he is born, he acts, he dies; but principles are eternal; and this has been a contest over a principle.

Never before in the history of this country has there been witnessed such a contest as that through which we have just passed. Never before in the history of American politics has a great issue been fought out as this issue has been, by the voters of a great party. On the fourth of March, 1895, a few Democrats, most of them members of Congress, issued an address to the Democrats of the nation, asserting that the money question was the paramount issue of the hour; declaring that a majority of the Democratic party had the right to control the action of the party on this paramount issue; and concluding with the request that the believers in the free coinage of silver in the Democratic party should organize, take charge of, and control the policy of the Democratic party. Three months later, at Memphis, an organization was perfected, and the silver Democrats went forth openly and courageously proclaiming their belief, and declaring that, if successful, they would crystallize into a platform the declaration which they had made. They began the conflict. With a zeal approaching the zeal which inspired the crusaders who followed Peter the Hermit, our silver Democrats went forth from victory unto victory until they are now assembled, not to discuss, not to debate, but to enter up the judgment already rendered by the plain people of this country. In this contest brother has been arrayed against brother, father against son. The warmest ties of love, acquaintance and association have been disregarded; old leaders have been cast aside when they have refused to give expression to the sentiments of those whom they would lead, and new leaders have sprung up to give direction to this cause of truth. Thus has the contest been waged, and we have assembled here under as binding and solemn instructions as were ever imposed upon representatives of the people.

We do not come as individuals. As individuals we might have been glad to compliment the gentleman from New York [Senator Hill] but we know that the people for whom we speak would never be willing to put him in a position where he could thwart the will of the Democratic party. I say it was not a question of persons; it was a question of principle, and it is not with gladness, my friends, that we find ourselves brought into conflict with those who are now arrayed on the other side.

The gentleman who preceded me [ex-Governor Russell] spoke of the State of Massachusetts; let me assure him that not one present in all this convention entertains the least hostility to the people of the State of Massachusetts, but we stand here representing people who are the equals, before the law, of the greatest citizens in the State of Massachusetts. When you [turning to the gold delegates] come before us and tell us that we are about to disturb your business interests, we reply that you have disturbed our business interests by your course.

We say to you that you have made the definition of a business man too limited in its application. The man who is employed for wages is as much a business man as his employer; the attorney in a country town is as much a business man as the corporation counsel in a great metropolis; the merchant at the cross-roads store is as much a business man as the merchant of New York; the farmer who goes forth in the morning and toils all day—who begins in the spring and toils all summer—and who by the application of brain and muscle to the natural resources of the country creates wealth, is as much a business man as the man who goes upon the board of trade and bets upon the price of grain; the miners who go down a thousand feet into the earth, or climb two thousand feet upon the cliffs, and bring forth from their hiding places the precious metals to be poured into the channels of trade are as much business men as the few financial magnates who, in a back room, corner the money of the world. We come to speak for this broader class of business men.

Ah, my friends, we say not one word against those who live upon the Atlantic coast, but the hardy pioneers who have braved all the dangers of the wilderness, who have made the desert to blossom as the rose—the pioneers away out there [pointing to the West], who rear their children near to Nature's heart, where they can mingle their voices with the voices of the birds—out there where they have erected schoolhouses for the education of their young, churches where they praise their Creator, and cemeteries where rest the ashes of their dead—these people, we say, are as deserving of the consideration of our party as any people in this country. It is for these that we speak. We do not come as aggressors. Our war is not a war of conquest; we are fighting in the defense of our homes, our families, and posterity. We have petitioned, and our petitions have been scorned; we have entreated, and our entreaties have been disregarded; we have begged, and they have mocked when our calamity came. We beg no longer; we entreat no more; we petition no more. We defy them.

The gentleman from Wisconsin has said that he fears a Robespierre. My friends in this land of the free you need not fear that a tyrant will spring up from among the people. What we need is an Andrew Jackson to stand, as Jackson stood, against the encroachments of organized wealth.

They tell us that this platform was made to catch votes. We reply to them that changing conditions make new issues; that the principles upon which Democracy rests are as everlasting as the hills, but that they must be applied to new conditions as they arise. Conditions have arisen and we are here to meet those conditions. They tell us that the income tax ought not to be brought in here; that it is a new idea. They criticize us for our criticism of the Supreme Court of the United States. My friends, we have not criticized; we have simply called attention to what you already know. If you want criticisms, read the dissenting opinions of the court. There you will find criticisms. They say that we passed an unconstitutional law; we deny it. The income tax law was not unconstitutional when it was passed; it was not unconstitutional when it went before the Supreme Court for the first time; it did not become unconstitutional until one of the judges changed his mind, and we cannot be expected to know when a judge will change his mind. The income tax is just. It simply intends to put the burdens of government justly upon the backs of the people. I am in favor of an income tax. When I find a man who is not willing to bear his share of the burdens of the government which protects him, I find a man who is unworthy to enjoy the blessings of a government like ours.

They say that we are opposing national bank currency; it is true. If you will read what Thomas Benton said, you will find he said that, in searching history, he could find but one parallel to Andrew Jackson; that was Cicero, who destroyed the conspiracy of Cataline and saved Rome. Benton said that Cicero only did for Rome what Jackson did for us when he destroyed the bank conspiracy and saved America. We say in our platform that we believe that the right to coin and issue money is a function of government. We believe it. We believe that it is a part of sovereignty, and can no more with safety be delegated to private individuals than we could afford to delegate to private individuals the power to make penal statutes or levy taxes. Mr. Jefferson, who was once regarded as good Democratic authority, seems to have differed in opinion from the gentleman who has addressed us on the part of the minority. Those who are opposed to this proposition tell us that the issue of paper money is a function of the bank, and that the Government ought to go out of the banking business. I stand with Jefferson rather than with them, and tell them, as he did, that the issue of money is a function of government, and that the banks ought to go out of the governing business.

They complain about the plank which declares against life tenure in office. They have tried to strain it to mean that which it does not mean. What we oppose by that plank is the life tenure which is being built up in Washington, and which excludes from participation in official benefits the humbler members of society.

Let me call your attention to two or three important things. The gentleman from New York says that he will propose an amendment to the platform providing that the proposed change in our monetary system shall not affect contracts already made. Let me remind you that there is no intention of affecting those contracts which according to present laws are made payable in gold; but if he means to say that we cannot change our monetary system without protecting those who have loaned money before the change was made, I desire to ask him where, in law or in morals, he can find justification for not protecting the debtors when the act of 1873 was passed, if he now insists that we must protect the creditors.

He says he will also propose an amendment which will provide for the suspension of free coinage if we fail to maintain the party within a year. We reply that when

we advocate a policy which we believe will be successful, we are not compelled to raise a doubt as to our own sincerity by suggesting what we shall do if we fail. I ask him, if he would apply his logic to us, why he does not apply it to himself. He says he wants this country to try to secure an international agreement. Why does he not tell us what he is going to do if he fails to secure an international agreement? There is more reason for him to do that than there is for us to provide against the failure to maintain the parity. Our opponents have tried for twenty years to secure an international agreement, and those are waiting for it most patiently who do not want it at all.

And now, my friends, let me come to the paramount issue. If they ask us why it is that we say more on the money question than we say upon the tariff question, I reply that, if protection has slain its thousands, the gold standard has slain its tens of thousands. If they ask us why we do not embody in our platform all the things that we believe in, we reply that when we have restored the money of the Constitution all other necessary reforms will be possible; but that until this is done there is no other reform that can be accomplished.

Why is it that within three months such a change has come over the country? Three months ago, when it was confidently asserted that those who believe in the gold standard would frame our platform and nominate our candidates, even the advocates of the gold standard did not think that we could elect a president. And they had good reason for their doubt, because there is scarcely a State here today asking for the gold standard which is not in the absolute control of the Republican party. But note the change. Mr. McKinley was nominated at St. Louis upon a platform which declared for the maintenance of the gold standard until it can be changed into bimetallism by international agreement. Mr. McKinley was the most popular man among the

Republicans, and three months ago everybody in the Republican party prophesied his election. How is it today? Why, the man who was once pleased to think that he looked like Napoleon—that man shudders today when he remembers that he was nominated on the anniversary of the battle of Waterloo. Not only that, but as he listens he can hear with ever-increasing distinctness the sound of the waves as they beat upon the lonely shores of St. Helena.

Why this change? Ah, my friends, is not the reason for the change evident to any one who will look at the matter? No private character, however pure, no personal popularity, however great, can protect from the avenging wrath of an indignant people a man who will declare that he is in favor of fastening the gold standard upon this country, or who is willing to surrender the right of self-government and place the legislative control of our affairs in the hands of foreign potentates and powers.

We go forth confident that we shall win. Why? Because upon the paramount issue of this campaign there is not a spot of ground upon which the enemy will dare to challenge battle. If they tell us that the gold standard is a good thing, we shall point to their platform and tell them that their platform pledges the party to get rid of the gold standard and substitute bimetallism. If the gold standard is a good thing, why try to get rid of it? I call your attention to the fact that some of the very people who are in this convention today and who tell us that we ought to declare in favor of international bimetallism—thereby declaring that the gold standard is wrong and that the principle of bimetallism is better— these very people four months ago were open and avowed advocates of the gold standard, and were then telling us that we could not legislate two metals together, even with the aid of all the world. If the gold standard is a good thing, we ought to

declare in favor of its retention and not in favor of abandoning it; and if the gold standard is a bad thing why should we wait until other nations are willing to help us to let go? Here is the line of battle, and we care not upon which issue they force the fight; we are prepared to meet them on either issue or on both. If they tell us that the gold standard is the standard of civilization, we reply to them that this, the most enlightened of all the nations of the earth, has never declared for a gold standard and that both the great parties this year are declaring against it. If the gold standard is the standard of civilization, why, my friends, should we not have it? If they come to meet us on that issue we can present the history of our nation. More than that; we can tell them that they will search the pages of history in vain to find a single instance where the common people of any land have ever declared themselves in favor of the gold standard. They can find where the holders of the fixed investments have declared for a gold standard, but not where the masses have.

Mr. Carlisle said in 1878 that this was a struggle between "the idle holders of idle capital" and "the struggling masses, who produce the wealth and pay the taxes of the country;" and, my friends, the question we are to decide is: Upon which side will the Democratic party fight; upon the side of "the idle holders of idle capital" or upon the side of "the struggling masses"? That is the question which the party must answer first, and then it must be answered by each individual hereafter. The sympathies of the Democratic party, as shown by the platform, are on the side of the struggling masses who have ever been the foundation of the Democratic party. There are two ideas of government. There are those who believe that, if you will only legislate to make the well-to-do prosperous, their prosperity will leak through on those below. The Democratic idea, however, has been that if you legislate to make the masses prosperous, their prosperity will find its way up through every class which rests upon them.

You come to us and tell us that the great cities are in favor of the gold standard; we reply that the great cities rest upon our broad and fertile prairies. Burn down your cities and leave our farms, and your cities will spring up again as if by magic; but destroy our farms and the grass will grow in the streets of every city in the country.

My friends, we declare that this nation is able to legislate for its own people on every question, without waiting for the aid or consent of any other nation on earth; and upon that issue we expect to carry every State in the Union. I shall not slander the inhabitants of the fair State of Massachusetts nor the inhabitants of the State of New York by saying that, when they are confronted with the proposition, they will declare that this nation is not able to attend to its own business. It is the issue of 1776 over again. Our ancestors, when but three millions in number, had the courage to declare their political independence of every other nation; shall we, their descendants, when we have grown to seventy millions, declare that we are less independent than our forefathers? No, my friends, that will never be the verdict of our people. Therefore, we care not upon what lines the battle is fought. If they say bimetallism is good, but that we cannot have it until other nations help us, we reply that, instead of having a gold standard because England has, we will restore bimetallism, and then let England have bimetallism because the United States has it. If they dare to come out in the open field and defend the gold standard as a good thing, we will fight them to the uttermost. Having behind us the producing masses of this nation and the world, supported by the commercial interests, the laboring interests, and the toilers everywhere, we will answer their demands for a gold standard by saying to them: You shall not press down upon the brow of labor this crown of thorns, you shall not crucify mankind upon a cross of gold.

Herbert Croly

"Hamiltonian means for Jeffersonian ends" was Herbert Croly's clarion call, which resulted in Progressivism (that is, using the social and political means of the state to strive for progress). Croly became an intellectual leader of the Progressive movement, entitling his ideology the "New Nationalism"—a union "between democracy and nationality," based on "the religion of brotherhood, not old-fashioned individualism." He believed that the old system would not cure itself, nor would the problem of corrupt people exploiting political and economic opportunities; the boss and the millionaire were inevitable results of the old system, not just abuses of it. Croly argued that his New Nationalism, with a strong, active, militarily powerful central government, would prepare the way for an American culture in which artists and intellectuals could feel at home.

Born in 1869 in New York City, Croly's father was an editor of *The World* and *The Graphic*. His mother edited *Demorest's Illustrated Monthly* and *Godey's Lady's Book*, two women's magazines. Croly studied for a year at the College of the City of New York and, thereafter, on and off at Harvard (influenced there, to some extent, by George Santayana). He then was employed with the *Architectural Record*, which he edited from

1900 to 1906 and worked for until 1913. He resigned as editor to write *The Promise of American Life* (1909), which was to have significant political influence. The book reinforced, if not stimulated, Theodore Roosevelt's New Nationalism (with ideas similar to Croly's) and, to a lesser extent, Woodrow Wilson's New Freedom. Croly argued for a "Hamiltonian principle of national responsibility" (Roosevelt's thrust also), moving beyond the mere "negative" governmental implications of Jeffersonian individualism (which was more Woodrow Wilson's thrust). Croly argued that Jefferson's "cant" about equal rights for all and special privileges for none obscured the need for a strong national state, and that Jefferson advocated "a government of and by the people" when he should have sought "a government for the people by popular but responsible leaders." According to Croly, laissez-faire liberalism was no longer sufficient for the industrial era. He believed big business and big labor required a strong government to balance and regulate them and to provide for the common good.

Upon reading *The Promise of American Life,* Theodore Roosevelt wrote to Croly: "I do not know when I have read a book which I feel profited me as much as your book on American life. I shall use your ideas freely in speeches I intend to make." Wealthy patrons were attracted by the book and supported Croly in founding the *New Republic* in 1914, which he edited until 1928. His other major work was *Progressive Democracy* (1914), which stressed democratic reforms such as referendum, recall, and initiative to offset possible abuses by the state. Croly died in 1930.

The Promise of American Life (1909)
(excerpts)

What is the Promise of American Life?

The average American is nothing if not patriotic. "The Americans are filled," says Mr. Emil Reich in his "Success among the Nations," "with such an implicit and absolute confidence in their Union and in their future success that any remark other than laudatory is inacceptable to the majority of them. We have had many opportunities of hearing public speakers in America cast doubts upon the very existence of God and of Providence, question the historic nature or veracity of the whole fabric of Christianity; but never has it been our fortune to catch the slightest whisper of doubt, the slightest want of faith, in the chief God of America—unlimited belief in the future of America." Mr. Reich's method of emphasis may not be very happy, but the substance of what he says is true. The faith of Americans in their own country is religious, if not in its intensity, at any rate in its almost absolute and universal authority. It pervades the air we breathe. As children we hear it asserted or implied in the conversation of our elders. Every new stage of our educational training provides some additional testimony on its behalf. Newspapers and novelists, orators and playwrights, even if they are little else, are at least loyal preachers of the Truth. The skeptic is not controverted; he is overlooked. It constitutes the kind of faith which is the implication, rather than the object, of thought, and consciously or unconsciously it enters largely into our personal lives as a formative influence. We may distrust and dislike much that is done in the name of our country by our fellow-country-men; but our country itself, its democratic system, and its prosperous future are above suspicion.

Of course, Americans have no monopoly of patriotic enthusiasm and good faith. Englishmen return thanks to Providence for not being born anything but an Englishman, in churches and ale-houses as well as in comic operas. The Frenchman cherishes and proclaims the idea that France is the most civilized modern country and satisfies best the needs of a man of high social intelligence. The Russian, whose political and social estate does not seem enviable to his foreign contemporaries, secretes a vision of a mystically glorified Russia, which condemns to comparative insipidity the figures of the "Pax Britannica" and of "La Belle France" enlightening the world. Every nation, in proportion as its nationality is thoroughly alive, must be leavened by the ferment of some such faith. But there are significant differences between the faith of, say, an Englishman in the British Empire and that of an American in the Land of Democracy. The contents of an Englishman's national idea tends to be more exclusive. His patriotism is anchored to the historical achievements of Great Britain and restricted thereby. As a good patriot he is bound to be more preoccupied with the inherited fabric of national institutions and traditions than he is with the ideal and more than national possibilities of the future. This very loyalty to the national fabric does, indeed, imply an important ideal content; but the national idealism of an Englishman, a German, or even a Frenchman, is heavily mortgaged to his own national history and cannot honestly

escape the debt. The good patriot is obliged to offer faithful allegiance to a network of somewhat arbitrary institutions, social forms, and intellectual habits—on the ground that his country is exposed to more serious dangers from premature emancipation than it is from stubborn conservatism.

France is the only European country which has sought to make headway towards a better future by means of a revolutionary break with its past, and the results of the French experiment have served for other European countries more as a warning than as an example.

The higher American patriotism, on the other hand, combines loyalty to historical tradition and precedent with the imaginative projection of an ideal national Promise. The Land of Democracy has always appealed to its more enthusiastic children chiefly as a land of wonderful and more than national possibilities. "Neither race nor tradition," says Professor Hugo Münsterberg in his volume on "The Americans," "nor the actual past, binds the American to his countrymen, but rather the future which together they are building." This vision of a better future is not, perhaps, as unclouded for the present generation of Americans as it was for certain former generations; but in spite of a more friendly acquaintance with all sorts of obstacles and pitfalls, our country is still figured in the imagination of its citizens as the Land of Promise. They still believe that somehow and sometime something better will happen to good Americans than has happened to men in any other country; and this belief, vague, innocent, and uninformed though it be, is the expression of an essential constituent in our national ideal. The past should mean less to a European than it does to an American, and the future should mean more. To be sure, American life cannot with impunity be wrenched violently from its moorings any more than the life of a European country can; but our American past, compared to that of any European country, has a character all its own. Its peculiarity consists, not merely in its brevity, but in the fact that from the beginning it has been informed by an idea. From the beginning Americans have been anticipating and projecting a better future. From the beginning the Land of Democracy has been figured as the Land of Promise. Thus the American's loyalty to the national tradition rather affirms than denies the imaginative projection of a better future. An America which was not the Land of Promise, which was not informed by a prophetic outlook and a more or less constructive ideal, would not be the America bequeathed to us by our forefathers. In cherishing the Promise of a better national future the American is fulfilling rather than imperiling the substance of the national tradition.

When, however, Americans talk of their country as the Land of Promise, a question may well be raised as to precisely what they mean. They mean, of course, in general, that the future will have something better in store for them individually and collectively than has the past or the present; but a very superficial analysis of this meaning discloses certain ambiguities. What are the particular benefits which this better future will give to Americans either individually or as a nation? And how is this Promise to be fulfilled? Will it fulfill itself, or does it imply certain responsibilities? If so, what responsibilities? When we speak of a young man's career as promising, we mean that his abilities and opportunities are such that he is likely to become rich or famous or powerful; and this judgment does not of course imply, so far as we are concerned, any responsibility. It is merely a prophecy based upon past performances and proved qualities. But the career, which from the standpoint of an outsider is merely an anticipation, becomes for the young man himself a serious task. For him, at all events, the better future will not merely

happen. He will have to do something to deserve it. It may be wrecked by unforeseen obstacles, by unsuspected infirmities, or by some critical error of judgment. So it is with the Promise of American life. From the point of view of an immigrant this Promise may consist of the anticipation of a better future, which he can share merely by taking up his residence on American soil; but once he has become an American, the Promise can no longer remain merely an anticipation. It becomes in that case a responsibility, which requires for its fulfillment a certain kind of behavior on the part of himself and his fellow-Americans. And when we attempt to define the Promise of American life, we are obliged, also, to describe the kind of behavior which the fulfillment of the Promise demands.

The distinction between the two aspects of America as a Land of Promise made in the preceding paragraph is sufficiently obvious, but it is usually slurred by the average good American patriot. The better future, which is promised for himself, his children, and for other Americans, is chiefly a matter of confident anticipation. He looks upon it very much as a friendly outsider might look on some promising individual career. The better future is understood by him as something which fulfills itself. He calls his country, not only the Land of Promise, but the Land of Destiny. It is fairly launched on a brilliant and successful career, the continued prosperity of which is prophesied by the very momentum of its advance. As Mr. H. G. Wells says in "The Future in America," "When one talks to an American of his national purpose, he seems a little at a loss; if one speaks of his national destiny, he responds with alacrity." The great majority of Americans would expect a book written about "The Promise of American Life" to contain chiefly a fanciful description of the glorious American future—a sort of Utopia up-to-date, situated in the land of

Good-Enough, and flying the Stars and Stripes. They might admit in words that the achievement of this glorious future implied certain responsibilities, but they would not regard the admission either as startling or novel. Such responsibilities were met by our predecessors; they will be met by our followers. Inasmuch as it is the honorable American past which prophesies on behalf of the better American future, our national responsibility consists fundamentally in remaining true to traditional ways of behavior, standards, and ideals. What we Americans have to do in order to fulfill our national Promise is to keep up the good work—to continue resolutely and cheerfully along the appointed path.

The reader who expects this book to contain a collection of patriotic prophecies will be disappointed. I am not a prophet in any sense of the word, and I entertain an active and intense dislike of the foregoing mixture of optimism, fatalism, and conservatism. To conceive the better American future as a consummation which will take care of itself,—as the necessary result of our customary conditions, institutions, and ideas,—persistence in such a conception is admirably designed to deprive American life of any promise at all. The better future which Americans propose to build is nothing if not an idea which must in certain essential respects emancipate them from their past. American history contains much matter for pride and congratulation, and much matter for regret and humiliation. On the whole, it is a past of which the loyal American has no reason to feel ashamed, chiefly because it has throughout been made better than it was by the vision of a better future; and the American of to-day and to-morrow must remain true to that traditional vision. He must be prepared to sacrifice to that traditional vision even the traditional American ways of realizing it. Such a sacrifice is, I believe, coming to be demanded; and unless it is made, American

life will gradually cease to have any specific Promise.

The only fruitful promise of which the life of any individual or any nation can be possessed, is a promise determined by an ideal. Such a promise is to be fulfilled, not by sanguine anticipations, not by a conservative imitation of past achievements, but by laborious, single-minded, clear-sighted, and fearless work. If the promising career of any individual is not determined by a specific and worthy purpose, it rapidly drifts into a mere pursuit of success; and even if such a pursuit is successful, whatever promise it may have had, is buried in the grave of its triumph. So it is with a nation. If its promise is anything more than a vision of power and success, that addition must derive its value from a purpose; because in the moral world the future exists only as a workshop in which a purpose is to be realized. Each of the several leading European nations is possessed of a specific purpose determined for the most part by the pressure of historical circumstances; but the American nation is committed to a purpose which is not merely of historical manufacture. It is committed to the realization of the democratic ideal; and if its Promise is to be fulfilled, it must be prepared to follow whithersoever that ideal may lead.

No doubt Americans have in some measure always conceived their national future as an ideal to be fulfilled. Their anticipations have been uplifting as well as confident and vainglorious. They have been prophesying not merely a safe and triumphant, but also a better, future. The ideal demand for some sort of individual and social amelioration has always accompanied even their vainest flights of patriotic prophecy. They may never have sufficiently realized that this better future, just in so far as it is better, will have to be planned and constructed rather than fulfilled of its own momentum; but at any rate, in seeking to disentangle and emphasize the ideal implications of the American national Promise, I am not wholly false to the accepted American tradition. Even if Americans have neglected these ideal implications, even if they have conceived the better future as containing chiefly a larger portion of familiar benefits, the ideal demand, nevertheless, has always been palpably present; and if it can be established as the dominant aspect of the American tradition, that tradition may be transformed, but it will not be violated.

Furthermore, much as we may dislike the American disposition to take the fulfillment of our national Promise for granted, the fact that such a disposition exists in its present volume and vigor demands respectful consideration. It has its roots in the salient conditions of American life, and in the actual experience of the American people. The national Promise, as it is popularly understood, has in a way been fulfilling itself. If the underlying conditions were to remain much as they have been, the prevalent mixture of optimism, fatalism, and conservatism might retain a formidable measure of justification; and the changes which are taking place in the underlying conditions and in the scope of American national experience afford the most reasonable expectation that this state of mind will undergo a radical alteration. It is new conditions which are forcing Americans to choose between the conception of their national Promise as a process and an ideal. . . .

Reconstruction; Its Conditions and Purposes

The best method of approaching a critical reconstruction of American political ideas will be by means of an analysis of the meaning of democracy. A clear popular understanding of the contents of the democratic principle is obviously of the utmost practical political importance to the American people. Their loyalty to the idea of democracy, as they understand it, cannot be questioned. Nothing of any considerable political importance is done or left undone in the United States, unless such action or inaction can be plausibly defended on democratic grounds; and the only way to secure for the American people the benefit of a comprehensive and consistent political policy will be to derive it from a comprehensive and consistent conception of democracy.

Democracy as most frequently understood is essentially and exhaustively defined as a matter of popular government; and such a definition raises at once a multitude of time-honored, but by no means superannuated, controversies. The constitutional liberals in England, in France, and in this country have always objected to democracy as so understood, because of the possible sanction it affords for the substitution of a popular despotism in the place of the former royal or oligarchic despotisms. From their point of view individual liberty is the greatest blessing which can be secured to a people by a government; and individual liberty can be permanently guaranteed only in case political liberties are in theory and practice subordinated to civil liberties. Popular political institutions constitute a good servant, but a bad master. When introduced in moderation they keep the government of a country in close relation with well-informed public opinion, which is a necessary condition of political sanitation; but if carried too far, such institutions compromise the security of the individual and the integrity of the state. They erect a power in the state, which in theory is unlimited and which constantly tends in practice to dispense with restrictions. A power which is theoretically absolute is under no obligation to respect the rights either of individuals or minorities; and sooner or later such power will be used for the purpose of oppressing the individual. The only way to secure individual liberty is, consequently, to organize a state in which the Sovereign power is deprived of any rational excuse or legal opportunity of violating certain essential individual rights.

The foregoing criticism of democracy, defined as popular government, may have much practical importance; but there are objections to it on the score of logic. It is not a criticism of a certain conception of democracy, so much as of democracy itself. Ultimate responsibility for the government of a community must reside somewhere. If the single monarch is practically dethroned, as he is by these liberal critics of democracy, some Sovereign power must be provided to take his place. In England Parliament, by means of a steady encroachment on the royal prerogatives, has gradually become Sovereign; but other countries, such as France and the United States, which have wholly dispensed with royalty, cannot, even if they would, make a legislative body Sovereign by the simple process of allowing it to usurp power once enjoyed by the Crown. France did, indeed, after it had finally dispensed with Legitimacy, make two attempts to found governments in which the theory of popular Sovereignty was evaded. The Orleans monarchy, for instance, through the mouths of its friends, denied Sovereignty to the people, without being able to claim it for the King; and this insecurity of its legal framework was an indirect cause of a violent explosion of effective popular Sovereignty in 1848. The apologists for the Second Empire admitted the theory of a Sovereign people, but claimed that the Sovereign power could be

safely and efficiently used only in case it were delegated to one Napoleon III—a view the correctness of which the results of the Imperial policy eventually tended to damage. There is in point of fact no logical escape from a theory of popular Sovereignty—once the theory of divinely appointed royal Sovereignty is rejected. An escape can be made, of course, as in England, by means of a compromise and a legal fiction; and such an escape can be fully justified from the English national point of view; but countries which have rejected the royal and aristocratic tradition are forbidden this means of escape—if escape it is. They are obliged to admit the doctrine of popular Sovereignty. They are obliged to proclaim a theory of unlimited popular powers.

To be sure, a democracy may impose rules of action upon itself—as the American democracy did in accepting the Federal Constitution. But in adopting the Federal Constitution the American people did not abandon either its responsibilities or rights as Sovereign. Difficult as it may be to escape from the legal framework defined in the Constitution, that body of law in theory remains merely an instrument which was made for the people and which if necessary can and will be modified. A people, to whom was denied the ultimate responsibility for its welfare, would not have obtained the prime condition of genuine liberty. Individual freedom is important, but more important still is the freedom of a whole people to dispose of its own destiny; and I do not see how the existence of such an ultimate popular political freedom and responsibility can be denied by any one who has rejected the theory of a divinely appointed political order. The fallibility of human nature being what it is, the practical application of this theory will have its grave dangers; but these dangers are only evaded and postponed by a failure to place ultimate political responsibility where it belongs.

While a country in the position of Germany or Great Britain may be fully justified from the point of view of its national tradition in merely compromising with democracy, other countries, such as the United States and France, which have earned the right to dispense with these compromises, are at least building their political structure on the real and righteous source of political authority. Democracy may mean something more than a theoretically absolute popular government, but it assuredly cannot mean anything less.

If, however, democracy does not mean anything less than popular Sovereignty, it assuredly does mean something more. It must at least mean an expression of the Sovereign will, which will not contradict and destroy the continuous existence of its own Sovereign power. Several times during the political history of France in the nineteenth century, the popular will has expressed itself in a manner adverse to popular political institutions. Assemblies have been elected by universal suffrage, whose tendencies have been reactionary and undemocratic, and who have been supported in this reactionary policy by an effective public opinion. Or the French people have by means of a plebiscite delegated their Sovereign power to an Imperial dictator, whose whole political system was based on a deep suspicion of the source of his own authority. A particular group of political institutions or course of political action may, then, be representative of the popular will, and yet may be undemocratic. Popular Sovereignty is self-contradictory, unless it is expressed in a manner favorable to its own perpetuity and integrity.

The assertion of the doctrine of popular Sovereignty is, consequently, rather the beginning than the end of democracy. There can be no democracy where the people do not rule; but government by the people is not necessarily democratic. The popular will must in a democratic state be expressed somehow in the interest of democracy itself; and we have not traveled very far towards a satisfactory conception of democracy until this democratic purpose has received some definition. In what way must a democratic state behave in order to contribute to its own integrity?

The ordinary American answer to this question is contained in the assertion of Lincoln, that our government is "dedicated to the proposition that all men are created equal." Lincoln's phrasing of the principle was due to the fact that the obnoxious and undemocratic system of negro slavery was uppermost in his mind when he made his Gettysburg address; but he meant by his assertion of the principle of equality substantially what is meant to-day by the principle of "equal rights for all and special privileges for none." Government by the people has its natural and logical complement in government for the people. Every state with a legal framework must grant certain rights to individuals; and every state, in so far as it is efficient, must guarantee to the individual that his rights, as legally defined, are secure. But an essentially democratic state consists in the circumstance that all citizens enjoy these rights equally. If any citizen or any group of citizens enjoys by virtue of the law any advantage over their fellow-citizens, then the most sacred principle of democracy is violated.

. . . Democracy must stand or fall on a platform of possible human perfectibility. If human nature cannot be improved by institutions, democracy is at best a more than usually safe form of political organization; and the only interesting inquiry about its future would be: How long will it continue to work? But if it is to work better as well as merely longer, it must have some leavening effect on human nature; and the sincere democrat is obliged to assume the power of the leaven. For him the practical questions are: How can the improvement best be brought about? and, How much may it amount to?

As a matter of fact, Americans have always had the liveliest and completest faith in the process of individual and social improvement and in accepting the assumption, I am merely adhering to the deepest and most influential of American traditions. The better American has continually been seeking to "uplift" himself, his neighbors, and his compatriots. But he has usually favored means of improvement very different from those suggested hereinbefore. The real vehicle of improvement is education. It is by education that the American is trained for such democracy as he possesses; and it is by better education that he proposes to better his democracy. Men are uplifted by education much more surely than they are by any tinkering with laws and institutions, because the work of education leavens the actual social substance. It helps to give the individual himself those qualities without which no institutions, however excellent, are of any use, and with which even bad institutions and laws can be made vehicles of grace.

The American faith in education has been characterized as a superstition; and superstitious in some respects it unquestionably is. But its superstitious tendency is not exhibited so much in respect to the ordinary process of primary, secondary, and higher education. Not even an American can over-emphasize the importance of proper teaching during youth; and the only wonder is that the money so freely lavished on it does not produce better results. Americans are superstitious in respect to education, rather because of the social "uplift" which they expect to achieve by so-called educational means. The credulity of the socialist in expecting to alter human nature

by merely institutional and legal changes is at least equaled by the credulity of the good American in proposing to evangelize the individual by the reading of books and by the expenditure of money and words. Back of it all is the underlying assumption that the American nation by taking thought can add a cubit to its stature,—an absolute confidence in the power of the idea to create its own object and in the efficacy of good intentions.

Do we lack culture? We will "make it hum" by founding a new university in Chicago. Is American art neglected and impoverished? We will enrich it by organizing art departments in our colleges, and popularize it by lectures with lantern slides and associations for the study of its history. Is New York City ugly? Perhaps, but if we could only get the authorities to appropriate a few hundred millions for its beautification, we could make it look like a combination of Athens, Florence, and Paris. Is it desirable for the American citizen to be something of a hero? I will encourage heroes by establishing a fund whereby they shall be rewarded in cash. War is hell, is it? I will work for the abolition of hell by calling a convention and passing a resolution denouncing its iniquities. I will build at the Hague a Palace of Peace which shall be a standing rebuke to the War Lords of Europe. Here, in America, some of us have more money than we need and more good will. We will spend the money in order to establish the reign of the good, the beautiful, and the true.

This faith in a combination of good intentions, organization, words, and money is not confined to women's clubs or to societies of amiable enthusiasts. In the state of mind which it expresses can be detected the powerful influence which American women exert over American men; but its guiding faith and illusion are shared by the most hard-headed and practical of Americans. The very men who have made their personal successes by a rigorous application of the rule that business is business—the very men who in their own careers have exhibited a shrewd and vivid sense of the realities of politics and trade; it is these men who have most faith in the practical, moral, and social power of the Subsidized Word. The most real thing which they carry over from the region of business into the region of moral and intellectual ideals is apparently their bank accounts. The fruits of their hard work and their business ability are to be applied to the purpose of "uplifting" their fellow-countrymen. A certain number of figures written on a check and signed by a familiar name, what may it not accomplish? Some years ago at the opening exercises of the Carnegie Institute in Pittsburgh, Mr. Andrew Carnegie burst into an impassioned and mystical vision of the miraculously constitutive power of first mortgage steel bonds. From his point of view and from that of the average American there is scarcely anything which the combination of abundant resources and good intentions may not accomplish.

The tradition of seeking to cross the gulf between American practice and the American ideal by means of education or the Subsidized Word is not [to] be dismissed with a sneer. The gulf cannot be crossed without the assistance of some sort of educational discipline; and that discipline depends partly on a new exercise of the "money power" now safely reposing in the strong boxes of professional millionaires. There need be no fundamental objection taken to the national faith in the power of good intentions and re-distributed wealth. That faith is the immediate and necessary issue of the logic of our national moral situation. It should be, as it is, innocent and absolute; and if it does not remain innocent and absolute, the Promise of American Life can scarcely be fulfilled.

A faith may, however, be innocent and absolute without being inexperienced and credulous. The American faith in education is by way of being credulous and superstitious, not because it seeks individual and social amelioration by what may be called an educational process, but because the proposed means of education are too conscious, too direct, and too superficial. Let it be admitted that in any one decade the amount which can be accomplished towards individual and social amelioration by means of economic and political reorganization is comparatively small; but it is certainly as large as that which can be accomplished by subsidizing individual good intentions. Heroism is not to be encouraged by cash prizes any more than is genius; and a man's friends should not be obliged to prove that he is a hero in order that he may reap every appropriate reward. A hero officially conscious of his heroism is a multilated hero. In the same way art cannot become a power in a community unless many of its members are possessed of a native and innocent love of beautiful things; and the extent to which such a possession can be acquired by any one or two generations of traditionally inartistic people is extremely small. Its acquisition depends not so much upon direct conscious effort, as upon the growing ability to discriminate between what is good and what is bad in their own native art. It is a matter of the training and appreciation of American artists, rather than the cultivation of art. Illustrations to the same effect might be multiplied. The popular interest in the Higher Education has not served to make Americans attach much importance to the advice of the highly educated man. He is less of a practical power in the United States than he is in any European country; and this fact is in itself a sufficient commentary on the reality of the American faith in education. The fact is, of course, that the American tendency to disbelieve in the fulfillment of their national Promise by means of politically, economically, and socially reconstructive work has forced them into the alternative of attaching excessive importance to subsidized good intentions. They want to be "uplifted," and they want to "uplift" other people; but they will not use their social and political institutions for the purpose, because those institutions are assumed to be essentially satisfactory. The "uplifting" must be a matter of individual, or of unofficial associated effort; and the only available means are words and subsidies.

There is, however, a sense in which it is really true that the American national Promise can be fulfilled only by education; and this aspect of our desirable national education can, perhaps, best be understood by seeking its analogue in the training of the individual. An individual's education consists primarily in the discipline which he undergoes to fit him both for fruitful association with his fellows and for his own special work. Important as both the liberal and the technical aspect of this preliminary training is, it constitutes merely the beginning of a man's education. Its object is or should be to prepare him both in his will and in his intelligence to make a thoroughly illuminating use of his experience in life. His experience,—as a man of business, a husband, a father, a citizen, a friend,—has been made real to him, not merely by the zest with which he has sought it and the sincerity with which he has accepted it, but by the disinterested intelligence which he has brought to its understanding. An educational discipline which has contributed in that way to the reality of a man's experience has done as much for him as education can do; and an educational discipline which has failed to make any such contribution has failed of its essential purpose. The experience of other people acquired at second hand has little value,—except, perhaps, as a means of livelihood,—unless it really illuminates a man's personal experience.

Usually a man's ability to profit by his own personal experience depends upon the sincerity and the intelligence which he brings to his own particular occupation. The rule is not universal, because some men are, of course, born with much higher intellectual gifts than others; and to such men may be given an insight which has little foundation in any genuine personal experience. It remains true, none the less, for the great majority of men, that they gather an edifying understanding of men and things just in so far as they patiently and resolutely stick to the performance of some special and (for the most part) congenial task. Their education in life must be grounded in the persistent attempt to realize in action some kind of a purpose—a purpose usually connected with the occupation whereby they live. In the pursuit of that purpose they will be continually making experiments—opening up new lines of work, establishing new relations with other men, and taking more or less serious risks. Each of these experiments offers them an opportunity both for personal discipline and for increasing personal insight. If a man is capable of becoming wise, he will gradually be able to infer from this increasing mass of personal experience, the extent to which or the conditions under which he is capable of realizing his purpose; and his insight into the particular realities of his own life will bring with it some kind of a general philosophy—some sort of a disposition and method of appraisal of men, their actions, and their surroundings. Wherever a man reaches such a level of intelligence, he will be an educated man, even though his particular job has been that of a mechanic. On the other hand, a man who fails to make his particular task in life the substantial support of a genuine experience remains essentially an unenlightened man.

National education in its deeper aspect does not differ from individual education. Its efficiency ultimately depends upon the ability of the national consciousness to draw illuminating inferences from the course of the national experience; and its power to draw such inferences must depend upon the persistent and disinterested sincerity with which the attempt is made to realize the national purpose—the democratic ideal of individual and social improvement. So far as Americans are true to that purpose, all the different aspects of their national experience will assume meaning and momentum; while in so far as they are false thereto, no amount of "education" will ever be really edifying. The fundamental process of American education consists and must continue to consist precisely in the risks and experiments which the American nation will make in the service of its national ideal. If the American people balk at the sacrifices demanded by their experiments, or if they attach finality to any particular experiment in the distribution of political, economic, and social power, they will remain morally and intellectually at the bottom of a well, out of which they will never be "uplifted" by the most extravagant subsidizing of good intentions and noble words. . . .

Theodore Roosevelt

Born in 1858, Theodore Roosevelt became the twenty-sixth U.S. president. During that Progressive era, he was known for advocating the doctrine of New Nationalism, which encouraged federal intervention in the economy to transcend laissez-faire liberalism for the sake of correcting economic abuses and social injustice.

After graduating from Harvard, Roosevelt took a law degree at Columbia University. His political career began as a Republican member of the New York State Legislature (1881–84). Thereafter, he served on the U.S. Civil Service Commission and then the New York City Police Board. He became assistant secretary of the navy in 1897. Recognition followed his organization of the "Rough Riders," a volunteer regiment that distinguished itself in Cuba during the Spanish-American War. After that war, Roosevelt became governor of New York for two years. Serving as vice president under McKinley in 1900, he became president the following year when McKinley was assassinated.

Roosevelt's administration sponsored reform legislation and contributed significantly to the cause of conservation. He advocated a New Nationalism to recover a sense of national purpose and a strong executive branch to offset the abuses of big business and big labor, spelled out in proposals for federal regulation of business, legislation to benefit labor, inheritance and income taxes, and attacks upon incompetence in the federal courts. In the presidential race of 1912, as head of the Progressive or "Bull Moose" party, he was defeated by Woodrow Wilson. Roosevelt died in 1919.

The New Nationalism (1910)

[Speech at Osawatomie, 31 August 1910]

We come here to-day to commemorate one of the epoch-making events of the long struggle for the rights of man—the long struggle for the uplift of humanity.[1] Our country—this great republic—means nothing unless it means the triumph of a real democracy, the triumph of popular government, and, in the long run, of an economic system under which each man shall be guaranteed the opportunity to show the best that there is in him. That is why the history of America is now the central feature of the history of the world; for the world has set its face hopefully toward our democracy; and, O my fellow citizens, each one of you carries on your shoulders not only the burden of doing well for the sake of your own country, but the burden of doing well and of seeing that this nation does well for the sake of mankind.

There have been two great crises in our country's history: first, when it was formed, and then, again, when it was perpetuated; and, in the second of these great crises—in the time of stress and strain which culminated in the Civil War, on the outcome of which depended the justification of what had been done earlier, you men of the Grand Army, you men who fought through the Civil War, not only did you justify your generation, not only did you render life worth living for our generation, but you justified the wisdom of Washington and Washington's colleagues. If this republic had been founded by them only to be split asunder into fragments when the strain came, then the judgment of the world would have been that Washington's work

was not worth doing. It was you who crowned Washington's work, as you carried to achievement the high purpose of Abraham Lincoln.

Now, with this second period of our history the name of John Brown will be forever associated; and Kansas was the theater upon which the first act of the second of our great national life dramas was played. It was the result of the struggle in Kansas which determined that our country should be in deed as well as in name devoted to both union and freedom; that the great experiment of democratic government on a national scale should succeed and not fail. In name we had the Declaration of Independence in 1776; but we gave the lie by our acts to the words of the Declaration of Independence until 1865; and words count for nothing except in so far as they represent acts. This is true everywhere; but, O my friends, it should be truest of all in political life. A broken promise is bad enough in private life. It is worse in the field of politics. No man is worth his salt in public life who makes on the stump a pledge which he does not keep after election; and, if he makes such a pledge and does not keep it, hunt him out of public life. I care for the great deeds of the past chiefly as spurs to drive us onward in the present. I speak of the men of the past partly that they may be honored by our praise of them, but more that they may serve as examples for the future.

It was a heroic struggle; and, as is inevitable with all such struggles, it had also a dark and terrible side. Very much

Isaak, *American Political Thinking.*

[1]The occasion for Roosevelt's speech was the dedication of a state park of the field at Osawatomie where John Brown had fought the Missouri raiders fifty-four years before. . . .

was done of good, and much also of evil; and, as was inevitable in such a period of revolution, often the same man did both good and evil. For our great good fortune as a nation, we, the people of the United States as a whole, can now afford to forget the evil, or, at least, to remember it without bitterness, and to fix our eyes with pride only on the good that was accomplished. Even in ordinary times there are very few of us who do not see the problems of life as through a glass, darkly; and when the glass is clouded by the murk of furious popular passion, the vision of the best and the bravest is dimmed. Looking back, we are all of us now able to do justice to the valor and the disinterestedness and the love of the right, as to each it was given to see the right, shown both by the men of the North and the men of the South in that contest which was finally decided by the attitude of the West. We can admire the heroic valor, the sincerity, the self-devotion shown alike by the men who wore the blue and the men who wore the gray; and our sadness that such men should have had to fight one another is tempered by the glad knowledge that ever hereafter their descendants shall be found fighting side by side, struggling in peace as well as in war for the uplift of their common country, all alike resolute to raise to the highest pitch of honor and usefulness the nation to which they all belong. As for the veterans of the Grand Army of the Republic, they deserve honor and recognition such as is paid to no other citizens of the republic; for to them the republic owes its all; for to them it owes its very existence. It is because of what you and your comrades did in the dark years that we of to-day walk, each of us, head erect, and proud that we belong, not to one of a dozen little squabbling contemptible commonwealths, but to the mightiest nation upon which the sun shines.

I do not speak of this struggle of the past merely from the historic standpoint.

Our interest is primarily in the application to-day of the lessons taught by the contest of half a century ago. It is of little use for us to pay lip loyalty to the mighty men of the past unless we sincerely endeavor to apply to the problems of the present precisely the qualities which in other crises enabled the men of that day to meet those crises. It is half melancholy and half amusing to see the way in which well-meaning people gather to do honor to the men who, in company with John Brown, and under the lead of Abraham Lincoln, faced and solved the great problems of the nineteenth century, while, at the same time, these same good people nervously shrink from, or frantically denounce, those who are trying to meet the problems of the twentieth century in the spirit which was accountable for the successful solution of the problems of Lincoln's time.

Of that generation of men to whom we owe so much, the man to whom we owe most is, of course, Lincoln. Part of our debt to him is because he forecast our present struggle and saw the way out. He said:—

> I hold that while man exists it is his duty to improve not only his own condition, but to assist in ameliorating mankind.

And again:—

> Labor is prior to, and independent of, capital. Capital is only the fruit of labor, and could never have existed if labor had not first existed. Labor is the superior of capital, and deserves much the higher consideration.

If that remark was original with me, I should be even more strongly denounced as a communist agitator than I shall be anyhow. It is Lincoln's. I am only quoting it; and that is one side; that is the side the capitalist should hear. Now, let the workingman hear his side.

Capital has its rights, which are as worthy of protection as any other rights. . . . Nor should this lead to a war upon the owners of property. Property is the fruit of labor; . . . property is desirable; is a positive good in the world.

And then comes a thoroughly Lincolnlike sentence:—

Let not him who is houseless pull down the house of another, but let him work diligently and build one for himself, thus by example assuring that his own shall be safe from violence when built.

It seems to me that, in these words, Lincoln took substantially the attitude that we ought to take; he showed the proper sense of proportion in his relative estimates of capital and labor, of human rights and property rights. Above all, in this speech, as in many others, he taught a lesson in wise kindliness and charity; an indispensable lesson to us of to-day. But this wise kindliness and charity never weakened his arm or numbed his heart. We cannot afford weakly to blind ourselves to the actual conflict which faces us to-day. The issue is joined, and we must fight or fail.

In every wise struggle for human betterment one of the main objects, and often the only object, has been to achieve in large measure equality of opportunity. In the struggle for this great end, nations rise from barbarism to civilization, and through it people press forward from one stage of enlightenment to the next. One of the chief factors in progress is the destruction of special privilege. The essence of any struggle for healthy liberty has always been, and must always be, to take from some one man or class of men the right to enjoy power, or wealth, or position, or immunity, which has not been earned by service to his or their fellows. That is what you fought for in the Civil War, and that is what we strive for now.

At many stages in the advance of humanity, this conflict between the men who possess more than they have earned and the men who have earned more than they possess is the central condition of progress. In our day it appears as the struggle of free men to gain and hold the right of self-government as against the special interests, who twist the methods of free government into machinery for defeating the popular will. At every stage, and under all circumstances, the essence of the struggle is to equalize opportunity, destroy privilege, and give to the life and citizenship of every individual the highest possible value both to himself and to the commonwealth. That is nothing new. All I ask in civil life is what you fought for in the Civil War. I ask that civil life be carried on according to the spirit in which the army was carried on. You never get perfect justice, but the effort in handling the army was to bring to the front the men who could do the job. Nobody grudged promotion to Grant, or Sherman, or Thomas, or Sheridan, because they earned it. The only complaint was when a man got promotion which he did not earn.

Practical equality of opportunity for all citizens, when we achieve it, will have two great results. First, every man will have a fair chance to make of himself all that in him lies; to reach the highest point to which his capacities, unassisted by special privilege of his own and unhampered by the special privilege of others, can carry him, and to get for himself and his family substantially what he has earned. Second, equality of opportunity means that the commonwealth will get from every citizen the highest service of which he is capable. No man who carries the burden of the special privileges of another can give to the commonwealth that service to which it is fairly entitled.

I stand for the square deal. But when I say that I am for the square deal, I mean not merely that I stand for fair play under the present rules of the game, but that I stand for having those rules changed so as to work for a more substantial equality of opportunity and of reward for equally good service. One word of warning, which, I think, is hardly necessary in Kansas. When I say I want a square deal for the poor man, I do not mean that I want a square deal for the man who remains poor because he has not the energy to work for himself. If a man who has had a chance will not make good, then he has got to quit. And you men of the Grand Army, you want justice for the brave man who fought, and punishment for the coward who shirked his work. Is not that so?

Now, this means that our government, national and state, must be freed from the sinister influence or control of special interests. Exactly as the special interests of cotton and slavery threatened our political integrity before the Civil War, so now the great special business interests too often control and corrupt the men and methods of government for their own profit. We must drive the special interests out of politics. That is one of our tasks to-day. Every special interest is entitled to justice—full, fair, and complete,—and, now, mind you, if there were any attempt by mob violence to plunder and work harm to the special interest, whatever it may be, that I most dislike, and the wealthy man, whomsoever he may be, for whom I have the greatest contempt, I would fight for him, and you would if you were worth your salt. He should have justice. For every special interest is entitled to justice, but not one is entitled to a vote in Congress, to a voice on the bench, or to representation in any public office. The Constitution guarantees protection to property, and we must make that promise good. But it does not give the right of suffrage to any corporation.

The true friend of property, the true conservative, is he who insists that property shall be the servant and not the master of the commonwealth; who insists that the creature of man's making shall be the servant and not the master of the man who made it. The citizens of the United States must effectively control the mighty commercial forces which they have themselves called into being.

There can be no effective control of corporations while their political activity remains. To put an end to it will be neither a short nor an easy task, but it can be done.

We must have complete and effective publicity of corporate affairs, so that the people may know beyond peradventure whether the corporations obey the law and whether their management entitles them to the confidence of the public. It is necessary that laws should be passed to prohibit the use of corporate funds directly or indirectly for political purposes; it is still more necessary that such laws should be thoroughly enforced. Corporate expenditures for political purposes, and especially such expenditures by public service corporations, have supplied one of the principal sources of corruption in our political affairs.

It has become entirely clear that we must have government supervision of the capitalization, not only of public service corporations, including, particularly, railways, but of all corporations doing an interstate business. I do not wish to see the nation forced into the ownership of the railways if it can possibly be avoided, and the only alternative is thoroughgoing and effective regulation, which shall be based on a full knowledge of all the facts, including a physical valuation of property. This physical valuation is not needed, or, at least, is very rarely needed, for fixing rates; but it is needed as the basis of honest capitalization.

We have come to recognize that franchises should never be granted except for a limited time, and never without proper provision for compensation to the public.

It is my personal belief that the same kind and degree of control and supervision which should be exercised over public service corporations should be extended also to combinations which control necessaries of life, such as meat, oil, and coal, or which deal in them on an important scale. I have no doubt that the ordinary man who has control of them is much like ourselves. I have no doubt he would like to do well, but I want to have enough supervision to help him realize that desire to do well.

I believe that the officers, and, especially, the directors, of corporations should be held personally responsible when any corporation breaks the law.

Combinations in industry are the result of an imperative economic law which cannot be repealed by political legislation. The effort at prohibiting all combination has substantially failed. The way out lies, not in attempting to prevent such combinations, but in completely controlling them in the interest of the public welfare. For that purpose the Federal Bureau of Corporations is an agency of first importance. Its powers, and, therefore, its efficiency, as well as that of the Interstate Commerce Commission, should be largely increased. We have a right to expect from the Bureau of Corporations and from the Interstate Commerce Commission a very high grade of public service. We should be as sure of the proper conduct of the interstate railways and the proper management of interstate business as we are now sure of the conduct and management of the national banks, and we should have as effective supervision in one case as in the other. The Hepburn Act, and the amendment to the Act in the shape in which it finally passed Congress at the last session, represent a long step in advance, and we must go yet further.

There is a widespread belief among our people that, under the methods of making tariffs which have hitherto obtained, the special interests are too influential. Probably this is true of both the big special interests and the little special interests. These methods have put a premium on selfishness, and, naturally, the selfish big interests have gotten more than their smaller, though equally selfish, brothers. The duty of Congress is to provide a method by which the interest of the whole people shall be all that receives consideration. To this end there must be an expert tariff commission, wholly removed from the possibility of political pressure or of improper business influence. Such a commission can find the real difference between cost of production, which is mainly the difference of labor cost here and abroad. As fast as its recommendations are made, I believe in revising one schedule at a time. A general revision of the tariff almost inevitably leads to logrolling and the subordination of the general public interest to local and special interests.

The absence of effective state, and, especially, national, restraint upon unfair money getting has tended to create a small class of enormously wealthy and economically powerful men, whose chief object is to hold and increase their power. The prime need is to change the conditions which enable these men to accumulate power which it is not for the general welfare that they should hold or exercise. We grudge no man a fortune which represents his own power and sagacity, when exercised with entire regard to the welfare of his fellows. Again, comrades over there, take the lesson from your own experience. Not only did you not grudge, but you gloried in the promotion of the great generals who gained their promotion by leading the army to victory. So it is with us. We grudge no man a fortune in civil life if it is honorably obtained and well used. It is not even enough that it should have been gained without doing damage to the community. We should permit it to be gained only so long as the gaining represents benefit to the community. This, I know, implies a policy of a far more active governmental interference with social and economic conditions in this country than we have yet had, but I think we have got to face the fact that such an increase in governmental control is now necessary.

No man should receive a dollar unless that dollar has been fairly earned. Every dollar received should represent a dollar's worth of service rendered—not gambling in stocks, but service rendered. The really big fortune, the swollen fortune, by the mere fact of its size acquires qualities which differentiate it in kind as well as in degree from what is possessed by men of relatively small means. Therefore, I believe in a graduated income tax on big fortunes, and in another tax which is far more easily collected and far more effective—a graduated inheritance tax on big fortunes, properly safeguarded against evasion and increasing rapidly in amount with the size of the estate.

The people of the United States suffer from periodical financial panics to a degree substantially unknown among the other nations which approach us in financial strength. There is no reason why we should suffer what they escape. It is of profound importance that our financial system should be promptly investigated, and so thoroughly and effectively revised as to make it certain that hereafter our currency will no longer fail at critical times to meet our needs.

It is hardly necessary for me to repeat that I believe in an efficient army and a navy large enough to secure for us abroad that respect which is the surest guarantee of peace. A word of special warning to my fellow citizens who are as progressive as I hope I am. I want them to keep up their interest in our internal affairs; and I want them also continually to remember Uncle Sam's interests abroad. Justice and fair dealing among nations rest upon principles identical with those which control justice and fair dealing among the individuals of which nations are composed, with the vital exception that each nation must do its own part in international police work. If you get into trouble here, you can call for the police; but if Uncle Sam gets into trouble, he has got to be his own policeman, and I want to see him strong enough to encourage the peaceful aspirations of other peoples in connection with us. I believe in national friendships and heartiest good will to all nations; but national friendships, like those between men, must be founded on respect as well as on liking, on forbearance as well as upon trust. I should be heartily ashamed of any American who did not try to make the American government act as justly toward the other nations in international relations as he himself would act toward any individual in private relations. I should be heartily ashamed to see us wrong a weaker power, and I should hang my head forever if we tamely suffered wrong from a stronger power.

Of conservation I shall speak more at length elsewhere. Conservation means development as much as it does protection. I recognize the right and duty of this generation to develop and use the natural resources of our land; but I do not recognize the right to waste them, or to rob, by wasteful use, the generations that come after us. I ask nothing of the nation except that it so behave as each farmer here behaves with reference to his own children. That farmer is a poor creature who skins the land and leaves it worthless to his children. The farmer is a good farmer who, having enabled the land to support himself and to provide for the education of his children, leaves it to them a little better than he found it himself. I believe the same thing of a nation.

Moreover, I believe that the natural resources must be used for the benefit of all our people, and not monopolized for the benefit of the few, and here again is another case in which I am accused of taking a revolutionary attitude. People forget now that one hundred years ago there were public men of good character who advocated the nation selling its public lands in great quantities, so that the nation could get the most money out of it, and giving it to the men who could cultivate it for their own uses. We took the proper democratic ground that the land should be granted in small sections to the men who were actually to till it and live on it. Now, with the water power, with the forests, with the mines, we are brought face to face with the fact that there are many people who will go with us in conserving the resources only if they are to be allowed to exploit them for their benefit. That is one of the fundamental reasons why the special interests should be driven out of politics. Of all the questions which can come before this nation, short of the actual preservation of its existence in a great war, there is none which compares in importance with the great central task of leaving this land even a better land for our descendants than it is for us, and training them into a better race to inhabit the land and pass it on. Conservation is a great moral issue, for it involves the patriotic duty of insuring the safety and continuance of the nation. Let me add that the health and vitality of our people are at least as well worth conserving as their forests, waters, lands, and minerals, and in this great work the national government must bear a most important part.

I have spoken elsewhere[2] also of the great task which lies before the farmers of the country to get for themselves and their wives and children not only the benefits of better farming, but also those of better business methods and better conditions of life on the farm. The burden of this great task will fall, as it should, mainly upon the great organizations of the farmers themselves. I am glad it will, for I believe they are all well able to handle it. In particular, there are strong reasons why the Departments of Agriculture of the various states, the United States Department of Agriculture, and the agricultural colleges and experiment stations should extend their work to cover all phases of farm life, instead of limiting themselves, as they have far too often limited themselves in the past, solely to the question of the production of crops. And now a special word to the farmer. I want to see him make the farm as fine a farm as it can be made; and let him remember to see that the improvement goes on indoors as well as out; let him remember that the farmer's wife should have her share of thought and attention just as much as the farmer himself.

Nothing is more true than that excess of every kind is followed by reaction; a fact which should be pondered by reformer and reactionary alike. We are face to face with new conceptions of the relations of property to human welfare, chiefly because certain advocates of the rights of property as against the rights of men have been pushing their claims too far. The man who wrongly holds that every human right is secondary to his profit must now give way to the advocate of human welfare, who rightly maintains that every man holds his property subject to the general right of the community to regulate its use to whatever degree the public welfare may require it.

But I think we may go still further. The right to regulate the use of wealth in the public interest is universally admitted. Let us admit also the right to regulate the terms and conditions of labor, which is the chief element of wealth, directly in the interest of the common good. The fundamental thing to do for every man is to give him a chance to reach a place in which he

---

[2] In a speech at Utica, New York.

will make the greatest possible contribution to the public welfare. Understand what I say there. Give him a chance, not push him up if he will not be pushed. Help any man who stumbles; if he lies down, it is a poor job to try to carry him; but if he is a worthy man, try your best to see that he gets a chance to show the worth that is in him. No man can be a good citizen unless he has a wage more than sufficient to cover the bare cost of living, and hours of labor short enough so that after his day's work is done he will have time and energy to bear his share in the management of the community, to help in carrying the general load. We keep countless men from being good citizens by the conditions of life with which we surround them. We need comprehensive workmen's compensation acts, both state and national laws to regulate child labor and work for women, and, especially, we need in our common schools not merely education in book learning, but also practical training for daily life and work. We need to enforce better sanitary conditions for our workers and to extend the use of safety appliances for our workers in industry and commerce, both within and between the states. Also, friends, in the interest of the workingman himself we need to set our faces like flint against mob violence just as against corporate greed; against violence and injustice and lawlessness by wage workers just as much as against lawless cunning and greed and selfish arrogance of employers. If I could ask but one thing of my fellow countrymen, my request would be that, whenever they go in for reform, they remember the two sides, and that they always exact justice from one side as much as from the other. I have small use for the public servant who can always see and denounce the corruption of the capitalist, but who cannot persuade himself, especially before election, to say a word about lawless mob violence. And I have equally small use for a man,

be he a judge on the bench, or editor of a great paper, or wealthy and influential private citizen, who can see clearly enough and denounce the lawlessness of mob violence, but whose eyes are closed so that he is blind when the question is one of corruption in business on a gigantic scale. Also remember what I said about excess in reformer and reactionary alike. If the reactionary man, who thinks of nothing but the rights of property, could have his way, he would bring about a revolution; and one of my chief fears in connection with progress comes because I do not want to see our people, for lack of proper leadership, compelled to follow men whose intentions are excellent, but whose eyes are a little too wild to make it really safe to trust them. Here in Kansas there is one paper which habitually denounces me as the tool of Wall Street, and at the same time frantically repudiates the statement that I am a Socialist on the ground that that is an unwarranted slander of the Socialists.

National efficiency has many factors. It is a necessary result of the principle of conservation widely applied. In the end it will determine our failure or success as a nation. National efficiency has to do, not only with natural resources and with men, but it is equally concerned with institutions. The state must be made efficient for the work which concerns only the people of the state; and the nation for that which concerns all the people. There must remain no neutral ground to serve as a refuge for lawbreakers, and especially for lawbreakers of great wealth, who can hire the vulpine legal cunning which will teach them how to avoid both jurisdictions. It is a misfortune when the national legislature fails to do its duty in providing a national remedy, so that the only national activity is the purely negative activity of the judiciary in forbidding the state to exercise power in the premises.

I do not ask for overcentralization; but I do ask that we work in a spirit of broad and far-reaching nationalism when we work for what concerns our people as a whole. We are all Americans. Our common interests are as broad as the continent. I speak to you here in Kansas exactly as I would speak in New York or Georgia, for the most vital problems are those which affect us all alike. The national government belongs to the whole American people, and where the whole American people are interested, that interest can be guarded effectively only by the national government. The betterment which we seek must be accomplished, I believe, mainly through the national government.

The American people are right in demanding that New Nationalism, without which we cannot hope to deal with new problems. The New Nationalism puts the national need before sectional or personal advantage. It is impatient of the utter confusion that results from local legislatures attempting to treat national issues as local issues. It is still more impatient of the impotence which springs from overdivision of governmental powers, the impotence which makes it possible for local selfishness or for legal cunning, hired by wealthy special interests, to bring national activities to a deadlock. This New Nationalism regards the executive power as the steward of the public welfare. It demands of the judiciary that it shall be interested primarily in human welfare rather than in property, just as it demands that the representative body shall represent all the people rather than any one class or section of the people.

I believe in shaping the ends of government to protect property as well as human welfare. Normally, and in the long run, the ends are the same; but whenever the alternative must be faced, I am for men and not for property, as you were in the Civil War. I am far from underestimating the importance of dividends; but I rank dividends below human character. Again, I do not have any sympathy with the reformer who says he does not care for dividends. Of course, economic welfare is necessary, for a man must pull his own weight and be able to support his family. I know well that the reformers must not bring upon the people economic ruin, or the reforms themselves will go down in the ruin. But we must be ready to face temporary disaster, whether or not brought on by those who will war against us to the knife. Those who oppose all reform will do well to remember that ruin in its worst form is inevitable if our national life brings us nothing better than swollen fortunes for the few and the triumph in both politics and business of a sordid and selfish materialism.

If our political institutions were perfect, they would absolutely prevent the political domination of money in any part of our affairs. We need to make our political representatives more quickly and sensitively responsive to the people whose servants they are. More direct action by the people in their own affairs under proper safeguards is vitally necessary. The direct primary is a step in this direction, if it is associated with a corrupt practices act effective to prevent the advantage of the man willing recklessly and unscrupulously to spend money over his more honest competitor. It is particularly important that all moneys received or expended for campaign purposes should be publicly accounted for, not only after election, but before election as well. Political action must be made simpler, easier, and freer from confusion for every citizen. I believe that the prompt removal of unfaithful or incompetent public servants should be made easy and sure in whatever way experience shall show to be most expedient in any given class of cases.

One of the fundamental necessities in a representative government such as ours is to make certain that the men to whom the people delegate their power shall serve the people by whom they are elected, and not the special interests. I believe that every national officer, elected or appointed, should be forbidden to perform any service or receive any compensation, directly or indirectly, from interstate corporations; and a similar provision could not fail to be useful within the states.

The object of government is the welfare of the people. The material progress and prosperity of a nation are desirable chiefly so far as they lead to the moral and material welfare of all good citizens. Just in proportion as the average man and woman are honest, capable of sound judgment and high ideals, active in public affairs,—but, first of all, sound in their home life, and the father and mother of healthy children whom they bring up well,—just so far, and no farther, we may count our civilization a success. We must have—I believe we have already—a genuine and permanent moral awakening, without which no wisdom of legislation or administration really means anything; and, on the other hand, we must try to secure the social and economic legislation without which any improvement due to purely moral agitation is necessarily evanescent. Let me again illustrate by a reference to the Grand Army. You could not have won simply as a disorderly and disorganized mob. You needed generals; you needed careful administration of the most advanced type; and a good commissary—the cracker line. You well remember that success was necessary in many different lines in order to bring about general success. You had to have the administration at Washington good, just as you had to have the administration in the field; and you had to have the work of the generals good. You could not

have triumphed without that administration and leadership; but it would all have been worthless if the average soldier had not had the right stuff in him. He had to have the right stuff in him, or you could not get it out of him. In the last analysis, therefore, vitally necessary though it was to have the right kind of organization and the right kind of generalship, it was even more vitally necessary that the average soldier should have the fighting edge, the right character. So it is in our civil life. No matter how honest and decent we are in our private lives, if we do not have the right kind of law and the right kind of administration of the law, we cannot go forward as a nation. That is imperative; but it must be an addition to, and not a substitution for, the qualities that make us good citizens. In the last analysis, the most important elements in any man's career must be the sum of those qualities which, in the aggregate, we speak of as character. If he has not got it, then no law that the wit of man can devise, no administration of the law by the boldest and strongest executive, will avail to help him. We must have the right kind of character—character that makes a man, first of all, a good man in the home, a good father, a good husband—that makes a man a good neighbor. You must have that, and, then, in addition, you must have the kind of law and the kind of administration of the law which will give to those qualities in the private citizen the best possible chance for development. The prime problem of our nation is to get the right type of good citizenship, and, to get it, we must have progress, and our public men must be genuinely progressive.

Woodrow Wilson

Born in 1856 in Staunton, Virginia, Woodrow Wilson was reared to be a great man by his stern, Presbyterian father, who imparted the belief that Calvinist salvation would come only to those who proved themselves worthy through moral service. Wilson became the ultimate self-righteous spokesman for American liberalism and its "manifest economic destiny." This culminated in his idealistic proposal for a league of nations to enforce liberal ideals through international law, which later became the basis for the United Nations.

Wilson first attended Davidson College and then graduated from Princeton. He distinguished himself on debating teams, believing that the mastery of oratory was critical for later political success. Wilson received a law degree from the University of Virginia, practiced law briefly, then studied political science and jurisprudence at Johns Hopkins University. In 1885 he published *Congressional Government,* a well-received book. He completed his Ph.D. and taught history and political economy at Bryn Mawr and Wesleyan University. Appointed professor of jurisprudence and political economy at Princeton University in 1890, his reputation spread through his writing and eloquent speaking. In 1902 he became president of Princeton, introducing a preceptorial system and other educational reforms aimed to individualize education. A quadrangle system that brought students of all classes to eat together met with stiff resistance from the Dean, who won the argument.

Wilson left Princeton and was elected governor of New Jersey as a "conservative" Democrat. Once elected, he dropped his conservative hedging and pushed through various liberal reforms: an employer's liability act, a corrupt practices act, the direct primary, and a restructuring of the state public utilities commission. These reforms made a national reputation for Wilson in time for the 1912 presidential election. He was nominated to represent his party on the forty-sixth ballot and won the election advocating a New Freedom domestic program against Theodore Roosevelt's New Nationalism. Wilson argued that federal authority must be expanded not so much to regulate industry as to free the people from the control of privileged groups. He followed through with legislative reforms: a federal income tax to counterbalance a downward revision in tariff rates; the Federal Reserve Act supplanting the so-called dictatorship of private banks with a public board; the creation of the Federal Trade Commission to keep conditions in trade competitive; and the far-reaching Clayton Antitrust Act limiting injunctions in labor disputes and declaring that labor strikes and boycotts were not violations of the law.

Maintaining neutrality in World War I as long as possible got Wilson reelected in 1916, carrying the pacificist vote. But his policy in Latin America led to American military interventions in Mexico, Cuba, the Dominican Republic, and Haiti and established protectorates over the last two. After many diplomatic efforts to achieve peace, German submarine violations of neutrality led Wilson to enter World War I in 1917, arguing that "the world must be made safe for democracy." Wilson drafted the famous "Fourteen Points" as the basis for a peace settlement after the Bolshevik Revolutionary government in Russia published the secret imperialistic war aims of the allies in 1918. When the war was over, Wilson refused to compromise and would not take any Republicans or senators with him to the Paris Peace Conference given their criticism of his policies. Wilson argued for a new world society characterized by "self-determination of peoples," free from secret diplomacy and wars, which would enforce international law through an association of nations—the future League of Nations. Coming back to the United States, Wilson refused to compromise again by adding clauses that would protect U.S. sovereignty. The Senate failed to ratify the Treaty of Versailles despite an exhausting national speaking tour that Wilson undertook to bring his case to the people. He suffered a stroke and died three years after his second term ended in 1920. His books include: *The State* (1889), *Division and Reunion, 1829–1889* (1893), *George Washington* (1896), *A History of the American People* (1902, 5 volumes), and *Constitutional Government in the United States* (1908).

ᦞᦞ

Campaign Address (1912)
(excerpt)

Buffalo, New York, September 2

. . . Why is it that the people of this country are in danger of being discontented with the parties that have pretended to serve them? It [is] because in too many instances their promises were not matched by their performances and men began to say to themselves, "What is the use [of] going to the polls and voting? Nothing happens after the election." Is there any man within the hearing of my voice who can challenge the statement that any party that has forfeited the public confidence, has forfeited it by its own nonperformance?

Very well then, when I speak to you today, I want you to regard me as a man who is talking business. I want in the first place to say that I shall be scrupulous to be fair to those with whom I am in opposition. Because there is a great deal to be said for the programs of hopeful men who intend to do things even if they haven't struck upon the right way to do them. And we ought not to divorce ourselves in sympathy with men who want the right thing because we do not think they have found the way to do them.

I want to speak upon this occasion, of course, on the interests of the workingman, of the wage earner, not because I regard the wage earners of this country as a special class, for they are not. After you have made a catalogue of the wage earners of this country, how many of us are left? The wage earners of this country, in the broad sense, constitute the country. And the most fatal thing that we can do in politics is to imagine that we belong to a special class, and that we have an interest which isn't the interest of the whole community. Half of the difficulties, half of the injustices of our politics have been due to the fact that men regarded themselves as having separate interests which they must serve even though other men were done a great disservice by their promoting them.

We are not afraid of those who pursue legitimate pursuits provided they link those pursuits in at every turn with the interest of the community as a whole; and no man can conduct a legitimate business, if he conducts it in the interest of a single class. I want, therefore, to look at the Nation as a whole today. I would like always to look at it as a whole, not divide it up into sections and classes, but I want particularly to discuss with you today the things which interest the wage earner. That is merely looking at the country as a whole from one angle, from one point of view, to which for the time being we will confine ourselves.

I want as a means of illustration, not as a means of contest, to use the platform of the third party as the means of expounding what I have to say today. I want you to read that platform very carefully, and I want to call your attention to the fact that it really consists of two parts. In one part of it, it declares the sympathy of the party with a certain great program of social reform, and promises that all the influence of that party, of the members of that party, will be used for the promotion of that program of social reform. In the other part, it itself lays down a method of procedure, and what I want you to soberly consider is whether the method of procedure is a suitable way of laying the foundations for the realization of that social program—with regard to the social program, the betterment of the condition of men in this occupation and the other, the protection of women, the shielding of children, the bringing about of social justice here, there, and elsewhere. With that program who can differ in his heart, who can divorce himself in sympathy from the great project of advancing the interests of human beings, wherever it is possible to advance them?

But there is a central method, a central purpose, in that platform from which I very seriously dissent. I am a Democrat as distinguished from a Republican because I believe (and I think that it is generally believed) that the leaders of the Republican party—for I always distinguish them from the great body of the Republican voters who have been misled by them—I say not the Republican party, but the leaders of the Republican party have allowed themselves to become so tied up in alliances with special interests that they are not free to serve us all. And that the immediate business, if you are to have any kind of reform at all, is to set your government free, is to break it away from the partnerships and alliances and understandings and [purchases] which have made it impossible for it to look at the country as a whole and made it necessary to serve special interests one at a time. Until that has been done, no program of social reform is possible because a program of social reform depends upon universal sympathy, universal justice, universal cooperation. It depends upon our understanding one another and serving one another.

What is this program? What is the program of the third party with regard to the

disentanglement of the government? Mr. Roosevelt has said, and up to a certain point I sympathize with him, that he does not object, for example, to the system of protection except in this circumstance—that it has [not] inured to the benefit of the workingman of this country. It is very interesting to have him admit that because the leaders of the Republican party have been time out of mind putting this bluff up on you men that the protective policy was for your sake, and I would like to know what you ever got out of it that you didn't get out of the better effort of organized labor. I have yet to learn of any instance where you got anything without going and taking it. And the process of our society instead of being a process of peace has sometimes too much resembled a process of war because men felt obliged to go and insist in organized masses upon getting the justice which they couldn't get any other way.

It is interesting, therefore, to have Mr. Roosevelt admit that not enough of the "prize money," as he frankly calls it, has gone into the pay envelope. He admits that not enough of the money has gone into the envelope. I wish it were not prize money, because dividing up prize money and dividing up earnings are two very different things. And it is very much simpler to divide up earnings than to divide up prize money, because the money is prize money for the [reason] that a limited number of men banded themselves together and got it from the Ways and Means Committee of the House and the Finance Committee of the Senate, and we paid the bills.

But Mr. Roosevelt says that his [object] will be to see that a larger proportion gets into the pay envelope. And how does he propose to do it? (For I am here not to make a speech; I am here to argue this thing with you gentlemen.) How does he propose to do it? I don't find any suggestion anywhere in that platform of the way in which he is going to do it, except in one plank. One plank says that the party will favor a minimum wage for women; and then it goes on to say by a minimum wage it means a living wage, enough to live on.

I am going to assume, for the sake of argument, that it proposed more than that, that it proposed to get a minimum wage for everybody, men as well as women; and I want to call your attention to the fact that just as soon as a minimum wage is established by law, the temptation of every employer in the United States will be to bring his wages down as close to that minimum as he dares, because you can't strike against the government of the United States. You can't strike against what is in the law. You can strike against what is in your agreement with your employer, but if underneath that agreement there is the steel and the adamant of Federal law, you can't tamper with that foundation. And who is going to pay these wages? You know that the great difficulty about wages, one of the great difficulties about wages now, is that the control of industry is getting into fewer and fewer hands. And that, therefore, a smaller and smaller number of men are able to determine what wages shall be. In other words, one of the entanglements of our government is that we are dealing not with a community in which men may take their own choice of what they shall do, but in a community whose industry is very largely governed by great combinations of capital in the hands of a comparatively small number of men; that, in other words, we are in the hands, in many industries, of monopoly itself. And the only way in which the workingman can gain more wages is by getting them from the monopoly.

Very well then, what does this platform propose to do? Break up the monopolies? Not at all. It proposes to legalize them. It says in effect: You can't break them up, the only thing you can do is to put them in charge of the Federal Government. It proposes that they shall be adopted and regulated. And that looks to me like a consummation of the partnership between monopoly and government. Because, when once the government regulates monopoly, then monopoly will have to see to it that it regulates the government. This is a [beautiful] circle of change.

We now complain that the men who control these monopolies control the government, and it is in turn proposed that the government should control them. I am perfectly willing to be controlled if it is I, myself, who control me. If this partnership can be continued, then this control can be manipulated and adjusted to its own pleasure. Therefore, I want to call your attention to this fact that these great combined industries have been more inimical to organized labor than any other class of employers in the United States. Is not that so?

These monopolies that the government, it is proposed, should adopt are the men who have made your independent action most difficult. They have made it most difficult that you should take care of yourselves; and let me tell you that the old adage that God takes care of those who take care of themselves is not gone out of date. No Federal legislation can change that thing. The minute you are taken care of by the government you are wards, not independent men. And the minute they are legalized by the government, they are protégés and not monopolies. They are the guardians and you are the wards. Do you want to be taken care of by a combination of the government and the monopolies? [*A voice from the audience: "No."*] Because the workingmen of this country are perfectly aware that they sell their commodity, that is to say labor, in a perfectly open market. There is free trade in labor in the United States. The laboring men of all the world are free to come and offer their labor here and you are similarly free to go and offer your labor in most parts of the world. And the world demand is what establishes for the most part the rate of wages, at the same time that these gentlemen who are paying the wages in a free-trade market are protected by an unfree market against the competition that would make them [bid] higher because [bid] in competition and not [bid] under protection. If I am obliged to refrain from going into a particular industry by reason of the combination that already exists in it, I can't become an employer of labor, and I can't compete with these gentlemen for the employment of labor. And the whole business of the level of wages is artificially and arbitrarily determined.

Now, I say, gentlemen, that a party that proposes that program cannot, if it carries out that program, be forwarding these other industrial purposes of social regeneration, because they have crystallized, they have hardened, they have narrowed the government which is to be the source of this thing. After all this is done, who is to guarantee to us that the government is to be pitiful, that the government is to be righteous, that the government is to be just? Nothing will then control the power of the government except open revolt, and God forbid that we should bring about a state of politics in which open revolt should be substituted for the ballot box.

I believe that the greatest force for peace, the greatest force for righteousness, the greatest force for the elevation of mankind, is organized opinion, is the thinking of men, is the great force which is in the soul of men, and I want men to breathe a free and pure air. And I know that these monopolies are so many cars of juggernaut which are in our very sight being driven over men in such ways as to crush their life out of them. And I don't look forward with pleasure to the time when the juggernauts are licensed. I don't look forward with pleasure to the time when the juggernauts are driven by commissioners of the United States. I am willing to license automobiles, but not juggernauts, because if

any man ever dares take a joy ride in one of them, I would like to know what is to become of the rest of us; because the road isn't wide enough for us to get out of the way. We would have to take to the woods and then set the woods afire. I am speaking partly in pleasantry but underneath, gentlemen, there is a very solemn sense in my mind that we are standing at a critical turning point in our [choice].

Now you say, on the other hand, what do the Democrats propose to do? I want to call your attention to the fact that those who wish to support these monopolies by adopting them under the regulation of the government of the United States are the very men who cry out that competition is destructive. They ought to know because it is competition as they conducted it that destroyed our economic freedom. They are certainly experts in destructive competition. And the purpose of the Democratic leaders is this: not to legislate competition into existence again—because statutes can't make men do things—but to regulate competition.

What has created these monopolies? Unregulated competition. It has permitted these men to do anything that they chose to do to squeeze their rivals out and to crush their rivals to the earth. We know the processes by which they have done these things. We can prevent those processes by remedial legislation, and that remedial legislation will so restrict the wrong use of competition that the right use of competition will destroy monopoly. In other words, ours is a program of liberty and theirs is a program of regulation. Ours is a program by which we find we know the wrongs that have been committed and we can stop those wrongs. And we are not going to adopt into the government family the men who forward the wrongs and license them to do the whole business of the country.

I want you men to grasp the point because I want to say to you right now the program that I propose doesn't look quite as much like acting as a Providence for you as the other program looks. But I want to frankly say to you that I am not big enough to play Providence, and my objection to the other program is that I don't believe that there is any other man that is big enough to play Providence. I have never known any body of men, any small body of men, that understood the United States. And the only way the United States is ever going to be taken care of is by having the voice of all the men in it constantly clamorous for the recognition of what is justice as they see life. A little group of men sitting every day in Washington City is not going to have a vision of your lives as a whole. You alone know what your lives are. I say, therefore, take the shackles off of American industry, the shackles of monopoly, and see it grow into manhood, see it grow out of the enshackled childishness into robust manliness, men being able to take care of themselves, and reassert the great power of American citizenship.

These are the ancient principles of government the world over. For when in the history of labor, here in this country or in any other, did the government present its citizens with freedom and with justice? When has there been any fight for liberty that wasn't a fight against this very thing, the accumulation of regulative power in the hands of a few persons? I in my time have read a good deal of history and, if I were to sum up the whole history of liberty, I should say that it consisted at every turn in human life in resisting just such projects as are now proposed to us. If you don't believe it, try it. If you want a great struggle for liberty that will cost you blood, adopt this program, put yourselves at the disposition of a Providence resident in Washington and then see what will come of it.

Ah, gentlemen, we are debating very serious things. And we are debating this: Are we going to put ourselves in a position to enter upon a great program of understanding one another and helping one another? I can't understand you unless you talk to me. I can't understand you by looking at you. I can't understand you by reading books. With apologies to the gentlemen in front of me, I couldn't even understand you by reading the newspapers. I can understand you only by what you know of your own lives and make evident in your own actions. I understand you only in proportion as you "hump" yourselves and take care of yourselves, and make your force evident in the course of politics. And, therefore, I believe in government as a great process of getting together, a great process of debate.

There are gentlemen on this platform with me who have seen a great vision. They have seen this, for example: You know that there are a great many foreigners coming to America and qualifying as American citizens. And if you are widely acquainted among them you will know that this is true: that the grown-up people who come to America take a long time in feeling at home in America. They don't speak the language and there is no place in which they can get together with the general body of American citizens and feel that they are part of them. But their children feel welcome. Where? In the schoolhouse. The schoolhouse is the great melting pot of democracy. And after the children of these men who have joined us in their desire for freedom have grown up and come through the processes of the schools, they have imbibed the full feeling of American life.

Now, somebody has said—somebody repeated to me the other day—the saying of one of these immigrants that when he went to a meeting or to a series of meetings in the evening in a schoolhouse where all the neighborhood joined to discuss the interests of the neighborhood, he for the first time saw America as he had expected to see it. This [was] America as he had imagined it, this frank coming together of all the people in the neighborhood, of all sorts and conditions, to discuss their common interests. And these gentlemen to whom I have referred have devoted their lives to this: to make the schoolhouses of this country the vital centers of opportunity, to open them out of school hours for everybody who desires to discuss anything and for making them, among other things, the clearinghouses where men who are out of jobs can find jobs and where jobs who are out of men can find men. Why shouldn't our whole life center in this place where we learn the fundamentals of our life? Why shouldn't the schoolhouses be the constant year-in-and-year-out places of assembly where things are said which nobody dares ignore? Because, if we haven't had our way in this country, it has been because we haven't been able to get at the ear of those who are conducting our government. And if there is any man in Buffalo, or anywhere else in the United States, who objects to your using the schoolhouses that way, you may be sure that there is something he doesn't want to have discussed.

You know I have been considered as disqualified for politics because I was a school teacher. But there is one thing a school teacher learns that he never forgets, namely, that it is his business to learn all he can and then to communicate it to others. Now, I consider this to be my function. I have tried to find out how to learn things and learn them fast. And I have made up my mind that for the rest of my life I am going to put all I know at the disposal of my fellow citizens. And I know a good many things that I haven't yet mentioned in public which I am ready to mention at the psychological moment. There is no use firing it off when there is nobody to shoot at, but when they are present, then it is sport to say it. And I have undertaken the duty of constituting myself one of the attorneys for the people in any court to which

I can get entrance. I don't mean as a lawyer, for while I was a lawyer, I have repented. But I mean in the courts of public opinion wherever I am allowed, as I am indulgently allowed today, to stand on a platform and talk to attentive audiences—for you are most graciously attentive—I want to constitute myself the spokesman so far as I have the proper table of contents for the people whom I wish to serve; for the whole strength of politics is not in the leader but in the followers. By leading I do not mean telling other people what they have got to do. I [mean] finding out what the interests of the community are agreed to be, and then trying my level best to find the methods of solution by common counsel. That is the only feasible program of social uplift that I can imagine, and, therefore, I am bound in conscience to fight everything that crystallizes things so at the center that you can't break in.

It is amazing to me that public-spirited, devoted men in this country have not seen that the program of the third party proclaims purposes and in the same breath provides an organization of government which makes the carrying out of those purposes impossible. I would rather postpone my sympathy for social reform until I had got in a position to make things happen. And I am not in a position to make things happen until I am part of a free organization which can say to every interest in the United States: "You come into this conference room on an equality with every other interest in the United States, and you are going to speak here with open doors. There is to be no whispering behind the hand. There is to be no private communication. What you can't afford to let the country hear had better be left unsaid."

What I fear, therefore, is a government of experts. God forbid that in a democratic country we should resign the task and give the government over to experts. What are we for if we are to be [scientifically] taken care of by a small number of gentlemen who are the only men who understand the job? Because if we don't understand the job, then we are not a free people. We ought to resign our free institutions and go to school to somebody and find out what it is we are about. I want to say I have never heard more penetrating debate of public questions than I have sometimes been privileged to hear in clubs of workingmen; because the man who is down against the daily problem of life doesn't talk about it in rhetoric; he talks about it in facts. And the only thing I am interested in is facts. I don't know anything else that is as solid to stand on. . . .

Frederick W. Taylor

Born in Germantown, Pennsylvania, Frederick Winslow Taylor (1856–1915) became known as the "father of scientific management." After attending a private school in New England, he became an apprentice machinist, sacrificing salary increments to get ahead faster. He soon became chief engineer at a steel company and received an engineering degree from the Stevens Institute of Technology. His theory of scientific management was based upon time-and-motion studies, reorganization of work, and maximization of efficiency. Taylor published numerous articles and spent a great deal of time consulting. His books include *Shop Management* (1911), *Principles of Scientific Management* (1911), *Concrete Costs* (with S. E. Thompson, 1912), and *Scientific Management* (C. B. Thompson, editor, 1914).

Taylor's work had widespread influence in modernizing management methods for shops, offices, industrial plants, and particularly the steel industry. But his ideas for increasing economic productivity to generate greater wealth created controversy in the press. From the viewpoint of organized labor, Taylor's ideas threatened to cause unemployment through labor-saving techniques, to keep job skills low, and to force workers to work faster. William B. Wilson of Pennsylvania, a member of the House of Representatives in tune with the concerns of the unions, chaired a committee for special inquiry into the concept of scientific management in 1912, calling Taylor as main witness. Excerpts from these congressional committee hearings follow.

Testimony before the Special House Committee

(excerpts)

Thursday, January 25, 1912.

The committee met at 10.40 o'clock a.m.,
Hon. William B. Wilson (chairman) presiding.

Testimony of Mr. Frederick Winslow Taylor

When you get almost any workingman to talking with you intimately and saying exactly what he believes and feels without reserve; I mean when he speaks without feeling that he is going to meet with an antagonistic opinion not in sympathy with him; to put this in still a third way, when you get that man to telling his real views, he will almost always state that he cannot see how it could be for the interest of his particular trade—that is, for the interest of those men associated with him, and with whose work he is familiar—to very greatly increase their output per day.

The question the workman will ask you, if you have his confidence, is: "What would become of those of us in my particular trade who would be thrown out of work in case we were all to greatly increase our output each day?" Each such man in a particular working group feels that in his town or section or particular industry there is, in the coming year, only about so much work to be done. As far as he can see, if he were to double his output, and if the rest of the men were to double their output tomorrow or next week or next month or next year, he can see no other outcome except that one-half of the workmen engaged with him would be thrown out of work. . . .

. . . I do not care what trade you go into, get back to the basic facts, the fundamental truths connected with that trade, and you will find that every time there has been an increased output per individual workman in that trade produced by any cause that it has made more work in the trade and has never diminished the number of workmen in the trade. All you have to do is to go back into the history of any trade and look up the facts and you will find it to be true; that in no case has the permanent effect of increasing the output per individual in the trade been that of throwing men out of work, but the effect has always been to make work for more men.

Now, that is the history of every trade, but in spite of that fact the world at large, both on the workman's side and on the manufacturer's side believes this fallacy

(and I find a great many men who ought to know better completely misinformed on the side of the management). And yet this is a fallacy, and a blighting fallacy, as far as the interests of the workingmen and the interests of the whole country are concerned. Now I feel it important or desirable to give just one illustration to show that an increase in output does not throw men out of work, and I could give thousands, simply thousands of such illustrations.

Take any trade, go back through the history of it, and see whether increase of output on the part of the workman has resulted in throwing men out of work. That is what people generally believe; that is what these working people who have testified here believe. They believe if they were to increase their output it would result in throwing a lot of them out of their jobs. And I have had much sympathy with the workingmen who have testified before your committee, because I feel that they firmly believe that it would not be for their best interests to turn out a larger output. I believe these men are honestly mistaken, just as the rest of the world has been honestly mistaken in many other instances.

Let us examine the actual facts in one trade—the cotton trade, for instance. It is as well known, perhaps, and as well understood as any trade in the whole list. The power loom was invented some time between 1780 and 1790, I think it was; I am not quite sure about that date, but it was somewhere about that time. It was very slow in coming into use. Somewhere about the year 1840—the exact date is immaterial, and I give that as about the time of the occurrence—there were in round numbers 5,000 cotton weavers in Manchester, England. About that time these weavers became convinced that the power loom was going to win out, that the hand looms which they were operating were doomed. And they knew that the power loom would turn out per man about three times the output.

That is a general figure. I do not wish to say that this ratio is exact, but in any case it is nearly so. Those men knew the possibilities of the power loom and realized that when it was introduced it would turn out a very much larger output per man than was being then turned out by the hand loom.

Now, what could they see? They were certain, those men were honestly certain, and it was a natural conviction on their part, that nothing could happen through the introduction of this power loom except that after it was in, after it was fully installed and doing three times the work that the hand loom did, that instead of there being 5,000 weavers in Manchester they would be reduced to 1,500 or 2,000, and that 3,000 weavers would be thrown out of a job. Now, these men felt fully convinced of that; with them there was no doubt about it; it was a matter of certainty, and they did in kind just what all of us would be apt to do in kind if we were convinced that three-fifths of our working body were to have our means of livelihood taken away from us. What I mean to say is that, broadly speaking, we would adopt the same general policy of opposition that they adopted. I am not advocating violence, arson, or any of the wrong things that were done by these men when I say that we would in a general way have done, broadly speaking, what they did. We would have opposed the introduction of any such policy by every means in our power. What the Manchester weavers did was to break into the establishments where these power looms were being installed. They smashed up the looms. They burned down the buildings in which they were being used. They beat up the scabs using them, and they did almost everything that was in their power to prevent the introduction of the power loom.

And even after that exhibition of fearful violence, gentlemen, I do not hesitate to say that I do not feel very bitterly toward those men. I believe that they were mis-guided. I feel a certain sympathy for them, not in their violence—I do not endorse that for one moment—but I cannot help but feel a certain sympathy for the men who believe, with absolute certainty, that their means of livelihood is being taken away from them. You cannot help but feel sympathy for men who believe that, even if you thoroughly disapprove of their acts. I do not want to be misquoted in this. These men did murder, violence, and arson. I do not believe in anything of that sort under any circumstances.

Now, gentlemen, the power loom came into use just as every labor-saving device that is a real labor-saving device is sure to come at all times. In spite of any opposition that may come from any source whatever, I do not care what the source is, I do not care how great the opposition, or what it may be, any truly labor-saving device will win out. All that you have to do to find proof of this is to look at the history of the industrial world. And, gentlemen, scientific management is merely the equivalent of a labor-saving device; that is all it is; it is a means, and a very proper and right means, of making men more efficient than they now are, and without imposing materially greater burdens on them than they now have, and if scientific management is a device for doing that it will win out in spite of all the labor opposition in the world; in spite of any opposition that may be brought to bear against it from any quarter whatever, from any class of people, or from the whole people, it will win out. If scientific management is right, and I believe it is right; if it is a labor-saving device for enabling men to do more work with no greater effort on their part, then it is going to win out.

Now, let us see what happened from the introduction of the power loom in 1840, or thereabouts. Did it throw men out of work; did it make work for a less number of men? In Manchester, England, now—

and, again, the figures I am giving are merely the broadest kind of general figures, as I am not personally familiar with the cotton industry. The data I have has been given to me by a man who is familiar with it, but I do not want to quibble over the exact figures, as they are not material. It is the broad general facts that count. In Manchester, England, today, the average weaver turns out, I am told, from 8 to 10 times the yardage of cotton cloth formerly turned out by the old hand weaver; the man who does his work with this modern machinery turns out 8 to 10 times the yardage formerly turned out by the hand weaver. The man who told me of the conditions said these figures were well within the limit. In Manchester, England, in 1840, there were 5,000 operatives, and in Manchester, today there are 265,000 operatives. Now, in the light of those figures has the introduction of the power loom, has the introduction of labor-saving machinery thrown men out of work?

What has happened in the cotton industry is typical of what happens in every industry, it makes no difference what that industry is. Broadly speaking, all that you have to do is to bring wealth into the world, and the world uses it. Now, real wealth, as you all know, has but very little to do with money; money is the least important element in wealth. The wealth of the world comes from two sources—from what comes out of the ground or from beneath the surface of the earth, on the one hand, and what is produced by man on the other hand. And the broad fact is that all you have to do is to bring wealth into the world and the world uses it. This is just what happened in the cotton industry.

If you will multiply the figures given in the Manchester illustration you will see that in each day now in Manchester there are 400 or 500 yards of cotton cloth coming out for every single yard that came out each day in 1840, whereas the population of England certainly has not more than doubled; I do not know exactly, but my impression is that it has not more than doubled since 1840. Suppose we even granted that it has trebled and the fact would still be astounding that there now comes out of Manchester, England, 400 to 500 yards of cotton cloth for every single yard that came out in 1840. The true meaning of this great production is that just that much more wealth is being unloaded on the world. This is the fundamental meaning of increase in output in all trades, namely, that additional wealth is coming into the world. Such wealth is real wealth, for it consists of those things which are most useful to man; those things that man needs for his everyday happiness, for his prosperity, and his comfort. The meaning of increased output, whether it be in one trade or another, is always the same, the world is just receiving that much more wealth.

Let us see, now, in a definite way what the increased output of cotton goods means to the American workman. None of us probably appreciate now that in 1840 the ordinary cotton shirt or dress made, for example, from Manchester cottons was a luxury to be worn only by the middle classes, as the English describe it, and that cotton goods were worn by the poor people only as a rare luxury. Now the cotton shirt and the cotton dress, cotton goods generally, have become an absolute daily necessity of all classes of mankind all over the civilized world. And this magnificent result (more magnificent for the working people than for any other portion of the community) has been brought about solely by this great increase in output so stubbornly fought against by the cotton weavers in 1840. It is in those changes which directly affect the poor—which give them a higher standard of living and make from the luxuries of one generation the necessities of the next that we can best see the meaning of an increase in the wealth of the world. And the most important fact of this whole subject is that any association of men, whether it be a group of workmen or a group of capitalists or manufacturers, a manufacturer's association, or whatever it may be, any men who deliberately restrict the output in any industry are robbing the people. And they rob the people of the wealth that justly belongs to them, whether they restrict output honestly, believing it to be for the interest of their trade, or dishonestly for any other reason. There is one point along this line which I want to make clear, gentlemen—that is, that many people believe the ridiculous nonsense that the wealth of the world is enjoyed by the rich. The fact is, that of the real wealth of the world, of the real necessities of life, of practically all the good things of this world, nineteen-twentieths are consumed and used by the working people, and only about one-twentieth by the rich people. Therefore that group of men who prevent wealth from coming into the world are robbing the working people of this nineteenth-twentieths and the rich people of but one-twentieth. In fact I doubt if they are robbing the rich people at all. That, after all, is the essence of the whole matter—the robbing of the poor through restriction of output—and I want to try and make it clear that I believe it is quite as much a crime for a manufacturer to restrict output for the sake of holding up prices as it is for the workman to restrict output for this or any other reason.

I don't mean to say for one instant that times may not come in every industry when it is wise to restrict output temporarily, but when that is true it is due merely to a lack of balance in the output of the world and lack of proper poise in industrial conditions. It is perfectly clear that there is such a thing as overproduction; that is no myth, but overproduction, in 99 cases out of 100, properly translated, means a lack of balance, a lack of evenness in production, a failure to maintain a fair balance between the necessities of life and production. It is a special condition, not a normal one. The world doesn't want, for example, 20 times the cotton goods that it has used in the past manufactured all at once. If there then were to be a fair balance maintained at all times between the various necessities of life and the amount of their production, then it would not be necessary to restrict output at any time. It is true, however, that the world seems to get out of kilter at certain fairly regular times; these periods appear to come at intervals of about 20 years. At such times we wake up to find that the world has attempted to start more new enterprises than there is available capital to handle these enterprises with. This condition is not confined to this country, but all over the world and in every class of trade and industry; men make their estimates in a reckless way about new things they will attempt. They start so many new enterprises and on such a large scale that the world's capital and credit is insufficient to carry them through, and then there is a panic. The whole world becomes overanxious, and there follows a period of depression.

No, I do not mean to say that overproduction does not at times exist and should be checked, but I do mean to say that, as a guiding policy—that is, a permanent policy on the part of workingmen or manufacturer to restrict the world's output to just so much and no more is mere robbery; it is deliberate robbery of the poor people of those things to which they are entitled and which they can get only from the real wealth of the world. . . .

Walter Rauschenbusch

Walter Rauschenbusch (1861–1918) was an American clergyman whom Reinhold Niebuhr called "the real founder of social Christianity in this country." Born in Rochester, New York, and ordained at twenty-five, he served as pastor of the Second German Baptist Church on the edge of Hell's Kitchen in New York City, working among German immigrants and observing firsthand the degradation people can suffer. Later he studied economics and theology at the University of Berlin and industrial relations in England, where he was introduced to the Fabian Society.

As a professor of church history at the Rochester Theological Seminary, Rauschenbusch became a leader in the Social Gospel movement, seeking a way to right social and economic injustice and adjusting theological assumptions accordingly. His books include: *Christianity and the Social Crisis* (1907), *Christianizing the Social Order* (1912), *The Social Principles of Jesus* (1916), and *A Theology for the Social Gospel* (1917), from which the following reading is taken from Chapter 1. Rauschenbusch's Social Gospel movement had a formative influence on religious political activists, particularly Norman M. Thomas, who headed the Socialist party after the death of Eugene Debs and ran for president six times as the Socialist candidate (1928–48).

A Theology for the Social Gospel (1917)
(excerpts)

The Challenge of the Social Gospel to Theology

We have a social gospel. We need a systematic theology large enough to match it and vital enough to back it. . . . If theology stops growing or is unable to adjust itself to its modern environment and to meet its present tasks, it will die. Many now regard it as dead. The social gospel needs a theology to make it effective; but theology needs the social gospel to vitalize it. . . .

We need not waste words to prove that the social gospel is being preached. It is no longer a prophetic and occasional note. It is a novelty only in backward social or religious communities. The social gospel has become orthodox.

It is not only preached. It has set new problems for local church work, and has turned the pastoral and organizing work of the ministry into new and constructive directions. It has imparted a wider vision and a more statesmanlike grasp to the foreign mission enterprise. In home missions its advent was signalized by the publication, in 1885, of "Our Country" by Josiah Strong. (*Venerabile nomen!*) That book lifted the entire home mission problem to a higher level. The religious literature uttering the social gospel is notable both for its volume and its vitality and conviction. The

---

emotional fervour of the new convictions has created prayers and hymns of social aspiration, for which the newer hymn books are making room. Conservative denominations have formally committed themselves to the fundamental ideas of the social gospel and their practical application. The plans of great interdenominational organizations are inspired by it. It has become a constructive force in American politics.

This new orientation, which is observable in all parts of our religious life, is not simply a prudent adjustment of church methods to changed conditions. There is religious compulsion behind it. Those who are in touch with the student population know what the impulse to social service means to college men and women. It is the most religious element in the life of many of them. Among ministerial students there is an almost impatient demand for a proper social outlet. Some hesitate to enter the regular ministry at all because they doubt whether it will offer them sufficient opportunity and freedom to utter and apply their social convictions. For many ministers who have come under the influence of the social gospel in mature years, it has signified a religious crisis, and where it has been met successfully, it has brought fresh joy and power, and a distinct enlargement of mind. It has taken the place of conventional religion in the lives of many outside the Church. It constitutes the moral power in the propaganda of Socialism.

All those social groups which distinctly face toward the future, clearly show their need and craving for a social interpretation and application of Christianity. Whoever wants to hold audiences of working people must establish some connection between religion and their social feelings and experiences. The religious organizations dealing with college men and women know that any appeal which leaves out the social note is likely to meet a listless audience. The most effective evangelists for these two groups are men who have thoroughly embodied the social gospel in their religious life and thought. When the great evangelistic effort of the "Men and Religion Forward Movement" was first planned, its organizers made room for "Social Service" very hesitatingly. But as soon as the movement was tried out before the public, it became clear that only the meetings which offered the people the social application of religion were striking fire and drawing crowds.

The Great War has dwarfed and submerged all other issues, including our social problems. But in fact the war is the most acute and tremendous social problem of all. All whose Christianity has not been ditched by the catastrophe are demanding a christianizing of international relations. The demand for disarmament and permanent peace, for the rights of the small nations against the imperialistic and colonizing powers, for freedom of the seas and of trade routes, for orderly settlement of grievances,—these are demands for social righteousness and fraternity on the largest scale. Before the War the social gospel dealt with social classes; to-day it is being translated into international terms. The ultimate cause of the war was the same lust for easy and unearned gain which has created the internal social evils under which every nation has suffered. The social problem and the war problem are fundamentally one problem, and the social gospel faces both. After the War the social gospel will "come back" with pent-up energy and clearer knowledge.

The social movement is the most important ethical and spiritual movement in the modern world, and the social gospel is the response of the Christian consciousness to it. Therefore it had to be. The social gospel registers the fact that for the first time in history the spirit of Christianity has had a chance to form a working partnership with real social and psychological science. It is the religious reaction on the historic advent of democracy. It seeks to put the democratic spirit, which the Church inherited from Jesus and the prophets, once more in control of the institutions and teachings of the Church.[1]

The social gospel is the old message of salvation, but enlarged and intensified. The individualistic gospel has taught us to see the sinfulness of every human heart and has inspired us with faith in the willingness and power of God to save every soul that comes to him. But it has not given us an adequate understanding of the sinfulness of the social order and its share in the sins of all individuals within it. It has not evoked faith in the will and power of God to redeem the permanent institutions of human society from their inherited guilt of oppression and extortion. Both our sense of sin and our faith in salvation have fallen short of the realities under its teaching. The social gospel seeks to bring men under repentance for their collective sins and to create a more sensitive and more modern conscience. It calls on us for the faith of the old prophets who believed in the salvation of nations.

Now, if this insight and religious outlook become common to large and vigorous sections of the Christian Church, the solutions of life contained in the old theological system will seem puny and inadequate. Our faith will be larger than the intellectual system which subtends it. Can theology expand to meet the growth of faith? The biblical studies have responded to the spiritual hunger aroused by the social gospel. The historical interpretation of the Bible has put the religious personalities, their spiritual struggles, their growth, and their utterances, into social connection with the community life of which they were part. This method of interpretation has given back the Bible to men of modernized intelligence and has made it the feeder of faith in the social gospel. The studies of "practical theology" are all in a process of rejuvenation and expansion in order to create competent leadership for the Church, and most of these changes are due to the rise of new ideals created by the social gospel. What, then, will doctrinal theology do to meet the new situation? Can it ground and anchor the social gospel in the eternal truths of our religion and build its main ideas into the systematic structure of Christian doctrine?

Theology is not superior to the gospel. It exists to aid the preaching of salvation. Its business is to make the essential facts and principles of Christianity so simple and clear, so adequate and mighty, that all who preach or teach the gospel, both ministers and laymen, can draw on its stores and deliver a complete and unclouded Christian message. When the progress of humanity creates new tasks, such as world-wide missions, or new problems, such as the social problem, theology must connect these with the old fundamentals of our faith and make them Christian tasks and problems.

The adjustment of the Christian message to the regeneration of the social order is plainly one of the most difficult tasks ever laid on the intellect of religious leaders. The pioneers of the social gospel have had a hard time trying to consolidate their old faith and their new aim. Some have lost their faith; others have come out of the struggle with crippled formulations of truth. Does not our traditional theology deserve some of the blame for this spiritual wastage because it left these men without spiritual support and allowed them to

---

[1] In his "Social Idealism and the Changing Theology," embodying the Taylor Lectures for 1912, Professor Gerald B. Smith has shown clearly the discrepancy created by the aristocratic attitude of authority in theology and the spread of democracy in modern ethical life, and has insisted that a readjustment is necessary in theology at this point to conform it to our ethical ideals. Professor Smith expresses the fear that our critical methods by themselves will lead only to a barren intellectualism. That feeling has been one motive in the writing of the present book.

become the vicarious victims of our theological inefficiency? If our theology is silent on social salvation, we compel college men and women, workingmen, and theological students, to choose between an unsocial system of theology and an irreligious system of social salvation. It is not hard to predict the outcome. If we seek to keep Christian doctrine unchanged, we shall ensure its abandonment.

Instead of being an aid in the development of the social gospel, systematic theology has often been a real clog. When a minister speaks to his people about child labour or the exploitation of the lowly by the strong; when he insists on adequate food, education, recreation, and a really human opportunity for all, there is response. People are moved by plain human feeling and by the instinctive convictions which they have learned from Jesus Christ. But at once there are doubting and dissenting voices. We are told that environment has no saving power; regeneration is what men need; we can not have a regenerate society without regenerate individuals; we do not live for this world but for the life to come; it is not the function of the church to deal with economic questions; any effort to change the social order before the coming of the Lord is foredoomed to failure. These objections all issue from the theological consciousness created by traditional church teaching. These half-truths are the proper product of a half-way system of theology in which there is no room for social redemption. Thus the Church is halting between two voices that call it. On the one side is the

voice of the living Christ amid living men to-day; on the other side is the voice of past ages embodied in theology. Who will say that the authority of this voice has never confused our Christian judgment and paralysed our determination to establish God's kingdom on earth?

Those who have gone through the struggle for a clear faith in the social gospel would probably agree that the doctrinal theology in which they were brought up, was one of the most baffling hindrances in their spiritual crisis, and that all their mental energies were taxed to overcome the weight of its traditions. They were fortunate if they promptly discovered some recent theological book which showed them at least the possibility of conceiving Christian doctrine in social terms, and made them conscious of a fellowship of faith in their climb toward the light. The situation would be much worse if Christian thought were nourished on doctrine only. Fortunately our hymns and prayers have a richer consciousness of solidarity than individualistic theology. But even today many ministers have a kind of dumb-bell system of thought, with the social gospel at one end and individual salvation at the other end, and an attenuated connection between them. The strength of our faith is in its unity. Religion wants wholeness of life. We need a rounded system of doctrine large enough to take in all our spiritual interests.

In short, we need a theology large enough to contain the social gospel, and alive and productive enough not to hamper it. . . .

Eugene Debs

Born in 1855 in Terre Haute, Indiana, son of immigrant Alsatian shopkeepers, Eugene Debs became the foremost Socialist party leader in the United States through devotion to union organization and the labor conditions of the working class. At age fourteen he started working on the railroad. When he was twenty-seven, the Brotherhood of Locomotive Fireman was organized and Debs was made secretary. An energetic union organizer, initially Debs was conservative in his approach, opposing strikes and merely trying to unite the railroad workers to confront management effectively at the bargaining table. Experience taught him that strikes did work, however, and so he gradually became a militant unionist.

Debs helped to form the American Railway Union in 1894, and came to believe that mere craft unions isolated groups of workers, who could then more easily be coopted by management. His solution was a wider industrial union made up of both skilled and unskilled workers. After union success in the Great Northern strike, the violent Pullman strike in 1894 landed Debs and other union organizers in jail in Chicago. The Pullman strike was a major story in the press, and socialists sent Debs reading material in jail, which he absorbed eagerly (writings of Bellamy, Blatchford, Gronlund, Kautsky, and Marx). After his jail term, Debs turned to politics and supported William Jennings Bryan in the 1894 election. When Bryan lost, Debs, together with Victor L. Berger, who had brought him Marx to read in jail, organized the Social Democratic party. Debs also played a role in the formation of the Industrial Workers of the World (IWW), a union soon plagued by internal bickering. He ran as Socialist party candidate for the presidency five times.

His leftist political views grew organically out of the experience of confrontations with corporate management, uncompromising judges, and the police. After giving a series of antiwar speeches during World War I, Debs was tried for sedition and sentenced to ten years in jail. The trial received a great deal of publicity and in the 1920 presidential election, Debs, while in jail, received the largest vote ever for a Socialist candidate for president. President Warren Harding pardoned Debs in 1921, and Debs continued his vocation of organizing until he died in 1926.

Industrial Unionism
(excerpts)

Address at Grand Central Palace, New York,
December 10, 1905

There is an inspiration in your greeting and my heart opens wide to receive it. I have come a thousand miles to join with you in fanning the flames of the proletarian revolution. (Applause.)

Your presence here makes this a vitalizing atmosphere for a labor agitator. I can feel my stature increasing, and this means that you are growing, for all my strength is drawn from you, and without you I am nothing.

In capitalist society you are the lower class; the capitalists are the upper class— because they are on your backs; if they were not on your backs, they could not be above you. (Applause and laughter.)

Standing in your presence, I can see in your gleaming eyes and in your glowing faces the vanguard; I can hear the tramp, I can feel the thrill of the social revolution. The working class are waking up. (A voice, "You bet.") They are beginning to understand that their economic interests are identical, that they must unite and act together economically and politically, and in every other way; that only by united action can they overthrow the capitalist system and emancipate themselves from wage-slavery. (Applause.)

I have said that in the capitalist society the working class are the lower class; they have always been the lower class. In the ancient world for thousands of years they were abject slaves; in the Middle Ages, serfs; in modern times, wage-workers; to become free men in socialism, the next inevitable phase of advancing civilization. (Applause.) The working class have struggled through all the various phases of their development, and they are today engaged in the last stage of the animal struggle for existence; and when the present revolution has run its course, the working class will stand forth the sovereigns of this earth.

In capitalist society the working man is not, in fact, a man at all; as a wage-worker, he is simply merchandise; he is bought in the open market the same as hair, hides, salt, or any other form of merchandise. The very terminology of the capitalist system proves that he is not a man in any sense of that term.

When the capitalist needs you as a workingman to operate his machine, he does not advertise, he does not call for men, but for "hands"; and when you see a placard posted, "Fifty hands wanted," you stop on the instant; you know that that means YOU, and you take a bee-line for the bureau of employment to offer yourself in evidence of the fact that you are a "hand." When the capitalist advertises for hands, that is what he wants.

He would be insulted if you were to call him a "hand." He has his capitalist politician tell you, when your vote is wanted, that you ought to be very proud of your hands because they are horny; and if that

is true, he ought to be ashamed of his. (Laughter and applause.)

What is your status in society today? You are a human being, a wage-worker. Here you stand just as you were created, and you have two hands that represent your labor power; but you do not work, and why not? For the simple reason that you have no tools with which to work; you cannot compete against the machinery of the capitalist with your bare hands; you cannot work unless you have access to it, and you can only secure access to it by selling your labor power, that is to say, your energy, your vitality, your life itself, to the capitalist who owns the tool with which you work, and without which you are idle and suffer all of the ills that idleness entails.

In the evolution of capitalism, society has been divided mainly into two economic classes; a relatively small class of capitalists who own tools in the form of great machines they did not make and cannot use, and a great body of many millions of workers who did make these tools and who do use them, and whose very lives depend upon them, yet who do not own them; and these millions of wage-workers, producers of wealth, are forced into the labor market, in competition with each other, disposing of their labor power to the capitalist class, in consideration of just enough of what they produce to keep them in working order. They are exploited of the greater share of what their labor produces, so that while, upon the one hand, they can produce in great abundance, upon the other they can consume but that share of the product that their meagre wage will buy; and every now and then it follows that they have produced more than can be consumed in the present system, and then they are displaced by the very products of their own labor; the mills and shops and mines and quarries in which they are employed close down, the tools are locked up and they are locked out, and they find themselves idle and helpless in the shadow of the very abundance their labor has created.

There is no hope for them in this system. They are beginning to realize this fact, and so they are beginning to organize; they are no longer relying upon someone else, but they are making up their minds to depend upon themselves and to organize for their own emancipation.

Too long have the workers of the world waited for some Moses to lead them out of bondage. He has not come; he never will come. I would not lead you out if I could; for if you could be led out, you could be led back again. (Applause.) I would have you make up your minds that there is nothing that you cannot do for yourselves.

You do not need the capitalist. He could not exist an instant without you. You would just begin to live without him. (Laughter and prolonged applause.) You do everything and he has everything; and some of you imagine that if it were not for him you would have no work. As a matter of fact, he does not employ you at all; you employ him to take from you what you produce, and he faithfully sticks to his task. If you can stand it, he can; and if you don't change this relation, I am sure he won't. You make the automobile, he rides in it. If it were not for you, he would walk; and if it were not for him, you would ride.

The capitalist politician tells you on occasion that you are the salt of the earth; and if you are, you had better begin to salt down the capitalist class.

The revolutionary movement of the working class will date from the year 1905, from the organization of the INDUSTRIAL WORKERS OF THE WORLD. (Prolonged applause.) Economic solidarity is today the supreme need of the working class. The old form of unionism has long since fulfilled its mission and outlived its usefulness, and the hour has struck for a change.

The old unionism is organized upon the basis of the identity of interests of the capitalist and working classes. It spends its time and energy trying to conciliate these two essentially antagonistic classes; and so this unionism has at its head a harmonizing board called the Civil Federation. This federation consists of three parts; a part representing the capitalist class; a part supposed to represent the working class, and still another part that is said to represent the "public." The capitalists are represented by that great union labor champion, August Belmont. (Laughter and hisses.) The working class by Samuel Gompers, the president of the American Federation of Labor (hisses and cries, "sic him"), and the public, by Grover Cleveland. (Laughter.)

Can you imagine a fox and goose peace congress? Just fancy such a meeting, the goose lifting its wings in benediction, and the fox whispering, "Let us prey."

The Civic Federation has been organized for the one purpose of prolonging the age-long sleep of the working class. Their supreme purpose is to keep you from waking up. (A voice: "They can't do it.")

The Industrial Workers has been organized for an opposite purpose, and its representatives come in your presence to tell you that there can be no peace between you, the working class, and the capitalist class who exploit you of what you produce; that as workers you have economic interests apart from and opposed to their interests, and that you must organize by and for yourselves; and that if you are intelligent enough to understand these interests you will sever your relations with the old unions in which you are divided and sub-divided, and join the Industrial Workers, in which all are organized and united upon the basis of the class struggle. (Applause.)

The Industrial Workers is organized, not to conciliate, but to fight the capitalist class. We have no object in concealing any part of our mission; we would have it perfectly understood. We deny that there is anything in common between workingmen and capitalists. We insist that workingmen must organize to get rid of capitalists and make themselves the masters of the tools with which they work, freely employ themselves, secure to themselves all they produce, and enjoy to the full the fruit of their labors. (Applause.)

The old union movement is not only organized upon the basis of the identity of interests of the exploited and exploiting classes, but it divides instead of uniting the workers, and there are thousands of unions, more or less in conflict, used against one another; and so long as these countless unions occupy the field, there will be no substantial unity of the working class. (Applause.)

And here let me say that the most zealous supporter of the old union is the capitalist himself. August Belmont, president of the Civic Federation, takes special pride in declaring himself a "union man" (laughter); but he does not mean by that that he is an Industrial Worker; that is not the kind of a union he means. He means the impotent old union that Mr. Gompers and Mr. Mitchell lead, the kind that keeps the working class divided so that the capitalist system may be perpetuated indefinitely.

For thirty years I have been connected with the organized labor movement. I have long since been made to realize that the pure and simple union can do nothing for the working class; I have had some experience and know whereof I speak. The craft union seeks to establish its own petty supremacy. Craft division is fatal to class unity. To organize along craft lines means to divide the working class and make it the prey of the capitalist class. The working class can only be unionized efficiently along class lines; and so the Industrial Workers has been organized, not to isolate the crafts but to unite the whole working class. (Applause.)

The working class has had considerable experience during the past few years. In almost every conflict between labor and capital, labor has been defeated. Take the leading strikes in their order, and you will find that, without a single exception, the organized workers have been defeated, and thousands upon thousands of them have lost their jobs, and many of them have become "scabs." Is there not something wrong with a unionism in which the workers are always worsted? Let me review hurriedly some of this history of the past few years.

I have seen the conductors on the Chicago, Burlington & Quincy Railroad, organized in a craft union, take the place of the striking union locomotive engineers on the same system.

I have seen the employees of the Missouri, Kansas & Texas Railway, organized in their several craft unions, stand by the corporation as a unit, totally wiping out the union telegraphers, thirteen hundred of them losing their jobs.

I have seen these same craft unions, just a little while ago, on the Northern Pacific and Great Northern systems—I have seen them unite with the corporation to crush out the telegraphers' union, and defeat the strikers, their own co-unionists and fellow employees.

Just a few weeks ago, in the city of Chicago, the switchmen on the Grand Trunk went out on strike. All their fellow unionists remained at work and faithfully served the corporation until the switchmen were defeated, and now those union switchmen are scattered about looking for jobs.

The machinists were recently on strike in Chicago. They went out in a body under the direction of their craft union. Their fellow unionists all remained at work until the machinists were completely defeated, and now their organization in that city is on the verge of collapse.

There has been a ceaseless repetition of this form of scabbing of one craft union upon another until the working man, if his eyes are open, is bound to see that this kind of unionism is a curse and not a benefit to the working class.

The American Federation of Labor does not learn by experience. They recently held their annual convention, and they passed the same old stereotyped resolutions; they are going to petition Congress to restrict the power of the courts; that is to say, they are going to once more petition a capitalist Congress to restrict the power of capitalist courts. That is as if a flock of sheep were to petition a pack of wolves to extract their own fangs. They have passed these resolutions over and over again. They have been totally fruitless and will continue to be.

What good came to the working class from this convention? Put your finger upon a single thing they did that will be of any real benefit to the workers of the country!

You have had some experience here in New York. You have plenty of unionism here, such as it is, yet there is not a city in the country in which the workers are less organized than they are here. It was in March last that you had here an exhibition of pure and simple unionism. You saw about six thousand craft union men go out on strike, and you saw their fellow unionists remain at work loyally until all the strikers were defeated and sacrificed. Here you have an object lesson that is well calculated to set you thinking, and this is all I can hope to do by coming here, set you thinking, and for yourselves; for when you begin to think, you will soon begin to act for yourselves. You will then sever your relations with capitalist unions and capitalist parties (applause), and you will begin

the real work of organizing your class, and that is what we of the Industrial Workers have engaged to do. We have a new mission. That mission is not merely the amelioration of the condition of the working class, but the complete emancipation of that class from slavery. (Applause.)

The Industrial Workers is going to do all for the working class that can be done in the capitalist system, but while it is engaged in doing that, its revolutionary eye will be fixed upon the goal; and there will be a great difference between a strike of revolutionary workers and a strike of ignorant trade unionists who but vaguely understand what they want and do not know how to get that. (Applause.)

The Industrial Workers is less than six months old, and already has a round hundred thousand of dues-paying members. (Applause.) This splendid achievement has no parallel in the annals of organized labor. From every direction come the applications for charters and for organizers, and when the delegates of this revolutionary economic organization meet in the city of Chicago, next year, it will be the greatest convention that ever met in the United States in the interest of the working class. (Applause.)

This organization has a world-wide mission; it makes its appeal directly to the working class. It asks no favors from capitalists.

No organization of working men has ever been so flagrantly misrepresented by the capitalist press as has been the Industrial Workers of the World; every delegate to the Chicago convention will bear testimony to this fact; and this is as it should be; the capitalist press is the mouthpiece of the capitalist class, and the very fact that the capitalist press is the organ, virtually, of the American Federation of Labor, is in itself sufficient to open the eyes of the working class.

If the American Federation of Labor were not in alliance with the capitalist class, the capitalist press would not pour its fulsome eulogy upon it.

This press has not one friendly word for the Industrial Workers, not one, and we do not expect it to have. These papers of the plutocrats know us and we know them (applause); between us there is no misunderstanding.

The workers of the country (the intelligent ones at least) readily see the difference between revolutionary and reactionary unionism, and that is why they are deserting the old and joining the new; that is why the Industrial Workers is building up so rapidly; that is why there is such a widespread demand for organizers and for literature and for all other means of building up this class-conscious economic organization. (Applause.)

As I have said, the Industrial Workers begin by declaring that there is nothing in common between capitalists and wage-workers.

The capitalists own the tools they do not use, and the workers use the tools they do not own.

The capitalists, who own the tools that the working class use appropriate to themselves what the working class produce, and this accounts for the fact that a few capitalists become fabulously rich while the toiling millions remain in poverty, ignorance and dependence.

Let me make this point perfectly clear for the benefit of those who have not thought it out for themselves. Andrew Carnegie is a type of the capitalist class. He owns the tools with which steel is produced. These tools are used by many thousands of working men. Andrew Carnegie, who owns these tools, has absolutely nothing to do with the production of steel. He may be in Scotland, or where he will, the production of steel goes forward just the same. His mills at Pittsburgh, Duquesne and Homestead, where these tools are located, are thronged with thousands of toolless wage-workers, who work day and night, in winter's cold and summer's heat, who endure all the privations and make all the sacrifices of health and limb and life, producing thousands upon thousands of tons of steel, yet not having an interest, even the slightest, in the product. Carnegie, who owns the tools, appropriates the product, and the workers, in exchange for their labor power, receive a wage that serves to keep them in producing order; and the more industrious they are, and the more they produce, the worse they are off; for the sooner they have produced more than Carnegie can get rid of in the markets, the tool houses are shut down and the workers are locked out in the cold.

This is a beautiful arrangement—for Mr. Carnegie; he does not want a change, and so he is in favor of the Civic Federation, and a leading member of it; and he is doing what he can to induce you to think that this ideal relation ought to be maintained forever.

Now, what is true of steel production is true of every other department of industrial activity; you belong to the millions who have no tools, who cannot work without selling your labor power, and when you sell that, you have got to deliver it in person; you cannot send it to the mill, you have got to carry it there; you are inseparable from your labor power.

You have got to go to the mill at 7 in the morning and work until 6 in the evening, producing, not for yourself, but for the capitalist who owns the tools you made and use, and without which you are almost as helpless as if you had no arms.

This fundamental fact in modern industry you must recognize, and you must organize upon the basis of this fact; you must appeal to your class to join the union that is the true expression of your economic interests, and this union must be large enough to embrace you all, and such is the Industrial Workers of the World.

Every man and every woman who works for wages is eligible to membership.

Organized into various departments, when you join you become a member of the department that represents your craft, or occupation, whatever it may be; and when you have a grievance, your department has supervision of it; and if you fail to adjust it in that department, you are not limited to your craft alone for support, but, if necessary, all the workers in all other departments will unite solidly in your defense to the very last. (Applause.) . . .

Karl Marx, the profound economic philosopher, who will be known in future as the great emancipator, uttered the inspiring shibboleth a half century ago: "Workingmen of all countries unite; you have nothing to lose but your chains; you have a world to gain."

You workers are the only class essential to society; all others can be spared, but without you society would perish. You produce the wealth, you support government, you create and conserve civilization. You ought to be, can be and will be the masters of the earth. (Great applause.)

Why should you be dependent upon a capitalist? Why should this capitalist own a tool he cannot use? And why should not you own the tool you have to use?

Every cog in every wheel that revolves everywhere has been made by the working class, and is set and kept in operation by the working class; and if the working class can make and operate this marvelous wealth-producing machinery, they can also develop the intelligence to make themselves the masters of this machinery (applause), and operate it not to turn out millionaires, but to produce wealth in abundance for themselves.

You cannot afford to be contented with your lot; you have a brain to develop and a manhood to sustain. You ought to have some aspiration to be free.

Suppose you do have a job and that you can get enough to eat and clothes enough to cover your body, and a place to sleep; you but exist upon the animal plane; your very life is suspended by a slender thread; you don't know what hour a machine may be invented to displace you, or you may offend your economic master, and your job is gone. You go to work early in the morning and you work all day; you go to your lodging at night, tired; you throw your exhausted body upon a bed of straw to recuperate enough to go back to the factory and repeat the same dull operation the next day, and the next, and so on and on to the dreary end; and in some respects you are not so well off as was the chattel slave.

He had no fear of losing his job; he was not blacklisted; he had food and clothing and shelter; and now and then, seized with a desire for freedom, he tried to run away from his master. Yo do not try to run away from yours. He doesn't have to hire a policeman to keep an eye on you. When you run, it is in the opposite direction, when the bell rings or the whistle blows.

You are as much subject to the command of the capitalist as if you were his property under the law. You have got to go to his factory because you have got to work; he is the master of your job, and you cannot work without his consent, and he only gives this on condition that you surrender to him all you produce except what is necessary to keep you in running order.

The machine you work with has to be oiled; you have to be fed; the wage is your lubricant, it keeps you in working order, and so you toil and sweat and groan and reproduce yourself in the form of labor power, and then you pass away like a silk worm that spins its task and dies.

That is your lot in the capitalist system and you have no right to aspire to rise above the dead level of wage-slavery.

It is true that one in ten thousand may escape from his class and become a millionaire; he is the rare exception that proves the rule. The wage-workers remain in the working class, and they never can become anything else in the capitalist system. They produce and perish, and their exploited bones mingle with the dust.

Every few years there is a panic, industrial paralysis, and hundreds of thousands of workers are flung into the streets; no work, no wages; and so they throng the highways in search of employment that cannot be found; they become vagrants, tramps, outcasts, criminals. It is in this way that the human being degenerates, and that crime graduates in the capitalist system, all the way from petty larceny to homicide.

The working millions who produce the wealth have little or nothing to show for it. There is widespread ignorance among them; industrial and social conditions prevail that defy all language properly to describe. The working class consist of a mass of human beings, men, women and children, in enforced competition with one another, in all of the circling hours of the day and night, for the sale of their labor power, and in the severity of the competition the wage sinks gradually until it touches the point of subsistence.

In this struggle more than five millions of women are engaged and about two millions of children, and the number of child laborers is steadily increasing, for in this system profit is important, while life has no value. It is not a question of male labor, or female labor, or child labor; it is simply a question of cheap labor without references to the effect upon the working class; the woman is employed in preference to the man and the child in preference to the woman; and so we have millions of children, who, in their early, tender years, are seized in the iron clutch of capitalism, when they ought to be upon the playground, or at school; when they ought to be in the sunlight, when they ought to have wholesome food and enjoy the fresh atmosphere they are forced into the industrial dungeons and there they are riveted to the machines; they feed the insatiate monsters and become as living cogs in the revolving wheels. They are literally fed to industry to produce profits. They are dwarfed and deformed, mentally, morally and physically; they have no chance in life; they are the victims of the industrial system that the Industrial Workers is organized to abolish in the interest, not only of the working class, but in the higher interest of all humanity. (Applause.)

If there is a crime that should bring to the callouts cheek of capitalist society the crimson of shame, it is the unspeakable crime of child slavery; the millions of babes that fester in the sweat shops, are the slaves of the wheel, and cry out in their agony, but are not heard in the din and roar of our industrial infernalism.

Take that great army of workers, called coal miners, organized in a craft union that does nothing for them; that seeks to make them contented with their lot. These miners are at the very foundation of industry and without their labor every wheel would cease to revolve as if by the decree of some industrial Jehovah. (Applause.) There are 600,000 of these slaves whose labor makes possible the firesides of the world, while their own loved ones shiver in the cold. I know something of the conditions under which they toil and despair and perish. I have taken time enough to descend to the depths of these pits, that Dante never saw, or he might have improved upon his masterpiece. I have stood over these slaves and I have heard the echo of their picks, which sounded to me like muffled drums throbbing funeral marches to the grave, and I have said to myself, in the capitalist system, these wretches are simply following their own hearses to the potter's field.

In all of the horizon of the future there is no star that sheds a ray of hope for them.

Then I have followed them from the depth of these black holes, over to the edge of the camp, not to the home, they have no home; but to a hut that is owned by the corporation that owns them, and here I have seen the wife,—Victor Hugo once said that the wife of a slave is not a wife at all; she is simply a female that gives birth to young—I have seen this wife standing in the doorway, after trying all day long to make a ten-cent piece do the service of a half-dollar, and she was ill-humored; this could not be otherwise, for love and abject poverty do not dwell beneath the same roof. Here there is no paper upon the wall and no carpet upon the floor; there is not a picture to appeal to the eye; there is no statue to challenge the soul, no strain of inspiring music to touch and quicken what Lincoln called the better angels of human nature. Here there is haggard poverty and want. And in this atmosphere the children of the future are being reared, many thousands of them, under conditions that make it morally certain that they will become paupers, or criminals, or both.

Man is the product, the expression of his environment. Show me a majestic tree that towers aloft, that challenges the admiration of man, or a beautiful rose-bud that, under the influence of sunshine and shower, bursts into bloom and fills the common air with its fragrance; these are possible only because the soil and climate are adapted to the growth and culture. Transfer this flower from the sunlight and the atmosphere to a cellar filled with noxious gases, and it withers and dies. The same law applies to human beings; the industrial soil and the soil climate must be adapted to the development of men and women, and then society will cease producing (cry of "down with capitalism") the multiplied thousands

of deformities that today are a rebuke to our much vaunted civilization, and, above all, an impeachment of the capitalist system. (Applause.)

What is true of the miners is true in a greater or less degree of all workers in all other departments of industrial activity. This system has about fulfilled its historic mission. Upon every hand there are the unerring signs of change, and the time has come for the education and organization of the working class for the social revolution (applause) that is to lift the workers from the depths of slavery and elevate them to an exalted plane of equality and fraternity. (Applause.)

At the beginning of industrial society men worked with hand tools; a boy could learn a trade, make himself the master of the simple tools with which he worked, and employ himself and enjoy what he produced; but that simple tool of a century ago has become a mammoth social instrument; in a word, that tool has been socialized. Not only this, but production has been socialized. As small a commodity as a pin or a pen, or a match involves for its production all of the social labor of the land; but this evolution is not yet complete; the tool has been socialized, production has been socialized, and now ownership must also be socialized; in other words, those great social instruments that are used in modern industry for the production of wealth, those great social agencies that are socially made and socially used, must also be socially owned. (Applause.) . . .

It is a very important thing to develop the economic power, to have a sound economic organization. This has been the inherent weakness in the labor movement of the United States. We need, and sorely need, a revolutionary economic organization. We must develop this kind of strength;

it is the kind that we will have occasion to use in due time, and it is the kind that will not fail us when the crisis comes. So we shall organize and continue to organize the political field; and I am of those who believe that the day is near at hand when we shall have one great revolutionary economic organization, and one great revolutionary political party of the working class. (Cheers and prolonged applause.) Then will proceed with increased impetus the work of education and organization that will culminate in emancipation.

This great body will sweep into power and seize the reins of government; take possession of industry in the name of the working class, and it can be easily done. All that will be required will be to transfer the title deeds from the parasites to the producers; and then the working class, in control of industry, will operate it for the benefit of all. The work day will be reduced in proportion to the progress of invention. Every man will work, or at least have a chance to work, and get the full equivalent of what he produces. He will work, not as a slave, but as a free man, and he will express himself in his work and work with joy. Then the badge of labor will be the only badge of aristocracy. The industrial dungeon will become a temple of science. The working class will be free, and all humanity disenthralled.

The workers are the saviours of society (applause); the redeemers of the race; and when they have fulfilled their great historic mission, men and women can walk the high-lands and enjoy the vision of a land without masters and without slaves, a land regenerated and resplendent in the triumph of Freedom and Civilization. (Long, continued applause.)

Individualism, Materialism, and Idealism   9

Herbert Hoover

Born in 1874 in West Branch, Iowa, Herbert Hoover became the thirty-first president of the United States (1929–33). He was known for his philosophy of voluntarism and for using the least government intervention possible in the economy, a policy that failed in the Great Depression and resulted in his replacement by Franklin D. Roosevelt.

After graduating from Stanford University, Hoover worked as a mining engineer in Australia, China, Burma, and Russia. He then became an independent mining consultant with offices in New York, San Francisco, and London. In 1909 he published *Principles of Mining*. When World War I started in 1914, Hoover was in London and was appointed chairman of the American Relief Commission. He organized the return of about 150,000 Americans stranded in Europe and then chaired the Commission for Relief in Belgium, bringing badly needed food and clothing to Belgium and northern France. When the United States entered the war, Hoover was made U.S. food administrator, a member of the War Trade Council, and chairman of the Interallied Food Council, successfully coordinating efforts to encourage Americans to voluntarily conserve food and to donate food and money to those in need abroad. Upon returning to the United States after the war, Hoover directed the American Relief Administration, which fed millions during the 1921–23 famine in the Soviet Union.

From 1921 to 1929, Hoover served as secretary of commerce under Presidents Harding and Coolidge, organizing conferences on unemployment, supporting trade organizations, and backing engineering projects such as the St. Lawrence Waterway and Hoover Dam. These activities made Hoover popular, and he became the Republican nominee for president in 1928, defeating Democrat Alfred E. Smith. As president, Hoover continued to advocate his philosophy of voluntarism. He believed in the basic soundness of the economy and that industries and labor unions could work things out. Creating the Federal Farm Board, Hoover pushed for revisions of tariffs, which led to the devastating protectionist Hawley-Smoot Tariff Act.

After the stock market crash of 1929, Hoover believed that the economy could be made stronger by keeping wages and prices high and cutting production to prevent overcapacity. State and local governments were encouraged in their relief efforts, but Hoover opposed giving them federal funds. However, in 1932 he backed federal creation of the Reconstruction Finance Corporation to stimulate industry by granting loans unavailable elsewhere. He also supported a large public works program. Despite losing to Roosevelt in the 1932 election, largely due to failure of his economic policies, Hoover continued to oppose government intervention in the economy and was in favor of as little involvement of the United States in foreign affairs as possible.

Apart from speeches at Republican conventions, Hoover largely retired from public life until after World War II. He then began coordinating food supplies for countries badly damaged by the war, and headed the Hoover Commission to study the executive branch of the government, which resulted in the establishment of the Department of Health, Education, and Welfare. He died in 1964.

Among Hoover's books are *The Challenge to Liberty* (1934), *The Ordeal of Woodrow Wilson* (1958), *An American Epic* (1959–61, 3 volumes), and *American Individualism* (1922), from which the following excerpts are taken.

American Individualism (1922)
(excerpts)

We have witnessed in this last eight years the spread of revolution over one-third of the world. The causes of these explosions lie at far greater depths than the failure of governments in war. The war itself in its last stages was a conflict of social philosophies—but beyond this the causes of social explosion lay in the great inequalities and injustices of centuries flogged beyond endurance by the conflict and freed from restraint by the destruction of war. The urgent forces which drive human society have been plunged into a terrible furnace. Great theories spun by dreamers to remedy the pressing human ills have come to the front of men's minds. Great formulas came into life that promised to dissolve all trouble. Great masses of people have flocked to their banners in hopes born of misery and suffering. Nor has this great social ferment been confined to those nations that have burned with revolutions.

Now, as the storm of war, of revolution and of emotion subsides there is left even with us of the United States much unrest, much discontent with the surer forces of human advancement. To all of us, out of this crucible of actual, poignant, individual experience has come a deal of new understanding, and it is for all of us to ponder these new currents if we are to shape our future with intelligence.

Even those parts of the world that suffered less from the war have been partly infected by these ideas. Beyond this, however, many have had high hopes of civilization suddenly purified and ennobled by the sacrifices and services of the war; they had thought the fine unity of purpose gained in war would be carried into great unity of action in remedy of the faults of civilization in peace. But from concentration of every spiritual and material energy upon the single purpose of war the scene changed to the immense complexity and the many purposes of peace.

Thus there loom up certain definite underlying forces in our national life that need to be stripped of the imaginary—the transitory—and a definition should be given to the actual permanent and persistent motivation of our civilization. In contemplation of these questions we must go far deeper than the superficials of our political and economic structure, for these are but the products of our social philosophy—the machinery of our social system.

Nor is it ever amiss to review the political, economic, and spiritual principles through which our country has steadily grown in usefulness and greatness, not only to preserve them from being fouled by false notions, but more importantly that we may guide ourselves in the road of progress.

Five or six great social philosophies are at struggle in the world for ascendency. There is the Individualism of America. There is the Individualism of the more democratic states of Europe with its careful reservations of castes and classes. There are Communism, Socialism, Syndicalism,

Capitalism, and finally there is Autocracy—whether by birth, by possessions, militarism, or divine right of kings. Even the Divine Right still lingers on although our lifetime has seen fully two-thirds of the earth's population, including Germany, Austria, Russia, and China, arrive at a state of angry disgust with this type of social motive power and throw it on the scrap heap.

All these thoughts are in ferment today in every country in the world. They fluctuate in ascendency with times and places. They compromise with each other in daily reaction on governments and peoples. Some of these ideas are perhaps more adapted to one race than another. Some are false, some are true. What we are interested in is their challenge to the physical and spiritual forces of America.

The partisans of some of these other brands of social schemes challenge us to comparison; and some of their partisans even among our own people are increasing in their agitation that we adopt one or another or parts of their devices in place of our tried individualism. They insist that our social foundations are exhausted, that like feudalism and autocracy America's plan has served its purpose—that it must be abandoned.

There are those who have been left in sober doubt of our institutions or are confounded by bewildering catchwords of vivid phrases. For in this welter of discussions there is much attempt to glorify or defame social and economic forces with phrases. Nor indeed should we disregard the potency of some of these phrases in their stir to action.—"The dictatorship of the Proletariat," "Capitalistic nations," "Germany over all," and a score of others. We need only to review those that have jumped to horseback during the last ten years in order that we may be properly awed by the great social and political havoc that can be worked where the bestial instincts of hate, murder, and destruction are clothed by the demagogue in the fine terms of political idealism.

For myself, let me say at the very outset that my faith in the essential truth, strength, and vitality of the developing creed by which we have hitherto lived in this country of ours has been confirmed and deepened by the searching experiences of seven years of service in the backwash and misery of war. Seven years of contending with economic degeneration, with social disintegration, with incessant political dislocation, with all of its seething and ferment of individual and class conflict, could but impress me with the primary motivation of social forces, and the necessity for broader thought upon their great issues to humanity. And from it all I emerge an individualist—an unashamed individualist. But let me say also that I am an American individualist. For America has been steadily developing the ideals that constitute progressive individualism.

No doubt, individualism run riot, with no tempering principle, would provide a long category of inequalities, of tyrannies, dominations, and injustices. America, however, has tempered the whole conception of individualism by the injection of a definite principle, and from this principle it follows that attempts at domination, whether in government or in the processes of industry and commerce, are under an insistent curb. If we would have the values of individualism, their stimulation to initiative, to the development of hand and intellect, to the high development of thought and spirituality, they must be tempered with that firm and fixed ideal of American individualism—*an equality of opportunity.* If we would have these values we must soften its hardness and stimulate progress through that sense of service that lies in our people.

Therefore, it is not the individualism of other countries for which I would speak, but the individualism of America. Our individualism differs from all others because it embraces these great ideals: *that while we build our society upon the attainment of the individual, we shall safeguard to every individual an equality of opportunity to take that position in the community to which his intelligence, character, ability, and ambition entitle him; that we keep the social solution free from frozen strata of classes; that we shall stimulate effort of each individual to achievement; that through an enlarging sense of responsibility and understanding we shall assist him to this attainment; while he in turn must stand up to the emery wheel of competition.*

Individualism cannot be maintained as the foundation of a society if it looks to only legalistic justice based upon contracts, property, and political equality. Such legalistic safeguards are themselves not enough. In our individualism we have long since abandoned the laissez faire of the 18th Century—the notion that it is "every man for himself and the devil take the hindmost." We abandoned that when we adopted the ideal of equality of opportunity—the fair chance of Abraham Lincoln. We have confirmed its abandonment in terms of legislation, of social and economic justice,—in part because we have learned that it is the hindmost who throws the bricks at our social edifice, in part because we have learned that the foremost are not always the best nor the hindmost the worst—and in part because we have learned that social injustice is the destruction of justice itself. We have learned that the impulse to production can only be maintained at a high pitch if there is a fair division of the product. We have also learned that fair division can only be obtained by certain restrictions on the strong and the dominant. We have

indeed gone even further in the 20th Century with the embracement of the necessity of a greater and broader sense of service and responsibility to others as a part of individualism.

Whatever may be the case with regard to Old World individualism (and we have given more back to Europe than we received from her) the truth that is important for us to grasp today is that there is a world of difference between the principles and spirit of Old World individualism and that which we have developed in our own country.

We have, in fact, a special social system of our own. We have made it ourselves from materials brought in revolt from conditions in Europe. We have lived it; we constantly improve it; we have seldom tried to define it. It abhors autocracy and does not argue with it, but fights it. It is not capitalism, or socialism, or syndicalism, nor a cross breed of them. Like most Americans, I refuse to be damned by anybody's word-classification of it, such as "capitalism," "plutocracy," "proletariat" or "middle class," or any other, or to any kind of compartment that is based on the assumption of some group dominating somebody else.

The social force in which I am interested is far higher and far more precious a thing than all these. It springs from something infinitely more enduring; it springs from the one source of human progress—that each individual shall be given the chance and stimulation for development of the best with which he has been endowed in heart and mind; it is the sole source of progress; it is American individualism. . . .

On the philosophic side we can agree at once that intelligence, character, courage, and the divine spark of the human soul are alone the property of individuals. These do not lie in agreements, in organizations, or institutions, in masses, or in groups. They abide alone in the individual mind and heart.

Production both of mind and hand rests upon impulses in each individual. These impulses are made of the varied forces of original instincts, motives, and acquired desires. Many of these are destructive and must be restrained through moral leadership and authority of the law and be eliminated finally by education. All are modified by a vast fund of experience and a vast plant and equipment of civilization which we pass on with increments to each succeeding generation.

The inherited instincts of self-preservation, acquisitiveness, fear, kindness, hate, curiosity, desire for self-expression, for power, for adulation, that we carry over from a thousand of generations must, for good or evil, be comprehended in a workable system embracing our accumulation of experiences and equipment. They may modify themselves with time—but in terms of generations. They differ in their urge upon different individuals. The dominant ones are selfish. But no civilization could be built or can endure solely upon the groundwork of unrestrained and unintelligent self-interest. The problem of the world is to restrain the destructive instincts while strengthening and enlarging those of altruistic character and constructive impulse— for thus we build for the future.

From the instincts of kindness, pity, fealty to family and race; the love of liberty; the mystical yearnings for spiritual things; the desire for fuller expression of the creative faculties; the impulses of service to community and nation, are moulded the ideals of our people. And the most potent force in society is its ideals. If one were to attempt to delimit the potency of instinct and ideals, it would be found that while instinct dominates in our preservation yet the great propelling force of progress is right ideals. It is true we do not realize the ideal; not even a single person personifies that realization. It is therefore not surprising that society, a collection of persons, a necessary maze of compromises, cannot realize it. But that it has ideals, that they revolve in a system that makes for steady advance of them is the first thing. Yet true as this is, the day has not arrived when any economic or social system will function and last if founded upon altruism alone.

With the growth of ideals through education, with the higher realization of freedom, of justice, of humanity, of service, the selfish impulses become less and less dominant, and if we ever reach the millennium, they will disappear in the aspirations and satisfactions of pure altruism. But for the next several generations we dare not abandon self-interest as a motive force to leadership and to production, lest we die.

The will-o'-the-wisp of all breeds of socialism is that they contemplate a motivation of human animals by altruism alone. It necessitates a bureaucracy of the entire population, in which, having obliterated the economic stimulation of each member, the fine gradations of character and ability are to be arranged in relative authority by ballot or more likely by a Tammany Hall or a Bolshevist party, or some other form of tyranny. The proof of the futility of these ideas as a stimulation to the development and activity of the individual does not lie alone in the ghastly failure of Russia, but it also lies in our own failure in attempts at nationalized industry.

Likewise the basic foundations of autocracy, whether it be class government or capitalism in the sense that a few men through unrestrained control of property determine the welfare of great numbers, is as far apart from the rightful expression of American individualism as the two poles. The will-o'-the-wisp of autocracy in any form is that it supposes that the good Lord endowed a special few with all the divine attributes. It contemplates one human animal dealing to the other human animals his just share of earth, of glory, and of immortality. The proof of the futility of these ideas in the development of the world does not lie alone in the grim failure of Germany, but it lies in the damage to our moral and social fabric from those who have sought economic domination in America, whether employer or employee.

We in America have had too much experience of life to fool ourselves into pretending that all men are equal in ability, in character, in intelligence, in ambition. That was part of the claptrap of the French Revolution. We have grown to understand that all we can hope to assure to the individual through government is liberty, justice, intellectual welfare, equality of opportunity, and stimulation to service.

It is in maintenance of a society fluid to these human qualities that our individualism departs from the individualism of Europe. There can be no rise for the individual through the frozen strata of classes, or of castes, and no stratification can take place in a mass livened by the free stir of its particles. This guarding of our individualism against stratification insists not only in preserving in the social solution an equal opportunity for the able and ambitious to rise from the bottom; it also insists that the sons of the successful shall not by any mere right of birth or favor continue to occupy their fathers' places of power against the rise of a new generation in process of coming up from the bottom. The pioneers of our American individualism had the good sense not to reward Washington and Jefferson and Hamilton with hereditary dukedoms and fixtures in landed estates, as Great Britain rewarded Marlborough and Nelson. Otherwise our American fields of opportunity would have been clogged with

long generations inheriting their fathers' privileges without their fathers' capacity for service.

That our system has avoided the establishment and domination of class has a significant proof in the present Administration in Washington. Of the twelve men comprising the President, Vice-President, and Cabinet, nine have earned their own way in life without economic inheritance, and eight of them started with manual labor.

If we examine the impulses that carry us forward, none is so potent for progress as the yearning for individual self-expression, the desire for creation of something. Perhaps the greatest human happiness flows from personal achievement. Here lies the great urge of the constructive instinct of mankind. But it can only thrive in a society where the individual has liberty and stimulation to achievement. Nor does the community progress except through its participation in these multitudes of achievements.

Furthermore, the maintenance of productivity and the advancement of the things of the spirit depend upon the ever-renewed supply from the mass of those who can rise to leadership. Our social, economic, and intellectual progress is almost solely dependent upon the creative minds of those individuals with imaginative and administrative intelligence who create or who carry discoveries to widespread application. No race possesses more than a small percentage of these minds in a single generation. But little thought has ever been given to our racial dependency upon them. Nor that our progress is in so large a measure due to the fact that with our increased means of communication these rare individuals are today able to spread their influence over so enlarged a number of lesser capable minds as to have increased their potency a million-fold. In truth, the vastly greater productivity of the world with actually less physical labor is due to the wider spread of their influence through the discovery of these facilities. And they can arise solely through the selection that comes from the free-running mills of competition. They must be free to rise from the mass; they must be given the attraction of premiums to effort.

Leadership is a quality of the individual. It is the individual alone who can function in the world of intellect and in the field of leadership. If democracy is to secure its authorities in morals, religion, and statesmanship, it must stimulate leadership from its own mass. Human leadership cannot be replenished by selection like queen bees, by divine right or bureaucracies, but by the free rise of ability, character, and intelligence.

Even so, leadership cannot, no matter how brilliant, carry progress far ahead of the average of the mass of individual units. Progress of the nation is the sum of progress in its individuals. Acts and ideas that lead to progress are born out of the womb of the individual mind, not out of the mind of the crowd. The crowd only feels: it has no mind of its own which can plan. The crowd is credulous, it destroys, it consumes, it hates, and it dreams—but it never builds. It is one of the most profound and important of exact psychological truths that man in the mass does not think but only feels. The mob functions only in a world of emotion. The demagogue feeds on mob emotions and his leadership is the leadership of emotion, not the leadership of intellect and progress. Popular desires are no criteria to the real need; they can be determined only by deliberative consideration, by education, by constructive leadership.

Sinclair Lewis

Sinclair Lewis wrote twenty-two novels and became the first American to win the Nobel Prize for Literature. Lewis was known for his biting wit and humorous, satiric attacks upon the mediocrity of mass culture and the standardization of habits and ideas, which he believed bogged down the promise of the New World. His writing flashes with critical, poetic thrusts in the tradition of Emerson, Thoreau, Whitman, and Twain, while still alluding to some of the hope and idealism of contemporaries Edward Bellamy and Henry George.

Born in 1884 in Sauk Centre, Minnesota, Lewis was a restless adventurer, spending much of his youth doing odd jobs and journalism. He caught cattle boats to Europe during the summers, finished his B.A. at Yale, and wrote for the *Yale Literary Magazine,* which he later edited. Working as a reporter and editor, selling short-story plots to Jack London, and in and out of different jobs in the publishing business in New York, Lewis wrote plays such as *It Can't Happen Here* and *Angela Is Twenty-Two,* some of which he produced, directed, or acted in. He is best known for his novels, particularly *Main Street* (1920), *Babbitt* (1922), *Arrowsmith* (1925), and *Elmer Gantry* (1927). When not traveling and lecturing in the United States and Europe, he lived on a farm in Massachusetts. Lewis refused a Pulitzer Prize for *Arrowsmith,* but accepted the Nobel Prize for Literature in 1930. He died in Rome in 1951.

His fictional character George Babbitt has taken on almost mythological status in symbolizing many typical beliefs of middle-class American social and political life as the excerpts here illustrate.

Babbitt (1922)
(excerpts)

I

This autumn a Mr. W. G. Harding, of Marion, Ohio, was appointed President of the United States, but Zenith was less interested in the national campaign than in the local election. Seneca Doane, though he was a lawyer and a graduate of the State University, was candidate for mayor of Zenith on an alarming labor ticket. To oppose him the Democrats and Republicans united on Lucas Prout, a mattress-manufacturer with a perfect record for sanity. Mr. Prout was supported by the banks, the Chamber of Commerce, all the decent newspapers, and George F. Babbitt.

Babbitt was precinct-leader on Floral Heights, but his district was safe and he longed for stouter battling. His convention paper had given him the beginning of a reputation for oratory, so the Republican-Democratic Central Committee sent him to the Seventh Ward and South Zenith, to address small audiences of workmen and clerks, and wives uneasy with their new votes. He acquired a fame enduring for weeks. Now and then a reporter was present at one of his meetings, and the headlines (though they were not very large) indicated that George F. Babbitt had addressed Cheering Throng, and Distinguished Man of Affairs had pointed out the Fallacies of Doane. Once, in the rotogravure section of the Sunday *Advocate-Times,* there was a photograph of Babbitt and a dozen other business men, with the caption "Leaders of Zenith Finance and Commerce Who Back Prout."

He deserved his glory. He was an excellent campaigner. He had faith; he was certain that if Lincoln were alive, he would be electioneering for Mr. W. G. Harding—unless he came to Zenith and electioneered for Lucas Prout. He did not confuse audiences by silly subtleties; Prout represented honest industry, Seneca Doane represented whining laziness, and you could take your choice. With his broad shoulders and vigorous voice, he was obviously a Good Fellow; and, rarest of all, he really liked people. He almost liked common workmen. He wanted them to be well paid, and able to afford high rents—though, naturally, they must not interfere with the reasonable profits of stockholders. Thus nobly endowed, and keyed high by the discovery that he was a natural orator, he was popular with audiences, and he raged through the campaign, renowned not only in the Seventh and Eighth Wards but even in parts of the Sixteenth.

II

Crowded in his car, they came driving up to Turnverein Hall, South Zenith—Babbitt, his wife, Verona, Ted, and Paul and Zilla Riesling. The hall was over a delicatessen shop, in a street banging with trolleys and smelling of onions and gasoline and fried fish. A new appreciation of Babbitt filled all of them, including Babbitt.

"Don't know how you keep it up, talking to three bunches in one evening. Wish I had your strength," said Paul; and Ted exclaimed to Verona, "The old man certainly does know how to kid these roughnecks along!"

Men in black sateen shirts, their faces new-washed but with a hint of grime under their eyes, were loitering on the broad stairs up to the hall. Babbitt's party politely edged through them and into the whitewashed room, at the front of which was a dais with a red-plush throne and a pine altar painted watery blue, as used nightly by the Grand Masters and Supreme Potentates of innumerable lodges. The hall was full. As Babbitt pushed through the fringe standing at the back, he heard the precious tribute, "That's him!" The chairman bustled down the center aisle with an impressive, "The speaker? All ready, sir! Uh—let's see— what was the name, sir?"

Then Babbitt slid into a sea of eloquence:

"Ladies and gentlemen of the Sixteenth Ward, there is one who cannot be with us here to-night, a man than whom there is no more stalwart Trojan in all the political arena—I refer to our leader, the Honorable Lucas Prout, standard-bearer of the city and county of Zenith. Since he is not here, I trust that you will bear with me if, as a friend and neighbor, as one who is proud to share with you the common blessing of being a resident of the great city of Zenith, I tell you in all candor, honesty, and sincerity how the issues of this critical campaign appear to one plain man of business—to one who, brought up to the blessings of poverty and of manual labor, has, even when Fate condemned him to sit at a desk, yet never forgotten how it feels, by heck, to be up at five-thirty and at the factory with the old dinner-pail in his hardened mitt when the whistle blew at seven, unless the owner sneaked in ten minutes on us and blew it early! (Laughter.) To come down to the basic and fundamental issues of this campaign, the great error, insincerely promulgated by Seneca Doane—"

There were workmen who jeered— young cynical workmen, for the most part foreigners, Jews, Swedes, Irishmen, Italians—but the older men, the patient, bleached, stooped carpenters and mechanics, cheered him; and when he worked up to his anecdote of Lincoln their eyes were wet.

Modestly, busily, he hurried out of the hall on delicious applause, and sped off to his third audience of the evening. "Ted, you better drive," he said. "Kind of all in after that spiel. Well, Paul, how'd it go? Did I get 'em?"

"Bully! Corking! You had a lot of pep."

Mrs. Babbitt worshiped, "Oh, it was fine! So clear and interesting, and such nice ideas. When I hear you orating I realize I don't appreciate how profoundly you think and what a splendid brain and vocabulary you have. Just—splendid."

But Verona was irritating. "Dad," she worried, "how do you know that public ownership of utilities and so on and so forth will always be a failure?"

Mrs. Babbitt reproved, "Rone, I should think you could see and realize that when your father's all worn out with orating, it's no time to expect him to explain these complicated subjects. I'm sure when he's rested he'll be glad to explain it to you. Now let's all be quiet and give Papa a chance to get ready for his next speech. Just think! Right now they're gathering in Maccabee Temple, and *waiting* for us!"

III

Mr. Lucas Prout and Sound Business defeated Mr. Seneca Doane and Class Rule, and Zenith was again saved. Babbitt was offered several minor appointments to distribute among poor relations, but he preferred advance information about the extension of paved highways, and this a grateful administration gave to him. Also, he was one of only nineteen speakers at the dinner with which the Chamber of Commerce celebrated the victory of righteousness.

His reputation for oratory established, at the dinner of the Zenith Real Estate Board he made the Annual Address. The *Advocate-Times* reported this speech with unusual fullness:

"One of the livest banquets that has recently been pulled off occurred last night in the annual Get-Together Fest of the Zenith Real Estate Board, held in the Venetian Ball Room of the O'Hearn House. Mine host Gil O'Hearn had as usual done himself proud and those assembled feasted on such an assemblage of plates as could be rivaled nowhere west of New York, if there, and washed down the plenteous feed with the cup which inspired but did not inebriate in the shape of cider from the farm of Chandler Mott, president of the board and who acted as witty and efficient chairman.

"As Mr. Mott was suffering from slight infection and sore throat, G. F. Babbitt made the principal talk. Besides outlining the progress of Torrensing real estate titles, Mr. Babbitt spoke in part as follows:

" 'In rising to address you, with my impromptu speech carefully tucked into my vest pocket, I am reminded of the story of the two Irishmen, Mike and Pat, who were riding on the Pullman. Both of them, I forgot to say, were sailors in the Navy. It seems Mike had the lower berth and by and by he heard a terrible racket from the upper, and when he yelled up to find out what the trouble was, Pat answered, "Shure an' bedad an' how can I ever get a night's sleep at all, at all? I been trying to get into this darned little hammock ever since eight bells!"

" 'Now, gentlemen, standing up here before you, I feel a good deal like Pat, and maybe after I've spieled along for a while, I may feel so darn small that I'll be able to crawl into a Pullman hammock with no trouble at all, at all!

" 'Gentlemen, it strikes me that each year at this annual occasion when friend and foe get together and lay down the battle-ax and let the waves of good-fellowship waft them up the flowery slopes of amity, it behooves us, standing together eye to eye and shoulder to shoulder as fellow-citizens of the best city in the world, to consider where we are both as regards ourselves and the common weal.

" 'It is true that even with our 361,000, or practically 362,000, population, there are, by the last census, almost a score of larger cities in the United States. But, gentlemen, if by the next census we do not stand at least tenth, then I'll be the first to request any knocker to remove my shirt and to eat the same, with the compliments of G. F. Babbitt, Esquire! It may be true that New York, Chicago, and Philadelphia will continue to keep ahead of us in size. But aside from these three cities, which are notoriously so overgrown that no decent white man, nobody who loves his wife and kiddies and God's good out-o'-doors and likes to shake the hand of his neighbor in greeting, would want to live in them—and let me tell you right here and now, I wouldn't trade a high-class Zenith acreage development for the whole length and breadth of Broadway or State Street!— aside from these three, it's evident to any one with a head for facts that Zenith is the finest example of American life and prosperity to be found anywhere.

" 'I don't mean to say we're perfect. We've got a lot to do in the way of extending the paving of motor boulevards, for, believe me, it's the fellow with four to ten thousand a year, say, and an automobile and a nice little family in a bungalow on the edge of town, that makes the wheels of progress go round!

" 'That's the type of fellow that's ruling America to-day; in fact, it's the ideal type to which the entire world must tend, if there's to be a decent, well-balanced, Christian, go-ahead future for this little old planet! Once in a while I just naturally sit back and size up this Solid American Citizen, with a whale of a lot of satisfaction.

" 'Our Ideal Citizen—I picture him first and foremost as being busier than a bird-dog, not wasting a lot of good time in day-dreaming or going to sassiety teas or kicking about things that are none of his business, but putting the zip into some store or profession or art. At night he lights up a good cigar, and climbs into the little old 'bus, and maybe cusses the carburetor, and shoots out home. He mows the lawn, or sneaks in some practice putting, and then he's ready for dinner. After dinner he tells the kiddies a story, or takes the family to the movies, or plays a few fists of bridge, or reads the evening paper, and a chapter or two of some good lively Western novel if he has a taste for literature, and maybe the folks next-door drop in and they sit and visit about their friends and the topics of the day. Then he goes happily to bed, his conscience clear, having contributed his mite to the prosperity of the city and to his own bank-account.

" 'In politics and religion this Sane Citizen is the canniest man on earth; and in the arts he invariably has a natural taste which makes him pick out the best, every time. In no country in the world will you find so many reproductions of the Old Masters and of well-known paintings on parlor walls as in these United States. No country has anything like our number of phonographs, with not only dance records and comic but also the best operas, such as Verdi, rendered by the world's highest-paid singers.

" 'In other countries, art and literature are left to a lot of shabby bums living in attics and feeding on booze and spaghetti, but in America the successful writer or pic-ture-painter is indistinguishable from any other decent business man; and I, for one, am only too glad that the man who has the rare skill to season his message with interesting reading matter and who shows both purpose and pep in handling his literary wares has a chance to drag down his fifty thousand bucks a year, to mingle with the biggest executives on terms of perfect equality, and to show as big a house and as swell a car as any Captain of Industry! But, mind you, it's the appreciation of the Regular Guy who I have been depicting which has made this possible, and you got to hand as much credit to him as to the authors themselves.

" 'Finally, but most important, our Standardized Citizen, even if he is a bachelor, is a lover of the Little Ones, a supporter of the hearthstone which is the basic foundation of our civilization, first, last, and all the time, and the thing that most distinguishes us from the decayed nations of Europe.

" 'I have never yet toured Europe— and as a matter of fact, I don't know that I care to such an awful lot, as long as there's our own mighty cities and mountains to be seen—but, the way I figure it out, there must be a good many of our own sort of folks abroad. Indeed, one of the most enthusiastic Rotarians I ever met boosted the tenets of one-hundred-per-cent pep in a burr that smacked o' bonny Scutlond and all ye bonny braes o' Bobby Burns. But same time, one thing that distinguishes us from our good brothers, the hustlers over there, is that they're willing to take a lot off the snobs and journalists and politicians, while the modern American business man knows how to talk right up for himself, knows how to make it good and plenty clear that he intends to run the works. He doesn't have to call in some highbrow hired-man when it's necessary for him to answer the crooked critics of the sane and efficient life. He's not dumb, like the old-fashioned merchant. He's got a vocabulary and a punch.

" 'With all modesty, I want to stand up here as a representative business man and gently whisper, "Here's our kind of folks! Here's the specifications of the Standardized American Citizen! Here's the new generation of Americans: fellows with hair on their chests and smiles in their eyes and adding-machines in their offices. We're not doing any boasting, but we like ourselves first-rate, and if you don't like us, look out—better get under cover before the cyclone hits town!"

" 'So! In my clumsy way I have tried to sketch the Real He-man, the fellow with Zip and Bang. And it's because Zenith has so large a proportion of such men that it's the most stable, the greatest of our cities. New York also has its thousands of Real Folks, but New York is cursed with unnumbered foreigners. So are Chicago and San Francisco. Oh, we have a golden roster of cities—Detroit and Cleveland with their renowned factories, Cincinnati with its great machine-tool and soap products, Pittsburgh and Birmingham with their steel, Kansas City and Minneapolis and Omaha that open their bountiful gates on the bosom of the ocean-like wheatlands, and countless other magnificent sister-cities, for, by the last census, there were no less than sixty-eight glorious American burgs with a population of over one hundred thousand! And all these cities stand together for power and purity, and against foreign ideas and communism—Atlanta with Hartford, Rochester with Denver, Milwaukee with Indianapolis, Los Angeles with Scranton, Portland, Maine, with Portland, Oregon. A good live wire from Baltimore or Seattle or Duluth is the twin-brother of every like fellow booster from Buffalo or Akron, Fort Worth or Oskaloosa!

" 'But it's here in Zenith, the home for manly men and womanly women and bright kids, that you find the largest proportion of these Regular Guys, and that's what sets it in a class by itself; that's why Zenith will be remembered in history as having set the pace for a civilization that shall endure when the old time-killing ways are gone forever and the day of earnest efficient endeavor shall have dawned all round the world!

" 'Some time I hope folks will quit handing all the credit to a lot of moth-eaten, mildewed, out-of-date, old, European dumps, and give proper credit to the famous Zenith spirit, that clean fighting determination to win Success that has made the little old Zip City celebrated in every land and clime, wherever condensed milk and pasteboard cartons are known! Believe me, the world has fallen too long for these worn-out countries that aren't producing anything but boot-blacks and scenery and booze, that haven't got one bathroom per hundred people, and that don't know a loose-leaf ledger from a slip-cover; and it's just about time for some Zenithite to get his back up and holler for a show-down!

" 'I tell you, Zenith and her sister-cities are producing a new type of civilization. There are many resemblances between Zenith and these other burgs, and I'm darn glad of it! The extraordinary, growing, and sane standardization of stores, offices, streets, hotels, clothes, and newspapers throughout the United States shows how strong and enduring a type is ours.' " . . .

" 'Yes, sir, these other burgs are our true partners in the great game of vital living. But let's not have any mistake about this. I claim that Zenith is the best partner and the fastest-growing partner of the whole caboodle. I trust I may be pardoned if I give a few statistics to back up my claims. If they are old stuff to any of you, yet the tidings of prosperity, like the good news of the Bible, never become tedious to the ears of a real hustler, no matter how oft the sweet story is told! Every intelligent person knows that Zenith manufactures more condensed milk and evaporated cream, more paper boxes, and more lighting-fixtures, than any other city in the United States, if not in the world. But it is not so universally known that we also stand second in the manufacture of package-butter, sixth in the giant realm of motors and automobiles, and somewhere about third in cheese, leather findings, tar roofing, breakfast food, and overalls!

" 'Our greatness, however, lies not alone in punchful prosperity but equally in that public spirit, that forward-looking idealism and brotherhood, which has marked Zenith ever since its foundation by the Fathers. We have a right, indeed we have a duty toward our fair city, to announce broadcast the facts about our high schools, characterized by their complete plants and the finest school-ventilating systems in the country, bar none; our magnificent new hotels and banks and the paintings and carved marble in their lobbies; and the Second National Tower, the second highest business building in any inland city in the entire country. When I add that we have an unparalleled number of miles of paved streets, bathrooms, vacuum cleaners, and all the other signs of civilization; that our library and art museum are well supported and housed in convenient and roomy buildings; that our park-system is more than up to par, with its handsome driveways adorned with grass, shrubs, and statuary, then I give but a hint of the all-round unlimited greatness of Zenith!

" 'I believe, however, in keeping the best to the last. When I remind you that we have one motor car for every five and seven-eighths persons in the city, then I give a rock-ribbed practical indication of the kind of progress and braininess which is synonymous with the name Zenith!

" 'But the way of the righteous is not all roses. Before I close I must call your attention to a problem we have to face, this coming year. The worst menace to sound government is not the avowed socialists but a lot of cowards who work under cover—the long-haired gentry who call themselves "liberals" and "radicals" and "non-partisan" and "intelligentsia" and God only knows how many other trick names! Irresponsible teachers and professors constitute the worst of this whole gang, and I am ashamed to say that several of them are on the faculty of our great State University! The U. is my own Alma Mater, and I am proud to be known as an alumni, but there are certain instructors there who seem to think we ought to turn the conduct of the nation over to hoboes and roustabouts.

" 'Those profs are the snakes to be scotched—they and all their milk-and-water ilk! The American business man is generous to a fault, but one thing he does demand of all teachers and lecturers and journalists: if we're going to pay them our good money, they've got to help us by selling efficiency and whooping it up for rational prosperity! And when it comes to these blab-mouth, fault-finding, pessimistic, cynical University teachers, let me tell you that during this golden coming year it's just as much our duty to bring influence to have those cusses fired as it is to sell all the real estate and gather in all the good shekels we can.

" 'Not till that is done will our sons and daughters see that the ideal of American manhood and culture isn't a lot of cranks sitting around chewing the rag about their Rights and their Wrongs, but a God-fearing, hustling, successful, two-fisted Regular Guy, who belongs to some church with pep and piety to it, who belongs to the Boosters or the Rotarians or the Kiwanis, to the Elks or Moose or Red Men or Knights of Columbus or any one of a score of organizations of good, jolly, kidding, laughing, sweating, upstanding, lend-a-handing Royal Good Fellows, who plays hard and works hard, and whose answer to his critics is a square-toed boot that'll teach the grouches and smart alecks to respect the He-man and get out and root for Uncle Samuel, U.S.A.!' " [. . .]

George Santayana

"I like to walk about amidst the beautiful things that adorn the world; but private wealth I should decline, or any sort of possessions, because they would take away my liberty," wrote George Santayana in *The Irony of Liberalism.* As an influential professor of philosophy at Harvard, Santayana evoked a worldly sense of aesthetic disillusionment, portraying the American mind as more ingenious than wise. To be an American, he thought, was a full-time occupation. In the essay included here, he writes "American life is a powerful solvent. It seems to neutralize every intellectual element, however tough and alien it may be, and to fuse it in the native good-will, complacency, thoughtlessness, and optimism."

Born in Madrid, Spain, in 1863, Santayana was the son of a Spanish father and an American mother. He arrived in the United States in 1872. In 1886, Santayana graduated from Harvard, studied in Berlin for two years, and then went to Cambridge University in England to complete his M.A. and Ph.D. He served as a lecturer before becoming a professor of philosophy at Harvard (1889–1911), but never really felt at ease there. In 1912 he had savings enough from a small inheritance to remain financially independent. He resigned his position and returned to Europe, taught briefly at the Sorbonne and at Oxford, and eventually resolved to spend the rest of his life in an Italian convent as a guest. Santayana died in 1952 without ever denouncing his professed materialism.

His many works range from volumes of poetry: *Sonnets and Other Verses* (1894), *The Hermit of Carmel and Other Poems* (1901); to aesthetic and literary criticism: *The Sense of Beauty* (1896), *Interpretations of Poetry and Religion* (1900), *Three Philosophical Poets: Lucretius, Dante and Goethe* (1910); to philosophy proper: *The Life of Reason* (1905–06, 5 volumes), *Egotism in German Philosophy* (1916), *Platonism and the Spiritual Life* (1927), *Realms of Being* (1920–40, 4 volumes); to political thought: *Character and Opinion in the United States* (1920), *Dominations and Powers: Reflections on Liberty, Society and Government* (1951). The following excerpt is a chapter from *Character and Opinion in the United States.* It represents the view of a worldly Hispanic intellectual whose perception of liberation was one of absorption in immediacy. Starting from "animal faith," people may, through great discipline, arrive at "the spiritual life," transcending (without abandoning) the endless instrumentalities of life to engage in the timeless contemplation or enjoyment of whatever essence may be presented. The discipline in Santayana's world view is summed up in his own words: "Perhaps the only true dignity of man is his capacity to despise himself."

Character and Opinion in the United States (1920)

(excerpt)

Materialism and Idealism in American Life

The language and traditions common to England and America are like other family bonds: they draw kindred together at the greater crises in life, but they also occasion at times a little friction and fault-finding. The groundwork of the two societies is so similar, that each nation, feeling almost at home with the other, and almost able to understand its speech, may instinctively resent what hinders it from feeling at home altogether. Differences will tend to seem anomalies that have slipped in by mistake and through somebody's fault. Each will judge the other by his own standards, not feeling, as in the presence of complete foreigners, that he must make an effort of imagination and put himself in another man's shoes.

In matters of morals, manners, and art, the danger of comparisons is not merely that they may prove invidious, by ranging qualities in an order of merit which might wound somebody's vanity; the danger is rather that comparisons may distort comprehension, because in truth good qualities are all different in kind, and free lives are different in spirit. Comparison is the expedient of those who cannot reach the heart of the things compared; and no philosophy is more external and egotistical than that which places the essence of a thing in its relation to something else. In reality, at the centre of every natural being there is something individual and incommensurable, a seed with its native impulses and aspirations, shaping themselves as best they can in their given environment. Variation is a consequence of freedom, and the slight but radical diversity of souls in turn makes freedom requisite. Instead of instituting in his mind any comparisons between the United States and other nations, I would accordingly urge the reader to forget himself and, in so far as such a thing may be possible for him or for me, to transport himself ideally with me into the outer circumstances of American life, the better to feel its inner temper, and to see how inevitably the American shapes his feelings and judgements, honestly reporting all things as they appear from his new and unobstructed station.

I speak of the American in the singular, as if there were not millions of them, north and south, east and west, of both sexes, of all ages, and of various races, professions, and religions. Of course the one American I speak of is mythical; but to speak in parables is inevitable in such a subject, and it is perhaps as well to do so frankly. There is a sort of poetic ineptitude in all human discourse when it tries to deal with natural and existing things. Practical men may not notice it, but in fact human discourse is intrinsically addressed not to natural existing things but to ideal essences, poetic or logical terms which thought may define and play with. When fortune or necessity diverts our attention from this congenial ideal sport to crude facts and pressing

Isaak, *American Political Thinking.*/Excerpts from *Character and Opinion in the United States* by George Santayana. Reprinted by permission of The MIT Press.

issues, we turn out frail poetic ideas into symbols for those terrible irruptive things. In that paper money of our own stamping, the legal tender of the mind, we are obliged to reckon all the movements and values of the world. The universal American I speak of is one of these symbols; and I should be still speaking in symbols and creating moral units and a false simplicity, if I spoke of classes pedantically subdivided, or individuals ideally integrated and defined. As it happens, the symbolic American can be made largely adequate to the facts; because, if there are immense differences between individual Americans—for some Americans are black—yet there is a great uniformity in their environment, customs, temper, and thoughts. They have all been uprooted from their several soils and ancestries and plunged together into one vortex, whirling irresistibly in a space otherwise quite empty. To be an American is of itself almost a moral condition, an education, and a career. Hence a single ideal figment can cover a large part of what each American is in his character, and almost the whole of what most Americans are in their social outlook and political judgements.

The discovery of the new world exercised a sort of selection among the inhabitants of Europe. All the colonists, except the negroes, were voluntary exiles. The fortunate, the deeply rooted, and the lazy remained at home; the wilder instincts or dissatisfaction of others tempted them beyond the horizon. The American is accordingly the most adventurous, or the descendant of the most adventurous, of Europeans. It is in his blood to be socially a radical, though perhaps not intellectually. What has existed in the past, especially in the remote past, seems to him not only not authoritative, but irrelevant, inferior, and outworn. He finds it rather a sorry waste of time to think about the past at all. But his enthusiasm for the future is profound; he can conceive of no more decisive way

of recommending an opinion or a practice than to say that it is what everybody is coming to adopt. This expectation of what he approves, or approval of what he expects, makes up his optimism. It is the necessary faith of the pioneer.

Such a temperament is, of course, not maintained in the nation merely by inheritance. Inheritance notoriously tends to restore the average of a race, and plays incidentally many a trick of atavism. What maintains this temperament and makes it national is social contagion or pressure—something immensely strong in democracies. The luckless American who is born a conservative, or who is drawn to poetic subtlety, pious retreats, or gay passions, nevertheless has the categorical excellence of work, growth, enterprise, reform, and prosperity dinned into his ears: every door is open in this direction and shut in the other; so that he either folds up his heart and withers in a corner—in remote places you sometimes find such a solitary gaunt idealist—or else he flies to Oxford or Florence or Montmartre to save his soul—or perhaps not to save it.

The optimism of the pioneer is not limited to his view of himself and his own future: it starts from that; but feeling assured, safe, and cheery within, he looks with smiling and most kindly eyes on everything and everybody about him. Individualism, roughness, and self-trust are supposed to go with selfishness and a cold heart; but I suspect that is a prejudice. It is rather dependence, insecurity, and mutual jostling that poison our placid gregarious brotherhood; and fanciful passionate demands upon people's affections, when they are disappointed, as they soon must be, breed ill-will and a final meanness. The milk of human kindness is less apt to turn sour if the vessel that holds it stands steady, cool, and separate, and is not too often uncorked. In his affections the American is seldom passionate, often deep, and always kindly. If it were given me to look into the depths of a man's heart, and I did not find goodwill at the bottom, I should say without any hesitation, You are not an American. But as the American is an individualist his good-will is not officious. His instinct is to think well of everybody, and to wish everybody well, but in a spirit of rough comradeship, expecting every man to stand on his own legs and to be helpful in his turn. When he has given his neighbour a chance he thinks he has done enough for him; but he feels it is an absolute duty to do that. It will take some hammering to drive a coddling socialism into America.

As self-trust may pass into self-sufficiency, so optimism, kindness, and goodwill may grow into a habit of doting on everything. To the good American many subjects are sacred: sex is sacred, women are sacred, children are sacred, business is sacred, America is sacred, Masonic lodges and college clubs are sacred. This feeling grows out of the good opinion he wishes to have of these things, and serves to maintain it. If he did not regard all these things as sacred he might come to doubt sometimes if they were wholly good. Of this kind, too, is the idealism of single ladies in reduced circumstances who can see the soul of beauty in ugly things, and are perfectly happy because their old dog has such pathetic eyes, their minister is so eloquent, their garden with its three sunflowers is so pleasant, their dead friends were so devoted, and their distant relations are so rich.

Consider now the great emptiness of America: not merely the primitive physical emptiness, surviving in some regions, and the continental spacing of the chief natural features, but also the moral emptiness of a settlement where men and even houses are easily moved about, and no one, almost, lives where he was born or believes what he has been taught. Not that the American has jettisoned these impedimenta in anger;

they have simply slipped from him as he moves. Great empty spaces bring a sort of freedom to both soul and body. You may pitch your tent where you will; or if ever you decide to build anything, it can be in a style of your own devising. You have room, fresh materials, few models, and no critics. You trust your own experience, not only because you must, but because you find your may do so safely and prosperously; the forces that determine fortune are not yet too complicated for one man to explore. Your detachable condition makes you lavish with money and cheerfully experimental; you lose little if you lose all, since you remain completely yourself. At the same time your absolute initiative gives you practice in coping with novel situations, and in being original; it teaches you shrewd management. Your life and mind will become dry and direct, with few decorative flourishes. In your works everything will be stark and pragmatic; you will not understand why anybody should make those little sacrifices to instinct or custom which we call grace. The fine arts will seem to you academic luxuries, fit to amuse the ladies, like Greek and Sanskrit; for while you will perfectly appreciate generosity in men's purposes, you will not admit that the execution of these purposes can be anything but business. Unfortunately the essence of the fine arts is that the execution should be generous too, and delightful in itself; therefore the fine arts will suffer, not so much in their express professional pursuit—for then they become practical tasks and a kind of business—as in that diffused charm which qualifies all human action when men are artists by nature. Elaboration, which is something to accomplish, will be preferred to simplicity, which is something to rest in; manners will suffer somewhat; speech will suffer horribly. For the American the urgency of his novel attack upon matter, his zeal in gathering his fruits, precludes meanderings in primrose paths; devices must be short cuts, and symbols must be mere symbols. If his wife wants luxuries, of course she may have them; and if he has vices, that can be provided for too; but they must all be set down under those headings in his ledgers.

At the same time, the American is imaginative; for where life is intense, imagination is intense also. Were he not imaginative he would not live so much in the future. But his imagination is practical, and the future it forecasts is immediate; it works with the clearest and least ambiguous terms known to his experience, in terms of number, measure, contrivance, economy, and speed. He is an idealist working on matter. Understanding as he does the material potentialities of things, he is successful in invention, conservative in reform, and quick in emergencies. All his life he jumps into the train after it has started and jumps out before it has stopped; and he never once gets left behind, or breaks a leg. There is an enthusiasm in his sympathetic handling of material forces which goes far to cancel the illiberal character which it might otherwise assume. The good workman hardly distinguishes his artistic intention from the potency in himself and in things which is about to realise that intention. Accordingly his ideals fall into the form of premonitions and prophecies; and his studious prophecies often come true. So do the happy workmanlike ideals of the American. When a poor boy, perhaps, he dreams of an education, and presently he gets an education, or at least a degree; he dreams of growing rich, and he grows rich—only more slowly and modestly, perhaps, than he expected; he dreams of marrying his Rebecca and, even if he marries a Leah instead, he ultimately finds in Leah his Rebecca after all. He dreams of helping to carry on and to accelerate the movement of a vast, seething, progressive society, and he actually does so. Ideals clinging so close to nature are almost sure of fulfilment; the American

beams with a certain self-confidence and sense of mastery; he feels that God and nature are working with him.

Idealism in the American accordingly goes hand in hand with present contentment and with foresight of what the future very likely will actually bring. He is not a revolutionist; he believes he is already on the right track and moving towards an excellent destiny. In revolutionists, on the contrary, idealism is founded on dissatisfaction and expresses it. What exists seems to them an absurd jumble of irrational accidents and bad habits, and they want the future to be based on reason and to be the pellucid embodiment of all their maxims. All their zeal is for something radically different from the actual and (if they only knew it) from the possible; it is ideally simple, and they love it and believe in it because their nature craves it. They think life would be set free by the destruction of all its organs. They are therefore extreme idealists in the region of hope, but not at all, as poets and artists are, in the region of perception and memory. In the atmosphere of civilised life they miss all the refraction and all the fragrance; so that in their conception of actual things they are apt to be crude realists; and their ignorance and inexperience of the moral world, unless it comes of ill-luck, indicates their incapacity for education. Now incapacity for education, when united with great inner vitality, is one root of idealism. It is what condemns us all, in the region of sense, to substitute perpetually what we are capable of imagining for what things may be in themselves; it is what condemns us, wherever it extends, to think *a priori;* it is what keeps us bravely and incorrigibly pursuing what we call the good—that is, what would fulfil the demands of our nature—however little provision the fates may have made for it. But the want of insight on the part of revolutionists touching the past and the present infects in an important particular their idealism about the future; it renders their dreams of the future unrealisable. For in human beings—this may not be true of other animals, more perfectly preformed—experience is necessary to pertinent and concrete thinking; even our primitive instincts are blind until they stumble upon some occasion that solicits them; and they can be much transformed or deranged by their first partial satisfactions. Therefore a man who does not idealise his experience, but idealises *a priori,* is incapable of true prophecy; when he dreams he raves, and the more he criticises the less he helps. American idealism, on the contrary, is nothing if not helpful, nothing if not pertinent to practicable transformations; and when the American frets, it is because whatever is useless and impertinent, be it idealism or inertia, irritates him; for it frustrates the good results which he sees might so easily have been obtained.

The American is wonderfully alive; and his vitality, not having often found a suitable outlet, makes him appear agitated on the surface; he is always letting off an unnecessarily loud blast of incidental steam. Yet his vitality is not superficial; it is inwardly prompted, and as sensitive and quick as a magnetic needle. He is inquisitive, and ready with an answer to any question that he may put to himself of his own accord; but if you try to pour instruction into him, on matters that do not touch his own spontaneous life, he shows the most extraordinary powers of resistance and oblivescence; so that he often is remarkably expert in some directions and surprisingly obtuse in others. He seems to bear lightly the sorrowful burden of human knowledge. In a word, he is young.

What sense is there in this feeling, which we all have, that the American is young? His country is blessed with as many elderly people as any other, and his descent from Adam, or from the Darwinian rival of Adam, cannot be shorter than that of his European cousins. Nor are his ideas always very fresh. Trite and rigid bits of morality and religion, with much seemly and antique political lore, remain axiomatic in him, as in the mind of a child; he may carry all this about with an unquestioning familiarity which does not comport understanding. To keep traditional sentiments in this way insulated and uncriticised is itself a sign of youth. A good young man is naturally conservative and loyal on all those subjects which his experience has not brought to a test; advanced opinions on politics, marriage, or literature are comparatively rare in America; they are left for the ladies to discuss, and usually to condemn, while the men get on with their work. In spite of what is old-fashioned in his more general ideas, the American is unmistakably young; and this, I should say, for two reasons: one, that he is chiefly occupied with his immediate environment, and the other, that his reactions upon it are inwardly prompted, spontaneous, and full of vivacity and self-trust. His views are not yet lengthened; his will is not yet broken or transformed. The present moment, however, in this, as in other things, may mark a great change in him; he is perhaps now reaching his majority, and all I say may hardly apply to-day, and may not apply at all to-morrow. I speak of him as I have known him; and whatever moral strength may accrue to him later, I am not sorry to have known him in his youth. The charm of youth, even when it is a little boisterous, lies in nearness to the impulses of nature, in a quicker and more obvious obedience to that pure, seminal principle which, having formed the body and its organs, always directs their movements, unless it is forced by vice or necessity to make them crooked, or to suspend them. Even under the inevitable crust of age the soul remains young, and, wherever it is able to break through, sprouts into something green and tender. We are all as young at heart as the most youthful

American, but the seed in his case has fallen upon virgin soil, where it may spring up more bravely and with less respect for the giants of the wood. Peoples seem older when their perennial natural youth is encumbered with more possessions and prepossessions, and they are mindful of the many things they have lost or missed. The American is not mindful of them.

In America there is a tacit optimistic assumption about existence, to the effect that the more existence the better. The soulless critic might urge that quantity is only a physical category, implying no excellence, but at best an abundance of opportunities both for good and for evil. Yet the young soul, being curious and hungry, views existence *a priori* under the form of the good; its instinct to live implies a faith that most things it can become or see or do will be worth while. Respect for quantity is accordingly something more than the childish joy and wonder at bigness; it is the fisherman's joy in a big haul, the good uses of which he can take for granted. Such optimism is amiable. Nature cannot afford that we should begin by being too calculating or wise, and she encourages us by the pleasure she attaches to our functions in advance of their fruits, and often in excess of them; as the angler enjoys catching his fish more than eating it, and often, waiting patiently for the fish to bite, misses his own supper. The pioneer must devote himself to preparations; he must work for the future, and it is healthy and dutiful of him to love his work for its own sake. At the same time, unless reference to an ultimate purpose is at least virtual in all his activities, he runs the danger of becoming a living automaton, vain and ignominious in its mechanical constancy. Idealism about work can hide an intense materialism about life. Man, if he is a rational being, cannot live by bread alone nor be a labourer merely; he must eat and work in view of an ideal harmony which overarches all his days, and which

is realised in the way they hang together, or in some ideal issue which they have in common. Otherwise, though his technical philosophy may call itself idealism, he is a materialist in morals; he esteems things, and esteems himself, for mechanical uses and energies. Even sensualists, artists, and pleasure-lovers are wiser than that, for though their idealism may be desultory or corrupt, they attain something ideal, and prize things only for their living effects, moral though perhaps fugitive. Sensation, when we do not take it as a signal for action, but arrest and peruse what it positively brings before us, reveals something ideal—a colour, shape, or sound; and to dwell on these presences, with no thought of their material significance, is an aesthetic or dreamful idealism. To pass from this idealism to the knowledge of matter is a great intellectual advance, and goes with dominion over the world; for in the practical arts the mind is adjusted to a larger object, with more depth and potentiality in it; which is what makes people feel that the material world is real, as they call it, and that the ideal world is not. Certainly the material world is real; for the philosophers who deny the existence of matter are like the critics who deny the existence of Homer. If there was never any Homer, there must have been a lot of other poets no less Homeric than he; and if matter does not exist, a combination of other things exists which is just as material. But the intense reality of the material world would not prevent it from being a dreary waste in our eyes, or even an abyss of horror, if it brought forth no spiritual fruits. In fact, it does bring forth spiritual fruits, for otherwise we should not be here to find fault with it, and to set up our ideals over against it. Nature is material, but not materialistic; it issues in life, and breeds all sorts of warm passions and idle beauties. And just as sympathy with the mechanical travail and turmoil of nature, apart from its spiritual fruits, is moral materialism, so the continual perception and love of these fruits is moral idealism—happiness in the presence of immaterial objects and harmonies, such as we envisage in affection, speculation, religion, and all the forms of the beautiful.

The circumstances of his life hitherto have necessarily driven the American into moral materialism; for in his dealings with material things he can hardly stop to enjoy their sensible aspects, which are ideal, nor proceed at once to their ultimate uses, which are ideal too. He is practical as against the poet, and worldly as against the clear philosopher or the saint. The most striking expression of this materialism is usually supposed to be his love of the almighty dollar; but that is a foreign and unintelligent view. The American talks about money, because that is the symbol and measure he has at hand for success, intelligence, and power; but as to money itself he makes, loses, spends, and gives it away with a very light heart. To my mind the most striking expression of his materialism is his singular preoccupation with quantity. If, for instance, you visit Niagara Falls, you may expect to hear how many cubic feet or metric tons of water are precipitated per second over the cataract; how many cities and towns (with the number of their inhabitants) derive light and motive power from it; and the annual value of the further industries that might very well be carried on by the same means, without visibly depleting the world's greatest wonder or injuring the tourist trade. That is what I confidently expected to hear on arriving at the adjoining town of Buffalo; but I was deceived. The first thing I heard instead was that there are more miles of asphalt pavement in Buffalo than in any city in the world. Nor is this insistence on quantity confined to men of business. The President of Harvard College, seeing me once by chance soon after the beginning of a term, inquired how my classes were getting on;

and when I replied that I thought they were getting on well, that my men seemed to be keen and intelligent, he stopped me as if I was about to waste his time. "I meant," said he, "*what is the number* of students in your classes."

Here I think we may perceive that this love of quantity often has a silent partner, which is diffidence as to quality. The democratic conscience recoils before anything that savours of privilege; and lest it should concede an unmerited privilege to any pursuit or person, it reduces all things as far as possible to the common denominator of quantity. Numbers cannot lie: but if it came to comparing the ideal beauties of philosophy with those of Anglo-Saxon, who should decide? All studies are good—why else have universities?—but those must be most encouraged which attract the greatest number of students. Hence the President's question. Democratic faith, in its diffidence about quality, throws the reins of education upon the pupil's neck, as Don Quixote threw the reins on the neck of Rocinante, and bids his divine instinct choose its own way.

The American has never yet had to face the trials of Job. Great crises, like the Civil War, he has known how to surmount victoriously; and now that he has surmounted a second great crisis victoriously, it is possible that he may relapse, as he did in the other case, into an apparently complete absorption in material enterprise and prosperity. But if serious and irremediable tribulation ever overtook him, what would his attitude be? It is then that we should be able to discover whether materialism or idealism lies at the base of his character. Meantime his working mind is not without its holiday. He spreads humour pretty thick and even over the surface of conversation, and humour is one form of moral emancipation. He loves landscape, he loves mankind, and he loves knowledge; and in music at least he finds an art which he unfeignedly enjoys. In music and land-scape, in humour and kindness, he touches the ideal more truly, perhaps, than in his ponderous academic idealisms and busy religions; for it is astonishing how much even religion in America (can it possibly be so in England?) is a matter of meetings, building-funds, schools, charities, clubs, and picnics. To be poor in order to be sim-ple, to produce less in order that the product may be more choice and beautiful, and may leave us less burdened with unnecessary duties and useless possessions—that is an ideal not articulate in the American mind; yet here and there I seem to have heard a sigh of it, a groan at the perpetual incubus of business and shrill society. Significant witness to such aspirations is borne by those new forms of popular religion, not mere variations on tradition, which have sprung up from the soil—revivalism, spiri-tualism, Christian Science, the New Thought. Whether or no we can tap, through these or other channels, some cos-mic or inner energy not hitherto at the dis-posal of man (and there is nothing incredible in that), we certainly may try to remove friction and waste in the mere process of living; we may relax morbid strains, loosen suppressed instincts, iron out the creases of the soul, discipline our-selves into simplicity, sweetness, and peace. These religious movements are efforts toward such physiological economy and hygiene; and while they are thoroughly plebeian, with no great lights, and no idea of raising men from the most vulgar and humdrum worldly existence, yet they see

the possibility of physical and moral health on that common plane, and pursue it. That is true morality. The dignities of various types of life or mind, like the gifts of vari-ous animals, are relative. The snob adores one type only, and the creatures supposed by him to illustrate it perfectly; or envies and hates them, which is just as snobbish. Veritable lovers of life, on the contrary, like Saint Francis or like Dickens, know that in every tenement of clay, with no matter what endowment or station, happi-ness and perfection are possible to the soul. There must be no brow-beating, with shouts of work or progress or revolution, any more than with threats of hell-fire. What does it profit a man to free the whole world if his soul is not free? Moral freedom is not an artificial condition, because the ideal is the mother tongue of both the heart and the senses. All that is requisite is that we should pause in living to enjoy life, and should lift up our hearts to things that are pure goods in themselves, so that once to have found and loved them, whatever else may betide, may remain a happiness that nothing can sully. This natural idealism does not imply that we are immaterial, but only that we are animate and truly alive. When the senses are sharp, as they are in the American, they are already half liber-ated, already a joy in themselves; and when the heart is warm, like his, and eager to be just, its ideal destiny can hardly be doubt-ful. It will not be always merely pumping and working; time and its own pulses will lend it wings. . . .

Conservative Critics of Democratic Liberalism

10

H. L. Mencken

Born in 1880 in Baltimore, Maryland, Henry Louis Mencken distinguished himself in the world of journalism through his biting wit as a conservative social and literary critic. He attended private school and Baltimore Polytechnic, then began his career as a reporter. He became editor of the Baltimore *Evening Herald* and then made his name as coeditor of *American Spectator* with drama critic George Jean Nathan (1914–23). The following decade he edited the open-minded *American Mercury,* his "royalist" iconoclasm somehow complementing the elitism of the youth movement at the time, which ranged from socialist to anarchist.

Mencken's *The Philosophy of Friedrich Nietzsche* (1910) was disdainful of democratic standards and conventions. Mencken was a strong advocate of Theodore Dreiser's fiction, which reflected sharp social criticism of American love and life. His other works demonstrated the breadth of his interests: *Ventures into Verse* (1903), *George Bernard Shaw: His Plays* (1905), *The Artist* (a play, 1912), *A Book of Burlesques* (1916), *A Little Book in C Major* (1916), *A Book of Prefaces* (1917), *In Defense of Women* (1917), *Damn: A Book of Calumny* (1917), *The American Language* (1918), *Prejudices* (in six series, 1919–27), *Treatise on the Gods* (1930), *Making a President* (1932), *Treatise on Right and Wrong* (1936), *Happy Days* (1940), *Newspaper Days* (1941), *Heathen Days* (1943), *Christmas Story* (1946), *A Mencken Chrestomathy* (1949), *A Minority Report* (1956), and *Notes on Democracy* (1926), from which the following excerpts are taken. Mencken died in 1956.

☙

Notes on Democracy (1926)
(excerpts)

. . . A great deal of paper and ink has been wasted discussing the difference between representative government and direct democracy. The theme is a favourite one with university pundits, and also engages and enchants the stall-fed Rousseaus who arise intermittently in the cow States, and occasionally penetrate to Governors' mansions and the United States Senate. It is generally held that representative government, as practically encountered in the world, is full of defects, some of them amounting to organic disease. Not only does it take the initiative in lawmaking out of the hands of the plain people, and leave them only the function of referees; it also raises certain obvious obstacles to their free exercise of that function. Scattered as they are, and unorganized save in huge, unworkable groups, they are unable, it is argued, to formulate their virtuous desires quickly and clearly, or to bring to the resolution of vexed questions the full potency of their native sagacity. Worse, they find it difficult to enforce their decisions, even when they have decided. Every Liberal knows this sad story, and has shed tears telling it. The remedy he offers almost always consists of a resort to what he calls a purer democracy. That is to say, he proposes to set up the recall, the initiative and referendum, or something else of the sort, and so convert the representative into a mere clerk or messenger. The final determination of all important public questions, he argues, ought to be in the hands of the voters themselves. They alone can muster enough wisdom for the business, and they alone are without guile. The cure for the evils of democracy is more democracy.

All this, of course, is simply rhetoric. Every time anything of the kind is tried it fails ingloriously. Nor is there any evidence that it has ever succeeded elsewhere, today or in the past. Certainly no competent historian believes that the citizens assembled in a New England town-meeting actually formulated *en masse* the transcendental and immortal measures that they adopted, nor even that they contributed anything of value to the discussion thereof. The notion is as absurd as the parallel notion, long held by philologues of defective powers of observation, that the popular ballads surviving from earlier ages were actually composed by the folk. The ballads, in point of fact, were all written by concrete poets, most of them not of the folk; the folk, when they had any hand in the business at all, simply acted as referees, choosing which should survive. In exactly the same way the New England town-meeting was led and dominated by a few men of unusual initiative and determination, some of them genuinely superior, but most of them simply demagogues and fanatics. The citizens in general heard the discussion of rival ideas, and went through the motions of deciding between them, but there is no evi-

dence that they ever had all the relevant facts before them or made any effort to unearth them, or that appeals to their reason always, or even usually, prevailed over appeals to their mere prejudice and superstition. Their appetite for logic, I venture, seldom got the better of their fear of hell, and the Beatitudes moved them far less powerfully than blood. Some of the most idiotic decisions ever come to by mortal man were made by the New England town-meetings, and under the leadership of monomaniacs who are still looked upon as ineffable blossoms of the contemporary *Kultur.*

The truth is that the difference between representative democracy and direct democracy is a great deal less marked than political sentimentalists assume. Under both forms the sovereign mob must employ agents to execute its will, and in either case the agents may have ideas of their own, based upon interests of their own, and the means at hand to do and get what they will. Moreover, their very position gives them a power of influencing the electors that is far above that of any ordinary citizen: they become politicians *ex officio,* and usually end by selling such influence as remains after they have used all they need for their own ends. Worse, both forms of democracy encounter the difficulty that the generality of citizens, no matter how assiduously they may be instructed, remain congenitally unable to comprehend many of the problems before them, or to consider al' of those they do comprehend in an unbiased and intelligent manner. Thus it is often impossible to ascertain their views in advance of action, or even, in many cases, to determine their conclusions *post hoc.* The voters gathered in a typical New England town-meeting were all ardent amateurs of theology, and hence quite competent, in theory, to decide the theological questions that principally engaged them; nevertheless, history shows that they were led facilely by professional theologians, most of them quacks with something to sell. In the same way, the great masses of Americans of today, though they are theoretically competent to decide all the larger matters of national policy, and have certain immutable principles, of almost religious authority, to guide them, actually look for leading to professional politicians, who are influenced in turn by small but competent and determined minorities, with special knowledge and special interests. It was thus that the plain people were shoved into the late war, and it is thus that they will be shoved into the next one. They were, in overwhelming majority, against going in, and if they had had any sense and resolution they would have stayed out. But these things they lacked. . . .

Whether or not democracy is destined to survive in the world until the corruptible puts on incorruption and the immemorial Christian dead leap out of their graves, their faces shining and their yells resounding— this is something, I confess, that I don't know, nor is it necessary, for the purposes of the present inquiry, that I venture upon the hazard of a guess. My business is not prognosis, but diagnosis. I am not engaged in therapeutics, but in pathology. That simple statement of fact, I daresay, will be accepted as a confession, condemning me out of hand as unfit for my task, and even throwing a certain doubt upon my *bona fides*. For it is one of the peculiar intellectual accompaniments of democracy that the concept of the insoluble becomes unfashionable—nay, almost infamous. To lack a remedy is to lack the very license to discuss disease. The causes of this are to be sought, without question, in the nature of democracy itself. It came into the world as a cure-all, and it remains primarily a cure-all to this day. Any boil upon the body politic,

however vast and raging, may be relieved by taking a vote; any flux of blood may be stopped by passing a law. The aim of government is to repeal the laws of nature, and re-enact them with moral amendments. War becomes simply a device to end war. The state, a mystical emanation from the mob, takes on a transcendental potency, and acquires the power to make over the father which begat it. Nothing remains inscrutable and beyond remedy, not even the way of a man with a maid. It was not so under the ancient and accursed systems of despotism, now happily purged out of the world. They, too, I grant you, had certain pretentions of an homeric gaudiness, but they at least refrained from attempts to abolish sin, poverty, stupidity, cowardice, and other such immutable realities. Medieval Christianity, which was a theological and philosophical *apologia* for those systems, actually erected belief in that immutability into a cardinal article of faith. The evils of the world were incurable: one put off the quest for a perfect moral order until one got to heaven, *post mortem*. There arose, in consequence, a scheme of checks and balances that was consummate and completely satisfactory, for it could not be put to a test, and the logical holes in it were chinked with miracles. But no more. Today the Holy Saints are deposed. Now each and every human problem swings into the range of practical politics. The worst and oldest of them may be solved facilely by travelling bands of lady Ph.D.'s, each bearing the mandate of a Legislature of kept men, all unfaithful to their protectors.

Democracy becomes a substitute for the old religion, and the antithesis of it: the Ku Kluxers, though their reasoning may be faulty, are not far off the facts in their conclusion that Holy Church is its enemy. It shows all the magical potency of the great systems of faith. It has the power to enchant and disarm; it is not vulnerable to logical attack. I point for proof to the appalling gyrations and contortions of its chief exponents. Read, for example, the late James Bryce's "Modern Democracies." Observe how he amasses incontrovertible evidence that democracy doesn't work—and then concludes with a stout declaration that it does. Or, if his two fat volumes are too much for you, turn to some school reader and give a judicious perusal to Lincoln's Gettysburg Address, with its argument that the North fought the Civil War to save self-government to the world!—a thesis echoed in falsetto, and by feebler men, fifty years later. It is impossible, by any device known to philosophers, to meet doctrines of that sort; they obviously lie outside the range of logical ideas. There is, in the human mind, a natural taste for such hocus-pocus. It greatly simplifies the process of ratiocination, which is unbearably painful to the great majority of men. What dulls and baffles the teeth may be got down conveniently by an heroic gulp. No doubt there is an explanation here of the long-continued popularity of the dogma of the Trinity, which remains unstated in plain terms after two thousand years. And no doubt the dogma of Transubstantiation came under fire in the Reformation because it had grown too simple and comprehensible—because even the Scholastic philosophy had been unable to convert its plain propositions into something that could be believed without being understood. Democracy is shot through with this delight in the incredible, this banal mysticism. One cannot discuss it without colliding with preposterous postulates, all of them cherished like authentic hairs from the whiskers of Moses himself. I have alluded to its touching acceptance of the faith that progress is illimitable and ordained of God—that every human problem, in the very nature of things, may be solved. There are corollaries that are even more naïve. One, for example, is to the general effect that optimism is a virtue in

itself—that there is a mysterious merit in being hopeful and of glad heart, even in the presence of adverse and immovable facts. This curious notion turns the glittering wheels of Rotary, and is the motive power of the political New Thoughters called Liberals. Certainly the attitude of the average American Liberal toward the so-called League of Nations offered superb clinical material to the student of democratic psychopathology. He began by arguing that the League would save the world. Confronted by proofs of its fraudulence, he switched to the doctrine that believing in it would save the world. So, later on, with the Washington Disarmament Conference. The man who hopes absurdly, it appears, is in some fantastic and gaseous manner a better citizen than the man who detects and exposes the truth. Bear this sweet democratic axiom clearly in mind. It is, fundamentally, what is the matter with the United States.

As I say, my present mandate does not oblige me to conjure up a system that will surpass and shame democracy as democracy surpasses and shames the polity of the Andaman Islanders or the Great Khan—a system full-blown and perfect, like Prohibition, and ready to be put into effect by the simple adoption of an amendment to the Constitution. Such a system, for all I know, may lie outside the farthest soarings of the human mind, though that mind can weigh the stars and know God. Until the end of the chapter the ants and bees may flutter their sardonic antennae at us in that department, as they do in others: the last joke upon man may be that he never learned how to govern himself in a rational and competent manner, as the last joke upon woman may be that she never had a baby without wishing that the Day of Judgment were a week past. I am not even undertaking to prove here that democracy is too full of evils to be further borne. On the contrary, I am convinced that it has some valuable merits, not often described, and I shall refer to a few of them presently. All I argue is that its manifest defects, if they are ever to be got rid of at all, must be got rid of by examining them realistically—that they will never cease to afflict all the more puissant and exemplary nations so long as discussing them is impeded by concepts borrowed from theology. As for me, I have never encountered any actual evidence, convincing to an ordinary jury, that *vox populi* is actually *vox Dei*. The proofs, indeed, run the other way. The life of the inferior man is one long protest against the obstacles that God interposes to the attainment of his dreams, and democracy, if it is anything at all, is simply one way of getting 'round those obstacles. Thus it represents, not a jingling echo of what seems to be the divine will, but a raucous defiance of it. To that extent, perhaps, it is truly civilized, for civilization, as I have argued elsewhere, is best described as an effort to remedy the blunders and check the cruel humours of the Cosmic Kaiser. But what is defiant is surely not official, and what is not official is open to examination.

For all I know, democracy may be a self-limiting disease, as civilization itself seems to be. There are obvious paradoxes in its philosophy, and some of them have a suicidal smack. It offers John Doe a means to rise above his place beside Richard Roe, and then, by making Roe his equal, it takes away the chief usufructs of the rising. I here attempt no pretty logical gymnastics: the history of democratic states is a history of disingenuous efforts to get rid of the second half of that dilemma. There is not only the natural yearning of Doe to use and enjoy the superiority that he has won; there is also the natural tendency of Roe, as an inferior man, to acknowledge it. Democracy, in fact, is always inventing class distinctions, despite its theoretical abhorrence of them. The

baron has departed, but in his place stand the grand goblin, the supreme worthy archon, the sovereign grand commander. Democratic man, as I have remarked, is quite unable to think of himself as a free individual; he must belong to a group, or shake with fear and loneliness—and the group, of course, must have its leaders. It would be hard to find a country in which such brummagem serene highnesses are revered with more passionate devotion than they get in the United States. The distinction that goes with more office runs far ahead of the distinction that goes with actual achievement. A Harding is regarded as genuinely superior to a Halsted, no doubt because his doings are better understood. But there is a form of human striving that is understood by democratic man even better than Harding's, and that is the striving for money. Thus the plutocracy, in a democratic state, tends to take the place of the missing aristocracy, and even to be mistaken for it. It is, of course, something quite different. It lacks all the essential characters of a true aristocracy: a clean tradition, culture, public spirit, honesty, honour, courage—above all, courage. It stands under no bond of obligation to the state; it has no public duty; it is transient and lacks a goal. Its most puissant dignitaries of to-day came out of the mob only yesterday—and from the mob they bring all its peculiar ignobilities. As practically encountered, the plutocracy stands quite as far from the *honnête homme* as it stands from the Holy Saints. Its main character is its incurable timorousness; it is for ever grasping at the straws held out by demagogues. Half a dozen gabby Jewish youths, meeting in a back room to plan a revolution—in other words, half a dozen kittens preparing to upset the Matterhorn—are enough to scare it half to death. Its dreams are of banshees, hobgoblins, bugaboos. The honest, untroubled snores of a Percy or a Hohenstaufen are quite beyond it.

The plutocracy, as I say, is comprehensible to the mob because its aspirations are essentially those of inferior men: it is not by accident that Christianity, a mob religion, paves heaven with gold and precious stones, *i.e.*, with money. There are, of course, reactions against this ignoble ideal among men of more civilized tastes, even in democratic states, and sometimes they arouse the mob to a transient distrust of certain of the plutocratic pretensions. But that distrust seldom arises above mere envy, and the polemic which engenders it is seldom sound in logic or impeccable in motive. What it lacks is aristocratic disinterestedness, born of aristocratic security. There is no body of opinion behind it that is, in the strictest sense, a free opinion. Its chief exponents, by some divine irony, are pedagogues of one sort or another—which is to say, men chiefly marked by their haunting fear of losing their jobs. Living under such terrors, with the plutocracy policing them harshly on one side and the mob congenitally suspicious of them on the other, it is no wonder that their revolt usually peters out in metaphysics, and that they tend to abandon it as their families grow up, and the costs of heresy become prohibitive. The pedagogue, in the long run, shows the virtues of the Congressman, the newspaper editorial writer or the butler, not those of the aristocrat. When, by any chance, he persists in contumacy beyond thirty, it is only too commonly a sign, not that he is heroic, but simply that he is pathological. So with most of his brethren of the Utopian Fife and Drum Corps, whether they issue out of his own seminary or out of the wilderness. They are fanatics; not statesmen. Thus politics, under democracy, resolves itself into impossible alternatives. Whatever the label on the parties, or the war cries issuing from the demagogues who lead them, the practical choice is between the plutocracy on the one side and a rabble of preposterous impossibilists on the other. One must either follow the New York *Times,* or one must be prepared to swallow Bryan and the Bolsheviki. It is a pity that this is so. For what democracy needs most of all is a party that will separate the good that is in it theoretically from the evils that beset it practically, and then try to erect that good into a workable system. What it needs beyond everything is a party of liberty. It produces, true enough, occasional libertarians, just as despotism produces occasional regicides, but it treats them in the same drum-head way. It will never have a party of them until it invents and installs a genuine aristocracy, to breed them and secure them. . . .

Reinhold Niebuhr

Reinhold Niebuhr (1892–1971) became well known as a philosophical theologian, teacher, and writer with a "realist's" moral stance, who went from being an active Socialist and leader in the Social Gospel movement of liberal Christians to becoming one of the foremost anti–Social Gospel theologians. Born in Wright City, Missouri, Niebuhr was ordained in 1915 and became pastor of an Evangelical church in Detroit, Michigan. As Detroit mushroomed into an industrial city, Niebuhr sided with labor against industrialists such as Henry Ford. At this time he was a Socialist and Social Gospel activist.

At age thirty-six, Niebuhr became an assistant professor of the philosophy of religion at Union Theological Seminary. Slowly he became disillusioned with Marxism, pacifism, and the Social Gospel theology movement, and by 1939 he was an influential anti–Social Gospel theologian. His aim was to maintain the reformation values of Martin Luther that were applicable to contemporary social problems. From 1950 to 1960 he served as dean of the Union Theological Seminary in New York City. He also edited the journal *Christianity and Society.*

Niebuhr's books include *Moral Man and Immoral Society* (1932), *Nature and Destiny of Man* (1941 and 1943, two volumes), and *Discerning the Signs of the Times* (1946). The following excerpts are taken from *Moral Man and Immoral Society,* in which he criticizes liberals who try to apply a belief in man's basic goodness to the behavior of states and calls for a skeptical realism that would permit moral distinctions in favor of democratic values.

ꙮ

Moral Man and Immoral Society (1932)
(excerpts)

The Preservation of Moral Values in Politics

Any political philosophy which assumes that natural impulses, that is, greed, the will-to-power and other forms of self-assertion, can never be completely controlled or sublimated by reason, is under the necessity of countenancing political policies which attempt the control of nature in human history by setting the forces of nature against the impulses of nature. If coercion, self-assertion and conflict are regarded as permissible and necessary instruments of social redemption, how are perpetual conflict and perennial tyranny to be avoided? What is to prevent the instruments of today's redemption from becoming the chain of tomorrow's enslavement? A too consistent political realism would seem to consign society to perpetual warfare. If social cohesion is impossible without coercion, and coercion is impossible without the creation of social injustice, and the destruction of injustice is impossible without the use of further coercion, are we not in an endless cycle of social conflict? If self-interest cannot be checked without the assertion of conflicting self-interests how are the counter-claims to be prevented from becoming inordinate? And if power is needed to destroy power, how is this new power to be made ethical? If the mistrust of political realism in the potency of rational and moral factors in society is carried far enough, an uneasy balance of power would seem to become the highest goal to which society could aspire. If such an uneasy equilibrium of conflicting social forces should result in a tentative social peace or armistice it would be fairly certain that some fortuitous dislocation of the proportions of power would ultimately destroy it. Even if such dislocations should not take place, it would probably be destroyed in the long run by the social animosities which a balance of power creates and accentuates.

The last three decades of world history would seem to be a perfect and tragic

Isaak, *American Political Thinking.*/Reprinted with the permission of Charles Scribner's Sons, an imprint of Macmillan Publishing Company, from *Moral Man and Immoral Society* by Reinhold Niebuhr. Copyright 1932 Charles Scribner's Sons; copyright renewed © 1960 Reinhold Niebuhr.

symbol of the consequences of this kind of realism, with its abortive efforts to resolve conflict by conflict. The peace before the War was an armistice maintained by the balance of power. It was destroyed by the spontaneous combustion of the mutual fears and animosities which it created. The new peace is no less a coerced peace; only the equilibrium of social and political forces is less balanced than it was before the War. The nations which pretended to fight against the principle of militarism have increased their military power, and the momentary peace which their power maintains is certain to be destroyed by the resentments which their power creates.

This unhappy consequence of a too consistent political realism would seem to justify the interposition of the counsels of the moralist. He seeks peace by the extension of reason and conscience. He affirms that the only lasting peace is one which proceeds from a rational and voluntary adjustment of interest to interest and right to right. He believes that such an adjustment is possible only through a rational check upon self-interest and a rational comprehension of the interests of others. He points to the fact that conflict generates animosities which prevent the mutual adjustment of interests, and that coercion can be used as easily to perpetuate injustice as to eliminate it. He believes, therefore, that nothing but an extension of social intelligence and an increase in moral goodwill can offer society a permanent solution for its social problems. Yet the moralist may be as dangerous a guide as the political realist. He usually fails to recognize the elements of injustice and coercion which are present in any contemporary social peace. The coercive elements are covert, because dominant groups are able to avail themselves of the use of economic power, propaganda, the traditional processes of government, and other types of non-violent power. By failing to recognise the real char-

acter of these forms of coercion, the moralist places an unjustified moral onus upon advancing groups which use violent methods to disturb a peace maintained by subtler types of coercion. Nor is he likely to understand the desire to break the peace, because he does not fully recognise the injustices which it hides. They are not easily recognised, because they consist in inequalities, which history sanctifies and tradition justifies. Even the most rational moralist underestimates them, if he does not actually suffer from them. A too uncritical glorification of co-operation and mutuality therefore results in the acceptance of traditional injustices and the preference of the subtler types of coercion to the more overt types.

An adequate political morality must do justice to the insights of both moralists and political realists. It will recognise that human society will probably never escape social conflict, even though it extends the areas of social co-operation. It will try to save society from being involved in endless cycles of futile conflict, not by an effort to abolish coercion in the life of collective man, but by reducing it to a minimum, by counselling the use of such types of coercion as are most compatible with the moral and rational factors in human society and by discriminating between the purposes and ends for which coercion is used.

A rational society will probably place a greater emphasis upon the ends and purposes for which coercion is used than upon the elimination of coercion and conflict. It will justify coercion if it is obviously in the service of a rationally acceptable social end, and condemn its use when it is in the service of momentary passions. The conclusion which has been forced upon us again and again in these pages is that equality, or to be a little more qualified, that equal justice is the most rational ultimate objective for society. If this conclusion is correct, a social conflict which aims at greater equality has a moral justification which must be denied to efforts which aim at the perpetuation of privilege. A war for the emancipation of a nation, a race or a class is thus placed in a different moral category from the use of power for the perpetuation of imperial rule or class dominance. The oppressed, whether they be the Indians in the British Empire, or the Negroes in our own country or the industrial workers in every nation, have a higher moral right to challenge their oppressors than these have to maintain their rule by force. Violent conflict may not be the best means to attain freedom or equality, but that is a question which must be deferred for a moment. It is important to insist, first of all, that equality is a higher social goal than peace. It may never be completely attainable, but it is the symbol for the ideal of a just peace, from the perspective of which every contemporary peace means only an armistice within the existing disproportions of power. It stands for the elimination of the inequalities of power and privilege which are frozen into every contemporary peaceful situation. If social conflict in the past has been futile that has not been due altogether to the methods of violence which were used in it. Violence may tend to perpetuate injustice, even when its aim is justice; but it is important to note that the violence of international wars has usually not aimed at the elimination of an unjust economic system. It has dealt with the real or fancied grievances of nations which were uniformly involved in social injustice. A social conflict which aims at the elimination of these injustices is in a different category from one which is carried on without reference to the problem of justice. In this respect Marxian philosophy is more true than pacifism. If it may seem to pacifists that the proletarian is perverse in condemning international conflict and asserting the class struggle, the latter has good reason to insist that the elimination of coercion is a futile ideal but that

the rational use of coercion is a possible achievement which may save society. It is of course dangerous to accept the principle, that the end justifies the means which are used in its attainment. The danger arises from the ease with which any social group, engaged in social conflict, may justify itself by professing to be fighting for freedom and equality. Society has no absolutely impartial tribunal which could judge such claims. Nevertheless it is the business of reason, though always involved in prejudice and subject to partial perspectives, to aspire to the impartiality by which such claims and pretensions could be analysed and assessed. Though it will fail in instances where disputes are involved and complex, it is not impossible to discover at least the most obvious cases of social disinheritance. Wherever a social group is obviously defrauded of its rights, it is natural to give the assertion of its rights a special measure of moral approbation. Indeed this is what is invariably and instinctively done by any portion of the human community which has achieved a degree of impartiality. Oppressed nationalities, Armenians fighting against Turkey, Indians against England, Filipinos against America, Cubans against Spain, and Koreans against Japan have always elicited a special measure of sympathy and moral approbation from the neutral communities. Unfortunately the working classes in every nation are denied the same measure of sympathy, because there is no neutral community which is as impartial with reference to their claims as with reference to the claims of oppressed nationalities. In the case of the latter there is always some group in nations, not immediately involved in the struggle, which can achieve and afford the luxury of impartiality. Thus Europeans express their sympathy for our disinherited Negroes and Americans have a special degree of interest in the struggle for the emancipation of India.

In spite of the partiality and prejudice which beclouds practically every social issue, it is probably true that there is a general tendency of increasing social intelligence to withdraw its support from the claims of social privilege and to give it to the disinherited. In this sense reason itself tends to establish a more even balance of power. All social power is partially derived from the actual possession of physical instruments of coercion, economic or martial. But it also depends to a large degree upon its ability to secure unreasoned and unreasonable obedience, respect and reverence. Inasfar as reason tends to destroy this source of its power, it makes for the diminution of the strength of the strong and adds to the power of the weak. The expropriators are expropriated in another sense beside the one which Marx analysed. Reason divests them of some of their moral conceit, as well as of some measure of the social and moral approbation of their fellows. They are not so certain of the approval of either their own conscience or that of the impartial community. Divested of either or both, they are like Samson with his locks shorn. A considerable degree of power has gone from them. The forces of reason in society are not strong enough to guarantee that this development will ever result in a complete equality of power; but it works to that end. The very fact that rational men are inclined increasingly to condemn the futility of international wars and yet to justify the struggles of oppressed nationalities and classes, proves how inevitably reason must make a distinction between the ultimate ends of social policies and how it must regard the end of equal justice as the most rational one.

We have previously insisted that if the purpose of a social policy is morally and rationally approved, the choice of means in fulfilling the purpose raises pragmatic issues which are more political than they are ethical. This does not mean that the issues lack moral significance or that moral reason must not guard against the abuse of dangerous political instruments, even when they are used for morally approved ends. Conflict and coercion are manifestly such dangerous instruments. They are so fruitful of the very evils from which society must be saved that an intelligent society will not countenance their indiscriminate use. If reason is to make coercion a tool of the moral ideal it must not only enlist it in the service of the highest causes but it must choose those types of coercion which are most compatible with, and least dangerous to, the rational and moral forces of society. Moral reason must learn how to make coercion its ally without running the risk of a Pyrrhic victory in which the ally exploits and negates the triumph.

The most obvious rational check which can be placed upon the use of coercion is to submit it to the control of an impartial tribunal which will not be tempted to use it for selfish ends. Thus society claims the right to use coercion but denies the same right to individuals. The police power of nations is a universally approved function of government. The supposition is that the government is impartial with reference to any disputes arising between citizens, and will therefore be able to use its power for moral ends. When it uses the same power against other nations in international disputes, it lacks the impartial perspective to guarantee its moral use. The same power of coercion may therefore represent the impartiality of society, when used in intra-national disputes, and a threat against the interests of the larger community of mankind when used in international disputes. Thus the effort is made to organize a society of nations with sufficient power to bring the power of individual nations under international control. This distinction between the impartial and the partial use of social and political coercion is a legitimate one, but it has definite limits.

The limits are given by the impossibility of achieving the kind of impartiality which the theory assumes. Government is never completely under the control of a total community. There is always some class, whether economic overlords or political bureaucrats, who may use the organs of government for their special advantages. This is true of both nations and the community of nations. Powerful classes dominate the administration of justice in the one, and powerful nations in the other. Even if this were not the case there is in every community as such, an instinctive avoidance of social conflict and such a superficiality in dealing with the roots of social disaffection, that there is always the possibility of the unjust use of the police power of the state against individuals and groups who break its peace, no matter how justified their grievance. A community may be impartial in using coercion against two disputants, whose dispute offers no peril to the life and prestige of the community. But wherever such a dispute affects the order or the prestige of the community, its impartiality evaporates. The prejudice and passion with which a staid, genteel and highly cultured New England community conducted itself in the Sacco-Vanzetti case is a vivid example. For these reasons it is impossible to draw too sharp a moral distinction between the use of force and coercion under the control of impartial tribunals and its use by individuals and groups who make it a frank instrument of their own interests.

The chief distinction in the problem of coercion, usually made by moralists, is that between violent and non-violent coercion. The impossibility of making this distinction absolute has been previously considered. It is nevertheless important to make a more careful analysis of the issues involved in the choice of methods of coercion in the social process. The distinguishing marks of violent coercion and conflict are usually held to be its intent to destroy either life or property. This distinction is correct if consequences are not confused with intent. Non-violent conflict and coercion may also result in the destruction of life or property and they usually do. The difference is that destruction is not the intended but the inevitable consequence of non-violent coercion. The chief difference between violence and non-violence is not in the degree of destruction which they cause, though the difference is usually considerable, but in the aggressive character of the one and the negative character of the other. Non-violence is essentially non-co-operation. It expresses itself in the refusal to participate in the ordinary processes of society. It may mean the refusal to pay taxes to the government (civil disobedience), or to trade with the social group which is to be coerced (boycott) or to render customary services (strike). While it represents a passive and negative form of resistance, its consequences may be very positive. It certainly places restraints upon the freedom of the objects of its discipline and prevents them from doing what they desire to do. Furthermore it destroys property values, and it may destroy life; though it is not generally as destructive of life as violence. Yet a boycott may rob a whole community of its livelihood and, if maintained long enough, it will certainly destroy life. A strike may destroy the property values inherent in the industrial process which it brings to a halt, and it may imperil the life of a whole community which depends upon some vital service with which the strike interferes. Nor can it be maintained that it isolates the guilty from the innocent more successfully than violent coercion. The innocent are involved with the guilty in conflicts between groups, not because of any particular type of coercion used in the conflict but by the very group character of the conflict. No community can be disciplined without affecting all its members who are dependent upon, even though they are not responsible for, its policies. The cotton spinners of Lancashire are impoverished by Gandhi's boycott of English cotton, though they can hardly be regarded as the authors of British imperialism. If the League of Nations should use economic sanctions against Japan, or any other nation, workmen who have the least to do with Japanese imperialism would be bound to suffer most from such a discipline.

Non-co-operation, in other words, results in social consequences not totally dissimilar from those of violence. The differences are very important; but before considering them it is necessary to emphasize the similarities and to insist that non-violence does coerce and destroy. The more intricate and interdependent a social process in which non-co-operation is used, the more certainly is this the case. This insistence is important because non-resistance is so frequently confused with non-violent resistance, Mr. Gandhi, the greatest modern exponent of non-violence, has himself contributed to that confusion. He frequently speaks of his method as the use of "soul-force" or "truth-force." He regards it as spiritual in distinction to the physical character of violence. Very early in his development of the technique of non-violence in South Africa he declared: "Passive resistance is a misnomer. . . . The idea is more completely expressed by the term 'soul-force.' Active resistance is better expressed by the term 'body-force.' "[1] A negative form of resistance does not achieve spirituality simply because it is negative. As long as it enters the field of social and physical relations and places physical restraints upon the desires and activities of others, it is a form of physical coercion. The confusion in Mr. Gandhi's mind is interesting, because it seems to arise from his unwillingness, or perhaps his inability, to recognise the qualifying influences of his

political responsibilities upon the purity of his original ethical and religious ideals of non-resistance. Beginning with the idea that social injustice could be resisted by purely ethical, rational and emotional forces (truth-force and soul-force in the narrower sense of the term), he came finally to realise the necessity of some type of physical coercion upon the foes of his people's freedom, as every political leader must. "In my humble opinion," he declared, "the ordinary methods of agitation by way of petitions, deputations, and the like is no longer a remedy for moving to repentance a government so hopelessly indifferent to the welfare of its charge as the Government of India has proved to be," an indictment and an observation which could probably be made with equal validity against and about any imperial government of history. In spite of his use of various forms of negative physical resistance, civil-disobedience, boycotts and strikes, he seems to persist in giving them a connotation which really belongs to pure non-resistance. "Jesus Christ, Daniel and Socrates represent the purest form of passive resistance or soul-force," he declares in a passage in which he explains the meaning of what is most undeniably non-violent resistance rather than non-resistance. All this is a pardonable confusion in the soul of a man who is trying to harmonise the insights of a saint with the necessities of statecraft, a very difficult achievement. But it is nevertheless a confusion.

In justice to Mr. Gandhi it must be said that while he confuses the moral connotations of non-resistance and non-violent resistance, he never commits himself to pure non-resistance. He is politically too realistic to believe in its efficacy. He justified his support of the British Government during the War: "So long as I live," he said, "under a system of government based

---

[1] *Speeches and Writings of M. K. Gandhi* (Mardas Edition, 1919), p. 132.

upon force and voluntarily partook of the many facilities and privileges it created for me, I was bound to help that government to the extent of my ability when it was engaged in war. . . . My position regarding that government is totally different today and hence I should not voluntarily participate in its wars." Here the important point is that the violent character of government is recognised and the change of policy is explained in terms of a change in national allegiance and not in terms of pacifist principles. His controversy with his friend C. F. Andrews over his policy of permitting the burning of foreign cloth and his debate with the poet Rabindranath Tagore about the moral implication of the first non-violent resistance campaign in 1919–21, prove that in him political realism qualified religious idealism, in a way which naturally bewildered his friends who carried less or no political responsibility. The first non-co-operation campaign was called off by him because it issued in violence. The second campaign also resulted in inevitable by-products of violence, but it was not called off for that reason. Gandhi is not less sincere or morally less admirable because considerations of political efficacy partly determine his policies and qualify the purity of the doctrine of "ahimsa" to which he is committed. The responsible leader of a political community is forced to use coercion to gain his ends. He may, as Mr. Gandhi, make every effort to keep his instrument under the dominion of his spiritual ideal; but he must use it, and it may be necessary at times to sacrifice a degree of moral purity for political effectiveness.

The use of truth-force or soul-force, in the purer and more exact meaning of those words, means an appeal to the reason and goodwill of an opponent in a social struggle. This may be regarded as a type of resistance, but it is not physical coercion. It belongs in the realm of education. It places no external restraints upon the object

of its discipline. It may avail itself of a very vivid and dramatic method of education. It may dramatise the suffering of the oppressed, as for instance Mr. Gandhi's encouragement to his followers to endure the penalties of their civil disobedience "long enough to appeal to the sympathetic chord in the governors and the lawmakers." But it is still education and not coercion.

It must be recognised, of course, that education may contain coercive elements. It may degenerate into propaganda. Nor can it be denied that there is an element of propaganda in all education. Even the most honest educator tries consciously or unconsciously to impress a particular viewpoint upon his disciples. Whenever the educational process is accompanied by a dishonest suppression of facts and truths, relevant to the point at issue, it becomes pure propaganda. But even without such dishonest intentions there is, in all exchange of ideas, a certain degree of unconscious suppression of facts or inability to see all the facts. That is the very reason the educational process alone cannot be trusted to resolve a social controversy. Since reason is never pure, education is a tool of controversy as well as a method of transcending it. The coercive elements in education do not become moral merely because they operate in the realm of mind and emotion, and apply no physical restraints. They also must be judged in terms of the purposes which they serve. A distinction must be made, and is naturally made, between the propaganda which a privileged group uses to maintain its privileges and the agitation for freedom and equality carried on by a disinherited group. It may be true that there is a difference in degree of coercive power between psychological and physical types of coercion, as there is between violent and non-violent types. But such differences would establish intrinsic moral distinctions, only if it could be assumed that the least coercive type of influence is naturally the best. This would be true only if freedom could be regarded as an absolute value. This is generally believed by modern educators but it betrays the influence of certain social and economic circumstances to a larger measure than they would be willing to admit. Freedom is a high value, because reason cannot function truly if it is under any restraints, physical or psychic. But absolute intellectual freedom is achieved by only a few minds. The average mind, which is molded by a so-called free educational process, merely accepts contemporary assumptions and viewpoints rather than the viewpoints which might be inculcated by an older or a newer political or religious idealism. The very education of the "democratic" educators is filled with assumptions and rationally unverifiable prejudices, taken from a rapidly disintegrating nineteenth-century liberalism. Psychic coercion is dangerous, as all coercion is. Its ultimate value depends upon the social purpose for which it is enlisted. . . .

Albert Jay Nock

Born in 1870, Albert Jay Nock was an eccentric conservative who became a leader of libertarian political opinion in the United States through his roles as critic, editor, scholar, and author. Brought up in a religious home, he worked out a classical education for himself and then became a minister from 1897 to 1909.

Nock dropped out of both the ministry and family life and went to work for *American Magazine.* During World War I, he developed an independent mix of political opinion, supporting Henry George's single-tax proposal, criticizing the repressive potential of the state in terms of individual freedom and how democracy worked, and believing that diplomats made war for the sake of economic imperialism. He was an elitist who became well known as editor of *The Freeman* (1920–24). Nock believed that only objective writing filtered through personal style would be of lasting significance. In addition to numerous essays in journals such as the *Atlantic, Harper's,* and *The American Mercury,* Nock wrote books, including *Myth of a Guilty Nation* (1922), *Journal of These Days* (1934), *The Theory of Education in the United States* (1932)—which praised the classics as the key to contemporary wisdom—and *Memoirs of a Superfluous Man* (1943). Nock found patrons so that he did not have to earn a living. He spent the latter part of his life in Brussels, but died in the United States in 1945. In his introduction to Herbert Spencer's *The Man versus the State,* Nock gives his interpretation of the significance of American liberalism.

Introduction to Herbert Spencer's the Man versus the State (1940)
(excerpts)

In 1851 Herbert Spencer published a treatise called *Social Statics; or, The Conditions Essential to Human Happiness Specified.* Among other specifications, this work established and made clear the fundamental principle that society should be

Isaak, *American Political Thinking.*/"Introduction" by Albert Jay Nock and excerpts taken from *The Man versus the State* by Herbert Spencer. Reprinted by permission of The Caxton Printers, Ltd., Caldwell, Idaho.

organised on the basis of voluntary coöperation, not on the basis of compulsory coöperation, or under the threat of it. In a word, it established the principle of individualism as against Statism—against the principle underlying all the collectivist doctrines which are everywhere dominant at the present time. It contemplated the reduction of State power over the individual to an absolute minimum, and the raising of social power to its maximum; as against the principle of Statism, which contemplates the precise opposite. Spencer maintained that the State's interventions upon the individual should be confined to punishing those crimes against person or property which are recognised as such by what the Scots philosophers called "the common sense of mankind"[1]; enforcing the obligations of contract; and making justice costless and easily accessible. Beyond this the State should not go; it should put no further coercive restraint upon the individual. All that the State can do for the best interests of society—all it can do to promote a permanent and stable well-being of society—is by way of these purely negative interventions. Let it go beyond them and attempt the promotion of society's well-being by positive coercive interventions upon the citizen, and whatever apparent and temporary social good may be effected will be greatly at the cost of real and permanent social good.

Spencer's work of 1851 is long out of print and out of currency; a copy of it is extremely hard to find. It should be republished, for it is to the philosophy of individualism what the work of the German idealist philosophers is to the doctrine of Statism, what *Das Kapital* is to Statist economic theory, or what the Pauline Epistles are to the theology of Protestantism.[2] It has no effect, or very little, on checking the riotous progress of Statism in England; still less in staying the calamitous consequences of that process. From 1851 down to his death at the end of the century, Spencer wrote occasional essays, partly as running comment on the acceleration of Statism's progress; partly as exposition, by force of illustration and example; and partly as remarkably accurate prophecy of what has since come to pass in consequence of the wholesale substitution of the principle of compulsory coöperation—the Statist principle—for the individualist principle of voluntary coöperation. He reissued four of these essays in 1884, under the title, *The Man versus the State;* and these four essays, together with two others, called *Over-legislation* and *From Freedom to Bondage,* are now reprinted here under the same general title.

The first essay, *The New Toryism,* is of primary importance just now, because it shows the contrast between the aims and

[1]These are what the law classifies as *malum in se,* as distinguished from *malum prohibitum.* Thus, murder, arson, robbery, assault, for example, are so classified; the "sense" or judgment of mankind is practically unanimous in regarding them as crimes. On the other hand, selling whiskey, possessing gold, and the planting of certain crops, are examples of the *malum prohibitum,* concerning which there is no such general agreement.

[2]In 1892 Spencer published a revision of *Social Statics,* in which he made some minor changes, and for reasons of his own—reasons which have never been made clear or satisfactorily accounted for—he vacated one position which he held in 1851, and one which is most important to his general doctrine of individualism. It is needless to say that in abandoning a position, for any reason or for no reason, one is quite within one's rights; but it must also be observed that the abandonment of a position does not in itself affect the position's validity. It serves merely to raise the previous question whether the position is or is not valid. Galileo's disavowal of Copernican astronomy, for example, does no more, at most, than send one back to a reexamination of the Copernican system. To an unprejudiced mind, Spencer's action in 1892 suggests no more than that the reader should examine afresh the position taken in 1851, and make his own decision about its validity, or lack of validity, on the strength of the evidence offered.

methods of early Liberalism and those of modern Liberalism. In these days we hear a great deal about Liberalism, Liberal principles and policies, in the conduct of our public life. All sorts and conditions of men put themselves forward on the public stage as Liberals; they call those who oppose them Tories, and get credit with the public thereby. In the public mind, Liberalism is a term of honour, while Toryism—especially "economic Toryism"—is a term of reproach. Needless to say, these terms are never examined; the self-styled Liberal is taken popularly at the face value of his pretensions, and policies which are put forth as Liberal are accepted in the same unreflecting way. This being so, it is useful to see what the historic sense of the term is, and to see how far the aims and methods of latter-day Liberalism can be brought into correspondence with it; and how far, therefore, the latter-day Liberal is entitled to bear that name.

Spencer shows that the early Liberal was consistently for cutting down the State's coercive power over the citizen, wherever this was possible. He was for reducing to a minimum the number of points at which the State might make coercive interventions upon the individual. He was for steadily enlarging the margin of existence within which the citizen might pursue and regulate his own activities as he saw fit, free of State control or State supervision. Liberal policies and measures, as originally conceived, were such as reflected these aims. The Tory, on the other hand, was opposed to these aims, and his policies reflected this opposition. In general terms, the Liberal was consistently inclined towards the individualist philosophy of society, while the Tory was consistently inclined towards the Statist philosophy.

Spencer shows moreover that as a matter of practical policy, the early Liberal proceeded towards the realization of his aims by the method of repeal. He was not for making new laws, but for repealing old ones. It is most important to remember this. Wherever the Liberal saw a law which enhanced the State's coercive power over the citizen, he was for repealing it and leaving its place blank. There were many such laws on the British statute-books, and when Liberalism came into power it repealed an immense grist of them.

Spencer must be left to describe in his own words, as he does in the course of this essay, how in the latter half of the last century British Liberalism went over bodily to the philosophy of Statism, and abjuring the political method of repealing existent coercive measures, proceeded to outdo the Tories in constructing new coercive measures of ever-increasing particularity. This piece of British political history has great value for American readers, because it enables them to see how closely American Liberalism has followed the same course. It enables them to interpret correctly the significance of Liberalism's influence upon the direction of our public life in the last half-century, and to perceive just what it is to which that influence has led, just what the consequences are which that influence has tended to bring about, and just what are the further consequences which may be expected to ensue.

For example, Statism postulates the doctrine that the citizen has no rights which the State is bound to respect; the only rights he has are those which the State grants him, and which the State may attenuate or revoke at its own pleasure. This doctrine is fundamental; without its support, all the various nominal modes or forms of Statism which we see at large in Europe and America—such as are called Socialism, Communism, Naziism, Fascism, etc.,—would collapse at once. The individualism which was professed by the early Liberals, maintained the contrary; it maintained that the citizen has rights which are inviolable by the State or by any other agency. This was fundamental doctrine; without its support, obviously, every formulation of individualism becomes so much waste paper. Moreover, early Liberalism accepted it as not only fundamental, but also as axiomatic, self-evident. We may remember, for example, that our great charter, the Declaration of Independence takes as its foundation the self-evident truth of this doctrine, asserting that man, in virtue of his birth, is endowed with certain rights which are "unalienable"; and asserting further that it is "to secure these rights" that governments are instituted among men. Political literature will nowhere furnish a more explicit disavowal of the Statist philosophy than is to be found in the primary postulate of the Declaration.

But now, in which direction has latter-day American Liberalism tended? Has it tended towards an expanding *régime* of voluntary coöperation, or one of enforced coöperation? Have its efforts been directed consistently towards repealing existent measures of State coercion, or towards the devising and promotion of new ones? Has it tended steadily to enlarge or to reduce the margin of existence within which the individual may act as he pleases? Has it contemplated State intervention upon the citizen at an ever-increasing number of points, or at an ever-decreasing number? In short, has it consistently exhibited the philosophy of individualism or the philosophy of Statism?

There can be but one answer, and the facts supporting it are so notorious that multiplying examples would be a waste of space. To take but a single one from among the most conspicuous, Liberals worked hard—and successfully—to inject the principle of absolutism into the Constitution by means of the Income-tax Amendment. Under that Amendment it is competent for Congress not only to confiscate the citizen's last penny, but also to levy punitive taxation, discriminatory taxation, taxation for "the equalization of wealth," or for any other purpose it sees fit to promote. Hardly could a single measure be devised which would do more to clear the way for a purely Statist *régime,* than this which puts so formidable a mechanism in the hands of the State, and gives the State *carte blanche* for its employment against the citizen. Again, the present Administration is made up of self-styled Liberals, and its course has been a continuous triumphal advance of Statism. In a preface to these essays, written in 1884, Spencer has a paragraph which sums up with remarkable completeness the political history of the United States during the last six years:

> Dictatorial measures, rapidly multiplied, have tended continually to narrow the liberties of individuals; and have done this in a double way. Regulations have been made in yearly-growing numbers, restraining the citizen in directions where his actions were previously unchecked, and compelling actions which previously he might perform or not as he liked; and at the same time heavier public burdens, chiefly local, have further restricted his freedom, by lessening that portion of his earnings which he can spend as he pleases, and augmenting the portion taken from him to be spent as public agents please.

Thus closely has the course of American Statism, from 1932 to 1939, followed the course of British Statism from 1860 to 1884. Considering their professions of Liberalism, it would be quite appropriate and by no means inurbane, to ask Mr. Roosevelt and his entourage whether they believe that the citizen has any rights which the State is bound to respect. Would they be willing—*ex animo,* that is, and not for electioneering purposes—to subscribe to the fundamental doctrine of the Declaration? One would be unfeignedly surprised if they were. Yet such an affirmation might go some way to clarify the distinction, if there actually be any, between the "totalitarian" Statism of certain European countries and the "democratic" Statism of Great Britain, France and the United States. It is commonly taken for granted that there is such a distinction, but those who assume this do not trouble themselves to show wherein the distinction consists; and to the disinterested observer the fact of its existence is, to say the least, not obvious.

Spencer ends *The New Toryism* with a prediction which American readers today will find most interesting, if they bear in mind that it was written fifty-five years ago in England and primarily for English readers. He says:

The laws made by Liberals are so greatly increasing the compulsions and restraints exercised over citizens, that among Conservatives who suffer from this aggressiveness there is growing up a tendency to resist it. Proof is furnished by the fact that the "Liberty and Property Defense League" largely consisting of Conservatives, has taken for its motto, "Individualism *versus* Socialism." So that if the present drift of things continues, it may by-and-by really happen that the Tories will be defenders of liberties which the Liberals, in pursuit of what they think popular welfare, trample under foot.

This prophecy has already been fulfilled in the United States. . . .

Adolf Berle

Adolf Berle, together with coauthor Gardiner Means, is known for the influential book *The Modern Corporation and Private Property* (1932). This book argues that the modern corporation is not an extension of its owners, but rather a complex organization run by neutral, technocratic managers who coordinate the concentration of economic power. Proving that corporate giantism contradicted the prevailing assumption of a self-regulating price system of small private enterprises in terms of supply and demand, the case became clear for increased government intervention in the private sector to protect the public interest.

Born the son of a pastor in 1895 in Boston, Massachusetts, Berle studied for his B.A., M.S., and law degrees at Harvard. At age twenty-one, he was the youngest to receive a law degree there. He practiced law on and off most of his life, among many other things. Serving in the Army during World War I at twenty-four years of age, he attended the Versailles Conference as an expert on northeastern Europe for the American commission to negotiate peace. He resigned in protest when a U.S. expeditionary force joined in the invasion of Russia. Specializing in corporate law and Latin American affairs, Berle taught at Harvard Business School and Columbia University Law School. He focused on the legal device of a corporation as an instrument of finance and business practice and on the social and ethical implications of an overconcentration of corporate power.

Publication of *The Modern Corporation and Private Property* brought Berle an invitation to join President Franklin D. Roosevelt's brain trust during the New Deal. His job was to explain the New Deal's aims to the public in articles. He was appointed city chamberlain of New York to clean up the city's finances. Under Roosevelt, he served as an assistant secretary of state and later as ambassador to Brazil. From 1947 to 1955, Berle served as chairman of New York State's Liberal party, which he described as a "pressure group on the Democratic party." His principles were based on hemispheric unity and on reform of the nation's corporate structure to bring the equalitarian principles of political democracy into economics.

Other books by Berle include: *The Twentieth Century Capitalist Revolution* (1954), *Power Without Property* (1959), *Latin America—Diplomacy and Reality* (1962), and *Power* (1963). He died in 1971.

Gardiner Means

Gardiner Means became well known as coauthor of *The Modern Corporation and Private Property*. Born in 1896 in Windham, Connecticut, Means received his B.A., M.A., and Ph.D. from Harvard. Afterward he served on the staff for Near East Relief in Turkey, returning to the United States to work as a textile manufacturer (1922–29) until he became resident economist at Columbia School of Law. A distinguished economist, Means served as economic adviser on finance to the U.S. secretary of agriculture, director of the industrial section of the National Resources Committee, chief fiscal analyst of the U.S. Bureau of the Budget, and associate director of research on the Committee for Economic Development. His books include *The Corporate Revolution in America* (1962), *Pricing Power and the Public Interest* (1962), and *The Structure of the American Economy* (1972). He died in 1988.

The Modern Corporation and Private Property (1932)
(excerpts)

Property, Production and Revolution

A Preface to the Revised Edition

More than thirty years ago, in the preface of this book, I wrote:

> The translation of perhaps two-thirds of the industrial wealth of the country from individual ownership to ownership by the large, publicly financed corporations vitally changes the lives of property owners, the lives of workers, and the methods of property tenure. The divorce of ownership from control consequent on that process almost necessarily involves a new form of economic organization of society.

Dr. Means and I had pointed out that the two attributes of ownership—risking collective wealth in profit-seeking enterprise and ultimate management of responsibility for that enterprise—had become divorced. Accordingly we raised the questions:

> Must we not, therefore, recognize that we are no longer dealing with property in the old sense? Does the traditional logic of property still apply? Because an owner who also exercises control over his wealth is protected in the full receipt of the advantages derived from it, must it *necessarily* follow that an owner who has surrendered control of his wealth should likewise be protected to the full? May not this surrender have so essentially changed his relation to his wealth as to have changed the logic applicable to his interest in that wealth? An answer to this question cannot be found in the law itself. It must be sought in the economic and social background of law.

We based these questions on the growing dominance of the corporate form, the increasing decision-making power of corporate management, the increasingly passive position of shareholders, and the increasing inapplicability of the ethical and economic justifications given (rightly enough at the time) by classic economics.

The object of this preface to the revised edition is to review some aspects of this conception in the light of a generation of experience and consequent developments.

The continuing current
of change to
"Collective Capitalism"

Factually, the trend toward dominance of that collective capitalism we call the "corporate system" has continued unabated. Evolution of the corporation has made stock-and-security ownership the dominant form by which individuals own wealth representing property devoted to production (as contrasted with property devoted to consumption). The last great bastion of individually owned productive property—agriculture—has been dramatically declining in proportion to the total production of the United States, and even in agriculture, corporations have been steadily making inroads. Outside of agriculture, well over 90 per cent of all the production in the country is carried on by more than a million corporations. In all of them, management is theoretically distinct from ownership. The directors of the corporation are not the "owners"; they are not agents of the stockholders and are not obliged to follow their instructions. This in itself is not determinative. Numerically most of the million corporations are "close"—the stockholders are also the directors or are so related to them that the decision-making power rests with the stockholders. Quantitatively, however, a thousand or so very large corporations whose stockholders' lists run from 10,000 up to 3,200,000, as in the case of American Telephone and Telegraph, account for an overwhelmingly large percentage both of asset-holders and of operations. *Fortune* Magazine tabulated the 500 largest United States industrial corporations and found their combined sales were 245 billion dollars in 1963 or about 62 per cent of all industrial sales. The factor of concentration is, of course, higher in the public-service industries: communications, transportation and public utilities. It is not unfair to suggest that if these industries were included

(they are not in the *Fortune* tabulation), 600 or 700 large corporations, whose control nominally is in the hands of their "public" stockholders (actually, of their managers), account for 70 per cent of commercial operation of the country—agriculture aside. There has been a slow but continuing trend toward corporate concentration reckoned by the percentage of industry thus controlled. Actually the total trend is more marked because, in contrast to total economic growth, the proportion of American economic activity represented by individually controlled agriculture has been relatively declining. American economics at present is dominantly, perhaps overwhelmingly, industrial.

The effect of this change upon the property system of the United States has been dramatic. Individually owned wealth has enormously increased. It is today reckoned at more than 1,800 billion dollars. Of more importance is the distribution of that figure. Relatively little of it is "productive" property—land or things employed by its owners in production or commerce—though figures are hazy at the edges. The largest item of individually owned wealth, exclusive of productive assets, is described as "owner-occupied homes" (approximately 520 billion dollars). These, of course, are primarily for consumption, though a fraction of them are probably farmsteads. The next largest item—consumer durables—accounts for 210 billion dollars more; these are chiefly automobiles and home equipment, again chiefly used for personal convenience and not for capital or productive purposes.

The property system as applied to productive assets breaks down (as of the end of 1963) as follows: 525 billion dollars of shares of corporate stock; 210 billion dollars in fixed income financial assets (federal, state and local government securities, corporate and foreign bonds, life insurance values, etc.); and 360 billion dollars in liquid assets, chiefly cash in banks. These figures mean that, far and away, the largest item of personally owned "property" representing productive assets and enterprise is in the form of stock of corporations. In addition, a substantial amount of other assets held by individuals consists of claims against intermediate financial institutions—banks, insurance companies and the like, whose holdings include large amounts of corporation stocks, bonds and securities. "Individually owned" enterprise is thus steadily disappearing. Increasingly, the American owns his home, his car, and his household appliances; these are for his consumption. Simultaneously, he increasingly owns stocks, life insurance, and rights in pension funds, social security funds and similar arrangements. And he has a job, paying him a wage, salary or commission.

Comparable figures do not run back to 1932; no one prior to Franklin D. Roosevelt had been vividly interested in developing a first-rate system of social statistics. My own crude figures, worked out in 1934 at the Columbia Law School in a little-noted volume, *Liquid Claims and National Wealth,* showed that the total of all domestic stocks and bonds reached a peak of 100.7 billion dollars in 1929—to which must be added 54 billion dollars of net

liquid claims (chiefly bank balances), and 12.6 billion dollars of life insurance values; but there was no division between individually owned and corporate-owned wealth at that time. My co-author, V. E. Pederson, and I estimated that in a single decade (1922–1932) more than one-sixth of the entire national wealth had shifted from individual hands into managerial—that is, corporate—hands, and we suggested that at that rate forty years would see the wealth of the entire country split, most of it being operated by corporate management, though its "ownership" would be represented by individual "holdings" of stocks, bonds, and other liquid claims.

Based on the figures to date, that development has gone far toward accomplishment. In crude summation, most "owners" own stock, insurance savings and pension claims and the like, and do not manage; most managers (corporate administrators) do not own. The corporate collective holds legal title to the tangible productive wealth of the country—for the benefit of others.

The word "revolutionary" has been justifiably applied to less fundamental change. The United States is no longer anticipating a development. It is digesting a fact. . . .

The Inadequacy of Traditional Theory

. . .Underlying the thinking of economists, lawyers and business men during the last century and a half has been the picture of economic life so skillfully painted by Adam Smith. Within his treatise on the "Wealth of Nations" are contained the fundamental concepts which run through most modern thought. Though adjustments in his picture have been made by later writers to account for new conditions, the whole has

been painted in the colors which he supplied. Private property, private enterprise, individual initiative, the profit motive, wealth, competition,—these are the concepts which he employed in describing the economy of his time and by means of which he sought to show that the pecuniary self-interest of each individual, if given free play, would lead to the optimum satisfaction of human wants. Most writers of the

Nineteenth Century built on these logical foundations, and current economic literature is, in large measure, cast in such terms.

Yet these terms have ceased to be accurate, and therefore tend to mislead in describing modern enterprise as carried on by the great corporations. Though both the terms and the concepts remain, they are inapplicable to a dominant area in American economic organization. New terms, connoting changed relationships, become necessary.

When Adam Smith talked of "enterprise" he had in mind as the typical unit the small individual business in which the owner, perhaps with the aid of a few apprentices or workers, labored to produce goods for market or to carry on commerce. Very emphatically be repudiated the stock corporation as a business mechanism, holding that dispersed ownership made efficient operation impossible. "The directors of such companies . . . ," he pointed out, "being the managers rather of other people's money than of their own, it cannot well be expected that they should watch over it with the same anxious vigilance with which the partners in a private copartnery frequently watch over their own. Like the stewards of a rich man, they are apt to consider attention to small matters as not for their master's honour, and very easily give themselves a dispensation from having it. Negligence and profusion, therefore, must always prevail, more or less, in the management of the affairs of such a company. It is upon this account that joint stock companies for foreign trade [at the time he was writing the only important manifestation of the corporation outside of banks, insurance companies, and water or canal companies] have seldom been able to maintain the competition against private adventurers. They have, accordingly, very seldom succeeded without an exclusive privilege, and frequently have not succeeded with one. Without an exclusive privilege they have commonly mismanaged the trade. With an exclusive privilege they have both mismanaged and confined it."

Yet when we speak of business enterprise today, we must have in mind primarily these very units which seemed to Adam Smith not to fit into the principles which he was laying down for the conduct of economic activity. How then can we apply the concepts of Adam Smith in discussing our modern economy?

Let us consider each of these concepts in turn.

Private property

To Adam Smith and to his followers, private property was a unity involving possession. He assumed that ownership and control were combined. Today, in the modern corporation, this unity has been broken. *Passive property,*—specifically shares of stock or bonds,—gives its possessors an interest in an enterprise but gives them practically no control over it, and involve no responsibility. *Active property,*—plant, good will, organization, and so forth which make up the actual enterprise,—is controlled by individuals who, almost invariably, have only minor ownership interests in it. In terms of relationships, the present situation can be described as including:— (1) "passive property," consisting of a set of relationships between an individual and an enterprise, involving rights of the individual toward the enterprise but almost no effective powers over it; and (2) "active property," consisting of a set of relationships under which an individual or set of individuals hold powers over an enterprise but have almost no duties in respect to it which can be effectively enforced. When active and passive property relationships attach to the same individual or group, we have private property as conceived by the older economists. When they attach to different individuals, private property in the instruments of production disappears. Private property in the share of stock still continues, since the owner possesses the share and has power to dispose of it, but his share of stock is only a token representing a bundle of ill-protected rights and expectations. It is the possession of this token which can be transferred, a transfer which has little if any influence on the instruments of production. Whether possession of active property,—power of control over an enterprise, apart from ownership,—will ever be looked upon as private property which can belong to and be disposed of by its possessor is a problem of the future, and no prediction can be made with respect to it.[1] Whatever the answer, it is clear that in dealing with the modern corporation we are not dealing with the old type of private property. Our description of modern economy, in so far as it deals with the quasi-public corporation, must be in terms of the two forms of property, active and passive, which for the most part lie in different hands.

Wealth

In a similar way, the concept "wealth" has been changed and divided. To Adam Smith, wealth was composed of tangible things,—wheat and land and buildings, ships and merchandise,—and for most people wealth is still thought of in physical terms. Yet in connection with the modern corporation, two essentially different types of wealth exist. To the holder of passive property, the stockholder, wealth consists,

not of tangible goods,—factories, railroad stations, machinery,—but of a bundle of expectations which have a market value and which, if held, may bring him income and, if sold in the market, may give him power to obtain some other form of wealth. To the possessor of active property,—the "control"—wealth means a great enterprise which he dominates, an enterprise whose value is for the most part composed of the organized relationship of tangible properties, the existence of a functioning organization of workers and the existence of a functioning body of consumers.[2] Instead of having control over a body of tangible wealth with an easily ascertainable market value, the group in control of a large modern corporation is astride an organism which has little value except as it continues to function, and for which there is no ready market. Thus, side by side, these two forms of wealth exist:—on the one hand passive wealth,—liquid, impersonal and involving no responsibility, passing from hand to hand and constantly appraised in the market place; and on the other hand, active wealth,—great, functioning organisms dependent for their lives on their security holders, their workers and consumers, but most of all on their mainspring,—"control." The two forms of wealth are not different aspects of the same thing, but are essentially and functionally distinct.

Private enterprise

Again, to Adam Smith, private enterprise meant an individual or few partners actively engaged and relying in large part

[1]Such would be the case, for instance, if by custom the position of director became hereditary and this custom were given legal sanction.

[2]The concept of the consumer as a functioning part of a great enterprise is one which may at first be difficult to grasp. Yet, just as a body of members is essential to the continued existence of a club, so a body of consumers is essential to the continued existence of an enterprise. In each case the members or consumers are an integral part of the association or enterprise. In each case membership is obtained at a cost and for the purpose of obtaining the benefits. The advertising slogan, "Join the Pepsodent Family," is perhaps unintended recognition of this fact.

on their own labor or their immediate direction. Today we have tens and hundreds of thousands of owners, of workers and of consumers combined in single enterprises. These great associations are so different from the small, privately owned enterprises of the past as to make the concept of private enterprise an ineffective instrument of analysis. It must be replaced with the concept of corporate enterprise, enterprise which is the organized activity of vast bodies of individuals, workers, consumers and suppliers of capital, under the leadership of the dictators of industry, "control."

Individual initiative

As private enterprise disappears with increasing size, so also does individual initiative. The idea that an army operates on the basis of "rugged individualism" would be ludicrous. Equally so is the same idea with respect to the modern corporation. Group activity, the coördinating of the different steps in production, the extreme division of labor in large scale enterprise necessarily imply not individualism but coöperation and the acceptance of authority almost to the point of autocracy. Only to the extent that any worker seeks advancement within an organization is there room for individual initiative,—an initiative which can be exercised only within the narrow range of function he is called on to perform. At the very pinnacle of the hierarchy of organization in a great corporation, there alone can individual initiative have a measure of free play. Yet even there a limit is set by the willingness and ability of subordinates to carry out the will of their superiors. In modern industry, individual liberty is necessarily curbed.

The profit motive

Even the motivation of individual activity has changed its aspect. For Adam Smith and his followers, it was possible to abstract one motive, the desire for personal profit,

from all the motives driving men to action and to make this the key to man's economic activity. They could conclude that, where true private enterprise existed, personal profit was an effective and socially beneficent motivating force. Yet we have already seen how the profit motive has become distorted in the modern corporation. To the extent that profits induce the risking of capital by investors, they play their customary role. But if the courts, following the traditional logic of property, seek to insure that all profits reach or be held for the security owners, they prevent profits from reaching the very group of men whose action is most important to the efficient conduct of enterprise. Only as profits are diverted into the pockets of control do they, in a measure, perform their second function.

Nor is it clear that even if surplus profits were held out as an incentive to control they would be as effective an instrument as the logic of profits assumes. Presumably the motivating influence of any such huge surplus profits as a modern corporation might be made to produce would be subject to diminishing returns. Certainly it is doubtful if the prospect of a second million dollars of income (and the surplus profits might often amount to much larger sums) would induce activity equal to that induced by the prospect of the first million or even the first hundred thousand. Profits in such terms bear little relation to those envisaged by earlier writers.

Just what motives are effective today, in so far as control is concerned, must be a matter of conjecture. But it is probable that more could be learned regarding them by studying the motives of an Alexander the Great, seeking new worlds to conquer, than by considering the motives of a petty tradesman of the days of Adam Smith.

Competition

Finally, when Adam Smith championed competition as the great regulator of industry, he had in mind units so small that fixed capital and overhead costs played a role so insignificant that costs were in large measure determinate and so numerous that no single unit held an important position in the market. Today competition in markets dominated by a few great enterprises has come to be more often either cut-throat and destructive or so inactive as to make monopoly or duopoly conditions prevail. Competition between a small number of units each involving an organization so complex that costs have become indeterminate does not satisfy the condition assumed by earlier economists, nor does it appear likely to be as effective a regulator of industry and of profits as they had assumed.

In each of the situations to which these fundamental concepts refer, the Modern Corporation has wrought such a change as to make the concepts inapplicable.[3] New concepts must be forged and a new picture of economic relationships created. It is with this in mind that at the opening of this volume the modern corporation was posed as a major social institution; and its development was envisaged in terms of revolution.

The New Concept of the Corporation

Most fundamental to the new picture of economic life must be a new concept of business enterprise as concentrated in the corporate organization. In some measure a concept is already emerging. Over a decade ago, Walther Rathenau wrote concerning the German counterpart of our great corporation:

"No one is a permanent owner. The composition of the thousand-fold complex which functions as lord of the undertaking is in a state of flux. . . . This condition of things signifies that ownership has been depersonalized. . . . The depersonalization of ownership simultaneously implies the objectification of the thing owned. The claims to ownership are subdivided in such a fashion, and are so mobile, that the enterprise assumes an independent life, as if it belonged to no one; it takes an objective existence, such as in earlier days was embodied only in state and church, in a municipal corporation, in the life of a guild or a religious order. . . . The depersonalization of ownership, the objectification of enterprise, the detachment of property from the possessor, leads to a point where the enterprise becomes transformed into an institution which resembles the state in character."

The institution here envisaged calls for analysis, not in terms of business enterprise but in terms of social organization. On the one hand, it involves a concentration of power in the economic field comparable to the concentration of religious power in the mediaeval church or of political power in the national state. On the other hand, it involves the interrelation of a wide diversity of economic interests,—those of the "owners" who supply capital, those of the workers who "create," those of the consumers who give value to the products of enterprise, and above all those of the control who wield power.

Such a great concentration of power and such a diversity of interest raise the long-fought issue of power and its regulation—of interest and its protection. A constant warfare has existed between the individuals wielding power, in whatever form, and the subjects of that power. Just

---

[3]It is frequently suggested that economic activity has become vastly more complex under modern conditions. Yet it is strange that the concentration of the bulk of industry into a few large units has not simplified rather than complicated the economic process. It is worth suggesting that the apparent complexity may arise in part from the effort to analyze the process in terms of concepts which no longer apply.

as there is a continuous desire for power, so also there is a continuous desire to make that power the servant of the bulk of the individuals it affects. The long struggles for the reform of the Catholic Church and for the development of constitutional law in the states are phases of this phenomenon. Absolute power is useful in building the organization. More slowly, but equally sure is the development of social pressure demanding that the power shall be used for the benefit of all concerned. This pressure, constant in ecclesiastical and political history, is already making its appearance in many guises in the economic field.

Observable throughout the world, and in varying degrees of intensity, is this insistence that power in economic organization shall be subjected to the same tests of public benefit which have been applied in their turn to power otherwise located. In its most extreme aspect this is exhibited in the communist movement, which in its purest form is an insistence that *all* of the powers and privileges of property, shall be used only in the common interest. In less extreme forms of socialist dogma, transfer of economic powers to the state for public service is demanded. In the strictly capitalist countries, and particularly in time of depression, demands are constantly put forward that the men controlling the great economic organisms be made to accept responsibility for the well-being of those who are subject to the organization, whether workers, investors, or consumers. In a sense the difference in all of these demands lies only in degree. In proportion as an economic organism grows in strength and its power is concentrated in a few hands, the possessor of power is more easily located, and the demand for responsible power becomes increasingly direct.

How will this demand be made effective? To answer this question would be to foresee the history of the next century. We can here only consider and appraise certain of the more important lines of possible development.

By tradition, a corporation "belongs" to its shareholders, or, in a wider sense, to its security holders, and theirs is the only interest to be recognized as the object of corporate activity. Following this tradition, and without regard for the changed character of ownership, it would be possible to apply in the interests of the *passive* property owner the doctrine of strict property rights, the analysis of which has been presented above in the chapter on Corporate Powers as Powers in Trust. By the application of this doctrine, the group in control of a corporation would be placed in a position of trusteeship in which it would be called on to operate or arrange for the operation of the corporation for the *sole* benefit of the security owners despite the fact that the latter have ceased to have power over or to accept responsibility for the *active* property in which they have an interest. Were this course followed, the bulk of American industry might soon be operated by trustees for the sole benefit of inactive and irresponsible security owners.

In direct opposition to the above doctrine of strict property rights is the view, apparently held by the great corporation lawyers and by certain students of the field, that corporate development has created a new set of relationships, giving to the groups in control powers which are absolute and not limited by any implied obligation with respect to their use. This logic leads to drastic conclusions. For instance, if, by reason of these new relationships, the men in control of a corporation can operate it in their own interests, and can divert a portion of the asset fund of income stream to their own uses, such is their privilege. Under this view, since the new powers have been acquired on a quasi-contractual basis, the security holders have agreed in advance to any losses which they may suffer by reason of such use. The result is, briefly, that the existence of the legal and economic relationships giving rise to these powers must be frankly recognized as a modification of the principle of private property.

If these were the only alternatives, the former would appear to be the lesser of two evils. Changed corporate relationships have unquestionably involved an essential alteration in the character of property. But such modifications have hitherto been brought about largely on the principle that might makes right. Choice between strengthening the rights of passive property owners, or leaving a set of uncurbed powers in the hands of control therefore resolves itself into a purely realistic evaluation of different results. We might elect the relative certainty and safety of a trust relationship in favor of a particular group within the corporation, accompanied by a possible diminution of enterprise. Or we may grant the controlling group free rein, with the corresponding danger of a corporate oligarchy coupled with the probability of an era of corporate plundering.

A third possibility exists, however. On the one hand, the owners of passive property, by surrendering control and responsibility over the active property, have surrendered the right that the corporation should be operated in their sole interest,— they have released the community from the obligation to protect them to the full extent implied in the doctrine of strict property rights. At the same time, the controlling groups, by means of the extension of corporate powers, have in their own interest broken the bars of tradition which require that the corporation be operated solely for the benefit of the owners of passive property. Eliminating the sole interest of the passive owner, however, does not necessarily lay a basis for the alternative claim that the new powers should be used in the interest of the controlling groups. The latter have not presented, in acts or words any accept-

able defense of the proposition that these powers should be so used. No tradition supports that proposition. The control groups have, rather, cleared the way for the claims of a group far wider than either the owners or the control. They have placed the community in a position to demand that the modern corporation serve not alone the owners or the control but all society.

This third alternative offers a wholly new concept of corporate activity. Neither the claims of ownership nor those of control can stand against the paramount interests of the community. The present claims of both contending parties now in the field have been weakened by the developments described in this book. It remains only for the claims of the community to be put forward with clarity and force. Rigid enforcement of property rights as a temporary protection against plundering by control would not stand in the way of the modification of these rights in the interest of other groups. When a convincing system of community obligations is worked out and is generally accepted in that moment the passive property right of today must yield before the larger interests of society. Should the corporate leaders, for example, set forth a program comprising fair wages, security to employees, reasonable service to their public, and stabilization of business, all of which would divert a portion of the profits from the owners of passive property, and should the community generally accept such a scheme as a logical and human solution of industrial difficulties, the interests of passive property owners would have to give way. Courts would almost of necessity be forced to recognize the result, justifying it by whatever of the many legal theories they might choose. It is conceivable,—indeed it seems almost essential if the corporate system is to survive,—that the "control" of the great corporations should develop into a purely neutral technocracy, balancing a variety of claims by various groups in the community and assigning to each a portion of the income stream on the basis of public policy rather than private cupidity.

In still larger view, the modern corporation may be regarded not simply as one form of social organization but potentially (if not yet actually) as the dominant institution of the modern world. In every age, the major concentration of power has been based upon the dominant interest of that age. The strong man has, in his time, striven to be cardinal or pope, prince or cabinet minister, bank president or partner in the House of Morgan. During the Middle Ages, the Church, exercising spiritual power, dominated Europe and gave to it a unity at a time when both political and economic power were diffused. With the rise of the modern state, political power, concentrated into a few large units, challenged the spiritual interest as the strongest bond of human society. Out of the long struggle between church and state which followed, the state emerged victorious; nationalist politics superseded religion as the basis of the major unifying organization of the western world. Economic power still remained diffused.

The rise of the modern corporation has brought a concentration of economic power which can compete on equal terms with the modern state—economic power versus political power, each strong in its own field. The state seeks in some aspects to regulate the corporation, while the corporation, steadily becoming more powerful, makes every effort to avoid such regulation. Where its own interests are concerned, it even attempts to dominate the state. The future may see the economic organism, now typified by the corporation, not only on an equal plane with the state, but possibly even superseding it as the dominant form of social organization. The law of corporations, accordingly, might well be considered as a potential constitutional law for the new economic state, while business practice is increasingly assuming the aspect of economic statesmanship. . . .

Franklin D. Roosevelt

Born in 1882 in Hyde Park, New York, into a wealthy family, Franklin D. Roosevelt became known as the president responsible for the "New Deal." As a response to the Great Depression, this policy pushed the United States permanently beyond laissez-faire liberalism into Keynesian state intervention into the economy. Roosevelt had graduated from Harvard and briefly practiced law in New York, but his vocation was always politics, and he became a New York state senator, an assistant secretary to the navy in World War I, and the Democratic vice-presidential candidate in 1920.

In 1921 Roosevelt contracted polio (infantile paralysis) and never fully recovered. But he made a remarkable comeback in politics and was elected governor of New York in 1928 and 1930. He then won the presidency as the Democratic candidate in the 1932 election against Herbert Hoover, who was unable to cope effectively with the Depression. The New Deal grew slowly from a mere campaign slogan to a patchwork of crisis-response programs designed to bring business and government together for the sake of economic recovery and the national interest. In his first hundred days in office, Roosevelt submitted a number of recovery and reform bills that passed easily through Congress.

Roosevelt was a traditional Democrat and reached to the past for ideas from Wilson's New Freedom and Croly's vision of nationalism. Guiding the United States through World War II successfully helped him consolidate the power of the executive branch of government. Though he never wrote a major book, the politics reflected in his speeches and actions were to dominate the U.S. political economy and foreign policy posture for decades after his death in 1945. Following is a 1932 campaign address given at the Commonwealth Club in San Francisco.

⊙‡⊙

Campaign Address at the Commonwealth Club, San Francisco (1932)
(excerpts)

The issue of Government has always been whether individual men and women will have to serve some system of Government or economics, or whether a system of Government and economics exists to serve individual men and women. This question has persistently dominated the discussion of Government for many generations. On questions relating to these things men have differed, and for time immemorial it is probable that honest men will continue to differ. . . .

When we look about us, we are likely to forget how hard people have worked to win the privilege of Government. . . . In many instances the victory of the central Government, the creation of a strong central Government, was a haven of refuge to the individual. The people preferred the master far away to the exploitation and cruelty of the smaller master near at hand.

But the creators of national Government were perforce ruthless men. They were often cruel in their methods, but they did strive steadily toward something that society needed and very much wanted, a strong central State able to keep the peace, to stamp out civil war, to put the unruly nobleman in his place, and to permit the bulk of individuals to live safely. The man

of ruthless force had his place in developing a pioneer country, just as he did in fixing the power of the central Government in the development of Nations. Society paid him well for his services and its development. . . .

There came a growing feeling that Government was conducted for the benefit of a few who thrived unduly at the expense of all. The people sought a balancing—a limiting force. There came gradually, through town councils, trade guilds, national parliaments, by constitution and by popular participation and control, limitations on arbitrary power.

Another factor that tended to limit the power of those who ruled, was the rise of the ethical conception that a ruler bore a responsibility for the welfare of his subjects.

The American colonies were born in this struggle. The American Revolution was a turning point in it. After the Revolution the struggle continued and shaped itself in the public life of the country. There were those who because they had seen the confusion which attended the years of war for American independence surrendered to the belief that popular Government was essentially dangerous and essentially

Isaak, *American Political Thinking.*

unworkable. They were honest people, my friends, and we cannot deny that their experience had warranted some measure of fear. The most brilliant, honest and able exponent of this point of view was Hamilton. He was too impatient of slow-moving methods. Fundamentally he believed that the safety of the republic lay in the autocratic strength of its Government, that the destiny of individuals was to serve that Government, and that fundamentally a great and strong group of central institutions, guided by a small group of able and public spirited citizens, could best direct all Government.

But Mr. Jefferson, in the summer of 1776, after drafting the Declaration of Independence turned his mind to the same problem and took a different view. He did not deceive himself with outward forms. Government to him was a means to an end, not an end in itself; it might be either a refuge and a help or a threat and a danger, depending on the circumstances. We find him carefully analyzing the society for which he was to organize a Government. "We have no paupers. The great mass of our population is of laborers, our rich who cannot live without labor, either manual or professional, being few and of moderate wealth. Most of the laboring class possess property, cultivate their own lands, have families and from the demand for their labor, are enabled to exact from the rich and the competent such prices as enable them to feed abundantly, clothe above mere decency, to labor moderately and raise their families."

These people, he considered, had two sets of rights, those of "personal competency" and those involved in acquiring and possessing property. By "personal competency" he meant the right of free thinking, freedom of forming and expressing opinions, and freedom of personal living, each man according to his own lights. To insure the first set of rights, a Government must

so order its functions as not to interfere with the individual. But even Jefferson realized that the exercise of the property rights might so interfere with the rights of the individual that the Government, without whose assistance the property rights could not exist, must intervene, not to destroy individualism, but to protect it.

You are familiar with the great political duel which followed; and how Hamilton, and his friends, building toward a dominant centralized power were at length defeated in the great election of 1800, by Mr. Jefferson's party. Out of that duel came the two parties, Republican and Democratic, as we know them today.

So began, in American political life, the new day, the day of the individual against the system, the day in which individualism was made the great watchword of American life. The happiest of economic conditions made that day long and splendid. On the Western frontier, land was substantially free. No one, who did not shirk the task of earning a living, was entirely without opportunity to do so. Depressions could, and did, come and go; but they could not alter the fundamental fact that most of the people lived partly by selling their labor and partly by extracting their livelihood from the soil, so that starvation and dislocation were practically impossible. At the very worst there was always the possibility of climbing into a covered wagon and moving west where the untilled prairies afforded a haven for men to whom the East did not provide a place. So great were our natural resources that we could offer this relief not only to our own people, but to the distressed of all the world; we could invite immigration from Europe, and welcome it with open arms. Traditionally, when a depression came a new section of land was opened in the West; and even our temporary misfortune served our manifest destiny.

It was in the middle of the nineteenth century that a new force was released and a new dream created. The force was what is called the industrial revolution, the advance of steam and machinery and the rise of the forerunners of the modern industrial plant. The dream was the dream of an economic machine, able to raise the standard of living for everyone; to bring luxury within the reach of the humblest; and to annihilate distance by steam power and later by electricity, and to release everyone from the drudgery of the heaviest manual toil. It was to be expected that this would necessarily affect Government. Heretofore, Government had merely been called upon to produce conditions within which people could live happily, labor peacefully, and rest secure. Now it was called upon to aid in the consummation of this new dream. There was, however, a shadow over the dream. To be made real, it required use of the talents of men of tremendous will and tremendous ambition, since by no other force could the problems of financing and engineering and new developments be brought to a consummation.

So manifest were the advantages of the machine age, however, that the United States fearlessly, cheerfully and, I think, rightly, accepted the bitter with the sweet. It was thought that no price was too high to pay for the advantages which we could draw from a finished industrial system. The history of the last half century is accordingly in large measure a history of a group of financial Titans, whose methods were not scrutinized with too much care, and who were honored in proportion as they produced the results, irrespective of the means they used. The financiers who pushed the railroads to the Pacific were always ruthless, often wasteful, and frequently corrupt; but they did build railroads, and we have them today. It has been estimated that the American investor paid for the American railway system more than three times over in the process; but despite this fact the net advantage was to the United

States. As long as we had free land; as long as population was growing by leaps and bounds; as long as our industrial plants were insufficient to supply our own needs, society chose to give the ambitious man free play and unlimited reward provided only that he produced the economic plant so much desired.

During this period of expansion, there was equal opportunity for all and the business of Government was not to interfere but to assist in the development of industry. This was done at the request of business men themselves. The tariff was originally imposed for the purpose of "fostering our infant industry," a phrase I think the older among you will remember as a political issue not so long ago. The railroads were subsidized, sometimes by grants of money, oftener by grants of land; some of the most valuable oil lands in the United States were granted to assist the financing of the railroad which pushed through the Southwest. A nascent merchant marine was assisted by grants of money, or by mail subsidies, so that our steam shipping might ply the seven seas. Some of my friends tell me that they do not want the Government in business. With this I agree; but I wonder whether they realize the implications of the past. For while it has been American doctrine that the Government must not go into business in competition with private enterprises, still it has been traditional, particularly in Republican administrations, for business urgently to ask the Government to put at private disposal all kinds of Government assistance. The same man who tells you that he does not want to see the Government interfere in business—and he means it, and has plenty of good reasons for saying so—is the first to go to Washington and ask the Government for a prohibitory tariff on his product. When things get just bad enough, as they did two years ago, he will go with equal speed to the United States Government and ask for a loan; and the Reconstruction Finance Corporation is the outcome of it. Each group has sought protection from the Government for its own special interests, without realizing that the function of Government must be to favor no small group at the expense of its duty to protect the rights of personal freedom and of private property of all its citizens.

In retrospect we can now see that the turn of the tide came with the turn of the century. We were reaching our last frontier; there was no more free land and our industrial combinations had become great uncontrolled and irresponsible units of power within the State. Clear-sighted men saw with fear the danger that opportunity would no longer be equal; that the growing corporation, like the feudal baron of old, might threaten the economic freedom of individuals to earn a living. In that hour, our anti-trust laws were born. The cry was raised against the great corporations. Theodore Roosevelt, the first great Republican Progressive, fought a Presidential campaign on the issue of "trust busting" and talked freely about malefactors of great wealth. If the Government had a policy it was rather to turn the clock back, to destroy the large combinations and to return to the time when every man owned his individual small business.

This was impossible; Theodore Roosevelt, abandoning the idea of "trust busting," was forced to work out a difference between "good" trusts and "bad" trusts. The Supreme Court set forth the famous "rule of reason" by which it seems to have meant that a concentration of industrial power was permissible if the method by which it got its power, and the use it made of that power, were reasonable.

Woodrow Wilson, elected in 1912, saw the situation more clearly. Where Jefferson had feared the encroachment of political power on the lives of individuals, Wilson knew that the new power was financial. He saw, in the highly centralized economic system, the despot of the twentieth century, on whom great masses of individuals relied for their safety and their livelihood, and whose irresponsibility and greed (if they were not controlled) would reduce them to starvation and penury. The concentration of financial power had not proceeded so far in 1912 as it has today; but it had grown far enough for Mr. Wilson to realize fully its implications. It is interesting, now, to read his speeches. what is called "radical" today (and I have reason to know whereof I speak) is mild compared to the campaign of Mr. Wilson. "No man can deny," he said, "that the lines of endeavor have more and more narrowed and stiffened; no man who knows anything about the development of industry in this country can have failed to observe that the larger kinds of credit are more and more difficult to obtain unless you obtain them upon terms of uniting your efforts with those who already control the industry of the country, and nobody can fail to observe that every man who tries to set himself up in competition with any process of manufacture which has taken place under the control of large combinations of capital will presently find himself either squeezed out or obliged to sell and allow himself to be absorbed." Had there been no World War—had Mr. Wilson been able to devote eight years to domestic instead of to international affairs—we might have had a wholly different situation at the present time. However, the then distant roar of European cannon, growing ever louder, forced him to abandon the study of this issue. The problem he saw so clearly is left with us as a legacy; and no one of us on either side of the political controversy can deny that it is a matter of grave concern to the Government.

A glance at the situation today only too clearly indicates that equality of opportunity as we have known it no longer exists. Our industrial plant is built; the problem just now is whether under existing conditions it is not overbuilt. Our last frontier has long since been reached, and there is practically no more free land. More than half of our people do not live on the farms or on lands and cannot derive a living by cultivating their own property. There is no safety valve in the form of a Western prairie to which those thrown out of work by the Eastern economic machines can go for a new start. We are not able to invite the immigration from Europe to share our endless plenty. We are now providing a drab living for our people. . . .

Just as freedom to farm has ceased, so also the opportunity in business has narrowed. It still is true that men can start small enterprises, trusting to native shrewdness and ability to keep abreast of competitors; but area after area has been preempted altogether by the great corporations, and even in the fields which still have no great concerns, the small man starts under a handicap. The unfeeling statistics of the past three decades show that the independent business man is running a losing race. Perhaps he is forced to the wall; perhaps he cannot command credit; perhaps he is "squeezed out," in Mr. Wilson's words, by highly organized corporate competitors, as your corner grocery man can tell you. Recently a careful study was made of the concentration of business in the United States. It showed that our economic life was dominated by some six hundred odd corporations who controlled two-thirds of American industry. Ten million small business men divided the other third. More striking still, it appeared that if the process of concentration goes on at the same rate, at the end of another century we shall have all American industry controlled by a dozen corporations, and run by perhaps a hundred men. Put plainly, we are steering a steady course toward economic oligarchy, if we are not there already.

Clearly, all this calls for a re-appraisal of values. A mere builder of more industrial

plants, a creator of more railroad systems, an organizer of more corporations, is as likely to be a danger as a help. The day of the great promoter or the financial Titan, to whom we granted anything if only he would build, or develop, is over. Our task now is not discovery or exploitation of natural resources, or necessarily producing more goods. It is the soberer, less dramatic business of administering resources and plants already in hand, of seeking to reestablish foreign markets for our surplus production, of meeting the problem of under consumption, of adjusting production to consumption, of distributing wealth and products more equitably, of adapting existing economic organizations to the service of the people. The day of enlightened administration has come.

Just as in older times the central Government was first a haven of refuge, and then a threat, so now in a closer economic system the central and ambitious financial unit is no longer a servant of national desire, but a danger. I would draw the parallel one step farther. We did not think because national Government had become a threat in the 18th century that therefore we should abandon the principle of national Government. Nor today should we abandon the principle of strong economic units called corporations, merely because their power is susceptible of easy abuse. In other times we dealt with the problem of an unduly ambitious central Government by modifying it gradually into a constitutional democratic Government. So today we are modifying and controlling our economic units.

As I see it, the task of Government in its relation to business is to assist the development of an economic declaration of rights, an economic constitutional order. This is the common task of statesman and business man. It is the minimum requirement of a more permanently safe order of things.

Happily, the times indicate that to create such an order not only is the proper policy of Government, but it is the only line of safety for our economic structures as well. We know, now, that these economic units cannot exist unless prosperity is uniform, that is, unless purchasing power is well distributed throughout every group in the Nation. That is why even the most selfish of corporations for its own interest would be glad to see wages restored and unemployment ended and to bring the Western farmer back to his accustomed level of prosperity and to assure a permanent safety to both groups. That is why some enlightened industries themselves endeavor to limit the freedom of action of each man and business group within the industry in the common interest of all; why business men everywhere are asking a form of organization which will bring the scheme of things into balance, even though it may in some measure qualify the freedom of action of individual units within the business. . . .

The Declaration of Independence discusses the problem of Government in terms of a contract. Government is a relation of give and take, a contract, perforce, if we would follow the thinking out of which it grew. Under such a contract rules were accorded power, and the people consented to that power on consideration that they be accorded certain rights. The task of statesmanship has always been the re-definition of these rights in terms of a changing and growing social order. New conditions impose new requirements upon Government and those who conduct Government. . . .

I feel that we are coming to a view through the drift of our legislation and our public thinking in the past quarter century that private economic power is, to enlarge an old phrase, a public trust as well. I hold that continued enjoyment of that power by any individual or group that must depend upon the fulfillment of that trust. The men who have reached the summit of American business life know this best; happily, many

of these urge the binding quality of this greater social contract.

The terms of that contract are as old as the Republic, and as new as the new economic order.

Every man has a right to life; and this means that he has also a right to make a comfortable living. He may by sloth or crime decline to exercise that right; but it may not be denied him. We have no actual famine or death; our industrial and agricultural mechanism can produce enough and to spare. Our Government formal and informal, political and economic, owes to everyone an avenue to possess himself of a portion of that plenty sufficient for his needs, through his own work.

Every man has a right to his own property; which means a right to be assured, to the fullest extent attainable, in the safety of his savings. By no other means can men carry the burdens of those parts of life which, in the nature of things, afford no chance of labor; childhood, sickness, old age. In all thought of property, this right is paramount; all other property rights must yield to it. If, in accord with this principle, we must restrict the operations of the speculator, the manipulator, even the financier, I believe we must accept the restriction as needful, not to hamper individualism but to protect it.

These two requirements must be satisfied, in the main, by the individuals who claim and hold control of the great industrial and financial combinations which dominate so large a part of our industrial life. They have undertaken to be, not business men, but princes of property. I am not prepared to say that the system which produces them is wrong. I am very clear that they must fearlessly and competently assume the responsibility which goes with the power. So many enlightened business men know this that the statement would be little more than a platitude, were it not for an added implication.

This implication is briefly, that the

responsible heads of finance and industry instead of acting each for himself, must work together to achieve the common end. They must, where necessary, sacrifice this or that private advantage; and in reciprocal self-denial must seek a general advantage. It is here that formal Government—political Government, if you choose—comes in. Whenever in the pursuit of this objective the lone wolf, the unethical competitor, the reckless promoter, the Ishmael or Insull whose hand is against every man's, declines to join in achieving an end recognized as being for the public welfare, and threatens to drag the industry back to a state of anarchy, the Government may properly be asked to apply restraint. Likewise, should the group ever use its collective power contrary to the public welfare, the Government must be swift to enter and protect the public interest.

The Government should assume the function of economic regulation only as a last resort, to be tried only when private initiative, inspired by high responsibility, with such assistance and balance as Government can give, has finally failed. As yet there has been no final failure, because there has been no attempt; and I decline to assume that this Nation is unable to meet the situation.

The final term of the high contract was for liberty and the pursuit of happiness. We have learned a great deal of both in the past century. We know that individual liberty and individual happiness mean nothing unless both are ordered in the sense that one man's meat is not another man's poison. We know that the old "rights of personal competency," the right to read, to think, to speak, to choose and live a mode of life, must be respected at all hazards. We know that liberty to do anything which deprived others of those elemental rights is outside the protection of any compact; and that Government in this regard is the maintenance of a balance, within which every individual may have a place if he will take it; in which every individual may find safety if he wishes it; in which every individual may attain such power as his ability permits, consistent with his assuming the accompanying responsibility. . . .

Faith in America, faith in our tradition of personal responsibility, faith in our institutions, faith in ourselves demand that we recognize the new terms of the old social contract. We shall fulfill them, as we fulfilled the obligation of the apparent Utopia which Jefferson imagined for us in 1776, and which Jefferson, Roosevelt and Wilson sought to bring to realization. We must do so, lest a rising tide of misery, engendered by our common failure, engulf us all. But failure is not an American habit; and in the strength of great hope we must all shoulder our common load.

Emma Goldman

Born in Russia in 1869, Emma Goldman came to the United States in 1886, settling in Rochester, New York. She worked in sweatshops in various eastern cities. Her long career as an anarchist and feminist found focus with the Haymarket Riot (1886), the culmination of a series of violently conducted and ruthlessly suppressed labor strikes that resulted in the judicial murder of four alleged anarchists. Soon "Red Emma" became one of the best-known authors and lecturers in the United States. As of the 1890s, she was constantly harassed by police and press. Yet despite opposition and successful efforts to prevent her from speaking, she published and edited the journal *Mother Earth* (1906–17), published *Anarchism and Other Essays,* and continued to speak out in the United States and abroad.

Goldman's advocacy of individualism and her belief that a meritocracy of the few was necessary to govern (rather than leaving it to the masses) distinguished her from the ideology of many of the anarchists she inspired. Her final essay, below, was written just before she died in 1940 and clarifies her vision of anarchism and liberation.

❦

The Individual, Society and the State (1940)

The minds of men are in confusion, for the very foundations of our civilization seem to be tottering. People are losing faith in the existing institutions, and the more intelligent realize that capitalist industrialism is defeating the very purpose it is supposed to serve.

The world is at a loss for a way out. Parliamentarism and democracy are on the decline. Salvation is being sought in Fascism and other forms of "strong" government.

The struggle of opposing ideas now going on in the world involves social problems urgently demanding a solution. The welfare of the individual and the fate of human society depend on the right answer to those questions. The crises of unemployment, war, disarmament, international relations, etc., are among those problems.

The State, government with its functions and powers, is now the subject of vital interest to every thinking man. Political developments in all civilized countries have brought the questions home. Shall we have a strong government? Are democracy and parliamentary government to be preferred, or is Fascism of one kind or another, dictatorship—monarchical, bourgeois or proletarian—the solution of the ills and difficulties that beset society today?

In other words, shall we cure the evils of democracy by more democracy, or shall we cut the Gordian knot of popular government with the sword of dictatorship?

My answer is neither the one nor the other. I am against dictatorship and Fascism and I am opposed to parliamentary regimes and so-called political democracy.

Nazism has been justly called an attack on civilization. This characterization applies with equal force to every form of dictatorship; indeed, to every kind of suppression and coercive authority. For what is civilization in the true sense? All progress has been essentially an enlargement of the liberties of the individual with a corresponding decrease of the authority wielded over him by external forces. This holds good in the realm of physical as well as of political and economic existence. In the physical world man has progressed to the extent in which he has subdued the forces of nature and made them useful to himself. Primitive man made a step on the road to progress when he first produced fire and thus triumphed over darkness, when he chained the wind or harnessed water.

What role did authority or government play in human endeavor for betterment, in invention and discovery? None whatever, or at least none that was helpful. It has

Isaak, *American Political Thinking.*/"The Individual, Society and the State" from *Red Emma Speaks: Selected Writing and Speeches* (1972) by Alix Kates Shulman. Reprinted by permission.

always been the individual that has accomplished every miracle in that sphere, usually in spite of the prohibition, persecution and interference by authority, human and divine.

Similarly, in the political sphere, the road of progress lay in getting away more and more from the authority of the tribal chief or of the clan, of prince and king, of government, of the State. Economically, progress has meant greater well-being of ever larger numbers. Culturally, it has signified the result of all the other achievements—greater independence, political, mental and psychic.

Regarded from this angle, the problem of man's relation to the State assumes an entirely different significance. It is no more a question of whether dictatorship is preferable to democracy, or Italian Fascism superior to Hitlerism. A larger and far more vital question poses itself: Is political government, is the State, beneficial to mankind, and how does it affect the individual in the social scheme of things?

The individual is the true reality in life. A cosmos in himself, he does not exist for the State, nor for that abstraction called "society," or the "nation," which is only a collection of individuals. Man, the individual, has always been and necessarily is the sole source and motive power of evolution and progress. Civilization has been a continuous struggle of the individual or of groups of individuals against the State and even against "society," that is, against the majority subdued and hypnotized by the State and State worship. Man's greatest battles have been waged against man-made obstacles and artificial handicaps imposed upon him to paralyse his growth and development. Human thought has always been falsified by tradition and custom, and perverted false education in the interests of those who held power and enjoyed privileges. In other words, by the State and the

ruling classes. This constant incessant conflict has been the history of mankind.

Individuality may be described as the consciousness of the individual as to what he is and how he lives. It is inherent in every human being and is a thing of growth. The State and social institutions come and go, but individuality remains and persists. The very essence of individuality is expression; the sense of dignity and independence is the soil wherein it thrives. Individuality is not the impersonal and mechanistic thing that the State treats as an "individual." The individual is not merely the result of heredity and environment, of cause and effect. He is that and a great deal more, a great deal else. The living man cannot be defined; he is the fountain-head of all life and all values; he is not a part of this or of that; he is a whole, an individual whole, a growing, changing, yet always constant whole.

Individuality is not to be confused with the various ideas and concepts of Individualism; much less with that "rugged individualism" which is only a masked attempt to repress and defeat the individual and his individuality. So-called Individualism is the social and economic *laissez-faire:* the exploitation of the masses by the classes by means of legal trickery, spiritual debasement and systematic indoctrination of the servile spirit, which process is known as "education." That corrupt and perverse "individualism" is the strait-jacket of individuality. It has converted life into a degrading race for externals, for possession, for social prestige and supremacy. Its highest wisdom is "the devil take the hindmost."

This "rugged individualism" has inevitably resulted in the greatest modern slavery, the crassest class distinctions, driving millions to the breadline. "Rugged individualism" has meant all the "individualism" for the masters, while the people are regimented into a slave caste to serve a handful of self-seeking "supermen." America is perhaps the best representative of this kind of individualism, in whose name political tyranny and social oppression are defended and held up as virtues; while every aspiration and attempt of man to gain freedom and social opportunity to live is denounced as "un-American" and evil in the name of that same individualism.

There was a time when the State was unknown. In his natural condition man existed without any State or organized government. People lived as families in small communities; they tilled the soil and practiced the arts and crafts. The individual, and later the family, was the unit of social life where each was free and the equal of his neighbor. Human society then was not a State but an association; a voluntary association for mutual protection and benefit. The elders and more experienced members were the guides and advisers of the people. They helped to manage the affairs of the life, not to rule and dominate the individual.

Political government and the State were a much later development, growing out of the desire of the stronger to take advantage of the weaker, of the few against the many. The State, ecclesiastical and secular, served to give an appearance of legality and right to the wrong done by the few to the many. That appearance of right was necessary the easier to rule the people, because no government can exist without the consent of the people, consent open, tacit or assumed. Constitutionalism and democracy are the modern forms of that alleged consent; the consent being inoculated and indoctrinated by what is called "education," at home, in the church, and in every other phase of life.

That consent is the belief in authority, in the necessity for it. At its base is the doctrine that man is evil, vicious, and too incompetent to know what is good for him. On this all government and oppression is built. God and the State exist and are supported by this dogma.

Yet the State is nothing but a name. It is an abstraction. Like other similar conceptions—nation, race, humanity—it has no organic reality. To call the State an organism shows a diseased tendency to make a fetish of words.

The State is a term for the legislative and administrative machinery whereby certain business of the people is transacted, and badly so. There is nothing sacred, holy or mysterious about it. The State has no more conscience or moral mission than a commercial company for working a coal mine or running a railroad.

The State has no more existence than gods and devils have. They are equally the reflex and creation of man, for man, the individual, is the only reality. The State is but the shadow of man, the shadow of his opaqueness, of his ignorance and fear.

Life begins and ends with man, the individual. Without him there is no race, no humanity, no State. No, not even "society" is possible without man. It is the individual who lives, breathes and suffers. His development, his advance, has been a continuous struggle against the fetishes of his own creation and particularly so against the "State."

In former days religious authority fashioned political life in the image of the Church. The authority of the State, the "rights" of rulers came from on high; power, like faith, was divine. Philosophers have written thick volumes to prove the sanctity of the State; some have even clad it with infallibility and with god-like attributes. Some have talked themselves into the insane notion that the State is "superhuman," the supreme reality, "the absolute."

Enquiry was condemned as blasphemy. Servitude was the highest virtue. By such precepts and training certain things came to be regarded as self-evident, as sacred of their truth, but because of constant and persistent repetition.

All progress has been essentially an unmasking of "divinity" and "mystery," of alleged sacred, eternal "truth"; it has been a gradual elimination of the abstract and the substitution in its place of the real, the concrete. In short, of facts against fancy, of knowledge against ignorance, of light against darkness.

That slow and arduous liberation of the individual was not accomplished by the aid of the State. On the contrary, it was by continuous conflict, by a life-and-death struggle with the State, that even the smallest vestige of independence and freedom has been won. It has cost mankind much time and blood to secure what little it has gained so far from kings, czars and governments.

The great heroic figure of that long Golgotha has been Man. It has always been the individual, often alone and singly, at other times in unity and co-operation with others of his kind, who has fought and bled in the age-long battle against suppression and oppression, against the powers that enslave and degrade him.

More than that and more significant: It was man, the individual, whose soul first rebelled against injustice and degradation; it was the individual who first conceived the idea of resistance to the conditions under which he chafed. In short, it is always the individual who is the parent of the liberating thought as well as of the deed.

This refers not only to political struggles, but to the entire gamut of human life and effort, in all ages and climes. It has always been the individual, the man of strong mind and will to liberty, who paved the way for every human advance, for every step toward a freer and better world; in science, philosophy and art, as well as in industry, whose genius rose to the heights, conceiving the "impossible," visualizing its realization and imbuing others with his enthusiasm to work and strive for it. Socially speaking, it was always the prophet, the seer, the idealist, who dreamed of a world more to his heart's desire and who served as the beacon light on the road to greater achievement.

The State, every government whatever its form, character or color—be it absolute or constitutional, monarchy or republic, Fascist, Nazi or Bolshevik—is by its very nature conservative, static, intolerant of change and opposed to it. Whatever changes it undergoes are always the result of pressure exerted upon it, pressure strong enough to compel the ruling powers to submit peaceably or otherwise, generally "otherwise"—that is, by revolution. Moreover, the inherent conservatism of government, of authority of any kind, unavoidably becomes reactionary. For two reasons: first, because it is in the nature of government not only to retain the power it has, but also to strengthen, widen and perpetuate it, nationally as well as internationally. The stronger authority grows, the greater the State and its power, the less it can tolerate a similar authority or political power alongside of itself. The psychology of government demands that its influence and prestige constantly grow, at home and abroad, and it exploits every opportunity to increase it. This tendency is motivated by the financial and commercial interests back of the government, represented and served by it. The fundamental *raison d'être* of every government to which, incidentally, historians of former days willfully shut their eyes, has become too obvious now even for professors to ignore.

The other factor which impels governments to become even more conservative and reactionary is their inherent distrust of the individual and fear of individuality. Our political and social scheme cannot afford to tolerate the individual and his constant quest for innovation. In "self-defense" the

State therefore suppresses, persecutes, punishes and even deprives the individual of life. It is aided in this by every institution that stands for the preservation of the existing order. It resorts to every form of violence and force, and its efforts are supported by the "moral indignation" of the majority against the heretic, the social dissenter and the political rebel—the majority for centuries drilled in State worship, trained in discipline and obedience and subdued by the awe of authority in the home, the school, the church and the press.

The strongest bulwark of authority is uniformity; the least divergence from it is the greatest crime. The wholesale mechanization of modern life has increased uniformity a thousandfold. It is everywhere present, in habits, tastes, dress, thoughts and ideas. Its most concentrated dullness is "public opinion." Few have the courage to stand out against it. He who refuses to submit is at once labelled "queer," "different," and decried as a disturbing element in the comfortable stagnancy of modern life.

Perhaps even more than constituted authority, it is social uniformity and sameness that harass the individual most. His very "uniqueness," "separateness" and "differentiation" make him an alien, not only in his native place, but even in his own home. Often more so than the foreign born who generally falls in with the established.

In the true sense one's native land, with its background of tradition, early impressions, reminiscences and other things dear to one, is not enough to make sensitive human beings feel at home. A certain atmosphere of "belonging," the consciousness of being "at one" with the people and environment, is more essential to one's feeling of home. This holds good in relation to one's family, the smaller local circle, as well as the larger phase of the life and activities commonly called one's country. The individual whose vision encompasses the whole world often feels nowhere so hedged in and out of touch with his surroundings than in his native land.

In pre-war times the individual could at least escape national and family boredom. The whole world was open to his longings and his quests. Now the world has become a prison, and life continual solitary confinement. Especially is this true since the advent of dictatorship, right and left.

Friedrich Nietzsche called the State a cold monster. What would he have called the hideous beast in the garb of modern dictatorship? Not that government had ever allowed much scope to the individual; but the champions of the new State ideology do not grant even that much. "The individual is nothing," they declare, "it is the collectivity which counts." Nothing less than the complete surrender of the individual will satisfy the insatiable appetite of the new deity.

Strangely enough, the loudest advocates of this new gospel are to be found among the British and American intelligentsia. Just now they are enamored with the "dictatorship of the proletariat." In theory only, to be sure. In practice, they still prefer the few liberties in their own respective countries. They go to Russia for a short visit or as salesmen of the "revolution," but they feel safer and more comfortable at home.

Perhaps it is not only lack of courage which keeps these good Britishers and Americans in their native lands rather than in the millennium to come. Subconsciously there may lurk the feeling that individuality remains the most fundamental fact of all human association, suppressed and persecuted yet never defeated, and in the long run the victor.

The "genius of man," which is but another name for personality and individuality, bores its way through all the caverns of dogma, through the thick walls of tradition and custom, defying all taboos, setting authority at naught, facing contumely and the scaffold—ultimately to be blessed as prophet and martyr by succeeding generations. But for the "genius of man," that inherent, persistent quality of individuality, we would be still roaming the primeval forests.

Peter Kropotkin has shown what wonderful results this unique force of man's individuality has achieved when strengthened by co-operation with other individualities. The one-sided and entirely inadequate Darwinian theory of the struggle for existence received its biological and sociological completion from the great Anarchist scientist and thinker. In his profound work, *Mutual Aid,* Kropotkin shows that in the animal kingdom, as well as in human society, co-operation—as opposed to internecine strife and struggle—has worked for the survival and evolution of the species. He demonstrated that only mutual aid and voluntary co-operation—not the omnipotent, all-devastating State—can create the basis for a free individual and associational life.

At present the individual is the pawn of the zealots of dictatorship and the equally obsessed zealots of "rugged individualism." The excuse of the former is its claim of a new objective. The latter does not even make a pretense of anything new. As a matter of fact "rugged individualism" has learned nothing and forgotten nothing. Under its guidance the brute struggle for physical existence is still kept up. Strange as it may seem, and utterly absurd as it is, the struggle for physical survival goes merrily on though the necessity for it has entirely disappeared. Indeed, the struggle is being continued apparently because there is no necessity for it. Does not so-called overproduction prove it? Is not the world-wide economic crisis an eloquent demonstration that the struggle for existence is being maintained by the blindness of "rugged individualism" at the risk of its own destruction?

One of the insane characteristics of this struggle is the complete negation of the relation of the producer to the things he produces. The average worker has no inner point of contact with the industry he is employed in, and he is a stranger to the process of production of which he is a mechanical part. Like any other cog of the machine, he is replaceable at any time by other similar depersonalized human beings.

The intellectual proletarian, though he foolishly thinks himself a free agent, is not much better off. He, too, has as little choice or self-direction, in his particular métier, as his brother who works with his hands. Material considerations and desire for greater social prestige are usually the deciding factors in the vocation of the intellectual. Added to these is the tendency to follow in the footsteps of family tradition, and become doctors, lawyers, teachers, engineers, etc. The groove requires less effort and personality. In consequence nearly everybody is out of place in our present scheme of things. The masses plod on, partly because their senses have been dulled by the deadly routine of work and because they must eke out an existence. This applies with even greater force to the political fabric of today. There is no place in its texture for free choice of independent thought and activity. There is a place only for voting and tax-paying puppets.

The interests of the State and those of the individual differ fundamentally and are antagonistic. The State and the political and economic institutions it supports can exist only by fashioning the individual to their particular purpose; training him to respect "law and order"; teaching him obedience, submission and unquestioning faith in the wisdom and justice of government; above all, loyal service and complete self-sacrifice when the State commands it, as in war. The State puts itself and its interests even above the claims of religion and of God. It punishes religious or conscientious scruples against individuality because there is no individuality without liberty, and liberty is the greatest menace to authority.

The struggle of the individual against these tremendous odds is the more difficult—too often dangerous to life and limb—because it is not truth or falsehood which serves as the criterion of the opposition he meets. It is not the validity or usefulness of his thought or activity which rouses against him the forces of the State and of "public opinion." The persecution of the innovator and protestant has always been inspired by fear on the part of constituted authority of having its infallibility questioned and its power undermined.

Man's true liberation, individual and collective, lies in his emancipation from authority and from the belief in it. All human evolution has been a struggle in that direction and for that object. It is not invention and mechanics which constitute development. The ability to travel at the rate of 100 miles an hour is no evidence of being civilized. True civilization is to be measured by the individual, the unit of all social life; by his individuality and the extent to which it is free to have its being, to grow and expand unhindered by invasive and coercive authority.

Socially speaking, the criterion of civilization and culture is the degree of liberty and economic opportunity which the individual enjoys; of social and international unity and co-operation unrestricted by man-made laws and other artificial obstacles; by the absence of privileged castes and by the reality of liberty and human dignity; in short, by the true emancipation of the individual.

Political absolutism has been abolished because men have realized in the course of time that absolute power is evil and destructive. But the same thing is true of all power, whether it be the power of privilege, of money, of the priest, of the politician or of so-called democracy. In its effect on individuality it matters little what the particular character of coercion is— whether it be as black as Fascism, as yellow as Nazism or as pretentiously red as Bol-

shevism. It is power that corrupts and degrades both master and slave and it makes no difference whether the power is wielded by an autocrat, by parliament or Soviets. More pernicious than the power of a dictator is that of a class; the most terrible—the tyranny of a majority.

The long process of history has taught man that division and strife mean death, and that unity and co-operation advance his cause, multiply his strength and further his welfare. The spirit of government has always worked against the social application of this vital lesson, except where it served the State and aided its own particular interests. It is this anti-progressive and anti-social spirit of the State and of the privileged castes back of it which has been responsible for the bitter struggle between man and man. The individual and ever larger groups of individuals are beginning to see beneath the surface of the established order of things. No longer are they so blinded as in the past by the glare and tinsel of the State idea, and of the "blessings" of "rugged individualism." Man is reaching out for the wider scope of human relations which liberty alone can give. For true liberty is not a mere scrap of paper called "constitution," "legal right" or "law." It is not an abstraction derived from the non-reality known as "the State." It is not the negative thing of being free from something, because with such freedom you may starve to death. Real freedom, true liberty is positive: it is freedom to something; it is the liberty to be, to do; in short, the liberty of actual and active opportunity.

That sort of liberty is not a gift: it is the natural right of man, of every human being. It cannot be given; it cannot be conferred by any law or government. The need of it, the longing for it, is inherent in the individual. Disobedience to every form of coercion is the instinctive expression of it. Rebellion and revolution are the more or less conscious attempt to achieve it. Those manifestations, individual and social, are fundamentally expressions of the values of man. That those values may be nurtured, the community must realize that its greatest and most lasting asset is the unit—the individual.

In religion, as in politics, people speak of abstractions and believe they are dealing with realities. But when it does come to the real and the concrete, most people seem to lose vital touch with it. It may well be because reality alone is too matter-of-fact, too cold to enthuse the human soul. It can be aroused to enthusiasm only by things out of the commonplace, out of the ordinary. In other words, the Ideal is the spark that fires the imagination and hearts of men. Some ideal is needed to rouse man out of the inertia and humdrum of his existence and turn the abject slave into an heroic figure.

Right here, of course, comes the Marxist objector who has outmarxed Marx himself. To such a one, man is a mere puppet in the hands of that metaphysical Almighty called economic determinism or, more vulgarly, the class struggle. Man's will, individual and collective, his psychic life and mental orientation count for almost nothing with our Marxist and do not affect his conception of human history.

No intelligent student will deny the importance of the economic factor in the social growth and development of mankind. But only narrow and willful dogmatism can persist in remaining blind to the important role played by an idea as conceived by the imagination and aspirations of the individual.

It were vain and unprofitable to attempt to balance one factor as against another in human experience. No one single factor in the complex of individual or social behavior can be designated as the factor of decisive quality. We know too little, and may never know enough, of human psychology to weigh and measure the relative values of this or that factor in determining man's conduct. To form such

dogmas in their social connotation is nothing short of bigotry; yet, perhaps, it has its uses, for the very attempt to do so proved the persistence of the human will and confutes the Marxists.

Fortunately even some Marxists are beginning to see that all is not well with the Marxian creed. After all, Marx was but human—all too human—hence by no means infallible. The practical application of economic determinism in Russia is helping to clear the minds of the more intelligent Marxists. This can be seen in the transvaluation of Marxian values going on in Socialist and even Communist ranks in some European countries. They are slowly realizing that their theory has overlooked the human element, *den Menschen,* as a Socialist paper put it. Important as the economic factor is, it is not enough. The rejuvenation of mankind needs the inspiration and energizing force of an ideal.

Such an ideal I see in Anarchism. To be sure, not in the popular misrepresentations of Anarchism spread by the worshippers of the State and authority. I mean the philosophy of a new social order based on the released energies of the individual and the free association of liberated individuals.

Of all social theories Anarchism alone steadfastly proclaims that society exists for man, not man for society. The sole legitimate purpose of society is to serve the needs and advance the aspiration of the individual. Only by doing so can it justify its existence and be an aid to progress and culture.

The political parties and men savagely scrambling for power will scorn me as hopelessly out of tune with our time. I cheerfully admit the charge. I find comfort in the assurance that their hysteria lacks enduring quality. Their hosanna is but of the hour.

Man's yearning for liberation from all authority and power will never be soothed by their cracked song. Man's quest for freedom from every shackle is eternal. It must and will go on.

III

The Contemporary Era
(1945–Present)

Introduction

At the end of World War II, American liberal capitalism was declared the winner in a militaristic ideological struggle with fascism or right-wing authoritarianism. The liberal consensus was established economically with the 1944 Bretton Woods agreement. However, the price of victory involved a temporary alliance with left-wing authoritarianism, the communist regime of Joseph Stalin in the Soviet Union. The hot war ended with a cold war in which American liberalism was frozen in a competition for ideological and geopolitical power with communism. Given the perceived necessity of a united ideological stance in this global superpower struggle, American administrations had difficulty admitting that their basic ideology might need adaptation or reform. Counterculture viewpoints were often ignored, overwhelmed, or even subverted through the tactics of the Federal Bureau of Investigation (particularly in the case of the black power movement). Postliberalism could become legitimate only when liberalism no longer required defense from foreign ideological threats. In the words of Louis Hartz in *The Liberal Tradition in America* (1955), "The psychic heritage of a nation 'born equal' is a colossal liberal absolutism, the death by atrophy of the philosophic impulse. ... An absolute national morality is inspired either to withdraw from 'alien' things or to transform them. The American liberal community contained far fewer radicals than any other Western society but the hysteria against them was much vaster than anywhere else. ... The red-scare mentality displays the American absolutism in its purest form."

This largely frozen black-and-white cold-war frame, which peaked in the Cuban missile crisis in 1962 during the Kennedy administration, fell suddenly into the background when the cold war ended with the disintegration of the Soviet Union in 1989. Many American political trends emerging in the second half of the twentieth century which were only partially visible when submerged in cold-war defensiveness came to the foreground as the cold war started to fade from the consciousness of the American people.

1. The Politics of Exclusion and Inclusion

What better way to begin to reveal the partially visible trends in political thinking than to tune in to the voice of the *Invisible Man* of Ralph Ellison. That which one does not see—or pretends not to see—is excluded from existential as well as political recognition. When the United States was born, blacks and women were excluded as voting citizens. Given the promise of America's liberal creed, it is surprising in some ways that not until the late twentieth century have blacks, women, and other minorities been fully recognized politically. That their economic and political power is still not equivalent to white males in American society explains the continuing potency of black's and women's political movements in demanding equal political representation and economic opportunity.

On the other hand, one could argue that it is the very conservatism of America's liberal creed that has kept minorities and women excluded for such a long time. To the extent that the liberal interpretation is one of minimal state protection for existing individual and property rights (call it "negative freedom"), its goal is not to redistribute political and economic advantages from those who have them to those who do not. If everyone is assumed to be born free, no one has to become so. And those born with the most freedom are naturally tempted to maintain a system designed to protect existing status, socioeconomic opportunities, and contracts rather than risk radical reforms that might redistribute their assets and opportunities to someone else. The whiteness and masculinity that characterized all those in political power kept racism and patriarchalism from being issues because they were taken for granted as social conventions.

In contrast, if the interpretation of liberalism demands active state intervention to ensure equal opportunity and equal justice under the law (call it "positive freedom"), aggressive attempts occur to reform the political system more fully to include those who have been excluded, or to level the playing field. The classic example of this is the "Warren Court," in which the Supreme Court under Chief Justice Earl Warren sought first to promote justice for all and second to find a constitutional rationale for so doing. The case *par excellence* of this use of the court system as a proactive agent to create equal opportunity rather than as a passive interpreter of the existing law is *Brown v. Board of Education* (1954), which introduced desegregation of the public schools.

2. The Concept of the Public Interest

To what extent the excluded can be included without destabilizing the existing constitutional balance of the American system is ultimately determined by some concept of the public interest that transcends particular interest groups or partisan politics as usual. A classic statement of such a nonpartisan, disinterested standard for liberalism is found in Walter Lippmann's *Public Philosophy* (1955).

Another vision of such a disinterested standard for American liberalism is embodied in John F. Kennedy's inaugural address (1961): "And so, my fellow Americans: ask not what your country can do for you—ask what you can do for your country. My fellow citizens of the world: ask not what America will do for you, but what together we can do for the freedom of man."

Kennedy's freedom-first vision, the ultimate liberal vision, put him at odds with communist ideology in the tensions of the cold war. This was not just a potential military conflict, but an economic one as well. By the 1960s the liberal consensus in international economic institutions was beginning to weaken as the United States lost its unilateral decision-making power. The debate over the best economic and political means to help alleviate global poverty was mentioned by Kennedy in his inaugural, but was largely postponed because of the distraction of cold war military confrontations. However, others were to take up with great vigor the theme of capitalist assumptions underlying the classical American view of liberalism.

3. Conservative Laissez-faire Capitalism

American conservatives believe that the corollary of individual political freedom is freedom in the economic markets. As even political economist Charles Lindblom, a critic of the dominating role of big business in the American political system, observed in *Politics and Markets* (1977): "Not all market-oriented systems are democratic, but every democratic system is also a market-oriented system." Perhaps economist Milton Friedman made the most persuasive case for contemporary laissez-faire liberalism, for keeping government intervention to a minimum in the economy, in *Capitalism and Freedom* (1962).

As a spokesman for the so-called neoconservative movement of the 1970s and 1980s (typified by many articles in the journal *The Public Interest*), Irving Kristol makes a strong case for defending the market in *Two Cheers for Capitalism* (1978). Kristol also notes that liberal capitalism may be in trouble for not sufficiently responding to spreading spiritual poverty and demands for social justice. As evidence for the importance of liberal capitalist beliefs for the existing social order in the United States, Kristol cites the extremely popular rags-to-riches stories of Horatio Alger in the mid–nineteenth century in which honesty, pluck, and hard work always paid off. America, after all, is widely perceived as the oasis of economic opportunity in the world where anyone can go from rags to riches, if not become president. Whether it is wiser to preserve this great range of economic freedom or to limit it for the sake of social equality and "fairness" is one of the great political questions of the twentieth century.

Another contemporary political thinker who, like Kristol, moved from the socialist to the capitalist direction as did a number of neo-conservatives is Michael Novak, the Catholic theologian. In *Will it Liberate? Questions About Liberation Theology* (1986), Novak brings back Adam Smith's laissez-faire economics alive from the past to show its vitality in "the liberal ethic" today. In a follow-up book, *Free Persons and the Common Good* (1989), Novak takes dead aim at his target:

> In recent decades, one of the greatest weaknesses of the liberal party is to have neglected the internal life of human beings: the struggle for character, the learning of moral and intellectual habits, the quest for God, and the battle against egoism, the flesh and the demons. The roots of this weakness probably lie in complacence. Far from sensing their own emptiness, many exhibit an unconscious reliance upon the spiritual capital of past ages, upon sound habits preconsciously passed from one generation to another, and upon a received body of ideas, stories, and images indispensable to the daily practice of liberty. This inheritance has been steadily squandered.

And so the conservative habit of the American liberal tradition is not enough to preserve individual freedom if the energy of liberation is not actively sought and awakened within the self. And such a search requires discipline, hard work, and humility.

4. Critiques from the Left

The anticommunist extremes of the 1950s fanned by the "Anti-American Hearings" led by Senator Joseph McCarthy and the defensive preoccupation with the cold war helped spark a reactionary "New Left" movement in the 1960s. The aim was to reform the capitalist liberal democracy for the sake of social equality and the establishment of "community." Paul Goodman's *Growing Up Absurd* (1960) is a scathing attack upon the consequences of existing American society for the young. They bear the burden of the missed and compromised revolutions of modern times and grow up in the confusion of phony sensationalism and broken traditions rather than in a coherent, viable society that makes healthy development possible. Rousseau has come back to roost: Americans are born free, yet everywhere they are in chains.

Herbert Marcuse's *One-Dimensional Man* (1964) poses an even starker scenario: the American "liberal" system is actually a systematic form of technological repression that Americans cannot think their way out of. America is like a huge shopping mall that one cannot psychologically escape because of "repressive desublimation." One thinks one's needs are "desublimated" or freed in this market of choice, but actually the choices themselves are "repressive" because one chooses between "false needs" promoted by mass media and markets. Another example of this subtle form of social control of human sexuality and eros is reading pornography, such as *Playboy,* for indirect "desublimation" of sexual desire in a repressive form, rather than going for the real thing, which might be disruptive to the social order. In reflecting on the creation of countercultures in the 1960s, such as the "hippies" who sought to free themselves from this kind of social repression, Theodore Roszak wrote in *The Making of a Counter Culture* (1969): "Most of what is presently happening that is new, provocative and engaging in politics, education, the arts, social relations (love, courtship, family, community) is the creation either of youth, who are profoundly, even fanatically, alienated from the parental generation, or of those who address themselves primarily to the young." Politically, the most well-known organization of the New Left was the Students for a Democratic Society (SDS). In their major public Port Huron Statement of 1962 (initially drafted by Tom Hayden), the SDS called for a new form of democratic idealism. The SDS vision went beyond corporate economics and the nuclear weapons military establishment to provide humanistic develop-ment for all Americans, particularly those excluded from mainstream opportunities. It was a collective call to have the courage to demand social justice.

Michael Walzer described himself to the editor as a "liberal socialist and critical communitarian." He asks in *Politics in the Welfare State* (1968) what will happen when the welfare state succeeds in extending its benefits to all and no one is invisible anymore. From the oppression of invisibility to the freedom of anonymity to . . . total bureaucratic exposure? The ideology of political utilitarianism little benefits a person who has become so included and integrated into a welfare state that all impetus to shape that system or to seize power for personal liberation has been sapped. Walzer's alternative is to reclaim the joy of politics from the administrative bureaucracy of government through the grassroots democracy of small groups.

5. Black Perspectives on Ends and Means

The Black Power movement also sprang up in the 1960s demanding social justice for African-Americans. Angela Davis, a student of Herbert Marcuse, was a dynamic feminist representative. H. Rap Brown and Stokely Carmichael articulated a strong antiestablish-ment black position. The movement inspired the formation of the Black Panthers (an extremist group constantly tracked by the FBI). Brown's famous motto sums up why the law enforcement authorities were nervous: "Violence is as American as apple pie."

Two of the most influential perspectives of African-American ends and means in American politics are provided by Martin Luther King, Jr. and Malcolm X. King was a catalyst for the civil rights movement, leading many mass nonviolent demonstrations and protest actions which, in turn, moved the government to pass desegregation legislation, and the courts to follow up. Malcolm X led the Black Muslim movement, which pressed for separation and autonomy from the white community. A gifted media politician, Malcolm X called for social justice for blacks "by any means." He later modified his position to ask for the races to work together for change.

Both King and Malcolm X were harassed by the FBI, and both died at the hands of assassins.

6. The Wisdom of Women

The search for social justice was not just limited to African-Americans. Women also were mobilized by the spirit of protest generated in the 1960s to demand social, economic and political equality. The publication of Betty Friedan's *The Feminine Mystique* (1963) started a social movement in which women demanded that they no longer be treated as second-class citizens. The National Organization of Women (NOW), founded and initially led by Friedan, became a power network for women's issues. Friedan's *The Second Stage* (1986) brings men back into the feminist political agenda with a focus on family stability.

However, the contribution of women to contemporary American political thought is by no means limited to interest-oriented action groups nor to writing that precipitates such action. Hannah Arendt, one of a number of intellectual refugees from Nazi Germany to enrich American political thought, argued that political thinking and political action must remain analytically distinct to avoid a mediocre muddle in either sphere. The "philosopher's philosopher," she demonstrated by her existence and work that women are fully capable of *being* philosophers, not just students demanding the opportunity to become them. One school of the 1990s women's movement is aimed at building women's self-confidence and enabling them to become what they want to be. Reading Arendt makes one aware that it is important not to confuse means with ends for fear that means become ends. She argues that one thinks alone (and should want to), while one acts collectively when one must.

Carol Gilligan pushes the search for the motivation for self-confidence and maturation even further than Arendt in *In A Different Voice* (1982). She discovers that to be healthy, women must seek a moral ethic of caring and interpersonal relationships more than the cool, abstract justice of men. If her empirical grounding holds up in the future, we may have to create different models of educational, philosophical, and moral development for men and women and adjust our conversations to the right state of consciousness accordingly to interact fruitfully with others, much less to judge them. Gilligan discovered her different moral voices while writing at her kitchen table; now she is writing at Harvard. Do not underestimate where you are sitting!

7. From Ecology to Anarchism and Back

The temptation to think alone is the temptation in the United States to take a long walk in the woods, perhaps in the direction of Walden Pond. This is very much the temptation of the ecological movement in American political thought, an evolution illustrated by *A Sand County Almanac* (1949)—the "thinking like a mountain" of Aldo Leopold, "father of wilderness conservation" in the United States. He is known for his strong advocacy of a land ethic, of a desire to have all human beings draw up their own rules for a reasonable use of their land and natural resources.

The unwillingness of people to follow the advice of those like Leopold suggests, however, that ecological *thinking* alone in the woods is not enough, even if the thinking gets published. Social ecologist and anarchist Murray Bookchin calls for radical *action* to counter the ecological and social insanity, manifest everywhere in the United States, that is ruining local American life. Bookchin would decentralize the government and return to the town meeting, explicitly undermining the power of the corporatists and military industrialists who have disempowered everyday people. It is time, he suggests, for another, more sophisticated "tea party."

Wendell Berry, poet, novelist, political essayist, and, not least, farmer, confirms this need to go back home to local roots, to the land, to cultivate your garden somewhere in particular. His *What Are People For?* (1990) asks the right question and gives a response of persuasive integrity based on commitment to specific people in a specific place. For him there is ultimately no such thing as "global thinking" (a meaningless abstraction) but only local thinking on the globe. This is a gentleman farmer's common sense. In *The Culture We Deserve* (1989), a work that prepared the way for Berry's, Jacques Barzun observed that in terms of the state, the outer shell or container of civilization, the global trend is against aggregation and toward disintegration. He noted that "Yearning and action alike are moving us toward the small, self-contained unit that can be free."

Berry describes "The Work of Local Culture" that naturally emerges from the global trend away from state-level aggregation and toward local autonomy.

8. Native-American Thinking

Native-American thinking is natural, metaphysical thinking, a oneness with land, river, sky. The Native American understands and disproves English poet Stephen Spender's observation (otherwise often on target) that "American learning is always haunted by the idea that there is an 'explication which is the ultimate reality.' Mystery is stripped from everything." (*Journals,* 1953).

Native Americans have been excluded from American liberal society, at times to the point of genocide. In addition to their diminished numbers, they face the challenge of communicating in a writing culture, because most of their wisdom flows from an oral tradition. Nevertheless, Vine Deloria, a Standing Rock Sioux, stands out among others as *A Sender of Words* (1984). Perhaps when the white people have fully explicated "the ecological perspective" they will get around to listening to the masters of ecological wisdom, the Native Americans. They could do worse than begin with Deloria's *We Talk, You Listen* (1970). Here he anticipates the new forms of communal individualism that are necessary in an economy of overcapacity. People are returning to small groups on the land, going back to values that transcend economic competitiveness, and embracing the integrity of the tribe and one's turf. Deloria makes the link with the hippie movement and New Left humanism of the 1960s, but he goes further to advocate educational reform. This would shorten schooling for those "doing time," those already skillful enough to cope with adult life. He seeks support for those for whom economic barriers block the learning that means access to fruitful careers. Status, in the Native American view, ultimately depends upon the individual's contribution to the community.

9. Dialogues on Liberalism and Justice

What of European critics who assume that the youth and pragmatic nature of American culture has spawned no worthwhile systematic philosophical thought on politics? Or, to put it as perhaps only a French academic might: what of Jacques Derrida's comment that "America *is* deconstruction"? That proposition is quickly disposed of if one considers the ongoing dialogue of living Americans at Harvard concerning the relationship between liberalism and justice. The dialogue not only illustrates the full range of the duality of America's conservative tradition of liberalism—from antistate laissez-faire to positive-state interventionism—but suggests that this tradition may be transcended in the future.

In 1971 John Rawls published his magnum opus, *A Theory of Justice.* Robert Nozick followed with his response, *Anarchy, State and Utopia* (1974). And Michael J. Sandel added another take on the problem of *Liberalism and the Limits of Justice* (1982).

Rawls brings the concept of moral duty back to American political thought through a social contract theory that resurrects a moral foundation for the liberal welfare state, but with some unpleasant consequences for those who believe in a disinterested standard of "the public interest." Imagine going back to the beginning of time, "beyond the veil of ignorance," before you were born. You would not vote for a political system in which the rules favored protecting the established interests of the few over the many, because odds are that you would be born among the many. This oversimplified illustration of Rawls's atemporal-thought experiment serves to introduce his "difference principle," the idea that in this land of newborn voters the only inequality that is justified is that which maximizes the interests of the least advantaged.

Those who find the moral consequences of Rawls's "utopian state" too demanding might try turning to Robert Nozick's utopia in *Anarchy, State and Utopia* (1974) where the state is transformed into a dominant insurance company set up to protect existing individual property rights. Nozick provides a conservative's critique of Rawls. Or if Nozick is too libertarian, go on to Michael Sandel's critique of unlimited justice and unlimited liberalism. For if, according to Sandel, one accepts the ethical assumption of the liberalism of Immanuel Kant, that "the right" precedes "the good," there must be some conception of "the right" or of justice that is so disinterested as to be unrelated to any particular person's notion of "the good." But if no such conception of disinterested justice or right is possible, one is stuck with concluding that it is necessary to accept a limited notion of justice and, in consequence, a limited version of liberalism. Sandel suggests that a totally disinterested self, unencumbered by property, obligations, or particular notions of the good, may not be a self at all, or at least not an identifiable person with character.

Clearly, American political thinking has been out of the woods for some time, and contemporary theorizing on liberalism and justice does not go against old European thought so much as it promises to transcend it. American political thought may have reached a watershed. It is reconstructing as much as it is deconstructing as it comes to grips with the limits of American liberalism in a muticultural state. But for a blueprint for a just and liberal new world to evolve out of all this would require that some Americans become as brilliant in their retrospection as the Founding Fathers were. Even if this high standard is not met, at the very least an attempt to understand the complexities of the ongoing American dialogue on the nature and limits of liberalism and justice can raise one's moral perceptions a notch.

An anthology of American political thinking should not end without examples that are challenging enough to raise the standard of excellence (such as Rawls, Nozick, and Sandel), especially when that standard is on the same level as some of the best contemporary thinking. Our political world is unmistakably becoming more complex and multilayered. Take, for example, the detail of the political economy "dialogue" between the perspectives of two contemporary presidents, both great communicators who are separated by more than just a generation. . . .

10. Political Economy Counterpoints

President Ronald Reagan's unique skills of persuasion enabled him to sell his economic program presented to Congress in 1981 almost intact. Congress even gave him much more in defense spending than he needed, boosting the base level of federal spending and causing a huge increase in the federal deficit despite Reagan's promise to trim it. His first two years in office were marked by a deep recession, which helped to lower the high rate of inflation. This was followed by a boom stimulated by tax cuts and federal government spending. His vision of supply-side economics, or "Reaganomics," focused on putting cash in people's pockets and on increasing the supply of goods and services to force demand to follow. It did, for most of the 1980s, as the rich became much richer and the poor were somewhat better off. In part the gap was caused by Reagan's decision to cut taxes of the rich more than those of the poor on the assumption that the rich will invest any surplus income, while the poor will consume it in food, rent, and debt repayment. And investment—provided it goes into equipment and processes that make the economy more productive—stimulates national economic growth. However, Reagan's theory of a modernized laissez-faire liberalism prevented him from having the government target where the investment should go. The rich invested largely in portfolios aimed at the highest short-term return rather than the long-term plant and equipment investments the country needed to update its infrastructure. And by helping to create so much "supply," by the end of the 1980s overcapacity and the large debt overhang threw the economy into recession. On the way, however, intense American defense spending and technological development served to break the financial back of the Soviet empire. In 1989 (under President George Bush, Reagan's former vice president) the Soviet Union fell apart, the cold war ended, and Germany was soon reunited. With the main superpower military threat gone, the Americans turned homeward to the problems of domestic economic competitiveness and social policy, which were not the main concerns of the Bush administration. This led to the reaction against Reaganomics and the election of Bill Clinton as president in 1992. By that time the American national debt had mushroomed to more than 4 *trillion* dollars with the government paying 200 *billion* dollars annually in interest.

Clinton spoke with Reagan about how he was able to get his economic program through Congress with such success. Clinton's economic program, summarized in his address to Congress in 1993 (printed here), represented a radical shift away from the classical laissez-faire liberalism revived by Reagan and Bush to a targeted, progressive, populist American liberalism dating back to Andrew Jackson and, particularly, to the New Deal of Franklin Roosevelt. Reforms of health care, education and training, job creation, and deficit reduction were Clinton's ends. Public investment in updating the infrastructure, capping health-care costs, stimulating small business growth, creating student national service and job-training programs, targeting federal spending cuts and tax increases were his means. Clinton's ends were many and his means few and politically contested. Nevertheless, in comparing the Reagan and Clinton economic programs, recall economist Rudolph Goldsheid's observation early in the twentieth century: "The budget is the skeleton of the state stripped of all misleading ideologies."

Selected Readings

Allen, Robert L. *Black Awakening in Capitalist America.* New York: Doubleday, 1969.

Banfield, Edward C. *The Unheavenly City Revisited.* Boston: Little, Brown, 1975.

Baran, Paul, and Paul M. Sweezy. *Monopoly Capital.* New York: Monthly Review Press, 1966.

Bartlett, Bruce R. *Reaganomics: Supply-Side Economics in Action.* New York: Quill, 1982.

Bay, Christian. *The Structure of Freedom.* Stanford, Calif.: Stanford University Press, 1958.

Bell, Daniel. *The Cultural Contradictions of Capitalism.* New York: Basic Books, 1976.

Benjamin, Jessica. *The Bonds of Love: Psychoanalysis, Feminism and the Problem of Domination.* New York: Pantheon, 1988.

Carmichael, Stokely, and Hamilton, Chares V. *Black Power.* New York: Vintage, 1967.

Cleaver, Eldridge. *Soul on Ice.* New York: McGraw-Hill, 1968.

Dahl, Robert A. *A Preface to Democratic Theory.* Chicago: University of Chicago Press, 1956.

Devine, Donald. *The Political Culture of the United States.* Boston: Little, Brown, 1972.

Dewey, John. *Individualism Old and New.* New York: Capricorn Books, 1962.

Domhoff, G. William. *Who Rules America?* Englewood Cliffs, N.J.: Prentice-Hall, 1967.

Eisenstein, Zillah, ed. *Capitalist Patriarchy and the Case for Socialist Feminism.* New York: Monthly Review Press, 1979.

Fromm, Erich. *Marx's Concept of Man.* New York: Ungar Publishing, 1961.

Gilligan, Carol, ed. *Making Connections.* Troy, N.Y.: Emma Willard School, 1989.

Hampden-Turner, Charles. *Radical Man: The Process of Psycho-social Development.* Garden City, N.Y.: Doubleday Anchor, 1971.

Hartz, Louis. *The Liberal Tradition in America.* New York: Harcourt, Brace and World, 1955.

Huntington, Samuel F. *American Politics: The Promise of Disharmony.* Cambridge, Mass.: Belknap Press, 1981.

Isaak, Robert. *American Democracy and World Power.* New York: St. Martin's Press, 1977.

Isaak, Robert, and Hummel, Ralph. *Politics for Human Beings.* Belmont, Calif.: Wadsworth Publishing Co., 1975.

Kirk, Russell. *The Conservative Mind.* Chicago: Regnery, 1953.

Kirk, Russell. *A Program for Conservatives.* Chicago: Regnery, 1954.

Kristol, Irving. *On the Democratic Idea in America.* New York: Harper & Row, 1972.

Lasch, Christopher. *The Culture of Narcissism.* New York: Norton, 1978.

Leinberger, Paul, and Bruce Tucker. *The New Individualists.* New York: HarperCollins, 1991.

Lipset, Seymour Martin. *Political Man.* (Garden City, N.Y.: Doubleday-Anchor, 1963.

Lowi, Theodore. *The End of Liberalism.* New York: Norton, 1979.

Novak, Michael. *The Spirit of Democratic Capitalism.* New York: Simon and Schuster, 1982.

Potter, David. *People of Plenty: Economic Abundance and the American Character.* Chicago: University of Chicago Press, 1968.

Rand, Ayn. *Capitalism: The Unknown Ideal.* New York: Signet, 1966.

Reich, Robert, and Ira Magaziner. *Minding America's Business: The Decline and Rise of the American Economy.* New York: Harcourt Brace Jovanovich, 1982.

Roelofs, H. Mark, *Ideology and Myth in American Politics: A Critique of a National Political Mind.* Boston: Little, Brown, 1976.

Roszak, Theodore. *The Making of a Counter Culture.* New York: Doubleday, 1969.

Schlesinger, Arthur M., Jr. *The Disuniting of America.* Knoxville, TN: Whittle Direct Books, 1991.

Skinner, B.F. *Walden II.* New York: Macmillan, 1948.

Snyder, Gary. *The Practice of the Wild.* San Francisco: North Point Press, 1990.

Steinfels, Peter. *The Neo-Conservatives.* New York: Simon and Schuster, 1979.

Thurow, Lester. *The Zero-sum Society*. New York: Basic Books, 1980.

Walzer, Michael. *What Does It Mean to Be an American?* N.Y.: Marsilio, 1992.

Will, George. *Statecraft as Soulcraft: What Government Does*. New York: Simon and Schuster, 1983.

Wolff, Robert Paul. *In Defense of Anarchism*. New York: Harper and Torchbooks, 1970.

Woods, Ellen M. *Mind and Politics*. Berkeley: University of California Press, 1972.

Ralph Ellison

Ralph Ellison rose to sudden prominence in 1952 with the publication of his first novel, *Invisible Man,* which won the National Book Award for fiction. The book has since become a contemporary classic, the tale of brutal social realities in the South and in Harlem as experienced by a young, disillusioned, black idealist. He moves first into underground invisibility and, then, into the light.

Ellison was born in 1914 in Oklahoma City, Oklahoma. After studying music at Tuskegee Institute in Tuskegee, Alabama, for three years, Ellison studied sculpture in New York City, where he met poet Langston Hughes and writer Richard Wright. Encouraged by the latter, Ellison wrote short stories, essays, and book reviews and briefly edited the *Negro Quarterly.* He served with the U.S. Merchant Marine during World War II. After the war, a Rosenwald Fellowship gave Ellison the opportunity to focus on writing *Invisible Man* (excerpted here). He also taught at Yale, Bard College, the University of Chicago, and Rutgers University.

Ellison said, "I propose that we view the whole of American life as a drama acted out upon the body of a Negro giant, who, lying trussed up like Gulliver, forms the stage and the scene upon which and within which the action unfolds." The racial crisis, still burning in the United States, is rendered in passionate intensity through *Invisible Man.* A good fiction, it is made of that which is real, which, once experienced, becomes impossible to forget as we come to realize how invisible we actually are to one another.

Invisible Man (1952)
(excerpts)

I am an invisible man. No, I am not a spook like those who haunted Edgar Allan Poe; nor am I one of your Hollywood-movie ectoplasms. I am a man of substance, of flesh and bone, fiber and liquids—and I might even be said to possess a mind. I am invisible, understand, simply because people refuse to see me. Like the bodiless heads you see sometimes in circus sideshows, it is as though I have been surrounded by mirrors of hard, distorting glass. When they approach me they see only my surroundings, themselves, or figments of their imagination—indeed, everything and anything except me.

Nor is my invisibility exactly a matter of a bio-chemical accident to my epidermis. That invisibility to which I refer occurs because of a peculiar disposition of the eyes of those with whom I come in contact. A matter of the construction of their *inner* eyes, those eyes with which they look through their physical eyes upon reality. I am not complaining, nor am I protesting either. It is sometimes advantageous to be unseen, although it is most often rather wearing on the nerves. Then too, you're constantly being bumped against by those of poor vision. Or again, you often doubt if you really exist. You wonder whether you aren't simply a phantom in other people's minds. Say, a figure in a nightmare which the sleeper tries with all his strength to destroy. It's when you feel like this that, out of resentment, you begin to bump people back. And, let me confess, you feel that way most of the time. You ache with the need to convince yourself that you do exist in the real world, that you're a part of all the sound and anguish, and you strike out with your fists, you curse and you swear to make them recognize you. And, alas, it's seldom successful.

One night I accidentally bumped into a man, and perhaps because of the near darkness he saw me and called me an insulting name. I sprang at him, seized his coat lapels and demanded that he apologize. He was a tall blond man, and as my face came close to his he looked insolently out of his blue eyes and cursed me, his breath hot in my face as he struggled. I pulled his chin down sharp upon the crown of my head, butting him as I had seen the West Indians do, and I felt his flesh tear and the blood gush out, and I yelled, "Apologize! Apologize!" But he continued to curse and struggle, and I butted him again and again until he went down heavily, on his knees, profusely bleeding. I kicked him repeatedly, in a frenzy because he still uttered insults though his lips were frothy with blood. Oh yes, I kicked him! And in my outrage I got out my knife and prepared to slit his throat, right there beneath the lamplight in the deserted street, holding him in the collar with one hand, and opening the knife with my teeth—when it occurred to me that the man had not *seen* me, actually; that he, as far as he knew, was in the midst of a walking nightmare! And I stopped the blade, slicing the air as I pushed

him away, letting him fall back to the street. I stared at him hard as the lights of a car stabbed through the darkness. He lay there, moaning on the asphalt; a man almost killed by a phantom. It unnerved me. I was both disgusted and ashamed. I was like a drunken man myself, wavering about on weakened legs. Then I was amused: Something in this man's thick head had sprung out and beaten him within an inch of his life. I began to laugh at this crazy discovery. Would he have awakened at the point of death? Would Death himself have freed him for wakeful living? But I didn't linger. I ran away into the dark, laughing so hard I feared I might rupture myself. The next day I saw his picture in the *Daily News,* beneath a caption stating that he had been "mugged." Poor fool, poor blind fool, I thought with sincere compassion, mugged by an invisible man!

Most of the time (although I do not choose as I once did to deny the violence of my days by ignoring it) I am not so overtly violent. I remember that I am invisible and walk softly so as not to awaken the sleeping ones. Sometimes it is best not to awaken them; there are few things in the world as dangerous as sleepwalkers. I learned in time though that it is possible to carry on a fight against them without their realizing it. For instance, I have been carrying on a fight with Monopolated Light & Power for some time now. I use their service and pay them nothing at all, and they don't know it. Oh, they suspect that power is being drained off, but they don't know where. All they know is that according to the master meter back there in their power station a hell of a lot of free current is disappearing somewhere into the jungle of Harlem. The joke, of course, is that I don't live in Harlem but in a border area. Several years ago (before I discovered the advantages of being invisible) I went through the routine process of buying service and paying their outrageous rates. But no more. I gave up all that, along with my apartment, and my old way of life: That way based upon the fallacious assumption that I, like other men, was visible. Now, aware of my invisibility, I live rent-free in a building rented strictly to whites, in a section of the basement that was shut off and forgotten during the nineteenth century, which I discovered when I was trying to escape in the night from Ras the Destroyer. But that's getting too far ahead of the story, almost to the end, although the end is in the beginning and lies far ahead.

The point now is that I found a home— or a hole in the ground, as you will. Now don't jump to the conclusion that because I call my home a "hole" it is damp and cold like a grave; there are cold holes and warm holes. Mine is a warm hole. And remember, a bear retires to his hole for the winter and lives until spring; then he comes strolling out like the Easter chick breaking from its shell. I say all this to assure you that it is incorrect to assume that, because I'm invisible and live in a hole, I am dead. I am neither dead nor in a state of suspended animation. Call me Jack-the-Bear, for I am in a state of hibernation.

My hole is warm and full of light. Yes, *full* of light. I doubt if there is a brighter spot in all New York than this hole of mine, and I do not exclude Broadway. Or the Empire State Building on a photographer's dream night. But that is taking advantage of you. Those two spots are among the darkest of our whole civilization—pardon me, our whole *culture* (an important distinction, I've heard)—which might sound like a hoax, or a contradiction, but that (by contradiction, I mean) is how the world moves: Not like an arrow, but a boomerang. (Beware of those who speak of the *spiral* of history; they are preparing a boomerang. Keep a steel helmet handy.) I know; I have been boomeranged across my head so much that I now can see the darkness of lightness. And I love light. Perhaps you'll think it strange that an invisible man should need light, desire light, love light. But maybe it is exactly because I *am* invisible. Light confirms my reality, gives birth to my form. A beautiful girl once told me of a recurring nightmare in which she lay in the center of a large dark room and felt her face expand until it filled the whole room, becoming a formless mass while her eyes ran in bilious jelly up the chimney. And so it is with me. Without light I am not only invisible, but formless as well; and to be unaware of one's form is to live a death. I myself, after existing some twenty years, did not become alive until I discovered my invisibility.

That is why I fight my battle with Monopolated Light & Power. The deeper reason, I mean: It allows me to feel my vital aliveness. I also fight them for taking so much of my money before I learned to protect myself. In my hole in the basement there are exactly 1,369 lights. I've wired the entire ceiling, every inch of it. And not with fluorescent bulbs, but with the older, more-expensive-to-operate kind, the filament type. An act of sabotage, you know. I've already begun to wire the wall. A junk man I know, a man of vision, has supplied me with wire and sockets. Nothing, storm or flood, must get in the way of our need for light and ever more and brighter light. The truth is the light and light is the truth. When I finish all four walls, then I'll start on the floor. Just how that will go, I don't know. Yet when you have lived invisible as long as I have you develop a certain ingenuity. I'll solve the problem. And maybe I'll invent a gadget to place my coffee pot on the fire while I lie in bed, and even invent a gadget to warm my bed— like the fellow I saw in one of the picture magazines who made himself a gadget to warm his shoes! Though invisible, I am in the great American tradition of tinkers. That makes me kin to Ford, Edison and Franklin. Call me, since I have a theory and a concept, a "thinker-tinker." Yes, I'll warm my shoes; they need it, they're usually full of holes. I'll do that and more.

Now I have one radio-phonograph; I plan to have five. There is a certain acoustical deadness in my hole, and when I have music I want to *feel* its vibration, not only with my ear but with my whole body. I'd like to hear five recordings of Louis Armstrong playing and singing "What Did I Do to Be so Black and Blue"—all at the same time. Sometimes now I listen to Louis while I have my favorite dessert of vanilla ice cream and sloe gin. I pour the red liquid over the white mound, watching it glisten and the vapor rising as Louis bends that military instrument into a beam of lyrical sound. Perhaps I like Louis Armstrong because he's made poetry out of being invisible. I think it must be because he's unaware that he *is* invisible. And my own grasp of invisibility aids me to understand his music. Once when I asked for a cigarette, some jokers gave me a reefer, which I lighted when I got home, and sat listening to my phonograph. It was a strange evening. Invisibility, let me explain, gives one a slightly different sense of time, you're never quite on the beat. Sometimes you're ahead and sometimes behind. Instead of the swift and imperceptible flowing of time, you are aware of its nodes, those points where time stands still or from which it leaps ahead. And you slip into the breaks and look around. That's what you hear vaguely in Louis' music. . . .

Meanwhile I enjoy my life with the compliments of Monopolated Light & Power. Since you never recognize me even when in closest contact with me, and since, no doubt, you'll hardly believe that I exist, it won't matter if you know that I tapped a power line leading into the building and ran it into my hole in the ground. Before that I lived in the darkness into which I was chased, but now I see. I've illuminated the blackness of my invisibility—and vice

versa. And so I play the invisible music of my isolation. The last statement doesn't seem just right, does it? But it is; you hear this music simply because music is heard and seldom seen, except by musicians. Could this compulsion to put invisibility down in black and white be thus an urge to make music of invisibility? But I am an orator, a rabble rouser—Am? I *was,* and perhaps shall be again. Who knows? All sickness is not unto death, neither is invisibility.

I can hear you say, "What a horrible, irresponsible bastard!" And you're right. I leap to agree with you. I am one of the most irresponsible beings that ever lived. Irresponsibility is part of my invisibility; any way you face it, it is a denial. But to whom can I be responsible, and why should I be, when you refuse to see me? And wait until I reveal how truly irresponsible I am. Responsibility rests upon recognition, and recognition is a form of agreement. Take the man whom I almost killed: Who was responsible for that near murder—I? I don't think so, and I refuse it. I won't buy it. You can't give it to me. *He* bumped *me, he* insulted *me.* Shouldn't he, for his own personal safety, have recognized my hysteria, my "danger potential"? He, let us say, was lost in a dream world. But didn't *he* control that dream world—which, alas, is only too real!—and didn't *he* rule me out of it? And if he had yelled for a policeman, wouldn't *I* have been taken for the offending one? Yes, yes, yes! Let me agree with you, I was the irresponsible one; for I should have used my knife to protect the higher interests of society. Some day that kind of foolishness will cause us tragic trouble. All dreamers and sleepwalkers must pay the price, and even the invisible victim is responsible for the fate of all. But I shirked that responsibility; I became too snarled in the incompatible notions that buzzed within my brain. I was a coward. . . .

It goes a long way back, some twenty years. All my life I had been looking for something, and everywhere I turned someone tried to tell me what it was. I accepted their answers too, though they were often in contradiction and even self-contradictory. I was naïve. I was looking for myself and asking everyone except myself questions which I, and only I, could answer. It took me a long time and much painful boomeranging of my expectations to achieve a realization everyone else appears to have been born with: That I am nobody but myself. But first I had to discover that I am an invisible man!

And yet I am no freak of nature, nor of history. I was in the cards, other things having been equal (or unequal) eighty-five years ago. I am not ashamed of my grandparents for having been slaves. I am only ashamed of myself for having at one time been ashamed. About eighty-five years ago they were told that they were free, united with others of our country in everything pertaining to the common good, and, in everything social, separate like the fingers of the hand. And they believed it. They exulted in it. They stayed in their place, worked hard, and brought up my father to do the same. But my grandfather is the one. He was an odd old guy, my grandfather, and I am told I take after him. It was he who caused the trouble. On his deathbed he called my father to him and said, "Son, after I'm gone I want you to keep up the good fight. I never told you, but our life is a war and I have been a traitor all my born days, a spy in the enemy's country ever since I give up my gun back in the Reconstruction. Live with your head in the lion's mouth. I want you to overcome 'em with yeses, undermine 'em with grins, agree 'em to death and destruction, let 'em swoller you till they vomit or bust wide open." They thought the old man had gone out of his mind. He had been the meekest of men. The younger children were rushed from the room, the shades drawn and the flame of the lamp turned so low that it sputtered on the wick like the old man's breathing. "Learn it to the younguns," he whispered fiercely; then he died.

But my folks were more alarmed over his last words than over his dying. It was as though he had not died at all, his words caused so much anxiety. I was warned emphatically to forget what he had said and, indeed, this is the first time it has been mentioned outside the family circle. It had a tremendous effect upon me, however. I could never be sure of what he meant. Grandfather had been a quiet old man who never made any trouble, yet on his deathbed he had called himself a traitor and a spy, and he had spoken of his meekness as a dangerous activity. It became a constant puzzle which lay unanswered in the back of my mind. And whenever things went well for me I remembered my grandfather and felt guilty and uncomfortable. It was as though I was carrying out his advice in spite of myself. And to make it worse, everyone loved me for it. I was praised by the most lily-white men of the town. I was considered an example of desirable conduct—just as my grandfather had been. And what puzzled me was that the old man had defined it as *treachery*. When I was praised for my conduct I felt a guilt that in some way I was doing something that was really against the wishes of the white folks, that if they had understood they would have desired me to act just the opposite, that I should have been sulky and mean, and that that really would have been what they wanted, even though they were fooled and thought they wanted me to act as I did. It made me afraid that some day they would look upon me as a traitor and I would be lost. Still I was more afraid to act any other way because they didn't like that at all. The old man's words were like a curse. . . .

❧

So there you have all of it that's important. Or at least you *almost* have it. I'm an invisible man and it placed me in a hole—or showed me the hole I was in, if you will—and I reluctantly accepted the fact. What else could I have done? Once you get used to it, reality is as irresistible as a club, and I was clubbed into the cellar before I caught the hint. Perhaps that's the way it had to be; I don't know. Nor do I know whether accepting the lesson has placed me in the rear or in the *avant-garde. That,* perhaps, is a lesson for history, and I'll leave such decisions to Jack and his ilk while I try belatedly to study the lesson of my own life.

Let me be honest with you—a feat which, by the way, I find of the utmost difficulty. When one is invisible he finds such problems as good and evil, honesty and dishonesty, of such shifting shapes that he confuses one with the other, depending upon who happens to be looking through him at the time. Well, now I've been trying to look through myself, and there's a risk in it. I was never more hated than when I tried to be honest. Or when, even as just now I've tried to articulate exactly what I felt to be the truth. No one was satisfied— not even I. On the other hand, I've never been more loved and appreciated than when I tried to "justify" and affirm someone's mistaken beliefs; or when I've tried to give my friends the incorrect, absurd answers they wished to hear. In my presence they could talk and agree with themselves, the world was nailed down, and they loved it. They received a feeling of security. But here was the rub: Too often, in order to justify *them,* I had to take myself by the throat and choke myself until my eyes bulged and my tongue hung out and wagged like the door of an empty house in a high wind. So I became ill of affirmation, of saying "yes" against the nay-saying of my stomach—not to mention my brain.

There is, by the way, an area in which a man's feelings are more rational than his mind, and it is precisely in that area that his will is pulled in several directions at the same time. You might sneer at this, but I know now. I was pulled this way and that for longer than I can remember. And my problem was that I always tried to go in everyone's way but my own. I have also been called one thing and then another while no one really wished to hear what I called myself. So after years of trying to adopt the opinions of others I finally rebelled. I am an *invisible* man. Thus I have come a long way and returned and boomeranged a long way from the point in society toward which I originally aspired.

So I took to the cellar; I hibernated. I got away from it all. But that wasn't enough. I couldn't be still even in hibernation. Because, damn it, there's the mind, the *mind.* It wouldn't let me rest. Gin, jazz and dreams were not enough. Books were not enough. My belated appreciation of the crude joke that had kept me running, was not enough. And my mind revolved again and again back to my grandfather. And, despite the farce that ended my attempt to say "yes" to the Brotherhood, I'm still plagued by his deathbed advice . . . Perhaps he hid his meaning deeper than I thought, perhaps his anger threw me off—I can't decide. Could he have meant—hell, he *must* have meant the principle, that we were to affirm the principle on which the country was built and not the men, or at least not the men who did the violence. Did he say "yes" because he knew that the principle was greater than the men, greater than the numbers and the vicious power and all the methods used to corrupt its name? Did he mean to affirm the principle, which they themselves had dreamed into being out of the chaos and darkness of the feudal past, and which they had violated and compromised to the point of absurdity even in their own corrupt minds? Or did he mean that we had to take the responsibility for all of it, for the men as well as the principle, because we were the heirs who must use the principle because no other fitted our needs? Not for the power or for vindication, but because we, with the given circumstance of our origin, could only thus find transcendence? . . .

I'm not blaming anyone for this state of affairs, mind you; nor merely crying *mea culpa.* The fact is that you carry part of your sickness within you, at least I do as an invisible man. I carried my sickness and though for a long time I tried to place it in the outside world, the attempt to write it down shows me that at least half of it lay within me. It came upon me slowly, like that strange disease that affects those black men whom you see turning slowly from black to albino, their pigment disappearing as under the radiation of some cruel, invisible ray. You go along for years knowing something is wrong, then suddenly you discover that you're as transparent as air. At first you tell yourself that it's all a dirty joke, or that it's due to the "political situation." But deep down you come to suspect that you're yourself to blame, and you stand naked and shivering before the millions of eyes who look through you unseeingly. *That* is the real soul-sickness, the spear in the side, the drag by the neck through the mob-angry town, the Grand Inquisition, the embrace of the Maiden, the rip in the belly with the guts spilling out, the trip to the chamber with the deadly gas that ends in the oven so hygienically clean—only it's worse because you continue stupidly to live. But live you must, and you can either make passive love to your sickness or burn it out and go on to the next conflicting phase.

Yes, but what *is* the next phase? How often have I tried to find it! Over and over again I've gone up above to seek it out. For, like almost everyone else in our country, I started out with my share of optimism. I believed in hard work and progress and action, but now, after first being "for" society and then "against" it, I assign myself no rank or any limit, and such an attitude is very much against the trend of the times. But my world has become one of infinite possibilities. What a phrase—still it's a good phrase and a good view of life, and a man shouldn't accept any other; that much I've learned underground. Until some gang succeeds in putting the world in a strait jacket, its definition is possibility. Step outside the narrow borders of what men call reality and you step into chaos—ask Rinehart, he's a master of it—or imagination. That too I've learned in the cellar, and not by deadening my sense of perception; I'm invisible, not blind.

No indeed, the world is just as concrete, ornery, vile and sublimely wonderful as before, only now I better understand my relation to it and it to me. I've come a long way from those days when, full of illusion, I lived a public life and attempted to function under the assumption that the world was solid and all the relationships therein. Now I know men are different and that all life is divided and that only in division is there true health. Hence again I have stayed in my hole, because up above there's an increasing passion to make men conform to a pattern. . . .

Whence all this passion toward conformity anyway?— diversity is the word. Let man keep his many parts and you'll have no tyrant states. Why, if they follow this conformity business they'll end up by forcing me, an invisible man, to become white, which is not a color but the lack of one. Must I strive toward colorlessness? But seriously, and without snobbery, think of what the world would lose if that should happen. America is woven of many strands; I would recognize them and let it so remain. It's "winner take nothing" that is the great truth of our country or of any country. Life is to be lived, not controlled; and humanity is won by continuing to play in face of certain defeat. Our fate is to become one, and yet many—This is not prophecy, but description. Thus one of the greatest jokes in the world is the spectacle of the whites busy escaping blackness and becoming blacker every day, and the blacks striving toward whiteness, becoming quite dull and gray. None of us seems to know who he is or where he's going. . . .

So why do I write, torturing myself to put it down? Because in spite of myself I've learned some things. Without the possibility of action, all knowledge comes to one labeled "file and forget," and I can neither file nor forget. Nor will certain ideas forget me; they keep filing away at my lethargy, my complacency. Why should I be the one to dream this nightmare? Why should I be dedicated and set aside—yes, if not to at least *tell* a few people about it? There seems to be no escape. Here I've set out to throw my anger into the world's face, but now that I've tried to put it all down the old fascination with playing a role returns, and I'm drawn upward again. So that even before I finish I've failed (maybe my anger is too heavy; perhaps, being a talker, I've used too many words). But I've failed. The very act of trying to put it all down has confused me and negated some of the anger and some of the bitterness. So it is that now I denounce and defend, or feel prepared to defend. I condemn and affirm, say no and say yes, say yes and say no. I denounce because though implicated and partially responsible, I have been hurt to the point of abysmal pain, hurt to the point of invisibility. And I defend because in spite of all I find that I love. In order to get some of it down I *have* to love. I sell you no phony forgiveness, I'm a desperate man—but too much of your life will be lost, its meaning lost,

unless you approach it as much through love as through hate. So I approach it through division. So I denounce and I defend and I hate and I love.

Perhaps that makes me a little bit as human as my grandfather. Once I thought my grandfather incapable of thoughts about humanity, but I was wrong. Why should an old slave use such a phrase as, "This and this or this has made me more human," as I did in my arena speech? Hell, he never had any doubts about his humanity—that was left to his "free" offspring. He accepted his humanity just as he accepted the principle. It was his, and the principle lives on in all its human and absurd diversity. So now having tried to put it down I have disarmed myself in the process. You won't believe in my invisibility and you'll fail to see how any principle that applies to you could apply to me. You'll fail to see it even though death waits for both of us if you don't. Nevertheless, the very disarmament has brought me to a decision. The hibernation is over. I must shake off the old skin and come up for breath. There's a stench in the air, which, from this distance underground, might be the smell either of death or of spring—I hope of spring. But don't let me trick you, there *is* a death in the smell of spring and in the smell of thee as in the smell of me. And if nothing more, invisibility has taught my nose to classify the stenches of death.

In going underground, I whipped it all except the mind, the *mind.* And the mind that has conceived a plan of living must never lose sight of the chaos against which that pattern was conceived. That goes for societies as well as for individuals. Thus, having tried to give pattern to the chaos which lives within the pattern of your certainties, I must come out, I must emerge. And there's still a conflict within me: With Louis Armstrong one half of me says, "Open the window and let the foul air out," while the other says, "It was good green corn before the harvest." Of course Louie was kidding, *he* wouldn't have thrown old Bad Air out, because it would have broken up the music and the dance, when it was the good music that came from the bell of old Bad Air's horn that counted. Old Bad Air is still around with his music and his dancing and his diversity, and I'll be up and around with mine. And, as I said before, a decision has been made. I'm shaking off the old skin and I'll leave it here in the hole. I'm coming out, no less invisible without it, but coming out nevertheless. And I suppose it's damn well time. Even hibernations can be overdone, come to think of it. Perhaps

that's my greatest social crime, I've overstayed my hibernation, since there's a possibility that even an invisible man has a socially responsible role to play.

"Ah," I can hear you say, "so it was all a build-up to bore us with his buggy jiving. He only wanted us to listen to him rave!" But only partially true: Being invisible and without substance, a disembodied voice, as it were, what else could I do? What else but try to tell you what was really happening when your eyes were looking through? And it is this which frightens me:

Who knows but that, on the lower frequencies, I speak for you?

Earl Warren

Earl Warren (1891–1974) served as chief justice of the Supreme Court from 1953 through 1969 and was responsible for key pro–civil rights decisions that so angered conservatives some wanted to impeach him. Appointed by Republican President Dwight Eisenhower, who later regretted his choice, Warren was initially known for favoring the expansion of citizens' rights but also, as governor of California, for accepting the supposed necessity of interning Japanese-Americans during World War II.

Eisenhower had no idea that Warren believed that justice should precede a precise or associated reading of the Constitution. A majority of the court consisted of fellow civil libertarians—William Douglas, Hugo Black, William Brennan, Arthur Goldberg (later replaced by Abe Fortas)—which made the influence of "the Warren Court" possible. The most momentous decision is the one excerpted here, *Brown v. Board of Education of Topeka* (1954), opening up the way for desegregation. Another blow to the established way of doing things was the reapportionment case, *Reynolds v. Sims* (1964), which eliminated traditional districts in all states and ruled that only population could be the basis for appointment. Typically, Warren began with the premise that the democratic norm was equal treatment of individual voters. He then asked what departures from absolute population equality the Constitution would permit. In his dissent, Justice Harlan said, "This view, in a nutshell, is that every major social ill in this country can find its cure in some constitutional principle, and that this Court should take the lead in promoting reform when other branches of government fail to act."

The Warren Court also struck out against unwarranted searches and seizures and self-incrimination, and guaranteed the right to counsel. It dropped the lines between state and federal law for the sake of constitutional rights. The culmination was the famous decision of *Miranda v. Arizona* (1966), which assured that police procedures would not violate the rights of those arrested.

BROWN ET AL. *v.* BOARD OF EDUCATION OF TOPEKA ET AL.

NO. 1.   APPEAL FROM THE UNITED STATES DISTRICT COURT FOR THE DISTRICT OF KANSAS.

Argued December 9, 1952.
Reargued December 8, 1953.
Decided May 17, 1954.

Segregation of white and Negro children in the public schools of a State solely on the basis of race, pursuant to state laws permitting or requiring such segregation, denies to Negro children the equal protection of the laws guaranteed by the Fourteenth Amendment—even though the physical facilities and other "tangible" factors of white and Negro schools may be equal. Pp. 486–496.

(a) The history of the Fourteenth Amendment is inconclusive as to its intended effect on public education. Pp. 489–490.

(b) The question presented in these cases must be determined, not on the basis of conditions existing when the Fourteenth Amendment was adopted, but in the light of the full development of public education and its present place in American life throughout the Nation. Pp. 492–493.

(c) Where a State has undertaken to provide an opportunity for an education in its public schools, such an opportunity is a right which must be made available to all on equal terms. P. 493.

(d) Segregation of children in public schools solely on the basis of race deprives children of the minority group of equal educational opportunities, even though the physical facilities and other "tangible" factors may be equal. Pp. 493–494.

(e) The "separate but equal" doctrine adopted in *Plessy* v. *Ferguson*, 163 U.S. 537, has no place in the field of public education. P. 495.

(f) The cases are restored to the docket for further argument on specified questions relating to the forms of the decrees. Pp. 495–496.

MR. CHIEF JUSTICE WARREN delivered the opinion of the Court.

These cases come to us from the States of Kansas, South Carolina, Virginia, and Delaware. They are premised on different facts and different local conditions, but a common legal question justifies their consideration together in this consolidated opinion.[1]

Isaak, *American Political Thinking.*

[1] In the Kansas case, *Brown* v. *Board of Education,* the plaintiffs are Negro children of elementary school age residing in Topeka. They brought this action in the United States District Court for the District of Kansas to enjoin enforcement of a Kansas statute which permits, but does not require, cities of more than 15,000 population to maintain separate school facilities for Negro and white students. Kan. Gen. Stat. §72–1724 (1949). Pursuant to that authority, the Topeka Board of Education elected to establish segregated elementary schools. Other public schools in the community, however, are operated on a nonsegregated basis. The three-judge District Court, convened under 28 U.S.C. §§2281 and 2284, found that segregation in public education has a detrimental effect upon Negro children, but denied relief on the ground that the Negro and white schools were substantially equal with respect to buildings, transportation, curricula, and educational qualifications of teachers. 98 F. Supp. 797. The case is here on direct appeal under 28 U.S.C. §1253.

    In the South Carolina case, *Briggs* v. *Elliott,* the plaintiffs are Negro children of both elementary and high school age residing in Clarendon County. They brought this action in the United States District Court for the Eastern District of South Carolina to enjoin enforcement of provisions in the state constitution and statutory code which require the segregation of Negroes and whites in public schools. S. C. Const., Art. XI, §7; S. C. Code §5377 (1942). The three-judge District Court, convened under 28 U.S.C. §§2281 and 2284, denied the requested relief. The court found that the Negro schools were inferior to the white schools and ordered the defendants to begin immediately to equalize the facilities. But the court sustained the validity of the contested

In each of the cases, minors of the Negro race, through their legal representatives, seek the aid of the courts in obtaining admission to the public schools of their community on a nonsegregated basis. In each instance, they had been denied admission to schools attended by white children under laws requiring or permitting segregation according to race. This segregation was alleged to deprive the plaintiffs of the equal protection of the laws under the Fourteenth Amendment. In each of the cases other than the Delaware case, a three-judge federal district court denied relief to the plaintiffs on the so-called "separate but equal" doctrine announced by this Court in *Plessy* v. *Ferguson,* 163 U.S. 537. Under that doctrine, equality of treatment is accorded when the races are provided substantially equal facilities, even though these facilities be separate. In the Delaware case, the Supreme Court of Delaware adhered to that doctrine, but ordered that the plaintiffs be admitted to the white schools because of their superiority to the Negro schools.

The plaintiffs contend that segregated public schools are not "equal" and cannot be made "equal," and that hence they are deprived of the equal protection of the laws. Because of the obvious importance of the question presented, the Court took jurisdiction.[2] Argument was heard in the 1952 Term, and reargument was heard this Term on certain questions propounded by the Court.[3]

Reargument was largely devoted to the circumstances surrounding the adoption of the Fourteenth Amendment in 1868. It covered exhaustively consideration of the Amendment in Congress, ratification by the states, then existing practices in racial segregation, and the views of proponents and opponents of the Amendment. This discussion and our own investigation con-

provisions and denied the plaintiffs admission to the white schools during the equalization program. 98 F. Supp. 529. This Court vacated the District Court's judgment and remanded the case for the purpose of obtaining the court's views on a report filed by the defendants concerning the progress made in the equalization program. 342 U.S. 350. On remand, the District Court found that substantial equality had been achieved except for buildings and that the defendants were proceeding to rectify this inequality as well. 103 F. Supp. 920. The case is again here on direct appeal under 28 U.S.C. §1253.

In the Virginia case, *Davis* v. *County School Board,* the plaintiffs are Negro children of high school age residing in Prince Edward County. They brought this action in the United States District Court for the Eastern District of Virginia to enjoin enforcement of provisions in the state constitution and statutory code which require the segregation of Negroes and whites in public schools. Va. Const., §140; Va. Code §22–221 (1950). The three-judge District Court, convened under 28 U.S.C. §§2281 and 2284, denied the requested relief. The court found the Negro school inferior in physical plant, curricula, and transportation, and ordered the defendants forthwith to provide substantially equal curricula and transportation and to "proceed with all reasonable diligence and dispatch to remove" the inequality in physical plant. But, as in the South Carolina case, the court sustained the validity of the contested provisions and denied the plaintiffs admission to the white schools during the equalization program. 103 F. Supp. 337. The case is here on direct appeal under 28 U.S.C. §1253.

In the Delaware case, *Gebhart* v. *Belton,* the plaintiffs are Negro children of both elementary and high school age residing in New Castle County. They brought this action in the Delaware Court of Chancery to enjoin enforcement of provisions in the state constitution and statutory code which require the segregation of Negroes and whites in public schools. Del. Const., Art. X, §2; Del. Rev. Code §2631 (1935). The Chancellor gave judgment for the plaintiffs and ordered their immediate admission to schools previously attended only by white children, on the ground that the Negro schools were inferior with respect to teacher training, pupil-teacher ratio, extracurricular activities, physical plant, and time and distance involved in travel. 87 A. 2d 862. The Chancellor also found that segregation itself results in an inferior education for Negro children (see note 10, *infra*), but did not rest his decision on that ground. *Id.,* at 865. The Chancellor's decree was affirmed by the Supreme Court of Delaware, which intimated, however, that the defendants might be able to obtain a modification of the decree after equalization of the Negro and white schools had been accomplished. 91 A. 2d 137, 152. The defendants, contending only that the Delaware courts had erred in ordering the immediate admission of the Negro plaintiffs to the white schools, applied to this Court for certiorari. The writ was granted, 344 U.S. 891. The plaintiffs, who were successful below, did not submit a cross-petition.

[2]344 U.S. 1, 141, 891.

[3]345 U.S. 972. The Attorney General of the United States participated both Terms as *amicus curiae.*

vince us that, although these sources cast some light, it is not enough to resolve the problem with which we are faced. At best, they are inconclusive. The most avid proponents of the post-War Amendments undoubtedly intended them to remove all legal distinctions among "all persons born or naturalized in the United States." Their opponents, just as certainly, were antagonistic to both the letter and the spirit of the Amendments and wished them to have the most limited effect. What others in Congress and the state legislatures had in mind cannot be determined with any degree of certainty.

An additional reason for the inconclusive nature of the Amendment's history, with respect to segregated schools, is the status of public education at that time.[4] In the South, the movement toward free common schools, supported by general taxation, had not yet taken hold. Education of white children was largely in the hands of private groups. Education of Negroes was almost nonexistent, and practically all of the race were illiterate. In fact, any education of Negroes was forbidden by law in some states. Today, in contrast, many Negroes have achieved outstanding success in the arts and sciences as well as in the business and professional world. It is true that public school education at the time of the Amendment had advanced further in the North, but the effect of the Amendment on Northern States was generally ignored in the congressional debates. Even in the North, the conditions of public education did not approximate those existing today. The curriculum was usually rudimentary; ungraded schools were common in rural areas; the school term was but three months a year in many states; and compulsory school attendance was virtually unknown. As a consequence, it is not surprising that there should be so little in the history of the Fourteenth Amendment relating to its intended effect on public education.

In the first cases in this Court construing the Fourteenth Amendment, decided shortly after its adoption, the Court interpreted it as proscribing all state-imposed discriminations against the Negro race.[5]

---

[4]For a general study of the development of public education prior to the Amendment, see Butts and Cremin, A History of Education in American Culture (1953), Pts. I, II; Cubberley, Public Education in the United States (1934 ed.), cc. II–XII. School practices current at the time of the adoption of the Fourteenth Amendment are described in Butts and Cremin, *supra,* at 269–275; Cubberley, *supra,* at 288–339, 408–431; Knight, Public Education in the South (1922), cc. VIII, IX. See also H. Ex. Doc. No. 315, 41st Cong., 2d Sess. (1871). Although the demand for free public schools followed substantially the same pattern in both the North and the South, the development in the South did not begin to gain momentum until about 1850, some twenty years after that in the North. The reasons for the somewhat slower development in the South (*e.g.,* the rural character of the South and the different regional attitudes toward state assistance) are well explained in Cubberley, *supra,* at 408–423. In the country as a whole, but particularly in the South, the War virtually stopped all progress in public education. *Id.,* at 427–428. The low status of Negro education in all sections of the country, both before and immediately after the War, is described in Beale, A History of Freedom of Teaching in American Schools (1941), 112–132, 175–95. Compulsory school attendance laws were not generally adopted until after the ratification of the Fourteenth Amendment, and it was not until 1918 that such laws were in force in all the states. Cubberley, *supra,* at 563–565.

[5]*Slaughter-House Cases,* 16 Wall. 36, 67–72 (1873); *Strauder* v. *West Virginia,* 100 U.S. 303, 307–308 (1880): "It ordains that no State shall deprive any person of life, liberty, or property, without due process of law, or deny to any person within its jurisdiction the equal protection of the laws. What is this but declaring that the law in the States shall be the same for the black as for the white; that all persons, whether colored or white, shall stand equal before the laws of the States, and, in regard to the colored race, for whose protection the amendment was primarily designed, that no discrimination shall be made against them by law because of their color? The words of the amendment, it is true, are prohibitory, but they contain a necessary implication of a positive immunity, or right, most valuable to the colored race,—the right to exemption from unfriendly legislation against them distinctively as colored,—exemption from legal discriminations, implying inferiority in civil society, lessening the security of their enjoyment of the rights which others enjoy, and discriminations which are steps towards reducing them to the conditions of a subject race."
See also *Virginia* v. *Rives,* 100 U.S. 313, 318 (1880); *Ex parte Virginia,* 100 U.S. 339, 344–345 (1880).

The doctrine of "separate but equal" did not make its appearance in this Court until 1896 in the case of *Plessy* v. *Ferguson, supra,* involving not education but transportation.[6] American courts have since labored with the doctrine for over half a century. In this Court, there have been six cases involving the "separate but equal" doctrine in the field of public education.[7] In *Cumming* v. *County Board of Education,* 175 U.S. 528, and *Gong Lum* v. *Rice,* 275 U.S. 78, the validity of the doctrine itself was not challenged.[8] In more recent cases, all on the graduate school level, inequality was found in that specific benefits enjoyed by white students were denied to Negro students of the same educational qualifications. *Missouri ex rel. Gaines* v. *Canada,* 305 U.S. 337; *Sipuel* v. *Oklahoma,* 332 U.S. 631; *Sweatt* v. *Painter,* 339 U.S. 629; *McLaurin* v. *Oklahoma State Regents,* 339 U.S. 637. In none of these cases was it necessary to re-examine the doctrine to grant relief to the Negro plaintiff. And in *Sweatt* v. *Painter, supra,* the Court expressly reserved decision on the question whether *Plessy* v. *Ferguson* should be held inapplicable to public education.

In the instant cases, that question is directly presented. Here, unlike *Sweatt* v. *Painter,* there are findings below that the Negro and white schools involved have been equalized, or are being equalized, with respect to buildings, curricula, qualifications and salaries of teachers, and other "tangible" factors.[9] Our decision, therefore, cannot turn on merely a comparison of these tangible factors in the Negro and white schools involved in each of the cases. We must look instead to the effect of segregation itself on public education.

In approaching this problem, we cannot turn the clock back to 1868 when the Amendment was adopted, or even to 1896 when *Plessy* v. *Ferguson* was written. We must consider public education in the light of its full development and its present place in American life throughout the Nation. Only in this way can it be determined if segregation in public schools deprives these plaintiffs of the equal protection of the laws.

Today, education is perhaps the most important function of state and local governments. Compulsory school attendance laws and the great expenditures for education both demonstrate our recognition of the importance of education to our democratic society. It is required in the performance of our most basic public responsibilities, even service in the armed forces. It is the very foundation of good citizenship. Today it is a principal instrument in awakening the child to cultural

---

[6]The doctrine apparently originated in *Roberts* v. *City of Boston,* 59 Mass. 198, 206 (1850), upholding school segregation against attack as being violative of a state constitutional guarantee of equality. Segregation in Boston public schools was eliminated in 1855. Mass. Acts 1855, c. 256. But elsewhere in the North segregation in public education has persisted in some communities until recent years. It is apparent that such segregation has long been a nationwide problem, not merely one of sectional concern.

[7]See also *Berea College* v. *Kentucky,* 211 U.S. 45 (1908).

[8]In the *Cumming* case, Negro taxpayers sought an injunction requiring the defendant school board to discontinue the operation of a high school for white children until the board resumed operation of a high school for Negro children. Similarly, in the *Gong Lum* case, the plaintiff, a child of Chinese descent, contended only that state authorities had misapplied the doctrine by classifying him with Negro children and requiring him to attend a Negro school.

[9]In the Kansas case, the court below found substantial equality as to all such factors. 98 F. Supp. 797, 798. In the South Carolina case, the court below found that the defendants were proceeding "promptly and in good faith to comply with the court's decree." 103 F. Supp. 920, 921. In the Virginia case, the court below noted that the equalization program was already "afoot and progressing" (103 F. Supp. 337, 341); since then, we have been advised, in the Virginia Attorney General's brief on reargument, that the program has now been completed. In the Delaware case, the court below similarly noted that the state's equalization program was well under way. 91 A. 2d 137, 149.

values, in preparing him for later professional training, and in helping him to adjust normally to his environment. In these days, it is doubtful that any child may reasonably be expected to succeed in life if he is denied the opportunity of an education. Such an opportunity, where the state has undertaken to provide it, is a right which must be made available to all on equal terms.

We come then to the question presented: Does segregation of children in public schools solely on the basis of race, even though the physical facilities and other "tangible" factors may be equal, deprive the children of the minority group of equal educational opportunities? We believe that it does.

In *Sweatt* v. *Painter, supra,* in finding that a segregated law school for Negroes could not provide them equal educational opportunities, this Court relied in large part on "those qualities which are incapable of objective measurement but which make for greatness in a law school." In *McLaurin* v. *Oklahoma State Regents, supra,* the Court, in requiring that a Negro admitted to a white graduate school be treated like all other students, again resorted to intangible considerations: ". . . his ability to study, to engage in discussions and exchange views with other students, and, in general, to learn his profession." Such considerations apply with added force to children in grade and high schools. To separate them from others of similar age and qualifications solely because of their race generates a feeling of inferiority as to their status in the commu-

nity that may affect their hearts and minds in a way unlikely ever to be undone. The effect of this separation on their educational opportunities was well stated by a finding in the Kansas case by a court which nevertheless felt compelled to rule against the Negro plaintiffs:

> "Segregation of white and colored children in public schools has a detrimental effect upon the colored children. The impact is greater when it has the sanction of the law; for the policy of separating the races is usually interpreted as denoting the inferiority of the negro group. A sense of inferiority affects the motivation of a child to learn. Segregation with the sanction of law, therefore, has a tendency to [retard] the educational and mental development of negro children and to deprive them of some of the benefits they would receive in a racial[ly] integrated school system."[10]

Whatever may have been the extent of psychological knowledge at the time of *Plessy* v. *Ferguson,* this finding is amply supported by modern authority.[11] Any language in *Plessy* v. *Ferguson* contrary to this finding is rejected.

We conclude that in the field of public education the doctrine of "separate but equal" has no place. Separate educational facilities are inherently unequal. Therefore, we hold that the plaintiffs and others similarly situated for whom the actions have been brought are, by reason of the segregation complained of, deprived of the equal protection of the laws guaranteed by the

---

[10]A similar finding was made in the Delaware case: "I conclude from the testimony that in our Delaware society, State-imposed segregation in education itself results in the Negro children, as a class, receiving educational opportunities which are substantially inferior to those available to white children otherwise similarly situated." 87 A. 2d 862, 865.

[11]K. B. Clark, Effect of Prejudice and Discrimination on Personality Development (Midcentury White House Conference on Children and Youth, 1950); Witmer and Kotinsky, Personality in the Making (1952), c. VI; Deutscher and Chein, The Psychological Effects of Enforced Segregation: A Survey of Social Science Opinion, 26 J. Psychol. 259 (1948); Chein, What are the Psychological Effects of Segregation Under Conditions of Equal Facilities?, 3 Int. J. Opinion and Attitude Res. 229 (1949); Brameld, Educational Costs, in Discrimination and National Welfare (MacIver, ed., 1949), 44–48; Frazier, The Negro in the United States (1949), 674–681. And see generally Myrdal, An American Dilemma (1944).

Fourteenth Amendment. This disposition makes unnecessary any discussion whether such segregation also violates the Due Process Clause of the Fourteenth Amendment.[12]

Because these are class actions, because of the wide applicability of this decision, and because of the great variety of local conditions, the formulation of decrees in these cases presents problems of considerable complexity. On reargument, the consideration of appropriate relief was necessarily subordinated to the primary question—the constitutionality of segregation in public education. We have now announced that such segregation is a denial of the equal protection of the laws.

In order that we may have the full assistance of the parties in formulating decrees, the cases will be restored to the docket, and the parties are requested to present further argument on Questions 4 and 5 previously propounded by the Court for the reargument this Term.[13] The Attorney General of the United States is again invited to participate. The Attorneys General of the states requiring or permitting segregation in public education will also be permitted to appear as *amici curiae* upon request to do so by September 15, 1954, and submission of briefs by October 1, 1954.[14]

It is so ordered.

---

[12]See *Bolling* v. *Sharpe, post,* p. 497, concerning the Due Process Clause of the Fifth Amendment.

[13] "4. Assuming it is decided that segregation in public schools violates the Fourteenth Amendment

"(*a*) would a decree necessarily follow providing that, within the limits set by normal geographic school districting, Negro children should forthwith be admitted to schools of their choice, or

"(*b*) may this Court, in the exercise of its equity powers, permit an effective gradual adjustment to be brought about from existing segregated systems to a system not based on color distinctions?

"5. On the assumption on which questions 4 (*a*) and (*b*) are based, and assuming further that this Court will exercise its equity powers to the end described in question 4 (*b*),

"(*a*) should this Court formulate detailed decrees in these cases;

"(*b*) if so, what specific issues should the decrees reach;

"(*c*) should this Court appoint a special master to hear evidence with a view to recommending specific terms for such decrees;

"(*d*) should this Court remand to the courts of first instance with directions to frame decrees in these cases, and if so what general directions should the decrees of this Court include and what procedures should the courts of first instance follow in arriving at the specific terms of more detailed decrees?"

[14]See Rule 42, Revised Rules of this Court (effective July 1, 1954).

Walter Lippmann

Walter Lippmann was the dean of twentieth-century American newspapermen, known for his objective biweekly column even more than for his numerous books on political philosophy. Born in 1889 in New York City, Lippmann was reared in a German-Jewish family. He later left Judaism for a classical Christian heritage.

Lippmann's orderly life reinforced his brilliance as a student. He picked up academic honors wherever he studied and completed his B.A. requirements *cum laude* in three years at Harvard. There he met his hero, William James, and assisted George Santayana in a course on the history of philosophy. Becoming head of the Harvard Socialist Club, he picked up the social reform concerns of the Fabian Socialists. He later became disenchanted with them and adopted a conservative, nonpartisan philosophy of liberalism. This shift was evident in his books: *A Preface to Politics* (1913), which accepted socialism with qualifications and was well received by liberals; *Drift and Mastery* (1914), which was increasingly critical of socialism and Marxism; and *The Good Society* (1937), where socialism and "free collectivism" are rejected, and liberalism is promoted as the opponent of all practices—industry or labor—that block the free movement of the market economy. In 1914 Herbert Croly asked Lippmann to help him found the progressive *New Republic*. Lippmann served as an assistant to the secretary of war in Woodrow Wilson's World War I administration and later did research for Edward ("Colonel") House for use at the peace conference. Thereafter, he returned to journalism and political philosophy, writing for *The New Republic*, the New York *World* and then the New York *Herald Tribune* until he died in 1974.

☙❦❧

Public Philosophy (1955)
(excerpt)

The Public Interest

1. What Is the Public Interest?

We are examining the question of how and by whom, the interest of an invisible community over a long span of time is represented in the practical work of governing a modern state.

In ordinary circumstances voters cannot be expected to transcend their particular, localized and self-regarding opinions. As well expect men laboring in the valley to see the land as from a mountain top. In their circumstances, which as private persons they cannot readily surmount, the voters are most likely to suppose that whatever seems obviously good to them must be good for the country, and good in the sight of God.

I am far from implying that the voters are not entitled to the representation of their particular opinions and interests. But their opinions and interests should be taken for what they are and no more. They are not— as such—propositions in the public interest. Beyond their being, if they are genuine, a true report of what various groups of voters are thinking, they have no intrinsic authority. The Gallup polls are reports of what people are thinking. But that a plurality of the people sampled in the poll think one way has no bearing upon whether it is sound public policy. For their opportunities of judging great issues are in the very nature of things limited, and the statistical sum of their opinions is not the final verdict on an issue. It is, rather, the beginning of the argument. In that argument their opinions need to be confronted by the views of the executive, defending and promoting the public interest. In the accommodation reached between the two views lies practical public policy.

Let us ask ourselves, How is the public interest discerned and judged? From what we have been saying we know that we cannot answer the question by attempting to forecast what the invisible community, with all its unborn constituents, will, would, or might say if and when it ever had a chance to vote. There is no point in toying with any notion of an imaginary plebiscite to discover the public interest. We cannot know what we ourselves will be thinking five years hence, much less what infants now in the cradle will be thinking when they go into the polling booth.

Yet their interests, as we observe them today, are within the public interest. Living adults share, we must believe, the same public interest. For them, however, the public interest is mixed with, and is often at odds with, the private and special interests. Put this way, we can say, I suggest, that the public interest may be presumed to be what men would choose if they saw clearly, thought rationally, acted disinterestedly and benevolently.

2. The Equations of Reality

A rational man acting in the real world may be defined as one who decides where he will strike a balance between what he desires and what can be done. It is only in imaginary worlds that we can do whatever we wish. In the real world there are always equations which have to be adjusted between the possible and the desired. Within limits, a man can make a free choice as to where he will strike the balance. If he makes his living by doing piece work, he can choose to work harder and to spend more. He can also choose to work less and to spend less. But he cannot spend more and work less.

Reality confronts us in practical affairs as a long and intricate series of equations. What we are likely to call "facts of life" are the accounts, the budgets, the orders of battle, the election returns. Sometimes, but not always, the two sides of the equations can be expressed quantitatively in terms of money, as supply and demand, as income and outgo, assets and liabilities, as exports and imports. Valid choices are limited to the question of where, not whether, the opposing terms of the equation are to be brought into equilibrium. For there is always a reckoning.

In public life, for example, the budget may be balanced by reducing expenditures to the revenue from taxes; by raising taxes to meet the expenditures, or by a combination of the two, by borrowing, or by grants in aid from other governments, or by fiat credit, or by a combination of them. In one way or another the budget is in fact always balanced. The true nature of the reckoning would be clearer if, instead of talking about "an unbalanced budget," we spoke of a budget balanced not by taxes but by borrowing, of a budget balanced by inflation, or of a budget balanced by subsidy. A government which cannot raise enough money by taxes, loans, foreign grants, or by getting its fiat money accepted, will be unable to meet its bills and to pay the salaries of its employees. In bankruptcy an involuntary balance is struck for the bankrupt. He is forced to balance his accounts by reducing his expenditures to the level of his income.

Within limits, which public men have to bear in mind, the choices as to where to balance the budget are open. In making these choices, new equations confront them. Granted that it is possible to bring the budget into balance by raising taxes, how far can taxes be raised? Somewhat but not ad infinitum. There are no fixed criteria. But though we are unable to express all the equations quantitatively, this does not relieve us of the necessity of balancing the equations. There will be a reckoning. Practical judgment requires an informed guess: what will the taxpayers accept readily, what will they accept with grumbling but with no worse, what will arouse them to resistance and to evasion? How will the taxpayers react to the different levels of taxes if it is a time of peace, a time of war, a time of cold war, a time of social and economic disturbance, and so on? Although the various propositions cannot be reduced to precise figures, prudent men make estimates as to where the equations balance.

Their decisions as to where to balance the accounts must reflect other judgments—as to what, for example, are the military requirements in relation to foreign affairs; what is the phase of the business cycle in relation to the needs for increased or decreased demand; what is the condition of the international monetary accounts; which are the necessary public works and welfare measures, and which are those that are desirable but not indispensable. Each of these judgements is itself the peak of a pyramid of equations: whether, for example, to enlarge or to reduce the national commitments at this or that point in the world—given the effect of the decision at other points in the world.

We may say, then, that public policy is made in a field of equations. The issues are the choices as to where the balance is to be struck. In the reality of things X will exact an equivalence of Y. Within the limits which the specific nature of the case permits—limits which have to be estimated—a balance has to be reached by adding to or subtracting from the terms of the equation.

Oftener than not, the two sides of the equation differ in that the one is, as compared with the other, the pleasanter, the more agreeable, the more popular. In general the softer and easier side reflects what we desire and the harder reflects what is needed in order to satisfy the desire. Now the momentous equations of war and peace, of solvency, of security and of order, always have a harder or a softer, a pleasanter or a more painful, a popular or an unpopular option. It is easier to obtain votes for appropriations than it is for taxes, to facilitate consumption than to stimulate production, to protect a market than to open it, to inflate than to deflate, to borrow than to save, to demand than to compromise, to be intransigent than to negotiate, to threaten war than to prepare for it.

Faced with these choices between the hard and the soft, the normal propensity of democratic governments is to please the largest number of voters. The pressure of the electorate is normally for the soft side of the equations. That is why governments are unable to cope with reality when elected assemblies and mass opinions become decisive in the state, when there are no statesmen to resist the inclination of the voters and there are only politicians to excite and to exploit them.

There is then a general tendency to be drawn downward, as by the force of gravity, towards insolvency, towards the insecurity of factionalism, towards the erosion of liberty, and towards hyperbolic wars.

John F. Kennedy

John Fitzgerald Kennedy became the youngest elected president in 1960 and the first Roman Catholic president. His assassination three years after his election raised his status to the mythical, although in many ways he had only begun to touch on his solutions to political problems and did not succeed in getting as much legislation through Congress as several presidents have since.

Born into a wealthy, closely competitive family in 1917 in Brookline, Massachusetts, Kennedy was reared for public service. He received a trust fund of one million dollars when he reached maturity. After briefly studying under Harold Laski at the London School of Economics, Kennedy graduated with a B.S. *cum laude* from Harvard. During a six-months leave from college, he visited his father, then ambassador to Great Britain, in London. There he wrote his thesis on England's preparedness for war. The thesis was expanded into the book *Why England Slept* (1940). Kennedy studied business briefly at Stanford and made a trip through South America. During World War II, he served in the navy, commanding a boat that was torpedoed by the Japanese. He saved several of his crewmen. After the war, he worked as a newspaper reporter covering European news and the United Nations Conference on International Organization in San Francisco.

In 1946 Kennedy was elected as a Democrat to the House of Representatives in Massachusetts, running as independently as possible of political bosses. After serving three terms, he defeated Henry Cabot Lodge in a race for the Senate in 1952, where he served eight years. While in the hospital for a back operation, Kennedy wrote *Profiles in Courage* (1956), which won the Pulitzer Prize in biography. Winning the closest election since 1916 against Republican Richard Nixon, Kennedy became the thirty-fifth U.S. president and gave the inaugural address printed here in 1961. It focuses largely upon the U.S. position in the cold war confrontation with the Soviet Union and the need to make private sacrifices for the public interest.

Inaugural Address

January 20, 1961

Vice-President Johnson, Mr. Speaker, Mr. Chief Justice, President Eisenhower, Vice-President Nixon, President Truman, Reverend Clergy, Fellow Citizens:

We observe today not a victory of party but a celebration of freedom—symbolizing an end as well as a beginning—signifying renewal as well as change. For I have sworn before you and Almighty God the same solemn oath our forebearers prescribed nearly a century and three-quarters ago.

The world is very different now. For man holds in his mortal hands the power to abolish all forms of human poverty and all forms of human life. And yet the same revolutionary beliefs for which our fore-bearers fought are still at issue around the globe—the belief that the rights of man come not from the generosity of the state but from the hand of God.

We dare not forget today that we are the heirs of that first revolution. Let the word go forth from this time and place, to friend and foe alike, that the torch has been passed to a new generation of Americans—born in this century, tempered by war, dis-ciplined by a hard and bitter peace, proud of our ancient heritage—and unwilling to witness or permit the slow undoing of those human rights to which this nation has always been committed, and to which we are committed today at home and around the world.

Let every nation know, whether it wishes us well or ill, that we shall pay any price, bear any burden, meet any hardship, support any friend, oppose any foe to to assure the survival and the success of lib-erty.

This much we pledge—and more.

To those old allies whose cultural and spiritual origins we share, we pledge the loyalty of faithful friends. United, there is little we cannot do in a host of co-operative ventures. Divided, there is little we can do—for we dare not meet a powerful chal-lenge at odds and split asunder.

To those new states whom we wel-come to the ranks of the free, we pledge our word that one form of colonial control shall not have passed away merely to be replaced by a far more iron tyranny. We shall not always expect to find them sup-porting our view. But we shall always hope to find them strongly supporting their own freedom— and to remember that, in the past, those who foolishly sought power by riding the back of the tiger ended up inside.

To those people in the huts and villages of half the globe struggling to break the bonds of mass misery, we pledge our best efforts to help them help themselves, for

whatever period is required—not because the Communists may be doing it, not because we seek their votes, but because it is right. If a free society cannot help the many who are poor, it cannot save the few who are rich.

To our sister republics south of our border, we offer a special pledge—to con-vert our good words into good deeds—in a new alliance for progress—to assist free men and free governments in casting off the chains of poverty. But this peaceful revolution of hope cannot become the prey of hostile powers. Let all our neighbors know that we shall join with them to oppose aggression or subversion anywhere in the Americas. And let every other power know that this hemisphere intends to remain the master of its own house.

To that world assembly of sovereign states, the United Nations, our last best hope in an age where the instruments of war have far outpaced the instruments of peace, we renew our pledge of support—to prevent it from becoming merely a forum for invective—to strengthen its shield of the new and the weak—to enlarge the area in which its writ may run.

Finally, to those nations who would make themselves our adversary, we offer not a pledge but a request: that both sides begin anew the quest for peace, before the dark powers of destruction unleashed by science engulf all humanity in planned or accidental self-destruction.

We dare not tempt them with weak-ness. For only when our arms are sufficient beyond doubt can we be certain beyond doubt that they will never be employed.

But neither can two great and powerful groups of nations take comfort from our present course—both sides overburdened by the cost of modern weapons, both rightly alarmed by the steady spread of the deadly atom, yet both racing to alter that uncertain balance of terror that stays the hand of mankind's final war.

So let us begin anew—remembering on both sides that civility is not a sign of weakness, and sincerity is always subject to proof. Let us never negotiate out of fear. But let us never fear to negotiate.

Let both sides explore what problems unite us instead of belaboring those problems which divide us.

Let both sides, for the first time, formulate serious and precise proposals for the inspection and control of arms—and bring the absolute power to destroy other nations under the absolute control of all nations.

Let both sides seek to invoke the wonders of science instead of its terrors. Together let us explore the stars, conquer the deserts, eradicate disease, tap the ocean depths, and encourage the arts and commerce.

Let both sides unite to heed in all corners of the earth the command of Isaiah— to "undo the heavy burdens . . . [and] let the oppressed go free."

And if a beachhead of co-operation may push back the jungle of suspicion, let both sides join in creating a new endeavor, not a new balance of power, but a new world of law, where the strong are just and the weak secure and the peace preserved.

All this will not be finished in the first one hundred days. Nor will it be finished in the first one thousand days, nor in the life of this administration, nor even perhaps in our lifetime on this planet. But let us begin.

In your hands, my fellow citizens, more than mine, will rest the final success or failure of our course. Since this country was founded, each generation of Americans has been summoned to give testimony to its national loyalty. The graves of young Americans who answered the call to service surround the globe.

Now the trumpet summons us again— not as a call to bear arms, though arms we need—not as a call to battle, though embattled we are—but a call to hear the burden of a long twilight struggle, year in and year out, "rejoicing in hope, patient in tribulation"—a struggle against the common enemies of man: tyranny, poverty, disease, and war itself.

Can we forge against these enemies a grand and global alliance, North and South, East and West, that can assure a more fruitful life for all mankind? Will you join in that historic effort?

In the long history of the world, only a few generations have been granted the role of defending freedom in its hour of maximum danger. I do not shrink from this responsibility—I welcome it, I do not believe that any of us would exchange places with any other people or any other generation. The energy, the faith, the devotion which we bring to this endeavor will light our country and all who serve it— and the glow from that fire can truly light the world.

And so, my fellow Americans, ask not what your country can do for you—ask what you can do for your country.

My fellow citizens of the world: ask not what America will do for you, but what together we can do for the freedom of man.

Finally, whether you are citizens of America or citizens of the world, ask of us here the same high standards of strength and sacrifice which we ask of you. With a good conscience our only sure reward, with history the final judge of our deeds, let us go forth to lead the land we love, asking His blessing and His help, but knowing that here on earth God's work must truly be our own.

Milton Friedman

Milton Friedman became perhaps the most influential American spokesman for unregulated, free-market capitalism in the United States. Born in 1912 in Brooklyn, New York, Friedman received his B.A. from Rutgers University and his Ph.D. from Columbia University. In his early years he worked for the National Resources Commission (1935–37), the National Bureau of Economic Research (1937–45), and the U.S. Treasury Department (1941–43). As a professor of economics at the University of Chicago (1946–82), he became well known as a monetarist through his clear writing and speaking. He argued that the money supply determines economic behavior. He served on President Reagan's Economic Policy Advisory Board from 1981–88. Among numerous books, perhaps his most important political work is *Capitalism and Freedom* (1962), an influential defense of modern laissez-faire liberalism, from which the following excerpts are taken.

Capitalism and Freedom (1962)
(excerpts)

The Relation between Economic Freedom and Political Freedom

It is widely believed that politics and economics are separate and largely unconnected; that individual freedom is a political problem and material welfare an economic problem; and that any kind of political arrangements can be combined with any kind of economic arrangements. The chief contemporary manifestation of this idea is the advocacy of "democratic socialism" by many who condemn out of hand the restrictions on individual freedom imposed by "totalitarian socialism" in Russia, and who are persuaded that it is possible for a country to adopt the essential features of Russian economic arrangements and yet to ensure individual freedom through political arrangements. The thesis of this chapter is that such a view is a delusion, that there is an intimate connection between economics and politics, that only certain combinations of political and economic arrangements are possible, and that in particular, a society which is socialist cannot also be democratic, in the sense of guaranteeing individual freedom.

Economic arrangements play a dual role in the promotion of a free society. On the one hand, freedom in economic arrangements is itself a component of freedom broadly understood, so economic freedom is an end in itself. In the second place, economic freedom is also an indispensable means toward the achievement of political freedom.

The first of these roles of economic freedom needs special emphasis because intellectuals in particular have a strong bias against regarding this aspect of freedom as important. They tend to express contempt for what they regard as material aspects of life, and to regard their own pursuit of allegedly higher values as on a different plane of significance and as deserving of special attention. For most citizens of the country, however, if not for the intellectual, the direct importance of economic freedom is at least comparable in significance to the indirect importance of economic freedom as a means to political freedom.

The citizen of Great Britain, who after World War II was not permitted to spend his vacation in the United States because of exchange control, was being deprived of an essential freedom no less than the citizen of the United states, who was denied the opportunity to spend his vacation in Russia because of his political views. The one was ostensibly an economic limitation on freedom and the other a political limitation, yet there is no essential difference between the two.

The citizen of the United States who is compelled by law to devote something like 10 per cent of his income to the purchase of a particular kind of retirement contract, administered by the government, is being deprived of a corresponding part of his personal freedom. How strongly this deprivation may be felt and its closeness to the deprivation of religious freedom, which all would regard as "civil" or "political" rather than "economic", were dramatized by an episode involving a group of farmers of the Amish sect. On grounds of principle, this group regarded compulsory federal old age programs as an infringement of their personal individual freedom and refused to pay taxes or accept benefits. As a result, some of their livestock were sold by auction in order to satisfy some claims for social security levies. True, the number of citizens who regard compulsory old age insurance as a deprivation of freedom may be few, but the believer in freedom has never counted noses.

A citizen of the United States who under the laws of various states is not free to follow the occupation of his own choosing unless he can get a license for it, is likewise being deprived of an essential part of his freedom. So is the man who would like to exchange some of his goods with, say, a Swiss for a watch but is prevented from doing so by a quota. So also is the Californian who was thrown into jail for selling Alka Seltzer at a price below that set by the manufacturer under so-called "fair trade" laws. So also is the farmer who cannot grow the amount of wheat he wants. And so on. Clearly, economic freedom, in and of itself, is an extremely important part of total freedom.

Viewed as a means to the end of political freedom, economic arrangements are important because of their effect on the concentration or dispersion of power. The kind of economic organization that provides economic freedom directly, namely, competitive capitalism, also promotes political freedom because it separates economic power from political power and in this way enables the one to offset the other.

Historical evidence speaks with a single voice on the relation between political freedom and a free market. I know of no example in time or place of a society that has been marked by a large measure of political freedom, and that has not also used something comparable to a free market to organize the bulk of economic activity.

Because we live in a largely free society, we tend to forget how limited is the span of time and the part of the globe for which there has ever been anything like political freedom: the typical state of mankind is tyranny, servitude, and misery. The nineteenth century and early twentieth century in the Western world stand out as striking exceptions to the general trend of historical development. Political freedom in this instance clearly came along with the free market and the development of capitalist institutions. So also did political freedom in the golden age of Greece and in the early days of the Roman era.

History suggests only that capitalism is a necessary condition for political freedom. Clearly it is not a sufficient condition. Fascist Italy and Fascist Spain, Germany at various times in the last seventy years, Japan before World Wars I and II, tzarist Russia in the decades before World War I—are all societies that cannot conceivably be described as politically free. Yet, in each, private enterprise was the dominant form of economic organization. It is therefore clearly possible to have economic arrangements that are fundamentally capitalist and political arrangements that are not free.

Even in those societies, the citizenry had a good deal more freedom than citizens of a modern totalitarian state like Russia or Nazi Germany, in which economic totalitarianism is combined with political totalitarianism. Even in Russia under the Tzars, it was possible for some citizens, under some circumstances, to change their jobs without getting permission from political authority because capitalism and the existence of private property provided some check to the centralized power of the state.

The relation between political and economic freedom is complex and by no means unilateral. In the early nineteenth century, Bentham and the Philosophical Radicals were inclined to regard political freedom as a means to economic freedom. They believed that the masses were being hampered by the restrictions that were being imposed upon them, and that if political reform gave the bulk of the people the vote, they would do what was good for them, which was to vote for laissez faire. In retrospect, one cannot say that they were

wrong. There was a large measure of political reform that was accompanied by economic reform in the direction of a great deal of laissez faire. An enormous increase in the well-being of the masses followed this change in economic arrangements.

The triumph of Benthamite liberalism in nineteenth-century England was followed by a reaction toward increasing intervention by government in economic affairs. This tendency to collectivism was greatly accelerated, both in England and elsewhere, by the two World Wars. Welfare rather than freedom became the dominant note in democratic countries. Recognizing the implicit threat to individualism, the intellectual descendants of the Philosophical Radicals—Dicey, Mises, Hayek, and Simmons, to mention only a few—feared that a continued movement toward centralized control of economic activity would prove *The Road to Serfdom*, as Hayek entitled his penetrating analysis of the process. Their emphasis was on economic freedom as a means toward political freedom.

Events since the end of World War II display still a different relation between economic and political freedom. Collectivist economic planning has indeed interfered with individual freedom. At least in some countries, however, the result has not been the suppression of freedom, but the reversal of economic policy. England again provides the most striking example. The turning point was perhaps the "control of engagements" order which, despite great misgivings, the Labour party found it necessary to impose in order to carry out its economic policy. Fully enforced and carried through, the law would have involved centralized allocation of individuals to occupations. This conflicted so sharply with personal liberty that it was enforced in a negligible number of cases, and then repealed after the law had been in effect for only a short period. Its repeal ushered in a decided shift in economic policy, marked by reduced reliance on centralized "plans" and "programs", by the dismantling of many controls, and by increased emphasis on the private market. A similar shift in policy occurred in most other democratic countries.

The proximate explanation of these shifts in policy is the limited success of central planning or its outright failure to achieve stated objectives. However, this failure is itself to be attributed, at least in some measure, to the political implications of central planning and to an unwillingness to follow out its logic when doing so requires trampling rough-shod on treasured private rights. It may well be that the shift is only a temporary interruption in the collectivist trend of this century. Even so, it illustrates the close relation between political freedom and economic arrangements.

Historical evidence by itself can never be convincing. Perhaps it was sheer coincidence that the expansion of freedom occurred at the same time as the development of capitalist and market institutions. Why should there be a connection? What are the logical links between economic and political freedom? In discussing these questions we shall consider first the market as a direct component of freedom, and then the indirect relation between market arrangements and political freedom. A by-product will be an outline of the ideal economic arrangements for a free society.

As liberals, we take freedom of the individual, or perhaps the family, as our ultimate goal in judging social arrangements. Freedom as a value in this sense has to do with the interrelations among people; it has no meaning whatsoever to a Robinson Crusoe on an isolated island (without his Man Friday). Robinson Crusoe on his island is subject to "constraint," he has limited "power," and he has only a limited number of alternatives, but there is no problem of freedom in the sense that is relevant to our discussion. Similarly, in a society freedom has nothing to say about what an individual does with his freedom; it is not an all-embracing ethic. Indeed, a major aim of the liberal is to leave the ethical problem for the individual to wrestle with. The "really" important ethical problems are those that face an individual in a free society—what he should do with his freedom. There are thus two sets of values that a liberal will emphasize—the values that are relevant to relations among people, which is the context in which he assigns first priority to freedom; and the values that are relevant to the individual in the exercise of his freedom, which is the realm of individual ethics and philosophy.

The liberal conceives of men as imperfect beings. He regards the problem of social organization to be as much a negative problem of preventing "bad" people from doing harm as of enabling "good" people to do good; and, of course, "bad" and "good" people may be the same people, depending on who is judging them.

The basic problem of social organization is how to co-ordinate the economic activities of large numbers of people. Even in relatively backward societies, extensive division of labor and specialization of function is required to make effective use of available resources. In advanced societies, the scale on which co-ordination is needed, to take full advantage of the opportunities offered by modern science and technology, is enormously greater. Literally millions of people are involved in providing one another with their daily bread, let alone with their yearly automobiles. The challenge to the believer in liberty is to reconcile this widespread interdependence with individual freedom.

Fundamentally, there are only two ways of co-ordinating the economic activities of millions. One is central direction involving the use of coercion—the technique of the army and of the modern totalitarian state. The other is voluntary co-operation of individuals—the technique of the market place.

The possibility of co-ordination through voluntary co-operation rests on the elementary—yet frequently denied—proposition that both parties to an economic transaction benefit from it, *provided the transaction is bi-laterally voluntary and informed.*

Exchange can therefore bring about co-ordination without coercion. A working model of a society organized through voluntary exchange is a *free private enterprise exchange economy*—what we have been calling competitive capitalism.

In its simplest form, such a society consists of a number of independent households—a collection of Robinson Crusoes, as it were. Each household uses the resources it controls to produce goods and services that it exchanges for goods and services produced by other households, on terms mutually acceptable to the two parties to the bargain. It is thereby enabled to satisfy its wants indirectly by producing goods for its own immediate use. The incentive for adopting this indirect route is, of course, the increased product made possible by division of labor and specialization of function. Since the household always has the alternative of producing directly for itself, it need not enter into any exchange unless it benefits from it. Hence, no exchange will take place unless both parties do benefit from it. Co-operation is thereby achieved without coercion.

Specialization of function and division of labor would not go far if the ultimate productive unit were the household. In a modern society, we have gone much farther. We have introduced enterprises which are intermediaries between individuals in their capacities as suppliers of service and as purchasers of goods. And similarly, specialization of function and division of labor could not go very far if we had to continue

to rely on the barter of product for product. In consequence, money has been introduced as a means of facilitating exchange, and of enabling the acts of purchase and of sale to be separated into two parts.

Despite the important role of enterprises and of money in our actual economy, and despite the numerous and complex problems they raise, the central characteristic of the market technique of achieving co-ordination is fully displayed in the simple exchange economy that contains neither enterprises nor money. As in that simple model, so in the complex enterprise and money-exchange economy, co-operation is strictly individual and voluntary *provided*: (*a*) that enterprises are private, so that the ultimate contracting parties are individuals and (*b*) that individuals are effectively free to enter or not to enter into any particular exchange, so that every transaction is strictly voluntary.

It is far easier to state these provisos in general terms than to spell them out in detail, or to specify precisely the institutional arrangements most conducive to their maintenance. Indeed, much of technical economic literature is concerned with precisely these questions. The basic requisite is the maintenance of law and order to prevent physical coercion of one individual by another and to enforce contracts voluntarily entered into, thus giving substance to "private". Aside from this, perhaps the most difficult problems arise from monopoly—which inhibits effective freedom by denying individuals alternatives to the particular exchange—and from "neighborhood effects"—effects on third parties for which it is not feasible to charge or recompense them. . . .

So long as effective freedom of exchange is maintained, the central feature of the market organization of economic activity is that it prevents one person from interfering with another in respect of most of his activities. The consumer is protected from coercion by the seller because of the presence of other sellers with whom he can deal. The seller is protected from coercion by the consumer because of other consumers to whom he can sell. The employee is protected from coercion by the employer because of other employers for whom he can work, and so on. And the market does this impersonally and without centralized authority.

Indeed, a major source of objection to a free economy is precisely that it does this task so well. It gives people what they want instead of what a particular group thinks they ought to want. Underlying most arguments against the free market is a lack of belief in freedom itself.

The existence of a free market does not of course eliminate the need for government. On the contrary, government is essential both as a forum for determining the "rules of the game" and as an umpire to interpret and enforce the rules decided on. What the market does is to reduce greatly the range of issues that must be decided through political means, and thereby to minimize the extent to which government need participate directly in the game. The characteristic feature of action through political channels is that it tends to require or enforce substantial conformity. The great advantage of the market, on the other hand, is that it permits wide diversity. It is, in political terms, a system of proportional representation. Each man can vote, as it were, for the color of tie he wants and get it; he does not have to see what color the majority wants and then, if he is in the minority, submit.

It is this feature of the market that we refer to when we say that the market provides economic freedom. But this characteristic also has implications that go far beyond the narrowly economic. Political freedom means the absence of coercion of a man by his fellow men. The fundamental threat to freedom is power to coerce, be it in the hands of a monarch, a dictator, an oligarchy, or a momentary majority. The preservation of freedom requires the elimination of such concentration of power to the fullest possible extent and the dispersal and distribution of whatever power cannot be eliminated—a system of checks and balances. By removing the organization of economic activity from the control of political authority, the market eliminates this source of coercive power. It enables economic strength to be a check to political power rather than a reinforcement.

Economic power can be widely dispersed. There is no law of conservation which forces the growth of new centers of economic strength to be at the expense of existing centers. Political power, on the other hand, is more difficult to decentralize. There can be numerous small independent governments. But it is far more difficult to maintain numerous equipotent small centers of political power in a single large government than it is to have numerous centers of economic strength in a single large economy. There can be many millionaires in one large economy. But can there be more than one really outstanding leader, one person on whom the energies and enthusiasms of his countrymen are centered? If the central government gains power, it is likely to be at the expense of local governments. There seems to be something like a fixed total of political power to be distributed. Consequently, if economic power is joined to political power, concentration seems almost inevitable. On the other hand, if economic power is kept in separate hands from political power, it can serve as a check and a counter to political power.

The force of this abstract argument can perhaps best be demonstrated by example. Let us consider first, a hypothetical example that may help to bring out the principles involved, and then some actual examples from recent experience that illustrate the way in which the market works to preserve political freedom.

One feature of a free society is surely the freedom of individuals to advocate and propagandize openly for a radical change in the structure of the society—so long as the advocacy is restricted to persuasion and does not include force or other forms of coercion. It is a mark of the political freedom of a capitalist society that men can openly advocate and work for socialism. Equally, political freedom in a socialist society would require that men be free to advocate the introduction of capitalism. How could the freedom to advocate capitalism be preserved and protected in a socialist society?

In order for men to advocate anything, they must in the first place be able to earn a living. This already raises a problem in a socialist society, since all jobs are under the direct control of political authorities. It would take an act of self-denial whose difficulty is underlined by experience in the United States after World War II with the problem of "security" among Federal employees, for a socialist government to permit its employees to advocate policies directly contrary to official doctrine.

But let us suppose this act of self-denial to be achieved. For advocacy of capitalism to mean anything, the proponents must be able to finance their cause—to hold public meetings, publish pamphlets, buy radio time, issue newspapers and magazines, and so on. How could they raise the funds? There might and probably would be men in the socialist society with large incomes, perhaps even large capital sums in the form of government bonds and the like, but these would of necessity be high public officials. It is possible to conceive of a minor socialist official retaining his job although openly advocating capitalism. It strains credulity to imagine the socialist top brass financing such "subversive" activities.

The only recourse for funds would be to raise small amounts from a large number of minor officials. But this is no real answer. To tap these sources, many people would already have to be persuaded, and our whole problem is how to initiate and finance a campaign to do so. Radical movements in capitalist societies have never been financed this way. They have typically been supported by a few wealthy individuals who have become persuaded—by a Frederick Vanderbilt Field, or an Anita McCormick Blaine, or a Corliss Lamont, to mention a few names recently prominent, or by a Friedrich Engels, to go farther back. This is a role of inequality of wealth in preserving political freedom that is seldom noted—the role of the patron.

In a capitalist society, it is only necessary to convince a few wealthy people to get funds to launch any idea, however strange, and there are many such persons, many independent foci of support. And, indeed, it is not even necessary to persuade people or financial institutions with available funds of the soundness of the ideas to be propagated. It is only necessary to persuade them that the propagation can be financially successful; that the newspaper or magazine or book or other venture will be profitable. The competitive publisher, for example, cannot afford to publish only writing with which he personally agrees; his touchstone must be the likelihood that the market will be large enough to yield a satisfactory return on his investment.

In this way, the market breaks the vicious circle and makes it possible ultimately to finance such ventures by small amounts from many people without first persuading them. There are no such possibilities in the socialist society; there is only the all-powerful state.

Let us stretch our imagination and suppose that a socialist government is aware of this problem and is composed of people anxious to preserve freedom. Could it provide the funds? Perhaps, but it is difficult to see how. It could establish a bureau for subsidizing subversive propaganda. But how could it choose whom to support? If it gave to all who asked, it would shortly find itself out of funds, for socialism cannot repeal the elementary economic law that a sufficiently high price will call forth a large supply. Make the advocacy of radical causes sufficiently remunerative, and the supply of advocates will be unlimited.

Moreover, freedom to advocate unpopular causes does not require that such advocacy be without cost. On the contrary, no society could be stable if advocacy of radical change were cost-less, much less subsidized. It is entirely appropriate that men make sacrifices to advocate causes in which they deeply believe. Indeed, it is important to preserve freedom only for people who are willing to practice self-denial, for otherwise freedom degenerates into license and irresponsibility. What is essential is that the cost of advocating unpopular causes be tolerable and not prohibitive.

But we are not yet through. In a free market society, it is enough to have the funds. The suppliers of paper are as willing to sell it to the *Daily Worker* as to the *Wall Street Journal*. In a socialist society, it would not be enough to have the funds. The hypothetical supporter of capitalism would have to persuade a government factory making paper to sell to him, the government printing press to print his pamphlets, a government post office to distribute them among the people, a government agency to rent him a hall in which to talk, and so on.

Perhaps there is some way in which one could overcome these difficulties and preserve freedom in a socialist society. One cannot say it is utterly impossible. What is clear, however, is that there are very real difficulties in establishing institutions that will effectively preserve the possibility of

dissent. So far as I know, none of the people who have been in favor of socialism and also in favor of freedom have really faced up to this issue, or made even a respectable start at developing the institutional arrangements that would permit freedom under socialism. By contrast, it is clear how a free market capitalist society fosters freedom.

A striking practical example of these abstract principles is the experience of Winston Churchill. From 1933 to the outbreak of World War II, Churchill was not permitted to talk over the British radio, which was, of course, a government monopoly administered by the British Broadcasting Corporation. Here was a leading citizen of his country, a Member of Parliament, a former cabinet minister, a man who was desperately trying by every device possible to persuade his countrymen to take steps to ward off the menace of Hitler's Germany. He was not permitted to talk over the radio to the British people because the BBC was a government monopoly and his position was too "controversial".

Another striking example, reported in the January 26, 1959 issue of *Time*, has to do with the "Blacklist Fadeout". Says the *Time* story,

> The Oscar-awarding ritual is Hollywood's biggest pitch for dignity, but two years ago dignity suffered. When one Robert Rich was announced as top writer for the *The Brave One*, he never stepped forward. Robert Rich was a pseudonym, masking one of about 150 writers . . . blacklisted by the industry since 1947 as suspected Communists or fellow travelers. The case was particularly embarrassing because the Motion Picture Academy had barred any Communist or Fifth Amendment pleader from Oscar competition. Last week both the Communist rule and the mystery of Rich's identity were suddenly rescripted.
>
> Rich turned out to be Dalton (*Johnny Got His Gun*) Trumbo, one of the original

"Hollywood Ten" writers who refused to testify at the 1947 hearings on Communism in the movie industry. Said producer Frank King, who had stoutly insisted that Robert Rich was "a young guy in Spain with a beard": "We have an obligation to our stockholders to buy the best script we can. Trumbo brought us *The Brave One* and we bought it". . . .

In effect it was the formal end of the Hollywood black list. For barred writers, the informal end came long ago. At least 15% of current Hollywood films are reportedly written by blacklist members. Said Producer King, "There are more ghosts in Hollywood than in Forest Lawn. Every company in town has used the work of blacklisted people. We're just the first to confirm what everybody knows."

One may believe, as I do, that communism would destroy all of our freedoms, one may be opposed to it as firmly and as strongly as possible, and yet, at the same time, also believe that in a free society it is intolerable for a man to be prevented from making voluntary arrangements with others that are mutually attractive because he believes in or is trying to promote communism. His freedom includes his freedom to promote communism. Freedom also, of course, includes the freedom of others not to deal with him under those circumstances. The Hollywood blacklist was an unfree act that destroys freedom because it was a collusive arrangement that used coercive means to prevent voluntary exchanges. It didn't work precisely because the market made it costly for people to preserve the blacklist. The commercial emphasis, the fact that people who are running enterprises have an incentive to make as much money as they can, protected the freedom of the individuals who were blacklisted by providing them with an alternative form of employment, and by giving people an incentive to employ them.

If Hollywood and the movie industry had been government enterprises or if in England it had been a question of employment by the British Broadcasting Corporation it is difficult to believe that the "Hollywood Ten" or their equivalent would have found employment. Equally, it is difficult to believe that under those circumstances, strong proponents of individualism and private enterprise—or indeed strong proponents of any view other than the status quo—would be able to get employment.

Another example of the role of the market in preserving political freedom, was revealed in our experience with McCarthyism. Entirely aside from the substantive issues involved, and the merits of the charges made, what protection did individuals, and in particular government employees, have against irresponsible accusations and probings into matters that it went against their conscience to reveal? Their appeal to the Fifth Amendment would have been a hollow mockery without an alternative to government employment.

Their fundamental protection was the existence of a private-market economy in which they could earn a living. Here again, the protection was not absolute. Many potential private employers were, rightly or wrongly, averse to hiring those pilloried. It may well be that there was far less justification for the costs generally imposed on people who advocate unpopular causes. But the important point is that the costs were limited and not prohibitive, as they would have been if government employment had been the only possibility.

It is of interest to note that a disproportionately large fraction of the people involved apparently went into the most competitive sectors of the economy—small business, trade, farming—where the market approaches most closely the ideal free market. No one who buys bread knows whether the wheat from which it is made was grown by a Communist or a Republican, by a constitutionalist or a Fascist, or, for that matter, by a Negro or a white. This illustrates how an impersonal market separates economic activities from political views and protects men from being discriminated against in their economic activities for reasons that are irrelevant to their productivity—whether these reasons are associated with their views or their color.

As this example suggests, the groups in our society that have the most at stake in the preservation and strengthening of competitive capitalism are those minority groups which can most easily become the object of the distrust and enmity of the majority—the Negroes, the Jews, the foreign-born, to mention only the most obvious. Yet, paradoxically enough, the enemies of the free market—the Socialists and Communists—have been recruited in disproportionate measure from these groups. Instead of recognizing that the existence of the market has protected them from the attitudes of their fellow countrymen, they mistakenly attribute the residual discrimination to the market.

The Role of Government in a Free Society

A common objection to totalitarian societies is that they regard the end as justifying the means. Taken literally, this objection is clearly illogical. If the end does not justify the means, what does? But this easy answer does not dispose of the objection; it simply shows that the objection is not well put. To deny that the end justifies the means is indirectly to assert that the end in question is not the ultimate end, that the ultimate end is itself the use of the proper means. Desirable or not, any end that can be attained only by the use of bad means must give way to the more basic end of the use of acceptable means.

To the liberal, the appropriate means are free discussion and voluntary co-operation, which implies that any form of coercion is inappropriate. The ideal is unanimity among responsible individuals achieved on the basis of free and full discussion. This is another way of expressing the goal of freedom emphasized in the preceding chapter.

From this standpoint, the role of the market, as already noted, is that it permits unanimity without conformity; that it is a system of effectively proportional representation. On the other hand, the characteristic feature of action through explicitly political channels is that it tends to require or to enforce substantial conformity. The typical issue must be decided "yes" or "no"; at most, provision can be made for a fairly limited number of alternatives. Even the use of proportional representation in its explicitly political form does not alter this conclusion. The number of separate groups that can in fact be represented is narrowly limited, enormously so by comparison with the proportional representation of the market. More important, the fact that the final outcome generally must be a law applicable to all groups, rather than separate legislative enactments for each "party" represented, means that proportional representation in its political version, far from permitting unanimity without conformity, tends toward ineffectiveness and fragmentation. It thereby operates to destroy any consensus on which unanimity with conformity can rest.

There are clearly some matters with respect to which effective proportional representation is impossible. I cannot get the amount of national defense I want and you, a different amount. With respect to such indivisible matters we can discuss, and argue, and vote. But having decided, we must conform. It is precisely the existence of such indivisible matters—protection of the individual and the nation from coercion are clearly the most basic—that prevents exclusive reliance on individual action through the market. If we are to use some of our resources for such indivisible items, we must employ political channels to reconcile differences.

The use of political channels, while inevitable, tends to strain the social cohesion essential for a stable society. The strain is least if agreement for joint action need be reached only on a limited range of issues on which people in any event have common views. Every extension of the range of issues for which explicit agreement is sought strains further the delicate threads that hold society together. If it goes so far as to touch an issue on which men feel deeply yet differently, it may well disrupt the society. Fundamental differences in basic values can seldom if ever be resolved at the ballot box; ultimately they can only be decided, though not resolved, by conflict. The religious and civil wars of history are a bloody testament to this judgment.

The widespread use of the market reduces the strain on the social fabric by rendering conformity unnecessary with respect to any activities it encompasses. The wider the range of activities covered by the market, the fewer are the issues on which explicitly political decisions are required and hence on which it is necessary to achieve agreement. In turn, the fewer the issues on which agreement is necessary, the greater is the likelihood of getting agreement while maintaining a free society.

Unanimity is, of course, an ideal. In practice, we can afford neither the time nor the effort that would be required to achieve complete unanimity on every issue. We must perforce accept something less. We are thus led to accept majority rule in one form or another as an expedient. That

majority rule is an expedient rather than itself a basic principle is clearly shown by the fact that our willingness to resort to majority rule, and the size of the majority we require, themselves depend on the seriousness of the issue involved. If the matter is of little moment and the minority has no strong feelings about being overruled, a bare plurality will suffice. On the other hand, if the minority feels strongly about the issue involved, even a bare majority will not do. Few of us would be willing to have issues of free speech, for example, decided by a bare majority. Our legal structure is full of such distinctions among kinds of issues that require different kinds of majorities. At the extreme are those issues embodied in the Constitution. These are the principles that are so important that we are willing to make minimal concessions to expediency. Something like essential consensus was achieved initially in accepting them, and we require something like essential consensus for a change in them.

The self-denying ordinance to refrain from majority rule on certain kinds of issues that is embodied in our Constitution and in similar written or unwritten constitutions elsewhere, and the specific provisions in these constitutions or their equivalents prohibiting coercion of individuals, are themselves to be regarded as reached by free discussion and as reflecting essential unanimity about means.

I turn now to consider more specifically, though still in very broad terms, what the areas are that cannot be handled through the market at all, or can be handled only at so great a cost that the use of political channels may be preferable.

Government as Rule-maker and Umpire

It is important to distinguish the day-to-day activities of people from the general customary and legal framework within which these take place. The day-to-day activities are like the actions of the participants in a game when they are playing it; the framework, like the rules of the game they play. And just as a good game requires acceptance by the players both of the rules and of the umpire to interpret and enforce them, so a good society requires that its members agree on the general conditions that will govern relations among them, on some means of arbitrating different interpretations of these conditions, and on some device for enforcing compliance with the generally accepted rules. As in games, so also in society, most of the general conditions are the unintended outcome of custom, accepted unthinkingly. At most, we consider explicitly only minor modifications in them, though the cumulative effect of a series of minor modifications may be a drastic alteration in the character of the game or of the society. In both games and society also, no set of rules can prevail unless most participants most of the time conform to them without external sanctions; unless that is, there is a broad underlying social consensus. But we cannot rely on custom or on this consensus alone to interpret and to enforce the rules; we need an umpire. These then are the basic roles of government in a free society: to provide a means whereby we can modify the rules, to mediate differences among us on the meaning of the rules, and to enforce compliance with the rules on the part of those few who would otherwise not play the game.

The need for government in these respects arises because absolute freedom is impossible. However attractive anarchy may be as a philosophy, it is not feasible in a world of imperfect men. Men's freedoms can conflict, and when they do, one man's freedom must be limited to preserve another's—as a Supreme Court Justice once put it," "My freedom to move my fist must be limited by the proximity of your chin."

The major problem in deciding the appropriate activities of government is how to resolve such conflicts among the freedoms of different individuals. In some cases, the answer is easy. There is little difficulty in attaining near unanimity to the proposition that one man's freedom to murder his neighbor must be sacrificed to preserve the freedom of the other man to live. In other cases, the answer is difficult. In the economic area, a major problem arises in respect of the conflict between freedom to combine and freedom to compete. What meaning is to be attributed to "free" as modifying "enterprise"? In the United States, "free" has been understood to mean that anyone is free to set up an enterprise, which means that existing enterprises are not free to keep out competitors except by selling a better product at the same price or the same product at a lower price. In the continental tradition, on the other hand, the meaning has generally been that enterprises are free to do what they want, including the fixing of prices, division of markets, and the adoption of other techniques to keep out potential competitors. Perhaps the most difficult specific problem in this area arises with respect to combinations among laborers, where the problem of freedom to combine and freedom to compete is particularly acute.

A still more basic economic area in which the answer is both difficult and important is the definition of property rights. The notion of property, as it has developed over centuries and as it is embodied in our legal codes, has become so much a part of us that we tend to take it for granted, and fail to recognize the extent to which just what constitutes property and what rights the ownership of property confers are complex social creations rather than self-evident propositions. Does my having title to land, for example, and my freedom to use my property as I wish, permit me to deny to someone else the right to fly over my land in his airplane? Or does his right to use his airplane take precedence? Or does this depend on how he flies? Or how much noise he makes? Does voluntary exchange require that he pay me for the privilege of flying over my land? Or that I must pay him to refrain from flying over it? The mere mention of royalties, copyrights, patents; shares of stock in corporations; riparian rights, and the like, may perhaps emphasize the role of generally accepted social rules in the very definition of property. It may suggest also that, in many cases, the existence of a well specified and generally accepted definition of property is far more important than just what the definition is.

Another economic area that raises particularly difficult problems is the monetary system. Government responsibility for the monetary system has long been recognized. It is explicitly provided for in the constitutional provision which gives Congress the power "to coin money, regulate the value thereof, and of foreign coin." There is probably no other area of economic activity with respect to which government action has been so uniformly accepted. This habitual and by now almost unthinking acceptance of governmental responsibility makes thorough understanding of the grounds for such responsibility all the more necessary, since it enhances the danger that the scope of government will spread from activities that are, to those that are not, appropriate in a free society, from providing a monetary framework to determining the allocation of resources among individuals. . . .

In summary, the organization of economic activity through voluntary exchange presumes that we have provided, through government, for the maintenance of law and order to prevent coercion of one individual by another, the enforcement of contracts voluntarily entered into, the definition of the meaning of property rights, the interpretation and enforcement of such rights, and the provision of a monetary framework. . . .

Irving Kristol

An intellectual leader of what has been called the neoconservative movement in the late twentieth century, Irving Kristol was born in 1920. As editor of the influential conservative journal *The Public Interest* since 1965, Kristol has written a number of books and spoken out on social issues, viewing America as "a continuing revolution."

As a student at City College of New York, Kristol was recruited into the Young People's Socialist League—an anti-Stalinist, leftist group from which he was later expelled for individualism. Upon returning from military service in World War II, he became editor of *Commentary*, a liberal intellectual journal. In 1953, he went to London where he cofounded and coedited *Encounter* with poet Stephen Spender. Upon returning to the United States in 1958, he served as editor of *The Reporter*, which was anticommunist and liberal. He then became an executive vice president and editor of Basic Books, where he collaborated with sociologist Daniel Bell on editing *Capitalism Today* (1971). During this period he also served as a corporate consultant. In 1967 he was appointed a professor of social thought at New York University, where he later taught in the Graduate School of Business. He contributed frequently to *Commentary* and the *Wall Street Journal*. His writings counter what he views as the political and social excesses of the 1960s and 1970s, emphasizing the importance of tradition and defending democratic capitalism with a tone of moderation. A typical example appears here, taken from his book of essays *Two Cheers for Capitalism* (1978).

◎Ж◎

Two Cheers for Capitalism (1978)
(excerpt)

Horatio Alger and Profits

Over these past few years, I have been attending many conferences of businessmen, and it almost always happens that someone will intervene to inquire plaintively: "What can we do to make the profit motive respectable once again?" Or: "Why, in view of the general prosperity which the free exercise of the profit motive has brought to our society, is it held in such low esteem—indeed, in contempt—by intellectuals, academics, students, the media, politicians, even our very own children?" Or: "Why is the profit-seeking businessman, who creates affluence for everyone, a somewhat less than reputable figure in American society today?"

Whatever the precise wording, it's a fascinating and important question. In some ways, it may be the most important question confronting our liberal-capitalist society. There can be no doubt that, if business as an occupation and businessmen as a class continue to drift in popular opinion from the center of respectability to its margins, then liberal capitalism—and our liberal political system with it—has precious little chance for survival.

But, as phrased, it is also the wrong question in the sense that it reveals how anti-business opinion has shaped the thinking and the language of businessmen themselves. For the idea that the businessman is ruled solely by the "profit motive," that he is simply an acquisitive creature lusting after the greatest possible gain, and that liberal-capitalist society is nothing more than an "acquisitive society," was originally proposed as *an indictment* of our socioeconomic system, and is still taken by many to be exactly that.

Indeed, if the description is true, the indictment is inevitable. Who on earth wants to live in a society in which all—or even a majority—of one's fellow citizens are fully engaged in the hot pursuit of money, the single-minded pursuit of material self-interest? To put it another way: Who wants to live in a society in which selfishness and self-seeking are celebrated as primary virtues? Such a society is unfit for human habitation; thus sayeth the Old Testament, the New Testament, the Koran, the Greek philosophers, the medieval theologians, all of modern moral philosophy. So if capitalism is what this indictment claims it is—if it is what so many businessmen today seem to think it is—then it is doomed, and properly.

But this is not what a liberal-capitalist society is supposed to be like, and it was only in recent decades that anyone thought it was supposed to be like that. As a matter of fact, if this had been the original idea of capitalism, it could never have come into existence—not in a civilization still powerfully permeated by Christian values and Christian beliefs. Certainly capitalism did free the spirit of commercial enterprise from its feudal and mercantilist fetters. It did legitimate the pursuit of self-interest *rightly understood.* And when this capitalist ethic is itself rightly understood *as an ethic,* it turns out to be something quite different from a mere unleashing of "the profit motive."

Businessmen as Heroes

If one wants to appreciate the moral dimensions of the liberal-capitalist perspective, there is no better place to look than in the Horatio Alger novels, the only substantial body of American literature where businessmen are heroes rather than villains. These novels, of course, are no longer read today. But prior to World War II, they were still in wide circulation and were being avidly read by adolescent boys. They had by then been enormously popular for half a century, so presumably they corresponded to certain deep American beliefs. And what does one discover when one returns to a reading of Horatio Alger? Well, one discovers nothing like a celebration of "the profit motive," pure and simple. Instead, one finds a moral conception of business as an honorable vocation for honorable men. A profitable vocation, to be sure. *But profitable because honorable,* not vice versa.

The basic assumption of Horatio Alger is that the life of business is a good life because it helps develop certain admirable traits of character: probity, diligence, thrift, self-reliance, self-respect, candor, fair dealing, and so on—all those "bourgeois virtues" which no one quite believes in any more. A young man who enters the vocation of business must have these virtues latent within him, or else he cannot succeed

honorably. And if he does succeed honorably, he will represent these virtues in their fullest form. Horatio Alger's success stories are also full-blooded morality tales.

It is also important to notice what Horatio Alger does not say. He does not say you cannot succeed otherwise; "speculators" and "freebooters" (wheeler-dealers) may indeed become wealthy, but such types are not honorable businessmen. Despite their wealth, they are never "success stories," since they have only enriched but not "bettered" themselves; their characters have been in no way improved by their active lives. Nor does he say that success under capitalism is an analogue to the "survival of the fittest" in nature: the law of the jungle is no suitable model for human association in society. He does not state that "private vices" (e.g., selfishness, greed, avarice) are justifiable because they may result in "public benefits" (e.g., economic growth); he insists on a continuity between private ethics and the social ethic of a good society. All of these other apologia for liberal capitalism, which we are familiar with, are curtly dismissed by him as unacceptable to anyone with a more than rudimentary moral sensibility.

Now, it is true that Horatio Alger wrote fiction, not fact. But it will not do to dismiss him as a mere fancifier and myth-maker. To begin with, he would never have been so popular, for so long, if his conception of American society had been utterly fanciful. His readers understood that he was writing stories, not sociology, but they apparently perceived some connection between his stories and the reality of their socio-economic order. There was in fact such a connection, which even we can still dimly perceive. Some of us are old enough to remember that there was a time when the only thing more reprehensible than buying on the installment plan was selling on the installment plan; it encouraged "fecklessness." And we still have some business institutions which could only have been founded in Horatio Alger's world. Thus, on the floors of our various stock and commodity exchanges, transactions involving millions of dollars take place on the basis of nothing more than mutual trust: there, a businessman's word is his bond. Imagine trying to set up such institutions today! A thousand lawyers, to say nothing of the SEC*, would be quick to tell you that such confidence in the honor of businessmen is inconsistent with sound business practices.

What the 20th century has witnessed is the degradation of the bourgeois-capitalist ethic into a parody of itself—indeed, into something resembling what the critics of liberal capitalism had always accused it of being. These critics, intellectuals and men of letters above all, never did like modern liberal society because it was "vulgar"; it permitted ordinary men and women, in the marketplace, to determine the shape of this civilization, a prerogative that intellectuals and men of letters have always claimed for themselves. (This is why so many intellectuals and men of letters naturally tend to favor some form of benevolent despotism, in our time called a "planned society.") But their criticism was relatively ineffectual so long as liberal capitalism was contained within a bourgeois way of life and sustained by a bourgeois ethos, the way of life and the ethos celebrated by Horatio Alger. The common man has always preferred bourgeois capitalism to its intellectual critics; in the United States, for the most part, he still does.

But the trouble is that capitalism outgrew its bourgeois origins and became a system for the impersonal liberation and satisfaction of appetites—an engine for the creation of affluence. And such a system, governed by purely materialistic conceptions and infused with a purely acquisitive ethos, is defenseless before the critique of its intellectuals. Yes, it does provide more food, better housing, better health, to say nothing of all kinds of pleasant conveniences. Only a saint or a snob would dismiss these achievements lightly. But anyone who naively believes that, in sum, they suffice to legitimize a socioeconomic system knows little of the human heart and soul. People can learn to despise such a system even while enjoying its benefits.

Placid Acceptance

Nothing more plainly reveals the moral anarchy that prevails within the business community today than the way in which it can placidly accept—indeed, participate in—the anti-bourgeois culture that is now predominant. How many businessmen walked out indignantly from a movie like *The Graduate*, which displayed them (and their wives) as hollow men and women, worthy of nothing but contempt? Not many, I would think. The capacity for indignation withers along with self-respect. How many businessmen refuse, as a matter of honor and of principle, to advertise in a publication such as *The Rolling Stone* or even *Playboy*, publications which make a mockery of their industry, their integrity, their fidelity, the very quality of their lives? The question answers itself.

If businessmen are nothing but merchants of affluence, then their only claim to their rights and prerogatives is that they can perform this task more efficiently than the government. This assertion is unquestionably true, but it really is irrelevant. Efficiency is not a moral virtue and by itself never legitimizes anything. It is the culture of a society—by which I mean its religion and its moral traditions, as well as its

---

*Editor's Note: Securities and Exchange Commission.

specific arts—which legitimizes or illegitimizes its institutions. For decades now, liberal capitalism has been living off the inherited cultural capital of the bourgeois era and has benefited from a moral sanction it no longer even claims. That legacy is now depleted, and the cultural environment has turned radically hostile.

Today, businessmen desperately try to defend their vocation as honorable because profitable. Without realizing it, they are standing Horatio Alger on his head. It won't work. That inverted moral ethos makes no moral sense, as our culture keeps telling us, from the most popular movie to the most avant-garde novel. This culture is

not, as it sometimes pretends, offended by some bad things that some businessmen do; it is offended by what businessmen are or seem to be: exemplars of the naked "profit motive." Businessmen, of course, are unaccustomed to taking culture seriously. They didn't have to, so long as it was mainly a bourgeois culture, with anti-bourgeois sentiments concentrated on the margins. Today, unless they start trying to figure out a way to cope with the new cultural climate, they are likely to catch a deathly chill. It may be a bad time for businessmen to sell stock (or buy stock) but it would seem to be a good time for them to take stock.

Michael Novak

A progressive, conservative Catholic theologian and political thinker, Michael Novak restores the links between the dynamism of the early capitalist economic thought of Adam Smith and contemporary liberation theology, between the Catholic notion of the "commonwealth" and the protestant liberal tradition, between capitalist growth and ethical freedom. Born in Johnstown, Pennsylvania, in 1933, Novak studied at Gregorian University in Rome and received an M.A. from Harvard and an LL.D. from Stonehill College.

Novak's career can be characterized as one of academic, intellectual, and ideological restlessness. Moving from university to university, he taught at Harvard, Stanford, the State University of New York at Old Westbury, Carleton College, Immaculate Heart College, the University of California at Santa Barbara, Syracuse University, and the University of Notre Dame, finally landing as a scholar of religion and public policy at the conservative American Enterprise Institute in Washington, D.C. He has been politically active as a speech writer in national political campaigns and served as U.S. representative on the human rights committee at the United Nations and on the presidential task force on economic justice under President Reagan. A prolific journalist, he has authored a syndicated column. Among his many books are: *A Theology for Radical Politics* (1969), *The American Vision* (1978), *The Spirit of Democratic Capitalism* (1982) *Confession of a Catholic* (1983), *Freedom with Justice* (1984), *Human Rights and the New Realism* (1986), *Free Persons and the Common Good* (1989), and *Will It Liberate? Questions about Liberation Theology* (1986), from which the following excerpt is taken. Here Novak resurrects Adam Smith's laissez-faire economics in contemporary liberalism and ethics.

৩|৫

Will It Liberate? Questions about Liberation Theology (1986)

(excerpt)

1. The Liberal Ethic

1. Every human being sometimes raises questions, sometimes merely by a look or by a gesture, sometimes in words. The capacity of the human being to raise questions is the fundamental drive both of the liberal society and of human progress. Whether one speaks of the internal voyage of the human soul, or of the progress or decline of the social order, the human drive to raise questions is fundamental. Until they question tyranny, citizens slumber. They will not yet have felt the stirrings of liberty.

2. This drive to raise questions is unrestricted, restless, infinite. Everything human may be questioned: a person's own state of soul, motives, ends; the structure of a social order; a received sense of reality. There is an infinity of new ways to look at things; of new potential standpoints; and of new directions for action.

3. Without a sense of reality (by which they select what is relevant from what is irrelevant, what is illusory from what seems solid); without a sense of the local scene and the larger drama within which their action "makes sense"; without a narrative purpose, human beings cannot act. For action is concrete, relational, purposive, and successive (one act follows another). Action must have "a point."

Humans gain this "point" from the narrative of which they are a part. In this respect, human action presumes prior choices: a vision of reality; an interpretation of the historical drama; one's own chosen role; images by which to define others and one's relations to them; a predilected future. All these choices must be fixed in mind, at least in a pre-conscious way, before action makes sense.

4. The unrestricted drive to raise questions can call each or all of these prior choices into question. When it does, the actor is momentarily disoriented. At such times, conversions or changes of direction, whether superficial or radical, may more easily take place.

5. When the process of raising questions disrupts one's sense of reality and assumed story radically, however, and when it calls into question even the alternatives one is tempted to put in its place, a human being begins to experience a certain dizziness, an emptiness, a loss of form and purpose. Action becomes, at least temporarily, impossible. This experience I call "the experience of nothingness," because it breaks down the forms through which we have habitually perceived, imagined, and acted. As Nietzsche put it: The "why" that we had put into reality we suddenly pull out. Then we are enveloped in the blooming, buzzing confusion (and the darkness) of raw experience.

6. The experience of nothingness has for humans a primordial character. It takes us back, first, to the primal chaos. Second, it brings us face-to-face with the profound unrestrictedness of our own drive to ask questions. *All* questions may be asked. When too many are asked at once, perplexity overwhelms us, we feel "at sea," vertigo seizes us, nausea arises. This experience is a crucial revelation of our own fundamental nature. We are *inquiring spirits*, embodied to be sure, but liable to question everything that formerly seemed solid. The experience of nothingness is, in the extreme, the ground of "brainwashing"—when everything formerly believed in, perceived, and imagined is broken down. Torture, intent upon "dehumanizing" us, "breaking" our spirits, and totally disorienting us, may reduce us to nothingness. As it were, it returns us to the *tabula rasa* at which we began.

The experience of nothingness is frightening. In a pluralistic age of rapid change and intense external (and internal) stimulation, however, it is far from rare. Even the young, perhaps especially the young, may often walk along its edges.

7. In an important way, this experience of nothingness lies at the heart of the liberal vision. We sense that under torture it might at any time be imposed upon us. In at least petty ways we ourselves, in our daily lives, are often cruel to others. But some persons—the torturers—make cruelty their profession. Given total and unchecked power, the number of torturers in any society may multiply. This has happened often in our own era and in every era. Even philosopher-kings, given total power, may sooner or later be tempted to torture others—for their own good, for state security, for the common good. Some pretext is always at hand.

8. Therefore, those who are called liberals cannot allow there to be a social system in which torture is permissible. For they are called liberals precisely because they desire a social order in which the only legitimate human relation is one of civil conversation, a mutually respectful questioning that preserves the dignity of each. They cannot allow there to be a social system in which torture is permissible, because they know that, under torture, they might not act as the self-determining and responsible agents they choose to be. For this

reason, liberalism is properly said to begin in fear of torture. Liberalism is a movement of *political* liberation because it seeks to construct institutions that delegitimate torture—that hold torture to be a crime, punishable by law. Liberals desire a state which is limited, one of whose primary limitations is that it may not torture, under any circumstances whatever.

9. This primal fear of torture moves liberals in two directions at once. In the depths of human experience, liberals perceive the indestructible light of human conscience, understanding, and responsibility. This light is "indestructible," not in the sense that no one can destroy it (for every person may be destroyed), but in the sense that this light belongs inalienably to the self. It may not lawfully be taken away by any other. So long as a person resists, that resistance is inalienable. When a person is "broken," self has been seized by another. No self remains.

10. What is the source, then, of this "light," this "inalienable self"? It comes not from other humans or the state. Dimly, one sees that it does not come solely from the self. It is experienced as "given." It is there. Yet it also holds everything about the self in question. It is, therefore, larger and deeper than the self. It holds the self under judgment. Persons become "religious" when they interpret this light as the presence of God—when they address it in personal terms, as if in conversation: "Our hearts are restless, Lord, until they rest in thee" (St. Augustine). Or as Jesus did in his "dark night": "Father, into thy hands I commend my spirit."

Perhaps no culture has explored the "dark night" more deeply than the Hispanic, especially through St. John of the Cross, who was himself submitted to dungeon and torture by the Inquisition. My own little volume, *The Experience of Nothingness*, is written as a commentary on the most famous of St. John's poems about *nada*.

11. The first direction of liberal thought, therefore, is inward, toward the inalienable rights endowed in each human person by the Creator—the mark of the Creator in his creature, that creature made in his own image. The possession of such rights is the mark of self, of personhood, of self-determination, and transcendent restlessness.

2. The Liberal Metaphysic in Politics

12. The second direction of liberal thought is outward, toward institutions. Of all political philosophies, liberalism is the most practical. Its foundational choice is to construct institutions that respect the image of the Creator in human beings. (I use Christian language, canonized for secular use in the U.S. Declaration of Independence.) The aim of liberalism is to construct institutions that respect such rights in a routine, regular, reliable way.

Many political philosophers of the past worried rather more about principles and concepts. Liberal political philosophy was the first to concentrate its attention upon *institutions*. For liberalism began with a concrete problem: How to construct a republic within which torture would no longer be legitimate? It set out—it was the first such philosophy—to build institutions of human rights, by design and in considerable detail. Liberalism thinks *institutionally*, not because it abandons "substantive" issues in order to deal with "procedural" issues, but because it recognizes the incarnate nature of human beings. Human beings are embodied persons. Therefore, one must take care to protect their bodies, which otherwise torturers will abuse in order to break their spirits. Earlier philosophies, intent on protecting principles, doctrines, and the spirit, had too often left the body vulnerable to Inquisitors.

Liberal philosophy, then, begins with the unrestricted drive to raise questions, with the experience of nothingness, with fear of torture. Therefore, liberals think institutionally. But there is another reason for liberals to think institutionally.

13. If the human spirit is to be free to inquire, then there are likely to be many provisional answers, many creeds, plural persuasions. Those who would think "substantively"—to decide what the shape of "the new man" ought to be, *for all the others*—will be tempted to apply torture to the recalcitrant whom they may "substantively" define as defective. Those who proceed by way of "substance" put themselves in the place of God. They alone, they think, possess the correct eschatology, envisage the appropriate utopia, are the intellectual vanguard of the true human destiny. Their "radical" criticism of others is with due probability likely to be murderous. They are much too likely not to "dialogue" with their critics, but to annihilate them.

14. When human inquiry is unrestricted, according to its inmost nature, pluralism will with virtual certainty result. Through which *procedures* then, in which *institutions*, according to which sets of *checks and balances*, will reasoned dialogue and civil disagreement be guaranteed? Liberal logic leads directly to the institutions of democracy, created for such purposes. Its direction is not to enforce one metaphysical vision upon all, but to set up checks and balances so that no one metaphysic may be obligatory for all.

15. It is important to note how antignostic, how anti-platonic, liberal realism is. The liberal realist recognizes the weakness of humankind, the frailty even of the philosopher-king, the fallibility of every "intellectual vanguard." It entrusts no one with political orthodoxy. The liberal trusts no one but God, lets God be God, puts no political apparatus in the place of God. The liberal society is prohibited from conferring transcendence upon itself. It is "under God."

16. The liberal ordinance, therefore, dictates a government that is self-denying. Thus, not even secular atheistic liberals may rightfully impose their unbelief upon the others; nor can believing liberals impose belief upon atheists. The liberal view does not require every person to be theologically or ideologically neutered. It requires only that the institutions and procedures of the public square allow each person (or group) to state his case as cogently, reasonably and civilly as each can.

17. In this respect, two forms of liberalism must be distinguished. In the beginning, some liberals held a highly optimistic vision of humans as perfectible, reasonable, moral animals, guided by reason and high ideals. This was liberal utopianism. To some extent, such utopianism had a good practical effect. When a society expects much of its citizens, particularly in their public roles, it is likely to elicit from them higher performance. The reverse is also likely.

But liberal *institutions* are not designed upon this utopian basis. On the contrary, checks and balances are established against every form of human power, precisely upon the ground that every human being sometimes sins. As individuals, in their own intimate behavior, human beings sometimes injure those they love; each sometimes sins. In *group* behavior, however, these human weaknesses are magnified. In *Moral Man and Immoral Society*, Reinhold Niebuhr discussed nearly a dozen reasons why this is so. Speaking of those who do not recognize this difference he wrote:

What is lacking among all these moralists, whether religious or rational, is an understanding of the brutal character of the behavior of all human collectives, and the power of self-interest and collective egoism in all intergroup relations. Failure to recognize the stubborn resistance of group egoism to all moral and inclusive social objectives inevitably involves them in unrealistic and confused political thought. They regard social conflict either as an impossible method of achieving morally approved ends or as a momentary expedient which a more perfect education or a purer religion will make unnecessary. They do not see that the limitations of the human imagination, the easy subservience of reason to prejudice and passion, and the consequent persistence of irrational egoism, particularly in group behavior, make social conflict an inevitability in human history, probably to its very end.

This view is that of the liberal realists.

18. Thus, a biblical theme extremely important to the metaphysic of liberalism is that of human earthiness, contingency, sin: the "modesty," the "lowliness," of the biblical view of man. *One ought not to expect humans to behave as if they are gods, angels, heroes, or saints.* One must understand, as God does, "what is in man."

The liberal metaphysic is opposed to utopianism of every sort. While it is future-oriented, open, and hopeful, liberal realism is also modest. In politics, Aristotle said, one must be satisfied with a "tincture of virtue": even in nature itself, natural laws only "work for the most part." One must expect from each field of study only the degree of certainty proper to it—and, in human affairs, that means: very little. The famous painting of Raphael, which shows Plato pointing to the heaven of ideas, and Aristotle pointing to the imperfect earth, captures liberal realism quite nicely. It does so in secular terms, quite compatible with the instruction given Jews and Christians in the Bible.

3. In Economics

19. As for politics, so for economics: the fundamental liberal principle in economics is that the drive to raise questions is and must be unrestricted. Herein lies the dynamism of the free economy. The future is as open as the mind of man. One must create an economic system worthy of the openness of human intellect: open to the radical criticism of the present, to invention, and to discovery.

Only after some years did the liberal economy come to be known as "capitalism." Insofar as *capital* was imagined to be inanimate—either as money or as machines—this name was chosen in error. For the free economy places money at risk through investing it in the uncertain future, and it places every generation of machinery upon the path of obsolescence. But insofar as *capital* designates the human mind (L., *caput*) the first of all economic resources, the name is aptly chosen.

20. It is absurd, then, to call capitalism a "conservative" idea. On the contrary, in the structure of daily life a capitalist economy precipitates one revolution after another. The discoverers of the steam engine, the locomotive, the automobile, and the airplane did not revolutionize transport alone but an entire way of life. Today's revolutions in electronics and computers are more profoundly altering the conditions of life than did the Industrial Revolution. Those who are in favor of human inventiveness—and, therefore, of the free mind-centered economy—are *inherently* "progressive."

The latter term, alas, has been inappropriately captured by socialists, nostalgic for the pre-human uniformity of nature. The central thrust of a capitalist economy is toward the future, is dynamic, is open-ended, and is characterized by rapid change. Alvin Toffler in his eccentricities was correct to describe the effect as *Future Shock*.

21. Institutionally, four fundamental changes have been introduced into the social order by the free or mind-centered economy: (1) the corporation; (2) elaborate techniques of budgeting and accounting that impose close disciplines over small losses and small gains; (3) the accessibility of credit and insurance; and (4) the legal protection of inventions, discoveries, new processes, and trademarks. . . . But it is crucial to point out that all of these advances are both social and institutional. To define capitalism in terms of the individual alone is a serious error. Moreover, each of these institutions requires for its proper functioning a certain integrity of character and an appropriate range of human virtues. Such institutions cannot function if the moral ethos necessary to make them work either perishes or is not yet in place in the habits of a people. Systematic dishonesty, corruption, favoritism, failure to keep one's word or to honor contracts, and other such vices vitiate such institutions at their source. Their source lies in human character.

22. In addition, the mind-centered economy rests upon a particular conception of economic intelligence. The first problem to be met is how to achieve an economic *order*. Intuitively, common sense imagines that if there is to be an order, someone must impose it. *Dirigisme* has always shaped the traditional economic order, and is today the order most often exemplified in the nations of the world. The capitalist insight, by contrast, is counterintuitive. It holds that the source of a maximally intelligent social order lies, not in the minds of directors or planners or other imposers of order, but rather in the concrete decisions of multitudes of individual economic agents using their own intelligence to the fullest.

23. Here the capitalist metaphysic begins with an empirical observation. As usual, this observation is modest, anti-utopian, realistic. When each economic agent makes the most intelligent decisions he or she can, taking into account all contingencies, those decisions are more likely than not to be economically fruitful; otherwise, intelligent economic agents would alter their behavior. Moreover, human agents are "mixed" creatures; they are not *purely* economic agents. They seek to follow their own life plans, to seek their own comforts, to accept civil and political responsibilities, to live as ethical, religious, and aesthetic beings. Thus, when they make economic decisions, they take into account their other life-purposes as well, and their own positions in their own life-cycles.

Furthermore, one may observe that when many economic agents are successful within the scope of their local decisions, cumulatively these successes add up to increases in national success. The individual agents may or may not *intend* such national success. Nonetheless, cumulatively, the *effect* of their personal successes adds up to national success. This difference between intention and effect is an important theoretical distinction; and it has important practical consequences.

24. Two metaphysical assumptions in market theory need to be mentioned. The first concerns world process, the second human knowing. (Together, these two are isomorphic.) Concerning world process, liberalism holds that history is dynamic, contingent, and open. History is ruled neither by random chance nor by determinism. Human will can affect it. Events happen according to schemes of probabilities, not according to necessity.

Concerning human knowing, liberalism holds that the realm of the unknown (and of the future) is immense, so that compared to it human minds seeking understanding are like tiny flashlights in immense darkness.

The openness of history—the range of immense possibility just beyond us—is the premise of all theories of liberation, including some versions of liberation theology. (Others are based on determinism.) The openness of human inquiry is a companion premise crucial to the liberal society. Only liberalism puts both together.

Since human action is itself dynamic, contingent, and open, human agents must act within a vast and dark horizon. Their actions occur within a rapidly shifting, dynamic context, in which other agents unknown to them are also acting, in ways unknown to them. Such actions have many unforeseeable consequences. Thus, human knowing penetrates the future weakly, if at all. Even the most carefully studied, monitored, and regulated actions often have unforeseen (and tragic) consequences.

On January 28, 1986, for example, after twenty-four successful and virtually routine space flights, the twenty-fifth, the space shuttle U.S. Challenger, carrying six crew members and a woman teacher, exploded in a ball of flame after just 74 seconds of ascent, its debris then falling in gentle tracers to the ocean far below. No one clearly anticipated—although some did fear—such consequences.

25. From these premises, two problems arise for economic order. How can a dynamic order become a coherent order? And how can that order realize values compatible with humanistic, Jewish and Christian values? Intuitively, to meet the first problem, most persons seem to believe that any coherent order must have a rational planner. Order, they hold, must be *ordered*. Intuitively, to meet the second problem, such persons would seem to want a rational planner to impose upon economic activity the desired values. The difficulty with these intuitive hypotheses is that, empirically, they do not seem to work. State-directed economies seem to suffer from incoherences and breakdowns far more pervasive than those of non-directed economies.

In addition, the assumption that private citizens cannot in their own economic actions embody humanistic, Jewish and Christian values, and that such values need to be imposed by *public officials*, leaves two facts out of consideration. First, what is to guarantee that public officials will act virtuously? The record of public officials in displaying personal virtue is not a happy one. *Quis custodes custodiet?* Second, why must it be supposed that private citizens will be moral only if coerced by political elites? State-directed economies seem to breed not personal virtue but personal cynicism. They do so by unchecked corruption, by selfish political motivations, and by economic incompetence.

This last point may be strengthened: Economic activities necessarily involve every citizen, every product, every service, and every exchange within the nation. Billions of transactions occur every day. It is strictly impossible for any group of planners to have sufficient information about such transactions, not only in advance but even after the fact. On this impossibility, statist regimes routinely falter. It is not merely difficult but quite impossible even in the age of the computer, to collect, process, and assess all the immensely detailed information that would be required if no use were to be made of the market. The Communist countries did not find it possible to do so. Thus, even socialist theoreticians have had to reconsider their antipathy to markets.

26. By contrast, the metaphysic of liberalism proceeds by a counterintuitive but empirically confirmed observation. Even when no economic agent intends, or even foresees, the order that will emerge from the accumulated sum of individual economic decisions, nonetheless, when free markets of a certain character are functioning, the unintended (and unforeseen) result of individual activities is a surprisingly coherent order. It may seem to intuition that this is impossible. To empirical obser-

vation, however, it is a fact. In free economies, schedules are met, things work, the economy as a system functions dynamically, shortages are quickly repaired, excessive production is quickly checked, etc. A coherent order emerges, apart from anyone's intention.

Many things, having full reference
To one consent, may work contrariously;
As many arrows, loosed several ways,
Fly to one mark; as many ways meet in one town;
As many fresh streams meet in one salt sea;
As many lines close in the dial's center;
So may a thousand actions, once afoot,
End in one purpose, and be all well borne
Without defeat.

There is, then, a crucial difference between the *ends* of economic agents and the common *result* of their activities. Free markets convey instantaneous information about transactions, desires, shortages, and overly optimistic forecasts. Markets are a social device for acquiring massive amounts of social information without massive information costs. The market system is designed to produce social order, counterintuitively. It does so by focusing upon results rather than upon intentions.

27. In a sense, Adam Smith misstated his initial formulation of this insight. When a person employs his own capital, Smith wrote, he is led "to promote an end which was not part of his intention. . . . By pursuing his own *interest*, he frequently promotes that of the society more effectively than when he really intends to promote it." The mistake here was to say "interest." Smith's true point is that in a market system, it is quite unnecessary for anyone to *know* everything. Such complete knowledge is impossible to achieve, and the belief that it can be achieved is doubly dangerous: "The statesman, who should attempt to direct private people in what manner they ought to employ their capitals, would not only load himself with a most unnecessary attention, but assume an authority which could safely be trusted, not only to no single person, but to no council or senate whatever, and which would nowhere be so dangerous as in the hands of a man who had folly and presumption enough to fancy himself fit to exercise it."

Intuitively, as we have seen, persons suppose that a coherent outcome requires a coherent plan. Not so, Smith. From observation, he saw in market *results* surprising coherence planned by no one, but suffused with considerable intelligence. We should accordingly reformulate Smith's observation in this way: "A very large number of actions taken by many people, often people removed from each other in time and place, can have *unforeseen results that nevertheless form a coherent pattern.*"

Smith's error was to say by pursuing his own "interest," where he should have said "by pursuing his own most intelligent judgment." The larger idea can be put this way: "When an economic activist follows his own most intelligent judgment in order to accomplish a fruitful economic outcome at his own station in the economic order, even without trying to imagine the finished whole of all similar acts by others, such an activist more effectively promotes the welfare of society than when he tries to think for, and to plan for, the whole society." A slightly different way of putting this point is as follows. When each person applies the maximal economic intelligence of which he is capable, at his own station and in matters for which he is responsible, the entire economic order is more suffused with accumulated acts of intelligence than if some one public official (or team of public officials) attempted to impose a coherent order.

It was on this principle that Abraham Lincoln supported the Homestead Act of 1862. Instead of opening the American West to a board of government planners, and instead of imitating the plantation and slave system of the American South (or of the *latifundia* and large estates of much of Latin America), Lincoln chose the path of multiplying the number of small owners, thus multiplying the number of individual economic decisionmakers. In a sense, this legislation anticipates the famous Catholic "principle of subsidiarity," enunciated in 1931 by Pius XI. It ensured that economic decisions would be made as close as possible to the concrete texture of immediate events. (One ought to note, though, that the Homestead Act—a fundamental *systematic* decision—was made at the national level, as a political decision. The "political" in political economy is often crucial.

28. Economics is the study of human action concerned with material scarcity and the creation of wealth, in the light both of social systems and of the actions of individuals. The field of such actions is governed neither by pure randomness nor by necessity; human actions can make a systematic difference in historical outcomes. Thus, Adam Smith's *Inquiry Into the Nature and Causes of the Wealth of Nations* suggests in its very title that human inquiry is crucial to economics, that a systematic knowledge of causes is possible, and that action informed by such knowledge can result at least in the diminishment of the poverty of all nations and, at its term, in the elimination of such poverty. In short, through human inquiry and action, a sound material base can be put in place under every single person on this planet. Put otherwise, the existing wealth of nations is neither random nor pre-determined by natural necessity but open to sustained and systematic development. Economics is the field of human action in which human beings achieve self-mastery over their own material conditions of scarcity and wealth.

29. Among the assumptions of this viewpoint are the following: (1) the *future* of human economic development is *open* to human action; (2) a decisive role in human development is to be played by *human judgment* separating illusions from realities, false perceptions from true, conventional understandings of the causes of wealth from more accurate and discerning understandings; (3) the critical factor in economic development is that form of human action described as *enterprise*, i.e., sustained alertness in detecting current errors of judgment and practice and an alertness to heretofore undetected ways to reduce current scarcities or to create new wealth. Enterprise is a habit of mind oriented to action, a specific human virtue either innate or acquired (or some combination of both) and natural to all human beings, although (as is the case in all the virtues) more highly developed in some cultures and in some persons than in others.

30. To understand *enterprise* more exactly, it is useful to distinguish among three forms of rationality. (1) *Calculative rationality* is the form of human reason whose perfection lies in deducing correct solutions (arriving at correct calculations), once ends, means, boundary conditions, basic operations, and existing states of affairs have been defined. This form of rationality is most useful to economics considered as a science, under conditions of equilibrium. Once all the relevant materials have been defined, correct actions consist in "summing" correctly the relevant factors and pursuing the course of action so defined.

(2) *Dialectical rationality* is that form of human reason whose perfection consists in rejecting false or inadequate *ultimate ends* in the definition of purposes for human action, and in arriving at appropriate or adequate ultimate ends.

Existentially, human beings disagree about ultimate ends. Some define the point of living in one way, some in another. Much depends upon the story each human being chooses as best descriptive of the narrative line he or she chooses to pursue in sequences of human action. Those who disagree may point out disadvantages in the definitions of ends given by others, while pointing out advantages in their own definition. Dialectical reasoning is highly useful to all individuals, since through it—especially in spirited dialogue with others—matters heretofore unnoticed are often brought to light, errors of perception or oversights or mistaken lines of reasoning may emerge, and possibilities heretofore unconsidered come into view.

If self-knowledge were ever instantaneous, complete, and entirely luminous, dialectical reasoning would not be necessary. But human beings are always ignorant, partially blind, or mistaken even in their knowledge of themselves, their own purposes, and the story they are currently pursuing. The Socratic injunction, "Know thyself," is intended to suggest the considerable darkness about themselves in which human beings always dwell. Self-knowledge is never complete. Therefore, dialectic reasoning is always necessary for personal progress in self-appropriation.

The same necessity is experienced by societies and cultures, as they learn from experience. From such considerations arise the possibilities of human moral progress. From them, as well, arise the utility—even the necessity—of the open society, through whose pluralistic and unfettered institutions dialectical reasoning is free to bring ever fresh criticism to bear. Societies, like persons, often do learn from history (its lessons articulated by dialectical reasoning) and often do change direction accordingly, choosing to pursue new ends or, at least, to proceed through new ways.

(3) *Prudential reasoning* is that form of human reasoning whose perfection consists in the wisest possible choice of proximate ends and means in the light of ultimate ends. There is no simple *definition* (that can be stated abstractly) concerning "the wisest possible choice." This is because

human individuals are unique and human circumstances are unique. What works for one person (a batter in baseball, for example) may not work for another. Each must choose the disposition of personal forces best suited both to the self at that moment and to the situation at hand. Since some persons do so characteristically and by habit—and since the fruits of their so doing usually become apparent to others—such persons become known as "wise." Others like to seek their advice. Such persons become the *criterion* for sound prudential reasoning. To act wisely in practice is to act *as such persons would act* (due account being taken of the differences between such persons in their own situations and oneself).

Such a definition of practical wisdom (or prudential reasoning) escapes circularity because not *all* persons are appropriate models; persons of practical wisdom are relatively rare and usually stand out among their peers, especially over time. While no one is perfect, such persons more often than not achieve their own ultimate ends through felicitous choices of proximate ends and means. They seem to have a facility for discerning quite early the errors into which others often fall and for discerning, as well, and with seeming ease, the most expeditious and fruitful choices amid the labyrinth of possibilities. Just as some persons may quickly solve a crossword puzzle, pass easily an academic test, solve a mathematical problem—and come thus to be distinguished as "bright" rather than "dull"— so also some persons show extraordinary discernment amid practical perplexities. They show "brightness" in practical discernment. Where others see difficulties, they discern opportunities. Experience shows that they are often correct. When they are not, they also have an extraordinary facility for seeing *why* not, and for correcting future judgments accordingly. Such persons are vital assets in any community.

31. Enterprise is, therefore, to be understood as a form of prudential reasoning as applied especially to reducing material scarcities and creating new material wealth. Israel Kirzner defines enterprise as "alertness," a term not distant from the classical term "discernment" of which I have been availing myself. One will note the alertness of the family cat when, at the end of a long afternoon, the refrigerator door is opened. Such alertness may be merely a form of instinct, hunger, and association. In human beings, alertness or discernment operates over fields far larger and often far more remote and abstract. In economic life, in particular, alertness or discernment comes clearly into evidence when a person of enterprise becomes aware of errors in the way current markets are functioning, aware of oversights and misperceptions and opportunities lost. Such a person may see earlier than others possibilities for new services or new good not heretofore available, or new methods for doing more cheaply or better things already done.

32. In this sense, the person of enterprise is an agent of disequilibrium. He or she brings into economic activities something new and destabilizing. In the past, no funds whatever may have been expended for the matter of his or her invention. Once the enterpriser has intervened, however, others in the market must adjust to new competition. Since new inventions create jobs never before available, and since the new invention provides either a new good or service or a cheaper, better way of providing older goods or services, new wealth is created. Older inefficiencies are overcome. New possibilities are launched. Typically, one achieved possibility opens the way to others, heretofore impossible.

In short, the distinctive factor in economic development—in creativity and progress—is the human action of enterprise, a form of practical wisdom applied to reducing scarcity or creating new wealth.

In enterprise we see the dynamic factor in economic progress. Without enterprise, there is repetition, stagnation, equilibrium.

33. Since scientific reasoning is designed for situations of equilibrium, in which terms and operations have a certain definable stability, economic science *qua* science has had little to say about the vital factor of enterprise. Von Mises and Hayek, proceeding upon the rather more ethical and humanistic plane of human action, have not failed to notice its decisive importance.

34. It is enterprise, indeed, that lies at the heart, not only of the capitalist spirit, but also of capitalism as a system. What is distinctive about capitalism as a novel form of economic activity is not markets, private property, exchange or profit, since all these existed under mercantilism, feudalism, and other pre-capitalist forms of economic activity. Nor is its distinctive factor "private ownership of the means of production," for such forms of ownership are by no means new to the capitalist era. In addition, mere private ownership of the means of production, without enterprise, would by no means yield the dynamic of capitalist discovery, invention, and creativity. What is precisely new in capitalism is the factor of enterprise. More exactly, it is the invention of *institutions* to encourage the virtue of enterprise among the widest possible range of citizens. As Servan-Schreiber observed in *The American Challenge*, the distinctive character of American institutions—the institutions *par excellence* of capitalism—is that they are designed to promote, to elicit, and to reward the habit of enterprise throughout the population. Capitalism is not simply the *sum* of private practices of the virtue of enterprise; it is a *social system* designed to encourage the broadest and most daring exercise of this habit.

35. Capitalism, therefore, as its name suggests, is best defined as *the mind-centered system*: a system designed to encourage the development of prudential reasoning applied to the reduction of scarcity and the creation of new wealth. Historians such as Daniel Boorstin in *The Discoverers* and Page Smith in *The Rise of Industrial America* have detailed how this characteristic design blazed an historical path. Israel Kirzner, as we have seen, has articulated the process in the terms of economic philosophy.

36. There are, then, two paths to enhancing the degree of intelligence and coherence in the economic order. The first is to hold that coherent intentions require a coherent plan, imposed from above. The second is to hold that coherent outcomes spring from maximizing the number of intelligent decisionmakers as close as possible to concrete transactions. The liberal metaphysic holds, on empirical grounds, that the second achieves a more intelligent and coherent result than the first. This hypothesis is subject to disconfirmation.

37. The free market, therefore, is a social institution, designed to effect the achievable maximum of social intelligence and social coherence. The market is not so much designed to enhance the individual responsibilities of economic decisionmakers, although it certainly does that, as to enhance the degree of social intelligence and social coherence. It is an achievement of social ethics, not of individual ethics.

38. This line of thought raises anew the second question mentioned above. How can a liberal social order realize values compatible with humanistic, Jewish, and Christian ethics? No one claims that any social order, short of the Kingdom of Heaven, will assure perfect human, Jewish, or Christian virtue. No earthly order guarantees that. The claim, rather, can only be comparative. It, too, is subject to empirical falsification. *Compared to any other economic order*, a liberal order will achieve a higher practice of humanistic, Jewish, and Christian values.

39. It does so in two ways. First, it maximizes the opportunity for every decisionmaker to act in the most humanistic, Jewish, and Christian way open to that individual. Strictly economic outcomes are almost never a person's sole interest. Second, it maximizes the reliance of each person upon the integrity and cooperation of others. Thus, Adam Smith writes: "In civilized society [any person] stands at all times in need of the co-operation and assistance of great multitudes, while his whole life is scarce sufficient to gain the friendship of a few."

A market system depends upon habits of cooperation and trust in others. When others must systematically be distrusted, costs of transactions are exorbitant; sclerosis sets in.

40. Moreover, the market obliges each of its participants to be other-regarding, not from motives of charity (although these are not excluded), but in order to win acceptance from others. In order to be successful over time, each economic agent must win a reputation for integrity, reliability, and service. Whatever the motives of individuals, the result is that each member of society is taught by markets to pay due regard to the wants and needs of others. That sellers sometimes take advantage of purchasers is reflected in the ancient saying *caveat emptor*. But those who depend upon broad markets and consistent loyalty down the years must prove worthy of trust.

41. The reason for this is that market transactions are voluntary. They consist essentially in free acts between consenting adults. Of course, no human beings enjoy pure, angelic liberty. Each is constrained by concrete realities. Without markets, however, individual liberties are far more constrained than they are with markets. If the state is the only effective payer of wages and purchaser of goods and services, citizens have only those choices permitted by the state. By contrast, as payers of wages and purchasers of goods and services are multiplied, freedom of choice expands. The larger the number of payers and purchasers, the freer the scope of economic choice. This is a sound economic, as well as a sound moral, principle.

42. Not all human goods and services are appropriately assigned to markets. The education of the young is so crucial to the conduct both of a democratic polity and of a mind-centered economy that the state may be assigned some responsibility for universal education. (Adam Smith so assigned it.) It does not follow that the state ought to be the *only* supplier of educational opportunity. In education, as in other fields, competition is the best ethical corrective for human laxity, incompetence, and tyranny. The case is similar with welfare provisions for those too young, too old, disabled, afflicted with illness or nervous disorder, etc., and unable to be self-reliant. A good society is properly judged by how well it cares for those unable to care for themselves. The state may play an important role in welfare policy as in education and other fields. But the state is not wisely allowed to be the *only* provider of care.

43. A similar logic applies to those other portions of social life that are not entirely amenable to the methods of the market. Markets are not a universal device for every purpose.

Questions of public goods and externalities, for example, may require attention from the political side of political economy more than from the strictly economic side. The practical question is: *What works best, with fewest evil consequences?* One may need to imagine special forms of markets, under special regulation by the state, to deal with complex matters. For example, the state may assume responsibilities for the supply of drinking water and sanitation, while "contracting out" portions of these responsibilities to privately owned and competitive services designed to meet them in regulated ways.

44. To sum up: the liberal society has a preference for an economic order based upon the social institution of markets because such an order is empirically best matched to a dynamic, contingent, open universe. In their very design, markets meet the demands of human action in a dynamic, contingent and open world. Markets liberate a maximal number of intelligent, responsible, individual economic actors, while binding each of them to habits of integrity, reliability, trust, cooperation, and other-regardingness. Such habits fall far short of saintliness. But they represent a basic moral minimum for civic virtue. Given this minimum, human beings may use their liberty to flower forth in generosity and saintliness—or, alas, in such mediocrity or wasted liberty as is our common lot. The call of sanctity may be heard.

45. These brief notes toward an appropriation of the basic presuppositions of the liberal society within the classic Catholic tradition of Aristotle and Aquinas illustrate the work yet to be done in Catholic social thought. Catholic thinkers have paid far too little attention to the great classics of economic thought: to Ludwig von Mises' *Human Action*; Friedrich von Hayek's *The Constitution of Liberty*; Wilhelm Roepke's *The Humane Economy*; Joseph Schumpeter's *The History of Economic Analysis; The Federalist*; and many other essential books concerning the foundations of the liberal society. An immense task of appropriation lies ahead of us. In my opinion, many of these classics cry out for critical inclusion within the tradition laid out by St. Augustine and that "first Whig," St. Thomas Aquinas. Rethinking the liberal classics in the context of the metaphysics of Bernard Lonergan and Karl Rahner would go far toward reconstructing both the intellectual and the social order of Western thought. In this task Lord Acton, too, has much to teach. And John Courtney Murray, S.J., in *We Hold These Truths*, has here as elsewhere anticipated us.

In these brief and fragmentary comments I have lingered longest upon the ideas of economic liberty, rather than political and civil liberty, and moral-cultural liberty. I have done so for two reasons. The constitution of economic liberty is less well known among intellectuals even in the West. And economic liberties deploy the instruments through which political and moral-cultural liberties are active in the world of time and matter. Private property, as Chesterton remarked, is the canvas and the paint by which Everyman exercises artistic creation. Economic liberties give material substance to political and civil liberties, and to intellectual and artistic liberties. To own printing presses—in general, to have autonomy over economic instruments—is an indispensable condition for other liberties, among incarnate creatures such as we.

... Maximizing the efficacy of that liberty is essential to human liberation. It is also the secret to economic creativity. Made in the image of the Creator, every human person bears the risk of using economic liberty in failure and in success, and the responsibility to create for posterity during his or her life more wealth than he or she consumes. Only so does human economic progress proceed.

In these intellectual struggles, much is at stake for the poor of the world. Ideas have consequences, especially for the poor. These days, the consequences of bad ideas are slowly leading more and more inquirers toward the rediscovery of the constitution of liberty: political liberty from torture, economic liberty from poverty, and liberty of conscience, information, and ideas. The best years of the liberal society are yet to come.

Slowly, God willing, liberal institutions will by trial and error be constructed around the world. It is a noble task to further them. The heart of Judaism and Christianity—their convictions about freedom and responsibility—is liberal.

Nothing so lifts up the poor as the liberation of their own creative economic activities.

"The God who gave us life gave us liberty.". . .

4

Paul Goodman

Paul Goodman became an underground hero of the New Left by representing communitarian anarchism and pacifism in an eclectic, prolific body of work—poetry, drama, novels, essays, and books on education and urban planning. His writing affirms humanism and respect for the dignity of human beings in their man-made environment and gives a radical critique of the institutionalized, affluent American way of life, which he claims stifles any sense of community and meaningful individual development.

Born in 1911 in New York City, after religious training in a Hebrew school and a good secondary school education, Goodman received his B.A. at the City College of New York. He first supported himself by reading movie scripts at home and continued his education by simply walking in on classes that interested him and sitting down. One such class was taught by Richard McKeon at Columbia University, who recognized Goodman's gifts and later arranged for him to lecture on English literature at the University of Chicago while earning a Ph.D. Forced to leave for nonconformist behavior, a way of living that later caused him to leave other teaching positions, he was not awarded his Ph.D. until 1954 when Chicago University Press published his doctoral thesis, *The Structure of Literature*. He supported himself as a gestalt therapist until he finally became well known enough to make a living lecturing and writing.

Among Goodman's major works are *The Empire City* (1959), a novel; *Communitas* (1947), a classic book on urban planning coauthored with his brother Percival; and *Growing Up Absurd: Problems of Youth in the Organized System* (1960), from which the following is excerpted.

ややや

Growing Up Absurd (1960)
(excerpts)
The Missing Community

1.

It is the argument of this book that *the accumulation of the missed and compromised revolutions of modern times, with their consequent ambiguities and social imbalances, has fallen, and must fall, most heavily on the young, making it hard to grow up.*

A man who has attained maturity and independence can pick and choose among the immense modern advances and somewhat wield them as his way of life. If he has a poor society, an adult cannot be very happy, he will not have simple goals nor achieve classical products, but he can fight and work anyway. But for children and adolescents it is indispensable to have a

Isaak, *American Political Thinking.*/From *Growing Up Absurd* by Paul Goodman. Copyright © 1956, 1957, 1958, 1959, 1960 by Paul Goodman. Reprinted by permission of Random House, Inc.

coherent, fairly simple and viable society to grow up into; otherwise they are confused, and some are squeezed out. Tradition has been broken, yet there is no new standard to affirm. Culture becomes eclectic, sensational, or phony. (Our present culture is all three.) A successful revolution establishes a new community. A missed revolution makes irrelevant the community that persists. And a compromised revolution tends to shatter the community that was, without an adequate substitute. . . .

2.

Let us start with the physical environment.

Technocracy. In our own century, philosophers of the new technology, like Veblen, Geddes, or Fuller, succeeded in making efficiency and know-how the chief ethical values of the folk, creating a mystique of "production," and a kind of streamlined esthetics. But they did not succeed in wresting management from the businessmen and creating their own world of a neat and transparent physical plant and a practical economics of production and distribution. The actual results have been slums of works of engineering, confused and useless overproduction, gadgetry, and new tribes of middlemen, promoters, and advertisers.

Urbanism. As Le Corbusier and Gropius urged, we have increasingly the plan and style of functional architecture; biological standards of housing; scientific study of traffic and city services; some zoning; and the construction of large-scale projects. But nowhere is realized the ideal of over-all community planning, the open green city, or the organic relation of work, living, and play. The actual results have been increasing commutation and traffic, segregated ghettos, a "functional" style little different from packaging, and the tendency [of] some basic urban functions,

such as recreation or schooling, to be squeezed out altogether.

Garden City. The opposite numbers, the Garden City planners after Ebenezer Howard, have achieved some planned communities protected by greenbelts. But they did not get their integrated towns, planned for industry, local commerce, and living. The result is that actual suburbs and garden cities are dormitories with a culture centering around small children, and absence of the wage earner; and such "plans" as the so-called shopping centers disrupt such village communities as there were. The movement to conserve the wilds cannot withstand the cars, so that all areas are invaded and regulated.

3.

Let us proceed to economic and social changes.

New Deal. The Keynesian economics of the New Deal has cushioned the business cycle and maintained nearly full employment. It has not achieved its ideal of social balance between public and private works. The result is an expanding production increasingly consisting of corporation boondoggling.

Syndicalism. Industrial workers have won their unions, obtained better wages and working conditions, and affirmed the dignity of labor. But they gave up their ideal of workers' management, technical education, and concern for the utility of their labor. The result is that a vast majority couldn't care less about what they make, and the "labor movement" is losing force.

Class Struggle. The working class has achieved a striking repeal of the iron law of wages; it has won a minimum wage and social security. But the goal of an equalitarian or freely mobile society has been given up, as has the solidarity of the underprivileged. The actual result is an increasing rigidity of statuses; some of the underprivileged tending to drop out of society altogether. On the other hand, the cultural equality that has been achieved has been the degradation of the one popular culture to the lowest common denominator.

Production for Use. This socialist goal has been missed, resulting in many of the other failures here listed.

Sociology. During the past century, the sociologists have achieved their aim of dealing with mankind in its natural groups or groups with common problems, rather than as isolated individuals or a faceless mass. Social science has replaced many prejudices and ideologies of vested interests. But on the whole, social scientists have given up their aim of fundamental social change and an open-experimental method determining its goal as it went along: the pragmatist ideal of society as a laboratory for freedom and self-correcting humanity. The actual result is an emphasis on "socializing" and "belonging," with the loss of nature, culture, group solidarity and group variety, and individual excellence.

4.

Next, political and constitutional reforms.

Democracy. The democratic revolution succeeded in extending formal self-government and opportunity to nearly everybody, regardless of birth, property, or education. But it gave up the ideal of the town meeting, with the initiative and personal involvement that alone could train people in self-government and give them practical knowledge of political issues. The actual result has been the formation of a class of politicians who govern, and who are themselves symbolic front figures.

The Republic. Correspondingly, the self-determination won by the American Revolution for the regional states, that should have made possible real political

experimentation, soon gave way to a national conformity; nor has the nation as a whole conserved its resources and maintained its ideals. The result is a deadening centralism, with neither local patriotism nor national patriotism. The best people do not offer themselves for public office, and no one has the aim of serving the Republic.

Freedom of Speech. Typical is the fate of the hard-won Constitutional freedoms, such as freedom of speech. Editors and publishers have given up trying to give an effective voice to important but unpopular opinions. Anything can be printed, but the powerful interests have the big presses. Only the safe opinion is proclaimed and other opinion is swamped.

Liberalism. The liberal revolution succeeded in shaking off onerous government controls on enterprise, but it did not persist to its goal of real public wealth as the result of free enterprise and honestly informed choice on the market. The actual result is an economy dominated by monopolies, in which the earnest individual entrepreneur or inventor, who could perform a public service, is actively discouraged; and consumer demand is increasingly synthetic.

Agrarianism. Conversely, the Jeffersonian ideal of a proud and independent productive yeomanry, with natural family morals and a co-operative community spirit, did in fact energize settling the West and providing the basis for our abundance. But because it has failed to cope with technological changes and to withstand speculation, "farming as a way of life" has succumbed to cash-cropping dependent on distant markets, and is ridden with mortgages, tenancy, and hired labor. Yet it maintains a narrow rural morality and isolationist politics, is a sucker for the mass culture of Madison Avenue and Hollywood, and in the new cities (e.g., in California, where farmers have migrated) is a bulwark against genuine city culture.

Liberty. Constitutional safeguards of person were won. But despite the increasing concentration of state power and mass pressures, no effort was made to give to individuals and small groups new means easily to avail themselves of the safeguards. The result is that there is no longer the striking individuality of free men; even quiet nonconformity is hounded; and there is no asylum from coast to coast.

Fraternity. This short-lived ideal of the French Revolution, animating a whole people and uniting all classes as a community, soon gave way to a dangerous nationalism. The ideal somewhat revived as the solidarity of the working class, but this too has faded into either philanthropy or "belonging."

Brotherhood of Races. The Civil War won formal rights for Negroes, but failed to win social justice and factual democracy. The actual result has been segregation, and fear and ignorance for both whites and blacks.

Pacifism. This revolution has been entirely missed.

5.

Let us proceed to some more general moral premises of modern times.

Reformation. The Protestant Reformation won the possibility of living religiously in the world, freed individuals from the domination of the priest, and led, indirectly, to the toleration of private conscience. But it failed to withstand the secular power; it did not cultivate the meaning of vocation as a community function; and in most sects the spirit of the churches did not spring from their living congregations but was handed down as dogma and ascetic discipline. The final result has been secularism, individualism, the subordination of human beings to a rational economic system, and churches irrelevant to practical community life. Meantime, acting merely as a negative force, the jealous sectarian conscience has driven religion out of social thought.

Modern Science. The scientific revolution associated with the name of Galileo freed thinking of superstition and academic tradition and won attention to the observation of nature. But it failed to modify and extend its method to social and moral matters, and indeed science has gotten further and further from ordinary experience. With the dominance of science and applied science in our times, the result has been a specialist class of scientists and technicians, the increasing ineptitude of the average person, a disastrous dichotomy of "neutral" facts versus "arbitrary" values, and a superstition of scientism that has put people out of touch with nature, and also has aroused a growing hostility to science.

Enlightenment. The Enlightenment unseated age-old tyrannies of state and church and won a triumph of reason over authority. But its universalism failed to survive the rising nationalisms except in special sciences and learning, and its ideal of encyclopedic reason as the passionate guide to life degenerated to the nineteenth-century hope for progress through science and learning. And we now have an internationalism without brotherhood or peace, even concealing science as a strategic weapon; and a general sentiment that the rule of reason is infinitely impractical.

Honesty. The rebellion for honest speech that we associate with Ibsen, Flaubert, etc., and also with the muckrakers broke down the hypocrisy of Victorian prudishness and of exploiting pillars of society; it reopened discussion and renovated language; and it weakened official censorship. But it failed to insist on the close relation between honest speech and corresponding action. The result has been a weakening of the obligation to act according to speech, so that, ironically, the real motives of public and private behavior are more in the dark than ever.

Popular Culture. This ideal, that we may associate in literature with the name of Sam Johnson and the Fleet Street journalists, in the plastic arts with William Morris and Ruskin, freed culture from aristocratic and snobbish patrons. It made thought and design relevant to everyday manners. But it did not succeed in establishing an immediate relation between the writer or artist and his audience. The result is that the popular culture is controlled by hucksters and promoters as though it were a saleable commodity, and our society, inundated by cultural commodities, remains uncultivated.

6.

Finally, some reforms directly connected with children and adolescents.

No Child Labor. Children have been rescued from the exploitation and training of factories and sweat shops. But, relying on the public schools and the apprentice-training in an expanding and open economy, the reformers did not develop a philosophy of capacity and vocation. Nor, since there were many small jobs, did they face the problems of a growing boy needing to earn some money. In our day, the result is that growing youths are idle and vocationally useless, and often economically desperate; and the schools, on the contrary, become apprentice-training paid for by public money.

Compulsory Education. This gave to all children a certain equality of opportunity in an open expanding industrial society. Formal elementary discipline was sufficient when the environment was educative and provided opportunities for advancement. In our circumstances, formal literacy is less relevant, and overcrowding and official interference make individual attention and real teaching impossible; so that it could be said that the schools are

as stupefying as they are educative, and compulsory education is often like jail.

Sexual Revolution. This has accomplished a freeing of animal functioning in general, has pierced repression, importantly relaxed inhibition, weakened legal and social sanctions, and diminished the strict animal-training of small children. The movement has not so much failed as that it is still in process, strongly resisted by inherited prejudices, fears, and jealousies. By and large it has not won practical freedom for older children and adolescents. The actual present result is that they are trapped by inconsistent rules, suffer because of excessive stimulation and inadequate discharge, and become preoccupied with sexual thoughts as if these were the whole of life.

Permissiveness. Children have more freedom of spontaneous behavior, and their dignity and spirit are not crushed by humiliating punishments in school and in very many homes. But this permissiveness has not extended to provide also means and conditions: Young folk might be sexually free but have no privacy; they are free to be angry, but have no asylum to escape from home, and no way to get their own money. Besides, where upbringing is permissive, it is necessary to have strong values and esteemed behavior at home and in the community, so that the child can have worth-while goals to structure his experience; and of course it is just these that are lacking. So permissiveness often leads to anxiety and weakness instead of confidence and strength.

Progressive Education. This radical proposal, aimed at solving the dilemmas of education in the modern circumstances of industrialism and democracy, was never given a chance. It succeeded in destroying the faculty psychology in the interests of educating the whole person, and in emphasizing group experience, but failed to introduce learning-by-doing with real problems.

The actual result of the gains has been to weaken the academic curriculum and foster adjustment to society as it is.

7.

Let us consider the beginning, the ending, and the middle of these little paragraphs.

The headings printed in bold type are, in their summation, a kind of program of modern man. It is evident that every one of these twenty-odd positions was invented-and-discovered as a response to specific historical conditions. The political positions were developed to oppose the absolutism of the kings who had unified the warring feudal states; the program for children and adolescents has been a response to modern industrialism and urbanism; and so forth. But it does *not* follow, as some sociologists think, that they can therefore be superseded and forgotten as conditions change.

Consider the following of C. Wright Mills: "The ideals that we Westerners associate with the classic, liberal, bourgeois period of modern culture may well be rooted in this one historical stage of this one type of society. Such ideals as personal freedom and cultural autonomy may not be inherent, necessary features of cultural life as such." This is like saying that tragic poetry or mathematics was "rooted" in the Greek way of life and is not "inherently" human. This kind of thinking is the final result of the recent social-scientific attitude that culture is added onto a featureless animal, rather than being the invention-and-discovery of human powers. This is effectually to give up the modern enterprise altogether. But we will not give it up. New conditions will be the conditions of, now, this kind of man, stubbornly insisting on the ideals that he has learned he has in him to meet.

Yet the modern positions are not even easily consistent with one another, to form a coherent program. There have been bitter conflicts between Liberty and Equality, Science and Faith, Technology and Syndicalism, and so forth. Nevertheless, we will not give up one or the other, but will arduously try to achieve them all and *make* a coherent program. And indeed, experience has taught that the failure in one of these ideals at once entails failure in others. For instance, failure in social justice weakens political freedom, and this compromises scientific and religious autonomy. "If we continue to be without a socialist movement," says Frank Marquart, "we may end up without a labor movement." The setback of progressive education makes the compulsory school system more hopeless, and this now threatens permissiveness and sexual freedom; and so forth. So we struggle to perfect all these positions, one buttressing another, if we are to fulfill our unique modern destiny.

There is no doubt, too, that in our plight new modern positions will be added to these, and these too will be compromised, aborted, their prophetic urgency bureaucratized and ironically transformed into the opposite. But there it is.

8.

If we now collect the actual, often ironical, results of so much noble struggle, we get a clear *but exaggerated* picture of our American society. It has: slums of engineering—boondoggling, production—chaotic congestion—tribes of middlemen—basic city functions squeezed out—garden cities for children—indifferent workmen—underprivileged on a dole—empty "belonging" without nature or culture—front politicians—no patriotism—an empty nationalism bound for a cataclysmically disastrous finish—wise opinion swamped—enterprise sabotaged by monopoly—prejudice rising—religion otiose—the popular culture debased—science specialized—science secret—the average man inept—youth idle and tru-ant—youth sexually suffering and sexually obsessed—youth without goals—poor schools.

This picture is not unjust, but it is, again, exaggerated. For it omits, of course, all the positive factors and the on-going successes. We have a persisting grand cul-ture. There is a steady advance of science, scholarship, and the fine arts. A steady improvement in health and medicine. An economy of abundance and, in many ways, a genuine civil peace and a stubborn affirm-ing of democracy. And most of all there are the remarkable resilience and courage that belong to human beings. Also, the Americans, for all their folly and confor-mity, are often thrillingly sophisticated and impatient of hypocrisy.

Yet there is one grim actuality that even this exaggerated picture does not reveal, the creeping defeatism and surren-der by default to the organized system of the state and semimonopolies. International Business Machines and organized psychol-ogists, we have seen, effactually determine the method of school examinations and per-sonnel selection. As landlords, Webb and Knapp and Metropolitan Life decide what our domestic habits should be; and, as "civic developers" they plan communities, even though their motive is simply a "long-term modest profit" on investment while millions are ill housed. The good of Gen-eral Motors and the nation are inseparable says Secretary Wilson—even though the cars are demonstrably ruinous for the cities, ruinous for the young, etc. Madison Ave-nue and Hollywood not only debauch their audiences, but they pre-empt the means of communication, so nothing else can exist. With only occasional flagrant breaches of legality, the increasingly interlocking police forces and the FBI make people cowed and speechless. That Americans can allow this kind of thing instead of demol-ishing it with a blow of the paw like a strong lion, is the psychology of missed revolutions.

9.

For our positive purposes in this book, it is the middle parts of our paragraphs that warrant study: the failures, the fallings-short, the compromises. Imagine that these modern radical positions had been more fully achieved: we should have a society where:

A premium is placed on technical improvement and on the engineering style of functional simplicity and clarity. Where the community is planned as a whole, with an organic integration of work, living, and play. Where buildings have the variety of their real functions with the uniformity of the prevailing technology. Where a lot of money is spent on public goods. Where workers are technically educated and have a say in management. Where no one drops out of society and there is an easy mobility of classes. Where production is primarily for use. Where social groups are labora-tories for solving their own problems experimentally. Where democracy begins in the town meeting, and a man seeks office only because he has a program. Where regional variety is encouraged and there is pride in the Republic. And young men are free of conscription. Where all feel them-selves citizens of the universal Republic of Reason. Where it is the policy to give an adequate voice to the unusual and unpopu-lar opinion, and to give a trial and a market to new enterprise. Where people are not afraid to make friends. Where races are factually equal. Where vocation is sought out and cultivated as God-given capacity, to be conserved and embellished, and where the church is the spirit of its congre-gation. Where ordinary experience is habit-ually scientifically assayed by the average man. Where it is felt that the suggestion of reason is practical. And speech leads to the corresponding action. Where the popular culture is a daring and passionate culture. Where children can make themselves useful and earn their own money. Where their sexuality is taken for granted. Where the community carries on its important adult business and the children fall in at their own pace. And where education is concerned with fostering human powers as they develop in the growing child.

In such an utopian society, as was aimed at by modern radicals but has not eventuated, it would be very easy to grow up. There would be plenty of objective, worth-while activities for a child to observe, fall in with, do, learn, improvise on his own. That is to say, it is not the spirit of modern times that makes our society difficult for the young; it is that that spirit has not sufficiently realized itself.

In this light, the present plight of the young is not surprising. In the rapid changes, people have not kept enough in mind that the growing young also exist and the world must fit their needs. So instead, we have the present phenomena of excessive attention to the children as such, in psychology and suburbs, and coping with "juvenile delinquency" as if it were an entity. Adults fighting for some profoundly conceived fundamental change naturally give up, exhausted, when they have achieved some gain that makes life tolerable again and seems to be the substance of their demand. But to grow up, the young need a world of finished situations and society made whole again. . . .

Tom Hayden

Born in 1939 in Royal Oak, Michigan, Tom Hayden became known for his Left-wing political activism and leadership in the Students for a Democratic Society (SDS) in the 1960s. He received a B.A. at the University of Michigan and began graduate work there, but his time was consumed with founding the SDS. He wrote the initial draft of the SDS policy manifesto, "The Port Huron Statement" (excerpted here), which was the first national declaration of the New Left and is seen as the classic statement of the goals of this influential political movement. It stresses the human potentiality that could flourish in a decent social context and rejects "trickle down" economics as a means of achieving social justice, calling instead for reduced military spending and increased worker participation in government and corporate decision making.

As president of SDS from 1962 to 1963, Hayden cofounded the Economic Research and Action Project (ERAP) to help the urban poor in the northeastern United States. This led to the Newark Community Union Project, which Hayden helped organize, and which pressured the city government to respond to the complaints of the poor. The project ended following the 1967 Newark race riots, which Hayden described in *Rebellion in Newark.* Hayden coauthored *The Other Side* with Straughton Lynd—a view of the North Vietnam enemy "as people" following a 1965 visit there. Hayden was one of the "Chicago Seven" arrested for antiwar demonstrations at the 1968 Democratic Convention. In 1976 in California he lost a respectable bid for a U.S. Senate seat, but was later elected to the California Legislature. Hayden published *The American Future,* a plan for economic democracy, in 1980.

The Port Huron Statement* (1962)
(excerpts)

Introduction: Agenda for a Generation

We are people of this generation, bred in at least modest comfort, housed now in universities, looking uncomfortably to the world we inherit.

When we were kids, the United States was the wealthiest and strongest country in the world: the only one with the atom bomb, the least scarred by modern war, and initiator of the United Nations that we thought would distribute Western influence throughout the world. Freedom and equality for each individual, government of, by, and for the people—these American values we found good, principles by which we could live as men. Many of us began maturing in complacency.

As we grew, however, our comfort was penetrated by events too troubling to dismiss. First, the permeating and victimizing fact of human degradation, symbolized by the Southern struggle against racial bigotry, compelled most of us from silence to activism. Second, the enclosing fact of the Cold War, symbolized by the presence of the Bomb, brought awareness that we ourselves, and our friends, and millions of abstract "others" we knew more directly because of our common peril, might die at any time. We might deliberately ignore, or avoid, or fail to feel all other human problems, but not these two, for these were too immediate and crushing in their impact, too challenging in the demand that we as individuals take the responsibility for encounter and resolution.

While these and other problems either directly oppressed us or rankled our consciences and became our own subjective concerns, we began to see complicated and disturbing paradoxes in our surrounding America. The declaration "all men are created equal . . ." rang hollow before the facts of Negro life in the South and the big cities of the North. The proclaimed peaceful intentions of the United States contradicted its economic and military investments in the Cold War status quo.

We witnessed, and continue to witness, other paradoxes. With nuclear energy whole cities can easily be powered, yet the dominant nation-states seem more likely to unleash destruction greater than that incurred in all wars of human history. Although our own technology is destroying old and creating new forms of social organization, men still tolerate meaningless work and idleness. While two-thirds of mankind suffers undernourishment, our own upper classes revel amidst superfluous abundance. Although world population is expected to double in forty years, the nations still tolerate anarchy as a major principle of international conduct and uncontrolled exploitation governs the sapping of the earth's physical resources. Although mankind desperately needs revolutionary leadership, America rests in national stalemate, its goals ambiguous and tradition-bound instead of informed and clear, its democratic system apathetic and

---

Isaak, *American Political Thinking.*/From *The Port Huron Statement* by Tom Hayden. Reprinted by permission of the author.

* "The Port Huron Statement" was . . . the first official statement of the Students for a Democratic Society (SDS) at their convention in Port Huron, Michigan, June 11–15, 1962. . . .

manipulated rather than "of, by, and for the people."

Not only did tarnish appear on our image of American virtue, not only did disillusion occur when the hypocrisy of American ideals was discovered, but we began to sense that what we had originally seen as the American Golden Age was actually the decline of an era. The worldwide outbreak of revolution against colonialism and imperialism, the entrenchment of totalitarian states, the menace of war, overpopulation, international disorder, supertechnology—these trends were testing the tenacity of our own commitment to democracy and freedom and our abilities to visualize their application to a world in upheaval.

Our work is guided by the sense that we may be the last generation in the experiment with living. But we are a minority— the vast majority of our people regard the temporary equilibriums of our society and world as eternally functional parts. In this is perhaps the outstanding paradox: we ourselves are imbued with urgency, yet the message of our society is that there is no viable alternative to the present. Beneath the reassuring tones of the politicians, beneath the common opinion that America will "muddle through," beneath the stagnation of those who have closed their minds to the future, is the pervading feeling that there simply are no alternatives, that our times have witnessed the exhaustion not only of utopias, but of any new departures as well. Feeling the press of complexity upon the emptiness of life, people are fearful of the thought that at any moment things might be thrust out of control. They fear change itself, since change might smash whatever invisible framework seems to hold back chaos for them now. For most Americans, all crusades are suspect, threatening. The fact that each individual sees apathy in his fellows perpetuates the common reluctance to organize for change. The dominant institutions are complex enough to blunt the minds of their potential critics, and entrenched enough to swiftly dissipate or entirely repel the energies of protest and reform, thus limiting human expectancies. Then, too, we are a materially improved society, and by our own improvements we seem to have weakened the case for further change.

Some would have us believe that Americans feel contentment amidst prosperity—but might it not better be called a glaze above deeply felt anxieties about their role in the new world? And if these anxieties produce a developed indifference to human affairs, do they not as well produce a yearning to believe there *is* an alternative to the present, that something *can* be done to change circumstances in the school, the workplaces, the bureaucracies, the government? It is to this latter yearning, at once the spark and engine of change, that we direct our present appeal. The search for truly democratic alternatives to the present, and a commitment to social experimentation with them, is a worthy and fulfilling human enterprise, one which moves us and, we hope, others today. On such a basis we offer this document of our convictions and analysis: as an effort in understanding and changing the conditions of humanity in the late twentieth century, an effort rooted in the ancient, still unfulfilled conception of man attaining determining influence over his circumstances of life.

Values

Making values explicit—an initial task in establishing alternatives—is an activity that has been devalued and corrupted. The conventional moral terms of the age, the politician moralities—"free world," "people's democracies"—reflect realities poorly, if at all, and seem to function more as ruling myths than as descriptive principles. But neither has our experience in the universities brought us moral enlightenment. Our professors and administrators sacrifice controversy to public relations; their curriculums change more slowly than the living events of the world; their skills and silence are purchased by investors in the arms race; passion is called unscholastic. The questions we might want raised— What is really important? Can we live in a different and better way? If we wanted to change society, how would we do it?— are not thought to be questions of a "fruitful, empirical nature," and thus are brushed aside.

Unlike youth in other countries we are used to moral leadership being exercised and moral dimensions being clarified by our elders. But today, for us, not even the liberal and socialist preachments of the past seem adequate to the forms of the present. Consider the old slogans: Capitalism Cannot Reform Itself, United Front Against Fascism, General Strike, All Out on May Day. Or, more recently, No Cooperation with Commies and Fellow Travelers, Ideologies are Exhausted, Bipartisanship, No Utopias. These are incomplete, and there are few new prophets. It has been said that our liberal and socialist predecessors were plagued by vision without program, while our own generation is plagued by program without vision. All around us there is astute grasp of method, technique—the committee, the *ad hoc* group, the lobbyist, the hard and soft sell, the make, the projected image—but, if pressed critically, such expertise is incompetent to explain its implicit ideals. It is highly fashionable to identify oneself by old categories, or by naming a respected political figure, or by explaining "how we would vote" on various issues.

Theoretic chaos has replaced the idealistic thinking of old—and, unable to reconstitute theoretic order, men have condemned idealism itself. Doubt has replaced hopefulness—and men act out a defeatism that is labeled realistic. The decline of utopia and hope is in fact one of the defining features of social life today. The reasons are various: the dreams of the older left were perverted by Stalinism and never recreated; the congressional stalemate makes men narrow their view of the possible; the specialization of human activity leaves little room for sweeping thought; the horrors of the twentieth century, symbolized in the gas ovens and concentration camps and atom bombs, have blasted hopefulness. To be idealistic is to be considered apocalyptic, deluded. To have no serious aspirations, on the contrary, is to be "tough-minded."

In suggesting social goals and values, therefore, we are aware of entering a sphere of some disrepute. Perhaps matured by the past, we have no sure formulas, no closed theories—but that does not mean values are beyond discussion and tentative determination. A first task of any social movement is to convince people that the search for orienting theories and the creation of human values is complex but worthwhile. We are aware that to avoid platitudes we must analyze the concrete conditions of social order. But to direct such an analysis we must use the guideposts of basic principles. Our own social values involve conceptions of human beings, human relationships, and social systems.

We regard *men* as infinitely precious and possessed of unfulfilled capacities for reason, freedom, and love. In affirming these principles we are aware of countering perhaps the dominant conceptions of man in the twentieth century: that he is a thing to be manipulated, and that he is inherently incapable of directing his own affairs. We oppose the depersonalization that reduces human beings to the status of things—if anything, the brutalities of the twentieth century teach that means and ends are intimately related, that vague appeals to "posterity" cannot justify the mutilations of the present. We oppose, too, the doctrine of human incompetence because it rests essentially on the modern fact that men have been "competently" manipulated into incompetence—we see little reason why men cannot meet with increasing skill the complexities and responsibilities of their situation, if society is organized not for minority, but for majority, participation in decision-making.

Men have unrealized potential for self-cultivation, self-direction, self-understanding, and creativity. It is this potential that we regard as crucial and to which we appeal, not to the human potentiality for violence, unreason, and submission to authority. The goal of man and society should be human independence: a concern not with the image of popularity but with finding a meaning in life that is personally authentic; a quality of mind not compulsively driven by a sense of powerlessness, nor one which unthinkingly adopts status values, nor one which represses all threats to its habits, but one which has full, spontaneous access to present and past experiences, one which easily unites the fragmented parts of personal history, one which openly faces problems which are troubling and unresolved; one with an intuitive awareness of possibilities, an active sense of curiosity, an ability and willingness to learn.

This kind of independence does not mean egotistic individualism—the object is not to have one's way so much as it is to have a way that is one's own. Nor do we deify man—we merely have faith in his potential.

Human relationships should involve fraternity and honesty. Human interdependence is contemporary fact; human brotherhood must be willed, however, as a condition of future survival and as the most appropriate form of social relations. Personal links between man and man are needed, especially to go beyond the partial and fragmentary bonds of function that bind men only as worker to worker, employer to employee, teacher to student, American to Russian.

Loneliness, estrangement, isolation describe the vast distance between man and man today. These dominant tendencies cannot be overcome by better personnel management, nor by improved gadgets, but only when a love of man overcomes the idolatrous worship of things by man. As the individualism we affirm is not egoism, the selflessness we affirm is not self-elimination. On the contrary, we believe in generosity of a kind that imprints one's unique individual qualities in the relation to other men, and to all human activity. Further, to dislike isolation is not to favor the abolition of privacy; the latter differs from isolation in that it occurs or is abolished according to individual will.

We would replace power rooted in possession, privilege, or circumstance by power and uniqueness rooted in love, reflectiveness, reason, and creativity. As a *social system* we seek the establishment of a democracy of individual participation, governed by two central aims: that the individual share in those social decisions determining the quality and direction of his life; that society be organized to encourage independence in men and provide the media for their common participation.

In a participatory democracy, the political life would be based in several root principles:

> that decision-making of basic social consequence be carried on by public groupings;
>
> that politics be seen positively, as the art of collectively creating an acceptable pattern of social relations;
>
> that politics has the function of bringing people out of isolation and into community, thus being a necessary, though not sufficient, means of finding meaning in personal life;

that the political order should serve to clarify problems in a way instrumental to their solution; it should provide outlets for the expression of personal grievance and aspiration; opposing views should be organized so as to illuminate choices and facilitate the attainment of goals; channels should be commonly available to relate men to knowledge and to power so that private problems—from bad recreation facilities to personal alienation—are formulated as general issues.

The economic sphere would have as its basis the principles:

that work should involve incentives worthier than money or survival. It should be educative, not stultifying; creative, not mechanical; self-directed, not manipulated, encouraging independence, a respect for others, a sense of dignity and a willingness to accept social responsibility, since it is this experience that has crucial influence on habits, perceptions, and individual ethics;

that the economic experience is so personally decisive that the individual must share in its full determination;

that the economy itself is of such social importance that its major resources and means of production should be open to democratic participation and subject to democratic social regulation.

Like the political and economic ones, major social institutions—cultural, educational, rehabilitative, and others—should be generally organized with the well-being and dignity of man as the essential measure of success.

In social change or interchange, we find violence to be abhorrent because it requires generally the transformation of the target, be it a human being or a community of people, into a depersonalized object of hate. It is imperative that the means of violence be abolished and the institutions—local, national, international—that encourage non-violence as a condition of conflict be developed.

These are our central values, in skeletal form. It remains vital to understand their denial or attainment in the context of the modern world.

The Students

In the last few years, thousands of American students demonstrated that they at least felt the urgency of the times. They moved actively and directly against racial injustices, the threat of war, violations of individual rights of conscience and, less frequently, against economic manipulation. They succeeded in restoring a small measure of controversy to the campuses after the stillness of the McCarthy period. They succeeded, too, in gaining some concessions from the people and institutions they opposed, especially in the fight against racial bigotry.

The significance of these scattered movements lies not in their success or failure in gaining objectives—at least not yet.

Nor does the significance lie in the intellectual "competence" or "maturity" of the students involved—as some pedantic elders allege. The significance is in the fact the students are breaking the crust of apathy and overcoming the inner alienation that remain the defining characteristics of American college life.

If student movements for change are still rarities on the campus scene, what is commonplace there? The real campus, the familiar campus, is a place of private people, engaged in their notorious "inner emigration." It is a place of commitment to business-as-usual, getting ahead, playing it cool. It is a place of mass affirmation of the Twist, but mass reluctance toward the controversial public stance. Rules are accepted as "inevitable," bureaucracy as "just circumstances," irrelevance as "scholarship," selflessness as "martyrdom," politics as "just another way to make people, and an unprofitable one, too."

Almost no students value activity as citizens. Passive in public, they are hardly more idealistic in arranging their private lives: Gallup concludes they will settle for "low success, and won't risk high failure." There is not much willingness to take risks (not even in business), no settling of dangerous goals, no real conception of personal identity except one manufactured in the image of others, no real urge for personal fulfillment except to be almost as successful as the very successful people. Attention is being paid to social status (the quality of shirt collars, meeting people, getting wives or husbands, making solid contacts for later on); much, too, is paid to academic status (grades, honors, the med school rat race). But neglected generally is real intellectual status, the personal cultivation of the mind.

"Students don't even give a damn about the apathy," one has said. Apathy toward apathy begets a privately-constructed universe, a place of systematic study schedules, two nights each week for beer, a girl or two, and early marriage; a framework infused with personality, warmth, and under control, no matter how unsatisfying otherwise.

Under these conditions university life loses all relevance to some. Four hundred thousand of our classmates leave college every year.

But apathy is not simply an attitude; it is a product of social institutions, and of the structure and organization of higher education itself. The extracurricular life is ordered according to *in loco parentis* theory, which ratifies the Administration as the moral guardian of the young.

The accompanying "let's pretend" theory of student extracurricular affairs validates student government as a training center for those who want to spend their lives in political pretense, and discourages initiative from the more articulate, honest, and sensitive students. The bounds and style of controversy are delimited before controversy begins. The university "prepares" the student for "citizenship" through perpetual rehearsals and, usually, through emasculation of what creative spirit there is in the individual.

The academic life contains reinforcing counterparts to the way in which extracurricular life is organized. The academic world is founded on a teacher-student relation analogous to the parent-child relation which characterizes *in loco parentis*. Further, academia includes a radical separation of the student from the material of study. That which is studied, the social reality, is "objectified" to sterility, dividing the student from life—just as he is restrained in active involvement by the deans controlling student government. The specialization of function and knowledge, admittedly necessary to our complex technological and social structure, has produced an exaggerated compartmentalization of study and understanding. This has contributed to an overly parochial view, by faculty, of the role of its research and scholarship, to a discontinuous and truncated understanding, by students, of the surrounding social order and to a loss of personal attachment, by nearly all, to the worth of study as a humanistic enterprise.

There is, finally, the cumbersome academic bureaucracy extending throughout the academic as well as the extracurricular structures, contributing to the sense of outer complexity and inner powerlessness that transforms the honest searching of many students to a ratification of convention and, worse, to a numbness to present and future catastrophes. The size and financing systems of the university enhance the permanent trusteeship of the administrative bureaucracy, their power leading to a shift within the university toward the value standards of business and the administrative mentality. Huge foundations and other private financial interests shape the underfinanced colleges and universities, not only making them more commercial, but less disposed to diagnose society critically, less open to dissent. Many social and physical scientists, neglecting the liberating heritage of higher learning, develop "human relations" or "morale-producing" techniques for the corporate economy, while others exercise their intellectual skills to accelerate the arms race.

Tragically, the university could serve as a significant source of social criticism and an initiator of new modes and molders of attitudes. But the actual intellectual effect of the college experience is hardly distinguishable from that of any other communications channel—say, a television set—passing on the stock truths of the day. Students leave college somewhat more "tolerant" than when they arrived, but basically unchallenged in their values and political orientations. With administrators ordering the institution, and faculty the curriculum, the student learns by his isolation to accept elite rule within the university, which prepares him to accept later forms of minority control. The real function of the educational system—as opposed to its more rhetorical function of "searching for truth"—is to impart the key information and styles that will help the student get by, modestly but comfortably, in the big society beyond.

The Society Beyond

Look beyond the campus, to America itself. That student life is more intellectual, and perhaps more comfortable, does not obscure the fact that the fundamental qualities of life on the campus reflect the habits of society at large. The fraternity president is seen at the junior manager levels; the sorority queen has gone to Grosse Pointe; the serious poet burns for a place, any place, to work; the once-serious and never-serious poets work at the advertising agencies. The desperation of people threatened by forces about which they know little and of which they can say less, the cheerful emptiness of people giving up all hope of changing things, the faceless ones polled by Gallup who listed "international affairs" fourteenth on their list of problems but who also expected thermonuclear war in the next few years—in these and other forms, Americans are in withdrawal from public life, from any collective effort at directing their own affairs.

Some regard these national doldrums as a sign of healthy approval of the established order, but is it approval by consent or by manipulated acquiescence? Others declare that the people are withdrawn because compelling issues are fast disappearing; perhaps there are fewer breadlines in America, but is Jim Crow gone, is there enough work and is work more fulfilling, is world war a diminishing threat, and what of the revolutionary new peoples? Still others think the national quietude is a necessary consequence of the need for elites to resolve complex and specialized problems of modern industrial society. But, then, why should business elites help decide foreign policy, and who controls the elites anyway, and are they solving mankind's problems? Others finally shrug knowingly and announce that full democracy never worked anywhere in the past—but why lump qualitatively different civilizations together, and how can a social order work well if its best thinkers are skeptics, and is man really doomed forever to the domination of today?

There are no convincing apologies for

the contemporary malaise. While the world tumbles toward the final war, while men in other nations are trying desperately to alter events, while the very future *qua* future is uncertain—America is without community, impulse, without the inner momentum necessary for an age when societies cannot successfully perpetuate themselves by their military weapons, when democracy must be viable because of the quality of life, not its quantity of rockets.

The apathy here is, first, *subjective*—the felt powerlessness of ordinary people, the resignation before the enormity of events. But subjective apathy is encouraged by the *objective* American situation—the actual structural separation of people from power, from relevant knowledge, from pinnacles of decision-making. Just as the university influences the student way of life, so do major social institutions create the circumstances in which the isolated citizen will try hopelessly to understand his world and himself.

The very isolation of the individual—from power and community and ability to aspire—means the rise of a democracy without publics. With the great mass of people structurally remote and psychologically hesitant with respect to democratic institutions, those institutions themselves attenuate and become, in the fashion of the vicious circle, progressively less accessible to those few who aspire to serious participation in social affairs. The vital democratic connection between community and leadership, between the mass and the several elites, has been so wrenched and perverted that disastrous policies go unchallenged time and again. . . .

Towards American Democracy

Every effort to end the Cold War and expand the process of world industrialization is an effort hostile to people and institutions whose interests lie in perpetuation of the East-West military threat and the postponement of change in the "have not" nations of the world. Every such effort, too, is bound to establish greater democracy in America. The major goals of a domestic effort would be:

1. America must abolish its political party stalemate. . . .
2. Mechanisms of voluntary association must be created through which political information can be imparted and political participation encouraged. . . .
3. Institutions and practices which stifle dissent should be abolished, and the promotion of peaceful dissent should be actively promoted. . . .
4. Corporations must be made publicly responsible. . . .
5. The allocation of resources must be based on social needs. A truly "public sector" must be established, and its nature debated and planned. . . .
6. America should concentrate on its genuine social priorities: abolish squalor, terminate neglect, and establish an environment for people to live in with dignity and creativeness. . . .

Alternatives to Helplessness

The goals we have set are not realizable next month, or even next election—but that fact justifies neither giving up altogether nor a determination to work only on immediate, direct, tangible problems. Both responses are a sign of helplessness, fearfulness of visions, refusal to hope, and tend to bring on the very conditions to be avoided. Fearing vision, we justify rhetoric or myopia. Fearing hope, we reinforce despair.

The first effort, then, should be to state a vision: what is the perimeter of human possibility in this epoch? This we have tried to do. The second effort, if we are to be politically responsible, is to evaluate the prospects for obtaining at least a substantial part of that vision in our epoch: what are the social forces that exist, or that must exist, if we are to be at all successful? And what role have we ourselves to play as a social force? . . .

The University and Social Change

. . . The civil rights, peace, and student movements are too poor and socially slighted, and the labor movement too quiescent, to be counted with enthusiasm. From where else can power and vision be summoned? We believe that the universities are an overlooked seat of influence.

First, the university is located in a permanent position of social influence. Its educational function makes it indispensable and automatically makes it a crucial institution in the formation of social attitudes. In an unbelievably complicated world, it is the central institution for organizing, evaluating, and transmitting knowledge. . . . Social relevance, the accessibility to knowledge, and internal openness—these together make the university a potential base and agency in the movement of social change.

1. Any new left in America must be, in large measure, a left with real intellectual skills, committed to deliberativeness, honesty, and reflection as working tools. The university permits the political life to be an adjunct to the academic one, and action to be informed by reason.

2. A new left must be distributed in significant social roles throughout the country. The universities are distributed in such a manner.

3. A new left must consist of younger people who matured in the postwar world, and must be directed to the recruitment of younger people. The university is an obvious beginning point.

4. A new left must include liberals and socialists, the former for their relevance, the latter for their sense of thoroughgoing reforms in the system. The university is a more sensible place than a political party for these two traditions to begin to discuss their differences and look for political synthesis.

5. A new left must start controversy across the land, if national policies and national apathy are to be reversed. The ideal university is a community of controversy, within itself and in its effects on communities beyond.

6. A new left must transform modern complexity into issues that can be understood and felt close-up by every human being. It must give form to the feelings of helplessness and indifference, so that people may see the political, social, and economic sources of their private troubles and organize to change society. In a time of supposed prosperity, moral complacency, and political manipulation, a new left cannot rely on only aching stomachs to be the engine force of social reform. The case for change, for alternatives that will involve uncomfortable personal efforts, must be argued as never before. The university is a relevant place for all of these activities.

But we need not indulge in illusions: the university system cannot complete a movement of ordinary people making demands for a better life. From its schools and colleges across the nation a militant left might awaken its allies, and by beginning the process towards peace, civil rights, and labor struggles, reinsert theory and idealism where too often reign confusion and political barter. The power of students and faculty united is not only potential; it has shown its actuality in the South, and in the reform movements of the North.

The bridge to political power, though, will be built through genuine cooperation, locally, nationally, and internationally, between a new left of young people, and an awakening community of allies. In each community we must look within the university and act with confidence that we can be powerful, but we must look outwards to the less exotic but more lasting struggles for justice.

To turn these possibilities into realities will involve national efforts at university reform by an alliance of students and faculty. They must wrest control of the educational process from the administrative bureaucracy. They must make fraternal and functional contact with allies in labor, civil rights, and other liberal forces outside the campus. They must import major public issues into the curriculum—research and teaching on problems of war and peace is an outstanding example. They must make debate and controversy, not dull pedantic cant, the common style for educational life. They must consciously build a base for their assault upon the loci of power.

As students for a democratic society, we are committed to stimulating this kind of social movement, this kind of vision and program in campus and community across the country. If we appear to seek the unattainable, as it has been said, then let it be known that we do so to avoid the unimaginable.

Herbert Marcuse

Born in Berlin in 1898 into a prominent, upper-class Jewish family, Marcuse became a major intellectual influence for New Left radicals of the 1960s. His original libertarian critique of the American political system was based upon a synthesis of the theories of Marx and Freud.

Marcuse studied at the Augusta Gymnasium in Berlin, the University of Berlin, and the University of Freiburg, where he received his Ph.D. in philosophy *magna cum laude* and wrote a study of Hegel's ontology and theory of history. Together with Theodor Adorno and Max Horkheimer, Marcuse founded the Frankfurt Institute of Social Research. Marcuse's world view was shaped by the heady development of the field of sociology, the failure of the Weimar democracy to contain the Nazis, and the Marxist school of psychoanalysis founded by Wilhelm Reich.

A Nazi target, the Frankfurt Institute of Social Research closed when Hitler came to power, and Marcuse fled to Geneva, Switzerland, where he spent one year at the Institut de Recherches Sociales. He was then appointed to lecture at Columbia University in New York and became a naturalized U.S. citizen in 1940. During World War II, Marcuse was a European intelligence analyst for the Office of Strategic Services (the U.S. espionage agency). After the war, this agency shifted its focus from Germany and fascism to the Soviet Union and communism. It was moved from the jurisdiction of the Joint Chiefs of Staff to the Department of State, where it became the Office of Intelligence Research.

Marcuse headed its Central European section for four years. Thereafter, he did research in Russian studies at Columbia and Harvard, then taught at Brandeis University (politics and philosophy) and then at the University of California at San Diego.

Marcuse's books include *Reason and Revolution* (1941), *Soviet Marxism* (1958), *Eros and Civilization* (1955), and his most popular book, *One-Dimensional Man* (1964), from which the following excerpts are taken. Marcuse's widespread influence among the young sprang in large part from his belief that technological society had become totalitarian in subtle ways that repressed not only erotic pleasure but also the individual's full humanity. He believed that the "sewer system" of television and other mass media "systematically moronize" most people and that established institutions and "needs" undermine the ability to liberate the self to satisfy one's own true needs.

One-Dimensional Man (1964)
(excerpts)

Introduction

... Confronted with the total character of the achievements of advanced industrial society, critical theory is left without the rationale for transcending this society. The vacuum empties the theoretical structure itself, because the categories of a critical social theory were developed during the period in which the need for refusal and subversion was embodied in the action of effective social forces. These categories were essentially negative and oppositional concepts, defining the actual contradictions in nineteenth century European society. The category "society" itself expressed the acute conflict between the social and political sphere—society as antagonistic to the state. Similarly, "individual," "class," "private," "family" denoted spheres and forces not yet integrated with the established conditions—spheres of tension and contradiction. With the growing integration of industrial society, these categories are losing their critical connotation, and tend to become descriptive, deceptive, or operational terms.

An attempt to recapture the critical intent of these categories, and to understand how the intent was cancelled by the social reality, appears from the outset to be regression from a theory joined with historical practice to abstract, speculative thought: from the critique of political economy to philosophy. This ideological character of the critique results from the fact that the analysis is forced to proceed from a position "outside" the positive as well as negative, the productive as well as destructive tendencies in society. Modern industrial society is the pervasive identity of these opposites—it is the whole that is in question. At the same time, the position of theory cannot be one of mere speculation. It must be a historical position in the sense that it must be grounded on the capabilities of the given society.

This ambiguous situation involves a still more fundamental ambiguity. *One-Dimensional Man* will vacillate throughout between two contradictory hypotheses: (1) that advanced industrial society is capable of containing qualitative change for the foreseeable future; (2) that forces and tendencies exist which may break this containment and explode the society. I do not think that a clear answer can be given. Both tendencies are there, side by side—and even the one in the other. The first tendency is dominant, and whatever preconditions for a reversal may exist are being used to prevent it. Perhaps an accident may alter the situation, but unless the recognition of what is being done and what is being prevented subverts the consciousness and the behavior of man, not even a catastrophe will bring about the change.

The analysis is focused on advanced industrial society, in which the technical apparatus of production and distribution (with an increasing sector of automation) functions, not as the sum-total of mere instruments which can be isolated from their social and political effects, but rather as a system which determines *a priori* the product of the apparatus as well as the operations of servicing and extending it. In this society, the productive apparatus tends to become totalitarian to the extent to which it determines not only the socially needed occupations, skills, and attitudes, but also individual needs and aspirations. It thus obliterates the opposition between the private and public existence, between individual and social needs. Technology serves to institute new, more effective, and more pleasant forms of social control and social cohesion. The totalitarian tendency of these controls seems to assert itself in still another sense—by spreading to the less developed and even to the pre-industrial areas of the world, and by creating similarities in the development of capitalism and communism.

In the face of the totalitarian features of this society, the traditional notion of the "neutrality" of technology can no longer be maintained. Technology as such cannot be isolated from the use to which it is put; the technological society is a system of domination which operates already in the concept and construction of techniques.

The way in which a society organizes the life of its members involves an initial *choice* between historical alternatives which are determined by the inherited level of the material and intellectual culture. The choice itself results from the play of the dominant interests. It *anticipates* specific modes of transforming and utilizing man and nature and rejects other modes. It is one "project" of realization among others.[1] But once the project has become operative in the basic institutions and relations, it tends to become exclusive and to determine the development of the society as a whole. As a technological universe, advanced industrial society is a *political* universe, the latest stage in the realization of a specific historical *project*—namely, the experience, transformation, and organization of nature as the mere stuff of domination.

As the project unfolds, it shapes the entire universe of discourse and action, intellectual and material culture. In the medium of technology, culture, politics, and the economy merge into an omnipresent system which swallows up or repulses all alternatives. The productivity and growth potential of this system stabilize the society and contain technical progress within the framework of domination. Technological rationality has become political rationality.

---

[1] The term "project" emphasizes the element of freedom and responsibility in historical determination: it links autonomy and contingency. In this sense, the term is used in the work of Jean-Paul Sartre. . . .

The New Forms of Control

A comfortable, smooth, reasonable, democratic unfreedom prevails in advanced industrial civilization, a token of technical progress. Indeed, what could be more rational than the suppression of individuality in the mechanization of socially necessary but painful performances; the concentration of individual enterprises in more effective, more productive corporations; the regulation of free competition among unequally equipped economic subjects; the curtailment of prerogatives and national sovereignties which impede the international organization of resources. That this technological order also involves a political and intellectual coordination may be a regrettable and yet promising development.

The rights and liberties which were such vital factors in the origins and earlier stages of industrial society yield to a higher stage of this society: they are losing their traditional rationale and content. Freedom of thought, speech, and conscience were— just as free enterprise, which they served to promote and protect—essentially *critical* ideas, designed to replace an obsolescent material and intellectual culture by a more productive and rational one. Once institutionalized, these rights and liberties shared the fate of the society of which they had become an integral part. The achievement cancels the premises.

To the degree to which freedom from want, the concrete substance of all freedom, is becoming a real possibility, the liberties which pertain to a state of lower productivity are losing their former content. Independence of thought, autonomy, and the right to political opposition are being deprived of their basic critical function in a society which seems increasingly capable of satisfying the needs of the individuals through the way in which it is organized. Such a society may justly demand acceptance of its principles and institutions, and reduce the opposition to the discussion and promotion of alternative policies *within* the status quo. In this respect, it seems to make little difference whether the increasing satisfaction of needs is accomplished by an authoritarian or a non-authoritarian system. Under the conditions of a rising standard of living, non-conformity with the system itself appears to be socially useless, and the more so when it entails tangible economic and political disadvantages and threatens the smooth operation of the whole. Indeed, at least in so far as the necessities of life are involved, there seems to be no reason why the production and distribution of goods and services should proceed through the competitive concurrence of individual liberties.

Freedom of enterprise was from the beginning not altogether a blessing. As the liberty to work or to starve, it spelled toil, insecurity, and fear for the vast majority of the population. If the individual were no longer compelled to prove himself on the market, as a free economic subject, the disappearance of this kind of freedom would be one of the greatest achievements of civilization. The technological processes of mechanization and standardization might release individual energy into a yet uncharted realm of freedom beyond necessity. The very structure of human existence would be altered; the individual would be liberated from the work world's imposing upon him alien needs and alien possibilities. The individual would be free to exert autonomy over a life that would be his own. If the productive apparatus could be organized and directed toward the satisfaction of the vital needs, its control might well be centralized; such control would not prevent individual autonomy, but render it possible.

This is a goal within the capabilities of advanced industrial civilization, the "end" of technological rationality. In actual fact, however, the contrary trend operates: the apparatus imposes its economic and political requirements for defense and expansion on labor time and free time, on the material and intellectual culture. By virtue of the way it has organized its technological base, contemporary industrial society tends to be totalitarian. For "totalitarian" is not only a terroristic political coordination of society, but also a non-terroristic economic-technical coordination which operates through the manipulation of needs by vested interests. It thus precludes the emergence of an effective opposition against the whole. Not only a specific form of government or party rule makes for totalitarianism, but also a specific system of production and distribution which may well be compatible with a "pluralism" of parties, newspapers, "countervailing powers," etc.

Today political power asserts itself through its power over the machine process and over the technical organization of the apparatus. The government of advanced and advancing industrial societies can maintain and secure itself only when it succeeds in mobilizing, organizing, and exploiting the technical, scientific, and mechanical productivity available to industrial civilization. And this productivity mobilizes society as a whole, above and beyond any particular individual or group interests. The brute fact that the machine's physical (only physical?) power surpasses that of the individual, and of any particular group of individuals, makes the machine the most effective political instrument in any society whose basic organization is that of the machine process. But the political trend may be reversed; essentially the power of the machine is only the stored-up and projected power of man. To the extent to which the work world is conceived of as a machine and mechanized

accordingly, it becomes the *potential* basis of a new freedom for man.

Contemporary industrial civilization demonstrates that it has reached the stage at which "the free society" can no longer be adequately defined in the traditional terms of economic, political, and intellectual liberties, not because these liberties have become insignificant, but because they are too significant to be confined within the traditional forms. New modes of realization are needed, corresponding to the new capabilities of society.

Such new modes can be indicated only in negative terms because they would amount to the negation of the prevailing modes. Thus economic freedom would mean freedom *from* the economy—from being controlled by economic forces and relationships; freedom from the daily struggle for existence, from earning a living. Political freedom would mean liberation of the individuals *from* politics over which they have no effective control. Similarly, intellectual freedom would mean the restoration of individual thought now absorbed by mass communication and indoctrination, abolition of "public opinion" together with its makers. The unrealistic sound of these propositions is indicative, not of their utopian character, but of the strength of the forces which prevent their realization. The most effective and enduring form of warfare against liberation is the implanting of material and intellectual needs that perpetuate obsolete forms of the struggle for existence.

The intensity, the satisfaction and even the character of human needs, beyond the biological level, have always been preconditioned. Whether or not the possibility of doing or leaving, enjoying or destroying, possessing or rejecting something is seized as a *need* depends on whether or not it can be seen as desirable and necessary for the prevailing societal institutions and interests. In this sense, human needs are historical needs and, to the extent to which the society demands the repressive development of the individual, his needs themselves and their claim for satisfaction are subject to overriding critical standards.

We may distinguish both true and false needs. "False" are those which are superimposed upon the individual by particular social interests in his repression: the needs which perpetuate toil, aggressiveness, misery, and injustice. Their satisfaction might be most gratifying to the individual, but this happiness is not a condition which has to be maintained and protected if it serves to arrest the development of the ability (his own and others) to recognize the disease of the whole and grasp the chances of curing the disease. The result then is euphoria in unhappiness. Most of the prevailing needs to relax, to have fun, to behave and consume in accordance with the advertisements, to love and hate what others love and hate, belong to this category of false needs.

Such needs have a societal content and function which are determined by external powers over which the individual has no control; the development and satisfaction of these needs is heteronomous. No matter how much such needs may have become the individual's own, reproduced and fortified by the conditions of his existence; no matter how much he identifies himself with them and finds himself in their satisfaction, they continue to be what they were from the beginning—products of a society whose dominant interest demands repression.

The prevalence of repressive needs is an accomplished fact, accepted in ignorance and defeat, but a fact that must be undone in the interest of the happy individual as well as all those whose misery is the price of his satisfaction. The only needs that have an unqualified claim for satisfaction are the vital ones—nourishment, clothing, lodging at the attainable level of culture. The satisfaction of these needs is the prerequisite for the realization of *all* needs, of the unsublimated as well as the sublimated ones.

For any consciousness and conscience, for any experience which does not accept the prevailing societal interest as the supreme law of thought and behavior, the established universe of needs and satisfactions is a fact to be questioned—questioned in terms of truth and falsehood. These terms are historical throughout, and their objectivity is historical. The judgment of needs and their satisfaction, under the given conditions, involves standards of *priority*—standards which refer to the optimal development of the individual, of all individuals, under the optimal utilization of the material and intellectual resources available to man. The resources are calculable. "Truth" and "falsehood" of needs designate objective conditions to the extent to which the universal satisfaction of vital needs and, beyond it, the progressive alleviation of toil and poverty, are universally valid standards. But as historical standards, they do not only vary according to area and stage of development, they also can be defined only in (greater or lesser) *contradiction* to the prevailing ones. What tribunal can possibly claim the authority of decision?

In the last analysis, the question of what are true and false needs must be answered by the individuals themselves, but only in the last analysis; that is, if and when they are free to give their own answer. As long as they are kept incapable of being autonomous, as long as they are indoctrinated and manipulated (down to their very instincts), their answer to this question cannot be taken as their own. By the same token, however, no tribunal can justly arrogate to itself the right to decide which need should be developed and satisfied. Any such tribunal is reprehensible, although our revulsion does not do away with the question: how can the people who have been the object of effective and productive domination by themselves create the conditions of freedom?

The more rational, productive, technical, and total the repressive administration of society becomes, the more unimaginable the means and ways by which the administered individuals might break their servitude and seize their own liberation. To be sure, to impose Reason upon an entire society is a paradoxical and scandalous idea—although one might dispute the righteousness of a society which ridicules this idea while making its own population into objects of total administration. All liberation depends on the consciousness of servitude, and the emergence of this consciousness is always hampered by the predominance of needs and satisfactions which, to a great extent, have become the individual's own. The process always replaces one system of pre-conditioning by another; the optimal goal is the replacement of false needs by true ones, the abandonment of repressive satisfaction.

The distinguishing feature of advanced industrial society is its effective suffocation of those needs which demand liberation—liberation also from that which is tolerable and rewarding and comfortable—while it sustains and absolves the destructive power and repressive function of the affluent society. Here, the social controls exact the overwhelming need for the production and consumption of waste; the need for stupefying work where it is no longer a real necessity; the need for modes of relaxation which soothe and prolong this stupefication; the need for maintaining such deceptive liberties as free competition at administered prices, a free press which censors itself, free choice between brands and gadgets.

Under the rule of a repressive whole, liberty can be made into a powerful instrument of domination. The range of choice open to the individual is not the decisive factor in determining the degree of human freedom, but *what* can be chosen and what *is* chosen by the individual. The criterion

for free choice can never be an absolute one, but neither is it entirely relative. Free election of masters does not abolish the masters or the slaves. Free choice among a wide variety of goods and services does not signify freedom if these goods and services sustain social controls over a life of toil and fear—that is, if they sustain alienation. And the spontaneous reproduction of superimposed needs by the individual does not establish autonomy; it only testifies to the efficacy of the controls.

Our insistence on the depth and efficacy of these controls is open to the objection that we overrate greatly the indoctrinating power of the "media," and that by themselves the people would feel and satisfy the needs which are now imposed upon them. The objection misses the point. The preconditioning does not start with the mass production of radio and television and with the centralization of their control. The people enter this stage as preconditioned receptacles of long standing; the decisive difference is in the flattening out of the contrast (or conflict) between the given and the possible, between the satisfied and the unsatisfied needs. Here, the so-called equalization of class distinctions reveals its ideological function. If the worker and his boss enjoy the same television program and visit the same resort places, if the typist is as attractively made up as the daughter of her employer, if the Negro owns a Cadillac, if they all read the same newspaper, then this assimilation indicates not the disappearance of classes, but the extent to which the needs and satisfactions that serve the preservation of the Establishment are shared by the underlying population.

Indeed, in the most highly developed areas of contemporary society, the transplantation of social into individual needs is so effective that the difference between them seems to be purely theoretical. Can one really distinguish between the mass media as instruments of information and entertainment, and as agents of manipulation and indoctrination? Between the automobile as nuisance and as convenience? Between the horrors and the comforts of functional architecture? Between the work for national defense and the work for corporate gain? Between the private pleasure and the commercial and political utility involved in increasing the birth rate?

We are again confronted with one of the most vexing aspects of advanced industrial civilization: the rational character of its irrationality. Its productivity and efficiency, its capacity to increase and spread comforts, to turn waste into need, and destruction into construction, the extent to which this civilization transforms the object world into an extension of man's mind and body makes the very notion of alienation questionable. The people recognize themselves in their commodities; they find their soul in their automobile, hi-fi set, split-level home, kitchen equipment. The very mechanism which ties the individual to his society has changed, and social control is anchored in the new needs which it has produced.

The prevailing forms of social control are technological in a new sense. To be sure, the technical structure and efficacy of the productive and destructive apparatus has been a major instrumentality for subjecting the population to the established social division of labor throughout the modern period. Moreover, such integration has always been accompanied by more obvious forms of compulsion: loss of livelihood, the administration of justice, the police, the armed forces. It still is. But in the contemporary period, the technological controls appear to be the very embodiment of Reason for the benefit of all social groups and interests—to such an extent that all contradiction seems irrational and all counteraction impossible.

No wonder then that, in the most advanced areas of this civilization, the social controls have been introjected to the point where even individual protest is affected at its roots. The intellectual and emotional refusal "to go along" appears neurotic and impotent. This is the socio-psychological aspect of the political event that marks the contemporary period: the passing of the historical forces which, at the preceding stage of industrial society, seemed to represent the possibility of new forms of existence.

But the term "introjection" perhaps no longer describes the way in which the individual by himself reproduces and perpetuates the external controls exercised by his society. Introjection suggests a variety of relatively spontaneous processes by which a Self (Ego) transposes the "outer" into the "inner." Thus introjection implies the existence of an inner dimension distinguished from and even antagonistic to the external exigencies—an individual consciousness and an individual unconscious *apart from* public opinion and behavior.[2] The idea of "inner freedom" here has its reality: it designates the private space in which man may become and remain "himself."

Today this private space has been invaded and whittled down by technological reality. Mass production and mass distribution claim the *entire* individual, and industrial psychology has long since ceased to be confined to the factory. The manifold processes of introjection seem to be ossified in almost mechanical reactions. The result is, not adjustment but *mimesis:* an

---

[2] The change in the function of the family here plays a decisive role: its "socializing" functions are increasingly taken over by outside groups and media. See my *Eros and Civilization* (Boston: Beacon Press, 1955), p. 96 ff.

immediate identification of the individual with *his* society and, through it, with the society as a whole.

This immediate, automatic identification (which may have been characteristic of primitive forms of association) reappears in high industrial civilization; its new "immediacy," however, is the product of a sophisticated, scientific management and organization. In this process, the "inner" dimension of the mind in which opposition to the status quo can take root is whittled down. The loss of this dimension, in which the power of negative thinking—the critical power of Reason—is at home, is the ideological counterpart to the very material process in which advanced industrial society silences and reconciles the opposition. The impact of progress turns Reason into submission to the facts of life, and to the dynamic capability of producing more and bigger facts of the same sort of life. The efficiency of the system blunts the individuals' recognition that it contains no facts which do not communicate the repressive power of the whole. If the individuals find themselves in the things which shape their life, they do so, not by giving, but by accepting the law of things—not the law of physics but the law of their society.

I have just suggested that the concept of alienation seems to become questionable when the individuals identify themselves with the existence which is imposed upon them and have in it their own development and satisfaction. This identification is not illusion but reality. However, the reality constitutes a more progressive stage of alienation. The latter has become entirely objective; the subject which is alienated is swallowed up by its alienated existence. There is only one dimension, and it is everywhere and in all forms. The achievements of progress defy ideological indictment as well as justification; before their

tribunal, the "false consciousness" of their rationality becomes the true consciousness.

This absorption of ideology into reality does not, however, signify the "end of ideology." On the contrary, in a specific sense advanced industrial culture is *more* ideological than its predecessor, inasmuch as today the ideology is in the process of production itself.[3] In a provocative form, this proposition reveals the political aspects of the prevailing technological rationality. The productive apparatus and the goods and services which it produces "sell" or impose the social system as a whole. The means of mass transportation and communication, the commodities of lodging, food, and clothing, the irresistible output of the entertainment and information industry carry with them prescribed attitudes and habits, certain intellectual and emotional reactions which bind the consumers more or less pleasantly to the producers and, through the latter, to the whole. The products indoctrinate and manipulate; they promote a false consciousness which is immune against its falsehood. And as these beneficial products become available to more individuals in more social classes, the indoctrination they carry ceases to be publicity; it becomes a way of life. It is a good way of life—much better than before—and as a good way of life, it militates against qualitative change. Thus emerges a pattern of *one-dimensional thought and behavior* in which ideas, aspirations, and objectives that, by their content, transcend the established universe of discourse and action are either repelled or reduced to terms of this universe. They are redefined by the rationality of the given system and of its quantitative extension. . . .

---

[3] Theodor W. Adorno, *Prismen, Kulturkritik und Gesellschaft.* (Frankfurt: Suhrkamp, 1955), p. 24f.

Michael Walzer

"Americans have no inwardness of their own; they look inward only by looking backward. . . . Someone who is only an American is, so far as our bureaucrats are concerned, ethnically anonymous. He has a right, however, to his anonymity; that is part of what it means to be an American."

These are the words of Michael Walzer in *What Does It Mean to Be an American?* He describes himself as a "liberal socialist and critical communitarian." Born in New York City in 1935, Walzer received his B.A. at Brandeis University, studied at Cambridge briefly, and completed his Ph.D. at Harvard. A teacher of political thought at Princeton and then Harvard, Walzer has been a faculty member at the Institute for Advanced Study at Princeton since 1980.

Walzer spends much of his time writing and editing; he serves as editor of *Dissent* (a journal of socialist criticism), as a member of the editorial board of *Philosophy and Public Affairs* and *Political Theory,* and as a contributing editor for *The New Republic.* Some of his books include *The Revolution of the Saints* (1965), *Obligations* (1970), *Regicide and Revolution* (1974), *Just and Unjust Wars* (1977), *Spheres of Justice* (1983), *Exodus and Revolution* (1985), *Interpretation and Social Criticism* (1987), and *Civil Society and American Democracy* (1992).

As the twentieth century comes to an end, Walzer argues for a stronger, more engaged sense of citizenship. In the essays that make up *What Does It Mean to Be an American?* (1992), he opposes ending immigration into the United States, advocates strengthening public schools, and argues for channeling health care through religious associations. Pressing for a decentralization of governmental activity and a "radical democratization of corporate government," Walzer praises the "incoherence" of pluralism. In "The Politics of Difference," he perceives three distinct historical moments dominating the end of the twentieth century: the moments of *articulation* (group demands for public recognition), *negotiation* (groups come to acknowledge limits set by the legitimacy of others), and *incorporation* (nonrepressive modes of citizenship in domestic society). Ultimately he argues that "the relation of individuals to the state will be more direct in national than in multinational settings; group mediations will be reduced in importance. And so privatization will be less of a threat to citizenship and culture."

In the early essay printed here, Walzer provides a classic critique of American liberalism and advocates local community political action as an alternative.

Politics in the Welfare State (1968)
(excerpts)

One day, not soon, the welfare state will extend its benefits to all those men and women who are at present its occasional victims, its nominal partial members. That day will not be the end of political history. But it will represent the end of a particular

Isaak, *American Political Thinking.*/From "Politics in the Welfare State" by Michael Walzer. Reprinted by permission of *Dissent.*

history, and one in which socialists have been very much involved, if not always on our own terms.

It is worth reflecting on what that day will be like—what will we want *then?*—even while we fight to perfect the system of benefits and argue among ourselves about the best strategies. For we are not entering, we are not going to enter, the new world of state-administered prosperity all at once. It is in the nature of the welfare state, I think, that men break into it in groups, some sooner, some much later, some with only moderate difficulty, some after long and bloody struggles. Many of us are inside already, better served by machines and bureaucrats than men ever were by servants and slaves. What do we want *now?*

Liberal theorists of the welfare state have always claimed to know what we want. Their work rests on two assumptions: first, that politics ought to be the instrument of human desire; second, that the nature of human desire is obvious. People want pleasure, but such pleasure as cannot be shared, individual delight, egoistic satisfaction. The state cannot at the moment provide any sort of direct delight; perhaps one day it will simply administer the appropriate chemicals to its members. Today it can provide only the material prerequisites of individual delight, that is, first security, and then all those services conveniently grouped under the rubric of "welfare"— education, public health, economic controls, relief for the aged and the unemployed, and so on. These are vitally important services, and liberal theory is vindicated, at least in part, by the fact that they are in great demand. Every attempt to restrict them to selected groups of people has been, and will surely continue to be, resisted. The welfare state has grown through invasion, a clear tribute to its attractiveness.

In the heat of battle, goals have sometimes been suggested which elude or tran-

scend the liberal definition of human desire. Wild hopes for equality and fraternity have been proclaimed. But each success has turned out to be a further triumph for what might best be called political utilitarianism. If we or our ancestors or our comrades in this or that struggle have sought the actuality of freedom and love, we have settled readily enough for the pursuit of private happiness, so readily, indeed, that it would be difficult to deny that private happiness is all we ever wanted.

The cumulative effects, the likely future effects, of these successive triumphs are now becoming visible, even though there are important victories yet to be won (and the last battles may be the hardest). What I propose in this essay is a theoretical examination of these effects, of the welfare state as our collective project, our common future. I want to argue that the success, or the likely success, of welfarism makes necessary (as it makes possible) a new and radical challenge to political utilitarianism. Whatever the nature of our past demands, what we want *next* is not on any of the liberal lists. But first I must try to suggest the enormous achievements and the special characteristics of welfare politics. For we cannot say what it is we want, until we have understood what we have got and are getting.

First of all, the development of the welfare state has generated a pervasive enlightenment about the functions of political organization. For the first time in history, masses of men know with absolute clarity that the state ought to be doing something for them. They are rationalists-of-everyday life, each one demanding, "What has it done for me?" Prewelfare theorists have generally denied the validity of this simple question, insisting that the state always *is* more than it *does*. They have described it as a closely knit body, dense and opaque, whose members were involved emotionally as well as materially, mysteriously as well as rationally, in the fate of the whole. The members ought to be involved it was said, not for the sake of concrete benefits of any sort, but, simply, for the sake of communion. Since loyalty was a gift for which there was to be no necessary return, it could not be predicted on anything so clear-cut as interest. It depended instead on all sorts of ideological and ceremonial mystification: anointed kings, oaths, rituals, divine laws; and so on.

The state still does depend on ideology and mystery, but to a far lesser degree than ever before. It has been the great triumph of liberal theorists and politicians to undermine every sort of political divinity, to shatter all the forms of ritual obfuscation, and to turn the mysterious oath into a rational contract. The state itself they have made over from a "body politic" into a machine, the instrument of its citizens (rather than their mythical common life), devoted to what Jeremy Bentham called "welfare production." It is judged as it ought to be, by the amounts of welfare it produces and by the justice and efficiency of its distributive system.

Political unreason survives, of course, and especially in the form of an extraordinary devotion to the modern nation-state and to its leaders, a collective zeal all-too-often unmitigated by individual interest or by any demand for functional transparency. But here too the direction of political utilitarianism is clearly marked out. Thus an eighteenth-century *philosophe*: "What is patriotism? It is an enlightened love of ourselves, which teaches us to love the government which protects us ... the society which works for our happiness." This definition suggests that many of us are patriotic, if we are, for wrong or inadequate reasons. I will try to describe some of these reasons a little later on.

Second, the expansion of welfare production gives to the state a new and thoroughly rational legitimacy. The state is always immoral when viewed from the standpoint of its invisible and degraded men. Whatever the ideologies of which they are the primary victims, oppressed classes come eventually to regard the claims of their rulers with a deep-rooted skepticism and hostility.

But the claims of the liberals are of a different sort, not mysterious but hypocritical. Therefore the hostility of the oppressed takes a new form: not sullen and inarticulate disbelief, but a positive demand that the claims be realized. Do the middle classes claim to increase the general prosperity? Let them increase *our* prosperity. Do the police claim to defend public security? Let them defend *our* security. Do the rulers of the welfare state claim to maximize the happiness of the greatest number? Let them maximize *our* happiness.

Now insofar as the state becomes a general welfare state, excluding nobody, it meets these demands and so generates a legitimacy such as no previous political system has ever achieved. If no man is invisible, the state is not immoral. The recognition of its members as concrete individuals with needs and desires may seem a minimal requirement of any political system and hardly capable of producing significant moral attachments. In fact, however, such recognition, when it is finally achieved, will be the outcome of centuries of struggle; the right to be visible is always hard won; and the liberal state which finally recognizes all men and grants them their humanity will inherit from those centuries an extraordinary moral power. The state will never again be so easy to challenge as it was in the days of mass invisibility.

Third, the development of the welfare state has gone hand-in-hand with a transformation in the scale of political organization. This is due not only to increase in the rates of infant and adult survival—the first benefit of the welfare state is life—but also to the progressive extension of political membership to previously invisible men. The tiny political public of an earlier period has been broken into by successive waves of lower-class invaders. It has expanded to absorb each wave; it will probably expand to absorb each future wave.

Liberal theorists and politicians have discovered that there are no necessary limits on the size of the public, so long as its members are conceived as individual recipients of benefits, so long as the problems of political communion, the sharing of a common life, are carefully avoided. Now that there really are concrete benefits to be divided, the first political problem is distribution. And the members of the state, precisely because they are recognized as needful persons, seen by the impersonal public eye and assisted by an impersonal administration, need no longer be able to recognize and assist one another. The size of the citizen body of a Greek polis, like that of an early modern aristocracy, was limited by the requirement that its members be known to each other and so distinguishable from the faceless mass. But once invisibility is banished, the need for political "friendship" is also banished. The members of the welfare state need not have even the most remote acquaintance with each other. And so the welfare state is potentially of infinite extent.

The fourth tendency of successful welfare production is to decrease the importance of politics itself and to turn the state from a political order into an administrative agency. This was always the goal of liberalism, and it is the key reason for the liberal insistence upon the transparent material purposes of the state. Beyond welfare the liberal state cannot go; the world of the mind, philosophy, art, literature, and religion; the world of the emotions, friendship, sex, and love—all these have been freed from politics protected against heavy-handed and intolerant magistrates. Simultaneously, liberal politics has been freed from philosophy, art, literature, religion, friendship, sex, and love.

Politics is now concerned only with the provision of a plentiful and enjoyable external world and with the promotion of longevity so that this world can be enjoyed as long as possible. And it has been the assumption of liberal theorists ever since Hobbes and Locke that once security and welfare were assured, once the utilitarian purposes of politics were achieved, men would turn away from public to private life, to business and family, or to religion and self-cultivation. Indeed, it was this turning away—which might be called legitimate apathy since it rests on the satisfaction of all recognized needs and desires—that would assure the stability of the liberal achievement. Conflict would disappear; the state would become a neutral agency for the administration of security and welfare. This was a liberal even before it was a Marxian vision, as Marx himself suggested when he wrote that political emancipation, as practiced by the liberals, "was at the same time the emancipation of civil society from politics."

The state is an instrument and not an end in itself. Politics is an activity with a purpose and not itself an enjoyable activity. These are axioms of liberal enlightenment; the attack upon the opacity of the traditional policy turns out to be an attack upon the value of political life. Why should we be active in politics? asked Thomas Hobbes, and his sarcastic reply suggests the central animus of liberal theory:

> to have our wisdom undervalued before our own facts; by an uncertain trial of a little vain-glory to undergo most certain enmities . . . to hate and be hated . . . to lay open our secret councils and advices to all, to no purpose and without any benefit; to neglect the affairs of our own families.

So long as the state establishes peace and, added later liberal writers, promotes welfare, public activity is a waste of time, positively dysfunctional in the economy of private life. Happiness begins and ends at home. One of the ways in which the welfare state promotes happiness is by encouraging men to stay home. Hence the crucial principles of welfare distribution are first, that benefits ought to be distributed to individuals and, second, that they ought to be designed to enhance private worlds. In the perfected welfare state, enjoyment will always be private; only administration will be public; the policeman and the welfare administrator will be the only public men.

Now obviously this is no description of our present experience. Never in human history has politics been so important to so many people, never have so many been active in politics as in the past century and a half. Never before has the state stood at the center of so large a circle of conflict, agitation and maneuver. Politics has been the crucial means of becoming visible, of winning recognition for mass needs and desires. Nor has it been only a means; political activity has also brought the first joyful sense of membership in a community. It has provided the positive pleasures of self-assertion and mutual recognition, of collective effort and achievement.

Unlike the welfare state itself, the struggle groups which have demanded and won the various benefits the state now provides—the unions, parties, and movements—have been shaped to a human scale; their members have also been colleagues; they have called one another brethren, citizens, comrades. For a brief moment in time they created a communion which was not mysterious or opaque precisely because it was a common creation.

As the organizations of the oppressed win their battles, however, they are gradually integrated into the system of welfare administration. Their purposes are not given up, or not wholly given up, but rather give rise, under new circumstances, to new organizational forms: the struggle groups become pressure groups. Public life ceases to engage the minds and emotions of their members; local activity drops off; popular participation declines sharply. The tenacious sense of detail peculiar to highly qualified bureaucrats replaces the enthusiasm of members: it is more useful, even to the members themselves.

The pleasures of political struggle cannot be sustained once victory has been won. And it is in the nature of the infinitely expandable welfare state that victories can, in fact, be won. Thus it happens that communion is replaced by distribution, generalized aspiration by concrete expectation. Erstwhile militants are isolated and immobilized by the sheer size of the state into which they have won admission, mollified by its apparent legitimacy, by the obvious sincerity of its administrators, and the transparency of their purposes. The history of the welfare state begins with the coerced passivity of invisible and degraded men, mystified by ideology. And it ends, or will one day end, with the voluntary passivity of enlightened men, their human desires recognized and (in part) gratified by the public authorities. So at any rate, we have been led to believe by liberal writers.

What more can we possibly ask?

All these developments—the growing rationality and legitimacy of the state, the vast increase in its size, and the decline of political life—are not only compatible with classical liberal theory, but actually represent its fulfillment. But there is one further corollary of welfare production which raises the most serious problems for liberalism: the growth of state power.

There can be no question that the development of welfare programs has involved (or required) an extraordinary expansion of the machinery of everyday state administration and therefore an increase in the degree, intensity, and detail of social control. In part, this increase stems directly from the progressive enlargement of bureaucratic systems and from improvements in the training and discipline of their personnel. But it is also closely related to the very nature of the utilitarian service state and to the character of the political struggles of the past century and a half.*

For all that time, liberals (and socialists, too) have been like that character of Gogol's who "wanted to bring the government into everything, even into his daily quarrels with his wife," though some of them would have stopped short at the seat of domestic bliss. Everywhere else the agents of government have been invited to roam. This was true even during the brief moment of *laissez-faire,* for the restrictions on commerce which were then overcome were largely local and corporate, and only the central government could overcome them.

Indeed, the state has been an instrument absolutely necessary to reformers of every sort: it shatters the authority of local and traditional elites; it destroys the old corporations and regulates the new ones; it establishes minimal standards for masses of men whose own organizations, however powerful, cannot do so by themselves; it protects racial and religious minorities. It is, so to speak, the crucial licensing agency of modern society, increasingly the only one; it accords recognitions, turning oppressed subjects into full-fledged members, and it absorbs the power of every defunct agency as it wins the support of every newly enfranchised member.

Nor is its usefulness at an end. Given the continued creation of new groups, the continued raising of the level of material desire, the perfection of welfare production may well be an asymptotic goal and the state an eternally progressive force. But this does not mean that the character of political struggle will remain unchanged as new groups and new desires replace the old. For from a certain point in time, the new groups will almost certainly cease to have the same communal structure as the old. The deprivations of their members are more likely to be experienced by each man in his private, state-protected world, experienced simultaneously but not shared.

Thus the Negro is one kind of invisible man, bound to his fellows in a community of suffering and anger and therefore capable of collective action. The man who drives a dangerous car or breathes polluted air is another kind, largely unaware of the risks he shares with others, only marginally aware of the existence of others, and probably incapable of significant efforts on his own behalf. Precisely because of the privatizing results of the benefits he has already won (his automobile, for example), he now stands alone and helpless in the face of one or another sort of corporate power. He is dependent upon the muckraking of freelance journalists and academic experts and, much more, upon the benevolence of the state.

This benevolence has its price: the increased power of the benevolent administrators, the increasing control over the recipients of benefits. Perhaps the most impressive feature of modern welfare administration is the sheer variety of its coercive and deterrent instruments. Every newly recognized need, every service received, creates a new dependency and so a new social bond.

"A wife and a child are so many pledges a man gives to the world for his good behavior," wrote Jeremy Bentham. This is true only insofar as the world—economy and state—actually provides or promises a decent living to the wife and child. If it does, the pledge is serious

---

*The single greatest factor in the expansion of state power has, of course, been external war, and it is probably true that the greatest dangers posed by the modern liberal state are not those which its own citizens must face. But I have, perhaps arbitrarily, excluded foreign policy and war from this discussion.

indeed. And the better the living the world promises, the more good behavior it requires. Welfare politics thus has a dialectical pattern: pressure from below for more protection or benefits meets pressure from above for better (more disciplined, or orderly, or sociable) behavior. A balance is struck, breaks down, is struck again. Each new balance is achieved at a higher level of welfare production, includes more people, provides new reasons (and new sanctions) for good behavior.

Eventually, every antisocial act is interpreted as a demand for increased benefits. So it is. And so welfare is the obvious and only antidote to delinquency and riot. For who would be unwilling, if actually given the chance, to pay the price of social discipline, orderly conduct, hard work, and public decency for the sake of the pursuit of happiness? Only much later does it turn out that the price and the purchase are very nearly the same thing. Happiness *is* good behavior, and this equation, fervently endorsed by the authorities, is the ultimate sanction.

Like the public recognition of needs, so the recognition of men, our hard-won visibility, becomes a source of intensified social control. Never have ordinary citizens been so well-known to the public authorities as in the welfare state. We are all counted, numbered, classified, catalogued, polled, interviewed, watched, and filed away. The IBM card is the very means of our visibility, the guarantee that we are not forgotten among so many millions, even as it is simultaneously a symbol of our bondage to the bureaucratic machine.

Invisible men are invisible first of all to the officials of the state (and that is a worse bondage). Precisely because they are not seen as citizens, they are exposed to arbitrary cruelty and neglect. Because they are not numbered, they are always treated *en masse*. Because they are never polled, they are thought to have no opinions. Even their crimes, so long as they injure only

one another, are not recorded. When their country goes to war, they are impressed (that is, kidnapped), but not conscripted. Gradually, with the development of the welfare state, all this changes. An extraordinary traffic opens up between the visible and the previously invisible sections of society. Individuals and groups win public recognition, learn good behavior, and march out of the slums and ghettos. At the same time, policemen, census takers, recruiting officers, tax collectors, welfare workers, radical organizers, and sociologists (in roughly that historical order) march in.

In the long run, the two parts of society will merge into one world of absolutely visible men (that does not mean a world of equals), known not to each other but to the specialists in such knowledge, not personally but statistically. The universal character of this new knowledge doubtless will protect individuals from magisterial whim and prejudice. That is one of its purposes. But it will also involve a new kind of exposure: to the developing administrative sciences of anticipation and prevention.

"It's the anarchy of poverty/Delights me ... " wrote William Carlos Williams. He was too easily delighted, or rather, his delight was that of an onlooker and not a participant in the "anarchic" culture of the poor. Few men who are actually poor would share it. But having said that, it is still worth adding: "It's the regiment of the contented/That haunts me."

Liberals have not been unaware of the dangers of administrative tyranny. Wherever possible they have sought to avoid even benevolent regimentation by giving those whose welfare is at stake "sovereign" power, that is, by establishing governments representative of everyone who receives benefits. In the past that has generally meant of all property owners, for they have been the most important welfare recipients. It obviously means more today, though just how much more is unclear.

The expansion of the range of state benefits and the extension of the ballot to new social groups have been parallel and related processes. Suffrage is the first badge of membership; it is a means of winning benefits and also, presumably, of determining their character and the nature of their administration. In practice, however, it is something less than this. "Welfare without representation," Sargent Shriver has said, "is Tyranny." That is certainly true. But it is not the case that the only alternative to tyranny is a full-scale democracy.

In theory, of course, the purpose of representative government is to make the mass of people all-powerful. Representatives are to be delegates, asserting popular desires, and then legislators, enacting the popular will. Administrators are to be nothing more than servants of the people, bound absolutely by legislative decree. The quality of security and welfare is thus popularly determined, at only one remove. The government of representatives cannot be made responsible to the people on a day-to-day basis, but its general responsibility can be maintained by periodic elections and, more importantly, by continuous political activity between elections. The ultimate defense against bureaucratic omnicompetence is the self-interested assertiveness of ordinary men.

If things have not worked out this way, and do not seem likely to, it is at least partly because liberals never developed a system of democratic activism sufficient to bind administrators to representatives and representatives to constituents. Political parties might have served this purpose, but in the U.S., at least, parties have not developed as membership organizations capable of stimulating commitment and action on the grass-roots level. Local politics has never been competitive with business and family. And it has been discovered that the enhancement of private life through public welfare really does not require any very

rigorous and energetic self-government. It may well require a period of sustained struggle, but once that has been won, continued political participation (beyond occasional voting) seems unnecessary and even uneconomical.

Nor is it obvious that the closely articulated representative system that might make such activity worthwhile is really feasible, given the potentially infinite size and the extraordinary administrative complexity of the modern state. Administration has already outdistanced every other branch of government in the sheer accumulation of resources: competent staff, statistical knowledge, patronage, fiscal controls, regulatory powers, secrecy when that is required, publicity when it is not, and so on. Legislative activity has ceased in virtually every respect to be the central feature of the governmental process. It has been replaced in part by administration itself, in part by bargaining between state bureaucrats and the (non-elected) representatives of a great variety of social constituencies.

Thus a modern worker or farmer is far more usefully represented, his interest more successfully defended, by the Washington-based lobbyist of his union than by his locally-based congressman. This is true even though his congressman is elected in a democratic fashion, while the officers of his union are probably coopted and the lobbyist appointed. It is virtually a law of political life that power be imitated, that those who seek benefits copy the organizational style of those who dispense benefits. Today it is palpably the executive rather than the legislative branch of government that is copied. At least, it is copied by those secondary associations already within the welfare system; outside, other models are still possible. In any case, the electoral process has gradually taken on the character of an outer limit, a form of ultimate popular defense rather than of popular self-government, while the day-to-day visibility of workers and farmers and the legitimacy of their government are both maintained by processes largely, though by no means entirely, independent of democratic elections. The modern welfare state is an example of limited government, but not yet of popular sovereignty.

The failure of self-government reveals the fundamental difficulty of liberal utilitarianism. Its standard of utility is the welfare of an individual absolutely free to make his own choices and measure his own happiness. In fact, however, no such individual has ever existed.

Men live in groups and always find that they have limited choices and share, without having chosen, social measurements. If they are ever free to choose new limits and measurements, they must do so in some cooperative fashion, arguing among themselves, reaching a common decision. But to do this, to act collectively like the sovereign individual of the utilitarians, they must share political power. Government must be responsive to their concrete wills and not merely (as at present) to their conventionally defined desires. If they do not share power, they inevitably become the prisoners of the established social systems which they invade or into which they are admitted.

State recognition of new groups obviously affects the structure of social power and value, but there is very little evidence to suggest that it does so in fundamental ways. It clearly does not do so in the ways anticipated during the long struggles for recognition, that is, it does not open the way to social and economic equality. The welfare state has turned out to be perfectly compatible with inequality. Bureaucratic benevolence even bolsters inequality insofar as it neutralizes the struggle groups, decomposing and privatizing popular willfulness. Fundamental social change would require that the state embody this willfulness, inviting its new members to choose their own limits and measurements. This it does not, perhaps cannot, do.

Instead, welfare administrators function, whether consciously or not, as double agents: serving the minimal material interests of the invaders and upholding at the same time the social system that is being invaded. That is why welfare administration, especially in its more direct forms (social work, for example), tends so generally toward paternalism. The administrators are committed in advance to the common limits and measurements, to the established modes of security and welfare. They are knowledgeable about these modes and patronizing toward anyone who is ignorant or uncommitted. But the invaders have burst into a world they never chose. They have to be helped, guided, educated in the acceptable forms of aspiration and action. They are, in a word, newly licensed to have needs, but not yet intentions or plans of their own.

The perfected welfare state will bring with it an end to the terrible oppressiveness of poverty and invisibility. Once all men are recognized as members (even if only by a distant and powerful government), the sheer magnitude of state terrorism and economic exploitation, and so of human misery, will be enormously reduced. At the same time, it needs to be said that security and welfare are not open-ended categories whose final character will be determined by the freedmen of the liberal state. The pursuit of private happiness may be endless, but its direction, for most of us, is given. The newer welfare recipients are not and are not likely to become self-determining men; they remain subject to the determinations of others, not only in the state, but in society and economy as well. Indeed, the established forms of social and economic (that is, corporate) power are likely to be strengthened just as state power has been strengthened: by the general expansion in scale, by the increase in legitimacy that derives from the admission, however reluctant, of all outsiders; by the universal improvement in everyday social behavior;

by the new forms of bureaucratic surveillance and record keeping. For these same reasons, the individual member is taken into account in a new way. When his rulers claim to serve him, the claim is not a lie; it is his political destiny to receive services. The reception of services brings freedom of a limited sort, but of a sort rare enough to be valuable. The citizen of the welfare state is free (and, in many cases, newly enabled) to pursue private happiness within the established social and economic system. He is not free to shape or reshape the system, for he has not seized and, except in minimal ways, he does not share political power.

. . . Individual men can still recognize the pleasures of politics, can still choose political life as an end-in-itself. For politics is something more than welfare production. It is a vital and exciting world of work and struggle; of aspiration, initiative, intrigue, and argument; of collective effort, mutual recognition, and *amour social*; of organized hostility; of public venture and social achievement, of personal triumph and failure.

The welfare state offers no satisfactory substitute for any of these. Its theorists claim that all the intellectual and emotional energies of political men can be rechanneled into private life and their creativity coopted by intelligent administrators. Neither of these claims is true. The welfare state requires the virtual withering away of political energy and the disappearance, at least from public life, of any very significant popular creativity. This requirement is first of all an extreme restriction upon the pursuit of happiness, because political activity is or might be one of the forms that pursuit takes for many people. Even more important, it involves a surrender of everyone's say in the determination of fur-

ther restrictions (or expansions), a surrender of any popular role in determining the shape and substance, the day-to-day quality, of our common life. This is the socialist indictment of liberal utilitarianism.

. . . Unlike the defenders of the welfare state, theorists of citizenship have always been concerned with the problem of social scale. If human emotional and intellectual needs are to be partially fulfilled within political society, they have argued, then that society cannot be of any size or shape. It must be built of a human scale, accessible to our minds and feelings, responsive to our decisions.

Exactly what constitutes a human scale is and ought to be a subject of debate, but this is a debate likely to be carried on chiefly among radical democrats and socialists; it is not a debate in which liberal utilitarians take much interest. For it cannot be established that security and welfare are more efficiently administered to 2 million or 50 million or 200 million people. In fact, it is virtually certain that the quality of security and welfare need not change with the size of the population.

But this is probably not the case with regard to the fulfillment of nonmaterial desires. The quality and authenticity of emotional commitment, for example, does appear to vary with population size, though not absolutely or without reference to other factors: human emotions are more easily manipulated the wider their focus and the more they are cut away from immediate personal experience. Participation in cultural life probably varies the same way: the larger the audience, the more passive its members, the more stereotyped the products they consume. Once again, the formula is too pat, but surely contains an element of truth, and its significance may plausibly be extended to politics as well.

The increasing size of the state, the growing power of administration, the decline of political life: all these turn politics from a concrete activity into what Marx once called the fantasy of everyday life. The state becomes an arena in which men do not act but watch the action and, like other audiences, are acted upon. Patriotic communion is always a fraud when it is nothing more than the communion of an audience with its favorite actors, of passive subjects and heroes of the stage. Our emotions are merely tricked by parades and pageants, the rise and fall of political gladiators, the deaths of beloved chiefs, the somber or startling rites of a debased religion. It could be done to anyone, whereas patriotism ought to be the pride of particular man, the enjoyment of particular activities.

When the modern state moves beyond welfare, it does not bring us the satisfactions of citizenship, but only vicarious participation, the illusion of a common life. We find ourselves as if in a dream, living once again in a world which is morally dense and opaque, mystified by ideologies, dominated by leaders whose purposes are not obvious. We are oppressed in the name of a public interest, a national purpose, a solemn commitment, which is neither yours, nor mine, nor ours, in any usual sense of those perfectly simple pronouns. It is difficult not to conclude, as the liberals do, that with the provision of individual material needs, the state reaches or ought to reach its limits. That is the end of its history, the culmination of its legitimacy. There is no state beyond the welfare state.

The struggle to control the modern state is a battle for the perfection of the welfare system. Any political leader who claims that it is more than this, who claims, for example, that citizens should do more for the state than the state does for them, is a dangerous man. He aims to avoid the problems of welfare production, or he seeks some sort of totalitarian "transcendence"

(or he is preparing the nation for one or another kind of imperial adventure).

The fight over welfare is important enough. Given the most immediate desires of the poor themselves, given the sheer avariciousness of the rich and the powerful, the fight for some minimal standards of distributive justice takes on all the moral significance that has been attributed to it in the past century and a half. Nevertheless, it is not the only fight; nor ought the state to be the only focus of contemporary political struggle.

Even if the welfare state were to be perfected under the best possible conditions and under socialist auspices, the dangers of bureaucratic omnicompetence and popular passivity would not be avoided. Nor would a socialist government create a socialist society. That requires a different kind of politics, not the kind to which we are all so well accustomed, aimed permanently at the state, but a politics of immediate self-government, a politics of (relatively) small groups.

. . . It is not the natural tendency even of liberal bureaucracy to encourage the formation of autonomous groups. This is so both because of the individualist bias of the welfare system and because of the perennial efforts of administrators to escape the system's utilitarian limits and meet the demand for meaningful citizenship in their own (fraudulent) fashion.

What socialism requires, then, is not that the welfare state be surpassed or transcended, whatever that would mean, but that it be held tightly to its own limits, drained of whatever superfluous moral content and unnecessary political power it has usurped, reduced so far as possible to a transparent administrative shell (overarching, protective, enabling) within which smaller groups can grow and prosper. The state is not going to wither away; it must be hollowed out.

What sorts of groups can fill the shell? Two are of especial interest here.

First, the great functional organizations, labor unions, professional associations, and so on: these are the crucial representative bodies of the present day. Their strength and inclusiveness is the best guarantee we can have of the benevolence of the welfare bureaucracy. Unorganized men are unrepresented and unprotected men, their claims unheard or but distantly heard at the centers of power. If they are benefited at all, they are subject to the most extreme paternalism.

The perfection of the welfare state will require the organization of all possible functional groups, even, or rather especially, the group of those who receive direct state assistance. In a society which still exploits masses of men, poverty is itself a function, and no one so desperately requires representation as the man without an adequate income. But all these organizations, as I have argued, tend to become integrated into the welfare system: for them, success *is* integration. They are then trapped in more or less stable bargaining arrangements with governmental or corporate bureaucracies and forced to discipline their own members. They are agents simultaneously of distributive justice and social control. They are not and probably cannot be expected to become arenas of democratic decision making (even though they will be the occasional focus of democratic revolts).

Second, all the local units of social life, work, education, and culture: cities and towns, factories, union locals, universities, churches, political clubs, neighborhood associations, theater groups, editorial boards, and so on. These might be conceived as overlapping circles of engagement and action, closed circles (though not closed in any coercive sense), whose members face inward at least some of the time, and within which resources are contained.

These are the most likely arenas of a genuinely democratic politics. The great danger of the perfected welfare state is that all or most of them would be broken open so that resources leak away, independence is lost, and the members turn outward to face the powerful state, where all the action is, from which all good things come. To some extent this has already happened. But the process is by no means so far advanced as some of the more extreme versions of the theory of "mass society" suggest. Associations and neighborhoods continue to provide important social space for agitation and activity. Indeed, it needs to be said that the advance of the liberal state often transforms traditional communities (like the old churches) into new political arenas.

At the same time, however, the same process cuts individuals loose, isolates them from communal ties, drives them into a material and then an emotional dependency on the central authorities. It is in response to the expectant faces of these "liberated" individuals that state administrators proclaim the mysteries of national purpose and decide that they must pursue "excellence" or promote culture (or defend freedom), rewarding their eager, needful and bored constituents with inflated rhetoric and byzantine artifacts, and all too often eliciting from them an irrational and unreflective patriotism.

Now all such pursuits and promotions lie outside the competence of the state; they belong to a different sphere of activity; they require a smaller scale of organization. To make these points and to make them stick is the major purpose of socialist politics in the welfare state. It amounts to saying that what we want *next,* and what we want to share, are the pleasures of power. This demand for local self-determination, since it is made in the face of a state whose power is unprecedented in human history, is sometimes called by the melodramatic but useful name "insurgency."

Any member of the welfare state who is willful as well as desirous and who seeks some local space in which to act out his willfulness can be called an insurgent. He insists on his intentions as well as his needs. He seeks to close the circle (not every circle) against bureaucratic intrusions. He reargues the old democratic proposition that decisions should be made by those who are most affected by them. He calls into question the omnicompetence of the service state and of all the organizations created in its image.

In schools, factories, and neighborhoods, where social workers pursue their errands of decency, or union officials defend the interests of their members, or provosts and deans plan the educational experiences of the young, insurgency is likely to be a perennial phenomenon. It takes the form of wildcat strikes, welfare unions, student rebellions. Already a sense of professional *esprit* is growing up among those who know, or think they know, how to "handle" such outbursts. They believe that insurgency is a repudiation of services rendered, stupidly self-destructive since the services are so obviously helpful, even if they are often ineptly or impersonally delivered.

But insurgency, is or ought to be, very different from this. Its participants are not concerned that bureaucrats be sensitive and warm, but that they be reticent and limited, less imposing, less intrusive than they often are. Insurgency is a demand that bureaucratic services make possible, instead of replacing, local decision making. Or rather, it is the acting out of a new dialectic, which denies conventional definitions of good behavior and seeks to make the "helpfulness" of the welfare bureaucracy into the starting point of a new politics of popular resistance and self-government.

In the long run, the issue for socialists is not state power, but power *right here,* on this shop floor, in this university, in this city. And the central assumption of insurgent politics is that such power must always be won "from below"—which is also to say, against all the odds. . . .

But insurgency is different from revolution (more limited, more immediate) precisely in that it seeks no more extensive unity, but calls instead for the multiplication of diverse and independent unities. And it begins this process with a modest but urgent demand for a share *right now* in the management of *this* community.

Martin Luther King, Jr.

Michael Luther King, Jr., was born in 1929 in Atlanta, Georgia, to the pastor of the Ebenezer Baptist Church (founded by King's grandfather). The father changed his own first name and his son's to Martin out of admiration for Martin Luther, leader of the Reformation. Martin Luther King, Jr., became the most influential black leader in the United States in the twentieth century, symbolizing nonviolent demonstration against segregation and discrimination of African-Americans.

King studied at Morehouse College in Atlanta and then the integrated Crozer Theological Seminary in Chester, Pennsylvania, where he was senior class president and received a fellowship to the university of his choice as the most outstanding student. He completed Ph.D. coursework at Boston College, took philosophy courses at Harvard, and was later awarded his degree. Previously ordained a minister in his father's church, his first parish was the Dexter Avenue Baptist Church. There he organized a political and social action committee and persuaded church members to join the National Association for the Advancement of Colored People (NAACP) and to become active in community affairs. King was influenced by Thoreau's "Essay on Civil Disobedience," Walter Rauschenbusch, Reinhold Niebuhr, Paul Tillich, Jesus of Nazareth, and Mahatma Gandhi, as well as Martin Luther. He realized that for Christianity to be relevant to the human condition it had to be concerned with the everyday socioeconomic environment as well as the spiritual realm.

When an African-American seamstress, Rosa Parks, was arrested for refusing to give up her bus seat to a white person, King applied ideas of nonviolent resistance and a 381-day boycott of the buses by African-Americans resulted. King was undeterred even by the bombing of his own home and became one of twenty-four pastors arrested. An Alabama circuit judge found the boycott illegal and sentenced King to a $500 fine or 140 days in jail. The consequence was postponed pending appeals. Finally, the Supreme Court confirmed an injunction ending Montgomery bus segregation, and blacks and whites rode Montgomery buses on an unsegregated basis starting in 1956. King's first book, *Stride Toward Freedom* (1958), is a history of the Montgomery bus boycott that had brought him international stature and also comparisons to Thoreau and Gandhi.

King organized the Southern Christian Leadership Conference (SCLC) "to carry on non-violent crusades against the evils of second-class citizenship throughout the South." He then left Montgomery to become copastor of Ebenezer Baptist Church with his father. He gave speeches throughout the United States and visited Ghana and India. The Student Nonviolent Coordinating Committee adopted his principles of nonviolent resistance, leading to successful sit-in campaigns to desegregate public facilities throughout the South.

King was arrested in a nonviolent demonstration against segregation in Birmingham, Alabama, in 1963. During his confinement he wrote "Letter from Birmingham Jail" (printed here). King's demonstrations encouraged federal intervention and helped lead to the passage of the 1964 Civil Rights Act. At one of his marches in Washington, D.C., he gave his famous "I Have a Dream" speech at the Lincoln Memorial. In 1964, he was awarded the Nobel Peace Prize. The next year, King helped organize a march that aided in the passage of the Voting Rights Act of 1965. In 1967, he began speaking out against the Vietnam War and called for a "Poor People's March on Washington" to change government priorities in 1968. In April 1968, King was assassinated in Memphis, Tennessee, while trying to help local sanitation workers strike for higher wages. Senate testimony in 1975 demonstrated that the Federal Bureau of Investigation had illegally harassed and discredited King for six years by trying to prevent colleges from giving him honorary degrees, by keeping him from accepting the Nobel Peace Prize, and by preventing him from meeting with the Pope. Nevertheless, King's principles of nonviolent resistance made the African-American movement for civil rights respectable, preparing the way to assimilate African-Americans into the mainstream of American life.

Letter from Birmingham Jail*
(1963)

April 16, 1963

My Dear Fellow Clergymen:

While confined here in the Birmingham city jail, I came across your recent statement calling my present activities "unwise and untimely." Seldom do I pause to answer criticism of my work and ideas. If I sought to answer all the criticisms that cross my desk, my secretaries would have little time for anything other than such correspondence in the course of the day, and I would have no time for constructive work. But since I feel that you are men of genuine good will and that your criticisms are sincerely set forth, I want to try to answer your statement in what I hope will be patient and reasonable terms.

I think I should indicate why I am here in Birmingham, since you have been influenced by the view which argues against "outsiders coming in." I have the honor of serving as president of the Southern Christian Leadership Conference, an organization operating in every southern state, with headquarters in Atlanta, Georgia. We have some eighty-five affiliated organizations across the South, and one of them is the Alabama Christian Movement for Human Rights. Frequently we share staff, educational and financial resources with our affiliates. Several months ago the affiliate here in Birmingham asked us to be on call to engage in a nonviolent direct-action program if such were deemed necessary. We readily consented, and when the hour came we lived up to our promise. So I, along with several members of my staff, am here because I was invited here. I am here because I have organizational ties here.

But more basically, I am in Birmingham because injustice is here. Just as the

*Author's Note: This response to a published statement by eight fellow clergymen from Alabama (Bishop C. C. J. Carpenter, Bishop Joseph A. Durick, Rabbi Hilton L. Grafman, Bishop Paul Hardin, Bishop Holan B. Harmon, the Reverend George M. Murray, the Reverend Edward V. Ramage and the Reverend Earl Stallings) was composed under somewhat constricting circumstances. Begun on the margins of the newspaper in which the statement appeared while I was in jail, the letter was continued on scraps of writing paper supplied by a friendly Negro trusty, and concluded on a pad my attorneys were eventually permitted to leave me. Although the text remains in substance unaltered, I have indulged in the author's prerogative of polishing it for publication.

prophets of the eighth century B.C. left their villages and carried their "thus saith the Lord" far beyond the boundaries of their home towns, and just as the Apostle Paul left his village of Tarsus and carried the gospel of Jesus Christ to the far corners of the Greco-Roman world, so am I compelled to carry the gospel of freedom beyond my own home town. Like Paul, I must constantly respond to the Macedonian call for aid.

Moreover, I am cognizant of the interrelatedness of all communities and states. I cannot sit idly by in Atlanta and not be concerned about what happens in Birmingham. Injustice anywhere is a threat to justice everywhere. We are caught in an inescapable network of mutuality, tied in a single garment of destiny. Whatever affects one directly, affects all indirectly. Never again can we afford to live with the narrow, provincial "outside agitator" idea. Anyone who lives inside the United States can never be considered an outsider anywhere within its bounds.

You deplore the demonstrations taking place in Birmingham. But your statement, I am sorry to say, fails to express a similar concern for the conditions that brought about the demonstrations. I am sure that none of you would want to rest content with the superficial kind of social analysis that deals merely with effects and does not grapple with underlying causes. It is unfortunate that demonstrations are taking place in Birmingham, but it is even more unfortunate that the city's white power structure left the Negro community with no alternative.

In any nonviolent campaign there are four basic steps: collection of the facts to determine whether injustices exist; negotiation; self-purification; and direct action. We have gone through all these steps in Birmingham. There can be no gainsaying the fact that racial injustice engulfs this community. Birmingham is probably the most thoroughly segregated city in the

United States. Its ugly record of brutality is widely known. Negroes have experienced grossly unjust treatment in the courts. There have been more unsolved bombings of Negro homes and churches in Birmingham than in any other city in the nation. These are the hard, brutal facts of the case. On the basis of these conditions, Negro leaders sought to negotiate with the city fathers. But the latter consistently refused to engage in good-faith negotiation.

Then, last September, came the opportunity to talk with leaders of Birmingham's economic community. In the course of the negotiations, certain promises were made by the merchants—for example, to remove the stores' humiliating racial signs. On the basis of these promises, the Reverend Fred Shuttlesworth and the leaders of the Alabama Christian Movement for Human Rights agreed to a moratorium on all demonstrations. As the weeks and months went by, we realized that we were the victims of a broken promise. A few signs, briefly removed, returned; the others remained.

As in so many past experiences, our hopes had been blasted, and the shadow of deep disappointment settled upon us. We had no alternative except to prepare for direct action, whereby we would present our very bodies as a means of laying our case before the conscience of the local and the national community. Mindful of the difficulties involved, we decided to undertake a process of self-purification. We began a series of workshops on nonviolence, and we repeatedly asked ourselves: "Are you able to accept blows without retaliating?" "Are you able to endure the ordeal of jail?" We decided to schedule our direct-action program for the Easter season, realizing that except for Christmas, this is the main shopping period of the year. Knowing that a strong economic-withdrawal program would be the by-product of direct action, we felt that this would be the best time to bring pressure to bear on the merchants for the needed change.

Then it occurred to us that Birmingham's mayoral election was coming up in March, and we speedily decided to postpone action until after election day. When we discovered that the Commissioner of Public Safety, Eugene "Bull" Connor, had piled up enough votes to be in the run-off, we decided again to postpone action until the day after the run-off so that the demonstrations could not be used to cloud the issues. Like many others, we waited to see Mr. Connor defeated, and to this end we endured postponement after postponement. Having aided in this community need, we felt that our direct-action program could be delayed no longer.

You may well ask: "Why direct action? Why sit-ins, marches and so forth? Isn't negotiation a better path?" You are quite right in calling for negotiation. Indeed, this is the very purpose of direct action. Nonviolent direct action seeks to create such a crisis and foster such a tension that a community which has constantly refused to negotiate is forced to confront the issue. It seeks so to dramatize the issue that it can no longer be ignored. My citing the creation of tension as part of the work of the nonviolent-resister may sound rather shocking. But I must confess that I am not afraid of the word "tension." I have earnestly opposed violent tension, but there is a type of constructive, nonviolent tension which is necessary for growth. Just as Socrates felt that it was necessary to create a tension in the mind so that individuals could rise from the bondage of myths and half-truths to the unfettered realm of creative analysis and objective appraisal, so must we see the need for nonviolent gadflies to create the kind of tension in society that will help men rise from the dark depths of prejudice and racism to the majestic heights of understanding and brotherhood.

The purpose of our direct-action program is to create a situation so crisis-packed that it will inevitably open the door to negotiation. I therefore concur with you in your call for negotiation. Too long has our beloved Southland been bogged down in a tragic effort to live in monologue rather than dialogue.

One of the basic points in your statement is that the action that I and my associates have taken in Birmingham is untimely. Some have asked: "Why didn't you give the new city administration time to act?" The only answer that I can give to this query is that the new Birmingham administration must be prodded about as much as the outgoing one, before it will act. We are sadly mistaken if we feel that the election of Albert Boutwell as mayor will bring the millennium to Birmingham. While Mr. Boutwell is a much more gentle person than Mr. Connor, they are both segregationists, dedicated to maintenance of the status quo. I have hope that Mr. Boutwell will be reasonable enough to see the futility of massive resistance to desegregation. But he will not see this without pressure from devotees of civil rights. My friends, I must say to you that we have not made a single gain in civil rights without determined legal and nonviolent pressure. Lamentably, it is an historical fact that privileged groups seldom give up their privileges voluntarily. Individuals may see the moral light and voluntarily give up their unjust posture; but, as Reinhold Niebuhr has reminded us, groups tend to be more immoral than individuals.

We know through painful experience that freedom is never voluntarily given by the oppressor; it must be demanded by the oppressed. Frankly, I have yet to engage in a direct-action campaign that was "well timed" in the view of those who have not suffered unduly from the disease of segregation. For years now I have heard the word "Wait!" It rings in the ear of every Negro with piercing familiarity. This "Wait" has almost always meant "Never." We must come to see, with one of our distinguished jurists, that "justice too long delayed is justice denied."

We have waited for more than 340 years for our constitutional and God-given rights. The nations of Asia and Africa are moving with jetlike speed toward gaining political independence, but we still creep at horse-and-buggy pace toward gaining a cup of coffee at a lunch counter. Perhaps it is easy for those who have never felt the stinging darts of segregation to say, "Wait." But when you have seen vicious mobs lynch your mothers and fathers at will and drown your sisters and brothers at whim; when you have seen hate-filled policemen curse, kick and even kill your black brothers and sisters; when you see the vast majority of your twenty million Negro brothers smothering in an airtight cage of poverty in the midst of an affluent society; when you suddenly find your tongue twisted and your speech stammering as you seek to explain to your six-year-old daughter why she can't go to the public amusement park that has just been advertised on television, and see tears welling up in her eyes when she is told that Funtown is closed to colored children, and see ominous clouds of inferiority beginning to form in her little mental sky, and see her beginning to distort her personality by developing an unconscious bitterness toward white people; when you have to concoct an answer for a five-year-old son who is asking: "Daddy, why do white people treat colored people so mean?"; when you take a cross-country drive and find it necessary to sleep night after night in the uncomfortable corners of your automobile because no motel will accept you; when you are humiliated day in and day out by nagging signs reading "white" and "colored"; when your first name becomes "nigger," your middle name becomes "boy" (however old you are) and your last name becomes "John," and your wife and mother are never given the respected title "Mrs."; when you are harried by day and haunted by night by the fact that you are a Negro, living constantly at tiptoe stance, never quite knowing what to expect next, and are plagued with inner fears and outer resentments; when you are forever fighting a degenerating sense of "nobodiness"—then you will understand why we find it difficult to wait. There comes a time when the cup of endurance runs over, and men are no longer willing to be plunged into the abyss of despair. I hope, sirs, you can understand our legitimate and unavoidable impatience.

You express a great deal of anxiety over our willingness to break laws. This is certainly a legitimate concern. Since we so diligently urge people to obey the Supreme Court's decision of 1954 outlawing segregation in the public schools, at first glance it may seem rather paradoxical for us consciously to break laws. One may well ask: "How can you advocate breaking some laws and obeying others?" The answer lies in the fact that there are two types of laws: just and unjust. I would be the first to advocate obeying just laws. One has not only a legal but a moral responsibility to obey just laws. Conversely, one has a moral responsibility to disobey unjust laws. I would agree with St. Augustine that "an unjust law is no law at all."

Now, what is the difference between the two? How does one determine whether a law is just or unjust? A just law is a man-made code that squares with the moral law or the law of God. An unjust law is a code that is out of harmony with the moral law. To put it in the terms of St. Thomas Aquinas: An unjust law is a human law that is not rooted in eternal law and natural law. Any law that uplifts human personality is just. Any law that degrades human personality is unjust. All segregation statutes are unjust because segregation distorts the soul and damages the personality. It gives the segregator a false sense of superiority and the segregated a false sense of inferiority. Segregation, to use the terminology of the Jewish philosopher Martin Buber, substitutes an "I-it" relationship for an "I-thou" relationship and ends up relegating persons to the status of things. Hence segregation is not only politically, economically and sociologically unsound, it is morally wrong and sinful. Paul Tillich has said that sin is separation. Is not segregation an existential expression of man's tragic separation, his awful estrangement, his terrible sinfulness? Thus it is that I can urge men to obey the 1954 decision of the Supreme Court, for it is morally right; and I can urge them to disobey segregation ordinances, for they are morally wrong.

Let us consider a more concrete example of just and unjust laws. An unjust law is a code that a numerical or power majority group compels a minority group to obey but does not make binding on itself. This is *difference* made legal. By the same token, a just law is a code that a majority compels a minority to follow and that it is willing to follow itself. This is *sameness* made legal.

Let me give another explanation. A law is unjust if it is inflicted on a minority that, as a result of being denied the right to vote, had no part in enacting or devising the law. Who can say that the legislature of Alabama which set up that state's segregation laws was democratically elected? Throughout Alabama all sorts of devious methods are used to prevent Negroes from becoming registered voters, and there are some counties in which, even though Negroes constitute a majority of the population, not a single Negro is registered. Can any law enacted under such circumstances be considered democratically structured?

Sometimes a law is just on its face and unjust in its application. For instance, I have been arrested on a charge of parading without a permit. Now, there is nothing wrong in having an ordinance which requires a permit for a parade. But such an ordinance becomes unjust when it is used to maintain segregation and to deny citizens the First-Amendment privilege of peaceful assembly and protest.

I hope you are able to see the distinction I am trying to point out. In no sense do I advocate evading or defying the law, as would the rabid segregationist. That would lead to anarchy. One who breaks an unjust law must do so openly, lovingly, and with a willingness to accept the penalty. I submit that an individual who breaks a law that conscience tells him is unjust, and who willingly accepts the penalty of imprisonment in order to arouse the conscience of the community over its injustice, is in reality expressing the highest respect for law.

Of course, there is nothing new about this kind of civil disobedience. It was evidenced sublimely in the refusal of Shadrach, Meshach and Abednego to obey the laws of Nebuchadnezzar, on the ground that a higher moral law was at stake. It was practiced superbly by the early Christians, who were willing to face hungry lions and the excruciating pain of chopping blocks rather than submit to certain unjust laws of the Roman Empire. To a degree, academic freedom is a reality today because Socrates practiced civil disobedience. In our own nation, the Boston Tea Party represented a massive act of civil disobedience.

We should never forget that everything Adolf Hitler did in Germany was "legal" and everything the Hungarian freedom fighters did in Hungary was "illegal." It was "illegal" to aid and comfort a Jew in Hitler's Germany. Even so, I am sure that, had I lived in Germany at the time, I would have aided and comforted my Jewish brothers. If today I lived in a Communist country where certain principles dear to the Christian faith are suppressed, I would openly advocate disobeying that country's antireligious laws.

I must make two honest confessions to you, my Christian and Jewish brothers. First, I must confess that over the past few years I have been gravely disappointed with the white moderate. I have almost reached the regrettable conclusion that the Negro's great stumbling block in his stride toward freedom is not the White Citizen's Counciler or the Ku Klux Klanner, but the white moderate, who is more devoted to "order" than to justice; who prefers a negative peace which is the absence of tension to a positive peace which is the presence of justice; who constantly says: "I agree with you in the goal you seek, but I cannot agree with your methods of direct action"; who paternalistically believes he can set the timetable for another man's freedom; who lives by a mythical concept of time and who constantly advises the Negro to wait for a "more convenient season." Shallow understanding from people of good will is more frustrating than absolute misunderstanding from people of ill will. Lukewarm acceptance is much more bewildering than outright rejection.

I had hoped that the white moderate would understand that law and order exist for the purpose of establishing justice and that when they fail in this purpose they become the dangerously structured dams that block the flow of social progress. I had hoped that the white moderate would understand that the present tension in the South is a necessary phase of the transition from an obnoxious negative peace, in which the Negro passively accepted his unjust plight, to a substantive and positive peace, in which all men will respect the dignity and worth of human personality. Actually, we who engage in nonviolent direct action are not the creators of tension. We merely bring to the surface the hidden tension that is already alive. We bring it out in the open, where it can be seen and dealt with. Like a boil that can never be cured so long as it is covered up but must be opened with all its ugliness to the natural medicines of air and light, injustice must be exposed, with all the tension its exposure creates, to the light of human conscience and the air of national opinion before it can be cured.

In your statement you assert that our actions, even though peaceful, must be condemned because they precipitate violence.

But is this a logical assertion? Isn't this like condemning a robbed man because his possession of money precipitated the evil act of robbery? Isn't this like condemning Socrates because his unswerving commitment to truth and his philosophical inquiries precipitated the act by the misguided populace in which they made him drink hemlock? Isn't this like condemning Jesus because his unique God-consciousness and never-ceasing devotion to God's will precipitated the evil act of crucifixion? We must come to see that, as the federal courts have consistently affirmed, it is wrong to urge an individual to cease his efforts to gain his basic constitutional rights because the quest may precipitate violence. Society must protect the robbed and punish the robber.

I had also hoped that the white moderate would reject the myth concerning time in relation to the struggle for freedom. I have just received a letter from a white brother in Texas. He writes: "All Christians know that the colored people will receive equal rights eventually, but it is possible that you are in too great a religious hurry. It has taken Christianity almost two thousand years to accomplish what it has. The teachings of Christ take time to come to earth." Such an attitude stems from a tragic misconception of time, from the strangely irrational notion that there is something in the very flow of time that will inevitably cure all ills. Actually, time itself is neutral; it can be used either destructively or constructively. More and more I feel that the people of ill will have used time much more effectively than have the people of good will. We will have to repent in this generation not merely for the hateful words and actions of the bad people but for the appalling silence of the good people. Human progress never rolls in on wheels of inevitability; it comes through the tireless efforts of men willing to be co-workers with God, and without this hard work, time itself becomes an ally of the forces of social stagnation. We must use time creatively, in the knowledge that the time is always ripe to do right. Now is the time to make real the promise of democracy and transform our pending national elegy into a creative psalm of brotherhood. Now is the time to lift our national policy from the quicksand of racial injustice to the solid rock of human dignity.

You speak of our activity in Birmingham as extreme. At first I was rather disappointed that fellow clergymen would see my nonviolent efforts as those of an extremist. I began thinking about the fact that I stand in the middle of two opposing forces in the Negro community. One is a force of complacency, made up in part of Negroes who, as a result of long years of oppression, are so drained of self-respect and a sense of "somebodiness" that they have adjusted to segregation; and in part of a few middle-class Negroes who, because of a degree of academic and economic security and because in some ways they profit by segregation, have become insensitive to the problems of the masses. The other force is one of bitterness and hatred, and it comes perilously close to advocating violence. It is expressed in the various black nationalist groups that are springing up across the nation, the largest and best-known being Elijah Muhammad's Muslim movement. Nourished by the Negro's frustration over the continued existence of racial discrimination, this movement is made up of people who have lost faith in America, who have absolutely repudiated Christianity, and who have concluded that the white man is an incorrigible "devil."

I have tried to stand between these two forces, saying that we need emulate neither the "do-nothingism" of the complacent nor the hatred and despair of the black nationalist. For there is the more excellent way of love and nonviolent protest. I am grateful to God that, through the influence of the Negro church, the way of nonviolence became an integral part of our struggle.

If this philosophy had not emerged, by now many streets of the South would, I am convinced, be flowing with blood. And I am further convinced that if our white brothers dismiss as "rabble-rousers" and "outside agitators" those of us who employ nonviolent direct action, and if they refuse to support our nonviolent efforts, millions of Negroes will, out of frustration and despair, seek solace and security in black-nationalist ideologies—a development that would inevitably lead to a frightening racial nightmare.

Oppressed people cannot remain oppressed forever. The yearning for freedom eventually manifests itself, and that is what has happened to the American Negro. Something within has reminded him of his birthright of freedom, and something without has reminded him that it can be gained. Consciously or unconsciously, he has been caught up by the *Zeitgeist*, and with his black brothers of Africa and his brown and yellow brothers of Asia, South America and the Caribbean, the United States Negro is moving with a sense of great urgency toward the promised land of racial justice. If one recognizes this vital urge that has engulfed the Negro community, one should readily understand why public demonstrations are taking place. The Negro has many pent-up resentments and latent frustrations, and he must release them. So let him march; let him make prayer pilgrimages to the city hall; let him go on freedom rides— and try to understand why he must do so. If his repressed emotions are not released in nonviolent ways, they will seek expression through violence; this is not a threat but a fact of history. So I have not said to my people; "Get rid of your discontent." Rather, I have tried to say that this normal and healthy discontent can be channeled into the creative outlet of nonviolent direct action. And now this approach is being termed extremist.

But though I was initially disappointed at being categorized as an extremist, as I continued to think about the matter I gradually gained a measure of satisfaction from the label. Was not Jesus an extremist for love: "Love your enemies, bless them that curse you, do good to them that hate you, and pray for them which despitefully use you, and persecute you." Was not Amos an extremist for justice: "Let justice roll down like waters and righteousness like an ever-flowing stream." Was not Paul an extremist for the Christian gospel: "I bear in my body the marks of the Lord Jesus." Was not Martin Luther an extremist: "Here I stand; I cannot do otherwise, so help me God." And John Bunyan: "I will stay in jail to the end of my days before I make a butchery of my conscience." And Abraham Lincoln: "This nation cannot survive half slave and half free." And Thomas Jefferson: "We hold these truths to be self-evident, that all men are created equal . . ." So the question is not whether we will be extremists, but what kind of extremists we will be. Will we be extremists for hate or for love? Will we be extremists for the preservation of injustice or for the extension of justice? In that dramatic scene on Calvary's hill three men were crucified. We must never forget that all three were crucified for the same crime—the crime of extremism. Two were extremists for immorality and thus fell below their environment. The other, Jesus Christ, was an extremist for love, truth and goodness, and thereby rose above his environment. Perhaps the South, the nation and the world are in dire need of creative extremists.

I had hoped that the white moderate would see this need. Perhaps I was too optimistic; perhaps I expected too much. I suppose I should have realized that few members of the oppressor race can understand the deep groans and passionate yearnings of the oppressed race, and still fewer have the vision to see that injustice must be rooted out by strong, persistent and determined action. I am thankful, however, that some of our white brothers in the South have grasped the meaning of this social revolution and committed themselves to it. They are still all too few in quantity, but they are big in quality. Some—such as Ralph McGill, Lillian Smith, Harry Golden, James McBride Dabbs, Ann Braden and Sarah Patton Boyle—have written about our struggle in eloquent and prophetic terms. Others have marched with us down nameless streets of the South. They have languished in filthy, roach-infested jails, suffering the abuse and brutality of policemen who view them as "dirty nigger-lovers." Unlike so many of their moderate brothers and sisters, they have recognized the urgency of the moment and sensed the need for powerful "action" antidotes to combat the disease of segregation.

Let me take note of my other major disappointment. I have been so greatly disappointed with the white church and its leadership. Of course, there are some notable exceptions. I am not unmindful of the fact that each of you has taken some significant stands on this issue. I commend you, Reverend Stallings, for your Christian stand on this past Sunday, in welcoming Negroes to your worship service on a non-segregated basis. I commend the Catholic leaders of this state for integrating Spring Hill College several years ago.

But despite these notable exceptions, I must honestly reiterate that I have been disappointed with the church. I do not say this as one of those negative critics who can always find something wrong with the church. I say this as a minister of the gospel, who loves the church; who was nurtured in its bosom; who has been sustained by its spiritual blessings and who will remain true to it as long as the cord of life shall lengthen.

When I was suddenly catapulted into the leadership of the bus protest in Montgomery, Alabama, a few years ago, I felt we would be supported by the white church. I felt that the white ministers, priests and rabbis of the South would be among our strongest allies. Instead, some have been outright opponents, refusing to understand the freedom movement and misrepresenting its leaders; all too many others have been more cautious than courageous and have remained silent behind the anesthetizing security of stained-glass windows.

In spite of my shattered dreams, I came to Birmingham with the hope that the white religious leadership of this community would see the justice of our cause and, with deep moral concern, would serve as the channel through which our just grievances could reach the power structure. I had hoped that each of you would understand. But again I have been disappointed.

I have heard numerous southern religious leaders admonish their worshipers to comply with a desegregation decision because it is the law, but I have longed to hear white ministers declare: "Follow this decree because integration is morally right and because the Negro is your brother." In the midst of blatant injustices inflicted upon the Negro, I have watched white churchmen stand on the sideline and mouth pious irrelevancies and sanctimonious trivialities. In the midst of a mighty struggle to rid our nation of racial and economic injustice, I have heard many ministers say: "Those are social issues, with which the gospel has no real concern." And I have watched many churches commit themselves to a completely otherworldly religion which makes a strange, un-Biblical distinction between body and soul, between the sacred and the secular.

I have traveled the length and the breadth of Alabama, Mississippi and all the other southern states. On sweltering summer days and crisp autumn mornings I have looked at the South's beautiful churches with their lofty spires pointing heavenward. I have beheld the impressive outlines of her massive religious-education buildings. Over and over I have found myself asking: "What kind of people worship here? Who is their God? Where were their voices when the lips of Governor Barnett dripped with words of interposition and nullification? Where were they when Governor Wallace gave a clarion call for defiance and hatred? Where were their voices of support when bruised and weary Negro men and women decided to rise from the dark dungeons of complacency to the bright hills of creative protest?"

Yes, these questions are still in my mind. In deep disappointment I have wept over the laxity of the church. But be assured that my tears have been tears of love. There can be no deep disappointment where there is not deep love. Yes, I love the church. How could I do otherwise? I am in the rather unique position of being the son, the grandson and the great-grandson of preachers. Yes, I see the church as the body of Christ. But oh! How we have blemished and scarred that body through social neglect and through fear of being nonconformists.

There was a time when the church was very powerful—in the time when the early Christians rejoiced at being deemed worthy to suffer for what they believed. In those days the church was not merely a thermometer that recorded the ideas and principles of popular opinion; it was a thermostat that transformed the mores of society. Whenever the early Christians entered a town, the people in power became disturbed and immediately sought to convict the Christians for being "disturbers of the peace" and "outside agitators." But the Christians pressed on, in the conviction that they were "a colony of heaven," called to obey God rather than man. Small in number, they were big in commitment. They were too God-intoxicated to be "astronomically intimidated." By their effort and example they brought an end to such ancient evils as infanticide and gladiatorial contests.

Things are different now. So often the contemporary church is a weak, ineffectual voice with an uncertain sound. So often it is an archdefender of the status quo. Far from being disturbed by the presence of the church, the power structure of the average community is consoled by the church's silent—and often even vocal—sanction of things as they are.

But the judgment of God is upon the church as never before. If today's church does not recapture the sacrificial spirit of the early church, it will lose its authenticity, forfeit the loyalty of millions, and be dismissed as an irrelevant social club with no meaning for the twentieth century. Every day I meet young people whose disappointment with the church has turned into outright disgust.

Perhaps I have once again been too optimistic. Is organized religion too inextricably bound to the status quo to save our nation and the world? Perhaps I must turn my faith to the inner spiritual church, the church within the church, as the true *ekklesia* and the hope of the world. But again I am thankful to God that some noble souls from the ranks of organized religion have broken loose form the paralyzing chains of conformity and joined us as active partners in the struggle for freedom. They have left their secure congregations and walked the streets of Albany, Georgia, with us. They have gone down the highways of the South on tortuous rides for freedom. Yes, they have gone to jail with us. Some have been dismissed from their churches, have lost the support of their bishops and fellow ministers. But they have acted in the faith that right defeated is stronger than evil triumphant. Their witness has been the spiritual salt that has preserved the true meaning of the gospel in these troubled times. They have carved a tunnel of hope through the dark mountain of disappointment.

I hope the church as a whole will meet the challenge of this decisive hour. But even if the church does not come to the aid of justice, I have no despair about the future. I have no fear about the outcome of our struggle in Birmingham, even if our motives are at present misunderstood. We will reach the goal of freedom in Birmingham and all over the nation, because the goal of America is freedom. Abused and scorned though we may be, our destiny is tied up with America's destiny. Before the pilgrims landed at Plymouth, we were here. Before the pen of Jefferson etched the majestic words of the Declaration of Independence across the pages of history, we were here. For more than two centuries our forebears labored in this country without wages; they made cotton king; they built the homes of their masters while suffering gross injustice and shameful humiliation—and yet out of a bottomless vitality they continued to thrive and develop. If the inexpressible cruelties of slavery could not stop us, the opposition we now face will surely fail. We will win our freedom because the sacred heritage of our nation and the eternal will of God are embodied in our echoing demands.

Before closing I feel impelled to mention one other point in your statement that has troubled me profoundly. You warmly commended the Birmingham police force for keeping "order" and "preventing violence." I doubt that you would have so warmly commended the police force if you had seen its dogs sinking their teeth into unarmed, nonviolent Negroes. I doubt that you would so quickly commend the policemen if you were to observe their ugly and inhumane treatment of Negroes here in the city jail; if you were to watch them push and curse old Negro women and young Negro girls; if you were to see them slap and kick old Negro men and young boys; if you were to observe them, as they did on two occasions, refuse to give us food because we wanted to sing our grace together. I cannot join you in your praise of the Birmingham police department.

It is true that the police have exercised a degree of discipline in handling the demonstrators. In this sense they have conducted themselves rather "nonviolently" in public. But for what purpose? To preserve the evil system of segregation. Over the past few years I have consistently preached that nonviolence demands that the means we use must be as pure as the ends we seek. I have tried to make clear that it is wrong to use immoral means to attain moral ends. But now I must affirm that it is just as wrong, or perhaps even more so, to use moral means to preserve immoral ends. Perhaps Mr. Connor and his policemen have been rather nonviolent in public, as was Chief Pritchett in Albany, Georgia, but they have used the moral means of nonviolence to maintain the immoral end of racial injustice. As T. S. Eliot has said: "The last temptation is the greatest treason: To do the right deed for the wrong reason."

I wish you had commended the Negro sit-inners and demonstrators of Birmingham for their sublime courage, their willingness to suffer and their amazing discipline in the midst of great provocation. One day the South will recognize its real heroes. They will be the James Merediths, with the noble sense of purpose that enables them to face jeering and hostile mobs, and with the agonizing loneliness that characterizes the life of the pioneer. They will be old, oppressed, battered Negro women, symbolized in a seventy-two-year-old woman in Montgomery, Alabama, who rose up with a sense of dignity and with her people decided not to ride segregated buses, and who responded with ungrammatical profundity to one who inquired about her weariness: "My feets is tired, but my soul is at rest." They will be the young high school and college students, the young ministers of the gospel and a host of their elders, courageously and nonviolently sitting in at lunch counters and willingly going to jail for conscience' sake. One day the South will know that when these disinherited children of God sat down at lunch counters, they were in reality standing up for what is best in the American dream and for the most sacred values in our Judaeo-Christian heritage, thereby bringing our nation back to those great wells of democracy which were dug deep by the founding fathers in their formulation of the Constitution and the Declaration of Independence.

Never before have I written so long a letter. I'm afraid it is much too long to take your precious time. I can assure you that it would have been much shorter if I had been writing from a comfortable desk, but what else can one do when he is alone in a narrow jail cell, other than write long letters, think long thoughts and pray long prayers?

If I have said anything in this letter that overstates the truth and indicates an unreasonable impatience, I beg you to forgive me. If I have said anything that understates the truth and indicates my having a patience that allows me to settle for anything less than brotherhood, I beg God to forgive me.

I hope this letter finds you strong in the faith. I also hope that circumstances will soon make it possible for me to meet each of you, not as an integrationist or a civil-rights leader but as a fellow clergyman and a Christian brother. Let us all hope that the dark clouds of racial prejudice will soon pass away and the deep fog of misunderstanding will be lifted from our fear-drenched communities, and in some not too distant tomorrow the radiant stars of love and brotherhood will shine over our great nation with all their scintillating beauty.

Yours for the cause of
Peace and Brotherhood,
Martin Luther King, Jr.

Malcolm X

Born in Omaha, Nebraska, on May 19, 1925, Malcolm Little later changed his name to "Malcolm X." "Little" was never his name, he said, but was inherited from his father, who inherited it from his grandfather, and so on back to the slave master who had given it to them after erasing the true family name. At age fifteen Malcolm X dropped out of school and became a hustler, pimp, drug dealer, and thief. He was convicted of burglary and sent to prison at twenty-one. While in prison, he did a great deal of reading and was converted to the Nation of Islam (Black Muslims), becoming a follower of Elijah Muhammad.

Upon leaving prison in 1952, he devoted himself to building up the Black Muslims. The Black Muslims became an important conduit for black self-esteem in the 1960s, growing from four hundred members to tens of thousands largely because of Malcolm's media efforts. They believed in self-determination of African-Americans "by any means necessary," culminating in the vision of a segregated black state. During this time, Malcolm Little became Malcolm X. In 1964 he withdrew from the Nation of Islam movement and organized the Muslim Mosque, Inc. Later he organized the Organization of Afro-American Unity, a nonreligious group, and traveled to Africa and Saudi Arabia, where he was received as if he were the official ambassador of black Americans. After a visit to Mecca, he rejected racist doctrines and stressed the importance of bringing world public opinion and pressure to bear upon the racist problems of the United States. Malcolm X was assassinated in New York City on February 21, 1965, three months after returning to the United States.

The Autobiography of Malcolm X (1964)
(excerpts)

. . . Once, one of my Mosque Seven Muslim brothers who worked with teenagers in a well-known Harlem community center showed me a confidential report. Some black senior social worker had been given a month off to investigate the "Black Muslims" in the Harlem area. Every paragraph sent me back to the dictionary—I guess that's why I've never forgotten one line about me. Listen to this: "The dynamic interstices of the Harlem sub-culture have been oversimplified and distorted by Malcolm X to meet his own needs."

Which of us, I wonder, knew more about that Harlem ghetto "sub-culture"? I, who had hustled for years in those streets, or that black snob status-symbol-educated social worker?

But that's not important. What's important, to my way of thinking about it, is that among America's 22 million black people so relatively few have been lucky enough to attend a college—and here was one of those who had been lucky. Here was, to my way of thinking, one of those "educated" Negroes who never had understood the true intent, or purpose, or application of education. Here was one of those stagnant educations, never used except for parading a lot of big words.

Do you realize this is one of the major reasons why America's white man has so easily contained and oppressed America's black man? Because until just lately, among the few educated Negroes scarcely any applied their education, as I am forced to say the white man does—in searching and creative thinking, to further themselves and their own kind in this competitive, materialistic, dog-eat-dog white man's world. For generations, the so-called "educated" Negroes have "led" their black brothers by echoing the white man's thinking—which naturally has been to the exploitive white man's advantage.

The white man—give him his due— has an extraordinary intelligence, an extraordinary cleverness. His world is full of proof of it. You can't name a thing the white man can't make. You can hardly name a scientific problem he can't solve. Here he is now solving the problems of sending men exploring into outer space— and returning them safely to earth.

But in the arena of dealing with human beings, the white man's working intelligence is hobbled. His intelligence will fail him altogether if the humans happen to be non-white. The white man's emotions supersede his intelligence. He will commit against non-whites the most incredible spontaneous emotional acts, so psyche-deep is his "white superiority" complex.

Where was the A-bomb dropped . . . "to save American lives"? Can the white man be so naive as to think the clear import of this *ever* will be lost upon the non-white two-thirds of the earth's population?

Before that bomb was dropped—right over here in the United States, what about the one hundred thousand loyal naturalized and native-born Japanese American citizens who were herded into camps, behind barbed wire? But how many German-born naturalized Americans were herded behind barbed wire? They were *white!*

Historically, the non-white complexion has evoked and exposed the "devil" in the very nature of the white man.

What else but a controlling emotional "devil" so blinded American white intelligence that it couldn't foresee that millions of black slaves, "freed," then permitted even limited education, would one day rise up as a terrifying monster within white America's midst?

The white man's brains that today explore space should have told the slavemaster that any slave, if he is educated, will no longer fear his master. History shows that an educated slave always begins to ask, and next demand, equality with his master.

Today, in many ways the black man sees the collective white man in America better than that white man can see himself. And the 22 million blacks realize increasingly that physically, politically, economically, and even to some degree socially, the aroused black man can create a turmoil in white America's vitals—not to mention America's international image.

I had not intended to stray off. I had been telling how in 1963, I was trying to cope with the white newspaper, radio, and television reporters who were determined to defeat Mr. Muhammad's teachings.

I developed a mental image of reporters as human ferrets—steadily sniffing, darting, probing, for some way to trick me, somehow to corner me in our interview exchanges.

Let some civil rights "leader" make some statement, displeasing to the white public power structure, and the reporters, in an effort to whip him back into line, would try to use me. I'll give an example. I'd get a question like this: "Mr. Malcolm

X, you've often gone on record as disapproving of the sit-ins and similar Negro protest actions—what is your opinion of the Montgomery boycott that Dr. King is leading?"

Now my feeling was that although the civil rights "leaders" kept attacking us Muslims, still they were black people, still they were our own kind, and I would be most foolish to let the white man maneuver me against the civil rights movement.

When I was asked about the Montgomery boycott, I'd carefully review what led up to it. Mrs. Rosa Parks was riding home on a bus and at some bus stop the white cracker bus driver ordered Mrs. Parks to get up and give her seat to some white passenger who had just got on the bus. I'd say, "Now, just *imagine* that! This good, hard-working, Christian-believing black woman, she's paid her money, she's in her seat. Just because she's *black*, she's asked to get up! I mean, sometimes even for *me* it's hard to believe the white man's arrogance!"

Or I might say, "No one will ever know exactly what emotional ingredient made this relatively trivial incident a fuse for those Montgomery Negroes. There had been *centuries* of the worst kind of outrages against Southern black people—lynchings, rapings, shootings, beatings! But you know history has been triggered by trivial-seeming incidents. Once a little nobody Indian lawyer was put off a train, and fed up with injustice, he twisted a knot in the British Lion's tail. *His* name was Mahatma Gandhi!"

Or I might copy a trick I had seen lawyers use, both in life and on television. It was a way that lawyers would slip in before a jury something otherwise inadmissible. (Sometimes I think I really might have made it as a lawyer, as I once told that eighth-grade teacher in Mason, Michigan, I wanted to be, when he advised me to become a carpenter.) I would slide right

over the reporter's question to drop into his lap a logical-extension hot potato for him.

"Well, sir, I see the same boycott reasoning for Negroes asked to join the Army, Navy, and Air Force. Why should we go off to die somewhere to preserve a so-called 'democracy' that gives a white immigrant of one day more than it gives the black man with four hundred years of slaving and serving in this country?"

Whites would prefer fifty local boycotts to having 22 million Negroes start thinking about what I had just said. I don't have to tell you that it never got printed the way I said it. It would be turned inside out if it got printed at all. And I could detect when the white reporters had gotten their heads together; they quit asking me certain questions.

If I had developed a good point, though, I'd bait a hook to get it said when I went on radio or television. I'd seem to slip and mention some recent so-called civil rights "advance." You know, where some giant industry had hired ten showpiece Negroes; some restaurant chain had begun making more money by serving Negroes; some Southern university had enrolled a black freshman without bayonets—like that. When I "slipped," the program host would leap on that bait: "Ahhh! Indeed, Mr. Malcolm X—you can't deny *that's* an advance for your race!"

I'd jerk the pole then. "I can't turn around without hearing about some 'civil rights advance'! White people seem to think the black man ought to be shouting 'hallelujah'! Four hundred years the white man has had his foot-long knife in the black man's back—and now the white man starts to *wiggle* the knife out, maybe six inches! The black man's supposed to be *grateful?* Why, if the white man jerked the knife *out,* it's still going to leave a *scar!*"

Similarly, just let some mayor or some city council somewhere boast of having "no Negro problem." That would get off the newsroom teletypes and it would soon be jammed right in my face. I'd say they didn't need to tell me where this was, because I knew that all it meant was that relatively very few Negroes were living there. That's true the world over, you know. Take "democratic" England—when 100,000 black West Indians got there, England stopped the black migration. Finland welcomed a Negro U.S. Ambassador. Well, let enough Negroes follow him to Finland! Or in Russia, when Khrushchev was in power, he threatened to cancel the visas of black African students whose anti-discrimination demonstration said to the world, "Russia, too. . . ."

The Deep South white press generally blacked me out. But they front-paged what I felt about Northern white and black Freedom Riders going *South* to "demonstrate." I called it "ridiculous"; their own Northern ghettoes, right at home, had enough rats and roaches to kill to keep all of the Freedom Riders busy. I said that ultra-liberal New York had more integration problems than Mississippi. If the Northern Freedom Riders wanted more to do, they could work on the roots of such ghetto evils as the little children out in the streets at midnight, with apartment keys on strings around their necks to let themselves in, and their mothers and fathers drunk, drug addicts, thieves, prostitutes. Or the Northern Freedom Riders could light some fires under Northern city halls, unions, and major industries to give more jobs to Negroes to remove so many of them from the relief and welfare rolls, which created laziness, and which deteriorated the ghettoes into steadily worse places for humans to live. It was all—it *is* all—the absolute truth; but what did I want to *say* it for? Snakes couldn't have turned on me faster than the liberal.

Yes, I will pull off that liberal's halo that he spends such efforts cultivating! The North's liberals have been for so long pointing accusing fingers at the South and getting away with it that they have fits when they are exposed as the world's worst hypocrites.

I believe my own life *mirrors* this hypocrisy. I know nothing about the South. I am a creation of the Northern white man and of his hypocritical attitude toward the Negro.

The white Southerner was always given his due by Mr. Muhammad. The white Southerner, you can say one thing—he is honest. He bares his teeth to the black man; he tells the black man, to his face, that Southern whites never will accept phony "integration." The Southern white goes further, to tell the black man that he means to fight him every inch of the way—against even the so-called "tokenism." The advantage of this is the Southern black man never has been under any illusions about the opposition he is dealing with.

You can say for many Southern white people that, individually, they have been paternalistically helpful to many individual Negroes. But the Northern white man, he grins with his teeth, and his mouth has always been full of tricks and lies of "equality" and "integration." When one day all over America, a black hand touched the white man's shoulder, and the white man turned, and there stood the Negro saying "Me, too . . . ," why, that Northern liberal shrank from that black man with as much guilt and dread as any Southern white man.

Actually, America's most dangerous and threatening black man is the one who has been kept sealed up by the Northerner in the black ghettoes—the Northern white power structure's system to keep talking democracy while keeping the black man out of sight somewhere, around the corner.

The word "integration" was invented by a Northern liberal. The word has no real meaning. I ask you: in the racial sense in which it's used so much today, whatever "integration" is supposed to mean, can it precisely be defined? The truth is that "integration" is an *image*, it's a foxy Northern liberal's smoke-screen that confuses the true wants of the American black man. Here in these fifty racist and neo-racist states of North America, this word "integration" has millions of white people confused, and angry, believing wrongly that the black masses want to live mixed up with the white man. That is the case only with the relative handful of these "integration"-mad Negroes.

I'm talking about these "token-integrated" Negroes who flee from their poor, downtrodden black brothers—from their own self-hate, which is what they're really trying to escape. I'm talking about these Negroes you will see who can't get enough of nuzzling up to the white man. These "chosen few" Negroes are more white-minded, more anti-black, than even the white man is.

Human rights! Respect as *human beings!* That's what America's black masses want. That's the true problem. The black masses want not to be shrunk from as though they are plague-ridden. They want not to be walled up in slums, in the ghettoes, like animals. They want to live in an open, free society where they can walk with their heads up, like men, and women!

Few white people realize that many black people today dislike and avoid spending any more time than they must around white people. This "integration" image, as it is popularly interpreted, has millions of vain, self-exalted white people convinced that black people want to sleep in bed with them—and that's a lie! . . .

The black masses prefer the company of their own kind. Why, even these fancy, bourgeois Negroes—when they get back home from the fancy "integrated" cocktail parties, what do they do but kick off their shoes and talk about those white liberals they just left as if the liberals were dogs. And the white liberals probably do the very same thing. I can't be sure about the whites, I am never around them in private—but the bourgeois Negroes know I'm not lying.

I'm telling it like it *is!* You *never* have to worry about me biting my tongue if something I know as truth is on my mind. Raw, naked truth exchanged between the black man and the white man is what a whole lot more of is needed in this country—to clear the air of the racial mirages, clichés, and lies that this country's very atmosphere has been filled with for four hundred years.

In many communities, especially small communities, white people have created a benevolent image of themselves as having had so much "good-will toward our Negroes," every time any "local Negro" begins suddenly letting the local whites know the truth—that the black people are sick of being hind-tit, second-class, disfranchised, that's when you hear, uttered so sadly, "Unfortunately now because of this, our whites of good-will are starting to turn against the Negroes. . . . It's so regrettable . . . progress *was* being made . . . but now our communications between the races have broken down!"

What are they talking about? There never was any *communication.* Until after World War II, there wasn't a single community in the entire United States where the white man heard from any local Negro "leaders" the truth of what Negroes felt about the conditions that the white community imposed upon Negroes.

You need some proof? Well, then, why was it that when Negroes did start revolting across America, virtually all of white America was caught up in surprise and even shock? I would hate to be general of an army as badly informed as the American white man has been about the Negro in this country.

This is the situation which permitted Negro combustion to slowly build up to the revolution-point, without the white man realizing it. All over America, the local Negro "leader," in order to survive as a "leader," kept reassuring the local white man, in effect, "Everything's all right, everything's right in hand, boss!" When the "leader" wanted a little something for his people: "Er, boss, some of the people talking about we sure need a better school, boss." And if the local Negroes hadn't been causing any "trouble," the "benevolent" white man might nod and give them a school, or some jobs.

The white men belonging to the power structures in thousands of communities across America know that I'm right! They know that I am describing what has been the true pattern of "communications" between the "local whites of good-will" and the local Negroes. It has been a pattern created by domineering, ego-ridden whites. Its characteristic design permitted the white man to feel "noble" about throwing crumbs to the black man, instead of feeling guilty about the local community's system of cruelly exploiting Negroes.

But I want to tell you something. This pattern, this "system" that the white man created, of teaching Negroes to hide the truth from him behind a façade of grinning, "yessir-bossing," foot shuffling and head-scratching—that system has done the American white man more harm than an invading army would do to him.

Why do I say this? Because all this has steadily helped this American white man to build up, deep in his psyche, absolute conviction that he is "superior." In how many, many communities have, thus, white men who didn't finish high school regarded condescendingly university-educated local Negro "leaders," principals of schools, teachers, doctors, other professionals?

The white man's system has been imposed upon non-white peoples all over the world. This is exactly the reason why wherever people who are anything but white live in this world today, the white man's governments are finding themselves in deeper and deeper trouble and peril.

Let's just face truth. Facts! Whether or not the white man of the world is able to face truth, and facts, about the true reasons for his trouble—that's what essentially will determine whether or not *he* will now survive.

Today we are seeing this revolution of the non-white peoples, who just a few years ago would have frozen in horror if the mighty white nations so much as lifted an eyebrow. What it is, simply, is that black and brown and red and yellow peoples have, after hundreds of years of exploitation and imposed "inferiority" and general misuse, become, finally, do-or-die sick and tired of the white man's heel on their necks.

How can the white American government figure on selling "democracy" and "brotherhood" to non-white peoples—if they read and hear every day what's going on right here in America, and see the better-than-a-thousand-word photographs of the American white man denying "democracy" and "brotherhood" even to America's native-born non-whites? The world's non-whites know how this Negro here has loved the American white man, and slaved for him, tended to him, nursed him. This Negro has jumped into uniform and gone off and died when this America was attacked by enemies both white and non-white. Such a faithful, loyal non-white as *this*—and *still* America bombs him, and sets dogs on him, and turns fire hoses on him, and jails him by the thousands, and beats him bloody, and inflicts upon him all manner of other crimes.

Of course these things, known and refreshed every day for the rest of the world's non-whites, are a vital factor in these burnings of ambassadors' limousines, these stonings, defilings, and wreckings of embassies and legations, these shouts of "White man, go home!," these attacks on white Christian missionaries, and these bombings and tearing down of flags.

Is it clear why I have said that the American white man's malignant superiority complex has done him more harm than an invading army?

The American black man should be focusing his every effort toward building his *own* businesses, and decent homes for himself. As other ethnic groups have done, let the black people, wherever possible, however possible, patronize their own kind, hire their own kind, and start in those ways to build up the black race's ability to do for itself. That's the only way the American black man is ever going to get respect. One thing the white man never can give the black man is self-respect! The black man never can become independent and recognized as a human being who is truly equal with other human beings until he has what they have, and until he is doing for himself what others are doing for themselves.

The black man in the ghettoes, for instance, has to start self-correcting his own material, moral, and spiritual defects and evils. The black man needs to start his own program to get rid of drunkenness, drug addiction, prostitution. The black man in America has to lift up his own sense of values.

Only a few thousands of Negroes, relatively a very tiny number, are taking any part in "integration." Here, again, it is those few bourgeois Negroes, rushing to throw away their little money in the white man's luxury hotels, his swanky nightclubs, and big, fine, exclusive restaurants. The white people patronizing those places can afford it. But these Negroes you see in those places can't afford it, certainly most of

them can't. Why, what does some Negro one installment payment away from disaster look like somewhere downtown out to dine, grinning at some headwaiter who has more money than the Negro? Those bourgeois Negroes out draping big tablecloth-sized napkins over their knees and ordering quail under glass and stewed snails—why, Negroes don't even *like* snails! What they're doing is proving they're integrated.

If you want to get right down to the real outcome of this so-called "integration," what you've got to arrive at is intermarriage.

I'm right *with* the Southern white man who believes that you can't have so-called "integration," at least not for long, without intermarriage increasing. And what good is this for anyone? Let's again face reality. In a world as color-hostile as this, man or woman, black or white, what do they want with a mate of the other race?

Certainly white people have served enough notice of their hostility to any blacks in their families and neighborhoods. And the way most Negroes feel today, a mixed couple probably finds that black families, black communities, are even more hostile than the white ones. So what's bound to face "integrated" marriages, except being unwelcomed, unwanted, "misfits" in whichever world they try to live in? What we arrive at is that "integration," socially, is no good for either side. "Integration," ultimately, would destroy the white race . . . and destroy the black race.

The white man's "integrating" with black women has already changed the complexion and characteristics of the black race in America. What's been proved by the "blacks" whose complexions are "whiter" than many "white" people? I'm told that there are in America today between two and five million "white Negroes," who are "passing" in white society. Imagine their torture! Living in constant fear that some black person they've known might meet and expose them. Imagine every day living a lie. *Imagine* hearing their own white husbands, their own white wives, even their own white children, talking about "those Negroes."

I would doubt if anyone in America has heard Negroes more bitter against the white man than some of those I have heard. But I will tell you that, without any question, the *most* bitter anti-white diatribes that I have ever heard have come from "passing" Negroes, living as whites, among whites, exposed every day to what white people say among themselves regarding Negroes—things that a recognized Negro never would hear. Why, if there was a racial showdown, these Negroes "passing" within white circles would become the black side's most valuable "spy" and ally.

Europe's "brown babies," now young men and women who are starting to marry, and produce families of their own . . . have their experiences throughout their lives, scarred as racial freaks, proved anything positive for "integration"?

"Integration" is called "assimilation" if white ethnic groups alone are involved: it's fought against tooth and nail by those who want their heritage preserved. Look at how the Irish threw the English out of Ireland. The Irish knew the English would engulf them. Look at the French-Canadians, fanatically fighting to keep their identity. . . .

Not long ago, the black man in America was fed a dose of another form of the weakening, lulling and deluding effects of so-called "integration." It was that "Farce on Washington," I call it.

The idea of a mass of blacks marching on Washington was originally the brainchild of the Brotherhood of Sleeping Car Porters' A. Philip Randolph. For twenty or more years the March on Washington idea had floated around among Negroes. And, spontaneously, suddenly now, that idea caught on.

Overalled rural Southern Negroes, small town Negroes, Northern ghetto Negroes, even thousands of previously Uncle Tom Negroes began talking "March!"

Nothing since Joe Louis had so coalesced the masses of Negroes. Groups of Negroes were talking of getting to Washington any way they could—in rickety old cars, on buses, hitch-hiking—walking, even, if they had to. They envisioned thousands of black brothers converging together upon Washington—to lie down in the streets, on airport runways, on government lawns—demanding of the Congress and the White House some concrete civil rights action.

This was a national bitterness; militant, unorganized, and leaderless. Predominantly, it was young Negroes, defiant of whatever might be the consequences, sick and tired of the black man's neck under the white man's heel.

The white man had plenty of good reasons for nervous worry. The right spark—some unpredictable emotional chemistry—could set off a black uprising. The government knew that thousands of milling, angry blacks not only could completely disrupt Washington—but they could erupt in Washington.

The White House speedily invited in the major civil rights Negro "leaders." They were asked to stop the planned March. They truthfully said they hadn't begun it, they had no control over it—the idea was national, spontaneous, unorganized, and leaderless. In other words, it was a black powder keg.

Any student of how "integration" can weaken the black man's movement was about to observe a master lesson.

The White House, with a fanfare of international publicity, "approved," "endorsed," and "welcomed" a March on Washington. The big civil rights organization right at this time had been publicly squabbling about donations. The *New York Times* had broken the story. The N.A.A.C.P. had charged that other agencies' demonstrations, highly publicized, had attracted a major part of the civil rights donations—while the N.A.A.C.P. got left holding the bag, supplying costly bail and legal talent for the other organizations' jailed demonstrators.

It was like a movie. The next scene was the "big six" civil rights Negro "leaders" meeting in New York City with the white head of a big philanthropic agency. They were told that their money-wrangling in public was damaging their image. And a reported $800,000 was donated to a United Civil Rights Leadership council that was quickly organized by the "big six."

Now, what had instantly achieved black unity? The white man's money. What string was attached to the money? Advice. Not only was there this donation, but another comparable sum was promised, for sometime later on, after the March . . . obviously if all went well.

That original "angry" March on Washington was now about to be entirely changed.

Massive international publicity projected the "big six" as March on Washington leaders. It was news to those angry grass-roots Negroes steadily adding steam to their March plans. They probably assumed that now those famous "leaders" were endorsing and joining them.

Invited next to join the March were four famous white public figures: one Catholic, one Jew, one Protestant, and one labor boss.

The massive publicity now gently hinted that the "big ten" would "supervise" the March on Washington's "mood," and its "direction."

The four white figures began nodding. The word spread fast among so-called "lib-eral" Catholics, Jews, Protestants, and laborites: it was "democratic" to join this black March. And suddenly, the previously March-nervous whites began announcing *they* were going.

It was as if electrical current shot through the ranks of bourgeois Negroes—the very so-called "middle-class" and "upper-class" who had earlier been deploring the March on Washington talk by grass-roots Negroes.

But white people, now, were going to march.

Why, some downtrodden, jobless, hungry Negro might have gotten trampled. Those "integration"-mad Negroes practically ran over each other trying to find out where to sign up. The "angry blacks" March suddenly had been made chic. Suddenly it had a Kentucky Derby image. For the status-seeker, it was a status symbol. "Were you *there?*" You can hear that right today.

It had become an outing, a picnic.

The morning of the March, any rickety carloads of angry, dusty, sweating small-town Negroes would have gotten lost among the chartered jet planes, railroad cars, and air-conditioned buses. What originally was planned to be an angry riptide, one English newspaper aptly described now as "the gentle flood."

Talk about "integrated"! It was like salt and pepper. And, by now, there wasn't a single logistics aspect uncontrolled.

The marchers had been instructed to bring no signs—signs were provided. They had been told to sing one song: "We Shall Overcome." They had been told *how* to arrive, *when, where* to arrive, *where* to assemble, when to *start* marching, the *route* to march. First-aid stations were strategically located—even where to *faint!*

Yes, I was there. I observed that circus. Who ever heard of angry revolutionists all harmonizing "We Shall Overcome . . . Suum Day . . ." while tripping and swaying along arm-in-arm with the very people they were supposed to be angrily revolting against? Who ever heard of angry revolutionists swinging their bare feet together with their oppressor in lilypad park pools, with gospels and guitars and "I Have A Dream" speeches?

And the black masses in America were—and still are—having a nightmare.

These "angry revolutionists" even followed their final instructions: to leave early. With all of those thousands upon thousands of "angry revolutionists," so few stayed over that the next morning the Washington hotel association reported a costly loss in empty rooms.

Hollywood couldn't have topped it.

In a subsequent press poll, not one Congressman or Senator with a previous record of opposition to civil rights said he had changed his views. What did anyone expect? How was a one-day "integrated" picnic going to counter-influence these representatives of prejudice rooted deep in the psyche of the American white man for four hundred years?

The very fact that millions, black and white, believed in this monumental farce is another example of how much this country goes in for the surface glossing over, the escape ruse, surfaces, instead of truly dealing with its deep-rooted problems.

What that March on Washington did do was lull Negroes for a while. But inevitably, the black masses started realizing they had been smoothly hoaxed again by the white man. And, inevitably, the black man's anger rekindled, deeper than ever, and there began bursting out in different cities, in the "long, hot summer" of 1964, unprecedented racial crises. . . .

Hannah Arendt

Born in 1906 in Hanover, Germany, Hannah Arendt left Hitler's Europe in 1941 for the United States, where she was to become a highly respected political theorist. Arendt clearly differentiated between thinking and doing and between the social and the political. She articulated the concept of "the banality of evil" as a universal threat to civilized society.

Arendt had studied at the universities of Konigsberg, Marburg, and Freiburg, and completed her Ph.D. at the University of Heidelberg under the tutelage of Karl Jaspers. Jaspers later introduced her to the notion of the banality of evil as it applied to the mass appeal of Nazism. Arendt was a social worker in Paris from 1934 through 1940, served as research director for the Conference on Jewish Relations in the United States from 1944 to 1946, and later worked briefly as chief editor of Schocken Books and then as executive director of Jewish Cultural Reconstruction. She was naturalized a U.S. citizen in 1951.

Arendt taught political philosophy at the University of California at Berkeley, Princeton, Columbia, the University of Chicago, and finally, The New School for Social Research until her death in 1975. Her books include *The Origins of Totalitarianism* (1957), *The Human Condition* (1958), *On Revolution* (1963), *Eichmann in Jerusalem* (1964), *Men in Dark Times* (1968), *Between Past and Future* (1968), and *Crises of the Republic* (1972).

Arendt believed that clear thinking and acting were two separate things, although the former influenced the latter. She once said, "I really believe that you can only act in concert, and I really believe that you can only think by yourself."

Crises of the Republic (1972)
(excerpt)

Civil Disobedience

I

The images of Socrates and Thoreau occur not only in the literature on our subject, but also, and more importantly, in the minds of the civil disobedients themselves. To those who were brought up in the Western tradition of conscience—and who was not?—it seems only natural to think of their agreement with others as secondary to a solitary decision *in foro conscientiae*, as though what they had in common with others was not an opinion or a judgment at all, but a common conscience. And since the arguments used to buttress this position are usually suggested by more or less vague reminiscences of what Socrates or Thoreau had to say about the "citizen's moral relation to the law," it may be best to begin these considerations with a brief examination of what these two men actually had to say on the matter.

As for Socrates, the decisive text is, of course, Plato's *Crito*, and the arguments presented there are much less unequivocal and certainly less useful for the demand of cheerful submission to punishment than the legal and philosophical textbooks tell us. There is first the fact that Socrates, during his trial, never challenged the laws themselves—only this particular miscarriage of justice, which he spoke of as the "accident" ($\tau\acute{\nu}\chi\eta$) that had befallen him. His personal misfortune did not entitle him to "break his contracts and agreements" with the laws; his quarrel was not with the laws, but with the judges. Moreover, as Socrates pointed out to Crito (who tried to persuade him to escape and go into exile), at the time of the trial the laws themselves had offered him this choice: "At that time you could have done with the state's consent what you are trying now to do without it. But then you gloried in being willing to die. You said that you preferred death to exile" (52). We also know, from the *Apology*, that he had the option of desisting from his public examination of things, which doubtless spread uncertainty about established customs and beliefs, and that again he had preferred death, because "an unexamined life is not worth living." That is, Socrates would not have honored his own words if he had tried to escape; he would have undone all he had done during his trial—

would have "confirmed the judges in their opinion, and made it seem that their verdict was a just one" (53). He owed it *to himself*, as well as to the citizens he had addressed, to stay and die. "It is the payment of a debt of honor, the payment of a gentleman who has lost a wager and who pays because he cannot otherwise live with himself. There has indeed been a contract, and the notion of a contract pervades the latter half of the *Crito*, but . . . the contract which is binding is . . . *the commitment involved in the trial*" (my italics).[1]

Thoreau's case, though much less dramatic (he spent one night in jail for refusing to pay his poll tax to a government that permitted slavery, but he let his aunt pay it for him the next morning), seems at first glance more pertinent to our current debates, for, in contradistinction to Socrates, he protested against the injustice of the laws themselves. The trouble with this example is that in "On the Duty of Civil Disobedience," the famous essay that grew out of the incident and made the term "civil disobedience" part of our political vocabulary, he argued his case not on the ground of a *citizen's* moral relation to the law, but on the ground of individual conscience and conscience's moral obligation: "It is not a man's duty, as a matter of course, to devote himself to the eradication of any, even the most enormous, wrong; he may still properly have other concerns to engage him; but it is his duty, at least, to wash his hands of it, and, if he gives it no thought longer, not to give it practically his support." Thoreau did not pretend that a man's washing his hands of it would make the world better or that a man had any obligation to do so. He "came into this world not chiefly to make this a good place to live in, but to live in it, be it good or bad." Indeed, this

---

[1]See N. A. Greenberg's excellent analysis, "Socrates' Choice in the *Crito*" (*Harvard Studies in Classical Philology*, vol. 70, no. 1, 1965), which proved that the *Crito* can be understood only if read in conjunction with the *Apology*.

is how we all come into the world—lucky if the world and the part of it we arrive in is a good place to live in at the time of our arrival, or at least a place where the wrongs committed are not "of such a nature that it requires you to be the agent of injustice to another." For only if this is the case, "then, I say, break the law." And Thoreau was right: individual conscience requires nothing more.[2]

Here, as elsewhere, conscience is unpolitical. It is not primarily interested in the world where the wrong is committed or in the consequences that the wrong will have for the future course of the world. It does not say, with Jefferson, "I tremble *for my country* when I reflect that God is just; that His justice cannot sleep forever,"[3] because it trembles for the individual self and its integrity. It can therefore be much more radical and say, with Thoreau, "This people must cease to hold slaves, and to make war on Mexico, *though it cost them their existence as a people*" (italics added), whereas for Lincoln "the paramount object," even in the struggle for the emancipation of the slaves, remained, as he wrote in 1862, "to save the Union, and . . . not either to save or destroy slavery."[4] This does not mean that Lincoln was unaware of "the monstrous injustice of slavery itself," as he had called it eight years earlier; it means that he was also aware of the distinction between his "official duty" and his "personal wish that all men everywhere could be free."[5] And this distinction, if one strips it of the always complex and equivocal historical circumstances, is ultimately the same as Machiavelli's when he said, "I

love my native city more than my own soul."[6] The discrepancy between "official duty" and "personal wish" in Lincoln's case no more indicates a lack of moral commitment than the discrepancy between city and soul indicates that Machiavelli was an atheist and did not believe in eternal salvation and damnation.

This possible conflict between "the good man" and "the good citizen" (according to Aristotle, the good man could be a good citizen only in a good state; according to Kant, even "a race of devils" could solve successfully the problem of establishing a constitution, "if only they are intelligent"), between the individual self, with or without belief in an afterlife, and the member of the community, or, as we would say today, between morality and politics, is very old—older, even, than the word "conscience," which in its present connotation is of relatively recent origin. And almost equally old are the justifications for the position of either. Thoreau was consistent enough to recognize and admit that he was open to the charge of irresponsibility, the oldest charge against "the good man." He said explicitly that he was "not responsible for the successful working of the machinery of society," was "not the son of the engineer." The adage *Fiat justicia et pereat mundus* (Let justice be done even if the world perishes), which is usually invoked rhetorically against the defenders of absolute justice, often for the purpose of excusing wrongs and crimes, neatly expresses the gist of the dilemma.

However, the reason that "at the level of individual morality, the problem of

---

[2] All quotations are from Thoreau's "On the Duty of Civil Disobedience" (1849).

[3] *Notes on the State of Virginia*, Query XVIII (1781–85).

[4] In his famous letter to Horace Greeley, quoted here from Hans Morgenthau, *The Dilemmas of Politics*, Chicago, 1958, p. 80.

[5] Quoted from Richard Hofstadter, *The American Political Tradition*, New York, 1948, p. 110.

[6] Allan Gilbert, ed., *The Letters of Machiavelli*, New York, 1961, letter 225.

disobedience to the law is wholly intractable"[7] is of still a different order. The counsels of conscience are not only unpolitical; they are always expressed in purely subjective statements. When Socrates stated that "it is better to suffer wrong than to do wrong," he clearly meant that it was better *for him*, just as it was better for him "to be in disagreement with multitudes than, being one, to be in disagreement with [himself]."[8] Politically, on the contrary, what counts is that a wrong has been done; to the law it is irrelevant who is better off as a result—the doer or the sufferer. Our legal codes distinguish between crimes in which indictment is mandatory, because the community as a whole has been violated, and offenses in which only doers and sufferers are involved, who may or may not want to sue. In the case of the former, the states of mind of those involved are irrelevant, except insofar as intent is part of the overt act, or mitigating circumstances are taken into account; it makes no difference whether the one who suffered is willing to forgive or the one who did is entirely unlikely to do it again.

In the *Gorgias*, Socrates does not address the citizens, as he does in the *Apology* and, in support of the *Apology*, in the *Crito*. Here Plato lets Socrates speak as the philosopher who has discovered that men have intercourse not only with their fellow men but also with themselves, and that the latter form of intercourse—my being with and by myself—prescribes certain rules for the former. These are the rules of conscience, and they are—like those Thoreau announced in his essay—entirely negative. They do not say what to do; they say what not to do. They do not spell out certain principles for taking action; they lay down boundaries no act should transgress. They say: Don't do wrong, for then you will have to live together with a wrongdoer. Plato, in the later dialogues (the *Sophist* and the *Theaetetus*), elaborated on this Socratic intercourse of me with myself and defined thinking as the soundless dialogue between me and myself; existentially speaking, this dialogue, like all dialogues, requires that the partners be friends. The validity of the Socratic propositions depends upon the kind of man who utters them and the kind of man to whom they are addressed. They are self-evident truths for man insofar as he is a thinking being; to those who don't think, who don't have intercourse with themselves, they are not self-evident, nor can they be proved.[9] Those men—and they are the "multitudes"—can gain a proper interest in themselves only, according to Plato, by believing in a mythical hereafter with rewards and punishments.

Hence, the rules of conscience hinge on interest in the self. They say: Beware of doing something that you will not be able to live with. It is the same argument that led to "Camus's . . . stress on the necessity of resistance to injustice *for the resisting individual's own health and welfare*" (my italics).[10] The political and legal trouble with such justification is twofold. First, it cannot be generalized; in order to keep

---

[7] *To Establish Justice, to Insure Domestic Tranquility*, Final Report of the National Commission on The Causes and The Prevention of Violence, December, 1969, p. 98.

[8] *Gorgias*, 482 and 489.

[9] This is made quite clear in the second book of the *Republic*, where Socrates' own pupils "can plead the cause of injustice most eloquently and still not be convinced themselves" (357–367). They are and remain convinced of justice as a self-evident truth, but Socrates' arguments are not convincing and they show that with this kind of reasoning the cause of injustice can just as well be "proved."

[10] Quoted by Christian Bay, "Civil Disobedience," in the *International Encyclopedia of the Social Sciences*, 1968, II, 486.

its validity, it must remain subjective. What I cannot live with may not bother another man's conscience. The result is that conscience will stand against conscience. "If the decision to break the law really turned on individual conscience, it is hard to see in law how Dr. King is better off than Governor Ross Barnett, of Mississippi, who also believed deeply in his cause and was willing to go to jail."[11] The second, and perhaps even more serious, trouble is that conscience, if it is defined in secular terms, presupposes not only that man possesses the innate faculty of telling right from wrong, but also that man is interested in himself, for the obligation arises from this interest alone. And this kind of self-interest can hardly be taken for granted. Although we know that human beings are capable of thinking—of having intercourse with themselves—we do not know how many indulge in this rather profitless enterprise; all we can say is that the habit of thinking, of reflecting on what one is doing, is independent of the individual's social, educational, or intellectual standing. In this respect, as in so many others, "the good man" and "the good citizen" are by no means the same, and not only in the Aristotelian sense. Good men become manifest only in emergencies, when they suddenly appear, as if from nowhere, in all social strata. The good citizen, on the contrary, must be conspicuous; he can be studied, with the not so very comforting result that he turns out to belong to a small minority: he tends to be educated and a member of the upper social classes.[12]

This whole question of the political weight to be accorded moral decisions—decisions arrived at *in foro conscientiae*—has been greatly complicated by the originally religious and later secularized associations that the notion of conscience acquired under the influence of Christian philosophy. As we use the word today, in both moral and legal matters, conscience is supposed to be always present within us, as though it were identical with consciousness. (It is true that it took language a long time to distinguish between the two, and in some languages—French, for instance—the separation of conscience and consciousness has never taken place.) The voice of conscience was the voice of God, and announced the Divine Law, before it became the *lumen naturale* that informed men of a higher law. As the voice of God, it gave positive prescriptions whose validity rested on the command "Obey God rather than men"—a command that was objectively binding without any reference to human institutions and that could be turned, as in the Reformation, even against what was alleged to be the divinely inspired institution of the Church. To modern ears, this must sound like "self-certification," which "borders on blasphemy"—the presumptuous pretension that one knows the will of God and is sure of his eventual justification.[13] It did not sound that way to the believer in a creator God who has revealed Himself to the one creature He created in His own image. But the anarchic nature of divinely inspired consciences, so blatantly manifest in the beginnings of Christianity, cannot be denied.

The law, therefore—rather late, and by no means in all countries—recognized religiously inspired conscientious objectors but recognized them only when they appealed to a Divine Law that was also

---

[11]*To Establish Justice . . . , op. cit.,* p. 99.

[12]Wilson Carey McWilliams, "Civil Disobedience and Contemporary Constitutionalism," in *Comparative Politics,* Vol. I, 1969, p. 223.

[13]Thus Leslie Dunbar, as quoted in "On Civil Disobedience in Recent American Democratic Thought," by Paul F. Power, in *The American Political Science Review,* March, 1970.

claimed by a recognized religious group, which could not well be ignored by a Christian community. The present deep crisis in the churches and the increasing number of objectors who claim no relation to any religious institution, whether or not they claim divinely informed consciences, have thus created great difficulties. These difficulties are not likely to be dissolved by substituting the submission to punishment for the appeal to publicly recognized and religiously sanctioned higher law. "The idea that paying the penalty justifies breaking the law derives, not from Gandhi and the tradition of civil disobedience, but from Oliver Wendell Holmes and the tradition of legal realism. . . . This doctrine . . . is plainly absurd . . . in the area of criminal law. . . . It is mindless to suppose that murder, rape or arson would be justified if only one were willing to pay the penalty."[14] It is most unfortunate that, in the eyes of many, a "self-sacrificial element" is the best proof of "intensity of concern,"[15] of "the disobedient's seriousness and his fidelity to law,"[16] for single-minded fanaticism is usually the hallmark of the crackpot and, in any case, makes impossible a rational discussion of the issues at stake.

Moreover, the conscience of the believer who listens to and obeys the voice of God or the commands of the *lumen naturale* is a far cry from the strictly secular conscience—this knowing, and speaking with, myself, which, in Ciceronian language, better than a thousand witnesses testifies to deeds that otherwise may remain unknown forever. It is this conscience that we find in such magnificence in *Richard III*. It does no more than "fill a man full

of obstacles"; it is not always with him but awaits him when he is alone, and loses its hold when midnight is over and he has rejoined the company of his peers. Then only, when he is no longer by himself, will he say, "Conscience is but a word that cowards use,/Devised at first to keep the strong in awe." The fear of being alone and having to face oneself can be a very effective dissuader from wrongdoing, but this fear, by its very nature, is unpersuasive of others. No doubt even this kind of conscientious objection can become politically significant when a number of consciences happen to coincide, and the conscientious objectors decide to enter the market place and make their voices heard in public. But then we are no longer dealing with individuals, or with a phenomenon whose criteria can be derived from Socrates or Thoreau. What had been decided *in foro conscientiae* has now become part of public opinion, and although this particular group of civil disobedients may still claim the initial validation—their consciences—they actually rely no longer on themselves alone. In the market place, the fate of conscience is not much different from the fate of the philosopher's truth: it becomes an opinion, indistinguishable from other opinions. And the strength of opinion does not depend on conscience, but on the number of those with whom it is associated—"unanimous agreement that 'X' is an evil . . . adds credence to the belief that 'X' *is* an evil."[17]

II

Disobedience to the law, civil and criminal, has become a mass phenomenon in recent

---

[14]Marshall Cohen, "Civil Disobedience in a Constitutional Democracy," *The Massachusetts Review*, 10: Spring, 1969, p. 214.

[15]Carl Cohen, "Civil Disobedience and the Law," *Rutgers Law Review*, vol. 21, Fall, 1966, p. 6.

[16]Thus Marshall Cohen, *op. cit.*

[17]Nicholas W. Puner, "Civil Disobedience: An Analysis and Rationale," *New York University Law Review*, 43: October, 1968, p. 714.

years, not only in America, but also in a great many other parts of the world. The defiance of established authority, religious and secular, social and political, as a world-wide phenomenon may well one day be accounted the outstanding event of the last decade. Indeed, "the laws seem to have lost their power."[18] Viewed from the outside and considered in historical perspective, no clearer writing on the wall—no more explicit sign of the inner instability and vulnerability of existing governments and legal systems—could be imagined. If history teaches anything about the causes of revolution—and history does not teach much, but still teaches considerably more than social-science theories—it is that a disintegration of political systems precedes revolutions, that the telling symptom of disintegration is a progressive erosion of governmental authority, and that this erosion is caused by the government's inability to function properly, from which spring the citizen's doubts about its legitimacy. This is what the Marxists used to call a "revolutionary situation"—which, of course, more often than not does not develop into a revolution.

In our context, the grave threat to the judicial system of the United States is a case in point. To lament "the cancerous growth of disobediences"[19] does not make much sense unless one recognizes that for many years now the law-enforcement agencies have been unable to enforce the statutes against drug traffic, mugging, and burglary. Considering that the chances that criminal offenders in these categories will never be detected at all are better than nine to one and that only one in a hundred will ever go to jail, there is every reason to be surprised that such crime is not worse than it is. (According to the 1967 report of the President's Commission on Law Enforcement and Administration of Justice, "well over half of all crimes are never reported to the police," and "of those which are, fewer than one-quarter are cleared by arrest. Nearly half of all arrests result in the dismissal of charges.")[20] It is as though we were engaged in a nationwide experiment to find out how many potential criminals—that is, people who are prevented from committing crimes only by the deterrent force of the law—actually exist in a given society. The results may not be encouraging to those who hold that all criminal impulses are aberrations—that is, are the impulses of mentally sick people acting under the compulsion of their illness. The simple and rather frightening truth is that under circumstances of legal and social permissiveness people will engage in the most outrageous criminal behavior who under normal circumstances perhaps dreamed of such crimes but never considered actually committing them.[21]

---

[18]Wilson Carey McWilliams, *op. cit.*, p. 211.

[19]*To Establish Justice . . . op. cit.*, p. 89.

[20]*Law and Order Reconsidered*, Report of the Task Force on Law and Law Enforcement to the National Commission on the Causes and Prevention of Violence. n.d., p. 266.

[21]Horrible examples of this truth were presented during the so-called "Auschwitz trial" in Germany, for whose proceedings see Bernd Naumann, *Auschwitz*, New York, 1966. The defendants were "a mere handful of intolerable cases," selected from about 2,000 S.S. men posted at the camp between 1940 and 1945. All of them were charged with murder, the only offense which in 1963, when the trial began, was not covered by the statute of limitations. Auschwitz was the camp of systematic extermination, but the atrocities almost all the accused had committed had nothing do with the order for the "final solution"; their crimes were punishable under Nazi law, and in rare cases such perpetrators were actually punished by the Nazi government. These defendants had not been specially selected for duty at an extermination camp; they had come to Auschwitz for no other reason than that they were unfit for military service. Hardly any of them had a criminal record of any sort, and none of them a record of sadism and murder. Before they had come to Auschwitz and during the eighteen years they had lived in postwar Germany, they had been respectable and respected citizens, undistinguishable from their neighbors.

In today's society, neither potential lawbreakers (that is, nonprofessional and unorganized criminals) nor law-abiding citizens need elaborate studies to tell them that criminal acts will probably—which is to say, predictably—have no legal consequences whatsoever. We have learned, to our sorrow, that organized crime is less to be feared than non-professional hoodlums—who profit from opportunity—and their entirely justified "lack of concern about being punished"; and this state of affairs is neither altered nor clarified by research into the "public's confidence in American judicial process."[22] What we are up against is not the judicial process, but the simple fact that criminal acts usually have no legal consequences whatsoever; they are not followed by judicial process. On the other hand, one must ask what would happen if police power were restored to the reasonable point where from 60 to 70 per cent of all criminal offenses were properly cleared by arrest and properly judged. Is there any doubt that it would mean the collapse of the already disastrously overburdened courts and would have quite terrifying consequences for the just as badly overloaded prison system? What is so frightening in the present situation is not only the failure of police power per se, but also that to remedy this condition radically would spell disaster for these other, equally important branches of the judicial system.

The answer of the government to this, and to similarly obvious breakdowns of public services, has invariably been the creation of study commissions, whose fantastic proliferation in recent years has probably made the United States the most researched country on earth. No doubt the commissions, after spending much time and money in order to find out that "the poorer you are, the more likely you are to suffer from serious malnutrition" (a piece of wisdom that even made the New York Times's "Quotation of the Day"),[23] often come up with reasonable recommendations. These, however, are seldom acted on, but, rather, are subjected to a new panel of researchers. What all the commissions have in common is a desperate attempt to find out something about the "deeper causes" of whatever the problem happens to be—especially if it is the problem of violence—and since "deeper" causes are, by definition, concealed, the final result of such team research is all too often nothing but hypothesis and undemonstrated theory. The net effect is that research has become a substitute for action, and the "deeper causes" are overgrowing the obvious ones, which are frequently so simple that no "serious" and "learned" person could be asked to give them any attention. To be sure, to find remedies for obvious shortcomings does not guarantee solution of the problem; but to neglect them means that the problem will not even be properly defined.[24] Research has become a technique of evasion, and this has surely not helped the already undermined reputation of science.

---

[22]The allusion is to the million-dollar grant made by the Ford Foundation "for studies of the public's confidence in the American judicial process," in contrast to the "survey of law-enforcement officials" by Fred P. Graham, of the New York Times, which, with no research team, came to the obvious conclusion, "that the criminal's lack of concern about being punished is causing a major and immediate crisis." See Tom Wicker, "Crime and the Courts," in the New York Times, April 7, 1970.

[23]On April 28, 1970.

[24]There is, for example, the well-known over-researched fact that children in slum schools do not learn. Among the more obvious causes is the fact that many such children arrive at school without having had breakfast and are desperately hungry. There are a number of "deeper" causes for their failure to learn, and it is very uncertain that breakfast would help. What is not at all uncertain is that even a class of geniuses could not be taught if they happened to be hungry.

Since disobedience and defiance of authority are such a general mark of our time, it is tempting to view civil disobedience as a mere special case. From the jurist's viewpoint, the law is violated by the civil, no less than the criminal, disobedient, and it is understandable that people, especially if they happen to be lawyers, should suspect that civil disobedience, precisely because it is exerted in public, is at the root of the criminal variety[25]—all evidence and arguments to the contrary notwithstanding, for evidence "to demonstrate that acts of civil disobedience . . . lead to . . . a propensity toward crime" is not "insufficient" but simply nonexistent.[26] Although it is true that radical movements and, certainly, revolutions attract criminal elements, it would be neither correct nor wise to equate the two; criminals are as dangerous to political movements as they are to society as a whole. Moreover, while civil disobedience may be considered an indication of a significant loss of the law's authority (though it can hardly be seen as its cause), criminal disobedience is nothing more than the inevitable consequences of a disastrous erosion of police competence and power. Proposals for probing the "criminal mind," either with Rorschach tests or by intelligence agents, sound sinister, but they, too, belong among the techniques of evasion. An incessant flow of sophisticated hypotheses about the mind—this most elusive of man's properties—of the criminal submerges the solid fact that no one is able to catch his body, just as the hypothetical assumption of policemen's "*latent* negative attitudes" covers up their overt negative record in solving crimes.[27]

Civil disobedience arises when a significant number of citizens have become convinced either that the normal channels of change no longer function, and grievances will not be heard or acted upon, or that, on the contrary, the government is about to change and has embarked upon and persists in modes of action whose legality and constitutionality are open to grave doubt. Instances are numerous: seven years of an undeclared war in Vietnam; the growing influence of secret agencies on public affairs; open or thinly veiled threats to liberties guaranteed under the First Amendment; attempts to deprive the Senate of its constitutional powers, followed by the President's invasion of Cambodia in open disregard for the Constitution, which explicitly requires congressional approval for the beginning of a war; not to mention the Vice President's even more ominous reference to resisters and dissenters as " 'vultures' . . . and 'parasites' [whom] we can afford to separate . . . from our society with no more regret than we should feel over discarding rotten apples from a barrel"—a reference that challenges not only the laws of the United States, but every legal order.[28] In other words, civil disobedience can be tuned to necessary and desirable change or to necessary and desirable preservation or restoration of the *status quo*—the preservation of rights guaranteed under the First Amendment, or the restoration of the proper balance of power in the government, which is jeopardized by the executive branch as well as by the enormous growth of federal power at the expense of states' rights. In neither case can civil disobedience be equated with criminal disobedience.

---

[25]Justice Charles E. Whittaker, like many others in the profession, "attributes the crisis to ideas of civil disobedience." See Wilson Carey McWilliams, *op. cit.*, p. 211.

[26]*To Establish Justice . . .* , *op. cit.*, p. 109.

[27]*Law and Order Reconsidered, op. cit.*, p. 291.

[28]*The New Yorker's* many excellent comments on the administration's almost open contempt of this country's constitutional and legal order, in its "Talk of the Town" column, are especially recommended.

There is all the difference in the world between the criminal's avoiding the public eye and the civil disobedient's taking the law into his own hands in open defiance. This distinction between an open violation of the law, performed in public, and a clandestine one is so glaringly obvious that it can be neglected only by prejudice or ill will. It is now recognized by all serious writers on the subject and clearly is the primary condition for all attempts that argue for the compatibility of civil disobedience with law and the American institutions of government. Moreover, the common lawbreaker, even if he belongs to a criminal organization, acts for his own benefit alone; he refuses to be overpowered by the consent of all others and will yield only to the violence of the law-enforcement agencies. The civil disobedient, though he is usually dissenting from a majority, acts in the name and for the sake of a group; he defies the law and the established authorities on the ground of basic dissent, and not because he as an individual wishes to make an exception for himself and to get away with it. If the group he belongs to is significant in numbers and standing, one is tempted to classify him as a member of one of John C. Calhoun's "concurrent majorities," that is, sections of the population that are unanimous in their dissent. The term, unfortunately, is tainted by proslavery and racist arguments, and in the *Disquisition on Government*, where it occurs, it covers only interests, not opinions and convictions, of minorities that feel threatened by "dominant majorities." The point, at any rate, is that we are dealing here with organized minorities that are too important, not merely in numbers, but in *quality of opinion*, to be safely disregarded. For Calhoun was certainly right when he held that in questions of great national importance the "concurrence or acquiescence of the various portions of the community" are a prerequisite of constitutional government.[29] To think of disobedient minorities as rebels and traitors is against the letter and spirit of a Constitution whose framers were especially sensitive to the dangers of unbridled majority rule.

Of all the means that civil disobedients may use in the course of persuasion and of the dramatization of issues, the only one that can justify their being called "rebels" is the means of violence. Hence, the second generally accepted necessary characteristic of civil disobedience is nonviolence, and it follows that "civil disobedience is not revolution. . . . The civil disobedient accepts, while the revolutionary rejects, the frame of established authority and the general legitimacy of the system of laws."[30] This second distinction between the revolutionary and the civil disobedient, so plausible at first glance, turns out to be more difficult to sustain than the distinction between civil disobedient and criminal. The civil disobedient shares with the revolutionary the wish "to change the world," and the changes he wishes to accomplish can be drastic indeed—as, for instance, in the case of Gandhi, who is always quoted as the great example, in this context, of nonviolence. (Did Gandhi accept the "frame of established authority," which was British rule of India? Did he respect the "general legitimacy of the system of laws" in the colony?) . . .

---

[29] *A Disquisition on Government* (1853), New York, 1947, p. 67.

[30] Carl Cohen, *op. cit.*, p. 3.

Carol Gilligan

Carol Gilligan contends that men and women often exhibit two different kinds of "moral voice"—an abstract "justice voice" for men, and a "connection and care voice" for women. Gilligan is a pathfinding feminist seeking to establish healthy models of moral development for women by matching male-dominated studies.

Born in 1936 and raised in Manhattan, Gilligan attended Swarthmore College and received her Ph.D. in clinical psychology from Harvard. Her thesis showed that young children who had been read stories about Andrew Carnegie and the robber barons were more likely to cheat than those who had been read tales of children who act honorably and loyally together. Gilligan left academe to have a family, but was active in the 1960s and 1970s in the peace and civil rights movements. She worked as a dancer with an interracial modern dance company and then returned to Harvard to teach as a section leader in psychologist Erik Erikson's life-cycle course. She is now a professor of education at Harvard.

Gilligan's reputation was established with the publication of *In a Different Voice* in 1982 (excerpted here). Preoccupied with the role of gender in psychological development and maturation, she noted that few landmark psychological studies included women. Using information from three research studies—one involving twenty-five Harvard students; another, women considering abortion; and the other, 144 males and females at nine different points in the life cycle—Gilligan developed data leading to her theory of the existence of two different interior moral voices for men and women. Previous studies found men more likely to achieve the highest plane of moral development based on abstract moral principles; they asked questions such as "should a poor man whose wife is dying steal the drugs she needs?" But women, who use a "care" voice concerned more with human relationships than with abstract principles, were not on a *lower* level of moral development, according to Gilligan, but simply *different*.

In 1989, Gilligan published *Making Connections*, based on an intensive empirical study of the relational world of adolescent girls at Emma Willard School in Troy, New York. Gilligan and her colleagues found that women go through two distinctive phases in their adolescence: a "moment of resistance" around age eleven, when they see things with self-confidence and clarity, and a phase of "resistance going underground" at fifteen or sixteen, when a crisis develops as the adolescent women confront a mainstream culture in which the message to women is: "Keep quiet, and notice the absence of women, and say nothing." She then worked to develop educational strategies to help prevent girls from "going underground."

Through her books and articles, Gilligan has created a great stir of controversy among psychologists, philosophers, and political thinkers who now must determine to what extent they assume that women develop and think differently about social and political issues at different stages in the life cycle. And she appears to be developing the basis for healthy models of successful moral maturation for women to match those already existing for men (such as Lawrence Kohlberg's theory of moral stages).

In a Different Voice (1982)*

(excerpts)

Women's Rights and Women's Judgment

When in the summer of 1848 Elizabeth Cady Stanton and Lucretia Mott convened a conference at Seneca Falls, New York, to consider "the social, civil and religious condition and rights of women," they presented for adoption a Declaration of Sentiments, modeled on the Declaration of Independence. The issue was simple, and the analogy made their point clear: women are entitled to the rights deemed natural and inalienable by men. The Seneca Falls Conference was spurred by the exclusion of Stanton and Mott, along with other female delegates, from participation in the World Anti-Slavery Convention held in London in 1840. Outraged by their relegation to the balconies to observe the proceedings in which they had come to take part, these women claimed for themselves in 1848 only what they had attempted eight years previously to claim for others, the rights of citizenship in a professedly democratic state. Anchoring this claim in the premise of equality and drawing on the notions of social contract and natural rights, the Seneca Falls Declaration argues no special consideration for women but simply holds "these truths to be self-evident: that all men and women are created equal; that they are endowed by their Creator with certain inalienable rights; that among these are life, liberty, and the pursuit of happiness."

But the claim to rights on the part of women had from the beginning brought them into a seeming opposition with virtue, an opposition challenged by Mary Wollstonecraft in 1792. In "A Vindication of the Rights of Women," she argues that liberty, rather than leading to license, is "the mother of virtue," since enslavement causes not only abjectness and despair but also guile and deceit. Wollstonecraft's "arrogance" in daring "to exert my own reason" and challenge "the mistaken notions that enslave my sex" was subsequently matched by Stanton's boldness in telling a reporter to "put it down in capital letters: SELF-DEVELOPMENT IS A HIGHER DUTY THAN SELF-SACRIFICE. The thing which most retards and militates against women's self-development is self-sacrifice." Countering the accusation of selfishness, the cardinal sin in the ladder of feminine virtue that reached toward an ideal of perfect devotion and self-abnegation, in relation not only to God but to men, these early proponents of women's rights equated self-sacrifice with slavery and asserted that the development of women, like that of men, would serve to promote the general good.

As in claiming rights women claimed responsibility for themselves, so in exercising their reason they began to address issues of responsibility in social relationships. This exercise of reason and the attempt of women to exert control over conditions affecting their lives led, in the latter half of the nineteenth century, to various movements for social reform, ranging from the social purity movements for temperance and public health to the more radical movements for free love and birth control. All of these movements joined in support of suffrage, as women, claiming

Isaak, *American Political Thinking.*/*For permission to photocopy this selection, please contact Harvard University Press. Reprinted by permission of the publishers from *In a Different Voice* by Carol Gilligan, Cambridge, Mass.: Harvard University Press, copyright © 1982 by Carol Gilligan.

their intelligence and, to varying degrees, their sexuality as part of their human nature, sought through the vote to include their voices in the shaping of history and to change prevailing practices that were damaging to present and future generations. While the disappointment of suffrage is recorded in the failure of many women to vote and the tendency of others in voting only to second their husbands' opinions, the twentieth century has in fact witnessed the legitimation of many of the rights the early feminists sought.

Given these changes in women's rights, the question arises as to their effect, a question pointed at present both by the renewed struggle for women's rights and by the centennial celebrations of many of the women's colleges to which the feminists' call for women's education gave rise. In tying women's self-development to the exercise of their own reason, the early feminists saw education as critical for women if they were to live under their own control. But as the debate over the current Equal Rights Amendment repeats many of those that occurred in the past, so the issue of women's self-development continues to raise the specter of selfishness, the fear that freedom for women will lead to an abandonment of responsibility in relationships. Thus the dialogue between rights and responsibilities, in its public debate and its psychic representation, focuses the conflicts raised by the inclusion of women in thinking about responsibility and relationships. While this dialogue elucidates some of the more puzzling aspects of women's opposition to women's rights, it also illuminates how the concept of rights engages women's thinking about moral conflict and choice.

The century marked by the movement for women's rights is spanned roughly by the publication of two novels, both written by women and posing the same moral dilemma, a heroine in love with her cousin Lucy's man. In their parallel triangles these novels provide an historical frame in which to consider the effects of women's rights on women's moral judgments and thus offer a way of addressing the centennial question as to what has changed and what has stayed the same.

In George Eliot's novel *The Mill on the Floss* (1860), Maggie Tulliver "clings to the right." Caught between her love for her cousin Lucy and her "stronger feeling" for Stephen, Lucy's fiancée [*sic*], Maggie is unswerving in her judgment that, "I must not, cannot, seek my own happiness by sacrificing others." When Stephen says that their love, natural and unsought, makes it "right that we should marry each other," Maggie replies that while "love is natural, surely pity and faithfulness and memory are natural too." Even after "it was too late already not to have caused misery," Maggie refuses to "take a good for myself that has been wrung out of [others'] misery," choosing instead to renounce Stephen and return alone to St. Oggs.

While the minister, Mr. Kenn, considers "the principle upon which she acted as a safer guide than any balancing of consequences," the narrator's judgment is less clear. George Eliot, having placed her heroine in a dilemma that admits no viable resolution, ends the novel by drowning Maggie, but not without first cautioning the reader that "the shifting relation between passion and duty is clear to no man who is capable of apprehending it." Since "the mysterious complexity of our life" cannot be "laced up in formulas," moral judgment cannot be bound by "general rules" but must instead be informed "by a life vivid and intense enough to have created a wide, fellow-feeling with all that is human."

Yet given that in this novel the "eyes of intense life" that were Maggie's look out in the end from a "weary, beaten face," it is not surprising that Margaret Drabble, steeped in the tradition of nineteenth century fiction but engaged in the issues of twentieth century feminism, should choose to return to Eliot's story and explore the possibility of an alternative resolution. In *The Waterfall* (1969) she recreates Maggie's dilemma in *The Mill on the Floss* but, as the title implies, with the difference that the societal impediment has been removed. Thus Drabble's heroine, Jane Grey, clings not to the right but to Lucy's husband, renouncing the renunciations and instead "drowning in the first chapter." Immersed in a sea of self-discovery, "not caring who should drown so long as I should reach the land," Jane is caught by the problem of judgment as she seeks to apprehend the miracle of her survival and to find a way to tell that story. Her love for James, Lucy's husband, is narrated by two different voices, a first and a third person who battle constantly over the issues of judgment and truth, engaging and disengaging the moral questions of responsibility and choice.

Though the balance between passion and duty has shifted between 1860 and 1969, the moral problem remains in both novels the same. Across the intervening century, the verdict of selfishness impales both heroines. The same accusation that compels Maggie's renunciation orchestrates Jane's elaborate plea of helplessness and excuse: "I was merely trying to defend myself against an accusation of selfishness, judge me leniently, I said, I am not as others are, I am sad, I am mad, so I have to have what I want." But the problem with activity and desire that the accusation of selfishness implies not only leads Jane into familiar strategies of evasion and disguise but also impels her to confront the underlying premise on which this accusation is based. Taking apart the moral judgment of the past that had made it seem, "in a sense, better to renounce myself than them," Jane seeks to reconstitute it in a way that could "admit me and encompass me." Thus she strives to create "a new ladder, a new virtue," one that could include activity, sexuality, and survival without abandoning the old virtues of responsibility and care: "If I need to

understand what I am doing, if I cannot act without my own approbation—and I must act, I have changed, I am no longer capable of inaction—then I will invent a morality that condones me. Though by doing so, I risk condemning all that I have been."

These novels thus demonstrate the continuing power for women of the judgment of selfishness and the morality of self-abnegation that it implies. This is the judgment that regularly appears at the fulcrum of novels of female adolescence, the turning point of the *Bildungsroman* that separates the invulnerability of childhood innocence from the responsibility of adult participation and choice. The notion that virtue for women lies in self-sacrifice has complicated the course of women's development by pitting the moral issue of goodness against the adult questions of responsibility and choice. In addition, the ethic of self-sacrifice is directly in conflict with the concept of rights that has, in this past century, supported women's claim to a fair share of social justice.

But a further problem arises from the tension between a morality of rights that dissolves "natural bonds" in support of individual claims and a morality of responsibility that knits such claims into a fabric of relationship, blurring the distinction between self and other through the representation of their interdependence. This problem was the concern of Wollstonecraft and Stanton, of Eliot and Drabble. This concern emerged as well in interviews with college women in the 1970s. All of these women talked about the same conflict, all revealed the enormous power of the judgment of selfishness in women's thought. But the appearance of this judgment in the moral conflicts described by contemporary women brings into focus the role that the concept of rights plays in women's moral development. These conflicts demonstrate the continuation through time of an ethic of responsibility as the center of women's moral concern, anchoring the self in a world of relationships and giving rise to activities of care, but also indicate how this ethic is transformed by the recognition of the justice of the rights approach.

The senior year interview with Nan, one of the women in the college student study, illustrates some of the dimensions of women's moral concern in 1973, the year that the Supreme Court decided that abortion is legal and that women have the right to choose whether or not to continue a pregnancy. Two years before, Nan chose to take a course on moral and political choice because she was "looking for different ways of thinking about things" and was interested "in arguments that protect individual freedom." Claiming to "suffer from a low self-image," she reports, in her senior year, a sense of moral progress and growth which she attributes to having had "to review a lot of what I thought about myself" as a result of having become pregnant and deciding to have an abortion. Attributing the pregnancy to "a lapse of self-control, decision-making, and very much stupidity," she considered abortion to be a desperate and life-saving solution ("I felt very much to save my own life that I had to do it"), but one which she viewed as, "at least in the eyes of society, if not my own, a moral sin."

Given her "personal feeling of being very evil," her discovery that "people would help me out anyway did great things for my feelings toward them and myself." In the month that she spent waiting and thinking about the abortion, she thought "a lot about decision-making, and for the first time I wanted to take control of and responsibility for my own decisions in life." As a result, her self-image changed:

Because now that you are going to take control of your life, you don't feel like you are a pawn in other people's hands. You have to accept the fact that you have done something wrong, and it also gives you a little more integrity, because you are not fighting off these things in yourself all the time. A lot of conflicts are resolved, and you have a sense of a new beginning, based on a kind of conviction that you can act in a situation.

Thus she "came out basically supporting myself, not as a good or bad human being, but simply as a human being who had a lot to learn either way." Seeing herself in the present as capable of choice, she feels responsible for herself in a new way. But while the experience of choice has led Nan to a greater sense of personal integrity, her judgment of these choices stays remarkably the same. Although she has come to a more inclusive and tolerant understanding of herself and a new conception of relationships that will, she believes, allow her to be "more obvious with myself and more independent," the moral issue remains one of responsibility.

In this sense, she considers the pregnancy to have "come to my aid" in illuminating her previous failure to take responsibility.

It was so serious that it brought to light things in myself, like feelings about myself, my feelings about the world. What I had done, I felt, was so wrong that it came to light to me that I was not taking responsibility where I could have, and I could have gone on like I was, not taking responsibility. So the seriousness of the situation brings the questions right up in front of your face. You see them very clearly, and then the answers are there for you.

Seeing her own irresponsibility as having led to a situation in which she could envision no way of acting that would not cause hurt, she begins "getting rid of old ideas" about morality that now seem an impediment to her goal of living in a way that will not "cause human suffering." In doing so, she calls into question the opposition of selfishness and morality, discerning that "the word *selfish* is tricky." Recognizing that "individual freedom" is not "all that incompatible with morality," she expands her conception of morality, defining it as "the sense of concern for another human being and your sense of concern for yourself." While the moral questions remain, "How much suffering are you going to cause?" and "Why do you have the right to cause human suffering?" these questions apply not only to others but also to herself. Responsibility, separated from self-sacrifice, becomes tied instead to the understanding of the causes of suffering and the ability to anticipate which actions are likely to eventuate in hurt.

The right to include oneself in the compass of a morality of responsibility was a critical question for college women in the 1970s. This question, which arose in differing contexts, posed a problem of inclusion that could be resolved through the logic of justice, the fairness of equating other and self. But it also posed a problem of relationships, whose solution required a new understanding of responsibility and care. Hilary, explaining at age twenty-seven how her thinking about morality has changed, describes her understanding of morality at the time she entered college:

I was much more simple-minded then. I went through a period in which I thought there were fairly simple answers to questions of right and wrong in life. I even went through a period that now strikes me as so simplistic: I thought that as long as I didn't hurt anybody, everything would be fine. And I soon figured out, or eventually figured out, that things were not that simple, that you were bound to hurt people, they were bound to hurt you, and life is full of tension and conflict. People are bound to hurt each other's feelings, intentionally, unintentionally, but just in the very way things are. So I abandoned that idea.

This abandonment occurred in her first years of college:

I became involved in a love affair with a guy who wanted to settle down and get married, and I could not imagine a worse fate, but I was really quite fond of him. And we broke up, and he was so upset by it that he left school for a year, and I realized that I had hurt him very badly and that I hadn't meant to, and I had violated my first principle of moral behavior, but I had made the right decision.

Explaining that she "could not have possibly married him," Hilary felt that there was, in that sense, an "easy answer" to the dilemma she faced. Yet, in another sense, given her moral injunction against hurting, the situation presented an insoluble problem, allowing no course of action that would not eventuate in hurt. This realization led her to question her former absolute moral injunction and to "figure that this principle [of not hurting] was not all there was to it." The limitation she saw pertained directly to the issue of personal integrity; "What that principle was not even attempting to achieve was, 'To thine own self be true.' " Indicating that she had started to think more about maintaining her personal integrity, she says that this experience led her to conclude that, "You can't worry about not hurting other people; just do what is right for you."

Yet, in view of her continuing equation of morality with caring for others and her continuing belief that "acts that are self-sacrificing and that are done for other people or for the good of humanity are good acts," her abandonment of the principle of not hurting others was tantamount to an abandonment of moral concern. Recognizing the rightness of her decision but also realizing its painful consequences, she can see no way to maintain her integrity while adhering to an ethic of care in relationships. Seeking to avoid conflict and compromise in choice by "just doing what is right for you," she is in fact left with a feeling of compromise about herself.

This feeling is apparent as she recounts the dilemma that she faced in her work as a lawyer when opposing counsel in a trial overlooked a document that provided critical support for his client's "meritorious claim." Deliberating whether or not to tell her opponent of the document that would help his client's case, Hilary realized that the adversary system of justice impedes not only "the supposed search for truth" but also the expression of concern for the person on the other side. Choosing in the end to adhere to the system, in part because of the vulnerability of her own professional position, she sees herself as having failed to live up to her standard of personal integrity as well as to her moral ideal of self-sacrifice. Thus her description of herself contrasts both with her depiction of her husband as "a person of absolute integrity who would never do anything he didn't feel was right" and with her view of her mother as "a very caring person" who is "selfless" in giving to others.

On her own behalf, Hilary says somewhat apologetically that she has become, since college, more tolerant and more understanding, less ready to blame people whom formerly she would have condemned, more capable of seeing the integrity of different perspectives. Though she has access, as a lawyer, to the language of rights and recognizes clearly the importance of self-determination and respect, the concept of rights remains in tension with an ethic of care. The continuing opposition of selfishness and responsibility, however, leaves her no way to reconcile the injunction to be true to herself with the ideal of responsibility in relationships.

... Among college students in the 1970s, the concept of rights entered into

their thinking to challenge a morality of self-sacrifice and self-abnegation. Questioning the stoicism of self-denial and replacing the illusion of innocence with an awareness of choice, they struggled to grasp the essential notion of rights, that the interests of the self can be considered legitimate. In this sense, the concept of rights changes women's conceptions of self, allowing them to see themselves as stronger and to consider directly their own needs. When assertion no longer seems dangerous, the concept of relationships changes from a bond of continuing dependence to a dynamic of interdependence. Then the notion of care expands from the paralyzing injunction not to hurt others to an injunction to act responsively toward self and others and thus to sustain connection. A consciousness of the dynamics of human relationships then becomes central to moral understanding, joining the heart and the eye in an ethic that ties the activity of thought to the activity of care.

Thus changes in women's rights change women's moral judgments, seasoning mercy with justice by enabling women to consider it moral to care not only for others but for themselves. The issue of inclusion first raised by the feminists in the public domain reverberates through the psychology of women as they begin to notice their own exclusion of themselves. When the concern with care extends from an injunction not to hurt others to an ideal of responsibility in social relationships, women begin to see their understanding of relationships as a source of moral strength. But the concept of rights also changes women's moral judgments by adding a second perspective to the consideration of moral problems, with the result that judgment becomes more tolerant and less absolute.

As selfishness and self-sacrifice become matters of interpretation and responsibilities live in tension with rights, moral truth is complicated by psychological truth, and the matter of judgment becomes more complex. Drabble's heroine, who sought to write "a poem as round and hard as a stone," only to find that words and thoughts obtrude, concludes that "a poem so round and smooth would say nothing" and sets out to describe the variegated edges of an event seen from angles, finding in the end no unified truth. Instead, through a final shift in perspective, she relegates her suspicions to "that removed, third person" and, no longer fending off the accusation of selfishness, identifies herself with the first person voice.

Visions of Maturity

. . . Thus in the transition from adolescence to adulthood, the dilemma itself is the same for both sexes, a conflict between integrity and care. But approached from different perspectives, this dilemma generates the recognition of opposite truths. These different perspectives are reflected in two different moral ideologies, since separation is justified by an ethic of rights while attachment is supported by an ethic of care.

The morality of rights is predicated on equality and centered on the understanding of fairness, while the ethic of responsibility relies on the concept of equity, the recognition of differences in need. While the ethic of rights is a manifestation of equal respect, balancing the claims of other and self, the ethic of responsibility rests on an understanding that gives rise to compassion and care. Thus the counterpoint of identity and intimacy that marks the time between childhood and adulthood is articulated through two different moralities whose complementarity is the discovery of maturity.

The discovery of this complementarity is traced in the study by questions about personal experiences of moral conflict and choice. Two lawyers chosen from the sample illustrate how the divergence in judgment between the sexes is resolved through the discovery by each of the other's perspective and of the relationship between integrity and care.

The dilemma of responsibility and truth . . . is reiterated by Hilary, a lawyer and the woman who said she found it too hard to describe herself at the end of what "really has been a rough week." She too . . . considers self-sacrificing acts "courageous" and "praiseworthy," explaining that "if everyone on earth behaved in a way that showed care for others and courage, the world would be a much better place, you wouldn't have crime and you might not have poverty." However, this moral ideal of self-sacrifice and care ran into trouble not only in a relationship where the conflicting truths of each person's feelings made it impossible to avoid hurt, but also in court where, despite her concern for the client on the other side, she decided not to help her opponent win his case.

In both instances, she found the absolute injunction against hurting others to be an inadequate guide to resolving the actual dilemmas she faced. Her discovery of the disparity between intention and consequence and of the actual constraints of choice led her to realize that there is, in some situations, no way not to hurt. In confronting such dilemmas in both her personal and professional life, she does not abdicate responsibility for choice but rather claims the right to include herself among the people whom she considers it moral not to hurt. Her more inclusive morality now contains the injunction to be true to herself, leaving her with two principles of judgment whose integration she cannot yet clearly envision. What she does recognize is that both integrity and care must be included in a morality that can encompass the dilemmas of love and work that arise in adult life.

The move toward tolerance that accompanies the abandonment of absolutes is considered by William Perry (1968) to chart the course of intellectual and ethical development during the early adult years. Perry describes the changes in thinking that mark the transition from a belief that knowledge is absolute and answers clearly right or wrong to an understanding of the contextual relativity of both truth and choice. This transition and its impact on moral judgment can be discerned in the changes in moral understanding that occur in both men and women during the five years following college (Gilligan and Murphy, 1979; Murphy and Gilligan, 1980). Though both sexes move away from absolutes in this time, the absolutes themselves differ for each. In women's development, the absolute of care, defined initially as not hurting others, becomes complicated through a recognition of the need for personal integrity. This recognition gives rise to the claim for equality embodied in the concept of rights, which changes the understanding of relationships and transforms the definition of care. For men, the absolutes of truth and fairness, defined by the concepts of equality and reciprocity, are called into question by experiences that demonstrate the existence of differences between other and self. Then the awareness of multiple truths leads to a relativizing of equality in the direction of equity and gives rise to an ethic of generosity and care. For both sexes the existence of two contexts for moral decision makes judgment by definition contextually relative and leads to a new understanding of responsibility and choice.

The discovery of the reality of differences and thus of the contextual nature of morality and truth is described by Alex, a

lawyer in the college student study, who began in law school "to realize that you really don't know everything" and "you don't even know that there is any absolute. I don't think that you ever know that there is an absolute right. What you do know is you have to come down one way or the other. You have got to make a decision."

The awareness that he did not know everything arose more painfully in a relationship whose ending took him completely by surprise. In his belated discovery that the woman's experience had differed from his own, he realized how distant he had been in a relationship he considered close. Then the logical hierarchy of moral values, whose absolute truth he formerly proclaimed, came to seem a barrier to intimacy rather than a fortress of personal integrity. As his conception of morality began to change, his thinking focused on issues of relationship, and his concern with injustice was complicated by a new understanding of human attachment. Describing "the principle of attachment" that began to inform his way of looking at moral problems, Alex sees the need for morality to extend beyond considerations of fairness to concern with relationships:

> People have real emotional needs to be attached to something, and equality doesn't give you attachment. Equality fractures society and places on every person the burden of standing on his own two feet.

Although "equality is a crisp thing that you could hang onto," it alone cannot adequately resolve the dilemmas of choice that arise in life. Given his new awareness of responsibility and of the actual consequences of choice, Alex says: "You don't want to look at just equality. You want to look at how people are going to be able to handle their lives." Recognizing the need for two contexts for judgment, he nevertheless finds that their integration "is hard to work through," since sometimes "no matter which way you go, somebody is going to be hurt and somebody is going to be hurt forever." Then, he says, "you have reached the point where there is an irresolvable conflict," and choice becomes a matter of "choosing the victim" rather than enacting the good. With the recognition of the responsibility that such choices entail, his judgment becomes more attuned to the psychological and social consequences of action, to the reality of people's lives in an historical world.

Thus, starting from very different points, from the different ideologies of justice and care, the men and women in the study come, in the course of becoming adult, to a greater understanding of both points of view and thus to a greater convergence in judgment. Recognizing the dual contexts of justice and care, they realize that judgment depends on the way in which the problem is framed. . . .

Like the stories that delineate women's fantasies of power, women's descriptions of adulthood convey a different sense of its social reality. In their portrayal of relationships, women replace the bias of men toward separation with a representation of the interdependence of self and other, both in love and in work. By changing the lens of developmental observation from individual achievement to relationships of care, women depict ongoing attachment as the path that leads to maturity. Thus the parameters of development shift toward marking the progress of affiliative relationship.

The implications of this shift are evident in considering the situation of women at mid-life. Given the tendency to chart the unfamiliar waters of adult development with the familiar markers of adolescent

separation and growth, the middle years of women's lives readily appear as a time of return to the unfinished business of adolescence. This interpretation has been particularly compelling since life-cycle descriptions, derived primarily from studies of men, have generated a perspective from which women, insofar as they differ, appear deficient in their development. The deviance of female development has been especially marked in the adolescent years when girls appear to confuse identity with intimacy by defining themselves through relationships with others. The legacy left from this mode of identity definition is considered to be a self that is vulnerable to the issues of separation that arise at mid-life.

But this construction reveals the limitation in an account which measures women's development against a male standard and ignores the possibility of a different truth. In this light, the observation that women's embeddedness in lives of relationship, their orientation to interdependence, their subordination of achievement to care, and their conflicts over competitive success leave them personally at risk in mid-life seems more a commentary on the society than a problem in women's development. . . .

Thus women not only reach mid-life with a psychological history different from men's and face at that time a different social reality having different possibilities for love and for work, but they also make a different sense of experience, based on their knowledge of human relationships. Since the reality of connection is experienced by women as given rather than as freely contracted, they arrive at an understanding of life that reflects the limits of autonomy and control. As a result, women's development delineates the path not only to a less violent life but also to a maturity realized through interdependence and taking care. . . .

Among the most pressing items on the agenda for research on adult development is the need to delineate *in women's own terms* the experience of their adult life. My own work in that direction indicates that the inclusion of women's experience brings to developmental understanding a new perspective on relationships that changes the basic constructs of interpretation. The concept of identity expands to include the experience of interconnection. The moral domain is similarly enlarged by the inclusion of responsibility and care in relationships. And the underlying epistemology correspondingly shifts from the Greek ideal of knowledge as a correspondence between mind and form to the Biblical conception of knowing as a process of human relationship.

Given the evidence of different perspectives in the representation of adulthood by women and men, there is a need for research that elucidates the effects of these differences in marriage, family, and work relationships. My research suggests that men and women may speak different languages that they assume are the same, using similar words to encode disparate experiences of self and social relationships. Because these languages share an overlapping moral vocabulary, they contain a propensity for systematic mistranslation, creating misunderstandings which impede communication and limit the potential for cooperation and care in relationships. At the same time, however, these languages articulate with one another in critical ways. Just as the language of responsibilities provides a weblike imagery of relationships to replace a hierarchical ordering that dissolves with the coming of equality, so the language of rights underlines the importance of including in the network of care not only the other but also the self.

As we have listened for centuries to the voices of men and the theories of development that their experience informs, so we have come more recently to notice not only the silence of women but the difficulty in hearing what they say when they speak. Yet in the different voice of women lies the truth of an ethic of care, the tie between relationship and responsibility, and the origins of aggression in the failure of connection. The failure to see the different reality of women's lives and to hear the differences in their voices stems in part from the assumption that there is a single mode of social experience and interpretation. By positing instead two different modes, we arrive at a more complex rendition of human experience which sees the truth of separation and attachment in the lives of women and men and recognizes how these truths are carried by different modes of language and thought.

To understand how the tension between responsibilities and rights sustains the dialectic of human development is to see the integrity of two disparate modes of experience that are in the end connected. While an ethic of justice proceeds from the premise of equality—that everyone should be treated the same—an ethic of care rests on the premise of nonviolence—that no one should be hurt. In the representation of maturity, both perspectives converge in the realization that just as inequality adversely affects both parties in an unequal relationship, so too violence is destructive for everyone involved. This dialogue between fairness and care not only provides a better understanding of relations between the sexes but also gives rise to a more comprehensive portrayal of adult work and family relationships. . . .

Betty Friedan

Born Betty Goldstein in 1921 in Peoria, Illinois, Betty Friedan continually reenergized the feminist movement through her writing and activism from the 1960s on. She graduated *summa cum laude* from Smith College in psychology and was editor of the college paper. She studied on a fellowship at The University of California at Berkeley before coming to New York to work as a reporter for the labor press.

Fired as the result of her second pregnancy, Friedan lived the life of a suburban housewife in the 1950s. She noted and shared the unhappiness widespread among her former Smith College roommates. After creating a questionnaire and studying its responses, Friedan wrote *The Feminist Mystique* (1963) detailing how American society forced women into traditional, subservient roles. The book triggered a major social movement. Friedan founded the National Organization of Women (NOW), the influential political organization for women in the United States, and became its president in 1966. On the cutting edge of reform legislation, she fought to increase the autonomy of women in issues of abortion, child support, divorce, and access to credit and insurance. In 1981, she published *The Second Stage*, from which the following excerpts are drawn. This book took mainstream feminism one step further by condemning the "feminine mystique" and calling for men and women to overcome the false polarization of feminism and family. In 1993 Friedan published *The Fountain of Age* examining social and political consequences of the thirty-year increase in life expectancy in the United States in the twentieth century.

The Second Stage (1981)
(excerpt)

The Limits and True Potential of Women's Power

As that process which began with the women's movement evolves into the second stage, it is necessary to understand the limits of women's power and the possibilities of transcending those limits and generating a new kind of power.

There *are* limits to women's power, as we discovered this past year. Even on the gut issues of women's rights—the Equal Rights Amendment and the right of choice to have a child or safe, legal access to abortion—on which there is an enormous consensus, as measured in the polls, cutting across lines of race, economic class, generation and political party, women's power, exercised to its fullest, seemed to provoke an equal and opposite reaction in the election results of 1980.

But the question must be asked: Is the new kind of power generated or implicit in the women's movement truly expressed or measured in single-issue, special-interest politics?

There is a discrepancy between the power of the women's movement, as a fundamental change in the consciousness of and about women and their role in society, and the deadlocks and failures of the organized political movement on these single issues. Of course, it could be argued that the Equal Rights Amendment—which would put half the population under the full protection of the Constitution and the Bill of Rights for the first time, guaranteeing inalienable equal opportunity for women in employment, education, and other spheres where laws against sex discrimination are now being gutted, and providing the basis for equality in social security, marriage and divorce law, pensions and military service—is more than a single issue. Surely, half the population is more than a special-interest group. But no matter: as the movement focused its energies on those issues, it took on, at least in part, the dominant, masculine mode of previous political special-interest groups, abstracting one issue from the total context, locking itself into a win-lose, zero-sum, linear, confrontational context that belied the generative power by which women, and men, have transformed themselves and their lives in the women's movement.

On the other hand, in the movement activity of fighting for the Equal Rights Amendment over the past ten years, women have grown, discovered unsuspected strengths and skills, and developed a consensus extending from traditional establishment groups like the Junior League and the YWCA, the Girl Scouts, the League of Women Voters, Catholic nuns, Jewish and Protestant churchwomen, union, business and professional women, to the new women's caucuses in every field, as well as newly organized black and Chicano, student and farm women, and the proliferating mainstream to radical feminist organizations. This consensus is infinitely broader than any special-interest group of men. In fact, the movement for women's equal rights has won the support not only of the majority of men, as reflected in the polls,

but specific political support, finally, from labor leaders and civil rights and other special-interest groups. As Eleanor Smeal, the effective president of NOW, has said, "Not a moment of it was wasted, even if we never win."

It was not a "single issue" to fight to get that Constitutional underpinning for the rights won over these years of the modern women's movement. We somehow knew that in periods of economic recession or political reaction, those laws wouldn't be safe—and our worst fears have been realized sooner than we imagined. If only we had won the Equal Rights Amendment in those heady first seven years—as we should and could have, if we hadn't been diverted by sexual politics or co-opted by "masculine" political power—it would not be so easy for right-wing Senators to dismantle affirmative-action programs against sex discrimination in education and employment, as they announced they intended to do, less than a week after the 1980 Reagan landslide election.

The women's movement did not fail in the battle for equality. Our failure was our blind spot about the family. It was our own extreme of reaction against that wife-mother role: that devotional dependence on men and nurture of children and housewife service which has been and still is the source of power and status and identity, purpose and self-worth and economic security for so many women—even if it is not all that secure any more. And not only for the 49 percent who are still housewives. Most of the other 51 percent still don't get as much sense of worth, status, power or economic security from the jobs they now have as they get, or think they could get, or still wish they could get, from being someone's wife or mother. And the more insecure—with inflation, with the increasing divorce rate—the more such a woman is threatened by the very idea that she needs ERA, that she might have to take care of herself, that, God forbid, she might not always have a husband to take care of her and a family to justify her existence.

Something very complex is involved here. Is there a real polarization between the feminist who wants equality and "choice," and the woman for whom "the family" is security? Aren't those feminists who most stridently deny the family trying to deny that woman's vulnerability in themselves? Do women who want equal rights really threaten that clean, pure, sacred family morality that once made her feel secure? Or are ERA advocates threatening because they make her aware of her real insecurity, and her buried wish for independence and autonomy? And if a man stands to lose his job, and the dollars he's worked for all his life are worth pennies now, where can *he* look for security, respect, identity except in the family? All these people who want equal rights for women, abortion rights, homosexual rights— they're destroying the family! (Safer to fight *them* than to understand and fight the powerful economic forces that really threaten family security today.)

It is remarkable, however, that the polls showed an increasing majority of women and men supporting the ERA—and the right to abortion—as inflation forced more and more women to work, their paycheck helping the family to survive even when the husband was laid off.

The Republicans, in fact, probably lost the votes of the single largest voting bloc in the 1980 election as a result of their extreme platform stand, repudiating the Equal Rights Amendment, vowing to amend the Constitution to outlaw abortion, and pledging to appoint judges who concurred with these views. It is noteworthy— though the media and most politicians still have such a blind spot about women that they didn't really note it—that there was a nearly 20 percent difference between the voting of women and men in the 1980 Pres-

idential election. Reagan defeated Carter by an incredible 54 to 37 percent among men, but only 46 to 45 percent among women (New York Times—CBS News Poll). *The majority of women (52 percent) voted against Reagan*—(45 percent for Carter, 7 percent for Anderson). There has never been such a discrepancy between men's and women's voting in all the years since exit polls have been taken. In the previous Presidential election the male and female percentages were identical. Further, women who were for the Equal Rights Amendment voted overwhelmingly against Reagan, 65 to 32 percent, more than two to one. This women's rights bloc constituted 22 percent of the total vote, a far larger bloc than blacks (10 percent), Hispanics (2 percent) and Jews (5 percent) combined, or even than blue-collar workers (17 percent). Women who opposed the ERA constituted only 15 percent of the total vote, and they supported Reagan even more avidly than men—66 percent to 29 percent for Carter.

For women as for men, inflation was an overriding issue. After all, women still do most of the shopping. Nevertheless, for the majority of women to have voted against Reagan, equality had to be an overriding gut issue for a great many of them. The issue of war and peace, supposedly also of greater concern to women, had been largely defused by the debate. Polltakers puzzling this difference between the voting of women and men in the 1980 election could not pin it down to the specific issues of ERA and abortion—only to a general impression that "Carter would be better for women."

After all, Carter had delivered only one state beyond the thirty-four which had ratified ERA before his election—and he had also opposed federal funds for poor women's abortions. ("Life is not fair.") Eleven months before the election, the NOW board had resolved: "Anybody but Carter." But the women's rights groups, in a rare demonstration of united power, had effectively defied Carter's own commandos at the Democratic convention and won a stronger support of ERA and poor women's right to legal medical aid in abortion in the Democratic platform. Would Carter run with this? Well, no, not really. . . . Only at the very end, some of the fine feminists and shrewd female politicians in the Carter Administration—Eleanor Holmes Norton, Anne Wexler—enlisted the help of Eleanor Smeal and myself and other feminist leaders, making a commitment to mobilize the full machinery of the White House for ERA and child care, next time. Too little, too late.

If the Democrats had spent the same amount of energy and serious attention courting women on the issue of equal rights as they spent courting blacks and Jews and other minorities—not only during the campaign, but during the four years in the White House—we might have had the Equal Rights Amendment, and the women's movement might have mobilized in earnest to reelect Carter. As it turned out, we mobilized in belated panic to defeat Reagan and contained our disgust with Carter. But our help was not seriously sought—nor deserved. It is hardly surprising that 43 percent of women in favor or ERA voted against Carter (32 percent for Reagan, 11 percent for Anderson). Women, and some men, told me personally of "walking around the block four times before I decided that if inflation keeps up, ERA will be worthless anyhow. Besides, I wouldn't trust Carter now, on ERA or inflation."

But the polarization that led to the sweep of the Senators on the Moral Majority hit list (Birch Bayh, Frank Church, John Culver, Gaylord Nelson, George McGovern) cannot be attributed solely to the disgust with Carter, or to Reagan's coattails. The women's movement has to assume

some responsibility. We underestimated the threat and did not mobilize ourselves in all-out defense of the men who were explicitly fingered by the National Conservative Political Action Committee supposedly because they supported ERA, abortion and homosexual rights.

Is a distorted sexual politics at work if the women's movement did not rise to the support of these men with the same passion as, for instance, it supported Bella Abzug or Liz Holtzman? Is a distorted sexual politics responsible for the lumping of these three issues together in such an inflammable, sexually charged package? It is all very well for leaders of the women's movement today to insist, correctly, that the Equal Rights Amendment has nothing to do with either abortion or homosexuality—in fact, it has nothing to do with sexual behavior at all. But the sexual politics that distorted the sense of priorities of the women's movement during the seventies made it easy for the so-called Moral Majority to lump ERA with homosexual rights and abortion into one explosive package of licentious, family-threatening sex.

There is no doubt that the radical right, with its mysterious sources of endless money behind that pious Moral Majority front, is using abortion and homosexuality as sexual red herrings in its frighteningly successful drive to take over the United States Government and repress dissent, whatever its real aims. It goes beyond the premise of this work—or my own wisdom—to figure out why *sexuality* becomes such a convenient battleground for reactionary political and economic power. Hysteria over sexual license, homosexuality, abortion—and the reduction of women from independent people with rights to passive sexual objects, segregated behind literal or figurative chadors—serves more sinister purposes of reactionary power. For surely homosexuality and abortion are not the main problems in America today (though woman's drive to equality and economic and political independence—for which control of her own reproductive process is, indeed, essential—does pose a real threat to reactionary power). But up through history to Hitler and the Ayatollah Khomeini of Iran—and not exempting Stalinist Russia and most Communist regimes today—control and manipulation of sexuality and the family, and suppression of the rights and personhood of women, have been key elements in authoritarian power.

The manipulation of sexual hysteria and the repression of women are more than diversionary: they build a reservoir of impotent rage and frustrated energies in the family which can be diverted into violence, for one thing. The emotions and repressions linked to sexuality are so powerful that it is relatively easy to divert people's attention from their own basic economic interests and even from asking the tough political questions simply by manipulating sexual hysteria (just as it is easier to sell people things they don't really need with those subliminal sexual messages).

Of course, the more real sexual liberation—and real satisfaction of people's needs for love and intimacy, which may be possible only when women and men can live as relatively secure, self-respecting equals—the less possible for any dictator or demagogue to manipulate people that way, against their own interests.

And, in another sense, our sexuality is a final frontier of privacy and autonomy any woman or man has the right, and need, to defend, according to personal values, in this invasive mass society where so little is left that we can control in our own lives. Beneath the hysteria of the Moral Majority, surely many of the women who respond to its message feel the same sense of basic human value and autonomy imperiled as other women feel when told they can no longer decide when and whether to have a child.

The founding fathers of this republic were not wrong when they wrote into the Bill of Rights the protection of certain basic areas of privacy for the individual conscience, exempt from the state's control, even if, in the beginning, they guaranteed such rights of privacy only for people who were men. Surely it is politically unwise to seem to threaten that area of inviolate sexual privacy now, as part of an effort to secure these basic rights for women. Tactics that smack of sexual exhibitionism, like the lesbians' balloons at the National Women's Conference at Houston proclaiming, "We are everywhere," and even slogans like "sexual preference," distort the basic principle; they seem to invade that very right of privacy for which we fight.

The abortion issue may have further overtones. It is significant that the final straw that reversed the trend in Congress and the courts upholding the right to safe legal medical access to abortion was the use of federal or state funds for abortion. There is a convergence here of sexual and economic threat. To release women from that final sexual control, to free her to move in the world and even to enjoy and control her own sexual behavior without punishment—and then to make the taxpayer pay for it to boot—that's going too far! Of course, it is only a matter of time until Kemp-Roth, *et al.*, figure out that it costs far more to raise an unwanted kid on welfare than to let a woman get an abortion under Medicaid. Then the piousness of Government not sanctioning abortion may become an openly punitive move to forced sterilization. There is an interesting case of a lobbyist even now in Washington who has moved from agitating against abortion rights to lobbying to lower the age of marriage to twelve, and to prohibit girls from going to school or getting any jobs! (*New York Times*, Nov. 12, 1980)

There is also a curious illogic in the fact that the same "Right to Life" crowd, who would sanctify the unborn fetus over the life of woman herself in the so-called Human Life Amendment, also advocates, in the Laxalt Family Protection Act, the right to beat a child in school and the elimination of all sanctions against child-battering and wife-beating.

Still, there was something that went wrong in the terms we used to discuss abortion. Such slogans as "free abortion on demand" had connotations of sexual licentiousness, not only affronting the moral values of conservatives but implying a certain lack of reverence for life and the mysteries of conception and birth which have been women's agony and ecstasy and defining value down through the ages. There is a mystique of motherhood; but the conception and bearing of children—the ongoing generation of human life—is surrounded, in all religions, by an awe and mystery that is more than a mystique. Being "for abortion" is like being "for mastectomy." It completely overlooks the life-enhancing value for women and families of the choice to have children.

Yet an evolution is taking place here. Younger feminists, now aware of the possible consequences of the Pill and the IUD to women's future health and future ability to bear children are promoting, in the women's health network, the diaphragm and even the new natural method, based on the mucous and temperature changes that signify the ovulation period. The Catholic priests at the White House Conference on Families were ready to join us on "the choice to have children." More importantly, the official American body of Catholic bishops, at the recent Synod on the Family at the Vatican, objected to the definition of birth control, as "sin," noting that 85 percent of American Catholics use birth control, motivated by human responsibility and moral conscience, not "sin."

It was a second-stage approach, when NOW president Eleanor Smeal invited leaders of the Right to Life movement to meet with feminists in Washington in 1980 to discuss how we might jointly work to further research that would enable women to transcend the divisive issue of abortion and be able to choose to bear children responsibly and joyously and with full respect for all of our values and rights to life.

The limits of women's power, and its true potential, were masked by the first-stage preoccupation with sexual issues. The power of issues like abortion in countries like Italy and France as well as America to ignite women into united action, across lines of class and race and political difference, was deceptive. Focusing on such single issues, no matter how basic, blinds one to the totality of women's movement to personhood in society, which is what the women's movement was all about. Preoccupation with sexual issues can blind us to the larger economic and political situation which affects both women and men, and which women now as persons can actively affect. On the issues of war or peace, or inflation in the United States, or revolution in Iran, or national survival in Afghanistan, or Israel, or Cambodia, I do not think that women have a different stake than men, nor a need to organize in a separate women's movement (except to protect or advance their own rights which the revolution itself may threaten or ignore). I do not believe that sexual issues, where women may indeed have a separate stake, or even women's rights, take precedence, even for women, over larger issues such as war and peace, or economic survival, or revolt against tyranny, or threats to basic human freedom, in any nation or system. But women's own freedom is one basic human right that women themselves can never ignore. . . .

Aldo Leopold

Born January 11, 1887, in Burlington, Iowa, Aldo Leopold is often called the "father of wildlife conservation" in America. While still young, he became absorbed with ornithology and natural history. After attending the Sheffield Scientific School at Yale, he became the first graduate of forestry in the United States, receiving his master's degree in 1909 from the Yale Forestry School.

Leopold worked for the U.S. Forest Service, supervising the million-acre Carson Natural Forest. He also served as associate director of the U.S. Forest Products Laboratory in Madison, Wisconsin (the main research and development institution for the Forest Service at the time). In 1933 he was appointed to a chair in game management at the University of Wisconsin, which established the Department of Wildlife Ecology. There he taught until he died in 1948 (while helping neighbors put out a grass fire).

The author of hundreds of articles on scientific and policy matters and a classic text, *Game Management*, Leopold was best known for *Round River* (published in 1949 by Oxford University Press) and for *A Sand County Almanac* (excerpted here), in which he specialized in "thinking like a mountain."

ঞ৻৻

A Sand County Almanac (1949)
(excerpt)

The Land Ethic

When god-like Odysseus returned from the wars in Troy, he hanged all on one rope a dozen slave-girls of his household whom he suspected of misbehavior during his absence.

This hanging involved no question of propriety. The girls were property. The disposal of property was then, as now, a matter of expediency, not of right and wrong.

Concepts of right and wrong were not lacking from Odysseus' Greece: witness the fidelity of his wife through the long years before at last his black-prowed galleys clove the wine-dark seas for home. The ethical structure of that day covered wives, but had not yet been extended to human chattels. During the three thousand years which have since elapsed, ethical criteria have been extended to many fields of conduct, with corresponding shrinkages in those judged by expediency only.

The Ethical Sequence

This extension of ethics, so far studied only by philosophers, is actually a process in ecological evolution. Its sequences may be described in ecological as well as in philosophical terms. An ethic, ecologically, is a limitation on freedom of action in the struggle for existence. An ethic, philosophically, is a differentiation of social from anti-social conduct. These are two definitions of one thing. The thing has its origin in the tendency of interdependent individuals or groups to evolve modes of co-operation. The ecologist calls these symbioses. Politics and economics are advanced symbioses in which the original free-for-all competition has been replaced in part, by co-operative mechanisms with an ethical content.

The complexity of co-operative mechanisms has increased with population density, and with the efficiency of tools. It was simpler, for example, to define the anti-social uses of sticks and stones in the days of the mastodons than of bullets and billboards in the age of motors.

The first ethics dealt with the relation between individuals; the Mosaic Decalogue is an example. Later accretions dealt with the relation between the individual and society. The Golden Rule tries to integrate the individual to society; democracy to integrate social organization to the individual.

There is as yet no ethic dealing with man's relation to land and to the animals and plants which grow upon it. Land, like Odysseus' slave-girls, is still property. The land-relation is still strictly economic, entailing privileges but not obligations.

The extension of ethics to this third element in human environment is, if I read the evidence correctly, an evolutionary possibility and an ecological necessity. It is the third step in a sequence. The first two have already been taken. Individual thinkers since the days of Ezekiel and Isaiah have asserted that the despoliation of land is not only inexpedient but wrong. Society, however, has not yet affirmed their

belief. I regard the present conservation movement as the embryo of such an affirmation.

An ethic may be regarded as a mode of guidance for meeting ecological situations so new or intricate, or involving such deferred reactions, that the path of social expediency is not discernible to the average individual. Animal instincts are modes of guidance for the individual in meeting such situations. Ethics are possibly a kind of community instinct in-the-making.

The Community Concept

All ethics so far evolved rest upon a single premise: that the individual is a member of a community of interdependent parts. His instincts prompt him to compete for his place in that community, but his ethics prompt him also to co-operate (perhaps in order that there may be a place to compete for).

The land ethic simply enlarges the boundaries of the community to include soils, waters, plants, and animals, or collectively, the land.

This sounds simple: do we not already sing our love for and obligation to the land of the free and the home of the brave? Yes, but just what and whom do we love? Certainly not the soil, which we are sending helter-skelter downriver. Certainly not the waters, which we assume have no function except to turn turbines, float barges, and carry off sewage. Certainly not the plants, of which we exterminate whole communities without batting an eye. Certainly not the animals, of which we have already extirpated many of the largest and most beautiful species. A land ethic of course cannot prevent the alteration, management, and use of these "resources," but it does affirm their right to continued existence, and, at least in spots, their continued existence in a natural state.

In short, a land ethic changes the role of *Homo sapiens* from conqueror of the land-community to plain member and citizen of it. It implies respect for his fellow-members, and also respect for the community as such.

In human history, we have learned (I hope) that the conqueror role is eventually self-defeating. Why? Because it is implicit in such a role that the conqueror knows, *ex cathedra*, just what makes the community clock tick, and just what and who is valuable, and what and who is worthless, in community life. It always turns out that he knows neither, and this is why his conquests eventually defeat themselves.

In the biotic community, a parallel situation exists. Abraham knew exactly what the land was for: it was to drip milk and honey into Abraham's mouth. At the present moment, the assurance with which we regard this assumption is inverse to the degree of our education.

The ordinary citizen today assumes that science knows what makes the community clock tick; the scientist is equally sure that he does not. He knows that the biotic mechanism is so complex that its workings may never be fully understood.

That man is, in fact, only a member of a biotic team is shown by an ecological interpretation of history. Many historical events, hitherto explained solely in terms of human enterprise, were actually biotic interactions between people and land. The characteristics of the land determined the facts quite as potently as the characteristics of the men who lived on it.

Consider, for example, the settlement of the Mississippi valley. In the years following the Revolution, three groups were contending for its control: the native Indian, the French and English traders, and the American settlers. Historians wonder what would have happened if the English at Detroit had thrown a little more weight into the Indian side of those tipsy scales which decided the outcome of the colonial migration into the cane-lands of Kentucky. It is time now to ponder the fact that the cane-lands, when subjected to the particular mixture of forces represented by the cow, plow, fire, and axe of the pioneer, became bluegrass. What if the plant succession inherent in this dark and bloody ground had, under the impact of these forces, given us some worthless sedge, shrub, or weed? Would Boone and Kenton have held out? Would there have been any overflow into Ohio, Indiana, Illinois, and Missouri? Any Louisiana Purchase? Any transcontinental union of new states? Any Civil War?

Kentucky was one sentence in the drama of history. We are commonly told what the human actors in this drama tried to do, but we are seldom told that their success, or the lack of it, hung in large degree on the reaction of particular soils to the impact of the particular forces exerted by their occupancy. In the case of Kentucky, we do not even know where the bluegrass came from—whether it is a native species, or a stowaway from Europe.

Contrast the cane-lands with what hindsight tells us about the Southwest, where the pioneers were equally brave, resourceful, and persevering. The impact of occupancy here brought no bluegrass, or other plant fitted to withstand the bumps and buffeting of hard use. This region, when grazed by livestock, reverted through a series of more and more worthless grasses, shrubs, and weeds to a condition of unstable equilibrium. Each recession of plant types bred erosion; each increment to erosion bred a further recession of plants. The result today is a progressive and mutual deterioration, not only of plants and soils, but of the animal community subsisting thereon. The early settlers did not expect this: on the ciénegas of New Mexico some even cut ditches to hasten it. So subtle has been its progress that few residents of the region are aware of it. It is quite invisible to the tourist who finds this wrecked landscape colorful and charming (as indeed it is, but it bears scant resemblance to what it was in 1848).

This same landscape was "developed" once before, but with quite different results. The Pueblo Indians settled the Southwest in pre-Columbian times, but they happened *not* to be equipped with range livestock. Their civilization expired, but not because their land expired.

In India, regions devoid of any sod-forming grass have been settled, apparently without wrecking the land, by the simple expedient of carrying the grass to the cow, rather than vice versa. (Was this the result of some deep wisdom, or was it just good luck? I do not know.)

In short, the plant succession steered the course of history; the pioneer simply demonstrated, for good or ill, what successions inhered in the land. Is history taught in this spirit? It will be, once the concept of land as a community really penetrates our intellectual life.

The Ecological Conscience

Conservation is a state of harmony between men and land. Despite nearly a century of propaganda, conservation still proceeds at a snail's pace; progress still consists largely of letterhead pieties and convention oratory. On the back forty we still slip two steps backward for each forward stride.

The usual answer to this dilemma is "more conservation education." No one will debate this, but is it certain that only the *volume* of education needs stepping up? Is something lacking in the *content* as well?

It is difficult to give a fair summary of its content in brief form, but, as I understand it, the content is substantially this: obey the law, vote right, join some organizations, and practice what conservation is

profitable on your own land; the government will do the rest.

Is not this formula too easy to accomplish anything worthwhile? It defines no right or wrong, assigns no obligation, calls for no sacrifice, implies no change in the current philosophy of values. In respect to land-use, it urges only enlightened self-interest. Just how far will such education take us? An example will perhaps yield a partial answer.

By 1930 it had become clear to all except the ecologically blind that southwestern Wisconsin's topsoil was slipping seaward. In 1933 the farmers were told that if they would adopt certain remedial practices for five years, the public would donate CCC labor to install them, plus the necessary machinery and materials. The offer was widely accepted, but the practices were widely forgotten when the five-year contract period was up. The farmers continued only those practices that yielded an immediate and visible economic gain for themselves.

This led to the idea that maybe farmers would learn more quickly if they themselves wrote the rules. Accordingly the Wisconsin Legislature in 1937 passed the Soil Conservation District Law. This said to farmers, in effect: *We, the public, will furnish you free technical service and loan you specialized machinery, if you will write your own rules for land-use. Each county may write its own rules, and these will have the force of law.* Nearly all the counties promptly organized to accept the proffered help, but after a decade of operation, *no county has yet written a single rule.* There has been visible progress in such practices as strip-cropping, pasture renovation, and soil liming, but none in fencing woodlots against grazing, and none in excluding plow and cow from steep slopes. The farmers, in short, have selected those remedial practices which were profitable anyhow, and ignored those which were profitable to the community, but not clearly profitable to themselves.

When one asks why no rules have been written, one is told that the community is not yet ready to support them; education must precede rules. But the education actually in progress makes no mention of obligations to land over and above those dictated by self-interest. The net result is that we have more education but less soil, fewer healthy woods, and as many floods as in 1937.

The puzzling aspect of such situations is that the existence of obligations over and above self-interest is taken for granted in such rural community enterprises as the betterment of roads, schools, churches, and baseball teams. Their existence is not taken for granted, nor as yet seriously discussed, in bettering the behavior of the water that falls on the land, or in the preserving of the beauty or diversity of the farm landscape. Land-use ethics are still governed wholly by economic self-interest, just as social ethics were a century ago.

To sum up: we asked the farmer to do what he conveniently could to save his soil, and he has done just that, and only that. The farmer who clears the woods off a 75 per cent slope, turns his cows into the clearing, and dumps its rainfall, rocks, and soil into the community creek, is still (if otherwise decent) a respected member of society. If he puts lime on his fields and plants his crops on contour, he is still entitled to all the privileges and emoluments of his Soil Conservation District. The District is a beautiful piece of social machinery, but it is coughing along on two cylinders because we have been too timid, and too anxious for quick success, to tell the farmer the true magnitude of his obligations. Obligations have no meaning without conscience, and the problem we face is the extension of the social conscience from people to land.

No important change in ethics was ever accomplished without an internal change in our intellectual emphasis, loyalties, affections, and convictions. The proof that conservation has not yet touched these foundations of conduct lies in the fact that philosophy and religion have not yet heard of it. In our attempt to make conservation easy, we have made it trivial.

Substitutes for a Land Ethic

When the logic of history hungers for bread and we hand out a stone, we are at pains to explain how much the stone resembles bread. I now describe some of the stones which serve in lieu of a land ethic.

One basic weakness in a conservation system based wholly on economic motives is that most members of the land community have no economic value. Wildflowers and songbirds are examples. Of the 22,000 higher plants and animals native to Wisconsin, it is doubtful whether more than 5 per cent can be sold, fed, eaten, or otherwise put to economic use. Yet these creatures are members of the biotic community, and if (as I believe) its stability depends on its integrity, they are entitled to continuance.

When one of these non-economic categories is threatened, and if we happen to love it, we invent subterfuges to give it economic importance. At the beginning of the century songbirds were supposed to be disappearing. Ornithologists jumped to the rescue with some distinctly shaky evidence to the effect that insects would eat us up if birds failed to control them. The evidence had to be economic in order to be valid.

It is painful to read these circumlocutions today. We have no land ethic yet, but we have at least drawn nearer the point of admitting that birds should continue as a matter of biotic right, regardless of the presence or absence of economic advantage to us.

A parallel situation exists in respect of predatory mammals, raptorial birds, and fish-eating birds. Time was when biologists somewhat overworked the evidence that these creatures preserve the health of game by killing weaklings, or that they control rodents for the farmer, or that they prey only on "worthless" species. Here again, the evidence had to be economic in order to be valid. It is only in recent years that we hear the more honest argument that predators are members of the community, and that no special interest has the right to exterminate them for the sake of a benefit, real or fancied, to itself. Unfortunately this enlightened view is still in the talk stage. In the field the extermination of predators goes merrily on: witness the impending erasure of the timber wolf by fiat of Congress, the Conservation Bureaus, and many state legislatures.

Some species of trees have been "read out of the party" by economics-minded foresters because they grow too slowly, or have too low a sale value to pay as timber crops: white cedar, tamarack, cypress, beech, and hemlock are examples. In Europe, where forestry is ecologically more advanced, the non-commercial tree species are recognized as members of the native forest community, to be preserved as such, within reason. Moreover, some (like beech) have been found to have a valuable function in building up soil fertility. The interdependence of the forest and its constituent tree species, ground flora, and fauna is taken for granted.

Lack of economic value is sometimes a character not only of species or groups, but of entire biotic communities: marshes, bogs, dunes, and "deserts" are examples. Our formula in such cases is to relegate their conservation to government as refuges, monuments, or parks. The difficulty is that these communities are usually interspersed with more valuable private lands; the government cannot possibly own or control such scattered parcels. The net effect is that we have relegated some of them to ultimate extinction over large areas. If the private owner were ecologically minded, he would be proud to be the custodian of a reasonable proportion of such areas, which add diversity and beauty to his farm and to his community.

In some instances, the assumed lack of profit in these "waste" areas has proved to be wrong, but only after most of them had been done away with. The present scramble to reflood muskrat marshes is a case in point.

There is a clear tendency in American conservation to relegate to government all necessary jobs that private landowners fail to perform. Government ownership, operation, subsidy, or regulation is now widely prevalent in forestry, range management, soil and watershed management, park and wilderness conservation, fisheries management, and migratory bird management, with more to come. Most of this growth in governmental conservation is proper and logical, some of it is inevitable. That I imply no disapproval of it is implicit in the fact that I have spent most of my life working for it. Nevertheless the question arises: What is the ultimate magnitude of the enterprise? Will the tax base carry its eventual ramifications? At what point will governmental conservation, like the mastodon, become handicapped by its own dimensions? The answer, if there is any, seems to be in a land ethic, or some other force which assigns more obligation to the private landowner.

Industrial landowners and users, especially lumbermen and stockmen, are inclined to wail long and loudly about the extension of government ownership and regulation to land, but (with notable exceptions) they show little disposition to develop the only visible alternative: the voluntary practice of conservation on their own lands.

When the private landowner is asked to perform some unprofitable act for the good of the community, he today assents only with outstretched palm. If the act costs him cash this is fair and proper, but when it costs only forethought, open-mindedness, or time, the issue is at least debatable. The overwhelming growth of land-use subsidies in recent years must be ascribed, in large part, to the government's own agencies for conservation education: the land bureaus, the agricultural colleges, and the extension services. As far as I can detect, no ethical obligation toward land is taught in these institutions.

To sum up: a system of conservation based solely on economic self-interest is hopelessly lopsided. It tends to ignore, and thus eventually to eliminate, many elements in the land community that lack commercial value, but that are (as far as we know) essential to its healthy functioning. It assumes, falsely, I think, that the economic parts of the biotic clock will function without the uneconomic parts. It tends to relegate to government many functions eventually too large, too complex, or too widely dispersed to be performed by government.

An ethical obligation on the part of the private owner is the only visible remedy for these situations. . . .

Murray Bookchin

Born in New York City in 1921, Murray Bookchin was active in anarchist, ecologist, and radical peace movements for most of his lifetime. He began as a free-lance writer and lecturer and wrote *Our Synthetic Environment* (1962) under the pseudonym Lewis Herber. Bookchin developed from the Old Left of the radical and labor movements of the 1930s into a spokesman for the New Left, represented in his later works: *Post Scarcity Anarchism* (1971), *The Limits of the City* (1973), *Toward an Ecological Society* (1980), and *The Ecology of Freedom* (1982). Serving as a professor at Ramapo College of New Jersey and as a founder and director of the Institute for Social Ecology at Goddard College in Plainfield, Vermont, he made his home in Burlington, Vermont. His writing illustrates his enthusiasm for the biological and social sciences as well as for natural history. The following excerpts from *The Modern Crisis* symbolize the synthesis of his anarchist and social ecological perspectives as represented by a call for decentralized democracy in the United States.

The Modern Crisis (1986)
(excerpts)

An Appeal for Social and Ecological Sanity

. . . It is precisely in the sphere of the republican institutions and democratic ethos that an authentic American radicalism can find the nourishment for a reempowerment of the American people and a revitalization of American social and political life.

Isaak, *American Political Thinking.*/From *The Modern Crisis* by Murray Bookchin. Reprinted by permission of New Society Publishers, 4527 Springfield Avenue, Philadelphia, PA 19143; (1-800-333-9093).

Here to use Reaganesque language, lies the "window of vulnerability" of the new totalitarians and militarists in American life. Ironic as it may seem to radicals who have been pastured on the economism of class war, technological growth, and "scientific socialism," be it libertarian or authoritarian, politics must now acquire a "supremacy" over economics, ethics over material interest, the claims of life over the claims of survival if any effective movement for radical renewal and change is to be achieved. Not that they must be counterposed to each other, but that each must be given its proper weight in the new balance of social events. The so-called superstructure, to use the language of Marxian "historical materialism," cannot be seen as an epiphenomenon of the "base" if there is to be any resistance to a market-oriented society that tends to make the ordinary individual, even the self-anointed revolutionary, into a mirror-image of itself. To the extent that *homo politicus* can replace *homo economicus*, and *homo collectivicus* can replace both, humanity still has a chance to rescue itself from a spiritual catastrophe in which social immolation and ecological breakdown will merely provide the shroud for an already decaying corpse.

What this reconnaissance into the real opening of American life means is that all thinking people must participate consciously in the tension between the American Dream conceived as utopia and the American Dream conceived as a huge shopping mall. This tension is compellingly real. Perhaps no people today is more conflicted over its commitment to individual rights, its freedom from governmental control, and its freedom of expression at one end of the spectrum, and its desire to surrender all public responsibility and autonomy to the siren-call of material comfort and the opiates of electronic mass culture at the other end. Within this area of conflict the Right has enjoyed a monopoly

of power unmatched by a largely indifferent Left. Herein lies a tragedy of monumental proportions. Still nourished by a classical image of radicalism and tormented by a searing guilt for America's role in the "Third World," American radicals have remained strangers in their own homeland, just like the European immigrants who transferred their own heroic struggles against monarchs, semi-feudal landlords, and corrupt bureaucracies into a world whose concerns differed profoundly from the lands of their origin. The association between the two is closer than American radicals care to recognize. Irish direct action, German Marxism, Italian anarchism, and Jewish socialism have always been confined to the ghettoes of American social life. Combatants of a precapitalist world, these militant European radical immigrants stood at odds with an ever-changing Anglo-Saxon society, initially rooted in yeoman-farmer traditions, communities of urban craftsmen, commercial buccaneers, and straying lawless frontiersmen, whose Constitution had been wrought from the struggle for "Englishmen's Rights," not against feudal satraps.

Admittedly, these "rights" were meant for white men rather than people of color, for Anglo-Saxons rather than Celts, Latins, Semites, and Europe's "riff-raff." But rights they were in any case—universal, "inalienable," and "natural rights" that could have expressed higher ethical and political aspirations than the myths of a "workers' party" or the daydreams of "One Big Union," to cite the illusions of socialists and syndicalists alike. Had the Congregationalist town-meeting conception of democracy been fostered over aristocratic proclivities for hierarchy, had political liberty been given emphasis over *laissez-faire, laissez-aller*; had individualism been given an ethical ideal instead of congealing into proprietary egotism; had the Republic been slowly reworked into a confederal democracy; had capital concentration been inhibited by cooperatives and small, possibly worker-controlled, enterprises; had the rights of localities been rescued from the centralized state; and finally, had the middle classes been joined to the working classes in a genuine people's movement such as the Populists tried to achieve [instead of being fractured into sharply delineated class movements]—in short, had this American vision of utopia supplanted the Euro-socialist vision of a nationalized, planned, and centralized economy, it would be difficult to predict the innovative direction American social, life might have followed.*

That this was not to be does not mean that it cannot be. Admittedly, for more than a century American radicalism was largely in the custody of millions of immigrants, most of whom could barely speak English. Radicalism remained a ghetto ideology in all its forms, or was simply unrecognizable to its vast immigrant population when it surged out of Texas into the midwest in its distinctively American populist form. New England democracy, so crucial in shaping the most radical forms of the Colonial and Revolutionary eras, slumbered in western Massachusetts, in central and northern New Hampshire, in Vermont, and in Maine—reduced, by sheer prejudice, to a mere village archaism in a world of burgeoning cities. Yet never did American radicals, foreign-born or native, ask why a mass workers' party failed to develop as it had on the European continent, or why socialist ideas never took root outside the confines of the ghettoes in this, the most industrialized country in the world.

But is it an "ideological lag" that explains American "backwardness" in the socialist firmament? Were the "real Americans," as Lenin called them in contrast to the Italians, Jews, and Irish, so distant from the high utopian ideals of humanity over centuries of history? Now that the old European immigrants are virtually gone, their parties disbanded, their periodicals closed, their beautiful roses faded, and even their unruly depression-era children aging, can we perhaps look back and ask where they erred and formed a branch of their own away from the historical flow of the utopistic American Dream as distinguished from the material one they cherished?

Certainly they erred when they believed that the world would be remade by the very industrial workers they so often became—a form of social narcissism that is, perhaps, understandable but now more archaic and certainly more irrelevant than the New England town meetings of which they were totally ignorant. These immigrant socialists and anarchists were largely unionists rather than revolutionary utopians. The rhetoric of the "isms" colored the harsh material interests of their class which a Franklin Delano Roosevelt brought to terms with the interest of capital. Once the reconciliation of wage labor and capital was achieved by the annealing effects of the Second World War, socialism became overtly identified with state capitalism and its parties ceased to be truly oppositional, much less revolutionary. When the last pontiff of American socialism, Norman Thomas, chidingly declared that the "late President Roosevelt adopted most of our ideas," the good Reverend said more than he realized. The New Deal lives on as a program for economic centralization and planning to a greater extent than its most hostile opponents are willing to concede. It is the "Pentagon, Inc.," to use Jessica Savitch's phrase, that has largely taken

*"Third World" peoples now face very similar alternatives. Will the Indians in Central America, for example, be free to establish autonomous communities rooted in their rich, pre-industrial, native cultural heritage? Or will they be colonized, ultimately even exterminated, by American-supported feudal juntas and Russian-supported technocratic "Ladinos" who conjointly seek to exploit their labor and resources?

over the functions that were reconnoitered by Roosevelt's NRA, AAA, WPA, CCC, *et al.*—that has devoured Norman Thomas's old-time Socialist Party as well. The scenario has been changed in many parts, but the plot is very much the same.

Perhaps even more decisive than the disappearance of the European immigrants and their children is the steady demise of their ideological hope: the industrial proletariat itself. The factory in its traditional form is gradually becoming an archaism. Robots will soon replace the assembly line as the agents of mass industrial production, just as they are expected to replace the typist-secretary-accountant as the agents of commercial activity. Cybernetic devices are even invading agriculture on a scale that threatens the miserable livelihood of the migrant farmworker. In time, even "service workers," from retail clerks to mechanics, may be victimized by so-called intelligent robots and throwaway units, even governmental employees, so politically vigorous by comparison with their counterparts in the "private sector," face technological extinction.

What is crucial here is that the centerpiece for the immigrant "isms," such as the blue- and white-collar working class, is being "phased out" historically, just as the small farmer and the European immigrant have disappeared from the American social landscape. They and their factories are confronted with the same destiny. In key industrial areas that do remain, the Japanese patronal system with its myth of "employee-employer" cooperation—the "participatory democracy" of multinational corporatism—is replacing even the supine unionism of the previous generation of workers. Hence future generations of industrial proletarians may be a marginal stratum—marking the end of American industrial society as we have known it since the post–Civil War era. The military technology that brought the classical Age of

Revolution to an end has claimed the constituency of the classical revolution of modern times—the working class itself.

In so sweeping a confrontation between past and future, where do we stand in the present?

The world we have known over the past centuries is undergoing changes that are unequalled by any we have known since humanity turned from the nomadic ways of hunters to the settled ways of agriculturists. To regard this judgement as an overstatement is to exhibit incredible parochialism in the face of a technological leap that by far exceeds the consequences of the traditional Industrial Revolution with its ensuing urbanism, population growth, ascendency of the industrial bourgeoisie, and profound changes in daily lifeways. Contemporary science has now opened the secrets of matter and life, of the atom and gene. Given this knowledge, technology has scarcely crossed the threshold of an era whose boundaries are utterly unforeseeable. Biotechnics and cybernetics alone could vastly alter the landscape of the mind as we have known it up to now. Yet this technology has merely entered the "Kitty Hawk" stage of the Wright brothers who initiated the flight of heavier-than-air machines, a stage that less than eighty years later seems as far removed from aircraft design and power as does the Bronze Age from the use of tools today.

The social impact these technological developments will produce and the political problems they will create are even more difficult to assess. How a market economy that exchanges wages for labor power can deal with tens of millions of men and women who will be displaced by tractable machines, much less the "intelligent" ones that are now on the drawing boards, raises the specter of vast social dislocations. This may well require an all-encompassing system of surveillance, the elimination of free speech, assembly, the most rudimentary forms of representation, in short, all the rights we associate with the word "democracy"—ultimately, complete militarization and population controls that could well lead to compulsory sterilization, conceivably genocide by calculated starvation if not outright extermination. If such measures had not already been used during this century, we would be hard put to believe that they were possible. Yet they did appear in the 1940s and the aftershock of their use has already worn off in a world inured to mass slaughter, death from hunger, and the ebbing of life by old and exotic diseases. The Four Horsemen of the Apocalypse ride routinely across our planet today, but with very limited promise of redemption.

Given these economic and political premises, the residue of the Republic, the Bill of Rights, and the visions of a democratic commonwealth hang like a millstone on the cybernated, robotized, and genetically engineered society that is aborning in our midst. Two visions of the American Dream have reached searing acuity; the contradiction between the American populist past and its totalitarian future could well become explosive. We can foresee what we want and must defend it, if merely as a reaction against the schemes that are emerging to deal with the imperatives of social control and centralized power. To corporate America, our "agrarian" Republic is worse than "obsolete"; it is an unyielding obstacle to the homogenization and management of the American people. To the emerging elites of a cybernetic America, the breach between the separate branches of government must be "healed" by giving preemptive powers to the executive branch over the legislative and judicial. The western republics of the modern world are being geared to accept a new Caesarism, indeed, a new imperium that potentially, at least, could beggar in its power to control and destroy the most commanding monolithic states in history. To guard against this Caesarist tendency has become the precondition for developing a social agenda for our time. And to ignore an overall trend toward a new Caesarism in the name of a "radicalism" so "purified" of all reality and historical understanding as to yield complete inertness would be capitulation to the powers that be.

Equally important is the need to recreate a democratic public, a body politic committed to the ideals of free expression and the right of every person to formulate social policy. Contemporary urban society and the mass media have subverted the very notion of an active citizenry—the soul of such a body politic. Its decline can be summed up in the most fundamental feature of American life: disempowerment.

Reempowerment presupposes that every individual can feel he or she has control over the decisions that affect our society's destiny. Such a sensibility can only be recreated and fostered by a radical change in the scale of everyday life, a *conscious* endeavor to bring the social environment within the purview of the individual, to render it as comprehensible and understandable as possible. No mere intuitive actions and explosive episodes will do for a society that threatens to replace "primitive" innocence and naiveté with a "sophisticated" cynicism and indifference. Decentralization of decision making, and the institutionalization of the "grass roots" into impregnable structures that are built on a face-to-face democracy, constitute the unavoidable challenges that can form a new, active citizenry in a real participatory democracy. Without this "unitary democracy," democracy of any kind may well disappear. Corporate America cannot assert itself over the existing and potential means of power by hybridizing even republican institutions with totalitarian ones. We do not know whether anything less than complete state control can avoid any threat to the corporate order as such and the deployment of a stupendous technological armory to deal with the problems of a historically new epoch in human relationships.

Despite the erosion of our libertarian institutions over the past few generations, American political life still bears the deep imprints of its revolutionary origins. Mythic or real, individual rights, juridical equality, free expression, and resistance to State encroachment still exercise a powerful hold upon the American mind. This is a genuine reality in its own right, all losses of such values notwithstanding. The ideal of "liberty," however varied its meanings to different citizens, looms over the Caesarist challenge to the Republic as a haunting memory that has yet to be uprooted from our national heritage and our political conscience. *Homo economicus* has not yet completely supplanted *homo politicus*. The "Bill of Rights" and the demands of the great Declaration of Independence for "life, liberty, and the pursuit of happiness" still beleaguer the authoritarians like a ghostly army from the past—a *living* past that can yet be galvanized to recreate an empowered, active citizenry and a democratic body politic.

But how can these ideals be given a palpable form at the base of a society already highly centralized politically and economically? Indeed, a society riddled by spectatorial "citizens" who seem like fair game for the mass media and the political star system?

We encounter here the problem of recovering our revitalizing forms of democratic practice already in existence which lie dormant in a political community. I refer to forms that are still structured around the idea of decentralization and human scale—notably, the municipality as the ultimate source of power, be it the neighborhood assembly in large cities or the town meeting in small communities. The United States has given greater moral authority than any other country today to the "grass roots,"

a distinctively American expression that stems from our traditional emphasis on local government and our uniquely libertarian revolution. If a radical practice of public reempowerment is to take itself seriously, it must initiate the act of reempowering the citizen in the environment in which he or she is most directly immersed—the neighborhood or town. On this basic level of political and social life, it must try to create at least exemplary forms of public assembly whose moral authority slowly can be turned into political authority at the base of society. It may not be given that such a sequence of steps is practical in every American municipality, much less every region of America. But where it is practical or even remotely possible, it must become the most important endeavor of a new radical populism—a new libertarian populism.

Some of the more impressive examples of this renewal, examples that have acquired great moral influence, have been decisions by Vermont town meetings to demand a nuclear freeze and to withdraw aid from the Salvadoran junta, and, in New Hampshire, to resolve the grave ecological problem of acid rain. These decisions, let it be emphasized, are not local "town issues" which traditionally fall within the province of New England town meetings. They are national and international issues which constitutionally fall within the province of the federal government. Aside from the growing tension such decisions produce between the centralized state and the "grass-roots" locality, the *processes* by which these decisions are made become ends in themselves—not merely means to an end. They create an ambience of popular politics, of participatory citizenship, of active involvement in historic issues. They provide that vital function that self-governance should always fulfill: the process of *educating* the citizen into citizenship and deepening one's sense of selfhood through self-governance. Empowerment, even if only moral in its initial phases, imparts the attributes of a greater sense of public activity in the citizen, of social involvement, reflection, discourse, and decision making—the traits of authentic judgement—not merely the episodic act of delivering one's power, political intelligence, and moral standards into the hands of professional power brokers whose names appear on ballots.

... There is no room for naiveté any longer. The Caeserists and corporatists are too sophisticated, however quarrelsome they may be, to be outmaneuvered by innocents. Their acute consciousness must be answered by a consciousness of our own. Such a consciousness presupposes the learning, study, discussion, debate, teachers, and organizers that can only be supplied by a coherent network of groups whose dedication to social change is single-minded in practice and utterly respectful of mind in theory. Whether the German Greens provide us with an example of such a network or not we have yet to ascertain. If nothing else, we can learn as much from their errors as from their successes. But a Green network we certainly require—one that speaks to Americans in their own tongue, not in European, Asian, or Latin languages and formulas. It must also be one that is spawned from American radical traditions: Yankee democracy, frontier individuality, a popular mistrust of governmental power, a dedication to "grass-roots" democracy, in short, a libertarian populism that is built on the reemergence of "the People" and the institutionalization of the "grass roots" by confederated popular assemblies.

The term "libertarian" itself, to be sure, raises a problem, notably, the specious identification of an anti-authoritarian ideology with a straggling movement for "pure capitalism" and "free trade." This movement never created the word; it appropriated it from the anarchist movement of the last century. And it should be recovered by those anti-authoritarians—whether socialistic or anarchic—who try to speak for dominated people as a whole, not for personal egotists who identify freedom with entrepreneurship and profit. It would be wiser to simply ignore this specious movement for "liberty" and restore in practice a tradition that has been denatured by new disciples of Adam Smith.

Lest the word "libertarian" be seen as a political capitulation to statism, we would do well to realize a flaw in the authentic libertarian tradition that confuses politics in its *Hellenic* sense with statecraft. The traditional libertarian counterposition of "society" to "the State" is not false as such. Social forms like families, clans, tribes, guilds, workshops, village communities, neighborhoods, and towns are the organic institutional forms by which humanity "naturally" developed toward consociation and by which it metabolized with nature in the form of production. It is within these forms that the great anarchic theorists hoped to structure a confederal libertarian society. The State, quite soundly, was seen as an exogenous institution—a professionalized class instrument of executives, legislators, bureaucrats, soldiers, judges, and police with their paraphernalia of barracks, courts, and prisons. This exogenous institution had to be consistently bypassed in daily social activity and disbanded in periods of sweeping social change.

For the present, however, what should be emphasized is that the historical landscape is composed of more than society and the State. We must move beyond this simplistic and Manichean dualism to focus on a generally unexplored arena of human activity, a public space or *political* arena in the classical Hellenic sense of the word *politika*, or activity of the *polis*, that cannot be subsumed by the word State, much less "city-state." Perhaps for the first time in history, but by no means the last, the Athenian democratic *polis* produced an entirely new institutional arena—an arena that was not specifically "social" like the family, clan, tribe, presumably workplace, and various "natural" forms of consociation like clubs, cultic communities, vocational collegia (later, "guilds"), and professional societies. Nor was this institutional arena identical to—or even an extension of—that class-controlled professionalized system of violence such as armies, police, bureaucrats, judges, legislators, and centralized executives we call "the State"—a constellation of structures which were few enough in Periclean Athens although they were quite common in the ancient world.

What the Athenian *polis* created was a uniquely *civic* sphere—a distinctly municipal arena—characterized by the *agora*, or civic center, where citizens could gather informally, discuss, trade, and engage in a richly textured interaction that prepared them for the weekly meetings of all the citizens in the *ecclesia*, or popular assembly, where they normally discussed the issues of the *polis* with a view toward arriving at a public consensus in a face-to-face manner, either with unanimity or by a vote. There, too, as in the *agora*, they were daily and subtly educated into the arts and attributes of active citizenship, or more precisely, into the sensibility, character-structure, and selfhood of participatory and self-governing citizens—a new, specifically municipal "class" in the spectrum of "classes" which Marx and our current bouquet of radical social theorists have so neatly arranged for us. The Athenian democracy, in effect, functioned as a school for personal and social development, and with its dramas, festivals, and pageants provided a unifying *cultural* milieu that knitted together the *polis* into a community unified

in sensibility and tradition. Economic strata Athens had in abundance: slaves, craftpersons, merchants, alien residents, or *metics*, who enjoyed none of the political rights of citizens—although there were free, independent farmers, tenant farmers, intellectuals who practiced what we today would call "professions," nobles of aristocratic lineages, and, finally, a stratum of demagogues who tried to manipulate the citizen body to suit their own personal and social interests.

But there was also the citizen body itself—the body politic—that, despite its mixed "class" character, often transcended its particularistic economic interests to arrive at an ethical consensus. This consensus was guided by a notion of the "public good," a "good" that cannot be dismissed as purely "ideological" or subtly class motivated, but which rested on a shared notion of what was transparently the public welfare, all particularistic frictions and conflicts aside. As expressed by the social philosophers of Greece, whether democratic or authoritarian, this notion of the "public good" consisted of the body politic's *aretē*, or virtue. In the Athenian democratic *polis*, politics, or *politika*, to use a safely Hellenized term, belonged neither to the realm of the "social" nor that of the "State," terms for which the Greeks significantly had no words. It comprised the realm of the *polis*, of the *civis*, to use a more familiar Latin word, in which men (the society, like all those around it, was firmly patricentric) formed a "social compact" or common *ethical* understanding—in no way to be confused with a juridical "social contract"—to order its life as a "commonweal" to try to transcend particular interests.

What the anarchic theorists have not seen clearly is a supra-social level of politics—literally, the activity of the *polis*—that can validly be distinguished from *statecraft*. Politics is the public realm of citizenship where citizens gather to discuss social problems, evaluate them, and, finally, decide on their solution, whether by consensus or by vote. This political arena, as distinguished from the largely social world of organic relationships at one end of the spectrum and the statist world of ruling-class controls at the other end, is the intermediate world of the community and the citizen—a municipal world based not on kin but on the *civic* association that so often surfaces in the writing of Proudhon and Kropotkin, only to be overlaid by the industrial world of syndicalism.

Tragically the liberatory side of community and municipal politics was never fully elaborated. Indeed, it was myopically subsumed by an "antipolitical" bias that brought the distinctions caused by statist and social infiltration into a twilight zone of radical social theory. Libertarian municipalism was further stigmatized by the crude betrayals of its most outstanding spokesman, Paul Brousse, the French anarchist who drifted in his later life toward conventional party politics. Cleansed of this stigma, libertarian municipalism *and* its politics, based on popular assemblies and confederal relationships, can be seen as a process that does not deny politics in its *classical* sense but rather serves to give it authenticity and contemporary relevance.

To be sure, recovered forms and structures like town meetings and neighborhood assemblies do not of themselves yield the reempowerment of the citizen, the body politic, and a democratic society, much less the ecological society we hope to achieve. The bottles are no better than the wine they contain. That wine, it is self-evident, must be fermented by a libertarian populist movement, a network or coalition of the classless "class." It must be guarded from pollution by a coherent, highly conscious theory and practice. No less than the theorists and organizers, it must be abetted by events—by contemporary history itself—which unite seemingly single issues into a nexus of general ones and enlarge their logic into historic programs for sweeping social change.

Thus the social movement outside must combine with the intellectual movement inside. Already, feminism tends to meld with ecologism under the common theme of the domination of nature. Countercultural lifeways tend to unite with political movements for freedom, all the more because restrictions on sexual life, behavior, medical strategies, midwifery, art, and perhaps even dress threaten to undermine the very ingredients of culture as such, not to speak of one "counter" to prevalent mores. Even the peace movement cannot confine itself to such single issues as the nuclear freeze, arms reduction, or opposition to relocation plans in the event of war. It is destined to face the fact that it is not just opposed to armaments, but to *militarism*. This old demand, which predates the outbreak of the First World War, has reappeared as a result of the encroaching Caesarist and corporate State and of the militarization of every facet of life from school to industry, from family to community, from sexual relations to social relations. The Pentagon is no longer merely the "command post" of the nation. It threatens through its vast command of resources and the allocation of funds to become the artificial heart of an increasingly bionic and militarized society.

However summarily these remarks have been advanced, they offer a theory and practice for social and ecological sanity. If they have not explored the issue of property rights and multinational corporatism, of imperialistic designs and the problems of nuclear war, of feminism and ethnic oppression, it is only because these issues have been fully explored in countless statements, articles, and books. Civic entities can "municipalize" their industries, utilities, and surrounding land as effectively as any socialist state. The difference would be that a municipally managed enterprise would be a worker-*citizen* controlled enterprise meant to serve human and ecological needs, not a bureaucratically and politically controlled enterprise that assumes an interest and ends of its own. Even more can be said about the replacement of the nation-state by the municipal confederation, the treatment of sexes and "strangers," and the like. To "touch every base" merely to signify one is aware of "every" issue would be hypocritical and manipulative. What I have advanced is a perspective that is different from those which normally appear in most radical social theories—a libertarian populism based on municipal freedom and confederation. This perspective speaks more directly and traditionally to American conditions than the immigrant "isms" that still linger on among radical sects and European traditions of radicalism. It makes no attempt to imperialize the ideological landscape—and it carries the warning that ages long past, both in American history and European, may be irrecoverable for people whose very spirit may be industrialized and reduced to spectatorial passivity.

If nothing else, however, it tries to speak to a more independent, politically concerned, and libertarian American spirit that may still lie latent in the national character-structure. And if nothing is left of that spirit, radicals may follow their own personal course, perhaps returning to the daydreams of dignity in defeat with the certain knowledge that defeat will end in biocide. But if something of that spirit is still left, even as embers, these remarks may be regarded as part of an effort to raise up the flames of protest and provide us with the means for reconstruction.

Here, at least, is a chance for humanity to regain its sanity and rebuild this ruined planet as a world for life. It is a chance that must arouse the very unconscious of the individual and redeem the spirit of life with which he or she was born to produce a new culture and consciousness, not only a new movement and program.

Wendell Berry

Born in 1934 and educated in Kentucky, Wendell Berry taught in California and New York before returning permanently to the Kentucky river region. There he made his name as a poet, novelist, and ecological thinker based on the integrity of traditional human attachment to the land. As a spokesman for conservation, sustainable agriculture, and American common sense, he published *The Unsettling of America* and *The Gift of Good Land.* Living for more than two decades farming seventy-five acres in Henry County, Kentucky, Berry balances physical work with work of the spirit. His writings include the novels *Nathan Coulter* (1960), *A Place on the Earth* (1968), and *The Memory of Old Jack* (1974); nine collections of poetry; and a number of essay collections including *What Are People For?* (1990), from which the following essay was drawn. His aim is to "Make the human race a better head. Make the world a better piece of ground."

What Are People For? (1990)
(excerpt)

The Work of Local Culture

For many years, my walks have taken me down an old fencerow in a wooded hollow on what was once my grandfather's farm. A battered galvanized bucket is hanging on a fence post near the head of the hollow, and I never go by it without stopping to look inside. For what is going on in that bucket is the most momentous thing I know, the greatest miracle that I have ever heard of: it is making earth. The old bucket has hung there through many autumns, and the leaves have fallen around it and some have fallen into it. Rain and snow have fallen into it, and the fallen leaves have held the moisture and so have rotted. Nuts have fallen into it, or been carried into it by squirrels; mice and squirrels have eaten the meat of the nuts and left the shells; they and other animals have left their droppings; insects have flown into the bucket and died and decayed; birds have scratched in it and left their droppings or perhaps a feather or two. This slow work of growth and death, gravity and decay, which is the chief work of the world, has by now produced in the bottom of the bucket several inches of black humus. I look into that bucket with fascination because I am a farmer of sorts and an artist of sorts, and I recognize there an artistry and a farming far superior to mine, or to that of any human. I have seen the same process at work on the tops of boulders in a forest, and it has been at work immemorially over most of the land surface of the world. All creatures die into it, and they live by it.

The old bucket started out a far better one than you can buy now. I think it has been hanging on that post for something like fifty years. I think so because I remember hearing, when I was just a small boy, a story about a bucket that must have been this one. Several of my grandfather's black hired hands went out on an early spring day to burn a tobacco plant bed, and they took along some eggs to boil to eat with their dinner. When dinner time came and they looked around for something to boil the eggs in, they could find only an old bucket that at one time had been filled with tar. The boiling water softened the residue of tar, and one of the eggs came out of the water black. The hands made much sport of seeing who would have to eat the black egg, welcoming their laughter in the midst of their day's work. The man who had to eat the black egg was Floyd Scott, whom I remember well. Dry scales of tar still adhere to the inside of the bucket.

However small a landmark the old bucket is, it is not trivial. It is one of the signs by which I know my country and myself. And to me it is irresistibly suggestive in the way it collects leaves and other woodland sheddings as they fall through time. It collects stories, too, as they fall through time. It is irresistibly metaphorical. It is doing in a passive way what a human community must do actively and thoughtfully. A human community, too, must collect leaves and stories, and turn them to account. It must build soil, and build that memory of itself—in lore and story and song—that will be its culture. These two kinds of accumulation, of local soil and local culture, are intimately related.

In the woods, the bucket is no metaphor; it simply reveals what is always happening in the woods, if the woods is let alone. Of course, in most places in my part of the country, the human community did not leave the woods alone. It felled the trees and replaced them with pastures and crops. But this did not revoke the law of the woods, which is that the ground must be protected by a cover of vegetation and that the growth of the years must return—or be returned—to the ground to rot and build soil. A good local culture, in one of its most important functions, is a collection of the memories, ways, and skills necessary for the observance, within the bounds of domesticity, of this natural law. If the local culture cannot preserve and improve the local soil, then, as both reason and history inform us, the local community will decay and perish, and the work of soil building will be resumed by nature.

A human community, then, if it is to last long, must exert a sort of centripetal force, holding local soil and local memory in place. Practically speaking, human society has no work more important than this. Once we have acknowledged this principle, we can only be alarmed at the extent to which it has been ignored. For although our present society does generate a centripetal force of great power, this is not a local force, but one centered almost exclusively in our great commercial and industrial cities, which have drawn irresistibly into themselves both the products of the countryside and the people and talents of the country communities.

There is, as one assumes there must be, a countervailing or centrifugal force

that also operates in our society, but this returns to the countryside not the residue of the land's growth to refertilize the fields, not the learning and experience of the greater world ready to go to work locally, and not—or not often—even a just monetary compensation. What are returned, instead, are overpriced manufactured goods, pollution in various forms, and garbage. A landfill on the edge of my own rural county in Kentucky, for example, daily receives about eighty truckloads of garbage. Fifty to sixty of these loads come from cities in New York, New Jersey, and Pennsylvania. Thus, the end result of the phenomenal modern productivity of the countryside is a debased countryside, which becomes daily less pleasant, and which will inevitably become less productive.

The cities, which have imposed this inversion of forces on the country, have been unable to preserve themselves from it. The typical modern city is surrounded by a circle of affluent suburbs eating its way outward, like ringworm, leaving the so-called inner city desolate, filthy, ugly, and dangerous.

My walks in the hills and hollows around my home have inevitably produced in my mind the awareness that I live in a diminished country. The country has been and is being reduced by the great centralizing process that is our national economy. As I walk, I am always reminded of the slow, patient building of soil in the woods. And I am reminded of the events and companions of my life—for my walks, after so long, are cultural events. But under the trees and in the fields I see also the gullies and scars, healed or healing or fresh, left by careless logging and bad farming. I see the crumbling stone walls and the wire fences that have been rusting out ever since the 1930s. In the returning woods growth of the hollows, I see the sagging and the fallen barns, the empty and ruining houses, the houseless chimneys and foundations. As I look at this evidence of human life poorly founded, played out, and gone, I try to recover some understanding, some vision, of what this country was at the beginning: the great oaks and beeches and hickories, walnuts and maples, lindens and ashes, tulip poplars, standing in beauty and dignity now unimaginable, the black soil of their making, also no longer imaginable, lying deep at their feet—an incalculable birthright sold for money, most of which we did not receive. Most of the money made on the products of this place has gone to fill the pockets of people in distant cities who did not produce the products.

If my walks take me along the roads and streams, I see also the trash and the junk, carelessly manufactured and carelessly thrown away, the glass and the broken glass and the plastic and the aluminium that will lie here longer than the lifetime of trees—longer than the lifetime of our species, perhaps. And I know that this also is what we have to show for our participation in the American economy, for most of the money made on these things too has been made elsewhere.

It would be somewhat more pleasant for country people if they could blame all this on city people. But the old opposition of country versus city—though still true, and truer than ever economically, for the country is more than ever the colony of the city—is far too simple to explain our problem. For country people more and more live like city people, and so connive in their own ruin. More and more country people, like city people, allow their economic and social standards to be set by television and salesmen and outside experts. Our garbage mingles with New Jersey garbage in our local landfill, and it would be hard to tell which is which.

As local community decays along with local economy, a vast amnesia settles over the countryside. As the exposed and disregarded soil departs with the rains, so local knowledge and local memory move away to the cities or are forgotten under the influence of homogenized salestalk, entertainment, and education. This loss of local knowledge and local memory—that is, of local culture—has been ignored, or written off as one of the cheaper "prices of progress," or made the business of folklorists. Nevertheless, local culture has a value, and part of its value is economic. This can be demonstrated readily enough.

For example, when a community loses its memory, its members no longer know one another. How can they know one another if they have forgotten or have never learned one another's stories? If they do not know one another's stories, how can they know whether or not to trust one another? People who do not trust one another do not help one another, and moreover they fear one another. And this is our predicament now. Because of a general distrust and suspicion, we are all now living in jeopardy of being sued.

We don't trust our "public servants" because we know that they don't respect us. They don't respect us, as we understand, because they don't know us; they don't know our stories. They expect us to sue them if they make mistakes, and so they must insure themselves, at great expense to them and to us. Doctors in a country community must send their patients to specialists in the city, not necessarily because they believe that they are wrong in their diagnoses, but because they know that they are not infallible and they must protect themselves against lawsuits, at great expense to us.

The government of my home county, which has a population of about ten thousand people, pays an annual liability insurance premium of about $34,000. Add to this the liability premiums that are paid by every professional person who is "at risk" in the country, and you get some idea of the load we are carrying. Several decent family livelihoods are annually paid out of the county to insurance companies for a service that is only negative and provisional.

All of this money is lost to us by the failure of community. A good community, as we know, insures itself by trust, by good faith and good will, by mutual help. A good community, in other words, is a good local economy. It depends on itself for many of its essential needs and is thus shaped, so to speak, from the inside—unlike most modern populations that depend on distant purchases for almost everything and are thus shaped from the outside by the purposes and the influence of salesmen.

I was walking one Sunday afternoon several years ago with an older friend. We went by the ruining log house that had belonged to his grandparents and great-grandparents. The house stirred my friend's memory, and he told how the oldtime people used to visit each other in the evenings, especially in the long evenings of winter. There used to be a sort of institution in our part of the country known as "sitting till bedtime." After supper, when they weren't too tired, neighbors would walk across fields to visit each other. They popped corn, my friend said, and ate apples and talked. They told each other stories. They told each other stories, as I knew myself, that they all had heard before, Sometimes they told stories about each other, about themselves, living again in their own memories and thus keeping their memories alive. Among the hearers of these stories were always the children. When bedtime came, the visitors lit their lanterns and went home. My friend told about this, and thought about it, and then he said, "They had everything but money."

They were poor, as country people have often been, but they had each other, they had their local economy in which they helped each other, they had each other's comfort when they needed it, and they had their stories, their history together in that place. To have everything but money is to have much. And most people of the present can only marvel to think of neighbors entertaining themselves for a whole evening without a single imported pleasure and without listening to a single minute of sales talk.

Most of the descendants of those people have now moved away, partly because of the cultural and economic failures that I mentioned earlier, and most of them no longer sit in the evenings and talk to anyone. Most of them now sit until bedtime watching TV, submitting every few minutes to a sales talk. The message of both the TV programs and the sales talks is that the watchers should spend whatever is necessary to be like everybody else.

By television and other public means, we are encouraged to believe that we are far advanced beyond sitting till bedtime with the neighbors on a Kentucky ridgetop, and indeed beyond anything we ever were before. But if, for example, there should occur a forty-eight-hour power failure, we would find ourselves in much more backward circumstances than our ancestors. What, for starters, would we do for entertainment? Tell each other stories? But most of us no longer talk with each other, much less tell each other stories. We tell our stories now mostly to doctors or lawyers or psychiatrists or insurance adjusters or the police, not to our neighbors for their (and our) entertainment. The stories that now entertain us are made up for us in New York or Los Angeles or other centers of such commerce.

But a forty-eight-hour power failure would involve almost unimaginable deprivations. It would be difficult to travel, especially in cities. Most of the essential work could not be done. Our windowless modern schools and other such buildings that depend on air-conditioning could not be used. Refrigeration would be impossible; food would spoil. It would be difficult or impossible to prepare meals. If it was winter, heating systems would fail. At the end of forty-eight-hours many of us would be hungry.

Such a calamity (and it is a modest one among those that our time has made possible) would thus reveal how far most of us are now living from our cultural and economic sources, and how extensively we have destroyed the foundations of local life. It would show us how far we have strayed from the locally centered life of such neighborhoods as the one my friend described—a life based to a considerable extent on what we now call solar energy, which is decentralized, democratic, clean, and free. If we note that much of the difference we are talking about can be accounted for as an increasing dependence on energy sources that are centralized, undemocratic, filthy, and expensive, we will have completed a sort of historical parable.

How has this happened? There are many reasons for it. One of the chief reasons is that everywhere in our country the local succession of the generations has been broken. We can trace this change through a series of stories that we may think of as cultural landmarks.

Throughout most of our literature, the normal thing was for the generations to succeed one another in place. The memorable stories occurred when this succession failed or became difficult or was somehow threatened. The norm is given in Psalm 128, in which this succession is seen as one of the rewards of righteousness: "Thou shalt see thy children's children, and peace upon Israel."

The longing for this result seems to have been universal. It presides also over *The Odyssey*, in which Odysseus's desire to return home is certainly regarded as normal. And this story is also much concerned with the psychology of family succession. Telemachus, Odysseus's son comes of age in preparing for the return of his long-absent father; and it seems almost that Odysseus is enabled to return home by his son's achievement of enough manhood to go in search of him. Long after the return of both father and son, Odysseus's life will complete itself, as we know from Teiresia's prophecy in Book XI, much in the spirit of Psalm 128:

> A seaborne death
> soft as this hand of mist will come
> upon you
> when you are wearied out with sick
> old age,
> your country folk in blessed peace
> around you.

The Bible makes much of what it sees as the normal succession, in such stories as those of Abraham, Isaac, and Jacob, or of David and Solomon, in which the son completes the work or the destiny of the father. The parable of the prodigal son is prepared for by such Old Testament stories as that of Jacob, who errs, wanders, returns, is forgiven, and takes his place in the family lineage.

Shakespeare was concerned throughout his working life with the theme of the separation and rejoining of parents and children. It is there at the beginning in *The Comedy of Errors*, and he is still thinking about it when he gets to *King Lear* and *Pericles* and *The Tempest*. When Lear walks onstage with Cordelia dead in his arms, the theme of return is fulfilled, only this time in the way of tragedy.

Wordsworth's poem "Michael," written in 1800, is in the same line of descent. It is the story of a prodigal son, and return is still understood as the norm; before the boy's departure, he and his father make a "covenant" that he will return home and carry on his father's life as a shepherd on their ancestral pastures. But the ancient theme here has two significant differences: the son leaves home for an economic reason, and he does not return. Old Michael, the father, was long ago "bound / In surety for his brother's son." This nephew has failed in his business, and Michael is "summoned to discharge the forfeiture." Rather than do this by selling a portion of their patrimony, the aged parents decide that they must send their son to work for another kinsman in the city in order to earn the necessary money. The country people all are poor; there is no money to be earned at home. When the son has cleared the debt from the land, he will return to it to "possess it, free as the wind / That passes over it." But the son goes to the city, is corrupted by it, eventually commits a crime, and is forced "to seek a hiding place beyond the seas."

"Michael" is a sort of cultural watershed. It carries on the theme of return that goes back to the beginnings of Western culture, but that return now is only a desire and a memory; in the poem it fails to happen. Because of that failure, we see in "Michael" not just a local story of the Lake District of England, which it is, but the story of rural families in the industrial nations from Wordsworth's time until today. The children go to the cities, for reasons imposed by the external economy, and they do not return; eventually the parents die and the family land, like Michael's, is sold to a stranger. By now it has happened millions of times.

And by now the transformation of the ancient story is nearly complete. Our society, on the whole, has forgotten or repudiated the theme of return. Young people still grow up in rural families and go off to the cities, not to return. But now it is felt that this is what they *should* do. Now the norm is to leave and not return. And this applies as much to urban families as to rural ones. In the present urban economy the parent-child succession is possible only among the economically privileged. The children of industrial underlings are not likely to succeed their parents at work, and there is no reason for them to wish to do so. We are not going to have an industrial "Michael" in which it is perceived as tragic that a son fails to succeed his father on an assembly line.

According to the new norm, the child's destiny is not to succeed the parents, but to outmode them; succession has given way to supersession. And this norm is institutionalized not in great communal stories, but in the education system. The schools are no longer oriented to a cultural inheritance that it is their duty to pass on unimpaired, but to the career, which is to say the future, of the child. The orientation is thus necessarily theoretical, speculative, and mercenary. The child is not educated to return home and be of use to the place and community; he or she is educated to *leave* home and earn money in a provisional future that has nothing to do with place or community. And parents with children in school are likely to find themselves immediately separated from their children, and made useless to them, by the intervention of new educational techniques, technologies, methods, and languages. School systems innovate as compulsively and as eagerly as factories. It is no wonder that, under these circumstances, "educators" tend to look upon the parents as a bad influence and wish to take the children away from home as early as possible. And many parents, in truth, are now finding their children an encumbrance at home, where there is no useful work for them to do, and are glad enough to turn them over to the state for the use of the future. The extent to which this order of things is now dominant is suggested by a recent magazine article on the discovery of what purports to be a new idea:

> The idea that a parent can be a teacher at home has caught the attention of educators. ... Parents don't have to be graduates of Harvard or Yale to help their kids learn and achieve.*

Thus the home as a place where a child can learn becomes an *idea* of the professional "educator," who retains control of the idea. The home, as the article makes clear, is not to be a place where children may learn on their own, but a place where they are taught by parents according to the instruction of professional "educators." In fact, the Home and School Institute, Inc., of Washington, D.C. (known, of course, as "the HSI") has been "founded to show . . . how to involve families in their kids' educations."

In such ways as this, the nuclei of home and community have been invaded by the organizations, just as have the nuclei of cells and atoms. And we must be careful to see that the old cultural centers of home and community were made vulnerable to this invasion by their failure as economies. If there is no household or community economy, then family members and neighbors are no longer useful to one another. When people are no longer useful to one another, then the centripetal force of family and community fails, and people fall into dependence on exterior economies and organizations. The hegemony of professionals and professionalism erects itself on local failure, and from then on the locality exists merely as a market for consumer goods and as a source of "raw material," human and natural. The local schools no longer serve the local community; they serve the government's economy and the economy's government. Unlike the local community, the government and the economy cannot be served with affection, but only with professional zeal or professional boredom. Professionalism means more interest in salaries and less interest in what used to be known as disciplines. And so we arrive at the idea, endlessly reiterated in the news media, that education can be improved by bigger salaries for teachers— which may be true, but education cannot be improved, as the proponents too often imply, by bigger salaries alone. There must also be love of learning and of the cultural tradition and of excellence—and this love cannot exist, because it makes no sense, apart from the love of a place and a community. Without this love, education is only the importation into a local community of centrally prescribed "career preparation" designed to facilitate the export of young careerists.

Our children are educated, then, to leave home, not to stay home, and the costs of this education have been far too little acknowledged. One of the costs is psychological, and the other is at once cultural and ecological.

The natural or normal course of human growing up must begin with some sort of rebellion against one's parents, for it is clearly impossible to grow up if one remains a child. But the child, in the process of rebellion and of achieving the emotional and economic independence that rebellion ought to lead to, finally comes to understand the parents as fellow humans and fellow sufferers, and in some manner returns to them as their friend, forgiven and forgiving the inevitable wrongs of family life. That is the old norm.

The new norm, according to which the child leaves home as a student and never lives at home again, interrupts the old course of coming of age at the point of

---

*Marianne Merrill Moates, "Learning . . . Every Day," *Creative Ideas for Living*, July/August 1988, p. 89.

rebellion, so that the child is apt to remain stalled in adolescence, never achieving any kind of reconciliation or friendship with the parents. Of course, such a return and reconciliation cannot be achieved without the recognition of mutual practical need. In the present economy, however, where individual dependences are so much exterior to both household and community, family members often have no practical need or use for one another. Hence the frequent futility of attempts at a purely psychological or emotional reconciliation.

And this interposition of rebellion and then of geographical and occupational distance between parents and children may account for the peculiar emotional intensity that our society attaches to innovation. We appear to hate whatever went before, very much as an adolescent hates parental rule, and to look on its obsolescence as a kind of vengeance. Thus we may explain industry's obsessive emphasis on "this year's model," or the preoccupation of the professional "educators" with theoretical and methodological innovation. Similarly, in modern literature we have had for many years an emphasis on "originality" and "the anxiety of influence" (an adolescent critical theory), as opposed, say, to Spenser's filial admiration for Chaucer, or Dante's for Virgil.

But if the new norm interrupts the development of the relation between children and parents, that same interruption, ramifying through a community, destroys the continuity and so the integrity of local life. As the children depart, generation after generation, the place loses its memory of itself, which is its history and its culture. And the local history, if it survives at all, loses its place. It does no good for historians, folklorists, and anthropologists to collect the songs and the stories and the lore that make up local culture and store them in books and archives. They cannot collect and store—because they cannot know—

the pattern of reminding that can survive only in the living human community in its place. It is this pattern that is the life of local culture and that brings it usefully or pleasurably to mind. Apart from its local landmarks and occasions, the local culture may be the subject of curiosity or of study, but it is also dead.

The loss of local culture is, in part, a practical loss and an economic one. For one thing, such a culture contains, and conveys to succeeding generations, the history of the use of the place and the knowledge of how the place may be lived in and used. For another, the pattern of reminding implies affection for the place and respect for it, and so, finally, the local culture will carry the knowledge of how the place may be well and lovingly used, and also the implicit command to use it *only* well and lovingly. The only true and effective "operator's manual for spaceship earth" is not a book that any human will ever write; it is hundreds of thousands of local cultures.

Lacking an authentic local culture, a place is open to exploitation, and ultimately destruction, from the center. Recently, for example, I heard the dean of a prominent college of agriculture interviewed on the radio. What have we learned, he was asked, from last summer's drouth? And he replied that "we" need to breed more drouth resistance into plants, and that "we" need a government "safety net" for farmers. He might have said that farmers need to reexamine their farms and their circumstances in light of the drouth, and to think again on such subjects as diversification, scale, and the mutual helpfulness of neighbors. But he did not say that. To him, the drouth was merely an opportunity for agribusiness corporations and the government, by which the farmers and rural communities could only become more dependent on the economy that is destroying them. This is as good an example as any of the centralized thinking of a centralized economy—to which the only effective answer that I know is a strong local community with a strong local economy and a strong local culture.

For a long time now, the prevailing assumption has been that if the nation is all right, then all the localities within it will be all right also. I see little reason to believe that this is true., At present, in fact, both the nation and the national economy are living at the expense of localities and local communities—as all small-town and country people have reason to know. In rural America, which is in many ways a colony of what the government and the corporations think of as the nation, most of us have experienced the losses that I have been talking about: the departure of young people, of soil and other so-called natural resources, and of local memory. We feel ourselves crowded more and more into a dimensionless present, in which the past is forgotten and the future, even in our most optimistic "projections," is forbidding and fearful. Who can desire a future that is determined entirely by the purposes of the most wealthy and the most powerful, and by the capacities of machines?

Two questions, then, remain: Is a change for the better possible? And who has the power to make such change? I still believe that a change for the better is possible, but I confess that my belief is partly hope and partly faith. No one who hopes for improvement should fail to see and respect the signs that we may be approaching some sort of historical waterfall, past which we will not, by changing our minds, be able to change anything else. We know that at any time an ecological or a technological or a political event that we will have allowed may remove from us the power to make change and leave us with the mere necessity to submit to it. Beyond that, the

two questions are one: the possibility of change depends on the existence of people who have the power to change.

Does this power reside at present in the national government? That seems to me extremely doubtful. To any one who has read the papers during the recent presidential campaign, it must be clear that at the highest level of government there is, properly speaking, no political discussion. Are the corporations likely to help us? We know, from long experience, that the corporations will assume no responsibility that is not forcibly imposed upon them by government. The record of the corporations is written too plainly in verifiable damage to permit us to expect much from them. May we look for help to the universities? Well, the universities are more and more the servants of government and the corporations.

Most urban people evidently assume that all is well. They live too far from the exploited and endangered sources of their economy to need to assume otherwise. Some urban people are becoming disturbed about the contamination of air, water , and food, and that is promising, but there are not enough of them yet to make much difference. There is enough trouble in the "inner cities" to make them likely places of change, and evidently change is in them, but it is desperate and destructive change. As if to perfect their exploration by other people, the people of the "inner cities" are destroying both themselves and their places.

My feeling is that if improvement is going to begin anywhere, it will have to begin out in the country and in the country towns. This is not because of any intrinsic virtue that can be ascribed to rural people, but because of their circumstances. Rural people are living, and have lived for a long time, at the site of the trouble. They see all around them, every day, the marks and scars of an exploitive national economy. They have much reason, by now, to know how little real help is to be expected from somewhere else. They still have, moreover, the remnants of local memory and local community. And in rural communities there are still farms and small businesses that can be changed according to the will and the desire of individual people.

In this difficult time of failed public expectations, when thoughtful people wonder where to look for hope, I keep returning in my own mind to the thought of the renewal of the rural communities. I know that one revived rural community would be more convincing and more encouraging than all the government and university programs of the last fifty years, and I think that it could be the beginning of the renewal of our country, for the renewal of rural communities ultimately implies the renewal of urban ones. But to be authentic, a true encouragement and a true beginning, this would have to be revival accomplished mainly by the community itself. It would have to be done not from the outside by the instruction of visiting experts, but from the inside by the ancient rule of neighborliness, by the love of precious things, and by the wish to be at home.

Vine Deloria

Born in 1933 in Martin, a border town on the Pine Ridge Indian Reservation in South Dakota, Vine Deloria is a Standing Rock Sioux. Emerging from an unusual family of scholars, churchmen, and warrior-chiefs, Deloria has become a well-known spokesman for a variety of Indian causes.

He received degrees from Iowa State University and the Lutheran School of Theology at Rock Island, Illinois, and studied for his LL.B. at the University of Colorado. As executive director of the National Congress of American Indians, a member of the Board of Inquiry on Hunger and Malnutrition in the United States, and a member of the National Office for the Rights of the Indigent, Deloria has helped a number of tribes in Alaska and the Northwest with their problems. He has taught ethnic studies at Western Washington State College in Bellingham, Washington, and political science at the University of Arizona in Tucson and has authored a number of articles, and books: *Custer Died for Your Sins* (1969), *We Talk, You Listen: New Tribes, New Turf* (1970), *The Metaphysics of Modern Existence* (1979), and *A Sender of Words* (1984). "The New Individualism" (printed here) was taken from *We Talk, You Listen*. It points to the human consequences of economic overcapacity and institutionalized education as generated by the priority of economic competitiveness, and suggests an inevitable return to tribalism and commitment to the land.

ର୍ଯଚ

We Talk, You Listen (1970)
(excerpt)

The New Individualism

We have two antithetical ideas of the individual in today's society. One stems directly from the ideas held in the founding days of the Republic. At that time people assumed that a person, given free will and the right to exercise it, would generally make the correct decisions for himself and for his community. The voting franchise was thus considered to be the best method of arriving at a determination of the desires of the community at large, since any decisions made would be the result of the conscious and intelligent decisions of a number of responsible people.

This concept was more than optimistic. We have seen in practice that each person makes decisions according to his own good and hopes that somehow society will arrive at a wise and just decision in its deliberations. Unless a political movement is triggered by a charismatic political leader, society generally limps along postponing fundamental decisions because a majority of people want small adjustments and not major changes in their lives.

One theory of individualism has risen in recent years and is best characterized by the saying "do your thing." It indicates a complete freedom of movement for the individual person without regard to social goals and political movements. The remarkable thing is that the latter form of individualism has proven to be catalytic, whereas the more traditional understanding of the individual has produced stagnation and inability to comprehend mass movements.

Indians have always been the utmost individualists, but American society has failed to absorb them in its mainstream and there has been a continual warfare between the Indian tribes and the rest of society over this question. Yet the extreme individualism of the Indian has made it appear as if he would be suited above all to enter into the American social and political system. People are stunned to find that Indians totally reject American political ideology and concepts of equality, all the while being unable to reach any kind of conclusion within their own tribes as to programs and policies.

The vital difference between Indians in their individualism and the traditional individualism of Anglo-Saxon America is that the two understandings of man are built on entirely different premises. White America speaks of individualism on an economic basis. Indians speak of individualism on a social basis. While the rest of America is devoted to private property, Indians prefer to hold their lands in tribal estate, sharing the resources in common with each other. Where Americans conform to social norms of behavior and set up strata for social recognition, Indians have a free-flowing concept of social prestige that acts as a leveling device against the building of social pyramids.

Thus the two kinds of individualism are diametrically opposed to each other, and it would appear impossible to reconcile one with the other. Where the rich are admired in white society, they are not particularly welcome in Indian society. The success in economic wars is not nearly as important for Indians as it is for whites, since the sociability of individuals with each other acts as a binding tie in Indian society.

It is thus very important to understand the advent of the hippie and his subsequent influence on American life styles. The hippie, like the Indian, does not depend upon economic competition for his identity. He is more relaxed, more sociable, less worried about material goods, and more concerned with creating a community of others who share his interests and values. Youth of today fall into all grades of commitment to the new life style. Broadway shows reflect the new mode of life, books and magazines and underground newspapers chronicle it, and popular music spreads it abroad like a raging forest fire. Clothing and hair styles are creeping forward into age groups that formerly rejected out of hand a change in values.

The important thing about the hippie, and one thing that has certainly been missed by older commentators, is that the release from economic competition has created the necessity to derive a new identity based on other than economic criteria. Thus some of the most active and enthusiastic people in the new movement have been children of affluent homes that have not had to face economic competition. Born into the good life, they have been at a loss for identity since early childhood, and they have been the first generation that has been able to examine itself purely on the basis of feelings and experiences.

Older people have been horrified because their children have rejected out of hand the riches and power that they have spent so much time accumulating. They grew up in the Depression, where a lack of economic power meant relegation to a long line of unemployed, broken, status-less people. Thus the older generation promptly sought and in many cases achieved a position of economic power in which they could express their identity as a person without suffering the demeaning indignity of being another man in a long line or another number in an endless list of numbers.

The generation gap is more than an age difference in many ways. It reflects a difference in views of the world. The younger generation sees the world as inhabited by persons who must in some way relate to each other. The older genera-tion understands the world as an economic jungle where, without allies, the individual is crushed by forces beyond his control. If the world of economic reality is destroyed, then the older generation will lose identities that it has struggled all its life to achieve. If there is continued economic definition of man, then the younger generation will feel hopelessly trapped with identities it does not accept or understand.

The ideological basis of society is thus shifting every year as the older generation dies off and the younger generation becomes more radical in its search for itself. Programs such as the Peace Corps, VISTA and poverty projects are mildly regarded by older people as a means of expending excess energy of the younger generation until such time as they enter the economic wars. But these programs are looked at primarily in terms of experiences by younger people, so that service in one of these programs acts as a catalyst in deter-mining life values, and only drives more people to reject an economic determination of their lives.

When competition becomes freed from its economic foundation, as it has been in the Indian tribes, then life takes on a whole new aspect. Status depends upon the manner in which a person contributes to his community. Knowledge for knowl-edge's sake becomes an irrelevant asser-tion, because it does not directly contribute to the elevation of people within the group. It becomes much more important that a person be wise and enter into the decisions of the group than that he know a great number of facts. Science is the handmaiden of economics because it creates tools by which men can climb the economic ladder, but it is useless in a noneconomic society because it is an abstraction of life.

Eliminating economic competition from a society thus creates a change of great dimensions. Wisdom with respect to the immediate situation is much more valu-able than is the ability to consume and dispense great gobs of knowledge. Depth rather than breadth characterizes the tribal society. In the younger generation we can already see a rabid devouring of esoteric works in search of wisdom, and their poetry reflects a more sophisticated understanding of life than does the work of previous gen-erations. Dylan's poetry, for example, cari-catures the procedures by which the older generation operates, warning the youth that this is ephemeral and perhaps a charade that may fascinate but also entrap.

The outrageous clothing worn by young people emphasizes the "beautiful" aspect of their lives. It corresponds in many ways to Indian war-bonnet vanity and the desire to demonstrate acceptance by the group and honored status. It is no accident that many hippies wear beads and buck-skin, because these combine simplicity of economic origin with advertisement of per-sonal worth. Beads are extraneous to cloth-ing, yet they become an integral part of personality.

The contemporary movement toward communes also emphasizes tribalistic life and is not competitive in economic terms.

The concept of massing great stores of wealth runs counter to the demand that a person be respected in his group because of what he is. For that reason Charlie Manson's charisma was much more important than his ability to provide an economic base for his "family." As communes gather, the standard of living is defined by the group and not by outside forces. Thus communes can exist because they provide an understanding of togetherness which then defines economic reality. The older generation views it differently, feeling that economic considerations come first and neighborhoods form on that basis. Thus the suburbs are settled according to economic ability to provide and not sociability of people. Families are isolated in the suburbs because all they have in common is a bank balance of a certain size and the ability to keep it replenished.

While advocating education as the sure means of climbing the socio-economic ladder, education has been anything but individual-oriented. Children are hustled from grade to grade, whether they understand or not. Tests periodically separate the talented from the untalented and the winnowing process continues through college and graduate school. It is a simple case of running an intellectual obstacle course that keeps narrowing as the end approaches. The goal is to be certified for a job within the system. Any suggestion that the course could be covered in less time appears heretical and unworthy of consideration.

Because college and graduate schools are so costly, and because the poorer families do not have the funds to keep their children in school, education is merely an aspect of the economic system. Any particular child can be kept in the race only as long as there are funds to keep him running. When the money runs out or proves too little to continue the race, the child is finished, unless he can borrow or earn the money to remain in the competition. Recent

studies have shown that children formerly considered ineligible for college have done about as well as children considered ready for college. What was needed was economic support for the college years, not additional training to prepare them for the great challenge.

When economic competition is seen in relation to land, the question becomes WHAT is the land used for, and not WHOSE land is it. There is consequently the tendency to regard land as a commodity for sale, and no attachment can be formed with the land. People buy and sell land as if it were another piece in a game of chess, rather than understanding that they have a relationship to it. Many pieces are bought and sold and never seen by the buyers and sellers. There is consequently no feeling of responsibility to keep the land fruitful, since it is recognized only to produce economic gain. Companies and individuals consume land for their own purposes without recognizing that they are depleting their own valued resources.

The tribal-communal way of life, devoid of economic competition, views land as the most vital part of man's existence. It is THEIRS. It supports them, tells them where they live, and defines for them HOW they live. Land does not have the simple sentimentality of purple mountains majesty or the artificial coloring of slides taken by tourists. It is more than a passing fancy to be visited on a vacation and forgotten. Rather it provides a center of the universe for the group that lives on it. As such, the people who hold land in this way always have a home to go to. Their identity is secure. They live with it and do not abstract themselves from it and live off it.

Economic competition in religious life defines denominations. Churches grade people and congregations according to income received. Sermons are tailored to fit the conceptions and beliefs held by the economic class to which they are addressed. The rise of a person economically often tells his life's theological journey, traveling from Baptist to Methodist to Presbyterian to Episcopalian as his fortunes rise. In some areas economic competition defines the very buildings in which religious services are held, with escalating wars between congregations and a corresponding rise in prices for electric organs, stained-glass windows, pews and pulpits, and fast-talking preachers.

Eliminating economic determination from religious life levels the whole structure of organized religion, There is no way to distinguish between the validity of religious beliefs except by experience. Thus spirituality defines religious constituencies, and not affluence and ostentatious display. God cannot be pleased or glorified by a $10,000 organ because he does not recognize the ability to purchase as a religious criterion. The drive of youth into esoteric religions, drugs, astrology, reincarnation, and mysticism only emphasizes the individualistic aspect of religion in a noncompetitive manner. Gathering together for experiences, young people have the option of accepting or rejecting religious ideas on the basis of their own experiences rather than accepting authority outside themselves as the criteria for judgments.

The result of the new individualism is that groups are formed that have experiences in common. Status is gained according to personal recognition by others of the trueness of the individual. Consistency of viewpoint is the hallmark of the new individualism, yet the world view held by younger peoples is so comprehensive that it often appears contradictory to people of the older generation who think in rigid categories of interest.

The Woodstock Nation is thus the result of a feeling of humanity shared by a substantial number of people. In a sense it did represent a gathering of the tribes in the same way that the old Sioux nation, in the days before the white men came, met every year near Bear Butte in northwestern South Dakota, to visit, exchange presents, and renew the existence of the tribe. Many people have downgraded the youth because there have not been a series of Woodstocks each greater than the previous one. But this would degrade the very basis for meeting in concert.

Identity derived from economic status will probably be with us to some degree for a great while. It serves as a means of distinguishing between people and in turn promotes economic growth necessary to keep society operating. That is, it is not all bad and has proven useful to all Americans in a number of ways. The real problem is that we have passed the point of no return with respect to economics. Machines and computers are now so efficient that they are eliminating the ability and opportunity of most people to compete economically. Whether we like it or not we have undertaken to remove ourselves from the economic equation that was designed to support American society.

Already conservatives are talking about the guaranteed annual income, and the major part of American industry is on subsidy or economic existence guaranteed by government support. Without the ability or necessity to compete economically as a means of distinguishing between individuals, society must necessarily change to another form of identity-formation. This is what the younger generation has largely done and it happens to coincide with tribalistic forms already present in Indian tribes. Thus social movement, after four centuries of economic determinism, is reverting to pre-Columbian expressions, although modified by contemporary technology.

With machines producing an overabundance of wealth, the primary task of people will be to consume what is produced, lest the system break apart by overproduction. Agriculture already has broken apart, with large areas held out of production, and the result has been the breakdown of rural society. Suicides range higher in those rural areas where affluence and support appears to be greatest, because the people have not yet adjusted to the vacuum created by the absence of economic competition. Thus Iowa, one of the richest farm states, has had a consistently high suicide rate for a state with an apparently stable rural population.

We can look forward to a tremendous drive for social reform in spite of ourselves. Already graduates of prestige colleges and universities are going into social service programs instead of business. Public-interest law firms are on the increase. Free universities are rising everywhere. The separate disciplines of former days are being torn out of the institutions that entrapped them and thrust into the street. The university as the "marketplace of ideas" has become an absurdity, but off-campus the ideas flow with increasing vigor and insight. Even the conservation movement is gearing up to demand a reevaluation of land use for the benefit of all of society instead of the profit of a few people.

Whether we like it or not, the movement is steadily in one direction. The best that we can do is to open up as many options as possible so that the polarization of groups and group values does not freeze movements into violent confrontations. This would mean dropping traditional ideas and getting behind them to discover what we think we have been trying to do. Persecution of one group for smoking pot while another group destroys itself via nicotine and alcohol is a refusal to face reality. Subsidization of large farms while quibbling over pennies in food stamps is ridiculous. Authorizing supersonic transport planes while cutting education budgets is absurd.

In the field of education alone, radical changes could be made to open the present system up to the challenges presented by individuals. The twelve years of primary and secondary school has become a sacred cow that really defines the nature of babysitting more than it does education. We continually build more schoolhouses to "seat" so many children. We should be providing an escape hatch for those who are ready and able to go forward. If a student can read, absorb, and retain a certain amount of knowledge in a week, he should receive credit for that achievement and be able to move on. The present educational system looks the other way at students who skip classes, study hard for finals, and score high in tests. It traps a number of capable people in an endless round of classroom boredom under the pretense that mere attendance is equal to education.

By opening up social structures to rapid change, we will be allowing people to group themselves according to their interests and experiences. Formal recognition of groups will mean a coming-together of society on the realistic basis of self-interest. Each group will be incapable of overriding other groups on an economic basis, and to maintain its identity and cohesion it will have to have internal integrity. Individual people will have the right and motivation to flow through groupings on the basis of their own experiences and interests, and neighborhoods and communities will reflect a new kind of social reality that has been experienced as yet only during crises situations when everyone was thrown together in order to surviv.

The "do-your thing" doctrine of youth presents the ultimate challenge to American society, for it challenges society to expand its conception of the individual beyond the field of economics. It creates criteria by which a total sense of person and humanity can be defined. "Doing-your-thing" speaks of what a man IS, not what he HAS. In this type of change Indians are far ahead of the rest of society and may be steadily pulling away from the rest of the pack. Hence the absurdity of studies on how to bring Indians into the mainstream when the mainstream is coming to the tribe.

The change in ideology is important to recognize. It means that eventually the land upon which people lives determines how they will live. Before the coming of the white man the land was untouched. It provided for everyone and people dared not disturb it since it was the property of all. There was no need for industry or tedious work, since the land provided.

Over a period of four hundred years the white man has completely changed the land. But the land has not given up its powers. Today society is almost completely industrialized and the land is almost completely settled. Yet the wealth of natural resources and technological innovations have created a type of society in which it will not require tedious work and everyone will be forced to live in small tribal groups because that will be the only way to survive.

Thus whether the land is developed or not, and whether the people desire it or not, the land determines the forms by which societies are able to live on this continent. An undeveloped land created tribes and a fully developed land is creating tribes. In essence Indians have really won the battle for cultural survival. It remains only for years to go by and the rise of youth to continue, and everyone will be in the real mainstream of American life—the tribe.

John Rawls

Perhaps America's most influential contemporary political philosopher, John Rawls was born February 21, 1921, in Baltimore, Maryland. He taught philosophy at Princeton University, Cornell University, and the Massachusetts Institute of Technology. A member of the Harvard University faculty since 1959, he was named James Bryant Conant University Professor in 1979. As the quintessential American philosopher and educator, his life is all of one piece. He was a Fulbright fellow at Oxford in 1952 and then coeditor of *Philosophical Review* for three years, beginning in 1959. With publication of "Justice as Fairness" in the *Philosophical Review* in 1958, Rawls first announced to the world a contract theory of "distributive justice." That theory became perhaps the ultimate justification for the kind of liberal politics associated with the welfare state and liberal capitalism (a state based on the liberal ideal of the equality of opportunity). Drawing upon Hume's notion of the circumstances of justice, Kant's conception of the self, and Rousseau's moral psychology, Rawls's theory stresses the position of John Stuart Mill that "accidents of birth" are morally arbitrary. This culminates in his "difference principle," which justifies social inequalities only to the extent that they maximize the prospects of the least advantaged. This principle is but one distinctive feature of Rawls's intricate, seminal book *A Theory of Justice,* which has served to shape the dialogue on justice among late-20th-century political thinkers. *A Theory of Justice* was published in 1971 by Harvard University Press (from which the excerpts here are taken), and in 1993 another book by Rawls, *Political Liberalism,* was published.

A Theory of Justice (1971)
(excerpts)

The Role of Justice

Justice is the first virtue of social institutions, as truth is of systems of thought. A theory however elegant and economical must be rejected or revised if it is untrue; likewise laws and institutions no matter how efficient and well-arranged must be reformed or abolished if they are unjust. Each person possesses an inviolability founded on justice that even the welfare of society as a whole cannot override. For this reason justice denies that the loss of freedom for some is made right by a greater good shared by others. It does not allow that the sacrifices imposed on a few are outweighed by the larger sum of advantages enjoyed by many. Therefore in a just society the liberties of equal citizenship are taken as settled; the rights secured by justice are not subject to political bargaining or to the calculus of social interests. The only thing that permits us to acquiesce in an erroneous theory is the lack of a better one; analogously, an injustice is tolerable only when it is necessary to avoid an even greater injustice. Being first virtues of human activities, truth and justice are uncompromising.

. . . Let us assume, to fix ideas, that a society is a more or less self-sufficient association of persons who in their relations to one another recognize certain rules of conduct as binding and who for the most part act in accordance with them. Suppose further that these rules specify a system of cooperation designed to advance the good of those taking part in it. Then, although a society is a cooperative venture for mutual advantage, it is typically marked by a conflict as well as by an identity of interests. There is an identity of interests since social cooperation makes possible a better life for all than any would have if each were to live solely by his own efforts. There is a conflict of interests since persons are not indifferent as to how the greater benefits produced by their collaboration are distributed, for in order to pursue their ends they each prefer a large to a lesser share. A set of principles is required for choosing among the various social arrangements which determine this division of advantages and for underwriting an agreement on the proper distributive shares. These principles are the principles of social justice: they provide a way of assigning rights and duties in the basic institutions of society and they define the appropriate distribution of the benefits and burdens of social cooperation.

Now let us say that a society is well-ordered when it is not only designed to advance the good of its members but when it is also effectively regulated by a public conception of justice. That is, it is a society in which (1) everyone accepts and knows that the others accept the same principles of justice, and (2) the basic social institutions generally satisfy and are generally known to satisfy these principles. In this case while men may put forth excessive demands on one another, they nevertheless acknowledge a common point of view from which their claims may be adjudicated. If men's inclination to self-interest makes their vigilance against one another necessary, their public sense of justice makes their secure association together possible. Among individuals with disparate aims and purposes a shared conception of justice establishes the bonds of civic friendship; the general desire for justice limits the pursuit of other ends. One may think of a public conception of justice as constituting the fundamental charter of a well-ordered human association.

Existing societies are of course seldom well-ordered in this sense, for what is just and unjust is usually in dispute. Men disagree about which principles should define the basic terms of their association. Yet we may still say, despite this disagreement, that they each have a conception of justice. That is, they understand the need for, and they are prepared to affirm, a characteristic set of principles for assigning basic rights and duties and for determining what they take to be the proper distribution of the benefits and burdens of social cooperation. Thus it seems natural to think of the concept of justice as distinct from the various conceptions of justice and as being specified by the role which these different sets of principles, these different conceptions, have in common.[1] Those who hold different conceptions of justice can, then, still agree that institutions are just when no arbitrary

---

[1] Here I follow H. L. A. Hart, *The Concept of Law* (Oxford, The Clarendon Press, 1961), pp. 155–159.

distinctions are made between persons in the assigning of basic rights and duties and when the rules determine a proper balance between competing claims to the advantages of social life. Men can agree to this description of just institutions since the notions of an arbitrary distinction and of a proper balance, which are included in the concept of justice, are left open for each to interpret according to the principles of justice that he accepts. These principles single out which similarities and differences among persons are relevant in determining rights and duties and they specify which division of advantages is appropriate. Clearly this distinction between the concept and the various conceptions of justice settles no important questions. It simply helps to identify the role of the principles of social justice.

Some measure of agreement in conceptions of justice is, however, not the only prerequisite for a viable human community. There are other fundamental social problems, in particular those of coordination, efficiency, and stability. Thus the plans of individuals need to be fitted together so that their activities are compatible with one another and they can all be carried through without anyone's legitimate expectations being severely disappointed. Moreover, the execution of these plans should lead to the achievement of social ends in ways that are efficient and consistent with justice. And finally, the scheme of social cooperation must be stable: it must be more or less regularly complied with and its basic rules willingly acted upon; and when infractions occur, stabilizing forces should exist that prevent further violations and tend to restore the arrangement. Now it is evident that these three problems are connected with that of justice. In the absence of a certain measure of agreement on what is just and unjust, it is clearly more difficult for individuals to coordinate their plans efficiently in order to insure that mutually beneficial arrangements are maintained. Distrust and resentment corrode the ties of civility, and suspicion and hostility tempt men to act in ways they would otherwise avoid. So while the distinctive role of conceptions of justice is to specify basic rights and duties and to determine the appropriate distributive shares, the way in which a conception does this is bound to affect the problems of efficiency, coordination, and stability. We cannot, in general, assess a conception of justice by its distributive role alone, however useful this role may be in identifying the concept of justice. We must take into account its wider connections; for even though justice has a certain priority, being the most important virtue of institutions, it is still true that, other things equal, one conception of justice is preferable to another when its broader consequences are more desirable.

The Subject of Justice

... For us the primary subject of justice is the basic structure of society, or more exactly, the way in which the major social institutions distribute fundamental rights and duties and determine the division of advantages from social cooperation. By major institutions I understand the political constitution and the principal economic and social arrangements. Thus the legal protection of freedom of thought and liberty of conscience, competitive markets, private property in the means of production, and the monogamous family are examples of major social institutions. Taken together as one scheme, the major institutions define men's rights and duties and influence their life-prospects, what they can expect to be and how well they can hope to do. The basic structure is the primary subject of justice because its effects are so profound and present from the start. The intuitive notion here is that this structure contains various social positions and that men born into different positions have different expectations of life determined, in part, by the political system as well as by economic and social circumstances. In this way the institutions of society favor certain starting places over others. These are especially deep inequalities. Not only are they pervasive, but they affect men's initial chances in life; yet they cannot possibly be justified by an appeal to the notions of merit or desert. It is these inequalities, presumably inevitable in the basic structure of any society, to which the principles of social justice must in the first instance apply. These principles, then, regulate the choice of a political constitution and the main elements of the economic and social system. The justice of a social scheme depends essentially on how fundamental rights and duties are assigned and on the economic opportunities and social conditions in the various sectors of society.

. . . I shall be satisfied if it is possible to formulate a reasonable conception of justice for the basic structure of society conceived for the time being as a closed system isolated from other societies. The significance of this special case is obvious and needs no explanation. It is natural to conjecture that once we have a sound theory for this case, the remaining problems of justice will prove more tractable in the light of it. . . .

The other limitation on our discussion is that for the most part I examine the principles of justice that would regulate a well-ordered society. Everyone is presumed to act justly and to do his part in upholding just institutions. Though justice may be, as Hume remarked, the cautious, jealous virtue, we can still ask what a perfectly just society would be like.[2] Thus I consider primarily what I call strict compliance as opposed to partial compliance theory. The latter studies the principles that govern how we are to deal with injustice. It comprises such topics as the theory of punishment, the doctrine of just war, and the justification of the various ways of opposing unjust regimes, ranging from civil disobedience and militant resistance to revolution and rebellion. Also included here are questions of compensatory justice and of weighing one form of institutional injustice against another. Obviously the problems of partial compliance theory are the pressing and urgent matters. These are the things that we are faced with in everyday life. The reason for beginning with ideal theory is that it provides, I believe, the only basis for the systematic grasp of these more pressing problems. The discussion of civil disobedience, for example, depends upon it. At least, I shall assume that a deeper understanding can be gained in no other way, and that the nature and aims of a perfectly just society is the fundamental part of the theory of justice. . . .

The Main Idea of the Theory of Justice

My aim is to present a conception of justice which generalizes and carries to a higher level of abstraction the familiar theory of the social contract as found, say, in Locke,

---

[2]*An Enquiry Concerning the Principles of Morals*, sec. III, pt. I, par. 3, ed. L. A. Selby-Bigge, 2nd edition (Oxford, 1902), p. 184.

Rousseau, and Kant.[3] In order to do this we are not to think of the original contract as one to enter a particular society or to set up a particular form of government. Rather, the guiding idea is that the principles of justice for the basic structure of society are the object of the original agreement. They are the principles that free and rational persons concerned to further their own interests would accept in an initial position of equality as defining the fundamental terms of their association. These principles are to regulate all further agreements; they specify the kinds of social cooperation that can be entered into and the forms of government that can be established. This way of regarding the principles of justice I shall call justice as fairness.

Thus we are to imagine that those who engage in social cooperation choose together, in one joint act, the principles which are to assign basic rights and duties and to determine the division of social benefits. Men are to decide in advance how they are to regulate their claims against one another and what is to be the foundation charter of their society. Just as each person must decide by rational reflection what constitutes his good, that is, the system of ends which it is rational for him to pursue, so a group of persons must decide once and for all what is to count among them as just and unjust. The choice which rational men would make in this hypothetical situation of equal liberty, assuming for the present

that this choice problem has a solution, determines the principles of justice.

In justice as fairness the original position of equality corresponds to the state of nature in the traditional theory of the social contract. This original position is not, of course, thought of as an actual historical state of affairs, much less as a primitive condition of culture. It is understood as a purely hypothetical situation characterized so as to lead to a certain conception of justice.[4] Among the essential features of this situation is that no one knows his place in society, his class position or social status, nor does any one know his fortune in the distribution of natural assets and abilities, his intelligence, strength, and the like. I shall even assume that the parties do not know their conceptions of the good or their special psychological propensities. The principles of justice are chosen behind a veil of ignorance. This ensures that no one is advantaged or disadvantaged in the choice of principles by the outcome of natural chance or the contingency of social circumstances. Since all are similarly situated and no one is able to design principles to favor his particular condition, the principles of justice are the result of a fair agreement or bargain. For given the circumstances of the original position, the symmetry of everyone's relations to each other, this initial situation is fair between individuals as moral persons, that is, as rational beginnings with their own ends

---

[3]As the text suggests, I shall regard Locke's *Second Treatise of Government*, Rousseau's *The Social Contract*, and Kant's ethical works beginning with *The Foundations of the Metaphysics of Morals* as definitive of the contract tradition. For all of its greatness, Hobbes's *Leviathan* raises special problems. A general historical survey is provided by J. W. Gough, *The Social Contract*, 2nd ed. (Oxford, The Clarendon Press, 1957), and Otto Gierke, *Natural Law and the Theory of Society*, trans. with an introduction by Ernest Barker (Cambridge, The University Press, 1934). A presentation of the contract view as primarily an ethical theory is to be found in G. R. Grice, *The Grounds of Moral Judgment* (Cambridge, The University Press, 1967).

[4]Kant is clear that the original agreement is hypothetical. See *The Metaphysics of Morals*, pt. I (*Rechtslehre*); and pt. II of the essay "Concerning the Common Saying: This May Be True in Theory but It Does Not Apply in Practice," in *Kant's Political Writings*, ed. Hans Reiss and trans. by H. B. Nisbet (Cambridge, The University Press, 1970), pp. 73–87. See Georges Vlachos, *La Pensée politique de Kant* (Paris, Presses Universitaires de France, 1962), pp. 326–335; and J. G. Murphy, *Kant: The Philosophy of Right* (London, Macmillan, 1970), pp. 109–112, 133–136, for a further discussion.

and capable, I shall assume, of a sense of justice. The original position is, one might say, the appropriate initial status quo, and thus the fundamental agreements reached in it are fair. This explains the propriety of the name "justice as fairness": it conveys the idea that the principles of justice are agreed to in an initial situation that is fair. The name does not mean that the concepts of justice and fairness are the same, any more than the phrase "poetry as metaphor" means that the concepts of poetry and metaphor are the same.

Justice as fairness begins, as I have said, with one of the most general of all choices which persons might make together, namely, with the choice of the first principles of a conception of justice which is to regulate all subsequent criticism and reform of institutions. Then, having chosen a conception of justice, we can suppose that they are to choose a constitution and a legislature to enact laws, and so on, all in accordance with the principles of justice initially agreed upon. ... No society can, of course, be a scheme of cooperation which men enter voluntarily in a literal sense; each person finds himself placed at birth in some particular position in some particular society, and the nature of this position materially affects his life prospects. Yet a society satisfying the principles of justice as fairness comes as close as a society can to being a voluntary scheme, for it meets the principles which free and equal persons would assent to under circumstances that are fair. In this sense its members are autonomous and the obligations they recognize self-imposed.

One feature of justice as fairness is to think of the parties in the initial situation as rational and mutually disinterested. This does not mean that the parties are egoists, that is, individuals with only certain kinds of interests, say in wealth, prestige, and domination. But they are conceived as not taking an interest in one another's interests. They are to presume that even their spiri-

tual aims may be opposed, in the way that the aims of those of different religions may be opposed. Moreover, the concept of rationality must be interpreted as far as possible in the narrow sense, standard in economic theory, of taking the most effective means to given ends. ...

In working out the conception of justice as fairness one main task clearly is to determine which principles of justice would be chosen in the original position. To do this we must describe this situation in some detail and formulate with care the problem of choice which it presents. These matters I shall take up in the immediately succeeding chapters. It may be observed, however, that once the principles of justice are thought of as arising from an original agreement in a situation of equality, it is an open question whether the principle of utility would be acknowledged. Offhand it hardly seems likely that persons who view themselves as equals, entitled to press their claims upon one another, would agree to a principle which may require lesser life prospects for some simply for the sake of a greater sum of advantages enjoyed by others. Since each desires to protect his interests, his capacity to advance his conception of the good, no one has a reason to acquiesce in an enduring loss for himself in order to bring about a greater net balance of satisfaction. In the absence of strong and lasting benevolent impulses, a rational man would not accept a basic structure merely because it maximized the algebraic sum of advantages irrespective of its permanent effects on his own basic rights and interests. Thus it seems that the principle of utility is incompatible with the conception of social cooperation among equals for mutual advantage. It appears to be inconsistent with the idea of reciprocity implicit in the notion of a well-ordered society. Or, at any rate, so I shall argue.

I shall maintain instead that the persons in the initial situation would choose two rather different principles: the first requires equality in the assignment of basic rights and duties, while the second holds that social and economic inequalities, for example inequalities of wealth and authority, are just only if they result in compensating benefits for everyone, and in particular for the least advantaged members of society. These principles rule out justifying institutions on the grounds that the hardships of some are offset by a greater good in the aggregate. It may be expedient but it is not just that some should have less in order that others may prosper. But there is no injustice in the greater benefits earned by a few provided that the situation of persons not so fortunate is thereby improved. The intuitive idea is that since everyone's well-being depends upon a scheme of cooperation without which no one could have a satisfactory life, the division of advantages should be such as to draw forth the willing cooperation of everyone taking part in it, including those less well situated. . . .

The Original Position and Justification

I have said that the original position is the appropriate initial status quo which insures that the fundamental agreements reached in it are fair. This fact yields the name "justice as fairness." It is clear, then, that I want to say that one conception of justice is more reasonable than another, or justifiable with respect to it, if rational persons in the initial situation would choose its principles over those of the other for the role of justice. Conceptions of justice are to be ranked by their acceptability to persons so circumstanced. Understood in this way the question of justification is settled by working out a problem of deliberation: we have to ascertain which principles it would be rational to adopt given the contractual situation. This connects the theory of justice with the theory of rational choice.

One should not be misled, then, by the somewhat unusual conditions which characterize the original position. The idea here is simply to make vivid to ourselves the restrictions that it seems reasonable to impose on arguments for principles of justice, and therefore on these principles themselves. Thus it seems reasonable and generally acceptable that no one should be advantaged or disadvantaged by natural fortune or social circumstances in the choice of principles. It also seems widely agreed that it should be impossible to tailor principles to the circumstances of one's own case. We should insure further that particular inclinations and aspirations, and persons' conceptions of their good do not affect the principles adopted. The aim is to rule out those principles that it would be rational to propose for acceptance, however little the chance of success, only if one knew certain things that are irrelevant from the standpoint of justice. For example, if a man knew that he was wealthy, he might find it rational to advance the principle that various taxes for welfare measures be counted unjust; if he knew that he was poor, he would most likely propose the contrary principle. To represent the desired restrictions one imagines a situation in which everyone is deprived of this sort of information. One excludes the knowledge of those contingencies which sets men at odds and allows them to be guided by their prejudices. In this manner the veil of ignorance is arrived at in a natural way. This concept should cause no difficulty if we keep in mind the constraints on arguments that it is meant to express. At any time we can enter the original position, so to speak, simply by following a certain procedure, namely, by arguing for principles of justice in accordance with these restrictions.

It seems reasonable to suppose that the parties in the original position are equal. That is, all have the same rights in the procedure for choosing principles; each can make proposals, submit reasons for their acceptance, and so on. Obviously the purpose of these conditions is to represent equality between human beings as moral persons, as creatures having a conception of their good and capable of a sense of justice. The basis of equality is taken to be similarity in these two respects. Systems of ends are not ranked in value; and each man is presumed to have the requisite ability to understand and to act upon whatever principles are adopted. Together with the veil of ignorance, these conditions define the principles of justice as those which rational persons concerned to advance their interests would consent to as equals when none are known to be advantaged or disadvantaged by social and natural contingencies.

. . . This is an order which requires us to satisfy the first principle in the ordering before we can move on to the second, the second before we consider the third, and so on. A principle does not come into play until those previous to it are either fully met or do not apply. A serial ordering avoids, then, having to balance principles at all; those earlier in the ordering have an absolute weight, so to speak, with respect to later ones, and hold without exception. We can regard such a ranking as analogous to a sequence of constrained maximum principles. For we can suppose that any principle in the order is to be maximized subject to the condition that the preceding principles are fully satisfied. As an important special case I shall, in fact, propose an ordering of this kind by ranking the principle of equal liberty prior to the principle regulating economic and social inequalities. This means, in effect, that the basic structure of society is to arrange the inequalities of wealth and authority in ways consistent with the equal liberties required by the preceding principle. . . .

Democratic Equality and the Difference Principle

. . . This principle removes the indeterminateness of the principle of efficiency by singling out a particular position from which the social and economic inequalities of the basic structure are to be judged. Assuming the framework of institutions required by equal liberty and fair equality of opportunity, the higher expectations of those better situated are just if and only

if they work as part of a scheme which improves the expectations of the least advantaged members of society. The intuitive idea is that the social order is not to establish and secure the more attractive prospects of those better off unless doing so is to the advantage of those less fortunate. . . .

The Problem of Justice Between Generations

We must now consider the question of justice between generations. There is no need to stress the difficulties that this problem

raises. It subjects any ethical theory to severe if not impossible tests. Nevertheless, the account of justice as fairness would be incomplete without some discussion of this important matter. The problem arises in the present context because the question is still open whether the social system as a whole, the competitive economy surrounded by the appropriate family of background institutions, can be made to satisfy the two principles of justice. The answer is bound to depend, to some degree anyway, on the level at which the social minimum is to be set. But this in turn connects up with how far the present generation is bound to respect the claims of its successors.

So far I have said nothing about how generous the social minimum should be. Common sense might be content to say that the right level depends upon the average wealth of the country and that, other things equal, the minimum should be higher when the average increases. Or one might say that the proper level is determined by customary expectations. But these suggestions are unsatisfactory. The first is not precise enough since it does not say how the minimum depends on average wealth and it overlooks other relevant aspects such as distribution; while the second provides no criterion for telling when customary expectations are themselves reasonable. Once the difference principle is accepted, however, it follows that the minimum is to be set at that point which, taking wages into account, maximizes the expectations of the least advantaged group. By adjusting the amount of transfers (for example, the size of supplementary income payments), it is possible to increase or decrease the prospects of the more disadvantaged, their index of primary goods (as measured by wages plus transfers), so as to achieve the desired result.

Now offhand it might seem that the difference principle requires a very high minimum. One naturally imagines that the greater wealth of those better off is to be scaled down until eventually everyone has nearly the same income. But this is a misconception, although it might hold in special circumstances. The appropriate expectation in applying the difference principle is that of the long-term prospects of the least favored extending over future generations. Each generation must not only preserve the gains of culture and civilization, and maintain intact those just institutions that have been established, but it must also put aside in each period of time a suitable amount of real capital accumulation. This saving may take various forms from net investment in machinery and other means of production to investment in learning and education. Assuming for the moment that a just savings principle is available which tells us how great investment should be, the level of the social minimum is determined. Suppose for simplicity that the minimum is adjusted by transfers paid for by proportional expenditure (or income) taxes. In this case raising the minimum entails increasing the proportion by which consumption (or income) is taxed. Presumably as this fraction becomes larger there comes a point beyond which one of two things happens. Either the appropriate savings cannot be made or the greater taxes interfere so much with economic efficiency that the prospects of the least advantaged in the present generation are no longer improved but begin to decline. In either event the correct minimum has been reached. The difference principle is satisfied and no further increase is called for.

The Two Principles of Justice for Institutions

... Having noted these cases of priority, I now wish to give the final statement of the two principles of justice for institutions.

For the sake of completeness, I shall give a full statement including earlier formulations.

First Principle

Each person is to have an equal right to the most extensive total system of equal basic liberties compatible with a similar system of liberty for all.

Second Principle

Social and economic inequalities are to be arranged so that they are both:

(a) to the greatest benefit of the least advantaged, consistent with the just savings principle, and

(b) attached to offices and positions open to all under conditions of fair equality of opportunity.

First Priority Rule (The Priority of Liberty)

The principles of justice are to be ranked in lexical order and therefore liberty can be restricted only for the sake of liberty. There are two cases:

(a) a less extensive liberty must strengthen the total system of liberty shared by all;

(b) a less than equal liberty must be acceptable to those with the lesser liberty.

Second Priority Rule (The Priority of Justice over Efficiency and Welfare)

The second principle of justice is lexically prior to the principle of efficiency and to that of maximizing the sum of advantages; and fair opportunity is prior to the difference principle. There are two cases:

(a) an inequality of opportunity must enhance the opportunities of those with the lesser opportunity;

(b) an excessive rate of saving must on balance mitigate the burden of those bearing this hardship.

General Conception

All social primary goods—liberty and opportunity, income and wealth, and the bases of self-respect—are to be distributed equally unless an unequal distribution of any or all of these goods is to the advantage of the least favored. . . .

Robert Nozick

Robert Nozick became known through his writing and teaching as an original spokesman for radical libertarianism and the minimal state. Born in 1938 in Brooklyn, New York, Nozick received his B.A. from Columbia University and his M.A. and Ph.D. in philosophy from Princeton. He began his teaching career at Princeton and then moved to Harvard. There, as a professor of philosophy, he distinguished himself by teaching a new course each year, reportedly never teaching the same course twice.

Countering the distributive theory of justice of John Rawls, Nozick pushed the position of liberalism to the extreme in *Anarchy, State and Utopia* (1974), arguing that individual rights are paramount and that the basic function of the state is to act as a dominant insurance agency to protect private property. Nozick resurrects the legitimacy of Adam Smith's notion of "the invisible hand." Smith believed that if all individuals rationally pursue their own self-interests, their activities will spill over into benefits for the community as if some invisible hand brought individual efforts together to ensure this result. In addition to a number of professional articles, Nozick also authored *Philosophical Explanations* (1982)—"A person's life goals can shine forth"—and *The Examined Life* (1989). The following excerpt from his first book, which won the National Book Award in 1975, is his response to John Rawls's theory of justice.

❦

Anarchy, State and Utopia (1974)
(excerpt)

Rawls' Theory

We can bring our discussion of distributive justice into sharper focus by considering in some detail John Rawls' recent contribution to the subject. *A Theory of Justice* is a powerful, deep, subtle, wide-ranging, systematic work in political and moral philosophy which has not seen its like since the writings of John Stuart Mill, if then. It is a fountain of illuminating ideas, integrated together into a lovely whole. Political philosophers now must either work within Rawls' theory or explain why not. The considerations and distinctions we have developed are illuminated by, and help illuminate, Rawls' masterful presentation of an alternative conception. Even those who remain unconvinced after wrestling with Rawls' systematic vision will learn much from closely studying it. I do not speak only of the Millian sharpening of one's views in combating (what one takes to be) error. It is impossible to read Rawls' book without incorporating much, perhaps transmuted, into one's own deepened view. And it is impossible to finish his book without a new and inspiring vision of what a moral theory may attempt to do and unite; of how *beautiful* a whole theory can be. I permit myself to concentrate here on disagreements with Rawls only because I am confident that my readers will have discovered for themselves its many virtues.

Social Cooperation

I shall begin by considering the role of the principles of justice. Let us assume, to fix ideas, that a society is a more or less self-sufficient association of persons who in their relations to one another recognize certain rules of conduct as binding and who for the most part act in accordance with them. Suppose further that these rules specify a system of cooperation designed to advance the good of those taking part in it. Then, although a society is a cooperative venture for mutual advantage, it is typically marked by a conflict as well as by an identity of interests. There is an identity of interests since social cooperation makes possible a better life for all than any would have if each were to live solely by his own efforts. There is a conflict of interests since persons are not indifferent as to how the greater benefits produced by their collaboration are distributed, for in order to pursue their ends they each prefer a larger to a lesser share. A set of principles is required for choosing among the various social arrangements which determine this division of advantages and for underwriting an agreement on the proper distributive shares. These principles are the principles of social justice: they provide a way of assigning rights and duties in the basic institutions of society and they define the appropriate distribution of the benefits and burdens of social cooperation.

Let us imagine n individuals who do not cooperate together and who each live solely by their own efforts. Each person i receives a payoff, return, income, and so forth, S_i; the sum total of what each individual gets acting separately is

$$S = \sum_{i=1}^{n} S_i$$

By cooperating together they can obtain a larger sum total T. The problem of distributive social justice, according to Rawls, is how these benefits of cooperation are to be distributed or allocated. This problem might be conceived of in two ways: how is the total T to be allocated? Or, how is the incremental amount due to social cooperation, that is the benefits of social cooperation $T - S$, to be allocated? The latter formulation assumes that each individual i receives from the subtotal S of T, his share S_i. The two statements of the problem differ. When combined with the noncooperative distribution of S (each i getting S_i), a "fair-looking" distribution of $T - S$ under the second version may not yield a "fair-looking" distribution of T (the first version). Alternatively, a fair-looking distribution of T may give a particular individual i less than his share S_i. (The constraint $T_i \geq S_i$ on the answer to the first formulation of the problem, where T_i is the share of the ith individual, would exclude this possibility.) Rawls, without distinguishing these two formulations of the problem, writes as though his concern is the first one, that is, how the total sum T is to be distributed. One might claim, to support a focus on the first issue, that due to the enormous benefits of social cooperation, the noncooperative shares S_i are so small in comparison to any cooperative ones T_i that they may be ignored in setting up the problem of social justice. Though we should note that this certainly is not how people entering into cooperation with one another would agree to conceive of the problem of dividing up cooperation's benefits.

Why does social cooperation *create* the problem of distributive justice? Would there be no problem of justice and no need for a theory of justice, if there was no social cooperation at all, if each person got his share solely by his own efforts? If we suppose, as Rawls seems to, that this situation does *not* raise questions of distributive justice, then in virtue of what facts about social cooperation do these questions of justice emerge? What is it about social cooperation that gives rise to issues of justice? It cannot be said that there will be conflicting claims only where there is social cooperation; that individuals who produce independently and (initially) fend for themselves will not make claims of justice on each other. If there were ten Robinson Crusoes, each working alone for two years on separate islands, who discovered each other and the facts of their different allotments by radio communication via transmitters left twenty years earlier, could they not make claims on each other, supposing it were possible to transfer goods from one island to the next? Wouldn't the one with least make a claim on ground of need, or on the ground that his island was naturally poorest, or on the ground that he was naturally least capable of fending for himself? Mightn't he say that justice demanded he be given some more by the others, claiming it unfair that he should receive so much less and perhaps be destitute, perhaps starving? He might go on to say that the different individual non-cooperative shares stem from different natural endowments, which are not deserved, and that the task of justice is to rectify these arbitrary facts and inequities. Rather than its being the case that no one *will* make such claims in the situation lacking social cooperation, perhaps the point is that such claims clearly would be without merit. Why would they clearly be without merit? In the social noncooperation situation, it might be said, each individual deserves what he gets unaided by his own efforts; or rather, no one else can make a claim *of justice* against this holding. It is pellucidly clear in this situation who is entitled to what, so no theory of justice is needed. On this view social cooperation introduces a muddying of the waters that makes it unclear or indeterminate who is entitled to what. Rather than saying that no theory of justice applies to this noncooperative case, (wouldn't it be unjust if someone stole another's products in the noncooperative situation?), I would say that it is a clear case of application of the correct theory of justice: the entitlement theory.

How does social cooperation change things so that the same entitlement principles that apply to the noncooperative cases become inapplicable or inappropriate to cooperative ones? It might be said that one cannot disentangle the contributions of distinct individuals who cooperate; everything is everyone's joint product. On this joint product, or on any portion of it, each person plausibly will make claims of equal strength; all have an equally good claim, or at any rate no person has a distinctly better claim than any other. Somehow (this line of thought continues), it must be decided how this total product of joint social cooperation (to which individual entitlements do not apply differentially) is to be divided up: this is the problem of distributive justice.

Don't individual entitlements apply to parts of the cooperatively produced product? First, suppose that social cooperation is based upon division of labor, specialization, comparative advantage, and exchange; each person works singly to transform some input he receives, contracting with others who further transform or transport his product until it reaches its ultimate consumer. People cooperate in making things but they work separately; each person is a miniature firm. The products of each person are easily identifiable, and exchanges are made in open markets with prices set competitively, given informational constraints, and so forth. In such a system of social cooperation, what is the task of a theory of justice? It might be said that whatever holdings result will depend upon the exchange ratios or prices at which exchanges are made, and therefore that the task of a theory of justice is to set criteria for "fair prices." This is hardly the place to trace the serpentine windings of theories of a just price. It is difficult to see why these issues should even arise here. People are choosing to make exchanges with other people and to transfer entitlements, with no restrictions on their freedom to trade with any other party at any mutually acceptable ratio. Why does such sequential social cooperation, linked together by people's voluntary exchanges, raise any special problems about how things are to be distributed? Why isn't the appropriate (a not inappropriate) set of holdings just the one which *actually occurs* via this process of mutually-agreed-to exchanges whereby people choose to give to others what they are entitled to give or hold?

Let us now drop our assumption that people work independently, cooperating only in sequence via voluntary exchanges, and instead consider people who work together jointly to produce something. Is it now impossible to disentangle people's respective contributions? The question here is not whether marginal productivity theory is an appropriate theory of fair or just shares, but whether there is some coherent notion of identifiable marginal product. It seems unlikely that Rawls' theory rests on the strong claim that there is no such reasonably serviceable notion. Anyway, once again we have a situation of a large number of bilateral exchanges: owners of resources reaching separate agreements with entrepreneurs about the use of their resources, entrepreneurs reaching agreements with individual workers, or groups of workers first reaching some joint agreement and then presenting a package to an entrepreneur, and so forth. People transfer their holdings or labor in free markets, with the exchange ratios (prices) determined in the usual manner. If marginal productivity theory is reasonably adequate, people will be receiving, in these voluntary transfers of holdings, roughly their marginal products.[1]

But if the notion of marginal product were so ineffective that factors' marginal products in actual situations of joint production could not be identified by hirers or purchasers of the factors, then the resulting distribution to factors would not be patterned in accordance with marginal product. Someone who viewed marginal productivity theory, where it was applicable, *as a patterned theory of justice,* might think that such situations of joint production and indeterminate marginal product provided an opportunity for some theory of justice to enter to determine appropriate exchange ratios. But an entitlement theorist would find acceptable whatever distribution resulted from the party's voluntary exchanges. The questions about the workability of marginal productivity theory are intricate ones. Let us merely note here the strong personal incentive for owners of resources to converge to the marginal product, and the strong market pressures tending to produce this result. Employers of factors of productions are not all dolts who don't know what they're doing, transferring holdings they value to others on an irrational and arbitrary basis. Indeed, Rawls' position on inequalities requires that separate contributions to joint products be isolable, to some extent at least. For Rawls goes out of his way to argue that inequalities are justified if they serve to raise the position of the worst-off group in the society, if without the inequalities the worst-off group would be even more worse off. These serviceable inequalities stem, at least in part, from the necessity to provide incentives to certain people to perform various activities or fill various roles that not everyone can do equally well. (Rawls is *not* imagining that inequalities are needed to fill positions that everyone can do equally well, or that the most drudgery-filled positions that require the least skill will command the highest income.) But *to whom* are the incentives to be paid? To which performers of what activities? When it is necessary to provide incentives to some to perform their productive activities, there is no talk of a joint social product from which no individual's contribution can be disentangled. If the product was all that inextricably joint, it couldn't be known that the extra incentives were going to the crucial persons; and it couldn't be known that the additional product produced by these now motivated people is greater than the expenditure to them in incentives. So it couldn't be known whether the provision of incentives was efficient or not, whether it involved a net gain or a net loss. But Rawls' discussion of justifiable inequalities

---

[1] Receiving this, we should note, is not the same as receiving the equivalent of what the person *causes* to exist, or *produces.* The marginal product of a unit of F_1 with respect to factor $F_2. \ldots , F_n$ is a *subjunctive* notion; it is the difference between the total product of $F_1. \ldots , F_n$ used most efficiently (as efficiently as known how, given prudence about many costs in finding out the most efficient use of factors) and the total product of the most efficient use of $F_2, \ldots , F_n$ along with a unit of F_1. But these two different most efficient uses of $F_2, \ldots , F_n$ along with a unit less of F_1 (one with the additional unit F_1, the other without it) will use them differently. And F_1's marginal product (with respect to the other factors), what everyone reasonably would pay for an additional unit of F_1, will not be what it *causes* (*it* causes) combined with $F_2, \ldots , F_n$ and the other units of F_1, but rather the difference it makes, the difference there would be if this unit of F_1 were absent and the remaining factors were organized most efficiently to cope with its absence. Thus marginal productivity theory is not best thought of as a theory of actual produced product, of those things whose causal pedigree includes the unit of the factor, but rather as a theory of the difference (subjunctively defined) made by the presence of a factor. *If* such a view were connected with justice, it would seem to fit best with an entitlement conception.

presupposes that these things can be known. And so the claim we have imagined about the indivisible, nonpartitionable nature of the joint product is seen to dissolve, leaving the reasons for the view that social cooperation creates special problems of distributive justice otherwise not present, unclear if not mysterious.

Terms of Cooperation and the Difference Principle

Another entry into the issue of the connection of social cooperation with distributive shares brings us to grips with Rawls' actual discussion. Rawls imagines rational, mutually disinterested individuals meeting in a certain situation, or abstracted from their other features not provided for in this situation. In this hypothetical situation of choice, which Rawls calls "the original position," they choose the first principles of a conception of justice that is to regulate all subsequent criticism and reform of their institutions. While making this choice, no one knows his place in society, his class position or social status, or his natural assets and abilities, his strength, intelligence, and so forth.

> The principles of justice are chosen behind a veil of ignorance. This ensures that no one is advantaged or disadvantaged in the choice of principles by the outcome of natural chance or the contingency of social circumstances. Since all are similarly situated and no one is able to design principles to favor his particular condition, the principles of justice are the result of a fair agreement or bargain.

What would persons in the original position agree to?

> Persons in the initial situation would choose two . . . principles: the first requires equality in the assignment of basic rights and duties, while the second holds that social and economic inequalities, for example, inequalities of wealth and authority are just only if they result in compensating benefits for everyone, and in particular

for the least advantaged members of society. These principles rule out justifying institutions on the grounds that the hardships of some are offset by a greater good in the aggregate. It may be expedient but it is not just that some should have less in order that others may prosper. But there is no injustice in the greater benefits earned by a few provided that the situation of persons not so fortunate is thereby improved. The intuitive idea is that since everyone's well-being depends upon a scheme of cooperation without which no one could have a satisfactory life, the division of advantages should be such as to draw forth the willing cooperation of everyone taking part in it, including those less well situated. Yet this can be expected only if reasonable terms are proposed. The two principles mentioned seem to be a fair agreement on the basis of which those better endowed, or more fortunate in their social position, neither of which we can be said to deserve, could expect the willing cooperation of others when some workable scheme is a necessary condition of the welfare of all.

This second principle, which Rawls specifies as the difference principle, holds that the institutional structure is to be so designed that the worst-off group under it is at least as well off as the worst-off group (not necessarily the same group) would be under any alternative institutional structure. If persons in the original position follow the minimax policy in making the significant choice of principles of justice, Rawls argues, they will choose the difference principle. Our concern here is not whether persons in the position Rawls describes actually would minimax and actually would choose the particular principles Rawls specifies. Still, we should question why individuals in the original position would choose a principle that focuses upon groups, rather than individuals. Won't application of the minimax principle lead each person in the original position to favor maximizing the position of the worst-off *individual?* To be sure, this principle would reduce questions of evaluating social institutions to the issue of how the unhappiest depressive fares. Yet avoiding this by moving the focus to groups (or representative individuals) seems *ad hoc,* and is inadequately motivated for those in the individual position. Nor is it clear which groups are appropriately considered; why exclude the group of depressives or alcoholics or the representative paraplegic?

If the difference principle is not satisfied by some institutional structure *J,* then under *J* some group *G* is worse off than it would be under another institutional structure *I* that satisfies the principle. If another group *F* is better off under *J* than it would be under the *I* favored by the difference principle, is this sufficient to say that under *J* "some . . . have less in order that others may prosper"? (Here one would have in mind that *G* has less in order that *F* prosper. Could one also make the same statement about *I*? Does *F* have less under *I* in order that *G* may prosper?) Suppose that in a society the following situation prevailed:

1. Group *G* has amount *A* and group *F* has amount *B*, with *B* greater than *A*. Also things could be arranged differently so that *G* would have more than *A*, and *F* would have less than *B*. (The difference arrangement might involve a mechanism to transfer some holdings from *F* to *G*.)

Is this sufficient to say

2. *G* is badly off *because F* is well off; *G* is badly off *in order that F* be well off; *F*'s being well off makes *G* badly off; *G* is badly off *on account of F*'s being well off; *G* is not better off *because of* how well off *F* is.

If so, does the truth of statement 2 depend on *G*'s being in a worse position than *F?* There is yet another possible institutional structure *K* that transfers holdings from the worse-off group *G* to *F*, making *G* even more worse off. Does the possibility of *K* make it true to say that, under *J, F* is not (even) better off because of how well off *G* is?

We do not normally hold that the truth of a subjunctive (as in 1) is alone sufficient for the truth of some indicative causal statement (as in 2). It would improve my life in various ways if you were to choose to become my devoted slave, supposing I could get over the initial discomfort. Is the cause of my present state your not becoming my slave? Because your enslaving yourself to a poorer person would improve his lot and worsen yours, are we to say that the poor person is badly off because you are as well off as you are; has he less in order that you may prosper? From

3. If *P* were to do act *A* then *Q* would not be in situation *S*.

we will conclude

4. *P*'s not doing *A* is responsible for *Q*'s being in situation *S; P*'s not doing *A* causes *Q* to be in *S*.

only if we *also* believe that

5. *P* ought to do act *A,* or *P* has a duty to do act *A,* or *P* has an obligation to do act *A,* and so forth.

Thus the inference from 3 to 4, in this case, *presupposes* 5. One cannot argue from 3 to 4 as one step in order *to get to* 5. The statement that in a particular situation some have less in order that others may prosper is often based upon the very evaluation of a situation or an institutional framework that it is introduced to support. Since this evaluation does *not* follow merely from the subjunctive (for example, 1 or 3) an *independent* argument must be produced for it.[2]

Rawls holds, as we have seen, that

> since everyone's well-being depends upon a scheme of cooperation without which no one could have a satisfactory life, the division of advantages should be such as to draw forth the willing cooperation of everyone taking part in it, including those less well situated. Yet this can be expected only if reasonable terms are proposed. The two principles mentioned seem to be a fair agreement on the basis of which those better endowed or more fortunate in their social position . . . could expect the willing cooperation of others when some workable scheme is a necessary condition of the welfare of all.

No doubt, the difference principle presents terms on the basis of which those less well endowed would be willing to cooperate. (What *better* terms could they propose for themselves?) But is this a fair agreement on the basis of which those *worse* endowed could expect the *willing* cooperation of others? With regard to the existence of gains from social cooperation, the situation is symmetrical. The better endowed gain by cooperating with the worse endowed, *and* the worse endowed gain by cooperating with the better endowed. Yet the difference principle is not neutral between the better and the worse endowed. Whence the asymmetry?

Perhaps the symmetry is upset if one asks *how much* each gains from the social cooperation. This question might be under-

stood in two ways. How much do people benefit from social cooperation, as compared to their individual holdings in a *non*-cooperative scheme? That is, how much is $T_i - S_i$, for each individual i? Or, alternatively, how much does each individual gain from general social cooperation, as compared, not with *no* cooperation, but with more limited cooperation? The latter is the more appropriate question with regard to general social cooperation. For failing general agreement on the principles to govern how the benefits of general social cooperation are to be held, not everyone will remain in a noncooperative situation if there is some other beneficial cooperative arrangement involving some, but not all, people, whose participants *can* agree. These people will participate in this more narrow cooperative arrangement. To focus upon the benefits of the better and the worse endowed cooperating together, we must try to imagine less extensive schemes of partitioned social cooperation in which the better endowed cooperate only among themselves and the worse endowed cooperate only among themselves, with no cross-cooperation. The members of both groups gain from the internal cooperation within their respective groups and have larger shares than they would if there were no social cooperation at all. An individual benefits from the wider system of extensive cooperation between the better and the worse endowed to the extent of his incremental gain from this wider cooperation; namely, the amount by which his share under a scheme of general cooperation is greater than it would be under one of limited intragroup (but not cross-group) cooperation. *General* cooperation will be of more benefit to the better or to the worse endowed if (to pick a simple criterion) the

---

[2]Though Rawls does not clearly distinguish 2 from 1 and 4 from 3, I do not claim that he makes the illegitimate step of sliding from the latter subjunctive to the former indicative. Even so, the mistake is worth pointing out because it is an easy one to fall into, and it might appear to prop up positions we argue against.

mean incremental gain from general cooperation (when compared with limited intragroup cooperation) is greater in one group than it is in the other.

One might speculate about whether there is an inequality between the groups' mean incremental gains and, if so, which way it goes. If the better-endowed group includes those who manage to accomplish something of great economic advantage to others, such as new inventions, new ideas about production or ways of doing things, skill at economic tasks, and so on,[3] it is difficult to avoid concluding that the *less* well endowed gain *more* than the better endowed do from the scheme of general cooperation. What follows from this conclusion? I do *not* mean to imply that the better endowed should get even more than they get under the entitlement system of general social cooperation.[4] What *does* follow from the conclusion is a deep suspicion of imposing, in the name of fairness, constraints upon voluntary social cooperation (and the set of holdings that arises from it) so that those already benefiting

most from this general cooperation benefit even more!

Rawls would have us imagine the worse-endowed persons say something like the following: "Look, better endowed: you gain by cooperating with us. If you want our cooperation you'll have to accept reasonable terms. We suggest these terms: We'll cooperate with you only if we get *as much as possible.* That is, the terms of our cooperation should give us that maximal share such that, if it was tried to give us more, we'd end up with less." How generous these proposed terms are might be seen by imagining that the better endowed make the almost symmetrical opposite proposal: "Look, worse endowed: you gain by cooperating with *us.* If you want our cooperation you'll have to accept reasonable terms. We propose these terms: We'll cooperate with you so long as *we* get as much as possible. That is, the terms of our cooperation should give us the maximal share such that, if it was tried to give us more, we'd end up with less." If these terms seem outrageous, as they are, why don't

---

[3]They needn't be *better endowed,* from birth. In the context in which Rawls uses it, all "better endowed" means is: accomplishes more of economic value, able to do this, has a high marginal product, and so forth. (The role that unpredictable factors play in this complicates imagining a prior partitioning of the two groups.) The text follows Rawls in categorizing persons as "better" and "worse" endowed only in order to criticize the considerations *he* adduces for his theory. The entitlement theory does not rest upon any assumption that the classification is an important one, or even a possible one, or upon any elitist presupposition.

Since the entitlement theorist does not accept the patterned principle "to each according to his natural endowment," he can easily grant that what an exercised endowment brings in the market will depend upon the endowments of others and how they choose to exercise them, upon the market-expressed desires of buyers, upon the alternate supply of what he offers and of what others may substitute for what he offers, and upon other circumstances summing the myriad choices and actions of others. Similarly, we saw earlier that the similar considerations Rawls adduces about the social factors upon which the marginal product of labor depends (*Theory of Justice,* p. 308) will not faze an entitlement theorist, even though they might undercut the rationale put forth by a proponent of the patterned principle of distribution according to marginal product.

[4]Supposing they could identify themselves and each other, they might *try* to exact a larger share by banding together as a group and bargaining jointly with the others. Given the large numbers of persons involved and the incentive for some of the better-endowed individuals to break ranks and reach separate agreements with the worse endowed, if such a coalition of the better endowed is unable to impose sanctions on its defectors it will dissolve. The better endowed remaining in the coalition may use boycott as a "sanction," and refuse to cooperate with a defector. To break the coalition, those less well endowed would have to (be able to) offer someone better endowed sufficient incentive to defect to make up for his loss through no longer being able to cooperate with the other better-endowed persons. Perhaps it would pay for someone to defect from the coalition only as part of a sizable group of defectors, which defecting group the initial coalition might try to keep small by special offers to individuals to defect *from it,* and so on. The problem is a complicated one, further complicated by the obvious fact (despite our use of Rawls' classificatory terminology) that there is no sharp line of cleavage between the endowments of people to determine which groups would form.

the terms proposed by those worse endowed seem the same? Why shouldn't the better endowed treat this latter proposal as beneath consideration, supposing someone to have the nerve explicitly to state it?

Rawls devotes much attention to explaining why those less well favored should not complain at receiving less. His explanation, simply put, is that because the inequality works for his advantage, someone less well favored shouldn't complain about it; he receives *more* in the unequal system than he would in an equal one. (Though he might receive still more in another unequal system that placed someone else below him.) But Rawls discusses the question of whether those *more* favored will or should find the terms satisfactory *only* in the following passage, where A and B are any two representative men with A being the more favored:

> The difficulty is to show that A has no grounds for complaint. Perhaps he is required to have less than he might since his having more would result in some loss to B. Now what can be said to the more favored man? To begin with, it is clear that the well-being of each depends on a scheme of social cooperation without which no one could have a satisfactory life. Secondly, we can ask for the willing cooperation of everyone only if the terms of the scheme are reasonable. The difference principle, then, seems to be a fair basis on which those better endowed, or more fortunate in their social circumstances, could expect others to collaborate with them when some workable arrangement is a necessary condition of the good of all.

What Rawls imagines being said to the more favored men does *not* show that these men have no grounds for complaint, nor does it at all diminish the weight of whatever complaints they have. That the well-being of all depends on social cooperation without which no one could have a satisfactory life could also be said to the less well endowed by someone proposing any other principle, including that of maximizing the position of the best endowed. Similarly for the fact that we can ask for the willing cooperation of everyone only if the terms of the scheme are reasonable. The question is: What terms *would be* reasonable? What Rawls imagines being said thus far merely sets up his problem; it doesn't distinguish his proposed difference principle from the almost symmetrical counterproposal that we imagined the better endowed making, or from any other proposal. Thus, when Rawls continues, "The difference principle, then, seems to be a fair basis on which those best endowed, or more fortunate in their social circumstances, could expect others to collaborate with them when some workable arrangement is a necessary condition of the good of all," the presence of the "then" in his sentence is puzzling. Since the sentences which precede it are neutral between his proposal and any other proposal, the conclusion that the difference principle presents a fair basis for cooperation *cannot* follow from what precedes it in this passage. Rawls is merely repeating that it seems reasonable; hardly a convincing reply to anyone to whom it doesn't seem reasonable.[5] Rawls has not shown that the more favored man A has no grounds

---

[5] I treat Rawls' discussion here as one concerning better- and worse-endowed individuals who know they are so. Alternatively, one might imagine that *these* considerations are to be weighed by someone in the original position. ("If I turn out to be better endowed then . . . ; if I turn out to be worse endowed then . . .") But this construal will not do. Why would Rawls bother saying, "The two principles . . . seem to be a fair agreement on the basis of which those better endowed or more fortunate in their social position could expect the willing

for complaint at being required to have less in order that another *B* might have more than he otherwise would. And he can't show this, since *A does* have grounds for complaint. Doesn't he?

The Original Position and End-Result Principles

How can it have been supposed that these terms offered by the less well endowed are fair? Imagine a social pie somehow appearing so that *no one* has any claim at all on any portion of it, no one has any more of a claim than any other person; yet there must be unanimous agreement on how it is to be divided. Undoubtedly, apart from threats or holdouts in bargaining, an equal distribution would be suggested and found plausible as a solution. (It is, in Schelling's sense, a focal point solution.) If *somehow* the size of the pie wasn't fixed, and it was realized that pursuing an equal distribution somehow would lead to a smaller total pie than otherwise might occur, the people might well agree to an unequal distribution which raised the size of the least share. But in any actual situation, wouldn't this realization reveal something about differential claims on parts of the pie? Who is it that could make the pie larger, and would do it if given a larger share, but not if given an equal share under the scheme of equal distribution? To whom is an incentive to be provided to make the larger contribution? (There's no talk here of inextricably entangled joint product;

cooperation of others" (*Theory of Justice*, p. 15). Who is doing the expecting when? How is this to be translated into subjunctives to be contemplated by someone in the original position? Similarly, questions arise about Rawls' saying, "The difficulty is to show that *A* has no grounds for complaint. Perhaps he is required to have less than he might since his having more would result in some loss to *B*. *Now what can be said to the more favored man? . . .* The difference principle then seems to be a fair basis on which those better endowed . . . could expect others to collaborate with them . . . " (*Theory of Justice*, p. 103, my italics). Are we to understand this as: someone in the original position wonders what to say to himself as he then thinks of the possibility that he will turn out to be one of the better endowed? And does he then say that the difference principle *then* seems a fair basis for cooperation despite the fact that, and even while, he is contemplating the possibility that he is better endowed? Or does he say then that even later if and when he knows he is better endowed the difference principle will seem fair to him at that later time? And when are we to imagine him possibly complaining? Not while in the original position, for then he is agreeing to the difference principle. Nor does he worry, while in the process of deciding in the original position, that he will complain later. For he knows that he will have no cause to complain later at the effects of whatever principle he himself rationally will choose soon in the original position. Are we to imagine him complaining against himself? And isn't the answer to any later complaint, "You agreed to it (or you would have agreed to it if so originally positioned)"? What "difficulty" does Rawls concern himself with here? Trying to squeeze it into the original position makes it completely mysterious. And what is thinking of what is a "fair agreement" (sect. 3) or a "fair basis" (p. 103) doing here anyway. in the midst of the rational self-interested calculations of persons in the original position, who do not then knowingly possess, or at any rate utilize, particular moral notions?

I see no coherent way to incorporate how Rawls treats and speaks of the issue of the terms of cooperation between the better and the worse endowed into the structure and perspective of the original position. Therefore my discussion considers Rawls here as addressing himself to individuals *outside* the original position, either to better-endowed individuals or to his readers, to convince *them* that the difference principle which Rawls extracts from the original position is fair. It is instructive to compare how Rawls imagines justifying the social order to a person in the worst-off group in an unequal society. Rawls wants to tell this person that the inequalities work out to his advantage. This is told to someone who knows who he is: "The social order can be justified to everyone, and in particular to those who are least favored" (p. 103). Rawls does not want to say, "You would have gambled, and you lost," or any such thing, even "You chose it then in the original position"; nor does he wish merely to address someone in the original position. He also wants a consideration apart from the original position that will convince someone who knows of his inferior position in an unequal society. To say, "You have less in order that I may prosper," would *not* convince someone who knows of his inferior position, and Rawls rightly rejects it, even though its subjunctive analogue for someone in the original position, if we could make sense of this, would not be without force.

it's known *to whom* incentives are to be offered, or at least to whom a bonus is to be paid after the fact.) Why doesn't this identifiable differential contribution lead to some differential entitlement?

If things fell from heaven like manna, and no one had any special entitlement to any portion of it, and no manna would fall unless all agreed to a particular distribution, and somehow the quantity varied depending on the distribution, then it is plausible to claim that persons placed so that they couldn't make threats, or hold out for specially large shares, would agree to the difference principle rule of distribution. But is *this* the appropriate model for thinking about how the things people produce are to be distributed? Why think the same results could obtain for situations where there *are* differential entitlements as for situations where there are not?

A procedure that founds principles of distributive justice on what rational persons who know nothing about themselves or their histories would agree to *guarantees that end-state principles of justice will be taken as fundamental.* Perhaps some historical principles of justice are derivable from end-state principles, as the utilitarian tries to derive individual rights, prohibitions on punishing the innocent, and so forth, from *his* end-state principle; perhaps such arguments can be constructed even for the entitlement principle. But no historical principle, it seems, could be agreed to in the first instance by the participants in Rawls' original position. For people meeting together behind a veil of ignorance to decide who gets what, knowing nothing about any special entitlements people may have, will treat anything to be distributed as manna from heaven. . . .[6]

Michael J. Sandel

A critic of the ability of liberalism to provide a sufficient basis for justice and social ethics, Michael J. Sandel represents the "communitarian movement." Born in 1953, Sandel has been a professor of government at Harvard University since 1980, teaching one of the most popular undergraduate courses, called "Justice." A *summa cum laude* graduate of Brandeis University in 1975, he received his doctorate in politics and philosophy in 1981 from Oxford University, where he was a Rhodes scholar.

In 1988, Sandel argued that President Reagan's political genius stemmed from bringing together two contending strands of American conservatism: (1) the individualistic, libertarian, laissez-faire; and (2) the communal, traditionalist, Moral Majoritarian. To seize the nation's political agenda, he maintained, the Democrats had to correct the failure of their progressive liberalism to provide a vision for the common good based on a public policy of self-government and community. In short, ideas alone won't wash without a moral communitarian edge.

Lecturing widely on ethics, political philosophy, and American politics, Sandel became well known through his critique of the moral and political philosophy of contemporary liberalism, *Liberalism and the Limits of Justice,* published by Cambridge University

---

[6]Do the people in the original position ever wonder whether *they* have the *right* to decide how everything is to be divided up? Perhaps they reason that since they are deciding this question, they must assume they are entitled to do so; and so particular people can't have particular entitlements to holdings (for then they wouldn't have the right to decide together on how all holdings are to be divided); and hence everything legitimately may be treated like manna from heaven.

Press in 1982. Here he extends the dialogue on the attempt of John Rawls to salvage the deontological (duty-based) tradition in political ethics, demonstrating that this vision may be not so much liberated as disempowered. As moral agents, Sandel argues, individuals are rarely in a social position to construct their own notion of "right" nor to choose their own ends (other than matching preexisting desires that are undifferentiated as to worth with the best-available means of satisfying them). Liberalism, in short, must be transcended.

❧

Liberalism and the Limits of Justice (1982)
(excerpts)

Introduction: Liberalism and the Primacy of Justice

This is an essay about liberalism. The liberalism with which I am concerned is a version of liberalism prominent in the moral and legal and political philosophy of the day: a liberalism in which the notions of justice, fairness, and individual rights play a central role, and which is indebted to Kant for much of its philosophical foundation. As an ethic that asserts the priority of the right over the good, and is typically defined in opposition to utilitarian conceptions, the liberalism I have in mind might best be described as "deontological liberalism," a formidable name for what I think will appear a familiar doctrine.

"Deontological liberalism" is above all a theory about justice, and in particular about the primacy of justice among moral and political ideals. Its core thesis can be stated as follows: society, being composed of a plurality of persons, each with his own aims, interests, and conceptions of the good, is best arranged when it is governed by principles that do not *themselves* presuppose any particular conception of the good; what justifies these regulative principles above all is not that they maximize the social welfare or otherwise promote the

good, but rather that they conform to the concept of *right,* a moral category given prior to the good and independent of it.

This is the liberalism of Kant and of much contemporary moral and political philosophy, and it is this liberalism that I propose to challenge. Against the primacy of justice, I shall argue for the limits of justice, and, by implication, for the limits of liberalism as well. The limits I have in mind are not practical but conceptual. My point is not that justice, however noble in principle, is unlikely ever fully to be realized in practice, but rather that the limits reside in the ideal itself. For a society inspired by the liberal promise, the problem is not simply that justice remains always to be achieved, but that the vision is flawed, the aspiration incomplete. But before exploring these limits, we must see more clearly what the claim for the primacy of justice consists in.

The Foundations of Liberalism: Kant versus Mill

The primacy of justice can be understood in two different but related ways. The first is a straightforward moral sense. It says that justice is primary in that the demands of justice outweigh other moral and political interests, however pressing these others may be. On this view, justice is not merely one value among others, to be weighed and considered as the occasion arises, but the highest of all social virtues, the one that must be met before others can make their claims. If the happiness of the world could be advanced by unjust means alone, not happiness but justice would properly prevail. And when justice issues in certain individual rights, even the general welfare cannot override them.

But the primacy of justice, in its moral sense alone, hardly distinguishes this liberalism from other well-known varieties. Many liberal thinkers have emphasized the importance of justice and insisted on the sanctity of individual rights. John Stuart Mill called justice "the chief part, and incomparably the most sacred and binding part, of all morality" (1863: 465), and Locke held man's natural rights to be stronger than any commonwealth could override (1690). But neither was a deontological liberal in the deeper sense that concerns us here. For the full deontological ethic is not only about morals but also about the foundation of morals. It concerns not just the weight of the moral law, but also the means of its derivation, what Kant would call its "determining ground" (1788).

On the full deontological view, the primacy of justice describes not only a moral priority but also a privileged form of justification; the right is prior to the good not only in that its claims take precedence, but also in that its principles are independently derived. This means that, unlike other practical injunctions, principles of justice are justified in a way that does not depend on any particular vision of the good. To the contrary: given its independent status, the right constrains the good and sets its bounds." The concept of good and evil is

not defined prior to the moral law, to which, it would seem, the former would have to serve as foundation; rather the concept of good and evil must be defined after and by means of the law" (Kant 1788: 65).

From the standpoint of moral foundations, then, the primacy of justice amounts to this: the virtue of the moral law does not consist in the fact that it promotes some goal or end presumed to be good. It is instead an end in itself, given prior to all other ends, and regulative with respect to them. Kant distinguishes this second-order, foundational sense of primacy from the first-order, moral sense as follows:

> By primacy between two or more things connected by reason, I understand the prerogative of one by virtue of which it is the prime ground of determination of the combination with the others. In a narrower practical sense it refers to the prerogative of the interest of one so far as the interest of the others is subordinated to it and is not itself inferior to any other (1788: 124).

The contrast might also be drawn in terms of two different senses of deontology. In its moral sense, deontology opposes *consequentialism*; it describes a first-order ethic containing certain categorical duties and prohibitions which take unqualified precedence over other moral and practical concerns. In its foundational sense, deontology opposes *teleology*; it describes a form of justification in which first principles are derived in a way that does not presuppose any final human purposes or ends, nor any determinate conception of the human good.

... Even if the desire for happiness were universally shared, it could not serve as basis for the moral law. Persons would still differ in their conceptions of what happiness consists in, and to install any particular conception as regulative would impose on some the conceptions of others, and so deny at least to some the freedom to advance their own conceptions. It would create a society where some were coerced by the values of others, rather than one where the needs of each harmonized with the ends of all. "Men have different views on the empirical end of happiness and what it consists of, so that as far as happiness is concerned, their will cannot be brought under any common principle nor thus under any external law harmonizing with the freedom of everyone" (Kant 1793: 73–4).

For Kant, the priority of right is "derived entirely from the concept of *freedom* in the mutual external relationships of human beings, and has nothing to do with the end which all men have by nature (i.e. the aim of achieving happiness) or with the recognized means of attaining this end" (1793: 73). As such, it must have a basis prior to all empirical ends. Even a union founded on some common end which all members share will not do. Only a union "as an end in itself which they all ought to share and which is thus an absolute and primary duty in all external relationships whatsoever among human beings" can secure justice and avoid the coercion of some by the convictions of others. Only in such a union can no one "compel me to be happy in accordance with his conception of the welfare of others" (1793: 73–4). Only when I am governed by principles that do not presuppose any particular ends am I free to pursue my own ends consistent with a similar freedom for all. . . .

But this raises the question what the basis of the right could possibly be. If it must be a basis prior to all purposes and ends, unconditioned even by "the special circumstances of human nature" (1785: 92), where could such a basis conceivably be found? Given the stringent demands of

the deontological ethic, the moral law would seem almost to require a foundation in nothing, for any material precondition would undermine its priority. "Duty!" asks Kant at his most lyrical, "What origin is there worthy of thee, and where is to be found the root of thy noble descent which proudly rejects all kinship with the inclinations?" (1788: 89).

His answer is that the basis of the moral law is to be found in the subject, not the object of practical reason, a subject capable of an autonomous will. No empirical end but rather "a subject of ends, namely a rational being himself, must be made the ground for all maxims of action" (1785: 105). Nothing other than "the subject of all possible ends himself" can give rise to the right, for only this subject is also the subject of an autonomous will. Only such a subject could be that "something which elevates man above himself as a part of the world of sense" and enables him to participate in an ideal, unconditioned realm wholly independent of our social and psychological inclinations. And only this thoroughgoing independence can afford us the detachment we need if we are ever freely to choose for ourselves, unconditioned by the contingencies of circumstance. On the deontological view, what matters above all is not the ends we choose but our capacity to choose them. And this capacity, being prior to any particular end it may affirm, resides in the subject. "It is nothing else than personality, i.e., the freedom and independence from the mechanism of nature regarded as a capacity of a being which is subject to special laws (pure practical laws given by its own reason)" (1788: 89).

The Transcendental Subject

. . . *Qua* object of experience, I belong to the sensible world; my actions are determined, as the movements of all other objects are determined, by the laws of nature and the regularities of cause and effect. *Qua* subject of experience, by contrast, I inhabit an intelligible or super-sensible world; here, being independent of the laws of nature, I am capable of autonomy, capable of acting according to a law I give myself.

Only from this second standpoint can I regard myself as free, "for to be independent of determination by causes in the sensible world (and this is what reason must always attribute to itself) is to be free" (Kant 1786: 120). Were I wholly an empirical being, I would not be capable of freedom, for every exercise of will would be conditioned by the desire for some object. All choice would be heteronomous choice, governed by the pursuit of some end. My will could never be a first cause, only the effect of some prior cause, the instrument of one or another impulse or inclination. In so far as we think of ourselves as free, we cannot think of ourselves as merely empirical beings. "When we think of ourselves as free, we transfer ourselves into the intelligible world as members and recognize the autonomy of the will" (Kant 1785: 121). And so the notion of a subject prior to and independent of experience, such as the deontological ethic requires, appears not only possible but indispensable, a necessary presupposition of the possibility of self-knowledge and of freedom.

. . . For justice to be primary, certain things must be true of us. We must be creatures of a certain kind, related to human circumstance in a certain way. In particular, we must stand to our circumstance always at a certain distance, conditioned to be sure, but part of us always antecedent to any conditions. Only in this way can we view ourselves as subjects as well as objects of experience, as agents and not just instruments of the purposes we pursue. Deontological liberalism supposes that we can, indeed must, understand ourselves as independent in this sense. I shall argue that we cannot, and that, in the partiality of this self-image, the limits of justice can be found.

Where, then, does the deontological theory of the person go wrong? How do its shortcomings undermine the primacy of justice, and what rival virtue appears when the limits of justice are found? These are the questions this essay seeks to answer. To set the stage for my argument it will be helpful first to consider two other challenges that might be made to the Kantian view.

The Sociological Objection

The first might be called the sociological objection, for it begins by emphasizing the pervasive influence of social conditions in shaping individual values and political arrangements. It claims that liberalism is wrong because neutrality is impossible, and that neutrality is impossible because try as we might we can never wholly escape the effects of our conditioning. All political orders thus embody *some* values; the question is *whose* values prevail, and who gains and loses as a result. The vaunted independence of the deontological subject is a liberal illusion. It misunderstands the fundamentally "social" nature of man, the fact that we are conditioned beings "all the way down." There is no point of exemption, no transcendental subject capable of standing outside society or outside experience. We are at every moment what we have become, a concatenation of desires and inclinations with nothing left over to inhabit a noumenal realm. The priority of the subject can only mean the priority of the individual, thus biasing the conception in favor of individualistic values familiar to the liberal tradition. Justice only *appears* primary because this individualism typically gives rise to conflicting claims. The limits of justice would therefore consist in the possibility of cultivating those co-operative virtues, such as altruism and benevolence, that render conflict less pressing. But these are precisely the virtues least likely to flourish in a society founded on individualistic assumptions. In short, the ideal of a society governed by neutral principles is liberalism's false promise. It affirms individualistic values while pretending to a neutrality which can never be achieved. . . .

Deontology with a Humean Face

The second challenge poses a deeper difficulty with the Kantian subject. Like the first, it comes from an empiricist direction. But unlike the first, it seeks to secure deontological liberalism rather than oppose it. In fact this second challenge is less an objection to the Kantian view than a sympathetic reformulation. It embraces the priority of the right over the good, and even affirms the priority of the self over its ends. Where this view departs from Kant is in denying that a prior and independent self can only be a transcendental, or noumenal subject, lacking altogether an empirical foundation. This "revisionist" deontology captures the spirit of much contemporary liberalism, and finds its fullest expression in the work of John Rawls. "To develop a viable Kantian conception of justice," he writes, "the force and content of Kant's doctrine must be detached from its background in transcendental idealism" and recast within the "canons of a reasonable empiricism" (Rawls 1977: 165).

For Rawls, the Kantian conception suffers from obscurity and arbitrariness, for it is unclear how an abstract, disembodied

subject could without arbitrariness produce determinate principles of justice, or how in any case the legislation of such a subject would apply to actual human beings in the phenomenal world. The idealist metaphysic, for all its moral and political advantage, cedes too much to the transcendent, and in positing a noumenal realm wins for justice its primacy only at the cost of denying it its human situation.

And so Rawls takes as his project to preserve Kant's deontological teaching by replacing Germanic obscurities with a domesticated metaphysic less vulnerable to the charge of arbitrariness and more congenial to the Anglo-American temper. His proposal is to derive first principles from a hypothetical choice situation (the "original position"), characterized by conditions meant to yield a determinate outcome fit for actual human beings. Not the kingdom of ends but the ordinary circumstances of justice—as borrowed from Hume—prevail there. Not an ever-receding moral future but a present firmly planted in human circumstance provides justice its occasion. If deontology be the result, it will be deontology with a Humean face.[1] . . .

The Priority of the Self

But what exactly is the sense in which justice, as the arbiter of values, "must" be prior with respect to them? One sense of this priority is a *moral* "must" which emerges from Rawls' critique of utilitarian ethics. From this point of view, the priority of justice is a requirement of the essential plurality of the human species and the integrity of the individuals who comprise it. To sacrifice justice for the sake of the general good is to violate the inviolable,

[1] I am indebted to Mark Hulbert for suggesting this phrase.

to fail to respect the distinction between persons.

> Each person possesses an inviolability founded on justice that even the welfare of society as a whole cannot override. For this reason justice denies that the loss of freedom for some is made right by a greater good shared by others. It does not allow that the sacrifices imposed on a few are outweighed by the larger sum of advantages enjoyed by many. Therefore in a just society the liberties of equal citizenship are taken as settled; the rights secured by justice are not subject to political bargaining or to the calculus of social interests (3–4).[2]

But there is another sense in which justice "must" be prior to the values it appraises—prior in the sense of independently derived—and this has to do with a problematic feature of standards of judgment generally. It is an epistemological rather than a moral requirement, and arises from the problem of distinguishing a standard of assessment from the thing being assessed. As Rawls insists, we need an "Archimedean point" from which to assess the basic structure of society. The problem is to give an account of where such a point could conceivably be found. Two possibilities seem to present themselves, each equally unsatisfactory: if the principles of justice are derived from the values or conceptions of the good current in the society, there is no assurance that the critical standpoint they provide is any more valid than the conceptions they would regulate, since, as a product of those values, justice would be subject to the same contingencies. The alternative would seem a standard somehow external to the values and interests prevailing in society. But if our experience were disqualified entirely as the source of such principles, the alternative would seem to be reliance on a priori assumptions

whose credentials would appear equally suspect, although for opposite reasons. Where the first would be arbitrary because contingent, the second would be arbitrary because groundless. Where justice derives from existing values, the standards of appraisal blur with the objects of appraisal and there is no sure way of picking out the one from the other. Where justice is given by a priori principles, there is no sure way of connecting them up.

These then are the perplexing and difficult demands of the Archimedean point— to find a standpoint neither compromised by its implication in the world nor dissociated and so disqualified by detachment. "We need a conception that enables us to envision our objective from afar" (22), but not *too* far; the desired standpoint is "not a perspective from a certain place beyond the world, nor the point of view of a transcendent being; rather it is a certain form of thought and feeling that rational persons can adopt within the world" (587). . . .

Liberalism without Metaphysics: The Original Position

The original position is Rawls' answer to Kant; it is his alternative to the route represented by the *Critique of Pure Reason* and the key to Rawls' solution to the perplexities we have considered. It is the original position that "enables us to envisage our objective from afar," but not so far as to land us in the realm of transcendence. It aims to satisfy these demands by describing an initial situation of fairness and defining as just those principles that rational parties subject to its conditions would agree to.

Two crucial ingredients equip the original position to solve the dilemmas described by the reconstructions and to answer the need for an Archimedean point.

---

[2]All page numbers given alone in round brackets refer to Rawls 1971, *A Theory of Justice*, Oxford.

Each takes the form of an assumption about the parties to the original position: one says what they do not know, the other, what they do know. What they do not know is any information that would distinguish any one of them from any other as the particular human beings they are. This is the assumption of the veil of ignorance. It means that the parties are assumed to be deprived of any knowledge of their place in society, their race, sex, or class, their wealth or fortune, their intelligence, strength, or other natural assets and abilities. Nor even do they know their conceptions of the good, their values, aims, or purposes in life. They know that they do in fact possess such conceptions and deem them worthy of advancement, whatever they are, but must choose the principles of justice in temporary ignorance of them. The purpose of this restriction is to prevent the choice of principles from being prejudiced by the contingency of natural and social circumstances, to abstract from all considerations deemed irrelevant from a moral point of view. It is the veil of ignorance that assures that the principles of justice will be chosen under conditions of equality and fairness. Since the parties to the contract are not distinguished by different interests, a further consequence of the veil of ignorance is to assure that the initial agreement be unanimous.

What the parties do know is that they, like everyone else, value certain primary social goods. Primary goods are "things which it is supposed a rational man wants whatever else he wants," and include such things as rights and liberties, opportunities and powers, income and wealth. Regardless of a person's values, plans, or ultimate aims, it is assumed there are certain things of which he would prefer more rather than less, on the grounds that they are likely to be useful in advancing all ends, whatever ends they happen to be. So while the parties to the original position are ignorant of their particular ends, they are all assumed to be motivated by the desire for certain primary goods.

The precise content of the list of primary goods is given by what Rawls calls the thin theory of the good. It is thin in the sense that it incorporates minimal and widely shared assumptions about the kinds of things likely to be useful to all particular conceptions of the good, and therefore likely to be shared by persons whatever their more specific desires. The thin theory of the good is distinguished from the full theory of the good in that the thin theory can provide no basis for judging or choosing between various particular values or ends. So while the veil of ignorance provides that the parties deliberate in conditions of fairness and unanimity, the account of primary goods generates the minimal motivations necessary to get a problem of rational choice going, and to make possible a determinate solution. Together, the two assumptions assure that the parties act only on those interests that are common interests, that is, common to all rational persons, the foremost of which turns out to be an interest in establishing terms of social cooperation such that each person will have the fullest liberty to realize his aims and purposes compatible with an equal liberty for others. . . .

Conclusion: Liberalism and the Limits of Justice

For justice to be the first virtue, certain things must be true of us. We must be creatures of a certain kind, related to human circumstance in a certain way. We must stand at a certain distance from our circumstance, whether as transcendental subject in the case of Kant, or as essentially unencumbered subject of possession in the case of Rawls. Either way, we must regard ourselves as independent: independent from the interests and attachments we may have at any moment, never identified by our aims but always capable of standing back to survey and assess and possibly to revise them (Rawls 1979: 7; 1980: 544–5).

Deontology's Liberating Project

Bound up with the notion of an independent self is a vision of the moral universe this self must inhabit. Unlike classical Greek and medieval Christian conceptions, the universe of the deontological ethic is a place devoid of inherent meaning, a world "disenchanted" in Max Weber's phrase, a world without an objective moral order. Only in a universe empty of *telos,* such as seventeenth-century science and philosophy affirmed,[3] is it possible to conceive a subject apart from and prior to its purposes and ends. Only a world ungoverned by a purposive order leaves principles of justice open to human construction and conceptions of the good to individual choice. In this the depth of opposition between deontological liberalism and teleological world views most fully appears.

Where neither nature nor cosmos supplies a meaningful order to be grasped or apprehended, it falls to human subjects to constitute meaning on their own. This would explain the prominence of contract theory from Hobbes onward, and the corresponding emphasis on voluntarist as against cognitive ethics culminating in

Kant. What can no longer be found remains somehow to be created.[4] . . .

It is important to recall that, on the deontological view, the notion of a self barren of essential aims and attachments does not imply that we are beings wholly without purpose or incapable of moral ties, but rather that the values and relations we have are the products of choice, the possessions of a self given prior to its ends. It is similar with deontology's universe. Though it rejects the possibility of an objective moral order, this liberalism does not hold that just anything goes. It affirms justice, not nihilism. The notion of a universe empty of intrinsic meaning does not, on the deontological view, imply a world wholly ungoverned by regulative principles, but rather a moral universe inhabited by subjects capable of constituting meaning on their own—as agents of *construction* in case of the right, as agents of *choice* in the case of the good. *Qua* noumenal selves, or parties to the original position, we arrive at principles of justice; *qua* actual, individual selves, we arrive at conceptions of the good. And the principles we construct as noumenal selves constrain (but do not determine) the purposes we choose as individual selves. This reflects the priority of the right over the good.

The deontological universe and the independent self that moves within it, taken together, hold out a liberating vision. Freed from the dictates of nature and the sanction of social roles, the deontological subject is installed as sovereign, cast as the author

[3]For discussion of the moral, political, and epistemological consequences of the seventeenth-century scientific revolution and world-view, see Strauss 1953; Arendt 1958: 248–325; Wolin 1960: 239–85; and Taylor 1975: 3–50.

[4]As one liberal writer boldly asserts, "The hard truth is this: There is no moral meaning hidden in the bowels of the universe. . . . Yet there is no need to be overwhelmed by the void. We may create our own meanings, you and I" (Ackerman 1980: 368). Oddly enough, he insists nonetheless that liberalism is committed to no particular metaphysic or epistemology, nor any "Big Questions of a highly controversial character" (356–7, 361).

of the only moral meanings there are. As inhabitants of a world without *telos,* we are free to construct principles of justice unconstrained by an order of value antecedently given. Although the principles of justice are not strictly speaking a matter of choice, the society they define "comes as close as a society can to being a voluntary scheme" (13), for they arise from a pure will or act of construction not answerable to a prior moral order. And as independent selves, we are free to choose our purposes and ends unconstrained by such an order, or by custom or tradition or inherited status. So long as they are not unjust, our conceptions of the good carry weight, whatever they are, simply in virtue of our having chosen them. We are "self-originating sources of valid claims" (Rawls 1980: 543).

Now justice is the virtue that embodies deontology's liberating vision and allows it to unfold. It embodies this vision by describing those principles the sovereign subject is said to construct while situated prior to the constitution of all value. It allows the vision to unfold in that, equipped with these principles, the just society regulates each person's choice of ends in a way compatible with a similar liberty for all. Citizens governed by justice are thus enabled to realize deontology's liberating project—to exercise their capacity as "self-originating sources of valid claims"—as fully as circumstances permit. So the primacy of justice at once expresses and advances the liberating aspirations of the deontological world view and conception of the self.

But the deontological vision is flawed, both within its own terms and more generally as an account of our moral experience. Within its own terms, the deontological self, stripped of all possible constitutive attachments, is less liberated than disempowered. As we have seen, neither the right nor the good admits of the voluntarist derivation deontology requires. As agents of

construction we do not really construct, and as agents of choice we do not really choose. What goes on behind the veil of ignorance is not a contract or an agreement but if anything a kind of discovery; and what goes on in "purely preferential choice" is less a choosing of ends than a matching of pre-existing desires, undifferentiated as to worth, with the best available means of satisfying them. For the parties to the original position, as for the parties to ordinary deliberative rationality, the liberating moment fades before it arrives; the sovereign subject is left at sea in the circumstances it was thought to command.

The moral frailty of the deontological self also appears at the level of first-order principles. Here we found that the independent self, being essentially dispossessed, was too thin to be capable of desert in the ordinary sense. For claims of desert presuppose thickly-constituted selves, being capable of possession in the constitutive sense, but the deontological self is wholly without possessions of this kind. Acknowledging this lack, Rawls would found entitlements on legitimate expectations instead. If we are incapable of desert, at least we are entitled that institutions honor the expectations to which they give rise.

But the difference principle requires more. It begins with the thought, congenial to the deontological view, that the assets I have are only accidentally mine. But it ends by assuming that these assets are therefore common assets and that society has a prior claim on the fruits of their exercise. This either disempowers the deontological self or denies its independence. Either my prospects are left at the mercy of institutions established for "prior and independent social ends" (313), ends which may or may not coincide with my own, or I must count myself a member of a community defined in part by those ends, in which case I cease to be unencumbered by constitutive attachments. Either way, the difference principle contradicts the liberating aspiration of the deontological project. We cannot be persons for whom justice is primary and also be persons for whom the difference principle is a principle of justice.

Character, Self-Knowledge, and Friendship

If the deontological ethic fails to redeem its own liberating promise, it also fails plausibly to account for certain indispensable aspects of our moral experience. For deontology insists that we view ourselves as independent selves, independent in the sense that our identity is never tied to our aims and attachments. Given our "moral power to form, to revise, and rationally to pursue a conception of the good" (Rawls 1980: 544), the continuity of our identity is unproblematically assured. No transformation of my aims and attachments could call into question the person I am, for no such allegiances, however deeply held, could possibly engage my identity to begin with.

But we cannot regard ourselves as independent in this way without great cost to those loyalties and convictions whose moral force consists partly in the fact that living by them is inseparable from understanding ourselves as the particular persons we are—as members of this family or community or nation or people, as bearers of this history, as sons and daughters of that revolution, as citizens of this republic. Allegiances such as these are more than values I happen to have or aims I "espouse at any given time." They go beyond the obligations I voluntarily incur and the "natural duties" I owe to human beings as such. They allow that to some I owe more than justice requires or even permits, not by reason of agreements I have made but instead in virtue of those more or less enduring attachments and commitments which taken together partly define the person I am.

To imagine a person incapable of constitutive attachments such as these is not to conceive an ideally free and rational agent, but to imagine a person wholly without character, without moral depth. For to have character is to know that I move in a history I neither summon nor command, which carries consequences none the less for my choices and conduct. It draws me closer to some and more distant from others; it makes some aims more appropriate, others less so. As a self-interpreting being, I am able to reflect on my history and in this sense to distance myself from it, but the distance is always precarious and provisional, the point of reflection never finally secured outside the history itself. A person with character thus knows that he is implicated in various ways even as he reflects, and feels the moral weight of what he knows.

This makes a difference for agency and self-knowledge. For, as we have seen, the deontological self, being wholly without character, is incapable of self-knowledge in any morally serious sense. Where the self is unencumbered and essentially dispossessed, no person is left for *self*-reflection to reflect upon. This is why, on the deontological view, deliberation about ends can only be an exercise in arbitrariness. In the absence of constitutive attachments, deliberation issues in "purely preferential choice," which means the ends we seek, being mired in contingency, "are not relevant from a moral standpoint" (Rawls 1975: 537).

When I act out of more or less enduring qualities of character, by contrast, my choice of ends is not arbitrary in the same way. In consulting my preferences, I have not only to weigh their intensity but also to assess their suitability to the person I (already) am. I ask, as I deliberate, not only what I really want but who I really am, and this last question takes me beyond an attention to my desires alone to reflect on my identity itself. While the contours of my identity will in some ways be open and subject to revision, they are not wholly without shape. And the fact that they are not enables me to discriminate among my more immediate wants and desires; some now appear essential, others merely incidental to my defining projects and commitments. Although there may be a certain ultimate contingency in my having wound up the person I am—only theology can say for sure—it makes a moral difference none the less that, being the person I am, I affirm these ends rather than those, turn this way rather than that. While the notion of constitutive attachments may at first seem an obstacle to agency—the self, now encumbered, is no longer strictly prior—some relative fixity of character appears essential to prevent the lapse into arbitrariness which the deontological self is unable to avoid.

The possibility of character in the constitutive sense is also indispensable to a certain kind of friendship, a friendship marked by mutual insights as well as sentiment. By any account, friendship is bound up with certain feelings. We like our friends; we have affection for them, and wish them well. We hope that their desires find satisfaction, that their plans meet with success, and we commit ourselves in various ways to advancing their ends.

But for persons presumed incapable of constitutive attachments, acts of friendship such as these face a powerful constraint. However much I might hope for the good of a friend and stand ready to advance it, only the friend himself can know what that good is. This restricted access to the good of others follows from the limited scope for self-reflection, which betrays in turn the thinness of the deontological self to begin with. Where deliberating about my good means no more than attending to wants and desires given directly to my awareness, I must do it on my own; it neither requires nor admits the participation of others. Every act of friendship thus becomes parasitic on a good identifiable in advance. "Benevolence and love are second-order notions: they seek to further the good of beloved individuals that is already given" (191). Even the friendliest sentiments must await a moment of introspection itself inaccessible to friendship. To expect more of any friend, or to offer more, can only be a presumption against the ultimate privacy of self-knowledge.

For persons encumbered in part by a history they share with others, by contrast, knowing oneself is a more complicated thing. It is also a less strictly private thing. Where seeking my good is bound up with exploring my identity and interpreting my life history, the knowledge I seek is less transparent to me and less opaque to others. Friendship becomes a way of knowing as well as liking. Uncertain which path to take, I consult a friend who knows me well, and together we deliberate, offering and assessing by turns competing descriptions of the person I am, and of the alternatives I face as they bear on my identity. To take seriously such deliberation is to allow that my friend may grasp something I have missed, may offer a more adequate account of the way my identity is engaged in the alternatives before me. To adopt this new description is to see myself in a new way; my old self-image now seems partial or occluded, and I may say in retrospect that my friend knew me better than I knew myself. To deliberate with friends is to admit this possibility, which presupposes in turn a more richly-constituted self than deontology allows. While there will of course remain times when friendship requires deference to the self-image of a friend, however flawed, this too requires insight; here the need to defer implies the ability to know.

So to see ourselves as deontology would see us is to deprive us of those qualities of character, reflectiveness, and friendship that depend on the possibility of constitutive projects and attachments. And to see ourselves as given to commitments such as these is to admit a deeper commonality than benevolence describes, a commonality of shared self-understanding as well as "enlarged affections." As the independent self finds its limits in those aims and attachments from which it cannot stand apart, so justice finds its limits in those forms of community that engage the identity as well as the interests of the participants. . . .

Not egoists but strangers, sometimes benevolent, make for citizens of the deontological republic; justice finds its occasion because we cannot know each other, or our ends, well enough to govern by the common good alone. This condition is not likely to fade altogether, and so long as it does not, justice will be necessary. But neither is it guaranteed always to predominate, and in so far as it does not, community will be possible, and an unsettling presence for justice.

Liberalism teaches respect for the distance of self and ends, and when this distance is lost, we are submerged in a circumstance that ceases to be ours. But by seeking to secure this distance too completely, liberalism undermines its own insight. By putting the self beyond the reach of politics, it makes human agency an article of faith rather than an object of continuing attention and concern, a premise of politics rather than its precarious achievement. This misses the pathos of politics and also its most inspiring possibilities. It overlooks the danger that when politics goes badly, not only disappointments but also dislocations are likely to result. And it forgets the possibility that when politics goes well, we can know a good in common that we cannot know alone.

Ronald Reagan

Known as "the great communicator," former actor Ronald Reagan, elected the fortieth president of the United States, paradoxically restored conservative laissez-faire liberalism simultaneously with increased presidential power and defense spending. Although no favorite of intellectuals, he was one of the most popular of American presidents, winning in a landslide against President Jimmy Carter in 1980 and reelected by an even larger margin in 1984 (with a historic record of 525 electoral votes).

Born in Tampico, Illinois, in 1911, Reagan graduated from Eureka College and worked as a radio sports announcer. Then he went in to the movies and was elected president of the Screen Actors Guild, an American Federation of Labor union branch for Hollywood personalities. In the late 1940s and early 1950s Reagan changed from being a New Deal Democrat to an anticommunist conservative. He became a spokesman for the General Electric Company, preached his conservative ideology, and joined the Republican party. Gaining attention by speaking on behalf of Barry Goldwater in 1964, Reagan was elected governor of California by a landslide. He attacked state spending, higher taxes, and student demonstrations against the Vietnam War while calling for welfare reform. He was reelected governor. Reagan tried twice unsuccessfully to gain the Republican nomination as presidential candidate and then finally succeeded in 1980 to win the election against Jimmy Carter.

In becoming president, Reagan benefited from an American economy with a 12 percent inflation rate and widespread unemployment. Reagan's stated goals were to reduce the growth of the federal government, restore power to the states through his "new federalism," cut government spending through massive budget reductions, and to lower taxes and increase defense spending to shift foreign policy regarding the Soviet Union from detente to "peace through strength" (see his speech below). To accomplish those goals, he strengthened the power of the presidency compared to that of Congress.

The media called Reagan's economic program, which was based on supply-side economics, "Reaganomics." This theory advocated generating growth by stimulating a greater supply of goods and services, thereby creating jobs. Controlling government spending deficits—particularly for domestic social spending—was the recipe for fighting inflation (helped by a tight-money policy at the Federal Reserve Bank). Early budget cuts were followed by a 25 percent tax cut for individual taxpayers and tax write-offs for capital investments for business. The economic results were mixed: initial high unemployment was followed by a marked decline. Inflation fell significantly. Many jobs were created. But massive federal deficits accumulated as a result of the tax cuts, heavy increases in defense spending, and other factors. The stock market plunged in 1987, setting off a world stock panic. Reagan reacted by offering to discuss reducing the deficit and national debt—even perhaps to raise taxes if necessary. The so-called federalism pushed services down to the state and local level where officials said they were underfunded. Efforts at deregulation resulted in criticism that they caused new hazards to public health and safety. Defense spending undoubtedly broke the financial back of the Soviet empire and helped end the cold war. But the cost was so enormous that the United States went from being a creditor to a debtor country, mortgaging the economic future of the young.

Reagan managed to combine laissez-faire supply-side liberal economics (in tax cuts) with positive government intervention (in defense spending) and a conservative, communitarian social agenda that appealed to the Right-wing "Moral Majority," which opposed abortion. And this he did with simple words and a unique oratorical style that cast him into the role of personifying the conservative tradition of American liberalism and made him one of the most popular of presidents.

❧

Address to Congress (1981)

Mr. Speaker, Mr. President, distinguished Members of Congress, honored guests, and fellow citizens. Only a month ago, I was your guest in this historic building and I pledged to you my cooperation in doing what is right for this Nation that we all love so much.

I am here tonight to reaffirm that pledge and to ask that we share in restoring the promise that is offered to every citizen by this, the last, best hope of man on earth.

All of us are aware of the punishing inflation which has, for the first time in some 60 years, held to double digit figures for 2 years in a row. Interest rates have reached absurd levels of more than 20 percent and over 15 percent for those who would borrow to buy a home. All across this land one can see newly built homes standing vacant, unsold because of mortgage interest rates.

Almost eight million Americans are out of work. These are people who want to be productive. But as the months go by, despair dominates their lives. The threats of layoffs and unemployment hang over other millions, and all who work are frustrated by their inability to keep up with inflation.

One worker in a Midwest city put it to me this way: He said "I'm bringing home more dollars than I thought I ever believed I could possibly earn, but I seem to be getting worse off." And he is. Not only have hourly earnings of the American worker, after adjusting for inflation, declined 5 percent over the past 5 years, but in these 5 years, Federal personal taxes for the average family increased 67 percent.

We can no longer procrastinate and hope that things will get better. They will not. Unless we act forcefully and now the economy will get worse.

National Debt

Can we who man the ship of state deny it is somewhat out of control? Our national debt is approaching $1 trillion. A few weeks ago I called such a figure—a trillion dollars—incomprehensible. I've been trying ever since to think of a way to illustrate how big a trillion is. The best I could come up with is that if you had a stack of $1,000 bills in your hand only four inches high you would be a millionaire, A trillion dollars would be a stack of $1,000 bills 67 miles high.

The interest on the public debt this year we know will be over $90 billion. And unless we change the proposed spending for the fiscal year beginning October 1, we'll add another almost $80 billion to the debt.

Adding to our troubles is a mass of regulations imposed on the shopkeeper, the farmer, the craftsman, professionals and major industry that is estimated to add $100 billion to the price of things we buy and it reduces our ability to produce. The rate of increase in American productivity, once one of the highest in the world, is among the lowest of all major industrial nations. Indeed, it has actually declined in the last 3 years.

I have painted a pretty grim picture but I think that I have painted it accurately. It is within our power to change this picture and we can act with hope. There is nothing wrong with our internal strengths. There has been no breakdown in the human, technological, and natural resources upon which the economy is built.

Four-point Proposal

Based on this confidence in a system which has never failed us—but which we have failed through a lack of confidence, and sometimes through a belief that we could fine tune the economy and get a tune to our liking—I am proposing a comprehensive four-point program. Let me outline in detail some of the principal parts of this program. You will each be provided with a completely detailed copy of the entire program.

This plan is aimed at reducing the growth in Government spending and taxing, reforming and eliminating regulations which are unnecessary and unproductive or counterproductive, and encouraging a consistent monetary policy aimed at maintaining the value of the currency.

If enacted in full, this program can help America create 13 million new jobs, nearly 3 million more than we would have without these measures. It will also help us gain control of inflation.

Tax Increase Rate Reduction

It is important to note that we are only reducing the rate of increase in taxing and spending. We are not attempting to cut either spending or taxing levels below that which we presently have. This plan will get our economy moving again, increase productivity growth, and thus create the jobs our people must have.

And I am asking that you join me in reducing direct Federal spending by $41.4 billion in fiscal year 1982, along with another $7.7 billion user fees and off-budget savings for a total savings of $49.1 billion.

This will still allow an increase of $40.8 billion over 1981 spending.

Full Funding for Truly Needy

I know that exaggerated and inaccurate stories about these cuts have disturbed many people, particularly those dependent on grant and benefit programs for their basic needs. Some of you have heard from constituents, I know, afraid that social security checks, for example, were going to be taken away from them. I regret the fear that these unfounded stories have caused and I welcome this opportunity to set things straight.

We will continue to fulfill the obligations that spring from our national conscience. Those who through no fault of their own must depend on the rest of us, the poverty stricken, the disabled, the elderly, all those with true need, can rest assured that the social safety net of programs they depend on are exempt from any cuts.

The full retirement benefits of the more than 31 million social security recipients will be continued along with an annual cost of living increase. Medicare will not be cut, nor will supplemental income for the blind, aged, and disabled, and funding will continue for veterans' pensions.

School breakfasts and lunches for the children of low income families will continue, as will nutrition and other special services for the aging. There will be no cut in Project Head Start or summer youth jobs.

All in all, nearly $216 billion worth of programs providing help for tens of millions of Americans—will be fully funded. But government will not continue to subsidize individuals or particular business interests where real need cannot be demonstrated.

And while we will reduce some subsidies to regional and local governments, we will at the same time convert a number of categorical grant programs into block grants to reduce wasteful administrative overhead and to give local government entities and States more flexibility and control. We call for an end to duplication in Federal programs and reform of those which are not cost effective.

Restore Programs to States and Private Sector

Already, some have protested that there must be no reduction in aid to schools. Let me point out that Federal aid to education amounts to only eight percent of the total educational funding. For this eight percent the Federal Government has insisted on a tremendously disproportionate share of control over our schools. Whatever reductions we've proposed in that eight percent will amount to very little in the total cost of education. They will, however, restore more authority to States and local school districts.

Historically the American people have supported by voluntary contributions more artistic and cultural activities than all the other countries in the world put together. I wholeheartedly support this approach and believe that Americans will continue their generosity. Therefore, I am proposing a

savings of $85 million in the Federal subsidies now going to the arts and humanities.

There are a number of subsidies to business and industry that I believe are unnecessary. Not because the activities being subsidized aren't of value but because the marketplace contains incentives enough to warrant continuing these activities without a government subsidy. One such subsidy is the Department of Energy's synthetic fuels program. We will continue support of research leading to development of new technologies and more independence from foreign oil, but we can save at least $3.2 billion by leaving to private industry the building of plants to make liquid or gas fuels from coal.

We are asking that another major industry, business subsidy I should say, the Export-Import Bank loan authority, be reduced by one-third in 1982. We are doing this because the primary beneficiaries of tax payer funds in this case are the exporting companies themselves—most of them profitable corporations.

High Cost of Government Borrowing

This brings me to a number of other lending programs in which Government makes low-interest loans. Some of them at an interest rate as low as 2 percent. What has not been very well understood is that the Treasury Department has no money of its own. It has to go into the private capital market and borrow the money. So in this time of excessive interest rates the government finds itself borrowing at an interest rate several times as high as the interest rate it gets back from those it lends the money to. This difference, of course, is paid by your constituents, the taxpayers. They get hit again if they try to borrow because Government borrowing contributes to raising all interest rates.

By terminating the Economic Development Administration we can save hundreds of millions of dollars in 1982 and billions more over the next few years. There is a lack of consistent and convincing evidence that EDA and its Regional Commissions have been effective in creating new jobs. They have been effective in creating an array of planners, grantsmen and professional middlemen. We believe we can do better just by the expansion of the economy and the job creation which will come from our economic program.

Welfare and Unemployment Programs

The Food Stamp program will be restored to its original purpose, to assist those without resources to purchase sufficient nutritional food. We will, however, save $1.8 billion in fiscal year 1982 by removing from eligibility those who are not in real need or who are abusing the program.

Even with this reduction, the program will be budgeted for more than $10 billion.

We will tighten welfare and give more attention to outside sources of income when determining the amount of welfare an individual is allowed. This plus strong and effective work requirements will save $520 million in the next year.

I stated a moment ago our intention to keep the school breakfast and lunch programs for those in true need. But by cutting back on meals for children of families who can afford to pay, the savings will be $1.6 billion in fiscal year 1982.

Let me just touch on a few other areas which are typical of the kinds of reductions we have included in this economic package. The Trade Adjustment Assistance program provides benefits for workers who are unemployed when foreign imports reduce the market for various American products causing shutdown of plants and layoff of workers. The purpose is to help these workers find jobs in growing sectors of our economy. There is nothing wrong with that. But because these benefits are paid out on top of normal unemployment benefits, we wind up paying greater benefits to those who lose their jobs because of foreign competition than we do to their friends and neighbors who are laid off due to domestic competition. Anyone must agree that this is unfair. Putting these two programs on the same footing will save $1.15 billion in just 1 year.

Federal Regulation Burden

Earlier I made mention of changing categorical grants to States and local governments into block grants. We know, of course, that the categorical grant programs burden local and State governments with a mass of Federal regulations and Federal paperwork.

Ineffective targeting, wasteful administrative overhead—all can be eliminated by shifting the resources and decision-making authority to local and State government. This will also consolidate programs which are scattered throughout the Federal bureaucracy, bringing government closer to the people and saving $23.9 billion over the next 5 years.

Our program for economic renewal deals with a number of programs which at present are not cost-effective. An example is Medicaid. Right now Washington provides the States with unlimited matching payments for their expenditures. At the same time we here in Washington pretty much dictate how the States are going to manage these programs. We want to put a cap on how much the Federal Government will contribute but at the same time allow the States much more flexibility in managing and structuring the programs. I know from our experience in California that such flexibility could have led to far more cost-effective reforms. This will bring a savings of $1 billion next year

Space and Postal Agencies

The space program has been and is important to America and we plan to continue it. We believe, however, that a reordering of priorities to focus on the most important and cost-effective NASA programs can result in a savings of a quarter of a billion dollars.

Coming down from space to the mailbox—the Postal Service has been consistently unable to live within its operating budget. It is still dependent on large Federal subsidies. We propose reducing those subsidies by $632 million in 1982 to press the Postal Service into becoming more effective. In subsequent years, the savings will continue to add up.

The Economic Regulatory Administration in the Department of Energy has programs to force companies to convert to specific fuels. It has the authority to administer a gas rationing plan, and prior to decontrol it ran the oil price control program. With these and other regulations gone we can save several hundreds of millions of dollars over the next few years.

Defense Spending

I'm sure there is one department you've been waiting for me to mention, the Department of Defense. It is the only department in our entire program that will actually be increased over the present budgeted figure.

But even here there was no exemption. The Department of Defense came up with a number of cuts which reduced the budget increase needed to restore our military balance. These measures will save $2.9 billion in 1982 outlays and by 1986 a total of $28.2 billion will have been saved. Perhaps I

should say will have been made available for the necessary things that we must do. The aim will be to provide the most effective defense for the lowest possible cost.

I believe that my duty as President requires that I recommend increases in defense spending over the coming years.

I know that you are aware but I think it bears saying again that since 1970, the Soviet Union has invested $300 billion more in its military forces than we have. As a result of its massive military buildup, the Soviets have made a significant numerical advantage in strategic nuclear delivery systems, tactical aircraft, submarines, artillery and antiaircraft defense. To allow this imbalance to continue is a threat to our national security.

Notwithstanding our economic straits, making the financial changes beginning now is far less costly than waiting and having to attempt a crash program several years from now.

We remain committed to the goal of arms limitation through negotiation. I hope we can persuade our adversaries to come to realistic balanced and verifiable agreements.

But, as we negotiate, our security must be fully protected by a balanced and realistic defense program.

New Inspectors General

Let me say a word here about the general problem of waste and fraud in the Federal Government. One government estimate indicated that fraud alone may account for anywhere from 1 to 10 percent—as much as $25 billion—of Federal expenditures for social programs. If the tax dollars that are wasted or mismanaged are added to this fraud total, the staggering dimensions of this problem begin to emerge.

The Office of Management and Budget is now putting together an interagency task force to attack waste and fraud. We are also planning to appoint as Inspectors General highly trained professionals who will spare no effort to do this job.

No administration can promise to immediately stop a trend that has grown in recent years as quickly as Government expenditures themselves. But let me say this: waste and fraud in the Federal budget is exactly what I have called it before—an unrelenting national scandal—a scandal we are bound and determined to do something about.

Tax Proposals

Marching in lockstep with the whole program of reductions in spending is the equally important program of reduced tax rates. Both are essential if we are to have economic recovery. It's time to create new jobs. To build and rebuild industry, and to give the American people room to do what they do best. And that can only be done with a tax program which provides incentive to increase productivity for both workers and industry.

Our proposal is for a 10-percent across-the-board cut every year for three years in the tax rates for all individual income taxpayers, making a total cut in tax rates of 30 percent. This 3-year reduction will also apply to the tax on unearned income, leading toward an eventual elimination of the present differential between the tax on earned and unearned income.

I would have hoped that we could be retroactive with this, but as it stands the effective starting date for these 10-percent personal income tax rate reductions will be called for as of July 1st of this year.

Again, let me remind you that while this 30 percent reduction will leave the taxpayers with $500 billion more in their pockets over the next five years, it's actually only a reduction in the tax increase already built into the system.

Unlike some past "tax reforms" this is not merely a shift of wealth between different sets of taxpayers. This proposal for an equal reduction in everyone's tax rates will expand our national prosperity, enlarge national incomes, and increase opportunities for all Americans.

Some will argue, I know, that reducing tax rates now will be inflationary. A solid body of economic experts does not agree. And tax cuts adopted over the past three-fourths of a century indicate these economic experts are right. They will not be inflationary. I have had advice that in 1985 our real production of goods and services will grow by 20 percent and will be $300 billion higher than it is today. The average worker's wage will rise (in real purchasing power) 8 percent, and this is in after-tax dollars and this, of course, is predicated on a complete program of tax cuts and spending reductions being implemented.

The other part of the tax package is aimed directly at providing business and industry with the capital needed to modernize and engage in more research and development. This will involve an increase in depreciation allowances, and this part of our tax proposal will be retroactive to January 1st.

The present depreciation system is obsolete, needlessly complex, and is economically counterproductive. Very simply, it bases the depreciation of plant, machinery, vehicles, and tools on their original cost with no recognition of how inflation has increased their replacement cost. We are proposing a much shorter write-off time than is presently allowed: a 5-year write-off for machinery; 3 years for vehicles and trucks; and a 10-year write-off for plant.

In fiscal year 1982 under this plan business would acquire nearly $10 billion for investment. By 1985 the figure would be nearly $45 billion. These changes are essential to provide the new investment which is needed to create millions of new jobs between now and 1985 and to make

America competitive once again in the world market.

These won't be make-work jobs, they are productive jobs, jobs with a future.

I'm well aware that there are many other desirable and needed tax changes such as indexing the income tax brackets to protect taxpayers against inflation; the unjust discrimination against married couples if both are working and earning; tuition tax credits; the unfairness of the inheritance tax, especially to the family-owned farm and the family-owned business, and a number of others. But our program for economic recovery is so urgently needed to begin to bring down inflation that I am asking you to act on this plan first and with great urgency. Then I pledge I will join with you in seeking these additional tax changes at the earliest date possible.

Overregulation

American society experienced a virtual explosion in Government regulation during the past decade. Between 1970 and 1979, expenditures for the major regulatory agencies quadrupled, the number of pages published annually in the *Federal Register* nearly tripled, and the number of pages in the *Code of Federal Regulations* increased by nearly two-thirds.

The result has been higher prices, higher unemployment, and lower productivity growth. Overregulation causes small and independent businessmen and women, as well as large businesses, to defer or terminate plans for expansion, and since they are responsible for most of our new jobs, those new jobs just aren't created.

We have no intention of dismantling the regulatory agencies—especially those necessary to protect [the] environment and to ensure the public health and safety. However, we must come to grips with inefficient and burdensome regulations—eliminate those we can and reform the others.

I have asked Vice President Bush to head a Cabinet-level Task Force on Regulatory Relief. Second, I asked each member of my Cabinet to postpone the effective dates of the hundreds of regulations which have not yet been implemented. Third, in coordination with the task force, many of the agency heads have already taken prompt action to review and rescind existing burdensome regulations. Finally, just yesterday, I signed an executive order that for the first time provides for effective and coordinated management of the regulatory process.

Much has been accomplished, but it is only the beginning. We will eliminate those regulations that are unproductive and unnecessary by executive order, where possible, and cooperate fully with you on those that require legislation.

The final aspect of our plan requires a national monetary policy which does not allow money growth to increase consistently faster than the growth of goods and services. In order to curb inflation, we need to slow the growth in our money supply.

We fully recognize the independence of the Federal Reserve System and will do nothing to interfere with or undermine that independence. We will consult regularly with the Federal Reserve Board on all aspects of our economic program and will vigorously pursue budget policies that will make their job easier in reducing monetary growth.

A successful program to achieve stable and moderate growth patterns in the money supply will keep both inflation and interest rates down and restore vigor to our financial institutions and markets.

"Economic Recovery" Proposed

This, then, is our proposal. "America's New Beginning: A Program for Economic Recovery." I don't want it to be simply the plan of my Administration—I'm here tonight to ask you to join me in making it our plan. [Applause, members rising]

I should have arranged to quit right there.

Well, together we can embark on this road, not to make things easy, but to make things better.

Our social, political and cultural as well as our economic institutions can no longer absorb the repeated shocks that have been dealt them over the past decades.

Can we do the job? The answer is yes, but we must begin now.

We are in control here. There is nothing wrong with America that we can't fix. I'm sure there will be some who will raise the familiar old cry, "Don't touch my program—cut somewhere else."

I hope I've made it plain that our approach has been evenhanded; that only the programs for the truly deserving needy remain untouched.

The question is, are we simply going to go down the same path we've gone down before—carving out one special program here, another special program there. I don't think that is what the American people expect of us. More important, I don't think that is what they want. They are ready to return to the source of our strength.

The substance and prosperity of our Nation is built by wages brought home from the factories and the mills, the farms and the shops. They are the services provided in 10,000 corners of America; the interest on the thrift of our people and the returns for their risk-taking. The production of America is the possession of those who build, serve, create and produce.

For too long now, we've removed from our people the decisions on how to dispose of what they created. We have strayed from first principles. We must alter our course.

The taxing power of government must be used to provide revenues for legitimate government purposes. It must not be used

to regulate the economy or bring about social change. We've tried that and surely must be able to see it doesn't work.

Proper Province of Government

Spending by Government must be limited to those functions which are the proper province of Government. We can no longer afford things simply because we think of them.

Next year we can reduce the budget by $41.4 billion, without harm to Government's legitimate purposes or to our responsibility to all who need our benevolence. This, plus the reduction in tax rates, will help bring an end to inflation.

In the health and social services area alone the plan we are proposing will substantially reduce the need for 465 pages of law, 1,400 pages of regulations, 5,000 Federal employees who presently administer 7,600 separate grants in about 25,000 separate locations. Over 7 million man and woman hours of work by State and local officials are required to fill out government forms.

I would direct a question to those who have indicated already an unwillingness to accept such a plan. Have they an alternative which offers a greater chance of balancing the budget, reducing and eliminating inflation, stimulating the creation of jobs, and reducing the tax burden? And if they haven't, are they suggesting we can continue on the present course without coming to a day of reckoning?

If we don't do this, inflation and the growing tax burden will put an end to everything we believe in and our dreams for the future. We don't have an option of living with inflation and its attendant tragedy, millions of productive people willing and able to work but unable to find a buyer for their work in the job market.

We have an alternative, and that is the program for economic recovery.

True, it will take time for the favorable effects of our proposal to be felt. So we must begin now.

The people are watching and waiting.

They don't demand miracles. They do expect us to act. Let us act together.

Thank you and good night.

Bill Clinton

"It is time to break the bad habit of expecting something for nothing, from our government or from each other," said President Bill Clinton in his 1993 inaugural address. Clinton represents a sea change in American political thinking from the modernized, conservative, laissez-faire liberalism of Reagan and Bush to a progressive, populist, interventionist liberalism. His statement: "Let us resolve to make our government a place for what Franklin Roosevelt called 'bold, persistent experimentation,'" sums up his heritage and his vision of the positive state (epitomized by the speech below).

Born in Hope, Arkansas, in 1946, Clinton was inspired by the time he was sixteen by heroes such as John F. Kennedy and Arkansas Senator J. William Fulbright to enter politics. He studied international affairs at Georgetown University, attended Oxford University as a Rhodes scholar, and received a law degree from Yale. He directed the unsuccessful presidential campaign of George McGovern in Texas, worked as a staff attorney for the House Judiciary Committee and then taught at the University of Arkansas School of Law. Losing a close race for the Arkansas House of Representatives, Clinton then directed Jimmy Carter's successful presidential campaign in Arkansas. He was elected Arkansas state attorney general, running as a consumer advocate and opponent of environmental pollution. At age thirty-two he was elected governor of Arkansas and attempted to upgrade the state's highway system. But the gas tax and license fees he charged to pay for it helped to cost Clinton reelection. Other contributing factors included a problem beyond his control, dealing with Cuban refugees. In addition there were voter suspicions that Clinton was using Arkansas as a springboard to higher office given his distractions serving as chairman of the National Conference of Democratic Governors. He joined a law firm and won reelection as governor in 1984. As governor Clinton fought the state and national teachers' unions to push through an educational reform program that made Arkansas the first state to test teachers for competence without regard to their years of service. He increased the state sales tax to fund the educational reforms, which raised teachers' salaries, expenditures per pupil, and standards for academic achievement. Clinton was then continually reelected governor until he won his campaign for president against George Bush in 1992.

Clinton was elected on a platform of reforming the health care system, renewing the infrastructure, introducing national service for university students and apprenticeship training, creating long-term growth through public investment to reduce unemployment, monitoring pollution, reducing the skyrocketing federal deficit, and raising taxes on the well-to-do and foreign corporations to pay for his reforms. Clearly Clinton's economic program in the 1993 speech below provides a counterpoint to the economic program of President Ronald Reagan (above), although both promised to reduce the federal deficit.

Address to Congress (1993)

Mr. President, Mr. Speaker, members of the House and the Senate, distinguished Americans here as visitors in this chamber—as am I—it is nice to have a fresh excuse for giving a long speech.

When Presidents speak to the Congress and the nation from this podium, typically they comment on the full range and challenges and opportunities that face the United States. But this is not an ordinary time, and for all the many tasks that require our attention, I believe tonight one calls on us to focus, to unite and to act, and that is our economy. For more than anything else, our task tonight as Americans is to make our economy thrive again. Let me begin by saying that it has been too long—at least three decades—since a President has come and challenged Americans to join him on a great national journey, not merely to consume the bounty of today but to invest for a much greater one tomorrow.

Like individuals, nations must ultimately decide how they wish to conduct themselves—how they wish to be thought of by those with whom they live, and, later, how they wish to be judged by history. Like every individual man and woman, nations must decide whether they are prepared to rise to the occasions history presents them.

We have always been a people of youthful energy and daring spirit. And at this historic moment, as Communism has fallen, as freedom is spreading around the world, as a global economy is taking shape before our eyes, Americans have called for change—and now it is up to those of us in this room to deliver for them.

Our nation needs a new direction. Tonight, I present to you a comprehensive plan to set our nation on that new course.

I believe we will find our new direction in the basic old values that brought us here over the last two centuries: a commitment to opportunity, to individual responsibility, to community, to work, to family and to faith. We must now break the old habits of both political parties and say that there can be no more something for nothing, and admit frankly that we are all in this together.

The conditions which brought us as a nation to this point are well known. Two decades of low productivity growth and stagnant wages; persistent unemployment and underemployment; years of huge Government deficits and declining investment in our future; exploding health care costs and lack of coverage for millions of Americans; legions of poor children; education and job training opportunities inadequate to the demands of this tough global economy. For too long we drifted without a strong sense of purpose on responsibility or community, and our political system so often has seemed paralyzed by special interest groups, by partisan bickering and by the sheer complexity of our problems.

I believe we can do better, because we remain the greatest nation on earth, the world's strongest economy, the world's only military superpower. If we have the vision, the will and the heart to make the changes we must, we can still enter the 21st century with possibilities our parents could not even have imagined, and enter it having secured the American dream for ourselves and for future generations.

I well remember—I well remember twelve years ago President Reagan stood at this very podium and told you and the American people that if our national debt were stacked in thousand dollar bills the stack would reach 67 miles into space. Well, today, that stack would reach 267 miles.

I tell you this not to assign blame for this problem. There is plenty of blame to go around—in both branches of the Government and both parties. The time has come for the blame to end. I did not seek this office to place blame. I come here tonight to accept responsibility and I want you to accept responsibility with me and if we do right by this country, I do not care who gets the credit for it.

Elements of Plan

The plan I offer you has four fundamental components:

First, it shifts our emphasis in public and private spending from consumption to investment initially by jump-starting the economy in the short term and investing in our people, their jobs and their incomes over the long run.

Second, it changes the rhetoric of the past into the actions of the present, by honoring work and families in every part of our public decision-making.

Third, it substantially reduces the Federal deficit, honestly and credibly, by using in the beginning the most conservative estimates of Government revenues, not as the Executive Branch has done so often in the past, using the most optimistic ones.

And finally, it seeks to earn the trust of the American people by paying for these plans first with cuts in Government waste and efficiency, second with cuts, not gimmicks, in Government spending, and by fairness, for a change, in the way additional burdens are borne.

Tonight, I want to talk with you about what government can do, because I believe government must do more. But let me say first that the real engine of economic growth in this country is the private sector. And second that each of us must be an engine of growth and change. The truth is that as government creates more opportunity in this new and different time, we must also demand more responsibility in turn.

Our immediate priority must be to create jobs—create jobs now. Some people say well we're in a recovery and we don't have to do that. Well, we all hope we're in a recovery. But we're sure not creating new jobs. And there's no recovery worth its salt that doesn't put the American people back to work.

To create jobs and guarantee a strong recovery, I call on Congress to enact an immediate package of jobs investments over $30 billion to put people to work now to create a half a million jobs: jobs to rebuild our highways and airports, to renovate housing, to bring new life to rural communities and spread hope and opportunity among our nation's youth. Especially I want to emphasize after the events of last year in Los Angeles and the countless stories of despair in our cities and in our poor rural communities, this proposal will create almost 700,000 new summer jobs for displaced unemployed young people alone this summer. And tonight I invite America's business leaders to join us in this effort so that together we can provide over one million summer jobs in cities and poor rural areas for our young people.

Second, our plan looks beyond today's business cycle, because our aspirations, extend into the next century. The heart of this plan deals with the long term. It is an investment program designed to increase public and private investment in areas critical to our economic future. And it has a deficit reduction program that will increase the savings available for the private sector to invest, will lower interest rates, will decrease the percentage of the Federal budget claimed by interest payments, and decrease the risk of financial market disruptions that could adversely affect our economy.

Over the long run, all this will bring us a higher rate of economic growth, improved productivity, more high-quality jobs and an improved economic competitive position in the world.

What Must Be Done

In order to accomplish both increased investment and deficit reduction—something no American Government has ever been called upon to do at the same time before, spending must be cut and taxes must be raised. Spending cuts I recommend were carefully thought through in a way to minimize any adverse economic impact, to capture the peace dividend for investment purposes, and to switch the balance in the budget from consumption to more investment. The tax increases and the spending cuts were both designed to assure that the cost of this historic program to face and deal with our problems will be borne by those who could readily afford it the most.

Our plan is designed, furthermore, and perhaps in some ways most important, to improve the health of American business through lower interest rates, more incentives to invest and better-trained workers.

Because small business has created such a high percentage of all the jobs in our nation over the last 10 or 15 years, our plan includes the boldest targeted incentives for small business in history. We propose—we propose a permanent investment tax credit for the smallest firms in this country with revenues of under $5 million. That's about 90 percent of the firms in America, employing about 40 percent of the work force but creating a big majority of the net new jobs for more than a decade. And we propose new rewards for entrepreneurs who take new risks. We propose to give small business access to all the new technologies of our time, and we propose to attack this credit crunch which has denied small business the credit they need to flourish and prosper.

With a new network of community development banks, and one billion dollars to make the dream of enterprise zones real, we propose to bring new hope and new jobs to storefronts and factories from South Boston to South Texas to South-Central Los Angeles.

This plan invests in our roads, our bridges, our transit systems; in high-speed railways and high-tech information systems, and it provides the most ambitious environmental cleanup in partnership with state and local government of our time to put people to work and to preserve the environment for our future.

Standing as we are on the edge of the new century, we know that economic growth depends as never before on opening up new markets overseas and expanding the volume of world trade. And so we will insist on fair trade rules in international markets as a part of a national economic strategy to expand trade, including the successful completion of the latest round of world trade talks and the successful completion of a North American Free Trade Agreement with appropriate safeguards for our workers and for the environment.

At the same time—and I say this to you in both parties and across America tonight, all the people who are listening, it is not enough to pass a budget or even to have a trade agreement. The world is changing so fast that we must have aggressive targeted attempts to create the high-wage jobs of the future; that's what all our competitors are doing. We must give special attention to those critical industries that are going to explode in the 21st century but that are in trouble in America today like aerospace. We must provide special assistance to areas and to workers displaced by cuts in defense budget and by other unavoidable economic dislocations.

And I say we must do this together. I pledge to you that I will do my best to see that business and labor and government work together for a change.

Focus on Health Care

But all of our efforts to strengthen the economy will fail—let me say this again—I feel so strongly about this. All of our efforts to strengthen the economy will fail unless we also take, this year, not next year, not five years from now, but this year, bold steps to reform our health care system

In 1992 we spent 14 percent of our income on health care; more than 30 percent more than any other country in the world, and yet we were the only advanced nation that did not provide a basic package of health-care benefits to all of its citizens. Unless we change the present pattern, 50 percent of the growth in the deficit between now and the year 2000 will be in health care costs. By the year 2000, almost 20 percent of our income will be in health-care. Our families will never be secure, our businesses will never be strong and our Government will never again be fully solvent until we tackle the health-care crisis. We must do it this year.

The combination of the rising costs of care, and the lack of care and the fear of losing care are endangering the security and the very lives of millions of our people, and they are weakening our economy every day. Reducing health-care costs can liberate literally hundreds of billions of dollars for new investment in growth and jobs. Bringing health costs in line with inflation would do more for the private sector in this country than any tax cut we could give and any spending program we could promote. Reforming health care over the long run is critically essential to reducing not only our deficit but to expanding investment in America.

Later this spring, after the First Lady and the many good people who are helping her all across the country complete their work, I will deliver to Congress a comprehensive plan for health-care reform that finally will bring costs under control and provide security to all of our families, so that no one will be denied the coverage they need but so that our economic future will not be compromised either.

We'll have to—we'll have to root out fraud and overcharges and make sure that paperwork no longer chokes your doctor. We'll have to maintain the highest American standards and the right to choose in a system that is the world's finest for all those who can access it. But first we must make choices. We must choose to give the American people the quality they demand and deserve with a system that will not bankrupt the country or further drive more Americans into agony.

Let me further say that I want to work with all of you on this. I realize this is a complicated issue. But we must address it. And I believe if there is any chance that Republicans and Democrats will disagree on taxes and spending or anything else, they'd agree on one thing—surely we can all look at these numbers and go home and tell our people the truth: We cannot continue these spending patterns in public or private dollars for health care for less and less and less every year. We can do better.

Children and Education

Perhaps the most fundamental change in the new direction I propose offers as its focus on the future and its investment which I seek in our children. Each day we delay really making a commitment to our children carries a dear cost. Half of the 2-year-olds in this country today don't receive the immunizations they need against deadly diseases. Our plan will provide them for every eligible child and we know now that we will save $10 later for every $1 we spend by eliminating preventable childhood diseases—that's a good investment no matter how you measure it.

I recommend that the Women, Infants and Children's nutrition program be expanded so that every expectant mother who needs the help gets it. We all know that Head Start, a program that prepares children for school, is a success story. We all know that it saves money, but today it just reaches barely over a third of all the eligible children. Under this plan, every eligible child will be able to get a head start.

This is not just the right thing to do; it is the smart thing to do. For every dollar we invest today we'll save three tomorrow. I've heard that somewhere.

We have to ask more in our schools of our students, our teachers, our principals, our parents. Yes, we must give them the resources they need to meet high standards, but we must also use the authority and the influence and the funding of the Education Department to promote strategies that really work in learning. Money alone is not enough. We have to do what really works to increase learning in our schools.

We have to recognize that all of our high school graduates need some further education in order to be competitive in this global economy. So we have to establish a partnership between businesses and education, the Government, for apprenticeship programs in every state in this country to give our people the skills they need.

Lifelong learning must benefit not just young high school graduates but workers too, throughout their career. The average 18-year-old today will change jobs seven times in a lifetime.

We have done a lot in this country on worker training in the last few years, but the system is too fractured. We must develop a unified, simplified, sensible, streamlined worker-training program so that workers receive the training they need regardless of why they lost their jobs or whether they simply need to learn something new to keep them. We have got to do better than that.

Finally, I propose a program that got a great response from the American people all across this country last year, a program of national service to make college loans available to all Americans; and to challenge them at the same time to give something back to their country—as teachers or police officers or community service workers. To give them the option to pay the loans back, but at tax time, so they can't beat the bill, but to encourage them instead to pay it back by making their country stronger and making their country better and giving us the benefit of their talents.

A generation ago, when President Kennedy proposed and the United States Congress embraced the Peace Corps, it defined the character of a whole generation of Americans committed to serving people around the world. In this national service program we will provide more than twice as many slots for people before they go to college to be in national service than ever served in the Peace Corps.

This program could do for this generation of members of Congress what the Land Grant College Act did and what the G.I. Bill did for former congressmen. In the future, historians who got their education through the national service loan will look back on you and thank you for giving America a new lease on life, if you meet the challenge.

If we believe in jobs and we believe in learning, we must believe in rewarding work. If we believe in restoring the values that make America special, we must believe that there is dignity in all work and there must be dignity for all workers.

For those who care for our sick and tend our children, who do our most difficult and tiring jobs, the new direction I propose will make this solemn simple commitment. By expanding the refundable earned income tax credit we will make history, we will reward the work of millions of working poor Americans by realizing the principle that if you work 40 hours a week and you've got a child in the house, you will no longer be in poverty.

Welfare and Families

Later this year we will offer a plan to end welfare as we know it. I have worked on this issue for the better part of a decade and I know from personal conversations with many people, that no one—no one wants to change the welfare system as badly as those who are trapped in it. I want to offer the people on welfare the education, the training, the child care, the health care they need to get back on their feet, but say after two years they must get back to work, too, in private business if possible, in public service if necessary. We have to end welfare as a way of life and make it a path to independence and dignity.

Our next great goal should be to strengthen our families. I compliment the Congress for passing the Family and Medical Leave Act as a good first step, but it is time to do more. This plan will give this country the toughest child-support enforcement system it has ever had. It is time to demand that people take responsibility for the children they bring in this world.

And I ask you to help to protect our families against the violent crime which terrorizes our people and which tears our communities apart. We must pass a tough crime bill.

I support not only the bill which didn't quite make it to the President's desk last year but also an initiative to put 100,000 more police officers on the street, to provide boot camps for first-time nonviolent offenders for more space for the hardened

criminals in jail. And I support an initiative to do what we can to keep guns out of the hands of criminals.

Let me say this, if—I will make you this bargain: If you will pass the Brady Bill, I'll sure sign it.

Let me say now, we should move to the harder parts, I think it is clear to every American, including every member of Congress and both parties, that the confidence of the people who pay our bills in our institutions in Washington is not high. We must restore it. We must begin again to make Government work for ordinary taxpayers, not simply for organized interest groups and that beginning must start with real political reform.

I am—I am asking the United States Congress to pass a real campaign finance reform bill this year. I ask you to increase the participation of the American people by passing the motor-voter bill promptly. I ask you to deal with the undue influence of special interests by passing a bill to end the tax deduction for lobbying and to act quickly to require all the people who lobby you to register as lobbyists by passing the lobbying registration bill.

Believe me, they were cheering that last section at home. I believe lobby reform and campaign finance reform are a sure path to increased popularity for Republicans and Democrats alike, because it says to the voters back home: "This is your House, this is your Senate; we're your hired hands, and every penny we draw is your money."

Next, to revolutionize Government we have to insure that we live within our means, and that should start at the top and with the White House. In the last few days I have announced a cut in the White House staff of 25 percent, saving approximately $10 million. I have ordered administrative cuts in budgets of agencies and departments; I have cut the Federal bureaucracy—or will over the next four years—

by approximately 100,000 positions, for a combined savings of $9 billion.

It's—it is time for Government to demonstrate in the condition we're in that we can be as frugal as any household in America, and that's why I also want to congratulate the Congress. I noticed the announcement of the leadership today that Congress is taking similar steps to cut its costs. I think that is important; I think it will send a very clear signal to the American people.

But if we really want to cut spending we're going to have to do more and some of it will be difficult. Tonight I call for an across-the-board freeze in Federal Government salaries for one year. And—and thereafter during this four-year period I recommend that salaries rise at one point lower than the cost-of-living allowance normally involved in federal pay increases.

Next, I recommend that we make 150 specific budget cuts, as you know, and that all those who say we should cut more, be as specific as I have been.

Finally let me say to my friends on both sides of the aisle, it is not enough simply to cut Government—we have to rethink the whole way it works. When I became President, I was amazed at just the way the White House worked in ways that added lots of money to what taxpayers had to pay: outmoded ways that didn't take maximum advantage of technology, and didn't do things that any business would have done years ago to save taxpayers money.

So I want to bring a new spirit of innovation into every Government department. I want to push education reform, as I said, not just to spend more money but to really improve learning. Some things work and some things don't. We ought to be subsidizing the things that work and discouraging the things that don't.

I'd like to use that Superfund to clean up pollution for a change and not just pay lawyers.

In the aftermath of all the difficulties with the savings and loans, we must use Federal bank regulators to protect the security and safety of our financial institutions—but they should not be used to continue the credit crunch, to stop people from making sensible loans.

I'd like for us to not only have welfare reform, but to re-examine the whole focus of all of our programs that help people to shift them from entitlement programs to empowerment programs. In the end, we want people not to need us anymore. I think that's important.

On the Deficit

But in the end, we have to get back to the deficit. For years there's been a lot of talk about it, but very few credible efforts to deal with it. And now I understand why, having dealt with the real numbers for four weeks. But I believe this plan does—it tackles the budget deficit seriously and over the long term. It puts in place one of the biggest deficit reductions and one of the biggest changes in Federal priorities from consumption to investment in the history of this country, at the same time, over the next four years.

Let me say to all the people watching us tonight who will ask me these questions beginning tomorrow as I go around the country, and who've asked it in the past. We're not cutting the deficit just because experts say it's the thing to do, or because it has some intrinsic merit. We have to cut the deficit because the more we spend paying off the debt, the less tax dollars we have to invest in jobs and education and the future of this country.

And the more money we take out of the pool of available savings, the harder it is for people in the private sector to borrow money at affordable interest rates for a college loan for their children, for a home mortgage, or to start a new business. That's why we've got to reduce the debt, because it is crowding out other activities that we ought to be engaged in and that the American people ought to be engaged in.

We cut the deficit so that our children will be able to buy a home, so that our companies can invest in the future and in retraining their workers, so that our Government can make the kinds of investments we need to be a stronger and smarter and safer nation.

If we don't act now, you and I might not even recognize this Government 10 years from now. If we just stay with the same trends of the last four years, at the end of the decade the deficit will be $635 billion a year, almost 80 percent of our gross domestic product, and paying interest on that debt will be the costliest Government program of all.

We'll still be the world's largest debtor and when members of Congress come here, they'll be devoting over 20 cents on the dollar to interest payments, more than half of the budget to health care and to other entitlements. And you will come here and deliberate and argue over six or seven cents on the dollar, no matter what America's problems are. We will not be able to have the independence we need to chart the future that we must and we'll be terribly dependent on foreign funds for a large portion of our investment.

This budget plan by contrast will, by 1997, cut $140 billion in that year alone from the deficit, a real spending cut, a real revenue increase, a real deficit reduction using the independent numbers of the Congressional budget office.

Well, you can laugh, my fellow Republicans, but I'll point out that the Congressional Budget Office was normally more conservative in what was going to happen and closer to right than previous Presidencies.

I did this—I did this—I did this so that we could argue about priorities with

the same set of numbers. I did this so that no one could say I was estimating my way out of this difficulty. I did this because if we can agree together on the most prudent revenues we're likely to get, if the recovery stays and we do right things economically, then it'll turn out better for the American people than we say in the last 12 years, because there were difference over the revenue estimates.

You and I know that both parties were given greater elbow room for irresponsibility. This is tightening the rein on the Democrats as well as the Republicans. Let's at least argue about the same set of numbers, so the American people will think we're shooting straight with them.

Cutting the Budget

As I said earlier, my recommendation makes more than 150 difficult reductions to cut the Federal spending by a total of $246 billion. We are eliminating programs that are no longer needed such as nuclear power research and development, we're slashing subsidies and canceling wasteful projects, but many of these programs were justified in their time and a lot of them are difficult for me to recommend reductions in. Some really tough ones for me personally.

I recommend that we reduce interest subsidies to the Rural Electric Administration—that's a difficult thing for me to recommend. But I think that I cannot exempt the things that are—exist in my state or in my experience if I ask you to deal with things that are difficult for you to deal with. We're going to have to have no sacred cows except the fundamental abiding interest of the American people.

I have to say that we all know our Government has been just great at building programs; the time has come to show the American people that we can limit them, too, that we can not only start things but we can actually stop things.

About the defense budget, I raise a hope and a caution. As we restructure our military forces to meet the new threats of the post–cold war world, it is true that we can responsibly reduce our defense budget. And we may all doubt what that range of reduction is, but let me say that as long as I am President, I will do everything I can to make sure that the men and women who serve under the American flag will remain the best-trained, the best-prepared, the best-equipped fighting force in the world. And every one of you should make that solemn pledge.

We still have responsibilities around the world, we are the world's only super-power and this is still a dangerous and uncertain time and we owe it to the people in uniform to make sure that we adequately provide for the national defense and for their interests and needs.

Backed by an effective national defense and a stronger economy, our nation will be prepared to lead a world challenged, as it is everywhere, by ethnic conflict, by the proliferation of weapons of mass destruction, by the global democratic revolution and by challenges to the health of our global environment.

Raising Taxes

I know this economic plan is ambitious but I honestly believe it is necessary for the continued greatness of the United States. And I think it is paid for fairly, first by cutting Government, then by asking the most of those who benefited the most in the past and by asking more Americans to contribute today so that all of us can prosper tomorrow. For the wealthiest, those earning more than $180,000 per year, I ask you all who are listening tonight to support a raise in the top rate for Federal income taxes from 31 to 36 percent.

We recommend a 10 percent surtax on incomes over $250,000 a year and we recommend closing some loopholes that let some people get away without paying any tax at all.

For businesses with taxable incomes in excess of $10 million, we recommend a rate raise in the corporate tax rate, also in the 36 percent, as well as a cut in the deduction for business entertainment expenses.

Our plan seeks to attack tax subsidies that actually reward companies more for shutting their operations down here and moving them overseas, than for staying here and reinvesting in America.

I say that as someone who believes an American company should be free to invest around the world and as a former Governor who actively sought investment of foreign companies in my state, but the tax code should not express a *preference* to American companies for moving somewhere else and it does in particular cases today.

We seek to insure that through effective tax enforcement, foreign corporations who do make money in America simply pay the same taxes that American companies make on the same income.

To middle-class Americans who have paid a great deal for the last 12 years and from whom I ask a contribution tonight, I will say again as I did on Monday night: You're not going alone anymore. You're certainly not going first and you're not going to pay more for less as you have too often in the past.

I want to emphasize the facts about this plan: 98.8 percent of America's families will have no increase in their income tax rates. Only 1.2 percent at the top.

Limiting Medicare

Let me be clear: There will also be no new cuts in benefits for Medicare. As we move toward the fourth year with the explosion in health-care costs, as I said, projected to account for 50 percent of the growth in the deficit between now and the year 2000, there must be planned cuts in payments to providers—the doctors, the hospitals, the labs— as a way of controlling health-care costs. But I see these only as a stop-gap until we can reform the entire health-care system. If you'll help me do that, we can be fair to the providers and to the consumers of health care.

Let me repeat this, because I know it matters to a lot of you on both sides of the aisle: This plan does not make a recommendation for new cuts in Medicare benefits for any beneficiary.

Secondly, the only change we are making in Social Security is one that has already been publicized: the plan does ask older Americans with higher incomes, who do not rely solely on Social Security to get by, to contribute more. This plan will not affect the 80 percent of Social Security recipients who do not pay taxes on Social Security now. Those who do not pay tax on Social Security now will not be affected by this plan.

Our plan does include a broad-base tax on energy. And I want to tell you why I selected this and why I think it's a good idea.

I recommend that we adopt a B.T.U. tax on the heat content of energy as the best way to provide us with revenue to lower the deficit, because it also combats pollution, promotes energy efficiency, promotes the independence economically of this country, as well as helping to reduce the debt.

And because it does not discriminate against any area. Unlike a carbon tax, it's not too hard on the coal states. Unlike a gas tax, it's not too tough on people who drive a long way to work. Unlike an ad valorem tax, it doesn't increase just when the price of an energy source goes up.

And it is environmentally responsible. It will help us in the future as well as in the present with the deficit.

Taken together, these measures will cost an American family with an income of about $40,000 a year less than $17 a month. It will cost American families with incomes under $30,000 nothing, because of other programs we propose, principally those raising the earned income tax credit.

Because of our publicly stated determination to reduce the deficit, if we do these things we will see the continuation of what's happened just since the election. Just since the election, since the Secretary of the Treasury, the director of the Office of Management and Budget and others who begin to speak out publicly in favor of a tough deficit reduction plan interest rates have continued to fall long-term.

That means that for the middle class who will pay something more each month, if they have any needs or demands, their increased energy costs will be more than offset by lower interest costs or mortgages, consumer loans, credit cards. This can be a wise investment for them and their country now.

I would also point out what the American people already know and that is because we're a big, vast country where we drive long distances, we have maintained far lower burdens on energy than any other advanced country. We will still have far lower burdens on energy than any other advanced country and these will be spread fairly with real attempts to make sure that no cost is imposed on families with incomes under $30,000 and that the costs are very modest until you get into the higher income groups where the income taxes trigger in.

Dangers of Inaction

Now I ask all of you to consider this: whatever you think of the tax program, whatever you think of the spending cuts—consider the cost of not changing. Remember the numbers that you all know.

If we just keep on doing what we're doing, by the end of the decade we'll have a $650 billion a year deficit. We just keep on doing what we're doing, by the end of the decade 20 percent of our national income will go to health care every year—twice as much as any other country on the globe. We just keep on doing what we're doing, over 20 cents on the dollar will have to go to service the debt.

Unless we have the courage now to start building our future and stop borrowing from it, we're condemning ourselves to years of stagnation interrupted by occasional recession, to slow growth in jobs, to poor growth in income, to more debt, to more disappointment. Worse, unless we change, unless we increase investment and reduce the debt to raise productivity so that we can generate both jobs and incomes, we will be condemning our children and our children's children to a lesser life than we enjoy.

Once Americans looked forward to doubling their living standards every 25 years. At present productivity rates it will take a hundred years to double living standards, until our grandchildren's grandchildren are born. I say that is too long to wait.

Tonight the American people know we have to change. They're also likely to ask me tomorrow, and all of you in the weeks and months ahead, whether we have the fortitude to make changes happen in the right way. They know that as soon as I leave this chamber and you go home, various interest groups will be out in force lobbying against this or that piece of this plan and that the forces of conventional wisdom will offer a thousand reasons why we well ought to do this but we just can't do it.

Our people will be watching and wondering, not to see whether you disagree with me on a particular issue, but just to see whether this is going to be business as usual or a real new day, whether we're all going to conduct ourselves as if we know we're working for them. We must scale the walls of the people's skepticism, not with our words but with our deeds.

After so many years of gridlock and indecisions, after so many hopeful beginnings and so few promising results, the American people are going to be harsh in their judgements of all of us if we fail to seize this moment. This economic plan can't please everybody. If the package is picked apart, there'll be something that will anger each of us, won't please anybody. But if it is taken as a whole, it will help all of us.

So I ask you all to begin by resisting the temptation to focus only on a particular spending cut you don't like or some particular investment that wasn't made and nobody likes the tax increases. But let's just face facts: for 20 years, through Administrations of both parties, incomes have stalled and debt has exploded and productivity has not grown as it should. We cannot deny the reality of our condition. We have got to play the hand we were dealt and play it as best we can.

My fellow Americans, the test of this plan cannot be what is in it for me. It has got to be what is in it for us.

If we work hard and if we work together, if we rededicate ourselves to creating jobs, to rewarding work, to strengthening our families, to reinventing our Government, we can lift our country's fortunes again.

Tonight I ask everyone in this chamber and every American to look simply into your own heart, to spark your own hopes, to fire your own imagination.

There's so much good, so much possibility, so much excitement in this country now that if we act boldly and honestly, as leaders should, our legacy will be one of prosperity and progress.

This must be America's new direction. Let us summon the courage to seize it.

Thank you. God bless America.

Author Index

Title Index